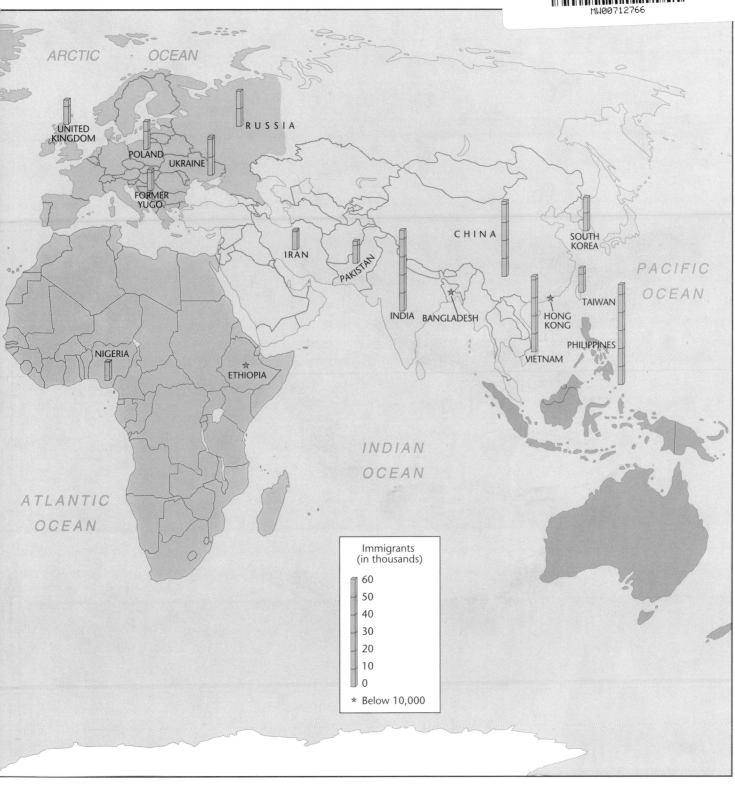

ARCTIC · OCEAN

UNITED
KINGDOM

RUSSIA

POLAND

UKRAINE

FORMER
YUGO.

IRAN

PAKISTAN

CHINA

SOUTH
KOREA

PACIFIC
OCEAN

INDIA BANGLADESH

HONG
KONG

TAIWAN

NIGERIA

ETHIOPIA

VIETNAM

PHILIPPINES

ATLANTIC

OCEAN

INDIAN
OCEAN

Immigrants
(in thousands)

60
50
40
30
20
10
0

★ Below 10,000

Run your *Living Sociology* **CD-ROM for more sociology maps and interactive map activities.**

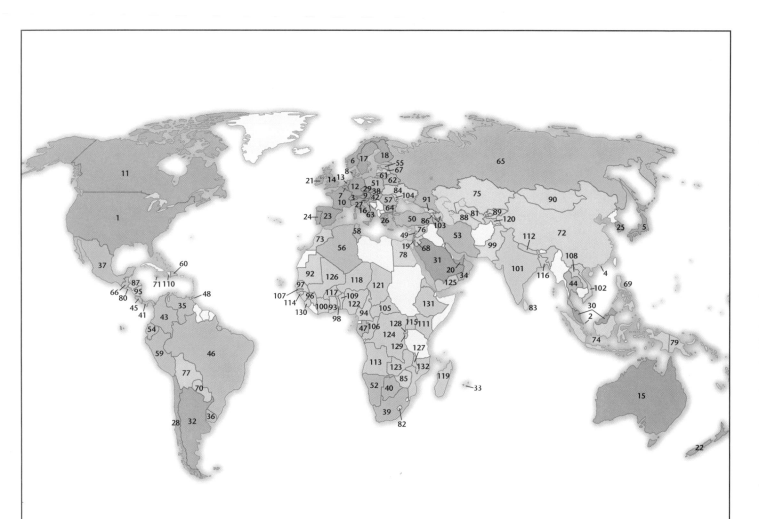

Most Parity	
Nation	Income per Person
1 United States	$28,020
2 Singapore	$26,910
3 Switzerland	$26,340
4 Hong Kong, China	$24,260
5 Japan	$23,420
6 Norway	$23,220
7 Belgium	$22,390
8 Denmark	$22,120
9 Austria	$21,650
10 France	$21,510
11 Canada	$21,380
12 Germany	$21,110
13 Netherlands	$20,850
14 United Kingdom	$19,960
15 Australia	$19,870
16 Italy	$18,890
17 Sweden	$18,770
18 Finland	$18,260
19 Israel	$18,100
20 United Arab Emirates	$17,000
21 Ireland	$16,750
22 New Zealand	$16,500
23 Spain	$15,290
24 Portugal	$13,450
25 Korea, Rep.	$13,080
26 Greece	$12,730
27 Slovenia	$12,110
28 Chile	$11,700
29 Czech Republic	$10,870
30 Malaysia	$10,390
31 Saudi Arabia	$9,700
32 Argentina	$9,530
33 Mauritius	$9,000

Second Tier	
Nation	Income per Person
34 Oman	$8,680
35 Venezuela	$8,130
36 Uruguay	$7,760
37 Mexico	$7,660
38 Slovak Republic	$7,460
39 South Africa	$7,450
40 Botswana	$7,390
41 Panama	$7,060
42 Hungary	$6,730
43 Colombia	$6,720
44 Thailand	$6,700
45 Costa Rica	$6,470
46 Brazil	$6,340
47 Gabon	$6,300
48 Trinidad and Tobago	$6,100
49 Lebanon	$6,060
50 Turkey	$6,060
51 Poland	$6,000
52 Namibia	$5,390
53 Iran, Islamic Rep.	$5,360
54 Ecuador	$4,730
55 Estonia	$4,660
56 Algeria	$4,620
57 Romania	$4,580
58 Tunisia	$4,550
59 Peru	$4,410
60 Dominican Republic	$4,390
61 Lithuania	$4,390
62 Belarus	$4,380
63 Croatia	$4,290
64 Bulgaria	$4,280
65 Russian Federation	$4,190
66 Guatemala	$3,820

Third Tier	
Nation	Income per Person
67 Latvia	$3,650
68 Jordan	$3,570
69 Philippines	$3,550
70 Paraguay	$3,480
71 Jamaica	$3,450
72 China	$3,330
73 Morocco	$3,320
74 Indonesia	$3,310
75 Kazakhstan	$3,230
76 Syrian Arab Rep.	$3,020
77 Bolivia	$2,860
78 Egypt Arab Rep.	$2,860
79 Papua New Guinea	$2,820
80 El Salvador	$2,790
81 Uzbekistan	$2,450
82 Lesotho	$2,380
83 Sri Lanka	$2,290
84 Ukraine	$2,230
85 Zimbabwe	$2,200
86 Armenia	$2,160
87 Honduras	$2,130
88 Turkmenistan	$2,010
89 Kyrgyz Rep.	$1,970
90 Mongolia	$1,820
91 Georgia	$1,810
92 Mauritania	$1,810
93 Ghana	$1,790
94 Cameroon	$1,760
95 Nicaragua	$1,760
96 Guinea	$1,720
97 Senegal	$1,650
98 Togo	$1,650
99 Pakistan	$1,600

Least Parity	
Nation	Income per Person
100 Cote d'Ivoire	$1,580
101 India	$1,580
102 Vietnam	$1,570
103 Azerbaijan	$1,490
104 Moldova	$1,440
105 Central African Rep.	$1,430
106 Congo Rep.	$1,410
107 The Gambia	$1,280
108 Lao PDR	$1,250
109 Benin	$1,230
110 Haiti	$1,130
111 Kenya	$1,130
112 Nepal	$1,090
113 Angola	$1,030
114 Guinea-Bissau	$1,030
115 Uganda	$1,030
116 Bangladesh	$1,010
117 Burkina Faso	$950
118 Niger	$920
119 Madagascar	$900
120 Tajikistan	$900
121 Chad	$880
122 Nigeria	$870
123 Zambia	$860
124 Congo, Dem. Rep.	$790
125 Yemen Rep.	$790
126 Mali	$710
127 Malawi	$690
128 Rwanda	$630
129 Burundi	$590
130 Sierra Leone	$510
131 Ethiopia	$500
132 Mozambique	$500

Global Stratification: Purchasing Power and Economic Development, 1996

Living Sociology

Living Sociology

SECOND EDITION

Claire M. Renzetti
St. Joseph's University

Daniel J. Curran
St. Joseph's University

Allyn and Bacon
Boston   London   Toronto   Sydney   Tokyo   Singapore

Series Editor: Jeff Lasser
Editor-in-Chief, Social Sciences: Karen Hanson
Development Editor: Mary Ellen Lepionka
Executive Marketing Manager: Lisa Kimball
Sr. Editorial Production Administrator: Susan McIntyre
Editorial Production Service: Kathy Smith
Composition Buyer: Linda Cox
Manufacturing Buyer: Megan Cochran
Cover Administrator: Linda Knowles
Text Design and Art: Glenna Collett
Photo Research: Helane Prottas
Electronic Composition: Omegatype Typography, Inc.

Library of Congress Cataloging-in-Publication Data

Renzetti, Claire M.
  Living sociology / Claire M. Renzetti, Daniel J. Curran.--2nd ed.
    p.   cm.
  Includes bibliographical references and index.
  ISBN 0-205-30910-0
  1. Sociology--Study and teaching.   I. Curran, Daniel J.   II. Title.

  HM571.R46 1999
  301.'071--dc21   99-045958

Brief Contents

Contents   *vi*

Preface   *xiv*

Contents

PART TWO   SOCIETY

7   *Deviance and Social Control*   163

PART THREE   STRUCTURES OF INEQUALITY

8   *Stratification and Social Class in the United States*   195

PART FOUR   SOCIAL INSTITUTIONS

PART FIVE   SOCIAL CHANGE

Preface

On a flight from Philadelphia to Miami, a fellow traveler asked us what we do for a living. "We are sociologists," we replied. "Oh, social workers! That must be interesting work," he said. "No, not social workers, sociologists," we said. "Oh, so you try to figure out what's wrong with people? You give them advice?" he asked. "No," we explained, "You're thinking of a counselor or a psychologist. We are sociologists." "So, just what do you do?" he asked again.

Since this book is all about what sociologists do, we won't go into our final answer to the traveler here. Suffice it to say that the inquisitor was happy it was only a two-hour flight. We mention the exchange now because it probably sounds familiar to most readers. The man's confusion is not uncommon. Indeed, we hear students express the same confusion when they're asked why they enrolled in an Introduction to Sociology course. Most are not sure exactly what sociology is, but know vaguely that it "has something to do with people."

Our responsibility to educate our students about sociology spans a quarter or a semester—a period considerably longer than a two-hour plane ride—and this responsibility includes not only ensuring that students know what sociologists do, but also equipping them with knowledge they can use in their everyday lives. Sociology is about *people* interacting with one another in their own society and, increasingly, across societies. These people, of course, include students, who, as we begin a new millenium, are confronting dramatic economic, political, and social change. The burgeoning service economy, for example, means that a college education is more important than ever, and that communication and critical thinking skills are more valuable than physical strength or endurance. However, the service economy also poses the threat of greater job insecurity for today's workforce, and for many, longer work hours without greater financial rewards.

Such changes are occurring not only in the United States, but also in most industrialized countries. Meanwhile, the nitty gritty aspects of manufacturing have moved to less economically developed countries, where workers' salaries are lower and there are few regulations of working conditions. It no longer makes sense to talk about the U.S. economy apart from other countries' economies. The United States is part of a global economy, supported by governments and other social institutions that are increasingly linked by sophisticated communications technology, thus breaking down cultural and geographic boundaries that formerly isolated countries. Each of us is a member not only of a single society, but also of a global community; we are citizens of the world as well as of the United States.

We wrote this book because we feel that introducing students to our discipline is one of the most exciting and satisfying things we do. But that isn't all. We wrote *Living Sociology* because we think it will help students meet the challenges of the twenty-first century by giving them an understanding of the relevance of sociology in their everyday lives. We have each taught sociology for more than twenty years. This is our fifth textbook. So we bring to this project a wealth of experience in classroom teaching and in teaching through writing. Our goal in this second edition of *Living Sociology* continues to be to demonstrate that sociology is not a set of loosely connected concepts, principles, and theories, as some critics of the discipline have charged, but a body of knowledge with tremendous practical importance. Herein lies sociology's contribution as well as its promise.

HOW THIS BOOK IS ORGANIZED

The second edition of *Living Sociology* is, like the first edition, organized in five parts. Part One, The Discipline of Sociology, provides an introduction to sociology. Chapter 1 presents an overview of the history of sociology and the development of the major sociological theories: structural functionalism, conflict theory, symbolic interactionism, and feminist theory. The historical roots of the theories are discussed, along with the central themes of each of the perspectives in their contemporary form. Most important, though, this opening chapter explains why the study of sociology is important, and encourages students to develop a sociological imagination. Chapter 2 explores the ways sociologists study the social world. This chapter reviews various research methods, but also covers significant methodological issues, such as inclusiveness of diverse groups in research samples and the ethical and political dimensions of sociological research. We've found that students sometimes have a preconceived notion of research methods as "dry" and unappealing, but we think this chapter will change their minds by conveying our enthusiasm for the research enterprise.

Part Two, Society, focuses on the "building blocks" of social life. At the suggestion of reviewers, Chapter 3 now focuses on social structure and types of societies, historically and in the contemporary world. Chapter 4 looks at culture, emphasizing that culture is a uniquely human creation and showing through many examples from everyday life the tremendous diversity across cultures in our own society and throughout the world. Chapter 5 explores the process of socialization throughout the life cycle and across cultural groups. Chapter 6 continues the discussion by examining human behavior in groups and how behavior changes as the type of group changes, spotlighting interaction in large social organizations. Finally, Chapter 7 discusses topics that our students over the years seem to find intrinsically interesting: deviance and social control. The emphasis in this chapter is on the social construction of deviance and variations in reactions to deviance. It is in this chapter that we also discuss criminal behavior and the criminal justice system.

The emphasis on diversity established in Part Two carries over to Part Three, Structures of Inequality. Chapter 8 introduces the concept of social stratification, which remains central throughout the text. This chapter zeroes in on social class inequality, with special attention to inequality and poverty in the United States. Chapter 9 points out that inequality characterizes social relations not only within a society, but between societies as well. This chapter introduces the World Bank system for examining global stratification and considers the extent and impact of differences in wealth, power, and prestige across countries. The remaining chapters in Part Three focus on inequalities between social groups. In Chapter 10, we examine gender inequality and heterosexism; in Chapter 11, racial and ethnic inequality; and in Chapter 12, age inequality. Each of these chapters examines not only the United States, but also numerous cross-cultural situations as well.

Part Four, Social Institutions, begins with Chapter 13, which looks at the economy as the central institution of any society. Included in this chapter is an introduction to many of the main themes in the sociology of work. Chapter 14 is an examination of politics and government, with a careful look at the political process not only in the United States, but elsewhere in the world as well. The intersection of U.S. politics with the politics of other countries is also emphasized in our discussion of the military and warfare. Chapter 15 turns attention to families and intimate relationships, emphasizing the diversity of family forms in our society and other societies. This chapter also examines some of the major problems families confront, including divorce and domestic violence. In Chapter 16, we look at education by considering the history of the development of our current education system, the way U.S. education compares with education in other countries, and various educational problems and their potential solutions. Chapter 17 investigates the diversity of religious beliefs and practices prevalent in our society and throughout the world, with an emphasis on the interrelationship between religion and other social institutions. Chapter 18 explores the growing and vibrant field of medical sociology, considering issues such as the social construction of health and illness, social factors that affect health and illness, the doctor-patient relationship, and the social structure of health care delivery.

In Part Five, Social Change, we concentrate on many aspects of social change. Chapter 19 examines several important sources of change—population growth, urbanization, and environmental factors—and their effects on social interaction and the organization of social life. In Chapter 20, we look at people's deliberate efforts to bring about or inhibit social change by engaging in various forms of collective behavior, including social movements.

MAKING SOCIOLOGY PART OF YOUR LIFE

Having written four other highly successful textbooks on social problems, the sociology of gender, and criminology, some of our colleagues were curious as to why we would want to write an introductory text. There are, after all, a number of fine introductory texts on the market. Quite frankly, we were motivated by our belief that we have something special to offer instructors and students alike. Reviewers' comments on the first edition of *Living Sociology* have reinforced this belief.

> I was very pleased to see the inclusion of feminist perspectives. Also, the "Intersecting Inequalities" feature caught my eye. Previously, many texts I have seen and used discussed these issues of utmost importance only in small, compartmentalized ways. The fact that the first chapter included sociologists such as Martineau, Du Bois, Wells-Barnett, and Addams were important to me. Additionally, I like the fact that there is a balance in each chapter between information about the chapter's subject and a theoretical overview. Too often, introductory texts focus on one or the other. This mixture allows students to both gain an understanding of the topic as well as see that theory is an integral part of all sociology. . . . The inclusion of gender, inequality, and computer technology makes this text seem cutting edge for our students. As most professors know, if students can associate the information with their own lives, they are more likely to see its purpose and understand its meaning. I also like the way the authors put themselves into the text. The chapters are sprinkled with personal reflection and example. . . . I also chose *Living Sociology* for its extraordinary supplements.
>
> —Carrie Uihlein Nilles, Marshall University, Huntington, WV

> The contents of *Living Sociology* are presented in a user-friendly, conversational, comprehensive way, and are geared toward the students involved in an Introduction to Sociology level course. I found it appropriate and motivating for both students and the instructor. . . . The openings, information boxes, and chapter summaries provide the students with a view and explanation of topics from real-life issues that aided in instruction. . . . I encourage student discussion and debate in all areas possible. I felt the format of the text and its content nicely provided for this enhanced learning process and opportunity.
>
> —George J. Ellefson, Bismarck State College, Bismarck, SD

The topical balance in *Living Sociology* is very good. The book does an excellent job of covering a large amount of information while providing up-to-date examples that students can easily follow. . . . The book is very current and accurate! All the research presented is very important and well chosen. I thought this was one of the stronger points of the text. . . . The book also does an excellent job of engaging students, forcing them to think critically about the material. Overall I find this text to be quite useful and an enjoyable read.

—Daniel Llanes, Pennsylvania State University, University Park, PA

I have found *Living Sociology* a very useful book, well written, and it incorporates gender/sexual orientation and race/ethnicity in every chapter. The addition of global perspectives gives it an added dimension that I particularly like. . . . Other books fail to adequately integrate global perspectives at all. . . . The text is written at an appropriate intellectual level for introductory students. It's down to earth and easy to follow. . . . The text also is colorful and has many things to hold student interest.

—Debra S. Allnock, University of New Mexico, Albuquerque, NM

Consider the following features of this edition:

An accessible writing style. *Living Sociology* has the same highly readable, jargon-free writing style that has won our other textbooks high praise. Based on reviewer comments, including those of students, we're delighted that so many instructors and students enjoy reading our books.

Putting it all in perspective. *Living Sociology* shows students how sociologists use theory to explain not only major social events, but also everyday occurrences. Students are given a theoretical foundation in Chapter 1, where each of the four major sociological theories—structural functionalism, conflict theory, symbolic interactionism, and feminist theory—are first introduced. In nearly every chapter, the approach of each theory to the subject at hand is presented and critically evaluated. Students learn the strengths and weaknesses of each theory for each topic, thus gaining a balanced view of our diverse discipline. Moreover, social theory comes alive in these pages through numerous examples that make the abstract more tangible and, therefore, more comprehensible.

Up-to-date information. In our age of information overload, it's almost impossible to keep up to date on the research and data in every subfield of our discipline. The time needed to search the databases in the average college or university library is simply prohibitive for most instructors, who have many other commitments. We've taken instructors' and students' time constraints into account in writing *Living Sociology*. Here, you'll find the latest available data, as well as hundreds of studies by sociologists, psychologists, anthropologists, biologists, and colleagues in a range of other disciplines. And to supplement what's here in print, check out our Web site, *http://www.abacon.com/renzetti,* where new information is added as soon as it's available.

The personal touch. We think it's important for readers to know us not only as sociologists, but also as individuals. Throughout the book, therefore, we often recount personal experiences to illustrate a sociological principle or concept. You'll sometimes read about our encounters with other cultures in Asia, Africa, Australia, and Europe, and you'll meet our sons, Sean and Aidan, as well as a few of our friends. We welcome you to share your experiences with us, too, by contacting us at St. Joseph's University, 5600 City Ave., Philadelphia, PA 19131, or by e-mail at *CRENZETI@SJU.EDU* and *DCURRAN@SJU.EDU*. After all, each of us is living sociology every day.

SPECIAL FEATURES

Attention to social diversity.   One of our goals in writing this book was to help all students see themselves in the pages. Consequently, while recognizing our common humanity, *Living Sociology* also highlights human diversity. Throughout the book, attention is given to inclusiveness of gender, race and ethnicity, social class, age, and sexual orientation. But diversity is emphasized in other special ways as well. There are, for example, *Intersecting Inequalities* boxes that draw attention to how people experience a particular aspect of social life differently because of their sex, race or ethnicity, social class, age, or sexual orientation. The boxes do not just present problems faced by members of different groups; they also celebrate our diversity. Students will read about experiences that are familiar to them, but the features will also give them a glimpse of social life that is often far different from what they're used to.

The world at your fingertips.   In keeping with our goal of developing students' understanding of their roles as world citizens, *Living Sociology* provides a global view of social life. Cross-cultural examples and international data are provided in every chapter to stretch students' perspectives beyond the boundaries of U.S. society to the world community. In addition, we've provided *Global Insights* boxes that focus specifically on social issues and experiences in many other countries. Students will learn the importance of framing in a global context what they see and hear about their own and other countries.

Learning by doing.   In a recent article in *Teaching Sociology,* Kathleen McKinney and colleagues (1998) identified one of the five key components of quality teaching as helping students learn to use what we teach them. A major theme of this book is helping students develop an appreciation of the value of applying sociology to their everyday lives. For this to happen, they must see sociology not as something you read or talk about, but rather as something you do. In *Living Sociology,* we invite students to *do* sociology, to become active participants in what they're studying. One way we foster active learning is through *Doing Sociology* boxes. These boxes introduce students to an important sociological concept or principle and then ask them to learn more about it by, for instance, surveying people on their campus, running a simple social experiment, or carrying out a brief content analysis. Our exciting new *Sociology Live* box involves actual students and instructors at various schools using our text in their introductory sociology courses. We invited students to conduct and report on their own sociological inquiries. Specifically, we asked the student research teams to respond to questions challenging them to link chapter concepts to their own campus and their own experiences as college students. The students did a wonderful job. Their essays perfectly reflect our continuing mission as the authors of *Living Sociology*.

Examining issues of social policy. *Social Policy* boxes show how sociological research can help shape public policy. These in-depth boxes present differing viewpoints on a social issue and examine how the research supports or refutes specific claims on each side. Students are then asked what they think about the issue and policy options.

Learning to think critically. We firmly believe that there is a reciprocal relationship between active learning and critical thinking. Thus, the *Doing Sociology* and *Social Policy* boxes play a dual role by promoting critical thinking skills through an active learning process. *Living Sociology* fosters critical thinking in other ways, too. At the end of each major section in every chapter, students are asked to reflect on what they've read. These *Reflecting On . . .* questions are not just for review. Rather, they challenge students to apply what they've read to their own experiences, to think about solutions to particular problems, or to evaluate a specific position or idea. Based on in-class trials, we're confident these questions will improve student participation and prompt lively classroom discussions that will often continue after a class has ended.

Comprehensiveness with flexibility. We have organized the book to give instructors flexibility. No one likes to be told what to teach or how they should teach it. The book covers the full range of topics that comprise the discipline, but it's arranged so instructors can craft their course to suit their personal, institutional, and pedagogical needs. Many instructors will choose not to assign all twenty chapters, but they needn't worry that students will miss out on something of interest to them because in each chapter there is a *Connections* chart that directs students to other places in the book where a specific issue or related topic is also discussed. Questions in the chart coach students in connecting, applying, and integrating their knowledge.

Help with teaching and learning. Instructors have different teaching styles and students learn in different ways. We want to do all we can to make the introductory sociology course an exciting, pleasurable teaching and learning experience. That's why we've included a number

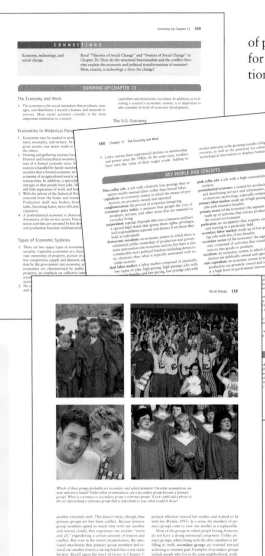

of pedagogical tools in this book. Besides the *Reflecting On* questions for each main section of text, and the *Connections* chart, three additional teaching/learning aids appear at the end of each chapter. **Summing Up** provides a brief review of chapter content, highlighting central points and ideas. **Key People and Concepts** is an end-of-chapter glossary of all the major names and concepts that were introduced in the chapter. And **Learning More** suggests additional sources of information for some of the major issues covered in the chapter. Both students and instructors will find *Learning More* helpful for identifying some of the best—and most controversial—new or recent books on a topic.

At the end of the book there is a **Glossary** that compiles all the key names and concepts introduced throughout the book and, of course, a complete list of **References**. A glance through the *References* for this book demonstrates that we remain committed to providing readers with a thorough and current review of the literature.

Thought-provoking visual images. We can learn much about sociology through visual images. Charts, graphs, and statistical tables are the visual images perhaps most often associated with sociological research. You'll find in *Living Sociology* numerous charts, graphs, and tables that summarize a wealth of data clearly and concisely. A great deal of information can be gleaned by studying these visual aids. But visual sociology is also encouraged through groupings of color photographs throughout the book. Great care has been taken in selecting photographs that are inclusive of diverse groups, that convey an important sociological message, and that are simply fascinating to look at.

SUPPLEMENTS FOR THE INSTRUCTOR

Instructor's Resource Manual

This teaching aid provides chapter-by-chapter learning objectives, lecture outlines, lists of key terms and people, suggested answers to the "Reflecting On" questions in the text, and correlation with other instructional resources available with *Living Sociology*.

Test Banks

The Test Bank and Alternate Test Bank each contain over 2,000 test questions in multiple-choice, true-false, fill-in, and essay formats. Answer justifications have been added to the answer keys. Computerized versions of both Test Banks, are available in both DOS/Windows and Macintosh.

Call-in Testing

Allyn & Bacon can run your tests for you and have a finished, ready-to-duplicate test on its way to you by mail or fax within forty-eight hours.

Learning by Doing Sociology: In-Class Experiential Exercises

This manual offers step-by-step procedures for numerous in-class activities, general suggestions for managing experiential learning, and trouble-shooting tips. It contains twenty-two exercises on a broad range of topics typically covered in the introductory sociology course.

Allyn & Bacon Transparencies for Introductory Sociology III

One hundred color acetates feature illustrations both from the text and from other sources. The majority of these transparencies are also available on the new Allyn & Bacon Digital Media Archive for Sociology III (CD-ROM).

Digital Media Archive for Sociology III

This exciting new CD-ROM contains hundreds of images and audio and video files that you can incorporate into your multimedia presentations in the classroom. The CD-ROM provides instructors with a broad selection of media to use to illustrate key sociological concepts.

PowerPoint Presentation and User's Guide

This PowerPoint presentation combines approximately three hundred graphic and text images into twenty modules that parallel the organization of the text. Using either Macintosh or DOS/Windows, instructors can easily create customized graphic presentations for lectures. PowerPoint software is not required to use this program; a PowerPoint viewer is included to access the images.

Allyn & Bacon Interactive Video and Video User's Guide

This custom video covers 16 key themes in sociology based on television news. The up-to-the-minute video segments are great to launch lectures, spark classroom discussion, and encourage critical thinking. The user's guide provides the script of each video segment, specific tie-ins to the text, and critical thinking questions for writing and discussion.

A&B Video Library

Qualified adopters may select from a wide variety of high quality videos from such sources as Films for the Humanities and Sciences and Annenberg/CPB.

Telecourse Faculty Guide

For instructors teaching a telecourse using the series *The Sociological Imagination: Introduction to Sociology,* this guide contains a complete syllabus that correlates use of the videos, textbook, *Telecourse Study Guide* (available from Allyn and Bacon), and *The Sociological Imagination Faculty Guide* (available from the telecourse producers).

The Blockbuster Approach: A Guide to Teaching Sociology with Video

By integrating commercially released video into the social sciences curriculum and using this manual, instructors can create an exciting new opportunity for learning both in and out of the classroom. This teaching guide describes selected commercial films in terms of relevance to sociological topics. Key terms are often noted in the video description to help integrate assignments. At least one sample assignment is provided within each topic category to assist instructors in applying the textbook material to the movie (or vice versa). The videos are organized by sociological topic and presented in an order common to most introductory textbooks.

SUPPLEMENTS FOR THE STUDENT

Study Guide

This comprehensive study guide offers a carefully structured learning system for all of the important concepts in the text. It includes chapter learning objectives, self-tests (in multiple-choice, true-false, and fill-in and essay formats), as well as answer feedback and extra vocabulary help for students who need it.

Telecourse Study Guide

A separate study guide is available for students enrolled in a telecourse using the series, *The Sociological Imagination: Introduction to Sociology.* This supplement connects reading assignments from the textbook with each of the videos, and helps students respond to and review material from both.

Practice Tests

Consisting of approximately twenty-five questions per chapter, these self-tests with answer justifications help students gain mastery of the material covered in the text—above and beyond their reading in the text and the study guide.

Companion Web Site

An extensive Web Site has been developed for this text at *http://www.abacon.com/ renzetti.* Features of the site include Learning Objectives; Practice Tests in an Online Study Guide (interactive multiple-choice, true-false, fill-in, and essay questions); Web Destinations; Exploring the Internet; Chapter Chats, and a special section for updates to the text.

Allyn & Bacon Quick Guide to the Internet for Sociology, 2000 Edition

This reference guide connects users with the basics of the Internet and the World Wide Web, and provides a multitude of sociology-specific references and links. Included in this Guide are sections on citing Internet sources and issues of privacy and security on the World Wide Web.

Careers in Sociology, 2e

This supplemental guide explores careers in sociology, explains how people working as sociologists entered the field, and discusses how a degree in sociology can be preparation for careers such as law, gerontology, social work, and public administration.

Living Sociology Interactive Companion

The new Interactive Companion on CD-ROM features a streamlined approach in which expanded pedagogical elements and media assets are linked to chapter summaries in outline form. Students use the Interactive Companion in conjunction with their text for study and review. The Interactive Companion contains chapter-by-chapter learning objectives, graphic and map activities, Internet activities, matching or association activities, reflective writing activities, critical thinking activities, audio, video, web links, and practice tests.

ACKNOWLEDGMENTS

Authors use many adjectives to describe the process of writing a textbook. Usually, *enjoyable* isn't one of them. We count ourselves among the lucky few who can say that we truly enjoy textbook writing, and we owe much of this good fortune to our friends and colleagues who offer us support and advice along the way.

For more than ten years we have worked with Karen Hanson, Editor-in-Chief, Social Sciences, for Allyn and Bacon. As we have said many times, Karen is the kind of editor authors wish for. She uses her wealth of editorial experience and creative energy to help make our books the best they can be. We wish to take this opportunity to welcome Jeff Lasser to our team. Jeff will be taking over from Karen as editor for this project. We always owe a special thanks to Susan McIntyre, Senior Editorial Production Administrator, whose patience with us over the years has only been matched by that of our parents while we were growing up. Mary Ellen Lepionka, our developmental editor, brought to this project a collaborative style and creativity for which we are very grateful. Her contributions include the "Sociology Live" feature, the "Connections" charts, and the photo caption program. We are convinced that Kathy Smith, who guides all of our books through the production process, can make a believer out of anyone. No matter how pressing the deadline or daunting the task, Kathy always says in her reassuring voice, "We can do this." Somehow she always convinces us. And to the marketing and sales staff at Allyn and Bacon we extend our sincere thanks. Your support and enthusiasm for our books over the years have been unflagging. We are very proud to have you representing our work.

We continue to be amazed by and thankful for the generosity of so many colleagues who, despite the numerous demands on their time, carefully review our manuscripts and make suggestions that improve them immeasurably. To the following individuals, who reviewed all or part of this book, our sincere thanks:

Debra S. Allnock, University of New Mexico
George J. Ellefson, Bismarck State College
Daniel Llanes, Pennsylvania State University
Carolyn Uihlein Nilles, Marshall University

We would also like to acknowledge the instructors using our text who worked with us on this edition to make our unique *Sociology Live* feature a reality. They are:

Susan Cooper, University of Kansas
Twyla Hill, Wichita State University
Irwin Kantor, Middlesex County College–Edison, New Jersey
Brenda Kowalewski, Weber State University
Stephen McNamee, The University of North Carolina–Wilmington
Carolyn U. Nilles, Marshall University
Lisa Riley, Creighton University
Stacey Sympson, Western Kentucky University
S. Rowan Wolf, Portland Community College–Portland, Oregon

Thank you so much for taking the time to present *Sociology Live* to students, encouraging and guiding them to participate, and forwarding their work.

We also remain indebted to reviewers who assisted us with the first edition. We have incorporated many of their thoughtful suggestions into the second edition:

Leonard Beeghley, University of Florida
Bruce L. Berg, California State University, Long Beach
Allan L. Bramson, Wayne County Community College
York Bradshaw, Indiana University
Clifford L. Broman, Michigan State University
Levon Chorbajian, University of Massachusetts, Lowell
Roberta L. Coles, Marquette University
William M. Cross, Illinois College
Mary L. Donaghy, Arkansas State University

Marlese Durr, Wright State University
Pamela Elkind, Eastern Washington University
Lorna E. Forster, Clinton Community College
Gary D. Hampe, University of Wyoming
Kate Hausbeck, University of Nevada, Las Vegas
Jill Heine, University of New Mexico
Charles B. Hennon, Miami University
Phillip R. Kunz, Brigham Young University
Frank Lechner, Emory University
Diane E. Levy, The University of North Carolina at Wilmington
Martin N. Marger, Michigan State University
Robert F. Meier, Iowa State University
Anthony M. Orum, The University of Illinois at Chicago
Anne R. Peterson, Columbus State Community College
Robert Ross, Clark University
Dale R. Spady, Northern Michigan University
James Sherohman, St. Cloud State University
Kathleen A. Tiemann, University of North Dakota
Theodore C. Wagenaar, Miami University

Finally, we are thankful to and for our sons, Sean and Aidan. They have let us use their books and recount stories about them in the pages that follow. They have unselfishly shared us with Allyn and Bacon for this project and the writing and revision of others. They model patience and good humor when we're frantic and grumpy, and display a level of maturity well beyond their years. Most important, they keep us focused on what's really important in life. And so to them we dedicate this book, with our unending love and gratitude.

About the Authors

Claire Renzetti is Professor and Chair of Sociology at St. Joseph's University in Philadelphia, where she has taught for nineteen years. She is editor of the international, interdisciplinary journal, Violence Against Women; coeditor of the Sage Violence Against Women Book Series; and editor of the Gender, Crime, and Law Book Series for Northeastern University Press. She has authored ten books and numerous book chapters and articles. It was in her introductory sociology course during her first semester of college that Claire decided to become a sociologist, a decision she has never regretted.

Dan Curran is Executive Vice President and Professor of Sociology at St. Joseph's University in Philadelphia, where he has taught for twenty years. He is the author of six books and many articles in professional journals. He is also a consulting editor in criminology and criminal justice for Sage Publications. After his first year in college, Dan left school and took a job in a plastics factory, where he labored side by side with the working poor. This experience inspired him to study sociology

because he saw in the discipline the opportunity to address serious social problems such as inequality.

Claire and Dan live in Drexel Park, Pennsylvania, with their sons, Sean and Aidan.

 Run Chapter 1 on your *Living Sociology* CD-ROM for interesting and informative activities, web links, videos, practice tests, and more.

Sociological Perspectives

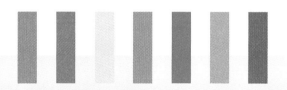

I magine, if you can, that you lost your eyesight in early childhood. Now, forty-five years later, doctors tell you that a new surgical procedure can restore your vision. You have the operation and are told it was successful. Today the bandages will be removed. The doctor slowly unwinds the gauze and you open your eyes. Everyone waits for you to exclaim, "I can see!" But you say nothing; you are bewildered and confused. Why?

Although this vignette sounds like a scene from an old movie, it is, in fact, based on a real case studied by neuro-anthropologist Oliver Sacks (1995). Sacks recounts the story of Virgil, who lost his sight at age six because of a serious illness. When Virgil was fifty, his vision was surgically restored. However, when the bandages were removed from Virgil's eyes, "He saw, but what he saw had no coherence" (Sacks, 1995, p. 114). As Dr. Sacks (1995) explains:

> When [the sighted] open [their] eyes each morning, it is upon a world [they] have spent a lifetime *learning* to see. . . . But when Virgil opened his eyes, after being blind for forty-five years—having had little more than an infant's visual experience, and this long forgotten—there were no visual memories to support a perception; there was no world of experience and meaning awaiting him. (p. 114)

Virgil's story reminds us that we are not merely biological beings, we are also fundamentally *social* beings. Even a basically physiological phenomenon such as seeing depends on social learning—learning in the context of the social groups to which we belong—to give it meaning. That is what *sociology* is about: our interactions as social beings and the meanings we give to these interactions. Let's consider these ideas more carefully.

WHAT IS SOCIOLOGY?

Sociology is the scientific study of human societies. Societies are composed of people, or, more specifically, *social actors*. In studying human societies, sociologists examine the collective interactions of social actors within a particular social structure and the collective meanings that these actors give to their interactions with one another.

Note the repeated use of the word *collective*. The sociologist is not concerned with the individual. Rather, the basic unit of analysis for the sociologist is the *social group*. Sociologists study how factors *external* to individuals give rise to particular behaviors or situations and how social actors, through their membership in specific social groups, experience and interpret these behaviors and situations.

To understand how a sociologist approaches the world, let's return for a moment to the story of Virgil. When Virgil couldn't make sense of what he saw following surgery, the physician treating him probably would have focused on his physical condition. Had the retinas or other structures of his eyes somehow been damaged? A psychologist called to the case would consider Virgil's emotional state, personality, and life history. Was some personal trauma keeping him from seeing normally despite his restored physical capacity? But a sociologist considering Virgil's situation would put him in the context of his social world. A sociologist would not be concerned with Virgil as an individual, but with Virgil as a member of a society—a society with particular rules and expectations. Virgil's problem, then, was not unlike that of a traveler in a foreign country: Everything was different from what he was used to. The problem was not just Virgil's, either; it affected others who shared his social circumstances and the people with whom they in turn interacted.

This is not to say that the sociologist's approach to Virgil's problem is *the* correct one or that it is better than the physician's or the psychologist's approach or anyone else's from another field. Each approach is simply a way of studying and understanding a particular problem or event. As sociologist Peter Berger (1963, p. 17) reminds us, the sociologist doesn't claim that her or his frame of reference is the only one to apply to a condition. "The point is not that one denies other people's games, but that one is clear about the rules of one's own."

Let's consider in greater detail several distinguishing themes that characterize the discipline of sociology: social locations, social inequality, cultural diversity, and the interdependence of the world community.

Social Locations

When we say that sociologists are not concerned with individuals, but with the interactions of individuals in social groups, we do not mean that they deny the importance of individuality. Sociologists fully appreciate individual differences, as you will see, but they recognize that individuals are shaped or constrained by their membership in particular groups in their society, especially group assignments over which individuals have little or no control.

Every society has some means by which its people are sorted into various categories, and each category has some kind of value attached to it. Typically, societies categorize their members by sex, race or ethnicity, class or economic standing, and age. In many societies, ability/disability and sexual orientation are also important categories. These categories serve as *social locators;* each bestows on an individual a particular *status* or position that tells others the individual's place in the society and, in turn, influences how others interact with that individual (such as with deference or superiority). These statuses also shape individual behavior and life experiences by bestowing or denying various privileges, opportunities, responsibilities, and rewards.

Sociologists, then, are fundamentally concerned with how social locating factors, such as sex, race, class, and age, affect the ways people think and act in particular situations and how they influence people's life chances. Emphasizing social locators does not deny individual choice, but rather recognizes that the choices we make—and the options available to us—may be limited by the social locations that we happen to hold. There are numerous examples of the effects of social locators in the chapters that follow. For instance, we'll see how our financial circumstances determine, to a large extent, where we live, whom we socialize with, and even the probability of being enrolled in an introductory sociology course. However, we'll also see that economic status varies not only among groups within a particular society, but also among the societies that make up the world community. Indeed, we will find that what is considered a below-average standard of living in the United States may be viewed as quite affluent in many developing countries.

Social Inequality

Our discussion of social locations raises the issue of *inequality.* **Inequality** refers to differences in the allocation of rewards, opportunities, and other social resources. We have already said that categories confer statuses, and some statuses are considered by the members of the society to be better or more desirable than others. Those who hold the most valued or highest positions in the status hierarchy receive or have access to a greater share of the society's rewards, opportunities, and other valued resources. Sociologists are concerned with both the causes and the consequences of inequality.

Although all societies have some system of categorization, the level of inequality that results varies from society to society. For example, in societies with little technology, where people rely primarily on hunting and gathering their food for survival, categorization is limited and tends to be based only on age and sex. Different tasks and expectations are placed on members of the society depending on how old they are and whether they are male or female. Men, for instance, are typically responsible for hunting, while women are usually assigned the job of gathering vegetation. Interestingly, there is little inequality between the sexes because "women's work" in these societies is considered just as important to the survival of the group as "men's work."

In contrast, in our own society, inequality is pervasive. Members of U.S. society are simultaneously categorized into many groups based on race or ethnic background, sex, social class, age, sexual orientation, and ability or disability. Consider, for example, that the income of African Americans is, on average, about 63 percent of that of White Americans; in other words, for every $100 of income enjoyed by a White person, a Black person has only about $63 (U.S. Department of Commerce, Bureau of the Census, 1997). Similarly, women workers in the United States earn on average only 75 percent of what male workers earn (U.S. Department of Commerce, Bureau of the Census, 1997). As these statistics show, in the United States, White people are accorded higher status than people of color, and men are privileged over women. However, it is not sufficient to examine categories separately. Sociologists emphasize how forms of inequality *intersect* and thus have a cumulative impact on the members of various groups. Consider, for instance, the combined effects of race and sex on income. We find that White women and African American men have similar earnings (about 75 percent of White men's earnings), while African American women's income is less than 63 percent of what White men earn (U.S. Department of Labor, 1998b). We see, then, that an individual's race *or* sex may place him or her in a disadvantaged position, but disadvantage is compounded when a person is both female and a member of a devalued racial group. The Intersecting Inequalities box provides another example of how inequalities may intersect to produce particular outcomes.

Cultural Diversity

A society, then, is characterized by differences among its members, and there are significant differences between societies. But difference does not necessarily produce inequality. Difference may be cause for celebration, since variations in skills, talents, approaches to problem solving, and so on may maximize the survival of the group as a whole. Consequently, sociologists want not only to examine inequality, but also to develop an appreciation of diversity.

One additional point about diversity: People typically regard their own values and ways of doing things as "right" or "best" and tend to judge others' values and practices as inferior. Sociologists refer to this as **ethnocentrism.** But sociologists do not judge any belief system or social practice as inherently better, more natural, or more "human" than any others. Rather, they try to see various beliefs and practices through the eyes of those who hold them dear, in other words, from the perspective of those who live them. At the same time, sociologists listen to voices outside the mainstream because it is often the case that those who have been excluded from

INTERSECTING INEQUALITIES

Violent Victimization: Do Age, Race, and Sex Make a Difference?

Why do sociologists examine social locators when they study social interaction? Factors such as age, race, and sex influence people's experiences. Consider a person's chances of becoming the victim of a violent crime. While many of us may worry about this, sociological research shows that the likelihood of violent victimization depends to a large extent on our membership in particular groups.

Young Americans are more likely than older Americans to be victimized by a violent crime. Those twelve to nineteen years old, in fact, have the highest rate of violent victimization: 107.4 violent victimizations for every 1,000 people in this age group. In contrast, se-

nior citizens, aged sixty-five and older, have the lowest rate of violent victimization: 5.9 violent victimizations per 1,000 people in this age group. And those fifty to sixty-four years old have the second lowest rate of violent victimization: 14.0 per 1,000 people in this age group.

The differences in violent victimization rates by race are also dramatic. African Americans are significantly more likely than White Americans to be violent crime victims in any given year. For every 1,000 African Americans in the population, 55.4 are victimized by a violent crime. For every 1,000 White Americans in the population, the rate of violent victimization is 43.1.

Finally, men are more likely than women to be victimized by a violent crime: For every 1,000 men in the population, 53.1 are violent crime victims, whereas just 36.5 of every 1,000 women in the population are violent crime victims.

However, if we look at all three social locators simultaneously, as we do in Table 1.1, we find that it is young African American men—African American men between the ages of twelve and twenty-four—who have the highest rates of violent victimization. Thus, we can see that taking social locators into account is important if we wish to get a more complete and accurate picture of social life.

particular experiences and opportunities—those who have been rendered "outsiders" within the culture—have the ability to see and understand a situation or problem with the greatest clarity. As one social scientist recently put it, "there is a link between where one stands in a society and what one perceives" (Frankenberg, 1993, p. 8).

It is not easy to adopt this sociological stance of openness to difference, but it is necessary if we are to develop an understanding of the rich diversity that characterizes human life on earth.

The Interdependence of the World Community

A student at a university in Canada writing a term paper on attitudes in Western European countries toward the death penalty sends a request for information on this topic via an international electronic mail forum; within minutes, students and researchers online throughout the world begin to respond. In Beijing, a Chinese father wipes tomato sauce from his young child's Lion King t-shirt as the family celebrates a special occasion at an upscale local restaurant, Pizza Hut. Villagers in Nakuru, Kenya, gather around a small portable television set powered by a battery-operated generator to watch a local resident compete in the summer Olympic games. In Honduras, representatives of a U.S. shoe manufacturer sign an agreement

with Honduran government officials, allowing the company to relocate a plant from Rhode Island to an area just outside the Honduran capital, Tegucigalpa. Six months later, several hundred Honduran citizens will be manufacturing shoes for sale in the United States and Europe at a wage rate of about $11 per week, while in Rhode Island, several hundred women and men who used to manufacture the same shoes for an average wage of $7 per hour will be out of work.

The world as we know it is composed of more than 200 political states and their territories. As the preceding examples make clear, the 5.8 billion people who inhabit the earth can hardly be thought of as isolated from one another. Through technology such as computers and the media, and through business and trade, our daily lives and the lives of people on the other side of the world are inextricably linked, although we and they typically are unaware of most of the linkages. Sociologists, on the other hand, are fundamentally concerned with our global connections.

At the basic level, the members of the world community are *environmentally interdependent*. We share the same biosphere—that zone of the earth's surface and atmosphere that sustains life. But human activity that produces nonbiodegradable waste and industrial pollution, and that leads to overharvesting forests and overhunting animals, is causing worldwide ecological changes that threaten the future sustainability of our planet. For ex-

TABLE 1.1 Violent Victimization Rates for Persons Age Twelve and Older, by Race and Sex

Sex, Race, and Age of Victim	Total Population	Rate of Violent Victimization (per 1,000 persons)
White Males		
12–15 years	6,257,840	135.6
16–19 years	5,873,320	146.0
20–24 years	7,527,480	123.3
25–34 years	17,326,480	65.0
35–49 years	24,922,090	44.5
50–64 years	14,319,810	15.2
65 years & older	11,780,640	5.7
White Females		
12–15 years	5,948,580	88.2
16–19 years	5,576,340	102.4
20–24 years	7,375,450	78.1
25–34 years	17,135,720	57.9
35–49 years	24,903,460	33.6
50–64 years	15,282,970	14.3
65 years & older	16,311,340	2.8
Black Males		
12–15 years	1,234,310	141.6
16–19 years	1,138,680	124.8
20–24 years	1,111,420	71.1
25–34 years	2,539,490	66.9
35–49 years	3,199,810	49.9
50–64 years	1,499,080	28.5
65 years & older	973,190	33.7
Black Females		
12–15 years	1,234,480	129.8
16–19 years	1,100,140	109.3
20–24 years	1,419,040	97.5
25–34 years	2,983,380	59.0
35–49 years	3,750,950	40.5
50–64 years	1,855,770	13.5
65 years & older	1,590,380	6.7

Source: U.S. Department of Justice, 1997b, p. 15.

ample, industrial chemicals released into the atmosphere during the manufacturing process not only cause smog and air pollution in the countries where they originate, but they also destroy the earth's protective ozone layer. In the Antarctic, where no manufacturing of any kind has ever taken place, scientists have found a "hole" in the ozone layer so severe that during the springtime, almost 50 percent of the ozone there is missing. Moreover, that hole extends to the southernmost region of South America, where elevated rates of skin cancer and eye diseases are being reported (Nash, 1991).

In addition to being environmentally connected, we are also connected globally through politics and economics. For instance, when the Soviet Union was dissolved and the Berlin Wall came down, the Cold War ended and relations between the West and the new Commonwealth of Independent States were fundamentally changed. The threat of nuclear warfare was replaced with optimistic prospects for world peace. However, internal ethnic rivalries that had been suppressed under communism resurfaced and bloody civil wars erupted in the countries that once made up the former Yugoslavia and elsewhere in Eastern Europe. At the same time, the economic instability of the new Russian federation transformed these countries from givers of international monetary aid to receivers of that aid, as they turned to Western nations for billions of dollars to overhaul their economies. Western countries, including the United States, must therefore allocate more money for international economic aid and distribute less to their long-standing aid recipients and allies in Asia, Africa, and Latin America—a difficult decision with far-reaching implications for our own economy as well.

On a smaller scale, our example of the shoe manufacturing enterprise in Honduras illustrates how international economic decisions affect the everyday lives of people, in this case, as jobs are created and eliminated. In fact, most of us make global economic connections daily when, for instance, we turn on our televisions (64 percent of which are imported from Mexico) or play a videocassette on the VCR (59 percent of which are imported from Malaysia) ("First-Half Imports Up for All Major Products," 1995). And chances are that most of your clothing bears labels that say, "Made in Korea," or "Made in Indonesia." About 55 percent of clothing currently sold in the United States is made in Asia, mostly in developing countries where wages are a fraction of those in the United States and there is little government regulation of industry.

The rapid proliferation of information technology has also forged links between societies worldwide. Television, in particular, plays a major role. Peace negotiations in Northen Ireland, the bombing of a suspected biological weapons facility in Iraq, a debate in the U.S. House of Representatives over whether to impeach the President—all can be seen as they happen, or shortly thereafter, thanks to satellite transmissions. In fact, television is such a popular medium that in many countries there are more people that have televisions in their homes than there are people that have telephones (U.S. Department of Commerce, U.S. Bureau of the Census, 1997). And although the United States imports most of the television sets sold here, television conveys one of our primary exports: U.S. popular culture. United States television programs, along with films and music produced here, enjoy tremendous popularity abroad. In 1997, for instance, the top grossing film in most countries throughout the world, including Argentina, Chile, France, Germany, Japan, and Sweden, which themselves produce a large number of films each year, was *Titanic*. Also popular were

GLOBAL INSIGHTS   Sociology in the People's Republic of China

In 1979, sociology became an officially recognized academic discipline in the People's Republic of China. The significance of this recognition ended more than a quarter century during which sociology could not be taught in China and sociological research could not be carried out. During the 1980s and 1990s, sociology grew quickly in China. Nevertheless, while sociological research is considered a valuable resource by many Chinese officials, it is still kept under a watchful eye because of the sensitive nature of the topics sociologists study. For example, studies of crime, discrimination against women, and government corruption can be sources of embarrassment to the government and could potentially fuel social unrest. Sociologists have often openly criticized the government and its policies, and sociologists were prominent members of the prodemocracy democracy movement that met violent repression on Tiananmen Square in 1989.

Chinese society is changing rapidly, largely due to globalization and the growth of the country's economy. Officials are increasingly turning to sociologists for advice on the best ways to handle the social consequences of this change. Today, many Chinese universities have departments of sociology, and a growing number of Chinese students are majoring in sociology, both at home and abroad. There is now a professional association for Chinese sociologists and other social scientists—the Chinese Academy of Social Sciences—and the Institute of Sociology conducts some of the most significant sociological research in China. Still, the discipline faces a number of problems, not the least of which is continued government oversight and intervention in sociological research and publications. Chinese sociologists do not enjoy the academic freedom that sociologists in the United States and other democratic societies enjoy. A number of sociological and social science periodicals, for instance, have recently come under intense pressure from the government because of their open criticism of various official policies. One journal, called *Way*, was warned in 1999 to publish only articles on scientific subjects or else it would be closed. Another periodical, *Cultural Times*, published by the Guangzhou Academy of Social Sciences, was put out of business in December 1998, because of government concerns about its "controversial" articles (Eckholm, 1999). Clearly, one of the greatest challenges for Chinese sociologists is devising a way to present a careful, empirically grounded evaluation of social policy and social change in their country while staving off government efforts to stifle social criticism.

Lost World and *Men in Black* (Yahoo! Box Office Reports, 1999). Unfortunately, the entertainment media frequently present distorted images of life in the United States, emphasizing extremes of affluence, sexual appetites, and violence.

United States popular culture may influence the clothing styles, musical tastes, and food preferences of people in other countries, but it is important to keep in mind that much of what we consider "U.S. culture" is actually a blend of cultures brought here throughout the years by immigrants. At the same time, we in the United States today enjoy the popular cultures of other countries: We listen to reggae music; decorate our homes with art and artifacts from Africa, Asia, and even Aboriginal Australia; and eat couscous one night and burritos the next.

In short, it is inaccurate at best, dangerous at worst, for us to consider ourselves citizens of a single country. Rather, we are members of a world community. Throughout this book, we will discuss the causes and consequences, as well as the advantages and disadvantages, of our global connections. We will ask, "Who benefits, who loses, and why?" In order to think sociologically, we must think globally (see the Global Insights box).

Stability and Change

Considering the diversity of our society and the even greater diversity of the world community, the question arises, "How is social order possible?" After all, if people are so different from one another and they belong to a number of different groups, why doesn't daily life just break apart with everyone doing her or his own thing?

As we will see shortly, sociologists have always tried to understand what factors create social stability. Indeed, a major reason sociology developed as a discipline was that nineteenth-century social thinkers wanted to make the Western European social world in which they lived— a world characterized by political and economic unrest— more orderly or stable. Not surprisingly, then, we will address the issue of social order throughout this book.

But if stability is one feature of social life, change is another. Change may be slow, taking place over many, sometimes hundreds, of years, or it may be rapid, producing dramatic alterations in the social landscape in a relatively short period of time. In any case, sociologists examine not only the stable operation of the social system, but also how social systems change over time and the factors that precipitate and shape change. Moreover, in studying social life, sociologists themselves often try to help bring about change—for example, by influencing public policy with their research. In the 1950s, the U.S. Supreme Court drew on sociological research documenting the detrimental impact of racial segregation in schools and reached a landmark decision in *Brown* v. *The Board of Education of Topeka* (1954), which struck down the

principle of "separate, but equal." During the 1960s, sociologist Lloyd Ohlin, who had spent years studying youth crime in Chicago, became a consultant to the White House and helped develop federal programs to prevent juvenile delinquency; one of the better-known programs that reflects Ohlin's influence is Head Start. Similarly, in the 1990s, sociological research on violence in intimate relationships was instrumental in getting the Violence Against Women Act (1994) passed.

Thus, sociologists do not just study things as they are, but also things as they were and what they may become. The study of sociology, in turn, not only gives us an understanding of how particular social arrangements are created and maintained, but it also *empowers us to* change those aspects of social life that are destructive. To paraphrase one early social theorist, Karl Marx, it is not enough to simply think about the world in different ways, we must also try to change it.

REFLECTING ON

Sociology

1. If your major is not sociology, how does it differ from sociology? If you were confronted with a case like Virgil's, how might you approach it based on the training you've had so far in your major?
2. Think of the various social locating factors that identify you, both as an individual and as a member of particular groups. What does this information tell others about you? How does it influence your personal life?
3. Can you think of any specific instances today in which sociologists might contribute to bringing about social change?

THE ORIGINS AND DEVELOPMENT OF SOCIOLOGY

Sociology itself is a social product. It grew out of major social, political, and economic changes that took place in Europe during the late eighteenth and early nineteenth centuries. These changes, along with major discoveries in the physical and natural sciences, led to a new way of thinking about the social world that came to be called *sociology*.

The Emergence of Sociology in Nineteenth-Century Europe

Sociology as a discipline emerged largely in response to the social problems that plagued Europe in the late 1700s and early 1800s. The French Revolution of 1789 had promised to end the reign of the aristocracy and the oppression of the peasantry, but instead of peace and a new government based on liberty and equality, France experienced more than fifty years of political revolts and popular uprisings.

It was also during the late 1700s and early 1800s that the Industrial Revolution began, drastically changing the way goods were produced and, consequently, the organization of social life. Cities developed around factories as peasants migrated from their villages in search of work and a higher standard of living. But even though the factories produced more goods than craftspeople had working alone, factory workers found that their incomes, along with their standard of living, declined instead of rose. Some simply gave up and returned to peasant farming in rural villages. For many, though, this was not an option. Most former craftspeople, for instance, could not compete with the lower cost and higher efficiency of factory production. To simply survive, then, everyone in the family who was able, including children, became wage earners. For the meager salaries they received, they labored long hours in unsafe and unsanitary conditions. But not everyone suffered; the industrialists and entrepreneurs, as well as bankers who helped finance production and invest profits, amassed great fortunes. Coser (1977, p. 31) provides a less than flattering description of the "new rich": "Their elemental greed was hardly tamed by the *noblesse oblige* that characterized older ruling classes. . . . What they lacked in refinement and status, they more than made up for by their ferocious energy and self-confidence."

Social philosophers—the social thinkers of the time—were openly concerned about these conditions. To them, social life had become disorganized and unpredictable. Nevertheless, advances in the natural sciences gave them reason to hope. Natural scientists were discovering an underlying order in the workings of the physical world. Just as Isaac Newton had demonstrated unvarying relationships of cause and effect in physics (what goes up must come down), perhaps a similar order could be discovered in the social world by using the methods of natural science. Once the operation of society was understood, stability could be restored and social life could be efficiently managed (Pickering, 1993).

Auguste Comte.   **Auguste Comte** (1798–1857) was one such social thinker. Comte is known as the founder of sociology because he outlined what a "science of society" should be and he called this new discipline *sociology.*

For Comte, it was most important that sociology be *scientific*; that is, sociologists must use the scientific method developed by the physical and natural scientists to study social life. Looking back on how knowledge about society had developed historically, Comte saw three distinct periods or stages. During the first stage—what he called the *theological stage,* which lasted through the

Middle Ages—people understood society in terms of their religious beliefs; social life and events were seen as manifestations of Divine will. The Renaissance marked the start of the second stage—the *metaphysical stage*—when people began to think of social life as an expression of human nature. The discoveries of seventeenth- and eighteenth-century scientists such as Newton and Galileo gave rise to the third stage—the *scientific stage*—in which science replaced religion and philosophy as the means of understanding society. Knowledge developed during the scientific stage is *positive knowledge* and Comte therefore espoused a position he termed **positivism**: that knowledge must be derived from observable facts, rather than from superstition, fantasy, or some other nonempirical (nonverifiable) source.

According to Comte, the various disciplines passed through these three stages at different rates, and sociology was the last to reach the scientific stage. As such, it represented the apex of the sciences, dealing with the most complex subject matter: human beings and their social interactions. Despite the complexity of the social world, however, it, like the natural world, was governed by a set of invariable laws. By applying the scientific method to the study of society, sociologists would not only discover these laws, but could use them to realign the everyday operation of society (Pickering, 1993). Thus, sociologists, equipped with their scientific knowledge, were among the best suited for positions of leadership. Indeed, Comte eventually claimed that sociologists comprised a "priesthood of humanity," able not only to explain social life, but also to guide society progressively toward improvement.

Many of Comte's contemporaries and near-contemporaries disagreed with his approach to the study of society. For example, Harriet Martineau (1802–1876) was a British sociologist who translated Comte's work from French into English in 1853. Her translation was faithful to Comte's original writing, but Martineau sharply disagreed with many of Comte's ideas, including his vision of sociologists as a "priesthood" that would save humanity (Hoecker-Drysdale, 1992; McDonald, 1993). Martineau made many important contributions of her own to sociology, including social analyses of such wide-ranging topics as religion, the social customs of England and the United States, industrialization, slavery, immigration, and the family (David, 1987). However, her work was ignored until relatively recently because she was a woman.

Certainly sociologists today don't think of themselves as saviors of the world the way Comte did, but the discipline has retained some important aspects of his original vision. Our goal is no longer to discover the "laws" that govern social life, but sociological research continues to be guided by scientific methods and principles. In addition, analyzing social problems in order to reduce or eliminate them remains a significant dimension of the

August Comte

Emile Durkheim

Karl Marx

Max Weber

Auguste Comte first outlined a "science of sociology" based on observable facts. Emile Durkheim identified social groups as the unit of analysis and the incidence and frequency of social behaviors as the unit of measurement. Sociology was influenced by the political philosophies of nineteenth-century Europe and by the economic transformations of the Industrial Revolution, most profoundly by Karl Marx's analysis of communism and Max Weber's analysis of capitalism. To what contemporary sociological perspectives did Marx and Weber contribute? What are the principal characteristics of those perspectives?

[handwritten note: Suicide - individual choice. Emile - 3 types. Social forces caused people to commit suicide.]

sociological enterprise (Rose, 1971; Turner & Turner, 1990).

Still, not all sociologists approach the scientific study of society in the same way. As the title of this chapter implies, there are different sociological perspectives. However, all of the perspectives are *sociological* in that they focus on social factors rather than individual ones and attempt to link the individual with the larger social structure. This can best be seen by examining the work of some of the early social theorists who came after Comte.

Emile Durkheim. Emile Durkheim (1858–1917) was, like his predecessor Comte, fundamentally concerned with the political instability, violence, and social upheaval that characterized the French society in which he lived. The major question on which he focused was: What makes social order possible? For Durkheim, the answer was not rational self-interest (a reasoned attempt to better one's personal circumstances), as philosophers such as Hobbes and Rousseau had suggested. Rather, the answer was an underlying set of moral rules that give the members of a society the shared feeling that they belong to something larger than themselves as individuals.

Durkheim referred to this set of moral rules as the **collective conscience.**

In a preindustrial society, the collective conscience is strong because all the society's members are pretty much alike, performing a small number of tasks that keep the society functioning. However, the collective conscience does not disappear with industrialization. In fact, according to Durkheim, it is through what he termed the **division of labor**—the greater specialization in tasks that accompanies industrialization—that the collective conscience is preserved. More specifically, as people perform more differentiated tasks, they simultaneously become more dependent on one another to meet the everyday needs that in the past they could generally provide for themselves. Thus, social interaction increases, and interaction creates and cements social bonds.

The collective conscience and the division of labor, then, are group phenomena that integrate individuals into the society. Interestingly, the best time to observe social integration is when rules or expectations are violated. When a crime is committed, for example, many members of the community express outrage even though they personally were not victimized. According to Durkheim, this is because the perpetrator harmed not only the victim, but also the community as a whole by violating its agreed-upon rules of behavior. In fact, Durkheim argued that crime is therefore functional in society because it highlights the society's moral order and brings law-abiding members together, thus ritually reinforcing their social bond.

Of course, Durkheim was not advocating that crime is good for society. Rather, he meant that some deviation from the rules is an inevitable part of social life and that, while certainly undesirable, it nevertheless serves a positive function by reaffirming social solidarity among a society's members. When this solidarity is weak and social integration is lacking, social order becomes fragile and eventually unstable.

Although Auguste Comte is considered the founder of sociology, Emile Durkheim must be credited with establishing sociology as an independent scientific discipline. Why? Durkheim explicitly distinguished sociology from other fields of study. He made clear that the subject matter of sociology is not the individual, but rather the social group. The focus of sociology, Durkheim said, is on social facts. **Social facts** are phenomena that have three distinct features: they endure over time, beyond the life span of particular individuals; they are caused by factors external to individuals; and they exercise a "coercive power" over individuals by constraining and influencing thought and behavior (Durkheim, 1966/1897).

Each of us experiences the influence of social facts repeatedly in our daily lives. Consider college, for instance. Each term, students enroll in a variety of courses at your school and others throughout the country, but despite the variation in interests, curriculum, and requirements, these students behave in remarkably similar ways. They go to class at a specified time, sit (often silently) and take notes while the instructor lectures, leave after a certain time has elapsed, and stop attending when the term ends. Each year, thousands of students graduate and are replaced by other students, but the courses—and the patterns of behavior—continue unchanged for the most part, because they are part of a larger social structure, the education system, which has its own rules and organization.

Perhaps the best illustration of the power of social facts over the individual is Durkheim's own study of suicide (Durkheim, 1966/1897). There is hardly a behavior more individual, solitary, or personal than suicide. Not surprisingly, then, when we think of the reasons why someone may commit suicide, we tend to think on an individual level—for example, the loss of a job, the breakup of a relationship, or some personal failure. Durkheim, however, showed that apart from any individual reason for suicide, there are social causes at work, and these can be uncovered not by studying a particular case of suicide, but rather by analyzing suicide *rates*.

Rates of behavior tell us the incidence of a particular phenomenon among a specific group of people. So, for example, in his study of suicide, Durkheim looked at government statistics that showed variations in the rate of suicide by religious affiliation. He found that Protestants had higher suicide rates than Catholics, and Catholics had higher suicide rates than Jews. Thus, although a Protestant and a Jew might have the same individual experience, say of losing their jobs, the Protestant would be more likely than the Jew to commit suicide as a result. Durkheim looked to the characteristics of these religious groups to explain the difference. He found that the rules and belief systems of both Catholicism and Judaism were stronger and more rigid than those of most Protestant denominations. This, he reasoned, produced closer social bonds among Catholics and Jews and gave them a greater sense of belonging or integration into the religious community. Stronger social ties lowered their probability of considering suicide during times of personal crisis. Consequently, an act as individual as self-destruction is influenced by a social factor, social integration.

Although some sociologists have since challenged Durkheim's conclusion that certain religions better protect their members against suicide than other religions (see, for example, van Poppel & Day, 1996), the underlying theme of his research—the relationship of the individual to society—is still a focal point of the discipline. Indeed, Durkheim's influence on sociology is nothing less than profound. We will discuss many of his ideas throughout this text. Later in this chapter, we will find his ideas mirrored in one of the contemporary sociological perspectives that we will discuss, structural functionalism. In Chapter 2, "Sociological Inquiry," we will see his influence on research methodology, as sociologists continue to analyze rates of behavior to gauge social trends. In Chapter 3, "Societies," we will revisit his concepts of the division of labor and social integration. In Chapter 17, "Religion," we will examine his sociology of religion.

Karl Marx. Karl Marx (1818–1883) spent the early part of his life in Germany and moved to France when he was in his twenties. He spent most of his adult life, however, in Great Britain. Marx shared Durkheim's interest in the massive social, economic, and political changes that were taking place during the mid-1800s, but he was far less optimistic than Durkheim, especially about the impact of the Industrial Revolution. While Durkheim saw the industrial division of labor leading to social integration, Marx saw it leading to inevitable inequality and conflict.

According to Marx, the rapid advances in technology that made the production of material goods so much more efficient and therefore more profitable than under the old guild system divided the population into two primary groups. One group, which he called the **bourgeoisie,** was composed of the wealthy factory owners, bankers, and other property holders. The second group consisted mostly of the workers, whom he called the **proletariat.**

The proletariat owned nothing but their labor power, which they were forced to sell to the bourgeoisie in exchange for wages in order to survive.

The difference in the living conditions between these two economic groups, or **social classes,** was conspicuous. While the bourgeoisie, relatively few in number, enjoyed tremendous wealth and the luxurious lifestyle this wealth could buy, the proletariat, the vast majority of the population, lived in squalor. For Marx, then, social relations were not characterized by mutual, harmonious interdependence and moral integration, but rather by social conflict and antagonism between the haves of society and the have-nots. This conflict centered chiefly on the unequal distribution of resources and rewards in this type of society, that is, a *capitalist* society, which is built on the principles of free enterprise and private ownership of property.

From Marx's perspective, it was the inherent inequality of the capitalist system that produced most of the other serious problems that plagued nineteenth-century society: rising rates of crime, alcoholism, and the breakup of families. The solution, as he saw it, was not to integrate people more fully into this social system, but rather to change the system altogether. Indeed, Marx was a social activist who gave numerous speeches and wrote many articles and books advocating revolutionary social change. Marx urged the proletariat to overthrow the bourgeoisie and adopt a new social system, *communism,* in which resources would be distributed equitably, and industry and science would benefit all instead of only the wealthy few.

In some places in the world, including the former Soviet Union, China, and Cuba, Marx's work did inspire radical social action and change. These societies, however, were not capitalistic, as Marx would have predicted, and critics have been quick to point to this as well as other "errors" in Marx's theory. Nevertheless, Marx's ideas have made an indelible mark on sociology. His emphasis on inequality, conflict, and change, as well as his call to activism, are echoed in a contemporary sociological perspective known as *conflict theory,* which we will discuss shortly. His theory of revolutionary social change will come up again in Chapter 3, "Societies." We will also discuss his analysis of social class relations (Chapter 8, "Stratification and Social Class in the United States") and his prediction of the global reach of capitalism (Chapter 9, "Global Stratification" and Chapter 13, "The Economy and Work").

Max Weber.   It has been said that the German sociologist **Max Weber** (1864–1920) was engaged in a "debate with Marx's ghost" (Zeitlin, 1968). This is because, like Marx, Weber (pronounced "*vay*-ber") devoted much of his energy to analyzing capitalism.

Weber shared Marx's pessimism about the effects of modern industrial capitalism as well as Marx's concern about the division of society into social classes. Nevertheless, he approached capitalism in a significantly different way. For example, while Marx believed economic factors were the primary driving force of society, Weber felt ideas and values were equally important. Indeed, as we will discuss in Chapter 17, "Religion," Weber argued that capitalism itself developed in part from the Protestant beliefs espoused by John Calvin and his followers in the sixteenth century. The Calvinists elevated hard work, success in business, and frugal living to the level of religious expression. Also, as we will find in Chapter 8, "Stratification and Social Class in the United States," Weber developed a complex definition of social class that went beyond Marx's focus on the role of individuals in the production process.

Weber did not hold out much hope for Marx's popular revolution and the overthrow of capitalism. In fact, he saw an increasing emphasis on rationality and efficiency in modern social life, manifested in the growth of bureaucracy. Weber used the term **bureaucracy** to describe a form of social organization based on written rules and procedures and designed to coordinate the actions of large numbers of people. Though efficient, bureaucracies are highly impersonal and rigid, and Weber therefore saw the growth of bureaucracies leading inescapably to a dehumanization of social life. As Coser (1977, p. 232) puts it, Weber "thought it more probable that the future would be an 'iron cage' rather than a Garden of Eden." We will revisit Weber's analysis of bureaucracy in Chapter 6, "Social Interaction in Groups and Organizations."

Weber was not only a social theorist, but also a research methodologist. Among his most important contributions to sociological research methods was his concept of *verstehen* (pronounced fersh-tay-en). *Verstehen* is a German word that means "understanding" or "insight." According to Weber, sociologists can understand social reality only by seeing the world empathically through the experiences of people who live in it. In other words, sociologists must put themselves in other people's shoes if they truly wish to grasp the meanings that interactions and events have for the people who live them.

With his emphasis on *verstehen*, Weber took a radically different approach from most social scientists of his day. Recall, for example, that Comte and others maintained that the social world could be understood in much the same way as the natural world—using objective scientific methods of observation. In contrast, Weber recognized that a subjective dimension sets the social world apart from the natural world. Sociologists must therefore try to capture the subjective meanings that people give to social life because this is the way that social reality is actually created.

In urging sociologists to use empathic understanding in studying social life, Weber was not abandoning the principle of objectivity in scientific research. On the contrary,

Weber wrote extensively about the importance of keeping personal bias out of research. But he recognized that in sociology, as well as in social life, there is a subjective as well as an objective dimension.

This *dualistic nature* of sociology comes up again in Chapter 2, "Sociological Inquiry." We will also see shortly how contemporary sociologists who call themselves *symbolic interactionists* have been influenced by Weber's concept of *verstehen*.

Sociology in the United States

Like their European colleagues, American sociologists at the turn of the century saw widespread problems developing in a rapidly urbanizing society. Thousands of women and men flocked to the new industrial cities of the young nation in search of work. Among these people were poor Southern Blacks and European immigrants whose skin color, language, and "foreign ways" immediately set them outside the "American mainstream." Those who got jobs, despite the widespread prejudice and discrimination against them, worked long hours under hazardous conditions for pennies a day. After work, they went home to equally unsafe, overcrowded tenement buildings.

The individuals who turned to sociology as a career at this time were mostly men who had been born and raised on farms or in small rural communities. Some were children of Protestant ministers, a few were ministers themselves, and almost all were members of the various social reform organizations that arose in late nineteenth- and early twentieth-century America. Indeed, most who were drawn to careers in sociology were political liberals who sought to bring about social reform (Lindner, 1996; Turner & Turner, 1990). Their focus came to rest on the social problems that beset city dwellers: crime, juvenile delinquency, alcoholism, poverty, mental illness, and homelessness.

The Chicago School.   The first academic department of sociology in the United States was established at the University of Chicago in 1892. For sociologists of the **Chicago School**, as it came to be called, the focal point of sociological research was social problems. The Chicago sociologists—Robert Park (1864–1944), Ernest Burgess (1886–1966), W. I. Thomas (1863–1947), and Florian Znaniecki (1882–1958), to name a few of the best known—believed social problems stemmed from the disorganized nature of life in big cities. They and their colleagues therefore conducted studies of all aspects of urban life, from juvenile gangs, immigrant experiences and adjustment, and race relations, to social interaction in public dance halls. Much of this research, which we call *ethnography* today, involved extensive observation and interviews, as the sociologists immersed themselves in the everyday experiences of the people they were studying.

Despite the liberal political leanings of the Chicago School sociologists, they were sometimes criticized for trying to impose their personal standards of rightness and morality on people who were different from themselves (Bramson 1961). Regardless of this criticism, however, the Chicago School introduced a distinctively sociological perspective to the study of social problems. Before this time in the United States, the causes of social problems were thought to lie within individuals—for example, in an immoral character or even in a "defective physical or mental constitution." Many, therefore, advocated "treatment" programs of various sorts—some humane, some not so humane—aimed at "curing," or at least containing, the "defective, dependent, and delinquent classes."

In contrast, the Chicago sociologists emphasized the *external* sources of social problems—that is, the social disorganization of city life—which implied that the solution rested not in the treatment of individuals, but rather in *social change* (see, for example, Lindner, 1996). Thus, the Chicago School made its mark on U.S. sociology and, for the first third of this century, was recognized throughout the country as one of the major centers—if not *the* center—of sociological research. That is not to say, however, that the only important sociological work was being done at Chicago and by White male sociologists.

W. E. B. Du Bois, Ida Wells-Barnett, and Jane Addams. While the University of Chicago is widely known as the locale of the first department of sociology in the United States, few are aware that the second department of sociology in this country was established at Atlanta University by an African American sociologist, W. E. B. Du Bois (1868–1963). After earning his doctorate at Harvard—the first African American to receive the degree from that university—Du Bois embarked on an extraordinarily productive career, establishing a sociology laboratory, organizing and participating in professional conferences, founding two scholarly journals, and publishing numerous books and articles. Throughout all of this, Du Bois remained true to his vision of the discipline: to seek truth through scientific research in order to apply the knowledge gained to the improvement of society. In his own work, he focused on racial inequality and refuted many of the myths about the inherent inferiority of Black people. He helped found the National Association for the Advancement of Colored People (NAACP), but as he aged, he grew increasingly pessimistic about the possibility of resolving the racial problems that plagued this country. Du Bois became increasingly radical in his political position, and finally left the United States in 1961 to live in Ghana as a Marxist advocating revolution. It was there that he died two years later (Lewis, 1993; Marable, 1986).

Harriet Martineau

Ida Wells-Barnett

W. E. B. Du Bois

Jane Addams

Harriet Martineau translated Comte into English and wrote sociological treatises on English and American customs and institutions. In the United States, W. E. B. Du Bois and Ida Wells-Barnett applied sociological analysis to the problems of racial inequality and gender inequality. In Chicago, the work of social reformer Jane Addams also reflected an American emphasis on applied sociology. Until very recently, however, histories did not mention these early contributors to the field of sociology. Why not?

Ida Wells-Barnett (1862–1931), a former slave from Mississippi, was also a founding member of the NAACP, but she is perhaps best known for her research and writing on the practice of lynching. Any Black person who offended a White person in any way could be hunted down by an angry mob of Whites and hanged, usually after being beaten and tortured. Lynchings were common throughout the United States during Wells-Barnett's lifetime, but were especially prevalent in the South. Wells-Barnett won international acclaim not only for her writing on this problem, but also for her public speeches against it. Moreover, Wells-Barnett recognized the intersection of racial and gender inequalities and was active in women's rights campaigns, especially the fight to win women the right to vote (Deegan, 1988; Lerner, 1972).

Jane Addams (1860–1935) was also a tireless social reformer whose activism on behalf of the poor, women, and immigrants won her the Nobel Peace Prize. Nevertheless, her contributions to the Chicago School of sociology were not recognized until recently. Addams is perhaps best known for establishing Hull House, a set-

tlement house in Chicago. Although she was a social worker by training, Addams was also an active member of the American Sociological Society, which is today the American Sociological Association, and her books and articles were widely used by sociologists, especially those of the Chicago School. In fact, according to sociologist Mary Jo Deegan (1988), Addams's book, *Hull-House Maps and Papers,* published in 1895, became the model that the Chicago School sociologists followed for more than forty years.

The Golden Era of Sociology. During the 1940s and 1950s—a period some have referred to as the "Golden Era" of sociology (Rhoades, 1981)—leadership in the discipline came less from Chicago and more from sociology departments on the east coast, particularly Harvard and Columbia. Sociologists such as Talcott Parsons (1902–1979) and Robert Merton (b. 1910) shifted the focus of the discipline from the level of disorganized neighborhoods to the level of the social system as a whole. Also, sociologists were less concerned with social intervention than with sociological theorizing. They developed complex social system models showing how all parts of a society fit together to compose the whole.

Sociologist Seymour Martin Lipset (1994) argues that despite the discipline's focus during this period, sociologists themselves remained politically liberal and were actively involved in social reform movements. One sociologist in particular, C. Wright Mills (1916–1962), labored against the conservative tide in the 1950s to keep a liberal perspective alive in sociology. Mills tried to raise people's awareness of the connections between their personal lives and the social world. By using what he called the *sociological imagination,* Mills believed that ordinary people could see the links between the personal troubles they experienced in their everyday lives and the public issues that plagued their society. Once they did this, they would come to understand that most of their problems were not caused by their own failings or limitations, but rather by broader social forces beyond their control as individuals. In other words, Mills said, the sociological imagination helps us to grasp the relationship between history and biography (Mills, 1959).

C. Wright Mills was only forty-six years old when he died in 1962. Had he lived, he probably would have relished what happened to sociology in the 1960s. Antiwar demonstrations, the civil rights and women's movements, Watergate, and the discovery of large pockets of poverty in the United States led some sociologists to see their field as being too conservative. They asked their colleagues, "Whose side are we on?" and called for more radical social activism (Becker, 1967). Bitter disagreements and ideological divisions erupted, which may have hurt sociology's prestige and credibility as a scientific discipline (Lipset, 1994). Nevertheless, disagreement led to the development of new sociological perspectives, which, as we will see shortly, included the voices of previously marginalized groups.

R E F L E C T I N G   O N

The Origins and Development of Sociology

1. How is sociology a social product?
2. Although similarities were drawn between Europe and the United States, what do you think are the most important differences between early European and American sociology?
3. If you had to pick a "sociology hero or heroine" from among those we have discussed so far, who would it be? Why?
4. If you think about the sociology department at your college or university, would you say that the participation of women and racial and ethnic minorities in sociology is different today than it was earlier in this century? In what ways? Have the changes been for better or for worse?

CONTEMPORARY SOCIOLOGICAL PERSPECTIVES

A **theory** is a set of interrelated statements that explain how two or more phenomena are related to one another. American sociology today is composed of several different theoretical perspectives, each of which has been influenced by the European founding theorists as well as by pioneering U.S. sociologists, and by various events in this country and abroad during the twentieth century. In this part of the chapter, we will discuss four contemporary sociological theories: structural functionalism, conflict theory, symbolic interactionism, and feminist theory. Each offers a lens through which to view the social world; however, just as changing the lenses on a camera alters the image that appears in a photograph, so do each of these theories provide differing insights into social life.

Structural Functionalism

If any one sociologist may be credited with the development of a particular theoretical perspective, it is Harvard sociologist Talcott Parsons. Parsons was the chief architect of the contemporary sociological theory known as **structural functionalism.** He was joined in this work by Robert Merton, one of his students who went on to be a prominent sociologist in his own right. Both theorists, as we will see, were strongly influenced by Emile Durkheim's ideas, especially Durkheim's emphasis on social order and social integration.

Parsons began with the assumption that a society is made up of interrelated parts. Essentially, these parts are social institutions or *structures.* They include the economy, government, family, education, religion, and the health care system. Each institution has a *function* or role to play in keeping society running smoothly. For example, each institution in its own way promotes cooperation among the members of society and helps preserve social order. Parsons saw these, in fact, as two of the most important functions of any society's major social institutions or structures.

Merton elaborated on this point by distinguishing between two types of functions: manifest functions and latent functions. **Manifest functions** are observable consequences or outcomes that are intended; that is, they are supposed to happen. **Latent functions** are observable consequences or outcomes that are unintended or unexpected. For example, parents send their children to kindergarten to learn some basic academic skills, such as the ABCs, and to acquire social skills such as learning to share with others; these are manifest functions of kindergarten. But in interacting with one another in kindergarten, many children also learn behaviors that their parents and teachers consider undesirable—calling each other names, for instance,

How might a structural functionalist describe what is happening in this picture? What concepts and questions would be most relevant? For instance, how does the scene depict normative consensus? In contrast, how might a conflict theorist describe what is happening in relation to the larger social context? For instance, what competing interests and social inequalities might be involved? How would a symbolic interactionist go about studying the situation?

or refusing to touch certain people or things because they have "cooties." *Peer socialization* or social learning from children their own age, whether positive or negative, is a latent function of kindergarten.

Usually, the institutions of a society function together to meet the society's basic needs, which results in social order or, as functionalists would say, a state of *equilibrium* or balance. In addition, the members of the society share a set of values, customs, and expectations for appropriate behavior that functionalists call the **normative consensus**. However, Merton recognized that at times various institutions and values of the social system may not function well for all the society's members, so he stressed the need to study dysfunctions as well as functions. **Dysfunctions** are any consequences or outcomes produced by a part of the social system that lower social integration. For example, in the United States we value family privacy, but the premium we place on privacy hides the abuse women and children often suffer in the home and leaves batterers unaccountable for their crimes.

Structural functionalists emphasize the orderly workings of a society and see the sociologist's job as studying specifically how particular structures contribute to order and stability—a task not without merit. However, it is their very emphasis on order and consensus that draws criticism. Critics point out that our society and many others are divided along lines of social class, race and ethnicity, sex, age, and sexual orientation. Rather than

producing equilibrium and agreed-upon values, these divisions generate considerable tension at best and widespread inequality, conflict, social unrest, and even violence at worst. By focusing on order and consensus, functionalists help to preserve the status quo instead of promoting social change, and overlook or downplay the many sources of strain and divisiveness in a society.

Conflict Theory

Structural functionalism enjoyed tremendous popularity from the 1940s to the early 1960s, when the social climate of the United States was decidedly conservative. However, as noted earlier, sociology was not untouched by the social unrest that swept the country during the 1960s. Certainly it appeared then that society was characterized more by conflict than by order, and there seemed to be little agreement among various segments of the population regarding values. In one study, for instance, people were asked whom they consider "deviant." The researcher received more than 250 different answers, including some we would expect, such as criminals, alcoholics, and drug addicts, but others that should surprise us: women, young people, Democrats, and men with beards (Simmons, 1969).

In the midst of antiwar protests, public demonstrations demanding equal rights for women and Black Americans, and a widespread questioning of what constituted core American values, many sociologists turned to the study of social conflict and inequality. The sociological perspective known as **conflict theory** developed from their work. Conflict theorists owe much to the writings of the classical social theorists Karl Marx and Max Weber, especially their analyses of social class. Conflict theory's emphasis on studying and solving social problems also bears the influence of the Chicago School. And although he wrote before the theory became popular, C. Wright Mills is often identified as a founding conflict theorist, largely because of his focus on the struggles between the powerful and the powerless. Mills (1956) argued that the political influence wielded by top corporate and military leaders—the power elite, as he called them—was undermining democracy because it drowned out the voices of the rest of the population, denying them any say in decision making. Although his research to back up his claims was later criticized for its lack of precision, his analysis of class conflict provided a strong foundation for conflict theorists to build on (Coser, 1977).

Conflict theorists begin with the observation that societies are characterized by inequality. That is, societies are arranged in such a way that resources and rewards are unevenly distributed among the population. This inequality gives rise to conflict. Conflict from this perspective is not necessarily bad for society since it is a source of social change, but inequality itself has serious consequences in the lives of individuals. Most people in our society suffer from the effects of inequality, while a few reap tremendous benefits from it. Moreover, those few at the top of the hierarchy can use their greater economic and political resources to preserve their advantageous position. Conflict theorists tell us that in studying society, sociologists must carefully consider the competing interests of the haves and have-nots.

Conflict theorists also argue that sociological research should not be separated from sociological practice. To the conflict theorist, separating sociological research from the ways in which the research can be used is irresponsible. The sociologist's job is not to study society just for the sake of increasing knowledge, but rather to use the knowledge gained to develop strategies for making society better. To the conflict theorist, a "good" society is a society in which resources, rewards, and opportunities are distributed equitably.

The conflict perspective, though popular, is not without its critics. Some sociologists argue that focusing on conflict and change exaggerates their importance in the overall workings of the social system while downplaying the significance of order, stability, and consensus. Others believe that in advocating the rights of the oppressed, conflict theorists lose objectivity and are thus blind to alternative points of view. Interestingly, still others charge that while conflict theory focuses on inequality, it does so in an unequal way, not giving sufficient attention to women and other oppressed groups.

Another criticism, though, has been leveled against *both* conflict theory and structural functionalism: Both perspectives study social relations at the **macro level**. In other words, both conceptualize society in broad, abstract terms and emphasize the role of institutional structures in shaping social life. There is nothing inherently wrong with a macro approach, but critics say it is incomplete. As Max Weber wrote, sociologists should also be concerned with the meanings that people give to events in their lives and how everyday, face-to-face human interaction reinforces social order. In other words, say these critics, the **micro level** of society—individual interactions that make up social life—must be taken into account.

Symbolic Interactionism

While structural functionalism and conflict theory may be characterized as top-down approaches to the study of social life and social organization, **symbolic interactionism** may be viewed as a bottom-up approach. By this we mean that symbolic interactionists start with the assumption that culture, organizations, and social structures are created through daily communications and interactions among people. As people interact with one another over time, *patterns* of interaction emerge, and *rules* governing interaction develop. These ritualized interac-

tions become so much a part of people's lives that they do them almost automatically, like actors playing a well-rehearsed part. It is only when the patterns or rules are broken as in the Doing Sociology box on page 17, that social actors become consciously aware of the rules' existence—and their importance in everyday life.

Social reality, then, is constructed. Thus, what we recognize as social life and, indeed, the social lives we lead, are largely products of a multitude of social interactions that have taken place over time. From a symbolic interactionist perspective, there can be no society without a group of individuals who routinely interact with one another. Moreover, interacting generates symbols that have a shared meaning among the members of the group. A symbol is anything that stands for something else. Symbols can take many forms—for example, words, sounds, gestures, objects—but no symbol has intrinsic meaning. Rather, the meaning of a symbol is assigned to it by the people who decide that the word, sound, gesture, or object has significance. For instance, there is nothing inherent in the color red that tells people they must stop their cars when they see a light that color. Instead, in particular societies, that meaning has been assigned to red lights by people who have decided to use them for this purpose.

It was sociologist George Herbert Mead (1863–1931) who first emphasized the importance of symbolic communication for understanding human interaction. However, it was Herbert Blumer who developed Mead's ideas into the theory of symbolic interactionism. Blumer (1969) pointed out that people's actions derive from their interpretation of what goes on around them, and much of this interpretation is learned through interacting with others. We do not create new meanings every day; this would make daily life burdensome at best, chaotic at worst. Instead, as we live in a society, we learn the meanings that have been assigned to particular symbols. This process of learning, which continues throughout our lives, is also a subject of intense interest to symbolic interactionists, as we will see later in the text.

Symbolic interactionism is a valuable approach because, among other things, it draws our attention to the ways in which routine behaviors and taken-for-granted beliefs help make social order possible. In addition, by emphasizing the role of social learning, it places the possibility of social change firmly in our grasp. That is, if a specific harmful behavior or belief has been learned, it can be unlearned; other behaviors and beliefs may be taught in its place.

Despite these important contributions, symbolic interactionism has also met with criticism, particularly that it does not give sufficient attention to the workings of social institutions and large social structures. Critics also argue that it is naive to assume that social learning by itself can bring about significant social change, since learning does not occur in a vacuum, but in the context of the larger society. Social learning is influenced by the domi-

DOING SOCIOLOGY

What Does Rule Breaking Teach You about Rules?

Social life, we have said, is governed by a set of rules about behavior that develops out of people's ongoing interactions with one another. These rules become so routine that most people are unaware of them—until they are broken. Indeed, some sociologists have devised experiments in which rules of social interaction are deliberately broken in order to reveal them for more careful study.

The leading advocate of this approach is Harold Garfinkel (1967), who asked his students to violate some of the most basic, unspoken rules of social interaction. In one experiment, for example, students behaved like strangers in their own homes: They knocked on the door and waited for an answer before entering the house; they addressed their parents or roommates by formal titles, such as "Mr." or "Mrs."; they asked for permission to watch television or take something from the refrigerator. In other experiments, Garfinkel's students would move closer and closer to the person they were talking to until they were practically touching, or they would board an elevator and instead of looking politely at no one, would stare directly at a fellow passenger.

None of these experiments took much time, either because the experimenter felt too uncomfortable to continue for long or because the unwitting participants in the experiments reacted so strongly. Regardless of the specific experiment, participants responded in much the same way: They were usually surprised and confused, but soon grew angry and impatient. Some seemed embarrassed, and others appeared afraid, questioning the experimenter's sanity. According to Garfinkel, such reactions reveal the significance of these taken-for-granted rules of interaction in everyday life—rules we don't realize we value until they are broken.

Garfinkels' experiments are straightforward and easy to replicate. Try one yourself. You could go into a department store and try to bargain for an item, or you could use one of the experiments we've discussed here. If you need more ideas, consult Garfinkel's book, *Studies in Ethnomethodology.* Whatever experiment you choose, be sure to record in a notebook the rule you broke and others' reaction to you, as well as how long you were able to carry out the rule breaking and your own feelings during the experiment. Sharing your results in class will generate some interesting discussion—and probably plenty of sympathetic laughs.

---

nant values and rules of the larger society and the very organization of the society. So, for example, we may teach our children that racism is wrong, but if they live in racially segregated neighborhoods and go to racially segregated schools where their textbooks teach only about the accomplishments of White people, they are likely to grow up with many of the same prejudices as previous generations. Thus, while social learning can contribute to social change, its effect is limited without simultaneous efforts to bring about macro-level change.

Feminist Sociology

You may have noticed that all of the mainstream sociologists we have discussed in this chapter shared several characteristics: With few exceptions, they were/are all White men of European ancestry. The fact that this social group has dominated the discipline means that to a large extent mainstream sociology has been both *Eurocentric* and *androcentric* (Chafetz, 1997). It is **Eurocentric** in that it has tended to focus on beliefs and concerns relevant to Western societies with European roots. It is **androcentric** because it traditionally has been *male-centered;* sociological research and writing has been done primarily by men, using mostly men as research subjects, producing findings and theories from a male perspective. Sociologist Lyn Lofland (1975), for instance, reviewed the sociological research on urban communities and found that it focused on settings in which men were likely to be present, such as city street corners or neighborhood taverns, whereas areas of urban life where women were likely to be found, such as playgrounds with their children or grocery stores, were almost entirely overlooked. Consequently, although these urban sociologists claimed to be studying community, they were studying male community, not *human* community. "Most of what we have formerly known as the study of society is only the male study of male society" (Millman & Kanter, 1975, p. viii).

During the 1960s, an increasing number of sociologists began to call for a more inclusive sociology, one giving voice to multiple perspectives, particularly those from groups that had historically been silenced or marginalized. Although some of these sociologists were men, the majority were women, inspired by their personal experiences in society and the discipline as well as by the writings and actions of those involved in the women's or feminist movement (Laslett & Thorne, 1997). Consequently, the perspective that these sociologists developed is called **feminist sociology.**

Feminist sociologists have found that their discipline traditionally has been androcentric, with research focusing on areas dominated by men. Sociologists tended to ignore settings where women congregate and to discount female experiences and views. In this picture, what settings, experiences, and views of women might a contemporary sociologist identify as potentially worthy of study?

There are many variations of feminist sociology, but all share the same view of gender and approach research in similar ways. **Gender** refers to the cluster of behavioral patterns and personality traits associated with masculinity and femininity. Traditionally, gender was thought to be innate, but feminist sociologists see gender as learned. In other words, while our **sex** (whether we are male or female) is determined by our genes, our gender (whether we look or behave masculinely or femininely) depends on what we are taught as we grow up. Feminist sociologists examine gender as a central organizing factor in the social world. Virtually all aspects of our social lives are gendered, so feminist sociologists include gender as a fundamental category of analysis, along with other social locators such as race and social class, in all their research (Chafetz, 1997).

It is important to emphasize that feminist sociologists do not focus exclusively on "women's issues." However, they do insist on including female experiences and perspectives in sociological research. They deliberately seek to make women's voices heard, and to do this, they often use research methods that allow the participants in a study to express their feelings openly and to speak for themselves. We'll discuss this approach to research in greater detail in Chapter 2.

The emphasis on personal experiences and interpretation in feminist sociology has been criticized as too subjective by nonfeminist sociologists. Critics charge that feminist sociologists often try too hard to be advocates for women and therefore lose their objectivity as scientists. However, feminist sociologists do not deny the partiality in their work; on the contrary, they acknowledge that it is both intended and desirable. This does not mean that feminist sociologists reject scientific standards in their research. Rather, they adopt the Weberian view

that in order to truly understand social relations, the researcher must adopt an empathic stance toward research participants.

Applying the Four Perspectives

To better understand the similarities and differences, as well as the strengths and weaknesses of the four major sociological perspectives, let's use them to explain a contemporary social problem—homelessness.

Although it's difficult to accurately count how many people are homeless in the United States, estimates range from 300,000 to 3 million. Why are people homeless? How can homelessness be explained sociologically?

Structural functionalists, we said, focus on social order and how social institutions function to keep the society running smoothly. Recall, too, that shared values, customs, and expectations—the normative consensus—play a major role in maintaining society's equilibrium. During periods of rapid social change, such as the downturns in the economy that the United States experienced during the 1980s, the normative consensus may weaken and various social institutions may not function as they should. The disruption produced ripples through the social system, generating serious social problems, including homelessness. Thus, homelessness is dysfunctional in that it is an outgrowth of lowered social integration.

Conflict theorists see homelessness as a product of the social inequality that is inherent in our society. From 1980 to 1996, the price of a new home rose by 116 percent, while the cost of an existing home rose by about 48 percent. Rents have also risen by about 31 percent since 1985 (U.S. Department of Commerce, Bureau of the Census, 1997). At the same time, the number of people in need of low-cost housing grew, but the number of low-

How would homelessness be viewed from each of the theoretical perspectives in sociology presented in this chapter?

cost housing units available declined. From the conflict perspective, therefore, the wealthy investors and landowners are the winners and the homeless are the most visible losers in a housing market where profits are more important than meeting basic human needs.

Both structural functionalists and conflict theorists approach homelessness from a structural angle because they espouse macro-level theories, but symbolic interactionists would look at homelessness at the micro level. Although there are a number of issues symbolic interactionists might address, we'll consider just one: homelessness as rule breaking. The homeless break numerous rules of everyday social interaction that we take for granted: they are not neat and clean; they lie down in public places; they root through trash cans in public view; they approach strangers and ask for money, or worse, talk out loud to themselves or to some invisible friend or foe. And how do the housed typically react to the homeless? Many try to ignore them; the homeless are rendered invisible because they make us feel uncomfortable, confused, angry, or frightened. Certainly, these interactions provide much fodder for the studies of symbolic interactionists.

Finally, there is feminist theory. We have said that feminist sociologists may undertake macro-level or micro-level research, but they always include gender as a fundamental category of analysis, along with other so-

cial locators such as race and social class. In studying homelessness, then, feminist sociologists would ask how the factors that propel people into homelessness differ by gender, and how women's and men's experiences of homelessness compare. For instance, in her recent study of homelessness, Sarah Golden (1992) found that although women and men share many of the same reasons for being homeless, women were more likely than men to become homeless because of relationship loss. Many of the homeless women Golden met during her research had been financially dependent on a husband, boyfriend, or father. When the relationships dissolved because of death or another reason, the women simply could not fend for themselves. Golden also found that women's experiences of homelessness are different from those of men in important ways. Women, for example, are more vulnerable to rape and other sexual assaults.

One problem, four perspectives. Each theory provides a lens through which to view the social world. Each offers unique insights, but each also has specific limitations. Throughout this text, we will use all four of these theories to develop a multidimensional understanding of our social world. Table 1.2 on page 20 provides a complete summary of the theories.

REFLECTING ON

Contemporary Sociological Perspectives

1. What do you think is the most pressing social issue confronting the United States today? How do you think sociologists using each of the four theories we have discussed would analyze this problem?
2. Why is it important to include women's perspectives and experiences in the study of society? What other perspectives should also be included?

BECOMING A SOCIOLOGIST

In light of our discussion of sociological perspectives, it should be clear that there is tremendous diversity within sociology. We have covered only four theories, but there are several others. Some observers have argued recently that the diversity in sociology is harmful to it as a discipline. These critics see sociology as fragmented, being spread too thin by its indiscriminate inclusion of so many different perspectives and its misplaced efforts to solve intractable social problems. As a result, they say, sociology lacks a core body of knowledge like that in the natural sciences (Cole, 1994; Davis, 1994; Molotch, 1994; Stinchcombe, 1994). We disagree. We see the diversity within sociology as one of its greatest strengths and essential to

TABLE 1.2 Contemporary Sociological Perspectives

Perspective	Level of Analysis	Assumptions	Basic Question	Key People	Key Concepts
Structural Functionalism	Macro level	Society is made up of interrelated parts, each of which contributes to the functioning of society as a whole.	What function does a specific institution provide for society as a whole?	Durkheim, Parsons, Merton	manifest functions, latent functions, normative consensus, dysfunctions
Conflict Theory	Macro level	Societies are arranged in such a way that resources and rewards are unevenly distributed among the population, and this inequality produces conflict.	Who benefits and who loses from a particular social arrangement?	Marx, Weber, Mills	inequality, conflict
Symbolic Interactionism	Micro level	Reality is socially created through people's everyday interactions and symbolic communication with one another.	What are the shared meanings of a particular interaction for the members of a social group?	Mead, Blumer	symbols
Feminist Sociology	Macro level or micro level	Gender is a central organizing factor of the social world.	How does gender shape people's social experiences?		gender, sex

the growth of the discipline. Diversity promotes dialogue, not always friendly, that can help us to see the social world in alternative ways. This is especially difficult because sociologists are part of what we study: We are participants in the social world. It's like the fish who doesn't know its environment is wet. This makes it even more important to include a plurality of voices in sociology, especially those of people who have traditionally been considered "outsiders," because they often understand with the greatest clarity the beneficial or problematic nature of a specific social situation (Collins, 1986; Feminist Scholars in Sociology, 1995; Frankenberg, 1993; West, 1993).

As our world grows ever smaller because of the increasing number of global ties that bind us, sociology grows ever more important. In fact, at least one observer has argued that sociology is entering a new "golden age" ("Sociology's New Golden Age," 1999). It is an essential tool for analyzing and understanding our personal lives and our social interactions and their interconnectedness. Our goal in this text, therefore, is to help you develop a sociological analysis of the world in which we live. Our hope is that when you finish this book, you will see everyday life, as well as extraordinary events, in an entirely new way: *as a sociologist.*

 For useful resources for study and review, run Chapter 1 on your *Living Sociology* CD-ROM.

CONNECTIONS

Impact of social locators	How do social locating factors such as age, sex, race, and class affect people's experiences as members of a society? In Chapter 8, for instance, how does occupation relate to wealth, power, and prestige? In Chapter 10, how does gender orientation relate to peer acceptance?
Impacts of sex and race in the workplace	Differences in social locating factors form the basis for social inequality. In Chapter 10, how do the concepts of glass ceiling and glass escalator illustrate gender inequality? In Chapter 11, how does the concept of job discrimination relate to racial inequality?

CONNECTIONS

Cultural diversity and ethnocentrism	Read the section on "Ethnocentrism and Cultural Relativism" in Chapter 4 and the section on "Racial, Ethnic, and Minority groups" in Chapter 11. How would you now redefine cultural diversity? What are three attitudes toward this diversity discussed in this text?
Environmental interdependence	What other examples can you find in the section on "The Natural Environment" in Chapter 19 of the fact that members of the world community are environmentally interdependent?
Cultural diffusion and culture change	Read the section on "Sources of Social Change" in Chapter 20. What elements of culture diffuse most rapidly? What role do computers play in cultural diffusion?
Durkheim's ideas about deviance and crime	Read about "Durkheim's Normality of Deviance" in the section on "Sociological Theories of Deviance" in Chapter 7. Why did Durkheim think that deviance, even homicide and suicide, can be functional for society?
The Chicago School	Read more about the Chicago School's analysis of urbanization in Chapter 19 in the section on "The Chicago School and Urban Ecology." What is human ecology?
C. Wright Mills's power elite	Read "The Elitist Perspective" in Chapter 14. What is an alternative elitist theory about the "ruling class"? What are the main criticisms of elitist perspectives on the political process?
Social interaction in small groups	How does group size relate to the dynamics of small group interaction? Read the section on "Behavior in Groups" in Chapter 6. What patterns of interaction can emerge in groups based on obedience to authority?
Feminist sociology	Read the section on "Feminist Sociology" in Chapter 10 and compare it with the section on "Feminist Sociology" in Chapter 1. How does one section build on the other? What do the authors mean when they refer to a "plurality of feminisms"?
Homelessness	Continue reading about "The Homeless" in Chapter 8. What are some assumptions and judgments about homelessness that sociological research and analysis can reveal?

SUMMING UP CHAPTER 1

What Is Sociology?

1. Sociology is the scientific study of human societies. Sociology is distinct from other disciplines in that sociologists focus on the social group, not the individual. They study the *collective* interactions of people within a particular social structure and the *collective* meanings that the actors give to their interactions with one another.

2. Every society has some system for categorizing its members. Sociologists are fundamentally concerned with how these categories or social locating factors affect how people think and act in particular situations and how they influence people's life chances.

3. Sociologists are also concerned with how categorizing produces inequality and the consequences this has in people's lives. Nevertheless, in studying diversity, sociologists take an appreciative stance, avoiding ethnocentrism.

4. Sociologists recognize that members of societies throughout the world are connected to one another in many ways—through environmental interdependence, politics, economics, technology, and popular culture. The causes and consequences of our global connections are a major theme in sociology.

5. Sociologists seek to answer the question, "What makes social order possible?" However, sociologists are also

concerned with social change, and may actively try to bring about change.

The Origins and Development of Sociology

1. Sociology originated in Europe during the nineteenth century in response to the serious social problems of the time. The founder of sociology was Auguste Comte (1798–1857), an advocate of positivism, the position that knowledge must come from verifiable sources. Three other European social theorists who were instrumental in the development of sociology as a discipline were Emile Durkheim (1858–1917), Karl Marx (1818–1883), and Max Weber (1864–1920).

2. Durkheim focused on the question of what makes social order possible. In preindustrial societies, the answer was the collective conscience, but in industrial societies, it is the division of labor. The greater specialization of tasks that accompanies industrialization causes people to be more dependent on one another to meet their everyday needs. Durkheim is also credited with establishing sociology as an independent scientific discipline because he distinguished it from other fields. The subject matter of sociology is the social group, not the individual.

3. Karl Marx was concerned with social class inequality and conflict under capitalism. He believed that these two problems produced other social problems, and he maintained that the solution was to replace capitalism with a more equitable social system, communism.

4. Max Weber also studied capitalism, but his concern was the increasing rationality and efficiency of modern social life as manifested in the growth of bureaucracy. Bureaucracies, though efficient, are highly impersonal and rigid and, according to Weber, lead to a dehumanization of social life. Weber was also a research methodologist who believed that sociologists can only understand social reality by seeing the world empathically through the experiences of people who live in it.

5. In the United States, sociology was first established as a distinct academic discipline at the University of Chicago in 1892. The sociologists of the Chicago School studied problems of urban life, and located the cause of these problems in the social disorganization of cities.

6. Although the recognized leaders of sociological research at the turn of the twentieth century were the men of the Chicago School, important work was also done by others, such as W. E. B. DuBois, Ida Wells-Barnett, and Jane Addams. But the work of these sociologists was overlooked until recently, largely because they were members of marginalized groups: African Americans and/or women.

Contemporary Sociological Perspectives

1. The development of the major contemporary sociological perspectives was influenced by European as well as U.S. sociology, by historical events, and by sociologists' own experiences.

2. Structural functionalists see society as being made up of interrelated parts or institutions that function to keep society running smoothly. These functions may be manifest or latent, but as long as they work properly, society will be in balance or equilibrium. But institutions and values may also be dysfunctional, which will weaken social integration.

3. Conflict theorists focus on inequality in society and how this inequality generates social conflict. They also believe that sociologists should use their research to bring about social change that improves society.

4. Symbolic interactionists start with the assumption that culture, organizations, and social structures are created through daily communications and interactions among people. Interacting generates symbols that have a shared meaning among members of the group. Through this symbolic communication, social reality is constructed.

5. Feminist sociologists examine gender as a central organizing factor in the social world, recognizing that virtually all aspects of our social lives are gendered. They insist on the inclusion of female experiences and perspectives in sociological research.

KEY PEOPLE AND CONCEPTS

androcentrism: a disproportionate focus on men's perspectives and concerns; male-centered

bourgeoisie: the social class composed of wealthy property holders and bankers

bureaucracy: a form of social organization, based on written rules and procedures, designed to coordinate the actions of large numbers of people

Chicago School: developed at the first academic department of sociology in the United States, the University of Chicago, and focused on the study of the problems of urban life experienced by particular segments of the population as a result of social disorganization

collective conscience: an underlying set of moral norms that gives the members of a society the shared feeling that they belong to something larger than themselves as individuals

Comte, Auguste (1798–1857): considered to be the founder of sociology

conflict theory: a contemporary sociological perspective that focuses on how inequality in society produces advantages or disadvantages for particular segments of the population, thus generating social conflict and sometimes social change

division of labor: the differentiation of people according to the roles and tasks for which they are responsible

Durkheim, Emile (1858–1917): the sociologist whose work essentially established sociology as an independent scientific discipline; focused on the fundamental question of what makes social order possible

dysfunctions: consequences or outcomes of institutional operations that lessen social adaptation and weaken the social system

ethnocentrism: judging others' values and practices as inferior as a result of regarding one's own values and practices as "correct" or "best"

Eurocentrism: a disproportionate focus on beliefs and concerns of relevance to Western societies with European roots

feminist sociology: a contemporary sociological perspective that examines gender as a central organizing factor in the social world

gender: the socially constructed cluster of behavioral patterns and personality traits associated with masculinity and femininity

inequality: the differential allocation of rewards, opportunities, and other resources among members of a society

latent functions: observable, unintended consequences or outcomes of institutional operations

macro-level theory: a theory that conceptualizes society in broad, abstract terms and emphasizes the role of institutional structures in shaping social life

manifest functions: observable, intended consequences or outcomes of institutional operations

Marx, Karl (1818–1883): the revolutionary social theorist whose life's work was dedicated to the study of class conflict, especially in capitalist societies; believed that a fundamental restructuring of the social system was necessary to end inequality

micro-level theory: a theory that focuses on contextualized patterns of social interaction and communication

normative consensus: a set of agreed-upon values, customs, and expectations for appropriate behavior shared by the members of a society

positivism: the position that knowledge must be derived from observable facts, not from superstition, fantasy, or some other nonempirical (nonverifiable) source

proletariat: the social class consisting mostly of workers who sell their labor to the bourgeoisie in exchange for wages

sex: maleness or femaleness, determined genetically

social class: as defined by Marx, one's socioeconomic position in society, which is determined by one's role in production

social facts: phenomena that endure beyond the life span of particular individuals, are caused by factors external to individuals, and exercise a coercive power over individuals

sociology: the scientific study of human societies; the scientific study of the collective interactions of social actors within a particular social structure and the collective meanings these actors give to their interactions with one another

structural functionalism: a contemporary sociological perspective that sees society as being made up of interrelated parts, each of which contributes to the overall functioning of the society as a whole

symbolic interactionism: a contemporary sociological perspective that focuses on how social reality is constructed through the daily communications and rituals in which people engage with one another

theory: a set of interrelated propositions that explain how two or more phenomena are related to one another

verstehen: in sociology, a research method requiring the sociologist to take an empathic stance toward understanding research subjects, thus interpreting the significance of specific interactions and events in terms of the meanings that they have for people who live them

Weber, Max (1864–1920): classical social theorist who, like Marx, studied the problems of capitalist society and who advocated the use of interpretative understanding (*verstehen*) in sociological research

LEARNING MORE

David, D. (1987). *Intellectual women and Victorian patriarchy.* Ithaca, NY: Cornell University Press. An account of the lives and experiences of some of the first female sociologists and social theorists.

Laslett, B., & Thorne, B. (Eds.). (1997). *Feminist sociology: Life histories of a movement.* New Brunswick, NJ: Rutgers University Press. Autobiographical accounts by feminist sociologists, chronicling their struggles in academic life as well as their accomplishments and significant contributions to the discipline.

Marable, M. (1986). *W. E. B. Du Bois: Black radical democrat.* Boston: Twayne Publishers. A thorough, accurate, insightful, and interesting biography of sociologist W. E. B. Du Bois.

Mills, C. W. (1959). *The sociological imagination.* New York: Oxford University Press. The inspirational classic that no student of sociology should miss.

Mohan, R. P., & Wilke, A. S. (Eds.). *International handbook of contemporary developments in sociology.* New York: Greenwood. A survey of significant developments in the field of sociology in thirty-one countries, written by some of the world's most prominent sociologists.

Turner, S. P., and Turner, J. H. (1990). *The impossible science.* Newbury Park, CA: Sage. A survey of the development of U.S. sociology from the late nineteenth century through the 1980s, highlighting its diverse strains and speculating on its future.

 Run Chapter 2 on your *Living Sociology* CD-ROM for interesting and informative activities, web links, videos, practice tests, and more.

Sociological Inquiry

Picture yourself at home on a Monday morning. There's a knock at your door, and you open it to find a neatly dressed young woman with briefcase in hand. She introduces herself and reminds you that she is there to ask you some questions, as the two of you had arranged by phone the previous week. You let her in, show her to a comfortable chair, and she explains to you once again the purpose of her visit. She is part of a privately funded research team that has randomly selected adults from the general population and is interviewing them about their sexual behavior. She then proceeds to ask you a series of questions, beginning with general questions about your health and family background, and moving on to questions about your first sexual experiences, your sexual orientation, and your current sexual practices. In all, you spend about forty-five minutes talking with the interviewer.

An unlikely scenario, you say? You would never discuss your sexual behavior with a total stranger, even one with academic credentials? In fact, chances are that you would answer all of the interviewer's questions—just as 18,876 citizens of Great Britain did in 1990 and 1991. This figure represents more than 63 percent of the 29,802 people selected to be surveyed. Researchers attributed the relatively high participation rate to several factors, including the credibility of being funded by a prestigious private foundation and the fact that survey questions were extensively tested to be sure they were easily understood and not offensive (Wellings et al., 1994).

The British study illustrates a number of important aspects of sociological research. First, it shows that if a study is carefully designed, researchers can obtain information about even the most sensitive topics. Second, it shows that the findings obtained through sociological research are not trivial, but often have serious social implications. Sociological research generates usable knowledge. For instance, among other information, the British researchers learned the percentage of the population engaging in behavior that put them at high risk of contracting AIDS and the percentage of young unmarried adults who were sexually active but used no contraception. The implications of this for public health officials developing sex education programs is enormous—and that's just one use of one study.

Finally, the British study shows that sociological research is scientific. What does that mean? Because the concept of science is so important, we will address it in detail in the section that follows. Then, in the remainder of the chapter, we will examine some of the methods sociologists use to collect data, and some of the important philosophical, ethical, and political issues that sociologists must consider in conducting their research.

THE SCIENCE OF SOCIOLOGY

At a conference recently, a colleague asked the audience, "What do you get if you a cross a sociologist with the head of an organized crime family?" The answer: "You get an offer you can't understand."

This joke plays on the widely held belief that sociologists take what everyone knows through common sense and transform it into incomprehensible theories. Certainly, it is true that some sociologists are guilty of spiking their writing with unnecessary jargon, but the fact is that sociology is such a critically important discipline precisely because common sense, or what "everyone knows," is typically a poor guide to understanding human behavior and social life. Let's consider more carefully why we can't rely on common sense to give us an accurate picture of the social world, and then we'll discuss what sociologists study and why.

Sociology and Common Sense

To distinguish common sense from sociology, let's begin with an example. "Everyone knows" that the availability of welfare encourages poor teenage girls to have children outside of marriage so they can collect benefits. Sociological research reveals, however, that the rate of nonmarital teen births is highest in states with the lowest welfare benefits (Children's Defense Fund, 1997). In fact, pregnancies among unmarried impoverished teens appear to have more to do with our country's inadequate system of sex education, problems with obtaining and consistently using contraceptives, and the lack of alternative avenues available to these young women for achieving status and self-esteem (Gilligan et al., 1995; Luker, 1996).

But surely, if welfare is available, poor people have no incentive to go out and find jobs. Why work if you can get a government handout? That's just common sense, right? Actually, sociological research shows that most poor people are working or looking for work, or are too young or too old to work. Nearly 15 million people in the United States live in working poor families. Among poor families about 70 percent had at least one member employed in 1998 (Center on Budget and Policy Priorities, 1999). Children account for almost 19.9 percent

If this unmarried couple separated, say, to attend different colleges, is their relationship more likely to be strengthened or weakened? Folk wisdom says that "absence makes the heart grow fonder," but also "out of sight, out of mind." How is sociology different from common sense understandings about human relationships? How would a sociologist go about answering the question about the couple?

of Americans living in poverty, and about 10.5 percent of the elderly aged sixty-five and older are poor. Overall, only about 33 percent of families with incomes under $15,000 a year even receive any cash welfare or unemployment benefits (U.S. Department of Commerce, Bureau of the Census, 1997).

Why does sociological knowledge often differ from common sense or what is often called "folk wisdom"? The answer lies in the fact that each kind of knowledge derives from a different source. Folk wisdom derives simply from *faith*. Frequently, the faith is based on religious teachings or beliefs. For instance, many people believe that everything that happens is a result of God's plan for them. Rarely do these people claim to have seen or talked to God directly, but they nevertheless accept this idea as Truth. More often, folk wisdom is information that is shared widely among groups of people and appeals because it matches their previous experiences or what they have been told or taught in the past. No attempt is made to test the accuracy of the information; it is simply accepted as true because those who supplied it are trusted and the information itself "makes sense."

In contrast, sociological knowledge is based on science. **Science** is a logically organized method of obtaining information through direct, systematic observation. In other words, scientific knowledge derives from **empirical evidence,** that is, information that is directly verifiable.

Does this mean that sociologists are areligious or that they never draw on common sense or folk wisdom? Cer-

tainly not; many sociologists practice a particular religion and hold specific religious beliefs as principles of faith. Sociologists may also draw on folk wisdom for solving everyday problems. They might, for example, sprinkle sugar on a child's burnt tongue, not because scientific data show that it stops the pain, but because others say it works. Sometimes a particular belief or piece of folk wisdom may inspire a sociological study. In such cases, sociologists empirically test the folk wisdom. When it comes to understanding social life—the collective interactions of social actors in particular settings—only scientific evidence satisfies the sociologist.

What Sociologists Study and Why

What do sociologists study? The list of topics researched in sociological studies is far too long to try to reproduce here, but suffice it to say that virtually any aspect of human behavior is subject to scrutiny by sociologists. Recall that in Chapter 1 we distinguished between macro-level sociology and micro-level sociology. Sociological research may examine macro-level issues, such as the effects of economic changes on work patterns (Vallas & Beck, 1996) and racial differences in marriage patterns (Raley, 1996). Or, sociological research may focus on the micro level, studying such topics as stylists' and customers' interactions in a beauty salon (Gimlin, 1996) and women's exchanges at garage sales (Herrmann, 1996). Even at the micro level, however, an underlying goal of the research is to uncover the links between the individual and society.

How do sociologists identify topics for research? This is one of the questions we will address in the section that follows as we examine the research process.

R E F L E C T I N G O N

The Science of Sociology

Can you think of a piece of folk wisdom or common sense understanding that you would like to test empirically? Why would it be important to test this particular idea? In other words, what are the practical implications of such research?

THE RESEARCH PROCESS

How do sociologists carry out their research? Table 2.1 on page 28 summarizes the research process. In this section we'll review each step of the research process; later, we'll discuss particular methods that sociologists use to conduct research.

TABLE 2.1 The Research Process

Step 1. Choose and define the problem to be studied.

Step 2. Review the research literature to learn about the findings of other researchers who have studied this problem.

Step 3. Design the study.

Step 4. Collect the data.

Step 5. Analyze the data.

Step 6. Share the research with others by reporting the findings and conclusions.

Choosing a Research Problem

The first step in the research process is deciding what you want to study. How do sociologists choose research topics? Often, when you ask a sociologist that question, the reply will be, "I've always been interested in. . . ." In other words, research problems frequently reflect the personal interests and experiences of the researcher. For example, when one of your authors was in college, a close friend was raped. Witnessing the friend's trauma and her treatment by police and others caused the author to wonder not only why rape occurs, but also how services for rape victims could be improved. Some answers to these questions were eventually obtained through a study of rape crisis counseling (Andersen & Renzetti, 1980).

As we noted earlier, sociologists may also develop a research project to test some common-sense understanding or folk wisdom. In addition, sociologists get ideas for research by reading other sociologists' work. Often, the purpose of a study is to address issues that other researchers have overlooked, to challenge or replicate others' findings, or to test a specific theory. For instance, sociologist Jody Brown (1997) has conducted research on women who leave abusive husbands. Her research calls into question many popular stereotypes about battered women, and, at the same time, tests a specific theory of behavior change which posits that we modify our behavior in progressive stages, but also experience frequent setbacks.

We will say more about the relationship between theory and research later. Now, however, we want to emphasize that regardless of the reason a research topic is chosen, the researcher must define the problem as clearly as possible. It is not sufficient, for example, to say you want to study juvenile delinquency. You must state what it is about juvenile delinquency that you want to study. Defining your research problem, then, is a matter of *specifying* precisely what it is you want to know.

Reviewing the Literature

Once you've identified what you want to study, the next step in the research process is to read about what other researchers have learned about your research problem. This step is called a **literature review.**

A thorough literature review is indispensable for a good research project. Reading others' work helps the researcher refine her or his research problem and clarify ideas; suggests ways of carrying out the study; highlights issues that have been overlooked in previous studies; and helps the researcher to avoid pitfalls that others have encountered. Today, reviewing the literature on a topic is much easier than it used to be, thanks to the widespread availability of online computer searches in libraries. If you haven't done so before, go to your college or university library and learn how to do an online search to identify research literature on a topic of your choice.

Designing the Project

The third step in the research process is research design. Designing a research project is in many ways no different from designing anything else; the researcher *develops a plan* for finding answers to the research problem. A sound research design is one that addresses several issues having to do with measurement and time. Let's consider these issues in turn.

Units of Analysis.   Let's say that you've just read a magazine article claiming that sociologists as a group tend to be more politically liberal than psychologists. This has sparked your curiosity, so you've decided to design a study to see if there is empirical support for the claim. One of the first questions you must answer is: Who or what will I study? In technical terms, you must identify the *units of analysis* for your study.

In sociological research, the most common units of analysis are individuals. Although sociologists study social groups, we typically do so by analyzing information obtained from individuals who belong to specific groups. Individuals, though, are not the only units of analysis found in sociological research. In fact, research methodologist Earl Babbie (1995) points out that the selection of units of analysis is limited only by the researcher's imagination. Units of analysis may be households, organizations, or even things, including sociology textbooks.

Because of the variety of units of analysis available for sociological study, it's important that the researcher be clear what the units of analysis are in his or her study. The researcher must always be on guard against drawing conclusions about one unit of analysis based on a study of a very different unit of analysis. For instance, in our example above, the conclusions that you'll eventually draw

SOCIOLOGY LIVE

Wichita State University, Wichita, KS
Course: Introduction to Sociology,
    Dr. Twyla Hill
Students: (not shown) Corie Barlow,
    Brandon Gunter, Robin Lintecum,
    Connie Mucci, and Tina Pham

What social behavior at our school could we study as a research team?

After much discussion, we decided that student drinking behavior would be a good subject for our sociological research. College students drink for many reasons, especially in social situations to relieve stress and win acceptance into a peer group. When people think of fraternities and sororities, they think of big "party animals" who drink all the time. This is the stereotype. Our question is: Are Greek students, in fact, heavier drinkers than non-Greek students?

We would say no, because both Greek and non-Greek students have equal access to alcoholic beverages. This would be our hypothesis prior to conducting research: That Greek students between the ages of 18 and 24 at our university drink just as much as non-Greek students because accessibility of alcohol is equal for both groups. To test our hypothesis, we would need to ask a large number of students about their group membership, drinking behavior, and amount of alcohol consumption. We realized

afterwards that we also needed to determine ease of access to alcohol!

We would need standardized data, which we could get by creating and distributing a questionnaire and conducting a survey. Because the scope of our study is restricted to our school, we could try to get data for all students rather than a representative sample. We could take our questionnaires to the head of each department to be distributed to professors, and professors could hand out the questionnaires for each student to complete. Students would be instructed not to take the survey more than once, but a drawback would be that we would be dependent on professors' cooperation to ensure that the information we get is correct and complete. We also would have to assume that students tell the truth in their answers.

The questions on our survey would be short and simple so that answering them would not be too time consuming. For example:

1. Do you consume alcoholic beverages?
2. On average, how many times in a week do you consume alcoholic beverages?

3. When you drink, how many drinks do you have?
4. How old are you?
5. Do you belong to a fraternity or a sorority?

After collecting and analyzing the data, we would share our findings with classmates and with the Wichita State University Student Affairs Department. This way, our findings could have a practical application by providing information about student drinking behavior. With our findings, the Student Affairs Department could be in a position to recruit speakers to inform our students of the dangers of alcohol abuse.

In conclusion, we have learned what goes into a research project. As a group, we had to decide on a specific topic. We learned that our questions on the questionnaire had to be exact. To come up with an effective research method, we had to meet twice a week or more to discuss all our ideas. Along the way, we had to debate what questions to ask, how to administer the questionnaires, and what group to target. As a group, we all felt that this was an interesting and challenging project.

---

from the study will likely be different depending on whether the units of analysis are individuals (sociologists and psychologists) or things (sociology and psychology textbooks).

Concepts and Variables.   In our daily lives, we communicate with one another using a set of shared and generally agreed upon terms that carry more or less the same meaning for each of us. When we hear a particular term, it produces a mental image. The image each of us sees may not be identical, but it is similar enough to allow us to understand one another. These mental images are concepts. More specifically, a **concept** is a mental representation of some aspect of our environment or the people

in that environment. Concepts help us describe one another and the world in which we live.

In doing scientific research, sociologists use a particular type of concept called **variables,** which are so named because their values vary or change. For instance, if you were to compare two friends, one of whom attends church or synagogue regularly and the other who repeatedly has told you that there is no God, you may say that the former is more religious than the latter. We can see, then, that the variable—in this case, religiosity—differs from case to case. We also see that variables are composed of **attributes,** that is, descriptive categories or values. So, in our example, we might say that the variable *religiosity* may be *high* or *low.* Or consider your friends

What macro-level sociological questions does this scene suggest to you? What micro-level questions might interest you about it as an amateur sociologist? What social fact or group or behavior would be your unit of analysis, and what concepts and variables would you consider in attempting to understand or explain it? What central question would you have, and what might be the best way to find your answer?

again: You may describe them using other variables, such as *sex,* which is composed of the attributes *male* and *female.*

Sociologists use variables as tools of *measurement.* In designing a research project, then, the researcher must also specify the variables that will be measured in the study. Many people are skeptical of sociologists' ability to measure those aspects of social life and human interaction that we are most interested in because these things tend to be abstract. For instance, you cannot see or touch prejudice, nor can you scoop up a handful of it. Nevertheless, you know it exists, and you know that some people are more or less prejudiced than others. Prejudice, then, is a concept (it produces a mental image) and it is a variable (its value may change or vary from individual to individual or from situation to situation). But how might sociologists measure it? That is, how can we determine its value in any specific case?

Like most variables, prejudice may be measured in a number of different ways. One sociologist may measure prejudice by asking a group of students enrolled in an introductory sociology course whether they agree or disagree with the statement, "Homosexuals should not be permitted to be teachers in elementary schools." Those who agree with the statement arguably may be more prejudiced than those who disagree. Another sociologist might ask the students how comfortable they would feel having a roommate who is homosexual. This sociologist would likely maintain that the more comfortable the student claimed to be, the less prejudiced that student is. In both instances, the sociologists are trying to measure prejudice by what they consider to be a specific indicator of it. An **indicator** shows the presence or absence of the variable being studied. Usually, sociologists use more than one indicator to measure a particular variable, since most of the variables we are interested in are complex and multidimensional.

In any case, in designing their research, sociologists must be careful to specify how they are going to measure any given variable. The process of developing the measures to be used to gauge the existence of a particular variable in the real world is called **operationalizing a variable.** Operationalizing variables is a critical element in scientific research, since the measures we develop in this process play a significant role in determining the quality of the data we obtain. Measures that are faulty or imprecise will yield data with limited utility—or worse, data that mislead us in our conclusions about what it is we are studying.

Reliability and Validity. Related to the process of operationalizing variables are the issues of reliability and validity. Not all measures are created equal. Some are better than others. How do we determine the quality of a particular measure? When operationalizing the variables of a study, sociologists must consider at a minimum whether the measures to be used are reliable and valid.

Reliability refers to the question of whether a measure yields consistent results. More specifically, when it is used repeatedly, does the measure produce the same results each time? Suppose, for instance, that we are interested in studying sexual harassment on college campuses. We define sexual harassment as any unwanted leers, comments, suggestions, or physical contact of a sexual nature, as well as any unwanted requests for sexual favors.

We decide to measure sexual harassment by stationing ourselves in a student center lounge on our campus and observing for one hour the interactions of male and female students there to see if any engage in this behavior. On our first day of observation, we record two instances of what appears to be sexual harassment: In one case, there is unwanted touching; in the second case, a male student promises a female student to help her with a course assignment if she agrees to go out with him. We leave the student center feeling satisfied with our research and stay out late that night celebrating. On our second day of observation, we are pretty sleepy and don't pay much attention to what is going on in the lounge; we record no instances of sexual harassment. On the third day of observation, we witness a young woman and young man sitting at a nearby table. They appear to be arguing. At one point, the young man stands up, pulls the woman to her feet and kisses her hard on the lips. The young woman storms from the room. We record one instance of sexual harassment and leave the student center, contemplating whether we should report the incident to university authorities. After our departure, however, the young woman returns to the lounge and the activity we witnessed occurs again; what we do not know is that this couple is practicing a scene from a play in which they have the lead roles. Our measure has yielded three instances of sexual harassment over three days, so we conclude that, on average, one incident of sexual harassment occurs each day in the student center lounge.

Unfortunately, the measure we used in this research project was not reliable. Had we been more awake on the second day, for example, we may have observed sexual harassment. Had we investigated further on the third day, we would have found out that what we observed was not sexual harassment at all. In fact, therefore, there may be more or less sexual harassment in the student center lounge than what our measure produced. Our conclusion about the rate of sexual harassment in the lounge is probably incorrect because it was derived from an unreliable measure. This is an issue that researchers must consider *before* they go out to collect data. In designing the research project, researchers must carefully think through the potential threat to reliability that each of their measures poses.

Now suppose that instead of making observations in the student center lounge, we decided to measure the level of sexual harassment on our campus by counting the number of complaints of harassment that have been filed with university authorities. No matter how many times we count the complaint forms, we arrive at the same number of incidents. This measure is obviously a more reliable one. However, we know that sexual harassment tends to be grossly underreported. Are these complaint forms, then, really measuring the level of sexual harassment on our campus, or are they simply a measure of *reported* sexual harassment? In this case, we are no longer questioning the reliability of our measure, we are questioning its

validity. The **validity** of a measure is the extent to which it actually measures what it was intended to measure. In designing a research project, therefore, sociologists must also try to ensure that their measures are valid.

Clearly, the questions of the reliability and validity of measurement are not insignificant ones for social researchers, and there are no easy solutions to the problem of how to develop measures that are at once reliable *and* valid. However, methodologist Earl Babbie (1995) advises that one way to handle the problem is to measure a concept in several different ways in the same study. Moreover, if the concept is made up of several parts or dimensions, try to measure all of them. The researcher's goal should always be to develop measures of concepts that help us better understand the world around us.

Time. One additional element of research design that must be considered is the time frame for the study. The researcher has two major options with respect to time: a cross-sectional study or a longitudinal study.

A **cross-sectional study** examines behavior or attitudes at one fixed point—a cross section—in time. For instance, if we wish to learn about marijuana use among teenagers, we could question a group of teenagers about whether they smoke marijuana and, if so, how often. We could even ask them if they have ever smoked marijuana. Such a study would give us an indication of the number of teenagers who currently smoke marijuana or who have smoked marijuana, but the study would miss all the teenagers in the group who start smoking marijuana after the study is completed.

A cross-sectional study is like a snapshot of time. In contrast, a **longitudinal study** is more like a motion picture or a series in time-lapse photography because in a longitudinal study, data are gathered over an extended period of time, either continuously or at specific intervals. For example, we could study teen marijuana use by asking the same group of teenagers each year, starting when they are thirteen and ending when they are nineteen, whether or not they smoke marijuana. This study design would allow us to map changes in marijuana use throughout the teen years and gauge trends in teen marijuana use by identifying, for instance, the ages at which teenagers are most likely to start smoking marijuana.

In deciding whether to conduct a cross-sectional study or a longitudinal study, researchers must consider several factors. First is the purpose of the study. If the researcher wishes to measure changes in behavior or attitudes over time, a longitudinal design would be the logical choice. However, other factors that should be taken into account are the researcher's time and financial resources, since longitudinal studies are typically more expensive than cross-sectional studies and they demand a greater time commitment on the part of the researcher, often several years (Babbie, 1995).

This is a sample of a population for a sociological study on American consumer behavior in the recreational vehicle market. This sample reveals at least three major errors in sampling, which would destroy the validity of the research. What are they? What kind of a sample would you need for this study to ensure validity?

Collecting the Data

When the research project is being designed, the researcher also has to select a method for collecting data. There are a variety of methods to choose from, including surveys, field research, experiments, content analysis, and secondary analysis. Because each method warrants a fairly detailed description, we'll postpone our discussion of research methods until later in the chapter. For now, we'll take up another important aspect of data collection: selecting the sources from which the data will be gathered.

We've already said that researchers must decide early on what their units of analysis will be. Obviously, though, a researcher cannot study every person or thing to which a particular topic applies. As a result, the sociologist faces a dilemma: Although some sociological studies are limited in their applicability to relatively small groups of people with unique characteristics or interests, most sociological research involves a topic of relevance to large numbers of people or to all members of a society. Limited time, money, and other resources also usually constrain

the number of people that can be included in a study. How do sociologists handle these problems?

The answer is **sampling:** the process of selecting a subgroup for study from the entire group of interest to the researcher. First, the researcher identifies the population of interest. In the context of research, a **population** is all the cases to which the research topic applies and about which the researcher seeks to draw conclusions. (We use the word *cases* in this definition because although sociologists most often study populations of people, they may study things—for example, television programs, laws, and speeches—as well.) From the population, the researcher then selects a subgroup, or **sample,** from whom data will be collected. Researchers draw conclusions about the characteristics, attitudes, or behavior of the population based on the findings obtained from the sample.

Consider the case of voter polling. Prior to any election, news reports offer predictions as to which candidate will win. These predictions are based on asking a sample of registered voters for whom they intend to vote. There are a total of about 100 million registered voters in the United States, but most of these surveys poll only about 2,000 of them. How good are the predictions based on these seemingly small samples? Well, on the day of the 1996 presidential election, ABC News said that 50 percent of those voting would vote for Clinton, 32 percent would vote for Dole, and 15 percent would vote for Perot. A *USA Today*/CNN/Gallup poll showed 51 percent for Clinton, 35 percent for Dole, and 8 percent for Perot. Actual election results showed that 49 percent of the votes cast were for Clinton, 41 percent were for Dole, and 8 percent were for Perot ("Portrait of the Electorate," 1996).

How can pollsters predict with such accuracy the outcome of an election if they only ask such a relatively small number of people about their voting intentions? Pollsters use **random sampling,** in which each member of the population has an equal chance of being selected for participation in the study. Using random sampling helps assure that the sample will be representative of the population. A **representative sample** is one that closely resembles the population in terms of aggregate characteristics that are important for a specific study, including race, age, sex, and income distribution. Random sampling is unnecessary if all the members of a population are identical because in that case, anyone chosen for inclusion in a study would represent the population as a whole. In the vast majority of cases, however, populations are diverse in their makeup. Because random sampling is governed by the laws of probability, it ensures that a representative sample will be selected and that researchers can even estimate the degree of bias in their samples. If a sample has been randomly selected, researchers can be reasonably confident that the conclusions they draw about the pop-

INTERSECTING INEQUALITIES

Why Do Sociological Studies Need Representative Samples?

When researchers conduct a study using a sample, they want to be able to generalize their findings to the entire population. It's important, therefore, that the sample be representative of the population. This means that if the population is made up of diverse groups, members of those groups must be included in the sample. If any group is excluded, researchers run the risk of making inaccurate statements about the population, and this could have serious implications. Consider, for example, a recent study that found that taking an aspirin every other day can prevent heart attacks. The study received a lot of media attention, with health reporters advising the public to start taking aspirin on a regular basis. However, since the sample studied included 22,000 men and no women, it is uncertain whether the aspirin regimen will have beneficial effects for both sexes (Nechas & Foley, 1994).

In order to select a sample that is inclusive of the diverse groups that make up a population, researchers should make certain they:

1. *Know the population.* Before sampling, researchers gather as much information as they can about the composition of the population.
2. *Identify the groups whose attitudes or behavior are relevant to the study.* It is not necessary for a sample to include members of all groups if the researcher does not intend to generalize the findings to all groups. For instance, if researchers want to study the attitudes of American men toward the women's movement, it would be appropriate to exclude women from the sample. However, the researchers must consider the diversity of the male population and include men from the various racial and ethnic groups that make up the population, as well as men from different age groups and social classes.
3. *Be certain that a sufficient number of study participants from each relevant group is included in the sample.* To do this, it is sometimes necessary to oversample underrepresented groups. If, for example, the population is 74 percent White, 16 percent African American, and 10 percent Hispanic American, and the desired sample size is 100, then it might be assumed that the sample selected should include roughly 74 White Americans, 16 African Americans, and 10 Hispanic Americans. However, it is doubtful whether meaningful comparisons could be made across racial and ethnic groups if data are obtained from so few African Americans and Hispanic Americans. To ensure racial and ethnic diversity in the sample, then, African Americans and Hispanic Americans are oversampled, producing a sample that includes roughly equal numbers of people from each group.

---

ulation based on data obtained from the sample are accurate. The Intersecting Inequalities box illustrates further the importance of careful random sampling when studying diverse populations.

Analyzing the Data

Once data have been collected, they must be analyzed. There are a number of ways this can be done, but in general there are two broad types of data analysis: quantitative and qualitative. The type of analysis used depends to a large extent on how the data were collected. We will discuss specific methods of data collection shortly. Here we will briefly distinguish between the two types of data analysis and also discuss how data analysis is used to determine how variables are related to one another.

Quantitative and Qualitative Analysis.   In **quantitative analysis,** data are reduced to numbers and analyzed using various statistical techniques, usually with the help of a computer. Studies that use questionnaires to ask people about their attitudes or behavior are particularly well suited to quantitative analysis. Each respondent's answer to a particular question is translated into a numerical code, and the coded data are entered into a computer. The answers are then tallied to see how many people responded to a specific question in a particular way. Responses to two or more questions can be compared to determine how many members of one group (for example, women) answered another question a certain way (for example, said they favor the death penalty). These comparisons, in turn, may be subjected to statistical tests to determine if there is a relationship between two or more variables. We will discuss the importance of identifying relationships between variables momentarily, but for now let us say that the purpose of the statistical tests is to answer the question, "Does a particular response to one question appear to affect the response to a second question?"

DOING SOCIOLOGY

Reading Tables and Understanding Descriptive Statistics

ow to Read a Table

Sociologists often present data using tables. A table can summarize a large amount of information quickly and efficiently. The table should be constructed in a way that helps people better understand the data.

One kind of table often used by sociologists is the **frequency distribution,** which shows the number of times each attribute of a variable occurs in the sample or population. The values, or frequencies, may be reported as raw numbers, percentages of the total, or both. Table A is an example of a frequency distribution for a single variable. What does this table tell us?

To read Table A, first look at the *title* of the table. You will see that this table will tell us the attendance status of people enrolled in college in the United States in 1994. Next, the table *headings* label the columns of the table, helping us locate specific information. In the

TABLE A
U.S. College Enrollment by Attendance Status, 1994

Attendance Status	Number	%
Part-time	6,141	43.0
Full-time	8,138	47.0
Total	14,279	100.0

Source: U.S. Department of Commerce, Bureau of the Census, 1997, p. 180.

first column is the *variable label*, attendance status, which has the attributes part-time and full-time. In the second column is the number of students who attended college either part-time or full-time in 1994. In the third column, these raw numbers are reported as a percentage of the total.

Recall, however, that sociologists typically want to make statements about the relationships between two or more variables. One way to begin to examine such relationships is to *cross-tabulate* the data for the two variables you are interested in. To cross-tabulate the data, compute the number of times the attributes of one variable occur simultaneously with the attributes of the second

variable. For instance, you might ask, "Are women more likely than men to attend college part-time?" Table B provides an answer to this question.

To read Table B, again begin by reading the title of the table, which in this case tells us that the data appearing in the table are college enrollments by attendance status and sex for 1994. The column headings on the table show the two variables being cross-tabulated. Reading down the attendance status column and then across the rows, you can find out how many part-time students are male and how many are female, as well as the percentages of part-time students who are male and female.

TABLE B
U.S. College Enrollment by Attendance Status and Sex, 1994

| Attendance Status | SEX | |
	Male	Female
Part-time	2,517 (35.9%)	3,624 (45.8%)
Full-time	3,855 (61.4%)	4,283 (54.2%)
Total	6,012 (100.0%)	7,907 (100.0%)

Source: U.S. Department of Commerce, Bureau of the Census, 1997, p. 180.

Data analyzed quantitatively are often presented in tabular form. The Doing Sociology box discusses how to read two different types of tables and introduces several commonly used statistics.

Qualitative analysis is more appropriate for analyzing data not easily reduced to numbers. For example, asking respondents to "tell their stories" generates data very different from that generated from questions allowing only a limited number of choices. Alternatively, think about a study in which the researcher watches people as they interact and records these observations without asking the people any questions. The observations are the researcher's data. Although it may be possible to count or quantify some aspects of the findings (for example, how many times respondents answered a certain way or how many times a particular behavior was observed), the rich

detail and nuances of meaning could never be captured in statistical analysis. In qualitative analysis, then, the researcher focuses on specific *qualities*—distinct descriptive categories—within the data. For example, the researcher would look for similarities and differences among the personal stories told or behaviors observed. Do women tell different stories from men, for instance? What themes are common in the women's stories? What themes are common in the men's stories? Do African American women and men tell different stories from White women and men? However, while qualitative analysis identifies similarities and differences, it does not make precise numerical statements about these similarities or differences.

Obviously, qualitative analysis is more subjective than quantitative analysis, but this does not mean that one type of analysis is inherently better than another. To reiterate

The same procedure allows you to consider the sex distribution of full-time students. By examining these data, you can conclude that female students are considerably more likely than male students to attend college part-time.

Notice that the table shows the total number of male and female students enrolled in college in 1994, but provides you with enough information to calculate the total number of part-time and full-time students. These numbers are referred to as *marginals*.

Describing Data Using Statistics

Sociologists also use a number of statistical techniques to analyze data. The most basic statistics are called **descriptive statistics** because they help the researcher describe specific variables, but they cannot be used for drawing conclusions about relationships between variables. The three most common descriptive statistics are the mean, the median, and the mode.

The **mean** is simply the average. To calculate the mean value of a variable in a sample, the values reported by each study participant are added together and then divided by the number of study participants. For example, suppose five students received the following scores on their first introduction to sociology exam: 65, 78, 84, 92, 97. To calculate the mean, add the scores (416) and then divide by 5 (416/5). The average score on the first exam was 83.2.

One problem with using the mean to describe a frequency distribution is that it can be distorted by extremely high and extremely low values. Suppose the lowest test score had been 45 instead of 65. The average score would be lowered to 79.2, which is not as accurate a description of the frequency distribution as a whole. Because of the potential for distortion by extreme values, sociologists also use the median to describe a frequency distribution. The **median** is the midpoint of the distribution; 50 percent of the distribution falls below this point and 50 percent falls above it. To calculate the median, the researcher arranges the values obtained from the study participants in numerical order and then identifies the midpoint. In our example, the midpoint is the same in both cases, 84. You can see that the median was not affected by the extremely low score and, therefore, provides a more accurate description of the test score distribution than the mean does when an extreme score is present.

The mean and the median can only be used to describe variables whose attributes have a zero point. Examples of such variables include not only test scores, but also age and income reported as raw numbers. But suppose you asked the question, "Do you think that abortion should be legal under all circumstances, only legal under certain circumstances, or illegal under all circumstances?" It would be impossible to calculate an average for this variable ("attitude toward legality of abortion") since there is no zero point. For these kinds of variables, sociologists can use another descriptive statistic, the **mode**, or most frequent response. If, for instance, out of 100 people questioned, 33 percent said abortion should be legal under all circumstances, 53 percent said abortion should be legal only under certain circumstances, and 14 percent said abortion should always be illegal, the mode would be "legal only under certain circumstances."

Try your hand at using descriptive statistics to analyze data. Calculate the mean, median, and mode for the following data set, which represents the answers of seven respondents to the question, "What is your total annual family income?": $11,296; $30,500; $209,222; $63,174; $36,125; $43,667; $30,500. Which statistic do you think best describes this sample in terms of annual family income? Why?

Remember, as we stated earlier, descriptive statistics such as the mean, median, and mode can only be used to describe one variable at a time. To examine the relationship between variables, sociologists rely on other statistical tests.

a point made earlier, the type of analysis chosen is largely dictated by the type of data collected.

Relationships among Variables.   When analyzing data, sociologists are first interested in the extent to which the values of any individual variable exist within a certain group [for example, how many women and men (variable = sex) in the United States identify themselves as members of the Republican Party]. Of greater concern, however, is the question of how specific variables are related to one another (for example, Does sex have any influence on political party affiliation?). Of course, variables may be related to one another in different ways.

One type of relationship is causal. In a **causal relationship,** a change in one variable causes a change in a second variable. The variable that causes the change is called the **independent variable.** The variable that changes is called the **dependent variable;** that is, its value depends on what the value of the independent variable is. Consider, for example, an employee who shows up for work two hours late each day until he is fired by the supervisor. The consistent lateness, the independent variable, causes the supervisor's behavior (the firing), which in this case is the dependent variable.

Establishing causal relationships would allow us to predict with great accuracy how people will behave in specific situations. But we know that, for better or for worse, human behavior is complex and diverse. Physical and natural scientists conducting research in a laboratory can usually isolate the effect of one variable on another by keeping out or neutralizing the effects of other variables that might interfere to produce a different result.

Rarely if ever can sociologists exercise similar control over all the variables operating simultaneously in a given social setting. Consequently, sociologists rarely establish cause-and-effect relationships with regard to human behavior.

Nevertheless, sociologists do try to gauge patterns of behavior and social trends. Doing so has important policy and practice implications. For example, if we discover that children who have completed preschool programs tend to have fewer academic problems in elementary school than children who do not complete such programs, then policy makers would be wise to invest more money and resources in preschool programs.

But if sociologists cannot establish cause and effect, how is even this type of prediction possible? Sociological research usually yields another type of relationship, **correlational relationships,** in which two or more variables change together. For instance, if when one variable increases in value, a second variable also increases in value, there is a direct or positive correlation between the two variables; they change together in the same direction. Note that a direct or positive correlation would also exist if, when the first variable decreased in value, the second variable also decreased in value. An inverse or negative correlation would occur if, when one variable increased in value, a second variable decreased in value, or vice versa.

There is an important difference between causal relationships and correlational relationships. With correlation, you cannot be absolutely certain that the change in the second variable (the dependent variable) was caused by the change in the first variable (the independent variable). It may be that the change observed in the dependent variable was caused only in part by the change in the independent variable and that a change in other variables also contributed to the change in the dependent variable. It may also be the case that the observed change in both variables was caused by a third variable. If the latter is true, then the relationship between the independent and dependent variables is said to be **spurious.** To understand the concept of spuriousness better, let's consider an example.

Researchers have long observed a correlation between alcohol abuse and domestic violence; this relationship is illustrated in Figure 2.1a on page 37. As a result of this finding, many people have come to assume that alcohol abuse causes men to behave violently toward their wives or girlfriends. Additional research, however, has shown that many men are abusive when they are sober and that some men who are abusive begin to drink heavily after a violent incident, not before it (Gelles, 1993). These findings indicate, then, that perhaps some other factor may be at work that causes both alcohol abuse and battering. Figure 2.1b on page 37 shows one such variable that researchers have examined in this regard: self-esteem. In-

dividuals who abuse alcohol often have low self-esteem. Similarly, research has shown that men who batter their intimate partners also have low self-esteem. If it is low self-esteem that is generating both alcohol abuse and domestic violence, then the correlation between alcohol abuse and domestic violence may be more apparent than real—that is, it may be spurious.

How can we determine if the relationship between alcohol abuse and domestic violence is spurious? To do so requires that we control for the effects of the third variable, level of self-esteem. To **control** a variable, we must neutralize its effects in some way. We may do this by preventing it from varying in the group of people we are studying; in other words, we could look at whether alcohol abuse contributes to domestic violence when level of self-esteem is held constant. If we find that men with low self-esteem who abuse alcohol are more likely to batter their partners than men with low self-esteem who do not abuse alcohol, then we can be pretty sure that the relationship we have observed between alcohol abuse and domestic violence is real, and, in fact, may even be causal. On the other hand, if we find that men with low self-esteem who do not abuse alcohol are just as likely as men with low self-esteem who do abuse alcohol to batter their intimate partners, then we should conclude that the relationship we have observed between alcohol abuse and domestic violence is spurious (see Figure 2.1c).

What actually happens to the relationship between alcohol abuse and domestic violence when we control for level of self-esteem? The correlation weakens considerably, but does not disappear altogether. Thus, level of self-esteem does appear to have significant effects on both alcohol abuse and domestic violence, but we still cannot be certain that the correlation between alcohol abuse and domestic violence is totally spurious (see Figure 2.1d).

When analyzing data, then, sociologists look not only for a relationship between two variables, but also for ways in which such relationships are impacted by the intervening effects of other social factors.

Reporting the Findings and Conclusions

It is not enough for a researcher to collect and analyze data; findings and the conclusions drawn from them must also be shared. Reporting research is important for several reasons. First, it gives the researcher an opportunity to tell others what has been learned from the study. Second, it may inspire others to undertake additional studies of the topic, particularly if the researcher identifies questions that future research should address. Third, it encourages replication of the research. That is, others repeat the study to see if they obtain the same results. Successful replications confirm earlier results, increasing researchers' confidence in the accuracy of their studies.

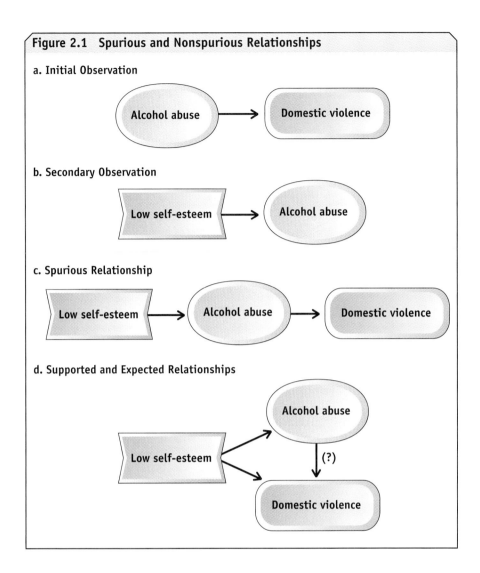

Figure 2.1   Spurious and Nonspurious Relationships

a. Initial Observation

Alcohol abuse → Domestic violence

b. Secondary Observation

Low self-esteem → Alcohol abuse

c. Spurious Relationship

Low self-esteem → Alcohol abuse → Domestic violence

d. Supported and Expected Relationships

Low self-esteem → Alcohol abuse
Low self-esteem → Domestic violence
Alcohol abuse (?) → Domestic violence

Finally, in reporting a study's findings and conclusions, researchers have the opportunity to discuss the policy implications of their research, fulfilling the goal of producing usable knowledge. The audience for a research report, then, may include government officials, policy makers, and the general public, in addition to the researcher's colleagues.

Sociologists report their research in many ways. Typically, though, they publish their findings in journal articles or books, or make presentations at professional meetings. However, the general public rarely reads scholarly papers. Moreover, as one former presidential advisor recently told a reporter, never during his twelve years of government service had he heard any policy maker refer to an article in an academic journal (Honan, 1994). Consequently, if sociologists want their research to have an impact beyond the academic community, they must take responsibility for getting their work into the hands of a broader audience.

The research process is circular. In other words, while a single study answers specific research questions, it also generates questions to be addressed in future research, thus starting the whole process anew. Figure 2.2 on page 38 summarizes the research process, showing its circular nature.

REFLECTING ON

The Research Process

1. If you were a sociologist, what research topic would you be most interested in studying? Why?
2. Can you think of an example of a variable? What are the attributes of the variable? How would you operationalize the variable?
3. Which step in the research process do you find most challenging? Why?

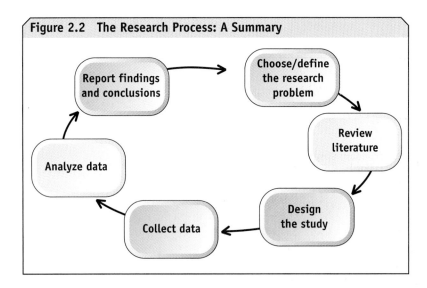

Figure 2.2 The Research Process: A Summary

METHODS OF SOCIOLOGICAL RESEARCH

A **research method** is a technique or procedure used to collect data. Sociologists use a variety of research methods, and we will examine several of them in this section. We'll discuss the strengths and weaknesses of each one, but ultimately, the decision as to which method is "best" depends on what the researcher is interested in studying. With each method, the researcher collects different types of data; thus, each method suits particular types of research questions.

Survey Research

If you are interested in people's attitudes, opinions, or experiences, the best data collection method is the **survey**. In a survey, the researcher selects a sample of respondents and asks them questions about specific topics. This may be done in two ways: using questionnaires or interviews.

Questionnaires. You have probably completed at least one questionnaire at some time; perhaps you have written and administered your own questionnaires. In either case, such experiences have likely driven home for you the importance of careful questionnaire construction. Consider, for example, that most questionnaires are self-administered, that is, respondents are expected to complete them on their own without the researcher present to provide instructions or clarify the meaning of particular questions. Most self-administered questionnaires are distributed and returned by mail. Consequently, the questionnaire must be accompanied by a cover letter that introduces the researcher and explains the purpose of the study and how respondents were selected. Directions for completing and returning the questionnaire must be pre-

cise and easy to understand. And of course, the questions themselves must be worded in such a way that they neither confuse respondents nor bias their answers. For example, ask a sample of your friends whether they think the government is spending too much, too little, or just the right amount of money on *helping the poor*. Then ask a comparable sample of your friends whether they think the government is spending too much, too little, or just the right amount of money on *welfare*. If your friends are like most Americans, they will answer "too little" to the first question, but "too much" to the second. Researchers have found that using the word *welfare* or the words *helping the poor* biases respondents' answers in different ways (Rasinski, 1989; see also Kasof, 1993).

One of the ways that researchers try to avoid such bias is by pretesting the questionnaire. A pretest is a dry run; before sending the questionnaire out to the study sample, the researcher gives it to a small group of people with the same characteristics as the sample. This allows the opportunity to identify any areas of confusion or bias in the questionnaire before the actual data collection gets underway.

The self-administered questionnaire is undoubtedly one of the most popular data collection techniques used by sociologists. It permits the researcher to collect extensive information from large numbers of people in a relatively quick and inexpensive manner. All respondents are asked the same questions in the same way, and they usually select their answers from a given set of response categories (such as strongly agree or strongly disagree), thus providing standardized data. However, such questionnaires have the disadvantage of being inflexible in that they typically allow respondents little if any opportunity to explain their answers or to put them in context. Many of us know the frustration of reading the response choices for a question on a questionnaire and feeling that

What four methods of sociological research are shown here? What are the general advantages and disadvantages of each method? Invent a research question that interests you for which each method (observation, survey, interview, experiment) might be especially appropriate.

none of them adequately expresses our opinion or that each of them expresses it under certain circumstances. This difficulty may be remedied by using an alternative survey method, interviewing.

Interviews. In an interview, the researchers personally ask respondents the questions they want answered. This may be done over the telephone, which has the advantage of allowing researchers to reach respondents geographically dispersed, just as they would with a self-administered questionnaire. However, many potential respondents are wary of answering questions posed by a stranger over the telephone, which means that researchers must contact a much larger sample of respondents in order to complete a sufficient number of interviews for analysis.

Alternatively, researchers may arrange to meet with respondents to ask them the survey questions in person. In the study on sexual behavior that opened the chapter, the

researchers used this kind of interview method, called the *in-person interview.* In-person interviews often provide both the researcher and the respondent with greater flexibility in questioning and answering. Researchers can ensure that the person they intended to complete the survey actually does it—something not possible with a mailed questionnaire. Researchers can also ask follow-up questions or probe the respondent for additional information. Respondents can provide greater detail in their answers and put their answers in context. And both researchers and respondents can ask each other for clarification if a question is confusing.

Despite the advantages of in-person interviewing, there are disadvantages as well. For one thing, few researchers have the funding needed to conduct in-person interviews with a large sample that is widely dispersed geographically. As a result, most studies involving in-person interviews are limited geographically. In-person interviewing is also more time-consuming than the other types of survey research. Moreover, interviewers run the risk of biasing respondents' answers simply by their presence. The characteristics of the interviewer (sex, race, age, mode of dress) may influence how a particular respondent answers. In general, the more dissimilar the interviewer is from the respondent, the greater the risk of the interviewer influencing or biasing the respondent's answers.

This latter point raises a drawback inherent in all types of survey research methods: the problem of artificiality. What people say they believe or what they say they do is sometimes not reflected in their actual behavior. Researchers may be told only what may be considered socially acceptable answers or what respondents think the researchers want to hear. Despite its drawbacks, however, survey research is the most popular research method in sociology.

Doing Survey Research on Intimate Violence: An Example.

Since the 1960s, a great deal of research has been done on violence in intimate relationships. Nearly all of this research, though, has studied violence in heterosexual relationships. In 1985, one of your authors undertook a study of violence in lesbian relationships (Renzetti, 1992). Participants for the study were recruited mainly through newspaper advertisements and announcements in the newsletters of gay and lesbian organizations throughout the country, so the sample was not random. More than two hundred women volunteered to participate in the study by mailing a card requesting a questionnaire from the researcher. The researcher then sent each volunteer a questionnaire with a postage-paid return envelope. One hundred questionnaires were eventually completed and returned to the researcher.

The twelve-page questionnaire that was developed for this study used a variety of closed-ended questions to learn about the participants, their partners, and the violence that occurred in the relationship. For example, participants were asked about which partner was responsible for doing various household tasks, sources of strain or conflict in the relationship, and how problems were usually resolved. They were also asked to identify from a list the different forms of physical violence and psychological abuse their partners had inflicted on them. They were asked if the abuse got worse over time, if they sought help from others, and if they ended the relationship. And they were asked a series of background questions, such as their own and their partner's ages, racial or ethnic identification, level of educational attainment, occupation, and income.

The study was not designed to find out how often violence occurs in lesbian relationships, but it did show that in lesbian relationships that are violent, the abuse is recurring and frequently severe. Nevertheless, from the outset of the study, the researcher had doubted whether closed-ended questions could adequately capture the complexity of the participants' interactions and feelings. Consequently, the researcher gave the respondents the opportunity on the questionnaire to volunteer for an interview by supplying their name and phone number. Seventy of the one hundred respondents volunteered to be interviewed, and forty interviews were completed.

The interviews, which allowed the respondents to talk freely about what they considered to be the most significant aspects of their abuse experiences, provided rich qualitative data that supplemented the questionnaire results. For example, the interview data called into question a longstanding theory of intimate violence: that abused children will grow up to be abusive adults. The partners of the women in this study were almost as likely to have grown up in nonviolent households as in violent ones.

This study illustrates how survey research can be used to study even highly sensitive topics, such as intimate violence. The anonymity afforded by the questionnaire also proved useful for obtaining information from a group of women who have been marginalized in our society because of their sexual orientation. And the research shows how interviews can be used with questionnaires in a single study to enrich the data.

Field Observation

One of the best methods for studying behavior and social interaction is **field observation.** In field observation, the researcher watches a social phenomenon unfold in its natural setting. For example, if you are interested in learning about how police typically respond to domestic violence calls, you would learn more by accompanying them on such calls and watching what they do, rather than simply sending them a questionnaire or talking to them about what they do.

There are two types of field observation: participant observation and nonparticipant observation. As the terms suggest, in participant observation, the researcher becomes actively involved in what he or she is studying, whereas in nonparticipant observation, the researcher simply watches the social interaction taking place, making no attempt to become personally involved in it.

Each of these approaches has advantages and disadvantages. As a participant observer, for instance, the researcher experiences firsthand what she or he is studying, thus obtaining a level of understanding of the phenomenon that is not possible with other methods. This is clearly an advantage. However, by participating directly in the interaction, the researcher unavoidably runs the risk of changing it or affecting it in some significant way. In addition, there is the danger that participant observers will become so personally involved in what they are studying that they will not be able to analyze their findings in an unbiased way. Nonparticipant observers are less likely to encounter these problems (an advantage of this method), but they are also less likely to gain as complete an understanding of what they are studying as participant observers do (a disadvantage).

The Hawthorne Effect. Both participant and nonparticipant observers must decide whether they will make their identities as researchers known to the people they are studying. On the one hand, it may be argued that by concealing her or his identity as a researcher and trying to pass as a member of the group being studied, the researcher is likely to get more valid data. If individuals know they are being studied, they may behave less naturally, or they may try to change their behavior to win the researcher's or others' approval. This problem is known as the **Hawthorne effect.** Specifically, the Hawthorne effect occurs when the participants in a study change their behavior to conform to what they perceive are the researcher's expectations of them. On the other hand, concealing one's true identity is a form of deception, a point we will discuss in more detail later in the chapter.

Humphrey's Controversial Study. One of the best-known observational studies in sociology was conducted by Laud Humphreys. Humphreys published his findings in a book called *Tearoom Trade* (1970), which won a prestigious award as a model of outstanding research.

Humphreys studied homosexual acts that occurred in men's rest rooms, which among the participants were known as "tearooms." Because such behavior was illegal and also often involved sex between an adult and a juvenile, the participants usually made sure that one person acted as a lookout for the police and any unsuspecting intruders. Humphreys decided to assume the role of lookout, since it would give him the opportunity to observe the interaction without directly engaging in it and without having to identify himself as a researcher. However, Humphreys wanted to know more about the participants in these impersonal sexual encounters than simple observation could tell him, so he also recorded the registration numbers on their cars and later identified their names and addresses. A year after he completed his observations, Humphreys contacted the tearoom customers and asked to interview them in their homes about a topic unrelated to his real research. During the interviews, Humphreys discovered that most of the men were married and lived with their wives. Many appeared to be mainstream members of their communities, involved in civic and church activities.

Humphreys's study was praised for calling into question some of the common stereotypes about individuals who engaged in homosexual sex. However, his research also generated considerable controversy, with critics charging that the deception he used to gain access to the participants was unethical and could have caused them serious harm. We'll return to the issue of research ethics later in the chapter.

Experiments

While survey and field methods are very popular among sociologists, a method less frequently used is the **experiment.** Although there are several experimental designs, usually experiments seek to test a **hypothesis:** a statement of the expected relationship between two variables, which we have already identified as the independent variable and the dependent variable. In order to increase the certainty that it is the independent variable that is causing any observed changes in the dependent variable and not some extraneous factor, the researcher tries to carefully control the conditions under which the experiment is conducted. This is usually done in two ways: by using experimental and control groups, and by pretesting and posttesting.

Experimental and Control Groups. Figure 2.3 on page 42 illustrates the most common experimental design. Research participants are divided into two groups, an *experimental group* and a *control group.* The members of each group are carefully matched, so that they are similar to one another with respect to all relevant characteristics; the only thing that is different is whether they are exposed to the independent variable.

First, both groups are measured in terms of the presence of the dependent variable. This measurement constitutes the pretest. Then, only the experimental group is exposed to the independent variable. Afterward, both groups are again measured in terms of the dependent variable. This second measurement is the posttest. The differences between the pretest and posttest results for each group are compared. If the difference for the experimental group is greater than the difference for the control group, the researcher can be reasonably certain that the independent variable had an effect on the dependent variable, and can go on to discuss the nature and extent of this effect.

Although the experiment has the advantage of precision because the researcher exercises extensive control over the research conditions, its greatest disadvantage is its artificiality. Experiments are especially prone to the Hawthorne effect. As we noted previously, when individuals know they are being studied, they may change

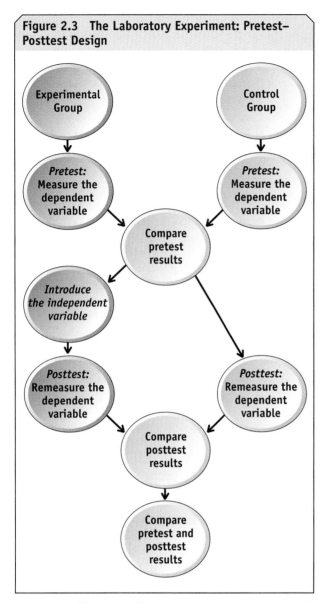

Figure 2.3   The Laboratory Experiment: Pretest–Posttest Design

Experimental Group

Control Group

Pretest: Measure the dependent variable

Pretest: Measure the dependent variable

Compare pretest results

Introduce the independent variable

Posttest: Remeasure the dependent variable

Posttest: Remeasure the dependent variable

Compare posttest results

Compare pretest and posttest results

Source: Adapted from E. Babbie. (1998). *The practice of social research.* Belmont, CA: Wadsworth, p. 243.

their behavior to conform to what they perceive to be socially acceptable, to please the researcher, or possibly in some cases to thwart the experiment. Moreover, we must also keep in mind that while an independent variable may actually have an effect on people's behavior under the controlled conditions of a research laboratory, one cannot be certain that it will elicit the same effect in a natural setting.

The Social Science Experiment: An Example.   What would happen if you brought a group of psychologically healthy young men into a laboratory designed to resemble a prison and told them that for the next two weeks half the group would be prisoners and the other half

would be guards? This is precisely what Stanford University psychologist Philip Zimbardo (1972) did in order to test the hypothesis that the structure of prison life itself, not abnormal personalities, generates violent and abusive behavior on the part of both guards and prisoners.

Although Zimbardo did not use the common pretest–posttest experimental design, he did strive to control experimental conditions as much as possible. Zimbardo sought to make his experiment realistic. Those volunteers who were designated prisoners were arrested at their homes by police officers; searched, handcuffed, and fingerprinted; and transported to the "prison," which was the basement of the Stanford University psychology building where cells had been constructed. Within a short time, the experiment turned into a nightmare, especially for those participants who were prisoners. The guards quickly took to humiliating and degrading the prisoners, treating them cruelly and appearing to enjoy it. Some of the prisoners responded with verbal and physical resistance, but others became withdrawn and depressed. In fact, after only four days, five of the twelve prisoners had to be "released" because they exhibited symptoms of extreme emotional disturbance. Within a week, Zimbardo called off the experiment for fear that the remaining prisoners would suffer irreparable harm.

Although this was a psychological experiment, Zimbardo's findings were important to sociologists. Zimbardo demonstrated the impact of environmental factors on people's behavior. More importantly, his work suggested that prison life can generate crime rather than reforming criminals (see, for example, Porter, 1998). However, Zimbardo's experiment also raised ethical questions because of the potential harm posed to participants. We'll return to this point shortly.

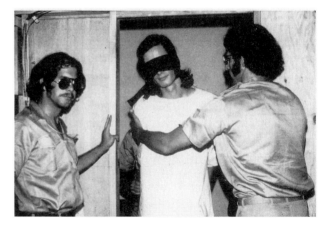

How did Zimbardo's famous "prisoners and guards" experiment illustrate ethical concerns about the use of human subjects in research? What sociological insight did the experiment provide about the influence of prison life on criminal behavior?

To what extent is this child being socialized to imitate violent behavior through televison exposure? How could you find out? Could you use the same method to determine the extent to which children learn prosocial behavior through television?

Content Analysis

Sometimes researchers do not have direct access to a population of people from which they can draw a sample or in some other way recruit people to participate in a study. Suppose, for instance, that you want to study attitudes, events, or social practices of a previous historical period. Unless the phenomena of interest are relatively recent, it would be impossible for you to observe, interview, or distribute questionnaires to individuals with firsthand experience. This does not mean, though, that you cannot conduct your study. You could do the study using a method called **content analysis,** which is common to historical research. Content analysis involves analyzing the content of some form of communication. In historical research, written documents—such as diaries, letters, speeches, laws, newspapers, and magazines—frequently are used, but virtually any form of communication can be examined, including photographs, recordings, videotapes, even mail-order catalogs and greeting cards.

Content analysis is a highly subjective method that requires the researcher to develop criteria for selecting representative material from the communications available and identifying indicators of the variables of interest in the study. For obvious reasons, content analysis is not only useful for historical research, but also for media studies and other types of communications research. Content analyses of violence on television, for example, have been used by both proponents and opponents of increased government regulation of television programming. How much violence is found in television programs depends on how violence is measured (Does verbal abuse count, or only physical action? Must the motive for the action be harm to another, or is the fact

that someone was harmed, even unintentionally, sufficient?). Rarely can researchers analyze all elements of the communication they are interested in, so they must also develop a sampling plan. In the case of television violence, for instance, researchers may sample programs only during certain periods of the day, such as Saturday morning children's programs or prime-time programming. Sample selection depends a great deal on the specific topic under investigation.

Advantages and Disadvantages of Content Analysis. Content analysis is usually a highly economical research method. It is also efficient in terms of time expenditure. Often, no special equipment is needed and expenses are minimal. Content analysis may be undertaken in one's own home or at a local library. When conducting a content analysis, the researcher need not fear that anything she or he does will change the subjects being studied. And finally, as we have already noted, content analysis is especially well-suited to research that involves the study of events, behaviors, or attitudes of a previous historical period or over several historical periods.

Despite these advantages, however, content analysis also has several disadvantages. Its highly subjective nature raises problems of validity. Moreover, in studying historical records and accounts, researchers must be cautious regarding their accuracy, whether these documents be official or unofficial, firsthand or secondary. As we noted in Chapter 1, "facts" may be seen or interpreted differently by different people, so it is wise for the researcher to try to verify individual accounts. If additional sources offer similar information, one can be more confident about the accuracy of the accounts. Similarly, researchers should be aware of the possible biases inherent in their data sources. For example, if one is interested in the lives of women in colonial America, the letters and diaries of wealthy women are likely to provide a very different perspective than diaries of poorer White women or enslaved Black women. The views of the latter two groups may be difficult to obtain, since these women were far less likely than the wealthy to be literate. Consequently, researchers must be careful about overgeneralizing from their data, since the information provided may be representative of only specific groups. To get a broader view, the researcher must collect data from sources that offer a variety of perspectives.

A Content Analysis of Children's Picture Books. In a now-classic content analysis of children's picture books, Lenore Weitzman and her colleagues (1972) found considerable gender stereotyping, with female characters usually depicted in household roles or excluded completely. Twenty years after the results of Weitzman's study were published, sociologist Roger Clark and his colleagues (1993) undertook another content analysis of children's picture books to see if anything had changed. While Weitzman had examined books that had won the prestigious Caldecott Medal during the five-year period 1967–1971, Clark and his colleagues examined Caldecott winners for the period 1987–1991. Importantly, however, Clark et al. expanded Weitzman's analysis by comparing books illustrated by African American artists with books illustrated by White artists. To do this, they included in their analysis books that had received the King award during the same period; the King award is given annually to African American illustrators and writers whose books promote world unity and peace and inspire young people to work toward their personal goals.

Clark and his colleagues found that in both recent Caldecott and King books, female characters were more visible and less stereotyped than Weitzman's study had found. However, they also found that in the King books, female characters are depicted as more independent and competitive, emotional, persistent, and nurturant than are the female characters in the Caldecott books. The researchers concluded that these depictions honor specific female traditions in the African American community: connectedness to and caring for others as well as an ethic of personal accountability.

This study by Clark and his colleagues not only exemplifies the method of content analysis, but also illustrates the principle of **replication** in sociological research. In replicating a study, researchers basically repeat a study that was done earlier. Like Clark and his colleagues, however, the replication often expands the earlier study by adding new variables.

Secondary Analysis

Another way that behavior or attitudes may be studied over periods of time is through **secondary analysis.** In secondary analysis, the researcher simply analyzes data that were gathered by others. Researchers who have collected data themselves often make these data sets available to other researchers for further analysis. One of the most popular sources of data for secondary analysis is the General Social Survey (GSS), a national survey conducted by the National Opinion Research Center (NORC) at the University of Chicago. The GSS is usually conducted biannually. In addition, government offices and agencies, such as the U.S. Bureau of the Census and various branches of the United Nations, as well as nongovernment organizations and businesses (such as the Worldwatch Institute, the Children's Defense Fund, and the Carnegie Foundation) routinely collect information that is published in the form of statistical reports and is available for use by the public, including researchers. In fact, you'll find data from many such sources throughout this book.

Problems with Secondary Analysis. Like content analysis, secondary analysis is economical in terms of both time and money. One of its major drawbacks, however, is the lack of control that the secondary analyst has over how the data were collected. Let's say, for instance, that you wish to study changes in the incidence of violent crime since 1960. To do this, you utilize the FBI's *Uniform Crime Reports* (UCR), which contain statistics on the number of crimes reported to law enforcement agents throughout the United States each year. You simply calculate from year to year whether the number of violent crimes went up or down and by how much. Obviously, such an approach is easier than many of the methods we've discussed so far, but consider whether it will necessarily produce reliable results. Reliability in secondary analysis is often problematic because of biases in the way the data were collected. In the case of the UCR, for example, secondary analysts must keep in mind that these data represent only crimes known to the police; there is a large amount of hidden crime, since it is estimated that only about one-third of all crimes committed come to the attention of law enforcement authorities. Moreover, the police themselves affect the crime rate in that they exercise considerable discretion in terms of how they respond when an offense is brought to their attention. They may be under political pressure to "get tough" on crime, so they act on every report, thus driving up the crime rate. Or, they may be under pressure to show that they have "cleaned up" a town, so they underreport offenses to the FBI, thus making it appear that the crime rate in their jurisdiction has gone down.

Secondary analysis also may raise problems of validity. How certain can you be that data collected for another purpose accurately capture the essence of what it is that *you* are interested in studying? We have already seen that the particular wording of a question may influence respondents' answers. Are another researcher's questions or operations adequate indicators of the variables you wish to measure? Ultimately, the secondary analyst must make the judgment as to whether the original variables and the way they were measured are good proxies for the variables she or he wishes to study.

Using Secondary Analysis to Study Female Criminality.

In 1975, criminologist Freda Adler shook the social science community with the publication of her research on female criminality, *Sisters in Crime*. Adler argued that women's crime was changing in both quantity and quality: Women were committing more crimes than they had in the past, and their criminality was becoming more like that of men, that is, more serious and violent. How did Adler arrive at these conclusions? A significant part of her research was a secondary analysis of female arrest rates recorded in the FBI *Uniform Crime Reports* for the period 1960–1972. Adler found that during this time women's arrests for robbery rose 277 percent, while men's arrests for robbery rose 169 percent. A wide gender gap was also found for embezzlement (a 280 percent increase for women and a 50 percent increase for men), larceny (a 303 percent increase for women and an 82 percent increase for men), and burglary (a 168 percent increase for women and a 63 percent increase for men). Women's and men's arrests for murder and aggravated assault were found to be roughly equal, although both were rising.

Adler's research generated considerable interest in female crime, a topic historically overlooked by criminologists. However, it also drew criticism because of the way the secondary analysis was conducted. Specifically, when Adler compared increases in male and female arrest rates, she did not control for the large difference in the absolute base numbers from which the rates of increase are calculated. If one base number is small, even a slight rise will exaggerate the rate change. Conversely, a sizable increase in a large base number is likely to appear as only a minor change (Smart, 1982; Terry, 1978). Thus, for example, between 1965 and 1970, the number of arrests of women for homicide increased almost 79 percent, while men's arrests for homicide increased 73 percent. The changes look about equal, but if we examine the actual numbers, the number of homicides committed by women during this period rose from 1,293 to 1,645, whereas for men the increase was from 6,533 to 8,858. Clearly, women's and men's homicide rates are not as comparable as Adler's analysis would lead us to believe.

Adler's study reminds us of the care that must be taken in secondary analysis to ensure not only that we are measuring precisely what we want to measure, but also that we are calculating our measurements accurately.

R EFLECTING ON

Methods of Sociological Research

1. Of all the research methods discussed here, which would you most like to try in a research project? Explain how you would use this method to study the topic of your choice. What are some specific benefits and disadvantages of using this method in your study?
2. Of all the research methods discussed here, which do you think is the most challenging? Why?
3. What advice would you give the researchers discussed in this chapter as to how they might remedy some of the problems they encountered in their studies?

LINKING THEORY AND RESEARCH: THE INDUCTIVE AND DEDUCTIVE MODELS

Table 2.2 on page 46 summarizes the various research methods we have discussed. However, there is more to sociological research than simply collecting data. Sociologists must also determine what the data mean. For this, they rely on theory. As we stated in Chapter 1, the purpose of theory is explanation.

Suppose, for example, that we asked a sample of college students if they had ever coerced a dating partner into having sex with them. Our findings end up showing that men are more likely than women to answer affirmatively and, what's more, men who belong to fraternities are more likely than other men to respond yes. Reading this, you might well ask, "So what?" Our findings are meaningless without a theory to explain them.

At the same time, however, we use research to test particular theories. If a sociologist were to state that fraternity members are more likely to engage in sexual assault than nonfraternity members because living in an all-male group generates antifemale attitudes, the statement would be nothing more than assertion because it has not been empirically tested. (For an empirical test of this theory, see Schwartz & DeKeseredy, 1997.)

Our examples suggest that there are actually two ways in which theory and research are linked: Research may help to generate theory in an effort to explain data or research may test an existing theory. These two approaches to the relationship between theory and research actually represent different models of logical thought known as the *inductive* and *deductive* models respectively.

TABLE 2.2 Research Methods: A Summary

Method	Advantages	Disadvantages	Example
Survey using questionnaires	Permits collection of data from a large number of people Can collect data from people geographically dispersed Relatively quick Relatively inexpensive Produces standardized data	Inflexibility: does not allow respondents to elaborate on or explain their answers Researcher cannot ensure that the questionnaire is completed by the appropriate respondent or under ideal conditions	Renzetti's study of violence in lesbian relationships
Survey using in-person interviews	Provides researcher with flexibility in asking questions Provides respondent with flexibility in answering questions Respondents can give more detailed answers to questions Questions may be clarified, reducing the possibility of misunderstanding Researcher can ensure that the person who is supposed to answer actually does	Usually requires a relatively small sample Limits ability to reach a geographically dispersed sample Relatively expensive Relatively time-consuming Risk of interviewer bias	Renzetti's study of violence in lesbian relationships
Field observation as a participant	Researcher can personally experience what she or he is studying, thus improving understanding of it	Risk of changing or significantly affecting what is being studied Potential ethical problem of deception	Humphreys's study of impersonal sex in public places
Field observation as nonparticipant	Researcher can watch what she or he is studying as it occurs	Potential risk of Hawthorne effect Potential ethical problem of deception	
Experiment	Researcher can exercise considerable control over the research conditions, adding to precision	Risk of Hawthorne effect Results may not apply to situations outside the laboratory setting	Zimbardo's prison experiment
Content analysis	Useful for historical research No risk of Hawthorne effect Economical Time efficient	Potential validity problems because of inaccurate records or data sources	Clark and colleagues' study of children's picture books
Secondary analysis	Useful for historical and longitudinal research No risk of Hawthorne effect Economical Time efficient	Potential reliability problems because of biases in the way the data were collected Potential validity problems because data collected for one purpose may not be accurate measure proxies for the variables of another study	Adler's study of change in male/female crime rates, using the FBI *Uniform Crime Reports*

In the **inductive model,** the researcher begins by collecting data on the topic of interest and subsequently builds theory through the data analysis. Laud Humphreys's study of impersonal sex in public places is an example of the inductive method. Humphreys did not begin his research with a set of hypotheses he wished to test, but rather relied on his data to suggest explanations for the interactions he had observed.

Compare, however, Humphreys's study with that of Philip Zimbardo. Zimbardo, we said, set out to test the hypothesis that it is the prison environment and not the individual personalities of prisoners or guards that gen-

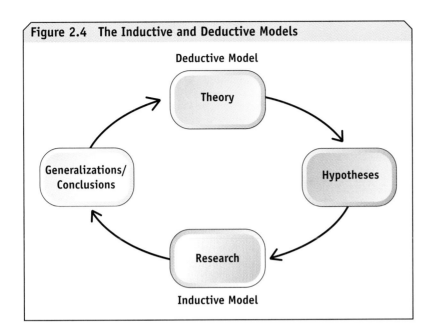

Figure 2.4 The Inductive and Deductive Models

Deductive Model

Theory

Hypotheses

Research

Generalizations/ Conclusions

Inductive Model

erates prison violence. Zimbardo, then, employed the deductive model. In the **deductive model,** the researcher develops hypotheses from a particular theory and conducts the research to test these hypotheses.

Figure 2.4 depicts the inductive and deductive models. Notice, however, the interplay between the two. The link between theory and research reminds us once again of the continuity of the research process.

REFLECTING ON

Linking Theory and Research: The Inductive and Deductive Models

Review the studies that were used in this chapter to illustrate specific research methods. Which studies follow the inductive method and which follow the deductive method?

OBJECTIVITY IN SOCIOLOGICAL RESEARCH

Every sociologist brings to her or his research a set of assumptions about the nature of scientific work. These assumptions inform the entire research enterprise. One important issue about which sociologists have held conflicting assumptions is the role of objectivity in sociological research.

All researchers approach their projects with basic assumptions about the role of objectivity in scientific work. **Objectivity** refers to the extent to which research is free

from the personal values and biases of the researcher. It is one thing to say, for example, that White Americans and African Americans have access to different opportunities in the United States. It is another thing to say that this is good or bad. The first statement is directly verifiable, whereas the second statement derives from a personal judgment. Most sociologists recognize that complete objectivity in research is impossible, since we are fundamentally part of what we study—the social world. Otherwise, however, they disagree on how much objectivity is possible or necessary.

Some claim, for instance, that apart from allowing their values to affect the research topic they choose, researchers should remain as detached as possible from the people they are studying. Others maintain that values should also affect how the research ultimately is used. These sociologists feel that research should raise awareness of social problems and help empower oppressed groups. In other words, rather than remaining detached, researchers should develop mutually beneficial relationships with the participants in their studies (see, for example, Maguire, 1987).

Feminist sociologists, in particular, strongly advocate the latter approach. They call for equity in the research process and greater attention to the needs of the people being studied. They maintain that because totally value-free research is impossible—and, most would add, undesirable—the researcher must openly acknowledge all assumptions, beliefs, sympathies, or biases that underlie the research, including biases deriving from the researcher's sex, race, social class, and sexual orientation.

In addition, feminist sociologists reject the traditional separation of the researcher from the researched, preferring self-disclosure and reciprocity. That is, feminist researchers feel an obligation to allow the people they are studying to "talk back" to them during the research—to ask personal questions of the researcher and have those questions answered honestly. This is self-disclosure. Feminist sociologists also think it's appropriate for study participants to seek help from the researcher and have that help be forthcoming and meaningful. This is reciprocity. Rather than presenting themselves as all-knowing experts, feminist researchers recognize that they have much to learn from the research participants and that they owe them a debt of gratitude (Bergen, 1993; Reinharz, 1992).

In sum, while all sociologists see the need for objectivity in their research, they disagree on how much is beneficial and necessary. Perhaps the best guideline continues to be Max Weber's principle of *value relevance*. Weber recognized that values always enter into the research process, particularly when the researcher decides on a topic of study. Researchers select a topic because personally we find it intriguing, or we think it is important, not trivial. The point is that personal backgrounds, interests, and experiences cannot help but enter into the research process, and it is appropriate for values to inform research in this way. However, Weber cautions that once research begins, sociologists must remain *value-neutral*; that is, they must not let their values influence the collection and analysis of the data, nor how the research is later used (Ringer, 1997). If, for instance, the researcher doesn't like what respondents are saying, or doesn't like the findings obtained, the researcher cannot change them so that they better conform to his or her wishes (see, for example, Swazey et al., 1993). Researchers must let their findings stand, even if the findings clash with their most cherished beliefs. This is the dualistic nature of sociology that we discussed in Chapter 1: The practice of sociology is both subjective and objective.

Weber's principles of value relevance and value neutrality raise questions regarding ethics in sociological research. They also raise questions about politics, because Weber maintained that sociologists should not advise a particular course of action based on research results. According to Weber, in undertaking empirical research, the sociologist studies what *is*, not what *ought to be*. As we have noted, however, some sociologists openly reject this aspect of value neutrality and actively seek to influence public policy with their research. It is also often the case that sociological research is put to a particular political use, whether the sociologist intends that or not.

R EFLECTING ON

Objectivity in Sociological Research

1. How would you respond to someone who states that sociological research should be completely value free?

2. What is a specific example of a researcher putting the principle of reciprocity into practice?

ETHICS AND POLITICS IN SOCIOLOGICAL RESEARCH

Ethics refers to principles of right or good conduct in research. Table 2.3 presents some of the guidelines for ethical research that have been adopted by the American Sociological Association. You may think that some of these guidelines are so obvious that they don't need to be stated. In many cases, however, the ethical course of action is not as clear-cut as you may assume.

The Ethics of Sociological Research

Suppose, for example, you responded to an ad soliciting volunteers to participate in what is described as a learning experiment. When you arrive at the research laboratory you are paired with another volunteer and are told that one of you will be the "teacher" in the experiment and the other the "learner." You draw lots to decide respective roles and you end up being the teacher. The learner is taken into a separate room and you watch as the experimenter straps the learner into a chair and attaches an electrical wire to the learner's arm. Both you and your partner are then instructed that the teacher will read a list of word pairs through a microphone to the learner; then, the teacher will go to the beginning of the list and read the first word of each word pair, giving the learner a choice of words from which to choose the word's match. The learner presses a switch (a, b, c, or d) to indicate the answer. If the match is correct, the teacher moves on to the next word on the list, but if the learner gives an incorrect answer, the teacher must press a switch to deliver an electrical shock as a "punishment" to the learner. With each wrong answer, the strength of the shock intensifies, going from 15 volts to more than 315 volts. Both you and the learner indicate that you understand the instructions, and the experiment gets underway. As the experiment proceeds, the learner starts getting a lot of matches wrong and you find yourself administering progressively stronger shocks. The learner begins to scream and asks that the experiment be stopped, but the experimenter instructs you to continue until the most intense shock has been administered. At one point the learner starts banging on the wall, complaining of chest pains; later, the learner stops answering. Nevertheless, the experimenter instructs you to continue.

What we have been describing here was an actual experiment conducted by social psychologist Stanley Milgram in the early 1960s. Motivated by the tales of Nazi soldiers during World War II who claimed to have carried

TABLE 2.3 ASA's Code of Ethics

The American Sociological Association (ASA), like most other professional organizations whose members engage in research, has developed a *code of ethics* to guide sociologists in designing and carrying out their research projects and reporting their findings. Among the twenty-four ethical principles the ASA has adopted to guide the practice of sociology are:

- Every sociologist should state explicitly at the outset of a project any personal limitations that may impact on the validity of their research findings or their ability to successfully conduct a specific research project.

- Sociologists must not misrepresent the findings of their research. Findings must be presented completely, without omitting significant data. Significant qualifications with respect to the findings or interpretation of the research should also be explicitly stated.

- Sociologists are obliged to disseminate their research findings, except when such dissemination might cause harm to research subjects, collaborators, or others involved in a research project.

- Once sociologists have completed a project, they should make the raw data available to other researchers, except when such disclosure violates confidentiality or research subjects' claims to proprietary information and privacy.

- Sociologists must be aware of situations in which their research or their influence and authority might be misused, and they should take efforts to address these potential problems and conflicts.

- Sociologists should not mislead those involved in their research about the purposes for which the research is being conducted.

- Research subjects are entitled to biographical anonymity and, to the extent possible, researchers must treat information confidentially, even if this information enjoys no legal protection or privilege and legal force is applied.

- The research process must not place research subjects at substantial risk of being harmed. If the risk of harm is greater than the risks posed by everyday life, researchers must obtain informed consent from research subjects. When especially vulnerable populations are involved, special steps may be necessary to secure informed consent and to avoid invasions of privacy.

Source: Code of Ethics of the American Sociological Association. Copies of the complete *Code of Ethics* may be obtained for a nominal charge from the American Sociological Association, 1307 New York Ave., NW, Suite 700, Washington, DC 20005-4107.

out their atrocities simply because they were ordered to do so, Milgram devised this experiment for the real purpose of learning the extent to which people would hurt others if they were ordered by some authority figure to do so. You might suppose that few of the "teachers" in Milgram's experiment would continue to administer shocks to the learner, especially when the learner began to scream and complain about the pain. In fact, however, two-thirds of the participants followed Milgram's orders completely, administering even the most severe shocks despite the learner's protests.

As it turns out, the shocks were not real, and the learner was one of Milgram's research assistants; the assignment of the roles for the research participants was rigged, so that the assistant was always the learner. Still, Milgram's experiment appears to violate two of the most important principles of ethical research: (1) do no harm to the research participants; and (2) participation in a research project should always be voluntary, not required or coerced.

In the film that Milgram made about the experiment, one sees clear and at times extreme distress on the faces and in the bodies of the research subjects. Milgram maintained afterward that the debriefing he gave the research subjects thoroughly allayed their anxieties, but one wonders whether being informed of the true purpose of the experiment and being reunited with the learner to see that no shocks were actually administered are sufficient to prevent psychological harm to these research subjects. How do you think you would have felt after participating in this experiment, especially if you had fully obeyed the experimenter's commands? Do you think you would have been psychologically harmed by participating in the experiment? Would simply knowing that the shocks were fake and seeing that the learner was uninjured be enough to prevent you from being harmed?

Apart from the question of psychological harm, we must ask whether you were really a voluntary participant in this experiment. While it is true that you willingly went to the laboratory to take part, you were unaware of

Figure 2.5 Announcement Placed by Stanley Milgram in a Local Newspaper to Recruit Subjects

Public Announcement

WE WILL PAY YOU $4.00 FOR ONE HOUR OF YOUR TIME

Persons Needed for a Study of Memory

*We will pay five hundred New Haven men to help us complete a scientific study of memory and learning. The study is being done at Yale University.

*Each person who participates will be paid $4.00 (plus 50¢ carfare) for approximately 1 hour's time. We need you for only one hour: there are no further obligations. You may choose the time you would like to come (evenings, weekdays, or weekends).

*No special training, education, or experience is needed. We want:

Factory workers	Businessmen	Construction workers
City employees	Clerks	Salespeople
Laborers	Professional people	White-collar workers
Barbers	Telephone workers	Others

All persons must be between the ages of 20 and 50. High school and college students cannot be used.

*You will be paid $4.00 (plus 50¢ carfare) as soon as you arrive at the laboratory.

Source: "Announcement" from *Obedience to Authority* by Stanley Milgram. Copyright © 1974 by Stanley Milgram. Reprinted by permission of HarperCollins Publishers, Inc.

the true purpose of the experiment. (See Figure 2.5, which is the advertisement Milgram published to solicit volunteers for the experiment.) In other words, Milgram deceived you. It is typically argued that such a study could not be conducted if full voluntary participation were solicited. It is also argued that even if those studied volunteered to participate, they probably would not be honest with the researcher, and therefore the findings would be seriously flawed. But when researchers fail to inform research participants of the true nature or subject of their studies (as Milgram did), they are engaging in deception, which, in principle, is unethical. Nevertheless, most professional associations, including the American Sociological Association, permit deception in research if it can be justified on compelling scientific or administrative grounds. Thus, Milgram argued that the social and political significance of his research outweighed any concerns about the unethical nature of his deception. In other words, the end justified the means. Still, some maintain that deceptive research is unethical under *any* circumstances, and if research participants must be deceived, the study should not be conducted (see, for example, Bok, 1979).

Certainly there are no pat solutions to the ethical problems that arise in sociological research. However, this does not absolve the researcher from the responsibility of identifying the problems and developing workable strategies for addressing them.

The Politics of Sociological Research

In addition to ethical difficulties, sociologists must also confront political issues related to their research. In contrast to ethics, the **politics of research** has to do with how the research may be used to promote or support a particular interest or partisan position.

Political issues may arise from research because of the topic studied, the findings obtained, or how the research may ultimately be used. For example, in 1990, two researchers released the findings from their study on adolescent drug use and psychological health (Shedler & Block, 1990). Not surprisingly, they found that adolescents who were frequent drug users showed symptoms of severe psychological maladjustment. Importantly, however, they also found that adolescents who had never experimented with any drugs seemed to have adjustment problems, too. It was the adolescents who had engaged in some drug experimentation, primarily with just marijuana, who showed the best level of psychological health and adjustment. In reporting their findings, Shedler and Block were careful to emphasize that their data should not be interpreted as encouraging drug use among adolescents or that drugs somehow improve an adolescent's psychological well-being. Nevertheless, these were precisely the messages that were implicitly—and sometimes explicitly—reported by the media. As a result, the study was condemned by drug counselors, politicians, parent groups, and others. The researchers' goals, then, were thwarted by the way their findings were used by various interest groups to promote partisan causes. Instead of the study being used to improve drug use prevention and treatment programs, as the researchers had intended, the study was inappropriately criticized and its findings were distorted (see also Sieber, 1993).

Unfortunately, there are no "codes of politics" akin to professional codes of ethics that provide guidelines for addressing such problems. Researchers simply must think through the political implications of their work and make every effort to ensure that their research find-

ings are interpreted correctly and that they are used for the intended purposes. Although researchers can probably never totally prevent misuse, they must respond to misuses of which they become aware and try to rectify the distortions.

R EFLECTING ON

Ethics and Politics in Sociological Research

1. What were some possible ethical and political issues in other studies described in this chapter?
2. Why do you think it is difficult for sociologists to keep their research value-neutral when it comes to politics?

 For useful resources for study and review, run Chapter 2 on your *Living Sociology* CD-ROM.

C O N N E C T I O N S

Sexuality and sexual behavior	Read about "Love, Romance, and Sex" and "Single-Parent Families" in Chapter 15. What social factors contribute to teen pregnancy? To intimacy in social relationships?
Domestic violence	In Chapter 15, the section on "Violence in Families" discusses partner abuse in heterosexual and homosexual relationships as well as child abuse and elder abuse. What social factors contribute to domestic violence?
Sexual harassment	Read more about "Sexual Harassment" in Chapter 10. In a given setting, what measure of sexual harassment probably would provide the greatest reliability? What situations might compromise the validity of the data?
Health risk behaviors	The section on "Health in the United States" in Chapter 18 analyzes the social parameters of common health risks. Is an epidemiological study more like a longitudinal study or a cross-sectional study?
Data on U.S. college enrollment	Read the "Intersecting Inequalities" section, "Who Goes to College?" in Chapter 16. Apply the information in this chapter's feature on "Reading Tables and Understanding Descriptive Statistics" to the data in the Chapter 16 feature. For instance, is the relationship between income and college attendance spurious?
Homosexual relationships	Read the sections on "Gay and Lesbian Singles and Domestic Partners" and "Partner Abuse in Gay and Lesbian Relationships" in Chapter 15. Why has so little research been done on these subjects?
Field observations	An ethnographic study is a form of field observation combined with interviewing that is especially used in cross-cultural research. For example, read the section on "Cross-Cultural Research" on gender in Chapter 10. What are the advantages and disadvantages of this method of obtaining data?

CONNECTIONS

Behavioral experiments	For another example of experimental behavioral research see the section on "Animal Studies" in Chapter 5. What were the pretest and posttest conditions in Harlow's study?
Content analysis of television programming	Read more in the section on "The Mass Media" in Chapter 5. What challenges did researchers face in studying people's viewing behavior and using content analysis?
Secondary analysis of crime statistics	Read the section on "Crime Statistics" in Chapter 7. How could you use secondary analysis in a study of violent crimes? What might be some drawbacks to this method?
Stanley Milgram's experiment	Read more about the Milgram experiment in Chapter 6 in the section "When Conformity Becomes Obedience." How does this research inform sociological perspectives on social groups at the micro level as well as on political systems at the macro level?

SUMMING UP CHAPTER 2

The Science of Sociology

1. Sociology is different from common sense because sociological knowledge is based on science, which derives from empirical evidence (information that is directly verifiable).
2. Sociologists study a wide range of topics, from the micro level to the macro level, but in all cases, an underlying goal is to identify links between the individual and society.

The Research Process

1. Research proceeds through steps. The first step is choosing a research problem. The problem chosen may represent a personal interest of the researcher, or it may be an attempt to test folk wisdom, a specific theory, or a topic that other researchers have overlooked.
2. The second step of the research process is reading what other researchers have learned about the research problem. This is called the literature review.
3. The third step of the research process is research design, when the researcher develops a plan for finding answers to the research problem. In designing the project, the researcher must specify the units of analysis, operationalize the variables, consider potential reliability and validity problems, and decide whether the study will be cross-sectional or longitudinal.
4. The fourth step of the research process is collecting the data, which may be done using several different methods. First, though, the researcher must select people to participate in the study. This is done by drawing a sample from the population of interest. The sample must be representative of the population. Random sampling increases representativeness.
5. The fifth step of the research process is analyzing the data. This may be done using quantitative or qualitative analysis. When analyzing the data, the researcher is interested in both how the values of individual variables are distributed within a group, and how specific variables are related to one another. Sociologists can rarely establish causal relationships from their research, but they do identify correlational relationships. The researcher tries to control for the influence of as many variables as possible in order to increase the likelihood that observed relationships are not spurious.
6. The sixth step of the research process is reporting the findings and conclusions to others. This may be done through publications or public presentations. Often, this step generates new ideas for research.

Methods of Sociological Research

1. A research method is a technique or procedure used to collect data. The method used depends largely on the research problem being studied.
2. Survey research is the most popular method in sociology. Survey researchers select a sample of respondents and ask them questions about specific topics. Surveys are done using questionnaires and interviews. Questionnaires allow the researcher to collect extensive standardized information from a large number of people relatively quickly and inexpensively. But questionnaires do not give respondents much flexibility in answering or allow them to explain their answers. While interviews have greater flexibility and thus provide more detailed data, they pose the risk

of interviewer bias and they are usually by necessity limited in size and geographic coverage.

3. Field observation allows the researcher to watch a social phenomenon unfold in its natural setting. The researcher must decide whether or not to participate in what is being studied. Participants may get a better understanding of the research problem, but run the risk of changing what's being studied or becoming so involved in it that they can't analyze it objectively. Nonparticipants do not experience these problems, but they may get a less complete understanding of the research problem. In either case, researchers must also decide whether they will reveal their true identities to study participants, weighing the risk of the Hawthorne effect against the ethical problem of deception.

4. Experiments are uncommon in sociological research. In general, the goal of the experiment is to test a hypothesis under controlled conditions. It is the control afforded the researcher that is the biggest advantage of the experiment, but control also produces artificiality, the biggest disadvantage of experiments.

5. Content analysis is a method that involves analyzing the content of some form of communication. Content analysis is especially valuable for historical research. Content analysis poses no risk of the Hawthorne effect, it is economical, and it is efficient. However, researchers must be careful that their categories of analysis are relevant and valid and that the documents they are analyzing are accurate.

6. Secondary analysis is a method in which researchers analyze data gathered by others. This method is economical in terms of time and money, but the researcher has no control over how the data were originally collected.

Linking Theory and Research: The Inductive and Deductive Models

1. Theory and research are interrelated. Theory inspires and explains research. Research both generates theory (the inductive model) and tests theory (the deductive model).

Objectivity in Sociological Research

1. Most sociologists recognize that complete objectivity in research is impossible, but they disagree on how much objectivity is possible or necessary. The traditional approach to the issue of objectivity has been for researchers to detach themselves from those they are studying. Feminist researchers, in particular, reject this model, replacing it with self-disclosure and reciprocity.

Ethics and Politics in Sociological Research

1. Ethics refers to principles of right or good conduct in research. Some of the most important ethical principles are: do no harm to study participants, do not deceive study participants, and do not force or coerce anyone to participate in a study. In practice, these principles are sometimes difficult to follow.

2. Political issues often arise from research and may result in a study being used, appropriately or inappropriately, to promote or support a particular interest or partisan position.

KEY PEOPLE AND CONCEPTS

attributes: the descriptive categories or values that comprise variables

causal relationship: an empirically measured relationship between two variables in which a change in one variable causes a change in a second variable

concept: a mental representation of some aspect of our environment or the people in that environment

content analysis: a research method in which the content of some form of communication is analyzed

control: to neutralize in some way the effects of a variable on the other variables being studied

correlational relationship: an empirically measured relationship between variables in which the variables are found to change together

cross-sectional study: a study that examines behavior or attitudes at one fixed point in time

deductive model: a method of conducting research in which the researcher develops hypotheses from a particular theory and conducts research to test these hypotheses

dependent variable: a variable whose value depends on the value of the independent variable; in a cause-and-effect relationship, this variable represents the effect

descriptive statistics: statistics used to describe specific variables; however, descriptive statistics cannot be used for drawing conclusions about the relationships between variables

empirical evidence: information that is directly verifiable

ethics: principles of right or good conduct in research

experiment: a research method through which the researcher tests hypotheses about the relationship between an independent variable and a dependent variable, while controlling for the effects of other variables; usually conducted in a laboratory setting

field observation: a research method in which the researcher watches the social phenomenon he or she is studying unfold in its natural setting

frequency distribution: a table that shows the number of times each attribute of a variable occurs in a sample or population

Hawthorne effect: when research participants change their behavior to what they perceive are the researcher's expectations of them

hypothesis: a statement of the expected relationship between two variables

independent variable: a variable that produces or causes change in another variable; in a cause-and-effect relationship, this variable is the cause

indicator: shows the presence or absence of the variable being studied

inductive model: a method of conducting research in which the researcher begins by collecting data on the topic of interest and subsequently builds theory through data analysis

literature review: reading what other researchers have learned about the research problem

longitudinal study: a study in which data are gathered over an extended period of time, either continuously or at specific intervals

mean: the average value in a distribution

median: the midpoint of a distribution; 50 percent of the distribution falls below this value and 50 percent falls above this value

mode: the most frequent value in a distribution

objectivity: the extent to which research is free from the personal values or biases of the researcher

operationalizing a variable: the process of developing measures to be used to gauge the existence of a particular variable in the real world

politics of research: the ways in which research may be used to promote or support a particular interest or partisan position

population: the entire group that a researcher is interested in studying; all possible subjects of relevance to a study

qualitative analysis: the analysis of data in which the researcher focuses on specific qualities (distinct descriptive categories) within the data that show patterns of difference or similarity among the study participants, but do not allow the formulation of precise numerical statements about or measurements of these similarities or differences

quantitative analysis: the analysis of data in which the researcher translates study participants' responses into numerical categories that subsequently can be analyzed using various statistical techniques, usually via a computer

random sampling: the method of selecting a sample for a study that ensures that each member of the population has an equal chance of being selected for participation in the study

reliability: the ability of a measure to yield consistent results each time it is used

replication: repeating a study that was conducted at an earlier time

representative sample: a sample that closely resembles the population in terms of aggregate characteristics that are important for a specific study

research method: a technique or procedure used to collect data

sample: a subgroup of the larger group one is interested in studying

sampling: the process of selecting a subgroup for study from the entire group of interest

science: a logically organized method of obtaining information through direct, systematic observation

secondary analysis: the analysis of data that were gathered by others

spurious: when an observed relationship between two variables is not real and the change in both is actually the result of a third variable

survey: a research method in which the researcher selects a sample of respondents and asks them questions about specific topics

validity: the extent to which a measure accurately gauges what it was intended to measure

variable: a concept whose value varies or changes

LEARNING MORE

Ferrell, J., & Hamm, M. S. (Eds.). (1998). *Ethnography at the edge: Crime, deviance and field research*. Boston: Northeastern University Press. A collection of essays that relates the field experiences of sociologists who have conducted their research by immersing themselves in the everyday lives of pimps, phone sex workers, terrorists, even skydivers. Readers get a firsthand account of the challenges of observational research.

Humphreys, L. (1970). *Tearoom trade: Impersonal sex in public places*. Chicago: Aldine. The book that did more than just report the findings of the author's field work on gay male prostitutes and their clients; it sparked a highly charged debate over research ethics within the discipline, with one side praising Humphreys and the other denouncing him. Read it and decide where you stand on the ethical issues it raises.

Lurie, A. (1991). *Imaginary friends*. New York: Avon. A funny novel about two sociologists who try to study a cult. The story highlights in a comic way some of the ethical problems sociologists confront in doing field observation.

Platt, J. (1996). *A history of sociological research methods in America, 1920–1960*. New York: Cambridge University Press. Platt, traces the development of research methodology in the discipline during a period when an increase in government interest in and funding of sociological research occurred. Her detailed historical account is not an easy read, but it is informative.

Reinharz, S. (1992). *Feminist methods in social research.* New York: Oxford University Press. A readable review of feminist takes on various research methods, with many interesting examples to illustrate major points.

Renzetti, C. M., & Lee, R. M. (Eds.). (1993). *Researching sensitive topics.* Newbury Park, CA: Sage. A collection of articles in which researchers from various fields, including sociology, discuss how they handled specific problems that arose from their study of a sensitive topic, including cults, child abuse, AIDS, women's secret societies in Africa, and crime in post–Tiananmen Square China.

 Run Chapter 3 on your *Living Sociology* CD-ROM for interesting and informative activities, web links, videos, practice tests, and more.

CHAPTER

3

Societies

It is midwinter on the northeastern Canadian peninsula of Labrador, a typically frigid day. A young man sits inside his small family dwelling, cradling his five-week-old son in his arms. The baby is sick, and this man has spent most of the day holding and soothing him. The baby's mother has come in intermittently to feed him, but she is otherwise busy tanning the skin of a caribou her husband killed during a hunt. Finally, the infant falls asleep, and the man gently places him in a small, blanket-lined basket. It's time to prepare the evening meal. The man wonders what his wife will make from the caribou skin. Tanning is extremely hard work, and he marvels at her skill. After all, men may know how to cook and care for babies, but they know little about tanning leather.

Does such a man really exist, or is he simply the figment of your authors' imagination? The man is real, and the story is taken from the field notes of anthropologist Eleanor Leacock (1972), who observed him and other members of his society of Naskapi Eskimos. The relations between Naskapi women and men are quite different from the relations between women and men in our society. But it is not only gender relations that differ from society to society, as we will learn in this chapter. We will find that although all people have basic needs that must be met, the way they organize social interaction to meet these needs—from feeding themselves to protecting themselves from enemies—varies tremendously from society to society.

SOCIAL STRUCTURE

Our focus in Chapter 3 is on types of societies. A **society** is a collectivity of interacting people who share the same culture. Thus, membership in a society may transcend geographic or territorial boundaries, since people living in different places may share the same culture. Our definition also implies that a society is an organized collectivity. In other words, the behavior and interactions of the members of a society are, for the most part, stable and patterned. Sociologists call these stable patterns of interaction **social structures.** For instance, when you enter a college classroom on the first day of a new term, you may not know the other students in the class or the instructor, and you may not even be sure what the course is about. Nevertheless, you can be fairly certain that the interactions that will take place in that classroom will be structured in a particular way, and that this pattern is also being followed more or less in classrooms all over campus—indeed, all over the United States—term after term. It is social structure that imbues the college classroom with a comforting familiarity.

Sociologists study social structure by examining the parts that compose it. A social structure is made up of institutions, statuses, roles, and groups. Let's look at each part in turn.

Institutions

A **social institution** is a set of stable rules and relationships that regulate the social activities in which a society's members engage to meet their survival needs. The major social institutions of a society are:

- *The economy,* the social institution that produces, manages, and distributes a society's human and material resources;
- *Government,* which has formal legal authority to regulate relationships among the society's members as well as relationships between the society itself and other societies;
- *Family,* or a long-term, exclusive, intimate relationship in which members are committed to one another emotionally as well as financially;
- *Education,* the social institution with responsibility for teaching a society's members the knowledge, skills, and values deemed most important for their own survival and the survival of the society;
- *Religion,* which is a set of beliefs and practices that a group of people deem sacred and use to guide their behavior as well as give meaning to their lives; and
- *Medicine,* the social institution dedicated to preventing and treating disease and promoting health.

Together with culture, institutions shape the social life of a society. Like culture, however, the rules and relationships that constitute a specific institution vary considerably from society to society, as well as over time within a single society. Consider the family, for instance. Families exist in every known society in the world and are made up of people who are bonded to one another socially, financially, and emotionally. However, the exact nature of these bonds, as well as the responsibilities, obligations, and privileges accorded to specific family members, vary widely. Even the composition of families shows dramatic variation cross-culturally and historically. Let's return for a moment to the Naskapi Eskimos. Although the composition of the Naskapi family is not unfamiliar to us—husband, wife, and child—it probably seems un-

What two human social institutions are represented in this picture? What roles and statuses of each are evident? How do social institutions, roles, and statuses operate to preserve a society?

usual for husbands to have primary responsibility for cooking and child care, while wives tan animal hides. In contrast, in most contemporary American households with children, women are working outside the home, but they also shoulder primary responsibility for housework and child care. A growing number of American women, in fact, are sole breadwinners and parents for their families, heading households without a husband/father present. Both of these developments—mothers in the labor force and single-parent households—are also relatively recent developments in the United States. Less than a hundred years ago, both were rare. In terms of composition, most American families in the early 1900s had more in

common with the Naskapi family than with contemporary American families. But in the U.S. home of the 1900s, it would definitely have been the wife who was tending to the sick child and preparing dinner, while the husband worked outside the home.

Institutions are so important to society that we have devoted an entire section of the book to them, with a separate chapter discussing each one. In this chapter, we will begin to examine how institutions vary by type of society. First, though, let's briefly discuss the other components of social structure.

Statuses and Roles

Institutions do not exist in a vacuum. They are social constructions, and the members of society who interact within them hold particular social positions, called **statuses.** When we think of status, we tend to think of prestige, but sociologically, all social positions are statuses; they simply vary in the level of prestige attached to them. Within the legal system, for instance, judge, attorney, and convicted felon are all statuses, but they clearly do not carry the same level of prestige.

Attached to every status is one or more roles. **Roles** are the behaviors, responsibilities, and privileges that are expected of individuals occupying a specific status. Returning to our example from the legal system, the status of judge suggests a variety of behavioral expectations, responsibilities, and privileges: A judge is expected to maintain fairness in the courtroom and to see that specific legal procedures are carried out; a judge makes decisions about a case; a judge instructs members of a jury before they begin their deliberations; a judge is shown deference by those present in a courtroom, so all stand when a

According to anthropologist Eleanor Leacock, what sex roles and gender relations distinguish the Eskimos in this traditional family group? In what other ways might roles, statuses, and groups vary from society to society?

judge enters and leaves the courtroom. Many of these expectations are formal; they are specified in written documents and are regulated by law. However, many of the behavioral expectations attached to statuses are informal and more flexible. The role of convicted felon, for instance, is not especially well defined. What expectations, responsibilities, or privileges can you think of that are attached to the status convicted felon?

SOCIOLOGY LIVE

The University of North Carolina at Wilmington, NC
Course: Introduction to Sociology,
Dr. Stephen J. McNamee
Students: (left to right) Jennifer Harvell, Travis Tice,
Rebecca E. Clodfeller, Michelle Weinberg, Carrie Warwick,
and April Boehm

What statuses define our school as a society?

Our response begins with the definitions for "status" and "society" as they appear in the glossary of our text, *Living Sociology*. "Status" is referred to as particular social positions held by members of a society who interact, while a "society" is a collective of interacting people who share the same general culture (Renzetti & Curran, 618). These definitions support our determination that the University of North Carolina at Wilmington (UNCW) is a society with administrative, nonadministrative, and student statuses.

Members of the administrative status have noninstructional, managerial functions organized toward providing support for the business of higher education. Examples are the Chancellor's Office—the most prestigious office in the administrative status—the Budget Office, and the Registrar's Office. These offices are directly and indirectly involved with students and set policies and procedures for the campus. Interactions between administrative statuses and students and nonadministrative statuses tend to be mainly informational or disciplinary.

Next, the nonadminstrative status includes the teaching faculty, maintenance crews, security personnel, clerical staff, athletic staff, and participating alumni. Nonadministrative positions are strongly service oriented and student oriented. Members of this status influence students through direct involvement and leadership, including mentoring and role modeling. Nonadministrative members also tend to reinforce the norms and expectations of administration.

The student status (see our bar graph) includes full-time, part-time, undergraduate, graduate, traditional, and nontraditional students. Structurally, students are low on the status hierarchy, but at UNCW the pro-student attitudes and values of administrative and nonadministrative status members empower students in many other ways.

All students are expected to behave according to the published Student Code of Ethics and to complete a minimum number of course hours to receive their undergraduate degree. Participation in enrichment activities and athletics is also encouraged. All categories of students interact, with slight differences from category to category. For example, part-time students may participate less than full-time students. Graduate students are both students and teachers when they serve as teaching assistants. And nontraditional students may have more roles and statuses to fulfill because of their family, employment, and community responsibilities. In any case, on the basis of our study, our university can be seen as a society composed of structured statuses.

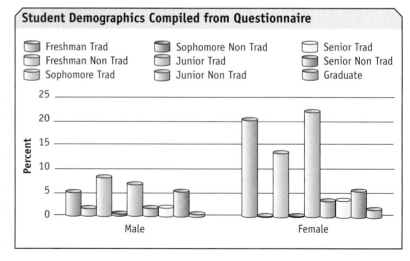

Student Demographics Compiled from Questionnaire

Freshman Trad | Sophomore Non Trad | Senior Trad
Freshman Non Trad | Junior Trad | Senior Non Trad
Sophomore Trad | Junior Non Trad | Graduate

We will discuss statuses and roles in greater detail in Chapter 6. In this chapter, we will learn about the various statuses and roles that are prevalent in particular types of societies, and how these statuses and roles emerge and change over time.

Groups

A **social group** is two or more people who interact with one another on a regular basis and share common expectations and a common identity. Each of us belongs to many groups simultaneously, but some groups are more important in our lives than others. Groups will be a central part of our discussion in Chapter 6. In this chapter, however, we must bear in mind that societies are composed of groups. The number and types of groups in a society will vary depending on the type of society in question. Let's turn our attention, then, to this notion of types of societies.

REFLECTING ON

Social Structure

1. Can you think of specific ways in which the rules and relationships that make up some of the central institutions of our society (government, education, medicine) have changed over time?
2. What are some of the statuses you hold? What roles are attached to each of these statuses?

TYPES OF SOCIETIES

Considering the dazzling diversity of societies throughout the world, you might suppose the task of studying them poses a daunting challenge. Thanks to sociologist Gerhard Lenski and writer Jean Lenski, however, this undertaking has been simplified (Lenski et al., 1995). The Lenskis developed a system for classifying all the societies in the world into just five basic types:

1. hunting and gathering societies;
2. pastoral societies;
3. horticultural societies;
4. agricultural societies; and
5. industrial societies.

To this list, we will add a sixth type:

6. postindustrial societies.

Before we look more closely at each type of society, two points must be made about this classification system. First, the basis for classification is the way the members of a society sustain themselves. It was the social theorist Karl Marx who pointed out over a hundred years ago that a society's economic system shapes other institutions in that society. Thus, when we discuss each type of society, we will focus first on the techniques used to meet the members' survival needs (the economy), and how the economy influences political decision making, spirituality, education, and interaction in the family.

The second point to remember as you read is that because societies are highly complex, any attempt to classify them runs the risk of oversimplifying reality. Indeed, given the enormous diversity of societies throughout the world, each society will fit only more or less into each of our available categories. Consequently, perhaps the best way to think of these categories is in terms of a concept that the early sociologist Max Weber gave us: the ideal type. An **ideal type** is an analytic tool. Sociologists construct an ideal type by carefully studying various examples of a particular phenomenon and identifying its essential features. We could construct, for example, an ideal type of college classroom by visiting a number of different classrooms and noting things that we consider essential. Our list might include desks, a blackboard, and a podium. Any individual classroom that we later visit may not conform precisely to our ideal type (for example, there may be rows of tables and chairs instead of desks), but we should be able to use our ideal type to recognize the room as a classroom and thus distinguish it from other rooms.

Notice that the concept of the ideal type does not refer to "the average" or the typical. The typical college professor, for example, may differ considerably from the ideal-type college professor. At the same time, the notion of ideal here does not refer to what's necessarily good or moral; you can develop an ideal-type thief as readily as you can an ideal-type police officer. Rather, the measure of any ideal type is how well it delineates the essential elements of some aspect of social reality and thereby allows sociologists to develop a more comprehensive understanding of that reality.

With these points in mind, then, let's consider each of the types of societies in our classification system. Table 3.1 on page 62 summarizes the distinguishing features of each type of society.

Hunting and Gathering Societies

In the **hunting and gathering society,** members meet their survival needs by hunting game (and often by fishing) and by gathering vegetation and other types of food from their surrounding environment. Hunting and gathering are the oldest known human subsistence strategies, dating back from the emergence of *Homo sapiens* (about 250,000 years ago). Hunting and gathering societies were the predominant type of society in the world until the development of agriculture approximately 12,000 years ago.

TABLE 3.1 Types of Societies

Type	Estimated First Developed	Subsistence Strategy	Population Characteristics	Institutions, Statuses, Roles, and Groups
Hunting and gathering	250,000 years ago	Hunting game, fishing, gathering vegetation	20–200 people, nomadic	All social life organized around the family; egalitarian roles; religion and government as we know them do not exist
Pastoral	10,000–12,000 years ago	Domesticating and herding animals	50–several hundred people, nomadic/semi-sedentary	Accumulation of wealth; emergence of various forms of social inequality; political leadership by hereditary chiefs; trade; emergence of specialized roles, such as craftspeople and religious leaders
Horticultural	10,000–12,000 years ago	Cultivating plants using the slash and burn technique and digging sticks	Several hundred thousand people, semisedentary/sedentary	Social inequality; rule by a single leader (hereditary monarchy); slavery; specialized roles; trade; religion focused on appeasing fickle gods
Agricultural	5,000–8,000 years ago	Cultivating plants using plows pulled by large draft animals	Millions of people, sedentary	Numerous individual communities spread over large regions, sharing a common economy and government; cultural diversity; social class inequality; slavery; trade; monetary system; written language
Industrial	250 years ago	Production of artifacts using machinery	Millions of people, sedentary	Separation of work from home; formal education and religion; improved standard of living, but widespread social class inequality; urbanization; bureaucracy
Postindustrial	currently developing	Production of services and information	Millions of people, sedentary	Too early to determine

Today, very few hunting and gathering societies remain. Contemporary examples of hunting and gathering societies include the !Kung bush-living people of the Kalahari Desert, the Mbuti Pygmies of Zaire, the Agta of the Philippines, and the Naskapi Eskimos, who were introduced at the beginning of this chapter (see Harris, 1993; O'Kelly & Carney, 1986; Shostack, 1981).

Not surprisingly, the focus of daily activity in hunting and gathering societies is on obtaining food, and everyone, except the very young and the very old, is expected to participate. The implements used by hunters and gatherers are simple: spears, bows and arrows, nets, and clubs. The yield from hunting and gathering rules out the possibility of anyone accumulating a **surplus** of resources, that is, more resources than are needed for daily subsistence. Material goods are few and may include woven baskets to carry gathered food; implements fashioned from stone, wood, grass, or vines; and vessels made by hollowing out vegetables and fruits or carving tree limbs. Shelter and clothing also come from whatever the natural environment has to offer: wood, grass, the hides of animals, and so on.

Hunters and gatherers depend on the resources of their natural environment for survival. Should food sources begin to dwindle because of drought, for instance, or unusual cold or a fire, the entire society moves to a more fruitful locale. Thus, hunting and gathering societies tend to be **nomadic,** although some may become relatively settled if their natural environment provides an abundance of food. Famine, however, is not a frequent problem for hunting and gathering societies.

In any event, depending on the vagaries of nature means that hunting and gathering societies must remain small. They may be composed of as few as twenty members, and rarely do their populations exceed two hundred. This type of society also tends to be highly egalitarian, treating every member pretty much the same, which is adaptive for the group. Just as everyone helps find food, so, too, is everyone expected to share. Typically, the food that is collected each day is distributed equitably among all the members of the group. Since most of these people are also related to one another through ancestry or marriage, family ties provide a kind of social insurance to hunters and gatherers. If bad luck or some disaster strikes, there is a strong support network to count on for help.

The egalitarian character of foraging societies and the high value placed on kinship or family ties are reflected in the societies' other institutions. As we saw in our opening example, for instance, within the family, men and women may be responsible for different tasks, but neither one's work is more highly regarded than the other's. Rather, the work of each is considered necessary to the survival of the group as a whole. To paraphrase O'Kelly and Carney (1986), in hunting and gathering societies, men and women are seen as essential *partners* in the economy. Among the Naskapi, like other hunters and gatherers, child care is the responsibility of both parents. Indeed, in most hunting and gathering societies, nurturing children is considered a community responsibility, and children are taught to be cooperative, generous, and peaceful as well as competent food providers.

Religion and government as we know them do not exist in foraging societies. Foragers do not worship a god, but rather believe in spirits that exist in nature—in plants, animals, the sea. These spirits may affect the lives of humans, but humans can interfere in the activities of the spirits through various rituals. Within these societies, some individuals are recognized for their spiritual powers and may serve as *shamans,* who perform the rituals. A particular individual may also serve temporarily as a kind of political leader. For instance, if a decision about moving must be made because of drought, the person considered most knowledgable about weather or the surrounding territory may be looked to for advice. However, all decisions that affect the group usually are arrived at consensually through community discussions. Moreover, even those who are considered shamans or who lead temporarily are not accorded a higher position than others in the society, nor are they excused from their responsibilities and obligations to the collectivity. What little inequality exists in foraging societies is based on age and kinship, with elders typically enjoying substantial respect and deference.

Although life in a hunting and gathering society seems difficult and risky, research indicates that for the most part, people lead relatively leisurely lives. Needs are simple and fairly easily met, and, with everyone pitching in, only a few hours of work per day per person is required to get necessary tasks accomplished (Sahlins, 1972). Better still, violence and aggression are uncommon in hunting and gathering societies. Contact with other societies has been infrequent, and because hunters and gatherers do not regard their few possessions or their environment as private property, they have had little to fight over or defend.

In short, the relatively peaceful and egalitarian lifestyle of hunters and gatherers is appealing on many levels. Unfortunately, their continued existence is threatened by more technologically developed societies. Some hunting and gathering peoples are trying to preserve their way of life by seeking protection through the governments and courts of the encroachers, as the Global Insights box on page 64 describes, but societies are quickly disappearing nonetheless. In fact, some observers predict that all will be gone early into the twenty-first century (Goleman, 1996; Lenski et al., 1995). We should be saddened by any loss of human and social diversity, but the peaceful and egalitarian character of hunting and gathering societies makes their pending extinction especially tragic.

Pastoral Societies

About 10,000 to 12,000 years ago, some hunters and gatherers discovered that instead of killing the animals they hunted and consuming them immediately, they could capture them and breed them, providing a more reliable food supply as well as a means of transportation. From this discovery, another type of society developed: the pastoral society. In a **pastoral society,** economic survival is based on domesticating and herding animals. Pastoral societies are especially suited to arid environments such as the deserts of Northern Africa and the Middle East, where cultivating plants is difficult at best, but where animals such as camels, goats, and sheep can be raised. Like hunters and gatherers, pastoralists tend to be nomadic. However, pastoral societies are also found in more fertile regions, such as Mediterranean Europe, where pastoralists not only herd, but also engage in gardening. These societies sometimes have to move to find grazing land and water for their livestock, but they tend to be at least **semisedentary,** or temporarily settled.

Pastoralism is typically a more dependable subsistence strategy than hunting and gathering, and thus it can sustain a larger number of people. Highly nomadic pastoral societies that rely almost totally on herding tend to have under fifty members, but camps or villages of semisedentary pastoralists may number several hundred.

Obviously, since the animals and crops raised in pastoral societies are not all for immediate consumption, surplus is accumulated, if only in the form of livestock. In fact, herd size in these societies is the primary measure of an individual's, but more typically a family's, wealth. Thus, in contrast to the egalitarianism characteristic of hunting and gathering societies, in pastoral societies we find social inequality and hierarchies of status, where some people are considered more prestigious than others. The accumulated wealth of individuals and families may be passed on from one generation to the next, consolidating the wealth over time. Moreover, this wealth usually translates into political power, as those with the greatest accumulated resources become the key decision makers in the society. This power, too, may be passed on in the form of hereditary chieftainships (Earle, 1997).

GLOBAL INSIGHTS   Can Aboriginal Australians Preserve Their Way of Life?

The first inhabitants of Australia are thought to have migrated there from Southeast Asia at least 50,000 years ago. Until the British arrived in 1788, about 300,000 Aboriginal Australians lived in over 500 distinct tribes, each with its own territory, history, language, and culture (Broome, 1982). But one factor that united all Aboriginal groups was their ties to the land; they were hunters and gatherers, and Aboriginal culture derived in large part from the attachment of Aboriginal people to the land (Sarre, 1994). When the British arrived in 1788 to claim Australia as a penal colony, they brought with them deep prejudices against Black people that they had developed as a result of participating in the African slave trade. To the British, Black people were "dirty" and "primitive," not really fellow human beings, but animals to be exploited and used. The British proclaimed Australia an uninhabited territory, without settlement or established law, at the time the continent was "peacefully annexed" to the British empire (Broome, 1982; Sarre, 1994).

In the ensuing decades, the British cleared forests, introduced European animals (such as rabbits and foxes) that ended up destroying much of the indigenous vegetation, and hunted to near-extinction many species of indigenous wildlife (Lines, 1991). At the same time, the introduction of diseases, such as smallpox, from which Aboriginal people had no immunity and no treatments, resulted in many Aboriginal deaths. The British colonists also deliberately tried to eliminate the Aboriginal people and their culture. Colonists went on "Aborigine hunts" to systematically kill Aboriginal people, or gave "gifts" of poisoned flour that sometimes resulted in the deaths of an entire Aboriginal camp. Although the Aborigines met violence with violence and actively resisted British encroachment on their land, the more "advanced" weaponry of the British meant that the Aborigines usually lost (Day, 1996).

By the mid-1800s, Aboriginal Australians were legally segregated from White Australians. Most lived on "reserves," where they were prohibited from hunting and gathering freely, from speaking their indigenous languages, and from following their traditional diets—in short, from practicing their culture. Their children were taken from them to be raised by White families, an action justified as a "welfare intervention" for the benefit of the children (Sidoti, 1997). Today, Aboriginal Australians experience significantly higher rates of social problems than other Australians: They are, as a group, "poorer, less formally educated, more likely to be unemployed, more likely to live on welfare, have shorter lifespans, and suffer more chronic illness" (Bessant & Watts, 1999, p. 208).

Aboriginal Australians have not ceased their resistance to colonization, however, and in recent years this resistance has taken the form of legal challenges to regain the land stolen from them. In 1992, in the case of *Mabo and Others* v. *State of Queensland,* the High Court of Australia ruled that the British land law was defective and that much of the land claimed by the British from 1788 on actually still belongs to the Aborigines. This famous decision, known as the *Mabo decision,* was followed in 1993 by the Native Title Act, in which the Australian Parliament set up a system so that Aboriginal people can register claims for specific tracts of land they believe rightly belong to them. A tribunal then investigates the claim to determine if it is valid and if the current landholders should be compensated before returning the land to its Aboriginal owners (Sarre, 1996).

Needless to say, the Mabo decision has generated a good deal of conflict and controversy in Australia, but many people, especially Aboriginal Australians, see it as an important first step in reclaiming and preserving not only Aboriginal land rights, but also Aboriginal culture. As one observer put it, "It is hoped that one day the Mabo decision will help all Australians to understand that a national culture that accommodates indigenous cultures grows more powerful, not weaker, by virtue of its diversity" (Sarre, 1998, p. 87).

The possibility of accumulating wealth leads to disputes within and between societies, for now there is something to fight over and defend. Animals may be stolen, or herds raided by competing families or societies. Disputes may also arise over grazing rights on specific land or over access to water sources. Consequently, fighting and aggression are not uncommon in pastoral societies, and the vanquished may be taken by the victors as slaves. Not surprisingly, gender relations in these societies are usually far less egalitarian than in foraging societies. Men assume responsibility for tending the large animals and for fighting, and women take responsibility for child care, cooking, and housekeeping tasks. Children are raised to be independent and self-reliant, with boys taught fighting skills.

Because men tend the livestock and thus travel away from the camps, it is they, rather than women, who come in contact with members of other societies. From these contacts, trading relationships may develop and new items may be introduced into a society, providing another

What type of society does each picture represent? In each case, how do the people make their living, and what are the principal characteristics of their population? What are the main institutions, statuses, roles, and groups in terms of which the people organize their social life?

source of wealth. Political alliances may also develop from these contacts, but so too can political disputes. However, not everyone in a pastoral society needs to tend livestock or the camp or household. Pastoralism's steady supply of food frees up some members of the society to pursue other activities, such as weaving cloth or carpets from the sheared coats of the animals, crafting jewelry and other items, and communicating with god. Indeed, the religion that emerges in pastoral societies is one based on a belief in a primary deity (although secondary deities

are often included as well), who is actively involved in the daily affairs of the humans who worship (usually) him. Some individuals in these societies, then, assume the role of leading the worship and serving as mediators between the people and their god, providing the people with advice. Most of us are quite familiar with this kind of religion since three of the major world religions of today—Judaism, Islam, and Christianity—are similar and originated in the pastoral societies of Africa and the Middle East. In fact, Christian churches continue to be led by *pastors* ("shepherds") and the leadership they provide is often called *pastoral* counseling.

Examples of contemporary pastoral societies are the Sheikhanzai of Afghanistan, the Shahsevan of Iran, and the Maasai of sub-Saharan Africa. Like hunters and gatherers, contemporary pastoralists are finding their way of life threatened. These societies exist in countries that have centralized national governments that often refuse to recognize the pastoralists' historic claims to grazing lands, requiring instead deeds and court-issued property titles. Moreover, governments committed to economic development often seek to "modernize" pastoral societies, which typically weakens traditional, community-based economic, political, and familial relationships (Galaty et al., 1994; O'Kelly & Carney, 1986; Tavakolian, 1984). Thus, as with hunting and gathering societies, the number of pastoral societies in the world is declining, not because pastoralism is not a viable way of life, but because of pressures and intrusions from more economically developed societies. On the other hand, following the collapse of communism in the former Soviet Union, there has been a resurgence of pastoralism in Mongolia. In the short span of five years, from 1990 to 1995, the number of families officially registered as herders rose from 74,000 to 170,000. When communism collapsed in the Soviet Union, unemployment in Mongolian towns increased dramatically, but the political change also resulted in the lifting of a legal ban on families owning more than fifteen animals. Unemployed Mongolians are now finding pastoralism a viable way of life (Faison, 1996).

Horticultural Societies

Horticultural societies cultivate plants using relatively simple technology as their subsistence strategy. These societies developed at about the same time as pastoral societies—10,000 to 12,000 years ago—when hunters and gatherers who lived in areas suitable to plant cultivation discovered that instead of just searching for food each day, they could produce it themselves by planting seeds and tending gardens. The methods they used then are much the same as the methods used today in simple horticultural societies. One of the most common techniques is known as *slash and burn*, in which trees and other plants are cut down and then set on fire to clear the land. Seeds are then planted using wooden poles called *digging sticks*. Although the ashes left from the fire serve as fertilizer, digging sticks do not turn the soil well, so it erodes rather quickly. Every few years, therefore, the members of the horticultural society move in search of uncleared, fertile land, allowing the previous garden to become overgrown and thus replenish the soil's nutrients.

Horticultural societies are sometimes devastated by droughts or floods, but, in general, plant cultivation provides a fairly dependable food supply. Consequently, as with pastoralism, horticulture as a subsistence strategy allows for population growth and a semi-sedentary lifestyle. Moreover, once horticulturalists learn metallurgy and develop hoes with metal blades, which turn the soil more deeply, gardens are more productive longer and periodic moves are no longer necessary. Thus, advanced horticultural societies become **sedentary,** or settled, and able to sustain populations that number several thousand.

Horticulture as a subsistence strategy affects other institutions in much the same way pastoralism does. In horticultural societies, land is a valued resource and land ownership, by individuals or families, is a form of wealth that is often passed on through inheritance and expanded through marriage. Differences in wealth and prestige emerge. Political institutions become more complex, particularly in large advanced horticultural societies where various communities may be ruled by a single leader. This political power, too, may be inherited. In fact, it is in horticultural societies that we see the emergence of hereditary monarchies. However, political rule may be shortlived, since leaders may be ousted by rivals from other horticultural societies (Earle, 1997).

In areas where fertile land for cultivation is scarce and there is strong population pressure, competition over land motivates frequent fighting among horticultural communities (Harris, 1977). The defeated often become the slaves of the victors. Child rearing in land-scarce societies thus focuses on training boys to be fierce warriors and girls to be good at domestic chores and child care. In areas where land is not scarce, however, and where women participate in cultivation, children are reared for more egalitarian roles. For instance, in simple horticultural societies where men take responsibility for clearing the land, but both men and women plant, tend, and harvest, there is more gender equality, as well as other forms of social equality. The more removed women are from economic production in these societies, the lower their status is likely to be (O'Kelly & Carney, 1986).

As in pastoral societies, specialized jobs and roles develop in horticultural societies, as some members are freed from the task of food production. They may become full-time warriors, craftspeople, or religious leaders. Religious beliefs and practices prevalent in horticultural societies reflect the main concerns of the societies' members: Gods are fickle and vindictive forces that must be satisfied and pleased with offerings and (in some societies, human) sacrifices to ensure good harvests and successful battles. Religious beliefs and practices also tend to reflect and support the inequality that characterizes these societies: Gods are supreme (often male) beings who favor those who can offer them the most and the best tribute.

Because horticultural societies are semisedentary or sedentary, their members can acquire not only a surplus of food, but also other material goods, such as clothing, jewelry, and furniture. Contact with other societies usually establishes trade relations. It also exposes the members of these societies to the others' cultures, which can affect the continued survival of a horticultural society. A more advanced society may dominate a less advanced society, or exposure to more advanced technology may lead horticulturalists themselves to abandon their methods of cultivation for other, more productive methods. As we will see next, many horticultural societies today are being transformed into agricultural societies, where cultivating crops is still the primary subsistence strategy, but the technology used is much more advanced. Nevertheless, many simple and advanced horticultural societies exist in the world today, including the Mundurucu and Yanamami of Brazil and Venezuela, the Truk of the Caroline Islands in the Western Pacific, the Udu of Nigeria, and the Hagen of New Guinea (see, for example, Peters, 1998).

Agricultural Societies

About 5,000 to 8,000 years ago, most likely in Mesopotamia and Egypt first, horticulturalists developed a new tool that could dig deeper into the soil, turn it over better, and thereby make it more fertile and productive. This tool was the plow, and its invention ushered in what has been called the *agricultural revolution*. **Agricultural societies,** also called **agrarian societies,** utilize plows, draft animals, and other methods such as irrigation to cultivate crops as a subsistence strategy.

Because a plow pulled by large draft animals, such as oxen, can cultivate a much larger area of land than the average horticulturalist's garden, and because the plow improves the fertility of the soil and land can be farmed indefinitely, agriculturalists can establish permanently settled communities. Their technology also produces un-

precedented surpluses of food, thereby allowing these societies to sustain much larger populations than the other types of societies we have discussed so far. Agricultural societies may number in the millions; for example, the population of mid-nineteenth century China, an agrarian society, was recorded as 400 million. These societies, then, spread over extremely large regions, and are composed of numerous individual communities that share a common economy and government. The larger size of agricultural societies, in terms of both population and geography, also means that they are more culturally diverse; their members may have different ethnic heritages and identities, for instance.

Agriculture is commonly lauded as the "dawn of civilization" (see, for example, Lenski et al., 1995). However, it is important to keep in mind that not everyone benefits from this new technology and the social changes it brings about. As we see in the Intersecting Inequalities box on page 68, for example, the status of women in agricultural societies tends to be dramatically lower than the status of women in simple horticultural, pastoral, and hunting and gathering societies. Agricultural societies are also characterized by extreme social class inequality. **Social class** is determined by a person's role in the production process. The production process in agricultural societies is highly labor-intensive, that is, concentrated and exhausting. Guiding an animal-drawn plow over large stretches of land is not easy work. Animals also must be broken in and consistently watered and fed. Their manure is frequently used as fertilizer, so it must be collected and spread over the fields. The land must also often be irrigated, so irrigation ditches must be dug and maintained. Consequently, agricultural workers typically put in more hours of work more days of the

How do the roles and statuses of women differ in the different types of society? For example, is the status of women in agricultural societies, such as those shown in this photo, generally higher or lower than that of women in hunting and gathering societies? Why? Does social inequality generally increase or decrease as societies industrialize?

INTERSECTING INEQUALITIES

How Did Agriculture Affect the Status of Women?

The invention of the plow is considered by many to be an advance over the subsistence strategies of horticulturalism and pastoralism, but, as we have noted, not everyone benefits from the change. For example, anthropologists argue that the subordination of women is greater in agricultural societies than in any other type of society (O'Kelly & Carney, 1986). Why is this the case?

As we have noted, agricultural work requires significant physical strength. It can also be dangerous in that workers must travel long distances, often alone, to the fields, and return home after nightfall. It is easy to see how such work is difficult, if not impossible, for pregnant women or women caring for young children. In agricultural societies, the birth rate is higher and birth spacing is shorter than in other types of societies because having children, especially sons, is a way to increase the labor supply—and, therefore, the income—of families. Consequently, the status of women in agricultural societies is low because women are no longer primary contributors to the production process.

Women's lack of a primary role in agricultural production does not mean that women in agricultural societies do not work. To the contrary, women often participate in planting and harvesting crops, although they do not usually help clear the land, plow it, or dig irrigation ditches. Women also spend many hours in the arduous labor of processing agricultural products: they cook and preserve food; spin, weave, and sew cloth. But these tasks are viewed as secondary to men's labor in agricultural societies. Moreover, most of women's work is done in the home, which isolates women from men, and also from other women.

Wealthy women in agricultural societies enjoy a more leisurely lifestyle than peasant women, but they are still subject to male control. This control is reinforced by the frequent military conflicts that characterize agricultural societies. Men fight wars, and women become one of the spoils of their battles. The exchange of women through arranged marriages is also a way to consolidate political power as well as land wealth. Consequently, women come to be seen as male property, and women of all social classes are considered men's inferiors. The religions prevalent in agricultural societies help legitimate men's control over women, with beliefs in an all-powerful male God and images of women as physically and morally weak. The legal system also supports male control through strict laws regulating marriage and especially female sexual behavior (O'Kelly & Carney, 1986).

The traditional view of the emergence of agriculture as "progress," therefore, must be reevaluated in light of the decline in the status of women that accompanies this social change. The question we must ask is, Who benefits and who loses in the "advance of civilization"?

---

year than horticulturalists, pastoralists, or hunters and gatherers (O'Kelly & Carney, 1986). However, not everyone in an agricultural society participates in this backbreaking labor. The enormous surpluses produced in agricultural societies allow a minority of the population to live well off the work of the masses.

Most workers in an agricultural society are *peasants*. Peasants by definition do not own land, but rather enter into an agreement with a landowner (or landlord), who gives them the right to live on and cultivate a specific parcel of land in exchange for part of the harvest or certain services. The rent extracted by the landlord is typically high enough that most peasants eke out only a meager existence, despite their arduous labor. Other workers may be servants or administrators of some kind, artisans, or merchants, but their numbers are much smaller than the peasants. Slavery is also a common practice in agricultural societies.

At the top of the social class hierarchy in agricultural societies is the *nobility,* from whose ranks the ruler of the society (the king or emperor) is drawn. The nobles are numerically the smallest segment of an agricultural population, but they control the vast majority, if not all, of the land and other wealth. Because others work for them, the rulers and nobles are free to pursue other interests, including literature and the arts. In fact, it was in agricultural societies that the distinction between "high culture" and "mass culture" or "popular culture" arose. Religious leaders are also drawn from the nobility. The religions popular in these societies support the widespread social inequality. The primary belief is in a supreme god or family of gods who rules over all. The rulers themselves often claim legitimacy through "divine right," that is, that they were chosen by their god as leaders.

The rulers and nobility of agricultural societies are also kept busy with internal and external struggles. Internally, members of this elite group vie with one another for power, forming alliances to oust the rulers and take charge themselves. Empire building also produces external conflicts and warfare as rulers try to conquer other societies and expand their wealth and power. Advances in technology are used for military and political ends as much as for economic purposes. Improvements in transportation, for instance, allow weapons and warriors, as well as products and crops, to be moved more quickly and efficiently, thus facilitating warfare in addition to trade. The invention of the sail, for example, allowed the rulers of European agricultural societies of the Middle Ages to not only expand their empires across vast oceans, but also to introduce to their societies new foods and goods from Asia, Africa, and the Americas, including rice, tea, silk, ivory, and tobacco.

The technology, size, cross-cultural contact, and increased diversity of agricultural societies ultimately leads to a centralized government and certain forms of social organization. For example, agricultural societies develop a monetary system of exchange. Instead of trading goods and services in kind (bartering), with each "deal" worked out anew between individuals, a monetary system assigns a price or value to each product or service. All transactions are thereby standardized and universalized through the exchange medium of money. The growth of trade, the use of rents and taxation, and the simple need to keep track of one's subjects also requires the development of some system of record keeping. Not surprisingly, therefore, we see the emergence of written language in agricultural societies. And the need to control the behavior of large numbers of people leads to codifying rules into laws, with a legal system to administer them.

Among the most extensively studied agricultural societies are those of ancient Egypt, China, Greece, and the Roman Empire, as well as feudal Japan and Western Europe. Egypt continues to be largely an agrarian society, as does contemporary India. Their social structure is far more complex than that of horticultural, pastoral, or hunting and gathering societies. But, as we noted, progress comes with a price: severe and rigid social inequality. Indeed, inequality appears to be a built-in feature of the agricultural social system.

Industrial Societies

The members of an **industrial society** use mechanized systems of production to meet their subsistence needs. This is the type of society with which you are most personally familiar, since the United States has been industrialized since the end of the eighteenth century. Industrialism emerged only about two hundred-fifty years ago, but it has been so enormously successful as an economic strategy that it is now found in all parts of the world, from England where it first began, throughout Europe and the Americas, to Australia, Asia, and Africa. One of the most amazing facts about industrialism is its rapid spread compared to other types of societies. The populations of industrial societies number in the millions and, in some cases, the hundreds of millions. However, as we will see, this form of economic progress has high costs. For one thing, it has become the dominant subsistence strategy worldwide largely by absorbing or destroying other types

of societies, most recently in Africa, Latin America, and Asia. It has also taken a huge toll on the natural environment and devastated the quality of life for segments of some populations. To better understand its effects, let's take a closer look at how industrialism developed.

Most historians date the start of the Industrial Revolution at around 1750, with the invention of machinery for spinning and weaving textiles. Power came from natural resources such as water and wood, and British weavers produced fabric and clothing far more quickly and efficiently than ever before. By 1769, production increased even more dramatically, thanks to the invention of the steam engine and fuel-powered machinery. Invention quickly followed invention, revolutionizing other areas of production and social life: transportation, communications, the military, education, medicine, the production and preparation of food, and so on. In contemporary industrial societies, few, if any, areas of life are not at least touched by mechanization, and technological innovations to "improve" all aspects of everyday living are continually being introduced. Indeed, a hallmark of industrial society is rapid technological and social change.

Industrialization also revolutionized social relationships. The tremendous surplus that industrialization produced translated into significantly increased wealth, but not all members of newly industrialized societies benefited from it. Factory owners, financiers, bankers, and

The Industrial Revolution was founded on the harnessing of new energy resources and technologies. Textile mills powered by moving water soon ran on steam turbines instead, and steam rapidly was applied to everything from steel production to transportation. How did mass production and the factory system transform agricultural Europe into industrial societies? How are these forces transforming industrializing nations today?

railroad magnates reaped tremendous profits, accumulated large fortunes, and lived in luxury. Most people, however, were propertyless; they worked in the factories for meager wages and lived in squalor. For example, between 1816 and 1829, cotton production in France increased 300 percent, but in 1830, the wages of French workers were two-thirds less than what they had been in 1810. As industrialization continued, though, its material benefits became more widespread and living standards for the majority of the population improved considerably. In fact, two major consequences of industrialization are improved health and longer life expectancy. At the same time, poverty remains a problem in most contemporary industrial societies. We will discuss the problem of economic inequality in industrial societies and between industrial societies and other societies in Chapters 8 and 9.

Industrial societies are highly urbanized. Most of the population lives in or around cities because this is where jobs are located. People migrate from outlying areas and even from other countries to find employment and raise their standard of living. One important consequence is that industrial societies tend to be highly culturally diverse, with members exposed to many different customs, practices, ideas, and beliefs. Another consequence of living in an urban industrialized society is that people tend to have greater autonomy or freedom to do what they want, although along with this comes greater anonymity. Unlike the tightly knit communities of hunting and gathering societies, or even pastoral and horticultural societies, much social interaction in urban industrial societies is impersonal. In many U.S. neighborhoods, residents often know only their immediate neighbors, and even those not very well. A sense of community is more difficult to foster in large, diverse, fast-paced industrial societies.

Family life also changed significantly as a result of industrialization. In other types of societies, the family was the center of economic production. When production moved out of the household and into factories, the family lost its function as a primary unit of production and family members instead went out to work, becoming wage earners. Early on, every family member who was physically able went to work, including children. Child labor laws and laws restricting the hours and jobs available to women reduced the presence of these two groups in the paid labor force and lowered their financial contributions to the household. Although many women continued to be employed outside the home primarily because of financial need, the full-time homemaker came to represent affluence and middle-class respectability. Home and work came to be seen as the centers of separate spheres of activity, the former private and the latter public. At the same time, industrialized production required a more literate and skilled labor force. The education and job training that traditionally had taken place in the home was no longer adequate, and the family was replaced by the school as the primary source of education.

In Parts IV and V of this text, we will discuss in detail the changes in social institutions and organization that industrialization brought about. Suffice it to say here that in industrial societies, social life is more bureaucratic than in other types of societies. **Bureaucracy** is a form of social organization, based on written rules and procedures, and designed to coordinate the actions of large numbers of people. In an industrial society with its millions of members, most activities—politics, law, medicine, education, and even religion—tend to be organized bureaucratically. This allows life in an industrial society to be more orderly and efficient, but bureaucracies tend be impersonal and rigid, and unable to deal with individual circumstances.

So where does our discussion of industrial societies leave us? To answer this question, let's consider the data in Table 3.2. The table compares industrial societies with preindustrial societies using four variables: per capita income, life expectancy at birth (the average number of years a person can expect to live), the infant mortality rate (the number of deaths of children under one year of age per 1,000 live births), and the adult illiteracy rate (the percentage of the adult population who cannot read or write). It appears that generally the members of industrial societies are much better off than people living in

TABLE 3.2 Comparing Preindustrial and Industrial Societies

	Preindustrial Societies	*Industrial Societies*
Per capita income (US$)	$1,250	$25,700
Life expectancy at birth	65	77.5
Infant mortality rate	59	6
Adult illiteracy rate	30%	< 5%

Source: Compiled from World Bank (1999). *World development report.* New York: Oxford University Press, pp. 192–193, 202–203.

preindustrial societies. People living in industrial societies enjoy higher incomes, longer lives, fewer infant deaths, and lower adult illiteracy than people living in preindustrial societies (see, however, Shephard & Rode, 1996). But as you have probably sensed from our discussion so far, industrialization is a kind of double-edged sword, with these positive consequences being offset by a number of social problems, including widespread inequality.

Remember that sociology as a discipline emerged in response to industrialization in the eighteenth century. Early sociologist Emile Durkheim emphasized the positive functions of the specialized division of labor and the growth of individualism in industrial societies. Comparing preindustrial and industrial societies, Durkheim said that preindustrial societies are distinguished by what he called *mechanical solidarity*. In societies characterized by **mechanical solidarity**, people feel a sense of belonging because of their similarity to one another. There are few individual differences among them; they do the same work, fulfill the same social roles, and share a strong belief in "right" and "wrong." As societies industrialize, social diversity increases, causing mechanical solidarity to decline. However, social integration is preserved because the growth of a diverse, specialized division of labor fosters interdependence among the society's members. Thus, mechanical solidarity is replaced in industrial societies by **organic solidarity**, or social integration built on a specialized division of labor. Importantly, however, Durkheim saw a potential dysfunction in industrialization. If industrialization occurs too quickly, triggering other social changes such as rapid population growth, a society won't have time to develop appropriate norms to guide behavior and *anomie* will develop. **Anomie** is a condition in which the society's norms are inadequate for regulating members' behavior, causing confusion and social disorganization.

In contrast to Durkheim, Karl Marx and Max Weber were more alarmed by the social inequality and increasing dehumanization of social life under industrialism. Marx urged industrial workers to unite to overthrow the owners of the means of production. Weber predicted that industrialization would continue to develop, with bureaucracy growing until people lost their uniquely human creativity and became as mechanized in their daily living as the production process itself. Both Marx and Weber thus saw the problems of industrial societies as problems of *capitalism*, an economic system in which the means of production is privately owned and the owners accrue the profits. While Weber saw no way out of the problems of industrial capitalism, Marx envisioned as an alternative the *socialist* industrial society, in which production would be owned and controlled by the government, with goods and services distributed equitably among all members of the society. Unfortunately, in countries that embraced socialism along with industrialization, the outcome has often been closer to Weber's vision than Marx's: The

What is the role and status of the worker in an industrial society? How did industrialization fundamentally change people's social relationships? What did Durkheim, Marx, and Weber identify as the chief problems of industrial societies?

bureaucratic governments of these countries usually hinder rather than help economic development.

Scholars continue to debate the merits of Durkheim's, Marx's, and Weber's analyses of industrial societies, and we will revisit many of their ideas throughout this text. We can only wonder at this point, however, how they would view the emergence of what some observers consider a distinctly new type of society, the postindustrial society. We will conclude our discussion of types of societies by considering this new form.

Postindustrial Societies

According to the Department of Labor (1991), employment in agriculture and manufacturing in the United States has declined steadily since 1970. The growing area of employment is in what is called the *service sector*. The basic difference between a service job and a job in agriculture or manufacturing is that service workers do not produce a product for sale. Instead, they do just as the job title describes: They provide some kind of service, from cleaning buildings and filling fast-food orders to investing money and selling real estate. Often, service jobs require producing, managing, and distributing information, or they involve the use of computers and similar technology. Employment in the service sector has more than doubled since 1970 (U.S. Department of Commerce, Bureau of the Census, 1997).

This change in the primary focus of work in our society and others like ours, such as Canada, Japan, and Australia, suggests the emergence of a new type of society: the postindustrial society (see, for example, Bell, 1973; 1989). In a **postindustrial society,** work consists of producing services and information, rather than physical goods. This does not mean that factories disappear completely from the landscape of postindustrial societies. Rather, the manufacture of goods simply becomes less important than the manufacture of ideas, knowledge, and information. As information and its associated technology become more important to a society, the manufacture of goods increasingly takes place elsewhere, in other societies, and the postindustrial society imports these goods for its people. At the same time, however, the knowledge and technology produced in postindustrial societies may itself be applied to the manufacture of goods, so that the manufacturing that does take place in these societies is increasingly computerized and automated.

We are only on the threshold of transformation into a postindustrial society, so we don't know yet whether the outcomes will be mostly positive or negative. On the one hand, the postindustrial society may be more prosperous than the industrial society, and the vast majority of the population could share in the fruits of this prosperity. According to this scenario, the skills required for work in a postindustrial society will increase the overall educational level of the population, requiring fewer people to work at physically demanding jobs. Many work tasks will be automated or performed by robots, with human workers simply sitting at a control panel, entering commands and data to be sure that a task is done properly. Already, the greater availability of computers and electronic communications allows people to perform many work tasks no matter where they are—at home, on a plane, or sitting on the beach. This, in turn, gives some workers greater flexibility in their work schedules and work sites, making it easier, for instance, for parents with very young children or individuals with particular physical limitations to continue to work. As the trend continues, it should also increase the amount of leisure time workers enjoy.

This optimistic scenario also envisions postindustrial societies contributing to greater global cooperation among nations. Just as postindustrial societies rely on less technologically advanced societies to supply them with basic goods such as clothing, so, too, will less advanced societies rely on postindustrial societies for knowledge to foster their development. Of course, this vision puts tremendous faith in the ability of science and technology to solve social problems. It also contains an implicit trust that those with technological knowledge and skills will use them for the benefit of everyone in the society and in the world. Not surprisingly, some harbor doubts about these prospects.

A more pessimistic picture sees postindustrial society contributing to greater divisions within as well as between societies. For one thing, many of the service jobs created by postindustrialism require few skills and are low paying. Although some workers may obtain high-status jobs in such "glamour" services as banking, finance, and insurance, many others will be able to find work only in unskilled jobs (requiring no training) or deskilled jobs (jobs that used to require some training or skill, but no longer do), such as counter clerks at a fast-food restaurant or janitors at an office building. For example, a cashier used to need to at least know how to enter the price of an item on the cash register and calculate the change owed a customer. But now, cash registers can scan

What features of a postindustrial society does this picture suggest? What are the workers doing who might have staffed this plant during an earlier industrial phase? What do you think might be the greatest benefits and the greatest costs of postindustrial life?

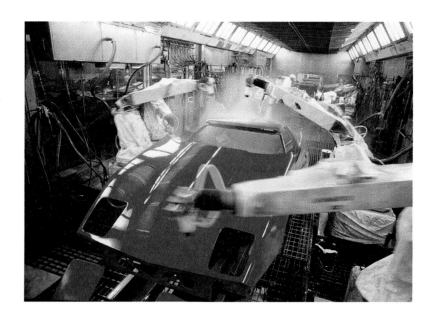

DOING SOCIOLOGY

What's in Store for the Future?

The ability to gauge trends from social scientific data has important implications. On a policy level, social forecasting can help politicians prepare for future demands by the population on various social institutions, such as the educational or health care systems. On a micro level, social forecasting can help individuals plan for their futures by, for instance, indicating which fields are likely to have the greatest job growth, or which areas of the country have the highest concentrations of particular types of employers.

The table below shows some recent population trends and projections for the United States. Based on these data, what advice would you give policy makers with respect to meeting the needs of the country's population in the next century? What services are likely to be most urgently needed? What current social policies or practices will have to be changed?

Resident Population Characteristics and Projections, 1980–2050

Year	SEX		RACE			Hispanic Origin	Median Age (years)
	Male	Female	White	Black	Other		
1980	48.6%	51.4%	85.9%	11.8%	2.3%	6.4%	30.0
1995	48.8	51.2	82.9	12.6	4.5	10.2	34.0
2000	48.9	51.1	81.9	12.8	5.3	11.3	35.5
2025	49.1	50.9	77.3	14.2	8.5	16.8	38.1
2050	49.0	51.0	72.8	15.7	11.4	22.5	39.0

Source: U.S. Department of Labor, Bureau of the Census, 1997, p. 14.

items for their price or cashiers can just push a button with the name or picture of the item on it, and the cash register not only totals the amount, but also calculates any change owed. The concern here is that the increasing technological know-how required in postindustrial society will allow the few who have such knowledge and skill to pull away from the majority who do not, creating an even greater gap between social classes in terms of education, income, and other resources. Moreover, while the technology of postindustrialism increases flexibility in work, it can also cause large numbers of people to lose their jobs. As workplaces become more automated, fewer human workers are necessary. The workers who join the ranks of the unemployed may eventually only find work in a deskilled or unskilled service occupation.

Those who hold this more pessimistic outlook are also concerned that instead of generating greater global cooperation, postindustrialism will widen the economic gap between societies. Although postindustrial societies will likely become increasingly dependent on other societies for producing goods, the relationship may not be mutually beneficial. Already, more goods production is taking place in less developed countries where workers are paid minimally and there are few health and safety regulations.

Often, traditional ways of life are being destroyed in those countries, as well as the physical and natural environment. And certainly, the economic dependence that results from this relationship is far more advantageous to the postindustrial societies than to the poorer ones.

It is still too early to determine which of these forecasts will come true, although the evidence at this stage seems to support the pessimistic view more than the optimistic one. Perhaps a bigger question at this point is whether, knowing what we do, we can or we will act to prevent the dire predictions from becoming reality. In the Doing Sociology box, we give you an opportunity to try your hand at social forecasting.

REFLECTING ON

Types of Societies

1. There are fewer hunting and gathering societies, pastoral societies, and horticultural societies than ever before. What do you think should be done to prevent the extinction of these types of societies?

Continued on p. 74

2. People live longer and are healthier in industrial societies than in other types of societies, yet poverty is a serious problem in most industrial societies. How would you explain this apparent contradiction?

3. Some people believe postindustrialism will improve social life, while others believe it will be detrimental to all but a small segment of the population. What is your assessment of postindustrial society?

4. If given a choice, what type of society would you prefer to live in? Why?

FUTURE PROSPECTS

Unlike Auguste Comte and his followers, predicting the future is no longer a goal of sociologists. Nevertheless, most sociologists today do try to gauge trends, such as fluctuations in population and economic changes, so that we can develop plans to address the potential consequences. To conclude this chapter, let's briefly consider some of the serious challenges that must be met as different types of societies confront the future.

One issue that repeatedly arose in this chapter is that some types of societies are diminishing in number and are even threatened with extinction. Hunting and gathering societies, in particular, but also pastoral, horticultural, and even agricultural societies are becoming more scarce as industrialism and postindustrialism spread. Although cross-cultural contact can contribute to the diversity of a society through cultural diffusion, it can also lessen diversity if it contributes to the destruction of particular ways of living. In fact, it appears that as hunting and gathering, pastoral, and agricultural societies are increasingly absorbed by the other societal types, the result may be that only industrial, postindustrial, and a few agricultural societies survive. These societies, especially the postindustrial, must begin to consider the consequences of their global expansion and the extent to which it is truly beneficial, not only to the societies they absorb, but also to their own societies. The culture and structure of most industrial and postindustrial societies owe a tremendous debt to those types of societies that preceded their emergence. The sophisticated tools and technology of industrial and postindustrial societies, for example, were built from knowledge painstakingly acquired throughout the

centuries by members of hunting and gathering, pastoral, horticultural, and agricultural societies. Many artifacts that we take for granted—our beds, clocks, eating utensils, even toilets—originated in preindustrial societies (Linton, 1937).

The technology that threatens to extinguish certain types of societies also threatens the survival of humans as a species. Indeed, the technology that produces such vast surpluses of goods can be applied just as easily to warfare and destruction, and in modern warfare, there are no winners. Should a nuclear war ever occur, there would likely be few survivors anywhere on the globe, not only because of the devastation of the nuclear blasts themselves, but also because the fallout would eventually destroy the planet's entire ecosystem.

The ecosystem, though, is even more directly threatened by the seemingly benign uses of technological innovation. Economic and technological advancement were first made possible to a large extent because of our ability to harness natural resources as energy. However, as technological development has increased, so too have our demands on our planet's natural resources, leading in many cases to serious depletion. This, in turn, has led to the extinction or threatened extinction of numerous animal, insect, and plant species, diminishing the earth's biological diversity. Moreover, industrial production is a primary source of environmental pollution, fouling the air, land, and water. Although postindustrialism holds the promise of a cleaner immediate environment for its members, this also means that industrial pollution is simply moved to other, less developed societies while continuing to have a global impact. Consequently, another major challenge confronting the world community in the twenty-first century is learning how to coexist in mutually beneficial ways with the natural environment. In trying to meet this challenge, perhaps we can learn a few lessons from hunting and gathering societies about respecting nature—instead of devaluing these societies' members as "primitive" people in need of our "enlightened" progress.

R E F L E C T I N G   O N

Future Prospects

In addition to the issues we have raised here, what other major challenges must be addressed as societies look to the future?

 For useful resources for study and review, run Chapter 3 on your *Living Sociology* CD-ROM.

CONNECTIONS

Family diversity	Chapter 15 describes family diversity in the section on "Families Throughout the World: Structures and Characteristics." For example, what terms are used to describe human diversity in marriage patterns?
Weber's "ideal types" of society	See "Types of Economic Systems" in Chapter 13. How is the concept of ideal types extended to the modern economic systems of capitalism and socialism?
Hunter gatherers	Read more about the !Kung, Mbuti, Agta, and other hunting and gathering peoples in the section on "Gender Relations in Contemporary Hunting and Gathering Societies" in Chapter 10. How do the gender relations of these peoples reflect the conditions of their type of society?
Organized religion	Chapter 17 describes the origins of Judaism, Islam, Christianity, and other "World Religions." What do they have in common? Why are organized or formal religions associated with the development of agrarian societies?
Global economic inequality	In "Global Stratification: An Overview," Chapter 9 explores the economic inequalities among low-, low-middle-, high-middle-, and high-income countries. How do these categories relate to the types of society?
Women and work	See "Gender and Global Poverty" in Chapter 9. How do gender inequalities intersect with economic inequalities in the different types of society?
Industrial societies	Trace the characteristics and processes of industrialization in the sections on "Economies in Historical Perspective" in Chapter 13 and "The Urban Environment" in Chapter 19. What transformation in ideal types of society does industrialization confer?
Bureaucratic organization	Weber's analysis of bureaucracy as a type of formal social organization is presented in Chapter 6. What were some benefits of bureaucracies for societies undergoing industrialization? What are some disadvantages of bureaucracies for postindustrial societies?
Capitalism and socialism	See "Types of Economic Systems" in Chapter 13 for further explanation of the development of socialism and capitalism. How do these types of economy relate to types of society?
Postindustrial service economies	The section in Chapter 13 on "Services: Where the Jobs Are" explores further the concept of a service economy, in the section on "Work in the United States." How does the idea of a dual labor market support the theory that social inequality increases in postindustrial societies?
Postindustrial futures	Read about "Theories of Social Change" in Chapter 20. What predictions for the future of postindustrial societies would you expect from the perspective of structural functionalism? What predictions would you expect from the perspective of conflict theory?

SUMMING UP CHAPTER 3

Social Structure

1. The stable patterns of interaction in a society are called *social structure*. Sociologists study social structure by examining the parts that compose it: institutions, statuses, roles, and groups.

2. A social institution is a set of stable rules and relationships that regulate the social activities in which the members of a society engage to meet their survival needs. The major social institutions of a society are: the economy, government, family, education, religion, and medicine.

Together with culture, institutions shape the social life of a society.

3. The members of a society interacting in institutions hold social positions called statuses. Attached to every status is one or more roles, that is, behaviors, responsibilities, and privileges that are expected of individuals occupying a specific status.

4. A social group is two or more people who interact with one another on a regular basis and share common expectations and a common identity. We all belong to many groups simultaneously, but they are not all equally important.

Types of Societies

1. There are six basic types of societies: hunting and gathering, pastoral, horticultural, agricultural, industrial, and postindustrial societies. However, these are ideal types; real societies throughout the world will fit only more or less into these categories.

2. In hunting and gathering societies, members meet their survival needs by hunting game, sometimes by fishing, and by gathering vegetation. Hunting and gathering societies are small, usually nomadic, and highly egalitarian. Religion and government as we know them do not exist.

3. In a pastoral society, economic survival is based on domesticating and herding animals. Wealth can be accumulated and passed on from one generation to the next and translated into political power. Accumulated wealth also leads to inequality and conflict. Pastoral societies are semi-settled, and contact with other societies leads to trade and cultural diffusion. The steady food supply frees people for other roles. The religion that emerges is based on a belief in a primary deity who is actively involved in the daily affairs of humans.

4. Horticultural societies cultivate plants using relatively simple technology, such as digging sticks and the slash-and-burn method, as their subsistence strategy. The stable food supply of horticultural societies allows populations to grow large and become sedentary. Land ownership is the primary source of wealth, and is passed on through inheritance and expanded through marriage. Political and religious institutions are more complex, and inequality produces conflict and warfare.

5. Agricultural societies use plows, draft animals, and other methods such as irrigation to cultivate crops as a subsistence strategy. Because agriculture can produce unprecedented surpluses of food, these can sustain very large, permanently settled populations. Agricultural societies

have a centralized government, a monetary system of exchange, a written language, and a legal system.

6. Industrial societies use mechanized systems of production to meet their subsistence needs. Industrialism spreads rapidly, sustaining large sedentary populations, while absorbing or destroying other types of societies. Hallmarks of industrial societies include rapid technological and social change, urbanization, widespread economic inequality, the spread of bureaucracy, improved health and longer life expectancy, and a rise in the population's level of education.

7. Durkheim emphasized the positive functions of industrialism, including the growth of individualism and the specialized division of labor. Preindustrial societies are characterized by mechanical solidarity (social integration results from members' similarities to one another), while industrial societies are characterized by organic solidarity (social integration is built on the interdependence growing out of the specialized division of labor). One potential dysfunction of industrialism is anomie, a condition in which the society's norms are inadequate for regulating members' behavior, causing confusion and social disorganization.

8. Karl Marx and Max Weber emphasized the social inequality and growing dehumanization of social life under industrialism. Marx believed that the problems associated with industrialism are the result of capitalism, and argued that the problems could be solved by replacing capitalist industrialism with socialist industrialism. Weber, on the other hand, could see no solutions to the problems of industrial societies.

9. In postindustrial societies, work consists of producing services and information, rather than physical goods. The manufacture of goods increasingly takes place elsewhere, in poorer countries. Some people believe postindustrialism will improve social life, while others believe it will be detrimental to all but a small segment of the population.

Future Prospects

1. There are several serious challenges that must be met as societies confront the future. Industrial and postindustrial societies must begin to consider the consequences of their global expansion and the extent to which it is beneficial to the societies they absorb as well as to their own societies. In addition, industrial and postindustrial societies must address the potential human and environmental destruction posed by technological innovation.

KEY PEOPLE AND CONCEPTS

agricultural society (agrarian society): a society in which the subsistence strategy is based on cultivating crops using plows, draft animals, and other technology such as irrigation

anomie: a condition in which the society's norms are inadequate for regulating members' behavior, causing confusion and social disorganization

bureaucracy: a form of social organization, based on written rules and procedures, designed for managing and coordinating the actions of large numbers of people

horticultural society: a society in which the subsistence strategy is based on cultivating plants using relatively simple technology such as digging sticks and the slash-and-burn method

hunting and gathering society: a society in which the subsistence strategy in based on hunting game, fishing, and gathering vegetation and other types of food from the surrounding environment

ideal type: an analytic tool that sociologists construct by carefully studying various examples of the phenomenon they are interested in, and from this, identifying what they consider to be its essential features

industrial society: a society in which the subsistence strategy is based on mechanized systems of production

mechanical solidarity: the sense of belonging that the members of a society develop because of their similarity to one another

nomadic: having to move from one locale to another, without permanent settlement

organic solidarity: social integration built on a specialized division of labor

pastoral society: a society in which the subsistence strategy is based on domesticating and herding animals

postindustrial society: a society in which work is devoted primarily to the production of services and information rather than to the physical production of goods

roles: the behaviors, responsibilities, and privileges expected of individuals occupying a specific status

sedentary: settled with respect to residence

semisedentary: semisettled with respect to residence

social class: an economic status determined by one's role in the production process

social group: two or more people who interact with one another on a regular basis and share common expectations and a common identity

social institution: a set of relatively stable rules and relationships that serve to regulate the social activities in which the members of a society engage in order to meet their survival needs

social structures: stable patterns of interaction in a society

society: a collectivity of interacting people who share the same culture

status: particular social positions held by members of a society interacting in social institutions

surplus: the accumulation of more resources than are necessary to meet daily subsistence

LEARNING MORE

Alfino, M., Caputo, J. S., & Wynyard, R. (Eds.). 1998. *McDonaldization revisited: Critical essays on consumer culture*. New York: Praeger. A reexamination of George Ritzer's theory (see Ritzer, 1993, below) that human behavior in emerging postindustrial societies is becoming more predictable and more homogeneous and, therefore, more dehumanized and controllable.

Kent, S. (Ed.). (1996). *Cultural diversity among twentieth-century foragers: An African perspective*. New York: Cambridge University Press. A collection of essays that examines some myths and truths about contemporary hunting and gathering societies in several African countries.

Ritzer, G. (1993). *The McDonaldization of society*. Thousand Oaks, CA: Pine Forge Press. A pessimistic look at the emergence of postindustrialism in the contemporary United States.

Sachs, C. E. (1996). *Gendered fields: Rural women, agriculture, and environment*. Boulder, CO: Westview. An analysis of women working in agriculture in various societies throughout the world, which addresses the impact of changes in agriculture on women's status.

 Run Chapter 4 on your *Living Sociology* CD-ROM for interesting and informative activities, web links, videos, practice tests, and more.

C H A P T E R

4

Culture

S
ome friends have invited you to a posh new restaurant for dinner. Sitting at the elegantly set table, you look with anticipation at the covered dish the server places before you. But when the cover is removed, you don't recognize what's on the plate. Your friends explain that this is one of the chef's specialties, sautéed scorpions. Not wishing to insult your hosts, you smile, serve yourself a few scorpions, and tentatively take a bite. Your taste buds tell you they aren't bad, but your mind tells you otherwise: One just doesn't eat scorpions, sautéed or otherwise. The second course arrives and your smile changes to a look of horror. You have been presented with a steamed chicken embryo. Your friends dig in enthusiastically, but you mumble something about having eaten a big lunch. You do better with the third course: sea slugs. They're mushy, but the taste is agreeable. You just wish their antennae weren't still attached. Course four is a hearty bowl of chicken feet soup. The feet stick right up out of the soup tureen, and your friends appear to particularly enjoy nibbling on the tiny toes in between spoonfuls of broth. Finally, the server brings a large platter of fresh fruit. Your friends are too filled for dessert, but you suddenly rediscover your appetite and devour the oranges and bananas.

Actually, this meal is quite real. All of these dishes have been served to—and eaten by—your authors during visits with friends and colleagues in China. Admittedly, we had to overcome our initial reactions, but as sociologists we know that what people consider edible is a matter of *culture*, not the food itself. Sautéed scorpions, sea slugs, and, yes, even steamed chicken embryos, tasted good as long as we didn't let cultural expectations override the objectivity of our palates.

Culture is the shared set of values, beliefs, behavioral expectations, and artifacts (material objects) that comprise the way of life of a people. Culture, then, distinguishes one group from another and gives group members a sense of belonging, a feeling of "we-ness." As you have seen, a **society** is composed of interacting people who share the same culture. That is, they hold the same values and beliefs, speak the same language, practice the same customs, and so on. Membership in a society, therefore, may transcend geographic or territorial boundaries, since people living in different places may nevertheless share the same culture just as people occupying a particular territory or geographic space may have different cultures. For example, Chinese immigrants to the United States may continue to eat the foods and practice the traditions that they enjoyed in China, but here in the United States they may live side-by-side in neighborhoods populated with people from many other countries—and cultures.

In this chapter, our discussion focuses on culture. We will consider the elements that make up a culture as well as the issues of cultural diversity and how cultures change. First, though, we'll discuss the relationship between biology and culture.

THE INTERACTION OF BIOLOGY AND CULTURE

Humans are the only species who have developed culture. Although scientists are unsure of when exactly in our evolutionary history culture first emerged, it was probably about 2 million years ago. Given that our universe is thought to be 15 billion years old and the earth about 4.5 billion years old, culture is a relatively recent phenomenon. Indeed, it was probably not until the brain of *homo sapiens* developed to full size—approximately 40,000 years ago—that culture as we know it today appeared (Bickerton, 1995; Lieberman, 1998).

Culture, then, makes us distinctively human. Most animals rely on instincts to direct them in meeting their survival needs. **Instincts** are biologically programmed directions for living. Consequently, all beavers build dams and construct them the same way; all hummingbirds in the United States and Canada fly to Venezuela for the winter and in a particular formation from which they never deviate; and all salmon swim upstream to spawn, with each generation returning to exactly the same breeding places as the generation before it. In each case, the animals have no choice; there is no thought involved. Their patterns of behavior are fixed. Very simply, their biology makes them do what they do.

In contrast, humans, having no instincts, rely on culture to guide them in their everyday lives. This is not to say biology has no effect on human behavior. Humans are undeniably biological creatures. But instead of instincts, we have biological **drives**, basic physiological needs that must be met in order for us to survive. Thus, all humans have a biological drive to eat, but, as our

This child in Beijing, China, is eating a snack—a deep fried grasshopper kabob. How does this example illustrate the interaction of biological and cultural determinism?

opening example illustrates, the way we satisfy this drive varies tremendously because, unlike other animals, our capacity for intelligent and creative thought enables us to make choices. We may, in fact, choose not to satisfy our hunger at all. We might, for example, go on a hunger strike to demonstrate our commitment to a particular cause.

The choices we make, however, are not made independently of the social group in which we live, and this is where culture comes in. Although we humans have what we call "free will," we are constrained by our culture, which tells us what is expected and what is acceptable in particular situations. Returning to the example of food, for instance, we would not be surprised to hear that someone paid $7.00 per pound for a piece of choice beef. In Malaysia, however, someone who can afford it is more likely to pay $7.00 for a prime queen termite, which measures about two inches. Indeed, wealthy residents of neighboring Singapore consider termites a prized and healthy snack, often eating them live. A good termite is "tough and firm on the outside, cool and creamy on the inside" ("Singapore's Snack?" 1995; see also Asimov, 1997; Schwabe, 1979; Smith, 1994).

Some people, of course, do reject some aspects of their culture, but what is rejected is replaced with a different belief, value, expectation, symbol, or artifact. *No human is ever totally without culture.* We emphasize this point because in everyday life, people tend to use the word *culture* to refer to the tastes and pursuits of "refined" individuals. That is, people who go to art museums, listen to classical music, and read fine literature are said to be cultured. While such pursuits may make up a society's **high culture**—the beliefs, values, expectations, and artifacts of the society's elite groups—they are not the whole of what sociologists refer to when they use the term *culture*. For sociologists, the term *culture* also encompasses what might be called **popular culture**—the beliefs, values, expectations, and artifacts of the society's masses. So, for example, while many people in the United States, elite and nonelite alike, may feel that eating steak tartare is "more cultured," that is, better, than eating a Big Mac, sociologists do not make such judgments. In fact, sociologists see such a judgment itself as a product of culture. There is nothing inherently better about steak tartare relative to a Big Mac, but one tends to be favored by individuals of high social standing and the other by "ordinary" people. However, Americans tend to value most highly whatever is associated with the wealthy and the powerful, a point we will take up later in the chapter and throughout the text.

In sum, to the sociologist, all aspects of a social group's way of life constitute culture. Culture interacts with biology to fundamentally shape who we are: We may have drives to survive and reproduce, but what we eat, how we dress, speak, and behave in specific situations, and how we interpret other people's words and gestures are determined by our culture.

REFLECTING ON

The Interaction of Biology and Culture

1. What might be a specific example of how culture makes us distinctively human?
2. How would you explain to someone how biology and culture interact to determine social behavior?
3. What would you say to a friend who argues that high culture is superior to popular culture?
4. What are two examples of the popular cultures of two different groups of ordinary people in the U.S.?

THE ELEMENTS OF CULTURE

Sociologists distinguish between two basic elements of culture: ideas and objects. Ideas are referred to as *non-*

material culture. More specifically, **nonmaterial culture** includes all the nontangible or nonphysical products that the members of a society create, including values, beliefs, and the language to express them. Thus, democracy, social classes, and Buddhism are examples of nonmaterial culture. **Material culture** includes all the tangible or physical products that the members of a society create, for instance, digging sticks, computers, wheels, and the space shuttle. Although it may at first seem these two dimensions of culture are separate or independent, in reality, the two are interdependent. Sociologists refer to the interdependence among the elements of a culture as **cultural integration.** Each dimension has an impact on the other; ideas spawn new objects (for example, a voting booth is invented so that democratic elections may be held), and objects produce ideas (every object is named).

Every society has both nonmaterial and material culture, but the content of each varies tremendously from society to society. All societies have language, but one speaks Spanish while another speaks Swahili. Similarly, members of all societies wear clothes, but in one, men wear kilts and in another, loin cloths.

Let's look now at the components of nonmaterial culture (symbols, language, values and beliefs, and norms) and material culture (artifacts and technology).

Symbols

We tend to think of communication in terms of what we say verbally to one another, but if you think about it, much of our everyday communication is unspoken. How, then, are we able to understand and interact in an organized way with one another? It is not because we occupy the same geographic space, but because we inhabit a shared *symbolic environment.* As we discussed in Chapter 1, humans give their actions and the world around them meaning. That is, actions and objects stand for something; they are symbols. A **symbol,** then, is anything that has been given representational meaning by the members of a cultural group.

The meaning given to a single object or action may vary tremendously from culture to culture. Take, for instance, the simple gesture of a head nod. In the United States, nodding one's head up and down signifies yes, while shaking one's head back and forth means no. In Bulgaria, however, the opposite is true (Axtell, 1991). Imagine the confusion between Americans and Bulgarians who meet for the first time and are unaware of this cultural difference.

Misunderstandings are common when individuals encounter different cultures, and the consequences may be minor or even humorous. Sometimes, though, the outcome can be more serious. At the 1988 Summer Olympics in Seoul, South Korea, for example, a U.S. television crew infuriated their hosts when they appeared wearing t-shirts

In what ways is this scene a symbolic environment? What kinds of symbols define the culture of a society? What are some social functions of cultural symbols? What are some connections between symbols and sentiments? What sentiments do you think are being evoked in the person in the photograph?

that proclaimed, "We're bad," above the South Korean flag and an image of two boxers. Their intent was to show support for the U.S. Olympic boxing team, but the South Koreans interpreted the slogan literally and considered it, and the use of their flag, a grave insult (Axtell, 1991). Some Americans felt the South Koreans overreacted to what was really an unintentional offense, but had the tables been turned and a South Korean news crew done something comparable, do you think most Americans would be forgiving? Consider the emotional reactions evoked when someone "mistreats" the U.S. flag by, for example, burning it to protest a government decision.

Religious symbols also tend to have strong emotional feelings attached to them, but again, what is adopted as a religious symbol and the specific meaning attached to it vary across cultures. The pig is a good example. Among Christians, pigs have no religious significance and evoke little, if any, emotion; at best, pigs are a food source. Among Jews and Muslims, however, pigs are considered unclean. Eating pork or even touching anything made from a pig pollutes the individual. So, for instance, to give a Muslim a pigskin wallet as a gift would be a serious insult. In contrast, in various tribes in New Guinea and Melanesia where religion takes the form of ancestor worship, pigs are holy. So beloved are pigs that they are named and raised as family members; they are fed what the rest of the family eats, and they sleep with the family as well. Devotion to the pig also requires that its flesh eventually be incorporated into the flesh of the human host. So, about once every twelve years, most of the adult pigs are sacrificed and consumed by the villagers at great feasts. If the celebrants become full, they make themselves vomit so they can eat more. The ritual pig feasts are believed to appease the village ancestors' craving for pork, to guarantee communal health, and to bring victory in future battles with enemy tribes (Harris, 1975).

But we do not have to travel to the South Pacific to find significant cultural differences in the meaning of symbols. Recently, for example, the citizens of Arthur Ashe's hometown announced that they wished to erect a statue in honor of the late tennis champion. However, a dispute arose when it was discovered that the statue would be placed in a park where confederate leaders of the Civil War were honored. To some Southerners, especially Whites, the confederate leaders were slain heroes, but to others, especially Black Southerners, the confederates' statues symbolized racial hatred, which was the antithesis of what Arthur Ashe had worked for during his life.

The meanings of symbols can also change over time. For example, sign language, the international communication system of the deaf based on symbolic gestures, is being revised to reflect growing sensitivity to the feelings of various groups. The traditional gesture to signify homosexual, for instance, was a swish of the wrist. Recently, however, deaf gays and lesbians have been substituting the letter *q*, for *queer*. Importantly, among gay men and lesbians, the word *queer*, which used to be considered demeaning, has come to signify pride in one's sexual orientation (Senior, 1994).

Clearly, the shared meanings that members of a culture attach to particular symbols are an important part of what binds them together as a group. At the same time, those who do not share a symbolic system are considered outsiders.

Language

Perhaps the most complex symbolic system in a culture is language. **Language** is a system of patterned sounds, often with corresponding written symbols, that the members of a society use to communicate their thoughts and feelings to one another. Notice that written language does not always accompany spoken language. Although every known culture has a spoken language, some, such as the Huaorani of Ecuador, have no written symbols that correspond to their vocalizations.

Even in a culture with a written language, some people may not be able to use it—that is, they are illiterate. In the United States, less than 5 percent of the population is illiterate, but in many economically underdeveloped countries, an average of 50 percent of the population is illiterate (World Bank, 1999), and United Nations experts predict that this number will grow steadily during the early decades of the twenty-first century (UNICEF, 1998).

Communication through language is an exclusively human trait, despite the claims of dog and cat owners, who believe that their pet not only can understand when it is spoken to, but also communicates with them nonverbally. Such uncanny understanding in animals has entertained movie audiences for years, leaving many shaking their heads and muttering, "If only that dog could talk." But despite appearances, research over the past half century shows that only the human brain has developed the capacity for language. Unlike other animals, humans not only can speak, but we also have the ability to put words together to form sentences (Bickerton, 1995; Lieberman, 1991; 1998).

All animals communicate with others of their kind by using sounds and physical posturing. Thus, one male lizard "tells" another male lizard that he is ready for a fight by bobbing his head and extending the orange flap of skin under his neck called a *dulap*. This, though, is instinctive behavior, uninfluenced by purposive thought or rational decision making. Other animals, such as chimps, may be taught a vocabulary of a few hundred words and be trained to communicate with humans by pointing to pictures or using a special typewriter, but they cannot learn to form grammatical sentences or understand even basic rules of syntax that the average human masters by the age of three. Moreover, neither chimps nor other animals can communicate to each other or to us creative thought; the ability to convey the products of our imagination—indeed, imagination itself—is uniquely human (Bickerton, 1995; Lieberman, 1991, 1998; see, however, Boxer, 1997; Brannon & Terrace, 1998).

Language is vital to the preservation of human societies because it is the primary means of **cultural transmission,** that is, the process by which culture is passed on from one generation to the next. Colonizers and conquerors have long recognized this. In Australia, for example, the British tried to destroy Aboriginal culture by taking children from their parents and putting them in "boarding schools" where White British culture was taught. American Indians were subjected to the same practice by the United States government in the 1800s. Although today we use books to tell us about our past, written accounts are a relatively recent part of human history. Moreover, even when books became available, they were accessible only to the elite since the masses could not read. For most of human history, and in many societies today, the average person relies on the oral teachings of previous generations

The Issue

In April 1995, Ana Dicklow went to an ice cream store to buy an ice cream cake for her father's eightieth birthday. When she asked the store manager to write "Happy Birthday" in Spanish on the cake, he refused. Assuming the manager didn't know Spanish, Ms. Dicklow offered to spell the Spanish words for him, but he still refused, telling her that this is America and he'd only write in English. Ms. Dicklow filed a formal complaint with the parent company of the store, and eventually, the manager was suspended pending the outcome of an investigation. However, the incident exemplifies the backlash against bilingualism in the United States and the growing popularity of what is called the *English-only movement*.

The Debate

Although bilingualism is a relevant issue for all non–English-speaking people in the United States, it is especially significant to Hispanic Americans, given that about half the U.S. population that speaks a language other than English speaks Spanish. In fact, the United States is one of the largest Spanish-speaking countries in the world (Portes & Truelove, 1991). Moreover, Spanish has been singled out by opponents of bilingualism, who have referred to the language as a "menace" and to speaking Spanish as "subversive" (Meier, 1990). In addition, the availability of bilingual programs affects the ability of non–English speakers to succeed in the United States. Hispanic immigrants most often cite language problems as the most serious obstacle to their successful integration into American society. Some Hispanic Americans see bilingual programs as a means for their

children to learn English quickly, while at the same time showing respect for the Spanish language and culture and fighting discrimination. Others, though, believe that immersion in the English language is the key to success in the United States, so they do not support bilingual programs (Meier, 1990; Puente & Morello, 1998).

In 1968, Congress passed the Bilingual Education Act, which provided federal funding for special school programs designed for non–English-speaking children. Six years later, the Supreme Court ruled unanimously that schools must provide programs to meet the special language needs of non–English-speaking children. During the remainder of the 1970s, federal funding for bilingual education rose steadily and many states passed bilingual education laws. At the same time, however, groups opposed to bilingualism began to organize and gain support. These groups seek to promote the passage of English-only laws to limit bilingual programs, to require ballots for elections to be printed only in English, and to establish English as the official language of the United States (Meier, 1990; Rodriguez, 1989).

In challenging the English-only movement, supporters of bilingual programs point out that the United States has a history of multilingualism. Bilingual education, for example, dates back to the 1700s (Rodriguez, 1989). It was not until after World War I that the United States abandoned bilingual education. Nevertheless, the English-only movement has successfully fostered xenophobia (fear of foreigners) among White Americans. Throughout the 1980s and into the 1990s, funding for bilingual programs was cut. By the end of the 1980s, seventeen states and more than forty towns had

passed laws making English their official language (Meier, 1990). In 1998, California voters passed Proposition 227, a law aimed at dismantling bilingual education in the state and requiring that all children be taught "overwhelmingly" in English (Puente & Morello, 1998). Observers expect other states to adopt similar laws, although they will likely be challenged in the courts.

What Do You Think?

The future of bilingual eduction is uncertain. What do you think about bilingualism? What would you say to policy makers to convince them to continue funding or to dismantle bilingual programs?

to learn the culture. Even in the contemporary United States and other technologically developed societies, we begin to learn our culture in infancy from our parents and other relatives, who teach us not by giving us something to read, but by telling and showing us. Without language,

then, a culture, and therefore a society, cannot survive (Bickerton, 1995). The Social Policy box discusses the struggle of nonnative English speakers in the United States to retain this important component of their culture (see also Gugliotta, 1999).

We have said that language allows us to express our thoughts, but does language influence how we think? That is, does language affect how we experience and understand reality? In the 1950s, two American linguists, Edward Sapir and Benjamin Whorf, theorized that language does shape perception. According to the **Sapir-Whorf hypothesis,** people tend not to notice or be aware of things for which they have no name in their language. It's not that we can't or don't see the things; it's that if we don't have a name or word for what we see, we tend to either ignore it or categorize it with something we know. So, for example, if we were standing in the middle of the Australian outback, we would likely call the reddish soil surrounding us *sand*. But, depending on the texture and shade of that particular soil, an Australian Aborigine would use one of twenty different words to name it. In other words, in this case, we have one reality and the Aborigine has twenty.

Of course, languages are constantly changing and evolving through use, the need to name new things, or sometimes because of conscious efforts. Just think of all of the words that are now part of our everyday vocabulary that did not exist, or at least were not in common use, twenty-five years ago; infomercial, CD-ROM, and fax are just a few examples. As Sapir and Whorf recognized, words are symbols that not only name and describe, but also influence how we see our world and ourselves.

Values

In the boardroom of a large U.S. corporation headquartered in downtown Manhattan, a group of executives debate the merits of a business proposal. Although everyone is participating in the discussion, two executives dominate and frequently interrupt the others. When it appears that neither side is being persuaded by the other's arguments, the chief executive calls for a vote and the majority decide the fate of the proposal. Meanwhile, deep in the Amazon rain forest, a group of Huaorani tribespeople sit in a circle debating the merits of setting off on a hunting expedition. Everyone participates in the discussion, each waiting patiently for another to stop speaking before taking a turn; no one's voice is ever raised. The discussion continues for hours until all agree on what to do and each is certain the other is content with the final decision.

Both of these groups are engaged in the same process, decision making. The way they carry out this activity, however, reflects a sharp difference in their values. **Values** are cultural standards or judgments of what is right, good, or desirable. In the first scenario, we see examples of what sociologists (e.g., Bellah et al., 1985; Williams, 1970) have identified as central values of American culture: individualism and personal freedom (each person is entitled to his or her own opinion and should be able to pursue personal goals); achievement and success through competition (life is a zero-sum game in which victory for one side means defeat for the other); democracy (one person, one vote; majority rules). In contrast, the values of Huaorani culture illustrated in the second scenario are egalitarianism (each member of the group is equal in all ways to every other member of the group—there is no status hierarchy); consensus (collective agreement—there are no losers, everyone wins); group harmony (the happiness and well-being of the group is more important than the interests of any individual) (Kane, 1995).

The central values of a culture are constantly being reinforced in its members, from their birth until their death. Not surprisingly, then, values powerfully influence how members of a culture conduct their everyday lives. We saw this in our discussion of U.S. and Huaorani decision making, but examples are abundant. In Japan, for instance, beliefs about the supernatural are often incorporated into the training of business executives. The top-ranking executives of some of Japan's largest corporations work with a *ki* master, who helps them harness the fundamental life force that allows the mind to overcome the limitations of the body. In Hong Kong, China, Bali, and other Asian countries, spiritual beliefs require that before a new building is constructed, religious advisors be consulted for the most cosmologically beneficial site (Pollack, 1995; Rosenthal, 1995). Lest we think ourselves above such "primitive" practices, consider that many of the most important events in the United States, such as the inauguration of the President, begin with a prayer—invoking the supernatural. Astrology is also extremely popular in this country, with most U.S. newspapers routinely printing daily or weekly horoscopes. Former First Lady Nancy Reagan even turned to astrology to determine the most advantageous travel schedule for her husband when he occupied the White House. An increasing number of Americans are using the principles of *fengshui* to decide on the best way to arrange the furniture in their homes or offices so as to maximize tranquility or productivity. *Fengshui* is the ancient Chinese system of positioning the body or objects in an environment in such a way as to maximize the flow of certain kinds of energy.

Interestingly, values within a culture may be contradictory. Most Americans value hard work and believe that success is the result of individual effort and responsibility, but many also say that success depends on luck or fate, being in the right place at the right time. Similarly, public opinion polls indicate that the majority of White Americans support equal opportunity and believe racial segregation is wrong, yet the polls also show that the majority of White Americans strongly resist racial integration of schools and residential neighborhoods (Hacker, 1992; Massey & Denton, 1993).

Contradictions such as these sometimes reflect efforts to bring about changes in values. The civil rights and

In this Balinese religious ceremony, food offerings are being made to an idol to obtain a blessing. Blessings are part of daily life, required for new construction, business activities, contracts, journeys, and other undertakings. What cultural values does this practice suggest? What values do you identify as most central in American culture?

Black Power movements, for instance, were instrumental in changing beliefs that support racial segregation, but their success has been less than total. In other cases, contradictory values are simply a built-in feature of the culture, sharing a peaceful coexistence. One value or belief may be emphasized over another depending on the circumstances, or the contradiction may be ignored altogether. Most Americans apparently have no difficulty believing that no one has the right to take another human life, while at the same time overwhelmingly supporting the death penalty (75 percent in favor) (U.S. Department of Justice, Bureau of Justice Statistics, 1998).

The contradictions within a culture extend beyond values and beliefs. As we will see in the next section, there are also gaps between cultural expectations for behavior and how people actually behave.

Norms

You have just been introduced to a visitor from Brazil who speaks English as well as Portuguese. After shaking hands and exchanging pleasantries, the two of you begin to talk. It's a casual conversation, but soon you are feeling intensely uncomfortable; your heartbeat has quickened, your voice is a bit jittery, and you are even perspiring a little. The source of your discomfort stems from the physical proximity of your visitor. When you began the conversation, you were standing a little more than two feet from each other; now, this person is only inches away from you. Every time you take a step back, the Brazilian takes a step forward. Finally, your back is against a wall, and the two of you are practically nose to nose. Your mind is no longer on the conversation, but on how to escape from this person.

Why would such a situation arouse so much anxiety in you? The answer has to do with norms. **Norms** are the rules of a culture; they tell the members of a culture how they are expected to behave in a given situation. They tell us what we should do under certain circumstances (*prescriptive norms*) and what we should *not* do (*proscriptive norms*). In our example, the Brazilian visitor was violating one of our culture's norms regarding personal space. You, however, were also violating one of Brazilian culture's norms regarding personal space. While you may have felt the Brazilian was being pushy or "fresh," the Brazilian was probably thinking that you were snobbish and rude (Axtell, 1991).

Like some of the other components of culture, norms are not all of one kind, and violating some norms is more serious than violating others. At the turn of the century, American sociologist William Graham Sumner drew a useful distinction between two types of norms: mores and folkways. **Mores** (pronounced "*more*-ays") are norms that carry a strong social sanction (such as imprisonment) if violated because the members of a culture consider adherence to them essential to the well-being of the society. In contrast, **folkways** are weaker norms, and violation brings only mild sanction (such as a cold stare), since adherence to them is not considered essential to the well-being of the society. The members of a society grant each other greater leeway in terms of conformity to most folkways. Thus, if a woman and man spread out a blanket in a public park on a warm spring day, lie down together, and spend the afternoon kissing, some observers might be offended and make disapproving remarks, but most passersby would simply ignore them. If, however, the couple removed even some of their clothing and engaged in sexual intercourse, they undoubtedly would be arrested. Kissing in public violates some people's standards of discretion or polite behavior, but sexual intercourse in public is considered an affront to societal standards of decency.

As the Global Insights box shows, the same behaviors may be regarded as folkways in one culture, but as mores in another. Our amorous couple would not bring official wrath on themselves for kissing in Central Park,

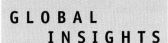

GLOBAL INSIGHTS   What's Proper?

What are your career plans? Perhaps you hope to land a job in marketing or finance. Or maybe you want to become a journalist, a counselor, or even a sociologist. Regardless of your chosen profession, you can expect to spend some of your time on the job interacting with people whose cultural backgrounds are different from your own. Understanding the folkways of other cultures may mean the difference between your professional success and failure. Are you prepared? To find out, let's test your knowledge of cross-cultural etiquette:

1. *True or False:* One of the nicest gifts you can give an Iranian client is a bouquet of yellow roses.
2. *True or False:* When doing business in Japan, you should try to make sustained eye contact with your Japanese colleagues.
3. *True or False:* When dining at a colleague's home in Zambia, you should always ask for food, rather than waiting for it to be offered to you.
4. *True or False:* In China, handkerchiefs make nice gifts, especially if wrapped in blue and white paper.
5. *True or False:* In Thailand, it is inappropriate to touch a person's—even a child's—head.
6. *True or False:* When visiting with a client or colleague in Saudi Arabia, you should always admire and lavishly praise their possessions.
7. *True or False:* After making a purchase in Korea, always hold out your hand so the shopkeeper can give you your change.
8. *True or False:* Once you've closed a deal with an Afghani client, you should smile broadly and signal your pleasure with the "thumbs-up" gesture.
9. *True or False:* You should always accept gifts from Saudi colleagues using only your right hand.
10. *True or False:* When you leave a meeting in Nigeria, you should always wave good-bye to your hosts.

Now let's see how you did:

1. *False*—unless you wish to send the message, "I hate you."
2. *False*—Looking someone straight in the eye and making sustained eye contact is considered disrespectful in Japan. To be polite, one should keep eyes lowered.
3. *True*—In Zambia, it is impolite for a guest to wait to be offered food, and it is equally impolite to refuse food.
4. *False*—The Chinese consider handkerchiefs a symbol of sadness, and blue and white are colors of mourning. A gift that comes in pairs—a pen and pencil set, two matching vases—would be more appropriate, since the Chinese believe that twins bring good luck.
5. *True*—In Thailand, the head is considered to be the most important part of the body, to be treated with utmost respect.
6. *False*—If you admire or lavishly praise an object belonging to a Saudi, you are putting that person in the awkward position of having to give it to you.
7. *False*—It is considered disrespectful for a Korean shopkeeper to place change directly in the hand of a customer.
8. *False*—The thumbs-up signal is to an Afghani the equivalent of raising your middle finger to an American.
9. *True*—The left hand is associated with toilet practices in the Middle East.
10. *False*—A hand wave is considered a menacing gesture in Nigeria.

Source: Adapted from R. E. Axtell. (1991). *Gestures: The do's and taboos of body language around the world.* New York: Wiley; and N. Dresser. (1996). *Multicultural manners.* New York: John Wiley and Sons.

but should they travel to Saudi Arabia, they are likely to find themselves under arrest for even more minor displays of affection. There, it is illegal for a single woman to be seen alone in public with a man who is not her father, brother, other male relative, or a man who has been designated by them to escort her, such as a chauffeur. (Women are also legally prohibited from driving cars in Saudi Arabia.) In most cultures, in fact, some norms are codified into laws. **Laws** are norms that the governing body of a society officially adopts to regulate behavior. For example, all societies have norms regulating mar-

riage. In the United States (and all other Western countries except Denmark), homosexuals are officially prohibited from marrying. This, though, appears to be a norm in transition, since efforts are underway in our country to lift the legal ban on homosexual marriages. In addition to laws, in all societies some norms are so strongly held that to violate them is virtually inconceivable. These norms are called **taboos;** an example from our own society would be eating human flesh.

Norms vary not only from culture to culture, but also situationally within a single culture. For instance, cracking open peanut shells and munching happily on their contents would be considered normative (expected) at a baseball game, but a norm violation if done in a church during a service. Norms also change over time. At the turn of the century, for example, gender norms dictated that a respectable married woman, especially one with young children, did not work outside the home for wages. Not surprisingly, therefore, in 1900, only a tiny percentage of married women with children under the age of eighteen were in the paid labor force. Indeed, only 20 percent of all working-age women were employed outside the home in 1900. These numbers did not change drastically, except during wartime, until the 1960s. In the late sixties, gender norms began to change, in large part because of the Women's Movement, but also in response to a number of other factors, including a downturn in the economy. As it became more socially acceptable for women to work and as economic conditions made it necessary for more families to have two wage earners in order to make ends meet, more women entered the labor force. Today, it is not only acceptable, it is expected that women, including married women with dependent children, will work outside the home for wages. The change in norms is reflected in women's labor force statistics: By 1996, 70 percent of married women with children under the age of eighteen were in the paid labor force; 67.1 percent of working-age women were employed (U.S. Department of Commerce, Bureau of the Census, 1997).

There are, of course, disparities between norms and actual behavior. In the United States, for example, we continue to frown on premarital sex by teenagers, although some would probably argue that this norm has become more of a folkway. But despite the normative prohibition, research shows that four out of five twenty-year-olds have had intercourse (Children's Defense Fund, 1997).

We will return to this point shortly. Suffice it to say for now that, as we saw in our discussion of values, these inconsistencies may arise out of broader social changes, or they may simply be incorporated into the culture itself. Nevertheless, most people in a society adhere more or less to most of the society's norms. Norms are a fundamental element of a society's system of social control. Without norms, social order would be impossible.

Artifacts and Technology

So far, our discussion has focused on nonmaterial culture, but cultures are also composed of physical products. We refer to these as *material culture.*

Material culture is composed of two elements: technology and artifacts. **Technology** is the body of knowledge that members of a society apply to their physical environment to meet their survival needs. We tend to think of technology in terms of scientific progress and industrial production, but using a stick to locate water un-

derground or to dig up tubers and larvae for food also constitutes technology.

The physical things that the members of a society make when they apply their technology to the physical environment are called **artifacts.** Artifacts may be technologically sophisticated (for example, an electron microscope or a robot that assembles cars), or they may be technologically simple (a spear for hunting or a sharpened stone for cutting meat or vines). What is important to remember is that newer (more sophisticated) is not always better. We like to think that we are helping "primitive" people when we introduce them to our modern technology. They will be better off, we argue, because our tools, machines, and weapons are so much more efficient than theirs. Keep in mind, however, that introducing advanced technology to a society that follows a simpler way of life does not necessarily improve living conditions there and, in some cases, actually does a good deal of harm.

Consider, for example, the case of the great hydroelectric dam in the West African nation of Ghana. Multinational aluminum manufacturers wanted to mine Ghana's rich bauxite deposits, but the country lacked the necessary technology. So, corporate representatives convinced Ghanian officials that building a hydroelectric dam would boost the nation's economy by attracting international businesses and also would improve Ghanians' standard of living by bringing them electricity. Unfortunately, although the dam has greatly benefited the aluminum companies, it has brought suffering to many of Ghana's people. For one thing, constructing the dam meant relocating 1 percent of the country's population. Whole villages were forced to move to make way for "progress." Second, the completed dam created a huge reservoir of stagnant water that became a haven for disease-carrying mosquitoes and an incubator for various tropical illnesses. Since the dam was completed in the 1960s, over 100,000 Ghanians have contracted river blindness (onchocerciasis), with 70 percent of these totally losing their sight. Another 80,000 people are permanently disabled as a result of schistosomiasis, another water-borne illness (Hancock, 1989). Schistosomes are a kind of worm that cause great pain as they lay eggs and multiply in different internal organs (see also Shephard & Rode, 1996).

Since material culture and nonmaterial culture are interrelated, the technology and artifacts that we prize reflect to a large extent the values that we hold dear. In the United States, for example, we value achievement, efficiency, and the ability of science to solve most problems. These values are not unrelated to the untiring effort in this country to develop smaller, lighter, but faster computers that can perform an enormous array of tasks, from sending faxes and composing music to painting pictures and transmitting pornographic images. Consider, too, the level of national pride that Americans felt during the Persian Gulf War as millions turned on their television sets to watch their coun-

These contemporary families in India, China, and England are posed with all their property and household artifacts. How would you characterize each material culture? How would you match each material culture with a type of society or level of socioeconomic development, as discussed in Chapter 3? Using these examples, what inferences might you draw about the strong links that exist in any society between material and nonmaterial culture?

try's computer-guided smart missiles seek out and destroy enemy targets with unprecedented precision. In contrast, among the Huaorani of Ecuador, whom we introduced earlier, the belief that humans exist in a mutually beneficial relationship with nature leads them to set off on long journeys into the rainforest with little more than the clothes on their backs, confident that the environment will supply all they need to survive. They kill with long, heavy spears for the purposes of obtaining food or defending themselves. As one Western observer commented, "When the Huaorani kill, there is a spiritual discipline to it. Americans kill without knowing they are doing it. You don't *want* to know you are doing it. . . . So you tell me: Who are the savages?" (quoted in Kane, 1995, p. 75).

The Ideal versus What Is Real

In discussing the components of culture, we have found that within any culture, values and beliefs are often in-

consistent or contradictory. Moreover, to no one's surprise we're sure, what the norms of a culture say *should* be done is sometimes very different from what people actually do. To recognize the gaps between the "oughts" and the "is's" of a society, sociologists draw a distinction between ideal culture and real culture. **Ideal culture** is made up of the shared values, beliefs, and norms that the members of a society claim as their culture. **Real culture,** on the other hand, refers to the values, beliefs, and norms reflected in the actual behavior and social practices of the society's members. To return to an earlier example, the prohibition against premarital sex among teenagers is part of American society's ideal culture, but the number of teenagers who report having had intercourse by the time they are twenty, as well as the high rate of teenage pregnancy in this country, indicate that premarital sex among teens is a norm of American society's real culture.

The gap between ideal culture and real culture also draws attention to the fact that within a single society

SOCIOLOGY LIVE

Middlesex County College, Edison, New Jersey
Course: Introduction to Sociology, Dr. Irwin Kantor
Students: (left to right) Will Robertson, Ed Strasz,
Mechelle Buksar, and (not shown) Jodi Greengarten

Is there a gap between the ideal and the real culture at our school?

At Middlesex County College, the ideal culture is presented as a great melting pot of many different people, including Indians, African Americans, Caucasians, Hispanics, and others from around the world, all with different religions, norms, and values. In this ideal culture, people of many different ethnic backgrounds and cultures come together on one campus with one purpose: to learn and achieve good grades. They accept one another's differences and mingle freely. They want only to better themselves and their society.

In the reality of campus life, however, the actual culture can be very different from the ideal culture. While Middlesex County College is diverse, groups do not easily "melt" together, and students often do not live up to the ideal of an academic community devoted exclusively to learning. Differences between the ideal and the real can cause friction. For example, from the faculty's view, poor class attendance suggests that students do not value their education or monetary contribution or the time professors put into creating lesson plans. Yet many outside factors affect student attendance.

Also, as one student reports, "There is a noticeable problem with the different groups of people blending on this campus. Although there are no fights or wars over the issue, there is a lack of effort to complete the melting pot and blend. For example, in the cafeteria it is not uncommon to see same-race cliques congregating together. They may even make jokes about those different than they are."

We have found that students tend to socialize with other students who have similar goals. According to the accumulation of responses in our survey, students attend Middlesex County College because they have other factors in their lives that must take precedence over school. Mothers, older students, and job holders are part of this group. Some come to Middlesex to expand their education in order to advance in their career, but their families are their first priorities. Also, a few students we spoke to informed us that holding down a job was necessary to help them pay for school. In this situation, the students' jobs take precedence over academic commitments.

Considering all the factors involved in attending college, most students do not have the time to make friends on campus and develop strong social bonds. Although the majority of the students we interviewed supported this fact, some students disagreed. These students made friends as a result of having a common area of interest. For example, involvement in a sports program at Middlesex makes it much easier to make friends because the group has a common goal—to win.

There is a gap between the real and ideal culture at Middlesex County College. We believe there would be a gap in all community colleges, because there are so many different people with different agendas as well as varied values, beliefs, and norms. Yet the ideal and the real meet at these facts: Diversity of culture is a normal and necessary part of a healthy and well-balanced society, and the main goal of a student is to learn.

there may be multiple ways of life. Although a certain culture may be dominant, with most members of the society more or less adopting it as their own, competing lifestyles and points of view may also exist. In general, the larger the society, the more likely this is the case. This point raises the issue of cultural diversity, our next topic. (See Table 4.1 for a summary of our discussion of the elements of culture.)

REFLECTING ON

The Elements of Culture

1. What is an example of a symbol that is especially important to you? What does it mean to you,

TABLE 4.1 The Elements of Culture

Element	Definition	Examples
NONMATERIAL CULTURE		
Symbols	Anything that has been given representational meaning by the members of a cultural group	Gestures, a flag, a statue
Language	A system of patterned sounds, often with corresponding written symbols, that the members of a society use to communicate their thoughts and feelings to one another	Swahili, English
Values	Cultural standards or judgments of what is right, good, or desirable	Personal freedom, egalitarianism
Norms	The rules of culture that tell the members of a culture how they are expected to behave in a given situation	Not talking out loud during a play, wearing black clothes to a funeral
Mores	Norms that carry a strong social sanction if violated because the members of a culture consider adherence to them essential to the well-being of the society	The prohibition against having sex in public, the prohibition against destroying other people's property
Folkways	Norms that carry only a weak social sanction if violated because the members of the society do not consider adherence to them essential to the well-being of the society	Washing one's clothes, eating with your mouth closed
Laws	Norms that the governing body of a society officially adopts to regulate behavior	Speed limits, not having sex with someone against their will (rape)
Taboos	Norms so strongly held by the members of a society that to violate them is virtually inconceivable	The prohibition against incest, the prohibition against cannibalism
MATERIAL CULTURE		
Technology	The body of knowledge that members of a society apply to their physical environment to meet their survival needs	Using a digging stick to plant seeds, using a robot to paint a car
Artifacts	The physical things that the members of a society make when they apply their technology to the physical environment	A bed, a hammer, a bracelet, a house

and what do you think it tells others about your values?

2. Does language define reality, or does reality create language? Explain your answer.
3. List the most important norms of a group to which you belong. What happens when a member of the group violates one of these norms?
4. What are some advantages and disadvantages of advanced technology for people in preindustrial societies?

CULTURAL DIVERSITY: WHAT'S THE DIFFERENCE?

So far, we've discussed examples from the cultures of many countries. Sometimes we've drawn contrasts between American culture and the cultures of other societies. These cultural differences constitute **cultural diversity.** How-

ever, cultural diversity encompasses not only variations in culture between societies, but also variations in culture within a society. We have identified, in fact, a number of symbols, linguistic conventions, values, beliefs, norms, and artifacts that dominate the cultural landscape of the United States. Let's look more closely at cultural diversity in our country.

Subcultures

A city magazine recently carried a story about a man who collects buttons with slogans. He has hundreds of them. The story was accompanied by a color photograph of some of the buttons. There was a large white button with a big green shamrock on it that said, "Kiss me, I'm Irish." A black button with an inverted pink triangle in the center bore the words, "Can't even see straight." And still another—a green and blue button decorated with different fruits and vegetables—proclaimed, "There's plenty to eat without choosing meat."

DOING SOCIOLOGY

What's in a Bumper Sticker?

Subcultures are often a source of pride for the people who belong to them. Members of subcultures may show their pride, for example, by wearing particular clothes (the gang colors) or by meeting at special places (the clubhouse). We can learn about a subculture—the values the members hold and the traditions they adhere to—by observing these displays of pride in membership.

Try to identify members of various subcultures by observing bumper stickers on cars. How many different subcultures can you identify? What does each bumper sticker tell you about the values of particular subcultures?

What sociological significance do these buttons have? To sociologists, each button identifies the person wearing it as a member of a particular subculture. A **subculture** is a group within a society's dominant culture. It shares in some of the dominant culture's elements, but at the same time, it differentiates itself from the dominant culture in a specific way. Wearers of the shamrock button, then, would likely be members of the subculture Irish Americans. Wearers of the inverted triangle button would be identifying themselves as members of the gay and lesbian subculture. And those who wear the third button in our example would probably be members of the subculture vegetarians.

Just as this man had hundreds of buttons in his collection, the United States has hundreds of subcultures. Ethnic and racial groups each constitute a subculture. There are Italian Americans, Latinos, African Americans, Japanese Americans, Native Americans, and so on. Members of each of these groups may further divide themselves into additional subcultures. Many Italian Americans, for example, distinguish themselves according to the region of Italy from which their ancestors came. Each region has its own customs and dialects, as well as other distinct features; consider, for instance, the differences in Northern

Italian and Sicilian cuisine. Among Native Americans, numerous subcultural differences exist between each Indian nation. The values, language, food, traditions, and ceremonies of the Zuni are different from the Hopi, which are, in turn, different from the Navajo, and so on.

Thus, although the United States claims to be a great "melting pot" of cultures and has adopted as its national motto, "*E pluribus unum*" ("One out of many"), our society is characterized by numerous divisions, which may be at once a source of pleasure and pride, as well as a source of tension and conflict. While many of us enjoy the sounds and flavors of ethnic festivals, for instance, multicultural neighborhoods can erupt in conflict and sometimes open hatred and violence. Serbs and Croats of the former Yugoslavia have demonstrated that conflicts between subcultures in a society can even lead to civil war. The Doing Sociology box gives you the opportunity to study subcultures.

Countercultures

Sometimes a subgroup within a society develops in opposition to the dominant culture. These groups openly reject the dominant culture and may try to change it in fundamental ways, or at least live alternative lifestyles. Such a subgroup is called a **counterculture.**

It has been argued that countercultures are typically composed of young people (Roszak, 1969; Spates & Perkins, 1982). This may be because teenagers and young adults often are not burdened with work and family responsibilities, so they have the time to explore countercultural lifestyles. It is also the case that adolescence and young adulthood are stages in the life cycle marked by a need to assert independence and establish an identity separate from parents and other generations. It is little wonder that experimenting with alternative norms and values is particularly attractive during this period of life.

Although numerous examples of youthful countercultures exist, the most frequently cited may be the hippies of the 1960s. The hippies rebelled against the dominant culture because they perceived it as too materialistic, competitive, and violent. Some expressed their opposition by joining organizations, such as the Weather Underground, that sought to overthrow the government. But most just withdrew from—or, as hippies themselves preferred to call it, dropped out of—the larger society, opting for simple communal living that encouraged personal growth and "expanded consciousness." Their rebellion was reflected in their clothing and hairstyles; their music; their use of marijuana, LSD, and other drugs; and the symbols and slogans they adopted such as "Make love not war." In short, the hippies rejected all of the basic norms and values of the dominant Western culture and replaced them with norms and values of their own. The hippie counterculture still exists today, although, like many countercultures, it has lost a large proportion of its following over time (see, for example, Niman, 1997).

Despite the attractiveness of countercultures to the young, it is inaccurate to conclude that all, or even most, countercultures are youth-oriented. Consider survivalists, for example. These right-wing separatists often live in armed compounds, where the leadership and the majority of the members are middle-aged or older. Their beliefs are typically a blend of fundamentalist Christianity and racism. They urge "true believers" to separate themselves from mainstream society, through armed conflict if necessary. Examples of survivalist countercultures include Elohim City (with a compound in Oklahoma) and the Twelve Tribes of Israel (with branches in about twelve U.S. cities) (Heard & Klebnikov, 1998).

For better or for worse, then, countercultures can have a profound effect on the larger society that they oppose. This observation leads us to consider the issue of cultural change more generally.

Cultural Change

It has been said that one of the few constants in life is change. Indeed, change is an ongoing part of social life, although it may occur so slowly that the members of the society do not notice the results immediately. Societies, in fact, change at different rates. The Huaorani of Ecuador, for instance, are thought to have lived much the same in 1965 as they did in 1865. In contrast, we live in a society where cultural change is both rapid and dramatic.

Within a single society such as ours, however, cultural change may occur unevenly. One dimension of culture may change faster than another. Typically, changes in material culture outpace changes in nonmaterial culture. Sociologist William Ogburn (1964) coined the term **cultural lag** to characterize this phenomenon. Consider, for instance, that it will soon be technologically possible to transplant the ovaries of aborted female fetuses into adult infertile women so that they can bear children. This essentially means that in the near future, some children may be born whose biological mothers are dead fetuses (Kolata, 1994). As much as the values, beliefs, and norms of family life and parenting have changed in the last few decades, it's hard to believe that they will quickly or easily accommodate this new technological possibility.

In addition to illustrating the phenomenon of cultural lag, the infertility treatment example also points to one of the primary triggers of cultural change in a society: *invention,* the creation of new things. Think for a moment

How is this picture an illustration of Ogburn's concept of cultural lag? How is it an illustration of the process of cultural change known as diffusion? In what sense do changes in technology necessitate changes in values? What might be some positive and negative consequences of this new technology for these people and their traditional way of life?

about how various inventions have revolutionized the way we communicate and disseminate information. Before the invention of the printing press by Johann Gutenberg in 1450, books were reproduced by hand and only an elite few had access to them. Gutenberg's invention not only made books more widely available, but also helped to promote literacy. Today, many of the tasks required to produce a book—from writing and editing to typesetting—have been streamlined as a result of another invention, the computer. In fact, textbooks such as the one you are reading now will soon be available electronically. Instead of opening the book in your hands, you can switch on a handheld pc to do your reading assignments (Bronner, 1998). You can use the electronic supplement to this text to e-mail your authors with questions, comments, or suggestions. Imagine how this single invention, the computer, has affected traditional norms of education. Now think about its impact on other aspects of social life and it is easy to understand how inventions stimulate cultural change.

A second source of cultural change is *discovery,* finding and gaining knowledge about something not previously recognized or understood. Unlike inventions, then, discoveries are not creations of something entirely new, but rather revelations of something that already exists. Discovery, though, is often helped by the use of inventions. For instance, the discovery of many stars in our galaxy would not have been possible without the invention of the telescope. The discovery of new galaxies in the universe would not have been possible without the invention of satellites, computerized cameras, and other devices. Obviously, many discoveries are made as a result of purposeful study, but important discoveries can occur by accident as well. We all are familiar with the story of how Christopher Columbus set out to map a new trade route from Europe to Asia, but instead ended up on the shores of what came to be called America—and we are all well aware of the tremendous cultural changes that his discovery brought about.

Another source of cultural change is **diffusion,** the spread of one society's culture to another. When members of different societies come into contact with one another, aspects of one society's culture may be absorbed or adopted by—or forced on—the members of the other society. In the United States, for example, a good deal of the music we listen to, the foods we eat, and the artifacts we use come from other cultures. Soap was invented by the ancient Gauls and glass by the ancient Egyptians; the umbrella was invented in India, and the spoon in ancient Rome, to name just a few examples (Linton, 1937).

Similarly, aspects of the dominant U.S. culture have found their way into other societies throughout the world—for better or for worse. Consider again the Huaorani.

Thought to be one of the few remaining intact indigenous peoples on the planet, they lived as an isolated group in the Amazon rainforest and had little contact with outsiders until the 1960s. Then U.S. oil companies discovered the rich natural resources of the Amazon and built an oil pipeline right through the rainforest. As a result, the Huaorani met "the Company"—what they have come to call anyone and anything associated with the oil industry. Because of the roads built by the oil companies to gain access to the inner rainforest areas, the Huaorani also began to have routine contact with many other groups as well, including wealthy developers and dispossessed peasants from nearby villages who came in search of work on the pipeline. Such contacts have produced far-reaching and irrevocable changes in the Huaorani way of life. No longer preferring to be naked, for example, the Huaorani now usually dress in shorts, t-shirts, and the black rubber boots commonly worn by oil drillers. Many wear wristwatches, even though their culture has no conception of future time, and their language contains no word for *later.* The word *oilspill,* however, has become part of their vocabulary (Kane, 1995; see also Goleman, 1996; Peters, 1998; Shephard & Rode, 1996).

There are numerous other—less disruptive and tragic—examples of the diffusion of U.S. culture throughout the world. In a public square in Shanghai, for instance, Chinese couples dance nightly to pop and big band music. You can quench your thirst with a Coca-Cola as easily in St. Petersburg, Russia, as you can in St. Petersburg, Florida. And although English is the first spoken language of only about 10 percent of the world's population, it is favored as a second language in most countries. So far and wide has the reach of the dominant U.S. culture spread that some observers wonder if we are witnessing the *globalization* of this culture. In other words, some analysts predict that in the future much of the rich cultural diversity that we find throughout the world today will be watered down or replaced by a single world culture highly influenced by the United States and other technologically advanced Western societies (see, for example, Featherstone, 1990).

While it cannot be denied that the technological, economic, and military might of the United States and other developed Western societies has more often made them the diffusers of their culture rather than the receptors of others' cultures, several factors inhibit the development of a global culture. For one thing, although it seems that technology has made planet Earth a smaller place, televisions and computers are not uniformly available throughout the world or even within a single society. For instance, people who live in cities generally have greater cross-cultural contact than people who live in rural towns or villages. The greater geographic isolation of rural areas

INTERSECTING INEQUALITIES

Why Is a Gap in Access to Technology a Problem?

In 1995, more than 22.9 million personal computers and workstations were shipped for sale in the United States (U.S. Department of Commerce, Bureau of the Census, 1997). Many were purchased by schools and businesses, but an increasing number of households— 23.3 percent of all U.S. households— also have at least one personal computer. People use them to plan the family budget, compose various documents from letters to wills, do homework, shop, and surf the Internet for a variety of services. But as the table shows, the availability of computers in American homes is largely limited to those with above average incomes. The cost of personal computers puts them beyond the reach of most poor and working-class families, who are also more likely than other Americans to lack the training needed to operate computers.

As an increasing number of personal services, such as banking, become computerized, many analysts are concerned that poor poeple will be more marginalized than ever before. Moreover, because racial and ethnic minorities are more likely than White Americans to be poor, they are also expected to be more seriously disadvantaged by the gap in access to technology. One recent study, for example, found that while

44.3 percent of White Americans own a home computer, only 29.0 percent of Black Americans own a home computer (Hoffman & Novak, 1998).

Already, various businesses, including banks, have closed their offices in poor neighborhoods with large numbers of non-White residents. Recent legislation designed to increase services available in poor communities has been inadequate largely because businesses have sought to economize on the services they make available. Supermarkets, for instance, may offer only minimarts in poor neighborhoods, while banks may provide little more than automatic teller machines. Electronic alternatives to staffed offices do not usually meet the needs of the poor for a

variety of reasons. For example, poor people often have bad credit histories and intermittent employment, making it difficult for them to even open accounts with banks and other businesses. In addition, poor neighborhoods often have a high number of residents who do not speak English or who have limited reading skills, both obstacles to using electronic services.

Thus, the increasing use of computers to handle many transactions previously done by people has not benefited the poor the way it has the more financially secure. What strategies would you suggest to close the gap across social groups in our society when it comes to access to computers?

Ownership of Personal Computers by Family Income

Family Income	Percentage of Households That Own a Personal Computer
Under $25,000	3.2
$25,000–$34,999	4.4
$35,000–$49,999	3.6
$50,000 and over	11.4

Source: U.S. Department of Commerce, Bureau of the Census, 1997, p. 728.

simply makes it harder for technology and goods, as well as other people, to get to them.

As the Intersecting Inequalities box shows, it is also the case that those who most benefit from cross-cultural influences are the economic elites of a society. In economically undeveloped countries, most Western commodities are extraordinarily expensive. A dinner at a Kentucky Fried Chicken Restaurant in Beijing may cost a typical Chinese family a week's wages. Nevertheless, multinational corporations often convince the populations of underdeveloped countries that Western products are the most desirable—sometimes with tragic results. In the 1970s and early 1980s, for example, U.S. and Western European infant formula manufacturers, faced with

declining sales in their own countries, launched a marketing campaign throughout much of Africa where birth rates are high, to convince women that formula feeding was better for their babies than breast feeding. Representatives of the companies gave out free samples of their formula to new mothers, as they do here. The problem, however, was that few of the women in these countries could afford to buy the formula; a single can was beyond the financial means of many families. Once the free sample was gone, the women could not resort to breast feeding because by then their bodies had stopped producing milk. Consequently, many would scrape together the money for a can of formula, but dilute it heavily with water so that it would last longer. The diluted formula, though, did not provide adequate nutrition. Moreover, the water used to dilute the formula was often contaminated, and the babies became ill. To make matters even worse, babies were not receiving immunities that they could have naturally obtained through their mothers' milk. Not surprisingly, many babies became seriously ill, and the death rate of bottle-fed babies was significantly higher than that of breast-fed babies. Eventually, international pressure forced the formula manufacturers to either drastically alter their marketing practices or stop sales altogether in these countries.

Even among the economically privileged, however, cultural traits from one society are not easily transposed onto another. Cultures that have been evolving over hundreds of years do not just absorb wholesale what another culture has to offer. Typically, what is being diffused gets modified, so its meaning or significance is different in the new culture. Language offers an obvious example. Although English is preferred as a second language throughout much of the world, many words and phrases do not translate well into other languages, and meanings become distorted. Many corporations have found this out the hard way. The makers of Pepsi, for instance, tried to promote their product in Taiwan with the slogan, "Come alive with the Pepsi Generation," but the translation came out as "Pepsi will bring your ancestors back from the dead." Similarly, the Kentucky Fried Chicken slogan, "finger-lickin' good" translated into "eat your fingers off." Ironically, the English language itself is a product of cultural diffusion, having its origins in Latin, Greek, French, and the Germanic languages.

Perhaps the greatest obstacle to the emergence of a global culture, however, is group resistance to it. Culture provides a people with a collective identity, a sense of belonging or "we-ness." Those who share a culture are often intensely proud of their heritage and resist efforts to suppress it. For example, in the former Soviet Union and the countries of Eastern and Central Europe, communist governments successfully suppressed age-old rivalries between the various ethnic and religious groups that made up their populations. Nevertheless, memories of prejudice, stereotypes, and antagonisms among groups were kept alive by members of each culture and were passed on from one generation to the next. With the demise of communism, the rivalries and bigotry surfaced, fueling open conflict and fighting in many of the independent Baltic states of the former Soviet Union, the Caucasus region of Russia, the Ukraine, Hungary, Albania, Bulgaria, Romania, Macedonia, and of course, the former Yugoslavia. Rather than seeing themselves as owing allegiance to the governments of their former communist states, each group wishes to be governed by leaders who share its heritage, speak its mother tongue, and practice its customs and traditions (Connor, 1993).

Within the United States there is a growing interest in cultural identity and heritage. Numerous festivals and parades celebrate a special event in a group's history or honor a particular group member. Kwanza is a good example. This African American cultural festival, celebrated annually from December 26 to January 1, was begun in 1966 to celebrate African heritage and to promote values esteemed in the African American community. In fact, given the diversity of cultures that are found in this country alone, it seems more appropriate to emphasize the phenomenon of multiculturalism than to speculate about a single world culture.

Multiculturalism

Multiculturalism emphasizes respect for and appreciation of the cultural contributions, practices, and experiences of diverse groups. Historically, in the United States, the cultural achievements of many segments of the population—such as African Americans, Asian Americans, and Native Americans—were downplayed or ignored, while the achievements of other groups, especially of the Anglo-Saxon heritage, were elevated. Think, for example, of your history lessons in elementary school. The focus was probably almost exclusively on the English and Western Europeans. Native Americans and Hispanic Americans were probably rarely mentioned apart from "Custer's last stand" or the Alamo, when it was clear who the "bad guys" were. Even today, most colleges and universities that have a history requirement continue to mandate "Western Civilization."

Critics of multiculturalism say it promotes separatism and intergroup conflict by encouraging people to identify with their "own kind" rather than with what members of society share in common. To a large extent, however, this criticism reflects a fundamental misunderstanding of multiculturalism. The purpose of multiculturalism is not to diminish the accomplishments of the English or Western Europeans or to deny that our contemporary culture owes a great deal to our Anglo-Saxon and Western European heritage. Rather, multiculturalism simply emphasizes that *many* groups have played a significant role in the cultural development of the United States, and that the historical and contemporary contributions of the many diverse cultural groups that make up the United States today should be recognized and appreciated.

Supporters of multiculturalism point out that the U.S. population is becoming more—not less—diverse, and a multicultural perspective is therefore increasingly necessary if the various subcultures are to forge a life together based on cooperation and mutual respect. Moreover, the rapid growth of international business and politics and the development of advanced communications technology mean culturally diverse societies have increased contact and are becoming more interdependent. This, too, should encourage us to adopt a multicultural perspective.

Ethnocentrism and Cultural Relativism

Despite the importance of multiculturalism in today's world, many people continue to believe their own values and ways of doing things are "right" or "best," thus judging others' values and practices inferior. This, we said in Chapter 1, is called **ethnocentrism.**

On a cognitive level at least, we all probably recognize that behaving ethnocentrically is wrong because it offends people from other cultures. However, as with many aspects of social life, practicing what we preach is not always easy. For example, we criticize the closed-mindedness of Americans traveling abroad who expect to be served only foods that they eat at home. "Why bother to even leave your house if you're not willing to try new things?" we might ask them. But would we be so unsympathetic if we learned that our travelers were served dog or monkey? After all, we "know" these are not foods; the thought of eating them is revolting to us. Keep in mind, however, that the American appetite for spare ribs, ham, and other pork dishes is equally disgusting to members of many other cultures.

Ethnocentrism is deeply ingrained in all people because their own specific culture is usually the only one they are exposed to from the time they are born. So much do we take for granted our own way of doing things, that any other way seems "unnatural." How, then, are we to respond to cultures different from our own? One answer is multicultural understanding, but ethnocentrism can be a formidable obstacle to our best intentions. Sociologists, who are by no means free of ethnocentrism themselves, address this dilemma by espousing cultural relativism. **Cultural relativism** refers to judging a cultural practice in terms of how well it helps the members of a society meet their survival needs. In other words, instead of applying our own standards to a particular practice, we consider the practice from the standpoint of the other culture's members.

For example, several years ago, while conducting research in the West African country of Guinea, your authors were invited by a physician to visit a hospital that had just been built in one of the rural villages. The physician, openly proud of the facility, greeted us in the hospital courtyard, surrounded by goats, cows, and other animals. Our first thought was that animals did not belong at a hospital, but the physician explained that people traveled great distances to get to the hospital, and often they brought at least some of their animals with them so that they would not wander off or be stolen in the owners' absence. Inside, we were shown a number of patients' rooms. As in any hospital, patients were lying

in the beds. What surprised us were the people lying on the floor. Our host explained that again, because many families lived a great distance away, a visit to a sick relative usually could not be accomplished in one day. There were no hotels or inns in the village, so unless visitors had other relatives living nearby, they usually stayed in the patient's room. As our tour ended, the physician escorted us to a back door of the building, opening it to show us where a new wing was planned. Our eyes fixed on another type of wing, however—the flapping wings of vultures. Seeing the stunned looks on our faces, the physician explained without any hesitation that the vultures served as a kind of waste disposal system. Most of the hospital waste, including waste from surgery, was put in the field behind the hospital where the vultures quickly disposed of it.

Needless to say, this hospital was like none we had ever encountered. Had we evaluated it by the standards of U.S. hospitals, we would have probably decided that it was doing its patients more harm than good. However, in the context of the culture it served, its practices made sense and indeed seemed beneficial. In a society where the loss of a farm animal could cause financial ruin, many people would forgo treatment if they could not bring their livestock to the hospital with them. Similarly, few patients would ever have visitors if no one were allowed to stay in the room with them. The prospect of being separated from family might also inhibit sick individuals from seeking treatment or might slow their recovery once admitted to the hospital. And although the sight of vultures waiting for their daily meal of hospital waste was initially shocking and repulsive, with some thought, we recognized this as a highly efficient and economical way of disposing of dangerous waste that could easily spread disease in a village with no sewage system.

Nevertheless, we must also emphasize that espousing cultural relativism does not mean that any and all cultural practices are acceptable just because some group somewhere in the world has adopted them. The basis of judgment is the extent to which a particular cultural practice contributes to the well-being of the members of the society. For example, among the Ewe people of Ghana, custom requires that when a serious offense such as murder, rape, or theft is committed, the offender's family must appease the gods by offering a young virgin daughter to the village priest. The young girl, usually not more than twelve years old, becomes the priest's slave. While the priests benefit from this practice of ritual slavery, the girls are clearly harmed by it, being deprived of education, the opportunity to marry, their very self-determination (French, 1997).

Of course, recognizing that it is reasonable to reject certain cultural practices as harmful probably will not be enough to relieve the strong emotional reactions we experience when we encounter a culture vastly different from our own. However, it does serve to remind us that we must always strive to understand another culture from the point of view of the people who share it, not solely from our own point of view.

REFLECTING ON

Cultural Diversity

1. Name one subculture to which you belong, and describe the traits that distinguish it from the dominant culture.
2. In what ways might a counterculture contribute to cultural change?
3. What is an example of a recent cultural change that you regard as significant? What have been the primary sources of this change?
4. Do you think that we will eventually see the emergence of a global culture? Why or why not?
5. Does the principle of cultural relativism mean that there are no moral absolutes? Explain your answer.

THEORETICAL PERSPECTIVES ON CULTURE

Sociologists working from the varying theoretical perspectives that we introduced in Chapter 1 emphasize different aspects of culture in their studies. Let's consider briefly how each theory analyzes culture.

Structural Functionalism

Because functionalists focus on social order, their analysis of culture emphasizes the way culture promotes stability in society. One function of culture is giving people a blueprint for conducting their lives. Culture, through norms, provides ground rules for interaction, so that members of a society can enter most situations with expectations of each other's behavior that allow encounters to proceed smoothly. In addition, culture contributes to stability by giving members of a society a sense of belonging or "we-ness." The shared language, values, and norms of a culture, which functionalists call *consensus,* form a kind of cement for the social bonds that hold the social group together. So, for example, when Americans celebrate Thanksgiving, they are doing more than feasting and watching football; the celebration provides the opportunity to recall a significant event in their history as a society and to reaffirm cherished values, including family cohesiveness and faith in a god.

Unfortunately, as we have noted, in multicultural societies where various subcultures are competing for dominance, the "we" feeling generated by culture can be dysfunctional. Native Americans, for instance, see Thanksgiving as a commemoration of the colonization of their land and the systematic destruction of their culture by White Europeans. Thus, culture may promote inequality if a culturally dominant group deems as inferior other groups and denies them access to society's resources, rewards, and opportunities. Even worse, it can produce violent confrontations between competing subcultures.

The functionalist perspective is valuable for highlighting the significance of culture in maintaining social order and generating social cohesion. However, functionalists tend to downplay the ways that culture can also contribute to conflict and serious social problems, such as racial and ethnic inequality.

Conflict and Feminist Perspectives

Both conflict and feminist theories focus on the social tensions produced by competing cultures and how cultural dominance may benefit some groups and disadvantage others. Cultural change is also important to conflict and feminist theorists.

Conflict theorists maintain that in any society made up of diverse groups, each group will create culture that serves its own interests. However, the strongest, most powerful groups will succeed in establishing their culture as dominant and impose it on everyone in the society. They deem the cultures of other groups inferior and resist cultural change that threatens their dominance. Recall, for instance, the arguments of supporters of the English-only movement discussed in the Social Policy box on page 84.

Feminist theorists give particular attention to the dominance of male culture. In many societies, they point out, elements of culture labeled masculine are prized, while those considered feminine are devalued. Language is a good example. For instance, masculine words (such as sir, bachelor, master, patron) are associated with positive, even esteemed things, while feminine words (such as madam, spinster, mistress, matron) are associated with negative things (Lakoff, 1991; Nilsen, 1991; Smith, 1985). Moreover, efforts to remedy the gender inequality of our language have had limited success, lending support to the position that cultural change that challenges the status of the dominant group will meet with resistance.

The conflict and feminist perspectives raise awareness of the role of culture in promoting inequality and generating conflict in a society, but both approaches have been criticized for not giving enough attention to the way culture contributes to social order.

Marriage is a cultural construction of which weddings often are emblems. Discuss this Laotian wedding and its cultural context from the perspectives of structural functionalism, conflict theory or feminism, and symbolic interactionism. In each case, what more would you need to know? What questions would you need to ask?

Symbolic Interactionism

Symbolic interactionists are concerned with the micro-level aspects of culture. Their focus is on how culture is generated, sustained, and changed in a society, not by social institutions, but by people interacting during the course of their daily lives. Symbolic interactionists study the basic elements of culture—symbols, values, norms, ideas, and objects—because these are the raw materials that humans use to create and reinforce social reality.

Consider weddings, for example. Structural functionalists would emphasize how weddings contribute to social order by, for instance, legitimating and regulating sexual relations between members of a society. Conflict and feminist theorists would focus on how weddings reinforce the dominance of particular groups. Weddings are a means for rich families to consolidate wealth, and the subordination of women to men is reinforced in wedding ceremonies when, for example, the bride is "given away" by her father to the groom. Symbolic interactionists, however, would analyze the subjective meanings that wed-

dings have for the participants. They would study the part each social actor plays as together the participants construct a shared reality they call marriage.

The symbolic interactionist perspective draws attention to micro-level processes of culture creation that are typically taken for granted. However, this theory has been criticized for failing to take into account how the social institutions that make up the macro level of society influence and constrain people's everyday lives.

REFLECTING ON

Theoretical Perspectives on Culture

Choose a particular value, norm, or practice and try to analyze it from the functionalist, conflict, feminist, and symbolic interactionist perspectives. What are the strengths and weaknesses of each approach?

CULTURE AND HUMAN NATURE

The differences among human cultures is truly astonishing, and most students find these differences intriguing. Sociologists also are not immune from the tendency to focus on cultural difference. After all, the overarching theme in this discussion has been cultural diversity. It seems fitting to ask, therefore, whether, despite all the cultural differences we encounter across societies, if there are any values, beliefs, norms, or practices that *humans as a group* share. That is, are there any cultural traits found in *all* cultures?

In fact, research shows that while the differences across cultures are great, similarities can be identified, too. Cultural traits common to all cultures are called **cultural universals.** Culturally universal traits include language; particular emotions (such as fear and happiness); the use of fire and tools; a need for shelter; a division of labor; standards of right and wrong (including a taboo against incest); and standards of physical/sexual attractiveness (Brown, 1991).

If cultural universals exist, does that mean there is a single set of human behaviors and characteristics that comprise what has been called *human nature*? On the pro side of this argument are the sociobiologists, who say the reason cultural universals can be found is that there is a genetic basis for certain human behaviors and personality traits. All humans have these behaviors and traits because they proved adaptive during the course of our evolution. Individuals who exhibited these behaviors and traits ended up with a reproductive advantage and were thus able to pass their genetic material on to their offspring, causing these traits to become dominant in the species as a whole (Wilson, 1978). The recent discovery of a gene for "novelty seeking" (extrovertedness, impulsivity, excitability, a willingness to take risks) was taken by many as evidence in support of sociobiology (Angier, 1996).

In opposition to the sociobiologists are the learning theorists who believe culture is almost wholly learned. Elements identified as cultural universals are nothing more than broad categories of social life. How these come to be expressed has as much to do with human inventiveness as it does with environmental adaptation, but the various expressions are taught to new generations, not passed on genetically. All humans, as we noted earlier in the chapter, have certain biological needs or drives, but these may be satisfied in multiple ways, or they may be modified or overridden altogether.

The debate about human nature is especially heated when it comes to the topic of human aggression. Sociobiologists argue that human males, in particular, are physically and sexually aggressive by nature because it is in their reproductive interests to behave this way. From this point of view, then, rape will always exist because it represents the human male's attempt to distribute his genetic material as widely as possible. In contrast, those who emphasize the role of learning—and this group includes the majority of sociologists—point to societies in which aggression by both men and women is discouraged. They see this as evidence against a universal human nature. Anthropologist Peggy Reeves Sanday (1981; 1996), for example, reports that rape does not occur in all cultures. In fact, in her cross-cultural research she has found societies that she characterizes as "rape-free."

Certainly, we cannot resolve this debate here. The point we wish to make, however, is that human social life is probably far more complex than either side makes it out to be. Both sociobiologists and learning theorists think of the issue in terms of biology *versus* culture, with one consistently and permanently dominating the other. Instead, it may be more useful—and more accurate—to think in terms of biology *and* culture. That is, how does biology influence culture and, conversely, how does culture influence biology? Also, how does this interaction between biology and culture occur continuously over the life course and throughout human evolutionary history (Birke, 1992)? Perhaps those questions can never be answered definitively, but in the long run, we suspect that efforts to understand the interaction between biology and culture may prove more valuable than our age-old attempts to demonstrate the dominance of one over the other.

R E F L E C T I N G   O N

Culture and Human Nature

1. What might be some cultural universals not mentioned in the text? Does the expression of the behavior or trait vary across cultures? If so, how?
2. What might be an example of how biology and culture interact to produce a certain outcome?

 For useful resources for study and review, run Chapter 4 on your *Living Sociology* CD-ROM.

C O N N E C T I O N S

Biology and culture	The discussion of biology and culture (nature and nurture) continues in Chapter 5 in the section on "The Interaction of Biology and Environment," and again in Chapter 10 in the sections on "The Biological Basis of Sexual Orientation" and "Culture and Sexual Orientation." Why is the nature-nurture issue unlikely to be resolved one way or the other?
Race relations in the United States	Chapter 11 describes the history of race relations in the United States. What examples can you find of the role and importance of symbols of racial identity and ethnic pride?
Literacy and cultural transmission	Read about "Education in Other Societies" in Chapter 16. Oral traditions are traditional means of transmitting culture, but literacy is globally prized. Why?
Values and norms	Social and cultural values permeate all aspects of societies and social behavior. See, for example, Chapter 18 on the significance of values in

CONNECTIONS

	matters of health and illness. How are the dominant values and norms of a society reflected in standards of health and medical practices?
Technology and material culture	Chapter 20 discusses material culture as a change agent in the section on "Sources of Social Change." For instance, what was the impact of the automobile on social behavior?
Adolescent subculture	"Peer Groups" in Chapter 5 refers to the forces of socialization that lead to a subculture of adolescence. How does the development of a subculture relate to the group dynamics of "Ingroups and Outgroups" (Chapter 6)? In what social contexts can youth ingroups become deviant subcultures (Chapter 7)?
Economic inequalities	Read more about Beijing's American-brand restaurants and similar cases in Chapter 9. How does "Modernization Theory" attempt to explain the effects of cross-cultural influences on global inequality?
Computer access	Read the section on "Culture" in Chapter 20. How does the information on computers and social change relate to the question of Internet access for low-income families and countries?
Projected racial and ethnic composition of the United States	See "The Racial and Ethnic Composition of the United States in the Twenty-First Century" in Chapter 11. About what percentage of the U.S. population is predicted to be members of minority groups by the year 2050?
Sociological perspectives	As you read in Chapter 1, structural functionalism, conflict theory, feminist theory, and symbolic interactionism are theoretical perspectives in sociology and unifying themes throughout this text. To trace applications of any one of these, see the Subject Index.
Sociobiology	See the section on "Sociobiology" in Chapter 10, which analyzes the sociobiological perspective on gender. According to this perspective, what is the source of all human social behavior?

SUMMING UP CHAPTER 4

Culture

1. Culture is the shared set of values, beliefs, behavioral expectations, and artifacts that comprise the way of life of a people, distinguishing one group from another and giving group members a sense of belonging. Culture permits membership in a society to transcend geographic boundaries.

The Interaction of Biology and Culture

1. Humans are the only species to have developed culture. While animals rely largely on instincts to direct their behavior, humans have biological needs called *drives,* which are satisfied in ways prescribed by their cultures.
2. No human is ever totally without culture. Although we may distinguish between high culture and popular culture, all aspects of a group's way of life constitute culture.

The Elements of Culture

1. The elements of culture are divided into two types: nonmaterial culture and material culture. These two dimensions of culture are interrelated.
2. Nonmaterial culture is composed of symbols, language, values, and norms. The specific content of each of these components varies tremendously across cultures.
3. Communication through language is an exclusively human trait. Language is vital to the preservation of human societies because it is the primary means by which culture is passed on from one generation to the next (cultural transmission). According to the Sapir-Whorf hypothesis, language not only allows us to express our thoughts, but also shapes our perceptions.
4. Norms are the rules of a culture that tell people what they should and should not do under certain circumstances.

There are four types of norms: mores, folkways, laws, and taboos. Norms vary not only across cultures, but also over time and situationally within a single culture.

5. Material culture is composed of technology and artifacts. Technology is the body of knowledge that members of a society apply to their physical environment to meet their survival needs. In applying technology, people create artifacts. Since material culture and nonmaterial culture are interrelated, the technology and artifacts we prize reflect our most cherished values.

6. Within any society, there are shared values and norms that members claim as their culture (ideal culture) and values and norms reflected in actual behavior (real culture). There is often a gap between a society's ideal and real cultures.

Cultural Diversity: What's the Difference?

1. Cultural differences, either between societies or within a single society, constitute cultural diversity. One way cultural diversity manifests itself is through subcultures, groups that share parts of the dominant culture, but also distinguish themselves in some way from the dominant culture. There are hundreds of subcultures in the United States.

2. Some subgroups in a society oppose the dominant culture. These subgroups are countercultures. Although much attention has been given to youth countercultures, most countercultures are not youth-oriented.

3. Cultures change over time, but within a society, cultural change may be uneven, with changes in material culture outpacing changes in nonmaterial culture. This is called cultural lag.

4. Cultural change may be triggered by inventions and discoveries. Cultural change may also be the product of cultural diffusion, the spread of one society's culture to another. Cultural diffusion typically benefits the economic elites of a society.

5. Multiculturalism emphasizes respect for and appreciation of the cultural contributions, practices, and experiences of diverse groups. Although some people see multiculturalism as divisive, other people maintain that multiculturalism fosters cooperation among different people.

6. All people tend to believe that their own culture is the "right" or "best" one. This attitude is called ethnocentrism. In contrast, cultural relativism refers to judging a cultural practice in terms of how well it helps the members of a society meet their survival needs. Although cultural relativism is often difficult to practice, it is the approach we should try to take when we encounter cultures different from our own.

Theoretical Perspectives on Culture

1. Because structural functionalists focus on social order, their analysis of culture emphasizes how culture promotes social stability and integration. However, functionalists' emphasis on social order leads to criticism that they neglect the ways culture can generate conflict.

2. Conflict theorists and feminist theorists focus on social tensions produced by competing cultures, the way cultural dominance benefits and disadvantages different groups, and how cultures change. Both perspectives emphasize the role of power in cultural dominance, but feminist theory gives particular attention to the dominance of male culture. Both approaches have been criticized for not giving enough attention to how culture contributes to social order.

3. Symbolic interactionists focus on how culture is generated, sustained, and changed through people's everyday social interactions. While symbolic interactionists highlight micro-level processes of culture creation, they have been criticized for overlooking macro-level cultural issues.

Culture and Human Nature

1. Cultural traits common to all cultures are called *cultural universals*. Researchers have identified several cultural universals. This has generated disagreement over the extent to which human behavior is genetically determined or learned through social interaction. However, instead of debating the relative contributions of biology versus culture, it is more useful to consider how biology and culture influence one another continuously over the life course and human history.

KEY PEOPLE AND CONCEPTS

artifacts: the physical things that the members of a society make when they apply their technology to the physical environment

counterculture: a subgroup within a society that develops in opposition to the dominant culture, openly rejecting it and sometimes attempting to change it or at least live an alternative lifestyle

cultural diversity: variations in culture between societies as well as within a society

cultural integration: the interdependence among the elements of a culture

cultural lag: when changes in one dimension of culture (typically material culture) outpace changes in another dimension of culture (typically nonmaterial culture)

cultural relativism: the practice of judging a culture in terms of how well it helps the members of a society meet their survival needs

cultural transmission: the process by which culture is passed on from one generation to the next

cultural universals: cultural traits common to all cultures

culture: the shared set of values, beliefs, behavioral expectations, and artifacts that comprise the way of life of a people

diffusion: the spread of one society's culture to another

drives: basic physiological needs that must be met in order for humans to survive

ethnocentrism: the practice of judging another culture by the standards of one's own

folkways: relatively weak norms that bring only mild sanctions when violated, since adherence is not considered essential to the well-being of the society

high culture: the beliefs, values, expectations, and artifacts of a society's elites

ideal culture: made up of the shared values, beliefs, and norms that the members of a society claim as their culture

instincts: biologically programmed directions for living

language: a system of patterned sounds, often with corresponding written symbols, that the members of a society use to communicate their thoughts and feelings to one another

laws: norms that a governing authority within a society officially adopts as rules to regulate the behavior of the members of that society

material culture: all the tangible or physical products that the members of a society create

mores: norms that carry a strong sanction if violated because the members of a culture consider adherence essential to the well-being of the society

multiculturalism: respect for and appreciation of the cultural contributions, practices, and experiences of diverse groups

nonmaterial culture: all the nontangible or nonphysical products that the members of a society create

norms: the behavioral rules of a culture

popular culture: the beliefs, values, expectations, and artifacts of a society's masses

real culture: the values, beliefs, and norms that are reflected in the actual behavior and social practices of a society's members

Sapir-Whorf hypothesis: the position that language shapes perception and affects how we experience and understand reality

society: composed of interacting people who share the same culture

subculture: a group within a society's dominant culture that shares some of its elements, but at the same time differentiates itself from the dominant culture in a specific way

symbol: anything that has been given representational meaning by the members of a cultural group

taboos: norms so strongly held that to violate them is inconceivable to virtually all members of the society

technology: the body of knowledge that the members of a society apply to their physical environment to help them meet their survival needs

values: cultural standards or judgments of what is right, good, or desirable

LEARNING MORE

Billson, J. M. (1995). *Keepers of the culture: The power of tradition in women's lives.* New York: Lexington Books. A feminist ethnography relating the challenges and triumphs of women of color, Native women, and rural and immigrant women as they attempt to deal with change and yet continue to maintain their indigenous cultures.

Dresser, N. (1996). *Multicultural manners.* New York: John Wiley and Sons. This etiquette book explains the customs of various racial and ethnic groups that together make up the U.S. population, from Vietnamese to Iraqis to Salvadorans. The author's goal is to promote understanding among diverse cultures.

Kane, J. (1995). *Savages.* New York: Alfred A. Knopf. An ethnographic account of the Huaorani of Ecuador that examines their history as well as the cultural changes wrought by multinational oil companies.

Kraybill, D. B., & Nolt, S. M. (1996). *Amish enterprise: From plows to profits.* Baltimore: Johns Hopkins University Press. Based on over 150 personal interviews with members of this subculture, the authors examine how Amish entrepeneurs reconcile their cultural traditions with business success, and explore the significant cultural changes that such success may bring to Amish households and communities.

Niman, M. I. (1997). *People of the rainbow: A nomadic utopia.* Knoxville: University of Tennessee Press. A participant-observation study of a utopian U. S. counterculture, the Rainbow Family, which practices decision making by consensus and places family ties above all others, including ties to government.

Rooks, N. M. (1996). *Hair raising: Beauty, culture, and African American women.* New Brunswick, NJ: Rutgers University Press. In her study of American "beauty culture," Rooks focuses on the cultural significance of hair in African American women's lives and discusses how beauty is socially constructed.

 Run Chapter 5 on your *Living Sociology* CD-ROM for interesting and informative activities, web links, videos, practice tests, and more.

C H A P T E R

5

Socialization

In the fall of 1970, social workers from a Los Angeles County welfare office made a grim discovery. They found a thirteen-year-old girl who had been kept a virtual prisoner in a small room in her parents' house from the time she was an infant. For most of each day, year after year, the girl, who was later called Genie, was harnessed to an infant's potty seat, able to move only her fingers, hands, toes, and feet. At night, she was taken off the potty seat and put into a sleeping bag that was fashioned like a straightjacket, so she could not move her arms, and then put in a large crib with wire mesh sides and a wire mesh cover. In other words, she slept in a cage. The room that served as her prison offered little in the way of visual or auditory stimulation. There were two windows, so Genie may have heard some sounds from outside. Periodically, her father would scream at her for some transgression and beat her with a board that he kept in the room. He would also sometimes stand outside the room and bark or growl like a dog to scare her. The only other interaction she had was with her mother, who fed her meals of baby food, cereal, and soft-boiled eggs. However, because the father wanted the child to have as little contact as possible with others, the mother would quickly stuff the food into Genie's mouth; if Genie choked and some of the food came out of her mouth, her face was rubbed in it.

The physical effects of this isolation were startling: Although Genie was thirteen years old when she was taken from her parents, she weighed only fifty-nine pounds and stood fifty-four inches tall. She was incontinent, could not chew solid food, had tremendous difficulty swallowing, could not focus her eyes on anything more than twelve feet away from her, and appeared unable to cry. She had two sets of teeth and salivated constantly. She could not perceive hot and cold, and could not perform any kind of physical activity that required her to fully extend her legs, such as hopping, skipping, and climbing. Genie also had numerous interpersonal and emotional problems. She could barely talk, although she did not appear to be physiologically unable. She did understand a few words that others said to her, but the only things she could say were "Stop it" and "No more." She spat frequently and indiscriminately. She seemed unable to express any emotions except frustration and anger, but even these were displayed in unconventional ways. When Genie was frustrated, she would scowl, tear paper, and scratch objects with her fingernails. When something made her angry, she would turn the anger on herself: scratching at her face, blowing her nose into her clothes, and urinating, but not making a single sound. One of the specialists called in to consult on Genie's case said she was the most "profoundly damaged" child he had ever seen (Rymer, 1993).

Genie's case is as enlightening as it is disturbing for the questions it raises about fundamental aspects of human development. Indeed, it speaks to the issue of what it means to be fully human. Genie's case underlines the point we have made numerous times in previous chapters: Human beings need more than physical sustenance to thrive; we need *social interaction*. In fact, one of our first tasks in life is to learn what it means to be human. This learning process, called *socialization*, is the focus of this chapter. Specifically, **socialization** is the process by which a society's culture is taught and learned and human personalities are developed. **Personality** is a set of behavioral and emotional characteristics that describe one's reactions to various situations or events.

Most of you probably have little difficulty accepting the first part of the socialization process as we've defined it, especially in light of what you have learned in Chapters 1 and 4. That is, culture is a social creation, so to behave according to the values and norms of one's culture, one must be taught what they are. However, the second part of our definition, that personality develops in response to socialization, may raise some questions in your mind. Many people assume that personality traits are largely present at birth, and that while environmental factors influence personality development, the hand dealt by genetics pretty much determines an individual's personality. In this chapter, though, we will see once again how the complex interaction of biology and environment produces not only cultural differences, but also personality differences across individuals and groups.

First, we will continue to review the debate about the relative influences of biology and culture on human development. We will then discuss theories of socialization, looking at how social theorists explain the process of human development. We will also discuss the groups and institutions responsible for socializing new members of a society and the types of socialization that occur. And finally, we will consider socialization as a life-long learning process by looking at how socialization takes place over the life course.

THE INTERACTION OF BIOLOGY AND ENVIRONMENT

We all probably have childhood memories of meeting some of our parents' friends for the first time and of having to stand quietly with a tolerant smile while they marveled at how much we resembled Mom or Dad or Aunt Tilly or Uncle Ned. You can also probably recall innumerable instances of being told you have your mother's eyes or your father's chin. Not only do we learn from others how much we physically resemble our kin, but also we often hear about the personality traits we have inherited. Perhaps you have been told, for instance, that you are stubborn like your father or outgoing like your mother. Most people incorporate the idea of inheritance into their understanding of the world around them. Of course, this kind of explanation for our appearance and actions can come in handy at times. It allows us to rationalize, for example, that our jeans don't fit properly because of the large bone structure passed on from our mother's side, rather than our recent overindulgences in pepperoni pizza.

The notion that genetics is responsible for who we are socially as well as physically holds considerable appeal, and it is not without research support. Some of the strongest evidence of the role of genetics in human social development comes from research with identical twins—known as *monozygotic twins*—who were reared apart. Identical twins originate from a single fertilized egg, so they share all (100 percent) of their genes. They are the same sex and they look very much alike. Moreover, they tend to have the same social interests and emotional dispositions, even if they do not grow up together in the same household. In one study, for instance, researchers located an identical twin pair who shared a phobia for the ocean; if they went into the water at all, they entered backwards and only up to their knees (Lykken et al., 1992). In another study, a pair of identical twins were found who dressed alike, read magazines from back to front, and wrapped rubber bands around their wrists (Holden, 1980; see also Wright, 1998). Since these twins were raised in different households, their uncanny likenesses could not be attributed to having grown up together or being influenced by the same caregivers. However, while the researchers who conducted these studies

Identical twins Gerald Levey and Mark Newman were separated at birth, raised in different families, and reunited when they were 31. They were surprised at how much they had in common, beginning with the fact that both had chosen to become fire fighters. What questions does their story raise about the interaction between genetic determinism and environmental determinism?

conclude that the observed similarities are products of genetics, heredity doesn't tell the whole story.

Genetics undoubtedly plays a critical role in laying the foundation of our individual human potential, but the extent to which we develop any of these traits or talents—competitiveness, say, or musical ability—has much, if not more, to do with the environment in which we live. Look, for example, at Genie. What talents or predispositions did she inherit? No one may ever know, since her isolation denied her any opportunity to discover and express them.

To better understand the interaction of biology and environment in human development, let's consider in more detail some of the research on the effects of social isolation.

Animal Studies

Some of the best-known research on the effects of social isolation was conducted in the 1950s and 1960s by psychologist Harry Harlow (1905–1981). In one experiment, Harlow and his colleagues at the University of Wisconsin took rhesus monkeys from their mothers after birth and raised them alone in bare wire cages. The monkeys were well fed, but they did not survive. In a second experiment, Harlow put newborn monkeys in cages with a "surrogate mother" made of wire and covered with soft terry cloth. These monkeys lived, and in observing them clinging to the terry cloth, Harlow and his colleagues hypothesized that the monkeys had an inborn need for comfort that the soft fabric seemed to satisfy (Harlow, 1962).

Harlow and his colleagues then did a third experiment. They put one group of newborn monkeys in a cage containing two surrogate mothers fashioned from wire; one surrogate was covered with terry cloth, and the bare-wire mother was fitted with a bottle for feeding. Another group of newborn monkeys was put in exactly the same kind of cage, but this time, the cloth mother was outfitted with the bottle. All of the monkeys preferred the cloth mother to the bare-wire mother, even when the bare-wire mother provided them with milk (Harlow & Zimmerman, 1958).

Harlow concluded that the need for physical comfort was as essential for the monkeys' survival as food. However, none of the monkeys—even those who had the comfort of a cloth surrogate—grew up behaving normally. They exhibited more fear and aggression than monkeys raised under normal conditions, and they were unable to engage in sexual relations.

Harlow believed the monkeys' abnormal behavior showed that particular emotions are innate, and that emotions develop in sequence during several critical periods in the early years of life. However, this development is not automatic. For development to occur properly, the infant needs particular types of social contacts during the critical developmental periods. Harlow's subsequent research showed, in fact, that various behaviors and emotions were affected differently by when social isolation was imposed, with early isolation most negatively affecting the ability to develop social and emotional attachments to others and to develop nurturing behaviors.

What did Harry Harlow's research and other animal studies show about the social and behavioral needs of animals in relation to their biological needs? What are the implications of this research for understanding the role of socialization in the human experience?

Harlow's research nicely demonstrates the interaction of biology and environment. Personality and social behavior may have a biological basis, but without appropriate social interaction, they cannot develop normally. The question now is, does research with humans yield similar results?

Studies of Children

Obviously, scientists are unable to conduct experiments like Harlow's using human subjects instead of monkeys. Consequently, data on the social isolation of children are limited to those fortunately rare cases in which children were deliberately kept in extreme isolation by their parents or other caregivers, or were abandoned as infants in wilderness areas and survived. In all, fifty such cases of abandoned children have been documented worldwide since 1800. However, research on these children, known as *wild* or *feral* children, has been unsystematic and plagued by serious methodological difficulties (Rymer, 1993). More successful research has been done with "closet children," children who, like Genie, were essentially imprisoned by their parents. Two well-known cases were discovered in the United States in the 1930s.

The first child, called Anna, was six years old when she was found in 1938. She had lived all but the first six months of her life isolated in the attic of her grandfather's farmhouse. Anna's mother, an unmarried, mentally retarded woman, had put Anna in an institution immediately following her birth because Anna's grandfather would not tolerate the presence of what he saw as a reminder of his daughter's immorality. But the family was unable to pay for institutional care, and Anna was returned to her grandfather's house, where she was subsequently kept hidden in the attic. During her five and a half years of isolation, Anna was fed enough to keep her alive, but she had virtually no social interaction.

When Anna was found by a social worker, she was physically debilitated. She was grossly underweight for a child her age, and she could not walk or talk or feed herself. She was also severely damaged emotionally and psychologically. Anna appeared incapable of emotion. She could not laugh or express anger; in fact, she was expressionless, totally indifferent to those around her.

After she was discovered, Anna was placed in an institution where she was given considerable social contact. Within a few years, she learned some words and phrases and could follow simple directions. She also learned to walk, to wash her hands and brush her teeth, to feed herself, and to build with blocks and string beads. However, at the age of ten she died from a disorder likely related to her early years of abuse and neglect. At that time, she still could not speak in sentences or run well; she had the social and motor skills of a two- or three-year-old child (Davis, 1940, 1947).

The second "closet child," also found in the late 1930s and also at age six, was called Isabelle. Like Anna, Isabelle had been imprisoned in a dark room by her grandfather. Unlike Anna, however, Isabelle was kept with her mother who, although deaf and mute, communicated with Isabelle using gestures. When Isabelle and her mother were discovered, the child had some of the same physical and social disabilities exhibited by Anna. In particular, though, she was wildly hostile toward men. Nevertheless, Isabelle responded well to the team of physicians and psychologists who took her case. Within a short period of time, she was speaking and her vocabulary grew rapidly. Indeed, by the time she was eight, just two years after she had been found, she achieved a normal enough level of intellectual and social functioning for her age that she was able to attend school (Davis, 1948).

Psychologists believe Isabelle's early social interaction with her mother was a major reason for her rapid and successful socialization. This interaction not only distinguishes Isabelle from Anna, but also from Genie. Like Isabelle, Genie was tended by a skilled team of physicians, psychologists, linguists, and other specialists. But despite their intensive efforts, she was permanently disabled in many ways. By the age of eighteen, Genie was only able to take care of her basic hygiene and perform some simple household tasks. She remained severely disturbed emotionally. Although her self-destructive behavior declined considerably, she still had trouble distinguishing appropriate from inappropriate social behavior; for example, she would masturbate, often using objects, whenever she felt like it, regardless of where she was or whom she was with (Curtiss, 1977).

One of Genie's greatest difficulties was language development. Although her vocabulary developed quickly and she learned to string words together to express an idea, she could not master grammar. Her speech always sounded like that of a very young child: "Think about Mama love Genie," "I want live back Marilyn house." The precise reasons for Genie's limitations are not well understood, but scientists hypothesize that language, like some emotions, is linked to critical developmental periods.

More specifically, scientists tell us that although we are born with the innate ability to speak and acquire language, our ability to master the grammar of language depends on the development of certain structures of the brain during critical periods of early life. By "development," scientists mean that particular organization patterns must be established. The brain structures are essentially "hardwired" (see Lieberman, 1998, however, for a somewhat different view). Furthermore, it is believed that by the time we reach puberty—the time in her life when Genie was discovered—all critical periods are over and the brain's organization is stable. For the organization to take place, the brain requires a particular type of stimulation: that provided by a logic sys-

tem such as language. The language system need not be spoken, for research shows that deaf individuals who are taught sign language as children show normal brain organization, whereas those without early exposure to sign language do not (Rymer, 1993). The gestures that Isabelle and her mother used to communicate apparently supplied the logic system that Isabelle's brain needed to stimulate growth and organization. Genie, in contrast, was deprived of this stimulation until after puberty, by which time her brain's organization had stabilized. Thus, she could be taught words, but her brain was unable to process grammar. As one observer put it, "even innate characteristics must be developed" (Rymer, 1993, p. 157).

In short, humans are born with a host of abilities and emotional capacities, but without a minimum of early cultivation, these abilities and capacities stagnate. Even though some may be revived through later intervention, they may not develop normally; others may be lost completely.

The cultivation we are speaking of is the process of socialization. For years, sociologists and psychologists have tried to map out the socialization process. Let's turn now to some of their theories about how we learn to be human, that is, *social* beings.

REFLECTING ON

The Interaction of Biology and Environment

1. The disagreement about how much of a person's personality is the result of biology and how much is the result of adaptation to the environment is called the *nature/nurture* debate. What is your position in this debate? Explain your answer.
2. Why are physical comfort and emotional attachment vital to normal human development?

EXPLAINING OUR HUMANITY

Socialization is a complex process, and explaining precisely how it takes place is a daunting enterprise at best. Nevertheless, a number of social scientists have risen to the challenge. As we will see in this section, a common theme in these theories is the idea that socialization takes place in *stages* over the life course. Table 5.1 on page 110 shows the major life stages and the approximate ages at which the stages occur. Although most of the theories we will consider focus on the early stages of development, one also includes the adult stages. We will begin with the

TABLE 5.1   Stages of the Life Course

Life Stage	Approximate Age
Infancy	Birth–2
Toddler	2–3
Early childhood	3–6
Middle childhood	6–13
Adolescence	13–20
Adulthood	20 and older
Young adulthood	20–40
Middle adulthood	40–65
Late adulthood	65 and older

work of Sigmund Freud, who emphasized the importance of early childhood experiences in the development of personality. Next, we will review the theories of Charles Horton Cooley and George Herbert Mead, who believed personality develops through social interaction. The work of Jean Piaget, who studied how children think, and Lawrence Kohlberg and Carol Gilligan, who examined moral development, will also be discussed. Finally, we will discuss the theory of Erik Erikson, who was equally interested in childhood and adult socialization.

Sigmund Freud

Probably no one reading this book has not heard of the Austrian psychologist, **Sigmund Freud** (1856–1939). We even speak of him and his ideas in everyday conversation. We call our overly neat roommate "anal retentive," and if we can't recall an embarrassing incident that all our friends seem to remember, we offhandedly laugh, "Oh, I must have repressed it." Being fixated on something and blocking unacceptable memories are both Freudian concepts. In fact, "few views in the social sciences have evoked stronger reactions, theoretically or emotionally, or provided as much controversy as Freud's" (Martin et al., 1990, p. 83). What's all the fuss about?

The Structure of the Personality.   According to Freud, the human personality has three interrelated parts: the id, the ego, and the superego. The **id** is present at birth. It is entirely unconscious and is composed of powerful forces, called *drives* and *wishes*. The two most important drives or wishes according to Freud are sex and destruction or aggression. The id operates on the *pleasure principle:* It wants immediate gratification so as to relieve the psychic tension produced by its powerful drives. In other words,

it seeks to maximize pleasure and minimize displeasure. It has no sense of reality, so it is not evil, but simply amoral.

The **ego** operates on the *reality principle:* It tries to satisfy the needs of the id in socially acceptable ways. The ego begins to develop when we are between six and eight months old. It develops as we come to understand that we are not part of our environment, but separate from the people and things around us. The ego is the part of the personality that is rational, oriented toward solving problems, and able to delay gratification. As the ego grows, so too does the individual's ability to deal with reality.

The **superego** is typically described as the *conscience.* It develops when we are three to five years old, as we internalize (make part of our own thinking) the values and norms of our society that we are taught initially by our parents or other caregivers and later by other authority figures. It is the superego that produces feelings of guilt.

Given the various functions and demands of these three components of the personality, the possibility for psychic conflict is obviously great. In a healthy individual, though, the ego successfully represses (blocks) id impulses or channels them into some acceptable outlet. Say, for example, you're angry over a test grade and feel an impulse to go to the professor's office and scream about how unfair the exam was. The impulse is coming from your id, but your healthy ego causes you to quickly put the thought out of your mind, or to challenge a friend to a vigorous game of racketball where you release your anger by hitting the ball as hard as you can. At the same time, the ego also keeps the superego in check, making sure it doesn't become too rigid or perfectionistic. However, the health of the ego depends on how well an individual passes through the five stages of personality development in childhood.

Stages of Personality Development.   Freud believed that the essential elements of personality are established in childhood and remain relatively stable throughout the life course. Everyone, he argued, must pass through five successive stages in the development of personality. During each stage, particular id impulses, primarily sexual in nature, seek satisfaction, and a specific part or *zone* of the body is the main source of pleasure. During each stage, the child must learn how to balance the competing forces of the personality, so as not to be too self-indulgent or too self-repressed.

The first stage of personality development is the **oral stage.** It spans from birth to one and a half years of age, and, as its name implies, the mouth, tongue, and lips are the areas of desire and gratification. Frustration and conflict arise because food is not always forthcoming when the baby demands it, and eventually the baby must give up the breast, the bottle, and its thumb in order to comply with societal norms.

Freud called the second stage the **anal stage.** At about one to one and a half years, children become fascinated by excretion and begin to realize that they can exercise control over their environment by expelling or retaining feces. Not surprisingly, the major source of frustration during this period is toilet training. At about age two or three, the child's parents and society believe it's time to learn to control bodily functions.

During these first two stages, boys and girls are alike in their behavior and experiences. For both, their mother is the chief object of their emotions, since she is their primary caregiver and gratifies most of their needs. However, during the third stage, the **phallic stage,** from about ages two to five, children become aware of their genitals and of the fact that the genitals of girls and boys are different. It is during this stage that **gender identification** takes place: Children begin to adopt the behavior and attributes of their same-sex parent. The process occurs differently, though, for boys and girls.

For boys, gender identification is motivated by what Freud called *castration anxiety.* Sometime around age two or three, a boy's love for his mother becomes more sexual, and he now views his father as a rival. Freud called this the *Oedipus complex,* after the Greek mythic figure, Oedipus, who unwittingly killed his father so he could marry his mother. What quickly cures the boy of his jealousy is a glimpse of the female genitalia. Reasoning that all girls have been castrated, he fears a similar fate if he continues to compete with his father, who is far more powerful than he is. Consequently, instead of competing, the boy begins to model his behavior after his father.

In contrast, a girl's identification with her mother is motivated by what Freud called *penis envy.* Penis envy in girls develops on first sight of the male genitals. Seeing the male's "far superior equipment," as Freud put it (1933, p. 88; 1983), the girl thinks she's been castrated. Overwhelmed by her sense of incompleteness, she becomes jealous of boys and disdainful of her mother and all women because they share her "deformity." She shifts her love to her father, who does possess the coveted penis, and begins to identify with her mother as a way to win him. Eventually, the girl realizes she can have a penis in two ways: briefly through intercourse, and symbolically by giving birth to a baby boy. However, according to Freud, the female never fully overcomes her feelings of inferiority and envy, and this leaves indelible marks on her personality.

Following the phallic stage is the **latency stage,** from five to twelve years of age, when sexual impulses become somewhat dormant. At around age twelve, the **genital stage** begins. This is the final stage in personality development. During this stage, children enter adolescence and become increasingly independent of their parents. They must also learn to relate socially and sexually to members of the opposite sex.

Each of Freud's stages poses particular challenges or conflicts that must be resolved in order to enter adulthood with a healthy personality. If any of these conflicts is not resolved and the psychic tensions that characterize a particular stage are not effectively handled by the ego, then an individual is likely to have personality problems in adulthood.

Evaluating Freud's Perspective. Freud focused the attention of the scientific community on the importance of childhood experience. He forced his colleagues to consider that children might have sexual feelings and desires and that what happens during childhood can leave an indelible imprint on an individual's personality. Furthermore, he offered an explanation of how individuals internalize the values and norms of their society.

Despite these significant contributions, Freud's theory has been criticized for several reasons. One is methodological. How do we go about empirically testing the theory? We must rely on an analyst's interpretations of an individual's words and behavior, but these are highly subjective and there is often substantial disagreement from one analyst to the next. Moreover, the idea that the personality is composed of three parts, instead of four or forty, is not empirically verifiable. Others object to Freud's depiction of the personality as established entirely in childhood and then remaining fixed or stable over time. As we will see later in this chapter, social learning continues throughout the life cycle, and we can modify our behavior and attitudes as we are exposed to new situations. Freud's emphasis on the biological roots of personality—innate wishes and drives—overlooks the significant impact that social and environmental factors have in shaping our desires and motivations. For example, all healthy humans have a sex drive, but how the sex drive is satisfied depends largely on a society's norms regulating sexual behavior. An individual may also choose to override the sex drive by remaining celibate.

Finally, it is impossible to ignore the antifemale bias in Freud's theory. Females are defined as inadequate and inherently jealous. By asserting that women are inferior to men, Freud's theory legitimates social inequality between women and men, and in that way it is clearly harmful to women.

Despite the criticisms, Freud must be credited with making important contributions to our understanding of human development, especially in terms of the impact of early childhood experiences on adult lives. For better or for worse, his ideas have influenced virtually every other major theorist.

Charles Horton Cooley and George Herbert Mead

Charles Horton Cooley (1864–1929) and **George Herbert Mead** (1863–1931) were American contemporaries of Sigmund Freud. However, both Cooley and Mead were social psychologists, and therefore placed their emphasis on social learning and social interaction in human development.

The Looking-Glass Self.   According to Cooley, who we are as individuals—that is, the development of the individual *self*—grows out of our interaction with others. We derive our concepts of ourselves from our perceptions of how others see us. Cooley called this self-concept the **looking-glass self**, likening it to the experience of seeing oneself in a mirror. When we look at ourselves in a mirror, we have some reaction to what we see—we are pleased or displeased depending on whether our reflection is what we would like it to be or what we imagined it to be. Something similar occurs in our interactions with other people. When we interact with another person, they react to us—to how we look, what we say, or what we do. We reflect on their reactions, learning from them how others see us, and this in turn affects how we see ourselves.

Cooley saw the development of the self-concept as a three-step process. First, we imagine how we appear to others. Each of us does this every day. Of course, we are more or less concerned about this "presentation of self," depending on who the others are and how important their opinions are to us. You are more likely to worry about how you look and what others think of you during a job interview than when your best friend stops by unexpectedly.

The second step in the development of the self-concept occurs during and after our interactions with others. We imagine how others judged us based on our perceptions of their reactions to our "presentation of self." Most of us have probably had the experience of saying something that we thought was funny, but no one laughed. If we're

with family or old friends, we don't give it a second thought, but if the others were new acquaintances whose opinions you value, you might later agonize over what they were thinking of you: "Did they think I was silly? Unprofessional? Maybe they saw me as more sophisticated than they are because they didn't get it."

Finally, based on how we interpret others' reactions, we get some kind of self-feeling. If we conclude that their reactions were positive, we think well of ourselves and this particular "presentation of self" will be reinforced. In the future, in similar situations, we will likely look, speak, and behave in much the same way again. However, if we perceive their judgments of us to be negative, our self-concept may be lowered and we feel bad about ourselves. When similar circumstances arise in the future, what we say and do, and perhaps even how we look, are likely to be different. You may resolve, for example, not to make jokes when you are introduced to new acquaintances.

According to Cooley, then, an individual's self-concept develops over time and is the product of numerous and neverending social interactions in everyday life. It is the case that sometimes we misread others' opinions or judgments. No doubt, each of us has at some time in our lives misinterpreted another person's reaction to the way we look or to something we've said or done. For example, when talking about an especially sensitive topic with others you don't know well, you may interpret silence as their agreement with what you are saying, when in fact they disagree, but remain silent to avoid an argument with you. Someone who repeatedly misperceives others' reactions or opinions may develop an overinflated, or, conversely, unrealistically poor conception of themselves. Of course, because our interactions are plentiful and our environments change, our self-concepts can change. In any event, whatever our self-concept, and however it changes from time

Charles Horton Cooley believed that social interaction is the key to our humanity. According to Cooley, what three steps in the development of self-concept will these children take. What does his mirror analogy—the looking-glass self—signify? What observations might George Herbert Mead have made about the behavior evident in this photograph?

to time, our self is created through social interaction. As Cooley (1964, p. 182) put it, "There is no sense of 'I' . . . without its correlative sense of you, . . . or they."

Taking the Role of the Other.   Mead's work elaborated on Cooley's ideas. Mead was especially interested in how language, gestures, and other symbolic systems of communication make social order possible. When people interact using symbols, particularly language and gestures, they must be able to interpret one another's intended meanings, and then they respond on the basis of their interpretations. Social order, then, is based on the ability of all members of the social group to visualize the world and themselves from the points of view of one another. Mead called this ability **taking the role of the other.** It is also through the process of taking the role of the other that the individual self emerges. In other words, the self and society mutually depend on one another for their existence. According to Mead, there can be no self without society, and there can be no society without the symbolic interactions of individuals. Because the members of a society share the same culture, they can anticipate each other's expectations and respond accordingly.

The self, then, is not biologically ordained; it is socially created. An especially critical period for the development of the self is childhood, when children gradually learn how to take the role of the other. They do this, according to Mead, in three stages of social learning or socialization. As children pass through each stage, they develop a stronger sense of who they are as individuals, and they master what others expect of them.

Mead called the first socialization stage **imitation.** From birth until about age three, children really do not see themselves as separate from others in the environment; they cannot yet distinguish individuals with different roles. But as they move through this stage, children acquire social experience and begin to imitate or mimic the people with whom they interact most. When Mommy or Daddy claps hands, for instance, baby also claps. In addition to learning gestures, children at this stage also begin to acquire language. First, they learn the names of the people and objects most important to them (Ma-Ma, Da-Da, bottle, and so on), and gradually they refine their pronunciation and build their vocabulary. Children under three cannot yet take the role of the other, but the learning that occurs during the imitation stage provides the foundation for acquiring that ability later.

Between ages three and six, children are in the **play stage** of development. They can now distinguish a wide variety of social roles and actually spend a good bit of their time in play that involves role taking. They may play "house," for example, with one child pretending to be the Mommy or another adult, and another child "the baby"; sometimes the children even take the role of family pets. They often use the same expressions and even the

same tone of voice as the adults they imitate. One of your authors, for instance, was taken aback several years ago when she asked her son, then four, what he was up to at his computer, and he responded in a rather exasperated (and familiar) tone of voice, "*Please,* I'm trying to get some work done here."

During the play stage, then, children develop the ability to take the role of the other, but according to Mead, it is the role of the **particular other.** That is, children at this stage see the world from the perspectives of people who are significant in their environment, such as their parents. They have not yet learned how to see the world from the perspective of the larger social group to which they belong: their society and its culture. Moreover, at this stage children have difficulty understanding the relationships between various roles. One of our sons, for example, at the age of five, was completely puzzled when we told him that his Uncle Mike was also his father's brother. How could this be? He understood the relationship between himself and his father, between himself and Uncle Mike, and between himself and his own brother, but the notion that his father and his uncle could also simultaneously hold the role of brother was difficult to grasp.

It is not until the third stage—which Mead called the **game stage**—that children internalize the values and expectations of the larger society (the **generalized other**) and come to understand the complex interrelationship among roles. When children enter this stage, they have also entered school, so much of their daily activity takes place in organized groups that are governed by rules of behavior. Children at this age also enjoy playing games and team sports that have elaborate rules and multiple roles for players. Each player must understand not only his or her own role, but also the roles of every other player and their relationships to one another. The successful team, like the successful workplace and the "successful society," is one in which the members interact as a unit, able to anticipate one another's attitudes and behavior in particular situations. To paraphrase Mead (1934, p. 154), each individual's actions are determined to some extent by what he or she assumes other players' actions will be.

The "I" and the "Me."   Like Cooley, Mead emphasized the social construction of the self, but at the same time, he valued individual autonomy, spontaneity, and creativity. Mead recognized that these elements are important components of the self that coexist with the generalized other in each of us. To make this point clearer, Mead distinguished two parts of the self as the "I" and the "Me." The **I** is the spontaneous, free-willed dimension of the self, whereas the **Me** is the dimension formed by the stable, internalized values and norms of one's community.

These two parts of the self are in continuous reaction to one another. For example, an individual may be born with musical talent, but the way that talent is expressed is limited to some degree by the culture into which the individual is born. Someone born into a West African society will have different musical instruments available than someone born into a Western European society. Of course, a musician may choose to defy the expectations of his or her culture, by for instance selecting unconventional objects for playing music or making unconventional sounds with the instruments available. In fact, such innovation can be found in the music of many well-known African American jazz musicians. The music these musicians made was, in turn, modified over the years in response to others' reactions. Built into Mead's theory of the development of self, then, is the idea of achieving balance between stability and change, between cooperation and conflict, and between individual autonomy and social control.

Evaluating Cooley and Mead.   Cooley and Mead draw attention to the *social* process of personality development. Cooley's work is valuable because it shows how a person's self-concept is not predetermined by biology; rather, it develops out of the person's interpretation of what others think of him or her. Mead's theory also emphasizes how social interaction influences the development of the self, but he adds the idea that the self develops in stages beginning in infancy.

Critics of Cooley and Mead argue that neither theorist takes into account how membership in various groups, such as particular racial and ethnic groups, might influence the development of the self. Cooley points out that individuals sometimes misinterpret others' judgments of them. However, what if others' judgments are incorrect? Suppose a person is a member of a devalued group—one that is viewed negatively by members of the dominant group in the society. How would these negative judgments influence the person's self-concept? African Americans, for instance, report that White Americans will sometimes cross the street if they see a young African American man approaching them. African Americans perceive this behavior as reflecting White Americans' fear of Black people stemming from a racist belief that African Americans are inclined to commit crimes. In this case, it is the perception of others' judgment that is correct and the judgment that is wrong. But the fact that the judgment is wrong may not lessen the impact it has on African Americans' self-concepts. Researchers also need to consider how efforts from within the African American community to foster racial pride can counter the negative influences of the dominant group's judgments (Poussaint & Comer, 1993).

Similarly, critics of Mead ask whether members of different groups experience the stages of development the same way (Hewitt, 1998). For example, some researchers argue that because boys and girls are treated differently by their parents, their experiences of the de-

velopmental stages may differ (Kaspar, 1986). However, Janice Hale-Benson (1986) and others have found fewer gender differences in socialization in African American families, with children of both sexes being taught to be self-reliant. Do African American children, then, experience Mead's developmental stages differently than White children? Empirical research is needed to answer this question.

Jean Piaget

Swiss psychologist **Jean Piaget** (1892–1980) devoted his life work to examining how children think. More specifically, Piaget was not interested in *what* children think (the content of their thinking), but rather in *how* children think (the mental processes they use to understand their observations and experience). He theorized that cognitive development—that is, the development of intellectual abilities—occurs over time and in stages. Although he identified particular ages for each stage, he cautioned that the age at which a child moves from one stage to the next varies greatly from child to child. Nevertheless, he maintained, all children, regardless of the society in which they live, pass through the same stages. Piaget stressed the biological foundations of cognitive development, but he did recognize that environment played a role in the first two years of life. Let's take a closer look at Piaget's work.

How Children Learn to Think.   For Piaget, cognitive development takes place over four sequential stages. In other words, the emergence of every new intellectual skill depends on the development of previous skills. No matter how intellectually gifted the child, she or he cannot skip any developmental stage.

The first developmental stage is the **sensorimotor stage,** which takes place from birth until about age two. Piaget considered this the most important stage because it establishes the essential foundation for all intellectual development. Ask any parent about the enormous changes that a child undergoes during the first half of this stage, the first year of life. Newborns are a bundle of needs and reflexes, but within just a couple months they develop a social smile, seek out and respond to visual and auditory stimulation such as a caregiver's voice or particular toys, and even develop basic memory skills. During the second half of their first year, their actions show intent: They know what they want and they do something to get it (for example, crawl to get a toy, climb to reach a cookie). A significant milestone of the sensorimotor stage takes place at about nine months; it is the development of what Piaget called **object permanence.** This is the ability to understand that when a person or object is out of sight, it still exists. For example, if you show a six-month-old infant a toy and then put the toy behind your back, the baby will quickly forget about it because for the baby, the toy no longer exists. By the age of one, however, the infant will understand that the toy is simply hidden, will remember where you put it, and will probably go in search of it.

The development of object permanence continues during the second half of the sensorimotor stage, when children also begin to walk and talk and learn some basic reasoning skills. With the acquisition of language, the two-year-old can talk about persons and objects that are not present. However, most thinking about others is only in relation to themselves; as parents and caregivers know well, children at this age are highly self-centered. They are unable to see the world or their environment from anyone else's perspective but their own. As the two-year-old niece of your authors explained, "Mommy's having a baby so I'll have a friend to play with me."

By the end of the sensorimotor stage, the foundation of intellectual development has been set. The child has developed memory skills, language, specific motor skills, some basic numerical reasoning skills, and some simple forms of logic. During the second stage, the **preoperational stage** (ages two to six or seven), the child builds on these skills and learns to represent the world symbolically. For example, they use their imaginations in play, pretending to be a mail carrier delivering invisible letters. It is during this stage as well that children learn how to interact with others. They learn sharing and cooperation, basic manners, and "right" versus "wrong" behavior in particular situations.

The third stage emerges at age six or seven and continues until about age twelve. This is the **concrete operations stage,** when children learn more complex rules of behavior and the reasons underlying them; develop the ability to see a situation from a number of different viewpoints besides their own and to evaluate these perspectives; and can anticipate events and other people's behavior. Operational thinking is logical thinking, and children at this stage can think logically about physical objects. In fact, the most significant marker of the concrete operations stage according to Piaget is **conservation,** or the understanding that an object may change in appearance, yet still maintain the same weight, substance, or volume. For example, if you present a four-year-old with two short, wide containers, each filled with exactly the same amount of water, but then pour the liquid from one of the containers into a tall, narrow container and ask the child which container now holds more water, the four-year-old will say the tall narrow one. To the four-year-old, there's more water in the narrow container because it *looks* like more. If you tried the same trick with a ten-year-old, though, he or she would not likely be fooled. By this age, conservation has developed, so the ten-year-old would understand that, regardless of appearances, the amount of water has not changed.

The child who has mastered conservation can distinguish appearances from reality. Still, it is not until the fourth and final stage of cognitive development, the **formal operations stage** which begins at about age twelve, that the child is fully capable of abstract thinking and uses deductive logic. The child in the formal operations stage moves beyond reasoning about immediate situations and can now think hypothetically, considering future possibilities, their relationships to one another, and their potential outcomes. In the early part of this stage, in adolescence, future-oriented thinking may be grandiose or idealistic—thinking, for example, that even if they do something risky, they won't be injured or killed because they're too young to die—but it becomes more realistic as the individual acquires more life experience.

Thus, in Piaget's model, refinements in thinking continue into adulthood. In fact, Piaget maintained that everyone, both children and adults, uses two mental strategies, **assimilation** and **accommodation,** to process the new information they continually receive throughout their lives. When we assimilate a piece of information or an experience, we incorporate it into our existing repertoire of thoughts and behaviors. In accommodation, however, we change or abandon an idea or behavior in our repertoire because of a new piece of information or an experience. We hope you will both assimilate and accommodate what you learn in this text and in your sociology classroom.

This child thinks that the tall thin glass has more water in it than does the other glass, when actually the amounts of water are the same. This means that she has not mastered Piaget's test for comprehension of the conservation of liquid volume. What do the results say about this child's stage of cognitive development?

GLOBAL INSIGHTS What Would Piaget Say about Japanese Cram Schools?

Japanese high school and college students consistently outperform their peers from around the world, including the United States, on international achievement tests. Many observers attribute the superior test performance of the Japanese to the number of hours they spend studying each day. For example, while the average U.S. high school student spends just 3.5 hours *a week* studying and 1.4 hours reading, the average Japanese student spends four hours *per night* studying and additional hours after school at private tutoring sessions called "cram schools" (Chira, 1991). In Japan, the best jobs are awarded to those individuals who have graduated from the most prestigious universities, and entrance to the schools is determined by a student's score on rigorous examinations as well as the prestige of the high school attended. To attend a prominent high school, however, one must study at a top-notch elementary school. Consequently, the competition for admission to the best schools has grown fierce in Japan, and many parents begin preparing their children for kindergarten entrance exams as young as age two (Wu Dunn, 1996).

Cram schools for toddlers and preschoolers may cost more than $9,000 a year. Each session is about two and a half hours long, and schools vary in the subjects they cover. Some schools focus on physical prowess, insisting that classes in gymnastics and karate teach young children discipline. Most schools, however, teach the skills needed to pass the kindergarten and first-grade entrance exams: counting, sorting objects by shape and other categories, memorizing stories, understanding the calendar. Many three- and four-year-olds attend four cram sessions per week in different subjects (Wu Dunn, 1996).

While Japanese youngsters are among the best test-takers in the world, the Japanese educational system has been criticized for stifling students' individualism and creativity and producing adults who have difficulty thinking independently. In addition, critics charge, the pressure to succeed turns peers into rivals, robbing children of enduring friendships and compassion for one another. According to some experts, student violence and rising teen suicide rates in Japan may be directly linked to the fierce competition and rigid rules of conformity that are traditional features of Japanese schooling (White, 1987; Wu Dunn, 1996). What do you think Jean Piaget would have to say about the Japanese cram schools for young children?

Evaluating Piaget. Piaget's work has had a substantial influence on parents and educators. Perhaps his greatest contribution was emphasizing the importance of giving very young children social and intellectual stimulation. This doesn't mean that children should be forced into activities beyond their developmental level or rushed through the early developmental stages. In fact, many psychologists argue that pushing children too fast and too hard actually does them more harm than good (Elkind, 1981; Zigler, 1987; see also the Global Insights box). However, Piaget warned against squandering the early years of children's intellectual development, especially the first two years, which affect children's chances of realizing their intellectual potential. Certainly, the importance of early stimulation in the first years of life was illustrated dramatically in the case of Genie.

Piaget does have his critics, however. Some point out that Piaget tended to underestimate the cognitive abilities of young children because of the limited ways in which he measured specific skills. In one study, for instance, researchers found evidence that children as young as two were able to adopt others' points of view. The two-year-olds in this study used shorter sentences when speaking to children younger than themselves, but increased the length of their sentences when speaking to those who were older (Shatz & Gelman, 1973). Consequently, some researchers argue that had Piaget used multiple measures or indicators of specific skills, or had he asked children of different ages to perform different types of tasks rather than the same tasks across age groups, he would have discovered the emergence of many cognitive abilities much earlier in life than he expected (Miller & Baillargeon, 1990). By rigidly focusing on children's abilities to perform the same task at different ages, Piaget's theory can result in some children being mistakenly labeled as intellectually deficient or "slow." In addition, Piaget has been criticized for downplaying the importance of environment in cognitive development (Rogoff & Morelli, 1989). Although he emphasized the importance of early stimulation, his critics do not believe he went far enough: Environment plays a critical role in cognitive development throughout childhood.

Lawrence Kohlberg and Carol Gilligan on Moral Development

Human beings do not just develop emotionally and intellectually, they also develop morally. *Morality* refers to the ability to evaluate attitudes and behaviors as good or bad, right or wrong, appropriate or inappropriate. Of course, moral development is related to intellectual development. One is not capable of moral reasoning until the intellect has developed to a certain level. Courts, for example, do not hold children under a certain age (in most states age twelve) responsible for their actions because children must learn to tell right from wrong. But when, and perhaps more importantly, *how,* do we develop a sense of morality? Answers to these questions are only suggested by the theories we have discussed so far. However, two psychologists—Lawrence Kohlberg and Carol Gilligan—have focused their work directly on moral development. Let's have a look at what each has to say.

Developing a Sense of Justice.   Suppose you know a very poor man—we'll call him Heinz—whose wife has cancer. There is only one drug that doctors think might save Heinz's wife's life, and it just so happens that the drug was developed by a pharmacist in the town where Heinz lives. The problem is that the drug is very expensive, mostly because the pharmacist is charging ten times more for the drug than it costs him to make it. Heinz needs $2,000 to buy the drug for his wife. He goes to everyone he can think of to borrow money, but only manages to scrape together $1,000. So Heinz goes to the pharmacist and pleads with him to sell the drug for less money or let Heinz pay the balance of the $2,000 later so that his wife can be treated in time. The pharmacist flatly refuses, telling Heinz that since he discovered the drug, he is entitled to make money from it. Heinz becomes desperate as his wife's condition worsens; finally, he breaks into the drug store and steals the drug for his wife.

Do you think Heinz acted morally or immorally? Was what he did just, or was it wrong? These are the questions that **Lawrence Kohlberg** (1927–1987) posed to individuals of various ages after telling them about Heinz's dilemma. Kohlberg found that young children tended to evaluate Heinz's actions differently than adolescents, and adolescents typically evaluated Heinz's actions differently than adults. Kohlberg, therefore, proposed three levels of moral development.

Level one, **preconventional morality,** is common in young children. Individuals at this level of morality evaluate behavior in terms of whether they will be punished or rewarded for it. Ask a five-year-old, for example, why she shouldn't hit her little brother and she's likely to tell you, "Because Mommy will give me a time-out."

Usually, the second level of morality, **conventional morality,** develops between the ages of seven and sixteen. At this level, consequences are considered in deciding whether an action is right or wrong, but in addition, the individual considers the expectations of others, trying to either please them or avoid their disapproval. The fourteen-year-old who doesn't drink at a party because his parents have told him not to is at the conventional level of morality.

The highest level of morality is called **postconventional morality.** Most people do not achieve this level until adulthood, and many adults only partially achieve it. In postconventional morality, people act on what they consider to be in the best interests of their community or their society. Postconventional individuals feel that murdering another person is immoral, not because they will be punished or incur the disapproval of others, but because such behavior contributes to the breakdown of social order and hurts the whole community, not just a

These children are in a dispute over playground turf, with both sides claiming that something is not fair. The boys are not concerned about the girls' disapproval, nor about adult intervention; they hold to the line they have drawn, as is their right. The girls feel an exception should be made to include everyone in the interests of greater fairness. According to Lawrence Kohlberg, in what stage of moral development are these children operating? What observations about the dispute might Carol Gilligan make? Do you agree that moral judgment is gendered? Why or why not?

single individual. In the most advanced stage of postconventional morality, an individual's judgments are guided by personal—rather than societal—moral belief systems. This personal morality may sometimes be at odds with the law or the established norms of society. Consider, for instance, those individuals who object to war on the ground that the taking of another human life is morally wrong under any circumstances. The conscientious objectors would go to prison or exile themselves rather than conform to their society's norm that killing in war is justifiable.

Evaluating Kohlberg. Kohlberg's work is provocative, but it is not without problems. Some critics, for example, argue that Kohlberg's theory is limited because he did not ask his subjects to evaluate realistic situations. Few of us have to decide between saving a loved one's life and stealing the cure. Confronted with a moral dilemma that they are more likely to experience in their everyday lives—for example, finding a wallet full of money and having to decide whether to keep it or return it to the owner—people, regardless of age, may respond differently than they would to Heinz's dilemma (Yussen, 1977). However, the strongest criticism of Kohlberg is that he based his research strictly on male subjects. To what extent do Kohlberg's findings hold when females are questioned about moral dilemmas?

Gender Differences in Moral Judgments. As we noted in Chapter 1, social science has traditionally been androcentric, that is, conducted by men on men. Yet findings from such studies are generalized to all people in similar situations. In other words, what men think and do has been taken as the standard way of thinking and behaving in a particular setting. Harvard psychologist **Carol Gilligan** was interested in moral development, but concerned about the omission of women as subjects and gender as a variable in the research that had already been done. She decided to replicate Kohlberg's study with female subjects (Gilligan, 1982).

Gilligan found that whereas boys tend to evaluate Heinz's dilemma in terms of laws and justice, girls tend to view it in terms of care and social relationships or connections among people. She argues that this gender difference manifests itself even in the way children play. Boys, she says, are concerned mostly about the rules of a game and are quick to point out individual violations and what they perceive as "cheating." In contrast, girls playing the same game—dodge ball, for instance—are less concerned with rule infractions and more concerned with their interactions with one another. Should a dispute arise, girls are less likely than boys to appeal to abstract principles or rules and more likely to find some way to compromise or talk through a situation. Consequently, Gilli-

gan concluded, while boys' moral reasoning is based on an *ethic of rights,* girls' moral reasoning is based on an *ethic of care.*

Evaluating Gilligan. In considering Gilligan's findings, the question arises: What is the source of the gender difference she observed? Does it reflect some basic biological difference in males and females? Or, does it reflect differences in the way boys and girls grow up in our society, learning to think and behave differently? Of course, answering these questions has provoked considerable controversy, with arguments being made in support of both positions (see, for instance, Hirsch & Keller, 1990; Kerber et al., 1986). Some critics, though, have charged that Gilligan's theory encourages gender stereotyping in that it portrays girls as more nurturing (a traditional image of femininity) and boys as more rational (a trait viewed traditionally as masculine).

Ironically, another problem with Gilligan's research was her choice of subjects. Initially, she studied White, middle-class children almost exclusively. Would the gender differences that Gilligan observed still hold true or be as pronounced if her samples included children from diverse racial, ethnic, and social class backgrounds? To answer this question, Gilligan and her colleagues (1995) studied a racially and ethnically diverse group of teenage girls from poorer backgrounds. Gilligan found support for her theory that girls see themselves relationally, regardless of race or ethnicity or social class. However, the girls' responses to relationality appear to differ by social class as well as race and ethnicity, with poor non-White girls becoming increasingly isolated, both psychologically and socially, compared with middle-class White girls (Gilligan et al., 1995).

Regardless of any weaknesses in Gilligan's work, it does highlight the importance of gender as a central variable in social science research. We cannot assume that the attitudes and behavior of one sex are generalizable to both sexes.

Erik Erikson: Identity Development across the Life Span

The final theoretical perspective on human development that we will consider is that of psychologist **Erik Erikson** (1902–1990). Erikson's work is often overlooked in sociology texts, which is unfortunate since he is one of the few major theorists who gave explicit attention to human development as a lifelong process. Erikson recognized that we continue to change and develop as individuals and as social actors during our adult years. In addition, he emphasized the importance of the interaction between biology and environment in shaping individuals' personalities. Indeed, Erikson, like Cooley and Mead, argued that our self-images develop not only from our own self

Interpret this photograph in terms of the theories of human development presented in this chapter. For instance, how might Freud have explained the baby's actions? How might Cooley and Mead have related these actions to the social construction of the self? How might Piaget have explained this baby's behavior in terms of a stage of cognitive development? Read ahead a bit and relate the section on Erik Erikson to the picture. According to Erikson, what is the first basic psychological conflict this baby will have to resolve?

perceptions, but also from the perceptions of others that are conveyed through social interaction.

Erikson outlined eight stages of human development, spanning the life course from birth through old age. At each stage, the individual must resolve a basic psychological conflict. How this conflict is resolved depends on the individual's inherent disposition, combined with her or his interactions with others and the social circumstances (such as the historical period) in which the individual is living.

Stages 1 through 4 cover the period from birth to age twelve. In stage 1 (birth to twelve to eighteen months), the individual learns to trust or distrust others. Infants depend entirely on others for their survival. If their needs are met, they learn that others are dependable and that their environment is safe. But if their needs are not met, they distrust others and find the world an unpredictable place.

In stage 2 (eighteen months to three years), the conflict centers on autonomy versus shame and doubt. Like Freud, Erikson saw toilet training as a critical identity-shaping event in a child's life. Toilet training involves learning self-control, so mastery leads to a personal sense of autonomy or independence. Difficulties during this stage, though, may result in an individual who is fearful, ashamed, and full of self-doubt.

During stage 3 (three to six years), independence should grow as children learn new skills such as how to

dress themselves, tie their shoes, and cooperate with others. Positive interactions during this stage encourage the child's initiative. Negative interactions foster dependence and a sense of guilt.

In stage 4 (six to twelve years), children take on increasingly more complex tasks such as reading, playing a sport, or in some societies, learning how to hunt or care for children. Depending on how well they meet the challenges of this stage, they develop a sense of either competence and industriousness or failure and personal inferiority.

Erikson is perhaps best known for his work with adolescents. Adolescence, said Erikson, is a time when individuals experience an "identity crisis"; that is, they are in conflict over who they are and what they want to do with their lives. The basic dilemma that Erikson proposes for stage 5, then, is identity versus role confusion. Adolescents must sort out their likes and dislikes, their political opinions, their feelings about sex and intimate relationships, and their ambitions and career goals. Although this stage is marked by rebellion for most, the adolescents who cannot adequately resolve the conflicts of this stage will remain confused and restless.

After adolescence, the individual enters young adulthood and stage 6 of Erikson's developmental model. At this point in life, intimacy becomes especially important, as individuals seek to form long-term relationships with others. Those who have difficulty with intimacy may end up socially and emotionally isolated.

In middle adulthood, stage 7, individuals strive to make their mark on the world, to make a difference in others' lives. They may do this through their relationships with their children, their careers, or their community involvement. People who have difficulty at this stage may question the meaning of their lives or experience a sense of stagnation or dullness.

Finally, in late adulthood or stage 8, individuals confront the conflict of what Erikson called *ego integrity* versus *despair*. During this stage, individuals look back over their lives, reflecting on their successes and failures. They also struggle to remain productive, contributing members of the society even though they may no longer be actively parenting or employed. As their lives come to a natural end, the way they meet these challenges determines whether they have feelings of fulfillment or personal regret. This final stage can be very difficult in our society, though, because we offer the elderly few productive roles.

Evaluating Erikson.   Erikson's theory and the other theories we have discussed are summarized in Table 5.2 on page 120. Erikson has been praised for taking the role of environment into account in his theory. At each stage, an individual's inherent personality traits influence how she or he resolves a conflict. But at the same time, there is

TABLE 5.2 Theories of Human Development

Theorist	Stages of Development (Ages)	Central Principles
Sigmund Freud (1856–1939)	oral (birth–1-1/2) anal (1-1/2–2) phallic (2–5) latency (5–12) genital (adolescence)	The essential elements of the personality are established in childhood and remain relatively stable throughout the life course. Everyone must pass through the five successive stages. During each stage, the individual must learn to balance the competing elements of the personality.
Charles Horton Cooley (1864–1929)		The development of the individual self grows out of interaction with others and derives from the individual's perceptions of how others see him or her (the looking-glass self).
George Herbert Mead (1863–1931)	imitation (birth–3) play (3–6) game (6–9)	The individual self is socially created through people's symbolic interactions with one another that allow them to anticipate each others' expectations and respond appropriately (taking the role of the other).
Jean Piaget (1892–1980)	sensorimotor (birth–2) preoperational (2–6 or 7) concrete operations (6 or 7–12) formal operations (12–adulthood)	Cognitive development takes place over four sequential stages. The emergence of every new intellectual skill depends on the development of previous skills. Early social and intellectual stimulation is essential for healthy cognitive development, but children must not be rushed through developmental stages.
Lawrence Kohlberg (1927–1987)	preconventional morality (birth–7) conventional morality (7–16) postconventional morality (adulthood)	Moral development occurs gradually over the life course as individuals acquire a sense of right and wrong, moving from an emphasis on the consequences of behavior to considering the expectations of others to considering the best interests of their community. Some individuals develop such a high level of morality that their judgments are guided by a personal rather than a societal belief system.
Carol Gilligan (b. 1936)		Morality develops differently in boys and girls. Boys' moral reasoning is based on an ethic of rights, whereas girls' moral reasoning is based on an ethic of care.
Erik Erikson (1902–1990)	1: trust versus mistrust (birth–1 or 1-1/2) 2: autonomy versus shame (1-1/2–3) 3: initiative versus guilt (3–6) 4: industry versus inferiority (6–12) 5: identity versus role confusion (adolescence) 6: intimacy versus isolation (young adulthood) 7: productivity versus stagnation (middle adulthood) 8: ego integrity versus despair (late adulthood)	Human development spans the life course from birth to old age. The life course is divided into eight stages. At each stage, the individual must resolve a basic psychological conflict.

input from others through social interaction. A teenager who is naturally easy-going, for instance, may have little difficulty resolving an identity crisis, but if her parents are divorcing while she is going through this developmental stage, the divorce will likely influence her feelings about intimate relationships.

Still, Erikson has been criticized for oversimplifying the developmental process. Although individuals at each stage may experience the conflicts Erikson highlighted, they certainly are not the only, nor even for many people, the primary focus of their lives at each stage. For example, many individuals in young adulthood postpone establishing long-term intimate relationships until they establish themselves in their careers. This does not mean that they have difficulty with intimacy or that they are socially and emotionally isolated. To the contrary, putting career first at this age may indicate a realistic attitude toward intimacy: An intimate relationship is more likely to thrive when both partners feel emotionally and financially secure.

Other critics see Erikson's portrayal of development as too rigid. In his scheme of things, the individual has either a positive or a negative outcome at each stage, but life is rarely so clear-cut. For instance, an increasing number of people in middle adulthood are assuming responsibility for the care of elderly parents. Adult caregiving may give them a sense of fulfillment in terms of making a difference in their parents' lives, but it can also be emotionally draining. In addition, the time it demands may inhibit their ability to "make their mark on the world" through their careers.

Erikson's model is valuable for its depiction of human development as a continuum of learning that occurs throughout the life cycle. However, it assumes that *all* humans experience development the same way. A complete picture of human development must consider how development experiences may vary among different types of societies as well as within a single society by sex, race and ethnicity, social class, and other social locating variables (see, for example, Mercer et al., 1989). It's possible that life stages are different for different groups of people, but more research is needed to show what, if any, life stage differences exist.

R E F L E C T I N G   O N

Explaining Our Humanity

1. Is there any way that Freud's theory could be empirically tested?
2. What is an example of how your perception of others' views of you affected your self-esteem and behavior?
3. How might young children respond if they are pushed to perform beyond their developmental level?
4. Why do you think gender may influence moral development and reasoning? What other characteristics might also make a difference?
5. How might people's responses to Erikson's psychosocial conflicts vary in relation to sex, race and ethnicity, and social class?

AGENTS OF SOCIALIZATION

The development of our social selves and our personalities is influenced by numerous factors and events that we experience over the course of our lives. Some of these are accidental. For instance, if you witness a murder or other traumatic event, it will undoubtedly have a strong effect on you, even though this influence was not intentional. However, other factors and events are quite deliberate and direct—they are intended to influence us. In every society, in fact, there are individuals, groups, and institutions that have as one of their primary functions the socialization of new members of the society by providing explicit instruction in or modeling (demonstrating) of social expectations. Sociologists call these individuals, groups, and institutions **agents of socialization.** In our society, and others like ours, the major agents of socialization are families, schools, peer groups, and the mass media. Let's look at each of these in detail and then at several other institutions that may also have a profound effect on our development.

Families

The family is our first social world. Infants and very young children depend entirely on the family for their emotional ties and their first exposure to their society's language and culture. Not surprisingly, then, sociologists consider families one of the most important—if not *the* most important—agents of socialization.

Much of the socialization that takes place in families is deliberate. Most parents, for example, try to teach their children "right" from "wrong," by using rewards and punishments. There is, however, an old adage that says, "Children learn what they live." In other words, children absorb what they observe in their immediate environment, incorporating it into their own repertoire of attitudes and behaviors. As a result, family members may unintentionally pass on numerous prejudices to their children. For instance, children who see only their mothers cooking dinner and only their fathers driving when the family goes out together may come to believe that it is inappropriate or "wrong" for men to cook or for women to drive if a man is present.

Several factors can affect the process—and content—of socialization in the family. The key factors are social class, religion, race and ethnicity, and family structure. The family provides the child with his or her social location for a substantial part, if not for all, of his or her life. Studies indicate that the way parents socialize children and what they teach them differs across social classes and racial and ethnic groups. For example, by virtue of their greater income, affluent parents can provide their children with more books, toys, and other resources, such as computers, that enrich the early learning environment. In addition, parents' views of appropriate child rearing techniques may vary by social class.

The classic research on this topic was conducted in the 1960s and 1970s by Melvin Kohn (1965, 1976, 1977). Kohn found that middle-class and working-class parents tend to rear their children differently. Middle-class parents in Kohn's studies tended to allow their children considerable freedom in decision making and encouraged their curiosity and initiative. They usually punished their children's transgressions by withholding privileges. Working-class parents, Kohn found, more often emphasized conformity to rules and respect for authority. These parents were more likely to use physical punishment to discipline their children. Kohn explained his findings in terms of the different kinds of jobs the parents usually hold. Middle-class parents tended to work at jobs that afforded them personal autonomy, opportunities for creativity, and decision-making power. In contrast, the jobs of working-class parents often involved rote performance of tasks that were overseen by a supervisor. Kohn thus concluded that parents socialize their children for life in the world as they know it. Middle-class parents taught their children to be independent, while working-class parents taught their children to respect authority.

Religion, however, appears to be an intervening variable that affects socialization practices. Researchers have found that the more conservative parents are in their religious beliefs, the more authoritarian they are in their childrearing practices. Authoritarian parents, for example, are more likely than other parents to emphasize child obedience, to favor strict discipline, and to approve of corporal punishment. They are also more likely to use corporal punishment to discipline their children (Ellison, et al., 1996; Ellison & Sherkat, 1993). Nevertheless, researchers warn that corporal punishment, even if imposed by warm, supportive parents, may eventually have the opposite effect of what parents desire. Recent studies show that the more children are spanked, the more likely they are to engage in antisocial behavior, such as cheating or lying, bullying or being mean to others, and disobeying teachers (Straus & Sugarman, 1997).

The Intersecting Inequalities box discusses how race and ethnicity as well as social class may influence how girls and boys are socialized. How we learn what is expected of us as males and females—that is, how we learn masculinity and femininity—occurs through a process called **gender socialization**. Traditionally, most studies of gender socialization in early childhood have only included participants from White, middle- and upper-middle class two-parent families. But the socialization practices of these families may not be representative of the practices of families from other races, ethnic backgrounds, and social classes (Mirandé, 1990).

Another factor that may shape socialization is the structure of the family itself. There are many different types of families in the United States today. As divorce rates have risen, so too have the number of single-parent families, especially those headed by women. Research indicates that the absence of a father may negatively affect

socialization, especially for boys. Most researchers, however, are quick to point out that there are detrimental socialization effects on children in families where parents are constantly arguing (Barber & Eccles, 1992; Hetherington, Stanley-Hagan, & Anderson, 1989; Wallerstein & Blakeslee, 1989). An increasing number of gay and lesbian couples are also choosing to have or adopt children and, importantly, research consistently shows that children raised by gay and lesbian parents are no more likely to experience psychological difficulties, such as confusion about their gender, than children raised by heterosexual parents (Golombok & Fivush, 1994; Mason et al., 1988; Patterson, 1992).

Schools

Children go to school specifically to be socialized—that is, to be taught the skills and information that will allow them to be productive, contributing adult members of the society. They learn to read, for example, and how to do math. They also learn values, such as the importance of cooperating with others, being on time, and following directions. Besides the formal curriculum that is taught in school, children also learn values through what sociologists call the **hidden curriculum**. The hidden curriculum refers to values children are implicitly taught in school. So, for instance, every time teachers ask girls in the class to water the plants or clean the chalkboard, but ask boys to rearrange the desks or operate a piece of audiovisual equipment, they are providing implicit gender socialization messages which, research shows, children learn quite well (Best, 1983; Sadker & Sadker, 1994; Thorne, 1993). If children are taught little or nothing about the work and achievements of racial and ethnic minorities, they receive the implicit message that members of these groups have done little worth knowing about.

Ideally, schools are supposed to expose children to social diversity. Recent studies show, however, that although racial and ethnic minority populations in the United States are increasing, our nation's schools appear to be growing less rather than more diverse. For example, in 1996, one-third of Black public school students attended schools where the enrollment is 90 to 100 percent Black (Keenen, 1996). If schools are racially and ethnically segregated, they cannot provide children with adequate exposure to diversity; yet students need to understand diverse groups to be prepared for life in our multicultural society.

At the same time, schools are supposed to reward students on the basis of merit. However, despite the ideological emphasis on rewarding individual achievement in school, research indicates that our nation's schools routinely stratify students into different ability groups based

How Do Race and Class Affect Gender Socialization?

Sociologist Janice Hale-Benson (1986) has studied the socialization goals and practices of African American families. She reports that in socializing both female and male children, African American parents stress heavily the importance of hard work, ambition, and achievement. Thus, African American children of both sexes learn to be more independent and self-reliant than their White peers. They also learn at an early age to take financial responsibility by being encouraged to earn money for themselves and their families. African American children of both sexes are also taught racial pride and strategies for responding to and overcoming racism (Poussaint & Comer, 1993).

Still, the socialization of African American boys and girls is not identical. Hale-Benson found, for example, that among the behaviors and skills taught to African American boys (largely in the context of their peer group) are the ways to move their bodies distinctively, athletic prowess, sexual competence, and street savvy, including how to fight. In contrast, preparing for motherhood is a priority in the socialization of Afri-

can American girls, although there is also an expectation that girls will grow up to work outside the home too. The development of personal uniqueness or distinctiveness is also emphasized for African American girls, with special attention given to sexuality, clothing, and body movement (see also McAdoo, 1988).

Given Hale-Benson's findings, it is not surprising that other researchers report that African American children hold fewer gender stereotypes than White children (Bardwell et al., 1986). Significantly, Isaaks (1980) reached the same conclusion about Hispanic American children after comparing them with a group of White peers. However, there is some research that shows opposite findings—that there is as much and sometimes more gender stereotyping in African American and Hispanic American households than in White households (Bronstein, 1988; Gonzalez, 1982; Price-Bonham & Skeen, 1982).

The picture becomes even less focused when social class is considered. For example, a number of studies have

shown that gender stereotyping decreases the higher a family's social class is (Burns & Homel, 1989; Lackey, 1989). However, researchers who have used parents' education as an indicator of a family's social class have found that, at least among White families, gender stereotyping is greater the higher a family's social class position (Bardwell et al., 1986). Unfortunately, most studies of African American and Hispanic American gender socialization practices recruit middle-class families as research participants (Bronstein, 1988; McAdoo, 1988). What is perhaps most needed is research that examines the combined effects of social class and race and ethnicity on socialization practices. One study that did look at the interaction of social class with race and ethnicity showed that the latter is the more important variable; that is, race and ethnicity have a stronger influence on childrearing practices than social class does (Hale-Benson, 1986). Hopefully, future research will explore these interrelationships further.

on their performance on tests that are culturally biased. Within these groups, students are exposed to different kinds of knowledge. Students in high-ability groups are taught subjects such as analytic geometry and are encouraged to think critically and creatively. Students in low-ability groups may be taught how to fill out forms, figure sales tax, and follow directions (Oakes, 1985). Reflecting on these differential socialization experiences, one researcher asks, "In essence, are we teaching kids at the bottom how to stay there and kids at the top how to get ahead?" (Oakes, 1985, p. 91).

Peer Groups

Throughout our lives, we spend a good deal of our time, particularly our social or leisure time, in the company of **peers**, that is, individuals who are about the same age and

who share our social position and interests. In childhood, our peers are playmates from our neighborhoods or child care centers. When we go to school, our peer group may widen; typically, its influence on our behavior becomes stronger at that time. The socializing influence of peers, in fact, is so strong, especially in adolescence, that at least one researcher has recently argued that peers are significantly more important than parents in socializing children (Harris, 1998). As we noted in our discussion of Erikson's developmental stages, preteens and teenagers struggle to establish greater independence from their parents and other adults and to craft an identity of their own. Peer groups provide a context for trying out new ideas, interests, ways of appearing, and even behaviors (Adler & Adler, 1998). For example, on a recent visit to a barber shop to have our sons' hair cut, we watched three teenage boys who were obviously close friends have their

Identify all the agents of socialization represented in these photos. What unique contribution does each type of agent make to an individual's socialization? What knowledge and skills do individuals learn from each type of agent? If you could add two more pictures to the set, what would they show?

heads shaved except for a small patch of hair around the crown.

Peer groups socialize through subtle and sometimes explicit pressure to conform to their standards of "rightness." Subtle pressure may take the form of simply excluding a nonconforming peer from group activities. More direct pressure often takes the form of dares, name-calling, or even threats if a peer does not conform to the group. For preadolescents and adolescents, who at this time in their lives are preoccupied with being autonomous from their families and anxious about "fitting in" or being accepted by others like themselves, this pressure can be difficult to resist (Adler & Adler, 1998). No wonder,

then, that parents express so much concern about their children's friends.

Although research shows that parents are highly influential agents of socialization in their children's lives—and public opinion polls indicate that most children greatly admire their parents (Farkas & Johnson, 1997)—studies also show quite clearly that peers, particularly during preadolescence and adolescence, can strongly influence a child's aspirations and behavior (Adler & Adler, 1998; Harris, 1998). This influence includes children's choice to engage in disapproved or even criminal behavior (Cernkovich & Giordano, 1987; Sebald, 1992). Researchers have found, for example, that young men who sexually assault women on college campuses (what is often called *acquaintance rape*) do so at least in part because they have been socialized by their male peers to see this behavior as acceptable (Schwartz & DeKeseredy, 1997).

Peer influence does not end with adolescence. As adults, too, our ideas, interests, behavior, and appearance are affected by the opinions and behavior of our friends or peers. Moreover, we may be influenced not only by the peer group to which we belong, but also by one to which we *aspire* to belong. For instance, a couple who wishes to be accepted into the social elite may buy a house in a particular neighborhood, drive a certain kind of car, send their children to a specific private school, and join a particular country club, in order to be welcomed as one of that "in-crowd." When we engage in this type of behavior, sociologists refer to it as **anticipatory socialization:** learning and adopting the behavior patterns and social traits of a group that we wish to join.

The Mass Media

The **mass media**—the means by which information is communicated to a large, sometimes global, audience—are a hallmark of modern societies. The media, though, are also often criticized for bias and inaccuracies, for reinforcing stereotypical thinking, and for promoting violence and other forms of undesirable behavior.

The mass media include newspapers, radio, and films, but it is television that draws the attention as a socializing agent. Television is a pervasive part of modern life. In the United States alone, 98.3 percent of households have television sets (about 4 percent more than have telephone service). Eighty-one percent have videocassette recorders (compared with just 1 percent in 1980), and about 63 percent subscribe to cable television (compared with only about 20 percent in 1980) (U.S. Department of Commerce, Bureau of the Census, 1997).

Television is a potent agent of socialization. It is free, it is available to just about everyone, and it does not even require that viewers leave the privacy of their homes, as movies and theater do. Watching television requires no special skills, such as literacy. And television broadcasts the same pictures and words into people's homes regardless of viewers' sex, race, age, social class, sexual orientation, and often geographic location. Importantly, however, factors such as viewers' sex, race, age, social class, sexual orientation, and geographic location influence how they interpret or relate to program content (Comstock, 1991; Gross, 1991; Press, 1991).

On any given day, the average American spends one-third of his or her leisure time watching television. Only about 7 percent of leisure time is spent socializing with other people, 6 percent reading, and about 2 percent in outdoor activities ("At Leisure," 1993). Average household consumption of television is fifty-five hours per week, with women watching more than men and adults watching more than children (Comstock, 1991). About 25 percent of children's leisure time each week is spent watching television, which represents a slight decline since 1981 (Hofferth & Sandberg, 1998).

Critics of television programming argue that it is biased and inaccurate in its portrayals of many groups, often reinforcing social stereotypes. A **stereotype** is an oversimplified summary description, usually negative, of a particular group. For example, women on television are usually depicted as being preoccupied with romantic relationships. While male characters tend to talk more about work, female characters talk more about romance. Women on television are more likely than men to use sex or romantic charm to get what they want, and they are more likely to cry and whine. Men, in contrast are more likely than women to use physical force (Condry, 1989; Fejes, 1992; Signorielli, 1997). Racial and ethnic stereotyping is also prevalent on television (Bianco, 1999; DeMott, 1996; Sterngold, 1998).

Even if media portrayals are sometimes inaccurate or stereotyped, defenders of television argue that television has little impact on people's real-life behavior and ways of thinking. "That only happens on television," they say. "People don't really believe that stuff." The evidence, though, shows that some people do believe that stuff. For instance, heavy television viewers tend to judge programs as more realistic than light viewers do (Wright et al., 1995; see also Comstock, 1991; Geis et al., 1984; Lanis & Covell, 1995). Studies investigating the influence of violent programming on people's behavior give cause for special concern. Although people rarely imitate exactly what they see on television, violent programming socializes viewers to accept violence in real life. People become desensitized to violence and its effects (Bok, 1998; Mifflin, 1998; Vivian, 1993; Walewski, 1999). Research on the effects of violent films has arrived at similar conclusions. For example, social psychologists Edward Donnerstein and Daniel Linz have found that men who view violent pornography on a regular basis are more likely than other men to condone violence against women and express a personal willingness to rape a woman (see also Krafka et al., 1996).

At the same time, however, television can have a positive influence on people's behavior. For instance, Geis and her colleagues (1984) found that female students who had watched commercials portraying women in nontraditional roles were more likely to describe their own futures in nonstereotyped ways than women who watched commercials with stereotyped female models. In other words, the content of the commercials seems to affect viewers' real-life aspirations. Additional research indicates that when the media, and television in particular, provide "pro-social" content, they can effectively reduce many forms of prejudice. The positive effects of pro-social media content appear to be stronger for young children (Corday, 1989; Mares, 1996). In short, it appears that for better or for worse, television is a powerful agent of socialization.

Other Socialization Agents

The family, school, peer group, and media are the four major agents of socialization that influence our lives, but there are others. For example, there are agents of socialization that are charged with the task of systematically stripping the individual of much of what she or he has learned in the past, replacing it with drastically different norms, values, behaviors, and attitudes. This kind of socialization is called **resocialization**, and it takes place in what is called a **total institution** (Goffman, 1961). A total institution is a place where individuals live, usually for a specific period of time, isolated from the rest of society and under the near-total control of officials charged with resocializing them. Total institutions include prisons, mental hospitals, army boot camps, and cloistered monasteries and convents.

The first step in resocialization is to strip away a person's established sense of self. To do this, a new resident's personal possessions are usually taken away as soon as they enter. Clothing, for instance, is replaced by an institutionally issued uniform so that all residents look the same. They may even be required to have their hair cut the same. Total institutions also have strict rules for behavior. Silence may be required during certain times or in certain places, and telephone calls or watching television may be either prohibited or permitted only during specific hours, and with monitoring. Some items or behaviors may be banned completely. For instance, on a recent visit to a retreat center of a cloistered order of nuns, one of your authors observed that mirrors were not permitted in individual rooms. In total institutions, rule violations are usually treated harshly. The few privileges a resident has may be taken away. Even worse, the rule violator may be placed in solitary confinement or subjected to physical punishment, such as a twenty-five-mile hike in the bitter cold or scorching heat.

People who undergo resocialization in a total institution are usually profoundly affected by it. The goal of resocialization is to replace a person's established self with a new self. However, specific outcomes depend to some extent on an individual's personality and background. For some, the experience may be quite positive, leading to rehabilitation, recovery, or personal and spiritual growth. For others, though, the experience may be permanently debilitating, leading to problems such as depression, an inability to express emotion, and violent outbursts (Irwin, 1980).

R EFLECTING ON

Agents of Socialization

1. Why is the family such an important socialization agent?
2. How do families, schools, and peers compete as socialization agents?
3. Is the socializing influence of television and other mass media getting stronger or weaker? Do you see this influence as positive or negative? Why?
4. How might you describe what a resocialization experience in a total institution would be like?
5. What other agents of socialization not discussed in this chapter have had an influence on your life?

SOCIALIZATION AS LIFELONG LEARNING

Resocialization is one way that socialization occurs in adulthood, but hardly the most common way. In fact, socialization is a constant in our lives, although the content and goals of the socialization vary depending on our stage of the life course. (You might want to review Table 5.1, which identifies the major life stages.) Since we have already spent considerable time discussing childhood socialization and adolescence, let's turn now to some common adult socialization experiences.

Adulthood

Table 5.1 divides adulthood into three stages: young adulthood, middle adulthood, and late adulthood. In a modern industrial society, *young adulthood* roughly spans ages twenty to about forty. A good deal of anticipatory socialization occurs in young adulthood, as we set out to pursue a career or to establish a long-term intimate relationship and perhaps start our own families. Young adulthood is a time when most people obtain their first "real" job, so work tasks must be learned. At the same time, every workplace has a "work culture," that is, informal rules about how employees are supposed to dress and interact with one another. A casual work culture may include, for instance, wearing jeans to work, celebrating coworkers' birthdays, or addressing one another by first names only.

Today, women and men are delaying marriage and childbearing longer than in the past, and some are choos-

DOING SOCIOLOGY

Learning about Reverse Socialization

Among families who emigrate to the United States from countries where the language and customs are different from ours, it is often the case that the children adjust to the new culture more quickly than their parents. Immigrant parents usually spend long hours working at jobs in the hope that they will improve the family's standard of living. They have little time to attend English classes. The cost of the classes also often puts them out of reach for many adult immigrants. Their children, however, enroll in public schools that expose them not only to the English language, but also to many of the routines of daily life in their new country (filling out forms, paying bills, even recycling paper and cans) (Zhou, 1998). As children absorb the new culture, traditional family relationships may be reversed, with parents becoming increasingly dependent on their children for the translation of the strange and unfamiliar.

This reverse socialization is often crucial to the survival of immigrant families, and many children are proud of being able to help their parents adjust to life in the United States. Nevertheless, reverse socialization can also be a source of strain for family members. Adults, for example, may feel they are losing parental control over their children, damaging their self-esteem as well as family harmony. The burden of helping parents with important tasks—and the fear of making a mistake with serious physical or financial consequences—can cause severe anxiety for youngsters (Alvarez, 1995).

Are there students in your class or peer group who are members of immigrant families and have experienced reverse socialization? If so, ask to interview them, focusing particularly on their relationship with their parents during the period of adaptation to their new country. What were the positive and negative aspects of their reverse socialization experiences? How did they cope with problems that arose? Did they receive any help from other sources, such as community groups or their teachers? What kinds of help do they think would be most useful for new immigrant families going through reverse socialization?

---

ing to forgo one or both of these possibilities altogether. But most women and men do usually marry and have at least one child during young adulthood. Furthermore, most married women who have children work outside the home. This means that for most people, young adulthood is a time of learning about an intimate partner's expectations of a permanent relationship and how to balance them with one's personal expectations. It is also a time of learning how to care for children and, especially for women, how to balance the conflicting demands of work and family.

Career goals or personal aspirations for a better life may require moving to another city or town, or even another country. Immigration to a foreign land entails much new learning, including language, customs, and laws. Some of this learning may involve a reversal of roles between parents and children, with children socializing their parents instead of the other way around (Alvarez, 1995; Zhou, 1998). The process by which children transmit culture to their elders is called **reverse socialization** (see the Doing Sociology box above). Another frequent instance of reverse socialization is when the young teach their elders how to use computers and video games (Verhovek, 1998).

Ages forty to sixty-five, roughly, constitute *middle adulthood*. This is frequently a time of personal assessment. One may take stock of intimate relationships and career, although this process may be different for women and men. Men, who traditionally have been socialized to derive self-esteem primarily from their jobs, may or may not be pleased with how far they've progressed in their chosen line of work. In this age of "downsizing" or "right-sizing" by many companies, some men may find themselves out of work in their middle adult years, having to learn how to cope not only with a significant loss of income, but also with the loss of a central component of their personal identities. Some may also have to learn new job skills to become reemployed. Men at this point in their lives also reexamine their family relationships, considering with satisfaction or regret how their relationships with their intimate partners and their children have developed over the years. If they feel they put too much time into work and not enough into family, they may have to learn ways of reestablishing closeness with their partners and children. Or if their intimate relationships have dissolved through divorce, they may have to learn how to live alone again and what the cultural expectations are about dating.

Women may confront similar dilemmas in assessing their lives in middle adulthood, particularly if they are divorced or laid-off from work, or if they feel they sacrificed family life for a career. Some women, though, may find middle adulthood a time to embark on new ventures, such as returning to school or pursuing a new career. They will have to learn the role of student or employee as the case may be. In addition, because of increases in life expectancy, many women in middle adulthood are caring for elderly parents. These women must

Does socialization stop once a person reaches adulthood? What are some examples of resocialization that might occur across a person's life span? How does this picture reflect the lifelong learning theme of this section of text? What role has this couple probably played in the socialization of others?

learn how to balance their caregiving responsibilities with other demands in their lives. They must also learn how to interact with the elderly as roles reverse and they "parent their parents."

From age sixty-five on, the stage of life is known as *late adulthood*. The aging process inevitably brings about some decline in physical prowess, so people in late adulthood must learn how to meet their everyday needs despite some physical limitations. They may also have to learn how to live alone if their partner dies, or how to live in a group setting should they move to a retirement community or nursing facility.

Most healthy women and men in late adulthood lead active and productive lives. The difficulties they confront in doing so often derive less from their own limitations than from the obstacles imposed by our youth-oriented society. The elderly in many non-Western, nonindustrialized societies are revered for the wisdom they have accumulated from their life experience. In contrast, in a society like ours, which emphasizes modernity and self-sufficiency, old people are negatively stereotyped as inflexible and dependent, and their ideas are deemed old-fashioned and obsolete.

For women and men in late adulthood, then, a major challenge is learning new social roles following retirement that they find meaningful and satisfying. In nonin-

dustrialized societies, young people are socialized by the elderly; the culture of the society is passed on, often by word of mouth, from the old to the young. In our society, we are just beginning to understand the value of intergenerational contacts to both old and young. This will perhaps grow in importance as the percentage of the population in late adulthood increases, rising from about 13 percent now to 22 percent by 2030 (Taeuber, 1992).

Death: Closure of the Life Course

Although death may occur at any stage of the life course, in modern industrial societies it is most likely to occur in old age. But despite our lifelong socialization experiences, we learn little in our society to prepare us for death.

In nonindustrial societies and until relatively recently in industrial ones, death usually took place at home with family and friends present. People of all ages witnessed death, and although they did not necessarily welcome it, perhaps they accepted it more readily than we do today. In our contemporary society, we sanitize death as much as possible; we do not discuss it openly and we do not want to expose children to it. But in wishing to avoid death, we often isolate the dying. The vast majority of people today die in hospitals and nursing homes with little preparation for the dying process.

Fortunately, researchers have begun to focus on the social and psychological dimensions of dying. This new area of study, called **thanatology,** examines death and dying from many perspectives, including sociology, psychology, law, and religious studies. One pioneering thanatologist is Elizabeth Kübler-Ross, whose interviews with dying people led her to develop a theory of how people deal with impending death.

According to Kübler-Ross (1969), terminally ill people go through five stages. First, there is *denial* ("There must be some mistake in the test results."). Next, they experience *anger* ("Why me?"). Third, they try to *bargain* ("God, if you give me a second chance, I'll lead a better life."). The fourth stage is *depression* ("I'm causing everyone a lot of trouble, and for what? I'll be dead soon anyway."). Finally, though, they develop *acceptance;* realizing that death is near, they do what they can to use whatever time that remains in a positive way and to gain peace of mind ("I must tell everyone in my family how much I love them and appreciate what they have done for me.").

Kübler-Ross's perspective has been criticized by other researchers, who say that not all dying people go through the stages she identified and that some experience these stages in a different order (see, for example, Schaie & Willis, 1986; and Stephenson, 1985). Nevertheless, Kübler-Ross and other thanatologists are providing us with anticipatory socialization toward death. We can see the influence of their work in the hospice movement. Hospices tend to the physical, social, psychological, and spiritual needs of the terminally ill and their families, either in special facilities or in the dying person's home. Essentially, while receiving hospice care, the dying person and her or his family are socialized about death (Christakis & Escarce, 1996). Thanatologists are now studying not only the dying, but also those who grieve for them. They are finding that, following the death of a loved one, survivors who emerge from their grief with a newfound respect for life and a commitment to live every day to the fullest experience a boost to their physical and emotional health not enjoyed by survivors who see death only as a negative aspect of life or who simply accepted their loved one's death and moved on (Bower et al., 1998).

Thus, in socializing us to see death as another challenge of the life course, thanatologists are helping us prepare for the closure of life—our own and that of those close to us.

R E F L E C T I N G   O N

Socialization as Lifelong Learning

1. What are the most important socialization agents in young adulthood?
2. What factors might influence whether an individual makes a positive life assessment in middle adulthood?
3. What social tasks or roles are well suited to the elderly? How might society promote these tasks or roles to give people in late adulthood more opportunities to contribute to their families and communities?
4. What might explain why death is such a taboo subject in this society?

For useful resources for study and review, run Chapter 5 on your *Living Sociology* CD-ROM.

C O N N E C T I O N S

George Herbert Mead	Review the information about Mead in Chapter 1 in the section that introduces symbolic interactionism. Why is this theoretical perspective especially suited to the sociological study of socialization across the life span?
Development of self-concept	Chapter 16 presents "The Symbolic Interactionist Perspective on Education," which emphasizes the influence of educational experiences on the development of self-concept. How does the concept of a self-fulfilling prophecy apply in this case?
Effects of labeling	The symbolic interactionist perspective also emphasizes the effects of labeling on children's self-image, performance, and life chances. How does the information on labeling theory in Chapter 7 relate to the context of socialization?
Gender socialization	Read the sections on gender socialization in Chapter 10, which includes the family, peers, and schools as agents of gender socialization. Which of these has the greatest effect on children's development?
Stereotyping	The section on "The Media" in Chapter 10 expands on the phenomenon of gender stereotyping. What exactly is a stereotype? What examples of age stereotyping can you find in Chapter 12?
Aging	Chapter 12 discusses aging as a social and cultural construction that is part of a lifelong socialization process. What specific examples of this process can you identify?
Family as an agent of socialization	Chapter 15 discusses the role of socialization in the gendered division of labor in families with children. What diverse socialization experiences can you identify in the section on "Racial and Ethnic Diversity in U.S. Families"?

CONNECTIONS

School as an agent of socialization	Chapter 16 presents "The Functionalist Perspective on Education," which emphasizes socialization and the direct and indirect transmission of culture. How are learners socialized through a hidden curriculum? What do children learn through practices such as ability grouping?
Total institutions	See the section on "The Criminal Justice System" in Chapter 7. What example of a total institution can you find? What might be some characteristics of the resocialization that occurs in that setting?

SUMMING UP CHAPTER 5

The Interaction of Biology and Environment

1. Findings from studies of identical twins reared apart indicate that genetics plays a critical role in laying the foundation of individual human potential, but the extent to which this potential is realized depends on environmental factors.
2. Animal studies and research with isolated children show that humans are born with many abilities and emotions, but without a minimum of early stimulation, these abilities and emotions stagnate.

Explaining Our Humanity

1. Sigmund Freud maintained that the human personality has three interrelated parts (the id, the ego, and the superego), which an individual must learn to keep in balance. The personality is established in childhood, as the individual passes through five successive stages of development: the oral stage, the anal stage, the phallic stage, the latency stage, and the genital stage. Once established, the personality remains stable over the life course. Freud's theory has been criticized because it is empirically untestable, too rigid in its view of the personality being unchangeable after childhood, and antifemale.
2. Charles Horton Cooley believed that the self develops and changes over time through people's interactions with one another as they interpret how others see them (the looking-glass self). To this, George Herbert Mead added an analysis of how individuals see the world and themselves from the points of view of others: by taking the role of the other. The self, therefore, is socially created and develops over time, but most especially in childhood during three stages: imitation, the play stage, and the game stage. The self is composed of two parts—the "I" and the "me"—that are in continuous reaction to one another. Critics argue that neither Cooley nor Mead considered how membership in various groups might influence the development of the self, and that Mead did not consider whether members of different groups pass through the stages the same way.

3. Jean Piaget focused on how children learn to think. He believed that cognitive development occurs over time and in four sequential stages: the sensorimotor stage, the preoperational stage, the concrete operations stage, and the formal operations stage. Piaget recognized the importance of social and intellectual stimulation for healthy cognitive development in children, but warned against pushing children into activities beyond their developmental level. Piaget has been criticized for underestimating the cognitive abilities of young children and for downplaying the role of environment in cognitive development.
4. Lawrence Kohlberg studied moral development. His research suggested three levels of moral development: preconventional morality, conventional morality, and postconventional morality. However, Kohlberg has been criticized for not studying moral judgments in realistic situations and for using only male subjects. Carol Gilligan replicated Kohlberg's research to specifically examine gender as a factor in moral development. Gilligan found that boys' moral development is based on an ethic of rights, while girls' moral reasoning is based on an ethic of care. Gilligan has been criticized for encouraging gender stereotypes and for only studying White, middle-class children.
5. Eric Erikson saw human development as a lifelong process. He proposed that people pass through eight stages of development, spanning the life course from birth to death. At each stage, the individual must resolve a basic psychological conflict. While Erikson has been praised for taking the role of environment into account, he has been criticized for oversimplifying the developmental process and for portraying development too rigidly.

Agents of Socialization

1. Individuals, groups, and institutions that have as one of their primary functions the socialization of new members of the society are called agents of socialization. The major agents of socialization in our society are: families, schools, peer groups, and the mass media.

2. Families are the most important agents of socialization. They socialize children in both direct and indirect ways. The process and content of socialization in the family varies by social class, race and ethnicity, and family structure.

3. The purpose of schools is to teach children the skills and information they need to be productive, contributing members of the society. Schools do this through the values and subjects taught deliberately and through the hidden curriculum. Although schools are supposed to expose students to cultural diversity and reward them on the basis of merit, there is evidence that calls into question how well schools achieve each of these goals.

4. Peers (individuals who are about the same age and who share social positions and interests) socialize through subtle and sometimes explicit pressure to conform to their standards of rightness. Peer socialization is especially strong in adolescence, when peer groups provide a context for trying out new ideas, interests, ways of appearing, and behaviors. But peer influence remains strong in adulthood.

5. The mass media are also agents of socialization, but television is the most powerful media socializer. Critics of television are concerned with television's often biased and stereotyped portrayals of many groups. Research suggests that frequent television viewers may internalize these attitudes and images. At the same time, however, nonstereotyped television images can have a positive influence on people.

6. A total institution is a place where individuals live, usually for a specific period of time, isolated from the rest of society and under the near-total control of officials charged with resocializing them. The goal of resocialization is to systematically strip an individual of his or her established self and replace it with a new self.

Socialization as Lifelong Learning

1. Socialization is a constant in our lives, but the content and goals of socialization vary depending on our stage of the life course. Much of the socialization that takes place in young adulthood is anticipatory socialization to prepare an individual for work and family roles. Middle adulthood is usually a period of personal assessment, but individuals may also embark on new ventures during this period. The major challenge of late adulthood is learning new social roles that are meaningful and satisfying following retirement.

2. Despite our lifelong socialization experiences, we receive little socialization to prepare us for death. The new area of study, thanatology, is currently trying to develop knowledge to help people deal with impending death. The work of Elizabeth Kübler-Ross is among the best known, and, despite criticisms, has had a significant influence on the hospice movement.

KEY PEOPLE AND CONCEPTS

accommodation: in Piaget's theory, the mental strategy by which we use a new piece of information or an experience to change or adapt an idea or behavior in our existing repertoire

agents of socialization: individuals, groups, and institutions that have as one of their primary functions the socialization of new members of the society by providing them with explicit instruction in or modeling of social expectations

anal stage: in Freud's theory, the second stage of personality development during which the focus of satisfaction as well as frustration centers on the child learning to control bodily functions

anticipatory socialization: learning and adopting the behavior patterns and social traits of a group one wishes to join

assimilation: in Piaget's theory, the mental strategy by which we incorporate a piece of new information into our existing repertoire of thoughts and behaviors and then use it later in situations we identify as similar or appropriate

concrete operations stage: the second stage of cognitive development in Piaget's theory, during which children learn more complex rules of behavior and the reasons underlying them; develop the ability to see and evaluate

a situation from a number of different viewpoints; and are able to anticipate events and other people's behavior

conservation: in Piaget's theory, the understanding that an object may change in appearance, but remain the same weight, substance, or volume

conventional morality: the second level of moral development in Kohlberg's theory, during which a behavior is evaluated not only in terms of its consequences, but also in terms of whether it will please others whose opinions are important to the actor

Cooley, Charles Horton (1864–1929): the social theorist who postulated that the development of the individual self grows out of our interactions with others and our perceptions of how others see us

ego: in Freud's theory, the element of the personality that operates on the reality principle, trying to satisfy the needs of the id in socially acceptable ways

Erikson, Erik (1902–1990): the psychologist who proposed a theory of human development as a lifelong process divided into eight stages, during each of which the individual struggles to resolve a basic psychological conflict

formal operations stage: the final stage of cognitive development in Piaget's theory, when children can think abstractly and use deductive logic and during which time children can engage in hypothetical or future-oriented thinking

Freud, Sigmund (1856–1939): the psychologist who developed a psychosocial theory of human development that focuses on the struggles between three interrelated components of the personality

game stage: the third stage of socialization in Mead's theory, during which children internalize the values and expectations of the larger society and come to understand the complex interrelationship of roles in the social network

gender identification: in Freud's theory of personality development, when children adopt the behavior and attributes of their same-sex parent

gender socialization: teaching individuals what is expected of them as males and females; teaching masculinity and femininity

generalized other: in Mead's theory, the values and expectations of the larger society

genital stage: in Freud's theory, the final stage in personality development, when children enter adolescence and become increasingly independent of their parents and learn to develop mature social and sexual relationships with members of the opposite sex

Gilligan, Carol: psychologist who critiqued and elaborated on Kohlberg's theory of moral development by replicating his research using female research subjects and thereby showing gender differences in moral reasoning

hidden curriculum: the value preferences that children are implicitly taught in school

I: in Mead's theory, the spontaneous, free-willed dimension of the self

id: in Freud's theory, the unconscious element of the personality, composed of powerful forces called *drives* and *wishes*

imitation stage: the first stage of socialization in Mead's theory, during which children begin to imitate or mimic the people with whom they interact most

Kohlberg, Lawrence (1927–1987): the social psychologist whose work focused on how children develop a sense of morality and engage in moral reasoning

latency stage: in Freud's theory, the period from five to twelve years of age, during which sexual impulses become dormant

looking-glass self: Cooley's notion that we derive our self-concepts from our perceptions of how others see us

mass media: the impersonal means by which information is communicated to a large audience

Me: in Mead's theory, the dimension of the self formed by the stable, internalized values and norms of one's community

Mead, George Herbert (1863–1931): the social theorist who focused on how language, gestures, and other symbolic systems of communication allow for the development of the individual and make social order possible

object permanence: in Piaget's theory, the ability to understand that when a person or object is out of sight, it still exists

oral stage: in Freud's theory, the first stage of personality development during which the mouth, tongue, and lips are the areas of gratification and desire

particular other: in Mead's theory, the perspectives of people who are significant in the child's environment

peers: those individuals who are about the same age, share the same social position in the status hierarchy, and have similar interests

personality: a set of behavioral and emotional characteristics that describe a person's reactions to various situations or events in the environment

phallic stage: in Freud's theory, the third stage of personality development during which gender identification takes place

Piaget, Jean (1892–1980): the social psychologist who focused his life's work on examining how children think and interpret the world around them

play stage: the second stage of socialization in Mead's theory, during which children distinguish a variety of social roles and spend time in play that involves role taking

postconventional morality: the highest level of moral development in Kohlberg's theory, during which people evaluate behavior in terms of whether they consider it to be in the best interests of their community or their society

preconventional morality: the first stage of moral development in Kohlberg's theory, during which behavior is evaluated in terms of whether it will be punished or rewarded

preoperational stage: the second developmental stage in Piaget's theory, during which the child builds on language and reasoning skills and learns to represent the world symbolically

resocialization: the systematic stripping of an individual of much of what she or he learned in the past and replacing it with drastically different norms, values, behaviors, and attitudes

reverse socialization: the process by which aspects of a culture are transmitted from the young to their elders

sensorimotor stage: the first (and most important) developmental stage in Piaget's theory, during which time the child begins to interact socially and develops object permanence

socialization: the process by which a society's culture is taught and learned and human personalities are developed

stereotype: an oversimplified summary description, usually negative in nature, of a particular group

superego: in Freud's theory, the element of the personality that represents the internalization of the values and norms of the society; also called the *conscience*

taking the role of the other: Mead's concept of the ability of all members of the social group to visualize the world and themselves from the points of view of one another

thanatology: the interdisciplinary study of death and dying

total institution: a place where individuals live for a specific period of time, isolated from the rest of society and under the near-total control of a group of officials charged, in part, with resocializing them

LEARNING MORE

Adler, P. A., & Adler, P. (1998). *Peer power: Preadolescent culture and identity.* New Brunswick, NJ: Rutgers University Press. A fascinating ethnographic study of the structure and dynamics of preadolescent peer groups.

Apter, T. (1995). *Secret paths: Women in the new midlife.* New York: W. W. Norton. A study of women in middle adulthood that examines the challenges they face in constructing their identities at midlife.

Mitford, J. (1998). *The American way of death revisited.* New York: Knopf. The revised and updated edition of Mitford's classic—and highly critical—analysis of the "business of death," undertaking, and how this industry plays on the average American's fear of death and feelings of guilt and remorse following the death of a loved one.

Rymer, R. (1993). *Genie: A scientific tragedy.* New York: HarperCollins. The story of Genie, the "closet child" whose tale opened this chapter, as told by a journalist who interviewed Genie's mother and the professionals who cared for her after she was found.

 Run Chapter 6 on your *Living Sociology* CD-ROM for interesting and informative activities, web links, videos, practice tests, and more.

Social Interaction in Groups and Organizations

et's begin with a riddle. It's a cold, rainy March night, and there's been a terrible car accident. A man is killed and his young son is critically injured. The boy is rushed to a nearby hospital and as attendants wheel him into the emergency room, the doctor on duty looks down at the child and says, "Oh no, it's my son!" What is the relationship of the doctor to the injured boy?

The answer is that the doctor is the boy's mother. But what does this riddle have to do with sociology? Quite simply, it illustrates some important sociological concepts. The riddle is based on a group of social actors and their relationships to one another. Each social actor occupies a specific **status** or social position; one is a father, another a son, and the third a doctor. Although we normally think of *doctor* as a prestigious status, we learned in Chapter 3 that in the sociological meaning of the word, prestige is just one element of a social position. All social positions occupied by individuals are statuses, whether one is a corporate president, a sociology student, or a street sweeper.

Of course, we do not hold social positions one at a time; our social identities are composed of many statuses that we hold simultaneously. Taken together, all the statuses held by an individual at one time is called a **status set.** In our riddle, the man who was killed was both a father and a husband; the woman was a doctor, a wife, and a mother. A status set also changes over time; for example, in this case, the woman's status as wife changed to widow. Everyone's status set expands and contracts many times over the course of life.

Attached to every status is one or more roles. **Roles** are the behaviors, responsibilities, and privileges that are expected of individuals occupying a specific status. Roles, then, are the *action* element of statuses. Indeed, as we see in the Doing Sociology box, some sociologists analyze social roles in terms of theatrical performances.

So, a mother's role is to take care of her children, and a physician's role is to take care of her patients. But what happens when, as in the case of the woman in our riddle, the behavioral expectations attached to one role interfere with one's ability to carry out the expectations of another role? A sociologist analyzing our riddle will tell you that this woman probably experienced **role conflict,** a clash between roles attached to different statuses occupied by the same individual. This woman was probably torn between comforting her son as a mother would and tending to his medical needs quickly and unemotionally, as a physician must. The role conflict would have been intensified if the woman had also been experiencing the role strain that often accompanies the status of emergency room physician. **Role strain** results from the fact that a single status is usually composed of multiple roles that at times may be incompatible, causing tension and stress. Thus, the emergency room physician may want to com-

fort and reassure patients, but at the same time, she must move them through examination and treatment quickly in order to tend to everyone. Unless the physician finds some happy medium between these two opposing roles—both of which she considers part of practicing good medicine—she is likely to experience considerable strain.

Finally, perhaps the most interesting aspect of our riddle from a sociological perspective is the difficulty many people have in arriving at the correct answer. Traditionally, in our society, physician was a status held almost exclusively by men. Even today, only about 26 percent of practicing physicians in the United States are women (U.S. Department of Commerce, Bureau of the Census, 1997). In many people's minds, the status *woman* is still incompatible with the status *physician.* Consequently, when asked about the relationship of the doctor to the injured

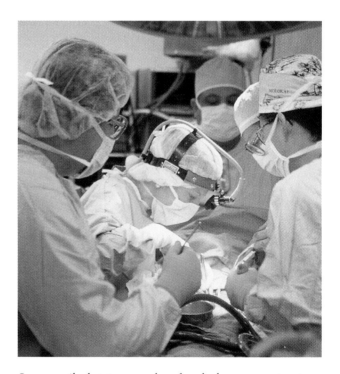

Some ascribed statuses, such as female, become master statuses, overshadowing achieved statuses, such as physician, and dictating people's role expectations. What sociological concepts concerning roles and statuses might explain why most people looking at this photo assume that the surgeon is a man?

DOING SOCIOLOGY

What Can You Learn from Dramaturgical Analysis?

Sociologist **Erving Goffman** (1922–1982) was interested in how social reality is constructed through everyday interaction. He believed that the social world is a human theater, with each individual both a performer (a social actor) and an audience member (Goffman, 1959). Each status a person holds can be thought of as a part in a play, and the roles attached to the status supply the script, prescribing how the person should look as well as what he or she should say and do. Social interaction, then, is a performance, and Goffman called the sociological study of these performances **dramaturgical analysis.**

In dramaturgical analysis, the social world is divided into two regions: frontstage and backstage. In the frontstage region, social actors carefully manage the images of themselves they project to others. This aspect of the performance Goffman called the **presentation of self.** In presenting ourselves to others, we carefully control our appearance and behavior because we want the self presented to have specific effects on what others think of us. So, for example, the

student who wishes others to see her as a serious scholar may be careful to never miss a class, always sit in the front row of the classroom, diligently take notes, nod approvingly when the instructor makes a specific point, participate in class discussions, and seek out the instructor outside of class.

At the same time, in backstage regions, social actors are less guarded in their performances. Backstage, they relax and their true selves may surface. With her roommates, for instance, the serious scholar may be the life of the party or an unrelenting prankster. In any event, Goffman maintained that those with whom we share a backstage are those with whom we have the closest social bonds. This bonding develops because we must be able to trust our backstage companions with often unflattering information about ourselves that we don't want others to know. In fact, embarrassment occurs, Goffman tells us, when our attempts to present a particular self are contradicted by the circumstances (Cupach & Metts, 1994). For example, the instructor glances down at the "serious" student's notebook and sees that it is filled with doodles instead of a careful recording of the instructor's words.

According to Goffman, there are two reasons why social interactions are

"performed." One is that performances make social life consistent and recognizable. In other words, the performance of social interaction creates and maintains social order. A second reason for the performance of social interaction is that people have learned that they can use the performances to enhance or at least preserve their position in the social group. Thus, for example, the student whose frontstage behavior gives the impression that she is a serious scholar may purposely design this presentation of self to get a better grade or to set the stage before asking for a letter of recommendation from the instructor.

Now, try your hand at dramaturgical analysis. Analyze a situation in which you are a participant as a theatrical performance. Who, besides yourself, are the social actors? What are the various statuses and roles of each actor? What impressions do the frontstage performances create? What are the differences between your frontstage performance and how you normally behave backstage? How can you explain this disparity? Are you aware of similar disparities for the other social actors involved? Share your analysis with your classmates, including any scenes that produced embarrassment for you or the other social actors.

---

boy, they often respond with a perplexed, "Didn't you say his father was with him in the accident and was killed?"

To understand why the status *woman* is incompatible with the status *physician* in many people's minds, consider that there are three different types of statuses that sociologists study. Two are determined by how an individual comes to hold the status. One way you can acquire a status is by being born into it or by having it imposed by nature or by chance; this is called an **ascribed status.** Examples of ascribed statuses in our riddle are male, female, and son. You may also come to hold a status by choice; in fact, some statuses require hard work to achieve. This kind of status is termed an **achieved status.** Achieved statuses in the riddle are mother, father, and physician. The third type of status is called a **master status,** a status that takes on greater significance in the eyes

of others than any other aspect of the individual's identity (Schur, 1984). It can be ascribed or achieved, but regardless of the other statuses an individual holds, the master status is the only one that matters, the only one that is used when a situation or an individual is evaluated by others. People who have trouble solving the riddle see the ascribed status *female* as the master status, so they have a hard time imagining someone with a devalued ascribed status holding the prestigious achieved status of physician.

The fact that we confer a master status on people highlights that statuses and roles have social meaning apart from the individuals who hold them. In fact, statuses and roles are given meaning only in terms of individuals' relationships and interactions with one another. Most of our relationships identify us as members of particular groups, and our interactions take place in the context of groups. Understanding social interaction in groups of varying sizes and the way various statuses and roles influence and are influenced by interaction in groups is therefore very important. In this chapter, we'll examine small groups first, and then turn our attention to larger, more complex groups.

SOCIAL GROUPS

You may have heard the saying, "Few things worth doing are ever done alone." Reflected here is the human *need* for companionship and interaction with others, a need so intense that our very survival depends on it, as Genie's story in Chapter 5 showed. Consequently, the majority of our everyday activities are carried out not in isolation, but in the company of others in social groups. Sociologically speaking, a **social group** is two or more people who interact with one another on a regular basis and share common expectations and a common identity.

Each of us belongs to numerous groups at any one time. You may be a member of a couple, a family, a drama club, a Neighborhood Watch group, a Wednesday night basketball league, and an introductory sociology class all at the same time. Although your level of active involvement in each of these groups varies and the people with whom you interact are also likely to vary from group to group, every group has statuses with roles attached so that group members know their responsibilities as well as the privileges they enjoy. Every group also has norms of behavior. These may be written down, but usually they don't have to be; every group member knows what is expected of her or him as well as what is expected of the other group members. In fact, in most small, informal groups, normative behavior is so taken for granted that the norms are not evident until they are violated. Belonging to many groups does not mean that we have no sense of individual identity. Rather, it means that in addition to having an individual self, we also have many group selves. The interaction we experience in social groups cannot help but shape who we are as individuals, but at the same time, our unique individual traits and talents inevitably have some impact on the groups to which we belong.

Groups vary in size, structure, purpose, and various other ways. But before we discuss the variations among groups, let's briefly look at what distinguishes social groups from other collections of people. Consider, for example, Jane Smith. Jane is married and so occupies the status *spouse*. Do spouses constitute a social group as we have defined it sociologically? No, sociologists consider *spouse* a **social category;** that is, it is a collection of people who occupy the same status. Jane certainly interacts regularly with her husband and therefore with

him forms a social group sometimes called a *couple,* and she may decide to join Spouses Support, a group of married people that meets each week to help one another with marital problems. However, she and the millions of other spouses in the world do not interact regularly and are not likely to share much of a common identity. Other examples of social categories are *immigrant, student,* and *child.*

What if each morning Jane Smith waits with several other people on a street corner by her house for the bus that transports them to work—is this collection of people a social group? No, these people just happen to be at the same place at the same time; sociologists refer to them as an **aggregate.** However, just as the category *spouse* is a criterion for membership in Jane's support group and a basis for group identification, so too could the aggregate on the street corner turn into a social group. If the people who wait for the bus with Jane every day begin to interact with one another (have conversations with each other, learn one another's names, share interests and concerns, check up on one another if someone fails to appear one morning, and so on), they may become less of an aggregate and more of a group. But, as we noted previously, there are different types of groups. Let's consider them now.

Primary and Secondary Groups

One of the fundamental ways that sociologists distinguish between different types of groups is in terms of the level of personal closeness or emotional attachment that members of the group feel toward one another. Think, for instance, about the difference in the way you have a conversation with your intimate partner compared to the way you converse with the person you sit next to in your introduction to sociology class. In both cases, you and the other person are members of social groups (a couple and a college class), but the level of attachment you feel in each case is likely to be very different—unless the person sitting next to you in class is your intimate partner or the only person you know who has the notes from the class you missed.

Charles Horton Cooley, whom we introduced in Chapter 5, was one of the first sociologists to study groups in terms of emotional attachment. Cooley used the term **primary group** for those social groups, almost always small in size, that are characterized by strong emotional attachments among the members and that endure over time. Examples of primary groups that easily come to mind are couples, families, and small, close-knit groups of friends.

Members of a primary group share a sense of responsibility for one another; they *care* about and for each other. They spend a lot of time with one another, typically because they want to, and they come to know one

Which of these groups probably are secondary and which primary? On what assumptions are your inferences based? Under what circumstances can a secondary group become a primary group? When is a primary or secondary group a reference group? If you could add a photo to the set representing a reference group that is important to you, what would it show?

another extremely well. This doesn't mean, though, that primary groups are free from conflict. Because primary group members spend so much time with one another and interact closely, they experience one another "warts and all," engendering a certain amount of tension and conflict. But even in the worst circumstances, the emotional attachment that primary group members feel toward one another fosters a strong bond that is not easily broken. Recall again the story of Genie in Chapter 5: Despite her mother's complicity in her abuse, Genie ex-

pressed affection toward her mother and wished to be with her (Rymer, 1993). In a sense, the members of primary groups come to view one another as irreplaceable.

Most of the groups to which people belong, however, do not have a strong emotional component. Unlike primary groups, where being with the other members is fulfilling in itself, **secondary groups** are oriented toward achieving a common goal. Examples of secondary groups include people who live in the same neighborhood, workers in a department store, members of an academic department in a college or university, and members of the local chapter of the League of Women Voters.

Secondary groups may be small, but they are usually large compared to primary groups. They may endure over time—for example, some people work in the same place all their adult lives—but typically they do not. The members of secondary groups may spend a good deal of time with one another, such as in a high-powered work setting where workers are expected to put in 60 to 70 hour weeks, but the nature of the time spent together is different from the time spent in primary groups. Specifically, time spent in secondary groups is oriented toward achieving some goal: getting a stop sign erected at a busy intersection, assembling an automobile, composing a clever jingle for a new product, performing a concerto at Carnegie Hall, or getting a particular candidate elected to office. Thus, the major feature distinguishing secondary groups from primary groups is the lack of emotional bonds or attachments among members.

This does not mean that members of secondary groups are emotionally flat. To the contrary, they may be quite passionate, but in the secondary group, the passion is likely derived from what the members *do* and not from their relationships to one another. Members of secondary groups may like one another and enjoy being together; they may also get to know one another fairly well. Still, in secondary groups, people rarely feel comfortable "letting their hair down." Recall Goffman's analysis in the Doing Sociology box on page 137. In secondary groups, we engage in a good deal of impression management, letting others see only those aspects of the self that are likely to elicit a favorable response.

Primary groups sometimes develop out of secondary groups. People who work side by side for many years may develop close friendships. Students who happen to sit near one another in a class may discover that they have much in common, and a relationship may bloom that endures well beyond the end of the semester. And, as we will see shortly, the larger a group is, the greater the potential for smaller "splinter" groups to form.

One final point about secondary groups: The more technologically developed the society, the greater the interaction in secondary groups. Think for a moment about our discussion of hunting and gathering societies in Chapter 3. In these societies, all social life—food acquisition, decision making, learning, and so on—is carried out in primary groups. However, as a society develops technologically and economically, and the number of statuses and accompanying roles multiply, fewer tasks are performed in the home. Work, governance, education, health care, and a wide range of other activities become part of the "public" domain, and social interaction grows more impersonal. Thus, in contemporary industrial societies like our own where most of our social interaction takes place in secondary groups, many of us place special value

on the time we do get to spend in primary groups such as our families.

Ingroups and Outgroups

How we identify as members of particular groups varies in intensity. Toward some groups we feel a minimal sense of loyalty, but toward others we feel strong allegiance. We actively support them and take great pride in being a member. Sociologists call social groups whose members express intense loyalty, respect, and pride in the group **ingroups.** Not surprisingly, however, ingroups perceive themselves in terms of competition or rivalry with other groups. These competing or rivalrous groups are called **outgroups.**

We are all familiar with friendly rivalries. Perhaps your college competes with another college in a friendly rivalry. Students, faculty, and alumni from both schools go to football or basketball games wearing their school colors and proudly waving banners bearing the name of their institution. Supporters of each team taunt the opposing supporters, yelling across the stands and holding up signs with clever insults. They may put bumper stickers on their cars like the one we recently saw, claiming that even God was a fan of their school's football team.

Colleges thrive on such friendly rivalries because they promote school spirit and loyalty to the institution even after graduation. Some ingroup/outgroup competitions are not so positive, however; groups may become openly hostile. Consider, for example, rival street gangs. Within each gang, the members perceive themselves as the ingroup; they think of themselves as having qualities, such as bravery and good fighting skills, that they think members of the rival gang (the outgroup) lack. In short, members of the ingroup consider themselves "better" than members of the outgroup, and when the two gangs meet and try to prove superiority, defend their turf, or uphold their honor, the outcome can be deadly.

Unfortunately, the daily newspaper and history books provide numerous examples of hateful and violent ingroup/outgroup relations on a global scale: Hitler's Germany; the "ethnic cleansing" of Muslims in the former Yugoslavia; the Hutu-Tutsi bloodbaths in Rwanda; the enslavement of South Korean women during World War II to provide sexual services for Japanese soldiers; street attacks and beatings of gay men and lesbians by straight teens who want to punish homosexuals for their "perversity"; and the spray painting of racial slurs on the homes of African American, Asian, and Hispanic families by neo-Nazi skinheads and other racist groups. Research indicates that the potential for hostile and violent conflicts between ingroups and outgroups increases under certain conditions. If, for example, an ingroup is politically, economically, or socially more powerful than an outgroup, its ability to inflict harm is greater. The likelihood of hostility and violence also increases if the groups perceive themselves in competition over scarce resources (Blackwell, 1982; Hardin, 1995; Noel, 1991).

Reference Groups

You are getting ready to go to an important job interview, and as you look through your closet, you think about how the people who work for this particular company are likely to dress. You choose your navy blue suit because that's what you think your interviewers and potential coworkers will probably be wearing. Later that night, when you're getting ready to go out to celebrate your new job with your friends, you reach for jeans and a t-shirt because that's what you and your friends always wear when you go out together. In both instances, you used **reference groups**—the perspectives of others as a point of reference for making a decision.

A reference group can be either primary or secondary. It can be composed of people you know well (your friends in the preceding example) or people you have never met (a prospective employer). In fact, we often take as reference points groups to which we *aspire* to belong. The media are a major source of such reference groups. Many

SOCIOLOGY LIVE

Weber State University, Ogden, Utah
Course: Sociology, Brenda Kowalewsky, Instructor
Students: (left to right) Alan Christensen, Carrie Wagner, Nicole Schneiter, Joseph W. White, Clint D. Shaw

What reference groups and role models do you use as a college student?

As college students at Weber State University, we identified two different types of reference groups commonly used by each of us. The first type of reference group may be described as a group we belong to, such as the aggregate of college students on our campus. We use other college students—those we know and those we don't know—as reference points to help us make decisions, to make judgments about ourselves, to learn from, and to compete against. The second type of reference group may be described as a group that we aspire to, such as professors, honor roll students, graduates, and professionals working in the disciplines we study. We look to these groups for motivation, inspiration, and direction. Both of these types of reference groups are examples of secondary groups.

The role models we have chosen to emulate are much more specific and individual than our reference groups. We have found that our role models are people we know and interact with on a regular basis, and that most of us have chosen role models from primary groups, namely our families. As role models, family members serve as valuable examples of what we hope to become. Their attitudes, opinions, personality traits, behaviors, values, and beliefs have a great impact on our own.

Alan, for example, identifies his "student" role model as his brother Scott. He observed the hard work, dedication, achievements, and rewards that Scott received in high school and now attempts to emulate this behavior in college. Through her mother's example, Nicole recognizes the importance of hard work and dedication in receiving her college education. As a parent, her mother also provided a structured learning environment, directing Nicole's interests toward the field of early childhood development.

Clint's role model for attending college is his wife, Valerie. Through hard work and effort, she received her master's degree while fulfilling responsibilities as a full-time teacher. Carrie hopes to become a sociologist one day, and so uses one of her professors at Weber State University as a role model for appropriate goals, values, opinions, and behavior. She looks to this professor as a guide for her academic ambitions.

As a student, Joseph looks to his brother Steve as a role model. Joseph was struggling with what he wanted to do with his life, and Steve inspired him to return to school. He helped Joseph realize that his goals could be met only through a college education.

After analyzing the use of reference groups and role models in our own lives, we have come to the conclusion that both are important for guiding our behavior as college students, but they function in our lives in different ways. Reference groups provide us with knowledge about our position as college students and the expectations that accompany that position. Role models provide us with the values, qualities, and characteristics for being successful college students that we take to that position.

young women, for example, adopt as a reference group for beauty standards the extremely thin models they see on television and in magazines. When they compare themselves to the models, they judge themselves to be overweight even if they actually aren't, and they try to diet to achieve the standard set by the reference group (Children Now, 1997).

Sometimes a single individual within a reference group becomes more important than others in the group. Again, we may or may not know this individual personally. What is significant is the value we attach to this person's opinions and behavior, and the consequent influence on our own opinions and behavior. We may try to dress like this person, wear our hair the same way, go to the same restaurants or hang-outs, or even talk and walk like the person. In short, we *model* what this person says or does. In sociological terms, this person is a **role model**, an individual who serves as an example to be emulated.

Our role models change over time as our reference groups change. Can you think of role models you had as a child? To what reference groups in your life did they belong?

Networks

A friend of ours who recently entered the job market reported that one of the best ways to land an interview is to attend the national conference of the major professional group in your field because conferences offer the opportunity to "network." Sociologists who study **networks**—chains of associations that link people with common interests who otherwise would not have the opportunity to interact—would agree with her. One researcher, for example, found that about 60 percent of the 399 jobseekers in his sample found employment by networking (Lin et al., 1981).

Most people belong to several networks simultaneously. We have friendship networks, for instance. We may go to a party with a group of friends and there be introduced to others who know our friends but whom we've never met before. They, in turn, may put us in touch with others who share our interests, and so the connections expand. We may also belong to professional networks. People with whom we work or who work in our field put us in touch with others in the field who may be working on the same type of project or who may have the answer to a problem we have. Those people may not only help with the problem at hand, but also go on to give us the names and phone numbers of others they know who might have further information for us.

Thus, a network is a series of social connections. In fact, we often say that a person who has an extensive friendship or professional network is "well connected." The problem with networks, however, is that they can function to exclude as well as include: We tend to build networks with people who are similar to ourselves not only in interests, but also in sex, race, and social class. So, for example, if jobs are obtained through networking and networks tend to be composed of similar people, then like will hire like. In other words, people of the same sex, same race, and same social class as the employer may have an unfair advantage over others who are equally qualified but who have no connections. In Lin et al.'s (1981) study, job seekers and employers were all men who shared high social standing. As more women and racial minorities have made inroads into the professions, they have begun to establish networks of their own, valuable resources for those who traditionally have lacked these kinds of connections (Ferguson & Dunphy, 1992).

Much of the research on networks has focused on a particular setting: large complex organizations. Before we examine complex organizations in depth, let's first look at some of the research findings on group behavior.

REFLECTING ON

Social Groups

1. Although we spend much of our daily lives interacting in secondary groups, primary groups appear to have a greater impact on shaping our individual identities. Why do you think this is the case?
2. Do you belong to any ingroups? What about outgroups? Compare your feelings and experiences as a member of each type of group.
3. Who are your three most important reference groups currently? What specific influence does each group have on your everyday life?
4. How can the exclusionary practices of some networks be counteracted?

BEHAVIOR IN GROUPS

We all know that we behave differently when we are alone than when we are in a group; it probably seems like such an obvious point that it doesn't merit further discussion. Precisely how do groups affect us? In the sections that follow, we will review various studies that offer answers to this question.

Size as a Variable

One important factor affecting how we behave in a group is the size of the group. Group size has been found to affect the stability of the group, the quality of interaction within the group, and the ability of the group to successfully accomplish specific tasks.

Consider the smallest of social groups, what the German sociologist Georg Simmel (1858–1918) called the **dyad,** made up of two people. According to Simmel, it is in the dyad that interaction is most intense, but intense interaction is exactly what makes the dyad one of the least stable social groups. If you think about this for a moment, Simmel's argument is not difficult to understand. In fact, it has served as the basis for many dramas and situation comedies. Two people are together, by choice or by chance, each with initial or perhaps longer-term impressions of the other. The present circumstances provide an opportunity for them to get to know one another. Early on, things seem to go well; they cooperate with one another, listen to each other, and ignore each other's quirks or habits. But as time passes, disagreements arise, they don't listen as well and even tune each other out, and the previously overlooked quirks can trigger explosive anger. Of course, dyads may also be the source of our greatest satisfaction, offering love, protection, loyalty, and emotional and financial support. In fact, recent research indicates that having one close dyadic relationship is a key to personal happiness (Reid, 1998). But sustaining and nurturing a dyad requires a substantial investment of time and energy on the part of both members, because of the intense intimacy. If one member pulls out, the group is no more. According to Simmel, that's why most societies create cultural and legal reinforcements for marriage.

What happens if a dyad becomes a **triad,** a group of three? Simmel thought the intensity of interaction in the group declined a bit, but this improved the group's stability. His equation makes sense since, with the addition of a third person, the burden of "relationship upkeep" is lessened a bit. If one member of the group tunes another out, the existence of the group is not threatened because there is a third person to listen. If two of the group members disagree, the third can intervene to help resolve the problem. Perhaps you've had this experience yourself with two of your closest friends; two have a falling out and the third tries, with phone calls and long talks with each, to restore the harmony of the group. The only danger in a triad is that two group members can develop an alliance and "gang up" on the third, or at least make the third person feel left out. Besides causing hurt feelings, such alliances can threaten the continuation of the group.

Figure 6.1 shows that, as groups grow in size beyond three members, the number of relationships within the group increases dramatically. According to Simmel's equation, larger groups are less emotionally intense and more stable than smaller groups. You probably understand this, too, from personal experience. You may belong to a club or a team that has fifteen or twenty members. You like some members more than others, and you tend to interact with them more. But your closeness to particular club

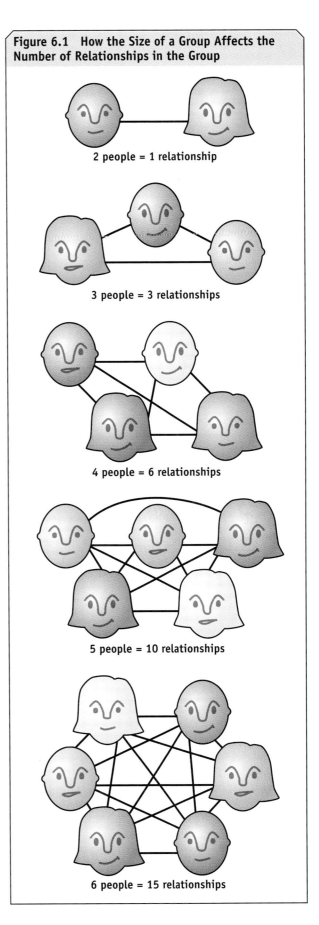

Figure 6.1 How the Size of a Group Affects the Number of Relationships in the Group

2 people = 1 relationship

3 people = 3 relationships

4 people = 6 relationships

5 people = 10 relationships

6 people = 15 relationships

According to Georg Simmel, what is the chief advantage of the triad as a variable in group size? What is its advantage over a dyad? over a larger group? What is the fundamental weakness of a triad? How does group size affect members' behavior?

or team members does not threaten the existence of the group as a whole, nor would your departure from the group cause it to dissolve.

Larger groups tend to be more complex than smaller groups, if only because the interaction needs to be "managed" more. Formal rules of behavior may even be necessary. These rules are usually written down and distributed to all members of the group. For example, at most colleges and universities, students, faculty, and staff have handbooks that state what they are required to do in specific situations and also what is forbidden.

Within large groups there is the potential for members to "broaden their horizons" a bit, simply because with more people there may be more diversity. Members of a sports team, for instance, share the same interest in the sport, but probably differ in their social class backgrounds or racial and ethnic backgrounds. Being members of the same team provides an opportunity for these diverse individuals to interact with and learn more about one another. At the same time, however, such groups often separate themselves from the larger environment, forming an ingroup. Team members, for example, may live, eat, and socialize together, excluding anyone not on the team or intimately associated with a team member. According to sociologists who study group behavior, the more diverse the membership of a specific group, the more likely group members are to interact with those outside the group (Levine & Moreland, 1998; Triandis, 1988). Just as important, though, is the social environment in which the group exists. If a group enjoys a spe-

cial or elite status, group members are substantially less likely to interact with nongroup members. An ingroup forms and fosters prejudice. If, on the other hand, the group exists in an environment where all groups enjoy basically equal status, then interaction between group members and nonmembers is likely and intergroup contact is strengthened (Hardin, 1995; Levine & Moreland, 1998; Triandis, 1988).

Are larger groups better than smaller groups at certain tasks? Consider, after all, the old saying that "Many hands make light work." Like most adages, there is at least partial truth in this one. The way sociologists answer this question is to distinguish between types of tasks. If there are only one or two correct ways to accomplish a task—what sociologists call a **determinate task**—then a larger group is usually more effective than a smaller one, especially when the task is complex and requires specialized knowledge. A good illustration of this is the scene in the film *Apollo 13*, when a group of engineers is told that they have just minutes to construct an air filter using only the materials that the stranded astronauts have available. Although a single individual or a dyad may have been able to accomplish this task, the possibility of success increased because of the combined skills and creativity of a larger number of people.

Suppose, however, there are many ways to accomplish a task—the kind of task sociologists call an **indeterminate task**. In such a case, a larger group may be effective, but the chances of success are greater with a small group. The more options available and the more individuals involved in completing the task, the more they are likely to argue over which option to take. Also, in any large group, some individuals are more dominant or persuasive than others, and they are likely to win out, even if their ideas are not the best.

This last point—who dominates in a group—raises two other topics that interest researchers studying group behavior: conformity and leadership. We'll consider each of these in turn.

Conformity

Conformity refers to an individual's willingness to go along with an opinion or action undertaken by others in a group. Researchers have found that conformity manifests itself in groups in several ways. Studies show, for example, that individuals in groups are generally more willing to adopt extreme opinions or engage in risky behaviors than they normally would on their own. For example, the individual members of a corporation's board of directors may not be pleased with the president's performance, but after an all-day meeting, they end up firing the president—an action no individual would have taken alone. Social psychologists refer to this phenomenon of a group taking more extreme actions than any single member would as **group polarization** (see Levine & Moreland, 1998; Zuber et al., 1992).

Although sociologists are not sure why group polarization occurs, some argue that it is a product of "safety in numbers." When a risky decision must be made, no one individual wants to assume the burden of responsibility should the decision prove wrong or harmful. Consequently, if it is understood that the decision is being made by the group as a whole, responsibility is diffused and no single individual bears the burden. This process of losing one's sense of personal responsibility and individuality to the group is called **deindividuation** (see Diener et al., 1980; Levine & Moreland, 1998; Prentice-Dunn & Rogers, 1984).

Sometimes individuals go along with a particular group decision to avoid "rocking the boat." In other words, their major concern is to ensure that everyone in the group gets along. If enough individuals adopt this stance, the result may be what social psychologist Irving Janis called **groupthink,** the process by which members of a group support one another during decision making in order to preserve group harmony and unity. According to Janis (1982), groupthink is most likely to occur when there is strong group cohesion, structural faults in the group (for example, an authoritarian leader), and a provocative situation (for example, an external threat). When groupthink occurs, information or opinions contrary to those held in common and expressed by group members are ignored or quickly dismissed. Disagreement within the group is not permitted; doubts and alternative points of view are suppressed (Janis, 1982; Kameda & Sugimori, 1993; Steiner, 1982).

A classic example of groupthink occurred during the presidential administration of John F. Kennedy. In 1961, Kennedy was presented with a CIA plan developed by exiles from Cuba to oust the communist government of Fidel Castro. With U.S. military support, the exiles would invade Cuba at the Bay of Pigs. In meetings with his chief advisors, Kennedy heard no opposition to the plan and decided to go ahead with it. As the history books tell us, the invasion was an abysmal failure and the President was widely criticized by the international community. Later, several advisors who attended the decision-making sessions with Kennedy admitted that they had had serious doubts about the plan, but that they'd kept their opinions to themselves so as not to disrupt the group support that seemed to be emerging (McCauley, 1989). Other unwise political decisions that have been attributed to groupthink include the escalation of U.S. involvement in Vietnam during the 1960s and 1970s and the Watergate break-in (Hart, 1991).

According to some researchers, groupthink is less likely to occur if group members understand effective methods of group decision making (see, for example, Aldag & Fuller, 1993; Mullen et al., 1994). Nevertheless,

pressure to conform within a group can be extremely potent. To understand this better, let's consider several groundbreaking studies on group conformity.

Seeing Is Believing?   Look at the line in Box A of Figure 6.2, then look at the lines in Box B of the figure. If we asked you which of the lines in Box B is the same length as the line in Box A, you would probably say it's the middle one and you would be correct. But suppose we brought you into a room with six or seven other people and we asked the same question of each person and, one by one, they replied that the first line in Box B was the same length as the line in Box A. Assuming we asked you last, would you disagree with everyone else and say it's the middle line, or would you simply go along with the group?

Presented with this scenario, most students maintain that they would insist the correct answer was the middle line, but the work of social psychologist Solomon Asch (1955) indicates that they would probably do otherwise. In the 1950s, Asch conducted the experiment we've just described here, bringing groups of seven to nine people into a laboratory under the ruse of testing their visual judgment. In reality, however, one of the group was really a research subject and the others were Asch's assistants who knew that the true purpose of the experiment was to study conformity. The first few times Asch's assistants answered correctly, but then they began giving obviously incorrect answers. The research participants, who were positioned to answer last each time, looked puzzled or confused, but in more than one-third of the cases, they ended up giving the same answer as the rest of the group members.

Later research revealed a number of factors that may influence the extent to which an individual conforms in a group situation such as the one Asch set up. Returning to a topic we discussed earlier in the chapter, for instance, it appears that the size of the group is important. The larger the group, the greater the pressure to

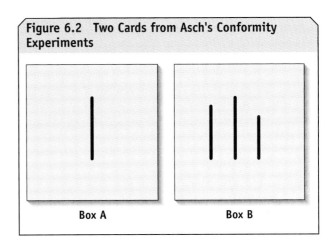

Figure 6.2   Two Cards from Asch's Conformity Experiments

Box A   Box B

conform. The presence of dissenters is also important. Although we will return to this issue shortly, suffice it to say here that variations on Asch's original experiment showed that when one or two of his assistants disagreed with the group, the level of conformity among research participants declined substantially. Conformity also varies to the extent that a behavior is public or private. The greater the privacy surrounding a behavior, the lower the level of conformity (Cialdini & Trost, 1998).

When Conformity Becomes Obedience.   Sometimes the pressure to conform is not as subtle as in Asch's experiments, but strong and direct. People may be told or ordered to do something. If they carry out orders, even when they know the behavior is wrong or harmful and they feel uncomfortable doing it, their conformity becomes *obedience.*

Stanley Milgram (1965), who was once a student of Solomon Asch, conducted a series of experiments to study obedience to perceived authority. You read about Milgram's work in Chapter 2, where we discussed the ethics of his research design. (You may want to reread pages 48–50, describing Milgram's experiment.) Here we will concentrate on what Milgram's study contributes to our understanding of obedience to authority.

Milgram was disturbed by the statements of Nazi soldiers, who claimed after the war that they had participated in murdering hundreds of thousands of Jewish women, men, and children because they had to "follow orders." Milgram wanted to learn more about people's willingness to obey authority figures, so he invited research participants into his laboratory for what he said was a learning experiment. Each participant was paired with another person, who was really one of Milgram's assistants. The research participant became the teacher, who was supposed to read a group of word pairs to the learner (the assistant), who was strapped to a machine in another room. Then the teacher would test the learner's memory by reading the first word in each pair and four other words to see if the learner could select the correct match. If the learner made a correct match, the teacher could move on to the next word, but if the learner got the match wrong, the teacher was told to press a switch on a machine called a *shock generator* that would deliver an electric shock to the learner as a punishment for answering incorrectly. With each wrong answer, the teacher had to increase the intensity of the shock, from "low shock" (15 volts) to "Danger: severe shock" (450 volts) to "XXX."

Initially, the learner did well, matching the word pairs correctly, but as the experiment went on, the learner gave more and more incorrect answers. The learner really wasn't receiving any shocks, but the teacher thought he was, and there were times when the learner cried in pain,

complained his heart was bothering him, told the teacher to stop the experiment, pounded on the wall, and finally refused to answer. Nevertheless, the experimenter, dressed in a white lab coat, instructed the teacher to keep going, increasing the intensity of the shock and treating a nonresponse as a wrong answer.

Before presenting his findings, Milgram asked a group of mental health specialists how many research participants they thought would fully obey the experimenter's orders despite the learner's cries and protests. The group thought very few would. In fact, however, 65 percent of the research participants obeyed the experimenter's orders completely. Although most participants asked several times to stop the experiment, and some asked the experimenter to check on the learner, they nevertheless continued to deliver the shocks at ever greater levels of intensity when told by the experimenter to do so.

In discussing these disturbing findings, Milgram pointed out that none of the participants in his study could be considered sadistic, which leads therefore to a very provocative question: If a stranger in a white lab coat could get ordinary people to inflict pain and possibly endanger another person's life, how much more potent would the influence of an authority such as the government be? How many times have we heard individuals claim that they are not responsible for their actions because they were simply doing what they were told? Indeed, this was the defense not only of Nazi soldiers in World War II, but more recently of Bosnian Serb soldiers on trial in

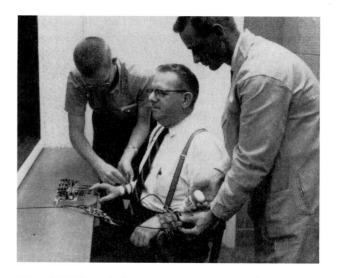

What did Milgram's famous experiment on conformity show about the dynamics involved in individual obedience to authority figures? What are some negative outcomes of this obedience? What are some implications of Milgram's findings for society? What are some implications for individuals in political institutions such as the military?

1996 for the mass murders of Muslims and Croats in the former Yugoslavia.

Milgram's research has been replicated in non-Western cultures with almost identical results (see, for example, Shanab & Yahya, 1978), and similar findings have been obtained across various age groups and between men and women. Thus, not only Milgram's classic study, but later research as well cautions us about the powerful influence others can have on our behavior, particularly people we perceive in a position of authority.

Dissenters. You may have seen the bumper sticker that reads, "Question Authority." Although ironically a command itself, this little maxim reflects the fact that conformity and obedience are not automatic. As rational beings, we always have the choice not to conform. And, as Asch's follow-up experiments and Janis's studies of groupthink show, even one or two people who dissent from the majority can greatly affect group decisions and behavior.

Our history books contain many examples of conformity and groupthink, but they also offer numerous dissenters as role models, individuals who courageously chose to oppose group practices or norms that they recognized as wrong, immoral, or harmful. Some are names you easily recognize—Mahatma Gandhi; Martin Luther King, Jr.; Nelson Mandela—but others are less well-known: Rosa Parks, an African American woman who in 1955, in Montgomery, Alabama, refused to sit in the back of a segregated city bus; Sr. Helen Prejean, who has taken a stand against the death penalty; and Sean McBride, the Irish lawyer who founded the human rights organization, Amnesty International. In the Global Insights box on page 148, you will learn about other "ordinary" people who became dissenters, Chinese students and scholars who took part in the prodemocracy movement in China in 1989.

Clearly, those who induce others to conform or obey and those who dissent can emerge as powerful leaders in a group. Let's turn our attention, then, to the issue of group leadership.

Leadership

A *leader* is a person who directs the activities of others in a group. Most groups have leaders, even if they don't bear an official title and the position is only temporary. In your family, among your friends, on your team or in your club, there are one or two individuals who usually take charge or to whom you and others look for direction about what to do. The larger and more complex the group, the more likely it is to have an officially recognized leader.

Much of the early research on leadership tried to identify the personality traits that characterized leaders. It was quickly discovered, however, that the personalities of leaders varied tremendously, so researchers turned instead to the question of how leaders lead. What they have learned is that there are several types of leaders. Leaders who are *task-oriented*—that is, they focus on getting a job done as efficiently and effectively as possible—are referred to as **instrumental leaders.** In contrast, leaders who are *people-oriented* are considered **expressive leaders.** It is not that expressive leaders don't wish to get work done, but rather that their primary concern is the well-being of the group as a whole.

Neither type of leader is necessarily better than the other, although each is better suited to lead in particular situations. Instrumental leaders are most effective in larger settings and during times of uncertainty or crisis within a group. Expressive leaders, on the other hand, function best in relatively small groups, where members are highly committed to the group, and day-to-day operations are informal. For example, at a small private college where most students know one another relatively well and student interaction with the faculty and administration is high, an expressive leader would probably be more successful in getting students involved in campus activities than an instrumental leader. However, if the college experienced a budget crisis and some student activities had to be cut, an instrumental leader might be better at representing students' interests.

Leaders can be distinguished not only in terms of their orientation to the group, but also in terms of their style of leadership. Let's assume, for instance, that a decision must be made. The individual or individuals in charge—the group leaders—have basically three options: make the decision and then tell the others in the group what it is and what they must do to carry it out (**authoritarian leadership**); bring the entire group together, present them with the matter to be decided, and get their advice or try to reach agreement about what to do (**democratic leadership**); or wait it out and see if the matter simply decides itself or fades in importance (**laissez-faire leadership**).

Leaders who are consistently authoritarian in style are not usually very popular, although they are prized in an emergency when quick, firm decisions are needed. If a terrorist is threatening to detonate a bomb in a crowded office, you wouldn't want the leader of the SWAT team to decide on a course of action by polling all those present. But in most situations, group members do want their voices heard, especially when a decision directly affects them. This is not to say they want prolonged discussion that produces nothing more than "analysis paralysis" or that they don't think their leaders are capable. Rather, most group members just want their opinions heard and respected by their leaders (Levine & Moreland, 1998).

What of the laissez-faire leaders who stand in the shadows, letting the group function on its own? In a

GLOBAL INSIGHTS What Are the Limits of Dissent in China?

During the 1980s, the People's Republic of China had increasingly opened its doors to the West, and, from an economic perspective, made significant progress in building a market economy. To many Chinese, especially scholars and students, the next logical step in this liberalization was more political freedom. In the late 1980s, discussions about democracy increased dramatically on university campuses throughout China, but primarily in the capital city, Beijing. Peking University, the most prestigious university in China, was the center of the democracy movement. In an area of the campus known as the Triangle because several pathways intersect there, students began posting announcements of democracy meetings in the spring of 1989. The death of a leading liberalization proponent in May 1989 became a catalyst for this student-led democracy movement.

The students believed that the time was right for a major public demonstration demanding more political freedom from China's Communist government. Tiananmen Square was chosen as the site for the protest not only because of its large size—it can accommodate thousands of people—but also because of its historical significance. The square is directly across from the Forbidden City, where over the gate hangs a portrait of Chairman Mao. Mao used to hold huge rallies in the square and delivered many of his most famous speeches to the crowds that assembled there. Mao's preserved body now lies in state in a memorial hall at the opposite end of the square, where each day thousands of people stand in long lines to file past and pay their respects.

According to students who planned and participated in the Tiananmen Square demonstration in June 1989, things went better than expected at first, thanks largely to widespread support from the general population and international media coverage. Word of the demonstration spread quickly, and within a short time, thousands of people from surrounding urban and rural areas joined the protestors in the square. Many of the newcomers did not

fully understand the students' plans and goals, and controlling the behavior of this large, diverse group became difficult. It was one thing for a relatively small group of students to protest, but quite another for several thousand citizens to take part. On June 4, 1989, the government ordered that Tiananmen Square be cleared. As the world watched, protestors were beaten and arrested by soldiers; some protestors were killed. After the square was cleared, the government imposed new restrictions on student gatherings, and those who were identified as participants were punished in various ways, such as being denied permission for further study, being denied permission to study abroad, and being sent to less prestigious universities. A number of movement leaders went into hiding to avoid arrest.

Although the Chinese government continues to send the most outspoken democracy proponents to prison or into exile, it has also eased many restrictions on scholars, students, and writers in recent years, allowing greater freedom of expression. There is less surveillence by the Public Security agents, and more open discussion of political alternatives. But this freedom appears to be more a result of economic change than a direct outgrowth of the events of June 1989, and it remains limited. In fact, while many Chinese books, magazines, and newspapers now examine politically sensitive topics, such as political corruption, the government has sent stern warnings about the dangers of overstepping boundaries. In 1999, for example, the Department of Propaganda shut down what was considered to be China's most influential book publisher, China Today Publishers, as well as a popular newspaper, *Cultural Times,* for interfering "with the work of the country by reporting too critically on economic goals" (Eckholm, 1999, p. A4). Many Chinese scholars and students vow they will use "every way possible to keep writing and publishing and discussing," so we can expect further tests of the limits of dissent in China (Eckholm, 1999, p. A4).

healthy group setting, this leadership style works fine. But most groups occasionally experience troubled times; goals become blurred and the direction of the group is uncertain. The lack of decisiveness inherent in the laissez-faire leadership style makes it the least effective of the three, and this style can, in a crisis, threaten the very survival of the group (Hersey et al., 1987; Ridgeway, 1983).

A leader's orientation to a group and leadership style are influenced by many factors, including whether the leader is paid to lead the group, the purpose of the group, and the sex of the leader. Some of the most interesting re-

cent research has been done on gender, as the Intersecting Inequalities box discusses. Regardless of orientation and style, however, a leader requires followers. An important question, then, is how do leaders get others to follow them? The answer lies in a topic we discussed earlier—authority—and a closely related concept, power.

Power and Authority. **Power** is the ability to get others to do one's will even if they do not want to do it. Its relationship to leadership is obvious: Leaders wield power in that they can get others in the group to carry out their

INTERSECTING INEQUALITIES

Do Women Lead Differently Than Men?

Do women lead differently than men? Researchers who study female and male leaders have discovered remarkable similarities: Both women and men enjoy being leaders and holding positions of influence. Both appear equally able to direct and organize the activities of groups, and their subordinates judge female and male leaders as equally effective (Eagly & Johnson, 1990; but see also Valian, 1998).

Nevertheless, research also reveals significant differences between female and male leaders. One area of difference is the reasons women and men give for seeking leadership positions. Women are more likely than men to seek a leadership position because of a desire to help others. In contrast, men more often cite high personal achievement motivation as their primary reason for aspiring to a leadership position (Bridges, 1989).

A second area of difference is the way women and men lead. Women leaders typically use collaborative, participatory communication in exercising leadership, whereas men lead with more directive, unilateral communication (Eagly & Karau, 1991). This doesn't mean that women are better or worse leaders than men. Assertiveness and directness are valued traits in leaders, but so are inclusiveness and collaboration. In fact, studies show that the most effective leaders are those who recognize when a situation calls for unilateral decision making and when it is best to foster team building (Cann & Siegfried, 1990).

Besides observed differences between female and male leaders, there is also the question of how their subordinates or followers judge them. In our society, there are prevalent stereotypes about how women and men are supposed to behave. Women are expected to be supportive, caring, and cooperative; men are expected to be assertive and to take charge of situations. Re-

search indicates that when the behavior of female and male leaders conforms to these stereotypes, they are judged effective regardless of sex. But when a female leader violates the gender stereotype by being highly assertive or directive, she is evaluated negatively by subordinates, jeopardizing her effectiveness (Basow, 1990; Butler & Geis, 1990; Eagly et al., 1995; Valian, 1998; Yoder et al., 1998). Interestingly, the violation of gender stereotypes by a male leader does not produce the same negative impact on his effectiveness rating. Instead, researchers report that supportiveness and a collaborative style by both female and male leaders tend to raise morale and enhance productivity (Eagly et al., 1995; Helgesen, 1990). Perhaps as findings such as these accumulate, we may see women's style of leadership becoming the norm in government and business.

---

wishes or directives. But what is the source of a leader's power?

We often think of power in physical terms. Certainly, one way leaders can get others to follow them is to use brute force or the threat of force. There are numerous examples of leadership by force, from dictatorial governments to abusive parents. In such cases, group members involuntarily yield to the will of their leader.

Leaders may also command a following because their leadership derives from **legitimate authority,** that is, power perceived as rightful by those being led. Max Weber, one of the founders of sociology, identified three types of legitimate authority. The first is **rational-legal authority,** which is bestowed on an individual by legally enacted rules, regulations, or contracts. The leadership of the President of the United States is derived from rational-legal authority, as is any club president's or team captain's if they were voted into the position by members of the group.

The second type of authority identified by Weber is **traditional authority,** which is authority bestowed on a person by custom. The British monarchy is an example of traditional authority bestowed at birth. When Queen Elizabeth dies, the throne passes to her eldest child, Prince Charles. Similarly, in Western societies, the husband/

father was considered the head of the household because it was customary for the adult man of the house to hold this position. When he died, his authority was passed to his eldest son, again by custom.

Finally, leadership may be grounded in what Weber called **charismatic authority.** Such leaders garner a following because of their extraordinary personal virtues or skills. They can perhaps best be described as inspirational (Bass, 1990). Many of those whom we identified earlier as dissenters—Martin Luther King, Jr., Nelson Mandela, Mahatma Ghandi—have led on the basis of charismatic authority. Other charismatic leaders include David Koresh, the late leader of the Branch Davidians; the late Ayatollah Khomeini; and even Jesus Christ. A charismatic leader develops an emotional bond with his or her followers, who, in turn, gain self-esteem through their relationship with the leader. Charismatic leaders "induce high levels of loyalty, identification, emulation, and trust in their followers" (Levine & Moreland, 1998, p. 443; see also Storr, 1996).

Recall, though, Weber's concept of the ideal type from Chapter 3: The ideal type is an analytic tool that identifies the essential features of a phenomenon. These three types of authority are ideal types; they are rarely, if ever,

This politician exhibits the qualities of effective leadership. According to sociological research, what attitudes and behaviors might those qualities include? How might the fact that the politician is a woman rather than a man affect her acceptance, style, communication, and performance as a leader? Do you think the fact that the politician is African American will affect her acceptance as a leader? How?

found in pure form. For instance, in many democracies, such as the United States, the individual elected to lead wins the position at least in part on the basis of charismatic character. And the traditional authority of the husband/father in the family was historically backed up by laws that deemed wife/mother and children his property and subject to his control.

We will revisit the concept of authority in Chapter 14, "Politics and Government." Now, however, let's turn to another of Weber's favorite topics, formal organizations.

R EFLECTING ON

Behavior in Groups

1. What are some ways the size of a group affects interactions within it? Can you provide specific examples from your own experience?
2. Why do you think it is so difficult to go against the opinions or decisions of a group?
3. What specific personal characteristics do you think distinguish dissenters? Do you think particular social circumstances help give rise to dissenters?
4. What do you think are the qualities of a good leader? Can you give an example of a leader who models these qualities?

FORMAL ORGANIZATIONS

A **formal organization** is a large, secondary group whose members interact for the purpose of achieving their common goals as efficiently and effectively as possible. In hunting and gathering societies (Chapter 3), there are no such groups; all social life takes place in the context of primary groups. But as societies grow, and especially once they industrialize, formal organizations proliferate. In a society such as ours—moving quickly, as many claim, into the postindustrial era—the better part of our daily lives is carried out in the context of formal organizations, including colleges and universities, banks and businesses, and government agencies. To understand this better, let's take a closer look at formal organizations.

Types of Formal Organizations

Given the prevalence of formal organizations, the thought of trying to classify them in some way seems daunting. But sociologist Amitai Etzioni (1975) looked at why people join organizations and discovered that there are just three major reasons. He used these as the basis of his classification system.

There are some organizations that nobody wants to join; they must be forced. Or, if they join by choice, they cannot easily withdraw. Etzioni calls these **coercive organizations.** Examples of these are the total institutions that we discussed in Chapter 5, such as mental hospitals and prisons. Because people don't want to be in these organizations, various measures are used to make them do what is expected of them. These measures include locking them in buildings or particular spaces (cells), isolation, barred windows, guards, and sometimes physical or psychological punishment.

The second reason people join organizations is to gain something. Membership is a means to an end. Etzioni calls these **utilitarian organizations.** For the most part, membership in utilitarian organizations is voluntary, but in some cases it is also a necessity. Going to college, for instance, is a means to acquire more knowledge and earn the credentials needed to get the kind of job you want. When you get the job, you join another utilitarian organization, which may bring you prestige and allow you to meet new people, but most importantly provides you with income. But while utilitarian organizations provide some gain, members must also make specific commitments to the organization and adhere to organizational policies and procedures. Thus, going to college and getting a job both require you to give up some portion of your leisure time and follow rules (such as an academic or workplace honesty policy, a performance or productivity standard, or a code of conduct).

Finally, some people join organizations simply for the personal satisfaction of participating in them or because

What type of formal organization is represented in this photo? What are some other examples of organizations of this type? What are their defining characteristics? As a sociologist, how might you go about explaining why membership of young people in this type of organization has declined in recent years?

they believe it is morally right. Etzioni calls these **voluntary** or **normative associations.** No one is forced to join, and no one materially benefits from membership. Voluntary associations encompass religious organizations and church groups, political parties, self-help groups, athletic associations, and civic groups. The United Methodist Church, Weight Watchers, the National Gay and Lesbian Caucus, the PTA, and Greenpeace are all examples of voluntary associations.

There are literally thousands of voluntary associations in the United States alone. In fact, it has long been argued

that Americans join more voluntary associations than people anywhere in the world (Curtis et al., 1992). Recently, however, political scientist Robert Putnam (1995) discovered that Americans' membership in voluntary associations has been declining significantly, and is especially low among young adults (see Figure 6.3). Although it is still unclear why this is happening, Putnam found an inverse relationship between the amount of television people watch and their memberships in voluntary associations. In other words, the more television a person watches, the fewer voluntary associations she or he belongs to. Putnam argues that television privatizes leisure time; people increasingly prefer to spend their leisure hours at home watching television rather than socializing or interacting with others in groups such as voluntary associations (see Roberts, 1995). Assuming Putnam is correct, his findings have important implications for the future. In voluntary organizations, people commit themselves to a particular cause and act together to bring about a result valued by the group. If the trend toward privatization continues, fewer voices will be heard and the opportunity for a small number of groups or individuals to dominate civic life increases, weakening the democratic foundation of our society.

Bureaucracies

It is not just the reasons people have for joining organizations that interest sociologists. We are also interested in how organizations are structured and how they function.

Max Weber was one of the first sociologists to draw attention to the structure and functioning of formal organizations. He observed that formal organizations existed

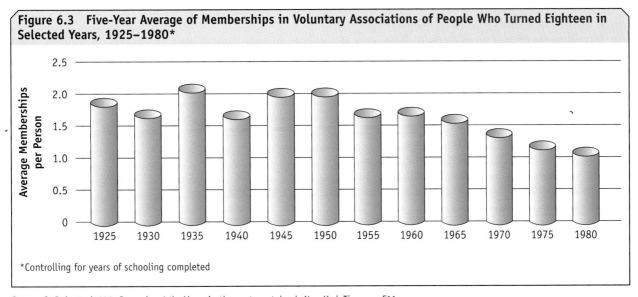

Figure 6.3   Five-Year Average of Memberships in Voluntary Associations of People Who Turned Eighteen in Selected Years, 1925–1980*

*Controlling for years of schooling completed

Source: S. Roberts (1995, December 24). Alone in the vast wasteland. *New York Times,* p. F11.
Copyright © 1995 by The New York Times Co. Reprinted by permission.

for thousands of years, but they functioned differently in preindustrial societies than they do in modern industrial ones because in preindustrial times, tradition or custom held greater sway in social life. People carried out tasks in a certain way not because it was most efficient, but because that was the way it had always been done, or that was the way "God" or the king or some other traditional authority said it was to be done. According to Weber, one of the major changes in social life wrought by the Industrial Revolution was a greater emphasis on efficiency. Industrial entrepreneurs needed a means for controlling the growing, more specialized labor force that characterized industrial production. No longer was tradition sufficient for maintaining order. Formal rules and procedures were necessary, and these were based not on custom, but on a plan of action specifying how to accomplish a task with minimal waste and expense. Weber called this emphasis on efficiency and logical planning the *rationalization* of social life. Rationalization produced not only a growth in formal organizations, but also fundamental changes in their structure and functioning. What emerged was an organizational model known as *bureaucracy.*

Weber's Ideal Type Bureaucracy.   You may remember from Chapter 3 that a **bureaucracy** is a form of organization based on written rules and procedures and designed to manage and coordinate the actions of large numbers of people. A central goal of a bureaucratic organization is to accomplish tasks at hand as efficiently as possible.

Weber's analysis of bureaucracy is significant because he showed how bureaucracies grow and come to permeate almost all aspects of daily interaction in modern societies, from education to government to work and even to religion. Weber was also the first to identify both the positive and negative consequences of bureaucratic organization. We will discuss the advantages and disadvantages of bureaucracy shortly. First, though, let's see how Weber analyzed bureaucracy. To study bureaucracy, Weber developed an ideal type. Weber's ideal type bureaucracy has six essential features:

1. *Specialization.* Bureaucracies have a clear division of labor. Statuses or offices in a bureaucratic organization are based on this division of labor, so that each status or office has one specific set of tasks and no others. Thus, if a member of a bureaucracy is asked to perform a task not within her realm of specialized duties, she may reply, "But that's not in my job description."

2. *Hierarchy.* The statuses or offices of a bureaucracy are hierarchical, arranged like a pyramid, so the higher up you go, the fewer the people there are who hold that status. Each person on the pyramid supervises those in positions below her or him and is supervised by those in superior positions. A good

way to understand this is to look at the organizational chart for your university.

3. *Written rules and regulations.* Efficiency requires predictability, and to ensure predictability, all members of the organization must know what is expected of them in specific situations. This information is typically spelled out in a handbook or manual that is issued when an individual joins the organization. Did you receive a student handbook when you arrived on campus? The administrators, faculty, and staff at your school also probably have handbooks that detail the rules and responsibilities governing their positions.

4. *Impartiality.* Employment in a bureaucracy is based on qualifications and merit, not on ascribed traits or "connections." Qualifications and performance standards are spelled out and consistently applied in hiring and promotion within the organization, so that individuals have a clear vision of their career track.

5. *Impersonality.* Rules and procedures are more important than individuals' feelings. Feelings or emotional attachments interfere with the operation of the organization because they result in inefficiency. If you have ever been told to wait your turn in line or fill out an application and leave it with the receptionist, you've experienced the impersonal nature of bureaucracies. You feel more like a number than a person. Such feelings are likely to grow, given today's trend toward using computer technology to automate transactions with customers and clients.

6. *Recordkeeping.* All transactions in a bureaucratic organization (including all memos, reports, and forms) are recorded and saved, usually in files. Computers allow bureaucratic recordkeeping to be done electronically, which means even greater amounts of information can be collected and stored. Of course, when we hear that "the computer is down," we know that information retrieval is virtually impossible and that further transactions must be put on hold.

Since Weber's bureaucracy is an ideal type, we know that in the real world most bureaucracies do not conform perfectly to his description. For instance, as we discussed in the section on networking, ascribed traits such as sex and race, as well as connections to powerful individuals within an organization often do make a difference in terms of who gets a job or promotion. Similarly, despite official rules and procedures, there is usually an informal side of operations in most bureaucracies. People working in bureaucratic organizations often disobey a rule or don't follow procedure because it doesn't make sense in a specific situation. Much information within bureaucracies is also circulated through informal channels, such as the office "grapevine." Deals, plans, and decisions may be made over lunch or on the racquetball court. And despite its impersonality, most people in bureaucratic organizations do establish personal relationships with others, even if only with those in their own office or department (Blau & Meyer, 1987).

Advantages and Disadvantages of Bureaucracy.

When Weber wrote about bureaucracy at the turn of the century, he believed the bureaucratic model dominated the social landscape of industrial societies because it was superior to other models for coordinating the activities of large numbers of people. As Weber saw it, bureaucratic organization was the only system that allowed government leaders and industrialists to mobilize the political and economic resources necessary for the large-scale planning and productivity required for the growth of industrialism. What is more, bureaucracy standardizes many aspects of social life, making daily interactions more predictable and therefore more manageable.

At the same time, however, Weber was concerned with the dysfunctions of bureaucracy. For him, the most serious was impersonalization. The standardization prized within bureaucracies makes it difficult, if not impossible, for a bureaucratic organization to handle special circumstances or the peculiarities of individual cases. As we learned in Chapter 3, in fact, Weber maintained that as bureaucracies grow, social life becomes so dehumanized that people's unique creative capacities wither, while social interaction grows more mechanical and less spontaneous. As a result, Weber was very pessimistic about the future of industrial societies, arguing that we would eventually be prisoners in the "iron cage" of dehumanization that we ourselves created.

Sociologists since Weber have continued to study the problems of bureaucracy. Besides impersonalization, to which we will return shortly, they have identified several other issues that deserve our attention: bureaucratic ritualism, bloat and secrecy, inequality, invasions of privacy, and incompetence.

Bureaucratic Ritualism.

If you ask people what first comes to mind when they hear the word "bureaucracy," most are likely to say, "Red tape." Being transferred from office to office, encountering one bureaucrat after another who seems more concerned with following official rules and procedures than with solving the problem at hand can be maddening. Sociologist Robert Merton (1968) referred to this problem as **bureaucratic ritualism:** The rules and procedures of the organization take on greater importance than the organization's purpose and goals.

Of course, sometimes doing things "by the book" is important for consistency. The risk is that people may become paralyzed by indecision when a situation arises that is not covered by the book (Blau & Meyer, 1987). Such

How many of the six characteristics of Weber's ideal type bureaucracy do you see in this photo of the lobby of a corporate headquarters? What are the advantages of bureaucracy for individuals and society, and what are some problems of bureaucracies? According to Robert Michels, how do bureaucracies become oligarchies, and with what consequences for society?

bureaucrats exhibit **trained incapacity,** a term coined by Thorsten Veblen at the turn of the century to describe what happens when jobs in an organization rob people of their ability to think independently and creatively.

Bloat and Secrecy.

Bureaucracies have a tendency to expand and perpetuate themselves. Offices or departments in bureaucracies often compete with one another for organizational resources, such as budget, staff, and work space. Growth does not necessarily mean more work gets done, however. In fact, as an organization gets larger, there is increased potential for incompetence to be overlooked and for employees to hide mistakes or problems. An organization bloated with too many workers, especially at the administrative level, undermines its own efficiency. The problem of secrecy can threaten the health and survival of the organization, since damaging mistakes or problems are left unaddressed.

Secrecy also manifests itself as a lack of communication across levels of the organizational hierarchy. For example, if people at the top of the hierarchy have an authoritarian leadership style, then people subordinate to them have little access to information that underlies important decisions. The subordinates' commitment to the organization weakens, and they "go through the motions" of their jobs, which reduces their productivity. At the same time, if people at the top are unwilling to listen to their subordinates' concerns and opinions, they miss a valuable alternative perspective and can be unaware of potentially disastrous problems in the organization.

Preserving Inequality. Bureaucratic organizations have historically been dominated by White, middle-class, wealthy men, and they have shown strong resistance to change in this respect. Legislation enacted in the 1960s and 1970s outlawed racial, ethnic, and sex discrimination in the workplace, but the formal structure of most bureaucratic organizations allows discrimination to continue, albeit in more subtle forms. Although more racial minorities and women hold positions in bureaucratic organizations that traditionally were closed to them, their experiences in these positions are typically different from—and more negative than—their White male counterparts (Valian, 1998).

The classic research on preserving inequality in organizations was conducted by Rosabeth Moss Kanter (1977). Kanter studied women and men in corporate management and found that women managers were regarded as *tokens:* They were treated as symbols or representatives of a category, rather than as individuals. Their work and behavior were more closely scrutinized than men's, which made their jobs more stressful since they felt greater pressure to "perform" well.

Kanter also found that men in these organizations often exaggerated differences between themselves and the women, treating the women as members of an outgroup. The women sometimes found themselves excluded from formal information networks needed for success in their jobs, but more often, they were shut out of informal social networks.

Similar findings have been reported in studies of minority professionals. Men and women of color state that White workers often treat them with hostility or coldness and exclude them from formal and informal information networks valuable for advancing in their careers (Cose, 1993; Feagin & Sikes, 1994; Reich & Nussbaum, 1994). Interestingly, however, White men who enter sex-atypical occupations do not have these experiences. Indeed, these men say they often receive preferential treatment in the workplace, being mentored and encouraged by their supervisors (Williams, 1995). Clearly, then, an employee's sex and race continue to serve as master statuses in contemporary bureaucratic organizations, thus preserving social inequality.

Invasions of Privacy. Recordkeeping, we have said, is a hallmark of bureaucracy, and today it is largely done electronically, thanks to the widespread use of computer technology. Corporations, hospitals, governments, and other bureaucratic organizations now have more information stored on individual citizens than was ever before possible (Flaherty, 1989). Just by typing in your name or any one of the numbers attached to your name (Social Security number, driver's license number, checking account number, credit card number), almost anyone in a bureaucracy can access a wide array of personal information about you, including whether you have ever been convicted of a crime, your medical history, your credit record, your shopping patterns, and who you call on the phone.

The rapid growth in the collection of information about individual citizens in our society as well as others has become a cause for alarm among many observers who worry that our privacy rights are increasingly jeopardized. Most of us have experienced this growth in our personal databases since it manifests itself in the annoying increase in the number of phone solicitations and junk mail we receive. When our first son was born, we were deluged with baby product samples, coupons, discounts on diaper services, and toy catalogs; our names, address, and the fact that we had had a baby had been sold by someone to various marketers (see also Hansell, 1998).

However, the collection and dissemination of information about particular individuals is not always benign, and there are currently few protections against these invasions of privacy. Consider, for example, that patients' medical records are now routinely stored in computer databases. Information about mental health, substance abuse, and AIDS may end up being shared with others who have less than noble intentions. In some cases, for instance, companies being sued for negligence have hired private investigators to access the medical records, credit histories, and other personal data of complainants and their families in order to obtain information that can be used to discredit the witnesses in court (Bernstein, 1997).

Congress has been considering legislation to protect the confidentiality of medical records, but because of the nature of the technology, it is doubtful that these laws will be effective in stopping abuses. What's more, there are other invasions of privacy that are winning approval in the courts. Employers, for example, may monitor employees' e-mail and phone conversations, under the claim that the electronic communications systems are the property of the company, thereby giving the company the right to control them. The outcome of monitoring for some workers has been the loss of their jobs (Samuels, 1996; see also Lambert, 1998).

As we see in the Social Policy box, the controversy surrounding this aspect of bureaucracy is a complex one that is not likely to be resolved soon, particularly given many people's mixed feelings about it. However, the erosion of privacy that appears to accompany bureaucratic expansion does call to mind Weber's pessimism about the future of industrial societies.

Social Policy
Protecting Privacy and Ensuring Security: Are the Two Goals Incompatible?

A blaring siren and flashing red lights from the car behind you signal that you should pull over. A police officer leans in your window and informs you that your car's left rear taillight is out. But instead of requesting your driver's license and registration, the officer asks to see your government-issued ID card. You hand over the card and then wait a bit anxiously as the officer checks you out using your card and the online computer in the police cruiser. Encoded on your card is a scan of your eye retina, a biological identity marker as unique as your fingerprints. Within seconds of reading your eye retina scan, the officer's computer retrieves from the national data bank all relevant information about you, including the date and place of your birth, your current address and all previous addresses over the last ten years, your current employer, and any history of arrests, criminal convictions, or outstanding warrants. Returning to your car, the officer hands you the ID card and issues a warning. The warning is now part of the national data bank's record of information about you, too.

The Issue

Does this sound more like a scene from a science fiction novel than real life? Actually, scientists, ethicists, lawyers, and government officials maintain that such encounters will be commonplace in the near future. Many members of Congress support the establishment of a national ID card system, largely for security purposes. Each citizen would be issued the card at birth or upon receiving citizenship, and the card would show the bearer's name, photo, and some other "counterfeit-proof" identity marker, such as a fingerprint or an eye retina scan. Stored

elsewhere, however, in a national computerized data bank, would be an ever-growing personal history of the cardholder.

The Debate

Supporters of the national ID card system see it as an effective way to reduce crime and protect national security. For example, the cards would allow the tracing of illegal cash transactions, provide on-the-spot verification that an adult accompanying a child is the child's parent or legal guardian, record the purchase of certain items such as guns or books about how to make bombs, let employers verify the citizenship or legal immigration status of prospective employees, and allow the police to quickly check the background of anyone behaving suspiciously. The security benefits of such a system, supporters maintain, more than make up for the minimal inconvenience it might cause "ordinary" citizens who have nothing to hide (Smith, 1996).

However, opponents of a national ID card system see it as a serious invasion of privacy and worry that it could cause more than a slight inconvenience for some groups of people. Would some people be stopped for security checks routinely, simply because their presence in a particular location is suspicious? Already, young African American men report that they are questioned by police if they are seen walking in a predominantly White neighborhood. What about people on the margins of social life, who don't have a permanent address or even a safe place to keep such a card? And would such a system really be foolproof, so that errors in identity or counterfeiting would be impossible (Smith, 1996)?

With technology developing more rapidly than ethical standards or laws to regulate it, some observers maintain that the controversy surrounding the establishment of a national ID card system may be moot before it is resolved. They point out that even more sophisticated systems of identification and recordkeeping are already being developed. One such system has been called the "Soul-catcher" by its inventors. The Soul-catcher is a computer chip that can be implanted into the optic nerve to record a person's physical state, emotions, behavior, words, and thoughts over the course of a lifetime. The information could then be transmitted to computers for storage and retrieval (The Soul Catcher, 1999).

What Do You Think?

Again, supporters of technology like Soul-catcher emphasize its security benefits. For example, police could play back what a crime victim or witness saw, heard, felt, said, and thought during the commission of a crime in order to more easily capture a criminal. Kidnapped children or Alzheimer's patients who wander away from caregivers could be easily located by tracking their computer-readable implants (Flanagan, 1996). But the notion that in just thirty years scientists will make available a device that can establish a complete record of a person's every action, word, feeling, and even memory makes us wonder about the meaning of "security." Is a society without personal privacy secure? Yes, computers and other information technology have numerous benefits, but will they eventually become the iron cage that Max Weber predicted would imprison us with impeccable rationality? What do you think?

Bureaucratic Incompetence.   When Laurence J. Peter looked at bureaucracies, what struck him was the incompetence of bureaucrats. To explain bureaucratic incompetence, Peter developed the *Peter principle* (Peter & Hull, 1969). According to the Peter principle, employees

in a bureaucratic organization are promoted to their individual level of incompetence. Thus, when bureaucratic employees do their jobs well, they get noticed by their superiors, who reward them with a promotion. The cycle of good job performance followed by promotion continues until eventually, an employee is promoted to a position for which he or she is not qualified and thus does not perform well. The employee has reached his or her individual level of incompetence and is unlikely to be promoted further. Then, the employee avoids demotion by taking credit for the accomplishments of his or her subordinates and passing blame for mistakes on to them as well.

Peter's analysis was intended to put bureaucratic incompetence in a humorous light. However, if bureaucracies actually operated according to the Peter principle, they would be paralyzed by inefficiency. As we've noted, one of the reasons bureaucracies have flourished is their success in managing the activities of large numbers of people in modern societies.

Oligarchy

The early decades of this century were especially tumultuous in Europe. Living through that period was a young historian named Robert Michels (1876–1936). Michels was a labor union activist in Germany and a member of the socialist party there; he gradually grew disillusioned with both as he watched these organizations espouse democratic ideals while becoming increasingly less democratic in practice. In 1911, he published *Political Parties*, an analysis of how large bureaucratic organizations transform themselves into oligarchies over time. **Oligarchy** occurs when the resources and decision-making authority of a bureaucracy are controlled by a tiny faction of members.

Michels's analysis is called the *Iron Law of Oligarchy*. Michels used the term "iron law" because he believed the concentration of power and authority in bureaucracies is inevitable. All organizations have leaders, so even if every member participates in discussions and has a vote, a few people usually dominate and tend to get their ideas adopted as the plan of action or policy. This arrangement is fine with most members, who are content to take a "back seat" and let others run the show. If leadership is formally recognized, members' personal involvement is likely to be even lower. Meanwhile, as the leaders devote more time and energy to the organization, they see themselves as having a greater stake in it than the membership. They grow apart from the membership and develop different values from the membership; in addition, they increasingly view themselves as being more knowledgeable than the membership. Most important, the leaders have control over organizational resources that they can mobilize to achieve their ends. Slowly but steadily, the leaders become corrupted; they grow less concerned with representing the interests of members and more concerned with maintaining their own positions of power. And even though they are outnumbered by the membership, their accrued power helps assure their victory in conflicts, including any attempt to remove them from office.

Research that has tested Michels's theory has found some support for it. According to Collins and Makowsky (1989), for example, control by the few can be found in organizations as diverse as trade unions, charities, and professional associations. As a prime example, they cite the major political parties in the United States, which have increasingly come under the control of "party bosses." This is not to say, of course, that members always relinquish control of their organizations to a handful of leaders whom they cannot remove from power, or that leaders always become corrupted. Rather, "Michels's theory tells how the different positions in an organization shape the interests of their holders and give them certain organizational weapons that they can use in the struggle with others for control of the organization" (Collins & Makowsky, 1989, p. 217).

Nevertheless, Michels was not hopeful about the future. He shared Weber's view that bureaucracy is the most efficient system of organization for contemporary industrial societies, but he also shared Weber's pessimism that as organizations grow, they exercise greater control over their members rather than vice versa. Are oligarchies an inevitable outgrowth of formal organizations? Some think not, as we discuss in the next section.

Reforming Bureaucracy

During the 1970s and 1980s, the United States showed serious slippage in its position as a world economic power. Many experts considered the rigid bureaucratic structure of major business organizations one of the causes of our economic woes.

The Japanese Alternative. Sociologists and business analysts took a close look at the organizational structures of countries who were outpacing the United States in the world market. Japan, in particular, commanded their attention. Japan's economy had been devastated by World War II, but less than forty years later, was at the top of the global economic pack.

One of the outstanding features of the Japanese organizational model is its emphasis on *teamwork*. U.S. companies tend to be organized top-down, promoting an ingroup/outgroup mentality between workers and management, but Japanese companies bring workers and management together. One way they do this is through *quality circles*, small groups of managers and workers who share ideas and strategies for solving problems and developing new products. Recall that earlier in the chapter we said that members of groups want their leadership to listen to and respect their opinions. This certainly appears to be the case in Japan (Matsui & Onglatco, 1990).

Various rituals reinforce team spirit. All members of the organization—managers and workers—gather for morning exercises, or the singing of the company

In what two ways does this photo at a Coca-Cola plant in Asahikawa, Japan, represent the Japanese ideal corporate model? What pictures might you add to represent other components of this model? In what ways might the Japanese model work and not work in U.S. corporations?

"anthem" or chanting of company slogans. Everyone proudly wears the company uniform or logo. More important than rituals, though, are the financial benefits of working for a Japanese company: guaranteed lifetime employment, promotions and pay raises based on seniority only, and a salary scale with relatively small gaps between the salaries of managers and workers compared to the United States (Ouchi, 1981).

So why aren't more U.S. business organizations adopting the Japanese model? One reason is the cultural differences between the two countries. Japanese culture emphasizes responsibility to the group, whereas in the United States, the cultural tradition is *individualism*. There is a prevalent attitude that one person's success comes as a result of another's failure. Those at the top of the organizational hierarchy are also not enthusiastic about sharing decision making with subordinates. Perhaps most importantly, managers and workers in the United States typically don't trust each other. Managers often believe that workers have little loyalty to the company and will try to get as much for themselves as possible while expending the least effort. Workers fear retaliation or job loss if they openly criticize management (Woodruff, 1982).

Some analysts argue that as the Japanese economy expands, the traditional organizational model will change. Benefits such as lifetime job security are expensive. In fact, to remain competitive in the world market where other countries offer workers fewer benefits and lower wages, many Japanese companies have been forced to rescind the very benefits that engender their employees' deep loyalty (Wu Dunn, 1997).

All of this is not to say that the Japanese organizational model doesn't have some of the same drawbacks as the bureaucratic model found in the United States. In particular, the preservation of social inequalities is a persistent problem. For example, most Japanese companies

prefer not to hire workers who belong to the outcast group known as the *Burakumin* (pronounced "BRA-ko-meen"). Burakumin are Japanese, but are regarded by the non-Burakumin population as physically and morally inferior. Some Japanese companies keep lists of Burakumin family names and even hire detectives to investigate a prospective employee's family background. Virtually no major corporation will hire a Burakumin for a management position (Chira, 1988; Upham, 1988).

Women, too, do not fare well in the Japanese labor market. Although Japanese women were hired in increasing numbers during the 1980s, that trend reversed during the 1990s. Moreover, women are typically hired for clerical positions, being referred to in many companies as "office flowers," and there are wide gaps between men's and women's salaries (Pollack, 1996; Sanger, 1994).

In general, the Japanese workplace does not allow married couples to balance time spent at work with time spent with family. Cultural norms mandate that married women care for the home and raise the children, and husbands are expected to be devoted to their jobs. Many men, in fact, are referred to as "7-11 husbands" because they leave for work at 7 A.M. and do not return home until at least 11 P.M. (Kristof, 1996).

A U.S. Alternative. Short of adopting the Japanese model, then, is there another choice? Yes, according to sociologists such as Rosabeth Moss Kanter, whose work we discussed earlier. Kanter (1977; 1983) and others call for *humanizing* bureaucracy; that is, making organizational environments more nurturing for all members. Just how can this be done?

One key element is that the organization must be responsive to the needs of its diverse membership. For example, companies must recognize that they have employees who have family responsibilities as well as work responsibilities, and that they must accommodate these employees. Companies must also foster an atmosphere of inclusiveness; no one should be made to feel like a "token" or an "outsider" because of race, ethnicity, sex, sexual orientation, or physical ability/disability.

A second essential element of humanizing the bureaucratic organization is *leveling*, replacing the rigid hierarchy of the traditional bureaucracy with team building. Team building requires open communication throughout the organization. It emphasizes group effort and responsibility over individual merit. The result is a flatter or horizontal organizational chart instead of a hierarchical pyramid (Byrne, 1993; George & Brief, 1992).

Third, positions in the organization must be enriching rather than stifling. The work to be done should be interesting and varied, so that it doesn't become routine. Everyone in the organization should have opportunities to innovate, and creativity should be rewarded (Shepperd, 1993).

In short, humanizing bureaucracy means making it more flexible. Moreover, say its proponents, humanizing bureaucracy will improve productivity. Morale is higher in a humanistic workplace, and high morale raises productivity, which, in turn, increases profits. However, it remains to be seen whether bureaucracies can be reformed. After all, the changes suggested here diminish the standardization and predictability that are hallmarks of bureaucratic organizations. Humanizing bureaucracies means that customers must be treated as individuals, not "cases." Although we complain about bureaucratic red tape, most people also get annoyed if they have to wait in line a long time because the customer in front of them needs extra attention because of "special circumstances." And well-seasoned bureaucrats cringe at the idea of their staff innovating on the job. All of this leads us to wonder: Will the ghosts of Weber and Michels say, "We told you so"?

REFLECTING ON

Formal Organizations

1. Can you think of any reasons besides those identified by Etzioni that a person might give for joining an organization? Would you add any new categories to Etzioni's classification system, or can you suggest an alternative classification system?
2. Describe some of your own experiences with bureaucratic organizations. If any of these experiences were negative, what suggestions would you make for reforming the bureaucracy? If your experiences were positive, what specific features of the bureaucracy contributed to this?

 For useful resources for study and review, run Chapter 6 on your *Living Sociology* CD-ROM.

CONNECTIONS

Role conflict and role strain	For another example of role conflict and role strain in a medical context, see the analysis of physicians' and patients' roles in the section "Sociological Perspectives on Health and Medicine" in Chapter 18.
Presentation of self	Review the social interactionist perspective on socialization in Chapter 5. How does Goffman's notion of dramaturgy build on Mead's concept of the I and the Me in explaining how people behave?
Social groups	The concepts of roles and statuses and social groups were introduced in Chapter 3 in the section on "Social Structure." In sociological analysis, is a group as defined in Chapter 3 a social category or a social aggregate?
Ingroups and outgroups	Read the section on "The Police" in Chapter 7. According to the information given in Chapter 6, what conditions favor the development of ingroups among law enforcement officers? For other examples of the significance of ingroup formation and outgroup labeling, see Chapter 11 on race and ethnic relations.
Milgram's experiment	Milgram's experiment on conformity and obedience was introduced in Chapter 2 in the discussion of research ethics. Survey Chapter 14 for examples of types of government and political activities in which obedience is a critical feature.
Conformity and dissent	Chapter 7 begins with an example of the power of social groups over the individual. How are nonconformity and dissent related to the concept of deviance?
Group leadership	See Chapter 14 for more examples of types of leadership and the characteristics of leaders. What kinds of power and authority do leaders have over groups? How are power and authority defined sociologically?
Formal organizations	For an example of the characteristics of a formal organization, read about the development of the American Medical Association in "Medicine in the United States" in Chapter 18. Is the AMA an example of a coercive, utilitarian, or voluntary association?

CONNECTIONS

Voluntary associations and social change	Survey Chapter 20 to find examples of social movements that began as voluntary associations. To what voluntary associations do you belong?
Bureaucracies	The concept of bureaucracy was introduced in Chapter 3 in the section on "ideal types" of societies. With which type of society is the development of bureaucracies associated? Survey Chapters 13 and 14 for examples of bureaucratic organizations involved in the U.S. economic and political systems.
Inequalities in the workplace	Sex discrimination in formal organizations is a topic in Chapters 10 and 13. Racial and ethnic discrimination in the workplace are discussed in Chapter 11. What examples can you find in those chapters that demonstrate the power of bureaucracies to preserve social inequalities?
Oligarchy	Read the section on "The Structure of the U.S. Economy" in Chapter 13. How does the concentration of power in an economy mirror the concentration of power in a bureaucracy?
Burakumin	See Chapters 8 and 11 for more information on the Burakumin. What are some other examples of the way corporations reflect their society's system of social stratification?

SUMMING UP CHAPTER 6

1. A status is a social position. Attached to every status is one or more roles, that is, behaviors, responsibilities, and privileges that are expected of individuals occupying a specific status. Individuals hold multiple statuses simultaneously; these multiple statuses comprise a status set. Sometimes, however, the roles attached to one status conflict with the roles attached to another, causing role conflict. Other times, the roles attached to a single status are incompatible, causing role strain.

2. Sociologists distinguish three types of statuses: a status acquired by birth, nature, or chance, called an *ascribed status;* a status acquired by choice, called an *achieved status;* and a status that takes on greater significance in the eyes of others than any other aspect of an individual's identity, called a *master status.* In all cases, statuses and roles have social meaning apart from the individuals who hold them. They are given meaning only in terms of individuals' relationships and interactions with one another.

Social Groups

1. A social group is two or more people who interact with one another on a regular basis and share common expectations and a common identity. Groups are different from social categories in that the members of different social categories do not interact regularly or share much of a common identity. Groups also differ from aggregates in that aggregates are a collection of people who just happen to be in the same place at the same time.

2. Groups may be distinguished by the level of personal closeness or emotional attachment that members feel toward one another. Primary groups are always small, they endure over time, and their members have strong emotional attachments to one another. However, most of the groups to which people belong are secondary groups, which do not have a strong emotional component. Secondary groups are oriented toward achieving a common goal. The more technologically developed the society, the greater the interaction in secondary groups.

3. Social groups whose members express intense loyalty, respect, and pride in the group are called *ingroups*. Those groups with whom ingroups see themselves in competition are called *outgroups*. The rivalry between specific ingroups and outgroups may be friendly, but sometimes it is openly hostile or violent. The possibility for conflict between an ingroup and an outgroup increases when the ingroup is politically, economically, or socially more powerful than the outgroup, and when the groups see themselves competing over scarce resources.

4. A reference group is one that a person uses as a point of reference for making a decision. It can be small or large, and it can be composed of people the person knows well or has never met. A single member of a reference group who becomes more important than others in the group in terms of the influence of his or her opinions and behavior is a role model.

5. A network is a series of social connections that functions to link people with common interests and also common social characteristics (sex, race and ethnicity, and social class). Consequently, networks may also exclude those who do not share similar characteristics.

Behavior in Groups

1. One important factor affecting how we behave in a group is group size, which affects group stability, quality of interaction, and the ability of the group to accomplish tasks. Interaction in dyads is most intense, but the intensity makes dyads unstable. In a triad, the intensity declines, but the group's stability improves. As groups grow in size, the number of relationships within the group increases dramatically, and large groups tend to be more complex than smaller groups. Larger groups are more effective at accomplishing determinate tasks, whereas smaller groups have greater success at accomplishing indeterminate tasks.

2. Researchers have found that conformity manifests itself in groups in several ways. One way is through group polarization, when a group takes more extreme actions than any single member would. Group polarization is thought to occur because of deindividuation, the process of losing one's sense of personal responsibility to the group. Another way that conformity manifests itself in groups is through *groupthink,* the process by which members of a group support one another during decision making in order to preserve group harmony and unity. A number of unwise political decisions have been attributed to groupthink.

3. Asch's experiments demonstrated the power of group pressure in bringing about conformity. Milgram's experiments showed that individuals perceived as authority figures can also induce conformity. However, if one or two people dissent from the majority, group decision making and behavior can be dramatically altered.

4. Most groups have leaders. Instrumental leaders are task-oriented, whereas expressive leaders are people-oriented. Neither type of leader is necessarily better than the other, although each is better suited to lead in particular situations. Leaders can also be distinguished by their style of leadership: authoritarian, democratic, or laissez-faire.

5. Group members may be led involuntarily, but leaders may also command a following because they have legitimate authority. Max Weber identified three types of legitimate authority: rational-legal, which is bestowed by legally enacted rules, regulations, or contracts; traditional, which derives from customs; and charismatic, which derives from a leader's extraordinary personal virtues or skills.

Formal Organizations

1. There are three types of formal organizations. Coercive organizations are those that people are forced to join. Utilitarian organizations are those people join to gain something. Voluntary organizations are those people join for the personal satisfaction of participating in them or because they believe it is morally right.

2. Max Weber studied a particular type of organizational bureaucracy and developed an ideal type bureaucracy with six essential features: specialization, hierarchy, written rules and regulations, impartiality, impersonality, and recordkeeping. The advantage of bureaucracy is that it standardizes social life, making interaction predictable and managable. But bureaucracy has several problems associated with it, including ritualism, bloat and secrecy, the preservation of inequality, invasion of privacy, and incompetence.

3. Robert Michels developed the Iron Law of Oligarchy to describe what he saw as the inevitable process by which resources and decision-making authority in a bureaucracy come to be controlled by a tiny faction of members.

4. Formal organizations in Japan are characterized by teamwork, bringing workers and managers together. Various rituals reinforce the team spirit, and workers receive significant financial benefits. In contrast, U.S. businesses emphasize individualism and a top-down organizational hierarchy. An alternative to adopting the Japanese model and retaining the traditional bureaucratic model is to humanize bureaucracy by making it more inclusive, team-oriented, and enriching. In short, bureaucracies may be humanized by making them more flexible.

KEY PEOPLE AND CONCEPTS

achieved status: a status one works to acquire

aggregate: a collection of people who happen to be in the same place at the same time

ascribed status: a status one acquires by birth or that is imposed on an individual by nature or by chance

authoritarian leadership: a leadership style in which leaders make decisions on their own and then inform group members what they are expected to do

bureaucracy: a form of organization based on written rules and procedures and designed for managing and coordinating the actions of large numbers of people

bureaucratic ritualism: when the rules and procedures of an organization take on greater importance than the organization's purpose and goals

charismatic authority: authority that is bestowed on an individual because of his or her extraordinary personal virtues or skills

coercive organization: an organization that one is forced to join, or that one joins by choice but cannot easily withdraw from

conformity: an individual's willingness to go along with an opinion or action undertaken by others in a group

deindividuation: the process of losing one's sense of personal responsibility and individuality to the group

democratic leadership: a leadership style in which leaders seek input from all group members before arriving at a decision

determinate task: a task that can be accomplished in only one or two correct ways

dramaturgical analysis: the sociological study of social interaction as theatrical performance

dyad: a group of two people

expressive leader: a leader who is people-oriented and whose primary concern is the well-being of the group as a whole

formal organization: a large, secondary group whose members interact for the purpose of achieving their common goals as efficiently and effectively as possible

Goffman, Erving (1922–1982): sociologist who studied the construction of social reality by developing dramaturgical analysis, the analysis of social interaction as theatrical performance

group polarization: the tendency for individuals in a group to adopt opinions or engage in behaviors that are more extreme or risky than those they would normally support or do alone

groupthink: the process by which the members of a group support one another during decision making, with the primary goal of preserving group harmony and unity

indeterminate task: a task that can be accomplished correctly in many different ways

ingroup: a social group whose members express intense loyalty, respect, and pride in the group

instrumental leader: a leader who is task-oriented and focuses on getting a job done as efficiently and effectively as possible

laissez-faire leadership: a leadership style in which leaders avoid intervention and simply wait for problems or crises to resolve themselves over time

legitimate authority: power that is perceived as rightful by those being led

master status: a status that takes on greater significance in the eyes of others than any other aspect of an individual's identity

network: a chain of associations that links people with common interests who otherwise would not have the opportunity to interact

oligarchy: occurs when the resources and decision-making authority of a bureaucracy are controlled by a tiny faction of members

outgroup: a group that is viewed as the competitor or rival of another group

power: the ability to get others to do one's will even if they do not want to do it

presentation of self: the careful control of one's appearance and behavior in order to convey to others a specific image of one's self

primary group: a social group, typically small in size, that is characterized by strong emotional attachments among the members and that endures over time

rational-legal authority: authority that is bestowed on an individual by legally enacted rules, regulations, or contracts

reference group: a group that serves as a point of reference in personal decision making

role: the behaviors, responsibilities, and privileges expected of individuals occupying a specific status

role conflict: the clash between roles attached to different statuses occupied by a single individual

role model: an individual who serves as an example to be emulated

role strain: the clash between multiple roles attached to a single status occupied by an individual

secondary group: a social group that may be large or small in size, but that is characterized by members' orientation to achieving the same goal rather than members' emotional attachments to one another

social category: a collective of people who occupy the same status

social group: two or more people who interact with one another on a regular basis and share common expectations and a common identity

status: a social position

status set: all the social positions held by an individual at any one time

traditional authority: authority bestowed on an individual by custom

trained incapacity: the inability to think independently and creatively, which results from the removal of autonomy in one's job within an organization

triad: a group of three people

utilitarian organization: an organization one joins because of the material gains to be had from membership

voluntary association: an organization one joins because of its moral appeal and the personal satisfaction attained from participating in it; also called *normative association*

LEARNING MORE

Ferguson, K. E. (1984). *The feminist case against bureaucracy.* Philadelphia: Temple University Press. Is bureaucracy a masculine construct? Is there a feminist alternative? This book offers answers to these questions while providing a fresh analysis of Weber's ideal type.

Kanter, R. M. (1993). *Men and women of the corporation.* New York: Basic Books. A revised edition of Kanter's classic study of gender relations in management that was originally published in 1977.

Kanter, R. M. (1989). *When giants learn to dance: Mastering the challenges of strategy, management and careers in the 1990s.* New York: Simon and Schuster. A look at the changes in corporations in the 1990s and beyond.

Nye, J. L., & Brower, A. M. (Eds.) (1996). *What's social about social cognition?* Thousand Oaks, CA: Sage. A collection of essays that looks at social interaction in small groups, including decision making, group boundaries, and the development of prejudices.

Scott, W. R. (1995). *Institutions and organizations.* Thousand Oaks, CA: Sage. A readable discussion of recent research and theoretical approaches to institutions and organizations.

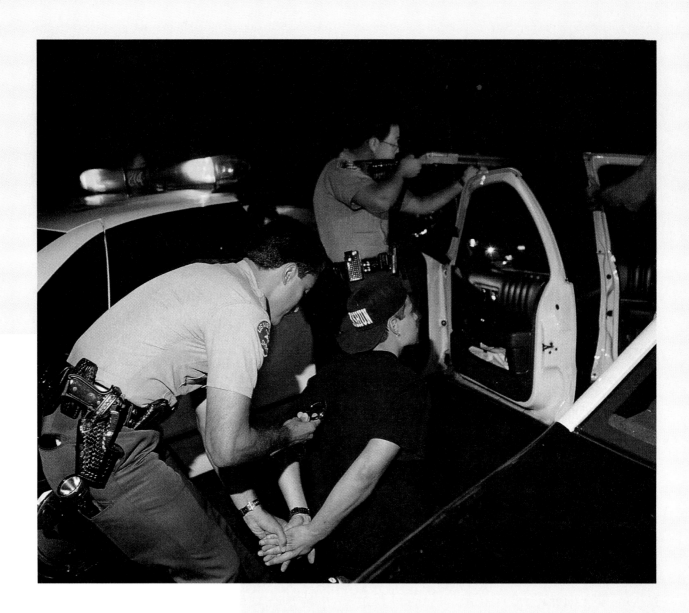

 Run Chapter 7 on your *Living Sociology* CD-ROM for interesting and informative activities, web links, videos, practice tests, and more.

Deviance and Social Control

One warm summer day, a mother duck sat atop six eggs, waiting for them to hatch. Gradually, cracks appeared in the eggs, and fluffy ducklings soon emerged—except for one. From the largest egg came a most unusual bird. Its neck was long and thin, and its feathers were dull in color. The mother duck was surprised, but she nevertheless led the strange-looking duckling to the water with her other offspring. All the other ducks and ducklings made fun of the unusual-looking bird. They taunted him endlessly and said, loud enough for him to hear, how ugly he was. Pretty soon, the unusual bird just couldn't stand the torment anymore, so he floated off, determined to make a life on his own. Summer turned to fall, and fall to winter. Finding enough food to stay alive during the cold winter months proved to be a challenge, and the bird was relieved and happy when spring arrived. Stretching his wings, the bird walked toward the water and there he saw, floating gracefully, several large white birds with long necks and bright orange bills. "How beautiful they are," thought the bird. "I wish I looked like them, but I'm the ugliest bird alive." The bird started to settle into the water, expecting the other birds to make fun of him, but instead they greeted him with cries of welcome. As he swam toward them bewildered, he glimpsed his reflection in the water's surface, but instead of an awkward skinny neck and dull feathers, he saw that he did look just like those other beautiful birds: He was a swan.

You may remember this tale from your childhood. It's the story of *The Ugly Duckling* by Hans Christian Andersen. We have read it to our children often to remind them that it's okay to be different and to encourage them to be themselves even if that means they don't look or behave like all their friends. It's an important message, for as we saw in Chapter 6, it's not easy to dissent from the group. The groups to which we belong—whether they're friends or neighbors or coworkers or teammates—put tremendous pressure on us to conform. And when one is "different" in some way, the outcome is not always as happy as it was for the ugly duckling.

This chapter is about nonconformity or *deviance*. **Deviance** is any act, attribute, or belief that violates a cultural norm and elicits from others a negative or positive reaction. Let's look at the different elements of this definition.

First, when we think of deviance, we typically think of someone *doing* something, such as robbing a bank or driving while drunk. Notice in our definition, though, that to be deviant one need do nothing. In some cases, one need only *be* a certain way for the label "deviant" to be applied. For example, people who are 25 percent above the average weight for their sex, age, and height are considered obese. Obesity may be the result of factors over which the person has little or no control; yet studies also indicate that people who are obese are discriminated against in the job market and are considered sloppy, stupid, and ugly by the general public (Attie & Brooks-Gunn, 1987; Crandall, 1995; Gortmaker et al., 1993). In other words, the person may well have done nothing to bring about the condition, but is labeled "deviant" nonetheless.

Second, reactions to deviance are usually negative, but notice that our definition allows for *positive* reactions. Recall the dissenters we discussed in Chapter 6, such as Martin Luther King, Jr., Nelson Mandela, and Mahatma Ghandi, who incurred negative reactions from some people, especially those whom they challenged, but whose extraordinary courage and revolutionary ideas made them heroes to the oppressed. Certain physical traits can also elicit positive reactions. Someone who is seven feet tall, for example, gets very positive responses from basketball coaches.

The fact that social reactions to particular acts, attributes, or beliefs can be positive or negative shows that nothing is *inherently* deviant. What is deviant depends not on the act, attribute, or belief itself, but on how others react to it. And reactions depend on many factors, including situational and historical context, the characteristics of the individual being reacted to, and the characteristics of the reactors. Wait just a minute, you say: Killing or forcing someone to have sexual intercourse are deviant regardless of who's doing it, who's reacting to it, or the context of the act. But killing is typically considered normative if it is done in the context of war or in self-defense. And opinion polls show that a majority of young men and women believe that under some circumstances it is appropriate for a man to force a woman to have sex (if the couple is married or if the woman "teased" the man) (Koss et al., 1987; Schwartz & DeKeseredy, 1997).

What is deviant, then, is not *absolute*, but culturally *relative*. It is relative first to situational context. Suppose, for example, someone sees your lips moving as if you are having a conversation, but there is no one visibly present

What groups or societies regard as deviant varies historically, cross-culturally, and situationally. Of these photos, all of which involve people killing people, which, if any, would you pick as deviant? What are the reasons for your decision? Which, if any, photos might you pick as representing "official" or sanctioned murder? If you could add two photos to the set, what would you show to clarify the meaning of deviance?

to whom you could be speaking. The observer asks you what you are doing, and you reply that you are talking to God. If you are in a church, synagogue, mosque, or other place of worship, your response would be appropriate. If, however, you are at the neighborhood deli eating lunch, your behavior would likely be viewed as at least odd, and the observer might react by politely ignoring you. What is defined as deviant is also relative to historical context. A woman who wore slacks in 1800 would have been considered scandalous, but a woman wearing slacks in 2000 would be met with indifference.

Another factor that influences what gets labeled deviant are the characteristics of those being reacted to. For example, behaviors considered normative for men are often considered deviant when they are engaged in by

women. If a man whistles at an attractive woman walking down a city street, others may disapprove or find the behavior annoying, but they would not likely consider it strange or unusual behavior. If, however, a woman whistles at an attractive man walking down a city street, she would almost certainly be considered deviant by most passersby. And what gets labeled deviant also depends on who is doing the reacting. A teenager who gets a favorite rock group's name tattooed on his arm may elicit the admiration of peers, but the wrath of his parents. The behavior has different meaning to different groups.

Crime is a special type of deviance. **Crime** is the violation of norms a society considers so important that it enacts laws to force compliance with them. Crime, like other forms of deviance, also varies situationally. For example, if a stranger breaks into your house and attacks you, the stranger has committed a crime. But if you fight back and kill the stranger, your behavior is considered self-defense, and not a crime. Crime also varies historically. Many behaviors which in the past were considered criminal, are now legal, and vice versa. In the nineteenth century, for instance, there were state and local laws prohibiting women from asking men out on dates, undressing in front of a photograph of a man, and appearing on a public highway wearing a bathing suit. Today we consider these laws, not the behaviors they prohibit, deviant.

The characteristics of social actors affect what is considered crime at a given time. When asked what they think is deviant, many people name street crimes such as dealing drugs or mugging. They rarely mention the kinds of crimes committed by high-ranking government officials or corporate executives, such as financial fraud, insider stock trading, illegal disposal of toxic waste, or the sale of unsafe products. There are, of course, significant differences, including racial and social class differences, between street offenders and corporate rule breakers. The low social standing of the average street offender makes it highly likely that he or she will be apprehended and processed through the criminal justice system, being officially defined and reacted to as deviant, while the high social standing of the average corporate offender protects him or her from this process.

Sociologists have shared the general public's preoccupation with street crime in their study of deviance, so we will spend a good bit of time in this chapter discussing criminal behavior. First, however, let's examine the various theories that sociologists and others have developed to account for why people deviate.

EXPLAINING DEVIANCE

There are two general approaches to explaining deviance. One approach focuses on deviants themselves; it assumes that most people comply with norms most of the time, so those who deviate must somehow be different from the rest of us. There must be something wrong with them. Just what that something is varies from theory to theory, but, taken together, these explanations look for factors *internal* to individual deviants to explain their rule breaking. These kinds of explanations tend to be nonsociological and can best be described as *kinds-of-people theories*.

The second approach to explaining deviance focuses not on rule breakers, but on the rules, or, more specifically, on the process by which someone or something comes to be defined as deviant. Instead of asking, "Why does Jack smoke marijuana?" this approach asks, "Why is smoking marijuana considered deviant? Has smoking marijuana always been considered deviant? If not, when

and how did it come to be defined as deviant? Is it deviant to everyone? If not, to whom is it deviant?" In short, this approach is concerned with how particular norms are established and how they are enforced. Theories taking this approach look for factors *external* to individual deviants to explain rule breaking and therefore are sociological in orientation. A good way to describe them is as *process theories*.

There are numerous kinds-of-people and process theories of deviance—far too many to discuss in detail here. We'll examine only the more popular theories from each approach, not only because they give us a sense of the various ways deviance has been studied and explained, but also because they suggest different methods of controlling or responding to deviance.

R E F L E C T I N G   O N

Explaining Deviance

At this point, which type of approach to explaining deviance makes the most sense to you? Why?

NONSOCIOLOGICAL THEORIES OF DEVIANCE

Biological Theories

You've probably heard the old saying, "Appearances are deceiving." Yet it is a fact of everyday life that we often judge others, at least initially, by how they look. We may try to strike up a conversation with someone because we find him or her attractive, or we may deliberately avoid someone who "looks weird." In short, we often make inferences about another person's *character* based on his or her *appearance*.

This is nothing new. In fact, the notion that an individual's character could be read from a physical examination dates back to the ancient Greeks and Romans. According to the "science" of *physiognomy*, faces, skulls, and other physical features revealed a person's natural disposition. For example, physiognomists warned against trusting beardless men and bearded women. In the Medieval period there was even a law stipulating that the uglier of two criminal suspects was probably the guilty party (Ellis, 1915).

By the middle of the eighteenth century, physiognomy had fallen into disrepute, but the idea that an individual's physical makeup determines his or her personality and behavior never disappeared completely. Not surprisingly, the notion found its way into various kinds-of-people theories of deviance.

Deviance and Physique. In the late 1800s, an Italian physician named Caesare Lombroso claimed that, based on his examination of prisoners, criminals and other deviants were physically different from the noncriminal population. Criminals were less biologically evolved than noncriminals, as evidenced by traits such as more than five fingers or toes, premature or excessive skin wrinkling, and tattooing. Lombroso's work was extensively criticized, of course, because many of the traits he identified as biologically based, such as tattoos, had obvious social origins. Even premature or excessive wrinkling could have a social cause, such as working in the sun for long hours. Nevertheless, Lombroso's theory inspired a long line of social scientists to pursue physiological causes for deviance.

In the 1940s, William Sheldon associated deviant behavior with body build. Sheldon identified three types of male physiques: soft and round, skinny and frail, and muscular and athletic. This last type—muscular athletic—he associated with a lustful, callous, aggressive temperament that predisposed a young man to violence and other criminal deviations (Sheldon, 1949). Supporting Sheldon were Eleanor and Sheldon Glueck (1956) and Juan Cortes (1972), who believed that body build interacts with particular social factors, such as relationships with parents, teachers, and friends, to predispose certain young men to deviant behavior.

While the work of these theorists is provocative, the data simply do not support their position (Vold & Bernard, 1986). Indeed, some critics consider the idea that deviance can be explained in terms of physique as fortune telling rather than science. However, these are not the only biological theories of deviance.

Deviance and Heredity. A number of researchers interested in explaining deviant behavior have looked to genetics as a cause. For example, in 1993, geneticist Dean Hamer announced that he had obtained the first empirical evidence of a genetic link to homosexuality. In a study of forty-four pairs of brothers who were homosexual, Hamer found that thirty-three pairs shared a unique piece of the X chromosome, a significantly greater incidence than one would expect by chance alone. He also found that these gay men were more likely to have gay male relatives on their mother's side than on their father's side. Hamer took this finding as further evidence of a genetic basis for homosexuality, since men, whose sex chromosomes consist of one X and one Y chromosome, receive the X chromosome from their mothers only (Hamer & Copeland, 1994).

Needless to say, Hamer's study has generated considerable controversy. One of the major criticisms is Hamer's use of small, nonrandom samples that are not necessarily representative of the general population. How much, for example, can a study of eighty-eight men tell us, given

that anywhere from 1 to 10 percent of the U.S. population is estimated to be homosexual, including at least 3 percent of women? Heredity studies like Hamer's are also criticized because they do not take into account possible social causes of the behavior in question. And, of course, many in the gay and lesbian community turn the tables on such research by questioning the appropriateness of defining homosexuality as deviant in the first place.

Psychological Theories

How many of us, when we hear about or see a particularly unusual or strange behavior, say, "You have to be crazy to do something like that," or "That person must be sick"? Kinds-of-people theories that explain deviance as a product of mental disorder date back to ancient Greece, when Pythagoras and his student Alcmaeon introduced the idea that the brain is the organ of the mind and "abnormal" behavior is a symptom of disease in that organ (Vold & Bernard, 1986).

One psychological approach tries to distinguish deviants from nondeviants on the basis of personality traits. Experiments and personality tests are used to identify personality differences. For example, one study asked a group of boys with arrest records what they would do if they were given $2. Most of the boys said they would spend the money. But when a group of boys without arrest records were asked the same question, most said they would save the money. The researchers maintain that these results show that deviants are less able than nondeviants to delay gratification (Wilson & Herrnstein, 1985). Additional studies report that deviants feel fewer emotional attachments to others, are hyperactive, and have less self-control than nondeviants (Megargee, 1972). But other researchers have been unable to find significant differences between the personality traits of deviants and nondeviants, and even when differences are identified, they do not indicate that deviants are psychologically abnormal (Kleinmuntz, 1982).

Mental illnesses such as psychosis are usually attributed as causes only in cases of extreme deviance, such as violent crime. The behavior of psychotics is erratic and illogical. They suffer from delusions and hallucinations, often claiming, for example, that they hear voices telling them to do certain things. One infamous deviant who was diagnosed as psychotic was David Berkowitz, who called himself "Son of Sam" and killed people because a creature who lived in the wall of his apartment told him to (Toch & Adams, 1989).

Still, while serious criminals may suffer from mental illnesses such as psychosis, the relative rarity of these disorders means that they can account for only a tiny fraction of all deviation. In fact, one problem that all psychological theories have in common is that they cannot explain deviance resulting from an attribute. For instance, they cannot explain why people who are overweight are labeled deviant. In these situations, it is not the person identified as deviant that warrants our attention, but those doing the identifying.

Psychological theories of deviance, like all kinds-of-people theories, are premised on a false dichotomy: that an individual *either* is deviant *or* is not deviant. As we will learn in the remainder of this chapter, however, deviance is better conceptualized in terms of a continuum. Few, if any, people are deviant all the time, and few, if any, always conform.

REFLECTING ON

Nonsociological Theories of Deviance

Do you see merit in any of the nonsociological theories of deviance?

SOCIOLOGICAL THEORIES OF DEVIANCE

There are numerous sociological theories of deviance, but they all have one thing in common: They focus on locating factors external to individuals that lead them into deviance or that prompt others to identify them as deviant. Some sociological theories also address the consequences of being identified as deviant. Most were developed to explain negative rather than positive deviance.

Structural Functionalism

There are several prominent structural functionalist theories of deviance. Emile Durkheim developed what may be considered the first structural functionalist theory of deviance. More recent functionalist theories include strain theory, subcultural theories, and control theory. Let's look at each in turn.

Durkheim's Normality of Deviance. Emile Durkheim, to whom we trace the origins of structural functionalist theory, observed that deviance is an inevitable part of social life. Since all societies have norms, there will always be individuals who violate those norms. Different types of societies exercise more or less control over their members, thereby influencing the amount of deviance, but no society is deviance-free.

Given his theoretical framework—that deviance is normal in a society—Durkheim went on to ask what the *functions* of deviance were. He arrived at a four-part answer. First, deviance clarifies the moral boundaries of a society. By reacting to specific acts, atttributes, and beliefs

as deviant, the conforming members of the society highlight for one another the normative line between what is acceptable and what is unacceptable. Second, deviance actually increases conformity in a society. Conforming members of the society receive reinforcement for their behavior through the negative reactions imposed on the deviant person. Third, public reactions to deviation, especially serious deviation, solidify social bonds between conforming members of the society. For example, acts of extraordinary and senseless violence, such as the school shootings in Littleton, Colorado in 1999, unify large segments of the population as they express their shared outrage and act to address the deviation and harm done.

Finally, deviance may promote social change by introducing new behaviors and ideas that at first seem strange or undesirable, but over time become normative. History books are filled with numerous examples, many spearheaded by dissenters who endured the hostility of others who considered them deviant. We need only look at the case of Steven Biko, who was South Africa's most important Black leader when he was arrested in 1977 on charges of terrorism. Biko died in police custody, but the five White security guards who had interrogated him were acquitted of his murder. Nonetheless, Biko's death became a rallying point for Black South Africans in their struggle for equality. It was not until 1997, however, that Biko's killers were finally brought to justice.

Durkheim's observation that deviance occurs in every society is valuable, as is his point that deviance benefits society. However, he overlooks the negative impact that being defined as deviant can have on deviants themselves, and he also does not consider the question of how certain acts, attributes, and beliefs come to be considered deviant to begin with.

Robert Merton's Strain Theory. Sociologist Robert Merton built on Durkheim's work in his own effort to explain deviance. Merton (1975) begins with the premise that every society has culturally defined *goals*—what the members of the society value and strive for. Every society also has a social structure composed of the institutionalized means for achieving these goals. In a well-balanced society, these two elements are integrated: All members know and accept the goals and have at their disposal the means to achieve them. Not everyone is uniformly successful in achieving the goals, but in the "ideal" society, people derive satisfaction simply from being in competition with others working toward the same ends.

What happens, though, if the culture and the structure of the society are not in balance? In the United States, for example, Merton observed that the most important goal is material success. American culture values money and the accumulation of wealth more than anything else. This would not be a problem if the institutionalized means to achieve material success were equally available to every-

How could you interpret this photo in terms of Robert Merton's strain theory? For instance, how does the picture suggest an imbalance between the society's goals and the means to achieve them? How does it suggest the use of illegitimate means as an adaptation strategy? According to Merton, which groups in a society are most likely to resort to illegitimate means?

gies that Merton identified. Taken together, they are referred to as his *typology of adaptations.* Three (innovation, retreatism, and rebellion) are considered deviant; the other two (conformity and ritualism) generally are not.

Conformity, according to Merton, is the most common adaptation. Conformists accept the goals and play by the rules to achieve them, no matter how difficult that may be. Conformity explains, for instance, why even in high-crime areas, many residents don't commit crimes. *Ritualism* also involves adhering to the rules, but scaling down the goals so that satisfaction may be obtained through a much lower level of "success." Ritualists "go through the motions" day in and day out, content with modest achievement and thereby avoiding the frustration that results from being unable to reach loftier aspirations.

Some people, though, adapt to the strain of anomie in deviant ways, such as *innovation.* Innovators accept the cultural goals, but, finding the institutionalized means blocked, turn to illegitimate means to achieve these ends. For example, some students who accept the emphasis our society places on grades and credentialism resort to cheating if they think they can't get a passing (or better) grade in a tough course.

Retreatism is another deviant adaptation used less often than innovation according to Merton. Retreatists have been socialized to accept the cultural goals as well as the institutionalized means to achieve them, but, failing to succeed, they simply drop out of the game. Drug addicts, alcoholics, and vagrants are examples of retreatists.

Finally, *rebellion* is the adaptation of those who reject both the established goals and means and seek to replace them with new ones. For example, it is alleged that the men charged with bombing the federal building in Oklahoma City in 1994 were motivated by their belief that the federal government had lost its legitimate authority and must be destroyed. But rebellion can also be

one. But some groups in the United States find the institutionalized means to success closed to them because of their race or ethnicity, for example, or because they are poor. Making matters worse is our country's belief in the American dream—that anyone who is honest and works hard will be successful.

Merton calls the imbalance between a society's goals and the means to achieve them **anomie,** a term he actually borrowed from Durkheim, but redefined. Anomie produces strain, which people must cope with in one way or another. Table 7.1 presents the different coping strate-

TABLE 7.1   Merton's Typology of Adaptations to Strain

Mode of Adaptation	Cultural Goals	Institutionalized Means
Conformity	Accepts (+)	Accepts (+)
Ritualism	Rejects (−)	Accepts (+)
Innovation	Accepts (+)	Rejects (−)
Retreatism	Rejects (−)	Rejects (−)
Rebellion	Rejects, but wishes to replace with new goals (±)	Rejects, but wishes to replace with new means (±)

Source: Adapted from R. K. Merton. (1968). *Social theory and social structure.* Glencoe, IL: Free Press, p. 194.

positive: Many of the dissenters we identified in Chapter 6 can be considered rebels.

Merton's strain theory is regarded as one of the most influential sociological theories of deviance (Clinard, 1964; Passas & Agnew, 1997). Nevertheless, critics question whether conformity is the most common adaptation. They maintain that if Merton's research had been more systematic, he would have found that total conformists are relatively few and far between, even in those groups such as the wealthy where one would expect strain to be minimal (Taylor, Walton, & Young, 1973). For example, some drug addicts are materially successful people—physicians, business people, and other professionals (Lindesmith & Gagnon, 1964). Some sociologists also point out that there is no single set of universally shared cultural goals in the United States or in most other societies, as Merton's theory assumes. Rather, these sociologists argue, to understand deviation one must understand the cultural diversity of a society (Lemert, 1964).

Subcultural Theories. Sociologists who explain deviance in terms of cultural diversity focus on the frustrations that particular groups experience as a result of their inability to "succeed" by the standards of the dominant culture. These groups develop independent value structures that better reflect their everyday experiences and give them opportunities to succeed. With a value system all its own, each group forms a unique **subculture.** Recall from Chapter 4 that a subculture is a group within the dominant culture that shares some elements of the dominant culture, but also distinguishes itself in specific ways. The way it differentiates itself—by language, dress, or patterns of behavior—is often considered deviant by the dominant culture.

There are several subcultural theories of deviance. Albert Cohen (1955), for example, focused on male street gangs in poor and working-class neighborhoods. The dominant culture of the society is middle class and consists of values such as delayed gratification, self-control, academic and occupational success, and good manners. Middle-class parents socialize their children to accept and abide by these values, but the socialization of lower-class children is more relaxed. As a result of this lack of restraint, lower-class children aren't very successful in school. Their parents' limited resources also do not give them a feeling of accomplishment. Instead, their lack of achievement by middle-class standards makes them feel frustrated. To cope with this frustration, Cohen argued, lower-class boys join gangs and develop their own set of values, against which they can be judged successful at least by their peers. Cohen identified five values as most important to the delinquent gang subculture:

1. *Nonutilitarianism*—Gang members commit crimes not as a means to an end, such as stealing for ma-terial gain or fighting to defend themselves, but "for the hell of it." Gang members get intrinsic satisfaction from committing crimes.
2. *Maliciousness*—Much delinquent activity, such as tearing down street signs or scratching people's cars, is "just plain mean." Its purpose is to create problems for people, or to make them unhappy or uncomfortable.
3. *Negativism*—The values of gang members are not just different from those of the dominant culture, they are the polar opposite. For example, the dominant culture values preserving property, whereas the delinquent subculture values destroying property.
4. *Short-run hedonism*—Gang members seek immediate gratification. They are out for fun and don't care about long-term goals or consequences.
5. *Group autonomy*—Gang members defy or ignore authority figures, including their parents and teachers. They resist any control on their behavior except that imposed informally by other gang members.

Why did Cohen focus only on boys and not on girls? Cohen believed that only lower-class boys experience the frustration that lack of achievement causes because achievement is a primary component of masculinity. Girls, he said, are preoccupied with developing romantic relationships, since marriage is their primary goal.

Although Cohen's theory of delinquent subcultures had some appeal, especially during the 1950s when it was published, it has also been extensively criticized. Before we discuss the criticisms, though, let's review some other subcultural theories.

Walter B. Miller (1958) also studied male street gangs. He believed that every social class develops its own value system. In other words, according to Miller, it's not just lower-class boys whose values are different from the dominant middle class, it's all members of the lower class. What are the values that make up the lower-class subculture? Miller identified six core values, or what he called *focal concerns:*

1. *Trouble*—Getting into and staying out of trouble are major preoccupations of lower-class people. For men, trouble includes fighting and sexual adventures; for women, it is sexual activity that results in unwanted pregnancy.
2. *Toughness*—Toughness is a focal concern of lower-class men. It refers to physical prowess and bravery in the face of physical threat.
3. *Smartness*—Smartness refers to a person's "street sense"—the ability to avoid being duped, outwitted, or conned, as well as the ability to dupe, outwit, and con others.

4. *Excitement*—Examples of excitement include the search for "thrills," "flirting with danger," and risk taking.
5. *Fate*—Fate is the idea that one's life is determined by forces beyond one's control. It is not a religious concept, but rather has to do with being "lucky" or "unlucky."
6. *Autonomy*—Autonomy refers to the desire of lower-class people to resist others' attempts to control their lives. But, Miller claims, the actual behavior of lower-class people often leads to the opposite result: Many lower-class people behave in ways that ultimately put them in restrictive environments, such as prisons.

In short, Miller believed that deviant behavior is concentrated among the poor and working class and that it reflects their values. Within their own communities, the

How do subcultural theories explain the development of deviance among low-income urban youths? In particular, how are frustration and lack of opportunity involved? According to Cohen and Miller, what roles might street values play? According to Cloward and Ohlin, under what circumstances might the youths in this photo develop a subculture based on conflict, criminal acts, or retreatism? According to Hirschi, what measures are most effective in preventing any of those things from happening?

behavior of lower-class people is normative, but by the standards of the dominant (middle-class) culture, it is deviant.

One other subcultural theory that was popular during the early 1960s is *differential opportunity theory*, developed by Richard Cloward and Lloyd Ohlin (1960). Cloward and Ohlin agreed with Merton's position that U.S. culture emphasizes material success, but not everyone has equal access to legitimate means for achieving success. They also agreed that those deprived of legitimate opportunities, especially the poor, may turn to illegitimate means to achieve material success. However, Cloward and Ohlin observed that even in the poorest neighborhoods, most people are conforming. Why? According to Cloward and Ohlin, the answer is differential access to illegitimate opportunities. It's not enough to simply be motivated to deviate; a person must know how to carry out particular forms of deviance (such as roll a marijuana cigarette or pick a lock) and also have a chance to actually deviate.

Cloward and Ohlin studied the differential opportunity structure of one deprived group: young men living in impoverished urban neighborhoods. Different neighborhoods produce different types of deviant subcultures. For example, in unstable neighborhoods with rapidly changing populations, a *conflict subculture* is likely to develop as boys use violence to establish a reputation. In more stable neighborhoods, where people know one another and adult criminal role models are plentiful, a *criminal subculture* is more likely to develop because young men can rely on the contacts and experience of older men who will "show them the ropes" of deviating. And in neighborhoods where residents are "double failures"—they can't succeed by legitimate or illegitimate means—a *retreatist subculture* will emerge. Members of a retreatist subculture withdraw from society by using alcohol or drugs.

Subcultural theories were developed to explain a specific form of deviance—street crime—which statistics show is especially prevalent in poor and working-class communities of color. One of the major criticisms of subcultural theories is that they portray deviance, especially criminal deviance, as a problem of only certain groups in society, while overlooking the deviance of the wealthy and socially more powerful. For example, the number of public officials charged with abusing the privileges of their office has increased by more than 600 percent since 1975, but few of these politicians have served time in prison or even repaid the money they embezzled (U.S. Department of Commerce, Bureau of the Census, 1995, 1997; see also Chambliss, 1973). This is not to say that deviant subcultures do not exist or that they do not reflect the life circumstances of their members. Rather, deviant subcultures, including those for whom crime is a favorite pastime, are present throughout the entire social structure, but we know little about many of them because sociologists have concentrated only on the deviations of the relatively powerless. In fact, poverty itself is frequently treated as deviant, with the poor being regarded as lazy and shiftless by those who are better off financially.

Like Merton's theory, subcultural theories also have been criticized for assuming that all members of a particular social class hold the same cultural values. Subcultural theorists argue that *all* lower-class people value toughness and excitement, but there is no empirical evidence that lower-class parents encourage their children to adopt these values. The data show just the opposite: Lower-class parents report as much and sometimes greater disapproval for interpersonal violence than higher-income parents (Erlanger, 1974). At the same time, many middle-class and wealthy people value excitement—that is, risk taking or thrill seeking—as evidenced by the popularity of casino gambling. Thus, subcultural theories may be a better reflection of stereotypes about the poor than an accurate depiction of a "lower-class lifestyle."

Hirschi's Control Theory. Travis Hirschi (1969) looks at deviance from a different angle than the other sociological theorists we have discussed. He starts out with the assumption that everybody is basically deviant at heart. Everyone is equally motivated to engage in deviance simply because fulfilling one's desires usually can be done most effectively, efficiently, and pleasurably in ways that are disapproved of or prohibited. Given this, the interesting question to Hirschi is not why people are deviant, but rather, why does anyone conform? Hirschi believes that it is a person's ties or *social bonds* to conventional institutions, such as family, school, or employer, that inhibit her or him from acting on deviant motivations. In short, individuals with strong social bonds are unlikely to deviate, whereas those whose social bonds are weak or broken probably will deviate.

At the center of Hirschi's **control theory**, then, is the social bond, composed of four interrelated elements. The most important element is *attachment*, an individual's sensitivity to the feelings of others. Attachment facilitates internalizing society's norms and developing a conscience. If a person doesn't care about the feelings of others, then he or she doesn't feel bound by the norms and is free to deviate.

The second element of the social bond is *commitment*, the stake that people have in playing by the rules. In other words, people invest their time, energy, money, and emotions in pursuing a specific activity such as getting an education or building a career. When considering whether or not to deviate—such as by cheating on a final exam or falsifying an expense account—the individual must factor in what he or she stands to lose if caught.

Involvement, the third element of the social bond, has to do with opportunity to deviate. People busy with conventional activities, such as studying, working, or playing a sport, simply do not have time to participate in deviant activities. This is the underlying rationale for many recreation-oriented delinquency prevention programs, such as the Police Athletic League (PAL) (see the Social Policy box).

The final element of the social bond is *belief,* which refers to the extent to which an individual believes he or she should obey the rules. The less a person believes a rule should be obeyed—that is, the lower the person's belief in the moral validity of the rule—the greater the likelihood that he or she will violate that rule.

Control theory is appealing. It makes sense to most people that someone with strong attachments to others, a high stake in conformity, intense involvement in wholesome activities, and strong belief in the moral validity of norms will not be deviant. Hirschi's theory also receives some support from juvenile delinquency studies (see, for example, Rankin & Wells, 1990; Rosenbaum & Lasley, 1990). Other studies, however, indicate that instead of the social bond influencing deviation, it is deviation that affects the social bond. For instance, Liska and Reed (1985) found that attachment to school had less impact on deviance than deviance had on attachment to school. A good bit of youthful deviance occurs in school or on school grounds. According to Liska and Reed, students who misbehave elicit negative responses from teachers and other school personnel and these reactions, in turn, lower students' attachment to school. Similarly, other studies have found that involvement in particular types of legitimate leisure activities, such as hanging out with friends, actually increases the likelihood that some people will engage in deviance (Agnew & Peterson, 1989).

Another problem with control theory, which it shares with other structural functionalist theories, is that it has not been applied to deviation much beyond the realm of crime and delinquency (crimes committed by juveniles). It is unclear, therefore, whether it adequately accounts for noncriminal forms of deviance, especially attributes that are frequently considered deviant, such as obesity.

Symbolic Interactionism

Symbolic interactionists believe the members of a society create social order through the meanings they give to their everyday interactions with one another. Applying this perspective to deviance leads us to focus on how people *learn* to deviate; how specific acts, attributes, and beliefs come to be defined as deviant; and the consequences of identifying someone as deviant.

Sutherland's Differential Association Theory. Edwin H. Sutherland (1883–1950) developed a theory of deviance

Social Policy
Community-Based Delinquency Prevention

The Issue

The rationale for community recreation programs, such as midnight basketball, in inner city neighborhoods is straightforward: If you give kids something fun and interesting to do, especially during the hours when they are most likely to get into trouble, they won't have the time, energy, or motivation to commit crime. Besides occupying children's time, these programs also establish partnerships between neighborhood residents, police, and local government. But the question remains, do the programs work?

The Debate

Research indicates that such programs can be successful in reducing crime, not only by taking kids off the streets, but also by providing them with opportunities to learn constructive problem-solving skills and to release tension and stress. The programs also give children a structured environment in which they learn to model the behavior of prosocial adults rather than antisocial peers (Moffitt, 1997; U.S. Department of Justice, Bureau of Justice Statistics, 1997). However, additional research shows that community recreation programs are just one small element of a larger crime prevention effort. According to some experts, community recreation programs must be established in conjunction with community development programs that include job training, employment opportunities, study groups and tutoring, improved public housing, and better police–community relations (U.S. Department of Justice, Bureau of Justice Statistics, 1997). Simply taking kids off the streets to play basketball from 10 P.M. to 1 A.M. will not reduce crime if they spend the remaining twenty-one hours of the day in violent, impoverished homes, schools, and neighborhoods. Indeed, without community economic and educational development, the gyms and recreation centers themselves can become sites for criminal activity, especially youth violence.

What Do You Think?

What do you think is the best strategy for ensuring the success of community-based delinquency prevention programs? Are you personally familiar with programs of this kind—for example, midnight basketball? If so, have they been successful in reducing youth crime and deviance in the community where they are located?

---

called *differential association theory,* which is generally regarded as one of the most influential theories of the twentieth century (Matsueda, 1988). According to Sutherland (1947), deviance is learned, and it is learned the same way any other behavior is learned: through interpersonal communication and social interaction in small, intimate groups (primary groups, such as family and friends). What is learned through this process includes not only the techniques for deviating, but also the attitudes and motivations that justify deviating. However, being exposed to deviant attitudes and motivations and even knowing how to deviate does not mean that a person will actually engage in deviation. For example, many people who desperately need money and who know various illegal ways to obtain it nevertheless persevere in solving their financial problems through entirely legal means. Indeed, before a person can become deviant, he or she must also learn specific situational meanings or definitions. According to Sutherland, a person becomes deviant because of an excess of definitions favorable to deviation over definitions unfavorable to deviation. Sutherland called the process of social interaction by which the definitions are acquired **differential association.**

Sutherland chose the term *differential association* to emphasize that in any society, both kinds of definitions—favorable and unfavorable—to deviation coexist. He also wished to show that all associations are not equal. In fact, Sutherland believed that associations vary in frequency, duration, priority, and intensity. Associations that occur often (frequency) and are long-lasting (duration) will have a greater impact on an individual than brief, chance encounters. Associations that occur early in a person's life, especially during childhood, are more important than those that occur later on (priority). And associations with prestigious people or those held in high esteem will be more influential than associations with people for whom one has little regard or who are socially distant (intensity). So, for example, definitions of a situation passed on by your mother will likely influence your behavior in that situation more than definitions communicated by someone you happen to sit next to on a public bus.

Differential association theory is appealing because it addresses questions that the strain and subcultural theories left unanswered: How can we account for the fact that individuals who have equal opportunities to deviate do not all deviate? Why is it that individuals who are equally pressured into nonconformity by factors such as poverty do not all become nonconformists? And why do some individuals who appear to have all their material needs met nevertheless embezzle business funds, defraud consumers, fix prices, and participate in insider stock trading? For Sutherland, the answer was clear: differential association. Other theorists, however, were less certain about the answers to these questions and criticized Sutherland's theory.

Perhaps the most serious criticism of differential association theory is that it is untestable. Sutherland hoped that ideally the theory could be quantified by calculating the ratio of an individual's exposure to weighted definitions favorable and unfavorable to deviation. However, Sutherland himself acknowledged that developing such a formula would be difficult.

One way researchers have tried to test differential association theory is to ask people not only about their own values and behavior, but also about those of their friends. The underlying assumption of these studies is that a person will most likely learn to be deviant from friends who approve of deviance and who are deviant themselves. The research shows a strong relationship between an individual's associations with deviant peers and his or her own likelihood of being deviant. The more deviant friends a person has, the more likely the person is to deviate (Johnson et al., 1987; Warr & Stafford, 1991). However, these studies do not prove that differential association has caused the deviance. Because the research relies on cross-sectional data, there is no way of knowing which came first, the associations or the deviance. It may be that people who are already deviant befriend others like themselves (Martin et al., 1990). There is, in fact, another interactionist theory that sees deviant associations as a *consequence* of being labeled deviant. Let's look at that theory—labeling theory—more closely.

Labeling Theory.   The most prominent symbolic interactionist theory of deviance is **labeling theory.** Labeling theory sees deviance not as the result of the quality of an act, attribute, or belief, but rather as the product of others applying rules or sanctions to a particular person. As one of the best known labeling theorists, Howard Becker (1973, p. 9), put it, "The deviant is one to whom that label has been successfully applied; deviant behavior is behavior that people so label." Labeling theorists emphasize the relativity of deviance, as we did at the opening of this chapter: What is labeled deviance varies according to context. But, as we shall see, of greater importance to labeling theorists is the impact of labeling. Labeling can occur informally, such as when one employee shares with another over lunch the rumor that their boss has been seeing a psychiatrist. The employees label their boss "mentally ill" or "emotionally unstable," even though the label is based solely on rumor. The boss may not have done anything, or may have seen a psychiatrist for any number of reasons, but the deviant label is applied informally nonetheless.

However, labeling theorists are more interested in labeling that takes place in what they refer to as public **status degradation ceremonies,** such as court hearings or

According to Howard Becker, "The deviant is one to whom that label has been successfully applied. . . ." What effect do you think this label had on the wearer? Under what circumstances might the label encourage rather than discourage the deviance? What is the purpose of public humiliation or degradation ceremonies? Are labels restricted to primary deviation as in this case of theft? According to Lemert, how is secondary deviation different?

trials. This public process attaches an *official* label of deviant. With an official label, individuals undergo a fundamental change in identity, in their own eyes as well as in the eyes of others, and this identity change restructures many of their social interactions.

To better understand official labeling, consider this example: Suppose the boss that the two employees had been talking about is admitted to a psychiatric hospital for treatment. The boss now bears the official label "mental patient," and when he is discharged, the label "ex-mental patient." People who have deeply ingrained, preconceived ideas of what a mental patient is like—emotionally unstable, delusional, unpredictably violent—begin to structure their interactions with the labeled individual on the basis of their stereotypes. They may even redefine the individual's past behavior so that it conforms to the stereotypes attached to the deviant label (for example, the time the boss lost his temper at a sales meeting is seen in a new light after it is discovered that he was once in a psychiatric hospital).

Now, imagine what such experiences may be like for the labeled person. It is not difficult to understand why he may eventually come to accept the label and even alter his behavior to conform to it (Crocker et al., 1998). What occurs is a **self-fulfilling prophecy:** Expectations about how the individual will behave are fulfilled, not so much because the person is truly "crazy" or irrational, but because both the person and others have come to believe that he or she is "crazy" or irrational and they act accordingly. The boss may begin to lose his temper more over insignificant matters, knowing that he is expected to behave this way.

In many degradation ceremonies, the individual is questioned publicly about his or her alleged deviance, witnesses are called to testify, and the individual is either acquitted or found guilty. If judged guilty, the individual is then publicly stripped of his or her membership in the group. Among the old-order Amish, for example, individuals guilty of violating a major rule, such as marrying an outsider, may be shunned by the community; that is, no member of the Amish community, including immediate family, may associate with, or even speak to, the guilty party (Kephart & Zellner, 1991). In our society, we send people found guilty of crimes to prison, where they may have their heads shaved, wear uniforms, and even be forced to work on chain gangs.

In short, labeling theorists see social reaction itself as the major cause of deviance. In fact, Edwin Lemert, one of the originators of labeling theory, drew a distinction between rule breaking and deviance to make this point. He referred to rule breaking as **primary deviation.** Individuals break rules for any number of reasons: They may choose to steal because they need money, smoke marijuana because it relieves tension, or preach from a soapbox to oppose a government policy. Or they may have no control over their rule breaking: It was accidental, or they were born with a specific condition. Whatever the specific reasons that underlie it, primary deviation is of little concern to labeling theorists *unless* it is detected and elicits a reaction.

Lemert used the term **secondary deviation** to refer to deviation that results from social reaction. Others' reactions may eliminate particular opportunities or interactions for the labeled individual. The alcoholic, for example, may not be invited to parties or to friends' homes anymore, thus adding to her or his isolation. This may leave the labeled individual with little choice but to seek out others similarly labeled or to pursue with even greater frequency deviant opportunities. The alcoholic is likely to spend an increasing amount of time in bars not only to drink, but also to seek the company of others. The reaction process may cause the *resocialization* of the labeled individual toward accepting the role attached to the deviant label. That is, the labeled individual becomes committed to a deviant identity and embarks on a deviant career.

Figure 7.1 summarizes the relationship between primary deviation and secondary deviation. According to labeling theorists, secondary deviation is an adaptive strategy on the part of the labeled individual. Indeed, one of the most important contributions of labeling theory to our understanding of deviance is that it draws attention to the way that labeling puts a person in circumstances that make it harder to carry on with normal everyday routines and thus propel her or him toward people and activities that reinforce the deviant status (Becker, 1973).

Labeling theory has its critics as well as its proponents, however. Some sociologists argue that labeling theorists give too much importance to the impact of public degradation ceremonies, and point to research that shows that informal labels imposed early in a person's life can have a far greater influence than formal labeling

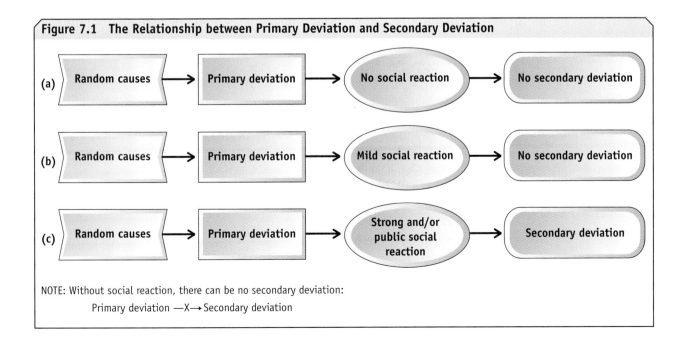

Figure 7.1 The Relationship between Primary Deviation and Secondary Deviation

(a) Random causes → Primary deviation → No social reaction → No secondary deviation

(b) Random causes → Primary deviation → Mild social reaction → No secondary deviation

(c) Random causes → Primary deviation → Strong and/or public social reaction → Secondary deviation

NOTE: Without social reaction, there can be no secondary deviation:
  Primary deviation —X→ Secondary deviation

later (Paternoster & Triplett, 1988). For example, parents who consistently tell their child she is bright may prevent damage to the child's self-concept when later a teacher labels the child a "slow learner." Other sociologists take issue with how labeling theory depicts individuals as passive, when, in fact, a deviant label is often strenuously resisted or rejected by those being labeled. Recall, for instance, the case of Steven Biko. White officials labeled Biko a terrorist, a label he, as well as his followers, rejected. Some labeled individuals join together to resist a deviant label, turning the tables on the labelers by proclaiming, for example, as one overweight women's group did, that "Big is better" and "Fat is beautiful." Such efforts can be successful. In addition, negative deviant labels are not indelible, and individuals can, and often do, overcome stigma (Crocker et al., 1998; Prus, 1975; Rogers & Buffalo, 1974).

Critics of labeling theory also point out that in some cases, the deviant label is valued, and even sought after. Akers (1968) uses the example of gang members whose deviant identity is formed before they are ever officially labeled. Gang members label themselves by adopting gang colors, wearing gang jackets, and even communicating by using secret hand signals only other gang members know. Political dissenters often adopt a deviant identity to set themselves apart from the authorities they challenge. In Northern Ireland, for example, Catholics who join the Sinn Fein movement in opposition to British rule are often arrested and imprisoned as suspects in terrorist activities. The process of being officially labeled deviant by the authorities is to many of them a symbol of accomplishment. Thus, labeling theory fails to recognize that individuals may choose to embark on a deviant career without ever having experienced social reaction to their behavior (Archer, 1985; Mankoff, 1971).

Finally, some sociologists criticize labeling theory for its lack of attention to how inequalities between various groups in society affect who gets labeled, who escapes labeling, and whose labels have the greatest impact. This is a topic taken up by conflict theorists.

Conflict Theory

Conflict theorists accept, as labeling theorists do, that deviance is relative. Nothing is inherently deviant; rather, it is deviant because it is defined as such by some members of the society. However, conflict theorists, who have their theoretical roots in Marxist sociology, go one step further by examining how particular structural conditions generate deviance. In other words, conflict theory is a theory of deviance, not deviants.

Conflict theorists begin with the assumption that one's position in the social hierarchy affects one's life chances and opportunities. With respect to deviance, this has at least two important implications. First, although deviance exists in all social groups, its visibility and the forms it takes vary from group to group. For instance, the poor may steal by muggings or break-ins, while the rich may steal by price fixing and insider stock trades. The type of deviance reflects the opportunities available to members of these groups, but the forms used by the poor have greater social visibility than the forms used by the rich.

Second, members of powerful social groups have a better chance than the less powerful or the powerless to either escape a negative deviant label or be awarded positive deviant status. For example, mental illness exists among all social groups, but people who are poor are more likely than the affluent to have their mental instability subjected to public scrutiny and reaction. Also, manifestations of mental illness among the poor are likely to invoke severe negative reactions, while similar actions among the wealthy may be brushed off as eccentricity. Should a poor man ride down a street in a tank, for instance, he would undoubtedly be arrested and quickly institutionalized, but when millionaire John Du Pont drove a tank from his personal arsenal to a neighbor's house one day several years ago, he was simply sent back to his own estate. In 1996, Du Pont stood accused of murdering a young man who worked for him, and many witnesses were called to testify about his history of bizarre behavior. Perhaps if others had reacted more strongly to Du Pont's behavior, his employee would still be alive.

For conflict theorists, then, the key to understanding deviance is not just relativism, but also *inequality* (Blau & Blau, 1982; Chasin, 1997; Hagan, 1989). Conflict theorists also emphasize that defining deviance is a *political* act. Behavior defined as acceptable may be redefined as deviant through political action. Smoking is a good example. Until recently, smoking was regarded neutrally by most people, although some considered it fashionable and others annoying. As more information about the ill effects of smoking became known and groups began lobbying against it, smoking was redefined as unhealthy, but it was still tolerated, with smokers simply being separated from nonsmokers in most public places such as airplanes and restaurants. Today, smoking is illegal in many places, including on airplanes and in public buildings. In California, smoking is banned in restaurants as well. Interestingly, however, other unhealthy behaviors, such as drinking, are not illegal.

In studying deviance, conflict theorists also take into account the social structure of a society. More specifically, conflict theorists argue that deviance varies not only across social groups in a particular society, but also across different types of societies. So, for example, in a hunting and gathering society, if a parent hits her child, the parent is quickly labeled deviant and dealt with accordingly, whereas in our own industrial society, most people regard hitting a child as an appropriate form of discipline necessary to punish or prevent the child's deviation.

Conflict theorists have given a good deal of attention to deviance in capitalist industrial societies (see, for example, Chasin, 1997; Krisberg, 1975; Spitzer, 1983). In fact, say some sociologists, conflict theorists depict capitalism as the "root of all evil" and overlook deviance in other types of societies, especially socialist societies (see, for instance, Klockars, 1979). It is true that there is little research by conflict theorists on deviance in noncapitalist societies. However, research in capitalist industrial societies does support conflict theory (Lynch & Groves, 1986).

In stressing the relativity of deviance and the importance of inequality and power relations in understanding deviance, conflict theorists also argue that the label "deviance" should be applied to such social phenomena as racism and sexism (Chasin, 1997). For example, when a company promotes White men over women or African Americans, the practice may be thought unfair, but it is not typically regarded deviant, as conflict theorists think it should be. Some sociologists consider this view overly broad and highly subjective (Toby, 1979). As we noted earlier, sociologists usually take a fairly circumscribed view of deviance, considering only that which is regarded negatively by the "conforming" population. However, one group of sociologists who do follow the conflict approach in examining racism and sexism with regard to deviance are feminist sociologists.

A Feminist Sociology of Deviance

Feminist sociologists agree with labeling theorists and conflict theorists about the relativity of deviance. But, while conflict theorists believe that social class affects who and what gets defined as deviant, feminist sociologists add that gender also plays a significant role in the defining process. For instance, historically, most criminologists ignored women as offenders because they assumed that criminality was "unfeminine" and, therefore, women simply didn't commit crimes (except for prostitution). Most women, then, escaped the deviant label "criminal," and those who were found guilty of crimes, especially violent crimes, were labeled "abnormal" because they had behaved more like men than women (Edwards, 1986).

Feminist sociologists argue that gender not only affects who gets labeled deviant, but also what opportunities are available to deviate. Until recently, for example, women rarely committed embezzlement and fraud because they are crimes most often committed in the workplace and most women did not work outside the home. Since the 1960s, an increasing number of women have entered the labor force, which gives them greater opportunities to embezzle and defraud, but the jobs they typically hold (low-paying clerical, sales, and service jobs) still do not afford them access to large sums of money. Feminist criminologist Kathleen Daly (1989) has found that when women commit fraud, they are most likely to defraud banks through loans and credit cards or the government by obtaining benefits they're not legally entitled to. Crimes such as insider stock trading and advertising fraud are still committed almost exclusively by men because men dominate the jobs that offer opportunities for these types of crimes.

Finally, gender influences how deviation is reacted to. For example, research shows that greater efforts are taken to control the sexual behavior of girls than boys. Meda Chesney-Lind, for example, reports that parents may go so far as to bring their daughter to court for sexual behavior they ignore or even endorse in their sons (Chesney-Lind & Sheldon, 1992). In fact, girls are more likely than boys to be arrested for all types of **status offenses**, that is, behavior which if engaged in by an adult would not be considered illegal, such as running away from home, incorrigibility, and being in danger of becoming "morally depraved." Girls charged with status offenses are treated more harshly and are more likely to be institutionalized than boys charged with status offenses.

In short, feminist sociologists maintain that to understand deviance it is not enough to simply examine social class inequality; one must also take into account *gender inequality*. Gender inequality intersects with social class inequality, as well as racial and ethnic inequality, to disadvantage certain groups in the struggle to avoid deviant labels and identities.

Table 7.2 on page 178 summarizes the feminist perspective of deviance, along with the other theories we have discussed in this section. Most of these theories focus rather narrowly on one specific type of deviance, crime. We'll take a more detailed look at crime in the next section.

R E F L E C T I N G   O N

Sociological Theories of Deviance

1. Do you agree that deviance—even serious criminal deviance—is functional for society?
2. How are Merton's anomie theory and the conflict theory of deviance alike and different?
3. What might be some other elements of the social bond not identified by Hirschi? How would you define these and how would they work to inhibit deviation?
4. Have you ever been influenced by your associations to engage in deviant behavior? Based on your experience, how would you evaluate Sutherland's theory?
5. How might a positive deviant label contribute to secondary deviation? Provide a specific example.

Continued on p. 179

TABLE 7.2 Theories of Deviance: A Summary

Theory	Major Proponent(s)	Basic Principles
Biological Theories	Lombroso, Sheldon, Glueck & Glueck, Cortes, Hamer	Deviance is caused by a physical abnormality in the individual.
Psychological Theories		Deviance is caused by certain personality traits (such as impulsiveness or the inability to defer gratification) or mental illness (psychosis).
Sociological Theories		
Structural Functionalism		
Deviance as normal social behavior	Durkheim	Deviance is an inevitable part of social life and serves specific functions for a society: clarifying moral boundaries, reinforcing conformity, solidifying social bonds between conformists, and promoting social change.
Strain theory	Merton	Deviance is the result of a gap between a society's culturally defined goals and the means available to achieve them.
Subcultural theories		
Status frustration	Cohen	Deviance is a response to the frustration lower-class males experience because they cannot succeed by middle-class standards. Young lower-class men develop their own set of values by which they can succeed.
Lower-class subculture	Miller	Every social class develops its own value system which reflects its position in society. The culture of lower-class people contains values considered deviant by the dominant (middle class) culture of the society.
Differential opportunity	Cloward and Ohlin	Deviance reflects the different opportunities (legitimate and illegitimate) available to people in different environments.
Control theory	Hirschi	Deviance occurs when social bonds to conventional institutions, such as family, school, or employer are weak.
Symbolic Interactionism		
Differential association theory	Sutherland	Deviance occurs when an individual receives more definitions favorable to norm violation than definitions unfavorable to norm violation.
Labeling theory	Lemert, Becker	Deviance is a result of social reactions to particular acts, attributes, or beliefs: "The deviant is one to whom that label has been successfully applied; deviant behavior is behavior that people so label."
Conflict Theory	Chambliss, Chasin	Deviance exists in all social groups, but its visibility and the forms it takes vary from group to group. Members of powerful social groups are more likely to escape a negative deviant label and be awarded a positive status. Deviance reflects inequality inherent in society.
Feminist Theory	Daly, Chesney-Lind	Gender plays a fundamental role in determining who and what get labeled deviant. Deviance is a product not only of social class inequality, but also of gender inequality and racial and ethnic inequality.

6. How might a conflict theorist explain injustices in criminal sentencing and imprisonment? Provide specific examples.
7. Has your gender ever made a difference in determining whether something you did was considered deviant or not deviant?

CRIMES AND CRIMINALS

One reason the study of deviance has largely been the study of crime is that crime is the form of deviance that is of greatest interest to the general public. Our preoccupation with crime reflects our continuing concern about safety. A recent national survey, for instance, found that 42 percent of the respondents are afraid to walk alone at night in their own neighborhood. Nearly one quarter worry about getting murdered; one-third worry about getting beaten up, knifed or shot; and almost half worry about themselves or someone in their family being sexually assaulted (U.S. Department of Justice, Bureau of Justice Statistics, 1998). These findings not only indicate a high level of public fear of crime, but also the fact that not all crimes are of equal concern. As you will see in this section, violent street crime arouses the greatest fear in most people, while corporate crime, which can be even more deadly in its consequences, is typically overlooked.

Before we examine these and other types of crime, however, let's first look at the sources of most of our information about crime.

Crime Statistics

There are two major sources of data on crime in the United States: the Uniform Crime Reports (UCR) and the National Crime Survey (NCS). We'll consider each in turn.

The Uniform Crime Reports. In 1930, the Federal Bureau of Investigation (FBI) established a system for compiling statistics on crimes that law enforcement authorities reported each year. The result is the **Uniform Crime Reports (UCR)**, which is published annually. Although participation by law enforcement agencies is voluntary, the FBI estimates that the UCR covers about 95 percent of the total U.S. population.

The FBI collects data on a variety of crimes, but it tends to concentrate on eight offenses that it considers representative of the overall crime picture in this country. These eight crimes constitute the **Crime Index Offenses.** As Table 7.3 shows, murder, nonnegligent manslaughter (killing without premeditation, but not accidentally), forcible rape, robbery, and aggravated assault are grouped as violent crime. Burglary, larceny-theft, motor vehicle theft, and arson are considered property crime.

According to the FBI, one index offense is committed every two seconds, which would seem to indicate that people have good reason to fear being a victim of a serious

TABLE 7.3   National Crime Rate, Index Crimes, 1996

Crime	Number	Rate per 100,000 Population
Violent crime total	1,682,280	634.1
Murder and nonnegligent manslaughter	19,650	7.4
Forcible rape	95,770	36.1
Robbery	537,050	202.4
Aggravated assault	1,029,810	388.2
Property crime total	11,791,300	4,444.8
Burglary	2,501,500	943.0
Larceny-theft	7,894,600	2,975.9
Motor vehicle theft	1,395,200	525.9
Arson*	89,859	n.a.

*Total for 1995; sufficient data are not available to estimate the rate for this offense.

Source: Federal Bureau of Investigation. (1997). *Crime in the United States.* Washington, DC: U.S. Government Printing Office, p. 62.

crime. However, many analysts are critical of the FBI and the UCR for concentrating on index crimes and thus overlooking offenses that have an injurious impact on society as a whole, such as corporate and organized crime. Moreover, the UCR represents only crimes known to the police, which, it is estimated, constitute only about one-third of all crimes committed. Crime often goes undetected or is not reported by victims. And even when a crime is reported, the police exercise considerable discretion in deciding which complaints warrant their attention and which should be ignored, so not even all reported crimes are passed along to the FBI (Fazlollah et al., 1998).

Despite these criticisms, the UCR does gauge trends in certain types of criminal activity. We get a clearer picture of the crime problem in the United States, though, when we examine the UCR in combination with other databases (see also the Global Insights box).

The National Victimization Crime Survey. The **National Crime Victimization Survey (NCVS)** is a measure of criminal victimization, established by the federal government in 1967 to learn more about crime regardless of whether it is reported to the police. Each year the NCVS asks a random sample of the general U.S. population about their own criminal victimization.

GLOBAL INSIGHTS How Do Crime Rates in Different Countries Compare?

Are high crime rates a problem unique to the United States, or are other industrialized countries experiencing a similar crime problem? A comparison of U.S. crime rates with those of Europe yields some interesting findings. Looking at the table below, for example, we find first that crime rates in Europe rose significantly between 1980 and 1990. The most dramatic increase occurred in the rate of burglaries, which doubled during the decade. The burglary rate in Europe exceeded that of the United States by 1990. However, it is important to keep in mind that burglary is a property crime. The other three crimes in this table—homicide, rape, and robbery—are violent crimes, and while U.S. rates showed more fluctuation than European rates, U.S. rates exceeded European rates

by a considerable margin. In fact, to say that violent crime in Europe increased dramatically from 1980 to 1990 is somewhat misleading, given that the base rates were so low to begin with. For instance, the incidence of rape increased 40 percent in Europe between 1980 and 1990, but the rate went from 4.2 per 100,000 population to just 7.2 per 100,000. While any increase in rape should be reason for concern, the European rate pales in comparison with the U.S. rate, which increased by only 14.4 percent between 1980 and 1990, but was still nearly six times greater than the European rate in 1990. Consequently, although crime appears to be increasing in Europe, the United States continues to be the most violent industrialized country in the world.

Number of Crimes per 100,000 Population: A Comparison of the United States and Europe for Selected Offenses

Crime	United States	Europe*	Crime	United States	Europe*
Homicide			Robbery		
1980	10.0	1.8	1980	244.0	38.4
1984	7.9	1.5	1984	205.4	49.1
1990	9.4	4.3	1990	257.0	74.0
Rape			Burglary		
1980	36.0	4.2	1980	1,669.0	893.1
1984	35.7	5.4	1984	1,263.7	1,055.3
1990	41.2	7.2	1990	1,235.9	1,655.0

*Figure represents the average for reporting countries; there were some differences in the countries reporting in 1980 and 1984.

Source: Interpol, 1981–1982, 1983–1984, 1990–1991.

NCVS data indicate that only about 44 percent of all violent crimes (excluding murder) and 37 percent of crime overall are reported to the police ("Lowest Violent U.S. Crime Rate," 1998). Why would someone not call the police after a violent crime? The most common reasons are that the event was a personal or a private matter (20.7 percent); the offender did not successfully complete the crime (18.6 percent); the event was reported to someone else, such as campus security (12.5 percent); the victim did not think the crime was important enough to report (6.3 percent); and the victim thought the police would not want to be bothered with their complaint (5.4 percent) (U.S. Department of Justice, Bureau of Justice Statistics, 1994). The NCVS also reveals that not all segments of the population have an equal probability of being victimized by crime, as the following sections show.

Violent Crime

The United States, it appears, is the most violent of all Western democracies. In 1990, for example, the homicide rate per 100,000 people in the United States was more than twice as high as the rates in other industrialized countries. The U.S. rates for rape and robbery also significantly exceed the rates of these crimes in other industrialized nations (see the Global Insights box).

Violence has historically held a prominent place in U.S. society. We view it as an essential, even glamorous part of our westward expansion. We revel in our military conquests, and we honor the soldiers who fight in our wars. Sometimes, we even exhibit a macabre fascination with violence. Consider, for example, the plan to sell at auction the tools of torture, murder, and cannibalism of the serial killer, Jeffrey Dahmer. Until pressure was brought to bear on the auction organizers and the sale was cancelled, items such as drills, handsaws, and an 80-quart kettle were expected to bring at least $1 million (Johnson, 1996). This fascination with violence is also evident in the media. Depictions of violence—*extreme* violence—are commonplace in film, television, and video games (Goldberg, 1998; Navarro, 1999). Recent research also indicates that filmmakers pepper scripts with increasingly more violent scenes in order to keep viewer interest—and profits—high (Gerbner, 1995). Add to all of this the widespread availability of guns in the United States—Americans spend about $3 million a year on firearms (U.S. Department of Commerce, Bureau of the Census, 1997) and we have three compelling reasons for the high rate of violent crime in this country.

When the subject of violent crime is raised, many people express fear of seemingly random acts of violence that injure or kill innocent bystanders. But statistics show that not everyone is equally at risk, and, in fact, for the majority of the U.S. population, the probability of becoming a victim of a violent act is declining (U.S. Department of Justice, Bureau of Justice Statistics, 1998). A person's social class, age, race, sex, and place of residence strongly influence the probability of becoming a victim. The poor are more likely than the middle class to be victims of violent crimes. Also, the chance of violent victimization for individuals between the ages of twelve and twenty-four is nearly twice that of the twenty-five to thirty-four age group, triple that of the thirty-five to forty-nine age group, six times that of the fifty to sixty-five age group, and nearly twenty times greater than that of people over sixty-five. Similarly, African Americans are more likely to be victims of violent crimes than White Americans, men are more likely to be victimized than women, and city-dwellers are more likely to be victimized than noncity dwellers (U.S. Department of Justice, Bureau of Justice Statistics, 1998).

The young are not only the most likely victims of violent crime, they are frequently the perpetrators of violence. In 1996, people under the age of eighteen accounted for nearly 19 percent of all violent crime and 15 percent of murder and nonnegligent manslaughter alone (U.S. Department of Justice, Bureau of Justice Statistics, 1998). Overall, the violent crime rate in the United States has declined since the 1980s, with the murder rate of 6.8 per 100,000 residents in 1997 being the lowest in thirty years. The rate of murders committed by juveniles declined as well to 16.5 per 100,000 in 1997 from a record high of 30.2 per 100,000 in 1993. However, analysts point out that the 1997 juvenile murder rate is still nearly double the 1984 juvenile murder rate of 8.5 per 100,000 (Cole, 1999; "Crime Drops in '97," 1998).

Business and Political Crime

In 1939, Edwin H. Sutherland introduced the term *white-collar crime* to a sociological community that had concentrated almost exclusively on crimes committed by poor people living in cities. Sutherland's work spotlighted offenses committed by people who enjoyed respectability and high status in their jobs. Today, sociologists prefer the term *business and political crime* to white-collar crime, because it covers a broader range of offenses, including employers' violations of workplace health and safety regulations, advertising and product fraud, and government or military violations of human rights.

There are three major categories of economic and political crime. One is **workplace crime,** crimes against employers by employees. Offenses in this category range from stealing small items such as pens and paper to not working a full day to stealing expensive tools and machinery from the workplace. Workplace crime costs U.S. businesses about $100 billion each year, and it is estimated that on average, companies must increase a product's cost between 2 and 5 percent to make up for lost income from workplace crime (Touby, 1994).

Dr. Thomas Frist, Jr., was named CEO of Columbia Hospital Association after Richard Scott (not pictured) was convicted of Medicare fraud in the 1990s. How does this case suggest the type of deviance that Edwin Sutherland termed white-collar crime? What are the characteristics of business and political crime? What are some recent examples in the news of workplace crime, occupational crime, and organizational crime? Why do some sociologists predict that business and political crime will increase over violent crime in postindustrial societies?

A second type of economic and political crime is **occupational crime,** an individual or group's illegal use of their professional position to secure something of value. This type of crime is found at all levels of the labor force, including the high-paying professions of medicine, law, public administration, and finance. Sutherland (1940), for example, studied fraud in the medical profession, documenting false reports and testimony in accident cases, unnecessary treatment, and fake specialists. More recent research shows that such criminal activities continue. One of the most common types of occupational crime in medicine is public insurance fraud, in which doctors either overcharge for services or bill the government for services never provided. One government investigation, for instance, found a doctor who billed the government for six tonsillectomies—performed on the same patient. Another physician submitted more than 25,000 bills for government reimbursement, but in order to have accumulated that many patient bills, the physician would have had to work 16 hours a day, 365 days a year, and spend only 10 minutes with each patient (Coleman, 1989; Pear, 1991).

Often the public does not think of occupational crime as a major problem, but its cost to society is substantial. A U.S. Judiciary Subcommittee estimated that if all forms of occupational crime are considered together, the cost to the public is between $174 billion and $231 billion a year. In contrast, the annual cost of street crime is about $15 billion (Livingston, 1992). Despite the serious costs of occupational crime, however, offenders are treated relatively leniently within the legal system. Convictions are few, and those convicted are typically fined or sentenced to prison terms averaging less than three years (Pizzo & Muolo, 1993).

One of the best-known cases of occupational crime is the savings and loan fraud perpetrated by Charles Keating and other banking executives in the late 1980s. Keating defrauded consumers and the government of millions of dollars by siphoning off savings and loan funds for personal profit. Eventually, this illegal activity resulted in the collapse of the savings and loan industry and will cost taxpayers, who are bearing the brunt of the losses, an estimated $500 billion by 2020 (Calavita et al., 1997; Labatan, 1998). Politicians also commit occupational crime. As Figure 7.2 indicates, in fact, the number of public officials convicted of such offenses has declined somewhat since the mid-1980s, but is still significantly higher than the 1970s and early 1980s. In the early 1990s, several major political figures in Washington were charged with misconduct, including Republican Senator Bob Packwood of Oregon, who was charged with sexual harassment, and Democratic Representative Dan Rostenkowski of Illinois, who was indicted on 17 counts of fraud and corruption.

The third type of economic and political crime is **organizational crime.** In organizational crime, the major decision makers of a corporation or government engage in illegal activity in the pursuit of profits or in the name of national security. For example, in 1988, the Beech-Nut Corporation pleaded guilty to 215 counts of violating federal law and agreed to pay $2 million, the largest fine in the history of the Food and Drug Administration. Beech-Nut had knowingly sold millions of bottles of sugar water as apple juice; the bottles were labeled "100% pure fruit juice" and "no sugar added" (Traub, 1988). In 1991, Pet, Inc. pleaded guilty to conspiring with other companies to rig bids on school milk contracts in several states. One of the most notable examples of organizational crime by government officials was the Iran-Contra scandal, in which the United States sold arms to Iran in an effort to free hostages, an activity that went counter to U.S. policy and did not achieve its goal. The profits from the sale were to be used to illegally finance activities to overthrow the government of Nicaragua (Walcott & Duffy, 1994). Organizational crime also includes acts of terrorism.

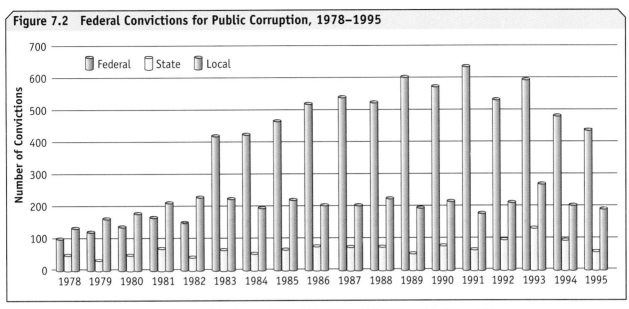

Figure 7.2 Federal Convictions for Public Corruption, 1978–1995

Sources: U. S. Department of Commerce, Bureau of the Census, 1991, p. 191; 1994, p. 212; 1995, p. 214; 1997, p. 217.

In sum, business and political crimes exact an enormous toll on the well-being of the general public, but the public usually ignores these types of offenses and the offenders do not consider themselves criminals. They rationalize that their behavior is within the limits of acceptable or necessary business practices or government decision making. These offenders are often well-educated and respected members of their communities. Their offenses are frequently overlooked or downplayed because their victims are not easily or immediately identifiable, or the victimization is considered justifiable. In the Iran-Contra case, for example, Oliver North was found guilty of three felonies, but he received a suspended sentence, was fined $150,000, and was required to do 1,200 hours of community service. Some people, however, didn't think North deserved even this sentence and sought instead to cast him as a national hero.

"Victimless" Crimes

Unlike violent crimes and business and political crimes, some offenses involve *willing* exchanges of strongly desired, but illegal goods and services, and none of those who participate see themselves as victims. Sociologists call these offenses **victimless crimes** (Schur, 1965). Victimless crimes include prostitution, gambling, and illegal drug use.

Although most people disapprove of these behaviors, there is widespread disagreement about which, if any, should be considered criminal. Some also question whether laws can successfully deter such behaviors, since they typically take place in private and, as we noted, the parties involved participate willingly. In fact, since crime by definition results in some type of injury to a specific party, some say these behaviors technically are not criminal. Others contend, however, that the community in general is victimized. Consider, for example, that drug dependency can motivate a person to rob a home or convenience store to get money to buy drugs (Meier & Geis, 1997; Roth, 1994). There are also those who maintain that the individuals involved in the acts may not perceive themselves as victims, but there are ways they are indeed being victimized. The Intersecting Inequalities box on page 185 addresses this point.

It isn't possible in an introductory text to cover all the different kinds of crime that sociologists study. Our discussion of violent crime, economic and political crime, and victimless crime, however, offers an overview of the range of criminal deviance in the United States as well as the diversity of both offenders and victims. Let's turn our attention now to the various ways people may respond to deviance.

R E F L E C T I N G   O N

Crimes and Criminals

1. What suggestions would you make for improving the UCR?
2. You probably have been the victim of some type of crime during your life. Did you report the crime to the police? Why or why not?

Continued on p. 184

3. Is there a relationship between media violence and actual violent crime? If so, what is the nature of this relationship? What other factors contribute to the high rate of violent crime in the United States?

4. Should business and political crime be treated more seriously? Why, and what should be done?

5. Should victimless crimes be decriminalized? What would be the advantages or disadvantages of decriminalizing prostitution, gambling, and marijuana use?

SOCIAL CONTROL

Deviance is socially constructed through social interaction. One dimension of this interaction is the social response to acts, attributes, or beliefs defined as deviant. Responses aimed at inhibiting or punishing deviation and promoting or rewarding conformity constitute forms of **social control.**

Social control is as diverse as deviance itself. It may be informal. Someone may take the deviant aside for a "friendly" chat, or people may do the opposite, and refuse to speak to the deviant. We often exercise informal social control with friends and others in our primary groups. A very powerful form of informal social control is simply not to associate with those whom one regards as deviant in some way.

Social control may also be formal, involving some official process for addressing deviation. An example of a formal type of social control is the shunning ritual, called the *Meidung,* practiced by old-order Amish communities. When a member of the Amish community is charged with violating a major rule, such as the prohibition on buying a car, and does not repent, the bishop may impose the *Meidung,* but only with the unanimous support of the congregation. The *Meidung* is a total ban on interaction with the offender. No one in the community, including the offender's family, may associate with him or her, and should the offender move to another Amish community, the *Meidung* will be honored there. Still, no matter how serious the violation, the *Meidung* may be lifted if the offender repents, asks the congregation's forgiveness, and returns to law-abiding behavior (Kephart & Zellner, 1991). A type of formal social control more familiar to us is the criminal justice system: the police, courts, and prisons.

The type of social control used in any given instance of deviation depends to a large extent on the characteristics of the deviant. There is strong evidence, for example, that a person's chances of being processed through the criminal justice system have less to do with the seriousness of her or his criminal deviation than with particular traits of offenders, including social class. For example, in his classic study of two adolescent gangs, one lower class (the "Roughnecks") and one middle class (the "Saints"), Chambliss (1973) found that the two groups did not differ in terms of their deviant activities, but the greater wealth and mobility of the Saints gave them opportunities to carry out their deviance with greater secrecy and less public visibility. But even when the Saints got caught deviating, their demeanor (the way they dressed and spoke) and their families' status in the community protected them from being labeled deviant. The Roughnecks, in contrast, had the opposite experience: Their demeanor immediately told authorities they were poor and their parents' status was low; when caught in a deviant act, they were quickly labeled deviant.

The type of social control invoked also depends on particular characteristics of the reactors. For instance, an adolescent girl who is sexually promiscuous may be called names or be ridiculed by her peers at school. But her parents may take her to juvenile court and ask that she be institutionalized in a juvenile detention facility, obtain psychological counseling for her, or, as seems to be popular nowadays, publicly humiliate her on a television talk show such as *Sally Jessy Raphael.*

A third major variable affecting social control is what reactors see as the reason underlying the deviation. For example, when people believed that deviation was caused by demon possession, exorcism was used, or more brutal methods, such as burning at the stake. If people believe an explanation for deviance is biological, then social control strategies are likely to involve some type of physical intervention or "treatment." During the first half of this century, for instance, at least thirty states enacted laws for forced sterilization of individuals considered "feebleminded" (having an IQ of 70 or below), because it was believed that feeblemindedness was hereditary. Sterilization would eventually eliminate the problem from the general population. In 1927, the U.S. Supreme Court upheld Virginia's compulsory sterilization law, and it is estimated that at least 20,000 forced sterilizations were performed in this country by 1940 (Gould, 1981; 1984). Given recent advances in gene therapy and genetic engineering, it is not surprising that some groups, such as homosexuals whose "deviance" has been explained in biological terms, express grave concern about these methods being used for social control (Zicklin, 1992).

As the idea that deviants are basically psychologically "disturbed" became more popular, psychiatrists and psychologists were increasingly recognized as the legitimate experts in "treating" deviants. This trend is referred to as

INTERSECTING INEQUALITIES

How Is Gender Related to Drug Use and Crime?

Pick up any U.S. newspaper and you are likely to find at least one story that links illicit drug use with other criminal behavior. Most likely, the story will be about someone who was arrested for a particular crime and later tests showed the suspect had recently used heroin, cocaine, or another illegal drug. Typically, readers infer from such stories that the drug use caused the person to commit other crimes, either because it lowered inhibitions or because the person was desperate for money to feed the drug habit. However, research indicates that the drugs/crime relationship is more complex than these stories would lead us to believe, and an important intervening factor is gender.

Consider, for example, the findings of criminologist James Inciardi and his colleagues (1993), who study street-addict lifestyles. In comparing male and female crack-cocaine addicts, Inciardi found some important similarities: The greater their drug use, the more likely they were to be involved in other types of crime. The crimes they were most likely to commit were property crimes and drug dealing because for both, the probability of arrest is low. However, male and female crack-cocaine addicts also differ in important ways. For one thing, male addicts are more likely than female addicts to commit violent crimes. Men also have a higher rate of violent victimization, but women's violent victimization rate is not low. Women's violent victimization is related to the fact that they often engage in prostitution

Arrests by Offense Charged and Sex of Offender, 1996

Offense Charged	Male	Female
Murder and nonnegligent manslaughter	12,062	1,719
Robbery	101,998	11,091
Aggravated assault	284,004	61,640
Burglary	209,076	27,190
Larceny-theft	655,775	297,624
Other assaults	695,386	177,644
Prostitution and commercialized vice	30,657	46,097
Drug abuse violations	857,057	173,831

Source: Federal Bureau of Investigation. (1998). *Crime in the United States.* Washington, DC: U.S. Government Printing Office, p. 219.

to earn money for drugs or in exchange for drugs. Inciardi and his colleagues found that the exchange of sex for drugs, particularly in crack houses, routinely included extreme physical and psychological abuse of women. In fact, the sex-for-drugs phenomenon that Inciardi and his colleagues observed so frequently on inner-city streets and in crack houses led them to conclude that crack addiction has a unique impact on women.

So the next time you read a story about drugs and crime, pay careful attention to who the story is about, what crimes were allegedly committed, and what the drugs/crime relationship is supposed to be. Then, ask yourself how the story might be different if the sex of the offender were changed.

the **medicalization of deviance**: assigning acts, attributes, and beliefs considered deviant to the realm of psychiatric medicine and psychology for treatment and "cure." Conditions such as alcoholism, drug abuse, obesity, and sexual promiscuity used to be considered "problems of living"; now, they are considered addictions, and are handled in therapeutic communities that emphasize resocialization. The soaring popularity of groups such as Alcoholics Anonymous, Overeaters Anonymous, and other

twelve-step self-help programs is a direct outgrowth of the medicalization of deviance.

Some view the medicalization of deviance as a positive change toward more humane treatment of deviants. Others, particularly sociologists, are critical of the trend because it attempts to remedy problems by changing individuals rather than the external social conditions that may have motivated their behavior. Thus, the sociological theories of deviance we discussed earlier suggest very different social control strategies. If, for example, one subscribes to Merton's view that deviance is caused by unequal opportunities to succeed, or to Hirschi's idea that weak social bonds cause deviance, then promising social control strategies include improving education and job training and offering parents flexible work hours so they can spend more time with their children.

In contrast, labeling theorists, who believe that secondary deviation (a commitment to a deviant career) is the result of social reaction to rule breaking, would respond to the question, "What is to be done about deviance?" with "Nothing," or at most, "Very little." Their approach is described as *nonintervention* (Schur, 1973). They favor, for instance, the legalization of victimless crimes, such as prostitution and drug use, pointing out that laws prohibiting such behaviors not only are difficult to enforce, but actually engender greater deviation, such as bribery and police corruption (Schur, 1965).

Labeling theorists also believe that social reaction isolates deviants from the "conforming" population, which further amplifies and promotes deviance. For example, under new laws, some states are now publishing the names and addresses of convicted sex offenders on the Internet. Police and public officials argue that these Web sites are a public information service that helps law-abiding citizens protect themselves and their children from potential crimes. However, a labeling theorist believes that this type of public degradation ceremony ostracizes former offenders by focusing attention on their deviance, thereby blocking their reintegration into the law-abiding community and encouraging further deviation.

Despite the protests of labeling theorists, however, the prevailing attitude of late has been a "get tough" approach, calling for harsher penalties, particularly for criminal offenders. As a result, an increasing number of deviants are being formally labeled by processing through the criminal justice system. To conclude this chapter, let's discuss the criminal justice system in the United States.

REFLECTING ON

Social Control

1. What forms of social control have you experienced, and what effects have these had on you?
2. How would a sociologist critique the medicalization of homosexuality as a curable form of deviance?
3. Do you see any merit in labeling theory's nonintervention solution to deviance? Support your argument with specific examples.

THE CRIMINAL JUSTICE SYSTEM

The U.S criminal justice system is composed of the police, the courts, and corrections. Each year, nearly $75 billion is spent on justice system activities, but most Americans—67 percent of respondents in a recent poll—feel that this amount is not enough. Most also want harsher penalties for convicted criminals (78 percent). And most Americans are displeased with the way the criminal justice system responds to crime: Only 23 percent of respondents said they have a great deal or quite a lot of confidence in the criminal justice system, while 35 percent said they have very little or no confidence in the system (U.S. Department of Justice, Bureau of Justice Statistics, 1998). Let's look at each of the three major components of the criminal justice system to see how it operates and to identify possible sources of the public's dissatisfaction.

The Police

Many of us have developed our ideas of the police from television programs that lead us to believe that most police departments are large, bureaucratic organizations. The fact is, however, that less than 2 percent of police departments employ more than 100 officers; almost 90 percent have fewer than twenty-five full-time sworn officers. Nevertheless, the police are the gatekeepers of the criminal justice system and the initial contact point for those suspected of violating a law; the police have a great deal of discretion in deciding how they respond to infractions. **Discretion** is the power of criminal justice officials to decide for themselves how to handle a specific case. For police officers, the most important discretionary decisions are when to arrest and when to use force.

What factors influence an officer's decision to arrest or use force against a suspect? Research shows that in addition to legal factors such as available evidence, the presence of a victim, and witnesses, the police also consider extralegal factors (see, for example, Fazlollah et al., 1998). The three most important extralegal factors are:

1. *The suspect's demeanor*—If officers think that an individual is being disrespectful to them (using obscenities, accusing them of unfair treatment, or refusing to answer questions), the probability of arrest increases.
2. *The suspect's social class* (determined by appearance)—Poor and working-class suspects are more likely to be arrested and subjected to force than middle- and upper-class suspects.
3. *The suspect's race*—Africans Americans are arrested more often for minor violations than White

Americans are, and the police use force more often with African American suspects.

The question of when police use of force is inappropriate or excessive has long been the subject of debate. However, several recent cases have brought increased attention to police brutality. Perhaps the best known case occurred in Los Angeles in 1990, when a group of police officers beat Rodney King, a motorist who had been stopped for a traffic violation. The incident was videotaped by a bystander and then broadcast on national television, which made the officers' brutality hard to deny, despite their claims that King had resisted arrest. In 1996, Los Angeles police were again videotaped beating a man and a woman suspected of being illegal immigrants. Also in 1996, a South Carolina state trooper was caught on film by the video camera in his own patrol car shoving, cursing, and threatening to cut the clothes off a woman he had stopped for speeding. In 1997, Abner Louima, a Haitian immigrant, was beaten and sodomized with a toilet plunger after being arrested by New York City police and taken to a Brooklyn station house ("Videotape," 1996; see also Kifner, 1998).

In each of these cases, the suspects were racial and ethnic minorities and the police officers were White. Some sociologists believe that racism is at the heart of police brutality. Consider, for instance, that African Americans are from five to thirteen times more likely than White Americans to die at the hands of police (Mann, 1993). Racial and ethnic minorities are underrepresented in police departments, even in regions with large minority populations. Of full-time sworn officers, 81 percent are White, 11.3 percent are African American, and 6.2 percent are Hispanic American (U.S. Department of Justice, Bureau of Justice Statistics, 1997). The lack of racial and ethnic diversity among police helps preserve racial and ethnic biases and keeps police culturally isolated from communities of color.

Policing can be dangerous and psychologically depressing. The police are paid to deal with the unsavory side of social life, including violence, and the stress of the job takes its toll in high rates of divorce, suicide, and alcoholism (Clancy, 1987; Gershon et al., 1999). One of the ways police officers cope with the stress of their jobs is turning to one another for support. The police adopt an *in-group mentality* to protect themselves from what they perceive as a hostile public. This in-group mentality includes a code of secrecy, whereby officers refuse to "rat" on fellow officers if they become aware of ethical or even criminal violations committed by their colleagues. But while an in-group mentality may help officers cope with stress, it also fosters an environment in which police brutality and corruption can thrive.

What happens after the police make an arrest? To answer this question, we need to examine the second component of the criminal justice system, the courts.

The Courts

After an arrest, the police take the suspect to a lower court or magistrate's court to begin judicial processing. The magistrate must decide if there is sufficient evidence to proceed to trial. If the magistrate rules that the suspect will be held for trial, the suspect is typically released on bail. **Bail** is a court requirement that the accused post a specified sum of money to guarantee his or her return to court for a hearing. Another option is to *release on recognizance,* which means that the judge believes that the person will not flee before trial and so just asks the accused to promise to return to court. Recent research indicates that about 60 percent of defendants are granted bail, while 35 percent are released on their own recognizance. However, of those granted bail, about 50 percent cannot afford to post it (Chiricos & Bales, 1991). If the bail cannot be posted, the defendant must await trial in jail. The bail system, then, puts poor defendants at a disadvantage because they are least likely to be able to afford bail. The average number of days between arrest and trial by a judge in felony cases is 235 days; it is 279 days between arrest and trial by a jury (U.S. Department of Justice, Bureau of Justice Statistics, 1998).

However, few cases—less than 10 percent, in fact, ever go to trial. Most are handled by **plea bargaining,** a process whereby the accused agrees to plead guilty in exchange for a reduction in the charges or the sentence. There are two major factors that contribute to the high incidence of plea bargaining: cost and system overload.

The first factor, cost, is a result of the fact that the farther a case goes in the criminal justice system, the more expensive it is. For example, the average cost per defendant for 100 days of detention while awaiting trial is $2,000 (Vaughn & Kappeler, 1987). The second factor, system overload, occurs when the number of cases being processed through the justice system exceeds the system's capacity to handle them. Each year, more than 80 million criminal cases are filed in state and local courts. Given that there are only 8,563 general trial court judges in the United States, if every defendant went to trial, each judge would have to hear 9,342 cases a year or about 25 a day, assuming each judge was on the bench 365 days a year.

Thus, plea bargaining benefits the system by improving efficiency in terms of both cost and time. Critics of plea bargaining argue that it subverts one of the central principles of the justice system by coercing defendants into surrendering their constitutional right to a jury trial in exchange for reduced charges or a less severe sentence.

The poor are especially vulnerable because they cannot afford the services of experienced, private attorneys and must rely instead on overworked and underpaid court-appointed attorneys. Private attorneys are more successful than public defenders in getting charges dismissed and winning acquittals for their clients (Champion, 1989).

Corrections

Once a defendant has been found guilty, through either a plea bargain or a trial, a sentence must be imposed. Maximum sentences for specific crimes are usually set by law, but judges often have considerable discretion in sentencing offenders. Like police, judges take into account legal and extralegal factors in deciding how to handle a specific offender. Legal factors include the severity of the crime and the defendant's number of prior convictions. Extralegal factors include the defendant's age, social class, race and ethnicity, and sex. For instance, studies have found that young, unemployed defendants receive harsher sentences than older, employed defendants (Chiricos & Bales, 1991). African American males receive harsher sentences than White males for similar violations (Mann, 1993; Reiman, 1995). And women deemed "disreputable" by the court receive harsher sentences than women who conform to a traditional model of femininity—they are married and living with their husbands, there is no evidence of drug or alcohol abuse, and they are not sexually promiscuous (Daly, 1989).

One sentencing option available to judges is *probation*. Offenders on probation live in their communities while under the supervision of a probation officer to whom they report periodically. Probation is cost efficient: The cost of probation ranges from $600 to $2,000 per client per year compared with $7,550 to $28,200 per prison inmate per year (U.S. Department of Justice, Bureau of Justice Statistics, 1994). Proponents of probation also believe that it is better than imprisonment because it gives the offender an opportunity to work and remain a productive member of the community. However, critics of probation argue that the heavy caseloads of probation officers, which sometimes exceed 200 clients per officer, make adequate supervision impossible, leaving offenders free to associate with criminal peers and to reoffend.

Judges seem to agree with probation's critics, since the number of offenders sentenced to prison has risen dramatically since the 1980s. By the close of 1998, there were over 1.8 million people confined in federal and state prisons and local jails, the highest number in U.S. history (U.S. Department of Justice, Bureau of Justice Statistics, 1999). More than half of those incarcerated are housed in facilities with a daily population over 1,000. Many prisons are old and were built to hold far fewer inmates. In fact, overcrowding—that is, each inmate has fewer than sixty square feet of floor space (the equivalent of the surface area of a pool table)—is a significant problem in forty-two states, as well as in the federal prison system. Adding to the problem of overcrowding is the fact that prisoners are serving longer sentences. The average time served in state prison by an individual convicted of a violent crime was forty-nine months in 1997, up from 43 months in 1993. Longer sentences are thought to have produced a 60 percent increase in the prison population (Butterfield, 1999).

Overcrowding is just one problem of prison life. Violence, including rape, is common. AIDS is also a growing problem in prisons: 3.9 percent of female inmates and 2.4 percent of male inmates are infected with HIV, the virus that causes AIDS (Brien & Beck, 1996).

The dramatic increase in the number of women sentenced to prison has created gender-specific problems. The number of women in state and federal facilities rose 375 percent between 1980 and 1992. By 1998, women were 6.5 percent of the state and federal prison population and 10.2 percent of the U.S. jail population (U.S. Department of Justice, Bureau of Justice Statistics, 1999). Women's prisons are often more geographically isolated than men's prisons, making visits from family and friends more difficult. In addition, women's prisons have fewer

The incarceration of women in U.S. prisons has increased exponentially in the last two decades. Is this because women are committing more crimes? What factors in society, in the criminal justice system, and in the social construction of crime do you think might help to account for the increase?

educational and occupational training programs than men's prisons (Chesney-Lind & Sheldon, 1992; Moyer, 1991).

Finally, the racial composition of the U.S. prison population raises questions about discrimination. Overall, the incarceration rate is 344 per 100,000 of the U.S. population. However, the rate for White males is 373 per 100,000, while the rate for African American males is 2,678 per 100,000. Some sociologists argue that this difference cannot be explained solely by a higher rate of offending for African American men; rather, it reflects racism inherent in the criminal justice system (Mann, 1993).

The Doing Sociology box discusses a third sentence strongly favored by the general public for the most serious crimes: the death penalty. In 1997, seventy-four convicted offenders were executed in the United States, the highest number since mid-century. By mid-1999, however, the number of U.S. prisoners executed that year had already reached sixty-four, providing perhaps the clearest evidence of the nation's growing support for a "get-tough" policy toward deviants (Amnesty International, 1999).

R E F L E C T I N G   O N

The Criminal Justice System

1. What policies would you recommend to prevent police brutality?
2. Do you think plea bargaining is fair to defendants? Why or why not? What might be some alternatives for handling case overload in the courts?
3. Do you think that current sentencing practices fulfill the constitutional principle that the punishment should fit the crime?
4. How would you explain the racial disparity in the nation's prison population? How might this disparity be remedied?

D O I N G   S O C I O L O G Y

Who Supports the Death Penalty?

Thirty-eight states and the federal government have death penalty statutes in effect. In the remaining states, efforts are underway to reinstate the death penalty. Moreover, the appeals process in capital cases has been curtailed and appeals that are filed are processed more quickly than in the past. According to a representative of the Death Penalty Information Center, a Washington-based group that studies inequality in the imposition of the death penalty, "There seems to be an impatience, a call for finality," in carrying out death sentences ("56 Executions," 1995).

In states with high execution rates, such as Texas and Virginia, officials argue that the death penalty reflects the will of "the people." It is certainly the case that a large percentage of the general public supports the death penalty: 73 percent of respondents in one recent national poll said they favor the death penalty for individuals convicted of murder (U.S. Department of Justice, Bureau of Justice Statistics, 1998). The most common reason people offer in support of the death penalty is its *deterrent value:* The possibility of being executed and the spectacle of an execution are believed to dissuade people from committing capital crimes. However, empirical evidence indicates that the death penalty actually has low deterrent value. Few, if any, offenders stop to consider the prospect of being executed before they commit a crime.

Despite the generally favorable attitude toward the death penalty among the public, support is not uniform throughout the population. Men are more supportive than women (80 percent versus 71 percent), and Whites are more supportive than racial and ethnic minorities (80 percent versus 46 percent) (U.S. Department of Justice, Bureau of Justice Statistics, 1998). One reason that minorities express less support for the death penalty is the uneven way it is applied. The race of both the victim and the offender influences the likelihood that the death penalty will be imposed: African Americans convicted of murdering Whites are most likely to receive the death penalty, while Whites convicted of murdering African Americans are least likely to receive the death penalty (Death Penalty Information Center, 1999).

What are the prevalent attitudes toward the death penalty on your campus? Survey a sample of your campus population to find out. Ask each respondent whether she or he favors the death penalty and the reason for the opinion. Do the responses differ by sex and race of the respondents? Compare your findings with others in your class.

For useful resources for study and review, run Chapter 7 on your *Living Sociology* CD-ROM.

CONNECTIONS

Conformity and dissent	Review the section on "Behavior in Groups" in Chapter 6. Why can we say that nonnormative or deviant behavior can be positive or negative? In what other ways is deviance a relative or subjective concept?
Rape and sexual assault	Read the section on "Gendered Violence" in Chapter 10. How would you describe the distinctions between acceptable, deviant, and criminal masculine sexual behavior? What beliefs and values might foster a "rape-prone" society such as the United States?
Deviance and heredity	Read more about Hamer's "homosexuality gene" research in Chapter 10 in the section on "The Biological Basis of Sexual Orientation." Also see the section on "Gay and Lesbian Rights" in Chapter 10. What do you think are some arguments for and against defining homosexuality as deviant?
Durkheim's explanation of deviance	Review Durkheim's basic sociological concepts in Chapter 1. According to Durkheim, how are deviance and crime related to social solidarity, a society's division of labor, and the collective conscience?
Merton's definition of anomie	Durkheim's concept of anomie, on which Merton's definition was based, was introduced in Chapter 3 in the section on "Industrial Societies." See also "Sociologists and the City" in Chapter 19. How do rapid urbanization and industrialization change social goals, which in turn creates strain, leading to anomie, which, according to Merton, leads to adaptations that include deviant behavior?
Subcultures and countercultures	Review the section on "Cultural Diversity" in Chapter 4. What examples can you find of groups whose deviance possibly can be explained in terms of subcultural theories of deviance?
Socialization and deviance	Review "Agents of Socialization" in Chapter 5. In what sense is deviance learned? How might agents of socialization affect individuals' conformity and deviance? How does Sutherland's theory of differential association rely on socialization as an explanation of deviance?
Social class and deviance	Chapter 8 describes the characteristics of "Social Classes in the United States" and the possibilities and barriers relating to "Social Mobility." What are some specific examples of the impact of social class factors on the incidence, frequency, and distribution of deviance and crime?
Labeling and self-fulfilling prophecy	Compare the symbolic interactionist view on deviance with the symbolic interactionist view on education in Chapter 16. In what ways do labels and self-fulfilling prophecies influence students' academic performance? Do labels and self-fulfilling prophecies promote deviant behavior in the same ways?
Sexism and racism as deviance	Read the section on "Gender and Sexual Orientation as Systems of Stratification" in Chapter 10 and the section on "Ethnocentrism and Racism" in Chapter 11. In what contexts can sexism and racism be seen as deviant? In what contexts can they be seen as normative?
Descriptive statistics and secondary analysis	Review "Analyzing Data" in Chapter 2. What cautions about data analysis would you need to apply in analyzing crime statistics? What might be some disadvantages of secondary analysis on UCR or NCVS data?

CONNECTIONS

Violent crime in the U.S.	Survey Chapters 10, 11, and 15 for additional examples of violent crime in the United States. How do gendered violence, hate crimes, and domestic violence interrelate?
Norms, sanctions, and social control	Review the discussion of "Norms" in Chapter 4. Which types of norms and sanctions are involved in systems of social control?

SUMMING UP CHAPTER 7

1. Deviance is any act, attribute, or belief that violates a cultural norm and elicits from others a negative or positive reaction. Nothing is inherently deviant; deviance is culturally relative. What is deviant depends not on the act, attribute, or belief itself, but on how others react to it. Factors that affect what is defined as deviant include situational context, characteristics of those being reacted to, and the characteristics of the reactors.
2. Crime is a special type of deviance. Crime is a violation of norms that a society considers so important it enacts laws to force compliance with them. Like other forms of deviance, what is considered crime is also influenced by situational context and the characteristics of social actors.

Explaining Deviance

1. There are two major approaches to explaining deviance: kinds-of-people theories that focus on deviants themselves, and process theories that focus on the process by which someone or something comes to be defined as deviant.

Nonsociological Theories of Deviance

1. Biological theories explain deviance in terms of a defect in the physical makeup of individuals. The defect may be physiological (body build) or genetic (a chromosomal abnormality).
2. Psychological theories explain deviance in terms of mental defects. One psychological approach distinguishes deviants from nondeviants on the basis of personality traits. Extreme forms of deviance, such as violent crime, are usually explained in terms of mental illness, such as psychosis.

Sociological Theories of Deviance

1. Sociological theories of deviance discuss factors external to individuals that lead them into deviance or that prompt others to define them as deviant. Each of the major sociological perspectives—structural functionalism, symbolic interactionism, conflict theory, and feminist theory—have developed explanations of deviance.
2. There are numerous structural functionalist theories of deviance. Emile Durkheim stressed the normality of deviance and identified four functions of deviance: clarify

moral boundaries, increase conformity, solidify social bonds, and promote social change. More recent functionalist theories of deviance include Merton's strain theory (deviance is one way an individual responds to the imbalance between society's cultural goals and the means available to achieve those goals); subcultural theories (deviance is a response to the frustration particular groups experience when they cannot succeed by the standards of the dominant culture), and Hirschi's control theory (deviance results from weak social bonds).
3. Symbolic interactionists focus on how people learn to deviate; how specific acts, attributes, and beliefs come to be defined as deviant; and the consequences of labeling someone deviant. Two interactionist theories are differential association and labeling theory. Sutherland's differential association theory maintains that deviance is learned the same way any other behavior is learned: through social interaction with others. When an individual receives more definitions favorable to deviation than definitions unfavorable to it, the individual will deviate. Labeling theorists distinguish between two types of deviance: primary (rule breaking caused by many different factors) and secondary (deviation caused by social reaction to rule breaking). From this perspective, it is social reaction that causes deviance.
4. Conflict theorists emphasize the relativity of deviance, but focus on how social class inequality affects a person's chances of being labeled deviant. Those who are wealthy are less likely to be defined as deviant than poor people are. Conflict theorists are especially concerned with deviance in capitalist societies.
5. Feminist theorists also emphasize the relativity of deviance, but focus on how gender affects who and what gets defined as deviant. According to feminist theorists, gender affects who gets labeled deviant, opportunities to deviate, and how deviation is reacted to. Gender intersects with social class as well as race and ethnicity to produce deviant labels and identities.

Crime and Criminals

1. There are two major sources of data on crime: the FBI Uniform Crime Reports (UCR) and the National Crime Victimization Survey (NCVS). Each has advantages and

disadvantages and provides a different view of the crime problem. The NCVS, in particular, highlights the extent to which crime is underreported to police.

2. The United States appears to be the most violent of all Western democracies. Fear of violent crime is a major concern for the majority of the U.S. population, but statistics show that not everyone has an equal chance of being victimized. Young African American males who live in urban areas are significantly more likely than members of other groups to be victimized by violent crimes. Young men are also overrepresented as perpetrators of gang violence.

3. There are three major types of economic and political crime: workplace crime (crimes against employers by employees), occupational crime (an individual or group's illegal use of their professional position to secure something of value), and organizational crime (the major decision makers of a corporation or government engage in illegal activity in the pursuit of profits or national security). Often the general public and even the perpetrators themselves do not think of these types of activities as crime, but research shows that they are more costly and harmful than traditional property crimes.

4. Victimless crimes are offenses involving willing exchanges of strongly desired, but illegal goods and services, and none of the participants see themselves as victims. There is widespread disagreement over whether such activities should be considered criminal.

Social Control

1. Social control involves any efforts to inhibit or punish deviation and promote or reward conformity. Social control may be informal or formal, but the type of social control used in any given instance of deviation depends to a large extent on the characteristics of the deviants and the reactors. Another factor influencing social control is what social reactors see as the reason underlying the deviation.

The Criminal Justice System

1. The police are the initial contact point in the criminal justice system. The police exercise considerable discretion in deciding how to handle specific cases. Factors affecting the decision to arrest include legal factors (seriousness, evidence) and extralegal factors (the suspect's demeanor, social class, and race). The discretion afforded police, coupled with the stress of the job and the development of an in-group mentality, contribute to police use of excessive force and police corruption.

2. The second component of the criminal justice system is the courts. Common judicial practices—bail and plea bargaining—although time and cost efficient, may also subvert a defendant's constitutional rights, especially if the defendant is poor.

3. Corrections, the third component of the criminal justice system, may take several forms. Probation involves community-based supervision, but it is less common than prison. Prisons are plagued by several serious problems, including overcrowding, violence, and AIDS. Female prisoners experience a unique set of problems. In addition, there is concern about racial discrimination in the imposition of prison sentences. Finally, the death penalty may be imposed for the most serious offenses.

KEY PEOPLE AND CONCEPTS

anomie: an imbalance between the goals of a society and the means to achieve these goals

bail: a court requirement that a defendant post a specified sum of money to guarantee his or her return to court for a hearing

control theory: a theory developed by Travis Hirschi that proposes that deviance results when an individual has weak social bonds to conventional institutions

crime: the violation of norms a society considers so important that it enacts laws to force compliance with them

Crime Index Offenses: eight crimes spotlighted by the FBI in the Uniform Crime Reports; these crimes are homicide and nonnegligent manslaughter, forcible rape, robbery, aggravated assault, burglary, larceny-theft, motor vehicle theft, and arson

deviance: any act, attribute, or belief that violates a norm and elicits from others a negative or positive reaction

differential association: the process of social interaction by which definitions favorable and unfavorable to deviation are taught and learned

discretion: the power of criminal justice officials to decide for themselves how to handle a specific case

labeling theory: a symbolic interactionist theory of deviance that sees deviance not as a result of some quality of an act, attribute, or belief, but rather as the product of others applying rules or sanctions to a particular person

medicalization of deviance: the assignment of various acts, attributes, and beliefs considered deviant to the realm of psychiatric medicine and psychology for treatment and "cure"

National Crime Victimization Survey (NCVS): a survey of a sample of the general population conducted by the U.S. Department of Justice that asks about experiences of criminal victimization during a specific period of time and whether these experiences were reported to the police

occupational crime: the willful attempt of an individual or group to take advantage of their professional position to illegally secure something of value

organizational crime: crimes committed by major decision makers of a corporation or government who, in the pursuit of profits or in the name of national security, engage in illegal activity

plea bargaining: a process whereby the accused agrees to plead guilty in exchange for a reduction in the charges or the sentence

primary deviation: rule breaking

secondary deviation: deviation that results from social reaction

self-fulfilling prophecy: expectations about how the individual will behave are fulfilled, not so much because the person is truly deviant, but because both the person and others have come to believe that he or she is deviant and behave accordingly

social control: responses aimed at inhibiting or punishing deviation and promoting or rewarding conformity

status degradation ceremony: the process of publicly attaching an official label of deviant to an individual

status offense: a behavior which if engaged in by an adult would not be considered illegal, such as running away from home, incorrigibility, and being in danger of becoming "morally depraved"

subculture: a group within the dominant culture that shares some of its elements, but at the same time differentiates itself from the dominant culture in a specific way

Uniform Crime Reports (UCR): statistics on the number of crimes reported to the police as compiled by the Federal Bureau of Investigation

victimless crimes: offenses that involve willing exchanges of strongly desired, but illegal goods and services in which none of the participants consider themselves victims

workplace crime: crimes against employers by employees

LEARNING MORE

Ermann, M. D., & Lundman, R. J. (Eds.). (1996). *Corporate and governmental deviance.* New York: Oxford University Press. A collection of articles that examines various forms of business and political crime, from the *Challenger* disaster to police use of force in the Rodney King case.

Inciardi, J. A., Lockwood, D., & Pottieger, A. E. (1993). *Women and crack-cocaine.* Boston: Allyn and Bacon. A disturbing look at crack addiction among women, based on the authors' field research in Miami's crack houses. A word of caution: Some readers may find the language in this book offensive.

Kauzlarich, D., & Kramer, R. C. (1998). *Crimes of the American nuclear state: At home and abroad.* Boston: Northeastern University Press. A thorough—and often frightening—study of governmental deviance typically perpetrated in the name of "national security."

Kephart, W. M., & Zellner, W. W. (1991). *Extraordinary groups.* New York: St. Martin's Press. A fascinating and highly readable analysis of eight social groups, including the Old-Order Amish, Gypsies, and Hasidic Jews, who are considered by many to be deviant because of their unconventional lifestyles.

Mann, C. R. (1993). *Unequal justice: A question of color.* Bloomington: Indiana University Press. An insightful and convincing analysis of the uneven application of criminal labels and sanctions to individuals based on their race.

 Run Chapter 8 on your *Living Sociology* CD-ROM for interesting and informative activities, web links, videos, practice tests, and more.

Stratification and Social Class in the United States

Martin Cook (a pseudonym) was a powerful executive at a major corporation headquartered in southern California. He was an American success story. Hired as a machinist, he had worked his way up the corporate ladder. He had earned a bachelor's degree in engineering management as he moved from the production floor to the executive office. He made the tough decisions a corporation expects of someone in a position of power, including cutting budgets and jobs when necessary. Cook found the personnel issues particularly difficult; once, an employee he'd fired killed himself shortly after their meeting. But in 1993, Cook was the one getting the bad news: He was no longer needed by the company after twenty-six years of employment. He, the executive, became a victim of corporate downsizing. In his early fifties, Martin Cook lost his $130,000-a-year job. He and his wife now depend on her salary from a secretarial job to pay their mortgage and other bills. But for Martin the situation is more than financial; it is about the loss of status, pride, and security. (Bragg, 1996).

Cook's plight offers insight into several of the concepts that are central to this chapter. The first is **social stratification**, a system of ranking people in a hierarchy according to certain attributes. Stratification is found in all societies, although the form it takes, how pervasive it is, and its effects vary substantially from society to society.

An important element of stratification is *difference*. Within any society, differences between individuals and groups are used as the basis for assigning them relative value. Often, the differences that are singled out for ranking have physical manifestations, such as sex, race, and age. We'll discuss these forms of stratification in later chapters, but in this chapter and the next, we're going to examine *economic* stratification. First, we'll look at economic stratification in the United States, and then, we'll place the United States in the global mix to look at economic stratification across societies. Although we discuss the forms of stratification—economic, sex, race, and age—separately, you'll see by the end of our discussion that they are interconnected, often in complex ways.

Difference is a central dimension of stratification, but keep in mind that we defined stratification as a ranking *system*. In other words, while differences between individuals are what get ranked, stratification itself is a built-in feature of the social structure, of how the members of a society organize themselves. For example, Martin Cook blamed himself for losing his job, but what happened to him was not the result of personal failure or a streak of bad luck, just as his initial success was not totally the product of individual merit or good luck. Rather, Cook's experience reflects a restructuring of the U.S. and global marketplaces. Changes in the U.S. and world economies have fundamentally altered many people's lives and life chances.

Differential ranking highlights another dimension of stratification: inequality. **Inequality**, as we defined it in Chapter 1, is the differential allocation of resources and privileges among the members of a society. Stratification does not necessarily produce widespread inequality. In fact, as we learned in Chapter 3, in hunting and gather-

Social stratification is both a cause and an effect of inequalities of wealth, power, and prestige. In the United States, what characteristics separate this beggar and the person passing by? What beliefs and values, or ideologies, rationalize their difference? In the U.S. class system, what are the beggar's chances for upward social mobility compared to other countries?

ing societies, where people are usually stratified only by sex and age, resources are distributed relatively equally, with everyone receiving what they need to survive. However, as societies become more technologically advanced, stratification becomes more complex and inequality simultaneously increases. Moreover, accompanying greater inequality is a set of beliefs or an **ideology** that serves to justify it. The content of these beliefs varies across societies, just as the form and extent of stratification varies. Regardless of specific content however, the ideology legitimates and reinforces the stratification system and its attendant inequality. It is not surprising, then, that Martin Cook blames himself for losing his job. In our society, there is a strong belief in individual initiative and hard work, so if someone loses his or her job, it's assumed the person must have done something wrong and is therefore at least partly at fault.

Finally, looking back at Martin Cook's story, we see that initially in his career he moved up in the stratification system, and then later, after he lost his job, he and his family plunged down. The personal changes Cook experienced illustrate the process of **social mobility**, that is, movement within the stratification hierarchy. Cook's case also shows that movement can be upward or downward, and the result of individual accomplishment or, as when he lost his job, because of structural changes in society. Thus, there are various types of social mobility that sociologists study, along with the degree to which mobility occurs within a society.

To begin our analysis of stratification, then, let's consider first the major components of economic stratification—class, status, and power—and the various types of stratification systems that coexist in the world.

SYSTEMS OF STRATIFICATION

In studying economic stratification, contemporary sociologists use Max Weber's three major components: class, status, and power. We will alter this trio only slightly, exchanging the term *wealth* for *class*. **Wealth** is the material component of stratification and refers to financial standing, as determined by income and other assets. **Status** is the prestige component of stratification and refers to how others perceive an individual or group in terms of respect and deference (see the Doing Sociology box). And **political power** is the decision-making component of stratification, referring to an individual's relationship to government and his or her ability to influence political decisions.

All three components of economic stratification exist along a continuum ranging from low to high. That is, individuals have more or less wealth, status, or power. Also, an individual's ranking in one area typically coincides with her or his rankings in the others, but in some cases, it may not. In other words, someone who is wealthy usually enjoys high prestige and political power as well. However, it is possible to be wealthy, but to rank low in

---

DOING SOCIOLOGY

How Prestigious Are Different Occupations?

Prestige is a subjective component of social class, based on people's perceptions. A person's prestige derives largely from her or his occupation. Usually, the most prestigious occupations are those that pay well or require extensive training and specialized education.

One way sociologists determine prestige is to ask a random sample of adults to rank various occupations relative to one another. The National Opinion Research Center (NORC), for example, periodically asks a random sample of

U.S. adults to evaluate 110 occupations according to their "social standing." The respondents' answers are averaged and NORC analysts convert the answers into prestige scores that range from 0 to 100.

You can do your own study of prestige ranking. Here is a list of twenty occupations. Ask family members and friends to rank order these occupations in terms of how prestigious they consider each one. Then compare your results with the findings of the National Opinion Research Center, which appear in Table 8.2 on p. 206. Although your findings will not be scored like those of NORC, you can examine the relative order of the rankings.

Occupations to Be Ranked

Accountant
Retail Salesperson (clothing)
Physician
Airline Pilot
Librarian
Garbage Collector
Food Server (Waiter/Waitress)
University/College Professor
Mail Carrier
Sociologist
Elementary School Teacher
Lawyer
Janitor
Childcare Worker
Realtor
Athlete
Architect
Secretary
Police Officer
Registered Nurse

prestige and political power: for example, a low-income worker who wins the lottery. It's also possible to have little wealth, but to rank high in prestige and power. Nelson Mandela, former president of South Africa, was by no means wealthy, but as an imprisoned social justice activist, he was respected throughout the world and his views significantly influenced international political decision makers.

Let's return to the idea that the form and extent of stratification in a society is related to the society's level of technological development. When we discussed types of societies, we noted that in hunting and gathering societies, where technology is limited to a few simple implements, there is little stratification and a high degree of equality among the society's members. Although those who are the best hunters or gatherers or who have some other talent that contributes in a special way to the survival of the group may win greater respect and admiration than others—that is, enjoy higher prestige—all members of the society tend to be equally valued. Moreover, given the simplicity of the technology available to hunter/gatherers, there is no opportunity for any single member to accumulate surplus resources or wealth.

In pastoral and horticultural societies, advances in technology do produce a surplus, and a small group of individuals typically emerges as the wealthy of the society. We observed this disparity in agricultural societies as well. A small, elite group comes to control the land, production, and decision making, while the vast majority of the population is subject to their rule and toil hard for a meager share of the resources. What is more, the elites institute various policies and practices that protect their privileged position; for example, wealth and nobility must be inherited, or only individuals sharing the same social standing may marry, which makes it virtually impossible for a "common" person to enter the elite ranks.

As societies industrialize, social roles become more numerous and more diverse. The rapid technological advances of industrial societies increase the need for specialized knowledge and training, which, in turn, makes it somewhat easier for people to move within the stratification system. Inequality remains, to be sure, but it is of a different nature than inequality in agricultural societies. In industrial societies, social mobility up and down the stratification system is possible. The mobility may be the result of individual merit (for example, a person acquired a high level of education to perform a highly valued job) or structural change (for example, a downturn in production causes people to lose their jobs).

In observing differences in stratification across types of societies, sociologists have come to distinguish two major types of stratification systems, based on how open they are, that is, the degree to which they allow mobility throughout the hierarchy. In a **caste system**, movement between strata is virtually closed, so individuals stay in the stratum into which they were born for their entire lives. In a **class system**, movement between strata is possible, so individuals can change strata over the course of their lives. Understanding these two basic types of stratification systems is important for comprehending stratification and inequality in the United States.

The Caste System

The hallmark of the caste system is that membership in a specific stratum or *caste* is ascribed. In other words, it is determined at birth by factors over which the individual has no control. (Recall our definition of *ascribed roles* in Chapter 6.) The basis for caste ascription may be skin color, parents' occupation, or parents' religion. Since movement between castes is virtually closed, a person remains in the caste into which she or he is born throughout life.

The caste system is preserved through laws and traditions that prohibit not only movement from one caste to another, but even physical contact between members of different castes. **Endogamy** is the prohibition against marriage or the formation of an intimate or sexual relationship with anyone outside one's own caste. Members of different castes may also be physically separated through **segregation**. For instance, lower caste individuals may be restricted in where they can live and the jobs they may hold. They may not be permitted to dine in the same restaurants or even eat the same foods as members of higher castes.

This Japanese Burakumin, like India's "untouchables," is an outcast, a victim of a traditional system of social stratification based on inherited status, endogamy, segregation, and restricted occupation. In all caste systems, lower caste people perform the most undesirable, dehumanizing, or "dirty" jobs. Caste systems are ill suited to modern industrial capitalist economies. Why?

The caste system is most frequently found in agricultural societies and, to a lesser extent, in horticultural and pastoral societies. One society well known for its caste system is India. The traditional Indian caste system is based on ancient Hindu teachings that describe four categories of people: the *Brahmins,* or intellectuals; the *Kshatriyas,* or warriors; the *Vaishyas,* or farmers; and the *Shudras,* or servants. But there is also a fifth group, the outcasts, who, according to ancient teaching, are the descendants of the offspring of a Brahmin woman and a servant man. Their union violated sacred laws, so all their descendants are considered impure, polluted, untouchable. They must perform the worst jobs, such as sweeping floors and cleaning toilets.

Today, it is estimated that 25 percent of the population of India (which numbers close to one billion people) are outcasts, who live in abject poverty. This situation continues even though India's Constitution abolished the untouchable caste and gave untouchables special protections. For example, a percentage of government jobs and university placements are reserved for former untouchables and members of other low castes. To openly discriminate against someone because of his or her caste is illegal, but enforcing the law is difficult, especially in rural India where adherence to traditional caste relations is much stronger than in the large cities.

Another example of a caste society is South Africa, where position in the stratification hierarchy is based on skin color. *Apartheid,* as this system is called, was legally in place for four decades (1950–1990), and official policies and practices were enacted to segregate the races. Twenty-three million Black South Africans—about 77 percent of the nation's population—were relegated to the bottom of the hierarchy. They had no political rights, including no right to vote. They had to carry identification cards at all times, and their movement was restricted. They were required to live in Black townships or "homelands," which were the most blighted areas of the country, and they could only hold the most menial (household servant) or most dangerous (miner) jobs. Just above Blacks in the South African caste system were "coloureds," whose racial ancestry is mixed, and Asians. At the top of the hierarchy were the White South Africans, or Afrikaners, of mostly Dutch ancestry. Although Whites made up less than 15 percent of South Africa's population, they controlled virtually all the wealth and political power and enjoyed the greatest prestige.

Apartheid fostered repression and violence in South Africa, and many people, mostly Blacks, lost their lives in the struggle to end the system. It was not until the late 1970s, however, that other countries began to exert pressure on White South Africa to dismantle apartheid. The countries imposed an arms embargo, divested multinational corporate holdings, and boycotted products made by South African companies. Finally, in 1990, then-Pres-

In this picture former presidents F. W. de Klerk and Nelson Mandela celebrate the end of apartheid in South Africa. In what ways was apartheid an example of a caste system? Why do many sociologists see the U.S. prior to the 1950s as essentially a caste system?

ident F. W. de Klerk was forced to repeal all apartheid laws. Mr. de Klerk subsequently negotiated with representatives of the country's Black population, and in 1994, the first political elections to include Blacks were held. Nelson Mandela, who had spent twenty-seven years in prison as an anti-apartheid activist, was elected the country's first Black president, and a racially representative government was installed. Of course, these changes do not mean that the caste system in South Africa has completely disappeared in practice, only that it is now illegal.

Americans who are appalled by apartheid forget that a similar caste system was in effect in this country for a much longer period of time—from the early 1600s until the 1960s. During slavery, Blacks were considered property or chattel, just like animals, furniture, or the slaveholders' other material possessions. The Emancipation Proclamation and the Reconstruction Acts, along with the Thirteenth Amendment, which abolished slavery, the Fourteenth Amendment, which guaranteed all citizens equal protection of the law, and the Fifteenth Amendment, which gave Black men the right to vote, were supposed to dismantle this racially based caste system. However, segregation of the races continued in Jim Crow laws and dominated all aspects of life: the workplace, schools, recreational facilities, public accommodations, restaurants, public transportation, and even cemeteries. Antimiscegenation laws also prohibited intimate relationships between women and men of different races. Beginning in 1954, with the Supreme Court ruling that segregated schools were unconstitutional, legislation finally put an end to the caste system in the United States. As in South Africa, though, remnants exist in practice, most notably in housing.

The Class System

In contrast to a caste system where membership in a stratum is ascribed, in a class system, membership in a particular stratum or *social class* is at least partly achieved. Individuals can move from one class to another, regardless of the class of their parents, as a result of their personal talents, how much effort they expend, and their educational attainment. Moreover, differences across strata, particularly strata neighboring one another on the hierarchy, are not rigid, so class distinctions can become blurred. It is not likely that an individual's level of wealth, prestige, and power will completely coincide in a class system as they usually do in caste societies. Thus, for example, while not everyone in a class system has equal political power, even those at the bottom of the hierarchy in terms of wealth and prestige are guaranteed certain political rights, such as the right to vote. Industrial societies have class systems of stratification because economic development and expansion depend to a large degree on a multiskilled population from different backgrounds who have freedom of movement within the marketplace from job to job, within the society, and across societies. The United States is an example of an industrial society with a class system of stratification.

We have described the class and caste system as ideal types. In reality, societies conform only more or less to one of these models, and most societies exhibit aspects of both systems. For example, in Great Britain, a landed aristocracy bearing titles of nobility (such as a Queen and King, prince and princess, and lord and lady) retains great wealth, prestige, and political power despite the fact that feudalism was replaced by democracy long ago. Although the United States is often considered the prime illustration of a class society, it too retains some caste-like characteristics. One study, for example, found that a person's family background—his or her parents' income, occupation, and level of educational attainment—played a greater role in determining adult social standing than the individual's own intelligence or educational attainment (Jenks et al., 1972).

An Alternative to Caste and Class

Stratification, we have said, is universal, existing in some form and to some extent in all known societies. However, one of sociology's founding theorists, Karl Marx, maintained that a nonstratified society was possible. According to Marx, a revolution of the working class in a capitalist country would lead to socialism, a transitional stage, and ultimately to a nonstratified or *classless* society that he called **communism.** In a communist society, all property, including the technology for production, is collectively owned and controlled. Every member contributes to the development and prosperity of the society according to her or his individual abilities, and each receives resources according to her or his individual needs.

Marx spoke and wrote passionately about communism, and his ideas inspired revolutions in countries throughout Europe, Asia, Africa, and Latin America. But the question that arises is whether any of the societies that emerged were classless. The Russian Revolution of 1917, for example, resulted in a government that called itself communist and took control of the means of production and all major institutions in the society in the interests of the masses. There was a massive redistribution of wealth that substantially leveled stratification. Nevertheless, inequalities remained. High government officials and party members enjoyed a standard of living and privileges unavailable to other citizens; they had access to restricted or scarce commodities and services, the best schools for their children, travel opportunities, luxury cars, and better quality, spacious housing. Virtually all political power was in the hands of these elites, yet they composed less than 7 percent of the country's population (Gordon, 1998; Lane, 1990). Even among the masses, blatant forms of stratification existed. For instance, although the majority of women were in the paid labor force, they were concentrated in low-level, poorly paying jobs, and they had little representation in decision-making positions (Gray, 1989). Inequalities such as these won popular support for economic reforms in the 1980s which, along with other complex factors, eventually led to the downfall of Soviet-style communism.

Similar economic inequality is evident in China, and problems appear to be growing as the country pursues "modernization." A tiny segment of the population has prospered in "special economic zones" established by the government. Some have even become millionaires. These individuals, who are now able to build new, single-family homes in the countryside and purchase luxury goods, such as Western-style clothing and imported cars, command considerable prestige and power. At the same time, they are arousing resentment in much of the rest of the population, particularly those who struggle to simply feed, clothe, and house their families (Eckholm, 1998; Tyler, 1995).

There is less economic disparity between the rich and the poor in contemporary Russia and China than in the United States and some other nations, but neither country matches up to Marx's vision of a classless society, and the revolutions caused tremendous human suffering (see also McKinley, 1999). To date, in fact, no industrial society has achieved the status of classless or nonstratified. Marx's prediction that all social classes in capitalist societies would be absorbed into just two, the rich and the poor, did not occur. Instead, a large middle class developed, whose members include doctors, lawyers, teachers, nurses, and managers. These workers enjoy better pay and higher prestige than factory workers, and they generally express satisfaction with their standard of living. Workers in capitalist societies also have legal protections and benefits programs that Marx never imagined: laws regulating hours and working conditions; the right to seek redress in court for employers' abuses; and Social Security, disability, and unemployment insurance. Even though many of Marx's predictions proved wrong, his concerns about the concentration of wealth and inherent inequality in capitalist society were not unfounded, an issue to which we will return later in the chapter.

The fact that no society is unstratified or classless has led some analysts to argue that stratification must be a necessary or essential feature of social organization. We'll address this topic next.

REFLECTING ON

Systems of Stratification

1. What are some examples of how the three components of stratification—wealth, status, and political power—do not coincide?
2. Why do changes in technology produce changes in stratification? How might today's rapid technological developments affect stratification in the future?
3. Does the United States retain traits of a caste system in areas besides housing?
4. Do you think it is possible to have a classless or nonstratified industrial society? Why or why not?

EXPLAINING STRATIFICATION

Sociologists have developed two very different explanations for the existence of stratification across societies. Let's look at each in turn.

The Structural Functionalist Explanation

If stratification is universal, structural functionalists reason, it must be beneficial in some way for a society. The most influential structural functionalist explanation is the *Davis-Moore hypothesis*, proposed more than fifty years ago by Kingsley Davis and Wilbert Moore (1945).

The Davis-Moore hypothesis begins with the assumption that the various tasks that must be done in a society are not of equal importance or difficulty. Some jobs are so easy and unskilled that just about anybody can do them, while others are complex and require unusual talent or specialized training. Compare, for example, the difference in skill level and education required to drive a truck versus pilot a space shuttle. Consequently, the jobs

that a society considers most important and/or difficult are given the greatest rewards, including money and prestige. According to the Davis-Moore hypothesis, then, stratification serves a motivating function. If all jobs were rewarded the same, no matter how easy or difficult they were to do, and no matter how well they were done, few people would be motivated to make the personal sacrifices—endure the stress, invest the time and money for the required education, give up time with family and friends—that doing the really difficult, but important jobs usually entails. Stratification encourages individual initiative and effort and ensures that those best qualified for specific positions fill them.

The Davis-Moore hypothesis is appealing because it makes sense. For instance, many observers have used it to explain why professionals such as doctors and scientists in former communist countries were not as productive as their counterparts in capitalist countries: Because they were rewarded the same as everyone else no matter what kind of job they did, they weren't motivated to excel. However, despite its widespread influence, the Davis-Moore hypothesis has been criticized for a number of reasons. One important criticism is that the rewards allotted to a particular job often do not coincide with that job's functional importance to the society (Tumin, 1953).

As Table 8.1 on page 202 shows, many entertainers and professional athletes are among the highest paid in our society, yet few would consider their work functionally more important than the work of the President or even a teacher. Although people enjoy watching Oprah Winfrey chat with guests on her show and may even be helped by what they have to say, a Supreme Court Justice makes decisions that affect the lives of millions of people. Some of the lowest-paid positions listed in Table 8.1 are extremely important to the well-being of our society. Consider, for instance, what happens when garbage collectors go on strike. The build-up and decomposition of the garbage is not only unpleasant, but also a serious health hazard to a large number of people.

A second problem with the Davis-Moore hypothesis is that it implies stratification is based on *meritocracy*, that rewards are differentially bestowed in a society on the basis of an individual's effort, ability, and talent, rather than on ascribed traits. Certainly, this is not the case in caste societies, but it is also problematic in class systems. In the United States and other class societies, for instance, wealth, prestige, and power can be passed on intergenerationally through inheritance. The name Rockefeller or Vanderbilt opens many doors, regardless of a particular individual's effort, ability, or talent. At the same time, members of many groups, because of ascribed traits such as sex, race, or ethnicity, find opportunities to move up the stratification hierarchy blocked because of discrimination. Hard work, education, and personal talent do not have the same payoffs for women and racial and

TABLE 8.1 Earnings for Selected Occupations, Athletes, and Entertainers, 1997

Occupation	Median Weekly Earnings ($)	Occupation	Median Weekly Earnings ($)
Lawyer	1,166	Carpenter	482
Physician	1,120	Secretary	410
Electrical engineer	987	Roofer	407
Architect	822	Bus driver	405
Firefighter	707	Bank teller	321
Police officer	697	Public sanitation worker	301
Mail carrier	677	Nursing aid	300
Elementary school teacher	662	Apparel salesperson	283
Accountant	652	Waiter/waitress	281
Social worker	522	Farm worker	273

Athlete/Entertainer	Weekly Earnings ($)*	Athlete/Entertainer	Weekly Earnings ($)*
Jerry Seinfeld (comedian/actor)	4,326,923 (225 million)	Michael Crichton (novelist)	1,250,000 (65 million)
Steven Spielberg (producer/director)	3,365,385 (175 million)	Master P (rap singer)	1,086,539 (56.5 million)
Oprah Winfrey (talk show hostess/actress)	2,403,846 (125 million)	Evander Holyfield (boxer)	1,044,230 (54.3 million)
James Cameron (producer/director)	2,211,539 (115 million)	Oscar de la Hoya (boxer)	730,769 (38 million)
Michael Jordan (basketball player)	1,505,769 (78.3 million)	Michael Schumacher (race car driver)	673,077 (35 million)
Tim Allen (comedian/actor)	1,480,769 (77 million)	Tiger Woods (golfer)	501,923 (26.1 million)

*Calculated by dividing annual earnings, shown in parentheses, by 52. Athletes' earnings include endorsements.

Sources: "Forbes Top 40 Athletes, 1997," Forbes on line (www.forbes.com); "Top 40 Entertainers," Forbes, September 21, 1998, pp. 220–224; U.S. Department of Labor (1998, January). Employment and earnings, pp. 209–214.

ethnic minorities as they do for men and for White people (Zweigenhaft & Domhoff, 1998).

Finally, by emphasizing the benefits of stratification, Davis and Moore overlook the devastating impact that inequality has on people at the bottom of the hierarchy. And, as you will see later in the chapter, not everyone has an equal chance to be at the bottom; some groups are more likely than others to live in poverty.

The Conflict Explanation

The second major sociological explanation of stratification is conflict theory. Conflict theorists begin with the observation that advances in technology allow for the accumulation of surplus goods and resources. Some individuals accumulate more than others, and their greater wealth affords them more prestige and power over others. These individuals act to preserve their higher social standing, while those below them struggle to maintain or improve their own situation. In other words, these groups are in conflict with one another, and stratification simply shows who has won and who has lost—the haves and have nots—in this ongoing conflict.

The conflict theory of stratification is based on Karl Marx's work. Marx saw the history of all societies as a history of class struggle, a struggle between those who

Do the people in these occupations directly compete for wealth, power, and prestige? Does your answer in this case support or question the conflict theory explanation of stratification? If you could add two pictures that would refute both of these explanations, what would you show?

own the means of production and those whose financial assets amount to little more than their labor power. In capitalist societies, this conflict is played out between the capitalists (or *bourgeoisie*) and the workers (or *proletariat*), and all the institutions of the society reflect this basic class division and serve to maintain it. Marx felt, in fact, that the capitalists were very aware of their class interests—that is, they had a strong *class consciousness*—and so used the system to protect their position. He hoped his work would raise the class consciousness of the workers so they could understand their exploitation by the capitalists and ultimately recognize that it was in their class interests to revolt and establish a classless or communist society.

As we've already discussed, Marx's predictions have not come to pass. Although there have been revolutions in highly stratified societies, none has occurred in a capitalist society. What is more, capitalism has been making significant inroads in formerly communist societies such as Russia and the Eastern Bloc nations, as well as in China, which retains its communist identification but is rapidly developing a market economy.

There is, however, plenty of evidence of class conflict in our society and other industrial societies throughout the world. Moreover, this conflict is made worse by other forms of stratification, such as that based on race and ethnicity as well as sex. Nevertheless, conflict theory has been criticized for depicting class antagonisms too simplisti-

cally. There are not just two conflicting social classes, but rather several classes whose interests sometimes coincide and other times collide. All workers, for instance, regardless of social class, benefit from disability insurance programs. In addition, there may be conflict between members of one class, not just between classes. Owners of health insurance companies, for example, may find themselves at odds with factory owners who expose workers to hazardous materials because such workplace conditions drive up the cost of health care.

To understand the complexity of social class, let's examine the social class structure of our society more closely.

REFLECTING ON

Explaining Stratification

1. What is an example of how meritocracy operates in our society? Do you have an example from your own life experience? How about an example of a situation in which ascribed characteristics were more important than merit?
2. Why has a socialist revolution never occurred in a capitalist country? Can you think of any reasons not suggested in this chapter?

SOCIAL CLASSES IN THE UNITED STATES

People tend to think of social class simply in terms of income or wealth, but dollars alone don't set boundaries between one class and another. For example, most people view a school teacher and a coal miner differently in terms of their class membership, although both have average incomes of about $35,000. Other factors are involved in determining class membership. This is why sociologists draw on the work of Max Weber that we discussed at the beginning of the chapter; in determining social class membership, they consider not only a person's income or wealth, but also the person's prestige and political power. Sociologists also consider lifestyle variables, such as education, consumption patterns, and leisure activities to get a better picture of the variations between classes. It is important to remember, however, that lifestyle variables exist in a reciprocal relationship with a person's economic standing, that is, how much wealth they have. For instance, a family's income determines to a large extent the amount and type of education the children can obtain; in turn, the children's education is a crucial element in determining their future income.

A pioneering study that attempted to empirically describe the social class structure of the United States was conducted in the 1930s by William Lloyd Warner (1963), who identified three basic classes (upper, middle, and lower), each with two subdivisions (upper and lower), yielding six classes altogether. Some sociologists today continue to use Warner's typology, while others collapse some of the categories, resulting in a typology of three or four social classes (upper, middle, working, lower or poor) (Gilbert & Kahl, 1993). Our discussion will focus on four social classes: the upper class, whom we label *the wealthy*; the middle class, the working class, and the poor. We will also highlight important divisions within these classes so that you can see differences not only between social classes, but within them as well.

The Wealthy

The **wealthy** are society's upper class, representing only about 3 percent of the U.S. population. Members of this social class have yearly incomes of hundreds of thousands, even millions of dollars. Their vast economic wealth affords members of this social class tremendous prestige and extensive political power at the national as well as state and local levels.

The wealthy may be divided into two groups: those whose wealth has accumulated over many years and derives primarily from inheritance, and those whose wealth is recent and derives mainly from earnings. People who have acquired their fortunes primarily through inheritance are often referred to as "blue bloods" or "high society." Their names—Rockefeller, DuPont, Getty—are found in the *Social Register*, an annual listing of elites that has been published since the late 1800s. They are White, usually Anglo-Saxon in ethnicity, and typically Protestant (Baltzell, 1979/58; 1988). They possess wealth not only as individuals, but more importantly as families, and this wealth is passed on from generation to generation. Hence, they are also referred to as "old-money" families.

Blue bloods include not more than 1 percent of the country's population, forming a kind of American aristocracy. This group tends to be highly *endogamous*, marrying or becoming intimate with only those who share their social standing. They are also a very exclusive group, associating and socializing with only their peers. They do this by living in residential areas where housing is prohibitively expensive for everyone except the very wealthy, and by sending their children to private schools where applicants are screened not only for academic achievement, but also for ancestry. They belong to exclusive clubs with similar screening procedures, sit on the boards of major cultural and charitable organizations, and participate in social rituals such as the annual International Debutante Ball, which brings together the young, unmarried sons and daughters in these families so that they can get acquainted (Domhoff, 1990; Ostrander, 1984). As one of the wealthy recently described these events, "It's all the people of the same caliber coming out to meet each other" (Goldberg, 1995, p. 44). One becomes a member of this social class almost solely by being born into it.

People with equally vast (or greater) fortunes but no lineage make up another subgroup of the wealthy. They are sometimes called the "new rich" because their wealth is recent and comes mainly from earnings. They often come from professional families, but some are from modest backgrounds and a few grew up in poor families. These people live in ostentatious homes and enjoy what many consider extravagant lifestyles, but their lack of "blue blood" ancestry means that they only infrequently, if ever, travel in the social circles of the blue bloods.

Many of the new rich are in health care, computer technology, and multimedia—the "boom industries" of the 1980s and 1990s that have created a mushrooming number of millionaires and billionaires in the United States over the past two decades. In 1950, for example, there were only about 13,000 people in the United States worth $1 million or more; less than fifty years later, there were 1.26 million people who were millionaires, and 36,000 of them were worth $10 million or more (U.S Department of Commerce, Bureau of the Census, 1995). In fact, the rich have gotten even richer in recent years, with the average wealth of U.S. billionaires climbing from $2.0 billion in 1994 to $6.4 billion in 1998 (Gorham et al., 1998).

To what social class do the people in each picture probably belong? On what observations and assumptions do you base your judgments? To what extent are your judgments based on stereotypes? What guidelines would you suggest for avoiding confusion between ideal types and stereotypes? If you could add three more pictures to the set to round out an objective representation of the U.S. social class system, what would you show?

Also adding to the swelling numbers of millionaires in this country are entertainers and professional athletes who command extraordinary salaries. Oprah Winfrey, for example, earned $125 million in 1997. Michael Jordan made over $300,000 *per game*. Jordan and other entertainers and professional athletes also earn millions each year through product endorsements alone; Jordan, for instance, made over $47 million in 1997 from endorsements ("*Forbes* Top 40 Athletes," 1998; "The Top 40 Entertainers," 1998). However, it is important to note that the growth in the number of millionaires and other wealthy people during the past two decades has not lessened overall social inequality in this country, as we will see later in the chapter.

The new rich, particularly those who have risen from modest beginnings, are less endogamous than the blue bloods, and although they enjoy considerable prestige, it is of a different kind than that of the blue bloods. Their political power is also more diverse, with some wielding much more than others. Nevertheless, their tremendous wealth affords them opportunities that are only imagined by those in the classes below them. Moreover, like the blue bloods, the new rich are typically White and male.

Each year, for example, *Forbes* magazine ranks the 400 wealthiest people in the United States. Many are the corporate elite who derive their fortunes from salaries, bonuses, and stock options; in 1997, about 58 percent derived their wealth from earnings rather than inheritance. In order to be included among the 400 wealthiest people in the United States in 1997, a person had to be a U.S. citizen and have a total net worth (assets minus liabilities) of at least a half billion dollars ($500 million). Of those who made the list, just 58 (14.5 percent) were women. Only one woman was not White: Oprah Winfrey, whose net worth in 1997 was $675 million. Among the men, just seven (1.75 percent of the total) were not White ("The *Forbes* 400," 1998).

The Middle Class

If you ask most people to which social class they belong, they are likely to say the middle class. Since the **middle class** is the largest social class, composed of 40 to 45 percent of the U.S. population, their answer would probably be correct. However, widespread identification with the middle class masks important sociological divisions within this class as well as between it and the classes that fall below it in the stratification hierarchy.

The middle class may be divided into two groups, although precise numerical boundaries are difficult to define. One group is the upper-middle class composed of highly paid professionals earning at least but often significantly more than $50,000 per year. Many in the upper-middle class are married to individuals who share their occupational standing, pushing family incomes upward to $200,000 or more per year. Typical occupations of members in this group require advanced degrees and include physicians, lawyers, engineers, professors, and high-level corporate managers and administrators. Also, as Table 8.2 shows, these occupations command high prestige rankings.

The high incomes of the upper-middle class allow them to enjoy very comfortable lifestyles. They usually have substantial savings and investments. The cars they drive are usually the more expensive makes and models and are purchased new. They typically live in spacious, well-furnished homes in the suburbs or trendy, gentrified urban neighborhoods. Their children may attend public schools in the most highly regarded school districts or be educated at private schools. Children of the upper-middle class almost certainly go on to college, and many follow their parents into the professions with advanced

TABLE 8.2   Prestige Rankings of Selected Occupations, United States

Occupation	Prestige Ranking	Occupation	Prestige Ranking
Physician	86	Electrician	51
Lawyer	75	Realtor	49
University/College Professor	74	Bookkeeper	47
Architect	73	Machinist	47
Aerospace Engineer	72	Mail Carrier	47
Dentist	72	Secretary	46
Clergy Member	69	Photographer	45
Psychologist	69	Bank Teller	43
Registered Nurse	66	Tailor	42
Secondary School Teacher	66	Welder	42
Accountant	65	Telephone Operator	40
Athlete	65	Carpenter	39
Electrical Engineer	64	Childcare Worker	36
Elementary School Teacher	64	Hairdresser	36
Airline Pilot	61	Baker	35
Computer Programmer	61	Retail Salesperson (clothing)	30
Sociologist	61	Truck Driver	30
Reporter	60	Cashier	29
Police Officer	60	Garbage Collector	28
Radio/Television Announcer	55	Food Server (Waitress/Waiter)	28
Librarian	54	Household Worker	23
Firefighter	53	Janitor	22
Social Worker	52		

Source: National Opinion Research Center (1994) *General social surveys, 1972–1994: Cumulative codebook.* Chicago: Author, pp. 881–889.

INTERSECTING INEQUALITIES

How Does Sex Affect Income?

Why distinguish between pink-collar jobs and other jobs? The data in the table below provide an answer. The table shows a list of lower-middle class and working class occupations in which either female or male workers predominate. Notice first that a number of female-dominated jobs have higher prestige rankings than male-dominated jobs (recall Table 8.2). Nevertheless, the female-dominated jobs pay, on average, less than the male-dominated jobs. Thus, our comparison of pink-collar jobs with male-dominated white-collar and blue-collar jobs provides a good example of how the prestige dimension of social class does not always coincide with the income dimension. In this case, the sex of the worker appears to have a greater effect on income than the perceived prestige of the job.

Median Weekly Earnings of Selected Female-Dominated and Male-Dominated Occupations, 1997

Occupation	Percent Female	Prestige Ranking	Median Weekly Earnings ($)
Secretary	98.7	46	410
Childcare Worker	97.4	36	202
Registered Nurse	92.4	66	710
Bank Teller	91.1	43	321
Bookkeeper	90.6	47	420
Elementary School Teacher	83.4	64	662
Librarian	82.6	54	638
Janitor	26.1	22	313
Mail Carrier	28.6	47	677
Police Officer	11.3	60	697
Truck Driver	4.1	30	506
Firefighter	3.0	53	707
Electrician	2.2	51	624
Carpenter	1.3	39	482

Source: U.S. Department of Labor (1998). *Employment and earnings, January.* Washington, DC: U.S. Government Printing Office, pp. 209–214.

degrees of their own. Despite their relatively high incomes and prestige, however, the upper-middle class does not wield substantial political power. They may be active in local and state politics, but political influence on the national level is usually limited to the lobbying efforts of the professional organizations to which they belong, such as the American Bar Association or the American Medical Association.

The upper-middle class is a small subdivision of middle America. They are more racially and ethnically diverse than the wealthy, but White Americans are still predominant. About 38 percent of White families have incomes above $50,000 per year, compared to 21 percent of Black families and 21 percent of Hispanic families (U.S. Department of Commerce, Bureau of the Census, 1998a). Instead, it is in the lower-middle class that one finds greater racial and ethnic diversity. This larger segment of the middle class is composed of families with incomes roughly between $25,000 and $50,000 per year. Among White families, about 30 percent have incomes in this range, compared to 29 percent of Black families and 32 percent of Hispanic families (Oliver & Shapiro, 1995; U.S. Department of Commerce, Bureau of the Census, 1998a).

The lower-middle class is composed of people who work primarily in white-collar service occupations, such as salespeople, skilled office workers, nurses, and teachers. **White collar jobs** traditionally require mostly mental labor, and usually require jobholders to have at least a high school education and some require additional specialized training or a college degree. **Blue collar jobs** require mostly physical labor. These jobs got their names because of the way workers who hold them usually dress for work. However, there is another category of work, **pink collar jobs,** that got its name not because of the way workers dress for the job, but because most of the workers who hold these jobs are women. Women are highly represented among lower-middle class jobholders, but as the Intersecting Inequalities box shows, there is often a significant difference between their salaries and those of lower-middle class men.

Besides their income, the largest financial asset of the lower-middle class is their homes, which are modest, although many in this group rent their housing. They typically own a car, perhaps two, but their cars are the more moderately priced makes and models and they get significant mileage on them before they are replaced. Members of the lower-middle class aspire to send their children to college, but the expense entails substantial sacrifice and hard work on the part of both parents and children. The political power of the lower-middle class is limited; they tend not to be politically active apart from voting in elections.

There has been a great deal of discussion in the media recently about what has been dubbed *voluntary downshifting* among the middle class, especially the upper-middle class. Basically, this refers to a trend toward restructuring one's life for greater simplicity—that is, buying only the necessities, increasing savings, eliminating all credit cards but one, and spending less time at work and more time with family and friends or pursuing hobbies. In short, "dumping what doesn't make you happy in order to have some time for what does" (Goldberg, 1995, p. C9). Interestingly, the move toward simplicity does not mean giving up luxuries, such as a vacation home or BMW. Indeed, what often goes unmentioned by the downshifting gurus is that the pursuit of greater simplicity assumes a certain level of financial comfort and security to begin with. Certainly, members of the strata below the middle class, and even many members of the lower-middle class, cannot afford to work less. Some, as we will see, already lead very basic lives, not because of voluntary downshifting, but because of involuntary, externally imposed financial constraints.

The Working Class

Between 30 and 35 percent of the U.S. population is **working class.** Members of this social class have annual incomes between $15,000 and $25,000, although some make slightly more. What distinguishes them from the classes directly above and below them in the stratification hierarchy is their full-time employment as skilled and semiskilled laborers. Blue-collar jobs held by members of this class include factory work, truck driving, and the construction trades. Pink-collar jobs include beautician, sales clerk, waitress, and many secretarial positions. Such jobs do not carry much prestige (see Table 8.2), nor do they require extensive education. Most members of the working class have graduated from high school or a trade school. Their children also are likely to follow this educational path; only about 30 percent of children from working-class families attend college (Children's Defense Fund, 1997).

Members of the working class tend to be inactive politically as individuals, apart from voting in elections. However, the working class as a group exerts some political influence through trade unions. Backed by large memberships that convert into large voting blocks, union leaders can sometimes successfully lobby politicians to support policies in workers' interests. Since the 1980s, though, unions have lost power; union membership has

declined and workers have been forced to make numerous concessions to industry.

In recent years, as housing costs have risen, it has become increasingly difficult for young, working-class families to purchase a home. The younger the head of the household, in fact, the more likely the family is to be living in rental housing (Children's Defense Fund, 1998). Working-class families who do purchase their homes, as well as those living in rental housing, live in low-income suburban or urban neighborhoods. They are likely to have a family car, but it may be purchased used, and it is almost certainly a moderately priced or low-priced make and model.

The narrow ratio between the income and expenses of the working class means that there is little money for discretionary spending, and savings are rare. This, in turn, makes the working class vulnerable to economic downturns, and a financial crisis, such as a layoff or a major illness, can easily propel them downward in social class, to the poor.

The Poor

The federal government classifies 13.3 percent of the population as officially poor (Porter, 1997; U.S. Department of Commerce, Bureau of the Census, 1998b), but many experts believe official counts underestimate the number of poor people in this country. They maintain that a more accurate estimate is that about 20 percent of the population is poor or teetering on the brink of poverty (DeParle, 1992; Institute for Research on Poverty, 1992).

The **poverty line** is a sum of money against which an individual's or family's income is compared to determine whether they are poor. The federal government calculates the poverty line by multiplying by three the cost of purchasing a minimally nutritional diet as specified by the U.S. Department of Agriculture. Also figured into the calculation is the number of people who live in the family. Consequently, there are actually several poverty lines. A family of four, for example, is considered poor if their annual income falls below $16,530, whereas the poverty line for a two-person family with family members younger than 65 is $10,915 (U.S. Department of Commerce, Bureau of the Census, 1999).

The incomes of poor families often fall well below the official poverty line because adults in the household may not be working or may only be able to find work sporadically. Many people, though, are working full time or part time, but hold jobs that pay minimum wage rates, which are not enough to lift them and their families out of poverty. At the current rate of $5.15 per hour, a minimum-wage worker, working full time, year round would only earn about $10,700, which is officially considered poverty level except for single adult and two-person households (U.S. Department of Commerce, Bureau of the Census, 1997).

The *working poor* are employed at jobs that are at best semiskilled, but usually unskilled. These are the most menial jobs in our society and include janitorial work, fast-food and similar unskilled service positions, as well as clothing assembly and other "sweatshop" manufacturing jobs. Not only do these jobs pay low or minimum wages, but they offer little job security and no benefits. The low educational attainment of the poor is often a barrier to obtaining better-paying jobs. Only 19.2 percent of the poor are high school graduates; less than 13 percent have attended college (U.S. Department of Commerce, Bureau of the Census, 1997).

The working poor do not usually live in poverty on a permanent basis; they drift in and out of poverty, but rarely do they live below the poverty line for a stretch of eight to ten years. Their poverty is often "event-driven," rather than persistent (Bane, 1986; Ellwood & Bane, 1994). In contrast, another subgroup of the poor is chronically unemployed, forming what some sociologists call the *underclass* (Wilson, 1987). Members of the chronically unemployed poor rely heavily on public assistance to survive. They usually lack the skills and training needed to get work and so are cut off from the mainstream labor force. The chronically unemployed are the poorest of the poor, living in isolation in urban ghettos and remote rural areas (Edin & Lein, 1997).

Unlike the other social classes, racial and ethnic minorities are disproportionately represented among the poor. In other words, although in raw numbers more White people than Black or Hispanic people are poor, given the total population of these groups, Blacks and Hispanics are significantly more likely to be poor than Whites: 26.5 percent of Black people and 27.1 percent of Hispanic people are poor compared with just 11 percent of White people (U.S. Department of Commerce, Bureau of the Census, 1998b).

The majority of poor families do not own their homes and rely on rental housing; some are homeless. Poor families spend a larger percentage of their income on housing and related expenses, such as utilities, than nonpoor families (Children's Defense Fund, 1998; Mergenhagen, 1996), and their housing is segregated into particular areas. About 42 percent of poor people live in inner city neighborhoods; 32 percent live in areas considered suburban, although these are not the pristine suburban neighborhoods inhabited by the social classes above them. The remaining 26 percent live in rural areas. The homes of the poor often have upkeep problems, and the poor often find it hard to meet their housing expenses (Short & Shea, 1995).

The poor who live in inner-city areas rely largely on public transportation, but those outside the cities often have a family car that has been bought used. Still, with insurance, registration, gas and oil, and repairs, transportation expenses are high (Mergenhagen, 1996). Although the majority of poor people have access to many consumer durables, such as a refrigerator, a television, and a washing machine, these too are likely to be used or old models. Clothing also is often purchased used from thrift shops, or if new, at discount stores (Mergenhagen, 1996; Short & Shea, 1995).

In short, the lifestyle of the poor stands in sharp contrast to the lifestyles of the middle class and the wealthy. We will consider the consequences of this inequality, but first, let's examine the extent to which individuals can move from one social class to another.

REFLECTING ON

Social Classes in the United States

1. Why do you think most people in the United States identify themselves as middle class despite the fact that by objective criteria only 40 to 45 percent of the population belong to this class?
2. What does it mean to say that racial and ethnic minorities are disproportionately represented among the poor? Why do you think this is the case?

SOCIAL MOBILITY

Just how open is the U.S. class system? This question takes us back to the concept of social mobility, which we introduced at the beginning of this chapter. Social mobility is movement within the stratification system, but there are various types of movement, so any answer to the question of openness is more complicated than it may first appear.

The first type of mobility is **vertical mobility**, movement up or down the stratification hierarchy. If our class system is open, we should expect a relatively high rate of vertical mobility. However, the question of whether vertical mobility is positive or negative depends on how much of it is upward and how much is downward. **Upward vertical mobility** involves movement to a higher position in the stratification hierarchy. Conversely, **downward vertical mobility** involves movement to a lower position in the stratification hierarchy. Martin Cook, whose personal story opened this chapter, illustrates both types of vertical mobility. Moving from machinist to manager was upward vertical mobility, but losing his managerial job resulted in downward vertical mobility.

Horizontal mobility is also possible: An individual moves from one position to another of equal income, status, and power. For example, a food service worker might take a job as an office cleaner.

In a class system, education is a primary means of achieving upward vertical social mobility. How might education affect intergenerational mobility? How might education affect intragenerational, positional, and structural mobility? How do intersecting inequalities of race or ethnicity and gender affect social mobility through access to education?

Mobility can also be measured across generations. This type of mobility, called **intergenerational mobility**, is studied by comparing the positions of parents and their adult children in the stratification hierarchy. For instance, when the daughter of a car salesman and homemaker, or the son of a truck driver and homemaker become college professors, **upward intergenerational mobility** has occurred. If, however, these children had become street sweepers, **downward intergenerational mobility** would have occurred.

The mobility that a single individual experiences in his or her lifetime is **intragenerational mobility**. Martin Cook, for example, moved from machinist to corporate manager to unemployed, but we hope his career trajectory takes an upward swing once again.

Finally, mobility may be studied in terms of its causes. The popular ideology in the United States is that individuals get ahead or fail largely because of innate talent, hard work, and luck (being in the right place at the right time). Movement through the stratification hierarchy as a result of these causes is called **positional mobility**. In contrast, if mobility is caused by factors external to individual control, such as changes in the economy or occupational structure of the society, we have **structural mobility**. Again, Martin Cook's experience illustrates both types of mobility. Cook worked on his engineering degree while being employed full time; his talent and hard work paid off with positional mobility. However, changes in the economy that led to his company's downsizing also caused his unemployment (structural mobility).

Before returning to our original question—how open is the U.S. class system—we must inject a qualifying statement. Most of the research on social mobility, regardless of the type examined, has used all-male samples. The traditional assumption has been that men are the head of the household, and women, even if they are employed outside the home, hold positions secondary to their husbands and therefore do not affect the social standing of the family. However, when women are included in mobility studies, we get a different picture. For one thing, the assumption that women's employment has no appreciable effect on a family's social standing is false, since a woman's income is sometimes high enough to pull the family up a notch on the stratification hierarchy or, more often, to keep the family from falling downward.

Feminist sociologists who study the economic status of women have also found that women face greater obstacles in the workplace than men, which makes upward vertical mobility in their careers much more difficult. Part of the problem is occupational sex segregation, the tendency for women and men to be concentrated in occupations in which members of their own sex predominate. And since "women's work" is systematically devalued in our society, women who hold traditionally female-dominated jobs, such as those we discussed in the Intersecting Inequalities box on page 207, are not likely to rise far in the social class hierarchy because, on average, they are paid less than men. At the same time, widespread stereotypes about women in general, and women workers in particular, limit women's promotions in the occupational structure (Reich & Nussbaum, 1994; Reskin & Hartmann, 1986; Zweigenhaft & Domhoff, 1998).

Racial and ethnic minorities, too, have historically experienced obstacles to upward vertical mobility. Although civil rights legislation dating from the 1960s resulted in some improvement, the threat of downward mobility is still much greater for racial and ethnic minorities than for White Americans. For example, considerable attention has been given recently in the popular and academic presses to the rising Black upper-middle class (see, for example, Garreau, 1987). The proportion of Black families with incomes above $50,000 increased from 15.7 percent in 1980 to 21 percent in 1997. At the same time, however, the percentage of Black families with incomes below $10,000 also increased, from 20.0 percent in 1980 to 21.4 percent in 1997 (Oliver & Shapiro, 1995; U.S. Department of Commerce, Bureau of the Census, 1998a). Hispanic Americans and Native Americans are at similarly greater risk of downward mobility, while Asian Americans have a higher probability of upward mobility.

With the limitations of the data in mind, then, let's attempt to answer our question about the openness of the U.S. class system.

Social Mobility in the United States

It is virtually impossible for individuals who are not born into the upper-upper class to break into it, although as the Global Insights box shows, the new rich and those at

GLOBAL INSIGHTS   Can Nobility Be Bought and Sold?

Although the new rich lack the ancestry of the blue bloods, technically disqualifying them from the ranks of nobility, their wealth may nevertheless allow them to purchase a noble title. British nobility, many of whom hold several noble titles simultaneously, have recently taken to selling them at auction to the highest bidder. For example, you can become the lord of a British manor for anywhere from $7,000 to $700,000. Most of the titles are bought by wealthy Britons, but Americans comprise the majority of non-British purchasers.

When a title is bought rather than inherited, the owner must include the preposition *of* when using it, so as to alert others to the fact that he or she is not entitled to a seat in the British House of Lords. So, for example, "Lord Langley" is more prestigious than "Lord

of Langley." But individuals who have purchased their nobility report that it does have advantages, allowing them, for instance, to socialize with other elites at balls and other special events. A noble title also bestows other perks on its owner, such as the right to wear the manorial coat of arms or a tiara to formal gatherings, the right to be paid royalties if public utility lines run through manorial land, and the right to decide if residents of one's village may remodel their homes in certain ways.

Once a title has been bought, the owner may deed the title to anyone. Many "new nobles," however, prefer to follow British rules of primogeniture by specifying in their will that their titles are to be inherited by their eldest child (McKee, 1996).

---

the top of the upper-middle class may use their wealth to try to pass as "blue bloods." Most Americans, though, would probably be satisfied with entering the ranks of the new rich or upper-middle class, if they could. The "rags to riches" dream fuels the lines of people who wait patiently to buy lottery tickets, taking a chance on becoming a millionaire overnight. It is a theme of movies and novels, and occasionally a nonfictional account of an individual who "made good." But while research shows that there has been significant mobility in the United States historically, most of it has not been dramatic. Typically, movement is to the social class directly above or below one's present class position.

The classic study of mobility was conducted by Peter Blau and Otis Dudley Duncan (1967), who examined the intergenerational mobility of a sample of White men. Blau and Duncan observed that about 40 percent of sons whose fathers were blue-collar workers moved up to white-collar jobs. This finding suggests substantial upward intergenerational mobility. However, Blau and Duncan also found downward intergenerational mobility: almost 30 percent of sons whose fathers were white-collar workers held blue-collar jobs. Most frequently, the intergenerational mobility Blau and Duncan observed was not vertical, but horizontal (see also Featherman & Hauser, 1978).

Much of the upward intergenerational mobility observed by Blau and Duncan was primarily structural: The post–World War II economic boom pushed many working-class families firmly into the middle class. Similar structural mobility occurred with the advent of the Industrial Revolution in the United States, when the labor force shifted from farming and agriculture to manufacturing. In more recent decades, another economic shift—

the decline in manufacturing jobs coupled with the simultaneous growth in service jobs—has resulted in structural mobility for the middle class, but this time it has more often been downward than upward, especially for "baby boomers," the generation of Americans born between 1946 and 1964 (Uchitelle, 1998).

Since 1970, there has been a gradual but steady decline in manufacturing jobs in the United States. Many of these jobs were unionized and had paid relatively well, but they have been exported to countries where wages and other production costs are much lower. At the same time, the number of service jobs in the United States has been increasing. This trend is expected to continue during the twenty-first century. According to U.S. Department of Labor estimates (1991), in fact, during the period 1970–2000, 40 percent of manufacturing jobs—that is, 10 million jobs—disappeared, and four out of five U.S. workers took employment in service occupations. Between March and December 1998, for example, 245,000 manufacturing jobs were lost, and most of these displaced workers subsequently took service jobs (Uchitelle, 1998).

At first glance, it might seem that a service job would be better than a manufacturing job. Service work sounds cleaner and easier than factory work. But keep in mind that service jobs are diverse. A relatively small number are in the "glamour professions" of commerce, banking, insurance, real estate, and law. Salaries in these jobs are high and traditionally quite secure, but they also require extensive education and technical expertise. These jobs are relatively few compared with other types of service jobs (Levy, 1998). However, even these jobs are not safe from downsizing. Recall the story of Martin Cook that opened this chapter. A growing number of white-collar professionals of the baby boom generation are being laid off, as large corporations try to lower costs by replacing these highly paid employees with younger workers at lower salaries.

The greatest growth in service jobs has occurred in the areas of state and semiprivate human welfare (for example, health care), retail and personal services (for example, food service), and building services (for example, cleaning and janitorial work). While health care often requires considerable education and training, on the whole, people in this category are not well paid. People in the second two areas—retail and personal services, and building services—tend to be unskilled and are poorly paid; their average wages are about half the average wages of people in manufacturing. Moreover, job benefits for service workers, regardless of the type of position they hold, are nearly 60 percent less than benefits in manufacturing, which significantly affects service workers' standard of living (Nelson, 1994; Uchitelle, 1996; 1998).

How, finally, should we answer our question: How open is the U.S. class system? We can say that substantial mobility continues to be characteristic of our society, although in recent years the chances of moving downward are greater than the chances of moving upward. In fact, as Figure 8.1 shows, the middle class has been shrinking in recent years, while the top and bottom ranks of the hierarchy have been increasing. Indeed, it appears that the rich are getting richer, while the poor are getting poorer. Let's continue our discussion, then, by turning from the issue of mobility to the issue of inequality.

R E F L E C T I N G   O N

Social Mobility

1. How do you think the overall picture of mobility in the United States would change if women and racial minorities were included in mobility studies?
2. How open is the U.S. class system? How would you explain your answer?

ECONOMIC INEQUALITY IN THE UNITED STATES

Throughout much of the world, the United States is regarded as a land of opportunity, a place where anybody can "make it big." But as we have seen, rags to riches success stories are relatively rare. Ours is a society of haves and have-nots, and the disparities between the wealthy and the poor in the United States are greater than in most other industrialized countries in the world (Shapiro, 1995).

How Unequal Are We?

One way sociologists and other social scientists study economic inequality is to break the population down into **income fifths** or **quintiles**: All families or households are

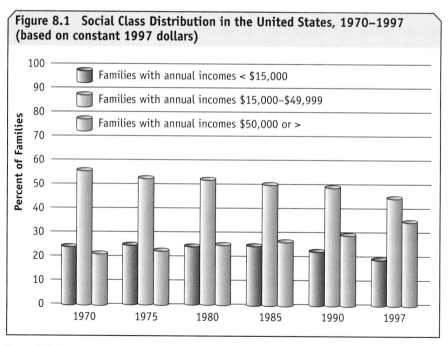

Figure 8.1   Social Class Distribution in the United States, 1970–1997 (based on constant 1997 dollars)

Families with annual incomes < $15,000
Families with annual incomes $15,000–$49,999
Families with annual incomes $50,000 or >

Source: U.S. Department of Commerce, Bureau of the Census, 1997, p. 465; 1998a, p. 5.

ranked according to their annual income, from the poorest to the wealthiest, and then the distribution is divided into five equal parts, from the lowest fifth to the highest fifth. This method allows us to compare income inequality over time so that we can see not only the current level of economic inequality, but also any historical patterns.

Table 8.3 shows the distribution of income fifths from 1948 to 1995. What we notice first is that the distribution of income has remained fairly constant over these four and a half decades; the percentages for each group do not fluctuate much. The wealthiest quintile has consistently earned more income than the lowest three quintiles combined. However, the small changes that have occurred have favored the wealthy and disadvantaged the poorer quintiles. For example, looking again at Table 8.3, we find that since 1968, the percentage of income held by the lowest quintile has declined by more than 1 percent, while the top quintile's share of income has increased 6 percent. The income of the top 5 percent of the U.S. population rose by 3 percent since the 1970s.

In fact, by 1995, the income of the wealthiest 1 percent of the population (just 2.5 million people) was nearly as much as the bottom 40 percent (approximately 100 million people). In other words, the top quintile enjoyed as much income as the bottom 80 percent of the population combined (Shapiro, 1995).

These data tell us that there has been virtually no redistribution of income from the wealthiest segments of the population to the poorer segments in nearly fifty years, and that in most recent years, the income gap between rich and poor has reached its widest point during this period.

Income inequality is an institutionalized feature of U.S. society; however, income figures tell only part of the story. Another way that sociologists measure economic inequality is by examining individual or family *wealth*, that is, the total assets of an individual or family. Assets include the value of one's home, stocks and bonds, and savings accounts. Personal wealth is more difficult to determine than income because some assets can be hidden and the value of others varies over time. However, the available data indicate that wealth is even more concentrated than income. For example, in Table 8.4 on page 214 we find that the top population quintile controls about 49 percent of the nation's wealth, more than double the next highest quintile and over thirteen times more than the lowest quintile. Put somewhat differently, the median net worth of the richest 20 percent of the U.S. population in 1993 was $118,996, while the median net worth of the poorest 20 percent of the U.S. population was just $4,249 (Eller & Fraser, 1995).

TABLE 8.3   Percent Share of Aggregate Income, Selected Years, 1948–1997, by Income Quintiles and Top 5 Percent of U.S. Population

Year	Lowest Fifth	Second Fifth	Middle Fifth	Fourth Fifth	Highest Fifth	Top 5 Percent
1997	3.6	8.9	15.1	23.2	49.4	21.7
1992	4.4	10.5	16.5	24.0	44.6	17.6
1988	4.6	10.7	16.7	24.0	44.0	18.3
1984	4.7	11.0	17.0	24.4	42.7	17.1
1980	5.1	11.6	17.5	24.3	41.6	16.5
1976	5.4	11.8	17.6	24.1	41.1	16.6
1972	5.4	11.9	17.5	23.9	41.4	17.0
1968	5.6	12.4	17.7	23.7	40.5	
1964	5.1	12.0	17.7	24.0	41.2	
1960	4.8	12.2	17.8	24.0	41.3	
1956	5.0	12.5	17.9	23.7	40.1	
1952	4.9	12.3	17.4	23.4	41.9	
1948	4.9	12.1	17.3	23.2	42.4	

Source: U.S. Department of Commerce, Bureau of the Census, 1998, p. xii; 1997, p. 470; 1994, p. 470; 1990, p. 30; 1984, p. 47.

TABLE 8.4 Distribution of Wealth by Income Quintiles, United States, 1993

Income Quintile	Median Measured Net Worth (Assets – Liabilities)	Distribution of Wealth (percent)
Total	$37,587	100.0
Lowest fifth	4,249	7.2
Second fifth	20,230	12.2
Middle fifth	30,788	15.9
Fourth fifth	50,000	20.6
Highest fifth	118,996	44.1

Source: T. J. Eller & W. Fraser. (1995). Asset ownership of households: 1993. *Current Population Reports.* Washington, DC: U.S. Department of Commerce, p. 5.

The data on the distribution of wealth by income fifths actually mask to some extent just how concentrated wealth is in the United States. Although about 44 percent of wealth is in the hands of just 20 percent of the population, the fact is that most of this wealth actually belongs only to the richest 1 percent of the population. The richest 1 percent, just 2.5 million people, own more than one-third of the nation's wealth (Nasar, 1992).

The gaps across quintiles grow when we consider other factors. For instance, if we look at wealth by gender, we find that even among the super-rich, women earn less than men. Among the 400 wealthiest people in the United States in 1997, the average net worth of men was $1.9 billion, whereas the average net worth of women was about 78 percent that sum or $1.5 billion ("By the Numbers," 1998). Race and ethnicity are also significant. In 1995, for example, only 8.7 percent of African American families and 7.3 percent of Hispanic American families were in the highest income quintile compared with 21.5 percent of White families (U.S. Department of Commerce, Bureau of the Census, 1997).

Inequality's Consequences

Income and assets are objective measures of economic inequality, but in wading through all the numbers it is easy to forget that they translate into important differences in people's everyday lives. Think back to our discussion of social classes in the United States. Financial standing affects virtually every aspect of a person's life, including where he or she lives, goes to school, and has fun—and even whom he or she will marry.

The work of Kathleen Short and Martina Shea (1995) illuminates the consequences of economic inequality for people's everyday lives. Short and Shea set out to measure differences in well-being between two basic segments of the population, the poor and the nonpoor. To do this,

they examined various quality-of-life indicators: ownership of and access to certain consumer goods, neighborhood crime rates, housing conditions, diet, and access to health care. Not surprisingly, they found that on all measures, the poor were worse off than the nonpoor. But consider what being poor means in real-life terms: If you are poor, you are three times more likely than someone who is not poor to live in a house or apartment that is infested with rats, mice, or roaches, and where the toilet, hot water heater, and other plumbing don't work. Your dwelling is four times more likely to have exposed wiring and holes in the floors. You are more than twice as likely to live in a neighborhood where trash and litter are a problem, there are run-down or abandoned buildings, and the crime rate is high. In fact, you are three times more likely to say you are afraid to go out at night. You are twice as likely as a nonpoor person to be evicted from your home, five times more likely to have your telephone disconnected, and eight times more likely to have gas and electric service turned off. If you or someone in your household gets sick, you are twice as likely as a nonpoor person to forgo needed medical care.

The consequences of being poor are especially detrimental for young children. Low income lowers the probability that mothers-to-be will receive timely prenatal care; this in turn increases the risk of low birth weight, which has been found to have long-term effects on school achievement, including grade failure, low test scores, and need for special education (Brooks-Gunn et al., 1997). Living in poverty during the preschool years has been found to be significantly related to low scores on intelligence and verbal assessment tests and to lower school readiness. In fact, studies show that living in a poverty-level household as a preschooler has a significantly greater effect on intellectual ability and educational achievement than either mother's education or family structure (that is, living in a two-parent or single-parent household). It appears that income is important to the cognitive development of young children because it allows parents to provide their children with more enriching learning environments. For instance, parents with higher incomes can purchase books and educational toys for their preschoolers and take the children to concerts and museums (Duncan et al., 1998; Smith et al., 1997).

The nonpoor are, for the most part, shielded from the direct consequences of poverty, but it is important to recognize that poverty as a social problem has a negative impact not only on the poor, but on society as a whole. As Jeanne Brooks-Gunn and her colleagues (1997, p. 16) point out:

> A life of poverty is statistically associated with higher rates of activities detrimental to individuals and to society, such as crime, violence, underemployment, unemployment, and isolation from the larger community. The costs of poverty are borne not only by the children reared in such circumstances but by society at large. In addition to direct government expenditures, these costs include a smaller number of educated citizens, an increase in neighborhoods characterized by danger, less social cohesion, and lower rates of social and political participation.

Not everyone, however, has an equal chance of being poor. Poverty, like wealth, tends to be concentrated among particular segments of the population, as we will see next.

REFLECTING ON

Economic Inequality in the United States

Do you think the level of income inequality in the United States is a problem? Why or why not? If so, what would you propose to help reduce income inequality?

POVERTY IN THE UNITED STATES

Who are the poor? This question is often answered by using the federal government's measure known as the *poverty line*, which we defined earlier as the income an individual or family needs to purchase a minimally nutritional diet and then multiplying that amount by three. Anyone having less than that income is officially defined as poor. The dietary standards are set by the U.S. Department of Agriculture, and the multiplier is based on the assumption that poor families spend about one-third of their income on food.

As we noted, there are actually several different poverty lines, because the necessary income varies according to a number of factors, including family size and the age of the head of the household. In 1995, the poverty line for a family of four was $15,569. By the government's count, about 13.8 percent of the population, or over 36 million people, are officially poor; an additional 10 million people are *near-poor*, that is, living on incomes below 125 percent of the poverty line (U.S. Department of Commerce, Bureau of the Census, 1997). However, these figures are hotly disputed and the government's answer to the question of who is poor is widely criticized.

Some critics point out, for example, that although the official calculation method takes factors such as family size, age of family head, and type of family into consideration, it ignores other important factors that have an impact on a family's finances. These factors include employment expenses (such as child care and transportation), the cost of medical insurance and health care, regional variations in the cost of living, and the cost of housing (Institute for Research on Poverty, 1998). Other critics argue that families today spend only about one-fifth to as little as one-seventh of their income on food, so the amount of money needed to meet the USDA's dietary standards should be multiplied by five, six, or seven. The greater the multiplier, the higher the number of people who are officially considered poor (Institute for Research on Poverty, 1998; Porter, 1997).

Keeping these criticisms in mind, then, let's take a look at that segment of our population that the government labels "officially poor."

Who Are the Poor?

The commonly held stereotype of the poor is a young, Black, unemployed man who lives in the inner city. However, this image describes what might be called the *visible poor*, those whom the media and other public information sources typically present as poor. When we compare the stereotype with empirical data from the Census Bureau (U.S. Department of Commerce, 1998b; 1997; 1996; 1995; 1994), we get a somewhat different picture of the poverty population:

- *In raw numbers, most poor people are White, not Black* (24.4 million White people versus 9.1 million Black people). However, the poverty *rate* is nearly two and a half times higher for Black people than for White people (26.3 percent versus 11.0 percent). Similarly, while only 8.3 million Hispanic Americans are poor, the poverty rate for the Hispanic population is 27.1 percent. Among Asian Americans, 1.5 million people are poor, which constitutes 14.0 percent of the Asian American population. In raw numbers, 585,273 Native Americans are poor, which looks at first like a relatively small group, but which actually represents 31.2 percent of the Native

American population. Racial and ethnic minorities are disproportionately represented among the poor.

- *Only 42 percent of the poor live in inner city neighborhoods.* As we saw earlier, 32 percent of the poor live in suburban areas and the remaining 26 percent live in nonurban settings. Areas of acute rural poverty include Appalachia and the southern United States.

- *The poverty rate of female-headed families is more than six times that of married couple families.* Of the 16.2 million female-headed, single-parent households with children under the age of eighteen, nearly half (49 percent) were living below the poverty line compared with just 9.5 percent of married couple households with children under eighteen.

- *Most poor adults are working or looking for work.* In 1995, among poor families, 62.6 percent had at least one member employed. Most poor people hold minimum-wage jobs that provide annual incomes well below the federal poverty line for a family of four, or they work part-time or only sporadically during the year (Fitzpatrick & Lazere, 1999).

- *A sizeable percentage of the poverty population is made up of children.* Of the 71 million children under the age of eighteen in the United States, over 14 million live in poverty-stricken households. Children make up about 40 percent of the poverty population.

- *Of the elderly aged sixty-five and older, 10.5 percent are poor.* The number of elderly poor is less than half as many as it was in 1970. Elderly women who live alone are at greatest risk of being poor: 73 percent of the elderly poor are female; 82 percent of the elderly poor who live alone are female. Elderly Black, Hispanic, and Native Americans are also

disproportionately represented among the elderly poor.

- *Only about one-third of officially poor families receive unemployment compensation or some form of public assistance.* Contrary to popular belief, most poor families do not receive unemployment benefits or welfare. In 1995, for example, of the 27.5 million families who were officially poor, only about 11 million received unemployment compensation, Supplemental Security Income (SSI), or public assistance. As a result of the 1996 welfare reform law, this number has dropped considerably (see the Social Policy box).

The Homeless

Some poor people are homeless. The **homeless** do not have a private living space or adequate shelter and, therefore, are forced to sleep in parks, train and bus stations, abandoned buildings and cars, and often on top of steam vents in the middle of the sidewalk. It is difficult to determine how many people in the United States are homeless; estimates range from 300,000 to 3 million (Barringer, 1991; Berke, 1988).

Like the poor in general, myths about the homeless abound. Many people falsely believe that the homeless are unemployed men and women who are mentally disturbed or addicted to drugs or alcohol. It is true that some homeless people have mental or emotional problems, but it is unclear whether these preceded their homelessness or were caused by the daily struggles of life on the streets (Golden, 1992). It is also the case that some are homeless because mental hospitals in many states were closed in the 1970s, a process known as *deinstitutionalization*.

Who are the poor in the United States? How is "poor" defined? Who are the homeless? How are the people in this photo different from the stereotype of homeless people? What economic factors and social policies in the United States are related to increases in homelessness?

Social Policy
Welfare versus Wealthfare

The Issue

In 1996, President Clinton signed the Personal Responsibility and Work Opportunity Reconciliation Act (PRWORA), a law that dramatically changed social welfare policy and practices in the United States. This law includes among its provisions a mandatory work requirement after two years of assistance, a cap of five years on the total time a family can receive assistance, permission for the states to deny additional benefits to women who have more children while on welfare, a requirement that mothers establish the paternity of their children so child support can be collected from absent fathers, and significant reductions in the Food Stamp program.

Early studies of the law's impact show a dramatic reduction in the number of welfare recipients, from 14.3 million in 1994 to 8 million in 1998, a decline of 44 percent ("Citing Drop in Welfare Rolls,"1999). Moreover, most states have met the law's requirement that 25 percent of welfare recipients hold jobs or actively prepare themselves for work. Overall, about 28 percent of adults on welfare are working, but the figures range from 13.5 percent in Louisiana to 96.7 percent in Oregon (Pear, 1998). However, in signing the PRWORA, President Clinton maintained

that the goal was to put people to work so they could earn enough money to live above the poverty line. Has the law succeeded in meeting this goal? In other words, has the PRWORA reduced poverty?

The Debate

Supporters of PRWORA say that the law lessens the dependency of the poor on the state and gives them a renewed sense of responsibility for their own well-being and the well-being of their families. Supporters also praise the law because it is helping to lower the federal deficit (Handler & Hasenfeld, 1997; Mink, 1998).

However, critics of PRWORA point out that although the law puts people to work, the jobs they are able to get do not pay enough to pull them out of poverty. Welfare recipients who find jobs typically earn between $8,000 and $10,800 a year, a sum well below the poverty line for a family of four. Moreover, these jobs do not provide benefits, such as paid vacation or sick leave, making it difficult for these workers to take time off from work if a child or other family member gets sick (Handler & Hasenfeld, 1997; Mink, 1998; Parrott, 1998). As for reducing the federal deficit, critics of PRWORA point out that there are other strategies available that do not harm the poor. For instance,

many more billions of dollars could be saved by eliminating various tax expenditures (popularly known as tax loopholes) that benefit wealthy individuals and corporations by substantially reducing the taxes they pay. Wealthy individuals often pay little or no income taxes because of tax loopholes (Associated Press, 1991; Lav, 1998). Tax loopholes that were enacted after 1950 have reduced the amount of money corporate taxes contribute to federal budget revenue from 26.5 percent to just 10.0 percent in 1994 (U.S. Department of Commerce, Bureau of the Census, 1997). In other words, critics of PRWORA see tax loopholes as a kind of entitlement given by the government to the nonpoor. In fact, so generous are these benefits that some analysts refer to them as "corporate welfare" or *wealthfare*.

What Do You Think?

Do you support or oppose the PRWORA? What do you see as the main strengths and weaknesses of this law? Do you agree with critics of PRWORA that the government should refocus its efforts to reduce the federal deficit by eliminating tax expenditures for the wealthy rather than cutting social spending that benefits the poor?

However, research indicates that most homeless people are not severely mentally disturbed, nor do they have drug and alcohol problems (Golden, 1992). The homeless are a far more diverse group than the stereotypes would lead us to believe.

What all homeless people do have in common is abject poverty. Since certain groups, such as racial and ethnic minorities, are disproportionately represented among the poor, they are at greater risk of becoming homeless. Rossi (1989), for example, found that nationally nearly 46 percent of the homeless are Black, almost 12 percent are Hispanic, and about 5 percent are Native Americans. Research also indicates that the majority of homeless adults are high school graduates and more than 24 percent have attended college. A considerable number of homeless adults have full-time jobs, but these are typi-

cally minimum-wage jobs that do not provide enough income to obtain housing, especially in major metropolitan areas. However, homelessness is not solely an urban problem; it is increasing in the nation's suburbs as factories close and in rural regions as a result of farm foreclosures (Kozol, 1988; Schmitt, 1988; Vanderstaay, 1992).

The most striking and dismaying fact about homelessness in the United States is that the fastest-growing segment of the homeless is families with dependent children. It is estimated that families with children now comprise about 43 percent of the homeless population (Children's Defense Fund, 1998; Kolker, 1998; Kozol, 1988; U.S. Conference of Mayors, 1993). The majority of homeless families are women with children. For most, their homelessness is a further reflection of the high rate of poverty among female-headed families. The primary reasons they are homeless are the rising cost of housing, the shortage of low-income housing units, and an inability to find a job that pays adequate wages (Children's Defense Fund, 1998). A growing number of women and children are also becoming homeless as a result of leaving an abusive husband/father. For abused women and children, living on the street is a survival strategy (Browne & Bassuk, 1997; Golden, 1992). But homelessness breaks up families too. In many cities, for example, women and children must stay in shelters separate from men (Kozol, 1988).

Explaining Poverty

How can we account for poverty and homelessness? There are several competing explanations of poverty, with some assigning responsibility to individuals, and others assigning responsibility to structural components of society.

Personal Inferiority.   Explanations of poverty that focus on the personal inferiority of poor people begin with the assumption that some people are naturally inferior to others. Inferiority thus prevents some individuals from socially advancing because they will inevitably fail in competition with people of superior ability. People with personal deficiencies invariably fall into the ranks of the poor in any given society.

Personal inferiority explanations have a long history in Western societies. Some of the earliest theories argued that poverty was caused by biological defect. For instance, Herbert Spencer, a nineteenth-century English philosopher, used the phrase "survival of the fittest" to argue that the poor were poor because they were the most biologically "unfit" members of the society. They lacked the innate talent to succeed. Many of these early theories also argued that particular racial and ethnic groups were biologically inferior to Americans of Anglo-Saxon descent, which explained their greater likelihood of being poor.

Twentieth-century theories tend to be more psychologically oriented, focusing on mental and emotional deficiencies as the primary causes of poverty. Among the most popular was a theory based on hereditary intelligence. The poor were poor because they were intellectually inferior, and this defect is passed on genetically from one generation to the next. This argument was recently revived by Richard Herrnstein and Charles Murray in their book, *The Bell Curve: Intelligence and Class Structure in American Life* (1994).

Personal inferiority explanations have been widely criticized. They are based on questionable data that typically distort the reality of poverty in the United States. Even worse, these theories have serious policy implications. Implicit in them is the idea that nothing can be done about poverty. If one accepts that the poor cannot be helped, then there is no reason to offer financial, educational, or other forms of assistance so that poor people might im-

prove their life circumstances. Of course, if poverty is seen as inevitable and ignored, the prophecy is fulfilled.

Cultural Inferiority.   A variation on the inferiority theme is the notion that the poor *as a group* hold beliefs, values, and goals that are significantly different from the nonpoor population, and this shared belief system reinforces and perpetuates the poverty lifestyle. In other words, the emphasis is on deficiencies in the group's *culture* rather than in the poor individual.

The chief proponent of this perspective, which has come to be known as the *culture of poverty* theory, was Oscar Lewis (1966). Lewis maintained that the poor develop a unique value system as a way of coping with their lack of success by middle class standards. Many of the negative attributes associated with poverty, Lewis claimed, are the products of poor people's unwillingness to aspire to the middle class. What is more, the poor socialize their children into this culture of poverty, thus ensuring that it persists over time.

Lewis's position was picked up by Edward Banfield (1974), who argued that a fundamental component of the culture of poverty was the poor's inability to defer gratification. Banfield believed the nonpoor are *future-oriented*, that is, focused on long-term goals, while the poor are *present-oriented*, living from moment to moment. Behavior among the poor is governed by impulse; they have no sense of the future and are incapable of sacrificing the satisfaction of an immediate desire in favor of fulfilling a future goal. Thus, the poor are destined to remain poor because of their hedonism. In addition, poor people's inability to control their basic drives leads to many other problems as well, including crime, violence, and sexual permissiveness.

Lewis's and Banfield's positions have been widely criticized (see, for example, Leacock, 1971; Pivan & Cloward, 1977; Ryan, 1981). For one thing, say critics, the poor do not have a different value structure from the dominant nonpoor culture. This is not to say that the poor do not develop unique beliefs as a result of living in poverty, but rather that this set of beliefs does not override or replace their acceptance of mainstream ideology. Research indicates, for instance, that the poor hold the same aspirations for success as people in more financially prosperous classes. Other studies that we discussed earlier show that there is not a large group of people who can be classified as "permanently poor." Rather, most poor people move in and out of poverty, reflecting changes in their personal circumstances as well as changes in the economy (Ellwood & Bane, 1994; Shea, 1995).

Despite the lack of solid evidence to support it, the culture of poverty explanation still enjoys considerable popularity. Many nonpoor Americans believe that the poor live by different moral standards and, consequently, will remain in poverty. Politicians and policy makers also use the culture of poverty explanation to justify reductions in assistance to the poor (see the Social Policy box on page 217).

Structural Poverty. Structural explanations of poverty look at society as the source of the problem. One structural argument follows from the structural functionalist position that stratification ensures the most qualified and talented people undertake the most difficult jobs in a society. The existence of a class of poor people also ensures that the dirty, menial jobs in society will get done because nonpoor people would simply refuse to do such work. Poverty also creates jobs for the nonpoor, from social workers to pawnbrokers (Gans, 1973). In short, structural functionalists maintain that some poverty is both necessary and beneficial to society as a whole.

This structural explanation of poverty has been criticized for a number of reasons. One important criticism, for example, is that this explanation assumes that stratification is based on *meritocracy*—that rewards are differentially bestowed on workers on the basis of their effort, talent, and individual ability. The nonpoor, the theory maintains, are those individuals with marketable skills and valued talents; conversely, the poor are unskilled and untalented. However, this position overlooks the fact that in our society, many people, because of ascribed traits such as sex, race, or ethnicity, find job opportunities blocked regardless of their training or talent. Hard work, education, and personal talent do not have the same payoffs for women and people of color as they do for men and White people because of discrimination (Zweigenhaft & Domhoff, 1998). Moreover, by emphasizing the positive functions of poverty, this explanation downplays the devastating impact that poverty has on people at the bottom of the social class hierarchy.

A second structural explanation of poverty derives from conflict theory, which sees poverty as rooted in various structural conditions over which poor people have no control. Among these conditions are the export of jobs to countries with lower production costs, automation, and the expansion of the service sector of the economy at the expense of the manufacturing sector. In other words, the poor are not poor because they lack ambition or talent, but because of the structural constraints of a society in which jobs and access to valued resources and rewards are limited (Harrington, 1984; Levy, 1998).

Perhaps the best known proponent of this type of structural explanation of poverty is William Julius Wilson (1996; 1990). Wilson's research focuses on impoverished residents of inner-city neighborhoods. Wilson maintains that well-paid manufacturing jobs are no longer available in most inner-city areas. Moreover, middle-class Black families have moved out of inner-city neighborhoods, leaving poor Blacks behind. The exodus of the Black middle class contributes to the weakening of social institutions such as churches, political organizations, and community groups that traditionally have helped the economically marginalized in the inner city. Although Wilson sees the lack of well-paying jobs as the chief structural cause of poverty, he also shows how racial discrimination and social isolation reproduce poverty.

This explanation of poverty has been criticized for placing too much emphasis on structural conditions and overlooking the role of individual factors as causes of poverty. Wilson's work has also been criticized for focusing on the inner-city poor to the neglect of the suburban and rural poor. Nevertheless, there is considerable research support for Wilson's argument and similar structural explanations (see, for example, Corcoran & Adams, 1997).

Poverty and Economic Inequality in Global Perspective

The conflict theory of poverty highlights how structural factors beyond the boundaries of the United States—such as lower production costs in other countries—influence inequality and poverty in this country. Indeed, it is impossible to consider conditions in the United States in isolation from the world context. We are members of a world community, not just individual citizens of a single country. Consequently, if we are to more fully understand economic inequality, we must examine our situation in relation to societies around the globe. This will be our focus in Chapter 9.

R E F L E C T I N G   O N

Poverty in the United States

1. How do empirical data on the poverty population refute popular stereotypes about the poor?
2. What do you think is the best way to calculate the poverty line?
3. Why has the concept of a "culture of poverty" fallen into disfavor?
4. What are the strengths and weaknesses of the two structural explanations of poverty?

For useful resources for study and review, run Chapter 8 on your *Living Sociology* CD-ROM.

CONNECTIONS

Global marketplaces	Preview the section on "Explaining Global Inequality" in Chapter 9. How do global economic inequalities affect employment and stratification in the United States?
Employment and unemployment	Survey the sections on "Unemployment Rate" in the U.S. economy and "Work in the United States" in Chapter 13. What factors lead to unemployment and underemployment in the United States? How do those factors contribute to the U.S. system of social stratification?
Occupational prestige and income	See the tables in Chapter 10, "Sex Segregation in the Workplace and Its Consequences." What were the top ten occupations for men and women in 1995? What are the characteristics of high-prestige and low-prestige jobs? How do these characteristics relate to the U.S. system of social stratification?
Types of social stratification	Review the types of societies in Chapter 3. How would you describe the system of stratification characteristic of each type of society? What is the role of technology and material culture in the development of systems of social stratification?
Apartheid and social change	For more information on apartheid, see the introduction to Chapter 20. In what sense was apartheid an example of a caste system of social stratification?
The African-American experience	Preview "African Americans" in Chapter 11. How have African Americans moved from a caste to a class system? What social factors strengthen and weaken class inequality for African Americans and other U.S. minorities?
Karl Marx and communism	Marx's basic philosophy was introduced in Chapter 1, and his focus on social inequality is highlighted in Chapter 3 in the section on "Industrial Societies." How does conflict theory explain systems of social stratification? Do you think a classless society could ever be achieved without conflict?
Types of economic systems	See "Types of Economic Systems" in Chapter 13. What effects do capitalism and socialism have on systems of social stratification? How does the level of economic development of a country affect its system of stratification?
Gender, race, and age inequalities	Survey Chapters 10, 11, and 12 to identify specific examples of the effects of social characteristics such as gender, race or ethnicity, and age on wages and social class membership. What is the impact of social inequality on people at the top and the bottom of the U.S. social class hierarchy?
U.S. labor force and trade unions	See "Work in the United States" in Chapter 13. What are the composition of the U.S. labor force and the main problems of employment? Why has there been a decline in the power of trade unions? How do labor issues affect the U.S. system of social stratification?
Residential segregation	Read "Segregation" in Chapter 11 about the "redlining" of neighborhoods according to characteristics of race and ethnicity. How does this practice help to preserve class inequality as well racial segregation? See also the section on "The Urban Environment" in Chapter 19. How might residential segregation help explain the decline of inner cities?

CONNECTIONS

Global disparities between rich and poor	Read "Rich and Poor: The Great Divide" and "Poverty in Global Perspective" in Chapter 9. In what ways does global stratification among countries mirror stratification within a class society such as the United States? See also the section on "Population: Growth and Control" in Chapter 19. In what ways does overpopulation contribute to global disparities between rich and poor?
Social mobility	Survey the sections on "Sources of Social Change," "Collective Behavior," and "Social Movements" in Chapter 20. What specific examples can you find of collective behavior that stemmed from frustrations over social inequality and lack of opportunities for upward social mobility?
Single-parent households	Read the section on "Single-Parent Families" in Chapter 15. What historical and social factors have contributed to increases in the number and relative poverty of single-parent families?
Poverty and homelessness	Review the analysis of homelessness in Chapter 1. How could you explain poverty in the United States from each of the main theoretical perspectives in sociology?

SUMMING UP CHAPTER 8

Systems of Stratification

1. Social stratification is a system of ranking people in a hierarchy according to certain attributes. The three major components of stratification are wealth, prestige, and political power. Usually a person's ranking on one area coincides with his or her rankings on the others, but not necessarily.
2. In a caste system, membership in a stratum is ascribed. The system is preserved by laws and traditions that prohibit movement across castes. Caste societies are endogamous and typically are characterized by physical segregation of people from different castes.
3. In a class system, membership in a stratum is at least partly achieved. There is mobility across social classes. Class systems are common in industrial societies.
4. Karl Marx wished to replace stratified societies with nonstratified or communist societies through a workers' revolution. Although such revolutions have occurred and have resulted in a lessening of economic inequality across groups, no communist revolution has ever taken place in a capitalist industrial society as Marx predicted, and no communist country is unstratified.

Explaining Stratification

1. Structural functionalists reason that if stratification is universal, it must be beneficial for a society. The Davis-Moore hypothesis states that stratification serves a motivating function by ensuring that the most talented people will make the sacrifices needed to do the most important and necessary jobs. However, critics point out that the rewards allotted to a particular job often do not coincide with the job's functional importance to society. In addition, the Davis-Moore hypothesis overlooks the extent to which stratification is ascribed in our society and its detrimental consequences.
2. Conflict theory, based on Karl Marx's work, states that as some individuals accumulate greater wealth than others, they also acquire higher social standing, which they try to preserve as those below them struggle to get ahead. However, critics argue that although there is considerable class conflict, it is not as simplistic as conflict theorists depict it. There are multiple classes, not just two, and their interests sometimes coincide rather than conflict. In addition, there is conflict within social classes as well as between them.

Social Classes in the United States

1. The wealthy may be divided into two groups. First, the blue bloods or old-money families derive their wealth mainly from inheritance. They are highly endogamous and exclusive, associating only with their peers. The second group, the new rich, may have even greater wealth, but it comes mainly from earnings. They are less endogamous than the old rich, but still travel in relatively exclusive social circles.
2. The largest social class is the middle class. The middle class may be divided into two groups. One small group is the upper-middle class, composed of highly paid professionals with advanced education, who enjoy very comfortable lifestyles. The larger group is the lower-middle

class, composed of families with incomes roughly between $25,000 and $50,000 per year from white-collar service occupations requiring at least a high school education.

3. The working class is composed of those who work full time as semiskilled and skilled laborers. Their jobs do not require extensive education and have low prestige and modest incomes. Members of the working class tend to be politically inactive as individuals, although they may wield political power collectively through trade unions.

4. The incomes of poor families fall below the official poverty line. Many poor people are working, but the jobs they hold are usually unskilled, paying low or minimum wages and offering little security and no benefits. Another subgroup of the poor is the chronically unemployed, who rely heavily on public assistance to survive. The chronically unemployed are the poorest of the poor.

Social Mobility

1. Social mobility is movement within the stratification system. There are different types of mobility, including vertical mobility, horizontal mobility, intergenerational mobility, intragenerational mobility, positional mobility, and structural mobility.

2. Most studies of mobility have focused on White males. Women and racial/ethnic minorities historically have faced significant obstacles to upward vertical mobility. Racial/ethnic minorities, in fact, are at great risk of downward mobility.

3. Overall, there is substantial mobility in U.S. society, although in recent years the chances of moving downward are greater than the chances of moving upward, resulting in a shrinking middle class.

Economic Inequality in the United States

1. The distribution of income has remained fairly constant since the late 1940s. The small changes that have oc-

curred have favored the wealthy while disadvantaging the poorer social classes. Wealth is even more concentrated than income. Economic inequality affects virtually every aspect of a person's life.

Poverty in the United States

1. There are many stereotypes of the poor, but available data show a somewhat different picture. Racial minorities, female-headed households, and children are disproportionately represented among the poor. Most poor adults are working or looking for work.

2. The homeless do not have a private living space or adequate shelter. Although many homeless people have mental or emotional problems, it is unclear whether these problems preceded their homelessness or occurred as a result of homelessness. Racial and ethnic minorities are disproportionately represented among the homeless. Most homeless people are high school graduates and many are working. The fastest-growing segment of the homeless is families with dependent children.

3. There are several competing explanations of poverty. Personal inferiority explanations assume that some people are naturally inferior to others and, therefore, will be poor because they cannot successfully compete with people of superior ability. Cultural inferiority explanations maintain that poor people as a group hold beliefs, values, and goals that are significantly different from the nonpoor population, and this shared belief system reinforces and perpetuates the poverty lifestyle. Structural explanations of poverty look at society as the source of the problems. The structural functionalist perspective sees poverty as both necessary and beneficial to society as a whole. The conflict perspective views poverty as the result of various structural conditions, including the concentration of wealth and the pursuit of profits.

KEY PEOPLE AND CONCEPTS

blue-collar jobs: jobs that require mostly physical rather than mental labor, which got their name because of the way most workers who hold them dress for work (in denim)

caste system: a stratification system in which movement between strata is virtually closed, so individuals stay in the stratum into which they were born for their entire lives

class system: a stratification system in which movement between strata is possible, so individuals can change strata over the course of their lives

communism: a classless or nonstratified society in which all property is collectively owned and controlled

downward intergenerational mobility: the movement of adult children to a social stratum lower than that of their parents

downward vertical mobility: movement to a lower position in the stratification hierarchy

endogamy: the prohibition against marriage or the formation of an intimate relationship with anyone outside one's own social stratum

homeless: the segment of the poverty population without private living space or adequate shelter

horizontal mobility: movement from one position to another of equal wealth, status, and political power

ideology: a set of beliefs

income fifths (quintiles): the division of a population into five equal segments, ranked according to their income, from the lowest or poorest 20 percent to the highest or wealthiest 20 percent

inequality: the differential allocation of rewards, opportunities, and other resources among the members of a society

intergenerational mobility: the degree to which the social standing of adult children is different from that of their parents

intragenerational mobility: movement across the stratification system during a single individual's lifetime

middle class: the largest social class in the United States, encompassing 40 to 45 percent of the population and composed of two groups: a small segment (the upper-middle class) and a large segment (the lower-middle class)

pink-collar jobs: jobs primarily in the service sector with a high concentration of women workers, which got their name not because of the way workers dress for work, but because the jobs are associated with females and femininity.

political power: the decision-making component of stratification, referring to an individual's relationship to government and the ability to influence political decisions

positional mobility: movement through the stratification hierarchy as a result of individual causes, such as hard work and luck

poverty line: the federal government's measure of poverty, calculated by multiplying by three the amount of money needed for a minimally nutritional diet, while also taking into account factors such as size of the family and age of the household head

quintile (see **income fifths**)

segregation: the physical separation of social groups or strata

social mobility: movement within the stratification system of a society

social stratification: a system of ranking people in a hierarchy according to certain attributes

status: the prestige component of stratification, determined by how others perceive an individual or group in terms of respect and deference

structural mobility: movement through the stratification hierarchy as a result of factors external to individual control, such as changes in the economy or occupational structure of the society

upward intergenerational mobility: movement of adult children to a stratum higher than their parents

upward vertical mobility: involves movement to a higher position in the stratification hierarchy

vertical mobility: movement up or down the stratification hierarchy

wealth: the material component of stratification, determined by income and other assets

the wealthy: the society's upper class, representing only about 3 percent of the U.S. population, with yearly incomes of hundreds of thousands of dollars

white-collar jobs: jobs that require mostly mental labor rather than physical labor, which got their name because of the way most workers who hold them dress for work (in suits)

working class: composed of 30 to 35 percent of the U.S. population, with average annual incomes between $15,000 and $25,000

LEARNING MORE

Burke, M. J. (1995). *The conundrum of class: Public discourse on the social order in America*. Chicago: University of Chicago Press. An analysis of the different ways social class has been conceptualized, measured, and explained historically, as well as some of the major issues of debate, including how many classes there are.

Duncan, G. J., & Brooks-Gunn, J. (Eds.). (1997). *The consequences of growing up poor*. New York: Russell Sage Foundation. An important collection of research reports that meticulously document the effects of poverty on children and their life chances.

Edin, K., & Lein, L. (1997). *Making ends meet: How single mothers survive welfare and low-wage work*. New York: Russell Sage Foundation. An in-depth study that combines qualitative and quantitative methods to refute many popular myths about "welfare moms."

Frank, R. H., & Cook, P. J. (1995). *The winner-take-all society*. New York: Martin Kessler Books/Free Press. A provocative analysis that explains the growth in income inequality in the United States in terms of the "star system," a rewards structure that attracts numerous competitors to exceptionally high-paying jobs where only a very few can reach the top.

Harrington, M. (1994). *The new American poverty*. New York: Holt, Rinehart, and Winston. The late sociologist, Michael Harrington, offers a conflict analysis of poverty in the United States and suggests strategies for reforming the "structures of misery." Although the statistics are dated, Harrington's discussion is an excellent example of the conflict explanation of inequality.

MacDonald, C. L., & Sirianni, C. (Eds.) (1996). *Working in the service society*. Philadelphia: Temple University Press. A collection of essays that look at the increasing number of service jobs and how the workers who hold them are stratified by sex as well as race and ethnicity.

Ostrower, F. (1995). *Why the wealthy give: The culture of elite philanthropy*. Princeton, NJ: Princeton University Press. Have you ever wondered what motivates wealthy people to give millions of dollars to universities, cultural organizations, and charities? This fascinating study, based on interviews with ninety-nine wealthy Americans, argues that one of the primary reasons elites give away large sums of money is to set themselves apart from those below them on the social class hierarchy.

Zweigenhaft, R. L., & Domhoff, G. W. (1998). *Diversity in the power elite: Have women and minorities reached the top?* New Haven, CT: Yale University Press. Packed with statistics, this research monograph analyzes why some social groups are better represented among the power elite than other groups, including women, African Americans, and gay men and lesbians.

 Run Chapter 9 on your *Living Sociology* CD-ROM for interesting and informative activities, web links, videos, practice tests, and more.

CHAPTER

9

Global Stratification

I t is an hour before dawn on a frosty December morning, but already most of the residents of Dongwang, a village in southwestern China, are at work. Chen Xianshe, thirty years old, is hauling water up the steep hillside to his open-air reed hut. He uses wooden buckets hanging from a pole draped across his shoulders. Later in the day, he will husk corn from the small plot that supplies most of the food he and his family eat year-round. The typical diet in the village is corn-based, but includes some dairy products since most villagers own a cow. Unfortunately, Mr. Chen must buy milk and other dairy products because his cow was killed in an accident and he has no money to replace her. In fact, he is not likely to be replacing her anytime soon because the local government requires that he contribute the equivalent of two years of his income (about $86) to install electricity in the village. For Mr. Chen and the other villagers, this "milestone of progress" means they will each have two 60-watt bulbs lighting their huts.

Mr. Chen has heard about the "economic miracle" that has made people rich in the big cities and coastal provinces of China. He has even considered leaving Dongwang to look for work in one of these areas, but stories about the "floating population" frighten him. In China, all individuals and families are required to register their households with the local government in order to receive government benefits. This system of household registration is a powerful form of social control that also keeps migration of the rural population in check. People who leave their villages without official permission to relocate often cannot find work and have difficulty getting housing without government help. They end up "floating" from place to place, sometimes in such desperate financial circumstances that they turn to crime to survive. For now, Mr. Chen has decided, it is probably best to remain in the village with its meager subsidies. At the end of the day, after yet another dinner of cornmeal gruel, Mr. Chen and his family will huddle under a thin quilt to sleep. As the cold air whips through their hut, they wish—as they do every night—that the government will do something to make their village rich (Curran, 1996; Tyler, 1995).

The grinding poverty lived daily by Mr. Chen, 70 to 80 million other Chinese, and about 720 million additional people in other countries throughout the world is very different from that experienced by the poor in the United States. Even the poor in the United States and other industrialized nations are relatively rich overall. Sociologists use the term **relative poverty** to describe the poor in industrialized countries because although the poor lack many of the resources available to the rest of the population, they nevertheless have the basic necessities of life. In countries such as China, however, where the average person has significantly less income than the average person in the United States, sociologists refer to **absolute poverty**, meaning that the poor lack even the basic resources necessary to sustain life. This is not to say that no one in the United States or other industrialized countries lives in absolute poverty, nor is the distinction in terms intended to minimize the misery of the people living in relative poverty. But when we consider that in the United States only about 11 percent of the people living below the poverty line say they do not have enough food to eat, whereas in Africa 50 percent of the *continent's* population is malnourished, we begin to realize that there are vast differences in life conditions across societies (Short & Shea, 1995; United Nations Development Programme, 1996).

Stratification, then, exists not only within a particular country, but also between countries. Just as there are wealthy, less wealthy, and poor people within a single country, so too are there wealthy, less wealthy, and poor countries throughout our world. In this chapter, we will continue the discussion of stratification that we began in Chapter 8, but our focus now will be on the stratification that exists between countries. Americans often believe that what happens in another country, particularly a poor country, has no impact on them. But consider, for example, the impact on workers in the United States when corporations move their manufacturing operations to poorer countries in order to undercut wages and bypass health and safety laws. Perhaps some day you will be working for one of those corporations, making decisions that affect not only profits and losses, but also people's lives. We are not citizens of a single country; we are members of a world community. And what happens "there," affects us here.

To understand global stratification, we must first learn how sociologists classify countries in the global stratification system.

GLOBAL STRATIFICATION: AN OVERVIEW

In Chapter 8 we defined stratification as a ranking system with three dimensions or elements: wealth, status, and political power. We use these same dimensions when we speak of **global stratification.** In stratifying countries, sociologists and other social scientists pay particular attention to each nation's wealth and political power. It is more difficult to measure a country's prestige, but it is certainly the case that some countries, like some people, are perceived as being more prestigious than others, and their status is closely related to the countries' relative wealth and political power. To say one is a citizen of Great Britain, for example, usually commands more respect around the world than to say one is a citizen of Belize. Not surprisingly, Great Britain is also a wealthier and more politically powerful country than Belize.

Traditionally, when sociologists studied global stratification, they used the *three worlds system* of classification. The three worlds system had three strata: first world, second world, and third world. Wealthy capitalist industrialized countries—the United States and Canada in North America, the countries of Western Europe, and Japan, Australia, and New Zealand in Asia and the Pacific Rim—made up the *first world*. The *second world* was made up of the less industrialized, socialist countries of Eastern Europe and the former Soviet Union, China, Cuba, and a few countries in Africa. Any country that did not fit into either of these categories was classified as *third world*. Third world countries were characterized by their lack of industrialization and greater poverty compared to countries of the first and second worlds.

The term "third world" is still frequently used in everyday speech and academic writing to refer to the large, poor nonindustrialized countries of Africa, Asia, and Latin America. But most sociologists object to this classification

On what basis do international organizations such as the World Bank and the United Nations rank countries into a system of global stratification? How would you classify countries based on visual cues in these photographs of a Canadian shopping mall, Mexican market, and Ukrainian yogurt shop. What picture might you add to represent the fourth World Bank classification? Why might purchasing power be a better indicator of global stratification than per capita GNP?

system for at least two major reasons. First, this system groups over one hundred highly diverse countries into the category "third world," masking not only significant variation in their relative wealth, but also important differences in culture and traditions that affect life conditions. Second, this system was immediately outdated in 1991 with the demise of socialism in the former Soviet Union and Eastern Europe.

Consequently, now when sociologists study global stratification, they generally use the classification system developed by the World Bank, an international organization that lends money for economic development projects in poorer countries. The World Bank system classifies countries as low-income, middle-income (subdivided into low middle-income and high middle-income), and high-income. Although the World Bank uses various measures to classify a country, the most basic is the **per capita gross national product (per capita GNP)**, the total value of the goods and services produced in a country each year divided by the number of people in the country's population. That is:

$$\frac{\text{Total value of goods and services produced}}{\text{Total population}} = \text{Per capita GNP}$$

For example, in 1997, the total value of goods and services produced in Canada was $583.9 billion. Given that Canada's population in 1997 was 30 million, Canada's per capita GNP that year was:

$$\frac{\$583.9 \text{ billion}}{30 \text{ million}} = \$19,463$$

Per capita GNP is far from a perfect measure. One problem is that it primarily counts goods and services that are produced for sale, but in every country, whatever the level of economic development, numerous goods and services are produced that are not sold. For example, in countries with a large population of farmers or pastoralists, a significant amount of what is produced is for immediate private consumption. Other "free work," such as volunteer services, child care, and work performed at home is not counted (Hershey, 1995). And in virtually every country there is an *underground* or *shadow economy* of goods and services, frequently illegal, that are bought and sold but not counted in the GNP. If they were counted, the GNPs of many countries would change significantly. For instance, the production and sale of illicit drugs in Bolivia is estimated to equal about 20 percent of that country's GNP. In Colombia, it is estimated that the cocaine trade is equivalent to 10 percent of that country's GNP, with rebel activity, including extortion and kidnapping for ransom, equivalent to an additional 4 percent (Ayres, 1996). Prostitution in Indonesia, Malaysia, the Philippines, and Thailand is estimated to equal between 2 percent and 14 percent of the GNPs of these

countries (Lim, 1998). Were uncounted economic activities included in the GNP, then, many countries would appear better off economically.

Other critics of the GNP point out that it does not take into account a country's natural wealth and human or social wealth. Natural wealth includes farmland, forests, minerals, and fossil-fuel deposits, whereas human or social wealth refers to the education and skill level of the population as well as the population's health status (Passell, 1995). Finally, other observers caution that GNP is plagued by biases in reporting, recording, and interpreting because it is based on government statistics and these are more or less reliable depending on the country.

Still, despite these weaknesses, per capita GNP provides useful insights into global stratification especially when combined with other measures. In our discussion, therefore, we will use the World Bank's global stratification system based on GNP, but also examine other variables to get a more complete picture.

The major strata in the World Bank's system are defined as follows. **Low-income countries**, which are also sometimes referred to as *underdeveloped*, have a per capita GNP of $785 U.S. dollars or less a year. **Lower-middle income countries**, which are also known as *developing countries*, have a per capita GNP of $786 to $3,125 U.S. dollars per year. **Upper-middle income countries** have an annual per capita GNP of $3,126 to $9,655 U.S. dollars. And finally, **high-income countries**, which are also known as *industrial countries*, have an annual per capita GNP above $9,656 U.S. dollars. Switzerland has the highest annual GNP of an industrial country, $44,320 (World Bank, 1999). Figure 9.1 shows the distribution of low-, middle-, and high-income countries in the world. Let's examine now the differences between categories as well as the level of inequality within each category.

Assessing Global Inequality

The GNP is a major indicator of levels of inequality between countries, but for a complete picture, we need to look at other standard-of-living indicators as well. Table 9.1 on page 230 compares eight basic standard-of-living indicators, including average per capita GNP, for each of the World Bank strata. It is important to keep in mind, though, that making comparisons based on aggregate statistics of any sort has its limitations. Every country has a unique historical and cultural background that contributes to the life experiences and expectations of its people. What we in the United States might consider an unbearably low standard of living might be considered comfortable by the standards of another society. For example, China's per capita GNP is $860. An American's first reaction to this figure is likely, "How can anyone live on $860 a year?" But our views are colored by our personal experiences, which take place within a specific economic,

Figure 9.1 Groups of Economies

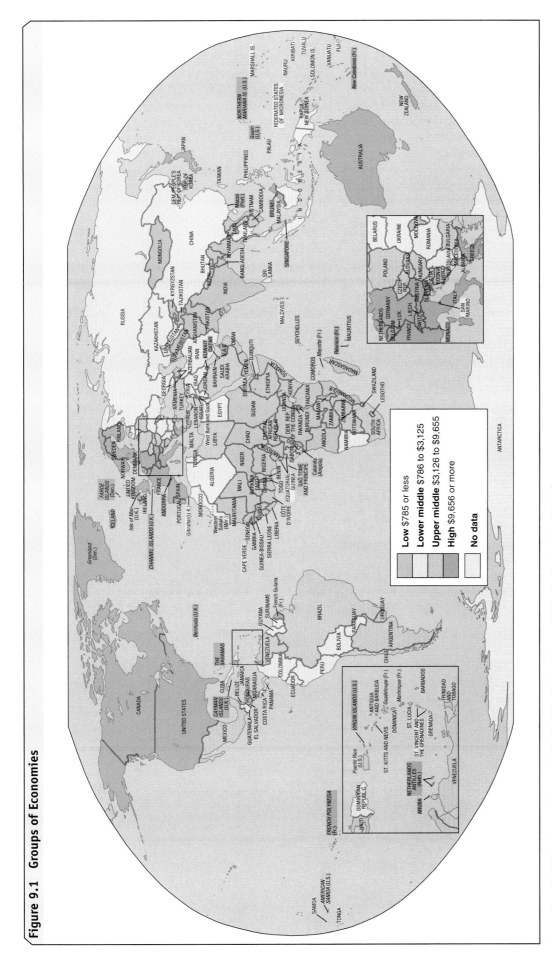

Source: From *World Development Report 1996* by World Bank. Copyright © 1996 by The International Bank for Reconstruction and Development/The World Bank. Used by permission of Oxford University Press, Inc.

229

political, and cultural context. In the United States, $860 would not be enough to pay for a single course in most universities, but in China, a person can live fairly well on such an income because the cost of basic needs is low: For example, average monthly expenditures for urban residents, including food, clothing, and rent, are $36 ("Expenditures," 1996). Consequently, while China's per capita GNP falls well below the U.S. official poverty line, Chinese people with this income do not consider themselves poor (World Bank, 1999).

Per Capita GNP. The first indicator in Table 9.1 is per capita GNP. Looking at average per capita GNP, we see that, not surprisingly, wealth increases dramatically as we move from the least economically developed countries to the most economically developed. To put these differences in wealth in perspective, though, we must realize that these figures tell us that the average person living in a low-income country enjoys only about one-sixtieth of the wealth of the average person living in a high-income country.

Figure 9.2 presents the data in yet another way, showing the distribution of global income among the three major strata. Here we see that low-income countries, which represent more than 35 percent of the world's population, possess just slightly more than 2 percent of the world's income. In contrast, high-income countries, with

only about 16 percent of the world's population, enjoy about four-fifths (79.5 percent) of the world's income (World Bank, 1999).

One important fact that Figure 9.2 does not reveal is that the gap in wealth between countries has widened in recent years. According to the United Nations, there has been a worldwide surge in economic growth over the past three decades, but it has benefitted only a handful of countries. More specifically, the benefits of global economic growth have been concentrated in just fifteen countries, whereas eighty-nine others—representing 1.6 billion people or one quarter of the world's population—are economically worse off than they were ten or more years ago. Of these eighty-nine countries, seventy are low-income and developing countries where income levels have fallen below those of the 1960s and 1970s. As a result, the poorest 20 percent of the world's population saw their meager share of global income cut by more than half over the past four decades, while the richest 20 percent of the world's population increased their share of global income by 17.3 percent in the same period. In other words, the income share ratio of the world's richest and poorest people has more than doubled during this time, increasing from 30:1 to 82:1 (U.N. Development Programme, 1998). These findings led the head of the United Nations Development Programme to conclude that, "In the past 15 years the world has become more economically

---

TABLE 9.1 World Development Indicators by World Bank Strata

Indicator	WORLD BANK STRATA			
	Low Income	Lower-Middle Income	Upper-Middle Income	High Income
Average GNP per capita in US$, 1997	350	1,230	4,520	25,700
Percentage of labor force working in agriculture/industry, 1990	69/15	36/27	21/27	5/31
Percent of children aged 10–14 in the labor force, 1997	21	8	9	0
Infant mortality (per 1,000 live births), 1996	80	37	31	6
Life expectancy at birth, males/females, 1996	58/60	66/71	66/73	74/81
Adult illiteracy (% population 15 and older), males/females, 1995	35/59	12/27	12/17	<5/<5

Sources: World Bank (1999). *World development report, 1998/99,* pp. 190–195, 202–203; (1997). *World Development Report, 1997,* pp. 220–221.

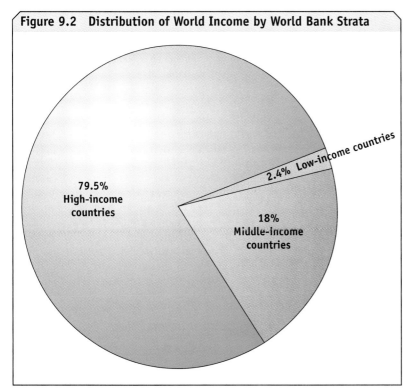

Figure 9.2   Distribution of World Income by World Bank Strata

79.5%
High-income
countries

2.4% Low-income countries

18%
Middle-income
countries

Source: Compiled from World Bank, 1998, p. 191.

polarized—both between countries and within countries. If present trends continue, economic disparities between the industrial and developing nations will move from inequitable to inhuman" (U.N. Development Programme, 1996, p. iii).

To better understand the issue of economic polarization between countries, let's consider some of the other standard-of-living indicators in Table 9.1.

Work.   The second standard-of-living indicator in Table 9.1 is work, gauged by the percentage of the population engaged in agriculture versus the percentage involved in industry. As we discussed in Chapter 8, one byproduct of economic development is a reduced number of workers in agricultural work. The same trend holds true worldwide. We find that 69 percent of the population in low-income countries labors in agriculture, while in high-income countries, the figure is 5 percent.

Agricultural production in the majority of low-income countries is *subsistence level* in that the volume of food produced does not normally exceed the immediate needs of those who farm the land. In many countries, however, subsistence farming is not adequate to feed even farmers and their families, resulting in food shortages. Many observers are concerned that the situation will grow worse over the next three decades (see the Social Policy box).

Another work-related standard-of-living indicator in Table 9.1 is the percentage of children aged ten to four-

teen in the labor work force. We find that about one-fifth of children in this age group are working in low-income countries, whereas, at least according to official records, no children work in high-income countries. Indeed child labor is illegal in the high-income, industrialized countries, although it does occur there. The extent of child labor is a reflection of the economic deprivation of many families. The meager wages children earn are nevertheless an important contribution to the family's survival. However, by keeping children out of school, child labor actually helps perpetuate poverty, a point to which we will return shortly.

Health.   The two health measures in Table 9.1—infant mortality and life expectancy at birth—reflect stark differences in well-being across the four strata of countries.

One basic health indicator is **infant mortality**, the number of deaths of children under one year of age per 1,000 live births. As Table 9.1 shows, infant mortality is dramatically higher in low-income countries—more than thirteen times the rate in high-income countries. It is important to note that substantial gains have been made in lowering the infant mortality rate in low-income countries in recent years, largely because of special programs, such as the World Health Organization's Expanded Programme on Immunization (EPI), which has eradicated many childhood diseases, such as measles, smallpox, and polio, that in the past claimed the lives of many children (U.N. World Development Programme, 1998). However,

The Issue

In the 1980s, world hunger emerged as a major international problem, brought to public attention around the world by media coverage of the famine in sub-Saharan Africa, especially Ethiopia and Somalia. Relief efforts were organized from sources as varied as religious groups, school children, and rock stars. This outpouring of human kindness undoubtedly saved thousands of lives. Famine—that is, a situation in which a sudden drop in food availability leads to widespread starvation and death—is relatively rare nowadays. However, hunger and malnutrition are not. People in virtually every country in the world suffer from hunger and malnutrition. The United States, for example, has the highest level of per capita food consumption in the world, yet 30 million Americans, including 13 million children under twelve, are hungry, unable to get adequate food on a daily basis (U.N. Development Programme, 1998). Nevertheless, hunger and malnutrition are most prevalent in low-income countries, where it is estimated that about 840 million people are undernourished (United Nations, 1997).

Children are the prime victims of hunger and malnutrition. Rates of child malnutrition declined during the 1990s in China, Southeast Asia, Latin America, and the Caribbean, but the decreases were small. In other parts of the world, particularly in sub-Saharan Africa and South Asia, child malnutrition worsened during the 1990s (United Nations, 1997). In North Korea, for instance, five years of extreme undernourishment due to food shortages has left 62 percent of children under the age of seven with stunted growth and extensive physical and mental impairment (Rosenthal, 1998). It is estimated that *each day* 40,000 children worldwide (but concentrated in low-income countries) die from hunger-related causes, and tens of thousands more incur irreversible health problems from malnutrition (World Bank, 1993). Only a small percentage of these deaths is the result of outright starvation. Instead, most victims die from what, under normal circumstances, would be mild infections—a common cold, a case of infectious diarrhea—that become fatal because their

bodies' immune systems have been weakened by hunger (Rosenthal, 1998; U.N. Development Programme, 1998).

The Debate

What causes such widespread hunger and malnutrition in this world of plenty? Most people think the answer to this question is crop failures from natural disasters, such as droughts, cyclones, or floods. However, most experts now believe that while natural disasters do sometimes play a part, hunger and malnutrition are most often caused by structural problems, including government policies that promote the production of food for export instead of internal consumption, and international and internal politics in which food is used as a weapon or to gain political leverage. For example, at the height of the Ethiopian famine in the early 1980s, the Ethiopian government exported revenue-producing goods, including vegetables and livestock, to Western Europe. At the same time, the United States and England deliberately delayed aid to Ethiopia in the hope that the food crisis would help topple the country's socialist government. When aid did arrive, the Ethiopian government, which was also fighting a civil war, withheld food from regions controlled by its enemies to try to force their surrender

(American Friends Service Committee, 1985; Korn, 1988).

A more recent example is North Korea. Although the food shortages there are partly a result of both floods and droughts, they are also the result of the collapse of the Soviet Union, which historically had been North Korea's main supplier of food, fuel, and fertilizer (Rosenthal, 1998). Some observers have also argued that North Korea has, in a sense, been held hostage since the United States and several other governments wanted to make aid contingent on specific political promises, such as better progress in the country's peace talks with South Korea (Kristof, 1997).

What Do You Think?

Is there a possibility of ending world hunger and malnutrition? Most experts agree that these problems are solvable, but only through international cooperation between low-income and high-income countries. One important part of the solution is the implementation of long-term educational, medical, and technical assistance programs that target the poor in low-income countries and provide them with the tools, knowledge, and skills to sustain independent economic production and viability (United Nations, 1997). In addition, the governments of low-income countries must provide local farmers with incentives to produce food for consumption in local, not foreign markets, and give the working poor sufficient wages to allow them to purchase adequate food (United Nations Development Programme, 1998). Also, all governments must stop using food as a weapon or political leverage tool. And some policy experts argue that democracy is necessary to eliminate hunger and malnutrition. Why? Because if no democratic elections existed, and no public criticism of leaders or their policies is permitted, then those in power can insulate themselves and their families from the deprivations of hunger and malnutrition, and they do not have to worry about the consequences of these problems for the rest of the population or the political fallout (U.N. Development Programme, 1996).

Can you think of other strategies for ending hunger and malnutrition?

this progress may be offset by the spread of new diseases such as AIDS, and the inability to control others, such as water-borne viruses. Each year, three million children under the age of five, the vast majority from low-income countries, die because of diarrhea, which induces dehydration and robs the body of necessary vitamins and minerals (World Health Organization, 1996).

The infant mortality rate affects another basic health indicator, **life expectancy at birth:** the average number of years a person can expect to live after birth. A high infant mortality rate lowers life expectancy for a population. According to Table 9.1, there is a twenty-one-year gap in life expectancy between the female populations of low-income and high-income countries, and a sixteen-year gap in male life expectancies. If we compare the wealthiest nations to some of the poorest, however, we find that life expectancy in many high-income countries is more than double that in low-income countries. For example, life expectancy in Japan and France is seventy-nine years and in the United States, it is seventy-six years. In Rwanda, it is just twenty-eight years and in Sierra Leone, thirty-five years. International agencies warn that this gap may widen over the next several decades because of political conflicts, such as civil war, and the rapid spread of infectious diseases, such as AIDS, the Ebola virus, the hepatitis C virus, and new strains of malaria and cholera that are appearing in low-income countries at an alarming rate (U.N. Development Programme, 1998; World Health Organization, 1996).

The disparity in life expectancy and infant mortality rates between low-income and high-income countries is also related to the population-to-physician ratio. Not surprisingly, significant health problems characterize countries where the pool of available doctors is limited. In many rural, isolated societies of low-income countries, the members of the population may never be seen by a physician. People in these areas rely on traditional treatments that may work for minor ailments, but are no match for highly infectious diseases such as the Ebola virus, the hepatitis C virus, and new strains of malaria and cholera that are appearing in low-income countries at an alarming rate (World Health Organization, 1996).

The remaining indicator in Table 9.1, the adult illiteracy rate (the percentage of the population aged fifteen and older who cannot read or write), is a measure of education across strata. Again, there are dramatic differences between low-income and high-income countries. There has been considerable progress made in lowering adult illiteracy in low-income countries, and between 1970 and 1995, illiteracy rates in these countries fell from 52 percent on average to 30 percent. Some of the largest gains were among women and girls, although we can see in Table 9.1 that women's illiteracy rates in low-income as well as middle-income countries remain significantly

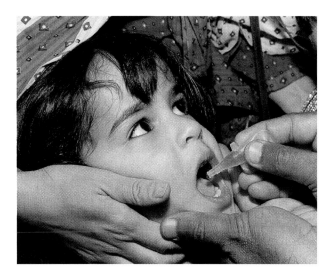

How is global stratification reflected in a country's economic activities, population size, infant mortality, life expectancy at birth, general health, and literacy? How does the Human Development Index show the link between these factors and global economic inequality?

higher than men's rates, a point that we'll come back to momentarily (U.N. Development Programme, 1998).

Analysts attribute improvement in adult literacy to increased enrollments in both primary and secondary schools during this period. Still, if we compare the illiteracy rates of wealthy nations with those of some of the poorest countries, the gap remains wide. Consider, for instance, that in the United States, Canada, and Japan, the adult illiteracy rate is 1 percent or less, while in Niger it is 86 percent and in Burkina Faso, it is 81 percent (U.N. Development Programme, 1998). Some of this discrepancy results from the fact that in low-income countries, there are numerous obstacles that stand in the way of establishing a comprehensive education system, including a lack of government funding, poor transportation and other problems in isolated rural areas, and a lack of qualified teachers.

One of the most serious consequences of high illiteracy is economic: When the opportunity arises to introduce advanced technology into these countries, the pool of indigenous skilled labor is very small, so foreign workers end up controlling the high-status, high-paying positions in the economy while the native population is relegated to the unskilled, low-paying jobs.

Global inequality manifests itself in many ways other than economic, although all the indicators we have discussed are closely interrelated with economic conditions. The United Nations has combined the six indicators we've examined with several others, such as consumer purchasing power, access to clean water, and sanitation services, to create the *human development index*. The United Nations ranks 174 countries in the world, and

Table 9.2 gives a partial listing for 1998. The top ten countries in the human development index are all high-income countries except one (Barbados, an upper middle-income country), while the bottom ten are all low-income countries. This is hardly a surprise, but it does underscore once again the deep disparities in quality of life that exist between countries globally. Moreover, a disturbing new pattern of inequality seems to be emerging *within* countries. Let's narrow our focus for a moment to look at inequality within countries.

Rich and Poor: The Great Divide

To examine inequality within nations, we use the same technique we used in Chapter 8 to look at economic inequality in the United States: income fifths or quintiles. All families or households in a country are ranked according to annual income, from poorest to wealthiest, and then the distribution is divided into five equal parts, from the poorest fifth to the wealthiest fifth. In this way, we see the range of economic strata within each country. Then we compare the distribution of income across income fifths for each of the four World Bank strata to see how income proportions vary and how a country ranks in a global stratification system.

Table 9.3 shows the distribution of income fifths for the four World Bank strata. It also gives a separate estimate of income distribution in the United States, calculated by averaging the distributions reported by the World Bank and the U.S. Department of Commerce. These data show first of all that, regardless of the stratum, inequality between income quintiles is extreme. On average, the lowest fifth earns only about 6.7 percent of total income, while the top fifth accounts for about 46 percent.

Notice, too, that although all the strata show a similar pattern of inequality, the disparity between rich and poor appears to be widest in middle-income countries. Apparently, during the transition from undeveloped to developing, especially during the initial stages of industrialization, the poor do not share in the economic advantages and thereby lose income. In other words, the poor in low-income (undeveloped) countries are better off than the poor in middle-income countries. Conditions improve somewhat when countries reach the industrial level. This pattern was first described in 1955 by the Nobel Prize-winning economist, Simon Kuznets, whose theory is known as the **Kuznets curve:** When countries are in the early stages of economic transformation from agriculture to industry, economic inequality increases.

TABLE 9.2 United Nations Rankings on the Human Development Index (HDI), Highest 25 and Lowest 25 Countries, 1998

Country	HDI rank	Country	HDI rank	Country	HDI rank
Canada	1	Denmark	18	Haiti	159
France	2	Germany	19	Uganda	160
Norway	3	Greece	20	Malawi	161
United States	4	Italy	21	Djibouti	162
Iceland	5	Israel	22	Chad	163
Finland	6	Cyprus	23	Guinea-Bissau	164
Netherlands	7	Barbados	24	Gambia	165
Japan	8	Hong Kong, China	25	Mozambique	166
New Zealand	9	Tanzania	150	Guinea	167
Sweden	10	Yemen	151	Eritrea	168
Spain	11	Nepal	152	Ethiopia	169
Belgium	12	Madagascar	153	Burundi	170
Austria	13	Central African Republic	154	Mali	171
United Kingdom	14	Bhutan	155	Burkina Faso	172
Australia	15	Angola	156	Niger	173
Switzerland	16	Sudan	157	Sierra Leone	174
Ireland	17	Senegal	158		

Source: U.N. Development Programme (1998). *Human development report, 1998,* pp. 128–130.

TABLE 9.3   Percent Distribution of Income by Quintile, World Bank Strata, and United States*

Income Category	Lowest Fifth	Second Fifth	Third Fifth	Fourth Fifth	Highest Fifth
Low income (29/61)	5.9	9.7	14.5	21.4	48.5
Lower-middle income (30/60)	6.2	10.4	14.7	21.2	47.4
Upper-middle income (11/35)	6.4	10.1	14.1	20.4	49.0
High income (19/55)	8.2	13.0	16.7	22.8	38.9
U.S. ESTIMATES AND COMPOSITE					
World Bank	4.8	10.5	16.0	23.5	45.2
U.S. Department of Commerce	3.6	8.9	15.0	23.2	49.4
Composite	4.2	9.7	15.5	23.4	47.3

*The statistics reflect data from all World Bank countries that report income distribution by quintiles. The numbers in parentheses show the number of countries for which these data are available in each income category over the total number of countries in the category.

Sources: U.S. Department of Commerce, Bureau of the Census, 1998a, p. xii; World Bank, 1999, pp. 198–199, 250–251.

Once industrialization takes hold, the inequality lessens somewhat, and when the country is fully industrialized, inequality stabilizes (see Figure 9.3).

The Kuznets curve has received some support from international research that shows that inequality in Western industrialized countries was high in the first half of the twentieth century, began declining at mid-century, and has since stabilized. However, major changes in the global economy and economic growth during the 1980s and 1990s indicate that Kuznets's theory may no longer apply. For example, in Chapter 8 we examined data that showed the gap between the rich and the poor in the United States reached record levels in the 1990s, and in Table 9.3, we see that income inequality is significantly greater in the

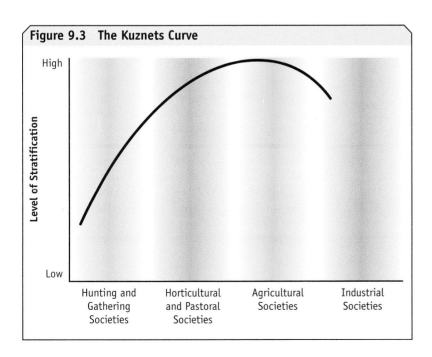

Figure 9.3   The Kuznets Curve

United States than in high-income industrialized countries as a group.

Moreover, according to the United Nations Development Programme (1998), the widening income gap between rich and poor that we see in the United States is becoming a pattern in many countries throughout the world, including industrialized countries. Among high-income industrialized countries, U.N. researchers found the widest gaps between rich and poor in Great Britain and Australia, where the richest quintile makes ten times more than the poorest quintile. In Switzerland, as in the United States, the richest quintile makes nine times more than the poorest quintile. These industrialized countries are now demonstrating the pattern of income inequality that has historically characterized developing countries.

However, this new pattern is not the norm in all industrialized countries, particularly not in those where economic growth has occurred fairly recently. For instance, in Japan, which enjoyed tremendous economic growth

One of the widest gaps between rich and poor occurs in Australia, where low-income traditional aboriginal Australians may live far from the modern high-income cities of the descendants of British colonists. How would this translate in terms of income quintiles? What is a quintile? If Simon Kuznets's theory of development held up, would you expect inequality to increase or decrease in Australia in the future?

over the past three decades, the average income of the poorest quintile is slightly less than half the national per capita income. Since the 1960s, the income gap between rich and poor in Japan has remained relatively unchanged (Kristof, 1998; U.N. Development Programme, 1996).

What, then, is the relationship between economic development and income inequality? Is economic development beneficial or detrimental to low-income countries and to the poor in those countries? Sociologists and other social scientists have given different answers to these questions, and we will examine them later in the chapter. First, let's continue our discussion of income inequality within and between countries by taking a closer look at the most disadvantaged segments of the world's population.

R E F L E C T I N G   O N

Global Stratification: An Overview

1. What standard-of-living indicators should sociologists examine to measure inequality between countries? Can you think of any additional indicators not mentioned in the chapter?
2. What do you see as the strengths and weaknesses of using the Kuznets curve as an explanation of global inequality?

POVERTY IN GLOBAL PERSPECTIVE

Sociologist Ruth Sidel (1986, p. xvi) once wrote that statistics are really "people with the tears washed off." It's important not to lose sight of the human face of poverty when discussing the problem. Poverty has real-life consequences for the poor, even though the consequences differ from country to country. For example, in the United States, poverty means living in housing where the plumbing and electricity are unreliable and the roof often leaks. For Chen Xianshe, whose story opened this chapter, poverty means living in a hut that has no plumbing or roof and having electricity that is only sufficient to light two 60-watt bulbs.

Nevertheless, when most sociologists talk about poverty, they rely on more "objective" measures. In Chapter 8, we saw that poverty in the United States is determined according to a government-constructed measure known as the *poverty line*. Individuals and families whose annual incomes fall below the amount of money specified by the poverty line are officially considered poor. As we discussed earlier in this chapter, however, such a standard is difficult to use internationally because living standards vary dramatically from one country to another. Nevertheless, some analysts have calculated an international poverty line below which individuals and families would not have enough money to obtain the most basic resources necessary for survival (World Bank, 1999).

Some analysts set the international poverty line at $1 per day or $365 per year. Using this standard, we find that 25 percent of the world's population—that is, 1.3 billion people—is poor, and the majority of the poor live in low-income and lower-middle income countries. Of these, almost half—more than 550 million people—live in South Asia, 215 million live in African countries south of the Sahara Desert, and 150 million live in Latin America (United Nations Development Programme, 1996).

Other analysts argue that measures of income poverty, in addition to being somewhat arbitrary, do not capture the multidimensional nature of poverty, just as GNP does not capture the multidimensional nature of stratification. Consequently, in assessing global poverty, the United Nations Development Programme measures what it calls **human poverty**, which examines deprivation in three essential elements of life: longevity, knowledge (education), and a decent standard of living. However, the U.N. uses different indicators to measure human poverty in undeveloped and developing countries than it does for industrialized countries. For low-income countries, the U.N. looks at such factors as the percentage of the population expected to die by age forty; the percentage of the population without access to safe water, health services, and sanitation; the percentage of underweight children younger than five years old; the percentage of children who leave school before grade five; and the adult illiteracy rate. For high-income countries, the U.N. measures human poverty by looking at the percentage of the population expected to die by age sixty; the percentage of the population that is functionally illiterate (unable to read and write adequately to meet the basic demands of their society); the proportion of people whose income is less than 50 percent of the median; and the long-term unemployment rate.

While these measures still do not give a complete picture of the extent of poverty in either undeveloped and developing countries or industrial countries, they do reveal an important point: Although the wealth of a country is certainly related to the level of impoverishment of its population, the extent of poverty in a particular country may not coincide with the average level of income in that country. For example, the United States, which has the highest per capita income in terms of purchasing power of any of the seventeen industrial countries ranked by the United Nations Development Programme, also has the highest level of human poverty (16.5 percent). Sweden, on the other hand, ranks thirteenth on per capita income in terms of purchasing power, but has the lowest level of human poverty (6.8 percent). Not surprisingly, though, the extent of human poverty in low-income countries is most severe, exceeding 50 percent in Mali, Ethiopia, Sierra Leonne, Burkina Faso, and Niger. This means that 50 per-

cent or more of the people of these countries suffer the deprivations of human poverty. According to the U.N., human poverty exceeds 33 percent in thirty-two of the seventy-seven undeveloped and developing countries for which it has data (U.N. Development Programme, 1998).

As we noted in Chapter 8, not all segments of a country's population are at equal risk of living in poverty. Just as in the United States, global poverty disproportionately affects women and children.

Gender and Global Poverty

Few societies in the world treat women as well as men. Moreover, inequalities between men and women are not necessarily less in high-income countries than in other countries because the inequality gap between men and women is not based strictly on high income. Nevertheless, in countries that are economically disadvantaged in the global scale, women are likely to be even more disadvantaged than men. In other words, women in these countries experience a *double deprivation*: the deprivation of living in a poor country and the deprivation imposed because they are women.

Earlier in the chapter we saw this double deprivation reflected in the significantly higher illiteracy rates of women in low-income and developing countries. Between 1970 and 1990, the difference in illiteracy rates of women and men was cut in half, and the gender gap in elementary school enrollment narrowed by 15 percent (United

Why are women and children among the poorest members of even high-income societies? The greatest burden of poverty, however, falls on women and children in low-income countries, especially widows, orphans, and the abandoned, who lack the safety net of family. These Muslim women also have the safety net of Islam, which requires charity toward the poor as one of the "seven pillars" of the faith.

Nations Development Programme, 1998). Nevertheless, the gender difference in adult illiteracy rates reflects the fact that of the 130 million children in low-income countries who either do not go to school or drop out before they finish fifth grade, 73 million (56 percent) are girls (United Nations Children's Fund, 1999).

Women's double deprivation is also evident in the areas of health and nutrition. Overall, life expectancy in low-income countries is considerably lower than life expectancy in high-income countries. Throughout most of the world, women on average live longer than men, and since 1970, women's life expectancy has improved 20 percent faster than men's life expectancy. However, in low-income countries, the sex difference in life expectancy is much smaller than in high-income countries. In some cases, such as Bangladesh and Pakistan, the life expectancies of women and men are the same, and in a few cases, such as Nepal, the sex difference in life expectancy is reversed—that is, men on average outlive women (United Nations Development Programme, 1998; World Bank, 1999).

We will consider the reasons why women usually outlive men in Chapter 18. Here, though, let's look at the factors that contribute to a smaller sex difference in life expectancy in low-income countries. First, women are responsible for securing water and fuel each day for their families. This usually means traveling great distances by foot and carrying back (typically on their heads) heavy loads while also often carrying babies or small children. Women are also involved in producing food for their families, usually through subsistence farming and without modern technology. Consequently, they cultivate and harvest crops by hand or by using crude tools, such as digging sticks. Grains must be husked and ground by hand, a long and physically exhausting process (U.N. Development Programme, 1998). In addition, cooking the food exposes women to unhealthy wood smoke or biomass fuels, such as cattle dung. "Emissions from biomass fuels are major sources of air pollution in the home, and studies have shown that cooks inhale more smoke and pollutants than the inhabitants of the dirtiest cities" (Doyal, 1990, p. 510).

Customs also contribute to sex differences in health and life expectancy. For instance, toilets are extremely rare in low-income countries; urination and defecation are done outside. But in some societies, women are prohibited by religious and moral teachings from being seen defecating. They must wait until dark to relieve themselves, which can lead to constipation and other bowel and intestinal problems, and also increases their risk of assault. In many countries, too, customs governing the distribution of food dictate that women eat less than men, even when pregnant. Food is distributed according to the prestige of family members, not according to family members' nutritional needs. Consequently, women

have higher rates of malnutrition, which in pregnant women can lead to anemia and other illnesses as well as harm the fetus (Doyal, 1990; United Nations Development Programme, 1998). In low-income countries, the maternal mortality rate (the number of women who die during or shortly after childbirth) averages about 1,100 per 100,000 births; in high-income countries, the average maternal mortality rate is just 30 per 100,000 births (United Nations Development Programme, 1998).

Custom also contributes to a higher mortality rate for female children in low-income countries. For example, in a number of Asian countries, such as China and India, there is such a strong preference for male children that female children may be selectively aborted or killed at birth, although infanticide has been outlawed (Hegde, 1999; Warren, 1985). Higher female infant and child mortality rates in some low-income countries are also attributed to the fact that boy babies tend to be breastfed considerably longer than girl babies and that girl children are fed less well than boys (Doyal, 1990; United Nations Development Programme, 1998).

The Intersecting Inequalities box discusses another disturbing manifestation of the intersection of global poverty with gender and age inequalities, child prostitution and sex tourism. Let's examine further the plight of poor children throughout the world.

Children and Global Poverty

We noted in Chapter 8 that a sizeable percentage of the U.S. poverty population consists of children under the age of eighteen. How does our child poverty rate compare with child poverty in other high-income countries? According to recent research conducted by a nonprofit international organization based in Western Europe, the child poverty rate in the United States is the highest among industrialized countries. Data gathered for the Luxembourg Income Study calculated the child poverty rate in the United States at 22 percent, even after taking into account various forms of government assistance. Two countries tied for the dubious honor of second place, Australia and Canada, but their child poverty rates were significantly less than the U.S. rate: 14 percent. Several countries would have higher child poverty rates than the United States were it not for their governments' assistance programs. For instance, the study showed that the child poverty rate in Ireland and Britain would be close to 30 percent, but government assistance programs reduce the rates to about 11 percent in Ireland and 10 percent in Britain. In fact, even though many social programs in European countries have suffered budget cuts in recent years, most European governments have expanded assistance programs for single-parent and low-income households with children. In contrast, in the United States a lower percentage of needy families re-

INTERSECTING INEQUALITIES

How Does Poverty Contribute to the Sexual Exploitation of Children?

One of the byproducts of the grinding poverty that characterizes life for most families in Asia and Latin America is a dramatic rise in the number of child prostitutes. According to children's rights advocates, an increasing number of children in countries such as Brazil, the Philippines, and Cambodia are being kidnapped and forced into prostitution or sold to pimps by their parents, most of whom are desperate for income. The children may be locked in the brothels if they are considered likely to try to escape, but usually such measures are unnecessary; beatings and threats are typically enough to convince the children to stay (Lim, 1998). Accurate estimates of the number of child prostitutes are difficult to come by, with some experts setting the lower limit in the tens of thousands and others maintaining that it is at least one million (Lim, 1998). The children involved are as young as six and as old as fifteen (the age of consent in most countries is sixteen) (Goering, 1996; Kristof, 1996; Sherry et al., 1995).

Who are the customers of child prostitutes? Some are local men, neighbors of the children, to whom the children are rented out by their parents. Most, however, are foreign businessmen and tourists. Some of the men are individual travelers, but others travel on organized sex tours. The tours, which first began in Japan, are now sold in such countries as Great Britain, South Korea, and Taiwan. If the child is a virgin, the fee may be as much as $500, but immediately following the loss of her virginity, a young girl may be hired for anywhere from $2 to $10, depending on her age and experience (Kristof, 1996; Lim, 1998; Sherry et al., 1995).

Many customers justify their behavior by claiming that they are actually helping the children, providing them with much-needed money for their families and preventing them from having to work at even more dangerous or menial occupations. The customers also often rationalize that children from impoverished countries become sexually active at early ages anyway.

Another motivation for seeking out young children, however, is the belief that they are less likely than adult prostitutes to be infected with HIV, the virus that causes AIDS (Sherry et al., 1995). According to international health experts, AIDS is spreading rapidly among prostitutes in many countries, especially in Asia. It is also spreading from country to country because of international trafficking in prostitutes and because of travelers who contract the disease abroad and bring it home with them. Prostitutes report that few of their customers use condoms, and the younger the prostitute, the more powerless she or he is to insist that a condom be worn. The fact is, however, that child prostitutes are at greatest risk of contracting HIV because of their age: A child's vagina or anus is more easily torn from intercourse, causing open cuts, sores, and bleeding that facilitate HIV transmission (Lim, 1998). Consequently, world health experts expect the incidence of AIDS in Asia as well as Latin America to continue to rise, with children making up an increasing percentage of those who become infected and eventually die from the disease.

ceive any form of government assistance, and the assistance they do receive is lower on average than what is given in many other industrialized countries (Pear, 1996; see also Cornia & Danziger, 1997; United Nations Children's Fund, 1999).

As we have seen in this chapter, the burden of poverty is spread unevenly throughout the world, with the populations of low-income countries suffering far greater rates and more severe poverty than other countries in the global stratification hierarchy. In low-income countries, the poorest households tend to be those with the greatest number of children or economically dependent members (elderly or disabled people). However, researchers disagree over whether family size contributes to poverty or vice versa. Obviously, the greater the number of mouths to feed, the more economic resources required, but having many children can also be a practical response to poverty. In fact, in low-income countries, elderly parents depend on their adult children for support. Therefore, given high infant and child mortality rates, parents have a relatively large number of children to ensure that a few survive into adulthood to provide economic security in old age. Even before reaching adulthood, children in impoverished households in low-income countries are often more of an economic asset than a liability to parents. At very young ages, children are expected to do domestic tasks, and many children contribute to the family's income by working (United Nations, 1997).

In the long run, however, child labor in low-income countries perpetuates poverty. Work takes the place of school for many children, particularly by the time they reach the age of ten. It is estimated that 128 million children of primary school age are in the paid labor force throughout the world. Although child labor can be found in virtually all countries, including the United States, it is particularly prevalent in Asia and Africa (United Nations, 1997). These children grow up to become the next generation of uneducated and untrained adults. The need to work closes off any avenue of opportunity that education might have provided (Jehl, 1997; United Nations Children's Fund, 1999).

The International Labor Organization also reports that children's work conditions are frequently exploitative and abusive. Many child laborers work extraordinarily long hours in unhealthy workplaces for subsistence wages at best. In Pakistan, for example, nearly 10,000 children under the age of fourteen work ten hours a day hand-stitching leather soccer balls for a daily wage of about $1.20 (Greenhouse, 1997). Children are especially susceptible to disease, so these conditions pose severe threats to their health. In addition, the children may be subject to beatings and live in virtual imprisonment. In fact, slave labor and debt bondage are not uncommon (Greenhouse, 1997). And, as the Intersecting Inequalities box reports, some children are sold into prostitution by their parents.

Impoverished children in low-income countries also face another problem: homelessness. Children may run away from or be abandoned by their families. A substantial number end up alone or with other children living on the streets. Estimates of the number of street children worldwide are difficult to come by. The most extensive documentation has come from Latin America, where it is estimated that there are nearly thirteen million street children. Children as young as six years old can be found on the streets of most Latin American cities begging, selling sex or drugs, or stealing in order to survive. They sleep on the sidewalks, in alleys, under bridges, and even in sewer tunnels (El Nasser, 1994). Many use

drugs themselves to cushion the brutality of their daily lives. Glue sniffing is extremely widespread among children in Latin America because it is cheap and readily available, but the effects are deadly. Early symptoms include nosebleeds and skin rashes, but as the addiction progresses, severe neurological dysfunction occurs and the brain simply atrophies (Griffin-Nolan, 1994; Henriques, 1995). Death may also come at the hands of adults, including the police. In Brazil and Colombia, for example, urban police periodically "clean" the streets of homeless children and other outcasts by systematically harassing and killing them. In Brazil, an estimated 3,000 street children have been killed by police since the mid-1980s, and in Colombia, the estimate is an average of thirty-five a month, although the number has been increasing since 1992 (Wilson & Greider, 1995).

REFLECTING ON

Poverty in Global Perspective

1. What are the advantages and disadvantages of using the United Nations's concept of human poverty as a measure of global poverty?
2. What is meant by the term *double deprivation,* and what is a specific example of this condition?
3. Why are children at such high risk for poverty? Why are homeless poor children treated so harshly in some countries and how are some poor children exploited? What do you think should be done about the "official" maltreatment and exploitation of children in these countries?

EXPLAINING GLOBAL INEQUALITY

What causes these glaring inequalities between countries? Social scientists have developed three major theories to explain global inequality. Let's consider each in turn.

Modernization Theory

One of the most popular explanations of global inequality is **modernization theory.** Modernization theory focuses on the conditions that are necessary for a country to become economically developed—that is, fully modern. Of course, many factors are involved, but the one that modernization theorists emphasize is what they call the country's **economic culture**, the system of values, beliefs, and traditions in which economic activities and economic institutions exist (Berger, 1986). In some countries, large extended families, devotion to ancestors, and a rigid adherence to custom leads people to embrace the past and reject new ways of doing things. These people tend to believe their lot in life is determined by fate. They resist modernization, so economic growth is inhibited. In contrast, in other countries, families push certain members to "get ahead," they are always looking for "better" ways of doing things, and they are future-oriented rather than focused on the past or the present. These people believe they are in charge of their own destinies. They welcome modernization, which, in turn, promotes economic growth.

The idea that a society's culture influences its economy is an old one in sociology. You'll recall from Chapter 1 that Max Weber connected culture and economic growth in analyzing capitalism. In *The Protestant Ethic and the Spirit of Capitalism* (1958/1904–05), Weber argued that the values promulgated by a particular Protestant sect, Calvinism, led to the emergence and phenomenal growth of capitalism in Western Europe. The cultural values of individualism, hard work, and deferred gratification provided an economic culture in which capitalism thrived. More recently, sociologist Peter Berger (1986) suggested that we can see modernization theory operating in many East Asian countries today. According to Berger, the economic culture of countries such as Singapore emphasizes productivity, savings, and devotion to work—values that translate into economic development.

In short, modernization theorists see a country's culture as largely to blame for poverty, but culture is not the

According to modernization theory, how should free enterprises, such as this McDonald's restaurant in Beijing affect China's economic development? Is it possible for a country to embrace capitalism and defend a socialist identity at the same time? How might China's governance of Hong Kong help to answer this question?

only culprit. Compounding the problem are governments that interfere with the operation of their countries' economies. That is, even if the economic culture is ripe for economic development, governmental attempts to control the marketplace will inhibit it. Again, Berger (1986) turns to East Asia to illustrate this point, citing China as a prime example. He asks why the Chinese who emigrate to other countries experience such phenomenal economic success, while China itself was economically underdeveloped (until recently). His answer is that in free market countries with little government control of the economy, the Chinese cultural values that we just described are able to take hold and the result is high economic achievement, often in less than a generation. In contrast, until recently, the Chinese government has determined what would be produced in the nation's fields and factories, how much would be produced, and what it would cost—total regulation. Once the Chinese government permitted free enterprise, the country's level of economic development skyrocketed.

At this point you may be remembering the story of Chen Xianshe that opened this chapter. Clearly, not everyone in China has reaped the benefits of the country's "economic miracle." Is this because Mr. Chen and his neighbors have a different economic culture than the Chinese living in more prosperous regions of the country? Some observers would answer by saying that the Chinese government chose to selectively develop only certain regions of the country, while totally neglecting others. But a modernization theorist would say that although initially the wealth derived from development is enjoyed by a relatively small portion of a country's population, as modern technology becomes more widely available and productivity continues to increase, even the poorest of the poor will see their lives improve.

Indeed, according to one of the most prominent modernization theorists, W. W. Rostow (1978), modernization takes place in four stages. Countries begin at the *traditional stage*, living in the present and revering the past. They resist change, but new technological discoveries weaken tradition and spur economic growth through the accumulation of a surplus. During this second, *take off stage*, the country is poised for modernization. In the third stage, the country *drives toward technological maturity*. Industrialization is fully underway, which has both positive and negative consequences. On the one hand, traditional beliefs and practices break down, and social life becomes more impersonal. On the other hand, the poverty rate declines, education becomes more widely available, and political life tends to be more democratic. Finally, when the country is fully modernized, the quality of life reaches a higher standard than ever before. This fourth stage is characterized by *high mass consumption*. More goods are produced at a faster rate more efficiently, and more people both demand and purchase these goods. Countries at this highest level of economic development are expected to help less developed countries progress through the earlier stages by offering low-interest loans and other types of economic aid, new technologies such as tractors and modern production equipment, and programs to reduce population growth.

The Strengths and Weaknesses of Modernization Theory.

Most observers agree that modernization theory does a good job of explaining economic development in East Asian countries such as Singapore. It is also the case that those countries that have followed the socialist path to development, such as Cuba, have seen their economies struggle or stagnate at best, while those who have actively embraced capitalism, such as Taiwan and South Korea, have developed most rapidly (Berger, 1986; McKinley, 1999; Warren, 1980). China represents a special case in which the government has adopted some capitalist principles, but has held fast to its socialist identity, so modernization theory's applicability to China is disputed.

Nevertheless, modernization theory is not without its harsh critics. Some, for example, criticize modernization theory as a victim-blaming perspective. These critics argue that by explaining a country's poverty in terms of its people's values and belief systems, modernization theorists downplay the structural factors that help shape culture in the first place and that affect people's as well as countries' economic opportunities. Consider, for example, poor countries' relationships with wealthy nations. Historically, wealthy countries plundered the human and natural resources of underdeveloped countries in Africa, Asia, and Latin America in order to enrich themselves. Today, exploitation occurs in the form of multinational corporations based in high-income countries. **Multinational corporations** are large corporations that engage in production and marketing in numerous countries throughout the world. Instead of promoting economic development in low-income countries, multinationals actually inhibit the growth of their domestic industries (George, 1990).

At the same time, modernization theorists appear to be incorrect in saying that the best catalyst for development is a "hands-off" approach by government. In fact, in many of the East Asian countries that modernization theorists cite as economic success stories—Singapore, for example—the government has taken a very active role in regulating the economy, assuring an equitable distribution of assets, and placing a high priority on social spending to improve education and other basic services (United Nations Development Programme, 1996; 1998).

Taking these criticisms into account, some sociologists offer alternative explanations for global inequality.

Dependency Theory

Instead of looking within poor countries to explain their poverty, some social scientists look at the relationship between wealthy countries and poor countries. From this perspective, low-income countries are poor because of the policies and practices that high-income countries pursue in order to amass an even greater share of global wealth. Because these policies and practices put low-income countries in a position of relative dependence on high-income countries, this perspective is known as **dependency theory**.

To support their argument, dependency theorists turn first to the historical record. There they find accounts of conquest of undeveloped societies in the Americas, Africa, and Asia by wealthy countries (primarily European). The wealthy countries would then rule the conquered countries, claiming the natural resources as their own and exploiting the population as cheap or slave labor. This practice, called **colonialism**, has virtually disappeared from the world today, but its effects can still be seen. Although it is impossible to know the course of development that the colonized countries would have taken had they not been conquered, dependency theorists maintain that colonization fueled the further economic development of already wealthy countries by keeping the economies of the colonized countries underdeveloped (Frank, 1969; Mamdani, 1996).

Today, dependency theorists argue, multinational corporations have replaced colonial governments as the "rulers" of low-income countries, a relationship called **neocolonialism:** The economic power of the multinationals dominates low-income countries in ways similar to the political control previously exercised by foreign governments. These corporations relocate production to low-income countries to keep their expenses (such as wages and materials) low and their profits high. Political leaders and a handful of wealthy individuals or families in the low-income countries are often coopted to protect the corporations' interests for a share of the foreign corporations' profits. Meanwhile, the vast majority of the population, including children, work long hours under poor conditions for subsistence wages. Consider, for example, the Nike corporation's factories in Indonesia, where indigenous workers earn slightly more than $2 a day. On such wages most workers can only afford to live in bamboo or tin huts without running water or any kind of household appliances. Many workers are women from rural areas who cannot afford to bring their children with them to the cities. Their wages are not enough to allow them to return to the villages more than once a year to see their children. Meanwhile, Nike's holdings in Indonesia are estimated at more that $5 billion, and Philip Knight, Nike's president, is one of the 400 wealthiest Americans, with a personal net worth of $3.5

billion ("The *Forbes* Four Hundred," 1998, p. 227; Herbert, 1996).

The goods produced cheaply by multinationals in low-income countries are exported for sale with significant price mark-ups in high-income countries, reaping high profits for the multinationals, but little profit for low-income countries. The multinationals reinvest their profits in themselves, not in the development of low-income economies. Local businesses do not have the resources to compete with the large international corporations, so their development is stifled as well. Compounding the problem are aid programs from high-income countries which, dependency theorists argue, actually inhibit economic growth rather than promote it because most aid is given in the form of loans. Low-income and developing countries are more than $1.3 trillion in debt. Even if this debt carries low-interest rates, the large sums of money lent (billions of dollars) mean that the annual interest due is itself beyond the means of many low-income countries. In sub-Saharan African countries alone, annual debt service amounts to 17 percent of all goods and services that they export (United Nations Development Programme, 1996). This kind of situation produces a debt crisis, forcing the low-income countries to renegotiate their payment terms with the lending nations, which, in turn, makes them more economically dependent on the high-income countries (George, 1990).

The Strengths and Weaknesses of Dependency Theory. The major strength of dependency theory is its emphasis on the interconnectedness of the world community. It reminds us that the practices and policies of one country can affect the lives and life chances of people in countries thousands of miles away. Dependency theory also brings to light the underside of global economic development—that some nations and corporations advance their own interests at the expense of others. This is a reality that should not be ignored.

Critics of dependency theory, however, see it as too simplistic, placing all the blame for global poverty on the shoulders of high-income countries and multinationals. Social scientists generally concede the negative impact of colonialism on the colonized, but they also point out that not all former colonies remain poor or underdeveloped today. Two of the most obvious examples are Singapore and Hong Kong. At the same time, a number of low-income countries were never colonies, for example, Ethiopia and Eritrea. Thus, the relationship between capitalist expansion and global inequality is more complex than dependency theory depicts.

World Systems Theory

Another perspective on global inequality is **world systems theory**, which was originally developed by sociologist Im-

These shoemakers in South Vietnam work for very low wages while contributing to the profits of multinational corporations in high-income countries. How does dependency theory explain this inequality? Why is this use of labor referred to as neocolonialism or economic imperialism? Are multinational corporations to blame for global inequality? How is Wallerstein's world systems theory different from dependency theory? How can the low-income country commodity chain hurt workers in high-income countries?

manual Wallerstein (1974, 1990). Like dependency theory, world systems theory emphasizes economic connections among countries. However, rather than dividing the world into rich and poor countries, world systems theory analyzes the global economy as an international network that is dominated by capitalism.

Initially, world systems theorists thought the global economy was composed of three levels: (1) the *core*, made up of high-income industrialized countries that profit most from worldwide production (e.g., Britain, the United States, Germany, and Japan); (2) the *semiperiphery*, made up of middle-income industrializing countries, which reap some profits from worldwide production, but which also generate profits for the core (e.g., China and Mexico); and (3) the *periphery*, made up of low-income countries that reap few of the profits from worldwide production but contribute to the profits of the core and semiperiphery (e.g., Pakistan and Honduras). This international network is both economic and political in nature, with alliances and conflicts having an impact on growth.

More recently, world systems theorists have focused on the production process itself, noting that the production of goods now typically takes place in stages that are completed in countries geographically dispersed throughout the globe. Consider once again the production of Nike athletic shoes. The shoes are designed in the United States. The materials from which the shoes are made come from countries as diverse as Mexico and Saudi Arabia. The shoes are sewn and assembled in Indonesian factories that are supervised by a Korean management firm. The finished products are then transported for sale to department stores in the United States, Great Britain, Europe, and Australia on cargo ships registered in Singapore.

World systems theorists call this production process a *commodity chain*, a network not just of countries, but of tasks that result in a finished product for sale. However, although each task is necessary to the completion of the product, some are more profitable than others. World systems theorists, therefore, speak of *core* and *peripheral activities*, rather than core and peripheral countries. Core activities are those that are the most profitable, whereas peripheral activities are less profitable or simply a source of profit. While many core activities, such as design and sales, take place in high-income countries such as the United States, peripheral activities, such as assembly, usually take place in low-income countries, such as Indonesia and Mexico. Some low-income and developing countries, such as Malaysia, have established themselves as centers for specific core activities, such as electronics assembly, which has helped them develop more rapidly than other low- and lower-middle income countries (Gereffi, 1992; Scott & Storper, 1986).

The Strengths and Weaknesses of World Systems Theory. World systems theory, even in its original form, responds to some of the simplicity of dependency theory by more accurately depicting the complexity of the interrelationships of the contemporary global economy. In its most recent form, world systems theory also captures the diversity in economic development throughout the world and offers a plausible explanation for why some countries in the same region, sometimes neighboring one another, may be experiencing dramatically different rates of development.

Nevertheless, world systems theory has its critics. Even though it takes into account that low-income countries can develop core activities, it still depicts the global network as largely one-way, with profits from low-income countries filling the coffers of multinational corporations based in high-income countries. But, say the critics, the populations of high-income countries do not necessarily benefit from the worldwide commodity chain. Workers in high-income countries lose good-paying jobs when factories are moved to low-income countries. Moreover, peripheral activities are not uniformly located in low-income and developing countries. Sweatshops can be found in virtually every major U.S. city, and peripheral tasks such as assembly take place in high-income European countries just as they do in low-income

Asian and Latin American ones (Applebaum & Gereffi, 1994).

R E F L E C T I N G O N

Explaining Global Inequality

1. What do you see as the strengths and weaknesses of Rostow's four stages of modernization? Give specific examples to support your views.
2. Dependency theorists have been accused of blaming capitalism for global inequality. Do you agree or disagree with this criticism?
3. What is a specific example of a commodity chain? Who in the chain benefits the most in your example?

WHAT DOES THE FUTURE HOLD?

Economic forecasters earn their living by predicting changes in the economy. As we've seen in this chapter, economic growth over the past several decades has not been balanced across the globe; some countries have witnessed tremendous growth, while others have not grown at all or have declined. This, we noted, has produced a widening gap between developed and developing countries. The Doing Sociology box gives you a chance to try some forecasting. But what do the expert economic forecasters say about the trend toward increasing global inequality?

According to economic forecasters, if the current pattern of uneven economic growth continues, the poorest countries of the world will grow even poorer, while the richest countries will become even richer. For example, by 2030, global production will triple. However, in sub-Saharan Africa, per capita income will fall to just $325 a year, whereas in high-income countries, average per capita income will approach $40,000. Many of the countries of East Asia are expected to catch up to the high-income countries in terms of per capita income by about 2050, but China's per capita income is not likely to approach that level until at least 2080 and India's will not reach the $40,000 per capita mark until about 2130—the twenty-second century (United Nations Development Programme, 1996).

Can the gap between rich and poor nations be narrowed rather than widened in the near future? A number of social scientists believe it is possible, but they stress that our goals must be reordered. Instead of concentrating on the *rate* of economic growth, social scientists and policy makers should pay more attention to the *quality* of economic growth. Economic growth that contributes to human development (improved health and education, a

DOING SOCIOLOGY

What Does the Future Hold?

The table below shows the 1995 population of the ten countries that are predicted to be the most populous countries in the world by 2015. The table also shows the Human Development Index (HDI) ranking of each country. Recall that the Human Development Index is a ranking system developed by the United Nations to measure how well individual countries are meeting the basic needs of their populations. It combines eight indicators, including consumer purchasing power, access to clean water and sanitation services, and school enrollments. Notice that only three countries—the United States, Brazil, and Russia—are in the top half of HDI rankings. The other seven countries, in fact, are well below the median.

Based on the trends we've discussed in this chapter, what are the implications of these data with respect to global inequality? What advice would you give to world leaders to help them prepare for the future and best meet the human needs of all the world's people?

Ten Most Populous Countries in 2015

Country	1995 Population (millions)	Projected Population 2015 (millions)	HDI Index Ranking
China	1,220.2	1,409.1	106
India	929.0	1,211.7	139
United States	267.1	310.8	4
Indonesia	197.5	251.8	96
Pakistan	136.3	224.5	138
Brazil	159.0	199.6	62
Nigeria	111.7	190.9	142
Bangladesh	118.2	162.7	147
Russia	148.5	138.1	72
Ethiopia	56.4	103.6	169

Sources: United Nations World Development Programme, *World Development Report 1998,* pp. 176–177, 200.

higher standard of living, and sustained natural resources) must become our top priority if we are to avoid a future world "gargantuan in its excesses and grotesque in its human and economic inequalities" (United Nations Development Programme, 1996, p. 8). If we continue to focus on the rate of economic growth, we will likely create a world where people are:

- *Jobless*—the economy grows, but there are few new or financially worthwhile employment opportunities. *Economic growth contributes to human development when it creates secure jobs that pay workers a living wage.*
- *Voiceless*—the economy grows, but political participation does not. *Economic growth contributes to human development when it is accompanied by democracy and political empowerment for all segments of the population.*
- *Rootless*—growth in the economy promotes the interests of dominant cultural groups within the population, but marginalizes or eliminates others. *Economic growth contributes to human development when cultural diversity is valued and governments are sensitive to the needs and interests of both dominant and minority groups.*
- *Futureless*—the economy grows, but through the destruction of natural resources needed for future generations. *Economic growth contributes to human development when it is accompanied by adequate conservation of natural resources, checks on environmental pollution, and greater access to usable land for poor people.*

- *Ruthless*—only the wealthiest segments of the population benefit, while everyone else struggles to survive. *Economic growth contributes to human development when all segments of the population share equitably in its benefits, and profits are used to finance basic social services for all* (United Nations Development Programme, 1996, pp. 2–4).

The final point on this list is related to another critical problem: gender inequality. Women and girls in low-income countries are the most disadvantaged segment of the most disadvantaged populations. Consequently, economic growth that contributes to *human* develop-

ment is economic growth that benefits women as well as men. We will take up the issue of gender inequality in Chapter 10.

R E F L E C T I N G   O N

What Does the Future Hold?

What strategies would you suggest for achieving the kind of development advocated by the United Nations?

 For useful resources for study and review, run Chapter 9 on your *Living Sociology* CD-ROM.

C O N N E C T I O N S

Global stratification and economic development	Review the definition and key indicators of social stratification in Chapter 8. How do the World Bank classifications of levels of economic development express the concept of social stratification? What standard-of-living indicators are used? In what sense do the World Bank classifications reflect the agenda of the richest countries? How is the United Nations measurement of poverty different?
Population and hunger	Preview the section on population in Chapter 19. What do Marx and Malthus predict about the relationship between population and hunger? What is the effect of economic development on population? Is overpopulation the principal cause of hunger and famines?
Infant mortality and life expectancy	Read the section on "Health and Economic Development" in Chapter 18 and see the tables on life expectancy and infant mortality in different countries. What are the characteristics of health care in low-income countries? How does global stratification relate to health, infant mortality, and life expectancy?
Education and literacy	Read the section on "Schools and Societies" in Chapter 16. What are the characteristics of education in low-income countries? How do economic development and global stratification relate to educational attainment and literacy?
Economic disadvantages of women	Review the status of women in different types of societies in Chapter 3. See also "Gender and Sexual Orientation in the Workplace" in Chapter 10. What are some economic disadvantages of women in low-income countries? How might a feminist sociologist explain these disadvantages?
Gender and health	Survey Chapter 18 for examples of how gender affects the social epidemiology of health and illness both within and among countries. What exactly is social epidemiology and how does it relate to global stratification in economic development?
Birth rates and population growth	See the sections on "Global Population Growth" and the tables on population growth in Chapter 19. What is a crude birth rate? What factors influence birth and death rates in a society? How are birth and death rates used to show a country's population pyramid? How do population pyramids reflect levels of economic development in different types of societies?

CONNECTIONS

Weber's *The Protestant Ethic and the Spirit of Capitalism*	Weber's contributions to sociology were introduced in Chapter 1. Read the section on "Conflict and Feminist Theories" of religion in Chapter 17. What might be some relationships between religion and global stratification? Also read "Max Weber on Religion and Social Change" in Chapter 17. What are some possible relationships between religion and social transformations?
Multinational corporations and the global economy	Review the discussion of corporations as "Formal Organizations" in Chapter 6, then read "The Postindustrial Age and the Global Economy" and "The Structure of the U.S. Economy" in Chapter 13. What roles can multinational corporations play in the global economy? In Chapter 14, find the discussion of the "Military-industrial complex." Based on this example, what impacts might multinational corporations have on global politics?

SUMMING UP CHAPTER 9

Global Stratification: An Overview

1. Stratification exists not only within a particular country, but also between countries. In stratifying countries, sociologists consider a country's wealth, status, and political power.
2. Typically, sociologists use the classification system developed by the World Bank to study global stratification. The World Bank stratification system is based on per capita gross national product and results in three strata: low-income or underdeveloped countries, middle-income countries (with two subdivisions—lower-middle and upper-middle), and high-income or industrial countries. To get a more complete picture of global stratification, however, sociologists also consider measures of work, population, health, and education, in addition to per capita GNP.
3. Global stratification may also be studied by dividing countries into income quintiles and comparing the distribution of income across quintiles for the four World Bank strata. This kind of analysis shows that, regardless of stratum, inequality between income quintiles is extreme. The gap between rich and poor is widest in lower-middle income countries, which, according to the theory of the Kuznets curve, is the result of the economic transition that such countries experience as they industrialize. However, major changes in the global economy and global economic growth in recent years cast the applicability of the Kuznets curve in doubt.

Poverty in Global Perspective

1. Because living standards vary dramatically from country to country, it is difficult to establish an international, monetary-based poverty line. Such measures assess income poverty, but, more recently, efforts to assess global poverty have focused on measures of human poverty. Income poverty and human poverty do not always coincide in a specific country.
2. Poverty is not equally distributed across population groups within a country. Throughout the world, females and children are at greater risk of poverty than males and adults. Gender and age are widely used as the bases for stratification within countries.

Explaining Global Inequality

1. One of the most popular explanations of global inequality is modernization theory, which focuses on the conditions necessary for a country to develop economically. One of the most important is economic culture: the system of values, beliefs, and traditions in which economic activities and institutions exist. Those countries that hold values of self-determination, a strong work ethic, and a future orientation typically welcome modernization and develop rapidly. Although modernization theory has done a good job of explaining economic development in many East Asian countries, it has been criticized for downplaying the role of structural factors in shaping culture and economic opportunities and for failing to recognize the importance of government regulation of the economy for promoting economic growth.
2. Dependency theory focuses on the relationship between wealthy countries and poor countries. Dependency theorists argue that the poverty of low-income countries is the result of the policies and practices that high-income countries pursue to amass an even greater share of global wealth. The major strength of dependency theory is its emphasis on the interconnectedness of the world community and some of the disadvantages of economic development for low-income countries. However, the theory has also been criticized for being too simplistic,

placing all the blame for global poverty on the shoulders of high-income countries and multinational corporations.

3. World systems theory emphasizes economic connections among countries, but focuses on the global economy as an international network dominated by capitalism. Currently, world systems theorists study how the production process itself is divided into stages, called a *commodity chain,* so that specific tasks are completed in geographically dispersed countries, with some countries profiting significantly more than others from their role in the process. World systems theory has been praised for depicting the complexity and diversity of interrelationships that make up the global economy. It has been criticized for depicting the process as one-way, even though the populations of high-income countries do not necessarily benefit from the worldwide commodity chain.

What Does the Future Hold?

1. According to economic forecasters, if current patterns of uneven economic growth continue, the world will become even more stratified; the poorest countries will grow even poorer, while the richest countries will become even richer.

KEY PEOPLE AND CONCEPTS

absolute poverty: the poor lack the basic resources necessary to sustain life

colonialism: the conquest of one country by another, resulting in the former ruling the latter, claiming its natural resources, and exploiting the population as cheap or slave labor

dependency theory: a theory that explains the poverty of low-income countries as the result of the policies and practices that high-income countries pursue to amass greater wealth while putting low-income countries in a position of relative dependency on them

economic culture: the system of values, beliefs, and traditions in which economic activities and economic institutions exist

global stratification: the ranking of the nations of the world in terms of wealth and political power and, to a lesser extent, prestige

high-income countries: industrial countries with an annual per capita GNP above US$9,656

human poverty: a measure used by the United Nations Development Programme to assess deprivation in three essential elements of life (longevity, knowledge [education], and a decent standard of living)

infant mortality: the number of deaths of children under one year of age per 1,000 live births

Kuznets curve: the theory that during the transitional stage of development from agriculture to industry, inequality will increase, but conditions will improve once industrialization is established

life expectancy at birth: the average number of years a person can expect to live after birth

lower-middle income countries: countries with an annual per capita GNP of between US$786 and US$3,125; also referred to as *developing countries*

low-income countries: countries with a per capita GNP of US$785 or less per year; also referred to as *underdeveloped countries*

modernization theory: a theory that focuses on the conditions that are necessary for a country to become economically developed—that is, fully modern

multinational corporations: large corporations that engage in production and marketing in numerous countries throughout the world

neocolonialism: the relationships between multinational corporations and low-income countries in which the economic power of the multinationals dominates low-income countries in ways similar to the political control previously exercised by foreign governments

per capita gross national product (per capita GNP): the total value of the goods and services produced in a country each year divided by the number of people in the country's population

relative poverty: the poor lack many of the resources available to the rest of the population, but nevertheless have the basic necessities of life

upper-middle income countries: countries with an annual per capita GNP between about US$3,126 and US$9,655 per year

world systems theory: a theory that emphasizes the interconnections of countries in the global capitalist production process, which results in an uneven distribution of profits across the countries depending on their participation in core or peripheral production activities

LEARNING MORE

Kurz, K. M., & Prather, C. J. (1995). *Improving the quality of life of girls.* New York: United Nations Children's Fund. A report prepared for the United Nations Children's Fund and the Association for Women in Development that looks at the intersecting inequalities of gender and age by examining current development programs and by suggesting alternative, more equitable development strategies.

Lappe, F. M., Schurman, R., & Danaher, K. (1987). *Betraying the national interest.* New York: Grove Press. A critical examination of how economic aid from high-income to low-income countries typically comes with strings attached and may even be used as a political weapon. Although the statistics are somewhat dated, the analysis continues to be relevant.

Lim, L. L. (Ed.). (1998). *The sex sector.* Geneva: International Labour Organization. An award-winning report by the International Labour Organization (ILO) on the economic and social factors that contribute to the mushrooming sex industry in Southeast Asia and the consequences for people there, especially women and children.

Thurow, L. C. (1996). *The future of capitalism.* New York: William Morrow and Company. A controversial analysis by a well-known economist who examines how particular events and factors, such as the collapse of communism and the rapid proliferation of technology, will affect the global economy of the future.

United Nations Development Programme. *Human development report.* New York: Oxford University Press. A valuable resource for anyone concerned with global inequality, this thorough analysis of economic changes worldwide is published each year and contains numerous tables and charts as well as insightful essays.

 Run Chapter 10 on your *Living Sociology* CD-ROM for interesting and informative activities, web links, videos, practice tests, and more.

Sex, Gender, and Sexual Orientation

C andles illuminate the old Episcopal church, and the smell of spring flowers fills the air. At the altar a woman and man exchange wedding vows, turn to face the congregation, and walk together down the aisle, smiling at the well-wishers who have come to celebrate this joyous occasion. Relatives and friends comment on the bride's beauty. Her mother and father, like many parents at their child's wedding, wonder where the time has gone. It seems like "only yesterday" that this child was born, though that day was much less happy than this one. You see, their child was born with an unusual condition known as *adrenogenital syndrome* or AGS. Adrenogenital syndrome occurs when the adrenal glands of the pregnant woman or her fetus malfunction, causing excessive exposure of the fetus to certain male hormones. If the fetus is genetically female, it will develop the internal reproductive organs of a female (ovaries, fallopian tubes, and a uterus), but when the baby is born, her genitals will appear masculine; the clitoris is enlarged and resembles a small penis. Because these children have normal internal reproductive organs and are often capable of having children, their external genitals are usually surgically redesigned to be consistent with their genetic sex. As these girls grow up, they also receive hormonal replacement therapy, so they experience normal female development at puberty. However, many researchers are interested in whether the excessive exposure to male hormones *in utero* affects AGS girls' femininity. Are they more likely to be tomboys? Do they have a difficult time developing intimate relationships with men?

Looking at our bride, one would have to answer no to both of these questions. But her story highlights an important distinction that sociologists and other scientists make when studying the behavior of women and men: the distinction between *sex* and *gender*. **Sex** refers to whether one is genetically male or female; it is biologically determined. **Gender,** in contrast, refers to the constellation of traits and behaviors that compose the categories *masculine* and *feminine;* gender is socially constructed. Central to this story also are two other sociological concepts. When researchers ask if an AGS girl is likely to be a tomboy, they are inquiring about her **gender identity,** the set of gendered characteristics that an individual adopts as an integral part of her or his self. And when researchers wonder whether an AGS girl will have difficulty developing intimate relationships with men, they are questioning her **sexual orientation,** the source of an individual's affectional preferences, sexual arousal, and sexual gratification. We will look at all of these issues in this chapter.

Later in the chapter, we will discuss differences in the behavior and experiences of women and men. A major issue of concern—one of heated debate—is the source of these differences. Let's begin, then, by looking at theoretical perspectives on gender, returning in the process to a more detailed discussion of AGS.

are certainly obvious and well known, but in our culture much is also made of personality and behavioral differences between women and men. "Everyone knows," for example, that men won't stop to ask for directions when they're lost; in fact, they rarely admit that they are lost. And "everyone knows" that women are sentimental, emotional romantics who cry at movies such as *You've Got Mail* or *Titanic.* Underlying these rather lighthearted characterizations, however, are firm beliefs in **gender stereotypes,** oversimplified descriptions of the supposedly "masculine male" and "feminine female." Most people conceive of these stereotypes in bipolar terms: A normal male lacks any feminine traits and a normal female lacks masculine traits (Deaux & Kite, 1987). Men are expected to be assertive, independent, and in control of their emotions, whereas women are expected to be passive, dependent, and emotional. Gender stereotypes are all-inclusive; every member of one sex is thought to share the characteristics that make up their respective gender stereotype. But to what extent do women and men actually conform to gender stereotypes? And what is the source of the sex differences we observe? Are behavioral differences, much like physical sex differences, innate? We will consider two sociological perspectives that diverge in fundamental ways in answering this question.

THEORETICAL PERSPECTIVES ON GENDER

It is hardly an earth-shattering observation to say that women and men are different. The physical differences

Sociobiology

In 1871, Charles Darwin wrote that the sexes can be distinguished on the basis of both primary and secondary sex characteristics. Primary sex characteristics are the genitals and reproductive organs, while secondary sex characteristics are other physical features such as amount of body hair and average height and weight. Darwin, though, included personality traits as secondary sex characteristics. For instance, "man is more courageous, pugnacious, and energetic than women, and has more inventive genius" (quoted in Hubbard, 1979, p. 19). For Darwin, these traits were as much the product of biology as genitals and body hair.

Today, more than a century later, we hear Darwin's words echoed in the **sociobiological perspective on gender,** which holds that the differences we observe in women's and men's personalities and behavior are directly traceable to differences in their physical makeup. There are many variations on this general theme that biological factors can be used to explain social phenomena. One that you are already familiar with is structural functionalism. In their analysis of gender, structural functionalists begin by highlighting what they consider the most significant physical differences between women and men. Men tend to be bigger and stronger than women, and women bear and nurse children. According to functionalists, these biological differences have led to the emergence of different **gender roles.** You'll recall from Chapter 6 that a social role consists of a set of behavioral requirements or expectations that the person who occupies the role is supposed to fulfill. Gender roles, then, refer to the behaviors that are prescribed for the female and male members of a society.

Functionalists maintain that for much of human history, women's reproductive role has dictated that their gender role should be domestic. Given that women bear and nurse children, it makes sense for them to remain at home to rear them. It follows then that if women are at home caring for children, they should assume other domestic duties as well. Their roles as childbearer, caregiver, and homemaker in turn reinforce their natural emotional capacity and ability for nurturing. In contrast, men's biology better suits them for the roles of economic provider and protector of the family. They are stronger not only physically, but also emotionally. They are more rational and better at problem solving.

This role division is functional for women and men and for society as a whole. In many ways, women's gender role reproduces society: by giving birth to new members, by teaching or socializing them to accept the culture's agreed-upon values and norms, and by providing men and children with affection and physical sustenance. Men's gender role ensures physical and financial security for the more vulnerable: women and children. It also allows the institutions of a society to function smoothly, since without the burden of childbearing and domestic tasks, men can devote their attention to the work world.

Some sociologists, however, raise two issues of concern that stem from functionalism's emphasis on gender

differences as *natural* phenomena deriving from human biology. First, the idea of gender differences as natural has been used to justify **gender inequality** or what is commonly called **sexism.** Gender inequality or sexism occurs when we differentially value people's traits or abilities on the basis of their sex and without regard for their attributes as individuals. Sexism, then, has both an *attitudinal* component and a *behavioral* component. The attitudinal component is **prejudice,** and the behavioral component is **discrimination.**

History is replete with examples of sexism. In the fifth century B.C.E. (Before the Common Era), for instance, the Chinese philosopher Confucius declared that while women are human beings, they are of a lower state than men (Peck, 1985). In 1873, Myra Bradwell was denied admission to the Illinois bar and the right to practice law because "the natural and proper timidity and delicacy which belong to the female sex evidently unfit it for many of the occupations of civil life" (quoted in Goldstein, 1979, p. 50). And more recently some scientists have argued that men inevitably outscore women on IQ tests because men's brains are slightly larger than women's brains (Blum, 1997). Thus, the structural functionalist idea of natural roles leads not only to sexism, but also to unequal access to resources. Moreover, even if biological factors are responsible for some personality and behavioral differences between women and men, *different* does not necessarily translate into *unequal.* The value attached to any difference between women and men is attached by society. In other words, it is up to society to decide that no one sex or gender is better than the other and that both deserve proportionate shares of society's resources, rewards, and opportunities.

Another serious consequence of portraying masculinity and femininity as natural is that *natural* suggests *immutability.* The implicit message is that if we find society's definitions of masculinity and femininity stifling, unfair, or unsuitable to us, any efforts to change the definitions will have no behavioral effects. The definitions are natural and therefore unchangeable. Moreover, from this perspective, men and women are opposites: What men are, women are not, and efforts to alter this natural dichotomy are at best futile or possibly harmful. But, in fact, gender is quite amenable to change, and what constitutes masculinity and femininity has varied tremendously throughout history and across cultures. Before we examine these data, let's first look at an alternative theoretical perspective.

Feminist Sociology

In contrast to the sociobiological model is the **feminist sociology of gender** model, and just as there are varieties of sociobiology, so too there are different strains of feminism within sociology (Delmar, 1986; Lorber, 1998).

Nevertheless, virtually all feminist-identified perspectives share several points, and these will be our focus here.

The feminist perspective acknowledges the importance of both biology and social learning in the acquisition of gender. However, feminist sociologists stress that it is virtually impossible to separate out the precise influence of biology because the learning process begins immediately after birth. They also emphasize the complex interrelation between biological and cultural factors. Our biology, they tell us, does not generate "specific bits and pieces" of our bodies, but rather provides the codes for a wide range of physical forms within a vast array of environmental conditions. Consequently, even when a specific trait has a biological basis, environmental intervention can suppress or modify it (Gould, 1981; Hubbard & Wald, 1993). For example, it is widely believed that men are more aggressive than women because they secrete more testosterone, a hormone that in laboratory tests has been linked with aggression. However, recent research indicates that the relationship between testosterone levels and aggression may be the opposite of what scientists traditionally thought—that is, increased aggressiveness raises testosterone levels instead of the other way around. In one study, for instance, researchers found that, following tennis matches, testosterone levels rose in young men who had won decisively and dropped in those who had lost (Booth et al., 1989; Mazur & Lamb, 1980). Such studies are leading scientists to reframe their understanding of the relationship between testosterone and aggression, but the findings also illustrate how biology can be affected by social events.

The feminist perspective, then, begins with the assumption that gender is essentially socially created, rather than innately determined. Feminists view gender, in part, as a set of social expectations that is reproduced and transmitted through the process of socialization. In this way, the expectations become fundamental components of our personalities.

Feminists also recognize that a complete comprehension of gender requires more than understanding this learning process. What we learn is itself a social product that is generated within the context of a particular social structure, the society's **sex/gender system.** Sex/gender systems vary historically and cross culturally, but each system includes at least three interrelated components:

1. the social construction of gender categories on the basis of biological sex,
2. a sexual division of labor in which specific tasks are allocated on the basis of sex, and
3. the social regulation of sexuality through positive and negative sanctions of particular forms of sexual expression (Rubin, 1975; Thorne, 1982).

Of special concern are the ways in which a sex/gender system operates as a system of **social stratification;** that is,

the extent to which women and men, and the traits and behaviors respectively associated with them, are valued unequally in a society. Given that social institutions are imbued with the power to reward and punish—to bestow privileges as well as impose obligations and restrictions—a sex/gender system has a profound impact on the lives and life chances of women and men. We have seen numerous examples of this throughout the text so far. Consider, for instance, the data presented in Chapter 9 showing that although women make up more than 50 percent of the world's population and perform nearly two-thirds of all work hours, they receive significantly less income, own less property, have lower levels of education, and often have poorer health and nutritional status than men.

These startling statistics reflect the fact that most women and men worldwide live in societies with patriarchal sex/gender systems. A **patriarchy** is a sex/gender system in which men dominate women, and anything considered masculine is more highly valued than anything considered feminine. In contrast, a **matriarchy** is a sex/gender system in which women dominate men, and anything considered feminine is more highly valued than anything considered masculine. There is disagreement over whether genuine matriarchal societies have ever existed (see, for example, Davis-Kimball, 1997; O'Kelly & Carney, 1986; Wilford, 1997), yet, as we will see shortly, patriarchy is by no means universal.

Feminist sociologists are fundamentally concerned with the differential consequences of particular social arrangements and social constructions of gender in the everyday lives of women and men. Feminists study sexism. At the same time, however, they recognize that the impact of sexism is not the same for all groups of women and men. Instead, the effects of gender inequality may be worsened by other types of inequality, including inequality based on race and ethnicity, age, sexual orientation, and physical ability/disability. It is more difficult, for example, to be a woman than a man in the United States, and more difficult still to be an African American woman than a White American woman, but the most difficult is to be a poor African American woman. Similarly, just as not all women are equally disadvantaged, not all men benefit equally from patriarchy because of the intersection of sexism, racism, classism, and other inequalities.

Finally, just as structural functionalism and other sociobiological theories have implications for social change, so does feminist sociology. Unlike sociobiologists, though, feminist sociologists are advocates of social change. They look for ways to eradicate gender inequality and change those aspects of our social constructions of gender that are harmful or destructive.

We'll return to the topic of feminist activism later in the chapter. Now, however, let's examine some of the empirical research that speaks to the issue of the biological versus social origins of gender.

Both of these families operated in social contexts based on a patriarchal tradition, although the photo of the contemporary American family suggests greater gender equality. What are some defining characteristics of a patriarchal family? Sex/gender systems vary historically and cross-culturally, but each system includes at least three interrelated components. What are they?

REFLECTING ON

Theoretical Perspectives on Gender

1. How is gender a product of the interaction between biology and culture? What is the significance of this interaction for explaining human social behavior? Can you think of an example to illustrate this point?
2. Have you ever experienced or witnessed sexism? What happened, and how did you feel about it?

SEX AND GENDER: THE INTERACTION OF NATURE AND ENVIRONMENT

Empirical research on the biological and social roots of gender comes from a rich variety of sources. We'll begin by returning to the story that opened this chapter to discuss research on AGS, a similar prenatal condition (androgen insensitive syndrome), and an unusual case involving identical twins. Based on this data, we'll draw some conclusions on the interaction of nature and environment in determining sex and gender. Finally, we'll look at cross-cultural research and consider studies of men's and women's brains.

What Does AGS Teach Us about Gender?

The story that opened this chapter described a condition called **adrenogenital syndrome** or **AGS,** which occurs

when the adrenal glands of a pregnant woman or her fetus malfunction, exposing the fetus to excessive amounts of male hormones. We noted that researchers are interested in whether AGS girls' *in utero* exposure to an excess of male hormones affects their gender identities or behavior. In most of these studies, girls who were receiving medical treatment for AGS or related health problems were questioned about such things as clothing, toy, and playmate preferences as well as their future goals. In comparing the AGS girls' responses with those of other girls similar in age and other social characteristics but without AGS, many researchers have found some striking differences between the two groups. For one thing, AGS girls describe themselves (and are described by their parents) as tomboys more often than normal girls are, and they prefer slacks and shorts over dresses and skirts. They are also more likely to prefer toys considered more for boys (trucks, building blocks), to prefer boys as playmates, and to enjoy rough-and-tumble play (Berenbaum & Hines, 1992; Dittman et al., 1990a, 1990b). Nevertheless, most researchers report that AGS girls are not more physically aggressive than normal girls, and that older AGS girls express a desire for romance, marriage, and motherhood in their futures (Baker, 1980; Money & Ehrhardt, 1972).

In a follow-up study with twelve AGS women who had been studied as adolescents, Money and Matthews (1982) reported that four had married and none showed any difficulty in establishing relationships with men. Other researchers, however, have noted that AGS women begin dating and engaging in sexual relations later than non-AGS women (Hurtig & Rosenthal, 1987), and that some report dreams or fantasies involving sexual relations with women as well as men (Ehrhardt & Meyer-Bahlburg, 1981). It may be that a delay in dating and sexual behavior is related to the extensive hormonal replacement therapy that these women undergo. In addition, there is no evidence that they have sexual dreams or fantasies involving same-sex partners more often than non-AGS heterosexual women.

Adrenogenital syndrome occurs when girls are exposed to male hormones, but what happens if a boy, who is supposed to be exposed to such hormones, is not? **Androgen-insensitive syndrome** is the condition that results when a genetically male fetus is unaffected by the male hormones to which it is exposed because its body is insensitive to them. When the baby is born, it is genetically a normal male, but externally, it has female genitals and internally undescended testes. Because androgen-insensitive individuals look like girls at birth, they are typically raised as girls by their parents. But do their genes predispose them to behave like boys? According to researchers, androgen-insensitive individuals are as feminine (and sometimes more feminine) than genetically normal females. In one study, for example, androgen-insensitive subjects expressed as strong an interest in dolls, dresses, housewifery, and motherhood as genetically normal girls who were identical in terms of age, race, social class, and IQ (Baker, 1980; Brooks-Gunn & Matthews, 1979; Money & Ehrhardt, 1972).

Finally, consider an unusual case of a boy initially studied by John Money and his colleagues at the Johns Hopkins University Gender Identity Clinic in Baltimore, Maryland. The boy, who, along with an identical twin brother, was born a chromosomally and physically normal male, had his penis almost completely destroyed when he was eight months old as a doctor tried to repair his foreskin. In consultation with physicians, the parents decided in favor of sex reassignment. At seventeen months, the boy was surgically reconstructed as a girl and lifelong hormone replacement therapy was planned. Money and his colleagues reported in 1973 that the reassigned twin had been "successfully" socialized as a girl. She preferred to wear dresses rather than slacks, had feminine toy and play preferences, and, in contrast to her brother, was neat, clean, and enjoyed helping with housework. However, a later study of the reassigned twin found that at about age twelve she began to experience serious emotional problems related to her sex and by age fourteen she refused to continue living as a girl. Some researchers claim that the girl's rebellion is proof that sexual identity is innate, but others point out that the girl's emotional difficulties stem at least in part from the fact that at puberty she developed a rather masculine appearance and was teased mercilessly by her peers because of it. Eventually, the young woman chose to live as a man and had a penis surgically constructed. Today, he is married and is the adoptive father of his wife's children from her previous marriage (Diamond & Sigmundson, 1997).

What do these cases teach us about gender? First, there is a lesson to be learned about the relationship of genetics and hormones to gender. Apparently, the development of a masculine or feminine gender identity is independent of one's genes or hormones. Although biology clearly plays a role in who we are as women and men, the components of an individual's sex (genes, hormones, reproductive organs, genitals) do not necessarily coincide with one's gender. What appears to be more important in the acquisition of gender is the sex our parents and others assign to us and use as a guide in rearing and interacting with us.

Even more importantly, these cases highlight the fact that neither sex nor gender is dichotomous. When we speak of sex, we may be referring to genetic sex, hormonal sex, reproductive sex, or genital sex. Although for most individuals these are consistent with the category male or the category female, the research we just discussed vividly shows that they can sometimes be inconsistent. Therefore, difficult as it may be for us, we should stop thinking of sex as a unidimensional characteristic with dichotomous attributes. Similarly, gender—what we generally call *masculinity* and *femininity*—is also far from being an either/or phenomenon. Gender includes a broad spectrum of attitudes, behaviors, and social expectations that we acquire during our lifetimes, through interactions with one another and experiences in various environments. Cross-cultural research underscores these points, but many researchers continue to search for the biological origins of gender, as the Intersecting Inequalities box shows.

Cross-Cultural Research

More than sixty years ago, the pioneering anthropologist Margaret Mead (1901–1978) did field research with three societies in New Guinea, an island in the South Pacific. Some of Mead's most significant findings concerned gender. For example, in one society, men were expected to be timid and passive, and women were aggressive and competitive. In another, both men and women were expected to be gentle and nurturant (Mead, 1935). Since Mead's work was published, numerous other cross-cultural studies have been done that reveal a rich assortment of gender relations throughout the world.

Every known society has a division of labor by sex (and also by age). However, what is considered men's work versus what is considered women's work varies dramatically from society to society. In some cultures, for instance, women build the houses; in others (including our own), this is men's work. In most societies, women do the cooking, but there are societies in which this is typically men's responsibility. Although there are very few societies

INTERSECTING INEQUALITIES

Do Women and Men Have Different Brains?

The notion that men and women have different brains is an old one. Nineteenth-century scientists believed that women were less intelligent than men because their brains were smaller. When it was pointed out that elephants should therefore be more intelligent than men, given the relative size of their brains, the argument was quickly modified. It was subsequently argued that the best estimate of intelligence could be obtained by dividing brain size by body weight. However, this hypothesis, too, was abandoned when it was discovered that by this measure women were more intelligent than men (Fausto-Sterling, 1985; Harrington, 1987). Today, the debate has simply changed form. The main issue now centers on how men's and women's brains are organized. It is hypothesized that the differential organization of the brain is not only the source of behavioral differences between women and men, but may also be responsible for the development of sexual orientation.

New Findings on Women's Brains

Research with human subjects has shown that the corpus collosum (the mass of tissue and nerve fibers that connect the two hemispheres of the brain) is as much as 23 percent larger in women than in men (Allen & Gorski, 1992). Scientists hypothesize that this may allow greater communication between the brain's two halves or hemi-

spheres. This would help to explain why women recover from strokes more quickly than men do, and why they are less likely to suffer certain types of brain damage (Witelson, 1989). Some researchers also think that these findings may also explain why women do better than men on tests of verbal ability and emotional expression, since verbal skills have been associated with communication between hemispheres. In one study, for instance, researchers found that women use both hemispheres of the brain when completing a rhyming task, thereby using a wider range of information to accomplish the task, while men use only the left hemisphere (Blum, 1997; Shaywitz et al., 1995). However, while the greater communication between the left and right hemispheres of women's brains may facilitate their verbal skills, it may also inhibit their visual-spatial skills. Men score higher on visual-spatial tests than women do (Gorman, 1992).

New Findings on Homosexuals' Brains

Neuroscientist Simon LeVay (1991) studied the post-mortem tissue of the brains of six women and sixteen men that he presumed had been heterosexual, and the tissue of nineteen men who had been homosexual. He found that one node of the anterior hypothalmus (an area of the brain that may affect sexual behavior) was three times larger

in the heterosexual men than in the homosexual men. The nodes of the homosexual men's hypothalmuses were closer in size to the ones found in the heterosexual women's brains.

In 1995, researchers in the Netherlands reported they had studied the brains of homosexual men, heterosexual women and men, and transsexuals (individuals who had undergone surgery and hormone treatments to change their sex), and had found significant size differences in a region of the hypothalmus for these groups. Men's hypothalmus is about 50 percent larger than women's hypothalmus, but 60 percent larger than the hypothalmuses of male-to-female transsexuals. The scientists who conducted this research think that the size of the hypothalmus is related to the feeling of being a man or a woman (Swaab et al., 1995). However, other scientists caution that the hormone treatments transsexuals receive may affect the size of their hypothalmus, and they also question whether findings obtained from such small samples (Swaab and his colleagues studied the brains of only six transsexuals; LeVay examined a total of just forty-one brains) are generalizable. Still other scientists say that the size of the hypothalmus may change as a result of a person's behavior during critical periods of the life course such as adolescence. This point again reminds us that social behavior can affect biology, just as biology can influence social behavior.

---

in which women do metalworking, lumbering, or hunt large land animals, there are exceptions. For example, among the Agta of the Philippines, women hunt deer and wild pigs with knives and bows and arrows (Estioko-Griffin, 1986). In most cases, though, women's hunting does not involve spears, bows and arrows, or heavy clubs (Harris, 1993). It has also been argued by some researchers that in virtually all societies men hold a monopoly on physical violence (see Harris, 1993; Konner, 1982), but others have reported on female warriors and soldiers (see

Davis-Kimball, 1997; McKinley, 1996; Sacks, 1979). Considerable evidence also exists that women may behave as aggressively as men when competitiveness and verbal abusiveness are included as measures of aggression (Bjorkqvist, 1994; Burbank, 1994; Lepowsky, 1994).

Particularly interesting, however, are gender relations in contemporary hunting and gathering societies. First, there is great diversity in the gender relations of these societies. Also, gender relations are usually very egalitarian. Let's take a closer look.

How does cross-cultural research, such as Margaret Mead's classic work in New Guinea and other places, inform our understanding of sex, gender, and sexual orientation? What are some examples of cross-cultural comparisons that help explain gendered behavior as a result of cultural construction rather than biological determinism?

Gender Relations in Contemporary Hunting and Gathering Societies.

As we discussed in Chapter 3, members of hunting and gathering societies meet their survival needs by hunting game (and often by fishing) and by gathering vegetation and other types of food from their environment. Just who performs each task, however, varies from society to society. In the pattern most frequently observed, men hunt large animals and go deep-sea fishing if the opportunity exists, while women take primary responsibility for gathering, hunting small animals, food preparation, home building, and child care (O'Kelly & Carney, 1986). In most societies, though, a clear division of labor by sex exists in principle, but in practice there is actually considerable overlap in what women and men do, and there are "crossovers in role" without shame or anxiety for either women or men (Gilmore, 1990).

O'Kelly and Carney (1986, p. 12–21) have identified six different patterns of the gendered division of labor among hunting and gathering societies:

1. men hunt, women process the catch;
2. men hunt, women gather;
3. men hunt, men and women gather;
4. men hunt and fish, women hunt and gather;
5. men and women independently hunt, fish, and gather;
6. men and women communally hunt and gather.

In the first pattern, which is common among Eskimo groups, meat and fish are the dietary staples, and men are the chief food providers. This puts women at a disadvantage to men because they must depend on men for food as well as for goods obtained through trade with non-Eskimos. Consequently, men in these societies have more power and prestige than women, but this does not mean that women are powerless or that women's work is considered unimportant. Women can secure power and prestige as shamans, and elderly women can act as political and military advisors. What is more, women are responsible for making the clothing and much of the equipment men need to hunt and fish (O'Kelly & Carney, 1986). As a result, "the skills of women are as indispensable to survival as those of men, and they are so perceived by men" (Sacks, 1979, p. 89).

Despite the complementarity of gendered behaviors in hunting and gathering societies of this first type, they are the least egalitarian of all hunter-gatherers. Women who live in societies characterized by one of the other five patterns take a more direct and active role in food acquisition, which in turn affords them more equal access to their societies' resources and rewards. Among the !Kung bush-living people of the Kalahari Desert, for example, women provide from 60 to 80 percent of the society's food through their gathering activities. The !Kung division of labor conforms to the second type on our list, but the game hunted by men is a much less dependable food source than the plant and small animal food obtained by women. Therefore, though the !Kung have a clear division of labor by sex, it is not rigidly adhered to and men and women sometimes do one another's chores without shame or embarrassment. Child care is considered the responsibility of both parents, and boys and girls generally are treated alike as they grow up. !Kung child-rearing practices are very relaxed, like !Kung social relations in general. Among the !Kung, aggressive behavior on the part of men or women is discouraged, and rarely is there organized armed conflict (Draper, 1975; Harris, 1993; Shostak, 1981). !Kung boys are taught early how to kill large animals, but no one is taught to kill other people (Harris, 1993).

Egalitarian gender relations like the !Kung's are also characteristic of the other types of hunting–gathering societies remaining on our list. In these societies, one sex is not intrinsically valued over the other. Rather, an individual wins respect and influence in the community based on his *or her* contribution to the group's well-being (Bleier, 1984).

While egalitarian gender relations are more common in hunting-gathering societies, they are found in other types of societies as well. The horticultural society of Vanatinai (a small island southeast of mainland Papua New Guinea) is one example (Lepowsky, 1990). Both Vanatinai women and men plant, tend, and harvest garden crops. Hunting with spears is a male activity, but women also hunt by trapping game. Women have primary responsibility for caring for children, but men share this task quite willingly. Members of both sexes learn and practice magic; participate in warfare, peacemaking, and community decision making; and go on sailing expeditions in search of ceremonial valuables. In short, Vanatinai society "offers every adult, regardless of sex or kin group, the opportunity of excelling at prestigious activities" (Lepowsky, 1990, p. 178).

Several important lessons can be learned from these cross-cultural data. First, they clearly show that our own society's definitions of masculinity and femininity are not cultural universals. Gender is constructed very differently in other societies, and in some societies, gender relations are highly egalitarian.

Second, the studies show that a gendered division of labor does not necessarily produce gender inequality. The key intervening variable is the *value* that the members of a society attach to a particular role or task. In our society, the work women do is typically considered less important than the work men do. But in the societies we just discussed, women are considered "essential partners" in the economy and in decision making, even though women and men may be responsible for different tasks or have different spheres of influence (Miller, 1993; O'Kelly & Carney, 1986).

A third point concerns women's capacity to bear children. Earlier in the chapter we said that some theorists believe women's reproductive role prevents them from fully participating in other activities, such as providing for their families. But in the cross-cultural studies reviewed in this section, women are not automatically excluded from certain activities because they bear children. Nor are men automatically excluded from childrearing simply because they cannot bear children. Childbearing and childrearing do not isolate mothers in the home, as is frequently the case in societies like our own. Survival tasks are carried out by a broader range of people, both male and female, and children are integrated early into the ongoing life of the community. At the same time, in these societies motherhood adds status, giving women greater say in decision making because they are considered mature adults after giving birth (Gailey, 1987).

It appears, then, that nonbiological factors—including environmental resources, size of the group, economy, and ideology—play at least as important a part, if not more important, than biological factors in determining what a society defines as masculine and feminine. This point is made even clearer when we consider examples of multiple genders.

Multiple Genders. Our discussions of prenatal conditions and gender roles in hunting and gathering and horticultural societies call into question the notion of gender as an either/or phenomenon. Indeed, in some societies there are three genders, and in others, four. The *berdache* of some Asian, South Pacific, and North American Indian societies are excellent examples. *Berdaches* are in-

dividuals who adopt the gender behavior ascribed to members of the opposite sex. While women may become *berdaches,* most of the research that has been conducted has focused on men who chose to be *berdaches.*

Berdaches live, work, and dress as members of the opposite sex, although they often specialize in tasks associated with both sexes (Roscoe, 1991; 1998; Whitehead, 1981; Williams, 1986). The Mohave, for instance, allowed men and women to cross genders. Boys who showed a preference for feminine toys and clothing would undergo an initiation ceremony at puberty to become *alyha.* As *alyha,* they adopted feminine names, painted their faces as women did, performed female tasks, and married men. When they married, *alyha* pretended to menstruate by cutting their upper thighs. They also simulated pregnancy. After the appropriate gestation period, they would drink a drug that caused "labor pains" and pretend to give birth to a stillborn child. When a Mohave

In what special social contexts do men and women in the United States adopt the behavior and dress ascribed to members of the opposite sex? How are they the same and different from Mohave or Zuni berdaches or from this female impersonator in India? In what way can there be multiple genders? In what way can gender be viewed as a process?

infant is stillborn, it is customary for the mother to bury it, so the return of the *alyha* to the community without a child is explained in this way (Martin & Voorhies, 1975).

A Mohave female who wished to pursue a masculine lifestyle underwent an initiation ceremony to become a *hwame*. *Hwame* dressed and lived much like men; they hunted, farmed, and became shamans, although they were not permitted to assume leadership positions or participate in warfare. They did, though, assume paternal responsibility for children; some women, in fact, became *hwame* after they had children. Most importantly, however, neither *hwame* nor *alyha* were considered abnormal or deviant within their cultures (Martin & Voorhies, 1975).

Other examples of gender crossing can be found in other Native American societies, including the Zuni, Diné, and Crow tribes (Roscoe, 1998); in Tahitian culture (Gilmore, 1990); among the Omani Muslims (Wikan, 1984); and with the Hijras of India (Nanda, 1990). However, there are also cultures in which gender is regarded as a *process* rather than a stable social category. To understand this better, consider the Hua of Papua New Guinea.

Among the Hua, gender is perceived as changing throughout an individual's life. The Hua bestow high status on masculine people, but view them as physically weak and vulnerable. Feminine people are regarded as invulnerable, but polluted. When children are born, they are all at least partially feminine because the Hua believe that women transfer some of their own femininity to their offspring. Thus, the more children a woman has, the more femininity she loses. After three births, she is no longer considered polluted. She may participate in the discussions and rituals of men and share their higher status and authority, but she must also follow their diet and sanitation customs since she is now more vulnerable.

Hua men, meanwhile, gradually lose their masculinity by imparting it to young boys in growth rituals. Thus, with each succeeding growth ritual, they become more physically invulnerable, but also more polluted. Consequently, old men work in the fields with young women and have little social authority. Among the Hua, then, gender is only indirectly related to sex, and it changes over time and can be transmitted from one person to another. "The process of engendering is lifelong, and through it males and females shed the gender they were born with and acquire the opposite characteristics" (Gailey, 1987, p. 36; see also Meigs, 1990).

These examples of multiple genders illuminate the fluidity of gender as well as the creativity that humans bring to the process of social organization. Our biology provides us with only very broad boundaries of the possible, out of which we craft our social reality, including our constructions of gender. However, these examples also raise questions about the origins of sexual orientation, the topic we will take up next.

REFLECTING ON

Sex and Gender: The Interaction of Nature and Environment

1. What social factors might contribute to masculinization in AGS girls?
2. How would a sociologist respond to the claim that sex, unlike gender, is relatively stable because an individual is either a male or a female?
3. What factors appear to contribute to the formation of egalitarian gender relations in some societies?
4. What does it mean to say that gender is a process? Give an example of this process from your own experience or observation.

SEXUAL ORIENTATION

Earlier we defined *sexual orientation* as the source of an individual's affectional preferences, sexual arousal, and sexual gratification. As with sex and gender, we also tend to think of sexual orientation as a dichotomous category with two attributes, *heterosexuality* and *homosexuality*. **Heterosexuality** is a sexual orientation in which the source of an individual's affectional preferences, sexual arousal, and sexual gratification are persons of the sex opposite that of the individual. Heterosexuals are sometimes also referred to as *straight*. **Homosexuality** is a sexual orientation in which the source of an individual's affectional preferences, sexual arousal, and sexual gratification are persons of the same sex as the individual. The term *gay* is sometimes used in reference to both men and women who are homosexual, though usually it refers to just homosexual men; homosexual women are usually referred to as *lesbians*.

Again, however, despite our tendency to think in either/or terms, research indicates that sexual orientation is more complex. For one thing, there are individuals who are sexually and affectionally attracted to members of both sexes. This sexual orientation is called **bisexuality,** and it may be expressed in various ways. For example, bisexuals may have affectional or sexual relationships with women and men simultaneously, or their relationships may be sequential—at one time with someone of the same sex, another time with someone of the opposite sex (Kelly, 1996).

Research also shows, however, that individuals who self-identify as heterosexual or homosexual are also more diverse than these labels may imply. For example, one recent study, the National Health and Social Life Survey (NHSLS), asked people who and what they find sexually attractive, the kinds of sexual behaviors in which they actually engage, and how they identify themselves in terms of sexual orientation. The researchers found that more people express sexual attraction to members of their same sex or both sexes than actually act on that attraction or self-identify as homosexual or bisexual (Laumann et al., 1994). Research also indicates that people may change their sexual behavior throughout their lives, making it difficult at best to pin specific sexual orientation labels on them (Michael et al., 1994).

For these reasons, and also because homosexuality and bisexuality are considered deviant in our society, it is difficult to determine what percentage of the U.S. population is gay, lesbian, or bisexual. Only a small percentage of the population self-identifies as exclusively homosexual, although researchers still disagree over precisely what that percentage might be. Since the 1940s, the accepted figure has been 10 percent, but research reported in the 1990s puts the estimate considerably lower—in some studies as low as 1 percent, in others as high as 5 percent, but in most slightly above 3 percent for women and 4 percent for men (Barringer, 1993). Research in Great Britain and France shows similar findings (Waite, 1992).

Researchers also disagree about how sexual orientation develops. As with gender, the dispute revolves primarily around the relative contributions of biology and culture.

The Biological Basis of Sexual Orientation

Research involving extensive interviews with gays and lesbians shows that most were aware of their sexual orientation prior to adolescence, and had heterosexual experiences but found them unsatisfying. They also reported that their parents played little or no part in the development of their sexual orientation (Bell et al., 1981). Based on such findings, researchers speculate that sexual orientation may have biological origins, perhaps hormonal, genetic, or physiological (resulting from the way the brain is organized or structured; see the Intersecting Inequalities feature). Until the early 1990s, however, there was little empirical evidence to support such a view. In the 1990s, a number of studies received widespread attention because they provided strong evidence of a biological basis for sexual orientation. Let's consider the hormonal and genetic studies.

There are two points at which hormones can affect sexual orientation: *in utero* and at adolescence. We discussed much of the data on effects of hormones *in utero* when we reviewed the research on prenatal conditions. There is currently little evidence indicating that exposure to particular hormones before birth predisposes an individual to a specific sexual orientation, although some researchers are testing the hypothesis that a gene or set of genes triggers prenatal hormonal secretions that organize the brain in such a way that a person is later at-

These males are self-identified as gay and resist being stigmatized or discriminated against because of their sexual orientation. How did they develop their sexual orientation as individuals? What is the biological basis? What roles do culture and socialization play? What are some examples of the effects of norms and sanctions on individuals' expressions of their sexual orientation?

tracted to the opposite or same sex (Blum, 1997; Macke et al., 1993). During adolescence, the production of hormones associated with sexual behavior increases, which has led some researchers to hypothesize that homosexuality and bisexuality may result from an over- or underproduction of hormones or from hormonal imbalances. Again, however, there is little empirical evidence at this time to support this idea (McWhirter, 1993).

Research on genetics and sexual orientation shows more promise, particularly studies on the sexual orientation of siblings and other relatives in a family. In one study, researchers compared the sexual orientations of twin brothers with the sexual orientations of genetically unrelated siblings (siblings by adoption), and found that if one identical twin is homosexual, the probability that the other is also homosexual is almost five times higher than if the pair were adopted. Results are similar in studies of lesbians and their siblings (Bailey & Pillard, 1991; 1993; Bailey et al., see also Hu et al., 1995).

Research by geneticist Dean Hamer has also been widely cited in support of a genetic theory of sexual orientation. Hamer and his colleagues studied forty-four pairs of homosexual brothers and found that thirty-three of the pairs shared a unique piece of the X chromosome. Moreover, these men were significantly more likely to have gay male relatives on their mother's side of the family, providing further evidence of a genetic link to sexual orientation since men receive the X chromosome from their mothers only (Hamer & Copeland, 1994; Hamer et al., 1993).

Needless to say, twin studies and Hamer's findings have generated a storm of controversy over whether sexual orientation is innate. One reason is that research on sexual orientation in our society carries not merely scientific implications, but also political and moral ones. Some worry, therefore, that findings supporting a genetic basis for sexual orientation could lead to interventionist strategies such as selective abortion of fetuses identified as carrying the "gay gene" or genetic engineering to eliminate the gene—and homosexuality—altogether (Zicklin, 1992). Keep in mind, though, that while these findings are provocative, they are hardly definitive. Most suffer from serious methodological flaws, such as sampling problems, and none has successfully *proven* a genetic basis for sexual orientation. Some scientists report that they have been unable to replicate the findings of these studies in subsequent research (Blum, 1997; Rice et al., 1999; Risch et al., 1993; Spanier, 1995). At best, this research suggests that sexual orientation may have a genetic component, as with most other human traits. However, as we have seen repeatedly in this text, how a particular trait is expressed—indeed, whether it finds expression at all—depends on a wide array of factors, most of which are social.

Culture and Sexual Orientation

Most sociologists do not deny that biology plays a part in sexual orientation, but they maintain that the way sexual and affectional preferences are manifested is strongly influenced by social norms and social learning experiences. In other words, even if sexual orientation has a biological foundation, like other dimensions of human personality and behavior, the way it is expressed is determined more by cultural and environmental factors than by biological dictates (Kitzinger, 1995).

Consider, for example, historical data. Kelly (1995) reports that in medieval Europe, sexual attraction and activities were viewed as independent of marriage and parenthood. People married and had children because it was every citizen's duty, while sexual expression only became an issue if it interfered with one's duties to the state or if it was in some way abusive. One's choice of sexual partners was not considered a reflection of some inherent trait, and people were not labeled as either homosexual or heterosexual. Rather, one's options for sexual expression were largely determined by such factors as age, social class, and prestige (see also Boswell, 1990).

Cross-cultural research also highlights the influence of social factors on sexual orientation. We have already discussed studies of *berdaches,* which show that in some societies women and men assume the dress and roles, including sexual roles, of members of the opposite sex without being labeled abnormal or deviant. In other societies, homosexual sex, especially among males, is looked on favorably. In some societies in Melanesia (in the South Pacific), boys are not only expected, but encouraged to have sex with older men, since it is believed that receiving semen makes the boys stronger and more virile. When these boys marry, they must engage only in heterosexual sex, though some continue to have sexual relationships with other men. Similarly, in some Hindu societies, males are expected to marry twice, first to another male and then to a woman. Both relationships are considered equally important in providing security and gratification, and both are expected to be enduring (Hopcke et al., 1994; Kelly, 1995).

In short, the social and biological research on sexual orientation shows the interconnectedness of nature and culture. Certainly, the findings we have examined here caution against ignoring either biology or environment in understanding complex human behavior. Instead, these studies on sexual orientation should prompt more research into the ways that culture and human free will impact on biology and vice versa.

REFLECTING ON

Sexual Orientation

1. What kinds of difficulties do researchers encounter when studying sexual orientation? How might these difficulties affect the outcome of their research?
2. What social factors might explain the findings from the twin studies discussed in this chapter?
3. What is the sociobiological explanation of sexual orientation? How do historical and cross-cultural data challenge this explanation?
4. How might biological and cultural explanations be integrated in a unified theory of sexual orientation?

GENDER AND SEXUAL ORIENTATION AS SYSTEMS OF STRATIFICATION

You learned in Chapters 8 and 9 that stratification is a system of ranking people. We saw how people are ranked, and therefore given differential access to societal rewards, resources, and opportunities on the basis of their wealth, prestige, and political power. But we can also rank people by sex and gender, and by sexual orientation—assigning differential value to one sex or gender over another, one sexual orientation over others. We have already noted that privileging one sex or gender over another is called *sexism.* When heterosexuality is privileged over homosexuality or bisexuality, we call this **heterosexism.** Although neither sexism nor heterosexism exists in all societies, it is prevalent in our own society, and the privileging process occurs throughout the life cycle, beginning at birth.

Gender Socialization in the Home

Imagine that you would like to start a family, but you and your partner have been told that you can have only one child. Which would you prefer that child to be, a boy or a girl?

If you are like most young people in the United States, you would prefer your only child to be a boy. Since the 1930s, researchers have documented that Americans in general have a slight "boy preference" (Coombs, 1977; Williams, 1976a). This boy preference is much stronger in other countries, such as China and India, where some parents use technology to choose the sex of their offspring or eliminate unwanted daughters by infanticide (Burns, 1994; Gargan, 1991; Kolker & Burke, 1992; Warren, 1985). In the United States, there is evidence that boy preference may be weakening since most American couples express a desire to have at least one child of each sex (Steinbacher & Gilroy, 1985; Teachman & Schollaert, 1989). Nevertheless, U.S. children continue to be born into a society that prefers boys over girls.

Some of the more common reasons that adults give for their boy preference are that boys carry on the family name (assuming that a daughter will take her husband's name at marriage), and that boys are both easier and cheaper to raise. The small minority that prefers girls seems to value them for their traditionally feminine traits: They are supposedly neater, cuddlier, cuter, and more obedient than boys (Williamson, 1976b). Although it isn't certain whether children perceive their parents' sex preferences (Williamson, 1976a), it is clear that parental preferences are closely associated with their children's behavior and that their preferences reflect gender stereotypes. Let's take a closer look at how parents transmit their expectations.

Parents as Gender Socializers.   If you ask parents whether they treat their children differently simply on the basis of sex, most would probably say "no." However, there is considerable evidence that what parents *say* they do and what they *actually* do are often not the same. Research shows, for instance, that the vast majority of comments parents make about their babies immediately following birth concern the babies' sex (Woollett et al., 1982). Moreover, when asked to describe their babies within twenty-four hours after birth, new parents frequently use gender stereotypes. Girls are described as tiny, soft, and delicate, while boys are described as strong, alert, and coordinated, even though there are few real physiological or behavioral differences between newborn males and females (Reid, 1994).

It is not unreasonable to suspect that parents' initial gendered perceptions of their children may lay the foundation for their differential treatment of sons and daughters. For example, research indicates that parents tend to engage in rougher, more physical play with sons than daughters, that they encourage sons to be more assertive

Gender concepts and role expectations often are communicated and legitimated through rites of passage such as this Quinceneria. This ceremony celebrates the femininity and acknowledges the sexual maturity of Hispanic girls at the age of 15. The powerful complex of Hispanic beliefs, values, and behaviors relating to femininity has been termed marianismo, *the opposite equivalent of* machismo. *What makes gender socialization so powerful?*

than daughters, and that they encourage greater independence in sons than in daughters (Burns et al., 1989; Golombuk & Fivush, 1994; MacDonald & Parke, 1986). It is important to note, however, that much of this research has involved White, middle-class families. The few studies that use more racially and ethnically diverse samples indicate that, at least in African American families, girls are encouraged to be independent, assertive, confident, and achievement-oriented (Hale-Benson, 1986; Reid, 1982). The findings for Hispanic families are not conclusive; and indications when social class is taken into account tend to be contradictory (Gonzalez, 1982; Isaaks, 1980; Lackey, 1989).

Gender socialization is generally a conscious effort by parents, in that expectations are reinforced with explicit rewards and punishments. While standing in line at a grocery store several years ago, we witnessed the following exchange between a father and his daughter: The little girl ran up to her father holding a small metal truck and asked him to buy it for her. "Put that back," said her father, "It's for boys. You aren't a boy, are you?" However, it is boys who receive the strongest explicit negative sanctions for engaging in what adults consider gender-inappropriate (feminine) behavior. Parents' concerns about their sons' feminine behavior stem to a large extent from homophobia. Many parents believe that if they let their sons play with dolls or do other feminine things, they are encouraging homosexuality. Gender socialization is typically heterosexist.

Gender socialization may be indirect, with gendered messages relayed implicitly through children's clothing, the way their rooms are decorated, and the toys they are given. Consider, for example, that the easiest and most accurate way for a stranger to determine the sex of an infant is by clothing. Madeline Shakin and her associates (1985) found that 90 percent of the children they observed in suburban shopping malls were dressed in sex-typed clothes. The color of the clothing alone supplied a reliable clue for sex labeling: The vast majority of girls wore pink or yellow, while most boys were dressed in blue or red. Clothing styles also vary by sex. On special occasions, girls wear dresses trimmed with ruffles and lace; at bedtime, they wear nighties with more of the same; for play, their slacks sets may be more practical, but chances are they are pastel and decorated with hearts and flowers. Boys, on the other hand, wear three-piece suits on special occasions; at bedtime, they wear astronaut, athlete, or super-hero pajamas; and for play, their overalls or slacks sets are in primary colors with sports or military decorations.

All of this may seem insignificant, even picky, to you, but clothing plays a significant part in gender socialization. First, by informing others about the sex of the child, clothing sends an implicit message about how the child should be treated (Shakin et al., 1986). Second, certain types of clothing encourage or discourage particular behaviors or activities. Frilly dresses, for example, discourage rough-and-tumble play, whereas boys' clothing rarely impedes their physical movement. Boys are expected to be more active than girls, and the styles of clothing designed for them reflect this gender stereotype. Clothing, then, serves as one of the most basic means by which parents organize their children's world along gender-specific lines.

Consider, too, children's environments and toys. Researchers who have gone into middle-class homes and examined the contents of children's bedrooms (Rheingold & Cook, 1975; Stoneman et al., 1986) have found that girls' rooms typically reflect traditional images of femininity, especially in terms of domesticity and motherhood. Their rooms are usually decorated with floral designs and ruffled bedspreads, pillows, and curtains. Their toys include dolls and related items (doll houses) as well as miniature appliances (toy stoves). Few of these items were found in boys' rooms, where the decor and contents reflect traditional notions about masculinity. Boys' rooms have more animal motifs and are filled with military toys and athletic equipment. They also have building toys and vehicles (blocks, trucks, and wagons). Importantly, boys have more toys overall, as well as more types of toys, including toys that are considered educational. The only objects girls are as likely to have as boys are musical instruments and books, although research shows that the content of children's books usually conveys traditional messages about masculinity and femininity (Clark et al., 1993; DeLoache et al., 1987).

The importance of these findings about the different nature and content of boys' environments versus girls' environments rests first with the fact that children spend a considerable amount of time at play. Toys not only entertain them, but also teach them particular skills and encourage them to explore through play various roles that they might one day occupy as adults. Thus, if parents provide boys and girls with very different kinds of environments and toys, they are essentially training them for separate (and in our society, unequal) roles as adults. What is more, they are subtly telling them that what they *may* do, as well as what they *can* do, is largely determined (and limited) by their sex. (See also the Doing Sociology box.) Importantly, however, parents are not the only gender socializers of children. Let's look at other agents of socialization.

Peers as Gender Socializers

Socialization is not a one-way process from adults to children. Rather, childhood socialization is a collective process in which children use information they receive from both adults and the world at large to generate their own unique peer subcultures (Corsaro & Eder, 1990).

DOING SOCIOLOGY

What Gendered Messages Do Toy Catalogs Convey?

Toy catalogs are directed primarily at parents because they are the major toy shoppers: In the United States, parents make over 70 percent of all toy purchases (Kutner & Levinson, 1978). However, children also spend a good bit of time looking at toy catalogs and often ask their parents to buy specific toys they see advertised. We did an unscientific survey of toy catalogs and found that they relayed very clear and stereotyped gender messages. The female models in the catalogs were usually shown playing with dolls, household appliances, or making craft projects. Although a little girl was also sometimes shown playing with a doctor kit, most of the toys for girls were very traditional, such as a "bridal kit" that included a gown and veil, an engagement

ring, wedding announcements, and two champagne flutes. In contrast, the male models in the catalogs were usually shown playing with building toys and completing science projects. Sometimes a little boy would be shown in a toy kitchen, but most of the toys shown with male models were also traditional, such as dress-up kits for police officers, ninjas, and knights.

Conduct your own content analysis of toy catalogs. Collect several toy catalogs and go through each, recording which toys are shown with male models, which are shown with female models, or both, and whether you consider these depictions to be gender stereotyped. What specific traits and abilities do you think each toy fosters in children? Share your results with classmates.

Research indicates, in fact, that children's same-sex peers are powerful agents of socialization (Fagot, 1985).

Children socialize one another through their everyday interactions in the home and at play, strongly rewarding gender-appropriate behavior (Goodenough, 1990). For example, boys and girls who choose gender-appropriate behavior are accepted by peers, while children who play with toys considered appropriate for the opposite sex are teased, criticized, or ostracized by their peers (Fagot & Leinbach, 1983; Golombuk & Fivush, 1994; Lobel et al., 1993; Martin, 1989).

One of young children's first attempts at social differentiation is through increasing sex segregation. Beginning at about age two or three, and increasingly as they move from early to middle childhood, children voluntarily segregate themselves into same-sex groups (Feiring & Lewis, 1987; Serbin et al., 1991). That is not to say that children play *only* with same-sex peers; sex-integrated play occurs in elementary school and is cooperative and friendly (Thorne, 1993). However, sex segregation is reinforced by teachers' treatment of children; let's look now at gender socialization in school.

Gender Socialization in the Schools

When teachers are asked about the way they treat students, they respond in much the same way that parents do—that they treat all their students fairly regardless of sex. Research indicates, however, that in practice teachers typically interact differently (and often inequitably)

with their male and female students and that these differences occur at all levels of the education system, from elementary school through graduate school. The interactions differ in at least two ways: the *frequency* of teacher–student interactions and the *content* of those interactions.

Studies on the frequency of teachers' interactions with their students show that regardless of the sex of the teacher, they interact with their male students more than with their female students (American Association of University Women [AAUW], 1992). Male students receive more teacher attention and more instructional time than female students. This may be because male students are more demanding of their teachers and because male students participate in class more than female students. However, research shows that even when boys do not voluntarily participate in class, teachers are more likely to solicit information from them than from girls (Hall & Sandler, 1985; Sadker & Sadker, 1994).

Apart from the frequency of teacher–student interactions, studies indicate that the content of these interactions also differs, depending on the sex of the student. For example, male students get more praise for the intellectual quality of their work and receive greater encouragement from teachers than female students (Jones & Wheatley, 1990; Sadker & Sadker, 1994). In addition, teachers give male students more detailed feedback about their work (AAUW, 1992). Teachers sometimes make remarks in class that disparage females (referring to single, middle-aged women as "old maids") or females' intellectual abilities ("You girls probably won't

Is there gender bias in teachers' interactions with students? In what ways might bias be manifested, intended or not? Why is it so important that schools and curricula are gender fair?

understand this") (Hall & Sandler, 1985; Myers & Dugan, 1996). Inequities such as these occur most often in fields of study traditionally dominated by males (mathematics and science), and they intensify as a student moves through the educational system, being especially prevalent in graduate school (Hall & Sandler, 1985; Rayman, 1993; Turner & Thompson, 1993).

Many education specialists believe the gender inequities embedded in teacher–student interactions lower female students' academic self-esteem and confidence. Moreover, these gendered messages from teachers are reinforced by traditional curriculum materials. Textbooks, for instance, contain both subtle and blatant gender biases, including language bias (use of only masculine pronouns and nouns) and gender stereotypes, omitting women, focusing on "great men," and neglecting scholarship by women (AAUW, 1992; Davis, 1995; Sadker & Sadker, 1994). The impact of biased instructional materials on students becomes clear when we compare them to gender-fair curriculum materials. Studies show that female and male students who are exposed to gender-equitable curricula are more likely than other students to have a broader knowledge of people in society, have more flexible attitudes about gender, and imitate the

gender-equitable behaviors presented to them (Scott & Schau, 1985).

What are some of the other impacts of gender inequality in education? In light of our discussion so far, it may be surprising to learn that girls earn higher grades than boys throughout their elementary school years (AAUW, 1992). However, girls' achievement test scores as well as their self-confidence decline as they progress through high school (Gilligan, 1990; 1995; Sadker & Sadker, 1994). In high school, the focus and interests of boys and girls diverge significantly. For boys, the single most important source of prestige and popularity is athletic achievement. It is the athlete who is looked to as a leader, not only by his peers, but also by teachers and parents. For girls, the most important source of prestige and popularity is physical attractiveness (Eder, 1995). Obviously, teenagers who are not heterosexual, both females and males, face tremendous obstacles in high school and, as the Social Policy box shows, often feel isolated and ostracized by both peers and adults.

It is in high school that young women and men are expected to begin formulating their career goals. Research indicates that high school girls and boys have equally high aspirations for themselves, although teenage girls tend to underestimate their academic abilities and express greater pessimism about their ability to achieve their career goals (Dennehy & Mortimer, 1992). In college, men and women generally pursue different fields of study. The data in Table 10.1 on page 268 illustrate this sex-specific pattern. Male students, we find, tend to pursue degrees in engineering, architecture, the physical and natural sciences, and computer science. Women are heavily concentrated in nursing, home economics, library science, education, social work, and psychology.

This imbalance persists and, in fact, worsens at the graduate level. In addition, two other disturbing trends emerge. First, the number of female Ph.D. degree recipients declines dramatically. Second, male Ph.D.'s outnumber female Ph.D.'s in several fields—including international relations, music, and mathematics—where there are either a higher concentration of women at the undergraduate level or a relative balance between the sexes (Commission on Professionals in Science and Technology, 1992).

Let's consider one more gender socializer, the media.

The Media

Women and men, and homosexuals and heterosexuals, are rarely treated equally in the media. In fact, the media are frequently accused of **symbolic annihilation** of women and homosexuals: ignoring, trivializing, ridiculing, and even condemning them. This is the case regardless of the medium examined. However, because television is the most important media socializer in our society, we will

Social Policy
The High School Experiences of Gay and Lesbian Youth

Adolescence is a period of tremendous physical and emotional change. It is a time when most young women and men begin to actively explore their sexuality and sexual identities. Historically, our schools have been woefully inadequate in educating young people about sex, but they have been most neglectful with respect to lesbian and gay youth. Although recent surveys show that teachers and school administrators express a willingness to treat homosexual students in a nonjudgmental way, they remain reluctant to proactively address the special needs of of homosexual students or to openly affirm their sexual identities (Sears, 1992). Most school personnel, in fact, assume the heterosexuality of their students and never raise the issue of sexual orientation.

The Issue

What are the consequences of this neglect? Researchers report that lesbian and gay adolescents have a disproportionately high rate of substance abuse, sexual abuse, risk-taking behaviors, academic problems, and homelessness (Lock & Kleis, 1998; Voelker, 1998). Lesbian and gay youth are also at especially high risk of dropping out of school (Uribe & Harbeck, 1992). While school could be a safe haven for gays and lesbians, it is usually the site of social rejection, harassment, and violence. In one study, 80 percent of gay and lesbian students reported being verbally insulted at school, 44 percent were threatened with violence, 31 percent were chased or followed, and 17 percent were physically assaulted (Lock & Kleis, 1998). The social rejection, harassment, and violence that these students experience from their heterosexual peers and often from parents and teachers as well contribute to low self-esteem, alienation, isolation, and a sense of inadequacy. Those who hide their sexual orientation may escape some of the physical and verbal harassment, but their secretiveness is likely to increase their feelings of loneliness and isolation. "By developing elaborate concealment strategies these young people are often able to 'pass as straight,' but at some significant, unmeasurable cost to their developmental process, self-esteem, and sense of connection" (Uribe and Harbeck, 1992, p. 11; see also Lock & Kleis, 1998).

The Debate

In order to better meet the needs of gay and lesbian students, over 170 organizations have been established nationwide, including schools for gay, lesbian, and bisexual students or children of gays, lesbians and bisexuals. Agencies, such as the Hetrick-Martin Institute in New York, the Gay and Lesbian Community Services Center in Los Angeles, and the Sexual Minority Youth Assistance League in Washington, DC, offer a variety of services, including counseling, tutoring, meals, and sometimes shelter for homosexual youth who have been forced to leave their homes after coming out to (or being found out by) their parents. A central goal of all of these organizations is to affirm the identities of homosexual teenagers and thereby raise their self-esteem. Some of the organizations also do programs, such as peer trainings, at local schools to help foster acceptance of homosexual youth and to help prevent harassment and violence. A number of them also lobby school boards and state departments of education to make school activities and curricula more inclusive of gay and lesbian youth (Green, 1993; Uribe & Harbeck, 1992; Woog, 1995).

What Do You Think?

Are separate schools for gay and lesbian youth a good idea? Or will separate schools just reinforce the isolation of gays and lesbians from straight society? What other strategies might be effective in improving the high school experiences of gay and lesbian youth?

---

focus on television, and in particular, on prime-time television programming.

A recent study conducted over a ten-year period by a research team from the Annenberg School of Communications at the University of Pennsylvania found that on prime-time television, women play only about one of every three roles—a figure, it should be added, that has not changed since 1954 (Gerbner, 1993; see also Metzger, 1992). This study, noteworthy for its magnitude as well as its findings, analyzed 19,645 speaking parts in 1,371 television programs on the three national networks, Fox Television, and eleven major cable networks.

Not only do women have fewer roles on television, but the characters played by women tend to be younger and less mature than male characters and therefore less authoritative (Fejes, 1992). Women on television age faster than men, and the older they are, the more likely they are to be portrayed as unsuccessful (Gerbner, 1993). As Condry (1989, p. 73) notes, "It is especially bad to be old on television, and it is terrible to be an old woman." Young female characters, usually thin and physically attractive, are four times more likely than male characters to be shown scantily dressed (dressed in nightclothes, underwear, or swimsuits) (Signorelli, 1997).

In some ways, the portrayal of women on television has changed over the years. For example, today's female television characters are more likely to be working outside the home. Nevertheless, the focus of their lives remains

TABLE 10.1 Percentage of Bachelor's, Master's, and Doctor's Degrees Conferred by U.S. Institutions of Higher Education to Women in Selected Fields of Study, 1993–1994

Major Field of Study	Percent Bachelor's Degrees Conferred to Women	Percent Master's Degrees Conferred to Women	Percent Doctor's Degrees Conferred to Women
Accounting	55.1	45.7	46.0
Agriculture & Natural Resources	35.0	38.9	23.2
Anthropology	63.5	61.4	53.3
Architecture	29.6	32.3	20.1
Art History	78.7	78.6	60.1
Astronomy	29.5	26.9	14.9
Banking & Finance	32.0	29.2	17.2
Biological & Life Sciences	52.1	52.6	41.1
Business Management	47.2	35.2	25.1
Chemistry	40.7	41.3	30.3
Communications	58.9	62.3	48.9
Computer & Information Sciences	28.4	25.8	15.4
Criminal Justice	38.8	38.0	44.0
Economics	29.5	32.7	24.1
Education	77.3	76.7	60.8
Engineering	16.4	15.4	11.1
English	65.8	65.6	57.7
Foreign Languages	70.1	66.9	59.9
Geology	33.9	31.2	17.7
Health Sciences	82.4	79.2	58.5
History	37.2	39.4	37.2
Home Economics	87.5	83.3	74.5
International Relations	56.5	45.1	21.2
Library Science	91.9	79.7	68.9
Mathematics	46.3	38.1	21.9
Music	51.7	51.6	37.9
Nursing	90.4	93.3	93.7
Philosophy	31.4	30.1	27.9
Physics	17.7	15.2	12.3
Political Science & Government	42.5	37.2	28.9
Psychology	73.1	72.1	62.2
Public Administration	48.7	48.9	33.8
Religion & Religious Studies	42.7	44.0	26.7
Social Work	85.8	82.9	69.5
Sociology	68.2	61.2	50.1
Visual & Performing Arts	57.0	60.1	44.4

Source: U.S. National Center for Education Statistics, 1996, pp. 258–265.

on their families and intimate relationships. Their male partners are now typically depicted as ideal family men—sensitive, supportive, and willing to do an equal share of housework—although men on prime-time television are rarely shown performing household chores (1 to 3 percent of men compared to 20 to 27 percent of women) (Metzger, 1992; Signorelli, 1997).

Clearly, stereotypes about gender (and age) are prevalent on prime-time television and compounded by stereotypes about race and ethnicity. In addition, people with physical disabilities are virtually invisible on prime-time television, representing just 1.5 percent of prime-time characters. Gay men and lesbians are nearly invisible as well, although there is evidence that this is changing. By 1997, there were eighteen regular gay or lesbian characters on prime-time television programs, all on situation comedies. These characters included Carter Heywood on *Spin City,* who is also TV's only African American gay character; Susan Bunch and Carol Wylick on *Friends,* the first lesbian couple on TV to become parents; and Ellen Morgan, the first homosexual character to come out on TV, although that show was canceled in 1998 (Bruni, 1996; "Since Coming Out Is In," 1997).

REFLECTING ON

Gender and Sexual Orientation as Systems of Stratification

1. In having children, would you (or did you) have a sex preference? If so, what is the reason for your preference? What is your preference for your child's sexual orientation, and why?
2. What is your first or most memorable experience of gender socialization? What did you learn from this experience, and how do you feel about it now?

GENDER AND SEXUAL ORIENTATION IN THE WORKPLACE

To some observers, paid employment outside the home is the path to equality between women and men. Their reasoning is based on the kinds of anthropological studies we discussed earlier in this chapter: In societies where women make a direct contribution to economic production, they enjoy relatively equal status with men. Unfortunately, such reasoning ignores the fact that, historically, a significant number of women, especially racial and ethnic minority women, have always worked in the paid labor force. Second, it overlooks the status of contemporary working women whose positions in the labor force are not equal to men's. Finally, it obscures the interrela-

Women's labor history is rife with instances of gender inequality and sex discrimination in the workplace. In what ways is gender inequality manifested? What forms can sex discrimination take? The woman in this picture is in a female-dominated occupation that is unskilled and lower paid. What difficulties might she find that a White woman would not? What difficulties might a man find in her job?

tionship between labor in the public work world and labor in the home. In this section, we will examine the first two of these three issues. In Chapter 15, we will discuss the relationship between household and family responsibilities and employment outside the home.

Historically, women's participation in the labor force has been determined to a large extent by changes in population and industrial patterns, as well as by stereotypes of the "proper place" for women and men. When production moved off farms and into factories during the nineteenth century, a substantial number of early factory workers were women. In the textile mills and garment industry, for example, the labor force was almost entirely female (Dublin, 1994; Stansell, 1986; Werthheimer, 1979). Jobs in manufacturing, however, were for many years available primarily to White women. Women of color, though more likely than White women overall to be in the paid labor force, found their employment opportunities limited to agricultural work (fruit and vegetable harvesters), domestic work (housekeepers), and laundry work (Amott & Matthaei, 1991). Although the dirtiest, most menial, and lowest paying jobs were given to minority men, they were still paid more than minority women.

Historically, women of color have been the lowest paid members of the labor force—a pattern that continues today (Glenn, 1992; Romero, 1992).

In general, however, women, especially married women, were much less likely than men to have paid employment until the outbreak of World War II. With men overseas in combat, women were given many of their jobs, including jobs in welding, riveting, shipfitting, and toolmaking. When the war ended, women were laid off to make room in the labor force for returning servicemen. Women who decided to continue working often had to take lower-paying jobs that were considered "women's work" (secretarial positions). Most women, though, married and stayed home with children.

It was in the mid-1960s that women began to enter the labor force in greater numbers than ever during peacetime. There were several reasons: Women were having fewer children; the divorce rate was rising and many women became the sole economic providers for themselves and their children; and downturns in the economy made two incomes necessary in many families in order to make ends meet. Also, political and social changes, such as the women's movement, which we will discuss later in the chapter, made women aware that they had options outside the home. By 1998, 59.9 percent of women sixteen years old and older were in the paid labor force (U.S. Department of Labor, 1998a). Today, the typical woman, like the typical man, is in the paid labor force and is working full-time, year-round.

There are important differences in women's and men's employment experiences, however. One of the most significant differences is the kinds of jobs they do. Women and men are largely segregated in different occupations that are considered "women's work" and "men's work," and the consequences are serious.

Sex Segregation in the Workplace and Its Consequences

Occupational sex segregation refers to the degree to which men and women are concentrated in occupations where workers of one sex predominate. Despite tremendous changes in the U.S. labor market historically as well as fluctuations during specific periods, occupational sex segregation was stable during most of the twentieth century, but it has declined somewhat since 1970 (Jacobs & Lim, 1995).

One easy way to measure occupational sex segregation is to look at the percentage of workers of each sex that holds a specific job. Table 10.2 shows the ten occupations that employ the largest numbers of men and women. Notice the lack of overlap in the jobs: Men are concentrated in the skilled trades and operative jobs, whereas women are primarily in teaching, clerical, and other service occupations.

As we noted, however, there has been improvement in occupational sex segregation in recent years. Sales jobs, in particular, have become relatively well-balanced in terms of the percentages of men and women employed. But improvements in occupational sex segregation are typically offset by other forms of workplace sex segregation, especially **industry sex segregation** and **establishment sex segregation.** In industry sex segregation, the representation of women and men is relatively balanced for an industry as a whole, but within the industry, women and men hold very different kinds of jobs. Women are usually concentrated in the lower-paying, lower-prestige specialties within the industry. For example, "in the case of bakers, women work mostly in supermarkets baking prepackaged dough, while men continue to monopolize the more skilled positions in bakeries" (Wright & Jacobs, 1995, p. 339; see also Tallichet, 1995).

With respect to establishment sex segregation, women and men hold the same job title at an individual establishment or company, but actually do different jobs. Again, women's jobs are usually lower paying and less prestigious. For instance, it is not uncommon in a law firm for women to be concentrated in the family law division, while men dominate the more lucrative corporate and commercial law department (Kay & Hagan, 1995; 1998).

A number of explanations have been offered for the persistence of occupational sex segregation. One of the most common is that women prefer and freely choose different occupations from men. The underlying assumption is that women's primary allegiance is to home and family, so they seek undemanding jobs that require little personal investment in training or skills acquisition in order to better tend to their household responsibilities.

There are several serious problems with this argument. One is that research simply does not support the claim that women's marital and motherhood statuses negate their desire to work in male-dominated jobs. On the contrary, studies show that while mothers of young children do try to avoid jobs with rotating shifts because of the child care problems they pose, having children is *positively* correlated with women's efforts to leave female-dominated jobs for male-dominated ones (Reskin, 1993). The logical explanation of this finding is that male-dominated jobs pay significantly better wages, have better benefits, and offer greater opportunities for promotion than female-dominated jobs, making such jobs especially attractive to women who must make a major financial contribution to their families' support (Padevic, 1992; Rosenfeld & Spenner, 1992).

A woman's decision to take a male-dominated job is also constrained by the availability of such jobs. *Availability* refers not only to a job opening, but also to the extent to which a job seeker perceives she or he has a fair chance of being hired for the job, feeling welcome on the job, and succeeding in the job. Some women "choose"

TABLE 10.2   Top Ten Occupations for Men and Women, 1997

Men	Number Employed	Percent Occupation Male
Construction worker (e.g., carpenter, dry wall installer)	3,365,000	98.3
Machine operator & tender, except precision	2,976,000	64.2
Truck driver	2,383,000	95.9
Sales supervisor or proprietor	1,836,000	60.3
Engineer	1,716,000	90.7
Protective service worker (e.g., police officer, detective, guard)	1,654,000	84.3
Vehicle/mobile equipment mechanic or repairer	1,504,000	98.6
Sales worker, retail & personal services	1,427,000	42.4
Janitor or cleaner	1,117,000	73.9
Material moving equipment operator (e.g., crane operator, bulldozer operator)	1,004,000	95.4

Women	Number Employed	Percent Occupation Female
Teacher, except college & university	2,830,000	74.3
Secretary	2,220,000	98.7
Miscellaneous administrative support worker (e.g., office clerk, bank teller)	2,111,000	82.8
Sales worker, retail & personal services	1,939,000	57.6
Machine operator & tender, except precision	1,658,000	35.8
Registered nurse	1,351,000	92.5
Sales supervisor or proprietor	1,210,000	39.7
Nursing aide	1,148,000	88.6
Sales counter clerk	1,034,000	77.1
Health technologist or technician (e.g., laboratory technician)	1,002,000	76.7

Source: U.S. Department of Labor, 1998b, pp. 209–214.

not to enter certain occupations that have a reputation for treating women poorly and fostering a hostile working environment (Reskin, 1993; Riger, 1988).

What are the consequences of occupational sex segregation for female and male workers? One of the most serious is economic impact. Female-dominated jobs tend to be less prestigious than jobs dominated by men; they also typically pay less. Table 10.3 on page 272 shows the median weekly earnings of selected occupations that are highly sex segregated. The table covers a broad range of jobs that require different levels of training, skill, effort, and responsibility, but across the board, most female-dominated jobs pay significantly less than male-dominated jobs. On average, women earn about 76 percent of what men earn. In other words, for every dollar a man makes, a woman makes 76 cents (Love, 1998). Research also indicates that occupational sex segregation acounts for about 20 to 40 percent of the difference in men's and

TABLE 10.3 Median Weekly Earnings of Selected Male-Dominated and Female-Dominated Occupations, 1997

Occupation	Female (%)	Median Weekly Earnings ($)
Child care worker	97.3	202
Dental assistant	96.4	366
Hairdresser or cosmetologist	87.7	311
Librarian	82.6	638
Social worker	67.4	522
Mail carrier	28.6	677
Architect	18.4	822
Engineer	9.4	977
Truck driver	4.1	506
Firefighter	3.0	707
Airplane pilot or navigator	1.1	1,079
Roofer	0.0	407

Source: U.S. Department of Labor, 1998b, pp. 209–214.

women's earnings (Kay & Hagan, 1995; Sorenson, 1994). "Women's work" is consistently devalued when job evaluators set wage rates for specific occupations (Reskin, 1993; Steinberg, 1990).

Researchers who have studied women in sex-atypical jobs report that women are usually disadvantaged in hiring and promotions and that they encounter a *glass ceiling*—an invisible barrier imposed because of their sex—that limits their upward occupational mobility. In contrast, men in sex-atypical occupations often receive preferential treatment in hiring and, instead of hitting a glass ceiling, often ride a *glass escalator* up the hierarchy of these professions, receiving subtle and sometimes not-so-subtle pressures to move up in their professions. These pressures may take positive forms, such as close mentoring and encouragement from supervisors (who, even in female-dominated fields, are often men), but they may also be the result of biased attitudes expressed by people outside the profession—the public and clients—who question the masculinity of men in traditional female occupations (Williams, 1992; 1995).

The glass ceiling and glass escalator phenomena highlight the heterosexism that characterizes most workplaces. For example, men interviewed by Christine Williams (1992; 1995) reported that their supervisors were more likely to discriminate against female employees than against them. However, openly gay men do not receive the favorable treatment afforded their straight male colleagues. Many lesbians and gay men report hostile and unfair treatment of homosexuals in the workplace, so a large number are not open to their employers or coworkers about their sexual orientation. Discrimination on the basis of sexual orientation is not prohibited by law in most states, so those men and women who are open about their sexual orientation are sometimes "punished" for it. One researcher found that known gay and lesbian employees were sometimes fired because their mere presence in the workplace was considered "disruptive" by their employers and fellow employees (Woods, 1993). Other forms of discrimination experienced by gays and lesbians in the workplace include being excluded from informal networks, overt harassment (sometimes based on coworkers' assumptions about their HIV status), and indirect insults or threats (such as antigay graffiti scribbled on the wall of the employees' restroom, or an antigay cartoon or joke posted on an office door or bulletin board) (Anastas, forthcoming). Surveys show that between 16 and 45 percent of gay and lesbian workers have encountered some form of employment discrimination (Woods, 1993).

REFLECTING ON

Gender and Sexual Orientation in the Workplace

1. Give examples of establishment sex segregation and industry sex segregation. What might be some consequences of this segregation for female and male workers?

2. How would you explain the systematic devaluation of jobs traditionally held by women?
3. What strategies can you suggest for breaking the glass ceiling?
4. What strategies can you suggest for preventing discrimination against homosexuals in the workplace?

GENDERED VIOLENCE

A number of factors influence one's chances of being the victim of a crime. Age and race are two variables that are strongly linked to likelihood of criminal victimization. Sexual orientation is also a factor. Gay men and lesbians are often singled out for violent criminal victimization because of their sexual orientation (Herek & Berrill, 1992; "High-Profile Violence Against Gays," 1998; "Negative Stereotypes," 1998).

Gender, too, influences the likelihood of criminal victimization. Men are more likely than women both to commit crimes and to be victimized by crime (U.S. Department of Justice, Bureau of Justice Statistics, 1997). However, women are particularly likely to be victims of domestic violence, sexual harassment, sexual assault, and other forms of violence that are directed almost exclusively against women because they are women. We will discuss domestic violence at length in Chapter 15. Here we will concentrate on the other two forms of violence against women.

Sexual Harassment

Sexual harassment refers to unwanted leers, comments, suggestions, or physical contact of a sexual nature, as well as unwelcome requests for sexual favors. Men rarely experience sexual harassment, although when a man is victimized, the case receives widespread media attention. Women, on the other hand, routinely experience sexual harassment in school and in the workplace. Studies conducted on college campuses throughout the United States, for example, indicate that between 20 and 49 percent of female faculty have experienced some form of sexual harassment, along with 20 to 30 percent of female students (Dzeich & Weiner, 1990; Reilly et al., 1986), although research also shows that many students don't recognize sexual harassment when it occurs and often blame the harassment on the victim (Corbett et al., 1993). Other research shows that from 42 percent to 88 percent of female workers have experienced sexual harassment at work (Ragins & Scandura, 1995).

Although women in all fields and types of occupations experience sexual harassment, some researchers believe the problem is especially pervasive in male-dominated fields where it serves as a means for men to assert dominance and control over women who are (or will soon become) their job equals (Gruber & Bjorn, 1982; Tallichet, 1995; Westley, 1982).

Regardless of the prevalence and reasons, the consequences of sexual harassment for female students and workers are serious and harmful. Harassed women report physical responses to the harassment, including chronic neck and back pain, upset stomach, colitis and other gastrointestinal disorders, and eating and sleeping disorders. They also report diminished academic or work performance, discouragement about continuing in the field, and lowered self-esteem. In other words, sexual harassment creates an unpleasant and hostile environment that affects women's performance and productivity, their personal and professional growth, and ultimately, the future of their careers.

Perhaps no other recent incident did more to highlight the problem of sexual harassment than the testimony of Anita Hill to the Senate Judiciary Committee during the confirmation hearings for Clarence Thomas's nomination to the U.S. Supreme Court in 1991. Although Thomas was ultimately confirmed to the Court, Hill's testimony raised public awareness of the problem and encouraged more women to report harassment. Between 1991 and 1995, the number of sexual harassment charges filed each year more than doubled, reaching 15,549 cases in 1995 ("Sexual Harassment," 1996). More recent cases involving top political figures, including Senator Bob Packwood (R-OR) and President Bill Clinton, have also helped keep the problem of sexual harassment in the public spotlight and perhaps encouraged women to bring formal charges.

Recent decisions by the U.S. Supreme Court have also made it easier for sexual harassment victims to press charges against perpetrators. First, in 1993, the U.S. Supreme Court, with Thomas as a member, approved a broad legal definition of sexual harassment that makes it easier for harassment victims to win lawsuits against their harassers: Sexual harassment is any action that creates an environment that would be reasonably perceived as hostile or abusive. Harassment victims no longer have to prove that the harassment caused them severe psychological injury. Then, in 1998, the Court unanimously agreed that federal law protects people in the workplace from being harassed by coworkers or supervisors of the same sex (Greenhouse, 1998).

Rape and Sexual Assault

Rape is the crime that women fear more than any other (Riger & Gordon, 1988; Warr, 1985). Their fear derives not only from the fact that rape is a serious crime, but also from its association with other serious offenses, such as robbery and homicide, and with gratuitous violence in addition to the rape itself (Riger & Gordon, 1988). The fear of contracting AIDS through rape also adds to women's fear (Center for Women Policy Studies, 1991).

Finally, women's fear of rape is also related to their perceived risk of being raped, and statistics on sexual assault indicate that their fears are well-founded. The U.S. Department of Justice, Bureau of Justice Statistics (1997) estimates that for every 1,000 persons age twelve and older in the U.S. population, two are victims of rape or sexual assault each year. According to the FBI (1997), a forcible rape occurs in the United States every six minutes. A recent study conducted by social scientists at the National Center for Policy Research found that nearly 18 percent of American women are victims of rape or attempted rape during their lifetimes (Tjaden & Thoennes, 1998). However, sexual assault is one of the violent crimes *least* likely to be reported to the police (Center for Women Policy Studies, 1991). Rape also has one of the lowest arrest and conviction rates of any crime. Almost two-thirds of victims of completed rapes do not report the crime to the police (U.S. Department of Justice, Bureau of Justice Statistics, 1997). Of the rapes that are reported, about half result in an arrest; only about 22 percent of those arrested are convicted (Federal Bureau of Investigation, 1997; Greenfeld, 1997). Of those convicted, about 66 percent receive prison sentences; the average prison sentence is slightly less than ten years, but most offenders serve less than five years (Greenfeld, 1997).

Rape occurs when a person uses force or the threat of force to have some form of sexual intercourse (vaginal, oral, or anal) with another person. This rather straightforward definition might lead us to conclude that the prosecution of rape cases is fairly simple, especially given current medical technology and modern evidence collection techniques. However, research indicates that widespread acceptance of rape myths among the general public, as well as police, prosecutors, and judges, often makes prosecution difficult (Bourque, 1989; Williams, 1985). These myths include the ideas that women enjoy forced sex, so if you don't really hurt them, it's not rape; that many women provoke men by teasing them, so these women get what they deserve; and that "real" rapes are committed by strangers who attack lone women on isolated streets or in dark alleys (Madriz, 1997). Consequently, rape victims face a predicament that victims of other crimes don't have to face: They must prove their innocence, whereas it is normally the state that has to prove the offender's guilt (Estrich, 1987).

The central issue in the majority of rape cases is not whether the complainant and the accused engaged in sexual intercourse, but rather whether the complainant consented to the act. It is the victim's lack of consent that is most difficult to prove in court, particularly when she and the accused know one another. A case involving a victim who knows or who is familiar with her assailant is called an **acquaintance rape.** Two-thirds of rapes are acquaintance rapes (U.S. Department of Justice, Bureau of Justice Statistics, 1997), and the younger the victim, the more likely she is to know her assailant (Langan & Harlow, 1994).

Acquaintance rapes are especially common on college campuses. Despite the claims of some observers (Gilbert, 1993; Roiphe, 1993) that the term "date rape" is widely misapplied to cases involving boyfriends who verbally coerce girlfriends or to intercourse that occurs when a woman is intoxicated and becomes "sexually confused," empirical research shows that the incidence of acquaintance rape on college campuses is hardly trivial. For instance, an extensive three-year study of college students found that one in eight female college students reported being victimized during the preceding twelve-month period, and 84 percent of the victims of completed rapes knew their assailants (Koss et al., 1987; see also Schwartz & DeKeseredy, 1997). Acquaintance rape is so prevalent that even if women do not go out alone at night, and even if they stay away from areas with high crime rates, they can still be sexually assaulted. More than 33 percent of rapes take place in the victim's home; 21.3 percent occur at, in, or near the home of a friend, relative, or neighbor (U.S. Department of Justice, Bureau of Justice Statistics, 1997).

Sociologists and anthropologists who have studied sexual assault in the United States and elsewhere have found important differences between societies with low rape rates (*rape-free societies*) and societies with high rape rates (*rape-prone societies*). The most outstanding feature of rape-free societies is their egalitarian gender relations. Although men and women do not perform identical duties, each is regarded as equally important, and both are considered powerful, although in different spheres of activity. Women in these societies also have considerable social and economic autonomy. Moreover, motherhood, nurturance, and passivity are revered, and women are valued not for their sexuality or physical attractiveness, but for their wisdom (Lepowsky, 1994; Sanday, 1981; 1996).

In contrast, in rape-prone societies such as our own, women are viewed as sexual property (Scully & Marola, 1985). There is also a prevalent conquest mentality toward sex, so that men view sex as something they "get," "take," or "win" from women. It is also widely accepted that under certain circumstances, a man may force a woman to have sex (Goodchilds & Zellman, 1984; Koss et al., 1987). In fact, it is not an exaggeration to say that in our society and other rape-prone societies, there is a very fine line between rape and acceptable masculine sexual behavior (Schwartz & DeKeseredy, 1997).

Rape and other forms of violence against women are major issues on the feminist agenda. The international community must recognize various forms of violence against women as human rights violations rather than as personal problems of individual women and men (see the Global Insights box).

GLOBAL INSIGHTS   Is Violence against Women a Violation of Human Rights?

Historically, the physical and psychological abuse of women, though widespread in many societies throughout the world, has not been considered a human rights problem. According to Chapman (1990), there has been a high level of official and social tolerance of violence against women, with most governments and official agencies viewing the problem as an individual matter or simply as a consequence of being female. For example, when nineteen teenage girls were killed and seventy-one others were raped by male classmates during a protest over fees at a boarding school in Kenya in 1991, school officials told reporters that rapes of female students by males were not unusual at their school or others. The deaths were accidental, they claimed; as the deputy principal of the school explained, "The boys never meant any harm against the girls. They just wanted to rape" (quoted in Perlez, 1991, p. A7). However, officials have not only excused or ignored such violence, they have participated in it. The rape and sexual abuse of female political prisoners while in official custody has been documented by human rights advocates (Amnesty International, 1991; Sontag, 1993).

Violence against women as a human rights issue began to command greater public attention when, in 1993, media in the United States and Europe began to report on the systematic rape, sexual enslavement, torture, and murder of Bosnian Muslim women and children by Serbian military forces in the former Yugoslavia. According to a report by a team of European Community investigators, an estimated 20,000 Muslim women were raped by Serb soldiers during the campaign against Muslim communities. The rapes were often carried out in especially sadistic ways with the intent of inflicting the greatest humiliation on the victims. Rape, the investigators concluded, was used as a weapon of war (Nikolic-Ristanovic, 1999; Riding, 1993).

Reports such as these rightfully produced widespread calls in the United States and abroad for international sanctions against the perpetrators of the rapes in Bosnia. But systematic violence against women is not unique to the former Yugoslavia, nor is it a new strategy. Twenty-five years ago, Susan Brownmiller (1975) showed that throughout history, sexual abuse of "enemy" women has been a common state-supported warfare tactic. This abuse has most frequently involved rape, but it has also taken other forms. During World War II, for example, the Japanese government coerced women into prostitution to sexually service Imperial Army soldiers. Though in reality the women were sex slaves, they were euphemistically called "comfort women." It is estimated that from 100,000 to 300,000 women were enslaved; most were from South Korea (McGregor & Lawnham, 1993).

More recently, attorneys assisting refugees seeking political asylum in the United States and Canada have documented extensive state-supported violence against women, including rape by police and military personnel in numerous countries, such as Haiti, Honduras, El Salvador, and Iran (Sontag, 1993). The United Nations High Commission on Refugees has issued special guidelines for government agencies to follow when evaluating women's applications for asylum. The United Nations has also issued a Convention on the Elimination of All Forms of Violence against Women which, although it doesn't include a specific provision on violence, does include a number of provisions that in effect impose sanctions for violence against women.

Rape and sexual assault are international human rights abuses in that they are sometimes used as a means to degrade and demoralize the enemy during wartime. In Bosnia, at least 20,000 Muslim women were raped by Serb soldiers.

REFLECTING ON

Gendered Violence

1. What factors do you think contribute to male students' and workers' beliefs that sexually harassing a female student or coworker is acceptable behavior?
2. How might the United States be transformed from a rape-prone to a rape-free society?

GENDER, SEXUAL ORIENTATION, AND SOCIAL CHANGE

Social movements are issue-oriented groups specifically organized to bring about or prevent social change through collective action. Such groups include feminism—which is more than just a theoretical perspective within sociology—and the gay and lesbian rights movement. Here, we provide a brief overview of each, outlining their historical roots, contemporary concerns, and their varied successes.

Working for Gender Equality

In the United States, women's efforts to secure equal rights with men date back to the Civil War era. At that time, many women joined organizations working to abolish slavery. Abolitionism brought women together and gave them valuable organizing skills. It also gave them a framework for understanding their own inequality with men because they were often prohibited from public speaking and required to sit in the balcony or at the back of the convention halls at abolitionist meetings (Banner, 1986).

When women first organized into women's rights groups, they addressed a variety of issues, including protecting women and children from violent men, securing changes in divorce and custody laws, acquiring property rights, and gaining the right to vote. But as time passed, they increasingly focused on voting rights for women, believing that if women could cast ballots, they would have the political clout to lobby for other social changes. They succeeded, and in 1920, the Nineteenth Amendment was passed, granting women the right to vote (Cott, 1987).

Unfortunately, after women were enfranchised, their activism greatly declined. For one thing, they thought they had achieved equality by getting the vote. Many women didn't vote and many of those who did, voted as men did. Young women ignored or rejected the women's movement, characterizing feminists as lonely single women who needlessly antagonized men. At about this time, too, the "cult of domesticity" was resurrected so that "femi-

ninity, not feminism, was increasingly the watchword" (O'Neill, 1969, p. 313; but see also Taylor, 1990).

In the 1960s women once again began to voice concern about gender inequality. Their interest arose from several factors, including the appointment of government bodies to investigate the problems of working women and the publication of books such as Betty Friedan's *The Feminine Mystique* (1963) that documented women's "second class citizenship." Women's involvement in civil rights and anti-war organizations also made them aware of gender inequality much the same way abolitionism had awakened women in the 1800s (Kramer, 1986). Since the mid-1960s, feminism has grown and matured, so that today there are many diverse organizations and groups. These organizations and groups often use different strategies for bringing about change, but the goal of the change is always gender equality (Lorber, 1998).

Feminism has achieved a great deal over the past thirty years and on many fronts. At the local level, feminists have established women's centers throughout the country that provide social services such as health care, rape crisis counseling, shelter from domestic violence, legal advice, and child care. Feminist lobbying efforts have exerted the political pressure necessary to effect substantial legislative and policy changes, including credit rights for women, legal prohibitions against sex discrimination in education and employment, and the enactment of laws, such as the Violence Against Women Act passed in 1994, that address violent victimization.

Today, an important dimension of feminism for young women is *inclusion*. Historically, feminism has focused on the interests of White, middle-class women, often neglecting the needs of women of color, poor and working-class women, immigrant women, and other disadvantaged groups of women. Although young feminist groups continue to draw their membership largely from the White middle class, many feminist organizations have a multicultural emphasis and attempt to address problems resulting from racial and ethnic inequality, social class inequality, and heterosexism as well as sexism. The inclusiveness of these groups may be the key to their viability, and the continued viability of feminism in general.

Gay and Lesbian Rights

Until recently, most of the information about homosexuality and homosexual relationships was written by nonhomosexuals, and most of it was heterosexist and grounded in myths and negative stereotypes. Because of the stigma attached to homosexuality, gays and lesbians themselves historically have been forced either to remain silent and hidden or to suffer severe consequences, including ostracism, job loss, violence, and imprisonment. This does not mean that efforts to secure equal rights for homosexuals have only begun recently. Groups for homosexuals were established in the United States in the 1920s, but their memberships were small and, rather than demanding equal rights, they worked to provide social support for homosexuals, correct widespread inaccuracies about homosexuals and homosexual relationships, and promote tolerance of homosexuals by heterosexuals (Cruikshank, 1992).

Like feminism, the contemporary gay and lesbian rights movement was influenced by the civil rights struggles and antiwar activism of the 1960s. However, the Stonewall riots of 1969 are generally considered the political spark that ignited widespread organized efforts to secure equality for homosexuals. On June 27, 1969, police in New York City raided the Stonewall Inn, a bar whose patrons were mostly lesbians and gay men. The patrons had been arrested in such raids before, but this time they voiced their anger about repeated harassment and brutality at the hands of the police and the heterosexual public. Joined by a crowd of about 2,000 others, they fought back in two nights of street rioting.

After Stonewall, a number of new, highly political activist groups emerged that continue today to organize public protests, parades of pride, and fundraising campaigns; publish newsletters and journals; provide various social services; and lobby for passage of equal rights laws. These groups, such as the National Gay and Lesbian Task Force, continue to face strong opposition and have experienced setbacks in recent years (Murray, 1996). For example, gays and lesbians continue to be denied basic rights including the right to marry and protection from employment and housing discrimination. Violent crime directed toward homosexuals is rising rather than declining, and there is the continuing controversy over gays and lesbians in the military. Today, more gays and lesbians are willing to be open about their sexual orientation and to demand that their rights be protected. But some observers predict that this increased openness will lead to greater social conflict on gay and lesbian rights as we move through the early decades of the twenty-first century (Murray, 1996).

REFLECTING ON

Gender, Sexual Orientation, and Social Change

1. What does the word *feminism* mean to you? How would you describe someone who is a *feminist*? Is your assessment of feminism positive or negative? Why? How do you explain the negative attention feminism has received since the 1980s?
2. How do you explain the continuing resistance to equal rights for gay men and lesbians? What do you think are the best strategies for reducing this resistance?

 For useful resources for study and review, run Chapter 10 on your *Living Sociology* CD-ROM.

CONNECTIONS

Gender roles and relations in the family	Review the section on "Families" as agents of gender socialization in Chapter 5, and explore this topic further in Chapter 15 in the section on "Families and Intimate Relationships in the United States." In what ways are gender roles expressed in family dynamics?
Prejudice and discrimination	Review the section on "Prejudice and Discrimination" in Chapter 11. What forms of discrimination have been displayed most prevalently against homosexuals? Who is most likely to express their prejudices through acts of discrimination?
Feminist sociology	This topic is introduced in Chapter 1; for example, see the feminist perspective on homelessness. In addition, Chapters 4 and 7 present feminist perspectives, respectively, on culture and deviance. How do feminist views on sex, gender, and sexual orientation compare with these earlier examples?
Biology and the social environment	Review "The Interaction of Biology and Environment" in Chapter 5. How do biology, socialization, and social interaction jointly influence gender development in individuals?

CONNECTIONS

Biology and culture	Review "The Interaction of Biology and Culture" in Chapter 4. How do biology and culture interact in sex identification, gender behavior, and sexual orientation in different societies?
Hunting and gathering societies	Review "Types of Societies" in Chapter 3 for more information on gender relations among contemporary hunter-gatherers. How do gender relations intersect with other characteristics of this type of society?
Sexual orientation	Chapter 15 describes gay and lesbian singles and domestic partners, gay and lesbian families, and partner abuse in gay and lesbian relationships. How do the myths and realities of homosexuality extend to family relations and domestic partnerships?
Gender bias in education	Read the sections on "The Hidden Curriculum" and "Gender Labels" in Chapter 16. How would you explain gender inequities from the conflict perspective? How would you explain it from the symbolic interactionist view?
Mass media as agents of socialization	Review "The Mass Media" in Chapter 5. How does television perpetuate gender stereotypes? Do you agree that the media symbolically annihilate women and homosexuals? Do you think the Internet is different?
Sex and gender issues in the workplace	See the section on "Work in the United States" in Chapter 13. How do sex and sexual orientation affect employment?
Violent victimization	Review the "Intersecting Inequalities" feature in Chapter 1. What do statistics show about the relationship between sex and gender and violence? How would you explain these facts? What is meant by gendered violence? How does this relate to the discussion of sexual harassment in the military in Chapter 14?
Women as leaders	Chapters 6 and 14 have sections describing the corporate and political leadership styles of women. What are the characteristics of women's leadership?
Social movements	Chapter 20 has a section devoted to the analysis of social movements and social change. According to that analysis, which type of social movement did Stonewall initiate? What stage in the life of a social movement is the gay and lesbian rights movement in?
Voting in the United States	See the "Doing Sociology" feature in Chapter 14. What is meant by a "gender gap" in political attitudes? How might this gap relate to voting patterns on issues of gender equality and gay and lesbian rights?
Gays and lesbians in the military	Chapter 14 discusses gays and lesbians in the military. How do opinions on this issue reveal homophobia? What do you think is the fate of the "Don't Ask, Don't Tell" policy?

SUMMING UP CHAPTER 10

Theoretical Perspectives on Gender

1. Two theories of gender differences were discussed. The sociobiological perspective on gender holds that the differences we observe in women's and men's personalities and behavior are directly traceable to differences in their physical makeup. One type of sociobiological theory is structural functionalism, which maintains that biological differences between men and women have led to the

emergence of different gender roles. The role division between women and men is considered functional for society as a whole. But structural functionalism has been criticized for justifying sexism and for suggesting that gender roles are immutable.

2. A second theory, the feminist perspective, acknowledges the importance of both biology and social learning in the acquisition of gender. But feminists believe it is impossible to separate the two influences, and they emphasize the complex interaction between biology and culture. Feminist sociology sees gender as socially created, rather than innately determined, and therefore amenable to change. This perspective is also concerned with the differential consequences of particular social arrangements and social constructions of gender in the everyday lives of women and men.

Sex and Gender: The Interaction of Nature and Environment

1. Studies of prenatal conditions such as AGS and androgen-insensitive syndrome show that the development of a masculine or feminine identity is independent of one's genes or hormones. In addition, these cases highlight the fact that neither sex nor gender is dichotomous.

2. Cross-cultural research shows that every society has a division of labor by sex, but what is considered men's work and women's work varies dramatically from society to society. Particularly interesting are gender relations in contemporary hunting and gathering societies because gender relations are very diverse in these societies and also highly egalitarian. Egalitarian gender relations are found in other types of societies as well. The cross-cultural data show that our own society's definitions of masculinity and femininity are not cultural universals. In addition, they show that a gendered division of labor does not necessarily produce gender inequality, and women's reproductive roles do not necessarily prevent them from fully participating in other activities.

3. The existence of multiple genders demonstrates the fluidity of gender and the creativity that humans bring to the process of social organization. In some societies, there are three genders; in others, more.

Sexual Orientation

1. A person's sexual orientation is the source of an individual's affectional preferences, sexual arousal, and sexual gratification. Heterosexuality, homosexuality, and bisexuality are the three most common sexual orientations. It is difficult to determine how many people are homosexual or bisexual in our society because these sexual orientations are considered deviant.

2. Researchers also disagree about how sexual orientation develops. Some believe that it is genetic, but others emphasize the role that culture and learning play in the development of sexual orientation. Biological and social research on sexual orientation show the interconnectedness of nature and culture.

Gender and Sexual Orientation as Systems of Stratification

1. Societies rank people by sex, gender, and sexual orientation. When one sex or gender is privileged over another, it is called *sexism;* the privileging of heterosexuality over other sexual orientations is called *heterosexism.*

2. Parents are the first gender socializers. Parents treat their children differently on the basis of sex: rewarding them for gender-appropriate behavior, punishing them for gender-inappropriate behavior, dressing them differently, and giving them different toys to play with. In these ways, parents essentially train male and female children for separate (and in our society, unequal) roles.

3. Peers are also gender socializers. Children socialize one another through their everyday interactions in the home and at play, strongly rewarding gender-appropriate behavior.

4. Children receive gender socialization in school as well. Teachers typically interact differently with their male and female students, interacting more often with males than females and giving them more praise and greater encouragement. Teachers also sometimes make remarks in class that disparage females and their intellectual abilities. Many education specialists believe the gender inequities embedded in teacher–student interactions lower female students' academic self-esteem and confidence. These inequities persist through high school and college.

5. The media are powerful gender socializers. Women and men, and homosexuals and heterosexuals, are rarely treated equally in the media. Television is the most important media socializer. Women have fewer roles on television than men do, and the characters played by women tend to be younger and less mature than male characters. Racial and ethnic stereotypes are also prevalent on prime-time television, as are stereotypes about homosexuals, although portrayals of homosexual characters are improving.

Gender and Sexual Orientation in the Workplace

1. Historically, women, especially married women, were much less likely than men to have paid employment, but today the typical woman, like the typical man, is in the paid labor force and working full-time, year-round. But there are important differences in women's and men's employment experiences. Most jobs, for example, are still sex segregated, and women's work on average pays less than men's work.

2. Women who hold sex-atypical jobs encounter limits to their upward occupational mobility. In contrast, men in sex-atypical jobs often receive preferential treatment in hiring and encouragement to move up in their professions. Neither gay men nor lesbians, however, receive favorable treatment in the workplace, but instead experience various types of discrimination, including harassment, being excluded from informal networks, and being fired because of their sexual orientation.

Gendered Violence

1. Men are both more likely than women to commit crimes and to be victimized by crime, but there are certain crimes that are directed against women because they are women. These crimes include sexual harassment and sexual assault.

2. Sexual harassment refers to unwanted leers, comments, suggestions, or physical contact of a sexual nature, as well as unwelcome requests for sexual favors. Men rarely experience sexual harassment, but studies show that between 20 and 49 percent of women on college campuses and 42 to 88 percent of female workers experience sexual harassment. Sexual harassment is especially prevalent in male-dominated fields, but in all cases it has serious consequences for victims.

3. Rape is the crime women fear more than any other, yet it is one of the violent crimes least likely to be reported to police and it has one of the lowest arrest and conviction rates of any crime. The widespread belief in rape myths makes the prosecution of rape cases difficult, and it is rape victims who must often prove their innocence in court. This is particularly true in cases of acquaintance rape, when the victim knows or is familiar with her assailant. The younger the victim, the more likely she is to know her assailant. Acquaintance rapes are especially common on college campuses.

4. Sociologists and anthropologists have found differences between societies with low rape rates (rape-free societies) and those with high rape rates (rape-prone societies). The most outstanding feature of rape-free societies is egalitarian gender relations and the high value accorded feminine traits and roles. In contrast, in rape-prone societies, women are viewed as sexual property and feminine traits and roles are devalued.

Gender, Sexual Orientation, and Social Change

1. In the United States, women's efforts to secure equal rights with men date to the Civil War era. The early women's movement concentrated on winning women the right to vote, but following enfranchisement in 1920, feminist activism declined. In the 1960s, there was a resurgence of feminism and over the past thirty years, feminism has achieved a great deal on many fronts. Today, an important dimension of feminism for young women is inclusion.

2. Groups for homosexuals were established in the United States in the 1920s, but their focus was on providing social support for homosexuals and promoting tolerance, rather than securing equal rights. The Stonewall riots of 1969 are generally considered the political spark that ignited widespread organized efforts to secure equality for homosexuals. These groups have achieved many successes, but they continue to face strong opposition and homosexuals are still denied basic rights.

KEY PEOPLE AND CONCEPTS

acquaintance rape: a case of sexual assault in which the victim knows or is familiar with her assailant

adrenogenital syndrome (AGS): a prenatal abnormality that occurs when the adrenal glands of a pregnant woman or her fetus malfunction, exposing the fetus to excessive amounts of male hormones and causing female babies to be born with female internal reproductive organs, but masculinized external genitalia

androgen-insensitive syndrome: a prenatal abnormality that occurs when a genetically male fetus is insensitive to male hormones, causing the baby to be born with female genitals and undescended testes even though it is a genetically normal male

berdache: individuals who adopt the gender behavior ascribed to members of the opposite sex; a part of the culture and gender relations of some societies in Asia and the South Pacific and among some North American Indian societies

bisexuality: a sexual orientation in which individuals are sexually and affectionally attracted to members of both sexes

discrimination: any actions, policies, or practices that have the effect of denying particular individuals or groups equal access to a society's resources and rewards

establishment sex segregation: a form of occupational sex segregation in which women and men have the same job, but they work for different types of establishments, which are unequal in pay and prestige

feminist sociology of gender: a theoretical perspective that acknowledges the importance of both biology and social learning in the acquisition of gender, but that sees gender as primarily a social construction

gender: the socially constructed constellation of traits and behaviors that compose the categories *masculine* and *feminine*

gender inequality: (see **sexism**)

gender identity: the set of gendered characteristics that an individual adopts as an integral part of her or his self

gender roles: the behavioral requirements or expectations that are prescribed for a society's members depending on their sex

gender stereotype: simplistic descriptions of the supposedly "masculine male" or "feminine female"

heterosexism: the privileging of heterosexuality over homosexuality

heterosexuality: a sexual orientation in which the source of an individual's affectional preferences, sexual arousal, and sexual gratification are persons of the sex opposite them

homosexuality: a sexual orientation in which the source of an individual's affectional preferences, sexual arousal, and sexual gratification are persons of their same sex

industry sex segregation: a form of occupational sex segregation in which the representation of women and men in a particular industry as a whole is relatively balanced, but within the industry, women and men hold different kinds of jobs that are unequal in pay and prestige

matriarchy: a sex/gender system in which women dominate men and that which is considered feminine is more highly valued than that which is considered masculine

occupational sex segregation: the degree to which men and women are concentrated in occupations in which workers of one sex predominate

patriarchy: a sex/gender system in which men dominate women and that which is considered masculine is more highly valued than that which is considered feminine

prejudice: biased beliefs or attitudes about individuals based on their membership in a particular group

rape: when a person uses force or the threat of force to have some form of sexual intercourse (vaginal, oral, or anal) with another person

sex: the genetic determination of maleness and femaleness

sex/gender system: the institutionalized traits, behaviors, and patterns of social interaction that are prescribed for a so-

ciety's members on the basis of their sex; composed of three interrelated components: the social construction of gender, a sexual division of labor, and the social regulation of sexuality

sexism: differentially valuing people's traits or abilities on the basis of their sex and without regard for their attributes as individuals

sexual harassment: any unwanted leers, comments, suggestions, or physical contact of a sexual nature, as well as unwelcome requests for sexual favors

sexual orientation: the source of an individual's affectional preferences, sexual arousal, and sexual gratification

social movements: issue-oriented groups established to bring about or prevent social change through social action

sociobiological perspective of gender: a theoretical perspective that holds that the differences we may observe in women's and men's personalities and behavior are directly traceable to the difference in their physical makeup, especially their reproductive abilities

symbolic annihilation: the practice of the media to ignore, trivialize, ridicule, or condemn women and homosexuals and the issues that are of particular concern to them

LEARNING MORE

Canary, D. J., Emmers-Sommer, T. M., with Faulkner, S. (1997). *Sex and gender differences in personal relationships*. New York: Guilford. A thorough review of the existing data on many sex and gender differences, which calls into question many common stereotypes about men and women.

Lepowsky, M. (1994). *Fruit of the motherland: Gender in an egalitarian society*. New York: Columbia University Press. A report on the results of the author's long and fascinating research with men and women on Vanitinai, an island southwest of New Guinea.

Murray, S. O. (1996). *American gay*. Chicago: University of Chicago Press. A very careful sociological analysis of trends within gay communities in the United States since the 1940s that includes some interesting predictions about the future.

Roscoe, W. (1998). *Changing ones: Third and fourth genders in Native North America*. New York: St. Martin's. A well-

researched analysis of the religious and economic importance of *berdaches* by a social scientist widely regarded as the leading expert on multiple genders.

Schwartz, M. D., & DeKeseredy, W. S. (1997). *Sexual assault on the college campus*. Thousand Oaks, CA: Sage. A thorough examination of the research—including the authors' own—on the problem of sexual assault of women at colleges and universities in the United States and Canada.

Williams, C. L. (1995). *Still a man's world: Men who do "women's work."* Berkeley: University of California Press. An elaboration of Williams's research with men in "nontraditional" occupations, this book refutes many stereotypes about men who hold "women's jobs," and documents the advantages that accrue to these men because of their sex.

 Run Chapter 11 on your *Living Sociology* CD-ROM for interesting and informative activities, web links, videos, practice tests, and more.

Race and Ethnicity

I magine that you are seated in the living room of your home with a U.S. government census-taker, who is asking you a series of questions. The questions are pretty easy to answer—how many people live in your household, what are their ages and relationship to one another, and so on. But then the census-taker asks about your racial identity, giving you five choices: White, Black, Asian/Pacific Islander, American Indian/Alaskan native, or other. You hesitate to answer. Although you are officially listed as "White" on your birth certificate, your mother's parents were from Western Europe, your father's father was the son of a Filipino woman and a Chinese man, and your father's mother was African American. What does that make you? The first answer that comes to mind is "other," but you don't like the sound of that. Who wants to be an "other"? So you decide not to answer that question and tell the census-taker so. The census-taker looks you over, observing your dark hair and eyes and your olive-toned skin, and notes that your last name is Spanish-sounding. The census-taker checks "White" on the form and underneath that also checks "Spanish/Hispanic origin." You've been "counted," although not as you would like and not accurately.

How would such an experience make you feel? For Teja Arboleda, the person to whom this actually happened, the experience aroused a mixture of confusion and anger. At a 1994 hearing on changing the racial classification system used by the Census Bureau, Mr. Arboleda emphasized that he sees himself as *multiracial*, not as a member of one race or as an "other" (Holmes, 1994). To some observers, a decision by the Census Bureau to include the category "multiracial" in the 2000 census would signal an important step toward doing away with the concept of *race* altogether. But others argue that the concepts of *race* and *ethnicity* are central to social interaction in this country and elsewhere (see, for example, Holmes, 1997).

In this chapter we will look at race and ethnicity in social relations. Let's begin by defining some key terms.

RACIAL, ETHNIC, AND MINORITY GROUPS

A sociological analysis of race and ethnic relations, like a sociological analysis of social class and gender, is critical to understanding social interaction both historically and in contemporary societies. Race and ethnicity are central organizing variables of social life. As we've seen in previous chapters, members of different racial and ethnic groups do not have equal experiences or opportunities. Race also intersects with class and gender in ways that advantage some groups while disadvantaging others socially, economically, and politically. Why? To begin to answer that question, we must first be clear on what we mean when we speak of races and ethnic groups.

Race

We tend to take the notion of race for granted. Certainly, we assume that it is real; we assume that everyone, even

if they can't define it, can at least name different races. Indeed, race is commonly understood as a fundamental basis of difference between people.

Sociologically, **race** refers to a group whose members share a real or supposed biological heritage that is thought to give rise to a set of fixed physical, mental, emotional, and moral characteristics. In addition, members of a race also typically share common customs, values, and traditions that give them a sense of peoplehood, or identification with one's "own kind of people."

Although today we often seem preoccupied with racial classifications, as the story that opened this chapter illustrates, the fact is that for much of human history people rarely assigned one another to different racial groups. It was not until the late eighteenth century, when biology achieved some stature in the scientific community and Western Europeans began exploring and colonizing Africa, Asia, and the Americas, that scientists set about classifying humans into racial categories (Jaret, 1995; Shipman, 1994).

Thus, since the late 1700s, race has been popularly thought of as a biological concept, even though most scientists today reject the notion that race has any biological basis (Shanklin, 1993). Nevertheless, most people continue to believe that "racial differences" reveal themselves in physical—that is, biological—differences that can be seen across groups. Members of one race typically point to a host of physical characteristics such as skin color, hair color and texture, height, and bone structure that they believe set them apart from other races. But despite the visible physical differences that people often use to distinguish races, scientists have been unable to isolate a "race gene." In both genetic and biological terms, there is more similarity than difference among humans, regardless of how they are racially classified (Gould, 1981, 1985; Jaret, 1995; Templeton, 1998).

Saying that race is not biologically based does not deny that biological differences exist between people. Skin color, for example, is an obvious difference among people that is genetically transmitted. But the heritability of skin color tells us nothing about the variability of personality or behavioral traits that we observe throughout the human population, nor does it imply that one group is superior to another group.

If race is not a biologically valid concept, then what is it? It is, in short, a *social* construct. People create the concept of race and racial categories as a way to describe and give meaning to the variations they see in humans. There is abundant evidence for the social foundations of race. Consider first that we emphasize physical differences between racial groups, but no real physical differences are necessary for racial categories to be developed, and the distinguishing physical traits are frequently arbitrary. "Often these [physical] differences are more imagined than real, sometimes they are entirely fictional and always a few physical traits are singled out for attention while most, including some which might differently divide the society if they were attended to, are ignored" (Berreman, 1991, p. 34). Recall once again, for example, the *Burakumin* of Japan, whom we have discussed in Chapter 6. *Burakumin* are physically indistinguishable from other Japanese, but are nonetheless considered a distinct—and inferior—"race" (Upham, 1988).

A look at racial labeling cross-culturally also illustrates how artificial and arbitrary it is. For instance, many people classified as Black in the United States would be considered "coloured" (a racial category distinct from Black) in South Africa. At the same time, in Peru, where hair texture, eye color, and stature are considered more indicative of racial heritage than skin color, many U.S. Blacks would be labeled White (Berreman, 1991; Yetman, 1991).

Even within a single society, racial labeling is often inconsistent. In the United States, for example, the racial classifications used by the Census Bureau have changed nearly every decade since the late 1800s. In the 1890 census, there were eight racial groups, with four distinguishing the Black population alone: Blacks were people with three-fourths or more Black ancestry; Mulattos had three-eighths to five-eighths Black ancestry; Quadroons had one-fourth Black ancestry; and Octoroons had one-eighth or "any trace" of Black ancestry. Just ten years later, there were only five racial categories because Mulatto, Quadroon, and Octoroon fell into disuse. However by 1930, the number of racial categories on the census swelled to ten: White, Negro, Indian (American Indian), Chinese, Japanese, Korean, Filipino, Hindu, Mexican, and Other. This was the first and only time that Mexicans were identified as a distinct race. Moreover, within twenty years, "Hindu" and Korean also disappeared as racial categories (Lee, 1993).

Professional golfer Tiger Woods calls himself a "Cablinasian" because his father's ancestry is African American, Chinese, and Native American, and his mother's is Thai, Chinese, and Caucasian. What is the significance of multiracialism for racial classifications? What is the significance of multiracialism for American society?

The changes in the census racial classifications over the years reflect the changing social, economic, and political concerns of the White population. Following the Civil War, White people were obsessed with the notion of "racial purity" and a desire to keep the races separate. Although such ideas did not disappear in the early twentieth century—indeed, for some they still have not disappeared—the revised census racial categories reflected a new concern: an influx of immigrants from Asia (Lee, 1993).

Thus, racial classification is a social and political process, not a biological or even a scientific process. Indeed, the fact that racial classification is arbitrary is what gives it its force in the eyes of people who rely on it. In other words, while racial categories have no intrinsic meaning, the meanings that members of a society give to the racial categories they create reinforce a hierarchy of privilege and power in that society. Individuals may be granted or denied resources, rewards, and opportunities simply on the basis of their membership in a particular racial group.

This is an important point to which we will return shortly. First, though, let's consider another social construct: the ethnic group.

Ethnicity

In everyday speech, the terms *race* and *ethnic group* are often used interchangably, and there is certainly overlap between them. Sociologically, however, the two kinds of groups may be considered distinct. In general, biological heritage is emphasized in defining racial groups, whereas culture and feelings of peoplehood are emphasized in identifying ethnic groups.

An **ethnic group**, then, is a group whose members share a common cultural heritage and a sense of peoplehood that they pass on from one generation to the next. The characteristics of an ethnic group—that is, the ways they express their cultural heritage and sense of belonging to the group—is referred to as **ethnicity**.

When many of us think of ethnic groups, it is the cultural manifestations that typically come to mind. We think of language, customs, music, styles of dress, and food preferences or prohibitions. But sociologists maintain that these cultural expressions of ethnicity are actually less important—and often inaccurate—indicators of ethnic identity. In the United States, for example, some members of ethnic groups know very little about their cultural heritage and yet they still identify as members of the group. Similarly, members of some ethnic groups sometimes complain that their ethnic identity is questioned by people who claim that they don't look, sound, or act like "real Indians," "real Italians," and so on (Jaret, 1995).

Consequently, most sociologists argue that rather than cultural expression, the critical defining feature of an ethnic group is a sense of peoplehood. Members of racial groups also share a sense of peoplehood, but as we said about classifying races, most people focus on physical or biological characteristics. The sense of peoplehood, or identification with one's "own kind of people," that members of an ethnic group share derives from their cultural ancestry, which members believe binds them to one another in a special way. Cultural expressions and symbols—a flag, a particular song, a story, a sporting event—usually evoke a very strong "we-feeling" in the members of an ethnic group. Peoplehood also provides a sense of affiliation and sometimes even obligation to others of "one's kind." It is the feeling that prompts two Italian Americans whose ancestors came from the same region of the "old country" to embrace as *paisons* even though they have never met before, or that motivates African Americans to raise clenched fists in solidarity with Black men and women in South Africa whom they call brothers and sisters even though they are not kin and have never seen one another.

Both the cultural characteristics and the sense of peoplehood that mark an ethnic group can be a source of great pride and cohesiveness. In fact, it is argued that culture and a sense of peoplehood are necessary for the continued existence of the group as a whole and for fostering positive self-images in individual members of the group (Fiske, 1998; Kitano, 1985). At the same time, ethnic pride and cohesiveness can also give rise to tremendous conflict, as we will see next.

Ethnocentrism and Racism

Earlier in the text we said that **ethnocentrism** was the belief that one's own group's values and behavior are "correct" or "best" and other groups' values and practices are inferior. We said that most of us would probably agree that ethnocentrism is wrong because it is unfair and shows a lack of respect for other groups' cultures. But saying and doing are two different things: The human tendency is to prefer the familiar, so what is unlike "ours" is often disliked and devalued. Some scientists think some degree of ethnocentrism is inevitable (Fiske, 1998). However, intense ethnocentrism can be volatile and destructive, and even the boundary between benign and harmful ethnocentrism is often blurry. To understand the difference between benign and harmful ethnocentrism, consider the extremes of the continuum. Taking pride in the accomplishments of one's ethnic group, for example, is quite different from claiming that these accomplishments are a result of the group's superiority and that other ethnic groups should therefore be disdained for their inferiority. Destructive ethnocentrism engenders various levels of conflict between ethnic groups. The conflict may take the form of avoidance, with members of different groups keeping to themselves, as in Australia where Aboriginal and White Australians live apart and have little contact with one another. Or the conflict may be violent, as in the former Yugoslavia where warring ethnic groups set out to systematically kill their opponents in a campaign of "ethnic cleansing."

While all ethnic groups have probably practiced and experienced ethnocentrism in varying degrees, the experiences of racial groups differ from those of ethnic groups in significant ways (see the Social Policy box on page 288). Recall that racial groups are typically distinguished on the basis of physical traits such as skin color and eye shape, whereas ethnic groups are usually distinguished by cultural markers. Many sociologists argue therefore that racial distinctiveness—particularly if the physical differences among groups are visible and not easily hidden—

SOCIOLOGY LIVE

Western Kentucky University—Bowling Green, KY
Course: Introduction to Sociology—Stacey Sympson, Instructor
Students: (left to right) Matthew Payne, Richard Cohen, Jodi Clinard-Pulley, Scott Wolfe, Andrei Makarevich, and (not shown) Nikita Havener.

What is the racial and ethnic composition of our school?

"The people were very friendly when I first came here. There were many different kinds of people: whites, blacks, and Asians. Everybody was really friendly and did not treat me any different." This is what Andrei Makarevich, a Russian student on a tennis scholarship at Western Kentucky University (WKU), had to say about his college experience.

In diversity, students at our university break down into the following percentages (for the number of students enrolled in the Fall 1998 semester).

White	91%
Black	7%
Asian	1%
Hispanic	.6%
Other	.6%
American Indian	.3%

As you can see from the composition of the student body, Whites are the majority. When compared to other schools in the state the numbers are similar except for the University of Louisville and Spalding University, both of which have an 80 percent White majority. However, Kentucky State University, with a historically larger Black population, has a student body with 54 percent Black students and 40 percent White students.

To understand the WKU chart and its distribution of different races, we decided to define ethnicity and race on our own. Race is a concept applied to different groups of people that share actual or assumed biological characteristics. Ethnicity is the different types of values, behaviors, and beliefs shared by a group with a common cultural identification. Diversity is the existence of different types of ethnicities and races.

We asked the President and the Dean of Student Life about WKU's policies and goals regarding student diversity. President Gary Ransdell responded that embracing diversity and achieving balance in diversity are major goals at the university. Howard Bailey, Dean of Student Life, pointed out that WKU is making progress in increasing diversity. However, "too often ethnic groups coexist separately, instead of inter-existing, as they probably should. Every university should embrace diversity to prepare students for the global work environment that they will find themselves in later on."

One student, however, sees things differently. She said that often she is the only African American female in a classroom, and instructors sometimes ask her what she thinks to get an African American perspective, as if her personal views were a reflection of her race and ethnicity. However, she said that on the whole, most people she knows are not prejudiced but often are ethnocentric.

Another person we talked to noted that Blacks tend to congregate together. Thinking about that brings up several questions. Do they socialize separately because they all get along, or because they feel unwanted, or do they have some hidden racism regarding Whites? In answer, one respondent said that our questions don't have anything to do with it. People hang around with others with whom they are good friends. Then she asked the same questions about White people, who seem to congregate together too!

Thus, our study has revealed that questions of diversity at our school are more complicated than we initially thought, and we have more questions than answers. Maybe in the end it has more to do with our perceptions and beliefs about people and life.

carries more negative consequences than cultural distinctiveness. In the United States, for example, compare the experiences of White European ethnic groups with various racial groups. Although some groups of White ethnics can cite encounters with ethnocentrism, the historical record, as we will see later in this chapter, indicates that they enjoyed better economic, political, and social op-portunities and privileges than Black Americans, Asian Americans, and Native Americans. Indeed, no ethnic group from Europe came to America enslaved as the ancestors of African Americans did, nor were White ethnics ever deprived of their land and forced to live on reservations as Native Americans were. And during World War II, only Japanese Americans were sent to U.S. concentra-

---

Social Policy
Affirmative Action

The Issue

Many European groups who immigrated to the United States faced prejudice and discrimination, but eventually, they integrated successfully into the dominant society. When members of these groups consider the circumstances of non-White racial and ethnic minorities today, they sometimes ask, "If we made it, why can't they?" The assumption is that non-White minorities "can or should make social, economic, and political progress the same way the White ethnic groups did (or at least the way they *believe* they did)" (Jaret, 1995, p. 79; see also Verhovek, 1997; Wolfe, 1998). Such a position has important public policy implications. For one thing, if we accept this assumption, we are likely to expect non-White minorities to succeed in the dominant society "on their own," without the assistance of government programs, such as affirmative action.

The Debate

In 1961, President John Kennedy issued Executive Order 10925, which we know as affirmative action. The purpose of the executive order was to ensure that employers holding contracts with the federal government do not discriminate on the basis of race, color, national origin, or religion in their hiring practices; in 1968, the order was amended to also prohibit sex discrimination. If discrimination was found, the guilty employer could lose its federal contract and be barred from future federal contracts. At the center of the controversy over affirmative action is the fact that the policy went beyond mere prohibition of discrimination by requiring employers to actively recruit, train, and promote minorities.

Opponents of affirmative action charge that it amounts to little more than reverse discrimination because it gives preferences in hiring and educational admissions to minorities. According to these critics, affirmative action perpetuates the practice of judging people on the basis of skin color (or sex) rather than on the basis of individual qualifications, so it inflicts the same harm it was designed to alleviate. In addition, critics argue that affirmative action results in unqualified minorities being hired or admitted to schools at the expense of qualified Whites (Belz, 1991; Sowell, 1990; see also Verhovek, 1997; Wolfe, 1998).

Supporters of affirmative action do not deny that individual merit should be weighted heavily in hiring and admissions decisions. But they also point out that discrimination is not an individual problem; rather, it is a systemic problem that requires an institutional remedy. Historically, employers and admissions personnel have overtly discriminated against minorities and women, or they have masked discrimination through the use of practices that appear neutral (such as seniority systems and aptitude tests), but are actually biased. Affirmative action, these supporters say, provides a fair way to redress the historical imbalance (Wigdor & Hartigan, 1990). Moreover, there is little evidence, if any, that affirmative action has resulted in highly qualified White men being displaced by unqualified minorities (Leonard, 1991; "Reverse Discrimination of Whites Is Rare," 1995; Davidson & Lewis, 1998).

Since the late 1970s, the federal government and the courts have sided with affirmative action's opponents, gradually eroding the provisions of the policy. In 1996, a majority of voters in California supported a proposition repealing the state's affirmative action program. In 1997, a federal appeals court ruled that the affirmative action program at the University of Texas at Austin's law school was unconstitutional because it allowed for reverse discrimination. University and professional school enrollments in both California and Texas are already showing the effects of these policy changes. For example, since 1997, entering classes at public law schools in both states have shown a sharp drop in minority students (Chavez, 1998; Holmes, 1998; Torry, 1997). A similar outcome is expected in Washington state where, in 1998, voters supported a ballot initiative to ban affirmative action (Bronner, 1998).

What Do You Think?

Do you agree with supporters of affirmative action that it is a fair way to address the problem of racism in the United States, a problem that White ethnics did not face and, in fact, often benefited from (Jaret, 1995)? Or, do you think there is a better way to eliminate racism in this country and to remedy our long history of racial discrimination?

tion camps, even though we were also at war with Italy and Germany (Takagi, 1989).

Consequently, when we speak of the unjust treatment of one group by another on the basis of race alone, we are discussing **racism,** which is different from ethnocentrism. Racism is a form of inequality in which one racial group dominates another and legitimates its dominance by proclaiming itself physically, intellectually, and/or socially superior, and instituting laws or practices to protect its dominance.

Racism is a word that evokes strong emotions in most people regardless of their racial identification, but researchers have found that members of different racial groups understand the word differently. White people tend to define *racism* rather narrowly, applying it only to those who explicitly claim that the "White race" is superior to all other races and favor restricting the rights of non-White people. Of course, if the term is applied only to extremists, then the majority of White people conveniently escape being labeled racist. In contrast, non-White people—people of color—tend to define racism more broadly to include anything, intentional or unintentional, that advantages one race over another. This definition, then, applies not only to explicit denials of rights and opportunities, but also to social situations such as when someone is made to feel unwelcome because her or his racial group is the brunt of a joke. Most sociologists also prefer this broader definition (Jaret, 1995; see also the Doing Sociology box). The racial differences in definitions of racism do not mean that only White people are racist. Non-White people may also be racist, but White people have greater power in our society, so their racism is more potent.

Some people say that a broad definition of racism allows individuals to deny personal responsibility. According to this argument, if a person of color does not get a particular job or is not admitted to a particular school, the individual can claim racism, even when the reason is a

Violence and defamation against minority groups and their property, such as this demonstration of anti-Semitism, are based on beliefs about innate superiority. Like other forms of racism, anti-Semitism has been expressed through institutional discrimination as well, for example through hiring and promotion, loans and mortgages, leases and housing, and political appointments (see p. 292). How might the case of Holocaust victims' bank accounts in Swiss banks be seen as an example of institutional discrimination?

lack of qualifications. Granted, claiming racism in such situations is manipulative, but the fear of such manipulation is exaggerated. At the same time, others point out that a narrow definition of racism excuses the objectionable attitudes and behavior of White people toward people of color, and also overlooks the harm caused by everyday, seemingly insignificant encounters with racial insensitivity and hostility. A narrow definition also ignores the extent to which racism can be an institutional as well as an individual phenomenon—that is, built into the practices and policies of the institutions that organize daily social life. We will explore the institutional manifestations of racism in the next section of this chapter.

DOING SOCIOLOGY

What Does Racism *Mean to You?*

Do members of different racial and ethnic groups on your campus define racism differently?

To find out, select a sample of people from your campus and ask them to define *racism.* Be sure your sample is diverse in terms of race and ethnicity. Besides defining racism, ask each person to give one or two examples of racism. Following the interviews, compare the answers of the White and non-White respondents. Do they differ? If so, how?

And how do your findings compare with those of your classmates? Taken together, what do you think these findings reveal about attitudes toward racism?

Racial and ethnic groups who are singled out for unfair treatment are referred to as **minority groups.** In the sociological sense, minority group status has nothing to do with a group's numerical representation in a society. In fact, minority group members may actually constitute the numerical majority of a society's population. In South Africa, for example, 77 percent of the population is Black, but until 1990, Black South Africans had none of the basic rights of citizenship enjoyed by White South Africans, and even today, Black South Africans are treated as less than full citizens by many Whites. The key to understanding the sociological distinction between a minority group and its counterpart, the majority group, is the level of inequality between the two (Essed, 1991). The majority group establishes a system of inequality through which it subordinates and exploits the minority. At the same time, it preserves its privileged position by controlling major institutions such as the economy, government, and the legal system, and promoting an ideology that justifies its dominance.

Some sociologists believe it would be more accurate to call minority groups *oppressed groups* and the majority group *oppressors,* arguing that these labels more vividly convey the inequalities of race and ethnicity. Regardless of the terms we use, the result is the same: Racism and ethnocentrism inequitably divide a society. Let's examine more carefully the ways of thinking and behaving that foster and perpetuate inequality between majority and minority groups.

R E F L E C T I N G   O N

Racial, Ethnic, and Minority Groups

1. Do you favor abandoning the use of racial classifications in the census and elsewhere? Why or why not? What would be the advantages and disadvantages of abandoning racial classifications?
2. What cultural symbols are significant to the ethnic group with which you identify most? What specific feelings or meanings do they evoke in you?
3. Do you favor a broad or a narrow definition of racism? Explain your position.

PREJUDICE AND DISCRIMINATION

In Chapter 10, we said that sexism has two dimensions: One is attitudinal and the other is behavioral. The same is true of racial and ethnic inequality: Each has an attitudinal and a behavioral component. The attitudinal component is prejudice, and the behavioral component is discrimination.

Prejudice

Prejudice refers to biased beliefs about individuals based on their membership in a particular racial or ethnic group. An integral element of prejudice is stereotyping, which we defined earlier in the text as an oversimplified, summary description of a group.

Although there are positive stereotypes (such as Asians are hard workers), in most cases stereotypes are overwhelmingly negative and hostile. Very few groups in the United States have not been stereotyped at one time or another, and the all-inclusive nature of the stereotypes means that few racial and ethnic group members have escaped their stigma. Claims have been made, for example, that all Blacks are lazy, all Chinese are sly, all Jews are miserly, all Italians are in the Mafia, and all Irish drink too much. Sometimes there are contradictory stereotypes of the same group: For instance, while Jews are often stereotyped as miserly, they are also stereotyped as "flashy."

What happens when a prejudiced person encounters Blacks, Chinese, Jews, Italians, or Irish who do not conform to the stereotypes? The research on this question shows the potency of prejudice: When prejudiced people encounter members of a group who do not conform to their biases about that group, they have one of two responses. The prejudiced person says there are always exceptions to the rule; depending on the group in question, there may be a couple of ambitious, honest, generous, law-abiding, or sober Blacks, Chinese, Jews, Italians, and Irish (Fiske, 1998). The alternative response, if the trait exhibited by the member of the stereotyped group is admired by the prejudiced person, is for the the prejudiced person to negatively redefine the behavior so that it conforms to the stereotype (Jenkins, 1994). For example, during World War II, combat behavior that was considered "courageous" when performed by White American soldiers was labeled "bloodthirsty" when displayed by Japanese soldiers.

In short, racial and ethnic prejudice are resilient, even in the face of evidence that refutes them. To a prejudiced person, race and ethnicity are more important than any other characteristic of the individual self in evaluating one's own behavior or that of others. Why? Most social scientists who have tried to answer this question have looked at the psychology of prejudiced individuals. One perspective states that when people become frustrated in their efforts to achieve a specific goal, they often blame others for their failure rather than looking inward at their personal limitations or outward at objective circumstances (Pettigrew & Meertens, 1995; Tyler & Smith, 1998). Those who are blamed are typically groups with little power to resist such unfair labeling. So, for example, during the economic downturn of the 1980s, some people blamed the Japanese for high U.S. unemployment. One Chinese American man, Vincent Chin, was even beaten to death by two White men who mistakenly assumed he was

Racist organizations such as the Ku Klux Klan and White supremacist groups such as the so-called skinheads have had a resurgence in recent years. Why? These movements are expressed in rallies, cross burnings, secret militias, and Internet propaganda. Civil liberties protect antisocial sentiments in a democracy, but not antisocial behavior that results in a crime. Why is this distinction sometimes hard to make when dealing with hate groups? Some observers have referred to Klansmen as an oppressed group oppressing other oppressed groups. What do they mean by that?

Japanese and therefore partly responsible for Americans' job losses (Chan, 1991). Chin and other Asian Americans were **scapegoats**, relatively powerless people whom others unjustly blame for their own or society's problems.

A related idea is that prejudiced people who scapegoat have a particular type of personality, which psychologist Theodore Adorno (1950) called the **authoritarian personality**. A person with an authoritarian personality is in-

secure and intolerant, rigidly conforming to tradition, superstitious, and submissive to authority. Individuals with this type of personality view the world as a competitive, hostile place, where superior people (like them) struggle with and inevitably win out over inferior people.

Social scientists who support the idea of the authoritarian personality believe this personality type develops when children are raised by domineering, unaffectionate parents. Children in such households grow up angry and insecure, with a need to blame others (whom they consider their inferiors) for personal and social problems. However, other social scientists point out that prejudice is common even among people who are not authoritarian. Consequently, these social scientists think that people learn prejudice like they learn other attitudes and beliefs, through the process of socialization (Devine, 1989; Devine & Monteith, 1993).

We will return to the role of socialization in explaining racism later in the chapter. But now let's see how prejudice translates into action, establishing a rationale for the unequal treatment of racial and ethnic minorities.

Discrimination

Discrimination refers to any actions, policies, or practices that deny an individual or group equal access to the society's resources, rewards, and opportunities. Notice that this definition focuses on the outcomes of behavior and policies governing behavior rather than on the intent that may underlie them. At least theoretically, then, discrimination can occur in the absence of conscious bigotry. In fact, sociologist Robert Merton (1949) identified four possible relationships between prejudice and discrimination (see Table 11.1). However, in real life, everyday thinking

TABLE 11.1   Merton's Typology of Prejudice and Discrimination

Type	Prejudiced	Discriminates
Unprejudiced nondiscriminator (*Example:* An Asian American teenager who dates teenagers from other racial and ethnic groups.)	No	No
Unprejudiced discriminator (*Example:* A White landlord who believes that people of all races should be able to live wherever they choose, but who does not rent to African Americans because the White tenants threaten to move out if he does.)	No	Yes
Prejudiced nondiscriminator (*Example:* An employer who believes Mexicans are lazy, but hires them because she fears a lawsuit if she is discovered discriminating.)	Yes	No
Prejudiced discriminator (*Example:* A banker who believes that Native Americans are bad credit risks and so turns down all Native Americans who apply to the bank for mortgages.)	Yes	Yes

is usually inseparable from everyday behavior and prejudice is one of the best predictors of discrimination (Dovidio et al., 1996; Essed, 1991).

Most conversations about discrimination focus on the behavior of individual discriminators. However, we shouldn't lose sight of the fact that institutions are discriminators, too. Institutions develop official policies and practices, as well as allocate societal resources and bestow societal rewards. In practical terms, then, **institutional discrimination** means that the central elements of the social structure—government, the economy, law, education, and so on—all systematically disadvantage particular racial and ethnic groups. Even more disturbing is the fact that, unlike individual discriminatory acts, institutional discrimination is more difficult to detect and harder still to eradicate. This is largely because, as a built-in feature of social arrangements, it easily goes unnoticed as discrimination. Instead, it is considered "business as usual." For example, when we hear that a group of White teenagers has spray-painted racist slurs on a house in their neighborhood newly occupied by a Black family, we are rightfully appalled. Nevertheless, while we are quick to express our reactions to such individual acts of discrimination, few of us question the residential segregation that systematically excludes Black families from specific neighborhoods. However, residential segregation as a form of institutional discrimination is more far-reaching and at least as harmful as any individual discriminatory act. In addition, institutional discrimination establishes a social context in which individual discrimination is not only possible, but condoned.

While institutional discrimination is often subtle, it may also be direct and explicit. The most widely practiced explicit form of institutional discrimination is **exclusion,** restricting the entry of a group into society or preventing its full participation in the society. The form of exclusion most widely practiced in this country is racial and ethnic **segregation**—physically and socially separating and keeping apart different racial and ethnic groups. Segregation was routine—and legal—in the United States until relatively recently. One example of this was the enactment of the *Jim Crow Laws* following the Civil War, which legally ensured racial segregation in the workplace, schools, recreational facilities, public accommodations, restaurants, public transportation, and even cemeteries. Today, explicit segregation is illegal, but it continues through such activities as *redlining,* the practice of identifying an area whose residents are considered ineligible for bank loans, homeowner's insurance, and other services. The residents of redlined neighborhoods are disproportionately racial and ethnic minorities. Consider, for instance, a recent investigation of home insurers in nine U.S. cities. Investigators, posing as prospective clients, called local offices of the country's three largest insurance companies to ask how much it would cost to

insure their homes. The callers didn't state their race or ethnicity, but an insurer could make a guess about it from the caller's name, voice, phone exchange, or address. In more than 50 percent of the calls, African American and Hispanic investigators were quoted higher rates for less coverage, were not given a rate quote at all, or were offered inferior policies compared with those offered White callers (Smith, 1995).

Exclusion may also involve keeping members of a particular group out of a country. In the late 1800s, the U.S. government enacted the Chinese Exclusion Act, prohibiting Chinese immigration to the United States for a ten-year period, although the law remained in effect until 1943. In 1996, in response to public perceptions that the United States was again accepting too many immigrants who are an economic burden on the country, Congress

Despite prejudice and discrimination, Chinese laborers in the United States helped to establish cities, such as San Francisco, shown in this 1925 photo. They also helped build transcontinental railroads and settle the West. Yet the Chinese Exclusion Act later prohibited Chinese immigration to the United States from the late 1800s until 1943—a form of institutional discrimination known as exclusion. What are the three other forms of institutional discrimination? What is a recent or historical example of each?

passed a law to sharply reduce the number of people who can legally emigrate to the United States each year. The law eliminates automatic entry privileges for siblings and adult children of legal residents and imposes an income test on sponsoring family members who must now prove that their earnings are greater than 125 percent of the poverty line ($20,622 for a family of four in 1998). The law obviously privileges middle-class and wealthy immigrant families, but makes it more difficult for working-class and poor families to reunite in the United States (Dugger, 1997).

Another direct and explicit form of institutional discrimination is **expulsion,** the forced removal of a group from an area or harassment to compel the group to migrate. Earlier in the chapter we mentioned the forced removal of Japanese Americans to U.S. concentration camps during World War II. Another example of expulsion in U.S. history was the Indian Removal Act in 1830, which required eastern American Indian tribes to relocate to the West. The most infamous event that occurred under this law was the "Trail of Tears," the forced march of the Cherokees from the southeastern United States to Oklahoma. Four thousand Cherokee men, women, and children died during the relocation (Snipp, 1989).

The most horrifying manifestation of institutional discrimination is **genocide,** the deliberate attempt to exterminate an entire race or ethnic group. When most of us think of genocide, we think of Adolf Hitler's Nazi Germany. In an attempt to establish an "Aryan nation," the Nazi regime systematically murdered more than six million Jews and other "non-Aryan" people such as the Romany (commonly referred to as "Gypsies") between 1933 and 1945. Genocide, however, is not something that has only happened in faraway places. In the United States, during the California gold rush (1848–1873), for example, the state government paid White settlers and prospectors for the heads of Indians, reimbursing individuals a total of about $1 million for the bullets they used. The Native American population in California declined from 150,000 to 30,000 (Ybarra, 1996).

More recent examples of genocide include Pol Pot's Cambodia and Idi Amin's Uganda. Between 1975 and 1979, Pol Pot implemented his policies for the "purification" of Cambodia, which included destroying anything foreign, including Cambodians who spoke foreign languages. An estimated two million people—one quarter of the country's population—were killed. During Amin's presidency (1971–1979), 300,000 Ugandans—one in every forty—were killed and thousands more were imprisoned in Amin's effort to eliminate everyone who was not Muslim and a member of his own group, the Kakwas. The populations of entire villages were murdered (Lamb, 1982). The most recent examples of genocide are in the former Yugoslavia, which we mentioned earlier (Hedges, 1998), and in Rwanda, where an estimated 1

Atrocities of the continuing civil war in former Yugoslavia often are given as an example of genocide. Bosnian Serb aggression against Muslim Croats and Albanians has been widely condemned, and in 1999 NATO intervened. In what sense is the murder of one racial or ethnic group by another institutional? Why is genocide within a society a threat to other countries as well?

million members of the Tutsi ethnic group have been killed by the Hutu ethnic group (Webb, 1997).

Discrimination may be prevalent in our society and others, but it is not inevitable. Interracial and interethnic contact can also lead to two other possible outcomes: assimilation and pluralism, which we will discuss next.

REFLECTING ON

Prejudice and Discrimination

1. Give an example from your personal experience of someone redefining behavior to fit a racial or ethnic group stereotype. What was the outcome of this redefinition?
2. Give an example of institutional discrimination, and explain how it establishes a social context for legitimating individual discrimination.

ASSIMILATION AND PLURALISM

The United States is often described as a "melting pot," a place where people from diverse cultures come together to form a distinctive "American" culture that blurs the differences among them. However, many observers question the extent to which such a blending is possible or even desirable. At the heart of this debate are the questions: How similar or alike should the members of a society be?

By what standards should we judge a group's integration into a society successful? Who sets these standards and passes judgment? What policies would have to be implemented to achieve the standards that are set? To understand the debate better and to try to answer these questions, we need to understand the concepts of assimilation and pluralism.

Assimilation

Assimilation is the process by which a racial or ethnic group gradually loses its distinctiveness and separateness and becomes absorbed into the culture and interaction of the host society. Assimilation as a goal underlies the popular melting pot metaphor. Sociologist Milton Gordon (1964) identified two main types of assimilation. One is **cultural** or **behavioral assimilation,** which is often referred to as simply **acculturation.** This form of assimilation involves cultural changes—in dress, language, food preferences, and the like. Such change occurs over the course of several generations, until eventually the cultural expression of the members of a specific racial or ethnic group is indistinguishable from the culture of the dominant group of the society.

For example, the grandparents of one of your authors emigrated to the United States from Italy shortly before the turn of the century. They spoke only Italian when they arrived, but, determined to be "Americans," they learned English fairly quickly. Furthermore, out of concern that others might think they were "unAmerican," they forbade their children to speak Italian in public. Over time, your author's parents spoke less and less Italian, and eventually they had difficulty expressing themselves in the language and understanding native Italian speakers. In addition, they did not teach their own children their ethnic language; your author can neither speak nor understand Italian (a fact that she considers unfortunate).

The second type of assimilation that Gordon identified is **structural assimilation,** which occurs when the members of a racial or ethnic group have full access to the same structural opportunities and social activities as the members of the dominant group. In other words, structural assimilation means that racial and ethnic group members are fully integrated into the ongoing life of the society. They are proportionately represented in the same jobs, political offices, and other critical social roles that other members of the society hold. They have open and equal access to all facilities, services, and institutions, such as health care, education, places of worship, and the like. Moreover, they are fully integrated on an interpersonal level: They form close friendships with members of the dominant group and other groups, belong to the same clubs, live in the same neighborhoods, and marry members of other racial or ethnic groups, including the dominant group.

It is not difficult to see the significance of Gordon's distinction. It is one thing to adopt the cultural characteristics of a group, but quite another to share in the collective identity of the society to the extent that the basic elements of one's daily personal life are indistinguishable from those of the dominant group. However, the process of structural assimilation is problematic for other reasons, too. For one thing, the burden of assimilating is usually placed on minority group members, but in reality, assimilation is an *interactive* process. The extent to which a specific group assimilates depends not only on their willingness, but also on the willingness of the dominant group to allow them to assimilate. If the members of a particular minority group do not succeed in the dominant society or by the standards of the dominant culture, they are accused of being "unassimilable" and incapable of "fitting in." Discrimination and exploitation by the dominant group and the ways these practices prevent assimilation are overlooked (Ringer, 1983; Steele, 1985).

Research shows that several factors can influence the extent and kind of assimilation a group experiences. One factor is whether the minority group voluntarily emigrated to the host society or whether the people were forcibly brought into the society. In general, people who voluntarily emigrate assimilate more quickly and completely than those who become a minority group because of conquest, colonialism, or forced migration (Blauner, 1972). The extent to which a minority group is visibly different from the majority group also affects assimilation. This factor makes race especially salient, so that racial groups usually do not assimilate (or are given less opportunity to assimilate) as fully as most ethnic groups.

Other factors that influence assimilation are the size of the minority group (small groups appear to assimilate more than large groups), geographical dispersion (when group members are geographically spread throughout the host society, they assimilate more than when members are concentrated in specific areas), the extent to which the members of the minority group view their stay in the host society as permanent (people who consider their stay temporary assimilate less than those who see it as permanent), and the timing of the group's arrival (groups that arrive in a new country when the economy is prospering have an easier time assimilating) (Yinger, 1985).

Some sociologists, however, question the desirability of assimilation. They argue that assimilation is really a guise for devaluing minority cultures, an attempt to transform "them" (minority group members) into "us" (members of the dominant group). The underlying assumption is that the minority group is inferior to the dominant group and has little to offer the host society. Critics of assimilation believe that abandoning or destroying one culture in favor of another is a disservice to both the minority group and the dominant group (Steele, 1985; Triandis,

These photos show immigrants taking the U.S. oath of citizenship, an African American family celebrating Kwanzaa, and people at a party in Boston. How might you describe these photos of minorities in the United States in terms of different kinds and degrees of assimilation and pluralism? For example, which picture most suggests Milton Gordon's concept of structural assimilation? Which most suggests equalitarian pluralism? If you could add two pictures to round out the set on assimilation and pluralism, what would they show?

1988). Maintaining racial and ethnic diversity within a society enriches the lives of *all* the society's members—a position associated with the pattern of interracial, interethnic contact known as *pluralism.*

Pluralism

Pluralism refers to racial and ethnic diversity in a society. Some analysts add that it also involves an appreciation of and respect for the cultures of groups other than one's own, an idea referred to as **equalitarian pluralism.** Thus, unlike assimilation, the goal of pluralism is not to minimize group differences, but rather to dispel the myth that difference from the dominant group means inferiority of the minority group. Instead of the melting pot metaphor, the underlying metaphor of pluralism is a salad bowl: The diverse ingredients mix together, but each retains its distinctive flavor, adding something unique to the dish.

The pluralist model enjoys considerable popularity in the United States today. For members of racial and ethnic groups, it means the opportunity to be structurally integrated into the society without having to abandon cherished cultural values and practices. The other side of the coin, some say, is that pluralist societies enjoy high productivity as well as artistic and scientific creativity because of the diverse skills and talents of their heterogenous populations.

Nevertheless, equalitarian pluralism is more of an ideal than a reality in most societies. In the United States, for instance, we find that as enthusiastically as pluralism is embraced, it exists at best in a watered-down form. The more unlike the White majority a group is, the more prejudice and discrimination they tend to experience. In fact, the United States and other societies have had such difficulties establishing equalitarian pluralism that some observers question the validity of the concept itself. Critics also point to the former Yugoslavia and Soviet Union, which were considered models of pluralism, but where, it turns out, historic ethnic hostilities and disputes were only being held in check by the tight controls of communist governments. With the fall of communism, these countries fractured into multiple independent states fueled by violent ethnic conflict and rivalries (Bohlen, 1998; Jaret, 1995).

INTERSECTING INEQUALITIES

Should Female Circumcision Be Tolerated or Outlawed?

Female circumcision is an ancient custom that today is practiced in about forty countries, primarily in East and West Africa, where it is not uncommon for as many as 90 to 98 percent of the female population to be circumcised (Ebomoyi, 1987; Renzetti & Curran, 1986). The custom has been imported to the United States and Western Europe by African immigrants. However, in the West, publicity regarding female circumcision has triggered angry protests by many feminists who consider the custom oppressive and barbaric and who insist that governments immediately outlaw it (Walker & Parmar, 1993). Few African governments have passed laws prohibiting female circumcision, but a number of governments in Western Europe, including France, Switzerland, and Great Britain, have outlawed it. In 1996, female circumcision was also legally banned in the United States (Dugger, 1996; Simons, 1993a). However, experts are uncertain whether such laws will prevent African immigrants from continuing the custom, which some view as a religious obligation and others practice because they believe it enhances a girl's beauty and, therefore, her marriage-

Cultural practices that cause harm pose a challenge to supporters of pluralism. Female circumcision, for example, causes tremendous physical harm to young girls, such as this six-year-old who is held by her sister as she screams from the excruciating pain. Yet many members of groups who practice female circumcision oppose outlawing it because they see such laws as obliterating a unique aspect of their cultural heritage.

ability as well as her moral reputation (MacFarquhar, 1996; Renzetti & Curran, 1986).

Why Outlaw Female Circumcision?

Why would Westerners, especially feminists, want female circumcision outlawed? The answer to this question lies in how the custom is usually performed and its consequences for girls. Female circumcision takes different forms. The mildest type is *Sunna*, in which the hood of the clitoris is cut analogous to male circumcision. The most extreme form,

infibulation, involves the removal of the clitoris and labia and stitching the vagina closed except for a small opening to allow urine and menstrual blood to pass. The most common form is excision, whereby the clitoris and part of the labia are removed (Lightfoot-Klein, 1989). Girls are usually circumcised when they are between the ages of seven and thirteen, although some are circumcised as infants. The circumcision is performed by an elder village woman or traditional birth attendant, who uses a nonsurgical instrument such as a razor, a knife, or even a piece of broken glass,

---

Other critics of the pluralist model of racial and ethnic relations think it is too narrow. They point out that societies may be diverse not only in terms of race and ethnicity, but also in terms of age, sex, and social class. Thus, emphasizing racial and ethnic equalitarian pluralism downplays the competition and conflict that may arise from age-based, sex-based, or class-based inequalities. In fact, some analysts argue that a great deal of racial and ethnic antagonism today actually grows out of—and disguises—social class conflict (Bonacich, 1991; Gans, 1992; Wilson, 1987).

Finally, critics of pluralism pose a difficult dilemma. While appreciating and respecting cultural diversity is a noble ideal, is it practical—and in some cases, humane—for the beliefs and practices of another culture to be preserved or honored even if they are harmful to some people? We addressed this issue in part in Chapter 4 when

we discussed cultural relativism. Here we will consider several examples in the context of racial and ethnic relations.

Sometimes the beliefs and practices of the dominant group are offensive to a minority group. In California, for instance, statues erected in the 1800s to commemorate historical events have prompted protests from Native Americans, who believe the statues glorify the brutality of European colonization and the gold rush and ignore the fact that hundreds of thousands of Indians were killed (Ybarra, 1996). Columbus Day and even Thanksgiving elicit similar responses from many Native Americans, who feel that history is being mistold; from their perspective, it is cruelty that is being celebrated. Should symbols, practices, and holidays be prohibited if they offend a racial minority? Should they be modified in some way so that alternative perspectives are presented?

and typically no anesthetics are available. After the girl has been cut, dirt, ashes, herbs, or animal droppings may be applied to the wound because they are believed to stop bleeding and aid healing. But not surprisingly, medical complications, including shock, hemorrhage, septicemia, and tetanus, often occur. At the very least, the custom ensures that a girl will never experience sexual pleasure; in fact, circumcision makes sexual intercourse painful (Ebomoyi, 1987; Lightfoot-Klein, 1989).

What Cultural Values Are at Stake?

Given the way the custom is carried out and the serious medical problems that often result, the angry and indignant responses of Westerners are understandable. A small, but growing number of African women has also begun working to eliminate the practice in their own countries (MacFarquhar, 1996; Simons, 1993b; Walker & Parmar, 1993). However, many African women have criticized their African sisters and Westerners for sensationalizing the custom and for presenting it out of cultural context. They are offended, too, when Westerners refer to the practice as "female genital mutilation," accusing them of cultural imperialism (imposing their own cultural values on the people of another culture) (French, 1997; Graham, 1986).

When we did field work in West Africa in the 1980s, we talked with many women about the practice of female circumcision. In the Republic of Guinea, where we were, women explained the custom in terms of cultural beliefs about female sexual desire. They saw circumcision as a way to protect girls from sexual temptations and preserve their marriageability. Although circumcision may cause severe psychological trauma for some young girls, these women emphasized that an uncircumcised girl may suffer even more serious social and psychological harm since she will be considered "dirty" and unmarriageable, and therefore unfit to carry out women's two most valued roles in the society, wife and mother. We talked with government officials and health care providers about outlawing the practice, but they responded in similar ways: Westerners should try to better understand the cultural significance of female circumcision, and they had "more serious" problems to worry about before they could address a custom that was supported by the majority of their people (Renzetti and Curran, 1986; see also Graham, 1986).

Who Is More Irrational?

To most Westerners, the custom of female circumcision, and the fact that women perpetuate this tradition, seems irrational at best. But what is often overlooked is the status of women in societies that practice female circumcision. It is through this custom that women exercise power and achieve recognition: They make themselves marriageable and worthy of motherhood. Interestingly, some African women pointed out that Westerners should see female circumcision as no more irrational than the behavior of Western women who undergo sometimes harmful treatments and "cosmetic" surgery or who follow unhealthy diets for the sake of "beauty" and attracting men. What do you think? Is female circumcision similar to these Western "beauty regimens"? If you disapprove of female circumcision, do you think laws banning it will be effective? What do you think is the best strategy for ending the custom?

Such questions are the topics of public debate, but it is unlikely that they will be quickly resolved.

What if a minority group's cultural practices are considered harmful by the host culture? Should they be banned, even if they are cherished by a particular racial or ethnic group? The Intersecting Inequalities box discusses female circumcision, a controversial custom that immigrants from East and West Africa have tried to continue after moving to Western societies, including the United States. A similar clash of cultures occurred recently when Iraqis who had fled Saddam Hussein's repression found themselves charged with a range of offenses stemming from what U.S. police and prosecutors consider child sexual abuse. In Iraq, arranged marriages of young girls to significantly older men is normative; in Nebraska, it is not. Consequently, following the marriages of two girls—one thirteen, the other fourteen—to a thirty-four-year-old man and a twenty-eight-year-old man respectively, the girls' parents and new husbands were arrested. The Iraqi community protested the arrests, saying that arranged marriages were part of their culture; that the girls had entered them not only freely but joyfully; and that the weddings were public, not secret, events. (In fact, the girls' parents had invited their entire neighborhood to the weddings.) Nevertheless, the marriages were annulled, the girls were returned to their parents' homes, and the parents and husbands faced the charges against them (Terry, 1996).

The dilemma is vexing. On one hand, as we noted in Chapter 4, we need not embrace a particular behavior just because it is part of another group's culture. In evaluating any belief or practice, we should take into account the extent to which it contributes to the well-being of the group or the society. Practices, beliefs, or symbols that are harmful or offensive should be called into question.

On the other hand, however, in judging a group's cultural practices, we run the risk of ignoring the group's perspective and harming the members by obliterating part of their heritage. Nevertheless, if we value pluralism as a model of racial and ethnic relations, we must grapple with these and the other issues we have raised so far.

R E F L E C T I N G   O N

Assimilation and Pluralism

1. What are the benefits and disadvantages of assimilation for a minority group? How might the manner and timing of arrival affect assimilation among immigrant groups?
2. How is pluralism more like a salad or salsa bowl than a melting pot? What kinds of programs and policies contribute to a pluralistic society?
3. How would you resolve the dilemma of pluralism: preserving cultural beliefs and practices while eliminating those that the dominant group regards as harmful?

RACE AND ETHNICITY IN THE UNITED STATES

The population of the United States is composed of a multitude of racial and ethnic groups, far more diverse than most of us probably imagine. Typically, when writers discuss social phenomena, they use the broad racial and ethnic categories of the census (see Table 11.2). We do the same in this book, so most statistics are given for Whites, African Americans, Hispanic Americans, Asian Americans, and Native Americans. Using the census categories, however, masks the significant differences that exist among the groups subsumed under these broad headings. Consider, for example, that the category Asian American includes at least eighteen different groups along with nine Pacific Islander groups. Each group has its own language and unique culture, and the different groups' experiences in the United States vary significantly. The other census categories also contain numerous groups that are actually more different than they are similar in terms of their cultural heritage and their history in this country.

Unfortunately, limited time and space mean we can't examine the diversity within each category in much detail. But we raise the issue because, as you read the sections that follow, it is important to remember that the groups we are discussing are not as homogenous as the data make them out to be.

With that caveat in mind, let's review some of the historic and recent collective experiences of various racial and ethnic groups in the United States, beginning with those who were the country's first residents.

Native Americans

Looking again at Table 11.2, we see that Native Americans are the smallest racial group in the United States, making up just under 1 percent of the total population. At the time of European settlement, however, Native Americans, or "Indians" as the Europeans called them, constituted more than 1 percent of the *world's* population (Murphy, 1985; Weyler, 1982). The North American natives were the descendents of people who had emigrated from Asia between 20,000 and 30,000 years before. By the time the Europeans arrived, there were at least four hundred tribes with distinct languages and cultures inhabiting the continent. But by 1800, the Native American population in what is now the United States had dwindled from 10 million to 600,000, and at the close of the nineteenth century, it was less than 250,000 (Snipp, 1989). A major cause of death was disease introduced by the European settlers; with no natural immunity, Native Americans died in great numbers. Many Native Americans were also killed in violent confrontations with Europeans (Mohawk, 1992).

At the center of many disputes between Europeans and Native Americans was land. European settlers believed in the principle of Right of Discovery, a European legal concept that basically amounted to "finders, keepers." Even when the European settlers—and later the U.S. government—negotiated with the Indians for land, they broke the treaties and formal exchange agreements. Between 1776 and 1871, the government ratified 371 treaties with Native tribes, promising them various goods (money, medical care, and education for their children) in addition to secure territory where they could live independently and peaceably. The government violated every one of these treaties (Weyler, 1982).

TABLE 11.2 Racial and Ethnic Composition of the U.S. Population

Racial/Ethnic Group	Number (in thousands)	Percentage of Total Population
All Groups	265,284	100.0
White	193,978	73.1
African American	31,912	12.0
Hispanic*	28,269	10.7
Asian, Pacific Islander	9,171	3.5
American Indian, Eskimo, Aleut	1,954	0.7

*People of Hispanic origin may be of any race, but in this table those classified in non-Hispanic groups did not identify themselves as of Hispanic origin.

Source: U.S. Department of Commerce, Bureau of the Census (1997), p. 22.

By 1871, most Native Americans were living within the confines of western reservations that the federal government had established on land that it thought was worthless. Their everyday lives were controlled by the Bureau of Indian Affairs (BIA), an office of the U.S. Department of the Interior, which continues to administer many aspects of Indians' lives today (Trimble, 1988). They were forbidden from practicing their tribal customs and religious ceremonies, and their children were taken to BIA boarding schools where they were forced to wear Western-style clothing and were severely punished for speaking their tribal languages (Noley, 1990).

It was not until 1924 that Congress granted Native Americans citizenship, although some states continued to deny citizenship rights until the late 1930s. Since the 1930s, the federal government has adopted various policies toward Native Americans. Usually, the stated goal is greater self-determination for Native American tribes, but many analysts think the real motivation is to reduce federal government funding of Indian assistance programs (Campbell, 1989; Snipp, 1991).

Today, the majority of Native Americans continue to live in the western and southwestern states, with about 54 percent of this number living in rural areas that include reservations. But 46 percent of Native Americans have left the reservations to live in or near large cities. Many who move off the reservations are young people seeking better job opportunities. Unemployment rates vary greatly from reservation to reservation, from 20 percent to over 75 percent with an average of 49 percent, about ten times the national average (Kilborn, 1997). Median household income is just $19,900. Not surprisingly, poverty rates on

Native Americans were not granted U.S. citizenship until the 1930s in some states. After a history of genocide and expulsion, Indians were segregated on reservations or were subjected to cruel forced assimilation. Why have Native Americans had to struggle to keep or win back their reservation lands? What factors limit opportunities for economic development? Why are poverty and unemployment on reservations so high?

the reservations are also exceptionally high. Depending on the reservation, anywhere from 20 percent to nearly 50 percent of the population may be living in poverty (Kilborn, 1997; U.S. Department of Commerce, Bureau of the Census, 1997). Educational attainment is also low; overall, 65.6 percent of Native Americans complete high school and just 9.4 percent complete college or postgraduate education. However, these rates vary across Indian nations, with high school completion rates ranging from 51 percent to 72 percent, and college/postgraduate completion rates ranging from 4.5 percent to 13 percent (U.S. Department of Commerce, Bureau of the Census, 1997).

Efforts to promote economic growth on Indian lands have intensified in recent years. Many of these strategies involve joint ventures between a specific tribe and an outside company or state government (De Palma, 1996). One source of economic revenue on reservations is gaming. Several tribes are operating successful casinos, but for most tribes (about 66 percent) this solution is unfeasible because the geographic isolation of their reservations makes them inaccessible to tourists (Cline, 1994; Kilborn, 1997). Some observers are also concerned that an increase in White-owned businesses and industries will only further destroy Native American culture as well as physically harm Native Americans themselves (Belluck, 1998; Churchill & LaDuke, 1992; Lane, 1995).

African Americans

African Americans, unlike any other racial or ethnic group in the United States, did not emigrate here freely. They were brought, primarily from West Africa, in bondage, beginning in 1619 with the arrival of the first slave ship at Jamestown, Virginia. Although millions of Africans were captured and sold into slavery, millions also died during the voyage. Those who entered the United States led a life of "social death"; they were considered property, not persons, and the conditions under which they lived and worked were totally at the discretion of their masters (Gordon, 1984; Kitano, 1985). There were "free" Blacks during slavery, but they never enjoyed the same privileges as Whites (Yetman, 1991).

From its inception, the institution of slavery was supported by a legal system that denied Black people even the most basic rights. A number of important legal reforms in the 1800s—including the Thirteenth Amendment, which abolished slavery, the Fourteenth Amendment, which guaranteed equal protection of the law, and the Fifteenth Amendment, which gave Black men the right to vote— were supposed to ensure equality for Black citizens. For the most part, however, these rights were bestowed on paper only. Jim Crow laws, for example, which we discussed earlier in this chapter, preserved in practice the historic system of racial oppression well into the twentieth century despite Black resistance and activism.

A significant step in reforming official policies occurred in 1954 when the U.S. Supreme Court, in the case of *Brown* v. *Board of Education of Topeka,* overturned an earlier decision (*Plessy* v. *Ferguson*) and declared that "separate but equal" was unconstitutional. This ruling was aimed directly at racial segregation, and, although it proved painfully difficult to put into practice, the *Brown* decision was a major victory for the civil rights movement. During the 1960s, civil rights activists also succeeded in securing other legal changes, including the 1964 Civil Rights Act, which, among other things, prohibited racial discrimination in employment, and the 1965 Voting Rights Act, which effectively removed any obstacles to Black voter registration. Also during the 1960s, a number of federally funded social programs were established to improve school performance and upgrade the job skills of the disadvantaged, a large percentage of whom were Black (Sudarkasa, 1988).

African Americans have made significant gains on many indicators of social well-being. Since the early 1960s, for instance, the gap in educational attainment between White and Black Americans has narrowed considerably. The Black high school completion rate in 1995 was less than 10 percent lower than the White high school completion rate that year, the smallest disparity between the two groups ever recorded by the Census Bureau. African Americans have also made record gains in their college enrollment rates (American Council on Education, 1998). In politics, there are now nearly 8,000 Black elected officials, whereas there were just 103 in 1964 (U.S. Department of Commerce, Bureau of the Census, 1997).

Perhaps most important, however, are the economic gains that Black Americans have made. Table 11.3 shows that the percentage of Black households in the middle class has risen considerably in little more than a decade. The percentage of Black households with incomes above $50,000 rose from 14.2 percent in 1980 to 21.0 percent in 1997. In 1997, the median household income of Black married couples was 87 percent as much as the median household income of White married couples, a narrowing of the income gap by 8 percent since 1989 when it was 79 percent. Still, the percentage of Black households with incomes under $10,000 remains significantly higher than White households in this income category, although in 1997, the Black poverty rate fell to 26.5 percent (U.S. Department of Commerce, Bureau of the Census, 1998b).

These economic changes have led some observers to argue that social class inequality is a better indicator than racism for explaining why some segments of the African American population are disadvantaged today. That is, government programs and antidiscrimination legislation have helped primarily middle-class, better-educated African Americans move into higher-status, higher-income positions, and, in turn, out of the inner city. Left behind in increasing isolation are impoverished African Americans. At the same time, the cities themselves have changed from manufacturing to service centers, leaving a mismatch between the skills of urban Black residents and available jobs (Wacquant & Wilson, 1991; Wilson, 1996; Wolfe, 1998).

This position receives a good deal of empirical support, but we must be careful not to lose sight of the fact that African Americans of all social classes continue to experience racial discrimination in this country. Even well-educated and wealthy African Americans report incidents of discrimination on the street or in other public places, such as stores and restaurants, as well as at work (see, for example, Feagin & Sikes, 1994; West, 1993). African Americans also still experience a high degree of residential segregation, regardless of class (Massey & Denton, 1993). And although public opinion polls show

TABLE 11.3 Percent Distribution of Family Income Levels and Median Family Income by Race, 1980–1997 (in constant 1997 dollars)

Income Level	1980 Black	1980 White	1990 Black	1990 White	1997 Black	1997 White
Under $10,000	26.7	11.7	26.8	10.6	21.4	9.5
$10,000–$14,999	13.2	8.1	11.2	7.7	10.5	7.8
$15,000–$24,999	20.3	16.1	17.4	15.3	17.9	14.6
$25,000–$34,999	12.9	14.8	13.5	14.5	14.2	13.2
$35,000–$49,999	13.9	19.9	14.1	18.2	14.9	16.5
$50,000–$74,999	9.8	18.3	10.7	18.5	13.1	18.8
$75,000 or more	3.4	11.1	6.2	15.1	7.9	19.7
Median	$19,932	$34,598	$21,777	$36,416	$25,050	$38,972

Source: U.S. Department of Commerce, Bureau of the Census, 1997, p. 465; 1998a, p. 5.

that the majority of White Americans favor racial integration, there is a glaring contradiction between what they say and what they do. Most White people continue to avoid close, frequent, or prolonged social contact with African Americans and strongly resist racial integration in their schools and neighborhoods (Fiske, 1998; Sigelman & Welch, 1991).

Thus, while many objective measures point to significant progress for African Americans, it is also clear that racial equality remains unrealized.

Asian Americans

Asian Americans are often referred to as a "model" minority group, largely because in the short span of less than a century, their aggregate level of educational attainment and income have surpassed those of the nation as a whole. Asian Americans have a high school completion rate of over 83 percent, compared to 86 percent for Whites, 74 percent for Blacks, and 53 percent for Hispanic Americans. Nearly 40 percent of the Asian American population completes four or more years of college, compared to 25 percent of the White population, 13 percent of the Black population, and 9 percent of the Hispanic population (Frederick D. Patterson Research Institute, 1997). The median annual income of Asian American families is $46,356, whereas the annual median income of U.S. families is $40,611 (U.S. Department of Commerce, Bureau of the Census, 1997). Nevertheless, these aggregate data hide tremendous differences among Asian ethnic groups in the United States, not only in terms of education and income, but in terms of other factors as well.

The first Asians to emigrate to the United States in sizable numbers were Chinese in the 1840s. Many opened small businesses in western towns and cities, while others worked in the gold mines or in railroad construction. Although initially they were welcomed by White Americans, they came to be viewed as competitors for jobs when the economy soured, and the growing hostility and resentment toward Chinese Americans often erupted into violence. In 1882, the federal government stepped in to halt Chinese immigration by passing the Chinese Exclusion Act, which, as we noted earlier, was supposed to remain in effect for ten years, but ultimately was not rescinded until 1943 (Chan, 1991).

The Japanese were the second major Asian ethnic group to emigrate to the United States, and, like the Chinese, settled primarily in the west. Their emigration began in the 1880s, so they also encountered a good deal of anti-Asian sentiment. In 1908, the federal government again acted to curtail Asian immigration by imposing severe restrictions on Japanese immigrants. Later, when Congress passed the 1924 Immigration Act, which established quotas on the number of immigrants allowed to enter the United States from specific countries, the Japanese were excluded totally (Hirschman & Wong, 1991).

After the Vietnam War, many Amerasian children like these —born to Vietnamese mothers by U.S. military fathers—were allowed to immigrate to the United States This was an effort of mercy, for racial prejudice and discrimination against them in their own country would have made life very difficult for them as adults. In what ways were the experiences of Asian Americans divergent? Why are Asian American groups often referred to as model minorities?

Although Chinese and Japanese Americans were treated similarly at first, they had very different experiences in the 1940s when, during World War II, China was a U.S. ally and Japan was an enemy. After the bombing of Pearl Harbor, President Franklin Roosevelt ordered the relocation of U.S. residents of Japanese descent (defined as anyone with at least one-eighth Japanese ancestry) to internment camps. Of the 120,000 Japanese who were interned, 81,000 were U.S. citizens. Relocation caused them tremendous financial hardship; most lost their homes and businesses as well as other valuable personal property. Even worse perhaps were the social and emotional effects of internment, including ill health, disrupted family life, and mental anguish (Nakanishi, 1988; Oishi, 1985).

The Asian ethnic groups that emigrated after the Chinese and Japanese include Filipinos, Koreans, Asian Indians, Vietnamese, Laotians, Hmong, and Cambodians. Their experiences also diverge. For instance, Filipinos were considered U.S. nationals when they began emigrating just before the turn of the twentieth century because the United States governed the Philippine Islands. Nevertheless, Filipinos were not permitted to become U.S. citizens and their immigration was curtailed in 1934 by the Filipino Exclusion Act, which was not lifted until 1965 (Chan, 1991). Koreans also began emigrating at the turn of the century, but at a slower rate than Filipinos. The Korean War in the 1950s brought more Koreans to the United States, but most Korean emigration has occurred since the 1970s (Yetman, 1991). War also spurred the emigration of about one million Indochinese refugees after 1975. At this same time, however, the United States was experiencing an economic downturn, which worsened in the 1980s, producing conflicts over job competition, fishing rights, and similar issues in areas with high refugee populations (Barringer et al., 1993; Chan, 1991; Zhou & Bankston, 1998).

Given their diversity of experience, significant differences exist among various Asian American ethnic groups today. For example, if we look at occupational distribution, we find that overall, Asian Americans compare favorably to White Americans, with a significant percentage holding executive, administrative, and managerial positions (jobs with relatively high status and earnings). But if we look at the occupational distribution of specific Asian American ethnic groups, we find that Asian Indian, Japanese American, and Chinese American men are somewhat more likely than White men to hold executive, administrative, and managerial positions, while Filipino men are 50 percent and Vietnamese men 150 percent less likely than White men to be employed in such jobs. Even within some Asian American ethnic groups, such as the Chinese and Filipinos, the occupational distribution is split, with a heavy concentration of workers in the professions and in unskilled service work (Barringer et al., 1993).

Employment patterns have an obvious impact on income, so that although overall Asian American median household income is high, there are disparities in median income across Asian American ethnic groups, with Japanese Americans having the highest median income and Vietnamese and Cambodians the lowest (Ong et al., 1994). Analysts also point out that the median income of Asian American ethnic groups is inflated because the households often contain multiple workers who pool their earnings. Such sharing is common in Asian cultures and has proven to be an effective economic survival strategy (Barringer et al., 1993).

The successes of Asian ethnic groups in the United States are undeniable, but we must be cautious in applying labels like "model minority." Not only do such notions mask differences across groups, but they also imply that Asian Americans as a whole no longer confront obstacles to equal opportunity, institutional access, and social acceptance (Nakanishi, 1988; Shiao, 1994). To the contrary, stereotypes of Asians remain prevalent and fuel discrimination against even the most successful (Noble, 1995; Onishi, 1996).

Hispanic Americans

Hispanic Americans are also a highly diverse group. As Figure 11.1 shows, most Hispanics in the United States are Mexican Americans or *Chicanos*. Some are the descendents of families who have lived in the Southwest since the mid-1800s, when land held by Mexico was conceded to the U.S. government after the Mexican–American

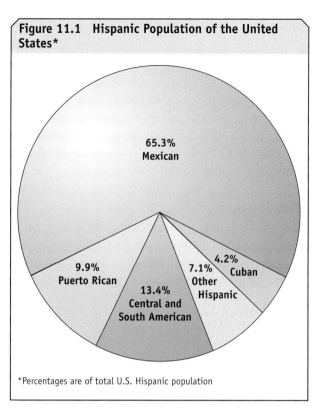

Figure 11.1 Hispanic Population of the United States*

65.3%
Mexican

9.9%
Puerto Rican

13.4%
Central and
South American

7.1%
Other
Hispanic

4.2%
Cuban

*Percentages are of total U.S. Hispanic population

Source: U.S. Department of Commerce, Bureau of the Census, 1997, p. 52.

War (1846–1848) or bought in the Gadsden Purchase (1853). Historically, Mexican Americans have been regarded by White Americans, including the federal government, as a source of inexpensive labor who, when they were no longer needed or were perceived as a threat to White job seekers, were sent back to Mexico. During the Great Depression of the 1930s, for example, 400,000 Mexicans, many of whom were U.S. citizens, were forced to repatriate to Mexico (Diaz, 1984; Estrada et al., 1981). The vast majority of Mexican Americans are recent immigrants, arriving in the past twenty-five years. In fact, since 1970, the largest number of immigrants to the United States have come from Mexico (U.S. Department of Commerce, Bureau of the Census, 1997).

Other Hispanic American groups have emigrated to the United States because of war and political conflict in their own countries. More than 750,000 immigrants from Central America have entered the United States since 1981, coming primarily from El Salvador, Guatemala, Honduras, and Nicaragua (U.S. Department of Commerce, Bureau of the Census, 1997). Earlier, nearly 700,000 Cubans emigrated to the United States when Fidel Castro overthrew the Batista Regime in 1959.

The second largest Hispanic group in the United States, however, is Puerto Ricans. Puerto Rico is a U.S. territory that was given commonwealth status by Congress in 1952. Puerto Ricans are considered U.S. citizens and are subject to most U.S. laws, including registration for the

These New Yorkers are celebrating at the Puerto Rican Day parade. Puerto Ricans are U.S. citizens and subject to most U.S. laws; yet Puerto Rico is not represented in Congress and Puerto Ricans cannot vote in presidential elections. Why is that? What characteristics unify and distinguish Hispanic Americans as a social aggregate? Why do many Mexican and Central Americans identify more with Native Americans than with Hispanic Americans?

military draft, but they have no formal political representation in Congress, nor can they vote in presidential elections. Puerto Rico is represented solely by a resident commissioner who has a say, but no vote in Congress, except on committees.

Again, in light of this diversity, it is hardly surprising that on measures of well-being, Hispanic American groups diverge greatly. For example, in educational attainment, Hispanic Americans have the lowest overall high school and college completion rates of any major racial or ethnic group. However, if we look at specific subgroups, we find that whereas just 46.5 percent of Mexican Americans have completed high school, 61.3 percent of Puerto Ricans, 64.7 percent of Cubans, 64.2 percent of Central and South Americans, and 68.4 percent of other Hispanics have completed high school. Similarly, while 19.3 percent of Cubans, 13.1 percent of Central and South Americans, and 14.2 percent of other Hispanics have earned a bachelor's degree or higher, only about half as many Mexican Americans (6.5 percent) and Puerto Ricans (10.7 percent) enjoy this level of educational attainment (U.S. Department of Commerce, Bureau of the Census, 1997).

Table 11.4 shows economic data for various Hispanic American ethnic groups. Here we see that Cuban Americans have the greatest financial security, with a median income in 1994 of about $3,000 less than that of the U.S. population as a whole in 1994; they also have the lowest poverty and unemployment rates of the Hispanic population. Their ranking probably reflects the fact that early Cuban immigrants were mostly former officials in the Batista government, landowners, professionals, industrialists, and managers of U.S.-owned companies based in Cuba. They were well-educated, with middle- and upper-class professional backgrounds, who brought with them highly marketable skills, business experience, and substantial capital for investment. Today, most of the approximately one million Cubans in the United States live in the Miami, Florida area, where many own businesses in manufacturing and construction as well as banking (Portes & Manning, 1991; Wilson & Portes, 1985). Although poor and working-class Cubans have emigrated to the United States more recently, their numbers remain small compared to more economically secure Cuban Americans (Yetman, 1991).

In contrast, the financial circumstances of Puerto Ricans and Mexican Americans are more precarious. The

TABLE 11.4   Economic Characteristics of the Hispanic American Population, 1995*

	ETHNIC GROUP				
Characteristic	Mexican	Puerto Rican	Cuban	Central and South American	Other Hispanic
Percent civilian labor force	66.9	57.9	60.2	70.2	63.8
Employed	60.4	51.4	55.7	64.6	58.8
Unemployed	6.5	6.5	4.4	5.6	5.1
Unemployment rate (percent of total civilian labor force)	9.7	11.2	7.4	8.0	7.9
Median family income	$23,609	$20,929	$30,584	$26,558	$28,658
Percent families below poverty line	29.6	33.2	13.6	23.9	21.4
Percent persons below poverty line	32.3	36.0	17.8	25.8	25.5

* Income data are for 1994.
Source: U.S. Department of Commerce, Bureau of the Census (1997), p. 52.

median household income of Puerto Ricans in 1994 was more than $10,000 less than that of the U.S. population as a whole, and the median household income for Mexican Americans was nearly $8,000 less. Unemployment rates were 6 percent higher for Puerto Ricans and 4 percent higher for Mexican Americans. Most disturbing, however, are the poverty rates. Mexican Americans are more than twice as likely as the general U.S. population to live in poverty, while the poverty rate of Puerto Ricans is more than 20 percent higher than U.S. rates as a whole (U.S. Department of Commerce, Bureau of the Census, 1997).

To some extent, these statistics reflect the fact that, unlike Cubans, neither Mexican Americans nor Puerto Ricans have entrepreneurial enclaves to which they can turn for jobs in this country (Portes & Truelove, 1991). They also reflect the persistent prejudice and discrimination that members of these groups face. For Mexican Americans, in particular, discrimination is fueled by concerns about illegal immigration. Although illegal immigrants represent about ninety different nationalities, Mexicans constitute the majority (about two-thirds) because of the close proximity of the border. Policing the border to prevent illegal entry has been sporadic, but has intensified since 1993. Mexicans make up about 90 percent of all undocumented immigrants apprehended by the Immigration and Naturalization Service (INS). In fact, employers report that INS officers often ignore workers who do not look Latino when they raid businesses (Meier, 1990). Most illegal immigrants settle in just seven states—California, New York, Texas, Florida, Illinois, New Jersey, and Arizona—and budget crises as well as the conservative political climates in these states have generated

Officers of the U.S. Immigration and Naturalization Service (INS) patrol the U.S.–Mexico border to detect illegal crossings and deter illegal immigration. Mexican immigrants, both legal and undocumented, are becoming majorities in the southwestern states. Why would you expect increases in prejudice and discrimination against Mexicans in that region? Why do Mexican families like the one in the picture risk a border crossing?

a strong anti-immigration movement with an underlying hostility toward Mexicans in particular (Clarke et al., 1994; Conover, 1997; Hershey, 1995).

White Americans

Much of the prejudice and discrimination that the racial and ethnic groups we have discussed so far experience is inflicted by White Americans, the dominant racial group in the United States. This is not to say that members of minority groups are not prejudiced against Whites or members of other groups, or that minorities never discriminate. As we have already said, prejudice and discrimination are found among all people. However, what cannot be denied is that White Americans enjoy a disproportionate share of the resources and rewards in our society, and that these privileges derive in large part from their race.

At the same time, the diversity among White Americans is great. The single largest ethnic group in the United States is English Americans, more commonly referred to as White Anglo-Saxons. Individuals with some English ancestry number about 50 million (Feagin & Feagin, 1993). Other groups preceded the English, but it was the English who first colonized North America. The early English settlers set out to establish permanent communities, subdue native people they encountered, and claim land for the Crown. Understanding their goals is critical to understanding how the language, customs, and values of this group became the core culture of our society, as well as why later immigrants from other countries faced prejudice and discrimination.

For example, English immigrants who came to the United States in the late nineteenth and early twentieth centuries assimilated rapidly because they shared the same language, religious practices, traditions, skin color, and physical features as the people in the dominant group whose ancestors had arrived more than two hundred years before. Consequently, the newcomers quickly moved into the professions where speaking English was necessary, and they easily socialized with and married other English Americans. Never did they experience residential segregation on the basis of race; it was social class that separated groups of English Americans from one another (Feagin & Feagin, 1993).

In contrast, consider the experiences of non-English European immigrants. The earliest French immigrants were Huguenots escaping religious persecution, but they did not share the language or religion of the English. The English colonists tried to prohibit their immigration and, failing that, imposed severe restrictions on them. Irish and German immigrants encountered similar reactions in the mid-1800s, as did Italians and Eastern Europeans at the turn of the century. At first, anti-immigrant sentiment focused primarily on religious differences—many immigrants were Catholic or Jewish—but by the 1890s, the theme was clearly perceived "racial" differences, with English Americans declaring themselves and other Northern Europeans the "superior race" (Feagin & Feagin, 1993). This position is known as **nativism.**

Nativism found its way into federal laws, such as the 1924 Immigration Act which, as we already noted, established quotas on immigrants from specific countries. The Immigration Act, which remained in effect for forty-four years, favored immigrants from northwestern Europe. Southern and Eastern European immigrants, along with immigrants from other countries who were admitted to the United States, were discriminated against in employment, housing, and other areas of social life. In response, they established ethnic neighborhoods and employment niches which, in turn, provided a supportive environment for their compatriots who emigrated later.

Despite the prejudice and discrimination against them, many early European immigrants enjoyed considerable success and were assimilated into the dominant group. It has been argued, though, that those who assimilated most quickly had physical features and skin tone closely resembling those of English Americans. Today, there is a high degree of cultural and structural assimilation among Americans of European descent, regardless of what part of the continent or Great Britain they are from. This is evidenced by the high degree of intermarriage between White Americans of different ethnic ancestries (Alba, 1985), which has led some observers to claim that social class is the primary source of social inequality among White Americans. While this position receives considerable empirical support, it is important to keep in mind that bias against Americans of Southern and Eastern European descent has not completely disappeared. For example, Feagin and Feagin (1993) point out that Geraldine Ferraro's Italian ancestry became an issue when she was a Democratic vice presidential candidate in 1984, as did Michael Dukakis's Greek ancestry when he became a presidential candidate in 1988. At the very least, non-English Americans often find themselves the brunt of ethnic slurs and jokes, although most take pride in their ethnic heritage.

The Racial and Ethnic Composition of the United States in the Twenty-First Century

White Americans are the dominant racial group in the United States not only socially and economically, but also numerically, making up nearly three-fourths (73.1 percent) of the population. However, as Figure 11.2 shows, their numerical dominance is expected to decline significantly by the middle of the twenty-first century. The African American population will increase slightly from 12 percent today to 13.6 percent in 2050, but it is the Asian American and Hispanic American populations that are expected to grow the most. The Asian American population is expected to almost triple by midcentury, al-

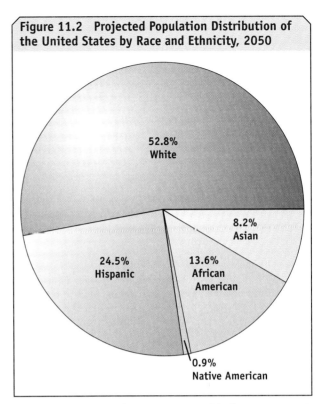

Figure 11.2 Projected Population Distribution of the United States by Race and Ethnicity, 2050

52.8% White

8.2% Asian

13.6% African American

24.5% Hispanic

0.9% Native American

Source: U.S. Department of Commerce, Bureau of the Census, 1997, p. 19.

though Asian Americans represent such a small proportion of the overall population that they will still constitute just 8.2 percent of the U.S. population. In contrast, Hispanic Americans will become the largest minority group in the United States and come to compose nearly a quarter of the country's population. The increase will come from immigration as well as higher birth rates among Hispanic American women compared to women in other racial and ethnic groups (U.S. Department of Commerce, Bureau of the Census, 1997).

Also adding to the growing diversity of the U.S. population is an increase in the number of interracial marriages, a trend that is expected to continue during the first half of the twenty-first century. Until 1967, marriages between individuals of different races were illegal in many states. Even after the United States Supreme Court declared such laws unconstitutional in the case of *Loving* v. *Virginia*, interracial marriages, especially between African Americans and Whites, remained rare. Since 1980, however, the number of interracial marriages has risen significantly, and the most dramatic increase has been in marriages of African American/White couples. In 1970, for example, fewer than 1 percent of all marriages were interracial, and the majority of these were Native American/White couples; 0.14 of marriages in 1970 were of African American/White couples. By 1995, the percentage of all marriages involving interracial couples had more than doubled to about 2.5 percent, and about 0.6 percent of marriages were of African American/White couples (Jaret, 1995; U.S. Department of Commerce, Bureau of the Census, 1996).

Some observers think that the rise in interracial marriages reflects greater structural assimilation of non-White racial and ethnic groups. But research shows that interracial marriage does not necessarily reduce conflict between different racial and ethnic groups, nor does it signal greater assimilation (Jaret, 1995). Although the number of interracial marriages has increased substantially in a relatively short period of time, there is still strong social disapproval of interracial marriage, not only among Whites, but among members of non-White racial and ethnic groups as well. And interracial couples continue to confront this disapproval in their daily lives.

Changes in racial and ethnic composition in the twenty-first century will certainly diversify what we consider "American" culture. But, as two sociologists suggest, on the basis of history and current events, we should probably think of the United States as a "boiling cauldron" rather than a "melting pot" or "salad bowl" (Feagin & Feagin, 1993). Indeed, there has been a resurgence of racist organizations in the United States in recent years, with many using computer technology to spread their messages. In 1998, there were 537 racial hate groups in the United States and over 163 Web sites devoted to racial hatred (Associated Press, 1998; Parker, 1999). There has also been an alarming increase in racially and ethnically motivated hate crimes. In 1996, three out of four hate crimes were motivated by race or ethnicity. (The remainder were motivated by sexual orientation and religion) (Federal Bureau of Investigation, 1997).

Will our future be characterized by racial and ethnic harmony and an appreciation of diversity? Or will it be plagued by racial and ethnic antagonism and conflict? Sociologists can't predict the form that race and ethnic relations will take in the United States or elsewhere, but the data they collect can help us develop strategies for achieving particular outcomes.

REFLECTING ON

Race and Ethnicity in the United States

1. In the history of race relations in the United States, "separate but equal" has meant "separate and unequal." Do you think this is still true today? Why or why not?
2. Do you think disparities experienced by racial and ethnic groups are caused more by racism or by class differences? What are your reasons?
3. In the mid-twenty-first century, what will be the composition of the United States population? What factors influence projections of the racial and ethnic composition of a population?

EXPLAINING RACIAL AND ETHNIC STRATIFICATION

Preparing for the future requires that we understand why specific forms of racial and ethnic stratification emerge. Let's conclude this chapter, then, by examining several sociological theories of race and ethnic relations.

The Primordialist Perspective

The prevalence of racial and ethnic stratification across societies has led some sociologists to explain it as a natural phenomenon. According to this view, called the **primordialist perspective**, people have an innate preference for people they perceive as like themselves, and racial classifications provide a quick and easy method for drawing the distinctions. An immutable bond forms between people who share a common racial or ethnic identity, producing not only a strong attachment among members of the group, but also equally strong feelings of dislike or repulsion toward others who are dissimilar (van den Berghe, 1978).

The primordialist perspective is appealing because it seems to explain what appear to be irrational attitudes and behavior by one racial or ethnic group toward another. Research by social psychologists has shown a strong human propensity to categorize other humans and to do so automatically and rapidly. This categorization is often dichotomous: "we" and "they." There is a strong favoritism toward those categorized as "we" and a negative bias toward those categorized as "they" (Fiske, 1998).

Nevertheless, this theory has several weaknesses. First, as we discussed at the beginning of this chapter, it is difficult, if not impossible, to delineate clear-cut boundaries between racial and ethnic groups. The primordialist perspective ignores or downplays the empirical evidence that shows that racial and ethnic stratification are the products of social decisions, not natural predispositions. People can and do choose not to be racist (Fiske, 1998).

Second, the existence of a primordial racial or ethnic bond is questionable, given the frequency of intraracial and intraethnic conflicts that occur in many societies, including our own. As we have already noted, conflicts may arise between members of different social classes, even though they share a common racial or ethnic ancestry (Bonacich, 1991).

Finally, the primordialist perspective discounts the role of human intervention in producing social change. If racial and ethnic antagonisms are biologically based, then there is little, if anything, we can do to resolve them. However, as we learned earlier in this text, what makes us distinctively human is our ability to evaluate a situation and make decisions about how to act to preserve or change it.

The Role of Socialization

The criticisms of the primordialist perspective all emphasize social rather than natural causes for racial and ethnic stratification. Some social scientists focus, therefore, on how socialization and social learning reproduce racial and ethnic attitudes and patterns of interaction from generation to generation. Research indicates that racial attitudes are learned and that they can be instilled early in childhood. Children as young as three can differentiate among racial groups, although their first positive or negative evaluations of the groups are not usually expressed until around age four or five. At this age, children tend to imitate adults and will repeat what they hear around them, often faithfully reproducing the feelings underlying the words even if they don't fully understand the ideas (Milner, 1983). By age nine, the child internalizes the attitudes and ideas as her or his own, and they become part of the child's worldview unless they are challenged through other socialization or personal experiences.

Looking at the role of socialization is important not only because it emphasizes the social roots of social phenomena, but also because it suggests potential solutions to racial and ethnic antagonism. One obvious solution is to teach people at an early age to appreciate and respect racial and ethnic diversity (Stephan & Stephan, 1984). Some even suggest that schools take up this task by incorporating cultural diversity into their curricula, such as teaching children Latino songs, reading them African or Native American folk tales, and letting them cook and eat Asian food in class.

Despite the fact that socialization and social learning obviously affect racial and ethnic attitudes and patterns of interaction, some sociologists think this approach is too limited. For one thing, focusing exclusively on socialization does not address the question of where specific attitudes and behaviors came from in the first place. That is, although socialization may help reproduce racial and ethnic stratification, how did the stratification originally develop?

A related criticism is that social scientists who focus on the role of socialization remain at the individual level and overlook the structural nature of racial and ethnic stratification. Socialization does not occur in a vacuum, but rather takes place under particular structural conditions. It is the conflict and feminist theories that examine the structural sources of racial and ethnic stratification.

Conflict and Feminist Theories

Conflict theorists recognize the importance of socialization in cultivating racial and ethnic attitudes and patterns of interaction. However, they also argue that socialization takes place in the context of a social structural framework that greatly influences what gets taught. The two dimensions of this structural framework that most affect the nature of racial and ethnic relations are competition over scarce resources and unequal distribution of power across groups.

According to conflict theorists, the contact between two physically and/or culturally dissimilar groups does not have to involve conflict or discrimination, but the likelihood increases when both groups seek a goal that is perceived to be attainable by only one group, or when one group tries to establish or maintain an advantageous position over the other. The group with more or better resources has an obvious edge in the struggle. In this context, racial differences become a convenient justification for subordination, and the more visible the differences, the easier it is to exploit them (Noel, 1991; Vander Zanden, 1983). In addition, racial and ethnic stereotypes are used by those at the top of the social class hierarchy to "divide and conquer" those on the lower rungs, making them easier to control and manipulate for the benefit of the "ruling class." Thus, from the conflict perspective, race and ethnicity are simply tools used by the powerful to preserve or enhance the status quo (Pettigrew, 1998).

Among the merits of the conflict perspective is that it is useful in explaining intraracial and intraethnic conflict, especially when it is class-based. The conflict perspective also receives some support from historical research, which shows how the exploitation of one racial or ethnic group by another helped establish and maintain a maldistribution of wealth, power, and privilege in the United States and other societies, and how supposed racial or ethnic differences have been used to legitimate systemic inequality. There is also considerable evidence that shows that racial and ethnic hostility increases during periods of economic decline (Blackwell, 1982), and decreases when groups enjoy equal status and share common goals and when racism is not institutionally supported (Miller & Brewer, 1984; Pettigrew, 1998).

Nevertheless, some sociologists are critical of the conflict perspective. First, by arguing that racial and ethnic stratification is simply a tool for preserving social class inequality, conflict theorists downplay the continuing significance of race in the lives of non-White women and men, regardless of their social class (Willie, 1989). As we have seen repeatedly in this chapter, economic success does not necessarily shield a person from racial or ethnic prejudice and discrimination. A second criticism is that the conflict perspective fails to consider how racism intersects with other forms of inequality—sexism and heterosexism, for example—in addition to social class inequality. An analysis of these intersecting inequalities is central to feminist sociology.

According to feminist sociologists, the category *race* overlaps with other social categories, including *social class*, but also *gender* and *sexual orientation*. Consequently, the effects of racism are made worse by other types of prejudice and discrimination: classism, sexism, and heterosexism. Together, these inequalities form what sociologist Patricia Hill Collins (1990) calls a **matrix of domination,** an interlocking system of control in which each type of inequality reinforces the others, so that the impact of one cannot be fully understood without also considering the others. For example, when a White male student at a prestigious Ivy League university yelled a racial slur at two African American women walking on campus several years ago, his insult was directed not only at their race, but also their sex. The elite environment in which the incident occurred also raises the issue of the social class of the students involved. In short, feminist sociologists caution against generalizing from the experiences of a particular racial or ethnic subgroup (such as White men or African American women) to all members of the race or ethnic group, since experiences differ in important ways depending not only on race, but also on social class, gender, and sexual orientation.

REFLECTING ON

Explaining Race and Ethnic Stratification

1. Is race and ethnic stratification "natural" or is it caused by social forces? Explain your answer.
2. How might a conflict theorist attempt to solve the problem of remedying race and ethnic stratification? How about if you were a feminist theorist?

For useful resources for study and review, run Chapter 11 on your *Living Sociology* CD-ROM.

CONNECTIONS

Social constructs	Compare the discussion in this chapter of race as a social construct with the discussion of gender as a social construct in Chapter 10 or of illness as a social construct in Chapter 18. Use your comparison to develop your own definition of a social construct.
Cultural diversity and multiculturalism	The topic of multiculturalism was introduced in Chapter 4 in the section on "Cultural Diversity." How does multiculturalism relate to the concept of cultural pluralism? What are the advantages of adopting a multicultural perspective?
Institutional racism	Read the section on "Warfare and the Military" in Chapter 14. What example of institutional racism is presented? What example of institutional discrimination can you identify?
Stereotyping	Review the definition and examples of stereotypes in the section on "The Mass Media" in Chapter 5. What are some media stereotypes of minorities not mentioned in the text? By what socialization processes do children learn prejudice?
Racial segregation	Review the discussion in Chapter 8 of the United States as a caste system of social stratification based on racial segregation. See also the section on sex segregation in the workplace in Chapter 10. What are the similar effects of these two forms of segregation?
Assimilation	Read the section on "Migration" in Chapter 19, and consider the case of refugees. What would determine if an immigrant group became assimilated or acculturated? What are all the factors that might influence the rate and effectiveness of a group's adaptation? What are the costs of assimilation compared to the benefits of pluralism?
Diversity in marriage patterns	See the section on "Families Throughout the World: Structures and Characteristics" in Chapter 15. What are some ways that cross-cultural differences in those family patterns could result in misunderstandings or problems adapting?

CONNECTIONS

School desegregation	Preview "Problems of Education" in Chapter 16, which describes racial segregation and desegregation issues in U.S. schools. How do issues of separatism or voluntary resegregation in the schools relate to the discussion in this chapter on cultural pluralism? How does the debate about affirmative action relate to issues of school resegregation?
Race and class	Review the section on "Social Mobility" in Chapter 8. What specific examples can you find of the intersecting inequalities between social class or income and race?
Race and education	Survey Chapter 16 for information on the "hidden curriculum," bilingual education debate, and the educational attainment of racial and ethnic minorities. What effect do you think multicultural education is having on the quality of education in the United States?
Nativism	Review the discussion of countercultures in Chapter 4. In what ways do the White-American survivalist militia groups described there illustrate the concept of nativism? Is nativism likely to increase or decrease as the composition of the U.S. population becomes more diverse?

SUMMING UP CHAPTER 11

Racial, Ethnic, and Minority Groups

1. Race is a social construct that people create to describe and give meaning to the variations they see in humans. The grouping of people into racial groups did not begin until the late eighteenth century. Racial groupings are artificial and arbitrary, and they vary from society to society. Even within a single society, racial labeling may be inconsistent.
2. Ethnic groups are distinguished from races in that ethnic groups are defined by their cultural characteristics, not by biological characteristics. The critical defining feature of an ethnic group is a sense of peoplehood, which provides members with a source of pride and cohesiveness.
3. Ethnocentrism is common, but when it is intense, it can be volatile and destructive, causing various levels of conflict between ethnic groups. Racism is different from ethnocentrism in that racism is a form of inequality in which one racial group dominates another and legitimates its dominance by proclaiming itself physically, intellectually, and/or socially superior, and by instituting laws or practices to protect its dominance. Members of different racial groups define racism differently, with people of color usually adopting a broader definition than White people.
4. Racial and ethnic groups singled out for unfair treatment are also called *minority groups*. A minority group may be a numerical majority, but they are oppressed in that they are subordinated and exploited by the dominant (majority) group.

Prejudice and Discrimination

1. Prejudice is the attitudinal component of racism and usually involves stereotyping. Most racial and ethnic stereotypes are negative, and people adhere to them even in the face of refuting evidence. Some social scientists think prejudice is the result of individuals' needs to scapegoat others; the need to scapegoat may derive from an authoritarian personality. But other social scientists point out that people without authoritarian personalities are often prejudiced and engage in scapegoating. These social scientists believe prejudice is learned through socialization.
2. Discrimination may occur independently of prejudice, but typically the two are interdependent. Discrimination may be individual or institutional. Institutional discrimination is more difficult to detect and harder to eliminate than individual discrimination because institutional discrimination is a built-in feature of social arrangements, it goes unnoticed, and it is taken for granted as "business as usual." There are various forms of institutional discrimination, all of which have occurred in the United States, including exclusion, expulsion, and genocide.

Assimilation and Pluralism

1. When a racial or ethnic group loses its distinctiveness and becomes absorbed into the culture and interaction of the host society, it has assimilated. Acculturation, which is a common form of assimilation, occurs when a group makes cultural changes that lead it to be indistinguishable from the dominant group in terms of dress, language, and the like. More difficult to accomplish is structural assimilation, in which a racial or ethnic group has full access to the same structural opportunities and social activities as members of the dominant group. Among the factors that affect the extent and kind of assimilation a group experiences are: whether the group voluntarily

joined the new society or was forced into it; the extent to which the minority group is visibly different from the majority; and the size of the minority group, its geographic dispersion, the extent to which its members view their stay in the host society as permanent, and the timing of their arrival. Some people, though, have questioned the desirability of assimilation, believing that it devalues and destroys diversity.

2. Unlike assimilation, the goal of pluralism is appreciation of and respect for the cultures of differing groups. Although the pluralist model is popular, social scientists have found that it often remains an ideal rather than a reality in most societies. Other critics see the pluralist model as too narrow because it downplays intragroup conflict that arises from social class, sex, age, and sexual orientation differences. Pluralism also poses the difficult dilemma of whether the beliefs and practices of a culture should be preserved and honored even if they are harmful or offensive to some people.

Race and Ethnicity in the United States

1. The population of the United States is composed of many diverse racial and ethnic groups, each of which has its own internal diversity. The Native American population, for example, is made up of several hundred tribes, most of which live in the western and southwestern states. About half of the Native American population lives on reservations. Unemployment and poverty rates on the reservations are high, and economic growth has been limited. A major concern of reservation residents is how to develop their economies without destroying their culture and physically harming themselves.

2. African Americans have a unique history in this country in that they are the only minority to have been forcibly brought here in slavery. Although racial discrimination has been outlawed, African Americans continue to experience both subtle and overt discrimination in their everyday lives. African Americans have made significant gains in social well-being during the past thirty years, but on most measures, they still lag significantly behind White Americans.

3. Asian Americans are often referred to as a "model" minority because their aggregate levels of educational attainment and income have surpassed those of Americans as a whole. But the model minority concept masks important differences among Asian American groups and overlooks the prejudice and discrimination that many Asian Americans continue to experience.

4. Hispanic Americans are also highly diverse, with Cubans enjoying the highest levels of well-being on most indicators and Puerto Ricans showing the lowest levels. These differences are largely a reflection of the different historical experiences of each group.

5. White Americans are the dominant racial group in the United States. English Americans or Anglo-Saxons were the first White people to establish permanent settlements here. Groups that emigrated after the English encountered varying levels of prejudice and discrimination, depending on how dissimilar they were to the English. Nevertheless, many European immigrants enjoyed considerable success, although some groups, especially those of Southern and Eastern European descent, still sometimes encounter prejudice and discrimination.

6. Although today White Americans are the numerical majority of the U.S. population, by the middle of the twenty-first century their numerical dominance is expected to decline considerably. The Asian American and Hispanic populations are expected to grow the most. These population changes will increase the cultural diversity of our country, but it remains to be seen whether this increased diversity will be welcomed by most people.

Explaining Racial and Ethnic Stratification

1. Some sociologists explain racial and ethnic stratification as a natural phenomenon. The primordialist perspective says that people have an innate preference for people they perceive as like themselves, and racial classifications provide a quick and easy method for drawing the distinctions. Critics of primordialism point out that it downplays evidence showing racial and ethnic categories as arbitrary social constructs; that it ignores intraracial and intraethnic conflicts, especially social class conflict; and that it discounts the role of human intervention in addressing racial and ethnic antagonisms.

2. Some social scientists who place greater emphasis on the social dimensions of racial and ethnic stratification explain it as a product of socialization and social learning. These social scientists point to research that shows that racial and ethnic attitudes are learned early in life and are passed down from generation to generation. They suggest that one obvious solution to racial and ethnic antagonism is to teach children at an early age, at home and in school, an appreciation of diversity. But critics of this model see it as too limited. While socialization is important, we must consider how the stratification originally developed, and we must look not only at individual factors, but also at structural factors.

3. Conflict theorists focus on structural causes of racial and ethnic stratification, especially competition over scarce resources and unequal distribution of power across groups. In the context of economic competition, racial and ethnic differences become a convenient justification for subordination of the powerless by the more powerful. Despite empirical support for the conflict model, some sociologists are critical of this position because they say that by depicting racial and ethnic stratification as a tool for preserving social class inequality, conflict theorists downplay the continuing significance of race in the lives of non-White women and men of all social classes. Feminist sociologists, in particular, are critical of the conflict perspective for failing to consider how racism intersects with other forms of inequality besides social class inequality. Feminist sociologists argue that racism overlaps with classism, sexism, heterosexism, and other inequalities to form a matrix of domination.

KEY PEOPLE AND CONCEPTS

assimilation: the process by which a racial or ethnic group gradually loses its distinctiveness and separateness and becomes absorbed into the culture and interaction of its host society

authoritarian personality: a personality type made up of traits including insecurity and intolerance, rigid conformity to tradition, superstition, and submission to authority

cultural assimilation (behavioral assimilation, acculturation): a form of assimilation that occurs over the course of several generations and involves cultural changes (such as changes in dress and language) until eventually the cultural expression of the members of a specific racial or ethnic group is indistinguishable from that of the dominant or core group

discrimination: any actions, policies, or practices that have the effect of denying an individual or group equal access to the society's resources, rewards, and opportunities

equalitarian pluralism: the maintenance of racial and ethnic diversity in a society that simultaneously involves the development of an appreciation of and respect for the cultures of groups other than one's own

ethnic group: a group whose members share a common cultural heritage and a sense of peoplehood that they pass on from one generation to the next

ethnicity: the characteristics of an ethnic group, that is, the ways they express their cultural heritage and sense of belonging to the group

ethnocentricism: regarding the values and behavior of one's own group as "correct" or "best" and judging other groups' values and practices as inferior

exclusion: a form of institutional discrimination that involves restricting the entry of a group into society or preventing its full participation in the society

expulsion: a form of institutional discrimination that involves the forced removal of a group from an area or the harassment of a group to compel migration

genocide: a form of institutional discrimination that involves the deliberate attempt to exterminate an entire race or ethnic group

institutional discrimination: policies and practices of the central institutions in a society that systematically disadvantage members of particular groups

matrix of domination: an interlocking system of control in which each type of inequality reinforces others, so that the impact of one cannot be fully understood without considering the others

minority groups: racial and ethnic groups who are singled out for unfair treatment

nativism: an anti-immigrant position that those already settled in an area are racially superior to newcomers

pluralism: the maintenance of racial and ethnic diversity in a society

prejudice: in the context of race and ethnic relations, biased beliefs about individuals based on their membership in a particular racial or ethnic group

primordialist perspective: a theory that explains race and ethnic stratification as a product of humans' natural preference for those whom they perceive as being most like themselves

race: a group whose members share a real or supposed biological heritage that is thought to give rise to a set of fixed physical, mental, emotional, and moral characteristics; members of a race also share common customs, values, and traditions and develop a sense of peoplehood

racism: a form of inequality in which one racial group dominates another and legitimates this domination by proclaiming itself physically, intellectually, and/or socially superior, and instituting laws or practices to protect its dominance

scapegoats: relatively powerless people whom others unjustly blame for their own or society's problems

segregation: physically and socially separating and keeping apart different racial and ethnic groups

structural assimilation: a form of assimilation that occurs when the members of a racial or ethnic group have full access to the same structural opportunities and social activities as the members of the dominant group

LEARNING MORE

Feagin, J. R., & Sykes, M. P. (1994). *Living with racism: The Black middle-class experience.* Boston: Beacon Press. An insightful analysis of everyday encounters with racism experienced by African Americans who are middle class or higher.

Min, P. G. (Ed.). (1994). *Asian Americans: Contemporary trends and issues.* Thousand Oaks, CA: Sage. A collection of essays that highlights the diversity among Asian American groups, examining each group's history while calling into question the notion of Asian Americans as a "model minority."

Nagel, J. (1996). *American Indian ethnic renewal: Red power and the resurgence of identity and culture.* New York: Oxford University Press. A study of the Red Power movement by a sociologist well known for her research on Native American culture and social organization.

Uriciuoli, B. (1996). *Exposing prejudice: Puerto Rican experiences of language, race, and class.* Boulder: Westview. An ethnography of bilingual working-class Puerto Ricans living in New York City that nicely illustrates the intersection of racism and social class inequality.

West, C. (1993). *Race matters.* New York: Random House. A highly readable and moving collection of essays by a prominent African American social thinker.

Wolfe, A. (1998). *One nation, after all.* New York: Viking. A fascinating look at the American middle class, based on research in eight communities throughout the country. Although Wolfe discusses middle-class attitudes and opinions on a variety of issues (e.g., gay rights, crime, and abortion), perhaps his most interesting findings are those on racism and immigration.

 Run Chapter 12 on your *Living Sociology* CD-ROM for interesting and informative activities, web links, videos, practice tests, and more.

C H A P T E R

12

Aging and the Life Course

A typical day in the lives of Martha and Tom Alexander might include swimming, an exercise class, a brisk ride on one of their twenty horses, a consultation with the farmhands who help with the work on their fifty-acre northern Virginia farm (until recently, they did most of the farm work themselves), entertaining friends, and two or three hours of ballroom dancing. For John Morris, a typical day includes sailing his small Boston whaler, clamming, shopping and cooking, and an hour and a half to two hours of tennis. Mr. Morris began playing what he calls "serious tennis" about eighteen years ago and has since won thirty-eight national championships in his age group. Herb Feldman spends most of his days teaching folk songs and dance to Alzheimer's patients and other elderly in Brooklyn, but he also jogs or walks for exercise on a daily basis (Brody, 1996; Goleman, 1996; Kolata, 1996).*

No doubt, many of us would find such days challenging, if not exhausting, so you may be surprised to learn that these three individuals are over eighty years old. They hardly fit the media images of the elderly, who are more often than not depicted as mentally feeble and physically frail, impaired by multiple chronic and disabling illnesses. While it is the case that elderly people—especially age seventy-five and older—are more likely than younger people to suffer from disabilities and chronic illness, for more than a decade, rates of disabilities and chronic illnesses have been slowly and steadily declining by 1 to 2 percent each year. Rates have declined across social classes and relatively equally for Whites and African Americans. Elderly Americans who do have disabilities can often take advantage of medical technology such as hip and lens replacements to improve the quality of their lives. These trends, not surprisingly, are contributing to a redefinition of old age in our society (Kolata, 1996).

In this chapter, we will explore what it means to be elderly in the United States and in other societies. Although we will focus on the segment of the population that is sixty-five and older, we will look at the values, beliefs, interactions, and problems of this age group in relation to other age groups at various stages of the life cycle.

Why devote an entire chapter to a single age group within the population? For one thing, as we have already learned, age is one way the population of a society may be stratified. Even hunting and gathering societies, which are characterized by relatively little social stratification, stratify by age. Second, the elderly constitute the fastest-growing segment of not only the U.S. population, but populations worldwide. Assuming that most elderly people are not employed, we need to assess the impact of their swelling ranks on the distribution of societal resources and social services across population groups.

To begin our discussion, then, let's look at the age distribution of the U.S. and world populations.

*These names are pseudonyms, but the vignette describes real people.

AGING AROUND THE WORLD

In 1900, 4 percent of the people in the United States were age sixty-five and older, while 40 percent were under age eighteen. Less than one hundred years later, 12.8 percent of the population was sixty-five and older, while only 26 percent of the population was under eighteen. Moreover, by the middle of the twenty-first century, the number of elderly Americans is expected to more than double, while the under-eighteen segment will shrink a bit more. By 2050, 20 percent of the total U.S. population will be sixty-five and older, while those under eighteen will make up 24 percent of the population (U.S. Department of Commerce, Bureau of the Census, 1997).

The U.S. population changes are being mirrored throughout the world (see Figure 12.1). In 1994, 357 million people worldwide, or 6 percent of the world's population, were sixty-five and older. More important, however, is that the growth rate for this population group is significantly higher than the growth rate for the population as a whole. Globally, the elderly population is growing by about 800,000 people each month (AARP, 1998; Kristof, 1996; Taeuber, 1992). Some of this dramatic growth in the elderly population is occurring in industrialized countries, such as Japan, which is currently considered the world's fastest-aging country, and Italy, which is expected to have the world's highest median age in 2025, when nearly half of its population will be over fifty (Kristof, 1996). However, the greatest growth is taking place in undeveloped and developing countries. Undeveloped and developing countries, particularly those in Asia and Africa, account for 74 percent of the monthly increase in the world's elderly population (Hobbs, 1996). Before the middle of the twenty-first century, it is projected that seven of the ten countries with the highest number of elderly will be developing and undeveloped countries: China, India, Brazil, Indonesia, Pakistan, Mexico, and Bangladesh (AARP, 1998; Mulenga, 1996).

A number of factors have contributed to these population changes. In the United States and in many other

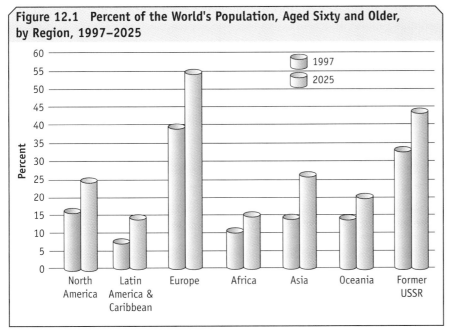

Figure 12.1   Percent of the World's Population, Aged Sixty and Older, by Region, 1997–2025

Source: American Association of Retired Persons (AARP). (1998). *Aging Everywhere*. Washington, DC: Author, p. 6.

industrialized countries, there was a surge in the birth rate—or, as it has come to be called, a *baby boom*—when World War II ended. Not until the 1960s did the birth rate begin to decline, and then finally, in the early 1990s, level off, although at a rate significantly below the mid-century rate. Today, people are delaying childbearing longer than in the past and they are having fewer children on average. So, the younger segment of the population is shrinking, but all the while, the baby boomers continue to age.

At the same time, advances in medical technology, the greater availability of health care, and basic improvements in diet and hygiene have lengthened life expectancy in much of the world. In developing and undeveloped countries, vaccination and other public health programs have particularly contributed to increased life expectancy, although the quality of a longer life in these countries is diminished by persistent, widespread, and severe poverty. In industrialized countries, rising levels of educational attainment also appear to play a role in the trend toward

The growth rate of the world's elderly population is significantly higher than the growth rate for the population as a whole, with the greatest growth occurring in pre-industrial and developing countries in Africa and Asia, even where up to half the population is under age 15. What is the impact of "baby booms" on a population?

longer life spans. Better educated people take better care of themselves; they also tend to be wealthier and so can afford more and better health care than less educated people (Kolata, 1996).

In sum, people throughout the world are living longer. Since the 1950s, for example, average life expectancy in developing countries has risen by about twenty years. The picture in the United States is even brighter: In 1850, a newborn baby girl could expect to enjoy forty years of life, two years more than a baby boy born that same year. But today, a baby girl born in the United States can expect to live about seventy-nine years, while a baby boy can expect to enjoy almost seventy-three years of life (U.S. Department of Health and Human Services, 1997). In fact, research shows that White and Black Americans who reach the age of eighty can expect to live longer than their peers in other industrialized countries (Manton & Vaupel, 1995).

Before we explore the various implications of these population shifts, let's get a better understanding of the aging process from several perspectives: biological, psychological, and sociological.

REFLECTING ON

Aging around the World

1. What are some social and economic implications of the rapidly increasing elderly population in undeveloped and developing countries?
2. What are some of the potential benefits and problems, for both the individual and society, of extending life expectancy?

AGING: MYTHS AND REALITIES

Browse through the birthday section of any greeting card store and you'll get a pretty good idea of how most people view aging: Aging is a process of physical and mental deterioration. The physical signs of aging are obvious: the skin wrinkles, hair turns gray, and hearing and vision diminish so that hearing aids and eyeglasses may become necessary. Along with the physical changes, we expect certain psychological and behavioral changes. For instance, we expect older people to not only move more slowly, but also think more slowly. We expect them to become increasingly inflexible, not just physically, but also intellectually and socially. We also commonly assume that elderly women and men are asexual, dependent, childish, conservative, and just plain "grumpy" (Fiske, 1998; Levin & Levin, 1980).

Given such an unflattering portrait, it's not surprising that in our society and many others, aging induces em-

barrassment and shame in many people. The desire to inhibit or prevent aging isn't a new phenomenon either. Think of Ponce de Leon's quest for the fountain of youth or the various potions and "treatments" concocted over the years by self-styled chemists and doctors. Today, most people simply try to conceal their age with the help of makeup, hair dye, and plastic surgery (see the Intersecting Inequalities box). Importantly, however, researchers in the biological sciences and psychology as well as sociology have found that much of the stereotypical decline associated with aging is not inevitable. The scientific study of the aging process is called **gerontology**. Gerontologists don't try to preserve youth, but rather better understand the aging process in order to improve the health and quality of life of the aged. Let's consider some of the findings from recent gerontological research.

Aging in Body and Mind

The physiological changes produced by aging occur gradually over the life course. For example, bones tend to lose calcium as aging progresses and so become more brittle, more easily fractured, and to take more time to heal. This is particularly a problem for women. However, studies show that how one lives when young greatly affects physiology in old age. Regular physical exercise and a low-fat diet of high-vitamin and calcium-rich foods not only keeps bones healthy, but also lowers blood pressure, reducing the risk of other life-threatening illnesses associated with aging such as heart disease and stroke (Brink, 1995). Remaining physically active as one ages is also important (Pereira et al., 1998). According to recent research, exercise that strengthens muscles is a key to good health in old age (Noble, 1998).

It is also often assumed that sexual performance declines with age. In fact, research shows this is true, but it is only individuals over seventy-five who report significantly lower levels of sexual activity than their younger counterparts, and even among them sexual desire is not extinguished. Some researchers have even found that while sexual activity may be less frequent in old age, sexual pleasure may actually increase for some, especially postmenopausal women (National Council on Aging, 1998; Riporetella-Muller, 1989.) There is also substantial evidence that the pattern of sexual activity in later life generally mirrors the pattern of one's younger years. In other words, a healthy interest in sex when one is young will likely continue into later years (Whitbourne, 1990). The factors that seem to most affect continued sexual activity in old age are a person's level of self-esteem, health, and the availability of a partner (Marsiglio & Donnelly, 1991; Purdy, 1995). The need for intimacy—for tenderness and close physical contact—is a fundamental human trait that persists throughout the life course.

INTERSECTING INEQUALITIES

How Do Men and Women of Means Try to Defeat the Aging Process?

In our society, the attractiveness of a woman is associated with her age: All other factors being equal, young women are generally considered more attractive than old women. Not surprisingly, the cosmetics industry has played on women's fear of losing their beauty as they age by marketing products and techniques that are supposed to make them look younger. Among the most popular cosmetics for women are anti-aging creams that reduce facial wrinkles. But for some women, cosmetics are not enough. These women have turned to surgery to make them look younger. The most common type of cosmetic surgery is liposuction, a procedure where a suction tube is inserted into the body through a tiny incision, usually in the thighs or abdomen, and fat is literally sucked out (Williams, 1992). Face lifts, vein surgery (to remove varicose veins), and "tummy tucks" are also popular, though expensive. (Depending on the procedure, the price of cosmetic surgery ranges from $190 for simple vein surgery to nearly $5,000 for a face lift.) But so strong is the dislike of looking old that 30 percent of women say they would undergo cosmetic surgery just to eliminate skin wrinkles if they could afford it (Freedman, 1986).

Traditionally, aging for men has not carried the stigma that it has for women. An older man with creased skin, graying hair, and even sagging muscles was often regarded as distinguished. Recently, however, analysts have noticed a surge in men's products and treatments promising a more youthful appearance. The analysts trace this trend to the phenomenon of corporate downsizing that began during the 1980s. Increasingly, businessmen in shrinking corporations are competing with younger men and women for jobs, and the perception among many employers is that the young, trim executive will have more energy, make a better impression on clients, and bring in more business (Spindler, 1996).

It's not surprising, then, that men are increasingly purchasing products and treatments to make them look younger. Among the available options are inexpensive undershirts ($19.95) to shape up sagging chests and stomachs, underpants ($24.95) to control the tummy and shape the buttocks, anti-wrinkle creams and gels, and hair dyes and thickeners (about 10 percent of men forty to sixty years old color their hair). But many men are also turning to surgery to get a more youthful appearance. The most popular cosmetic surgery for men is hair transplant and restoration, performed on almost 200,000 men annually. Liposuction to reduce stomach, chest, and breast fat is the second most popular procedure. Growing in popularity are face lifts and eyelid surgery, chin and jaw augmenta-tion or reduction, and pectoral and calf implants (to make the chest and calves look more muscular). Men were 10 percent of cosmetic surgery patients in 1980, but by 1994 they were 26 percent of cosmetic surgery patients (Spindler, 1996).

Perhaps the most popular youth-enhancer for men, however, is Viagra, a drug developed to treat impotence. Within its first two weeks on the market, doctors wrote nearly 37,000 Viagra prescriptions, at prices ranging from $8 to $12 a pill. Despite the possibility of side effects, even men without erectile dysfunctions have sought Viagra prescriptions in the belief that the drug will make them more virile and enhance their sexual experiences.

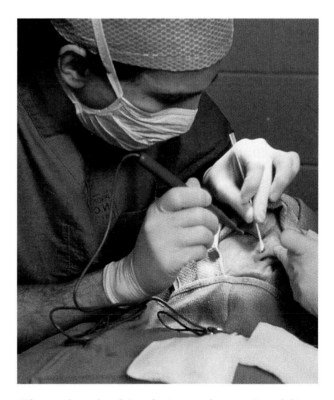

What myths and realities of aging may have motivated this woman to undergo cosmetic surgery? What American values and norms support this motivation, and what part might gender role expectations play? What practices aside from plastic surgery may also be responses to ageism in American society and culture?

At any age, a low-fat diet and regular exercise reduce risk for many life-threatening illnesses and also improve memory retention and reaction time. To what extent is it true that old age results in health problems such as debilitation and senility?

The greatest concern of most people about aging is a fear of mental or intellectual decline. Many assume that as we age, we become *senile*—intellectual functioning, including memory, reasoning, creativity, and the ability to learn deteriorates. Despite numerous role models, such as the individuals we introduced at the beginning of the chapter, who refute this idea, it remains a widely held stereotype.

Only about 5 percent of the population over sixty-five is impaired by senility, but the prevalent belief that senility is inevitable has serious consequences for the elderly. For example, some physical illnesses may go undiagnosed because the symptoms are interpreted as simply signs of aging. Memory loss, sharply reduced reaction time, and similar changes may be symptomatic of serious illnesses such as arteriosclerosis and Alzheimer's disease or may indicate a misuse or overuse of prescription drugs. Ignoring such symptoms can produce unnecessary suffering and ultimately death. Some elderly people exhibit aspects of senility because their family members and others treat them as if they were senile, producing a self-fulfilling prophecy (Levin & Levin, 1980). As symbolic interactionists point out, our perceptions of ourselves derive mainly from our interactions with others and the way we think they view us.

While it is not true that senility is an inevitable part of aging, most stereotypes are built on at least a grain of truth, and research does indicate certain types of decline in intellectual functioning in old age. As we age, our brains actually shrink a bit in size; we lose about 10 percent of our brain mass between the ages of twenty and seventy. The number of connections between cells in the brains of older people also appear to decrease. These physiological changes and others can affect such mental functions as memory. Importantly, however, it is speed of recall that is affected, not accuracy. Intellectual tasks that younger people complete quickly seem to require increased mental effort in the elderly, but if given enough time, elderly men and women are just as likely as their younger peers to complete the tasks successfully. Moreover, as long as the individual remains physically healthy, overall knowledge and vocabulary continue to grow with age; the capacity for learning does not diminish. In fact, researchers tell us that one of the best ways to retain and even improve intellectual functioning regardless of age is through mental exercise: reading, playing intellectually challenging games such as chess, working on jigsaw puzzles that stimulate inductive reasoning and spatial skills, and doing crossword puzzles. Physical exercise is also critical; studies show that regular physical exercise inhibits memory loss and improves reaction time in older women and men (Brink, 1995; Morris, 1996; Schaie, 1994).

Some gerontologists have wondered whether the way a person ages is genetically determined, since individuals whose parents had long lives tend to live long themselves. Recent research shows, however, that only about 30 percent of what we identify as characteristics of aging are genetically based (Brody, 1996). This does not mean that aging is not a biological process, but rather that once again, in aging we see an interaction of the biological and the social. Factors such as resilience (the ability to recover from distressing events) and productivity (making a social contribution through activity) are as important as exercise and diet to healthy aging (Shaie, 1994).

Having looked at biological and psychological aspects of aging, let's now consider how age may serve as a basis for stratification in a society.

R E F L E C T I N G   O N

Aging: Myths and Realities

1. As a sociologist, how would you respond to someone who says, "Life is all downhill after forty"?
2. How do biological and cultural factors interact to affect the aging process?

THEORETICAL PERSPECTIVES ON AGING

You have probably heard of the brothers Grimm, who are famous for the fairy tales they wrote for children. One brother, Jacob Grimm, once told a story that you aren't likely to have heard as a child. It was about a man whose elderly father lived with him and his family, but the man mistreated his father. He wouldn't let his father eat with the rest of the family, and he made him eat the food out of a small wooden trough. Then one day the man discovered his son fitting together some small boards. When he asked his son what he was doing, the boy replied, "It's for you father, for when you are old."

Grimm's chilling tale reminds us that aging and death are inescapable facts of life. But while aging is universal, the value attached to specific ages or periods of the life course varies from society to society. We know from previous chapters that stratification occurs when differential rankings are attached to ascribed traits and people at each rank are given unequal access to resources, rewards, or opportunities. Thus, **age stratification** is the social ranking of individuals at different stages of the life course who, in turn, are given differential access to society's resources, rewards, and opportunities on the basis of their age. **Ageism** is the social inequality that results from age stratification. When people practice ageism, they use age to define an individual's capabilities and social roles, and to determine the individual's access to societal resources, rewards, and opportunities.

All types of societies stratify their populations by age, making age stratification a cultural universal. However, as we have already noted, the form that the stratification takes—that is, whether old or young are revered or cursed—varies across cultures and even among societies of the same type. For example, in many hunting and gathering societies, old age—meaning the late thirties and forties—is looked on very favorably. The young respect the old as valued advisors because of their experience. The old are not expected to participate in the daily task of acquiring food, but they continue to contribute to the group as advisors and by helping to care for the children. In such societies, the different generations of a family live together, so there is close contact between young and old. From this day-to-day proximity, a reciprocal relationship develops between the generations: The old care for and advise the young, and as children grow up, they learn that they have obligations to the elderly (Keith, 1990; Keith et al., 1994; Rhoads, 1984). In some hunting and gathering societies, however, the elderly are considered an economic burden when they are no longer physically able to help gather daily food (Keith, 1990; Sheehan, 1976).

Once the accumulation of a surplus of food and material resources becomes possible, as in pastoral, horti-

cultural, and agricultural societies, the status of the elderly seems to be more uniformly high. This is because wealth tends to build up as one ages. The oldest members of these societies usually have the greatest wealth and prestige, as well as the greatest political power. Colonial America is a good example. When the economy of the United States was largely agrarian, the elderly were considered God's favorites. It was the old—more specifically, the old men—who controlled family property and held positions of authority in religious organizations and in government. In fact, young men of the colonies often colored their hair with white powder or wore gray wigs to look older and lied about their age to census takers, claiming to be older than they really were to enhance their status (Fischer, 1977).

Societies that respect and revere the aged are called **gerontophilic**. With industrialization, the pattern often reverses. Although for many, wealth continues to accumulate with age in industrialized societies, the technological demands of industrialization favor the young. In fully industrialized societies, technological change tends to be extraordinarily rapid, making it difficult for older workers to keep pace with the demand for new skills and knowledge. That is, it's easier to train young, upcoming workers than to remove established workers from the workforce to retrain them. Moreover, industrial societies don't need every individual to work in order to support the entire population. Consequently, in industrial societies children are exempt from work—indeed, in most industrial societies it is considered morally wrong for children under sixteen to work—and older workers are expected to retire to make room for younger workers. Instead of being gerontophilic, then, industrial societies are typically **gerontophobic**. Literally, the term means fear of aging and the aged, but sociologically it may be defined as a strong dislike or hatred of aging and the aged.

The idea that the economic transformation of a society from agriculture to industry progressively devalues aging stems from **modernization theory**. Modernization theory enjoys considerable popularity, so it deserves a closer look.

Modernization Theory

According to modernization theorists, the growth of a modern industrial society depends to a large extent on a literate, largely urban-based wage-labor force. Control of land is less important than technological expertise and geographic mobility, which puts older workers at a disadvantage in competing with younger workers for prestigious, better-paying jobs (Cowgill & Holmes, 1972).

At first glance, modernization theory makes sense. It's easy to understand how the technological demands of

What is the social status of this Navaho grandmother? Native American elders traditionally are accorded high status and great respect. In these gerontophilic societies, the aged also hold greater legitimate political and religious power and authority. What attitudes and practices characterize gerontophobic societies? How could you show the concept of age stratification as a continuum?

industrial production, especially today, make older people's knowledge seem obsolete, forcing them into retirement. Also, geographic mobility and urbanization contribute to changes in family structure, which in turn can lead to residential segregation and social isolation of the elderly.

Still, many sociologists and other social scientists find fault with modernization theory. For instance, as we have already learned, negative attitudes and behavior toward the elderly occur in preindustrial as well as industrial societies (Achenbaum, 1985; Keith, 1990). In addition, cross-cultural research indicates that a society's social or political ideology can have a mediating effect on modernization, preventing or lessening an adverse impact on the elderly (Keith et al., 1994).

For example, the modernization of China is rapidly occurring at the same time that the elderly population is growing and the Communist government's extensive system of welfare benefits is being cut back. To ensure that the ancient Chinese traditions of respect and care for elderly parents do not diminish as a result, several provincial governments in China have developed parental care contracts that spell out the obligations of adult children to their aging parents as well as the elders' rights. The contracts can be amended if family circumstances change, and arbitors and even the courts can be brought in to settle disputes. Although families are not currently required to enter into these contracts, the government hopes they will become popular ("China's Growing Reliance," 1998).

Japan is another society cited as a counterexample to modernization theory. Traditional Japanese society accords great respect and deference to elders, and this cus-

tom continued through the country's phenomenal industrial growth after World War II. Japanese culture includes honorific language to be used when speaking to or about one's elders; rules of etiquette that give precedence to elders in seating arrangements, serving order, bathing order, and entryways; a national holiday, Respect for Elders Day; and unquestioned authority of one's elders in family and household decision making (Palmore, 1981). The common Japanese word for the aged is *Otoshiyori*, which means "honorable elders." Today, life expectancy in Japan is among the highest in the world, and the majority of the elderly (57 percent) live with their adult children and grandchildren, with grandparents taking an active role in rearing grandchildren (Kristof, 1996).

There are signs, however, that Japan's gerontophilic traditions may be diminishing somewhat. (Some analysts question the extent to which Japan has ever been a gerontophilic society. After all, Japan used to have *ubasuteyama*, "mountains to dump a granny," where elderly and unwanted women were abandoned to die of starvation or hypothermia.) The decline in honoring the elderly appears to be prompted by economic and population changes. Living space in Japan is limited, and housing is very expensive. With elderly Japanese living longer, a growing trend is for younger households to be made up of four grandparents, two parents, and one grandchild (many Japanese are choosing to have only one child). Not only are such living conditions very crowded, but also they are a financial strain. The result seems to be that increasing numbers of elderly Japanese see themselves as a burden to the young, and the suicide rate of older Japanese is on the rise (Kristof, 1996; but for a potential solution to the housing problem, see "Stimulating Supply," 1998).

Modernization, then, does not necessarily lead to lower status for the aged, although it certainly may be a contributing factor. Modernization theory is only one of the theoretical perspectives on aging available. Let's consider what other sociological perspectives have to say.

Structural Functionalism

The major structural functionalist perspective on aging is referred to as **disengagement theory** (Cumming & Henry, 1961). Structural functionalists begin with the assumption that no matter how much people continue to learn and exercise, the aging process results in declining physical ability, slowed mental functioning, and eventually death. Aging is potentially disruptive to the smooth functioning of a society because it can interrupt the performance of socially necessary roles and tasks. Consequently, societies have built-in mechanisms for systematically transferring particular roles and responsibilities from one generation to the next. Retirement is such a mechanism in our society. When individuals reach a specific age, they relinquish—or *disengage* from—their work roles and responsibilities, which are in turn assumed by younger members of the society.

According to this structural functionalist perspective, disengagement not only benefits society by providing an orderly transition of roles and responsibilities, but it also benefits elderly people by giving them more leisure time and personal freedom. A number of analysts are skeptical of this claim, however. As we have already noted, an important key to successful aging is remaining socially productive. Removing older people from jobs they enjoy while providing few other socially valued outlets for productivity is more detrimental than beneficial, say critics. And for older people with limited financial resources, disengagement does not mean a life of leisurely comfort, but rather a life of poverty. Finally, it is questionable whether disengagement actually benefits society either. Removing experienced, able-bodied older people from the workforce and adding them to a growing population of people who are financially dependent on a shrinking labor pool puts considerable strain on workers and the economy overall.

Symbolic Interactionism

Symbolic interactionists shift the discussion from the structural level to the individual level, drawing our attention to the elderly themselves. Symbolic interactionists agree that for people to age successfully—that is, to lead satisfying lives throughout the life course—they must remain socially active. Consequently, the major symbolic interactionist perspective on aging is referred to as **activity theory.**

Activity theory does not propose that elderly people remain in the labor force until they are physically incapable of working. Rather, activity theory recognizes that in any society social roles are imbued with specific meanings or values, and individuals derive a sense of self-worth from the roles they hold. In our society, for example, productivity is highly valued, but a person can be productive in many ways: by participating in the labor force, performing household chores, caring for children, or doing volunteer work (see, for example, Hübler, 1999). Thus, activity theory holds that individuals should remain socially active throughout the life course, and their specific

This volunteer storyteller in a kindergarten makes a good illustration for the activity theory of aging proposed by the symbolic interactionists. How is this so? How might a structural functionalist theory of aging differ?

activities should reflect their personal choices, needs, and abilities.

One of the strengths of activity theory is its recognition of diversity. Old people are not a homogenous group; they are as diverse as younger segments of the population. Nevertheless, critics charge that activity theory places too much emphasis on individualism. It overlooks the constraints imposed by social structural factors on the choices available to various groups of older people. For example, the elderly poor, most of whom are women, are at greatest risk of suffering disability and chronic illness, which restrict their activity level. So, no matter how talented, capable, or willing an individual may be, that individual's opportunities may be blocked by problems, such as poverty, that are a built-in feature of the society.

Conflict Theory and Feminist Theory

Conflict theorists have not given as much explicit attention to aging as it deserves. For the most part, they have focused on ageism, pointing out that in an advanced capitalist society such as our own, the elderly are disadvantaged because they drive up production costs and lower profits. More specifically, older workers typically command higher wages than workers just entering the labor market; they also cost more in benefits, such as health insurance, since they tend to use medical services more than the young. At the same time, it is widely believed that older workers are less productive than younger workers, so employing older workers reduces profits (Dannefer, 1989; Hendricks, 1992).

Although conflict theorists put forth this general pattern for capitalist societies, they do recognize that not all groups of elderly are equally disadvantaged. Rather, conflict theorists emphasize that age intersects with social class to produce different outcomes. So, for example, conflict theorists point out to symbolic interactionists that the elderly in the upper social classes have significantly greater freedom of choice in the activities they pursue than the elderly at the bottom rungs of the social class hierarchy.

A major problem with conflict theory is its almost exclusive focus on ageism as a product of contemporary capitalist societies. But as we found in our discussion of modernization theory, ageism is found in precapitalist, preindustrial societies as well. Still, to its credit, conflict theory, like symbolic interactionism, draws attention to the diversity of the elderly population. Feminist theorists take the emphasis on diversity a step further by showing how age intersects not only with social class, but also with sex to produce unequal life chances for the elderly. Let's take a closer look at how gender, race and ethnicity, and social class combine to produce diverse aging experiences.

R E F L E C T I N G   O N

Theoretical Perspectives on Aging

1. Why is gerontophobia harmful? What strategies would you suggest for making the United States more gerontophilic?
2. Which theoretical perspective discussed in this chapter do you think best explains the aging experiences of most Americans? What are your reasons?

DIVERSITY IN AGING

Although we cannot explore all facets of social life, we will consider several that seem to be of paramount concern to individuals as they progress through the life course.

Poverty, Gender, Race and Ethnicity: Intersections with Age

It is commonly assumed that most old people are poor. The data show, however, that overall, the financial circumstances of the elderly population have improved considerably since the 1950s. Until the 1980s, the old were more likely than the young to live in poverty. In 1959, in fact, over a third of Americans age sixty-five or older lived below the poverty line. But in 1982, the elderly turned the corner with a lower rate of poverty than the under-eighteen population, and by 1993, the trend had reversed. In 1997, only 10.5 percent of the elderly population lived below the poverty line, compared to nearly 20 percent of children under eighteen (Davis et al., 1990; U.S. Department of Commerce, Bureau of the Census, 1998b).

There are, however, dramatic differences between the poverty rates of older women and men as well as between Whites and racial and ethnic minority groups. Consider the data in Table 12.1. Here, we see first a wide gap in the median incomes of older women and men. Men over sixty-five enjoy a significantly higher median income than women over sixty-five, continuing the gender gap in income that we observe for younger segments of the population. Because women have a longer life expectancy than men, there are more women over sixty-five than men in this age group. Nevertheless, although women make up about 58 percent of the elderly population, they are more than 70 percent of the elderly poor.

The elderly who live alone are more likely to be poor. The poverty rate of elderly people who live alone is 22 percent, which is over four times greater than that of elderly people who live with an intimate partner and nearly double the rate of elderly people who live with others.

TABLE 12.1   Median Income for Americans Age Sixty-Five or Older by Sex and Race

Sex and Race	Median Annual Income ($)
Males, White	15,276
Females, White	8,579
Males, Black	8,031
Females, Black	6,220
Males, Hispanic	9,253
Females, Hispanic	5,968

Source: F. B. Hobbs (1996). *65+ in the United States.* Washington, DC: U.S. Government Printing Office, pp. 4–13.

However, sex is again an intervening variable: 84 percent of the elderly poor who live alone are women. Put another way, only about 16 percent of elderly men who live alone are poor, but nearly 26 percent of elderly women who live alone are poor (U.S. Department of Commerce, Bureau of the Census, 1998b).

The poverty rate for elderly women is of particular concern to policy makers because as women on average continue to outlive men and the number of people over sixty-five continues to grow, the number of old women living in poverty is expected to grow as well. Although the elderly population as a whole should find itself in good financial circumstances in the twenty-first century, the segment of the elderly population that is poor is likely to be composed almost exclusively of women who live alone (Davis et al., 1990). The challenge confronting policy makers and gerontologists, then, is how to improve the financial security of elderly women.

Returning to Table 12.1, we see that median income also varies by race and ethnicity. Elderly White men enjoy a substantially higher median income than elderly people in any other category. White women have a higher median income than Black and Hispanic women, but a lower median income than Black and Hispanic men. Older Native Americans also have high rates of poverty, although their median incomes do not appear in the table. An estimated 34 percent of elderly Native American women and 29 percent of elderly Native American men are living in poverty. Some groups of elderly Asian Americans —in particular, those of Chinese, Vietnamese, and Cambodian descent—have high poverty rates, but others, such as Japanese and Korean Americans, have lower poverty rates than elderly White Americans (John, 1991; Taeuber, 1992). The proportion of the elderly population made up of racial and ethnic minorities is expected to swell in the next century, giving policy makers and gerontologists still another challenge.

To better understand the financial gaps between older women and men and between elderly White and minor-ity Americans, let's briefly examine some of the major income sources.

Employment and Retirement.   One source of income for the elderly is wages, although wages make up only about a fifth of the total income of elderly couples and a tenth of the income of elderly who live alone since few people remain in the labor force after their sixty-fifth birthday. In 1996, for instance, just 15.6 percent of men over sixty-five and 7.6 percent of women were still working. Just four decades ago, a third of all men over sixty-five remained in the paid labor force (U.S. Department of Commerce, Bureau of the Census, 1997).

Because many employers think older workers are unproductive, accident prone, expensive to train in new technologies and skills, and inclined to miss work because of health problems, many offer incentives to retire rather than stay on the job (Quadagno & Hardy, 1991). In fact, though, labor studies show that older workers tend to have lower absenteeism, greater job stability, and a more positive attitude toward their jobs than workers aged eighteen to thirty-five (Teltsch, 1991).

When people do retire, some draw on pensions for income. Many young people assume that pensions are an automatic benefit of most jobs today, but that is hardly the case. Less than two-thirds of the private labor force receives pension benefits. In 1995, about 56 percent of households headed by someone sixty-five or older received pension benefits. Although this figure represents a significant increase over just a generation ago, it still means that more than 9 million elderly households in the United States receive no pension benefits (U.S. Department of Commerce, Bureau of the Census, 1997). Moreover, most pensions are relatively small. Retirees with the highest pensions tend to have worked in high-income jobs in large companies or in government. Retirees who are least likely to receive pension benefits—especially part-time and seasonal workers—are also at high risk of living in poverty. Women and racial and ethnic minorities are disproportionately represented in this group. However, although women are less likely than men to receive pension benefits at work, White women married to White men are more likely to have access to pensions through their spouses' benefits than minority women married to minority men (Dressel, 1988; U.S. Department of Commerce, Bureau of the Census, 1997). Overall, pensions provide less than a fifth of the income of all elderly Americans.

Another income source for the elderly derives from assets. Elderly households have greater assets than nonelderly households simply because the longer one lives, the greater the opportunity to accumulate savings, home equity, and personal property. The median net worth of households headed by a person sixty-five or older was $99,550 in 1995, whereas the median net worth of U.S.

These images suggest contrasts in the aging experience relating to the variables of poverty and affluence, racial and ethnic diversity, and males and females. How, specifically, do sex, race and ethnicity, and income affect aging and the elderly in the United States?

households was $56,400 (U.S. Department of Commerce, Bureau of the Census, 1997). However, the assets of the majority of older Americans are not income-producing. The largest portion (70 percent) of the net worth of the elderly is home equity. (About 75 percent of elderly Americans own their homes.) To turn home equity into income would mean that many would have to sell their homes. Consequently, many elderly Americans are "house rich," but "cash poor" (U.S. Senate, Special Subcommittee on Aging, 1991). Elderly people who live alone have fewer assets and a significantly lower net worth than elderly couples. Given that the majority of elderly who live alone are women, their substantially fewer assets help explain their higher poverty rate. Minority elderly also have fewer assets and lower net worth than White elderly: The median net worth of elderly White households was $81,648 in 1988 (the most recent year for which data are available). In contrast, the median net worth of elderly Hispanic American households was

$40,371, and for elderly African American households, it was $22,210 (U.S. Senate, Special Subcommittee on Aging, 1991).

Another major source of income after retirement is Social Security, a federal program that provides workers who have contributed to it a guaranteed minimum income. Currently, over 90 percent of the elderly population is eligible for Social Security benefits, and it is estimated that without Social Security, between 48 and 60 percent of the elderly would be living in poverty (Clark, 1990; Olson, 1982). Nevertheless, the Social Security program has been at the center of political debate in recent years.

The Social Security program is far too complex to analyze in detail here. Suffice it to say that the most serious concerns are whether the program is equitable and whether it can meet the financial demands placed on it in the future. Critics of Social Security say it advantages high-wage earners. Wages are subject to a Social Security tax of 7.65 percent only up to a certain amount ($72,600 in 1999), so a secretary who earns $30,000 a year, for example, pays $2,295 in Social Security tax, or 7.65 percent of her income, while her boss, a physician who earns $175,000 a year, pays $5,553.90 in Social Security tax. But this is just 3.2 percent of the physician's income because only the first $72,600 is taxed. Not only does the wealthier person contribute a smaller portion of income, but he or she may also draw a larger Social Security payment on retirement since benefits are not based on need, but on a person's total career earnings. Individuals who have high lifetime earnings get larger Social Security checks. At the same time, income-producing assets such as stock dividends and capital gains are not subject to Social Security tax, again benefitting the wealthiest segments of the population since they are most likely to have such assets.

Critics also maintain that women are disadvantaged by the Social Security program. Women are 60 percent of Social Security beneficiaries, but on average, receive lower benefits than men. One reason is that, as we've noted, Social Security benefits are determined by one's career earnings, and women are paid less than men. In addition, women are more likely than men to have sporadic work histories because of caregiving responsibilities. No Social Security credit is given for housework. When women who have been full-time homemakers reach retirement age, they are entitled to benefits equal to half their husbands' benefits. If their husbands were low-wage workers, these benefits may not meet their financial needs. Even worse, when their husbands die, the benefits of these women are reduced by 33 to 50 percent, increasing their economic hardship.

The concern that the Social Security program may not be able to handle future demands is fueled by the financial strain of demographic changes. As more people retire, more become beneficiaries rather than contributors (Achenbaum, 1991). Some analysts therefore predict that unless employers develop ways to keep older workers in the paid labor force longer, or the federal government increases Social Security taxes or reduces benefits, the program will be bankrupt by 2032, leaving the majority of elderly without an important source of income. A number of competing plans are being considered by the federal government in an effort to keep Social Security solvent well into the twenty-first century (see, for example, Elkin & Greenstein, 1998; Kijakazi & Greenstein, 1998; Rosenbaum, 1999). As the Global Insights box on page 326 shows, this is a challenge facing many countries today.

The government can't significantly change the Social Security program without voter approval, and the elderly have so far strongly protested changes. How politically powerful is the elderly segment of the population? We will answer that question next.

Political Power

Political power is one of the three major dimensions of social stratification. The question of how much political power the elderly wield as a group is hotly debated. Some maintain that the elderly are a politically powerful group that is courted by politicians and special-interest groups because they are viewed as a significant voting bloc. Consider, for example, the political battle over cleaning up the Everglades in Florida in 1996. Environmental groups managed to get a referendum on the ballot that would levy a tax on sugar growers, who are generally considered the chief polluters of the area and thus should be responsible for the cleanup costs. Not surprisingly, the

Are these seniors likely to win their demand for continued and better funding of senior programs? Why or why not? What issues do sociologists examine in the study of people's political attitudes and political power? To what extent and in what ways are elders likely to become more politically active in the future?

GLOBAL INSIGHTS   How Do Other Countries Care for the Elderly?

The United States was one of the last Western industrialized countries to establish old-age insurance for its citizens. As we have already stated, the projected growth of the elderly population, coupled with the decrease in fertility, means that subsequent generations will become increasingly dependent on a shrinking labor pool to fund some of the most important benefits programs, such as Social Security (Taeuber, 1992). However, analysts point out that relying on current workers to pay for current retirees is likely to bankrupt the system, since the ratio of workers to retirees is narrowing considerably.

The United States is not the only industrialized country facing this crisis. Most countries in Western Europe, as well as Japan, and some Latin American countries have public pension programs similar to ours. But as the table shows, in many of these countries, the ratio of retirees to workers will grow even smaller than in the United States. The problem of bankruptcy of public pension programs in these countries is also more severe because historically, most Western European countries have given their elderly citizens more generous benefits than we do in the United States. In many European countries, public pensions account for 90 percent or more of elderly citizens' income (Greenhouse, 1987). Economists estimate that if the current retirement age in Western Europe remains the same, along with the current level of old-age benefits, the cost of financing public pension programs in most countries will more than double before the middle of the twenty-first century (Greenhouse, 1987; Torry et al., 1987; see also "Progress Report," 1998).

Like the United States, the countries of Western Europe, along with Japan, Brazil, and others, are trying to develop solutions to their public pension funding crisis. One solution is to raise the retirement age; this makes sense to many people because an increasing number of jobs are service occupations that do not involve physical labor, so the physical fitness and stamina associated with youth are no longer necessary to remain in the labor force (Kristof, 1996; "The Perilous Cost," 1998). Employers,

however, must overcome their bias toward youthful workers in order for this solution to succeed. Another solution is to lower benefits. While lowering benefits is politically risky, it has already been done in some countries, including Great Britain and Japan. Both countries are also implementing a third solution: encouraging individuals and employers to establish private pension and savings plans. In Japan, for instance, citizens are being advised to save for retirement. Japan already has one of the highest savings rates in the world, but economists estimate that less than 20 percent of elderly Japanese have sufficient savings to live comfortably. In the United States, it is estimated that about 30 percent of workers now thirty-three to fifty years old are saving what they need for retirement (Kristof, 1996; Haberman, 1987).

Ratio of Retirement-Age People to 100 Working-Age Adults, Selected Countries, 1990 and 2025

Country	RATIO OF RETIREMENT-AGE PEOPLE TO 100 WORKING-AGE ADULTS	
	1990	2025
Austria	36.7	61.4
Japan	24.9	55.8
Belgium	32.2	55.2
Germany	29.6	54.1
France	28.8	45.9
Finland	21.9	44.0
Britain	29.5	42.0
Spain	23.4	37.9
Canada	18.8	35.9
United States	22.3	35.1

Source: N. D. Kristof (1996, February 27). "Aging world, new wrinkles," *New York Times*, pp. C1, C3. © 1996 by The New York Times Co. Reprinted by Permission.

sugar growers opposed the tax, but they knew that to defeat it, they had to woo senior citizens, who make up 34 percent of the state's population. Their lobbying efforts, therefore, included taking busloads of elderly residents on tours of the Everglades with guides who not only pointed out the natural wonders but also proclaimed that a tax would cripple sugar production. Following the tour, lunch was provided. The strategy proved successful, and the referendum was defeated.

Such incidents cause some analysts to worry that as the percentage of aged people in the population grows, se-

nior citizens will come to exercise excessive power in political decision making. The concern is that the retired elderly will make increasing demands for financial benefits that the shrunken workforce will be unable to bear (Williamson et al., 1982). And as we see in the Social Policy box, other segments of the population, especially children, will be deprived of health and welfare benefits that are crucial to both the quality of their lives and their life chances (Thurow, 1996).

Other analysts, however, think the political power of the elderly is more limited (Jacobs, 1990). The basis for

Social Policy
Fiscal Policies and Intergenerational Conflict

The Issue

In Kalkaska, Michigan, where the majority of residents are over sixty-five, there's been a budget crunch. This is hardly unusual in U.S. communities, but what makes Kalkaska stand out is that its elderly citizens voted to use the school budget to pay for snow plowing and similar expenses. Then, when the schools ran out of money, these same citizens voted against additional funding allocations, forcing the schools to close early (Thurow, 1996). Incidents like this one in Kalkaska, Michigan, have prompted some analysts to raise the question of intergenerational equity: Are society's resources being fairly distributed across generations?

The Debate

Until the 1980s, the elderly were considered a disadvantaged group in need of assistance. During that decade, this image began to change. Fueled by media reports of increasing wealth among the elderly,

the stereotype was reversed: Instead of being considered disadvantaged, the elderly came to be regarded as prosperous and self-interested. Some children's advocates argued that elderly voters saved their own benefits programs from budget cuts by sacrificing benefits programs for children, and they began blaming elderly voters for the growing number of children who lack adequate nutrition, health care, education, and other social supports (Streib & Binstock, 1990). Some analysts even warn that as the elderly population grows, children will suffer more and the widest gaps in future resourcing will not be on the basis of race, class, or sex, but age, pitting young against old (Thurow, 1996).

While it is true that a number of benefits programs for the elderly have escaped severe budget cuts in recent years and some programs were even expanded, it is also the case that the elderly are not a homogenous population that has uniformly prospered. In fact, some subgroups of the elderly population, especially mi-

nority women, have been hurt by the recent elimination or reduction of social programs. Indeed, other analysts maintain that the question of intergenerational equity has been incorrectly framed because it treats all elderly people, as well as all children, as homogenous groups. There are advantaged and disadvantaged children just as there are advantaged and disadvantaged elderly. Consequently, these analysts warn that we must be careful not to let the issue of intergenerational equity mask other inequities, especially those based on race, class, and sex (Streib & Binstock, 1990).

What Do You Think?

Is economist Lester Thurow (1996) correct when he says that in the twenty-first century, class warfare will not mean rich versus poor, but rather young versus old? What do you think is the best way to address the question of intergenerational equity?

---

this view is a point we made earlier: The elderly are diverse, not homogenous. They differ among themselves, just as the young do, in terms of social class, educational attainment, geographic location, and other social locating variables—all of which influence political values and behavior considerably more than age (Binstock, 1978; Hudson & Gonyea, 1990). Let's examine the political attitudes of the elderly more closely.

Sociologists use the term **political socialization** to describe how political values and attitudes develop over time in response to various environmental influences, including one's social locations and experiences of political events. Thus, although it is commonly believed that old people are politically conservative, there is no evidence that people's attitudes automatically grow more conservative as they age. Rather, older people generally maintain the political attitudes they developed when they were younger, so that their current attitudes tend to reflect the political climate in which they grew up and matured. This has important implications for the future, since those who received their political socialization during the rebellious 1960s start becoming senior citizens in less than two decades.

At the same time, however, the idea that the elderly's political attitudes reflect their early political socialization should not be taken to mean that the elderly are "set in their ways," that once they form a political opinion, they refuse to change it under any circumstances. Studies show that the elderly do change their political opinions on some issues over time, often in the same direction and to the same extent as younger segments of the population (Dobson, 1983). However, as people mature, they become less inclined to adopt extreme positions, liberal or conservative. Instead, they grow more moderate, stable, and pragmatic as they age (Williamson et al., 1982).

Whether the elderly are liberal or conservative in their political views depends more on race and ethnicity, social class, and, to a lesser extent, sex, than on age. For example, gender differences in political attitudes persist regardless of age. Also, we have seen that racial and ethnic identification are closely associated with social class, so, like their younger counterparts, the politically conservative elderly tend to be White and relatively well off financially (Hudson & Gonyea, 1990).

Of course, translating political attitudes into political power implies a high level of political activism. To what extent are the elderly politically active? The answer depends on the way political activism is measured. Perhaps the most obvious measure of political activism is voting. Past studies of voting behavior showed that voter participation increases from age eighteen, peaks among people in their forties, and then gradually declines after age sixty. More recent research, however, reveals that when various other factors are taken into account, this pattern does not hold. For instance, when education, marital status, sex, income, occupation, and labor force participation are controlled for, making all age groups comparable except for age, the elderly are more likely to vote than members of younger age groups (Jacobs, 1990; U.S. Department of Commerce, Bureau of the Census, 1997).

If we consider other political activities—attending rallies or meetings, volunteering to work for a candidate or political party, joining community organizations, participating in petition drives or letter-writing campaigns—we obtain similar results. At first, it appears that these kinds of political participation decline with age, but when young and old people of the same sex, educational background, and social class are compared, levels of political participation are virtually identical across age groups (Jacobs, 1990; Williamson et al., 1982).

In sum, the political power of the elderly could increase over the next several decades simply because of the rising percentage of the population that will be sixty-five years or older. Adding to this potential is the fact that technology may remove some of the traditional barriers to political participation by the elderly. Physical restrictions caused by disability or illness, for example, may no longer

According to sociological research, controlling for factors such as education, marital status, sex, income, occupation, and labor force participation—making all groups comparable except for age—the elderly are more likely to vote in political elections than members of younger age groups. How would you explain this finding?

be a problem, because of advances in telecommunications and computer technology. Teleconferencing, home computers, and similar communications tools will make it possible for people of all ages to engage in political organizing and opinion polls, and perhaps even vote in elections without having to leave their homes (Williamson et al., 1982). It is already possible to register to vote online and to visit various web sites to become informed about candidates' voting records and positions on specific issues ("NetVote '98," 1998). And in the future, more elderly people will be familiar with such technology and know how to use it, increasing the likelihood that they will draw on it to meet their needs.

Social Integration versus Social Isolation

At the beginning of this chapter, we said that young and old alike associate aging with increasing frailty and dependence on others for personal care. As a result, many fear they will eventually be institutionalized. In the typical scenario, the elderly person's needs eventually become too great a burden on family members, who are then forced to move their aged relative to a nursing home. Nursing homes are pictured as little more than "human warehouses" where the elderly, isolated from family and friends, become lonely and depressed and wait docilely for death.

The fact is that about 5 percent of the elderly population lives in nursing homes (Hobbs, 1996) although the average person stands a 40 percent chance of being institutionalized as they age (AARP, 1998). Most of those who live in nursing homes are over seventy-five years old and have debilitating medical conditions that require round-the-clock medical attention. The majority of nursing home residents are women. Although the move to a nursing home can be traumatic for all involved, gerontologists point out that as long as elderly residents retain the right to make their own decisions, feelings of helplessness and loss of control can be minimized (AARP, 1998; Butler & Lewis, 1972).

Most elderly people, though, simply **age in place**, continuing to live in the homes they occupied while still in the labor force. Most of these are houses that they own in urban, middle-class, and working-class neighborhoods. Almost 75 percent of U.S. senior citizens live in metropolitan areas (Taeuber, 1992). About 79 percent live in homes they own (U.S. Department of Commerce, Bureau of the Census, 1997). Keeping their houses in good repair can be a financial burden for elderly homeowners, especially since their homes tend to be older than the houses in which younger people live. Another challenge is keeping houses safe, since most homes are not built to accommodate the changing physical needs of people as they get older. Nevertheless, most old people take pride in their homes and associate them with pleasant memories (Golant, 1984; Keith et al., 1994; "Words That Work," 1998).

The tendency for most people to age in place has given rise to what gerontologists call **naturally occurring retirement communities (NORCs)**. These are neighborhoods, single apartment buildings, or even entire towns that were not intended as residential areas for older people but where, because of the population's aging, at least half of the residents are over sixty. More than 25 percent of the elderly in the United States live in NORCs (Keith et al., 1994; Lewin, 1991).

Most elderly, whether they live in NORCs or elsewhere, say they are very satisfied with the communities where they live. They report having easy access to stores, banks, and other services (Lewin, 1991; Taeuber, 1992). More importantly, most older people live close to family members, other relatives, and friends, which allows them to maintain social contact even if they live alone (Hobbs, 1996). Maintaining social contacts contributes to a fairly high level of life satisfaction for most old people. In one study, for instance, 45 percent of respondents aged sixty-five and older agreed with the statement, "Life could be happier than it is now," but 49 percent of respondents under the age of sixty-five also agreed with this statement (Kart, 1985). Elderly members of racial and ethnic minority groups tend to express greater life satisfaction than elderly Whites, a finding that has been attributed to the stronger sense of responsibility and obligation toward the elderly among some minority cultures (Keith et al., 1994; Kunitz & Levy, 1991; Yee, 1990).

Thus, despite the stereotype that old people are lonely, isolated, and alone, empirical research indicates that the majority are well integrated into social life. Still, for a sizeable minority of the elderly segment of the population, life is not very satisfying. For instance, an estimated 10 percent of the elderly population has a drinking problem. Two-thirds of these people drank heavily when they were younger, but for the others, alcohol dependence emerged after retirement, the loss of a loved one, the onset of ill health, and increasing social isolation (Stock, 1996). In addition, the suicide rate of the elderly is rising, nearly doubling between 1980 and 1995. In 1995, the suicide rate for those sixty-five and older was 58.1 per 100,000, significantly higher than for any other age group in the population (U.S. Department of Health and Human Services, 1997). Some gerontologists estimate that the rate would increase more than four times if intentional life-threatening behavior (such as refusing to eat or take necessary medication) was also included in the calculation.

Not all groups of elderly are at equal risk of becoming suicidal. Men, for instance, are about five times more likely than women to commit suicide, and widowed men are more likely than men still living with a spouse to kill themselves. The rate of suicide among the oldest old—age seventy-five and older—is higher than the sixty-five

Sociological studies reveal that most elderly people live in naturally occurring retirement communities that develop over many years and that most are very satisfied with their housing and their neighborhood. At the same time, elders increasingly participate more in group recreations in the wider community. What are the forces for social integration and for social isolation in the lives of elders?

to seventy-four group (U.S. Department of Health and Human Services, 1997). Also, suicide is especially likely among elderly people who feel that their lives have been trivialized (O'Connell, 1996).

It is also the case that the suicide rate of the elderly has risen with the growing popularity of the right-to-die movement. The Doing Sociology box on page 330 discusses the debate surrounding the movement. The right-to-die controversy cannot be ignored. As the number of elderly in our population continues to grow and suicide becomes less stigmatized, we can expect the suicide rate of the elderly to continue to increase, unless we can ensure that their older years will be meaningful and productive. The issue is not simply prolonging life, but improving the *quality* of life for all segments of the elderly population. Ultimately, we will all benefit, since each of us, after all, is aging.

R E F L E C T I N G   O N

Diversity in Aging

1. What strategies would you suggest for making the Social Security program more equitable?
2. To what extent do you think the elderly as a group influence the political process? What are the implications for political representation?
3. Why are alcoholism and suicide rates comparatively high among the elderly? What can be done to lower those rates?
4. Should an elderly person with a degenerative or terminal illness have the right to physician-assisted suicide? Why or why not?

Do People Have a Right to Die?

Medical technology has changed not only how long people may live, but also how they will die. Until relatively recently, people with fatal, degenerative, or debilitating illnesses died fairly quickly at home in the company of relatives, friends, and perhaps their family physician. Today, such patients are likely to die slowly in a hospital intensive care unit, plugged into several machines, and tended to by a cadre of medical specialists and other health care workers. In many cases, these efforts to prolong life—or prolong death, as some people see it—take place against the will of the patient and his or her family. Moreover, an expert panel from the Institute of Medicine has concluded that the majority of dying patients—70 percent of whom are over sixty-five—experience severe undertreated pain and inappropriate aggressive treatments, while their physicians and other health care personnel do not discuss death with them and their families to better prepare them for this inevitable outcome (Cassel, 1995). Consequently, an increasing number of people are stipulating preferences regarding their medical care and the conditions under which they wish to die *before* the need for the decisions arises.

In 1990, the U.S. Supreme Court upheld citizens' constitutional right to refuse medical treatment, but also stipulated that states can require clear and convincing evidence that the refusal is truly what the patient would want to do. In 1991, Congress passed the Patient Self-Determination Act, requiring hospitals to provide patients being admitted for any procedure with information about "living wills" and to offer help in planning for death if the patient wants this assistance. The problem, however, is that few people make such plans. Furthermore, while the laws allow people to refuse treatment, they do not permit physician-assisted suicide. Consider, for example, an elderly, terminally ill patient who decides that she would prefer to commit suicide rather than continue life unable to care for herself and endure a slow, painful death. In this case, the issue is not simply the right to refuse aggressive and extraordinary treatment, but rather the right to end one's life in a pain-free, comfortable way, with the help of a physician who can provide the means (a lethal dose of a drug). In 1996, a Federal Appeals Court struck down a law in the state of Washington that made assisted suicide a felony, upholding the individual citizen's right to decide how and when to die.

Critics of the right-to-die movement and physician-assisted suicide worry about potential abuses. For example, given the high costs of caring for the elderly and terminally ill, such patients might be pressured into agreeing to physician-assisted suicide by a cost-conscious medical establishment or by family and friends who don't want to be burdened financially or emotionally. Another concern is that physician-assisted suicide might eventually become an easy solution for dealing with the elderly poor or medically uninsured (Covinsky et al., 1996). Some analysts think that physician-assisted suicide is a further manifestation of ageism and our culture's preoccupation with youthfulness and fear of mortality. One recent study found, for instance, that already, physicians write do-not-resuscitate orders for extremely sick patients over age seventy-five more often than for equally sick patients under seventy-five. This is not because the older patients insist on the orders or because their prognoses are worse, but simply because of their age (Hakim et al., 1996).

Public opinion polls show that most people in the United States support an individual's right to decide when and how to die and favor physician-assisted suicide. One national study, for example, showed that 53 percent of respondents supported physician-assisted suicide for the terminally ill. Support varied, however, by age of the respondents. Respondents aged thirty to forty-nine expressed the greatest support (62 percent), while respondents aged eighteen to twenty-nine showed the second highest level of support (56 percent). Interestingly, though, respondents aged sixty-five and older expressed the lowest level of support for physician-assisted suicide for even the terminally ill, with only 40 percent in favor (U.S. Department of Justice, Bureau of Justice Statistics, 1998).

What are students' opinions on your campus on the right to die and physician-assisted suicide? To find out, develop a brief survey and poll a sample of students. Afterward, share your findings with your class. What do the combined results indicate about views on your campus?

 For useful resources for study and review, run Chapter 12 on your *Living Sociology* CD-ROM.

CONNECTIONS

Aging population	Preview the discussion of demography in Chapter 19. Do you think the general aging of the world's population supports the theory of demographic transition? Why or why not?
Comparative health indicators	Review the section on "Health" in Chapter 9. What is the age gap in life expectancy between high-income countries such as the United States and low-income countries? Now read the list of factors that connect health to

CONNECTIONS

Comparative health indicators *(Continued)*	culture and social structure in "Health and Society" in Chapter 18. How might each of those factors affect life expectancy and the experience of aging and old age in the United States?
Ageism	Review Chapters 10 and 11. How is ageism like sexism and racism? How could you argue that elderly African-American females are among the most disadvantaged groups in U.S. society?
Aging and the life course	Review Erikson's stages of adult development in Chapter 5. According to Erikson, how does aging affect the development of personal identity? Also reread the section on "Adulthood." What significant life changes are part of the aging process?
Modernization theory	Review the section on "Explaining Global Inequality" in Chapter 9. How does the modernization theory of global inequality relate to the modernization theory of aging? Do you think these theories have similar strengths and weaknesses? Why or why not?
Age and poverty	Review the section on "The Poor" in Chapter 8. Why are many elderly at risk for being included in this category in the United States? What are some possible pathways from poverty to adverse outcomes for elders? Also see the section on "Poverty in the United States." What percentage of people aged sixty-five and older are poor?
Age differences in employment	Preview the section on "Work in the United States" in Chapter 13. What percentage of the labor force is made up of people aged sixty-five and older? Is this a higher or lower percentage than in the past? How would you account for the difference? In addition, what aspects of a postindustrial economy would contribute to a decline?
Aging and voting behavior	Preview the section on "Politics and Government in the United States" in Chapter 14. Is there an age gap in voting behavior just as there is a gender gap? Are older voters more conservative in their choices?
Closure of the life course	Reread the section on "Death" in Chapter 5. In what sense is preparation for death an example of resocialization? What concerns might thanatologists have about the quality of life and death for the elderly?
Aging and social change	Read the section on "Social Movements" in Chapter 20. What type of social movement would occur if taxpayers withheld their social security taxes to protest the state of the Social Security system? Which theory— mass society, relative deprivation, resource mobilization, or new social movements—do you think would best explain this social movement?

SUMMING UP CHAPTER 12

Aging around the World

1. The elderly make up the fastest-growing segment of not only the U.S. population, but also populations worldwide. These population changes are the result of a number of factors, including the aging of the baby boom generation and the lower birth rate of people of childbearing age today, advances in medical technology, greater availability of health care, improvements in diet and hygiene, and rising levels of educational attainment.

Aging: Myths and Realities

1. The scientific study of aging is called *gerontology*. Gerontologists have found that the stereotypical physical and mental decline associated with aging is not inevitable. Regular physical exercise, a healthy low-fat diet, a positive attitude toward sex, and regular mental exercise slows or counters many of the negative changes we commonly associate with aging. Although aging is a biological process, research shows that it is also affected by social factors.

Theoretical Perspectives on Aging

1. Stratification by age occurs in all societies. In some societies, especially hunting and gathering societies, the aged are highly valued for their wisdom, which derives from life experience. In some pastoral, horticultural, and agricultural societies, the elderly also have high status because they have accumulated the most wealth. The economic structure of industrialized societies, however, favors the young, so in many industrialized societies, a person's status declines when he or she is old.

2. One explanation of the changing status of the elderly across societies, modernization theory, says that the technological demands of industrial production make the knowledge and skills of the elderly obsolete, lowering their status. Critics of modernization theory, though, point out that in some preindustrial societies, the elderly also have low status. Moreover, modernization does not always lower the elderly's status, since other factors, such as the society's social or political ideology, may have a mediating effect.

3. The major structural functionalist perspective on aging, disengagement theory, maintains that aging is potentially disruptive to the smooth functioning of a society because the physical and mental declines that result from it can interrupt the performance of socially necessary roles and tasks. Consequently, social mechanisms such as retirement benefit society by providing an orderly transfer of roles and responsibilities from old to young, and also gives elderly people more leisure time and personal freedom. However, critics say that disengagement is actually detrimental to the elderly, who benefit more from remaining socially productive. In addition, critics point out that functionalists overlook the negative economic consequences of disengagement for both society and the elderly.

4. The major symbolic interactionist perspective on aging is called *activity theory*, which posits that individuals should remain socially active throughout the life course, and their specific activities should reflect their personal choices, needs, and abilities. The strength of activity theory is that it recognizes the diversity of the elderly population. However, it has been criticized for placing too much emphasis on individualism, overlooking social structural constraints on activities and individual choices.

5. Conflict theorists have not addressed the issue of aging in depth. They focus on ageism as a form of inequality, particularly in capitalist societies where the elderly are disadvantaged because they are seen as driving up production costs and lowering profits. Conflict theorists also recognize that the elderly of some social classes may be more disadvantaged than others. A serious weakness of conflict theory is that it focuses too heavily on capitalist societies, to the neglect of other types of societies. Feminist sociologists also emphasize diversity in aging experiences, looking at how age intersects with social class as well as sex and race and ethnicity to produce unequal life chances for various segments of the elderly population.

Diversity in Aging

1. The financial circumstances of the elderly population as a whole have improved substantially since the 1950s, and the elderly now have a lower poverty rate than the under-eighteen population. But poverty remains a problem for specific segments of the elderly population: women and racial and ethnic minorities.

2. The elderly draw on various sources of income, including wages, pensions, assets, and Social Security. Wages are only a small part of the elderly's income because most retire on or near their sixty-fifth birthday. Although the number of elderly with pensions has grown, many still receive no pension benefits, and among those receiving benefits, the pensions are often small. The elderly have greater assets than younger people, but these are typically not income-generating. The largest portion of the elderly's net worth is equity in their homes, making many "house rich," but "cash poor." The primary source of income for the elderly is Social Security, but critics of this federal program think it is inequitable, and they question whether it can meet the financial demands that will be placed on it in the future.

3. The question of how much political power the elderly wield as a group is hotly debated. Some experts see the elderly as a politically powerful group, but others see their political power as limited because of diversity among the elderly. Research shows that the political attitudes held by elderly people are largely a product of political socialization during their younger years. The political views of the elderly are also influenced by race and ethnicity, social class, and sex. But the political power of the elderly could increase in the future as their numbers grow and as technological innovations remove many traditional barriers to their political participation.

4. Most elderly people age in place, continuing to live in the homes they occupied while still in the labor force, and sometimes forming naturally occurring retirement communities. The majority of the elderly express high satisfaction with their homes and neighborhoods.

5. Contrary to the popular stereotype of the elderly as lonely and isolated, studies show most elderly people are socially connected to others and express high life satisfaction. Elderly members of racial and ethnic minority groups tend to express greater life satisfaction than elderly Whites. But some elderly do not find life satisfying and are at high risk of commiting suicide. Men are more likely that women to commit suicide, as are the oldest old and those elderly who feel their lives have been trivialized.

KEY PEOPLE AND CONCEPTS

activity theory: the symbolic interactionist position that in order for people to age successfully, they must remain socially active throughout the life course

age in place: the phenomenon of continuing to live in the home one occupied while still in the labor force after one reaches retirement age

ageism: the use of age to define an individual's capabilities and social roles, and to determine the individual's access to societal resources, rewards, and opportunities

age stratification: the social ranking of individuals at different stages of the life course who, in turn, are given differential access to society's resources, rewards, or opportunities

disengagement theory: a structural functionalist position that when people reach old age they disengage from their work roles and responsibilities, relinquishing them to younger workers so as to keep the society running smoothly

gerontology: the scientific study of aging

gerontophilia: respect and reverence for the aged

gerontophobia: a strong dislike or hatred of aging and the aged

modernization theory: the idea that the economic transformation of a society from agriculture to industry produces a progressive devaluation of aging

naturally occurring retirement communities (NORCs): neighborhoods, towns, or even just single apartment buildings that were not intended as residential areas for older people but where, because of the population's aging, at least half the residents are over sixty years old

political socialization: the development of political values and attitudes over time in response to various environmental influences, including one's social locations and experiences of political events

LEARNING MORE

Keith, J., Fry, C. L., Glascock, A. P., Ikels, C., Dickerson-Putnam, J., Harpending, H. C., & Draper, P. (1994). *The aging experience: Diversity and commonality across cultures.* Thousand Oaks, CA: Sage. A fascinating look at aging experiences in a variety of societies throughout the world that underlines the point that the aging process is a product of intersecting biological and social influences.

Olson, L. K. (1994). *The graying of the world.* New York: Haworth. Edited by one of the best-known experts on aging, this book looks at policies and programs for the elderly, in particular, the frail elderly, in eleven different countries, including Sweden, Israel, Germany, China, and the United States.

Posner, R. A. (1996). *Aging and old age.* Chicago: University of Chicago Press. A socioeconomic analysis of a variety of issues discussed in this chapter, including age discrimination, Social Security, retirement, and physician-assisted suicide.

Vincent, J. A. (1995). *Inequality and old age.* New York: St. Martin's Press. A clearly written book that considers such topics as intergenerational equity and cross-cultural differences in the status of the elderly in the context of the intersecting inequalities of race, class, and gender.

 Run Chapter 13 on your *Living Sociology* CD-ROM for interesting and informative activities, web links, videos, practice tests, and more.

The Economy and Work

P icture yourself twenty years after college graduation. If you are a traditional-age college student, you will be in your forties then. And if you are like most college students, you picture yourself at that time as a success in your chosen career, earning on average $89,000 a year and living better than your parents did in their forties. If you are somewhat older than the traditional college student, however, your image of the future may be a bit different. You are likely to be less optimistic about what the contemporary work world has to offer; you may, in fact, be in college because you've been laid off from your job, cannot find another, and have decided to upgrade your marketable skills. Twenty years from now, you hope to be secure in a new career or close to a comfortable retirement, but unlike your younger peers, you are less certain that their generation will be enjoying a better standard of living than their parents (Johnson, 1996; "Surprisingly Sunny" 1996; Uchitelle, 1998).

These different visions of life in the early twenty-first century reflect different generational experiences not only of work, but also of the economy. The **economy** is the social institution that produces, manages, and distributes a society's human and material resources. Indeed, the economy is viewed by many sociologists and other social scientists as the most important social institution in a society. On an individual level, the economy shapes our lives in fundamental ways, determining, for example, where and how we live, the types of jobs available to us, even the probability of being enrolled in college and in this sociology course. On the societal level, the economy critically influences the operation and stability of every other major social institution—government, family, education, religion, and health care. In this section of the text, then, where we analyze social institutions, let's begin by taking a closer look at the economy and the world of work.

ECONOMIES IN HISTORICAL PERSPECTIVE

When we think of the economy of the United States, what springs to mind are industry or manufacturing and various services, such as banking and insurance. These, in fact, constitute two of the three parts or *sectors* of the economies of many societies in the world today. The three sectors of an economy are called the primary, secondary, and tertiary sectors. More specifically, the **primary sector** of an economy is made up of activities that extract products directly from the natural environment. Thus, the primary sector includes agriculture, fishing, forestry, mining, and animal husbandry. The **secondary sector** of an economy is the *manufacturing sector,* and is composed of activities that transform material resources into goods or products. Finally, the **tertiary sector** of an economy is the *service sector,* and includes economic activities that provide services rather than produce tangible goods.

At any given time, in any given society, one sector of the economy tends to predominate relative to the others.

For example, consider the data in Figure 13.1. Here we see the countries of the world divided into three major strata we introduced in Chapter 9 ("Global Stratification"). As we move from low-income countries to high-income countries, primary economic activities decline in importance, while tertiary economic activities become substantially more important. The secondary sectors of many low-income countries have grown significantly since the 1970s as corporations based in high-income countries transferred manufacturing there to lower their costs. Considerably lower wages and less government regulation of industry in low-income countries make them

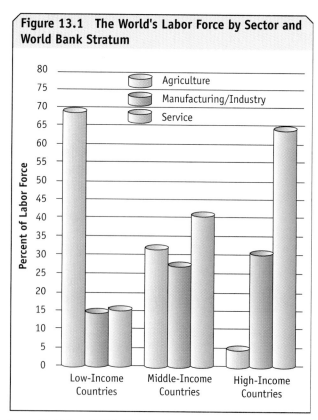

Figure 13.1 The World's Labor Force by Sector and World Bank Stratum

Source: World Bank (1997). *World development report,* pp. 220–221.

attractive to many businesses—a point that we will take up again later in this chapter. Now, though, we simply want to draw attention to the fact that, despite recent growth in the secondary sector of low-income countries, the primary sector still remains dominant, whereas in high-income countries such as the United States, the primary and secondary sectors are much smaller than the service sector.

Today, not surprisingly, the United States and most other high-income countries are often described as "service economies." But this was not always the case. To better understand economic transformation, let's briefly review what we have learned about different types of societies and, in particular, look at the economic history of the United States.

From Agriculture to Industry

Recall that in Chapter 3 we observed that sociologists and anthropologists classify all the societies of the world into six basic types: hunting and gathering societies, pastoral societies, horticultural societies, agricultural (agrarian) societies, industrial societies, and postindustrial societies. This system of classification is based on the predominant way in which the members of a society provide for their sustenance; in other words, it is based on the economy of a society.

In hunting and gathering societies, almost all members participate in food acquisition, which is the sole economic activity of these societies. In fact, these societies have no formal economic structure because there really are no resources other than food that must be distributed; there is no surplus of goods that can be accumulated by an individual or family. Just as food acquisition is a collective enterprise in hunting and gathering societies, so too is food distribution, and, given their small population, an equitable distribution is easily accomplished.

With the discovery of animal husbandry and plant cultivation 10,000 to 12,000 years ago, it became possible for some members of pastoral and horticultural societies to accumulate surplus resources. Even then, however, there was little in the way of formal economic organization because the distribution of resources (animals, land) was done along kinship lines and handled by family members.

It was not until agricultural societies arose 5,000 to 8,000 years ago that formal economic structures appeared. In agricultural societies, the development of technology, such as animal-driven plows and irrigation systems, permits the production of large quantities of food that can sustain sizeable populations. In other words, the technology allows the land to be farmed indefinitely, so permanently settled communities become established. The technology also frees up some people so that a specialized division of labor emerges to meet the needs and demands

What characteristics of an agriculture-based society permit specialization of labor, such as this blacksmith's job in Punjab, India? What other kinds of jobs does agriculture support? What features in this photograph suggest a transition from agriculture to industry?

of a more diverse population. In addition to farmers, then, agricultural societies include various craftspeople: blacksmiths, carpenters, potters, artists, and so on. Trade increases, but unlike pastoral and horticultural societies where trade is conducted through bartering (the exchange of goods and services in kind on an individual basis), the size and complexity of agricultural societies—as well as their increasing contact with other societies—necessitates a monetary system of exchange. Every good or service is assigned a value that is reflected in its price, so that transactions become standardized.

In agricultural societies, then, people hold jobs. Nevertheless, most work still takes place at home. The farmer's, craftperson's, artisan's, or merchant's workplace is also often their residence, and everyone in the family who is able contributes to the work. The fruits of their labor are for personal consumption as well as for sale to the public. There is little, if any, separation of work from home.

The U.S. economy was agricultural from colonization until the 1800s. The majority of the population worked in agriculture, mining, and forestry—that is, in the primary sector. Manufacturing was limited and usually took place in the home or cottage, so it is referred to as *cottage industry*. This pattern persisted until after the Civil War, when the Industrial Revolution dramatically altered the economy and occupational profile of the United States.

Industrialization

In an industrial society, people use mechanized systems of production—machines—to meet their subsistence needs. The invention of machinery to produce goods is considered revolutionary because, for one thing, it fundamentally altered the nature of work. Work became something people went to; it was separate from and took place away from home. Production was centralized in factories and work itself became more highly specialized than ever before.

Consider, for instance, the production of a chair. In an agricultural society, a carpenter would design the chair, collect the materials to make it, fashion each part individually, assemble them into the finished product, and then sell it personally. But in a chair factory in an industrial society, no single worker would produce a chair from start to finish. One worker would design the chair, another would cut out seats, another would cut out legs, another backs. Yet another worker would attach the legs to the seat, and pass this piece on to another worker who attached the back. Then other workers package the final product and transport it to the furniture store, where it

would be sold by still another worker who had no hand in making it.

You can see from this simplified example that not only is industrial work more specialized, but for many workers it is also highly repetitive. The repetition and specialization may also lead to a "deskilling" of many workers, because they have expertise in the performance of very few tasks and little knowledge of the overall production process. At the same time, workers don't reap the full benefits of production since they no longer directly sell what they produce. Instead, they sell their labor power in exchange for wages or a commission (a percentage of the product's selling price).

Industrialization was also revolutionary in the sense that it allowed the production of more goods less expensively and at a faster rate than ever before. The invention of the steam engine and other fuel-powered machines in the late 1700s not only raised production efficiency, but also improved transportation and communication, so that goods could be marketed more widely, even on a global scale as they are today. Finally, as you will learn in the following chapters, industrialization revolutionized not only the structure of the eonomy and work, but also most other social institutions, including government and the military, education, and family life.

England was the first country to experience the Industrial Revolution, which began there in the middle of the eighteenth century. In the United States, the Industrial Revolution was not in full swing until after the Civil War. However, within the short span of seventy years, primary sector economic activity declined significantly, while secondary sector economic activity rose. In 1850, for example, 54.8 percent of the labor force was in agriculture, and 14.5 percent in manufacturing. But by 1900, only 25.9 percent of the labor force was in agriculture, while 26.9 percent held manufacturing jobs (U.S. Department of Commerce, Bureau of the Census, 1975). Agriculture has continued to decline over the last century. In the 1970s, manufacturing began to precipitously decline while the service sector mushroomed. We are witnessing, many analysts tell us, the dawning of postindustrialism.

The Postindustrial Age and the Global Economy

In a postindustrial society, the majority of the members provide services, including generating and managing information. Thus, a **postindustrial economy** is a system for producing, managing, and distributing services and information, with the help of electronic technology, especially computers.

In postindustrial societies, primary and secondary sector activities are not totally lost, but they play a significantly diminished role in the overall economy. In fact,

These boys are sorting coal by hand at a Pennsylvania coal mine prior to the introduction of child labor laws in 1913. How is the production shown in this scene of early industrialization different from production in an agricultural society? What might be different about this scene if the photograph were taken today in a postindustrial society?

In fully industrialized societies, domestic and multinational corporations invite private investment in their businesses through stock exchanges. Stock market activity, in turn, both reflects and influences the global economy as well as the particular markets companies serve. How would you describe the economic activities of high-income nations in a global economy? What features other than globalization characterize postindustrial economies?

many of these activities are taken up by the workforces of other countries, so that instead of looking at the division of labor within a single country, we need to consider division of labor in a broader context—namely, how the divisions of labor across countries are interconnected. In fact, one of the hallmarks of a global economy is that the production process takes place in various stages not just within a single factory in a single country, but rather in offices and factories and stores spread throughout the world. Recall our discussion of Nike athletic shoes in Chapter 9: The shoes are designed in the United States and made from materials produced in a number of countries, including Mexico and Saudi Arabia. They are sewn and assembled in Indonesia, where the factories are supervised by a Korean management company. The finished shoes are transported on cargo ships registered in Singapore and sold in department stores and specialty shops in the United States, Great Britain, Europe, and Australia.

Notice in this Nike example the types of activities that take place in different countries, and think back to Figure 13.1. The primary and secondary economic activities are mostly carried out in lower-income countries, while the tertiary economic activities (product design, advertising, and sales) are mostly conducted in high-income countries. The service activity, management, is handled by workers from Korea, a country that in 1998 attained high-income status (World Bank, 1999). Finally, the corporate headquarters of Nike, which oversees and manages the entire production process, is located in a high-income country, the United States. The global reach of Nike and similar corporations has earned them the title *multinational*. Today, nearly 40 percent of the world's total economic activity is produced by just five hundred multinational corporations; 59 percent of these are based in Japan and the United States (U.S. Department of Commerce, Bureau of the Census, 1997; World Bank, 1999).

Figure 13.2 shows the transformation of the U.S. labor force since 1970. Employment in the service sector of the

Figure 13.2   U.S. Employment Distribution by Sector, 1970, 1980, 1990, 2000

Source: U.S. Department of Labor, 1991, p. 75.

economy far outpaces employment in either the primary or secondary sectors. In fact, according to the U.S. Department of Commerce (1997), six of the ten fastest-declining occupations are in the primary and secondary sectors, while all of the ten fastest-growing occupations are in the service sector (see Table 13.1). Among the top five fastest-growing occupations are computer engineers and scientists, and systems analysts. In fact, it is in the field of global information technology that the change from manufacturing to service seems to be occurring most rapidly. Companies such as IBM, Unisys, and Hewlett-Packard still make computers and copying machines, but their employees are increasingly moving into tertiary sector activities such as designing and running other businesses' copy centers, electronically tracking sales, and computerizing payrolls. In short, these companies are increasingly selling their expertise rather than physical products (Deutsch, 1997).

However, as Table 13.1 shows, not all fast-growing service occupations are in high-status, high-paying fields such as computer science. To the contrary, many of the service jobs generated by the postindustrial economy are low-skilled and pay significantly less than traditional jobs in manufacturing. We will return to this issue shortly when we continue our discussion of employment in the global economy. First, however, let's look at the major economic systems in the world, since the economies of different countries can be interconnected without having the same economic system.

REFLECTING ON

Economies in Historical Perspective

1. What do you consider the most important change in economic history? Why?
2. To what extent and in what ways do you think the United States is a postindustrial society? Explain your answer.

TYPES OF ECONOMIC SYSTEMS

Although there are nearly 200 countries on earth, social scientists typically divide their economies into just two basic types: capitalist and socialist. Although the terms *capitalist* and *socialist* refer to economic systems, they also carry political and ideological connotations. Most Americans, for example, think capitalism is the "best" economic system, far superior to what they usually think of as its polar opposite, socialism. The fact of the matter is, however, that the two categories, capitalism and socialism, are really *ideal types*, that is, analytic tools constructed by social scientists to help them study the essential features of different forms of a phenomenon, which in this case is the economy. In reality, the structure of a country's economic system is not a choice between two extremes, but rather a decision as to the *degree* to which the coun-

TABLE 13.1   Ten Fastest-Growing and Fastest-Declining Occupations in the United States

Ten Fastest-Growing Occupations	*Ten Fastest-Declining Occupations*
1. Personal and home health care aides	1. Letterpress operators
2. Home health aides	2. Typesetting and composing machine operators
3. Systems analysts	3. Directory assistance operators
4. Computer engineers	4. Telephone station installers and repairers
5. Physical and corrective therapy assistants and aides	5. Central office operators
6. Electronic pagination systems workers	6. Billing, posting, and calculating machine operators
7. Occupational therapy assistants and aides	7. Data entry keyers, composing
8. Physical therapists	8. Shoe sewing machine operators and tenders
9. Residential counselors	9. Roustabouts
10. Human services workers	10. Peripheral EDP equipment operators

Source: U.S. Department of Commerce, Bureau of the Census, 1997, p. 414.

try will adhere to the basic principles of one type or the other in its economic activities. In addition, a country's commitment to a particular type of economic system can change over time, as we have seen in the former Soviet Union and Eastern Europe.

Let's look at what are considered the essential features of each type of economic system. Keep in mind, though, that there is no pure capitalist society and no pure socialist society in the world today.

Capitalism

In general, **capitalism** may be defined as an economic system in which the means of production are privately owned and operated. Indeed, private property is a building block of capitalism, as is the pursuit of personal profit. In other words, in a capitalist economy, each individual seeks to maximize his or her individual position in relation to others by accumulating as large a share of the society's resources (wealth) as possible. Individuals can amass wealth because they own the means of production and accrue the profits after costs have been deducted.

A capitalist economy, then, is characterized by competition among members of the society who seek an ever-greater share of resources and profit. Theoretically at least, this competition regulates product quality and prices. To stay in business, a person must offer goods or services that are comparable to goods and services offered by others in the same business. Competition not only benefits consumers, though, it also ensures that no single individual gets control of an entire market.

These entrepreneurs are intent on making a profit through the buying and selling of Beanie Babies, collectable stuffed toys that became a consumer fad in 1997. According to the principles of capitalism, how will the market for Beanie Babies affect their ability to reach their goals? How might the market for Beanie Babies change in a socialist economy?

The notion of free competition relates to another feature of capitalism: limited regulation of economic activity by government (see Epstein, 1998). This is the principle known as *laissez-faire*. As the founder of laissez-faire capitalism, Adam Smith (1723–1790), put it, an "invisible hand" guides the market in response to public need, making capitalism self-regulating. Besides competition, then, regulation occurs naturally through the equally important market function of supply and demand. That is, the market responds to public needs and desires. If consumers want a certain product and the supply is scarce, the product will be expensive. So the market adjusts to the demand by producing more of the desired product which, in turn, lowers the price. If the supply of the product ends up exceeding the demand for it, the price will drop significantly.

In sum, the essential features of capitalism are private ownership of property, pursuit of personal profit, free competition, supply and demand, and nonintervention by government in economic activity.

Socialism

In contrast to capitalism, **socialism** may be defined as an economic system in which the means of production are publically owned and operated. The socialist model derives largely from the work of Karl Marx (1818–1883).

In a socialist economy, private enterprise and individual ownership of property are severely restricted. Most resources, including the means of production, are controlled by the government, which manages and distributes them in the collective interests of all members of society.

Thus, under socialism, the pursuit of personal profit is replaced, at least theoretically, by a state-operated system that acts to ensure that all members of the society have equal access to resources. There is, by design, little or no competition. The government is expected not only to monitor the economy, but also to actively engage in economic planning.

To summarize, the essential features of socialism are public ownership of property, an emphasis on collective interests over individual or personal gain, and government regulation and control of economic activity.

The Global Distribution of Economies

Our discussion of the essential features of capitalism and socialism would seem to suggest that they are diametrically opposed systems. But as we have already stated, in the real world there are no countries whose economies conform totally to either ideal type. For instance, while the United States is considered the paramount example of capitalism because it has the least government regulation of business among high-income capitalist countries, it nonetheless has direct government involvement in a number of areas, such as postal services, railways, some utilities, and public education. There is also considerable indirect government involvement through legal regulations; we have laws, for example, specifying wages and hours, establishing minimum safety standards, and prohibiting child labor.

In other high-income capitalist countries, the government takes an even more active role in economic activity. France and Australia, for instance, have greater public ownership of industries and services than the United States. Singapore offers another example. One of only nine Asian countries to be classified as high-income, Singapore's government has taken an aggressive role in promoting capitalism. In fact, Singapore is often used as the exemplary case of a hybrid economic system that social scientists call **state capitalism:** an economic system in which the means of production are privately owned and operated, but there is a high level of government intervention in economic activity.

Most experts would say the paramount example of a socialist economy is the People's Republic of China. For several decades under the leadership of Mao Tse-tung, China followed a national policy of isolationism, not trading with the West. Virtually all economic activity was state-controlled, and any surplus belonged to village collectives, not individuals. Since Mao's death in 1976, however, the Chinese government has increasingly entered into business ventures with corporations from many countries, including the United States. In fact, China ranks fourth among countries that export goods to the United States

(U.S. Department of Commerce, Bureau of the Census, 1997). Since Mao's death, China has also gradually eased internal government controls, permitting individuals to acquire private property, such as land and houses, and to produce goods above the collective quota and sell them for personal gain (Curran, 1996). Throughout, though, China has continued to be strongly socialist, with many companies and enterprises, including banking, remaining public and state-controlled (Eckholm, 1998).

Many other countries have more limited socialist economies. Sweden is a good example. There, most major services and many industries are state-owned and operated, including health care and the media. In addition, the government actively regulates privately owned industries and attempts to distribute resources equitably through various programs, including progressive taxation, which places the greatest tax burden on the wealthiest individuals. Sweden's economic system, like Singapore's, is also a hybrid. It is called **democratic socialism** because there is substantial public ownership of production and government intervention into economic activity, but also considerably more political freedom (including democratic elections) than what is typically associated with socialist countries.

Our discussion of the United States, China, Singapore, and Sweden suggests that any attempt to classify the economies of the world should be in terms of a continuum, with capitalism and socialism as the endpoints. Such a continuum is depicted in Figure 13.3. Here we see that no country occupies either endpoint, but we can position a country as more or less of an example of the ideal type.

These factory workers are working in a socialist state—China, a low-income country that does business with high-income capitalist countries. What are the principal features of socialism? What factors in the global economy are encouraging the development of capitalism and democratic socialism in countries like China?

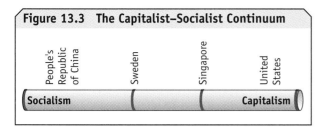

Figure 13.3 The Capitalist–Socialist Continuum

At the same time, thinking in terms of a continuum gives us only part of the picture. Recall what you learned about global stratification in Chapter 9. Three of the four countries on this continuum are high-income industrialized nations, regardless of their type of economic system. In fact, the United States and Sweden have nearly identical per capita gross national products (GNPs) of US$28,740 and US$26,220 respectively. The per capita GNP of Singapore is even higher at US$32,940. In contrast, the per capita GNP of China is US$860.

It is important to keep in mind that there are significant differences in the capitalism and socialism of economically undeveloped countries compared to economically developed ones. For instance, whether a poor country is capitalist or socialist, it must rely heavily on aid from wealthier countries for economic support. In addition, in an undeveloped capitalist country, the gap in wealth between the rich and the poor will be much smaller than in a developed capitalist country. On the other hand, in an undeveloped socialist country, the weak infrastructure will make it extremely difficult for the government to adequately provide for the needs of all the people, thereby limiting its ability to meet many socialist goals. Consequently, when analysts evaluate a country's economic system, the level of economic development is a critical intervening variable to be considered. In fact, instead of thinking of economic systems in terms of a continuum, it's more accurate to think of them in terms of a *matrix*, which takes economic development into account. Figure 13.4 depicts this matrix, and we can see how the positions of the four countries we've discussed compare when economic development is factored in.

Finally, as we said at the beginning of this section, a country's economic system may change over time. Such economic transformation brings benefits, but also new problems, as we see in the Global Insights box on page 344.

Now, let's turn to economic life and work in our own society. How healthy is the U.S. economy? What is work like in our increasingly postindustrial society? What can we expect in the future?

REFLECTING ON

Types of Economic Systems

1. How is communisim different from socialism? Why do you think that Americans prefer capitalism to socialism?
2. Identify countries other than those mentioned in this chapter that can be described as state capitalist or as democratic socialist.

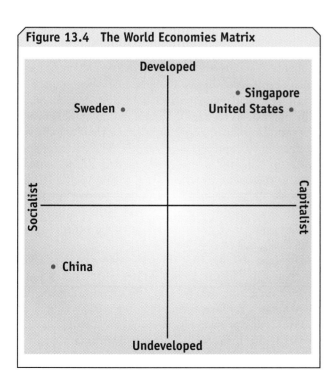

Figure 13.4 The World Economies Matrix

THE U.S. ECONOMY

While some industries in the United States are owned and operated by the government, the great majority are privately owned and operated, either by individuals or corporations. Although we often think of a **corporation** as a "thing," it is really a group of people who own a business, but who have received special legal status that grants them rights, privileges, and responsibilities separate and distinct from those they hold as individuals. We will take up our discussion of the U.S. economy by examining its structure more closely.

The Structure of the U.S. Economy

Although the U.S. economy is composed of numerous enterprises of various types and sizes, for the most part, actual economic activity is dominated by relatively few corporations. No single corporation controls an entire

GLOBAL INSIGHTS

Life after Socialism in Eastern Europe and the Commonwealth of Independent States (CIS)

The collapse of socialism in Eastern Europe and the former Soviet Union brought new opportunities for freedom and political participation for citizens of those countries. Democratic elections are being held, and people are free to express their political opinions. Public meetings and church services, once prohibited, now take place openly. Citizens are free to travel to countries formerly closed to them, such as the United States, and many university students now participate in educational exchanges not only in the United States, but also in Australia, Asia, and Latin America.

Nevertheless, the collapse of socialism has also come with costs, most of them economic. The privatization of many industries, for example, resulted in a disruption in production which, in turn, slowed economic growth and, in some countries, actually caused economic decline. Georgia appears to have been hardest hit, experiencing a growth rate of –28 percent a year since the demise of socialism. Armenia and Azerbaijan have experienced growth rates of –16 percent a year. Unemployment rates are also rising; in 1993, unemployment was 23 percent in Albania, 17 percent in Bulgaria, and 13 percent in Hungary (U.N. Development Programme, 1996). Because unemployment benefits are very small or nonexistent in these countries, poverty rates have soared. In Romania, for instance, poverty rose from 6 percent prior to the fall

of socialism to 32 percent in the post-socialist period. In Russia, about 30 percent of the population is poor (U.N. Development Programme, 1996; "Younger Workers," 1998).

As we saw in Chapters 8 and 9, unemployment and poverty are related to other serious problems. For example, malnutrition and undernutrition are rising, accompanied by increases in adult and infant mortality (U.N. Development Programme, 1996; Wines, 1998). Children are among those suffering the most. In Russia, for instance, outbreaks of diseases such as diphtheria among children rose from 500 in 1989 to over 15,000 in 1993. It is estimated that two million Russian children are orphans, although only about one-third live in orphanages. Two-thirds of Russian orphans live on the streets, finding shelter in abandoned houses and in city sewers. The suicide rate among children in Russia has doubled since 1988 ("2 Million Orphans," 1998; U.N. Development Programme, 1996).

Clearly, a major challenge for Eastern European and CIS countries is solving these serious social problems, but to do so will require much assistance from wealthier nations, including the United States, and sound economic planning that not only rebuilds crumbling infrastructures but also addresses human development issues.

market, constituting a pure monopoly, but it is the case that a small group of corporations—sometimes just two or three—enjoys a disproportionate share of the market for specific goods or services. This is called an **oligopoly** or **shared monopoly**, and it is one of the central elements of the U.S. economy.

Oligopolies composed of U.S. multinational corporations span the global marketplace. For example, General Motors, Ford, and Chrysler account for 86 percent of the motor vehicles and parts made by U.S. corporations. Indeed, the annual sales revenues of General Motors alone are greater than the gross national product (GNP, the total value of all goods and services produced) of all but twenty-three countries ("The *Fortune* 500," 1998; World Bank, 1999). Hasbro, Mattel, and Tyco account for almost 100 percent of the toys produced by U.S. companies. Pepsico, Coca-Cola, and Anheuser-Busch control 76 percent of the beverage industry, with Coke being the most widely recognized product in the world.

Although competition is supposed to be a hallmark of capitalism, the existence of oligopolies reduces competi-

tion. For one thing, the tremendous assets of corporations in oligopolies allow them to carry out very savvy but expensive business strategies and production programs. For example, a small company with limited assets must gradually upgrade its technology, but a multinational corporation can rapidly upgrade and thereby rapidly improve production to capture a new market. The concentrated wealth of oligopolies also protects them during downturns in the economy. Moreover, during such difficult times, the demise of smaller businesses further enhances the already superior position of oligopolies in the marketplace, since even greater economic concentrations end up in the hands of very few.

The data in Table 13.2 show the extent of economic concentration in the United States today. Each year, *Fortune* magazine lists the top 500 corporations in the United States, ranking them according to such factors as total revenues, profits, and assets. At the top of this elite hierarchy are firms that control extraordinary wealth. The top 1 percent—just five corporations—account for 12 percent of revenues and 10 percent of total profits. To-

TABLE 13.2   Ten Largest U.S. Corporations, 1998

Corporation	Revenue (millions)	Profits (millions)	Assets (millions)	Market Value (millions)
General Motors	$178,174.00	$6,698.00	$228,888.00	$54,243.80
Ford	$153,627.00	$6,920.00	$279,097.00	$73,923.00
Exxon	$122,379.00	$8,460.00	$96,064.00	$158,783.60
Walmart	$119,299.00	$3,526.00	$45,525.00	$113,730.60
General Electric	$90,849.00	$8,203.00	$304,012.00	$260,147.20
IBM	$78,508.00	$6,093.00	$81,499.00	$98,321.90
Chrysler	$61,147.00	$2,805.00	$60,418.00	$28,366.80
Mobil	$59,978.00	$3,272.00	$43,559.00	$58,409.60
Philip Morris	$56,114.00	$6,310.00	$55,947.00	$102,931.60
ATT	$53,261.00	$4,638.00	$58,635.00	$105,878.70
Average Top Five	$132,865.60	$6,671.40	$190,717.20	$132,165.64

Source: Fortune, April 27, 1998, pp. F-1, F-2.

gether, the revenues in 1998 totaled more than $664 billion, which is greater than the GNP of all but eight *countries* in the world (World Bank, 1998).

A second, related feature of our economy is the tendency for corporations to merge into a single, huge corporation. The process of corporate mergering is called **conglomeration.**

Many of today's large corporations started out as small businesses that competed with others such as themselves for a share of a particular market. Companies that attracted the largest number of customers gained a financial edge over their competitors, and when a competitor began to flounder financially, a more successful company often bought it out. When one company buys another company in the same industry or business, it is called a **horizontal merger.** However, sometimes a company buys another company that is not a direct competitor, but is engaged in a related business—say, for example, a supplier. Thus, a utility company might buy a mining company that provides fuel for its coal-burning electrical plants. A company may also try to diversify its business by buying companies only marginally related or completely unrelated to its own business. These acquisitions are called **vertical mergers.** Small mergers still occur, but in today's economic environment, conglomeration is the norm, with *megamergers* producing what might be called *megaconglomerates.* During the 1990s, the number of mergers rose dramatically and so did their value. Between 1992 and 1998, for example, the number of mergers increased 300 percent to 4,728, a record. The total value of mergers during this period increased from less than $150

billion to about $1.1 trillion. In 1998 alone, the five largest mergers in American history occurred: Mobil Corporation acquired Exxon ($80 billion), Ameritech purchased SBC Communications ($62 billion), Bell Atlantic bought GTE ($52 billion), AT&T acquired Tele-Communications Inc. ($32 billion), and British Petroleum bought Amoco ($48 billion) (Labaton, 1998; Sanger, 1998).

A third feature of our economy is growing **intercorporate control,** that is, a network of connections among corporations that allows them to coordinate their activities in order to enhance their economic position. Even without merging, many corporations are strongly tied to one another in various ways. One way is through investment; one corporation may own stock in another corporation. Corporations are also connected through their boards of directors. A corporation's board of directors is a group of individuals who collectively oversee the running of the business. They serve as a kind of line of defense for stockholders, monitoring the decisions of top corporate executives, scrutinizing company policies and practices, and offering advice on how to improve business. When serving on a board, members have access to vital information about a corporation, such as its marketing strategies, plans for product development or market expansion, finances, and so on. In addition, board members network among themselves, so they may develop relationships that are personally or professionally profitable. They may exchange information about their businesses or provide one another with introductions to potential clients or investors. This network of

What key economic indicators do these photographs represent? How is each of these indicators used to evaluate the economic well-being of a country and to make predictions about the country's future well-being? For each indicator, what conditions contribute to the health of an economy, and why?

associations through membership on the boards of directors of multiple corporations is called an **interlocking directorate.**

One safeguard against the misuse of board membership is federally enacted legislation that prohibits individuals from simultaneously serving on the boards of corporations that directly compete with one another. Information obtained through such memberships could lead, for example, to *price fixing*, in which corporations agree in advance on a set price for their products and they all charge consumers the same. Nevertheless, individuals can and usually do serve on boards with related business interests. For instance, an insurance company

and a manufacturer of medical equipment may have overlapping board memberships.

Although business analysts argue that the time and effort required to be a fully contributing board member should prohibit anyone from holding more than two board seats at a time, reports indicate that the number of individuals with multiple board memberships has increased during the 1990s. Holding positions on boards of nine or more corporations is not uncommon (Dobrzynski, 1996).

In sum, then, the structure of the U.S. economy is characterized by economic concentration in the forms of oligopolies, conglomerates, and intercorporate control, as well as rapid growth of the service sector, which we discussed earlier. How healthy is this economy? To answer this question, we will need to examine three key indicators.

Key Economic Indicators

Sociologists, economists, and other social scientists use a wide range of measures called *economic indicators* to analyze economic trends, make predictions about the future, and evaluate current economic well-being. Among the most commonly used indicators are inflation, the trade deficit, and the unemployment rate. Let's look at each briefly in turn.

Inflation.   **Inflation** refers to an increase in the price of goods and services. There are various ways to determine the rate of inflation, but the one most often used in the United States is the **consumer price index,** which gauges the cost of products, services, and other items (such as fuel) that are essential to everyday life. In other words, it measures the cost of living.

We feel the impact of inflation when we go shopping and find that the price of an item has gone up since the last time we bought it. But what causes the increase? Many factors contribute to inflation. One is a decrease in market competition. When relatively few companies compete for purchasers of their products and services, they can raise prices—and therefore increase their profits—regardless of supply and demand. A second factor that contributes to inflation is called *price reverberation.* This occurs as a result of increases in the cost of production.

For instance, suppose the cost of mining coal goes up because the extraction process has gotten more difficult, leading miners to demand higher wages and forcing mine owners to purchase new, expensive equipment. Rather than take a decrease in profits, the coal company owners pass their cost increases on to their customers, which include a number of industries and public utilities. These industries and utilities pass their increased costs along to their customers, and a chain reaction of price increases is in place. The profit margins of industries are secure because the general public makes up the difference by paying more for basic goods and services.

Figure 13.5 shows inflation rates from 1960 to 1996. Before 1970, inflation was relatively low, averaging 2.6 percent a year from 1960 to 1969. But then there was a dramatic jump, so that double-digit inflation was common from 1974 to 1981. Since 1983, the inflation rate has exceeded 5 percent just once, in 1990 (5.4 percent). In 1994, the inflation rate was just 2.6 percent, the lowest since 1986. Although inflation has risen since 1994, it remains relatively low. Generally, the rate of inflation in the United States in recent years has been comparable to that of other high-income countries (U.S Department of Commerce, Bureau of the Census, 1997).

If low inflation is an indicator of economic health, the U.S. economy appears to be in good shape. However, it would be unwise to judge the health of the economy by just one measure. Let's look at two others.

Trade Deficit.   A **trade deficit** or **trade gap** occurs when a country imports more goods than it exports. When people talk about the U.S. trade deficit, the phrase that

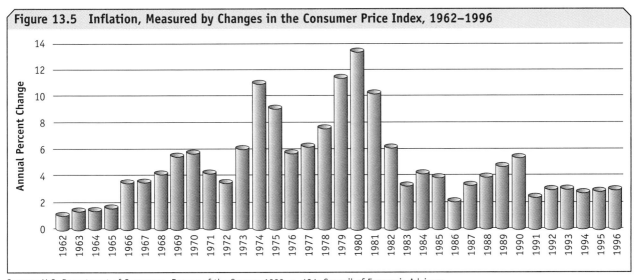

Figure 13.5   Inflation, Measured by Changes in the Consumer Price Index, 1962–1996

Sources: U.S. Department of Commerce, Bureau of the Census, 1999, p. 494; Council of Economic Advisors, 1991, p. 356.

often comes to mind is "Made in Japan." However, Japan is only one of seventy-two countries that holds an advantage in trade with the United States; twenty-seven of these countries have a trade advantage that exceeds $500 million.

Table 13.3 shows trends in the U.S. trade deficit from 1989 to 1996. Here we see that although the trade deficit narrowed during 1991 and 1992, it has grown dramatically since then, reaching a record level in 1996. A downturn in the global economy, especially in Asia in 1998, increased out trade deficit even more, since these countries had to lower their imports from the United States. The estimated trade deficit for 1998 was $170 billion (Sanger, 1998). While the gap in trade between the United States and Japan is still the largest, the gap with China has grown significantly, increasing more than 500 percent since 1989. In fact, imports into the United States from China now surpass imports from Taiwan, Mexico, and Indonesia (U.S. Department of Commerce, Bureau of the Census, 1997). Imported products include toys, clothing, housewares, paper products, and even Christmas decorations.

Many observers see this growth in foreign competition in the United States and international marketplaces as evidence that U.S. dominance of the world industrial market is eroding. Why is this occurring? As with most complex phenomena, the growth in foreign competition and the trade deficit are the result of multiple factors. Ironically, the United States, as one of the Allies deciding the fate of defeated nations after World War II, promoted the growth of two of its biggest competitors. In forbidding Japan and Germany from remilitarizing, the

Allies forced both countries to focus on industrial research, development, and production, spurring their rapid economic growth.

U.S. corporations themselves have also contributed to the growing trade deficit and increased foreign competition. To gain entry to overseas markets, they often sold manufacturing licenses and technology to foreign corporations or entered into joint production agreements with foreign firms. Many analysts also blame the federal government for not adequately regulating the flow of foreign-made goods into the U.S. market, since other countries impose tariffs and trade barriers against products made in the United States. In addition, production costs in the United States are significantly higher than in many other countries with whom we hold a trade disadvantage. The lower cost of production in these countries means that the products they make are less expensive than the same products made here, giving foreign-made goods an edge with consumers seeking lower prices. Finally, we have already noted that the ties that bind the global marketplace cause downturns in the economies of countries on the other side of the world to seriously impact our economy. If the economies of other countries weaken, they cannot afford to import many goods from the United States.

When the trade deficit is taken into account, then, the health of our economy appears less robust. Let's look at the third indicator on our list to try to make a more precise diagnosis.

Unemployment Rate. The **unemployment rate** is officially defined as the percentage of the working-age pop-

TABLE 13.3   U.S. Merchandise Trade Balances with Selected Countries, 1989–1996 (billions of dollars)

Year	Total	European Community	Japan	Canada	China	Rest of World
1989	−109.4	1.2	−49.1	−9.1	−6.2	−46.2
1990	−101.7	6.3	−41.1	−7.7	−10.4	−48.8
1991	−65.4	17.0	−43.4	−5.9	−12.7	−20.4
1992	−84.5	9.0	−49.6	−8.0	−18.3	−17.6
1993	−115.7	−0.6	−59.3	−10.7	−22.8	−32.3
1994	−151.1	NA	−65.7	−14.5	−29.5	NA
1995	−158.7	−21.2	−59.1	−18.1	−33.8	NA
1996	-166.6	NA	−47.7	−22.8	−39.5	NA

Source: U.S. Department of Commerce, Bureau of the Census, 1997, pp. 803–806; 1995, pp. 819–822.

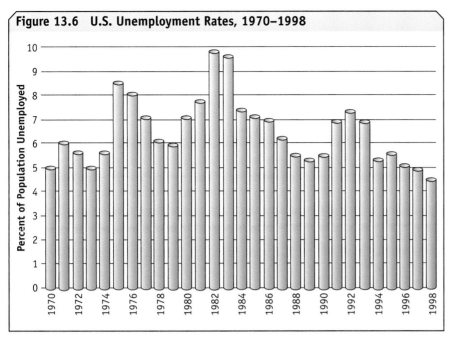

Figure 13.6   U.S. Unemployment Rates, 1970–1998

Sources: Council of Economic Advisors, 1994, p. 314; Stevenson, 1996, p. 35; "How the U.S. Consumer Feels," 1999, p. C7.

ulation that is currently out of work but actively looking for a job. This definition is somewhat misleading, though, because it excludes certain groups. For instance, discouraged workers—those who have given up hope of finding a job because they believe none is available or because they lack marketable skills—are not included among the officially unemployed. The unemployment rate also does not count people who are working only part time because they cannot obtain full-time work, as much as they wish they could. In 1996, more than 1.4 million people who usually work full time held only part-time employment because of economic factors such as slack business conditions (U.S. Department of Commerce, Bureau of the Census, 1997).

Despite these limitations, what does the unemployment rate tell us about the health of the economy? Figure 13.6 shows unemployment rates from 1970 to 1998. We can see that the unemployment rate was exceptionally high during the early to mid-1980s. In the late 1980s it declined somewhat, but rose again to 7.4 percent in 1992. Most economists consider an unemployment rate of around 6 percent "natural" for a healthy economy, but since 1994 the unemployment rate has been below 6 percent ("How the U.S. Consumer Feels," 1999; Stevenson, 1996).

Such low unemployment rates certainly cast the state of our economy in a positive light, and one would therefore expect that most workers are optimistic about their economic futures. Surprisingly, however, studies show

that some Americans still feel economically insecure and are worried about losing their jobs. For example, in a 1996 national opinion poll conducted by the *New York Times*, 37 percent of respondents said they felt somewhat or very economically insecure. In addition, 46 percent were somewhat or very worried that in the next year they or someone in their household would be out of work. These fears appear to be fueled by statistics showing that since 1990, about one in every twenty workers has lost her or his job in any two-year period (*"New York Times Poll,"* 1996).

These paradoxical findings—lower than normal unemployment rates and great personal job insecurity—indicate that the employment segment of our economic picture requires more detailed analysis. Let's look more carefully, then, at work in the United States today.

R E F L E C T I N G   O N

The U.S. Economy

1. How are interlocking directorates advantageous for corporations? How are interlocking directorates disadvantageous for consumers and small businesses?
2. Based on what you've read so far, how would you judge the health of the U.S. economy?

Our discussion of work in the United States will begin with a look at the composition of the labor force and the types of jobs that people hold. We'll then consider the problem of underemployment and the decline of trade unions. Finally, we'll discuss wages and the impact of technological innovations on work in the United States.

The Composition of the Labor Force

There are several different ways we can describe the U.S. labor force. One way is to look at the characteristics of workers. Table 13.4 shows the composition of the labor force by sex, race and ethnicity, and age. First, we see that the labor force participation rates of both males and females are high. This is a relatively recent historical development. Less than half a century ago (1960), two-thirds of the labor force was male. During the 1970s, women's labor force participation rates began to increase significantly. By the 1990s, although men's labor force participation rate remained higher than women's, the typical woman, like the typical man, was working full time, year round, even if she had children under the age of six.

TABLE 13.4   Labor Force Participation Rates by Sex, Race/Ethnicity, and Age, 1996

Characteristic	Percent of Population in the Labor Force
Sex*	
Male	87.5
Female	71.8
Race/Ethnicity*	
White	80.4
African American	73.7
Hispanic American	74.2
Age	
16–19 years	34.8
20–24 years	69.1
25–34 years	79.5
35–44 years	80.8
45–54 years	78.8
55–64 years	54.9
65 or older	10.9

* Adults aged 25–65.

Source: U.S. Department of Commerce, Bureau of the Census, 1997, pp. 399, 405.

The majority of workers in the United States are White. However, the racial and ethnic composition of the labor force corresponds roughly to the racial and ethnic composition of the population as a whole, so difference is to be expected. Nevertheless, as Table 13.4 shows, the labor force participation rates of African Americans and Hispanic Americans are somewhat lower than those of White Americans: 73.7 percent, 74.2 percent, and 80.4 percent respectively. Some analysts attribute these differences to the effects of racial and ethnic discrimination. As minority populations continue to grow in relation to the White population, we are likely to see dramatic changes in the racial and ethnic composition of the labor force. In the first half of the twenty-first century, racial and ethnic minorities will make up a larger percentage of the working population.

Finally, let's consider labor force participation by age. Although the rates may be what you would expect, with fewer workers in both the youngest and oldest categories, what the table does not show is that these percentages have dropped in recent years. In 1980, for example, 37.5 percent of sixteen- to nineteen-year-olds were in the labor force, as were 11.3 percent of those sixty-five and older (U.S. Department of Commerce, Bureau of the Census, 1997).

Change in the age composition of the labor force is partly the result of changes in the age structure of the population. For instance, one would expect fewer workers in the youngest age groups because the birth rate declined between 1960 and 1995, while the large baby-boomer generation got older. But demographic change is not the entire answer. It appears that to some extent, the youngest segments of the working-age population have difficulty getting jobs, while the oldest segments are opting out—or are being forced out—of the labor force in greater numbers. The decline in older workers may lead to a critical shortage of skilled, experienced workers in the future.

Another way to describe the labor force is to look at the types of jobs workers hold, although as the Intersecting Inequalities feature shows, sex and race or ethnicity are often related to a person's job type. Jobs are generally categorized as white-collar or blue-collar. **White-collar jobs** traditionally carry high prestige and require mental labor rather than physical labor. Included among white-collar jobs are the professions. A **profession** is an occupation that requires extensive, specialized training in a particular field. Professionals, however, don't just learn the "how to's" of their field; they must also learn the theoretical knowledge on which the field is based and keep abreast of new developments. Because of their highly specialized knowledge, professionals are experts in their chosen fields. Indeed, their clients hire them because of this knowledge and typically defer to their judgment on any matter pertaining to their area of expertise.

You may have few qualms about second-guessing your plumber, for instance, but you're likely to think carefully about ignoring the advice of your doctor or lawyer. Professionals also usually form associations that regulate entry into the profession; standards of conduct for members of the profession; and the profession's interests and image to outsiders. Such associations, for example, serve as gatekeepers by controlling who gets admitted into the profession. No one enters a profession without the proper credentials, such as advanced degrees. Some professional associations may require special examinations (such as the bar exam) and issue licenses (such as those physicians must obtain to practice medicine). They may also expel members not only from the association but also from the profession for unethical or unlawful conduct.

Blue-collar jobs have little prestige and require mostly manual labor rather than mental labor. These categories got their names from the way workers usually dressed for such jobs. However, in the 1970s, sociologists studying the sex composition of the labor force noticed that women workers were heavily concentrated in a small number of jobs. Consequently, they created a third category of jobs, **pink-collar jobs**, named not for the type of clothes women workers wear on the job, but because pink is the color associated with femininity in our culture.

Still another way to categorize jobs is in terms of the economic sector in which the job is located. We have already discussed the fact that the distribution of workers across sectors of the economy has shown marked changes in the past several decades, with about 80 percent of the labor force now employed in the service sector. Given its dominance in the economy, the service sector deserves a closer look.

Services: Where the Jobs Are. The service sector is nonindustrial; workers who hold service jobs do not produce a physical product for sale, but instead perform activities that help, or serve, the general public or specific segments of the public. Employment in the service sector can be divided into three categories: jobs that provide services for the affluent, welfare services, and services provided by the poor.

Services for the affluent are often thought of as "glamour jobs." These are white-collar jobs in fields such as commercial banking, finance, insurance, real estate, and law. Employees who hold these jobs tend to be highly paid, and as the Intersecting Inequalities feature shows, they are typically White men. For example, African Americans and Hispanic Americans are underrepresented in the fields of finance, insurance, and real estate. Only 3.1 percent of commodities sales positions are held by African Americans and 5.0 percent by Hispanic Americans. In securities and other financial services, just 4.5 percent of sales representatives are African American; 3.5 are Hispanic American. And in real estate, 3.3 percent of sales

positions are held by African Americans and 4.5 percent by Hispanic Americans (U.S. Department of Commerce, Bureau of the Census, 1997). Racial and ethnic minorities are also underrepresented among the consumers of these services.

The second category, *welfare services*, includes occupations in fields such as health care, education, government, and social services. Some of these jobs require specialized training and skills and carry high prestige. A few jobs also pay well, but most people in this category of service employment are not well paid. Some analysts maintain that wages in this segment of the service sector are low because a high percentage of the workers are women, who historically have been paid significantly less than men.

The third category of jobs in the service sector is *services provided by the poor*. These jobs have little prestige and pay low wages. In fact, most workers who hold these jobs earn on average substantially less than workers employed in manufacturing ($304 per week versus $475 per week) (U.S. Department of Labor, 1998). Jobs in this category are concentrated in two major industries: services to buildings, such as cleaning and janitorial services; and retail/personal services, such as clerking at a fast-food restaurant or other business that requires little skill.

The growth of the service sector has played a major role in the development of a **dual labor market** in the United States, that is, a labor market composed of essentially two types of jobs: high-paying, high-prestige jobs with extensive benefits, and low-paying, low-prestige jobs with few if any benefits. The first category is referred to as the **primary labor market**, and the latter is called the **secondary labor market**.

Although there was a significant increase in employment during the first half of the 1990s, most of the jobs created were in the secondary labor market. At the same time, as we will see shortly, major corporations trimmed their payrolls, eliminating many jobs in the primary labor market where jobs were traditionally considered secure. Overall, workers' benefits in the service sector are about 60 percent less than workers' benefits in manufacturing (Nelson, 1994; Uchitelle, 1998).

The growth of the dual labor market, coupled with fewer jobs in the primary labor market, has significantly altered the U.S. work world. One of the most important ways is underemployment.

Underemployment

Since World War II, the average education level of workers has risen. By 1970, 25.9 percent of the labor force had at least attended college; in 1996, this figure had risen to 57.2 percent (U.S. Department of Commerce, Bureau of the Census, 1997). However, this better-educated labor force has found that, on leaving college, they are often

INTERSECTING INEQUALITIES

How Do Sex, Race, and Ethnicity Affect Professional Employment?

What are your career aspirations? Perhaps you are attending college so that one day you can enter one of the professions. The professions are considered by many to be among the most desirable occupations in our society. Because of the unique features of professional occupations that we have already discussed, professionals enjoy a good deal of autonomy (they can be their own boss to a large extent) as well as high prestige and high pay.

Who holds these jobs? The majority of professionals are men and they are White. In the table, for example, we see the sex and racial/ethnic composition of some of the most popular—and most prestigious—professions. The dominance of Whites and men is staggering. Moreover, these numbers have not improved much since the 1980s, although women have fared somewhat better than racial and ethnic minorities. For instance, in 1983, 12.7 percent of architects were women, while 1.6 percent were African American and 1.5 percent were Hispanic American (U.S. Department of Commerce, Bureau of the Census, 1997).

Some analysts blame the poor representation of women and minorities in the professions on the fact that few members of these groups choose to pursue these fields in college. While it is true that smaller numbers of women and minorities than men and Whites major in fields such as engineering and architecture, the reasons underlying their choices are less clear. They may be reluctant to enter these fields, for example, because they do not perceive their chances for success as high. Research shows that occupational choice depends to some extent on a job seeker's perceptions of whether she or he has a fair chance of being hired for a job, feeling welcome on the job, and succeeding in the job (Reskin & Hartmann, 1986). Moreover, the historical underrepresentation of women and minorities in the professions has perpetuated the problem. Research also shows that the representation of a group already in the field affects the likelihood of others entering the field since those already there can serve as role models and mentors to job aspirants (Ferguson & Dunphy, 1992; U.S. Department of Labor, 1997).

Women, African Americans, and Hispanic Americans in Selected Professions, 1996

Profession	Women (%)	African Americans	Hispanic Americans
Architect	16.7	2.7	4.3
Engineer	8.5	4.2	3.8
Physician	26.4	4.5	5.1
Dentist	13.7	1.2	0.9
Psychologist	61.4	12.2	3.1
Lawyer	29.5	3.5	2.8

Source: U.S. Department of Commerce, Bureau of the Census, 1997, p. 410.

forced to take jobs that fall not only below their expectations, but also below their training and competence. During the 1990s, an additional problem has developed: College-educated and experienced workers already in the labor force were being laid off because of corporate cutbacks or "downsizing," as such layoffs are often called. These workers also have difficulty finding suitable jobs. Taking a job below one's educational background, abilities, or experience is termed **underemployment.**

It is estimated that during the 1990s, 20 to 25 percent of college graduates were working in jobs for which they were clearly overeducated. Faced with a shrinking number of entry-level corporate jobs in particular, some college grads—about 25 percent—opted to pursue even more education in graduate or professional schools (Arenson, 1998; McFadden, 1991). This trend, though, may only worsen the underemployment problem: College graduates who do not have advanced degrees could be perceived as less qualified, leading them to take positions for which they are overqualified. There is also growing concern that universities are graduating more Ph.D.'s than the market can absorb (Arenson, 1998).

As if underemployment at the top of the job market weren't bad enough, it sets off a chain reaction that ripples down to lower levels. When college-educated workers take jobs below their skill level, high school graduates who typically would have held these jobs are forced themselves to take work for which they are overqualified, or not work at all. The unemployment rate of high school graduates is more than double the unemployment rate of college graduates (U.S. Department of Commerce, Bureau of the Census, 1997; see also Kilborn, 1994). As the rippling effect continues, the least skilled and least educated individuals are not likely to find work at all, or to find jobs that do not provide adequate financial support ("Vanishing Act," 1998).

Not only do workers newly entering the labor force face underemployment, so do experienced workers who have been laid off. During the 1990s, layoffs occurred in nearly every field. Although blue-collar workers, especially in manufacturing, are still more likely than white-collar workers to be laid off, the number of white-collar workers losing their jobs increased significantly in the 1990s. Between 1979 and 1996, 24.8 million workers in blue-collar jobs such as mining, construction, and manufacturing lost their jobs, while 18.7 million white-collar workers in fields such as law, health care, education, and engineering lost their jobs. Most white-collar job loss occurred during the 1990s. During this period, the share of lost jobs with salaries of $50,000 or more doubled (Uchitelle, 1998; Uchitelle & Kleinfield, 1996).

A recent national survey of workers who lost their jobs in 1991 or 1992 found that by 1994, only 35 percent had obtained full-time employment at a job paying the same as or more than their previous job. Among the 65 percent who were less fortunate, 25 percent had found another full-time job that paid less, with the median loss of $85 per week. Eight percent were working only part-time and usually earning considerably less than in their previous job, and 24 percent remained unemployed (Uchitelle & Kleinfield, 1996). A 1998 report confirmed that although most laid-off workers find other jobs fairly quickly, few regain their former wage rate (Uchitelle, 1998).

Underemployment helps explain workers' pessimism about job security even when the unemployment rate is low and the economy appears to be strong. Some workers respond to the prospect of underemployment by employing themselves, a trend that has also grown during the 1990s.

Alternative Employment

From 1970 to 1996, the number of self-employed workers in the United States grew by more than 50 percent, from about 7 million to about 10.5 million (U.S. Department of Commerce, Bureau of the Census, 1997). Traditionally, the self-employed were shop and restaurant owners, but increasingly they are what are called *independent contractors, consultants,* or *freelancers.* These individuals sell their services to various clients to do a particular job. A high percentage (13.9 percent) of independent contractors and consultants work in the construction industry, but most (46 percent) are in services, including finance, insurance, and real estate. They include administrative, managerial, professional, and technical specialists (52.4 percent). They are more likely than workers in traditional employment arrangements to hold a college degree (U.S. Department of Labor, 1995).

Independent contractors and consultants currently make up about 6.7 percent of the total U.S. labor force. But other forms of nontraditional employment are also increasing; these include what is called *contingent work.*

How does this photograph suggest changes in the nature of work and the workplace in a high-tech service economy? How does this kind of economy affect the status of workers? How does this kind of economy affect the structure of occupations and wages? Do you think this trend will continue in postindustrial societies? Why or why not?

Contingent workers do not have continuous ongoing employment, but rather work at a job for a fixed period of time, usually a year or less; their employment is contingent on employers' needs for their services. Contingent workers make up 2.2 percent of the labor force. Individuals who work for firms such as temporary help agencies (1.5 percent of the labor force) are officially considered continuously employed because technically they work for the contract firm or temp agency. However, they typically work only sporadically throughout the year and move from job site to job site as demand requires. On-call workers and day laborers (1.7 percent of the labor force) are likely to work even less regularly, going to a job only when called. Unlike independent contractors and consultants who are typically White men, contingent workers, temps, and on-call and day laborers are more likely than workers in traditional employment arrangements to be female, young, and African American (U.S. Department of Labor, 1995).

Some analysts argue that alternative work arrangements have a number of advantages over traditional employment. For instance, they offer more flexible hours and some allow workers to do the job at home. But the disadvantages of alternative employment are great. Most alternative employment pays less to considerably less than traditional employment, and employment benefits, such as health insurance, often are unavailable. For instance, 57 to 65 percent of contingent workers have health insurance and they have purchased it themselves; in contrast, 82 percent of noncontingent workers have health insurance, with premiums paid in part or completely by their employees. Similarly, nearly 73 percent of contract workers have health insurance, compared to only 45 percent of temps who obtain work assignments from temporary help agencies (U.S. Department of Labor, 1995; see also Abelson, 1998).

Most independent contractors (82.5 percent) prefer their current employment arrangements over traditional employment, but most contingent, on-call, and day workers prefer traditional employment over their current alternative situations (nearly 61 percent) (U.S. Department of Labor, 1995). Regardless of worker preferences, however, many sociologists maintain that the increase in alternative work arrangements signals a fundamental change in employer–employee relations that is not likely to be reversed. Indeed, so strong is the trend toward alternative employment that some sociologists refer to the "permanently temporary" work force (see, for example, Moore, 1994; Uchitelle, 1996).

The Decline of Unions

A **labor union** is an organization of workers who seek to improve wages and working conditions in their trade.

Labor unions are led by representatives elected by and from the union membership. Union leaders then try to achieve the goals of the union in two ways—by negotiating with management or by calling on workers to *strike,* that is, refuse to work until management agrees to at least some of their demands.

The history of labor unions in the United States dates back to the late 1800s when unions arose as a means of combatting the poverty wages and hazardous working conditions of burgeoning industrialism. Business, joined by government, tried to suppress unions, often through violent confrontations with workers, and by and large, they succeeded. By the 1930s, however, unions were strong enough to become the established bargaining agents for workers in many fields, but especially the big "smokestack" industries—steel, automaking, and garment manufacturing—located primarily in the northeastern and midwestern states. Union membership grew steadily until by 1980, unions represented 25 percent of the total labor force (Kilborn, 1996).

Over the years, relations between unions and corporations normalized so that except for isolated strikes, most labor disputes could be negotiated without disrupting production. When a strike did occur, companies often hired interim workers until a settlement was arrived at, and then striking workers returned to their jobs. In 1981, however, this pattern changed. That year, President Ronald Reagan dismissed hundreds of striking air traffic controllers and hired permanent replacements. The president's action set a precedent, and in later strikes during the 1980s, employers followed Reagan's example by hiring permanent replacement workers (Greenhouse, 1996).

The threat of replacement workers added to workers' feelings of job insecurity and disarmed unions of their most powerful weapon, the strike. Not surprisingly, the number of labor strikes has dropped precipitously in recent years. In 1975, there were 3,005 strikes. In 1985, the number declined to 1,016, and in 1995, there were only 385 strikes, the lowest number since World War II (Greenhouse, 1996; see also Kilborn, 1995). At the same time, union membership has declined; in 1998, just 13.9 percent of workers were union members (Greenhouse, 1999).

In an effort to revitalize labor unions, many union leaders are trying to organize workers they traditionally ignored: workers in the South and Southwest, workers in smaller industries such as poultry processing, and the growing service sector. Unions are also trying different strategies in their negotiations with management. One approach, for example, is to alert a company's customers and suppliers to a particular labor problem in order to get them to pressure management to make concessions to workers. So far, however, the results are mixed and the future of unions is uncertain (Greenhouse, 1999; Kilborn, 1996; Smothers, 1996).

In 1998, Continental Airlines pilots threatened to strike in Houston, Texas, in a contract dispute calling for higher pay. What economic and political factors make strikes increasingly rare in the United States? Why is the future of labor unions uncertain in a postindustrial society?

Wages

The wages attached to a particular job are determined by a number of factors, including the level of skill, effort, and responsibility that the job entails. We expect workers in jobs involving high levels of skill, effort, and responsibility to be paid more than workers in less demanding jobs. But wage rates are a complex phenomenon. In addition to such "objective" measures as skill, effort, and responsibility, wages are also influenced by the sex and race or ethnicity of the majority of workers holding a particular job. Lawyers, for example, earn a median salary of $1,166 a week before taxes, while child care workers earn only a small fraction of that amount, $202 a week. Besides arguable differences in the levels of skill, effort, and responsibility each job entails, there are also significant differences in the sex and racial/ethnic composition of lawyers and child care workers. About 70 percent of all lawyers are male and about 93 percent are White. In contrast, although about 70 percent of child care workers are White, 97.1 percent are also female (U.S. Department of Commerce, Bureau of the Census, 1997; U.S. Department of Labor, 1998). "Women's work" is systematically devalued by job evaluators who set wage rates.

Aside from the question of fairness in wage rates, there is the matter of whether a specific wage is sufficient for meeting individual and family everyday needs. Historically, workers in even low-paying jobs have relied on periodic wage increases to help them keep pace with the rising cost of living. During the 1990s, however, pay in-creases for workers in many occupations were lower than during the 1980s. As a result, although workers in private industry now earn on average $407 per week compared with $299 per week in 1985, their money actually buys less because annual increases in the cost of living are greater than their small incremental gains. More specifically, the $407 a week that today's worker earns is actually worth just $256, whereas the $299 earned in 1985 was worth $271 (using constant 1982 dollars) (U.S. Department of Commerce, Bureau of the Census, 1997). Also, for the most part, the wages of low-skilled, less educated workers have not increased as much as the wages of better educated workers in high-skilled jobs.

About 7 percent of workers who are paid hourly wages receive the *minimum wage*. The minimum wage was established by the federal government in 1938 in an effort to lift as many workers as possible out of poverty. However, because the minimum wage has never been indexed to inflation, its erosion in value, especially in recent years, has been substantial. In fact, the 1956 minimum wage of $1.00 per hour was actually worth 88 cents more in terms of buying power than the 1995 minimum-wage of $4.25. More than a third of all minimum wage workers work full time (36 percent), eight of every ten are service workers, and nearly two-thirds (64 percent) are women (U.S. Department of Commerce, Bureau of the Census, 1997).

Even with the government's tax credit for low-wage earners and food stamp eligibility, workers making $4.25 an hour who worked full time, year round could not earn enough to raise themselves and their families above the official poverty line (Greenstein, 1996). So in 1996, Congress voted to raise the minimum wage. On September 1, 1997 minimum wage workers began earning $5.15 an hour. The increase was designed to narrow the income gap between highly paid workers and those at the bottom of the wage scale, a gap that is several times wider in the United States than in other large industrialized countries. It was also hoped that the increase will help keep the earnings of low-wage workers from being further eroded by inflation. However, some analysts doubt that the rise in the minimum wage will actually lower the poverty rate because so many new jobs are low paying. As the Social Policy box on page 356 reports, they favor the adoption of a *living wage* in place of the minimum wage.

The High-Tech Revolution

Work in the United States is not only characterized by underemployment, alternative employment, a decline in unions, and eroding wages, but also there is the high-tech revolution. The invention of computers, other information technology, and robots has revolutionized production and the overall economy as much, if not more, than the in-

Social Policy
A Living Wage versus the Minimum Wage

The Issue

In 1996, the Minnesota state legislature enacted a law requiring businesses that have more than twenty employees and that receive at least $25,000 a year in state or local subsidies to pay workers whose jobs were created by the public subsidies at least $7.28 an hour in wages and benefits. The law was in part the end product of tireless campaigning on the part of labor unions, church groups, and advocates for the poor and homeless, who argued that the minimum wage condemned families to a life of poverty, even when one member was working full time, year round. These groups successfully convinced the legislature that businesses should start giving something back to the community in exchange for the financial support they received from government, much of which comes from citizens' tax payments. Paying workers $7.28 per hour, which these groups consider a wage rate that families can reasonably live on, benefits the entire community by reducing poverty and the problems associated with it (Terry, 1996).

The Debate

Similar "living wage campaigns" are underway in other states and cities, including Los Angeles, Chicago, and Baltimore. However, living wage bills are also meeting fierce opposition from business groups, who argue that mandating the wage rates that employers must pay inhibits business growth and could force some companies to close. According to opponents of the bills, living wage laws will hurt communities because businesses will move to areas where wages are not government-mandated (Terry, 1996).

Even supporters of living wage bills concede that such laws are not an adequate solution to poverty, since even the higher wage rate still puts a family of four just above the official poverty line. But supporters see the living wage as a first step in the right direction by giving low-wage workers and their families better financial security (Terry, 1996).

What Do You Think?

Do you support the living wage concept? Do you think that if the government were to mandate payment of a living wage, many businesses would be forced to close? Would mandating a living wage make U.S. companies even less competitive in the global marketplace? As a consumer, would you be willing to pay more for a product if you knew that the increased cost reflected better pay for low-wage workers who could, in turn, better support their families?

---

vention of the steam engine in the eighteenth century. Computers, in particular, have fundamentally altered the way business is conducted, allowing corporations to conduct business simultaneously in multiple countries around the world with strokes on computer keyboards. For corporations, high technology is considered a blessing: a means of cutting costs and improving productivity through multipurpose, reprogrammable equipment and systems (Malmgren, 1990). But what is the impact of the high tech revolution on workers?

Today, jobs related to computer technology are among the fastest growing, including fields such as computer electronics, software, communications equipment, fiber optics, medical instruments, and biotechnology. According to some estimates, even modest growth in the computer industry over the next several years is likely to result in the hiring of 53 to 65 percent more systems analysts and 48 to 60 percent more programmers (U.S. Department of Commerce, Bureau of the Census, 1990). However, this job growth will not necessarily benefit workers in the United States. Just as multinational corporations have moved most of their basic manufacturing operations to countries where wages and materials are significantly lower than in the United States, so they are now increas-

ingly "outsourcing" much of their high-tech work (including document and data conversion services and data processing) overseas. Companies in India and Ireland are especially popular since both have an educated, English-speaking, low-wage labor force. For example, computer specialists with a master's degree in India earn $5,000 to $6,000 a year, while their U.S. counterparts would command $50,000 to $70,000 (Barlett & Steele, 1996).

Many computer-based companies also do not require large workforces to get jobs done. Internet companies, for example, have shown tremendous growth in the last few years because the number of Internet users has increased extremely fast—from about 5 million in 1995 to an estimated 115 million in 2000. Most of these companies, whose market value often rivals that of companies such as General Motors, Boeing, and Sears, Roebuck, have a significantly smaller labor force: For example, America Online, with a market value of $66.4 billion, has 10,000 employees; Yahoo!, with a market value of $33.9 billion, has 673 employees; and Amazon.com, with a market value of $25.4 billion, has 1,600 employees. In comparison, General Motors, with a market value of $52.4 billion, employs 600,000 workers; Boeing, with a market value of $35.8 billion, employs 230,000 workers;

DOING SOCIOLOGY

Are You Optimistic about the Future of the Economy?

In this chapter, you have read various predictions about the future of the U.S. economy, some of which are contradictory. Based on what you've learned, do you share the optimism of the students whose opinions we discussed at the chapter's opening? How do your friends feel?

To answer these questions, sample the students on your campus and ask them how they envision the country's economic future. What will economic conditions be like in 2025? What do they expect their careers and financial circumstances to be like at the close of the first quarter of the twenty-first century?

In analyzing your results, consider how responses differed between men and women, and by race and ethnicity. If you had a sample of older, nontraditional, or returning students, how did their answers differ from those of eighteen-to-twenty-one-year-old students? Were there differences by major? How can you and your classmates explain these findings?

---

and Sears, Roebuck, with a market value of $16.7 billion, employs 296,000 workers (Barboza, 1999).

The impact of robotics on jobs and the workplace is uncertain, although one thing is clear: The models in industry clearly lack the charm, creativity, and humanness of R2D2 and other robots in film and television. For the most part, robots are used on production lines to perform unskilled tasks, such as lifting, spray painting, and spot welding. From the perspective of manufacturers, robots have many advantages over human workers: They can complete basic production tasks accurately, dependably, inexpensively, and over a longer period of time. The potential therefore exists for robots to further displace human workers in the manufacturing sector. However, on the positive side, robots are currently being used in hazardous work settings, such as toxic and nuclear cleanups, that pose a serious threat to the health and safety of human workers (Holusha, 1995).

Analysts predict that the high-tech revolution will eventually have its greatest impact in the service sector, especially financial services and communications. These are the "glamour services," but even services provided by the poor are likely to be affected by high-tech innovations. For example, over the next several years, the fast food industry is expected to undergo a technological revolution with robots performing tasks such as cooking hamburgers, bagging fries, stuffing buritos, and delivering drive-thru orders to cars (Sims, 1988). Robots are also being designed to take the place of home health care assistants. The robots would help the ill or frail elderly move about

their homes, remind them to take medications, monitor their physical condition, and alert medical personnel in an emergency (Holusha, 1995).

There is no question that the high-tech revolution is transforming the U.S. economy, the workplace, and everyday life, but the ultimate outcome—positive or negative—remains to be seen. The Doing Sociology box asks you to return to the question that opened this chapter and to reconsider your future in light of what you have read. What do you think the economy of the early twenty-first century will look like, and what will your place be in that economy?

REFLECTING ON

Work in the United States

1. Why is underemployment a problem, and what specific strategies would you suggest for addressing this problem?
2. How does the growth of alternative employment change employer–employee relations? Would you be interested in alternative employment? Why or why not?
3. Which do you favor: the minimum wage or the living wage? Why?
4. What is your major or planned career path at this time? How could robotics and other high technology play a part in your field? What other trends will influence your future work world?

 For useful resources for study and review, run Chapter 13 on your *Living Sociology* CD-ROM.

CONNECTIONS

Types of societies	Review Chapter 3 on the six types of societies. On what kinds of economic activity is each type of society based? How did the economy affect the division of labor and the nature of work?
Industrialization	After reviewing Chapter 3, see the section on "Population in Industrialized and Developing Countries" in Chapter 19 and "Cities and the Industrial Revolution." Historically, how has industrialization affected population and urbanization?
Multinational corporations	Review the discussion in Chapter 9 on the foreign manufacture of U.S. products. In what ways are examples such as Nike emblematic of the postindustrial global economy? Also review the discussion of corporations in the section on "Formal Organizations" in Chapter 6. What role do multinational corporations play in the transformation from industrial to postindustrial societies?
Service economy	The concept of a service sector was introduced in Chapter 3 in the section on "Postindustrial Societies." What factors lead to a service economy? How does a service economy affect the labor force and jobs?
Types of economy in relation to types of political systems	Preview the section on "Types of Political Systems" in Chapter 14. In what ways do economic and political systems interrelate? How does the role of government in the economy shape a society's economic system?
Socialism and communism	Review the discussion of Marx's concept of communism as "An Alternative to Caste and Class" in Chapter 8. How are communism and socialism interrelated? What is state capitalism?
Capitalism and democracy	Based on your preview of Chapter 14 on types of political systems, in what ways would you say that democracy and capitalism are interrelated? What is democratic socialism?
Economic development	Review the discussion of economic development in Chapter 9 and the various means of describing and measuring economic development. Where would you place the following countries on the World Economies Matrix in Chapter 13: Iceland, Niger, Israel, Cambodia, New Zealand, Hong Kong, Angola?
Economic stratification	Review the discussion in Chapters 8 and 9 on the distribution of wealth in U.S. society and among societies worldwide. How does the concentration of wealth in a comparatively small number of interlocking corporations reflect both U.S. class structure and global stratification?
Labor force composition and participation	Review the discussions in Chapters 10, 11, and 12 on the labor force participation of males and females, ethnic and racial groups, and people over sixty-five. How do factors of sex and gender, race and ethnicity, and age affect the distribution of the labor force in the United States among white-collar, blue-collar, and pink-collar jobs? How do these factors affect occupation and income?
Technology	Review the definition of technology in Chapter 4. What are some examples of the knowledge, skills, and artifacts that make up the technology of postindustrial societies? What is the significance of this technology for the way of life of members of a society? for a society's economy?

CONNECTIONS

Economy, technology, and social change	Read "Theories of Social Change" and "Sources of Social Change" in Chapter 20. How do the structural functionalists and the conflict theorists explain the economic and political transformations of societies? How, exactly, is technology a force for change?

SUMMING UP CHAPTER 13

The Economy and Work

1. The economy is the social institution that produces, manages, and distributes a society's human and material resources. Most social scientists consider it the most important institution in a society.

Economies in Historical Perspective

1. Economies may be studied in terms of three sectors: primary, secondary, and tertiary. At any given time, in any given society, one sector tends to be predominant over the others.
2. Hunting and gathering societies have no formal economy. Pastoral and horticultural societies also have little in the way of a formal economy since the distribution of resources is handled by family members. It is in agricultural societies that a formal economic structure develops. The economy of an agricultural society standardizes financial transactions. In addition, a specialized division of labor emerges so that people have jobs. Nevertheless, there is still little separation of work and home.
3. With the advent of the Industrial Revolution, work was removed from the home and transferred to factories. Production itself was broken down into specialized tasks, becoming faster, more efficient, and generally less expensive.
4. A postindustrial economy is characterized by the predominance of the service sector. Primary and secondary sector activities are assumed by less developed countries, and production becomes multinational.

Types of Economic Systems

1. There are two major types of economies: capitalist and socialist. Capitalist economies are characterized by private ownership of property, pursuit of personal profit, free competition, supply and demand, and nonintervention by the government into economic activity. Socialist economies are characterized by public ownership of property, an emphasis on collective interests over personal gain, and government regulation of economic activity.
2. No country conforms perfectly to either economic type, and some countries have hybrid systems, such as state capitalism and democratic socialism. In addition, in evaluating a country's economic system, it is important to also consider its level of economic development.

The U.S. Economy

1. The structure of the economy in the United States today is characterized by economic concentration reinforced by the growth of oligopolies, conglomeration, growing intercorporate control, and rapid growth of the service sector.
2. The United States has experienced low inflation and low unemployment during the 1990s. At the same time, however, the trade gap with other countries has widened and workers are increasingly pessimistic about the security of their jobs.

Work in the United States

1. The U.S. labor force is made up of nearly equal numbers of men and women, but racial and ethnic minorities have somewhat lower labor force participation rates than Whites. A person's sex and race or ethnicity often affect the types of jobs available to him or her. In addition, the data indicate that the youngest segments of the working-age population are having difficulty getting jobs, while the oldest segments are leaving the labor force in numbers greater than expected.
2. Employment in the service sector may be divided into three categories: jobs that provide services for the affluent, welfare services, and services provided by the poor. The sex, race and ethnicity, and education level of workers in each of these categories differ markedly, as do the wages and prestige attached to the jobs.
3. Underemployment is a growing problem for the U.S. labor force. This problem is made worse by the increasing number of well-educated and experienced workers who are being laid off from high-paying, high-skilled jobs.
4. Contract and contingent employment are nontraditional work arrangements that have been growing in recent years. Although some workers like the flexibility of alternative employment, they often receive lower compensation and do not get benefits.

5. Labor unions have experienced declines in membership and power since the 1980s. At the same time, workers have seen the value of their wages erode. Adding to worker insecurity is the growing transfer of high-tech jobs overseas, as well as the potential for robots and other technological innovations to displace human workers.

KEY PEOPLE AND CONCEPTS

blue-collar job: a job with relatively low prestige that requires mostly manual labor rather than mental labor

capitalism: an economic system in which the means of production are privately owned and operated

conglomeration: the process of corporate mergering

consumer price index: a measure that gauges the cost of products, services, and other items that are essential to everyday living

corporation: a group of people who own a business and have a special legal status that grants them rights, privileges, and responsibilities separate and distinct from those they hold as individuals

democratic socialism: an economic system in which there is substantial public ownership of production and government intervention into economic activity, but there is also considerably more political freedom (including democratic elections) than what is typically associated with socialist societies

dual labor market: a labor market composed of essentially two types of jobs: high-paying, high-prestige jobs with extensive benefits, and low-paying, low-prestige jobs with few, if any, benefits

economy: the social institution that produces, manages, and distributes a society's human and material resources

horizontal merger: the acquisition of a company by another company in the same industry or business

inflation: an increase in the price of goods and services

intercorporate control: a network of connections among corporations that allows them to coordinate their activities so as to maintain or enhance their economic position

interlocking directorate: a network of associations formed through simultaneous memberships on the boards of directors of multiple corporations

labor union: an organization of workers who seek to improve wages and working conditions in their trade

oligopoly (shared monopoly): a small group of corporations that enjoys a disproportionate share of the market for specific goods or services

pink-collar job: a job with a high concentration of women workers

postindustrial economy: a system for producing, managing, and distributing services and information, with the help of electronic technology, especially computers

primary labor market: made up of high-paying, high-prestige jobs with extensive benefits

primary sector (of the economy): the segment of the economy made up of activities that extract products directly from the natural environment

profession: an occupation that requires extensive, specialized training in a particular field

secondary labor market: made up of low-paying, low-prestige jobs with few, if any benefits

secondary sector (of the economy): the segment of the economy composed of activities that transform material resources into goods or products

socialism: an economic system in which the means of production are publically owned and operated

state capitalism: an economic system in which the means of production are privately owned and operated, but there is a high level of government intervention in economic activity

tertiary sector (of the economy): the segment of the economy devoted to providing services rather than producing tangible goods; also called the *service sector*

trade deficit (or **trade gap**): occurs when a country imports more goods than it exports

underemployment: taking a job below one's educational background, abilities, or experience

unemployment rate: the percentage of the working-age population currently out of work but actively looking for a job

vertical merger: the acquisition of a company by another company whose business activities are unrelated or only marginally related

white-collar job: a well-paying job with high prestige that requires mental labor rather than physical labor

LEARNING MORE

Barlett, D. L., & Steele, J. B. (1996). *America: Who stole the dream?* New York: Anchor/Doubleday. A highly readable analysis of the economic reasons underlying contemporary U.S. workers' feelings of job insecurity, which examines such issues as the transfer of jobs overseas by U.S. corporations, immigration and naturalization policies, and the role of the federal government.

Rifkin, J. (1995). *The end of work.* New York: G. P. Putnam's Sons. A provocative analysis of some of the most significant changes in the economy and work in recent years, in which the author predicts that the "new elite" of professionals in high-tech industries will be a highly mobile group of workers with few ties to any one place, resulting in a lowered sense of civic responsibility.

Webster, J. (1996). *Shaping women's work: Gender, employment and information technology.* New York: Longman. An analysis of how the revolution in information technology is transforming women's employment and experiences on the job, not only in the United States and other high-income countries, but in developing countries as well.

Wilson, W. J. (1996). *When work disappears: The world of the new urban poor.* New York: Knopf. Focuses on unemployment in the urban ghettos of the United States and suggests measures the government could take to remedy the problem.

 Run Chapter 14 on your *Living Sociology* CD-ROM for interesting and informative activities, web links, videos, practice tests, and more.

Politics and Government

In the popular film *Independence Day*, space aliens attempt to take over earth by first invading the United States. A central goal of the invasion strategy is to render the federal government powerless. A huge space ship is shown hovering over the White House, then destroying the building and much of the nation's capital with deadly explosions. Many high-level officials are killed and the President narrowly escapes death himself. But despite the violence and mayhem, the aliens fail to destroy the government. Why?

The makers of the movie—and patriotic Americans—would probably answer that the United States is too strong and resilient to be conquered, even by aliens. But a sociologist would answer that government is more difficult to destroy than one might think. **Government** is the social institution that has formal authority to distribute power, allocate resources, make decisions for the society, and regulate relationships between the society's members as well as between the society itself and other societies. As we learned in Chapters 3 and 6, a social institution is made up of organized patterns of behavior that have an objective reality apart from the lives of particular individuals. So in the film, when top-level politicians were killed, government did not die with them; others stepped in to distribute power, allocate resources, make decisions, and so on—behaviors that kept the society operating with a semblance of order during an extraordinarily chaotic time.

Of course, governments rarely have to deal with crises of the magnitude of an invasion of space aliens, but there are periodic challenges to the stability of government from both within a society and external to it. In this chapter, we'll consider the role of government in society by looking at types of governments and and key government activities. Let's begin by revisiting the concepts of power and authority, which we introduced in Chapter 6.

POWER, AUTHORITY, AND THE STATE

What makes a person or group powerful? Is a father who makes his child go to the same college he did powerful? Is a city council powerful if it passes a law that teens wearing gang jackets cannot gather in groups larger than three? Is a country powerful if it gets another country to stop imprisoning its citizens because of their dissenting beliefs? According to sociologists, each of these is an example of **power**, the ability to get others to do one's will even if they do not want to. Power can be exercised by force or the threat of force ("If you don't go to my alma mater, I won't pay for your education," "If more than three teens wearing gang jackets are gathered publicly, the group will be jailed," "If your country doesn't stop imprisoning dissenters, my country will no longer import your products"), so that people comply with demands out of fear or because they are unable to resist. Their compliance is involuntary.

Max Weber, whose work will receive a good bit of attention in this chapter, was especially interested in power and how it is exercised. In his analysis of power, Weber distinguished government from other political entities such as political parties, by labeling it the *state*; Weber defined the **state** as the sole political entity with the legally recognized right to use force within its territory. To say the state has the right to use force does not mean that all or even most governments rely on coercion or fear to maintain order. Rather, if it ultimately becomes necessary, the state may legally resort to force to preserve its sovereignty (its power to govern citizens). Weber recognized that compliance obtained involuntarily, through the use of force or threats of force, is shortlived at best. People who are ruled by force, he warned, do not respect their rulers because they don't regard them as legitimate. Eventually, they rebel, and the rulers are deposed and replaced. Consequently, Weber said, most rulers, even if they obtain their position by force, seek to legitimate themselves as rulers. To achieve legitimacy—that is, to justify their leadership in the eyes of those they lead—rulers must transform power derived from force into power derived from authority. **Authority** is power perceived as rightful or legitimate by those being led. Weber distinguished three ideal types of authority: rational-legal, traditional, and charismatic. Let's consider each in turn.

Rational-Legal Authority

Rational-legal authority is bestowed by legally enacted rules, regulations, or contracts. Rational-legal authority is most often found in governments and organizations that are organized bureaucratically. Recall from our discussion of bureaucracy in Chapter 6 that one hallmark of bureaucratic organizations is a hierarchy of authority in which all members know the responsibilities and privileges of their positions as well as the positions of others directly above and below them. Another hallmark is a set of written rules and procedures specifying the organization's norms (what members should do and how they should do it, and what they shouldn't do).

In a state, the rules and procedures specify how people are to be selected for particular positions: by election, for example, or by appointment. The established rules and procedures, then, are the source of legitimacy for rational-legal authority. People attain positions of leadership only after certain procedures have been carried out. When you vote in an election, for instance, you are following an established procedure for bestowing rational-legal authority on officials, whether the President of the United States or the mayor of your town. Sometimes, a losing candidate contests the results of an election by arguing that a procedure was violated. In other words, the candidate is challenging the legitimacy of the person elected to lead.

The rules and regulations of a bureaucracy are impersonal. They apply to a position, so if someone leaves or is removed from a position, that person is stripped of the responsibilities and privileges of the position, which are then assumed by the person who takes their place in the hierarchy. In other words, the office has rights and responsibilities attached to it apart from any individual who may hold the office, and these rights and responsibilities endure over time, even though particular officeholders come and go.

Rational-legal authority predominates in modern, industrial societies because it provides the efficiency and predictability that such societies require. Even in times of crisis, written procedures assume a smooth transition of leadership and no power struggles. When President John Kennedy was assassinated, for example, leadership was transferred immediately to Vice President Lyndon Johnson, as specified in our country's constitution. In fact, Johnson took the oath of office aboard Air Force One en route to Washington with the slain President's body on board.

Thus, for a leader, the fact of assuming a position in a bureaucratic hierarchy confers legitimacy in a rational-legal system. The downside of rational-legal authority, however, is that no individual is considered indispensable. Any leader found wanting by the standards of the rational-legal government can simply be removed and replaced, as long as a clear and sufficient reason is offered for the action (Collins & Makowsky, 1989). For example, following an investigation by Special Prosecutor Kenneth Starr into President Clinton's extramarital relationship with former Washington intern Monica Lewinsky, a majority of the House of Representatives voted to impeach the President, although the Senate later acquitted him of all charges.

Traditional Authority

Traditional authority is bestowed by custom. The legitimacy of a leader's authority, therefore, derives from members' adherence to a belief in the sanctity of tradition. In the ideal type, traditional authority is not vested in a position by impersonal rules and procedures as rational-legal authority is, but rather is vested in a particular individual who either inherits it or has it bestowed by a higher authority, such as a god. Consider, for example, the British monarchy. Queen Elizabeth II inherited her authority from her father, King George VI, and tradition dictates that this authority pass to her eldest child, Prince Charles, upon her death. The legitimacy of the British monarchy derives not only from the tradition of inheritance, but also from the belief that this authority was bestowed by God.

Traditional authority flourishes in homogeneous societies—those with little diversity among the population. That's why traditional authority is commonly found in preindustrial societies. As societies industrialize, their populations—and the belief systems and customs of their populations—grow more diverse, requiring the standardization that rational-legal authority provides. In addition, traditions are open to interpretation, so leaders vested with traditional authority may find themselves battling with their advisers, many of whom aspire to lead themselves, over interpreting tradition in a way that preserves their leadership (Collins & Makowsky, 1989).

Charismatic Authority

Charismatic authority derives legitimacy from the extraordinary personal virtues or skills of the people on whom it is bestowed. In other words, charismatic leaders command allegiance from their followers because of their extraordinary personalities, heroics, or ethics. History is filled with examples of charismatic leaders: Buddha, Jesus Christ, Joan of Arc, Mahatma Ghandi, Adolf Hitler, Vladimir Lenin, Malcom X, Martin Luther King, Jr., Nelson Mandela. Notice that a charismatic leader can be either a villain or a savior. The outcome didn't matter as much to Weber as the fact that charismatic authority inheres in a particular individual, not in formal rules and procedures or custom.

Notice, too, that there is only one woman on our list. This is not because historically there have been few charismatic women, but rather because women were forced by gender norms to channel their leadership abilities into such pursuits as social work or health care that were considered feminine and, therefore, appropriate or permissible for them. Mother Teresa of India was one example of a charismatic female leader in these areas. Her activism on behalf of the poor, the sick, and the outcast earned her an international following. We are now seeing more charismatic women leaders, such as Benazir Bhutto of Pakistan, emerge in the political arena, but history is not without charismatic female political leaders. Consider Indira Ghandi of India, Golda Meier of Israel, and Eva Peron of Argentina, for instance.

What personal, cultural, and historical factors contributed to Slobodan Milosovic's charismatic authority as Yugoslavia's chief of state? How might traditional authority have contributed to his power and prestige? How did his exercise of power and authority lead to his downfall? What changes might you predict for the post-Milosovic future of governance in Yugoslavia?

A charismatic leader develops a strong emotional bond with his or her followers. Charismatic leaders have followers who are intensely loyal, but this loyalty can be shaken, a fact related to one of the main problems with charismatic authority. As Weber pointed out, because charismatic authority derives legitimacy from the characteristics of a single individual, it tends to be unstable and shortlived. For one thing, charismatic leaders face tremendous pressure to always demonstrate the outstanding personal qualities that made them leaders in the first place. Faced with a crisis, such as a natural disaster or an attack from a rival nation, for example, the charismatic leader runs the risk of losing legitimacy in the eyes of followers if his or her response falls short of expectations.

Moreover, charismatic leaders are hard to come by, so when one dies, it's very difficult to find a suitable replacement. Some simply cannot be replaced, and the followers disband. However, another potential outcome is the **routinization of charisma,** that is, the replacement of charismatic authority with some combination of traditional and rational-legal authority. For example, Lutheranism began in the sixteenth century as a protest movement against the Roman Catholic Church and was led by the charismatic German theologian, Martin Luther. When Luther died in 1546, his followers continued his work, thereby establishing traditions that took hold and grew until Lutheranism became a recognized religious denomination. Today, Lutheranism is the largest Protestant denomination in the world, with approximately 80 million members. Tradition is now combined with rational-legal principles, and the Lutheran World Federation, head-

quarted in Geneva, Switzerland, manages the activities of its membership by overseeing theological studies, religious practices, and church policies for Lutheran churches around the globe.

It bears repeating that Weber's three types of authority are ideal types, that is, in real life they are rarely found in pure form. Many leaders with rational-legal authority, for instance, attained their positions at least in part because of their charisma. Nelson Mandela's heroism on behalf of oppressed Black South Africans no doubt played a major role in his becoming President of South Africa through the rational-legal process of election. Sometimes, too, rational-legal authority is backed up by tradition. In the United States, for example, members of the Kennedy family, although elected to office, also carry the air of authority bestowed by the traditions of their aristocratic background.

REFLECTING ON

Power, Authority, and the State

1. Which type of authority do you consider the most effective? Which do you consider most dangerous or potentially harmful? Why?
2. Think of the organizations that you belong to. Can you identify an example of each type of authority in any of these organizations?

TYPES OF GOVERNMENT

A survey of political systems throughout history and the world today reveals that different types of political systems tend to be prevalent in particular types of societies. In hunting and gathering societies, no formal political institution exists. These small, egalitarian societies are organized around kinship or family ties. Decision making is usually communal, although a particular individual may serve temporarily as a kind of political leader when the group must make important decisions, such as whether to move camp. For the most part, the person who emerges as leader in such situations is someone with special knowledge of the problem. So, for example, if the group must decide where to move camp, members seek advice from the person who has most knowledge of the surrounding territory or who has traveled farthest on hunting or gathering expeditions. However, the final decision is still arrived at by consensus, and the person considered the leader in one situation is just one of the group in a different situation. In hunting and gathering societies, formally organized government as we know it simply does not exist (Murdock, 1949; O'Kelly & Carney, 1986).

In pastoral and horticultural societies where the economy allows for accumulating wealth in the form of live-

Which type of government discussed in this chapter does each photograph most likely represent? What are the principal characteristics of each of these types? What are some examples of the effects a society's political system has on its economy and other social institutions?

stock and land, social inequality and status hierarchies emerge. Wealth is safeguarded and consolidated through rules of inheritance. In these societies, wealth translates into political power: Those with the greatest wealth typically become the primary decision makers, using their surplus resources to buy and reward allies and punish enemies. Hereditary chieftainship is the political system prevalent in pastoral and horticultural societies, as political power is passed on with wealth from one generation to the next.

Political systems more familiar to us today developed in agricultural societies. As some landowners in agricul-

tural societies accumulated significant surplus wealth, they developed into an elite class, living well off the work of the majority of the population and monopolizing political power. In agricultural societies we thus see the emergence of a *ruling class*, the nobility. Because others work for them, the nobles are free to pursue such interests as empire building and political intrigue. It is from the nobility that the primary ruler of the society—the emperor or king—is drawn, as well as the ruler's advisors. The desire to accumulate even more wealth and power leads to wars as rulers try to conquer the territory of others. However, because technology limits the speed of transportation and communication, rulers in agricultural societies can directly govern only relatively small areas, often emanating from an urban area out to the hinterland to form a *city-state*. Some political empires, such as the Mesopotamian and Roman empires, were composed of a number of city-states.

As technological developments improved transportation, communication, and defense, governing became more manageable, and the geographic boundaries of territories were more clearly defined and more easily protected from invaders. The result was the emergence of the **nation-state**, a unit of political organization in which the governed are considered citizens with specific legal rights and responsibilities who reside within recognized national boundaries. The first European nation-states developed in the twelfth century.

The modern nation-state has several distinguishing characteristics. First, the nation-state attempts to unify its citizens under the banner of a single governmental authority. The reason we say *attempts* is because many nation-states have tremendous difficulty accomplishing this task since their populations are usually composed of groups that differ by race, ethnicity, religion, and other factors that can lead to internal conflict. For example, although Great Britain includes Northern Ireland, the Catholic population strongly resists British rule. In Canada, the French-speaking population of Quebec has long sought—and nearly succeeded in 1995—to gain independence from the rest of the English-speaking country. And in the former Yugoslavia, ethnic and religious animosities resulted in a war that divided the country into five new nation-states (Bosnia-Herzegovenia, Croatia, Slovania, Serbia and Macedonia).

The modern nation-state is also characterized by the rule of law. Every aspect of social life in the modern nation-state—birth, marriage, even death—is regulated by law. Most disputes in a nation-state are settled formally by law, with the government prosecuting and punishing law violators. The law also bestows specific rights on the citizens of the nation-state. These rights may be civil, such as the Equal Pay Act in our country which guarantees that workers doing jobs requiring the same skill, effort, and responsibility are paid the same. Other rights may be social (entitlements such as Social Security) and political (how much the public can participate in governance). Citizens of a nation-state, in turn, must fulfill certain obligations to their government; military service and tax payments are two common obligations of citizenship. In practice, however, the extent to which citizens can exercise their rights or are forced to meet their obligations can vary in a nation-state. For instance, a frequent complaint in the former Soviet Union was that while all adult citizens were guaranteed a job, the most desirable jobs were reserved for party members and their relatives. In the United States, all citizens are subject to taxation, but some of the wealthiest individuals pay little or no taxes because they can use deductions and shelter income.

Today, there are over 200 independent nation-states in the world. Does this mean there are over 200 distinct governments? Although the government of each nation-state may be unique in some ways, it is possible to classify all governments into four basic types: monarchy, authoritarianism, totalitarianism, and democracy. These types of governments are summarized in Table 14.1, but let's take a closer look at each one.

Monarchy

Monarchy is a political system in which one family rules from one generation to the next, inheriting political power. Monarchies are typically grounded in traditional authority and are common in agricultural societies.

There are two types of monarchies, distinguishable by the degree of political control exercised by rulers. In an *absolute monarchy*, rulers claim divine right to rule. In fact, the kings of ancient Egypt were considered gods themselves. Absolute monarchs perceive themselves as being above the law. They exercise near-total control over their subjects. Absolute monarchies have existed for thousands of years and are not unknown today. Saudi Arabia can be considered an example of a contemporary country with an absolute monarchy.

TABLE 14.1 Types of Political Systems: A Summary

Type of Political System	*Defining Characteristics*	*Examples*
Monarchy (a) absolute (b) constitutional	One person or family rules from one generation to the next because political power is inherited.	Saudi Arabia (absolute), Sweden (constitutional)
Authoritarianism	Authority is concentrated in the hands of rulers who deny citizens any participation in government.	Ethiopia, Albania
Totalitarianism	Government regulates nearly all aspects of people's lives.	People's Republic of China, Chile
Democracy	Government by the people, either directly or through elected representatives.	United States, Israel

In a *constitutional monarchy*, the monarchs serve primarily as symbolic rulers or heads of state, while the actual business of governing is carried out by elected officials, such as a prime minister and a parliament, who rule according to provisions specified in a constitution. The monarchies that exist in Europe today are this type. In Great Britain, Sweden, and Spain, for example, the royal families command the loyalty and admiration of their subjects, but they largely perform ceremonial functions, leaving the day-to-day operation of government to elected officials (see, for example, Hoge, 1998).

Authoritarianism

Authoritarianism is a political system in which authority is concentrated solely in the hands of rulers who severely restrict popular participation in government. Authoritarian rulers willfully disregard the needs and concerns of their people. They are also repressive in that there is little or no opportunity for people to express their opinions on issues or remove rulers from power. Consequently, authoritarian regimes are often unpopular and generate political disaffection. Nevertheless, there are numerous contemporary examples of authoritarian governments, including that led by Serbian President Slobodan Milosovic.

Totalitarianism

Totalitarianism is a political system in which government regulates nearly all the significant aspects of people's lives. Totalitarian governments are far more repressive than authoritarian governments. Control is maintained by creating an atmosphere of deep-seated fear and mistrust. Freedom of assembly, a right taken for granted in our society, is unknown in totalitarian societies, and access to information, such as what's printed in newspapers and textbooks, is severely restricted. The police, who are typically a branch of the military in these countries, monitor people's movements and enforce conformity.

Although authoritarian governments have existed for centuries, totalitarian political systems did not develop until modern times because they rely on surveillance technology and the dissemination of propaganda to establish and maintain control. The widespread availability of computers has given totalitarian rulers unprecedented potential to regulate the lives of their citizens.

Totalitarian governments are usually highly bureaucratic because bureaucracy is the most efficient organizational model for managing the behavior of large groups of people. Totalitarian governments bureaucratize even the most private aspects of people's lives. In the People's Republic of China, for example, couples who wished to have a child were required to apply to their local cadre and wait for approval before attempting conception. In fact, China's one-child population policy has long been cited as an infamous example of totalitarian control. There are indications, however, that the Chinese government is beginning to soften its population control policy (Rosenthal, 1998).

Dissent in totalitarian societies is quickly and often violently put down. Again, the People's Republic of China provides an example: Consider the government's brutal response to the student prodemocracy demonstrations in Tiananmen Square in 1989. Some protestors were killed during the demonstrations, while others were arrested and sentenced to long prison terms. As an extra measure of control, the government ordered all university students to take courses to ensure their "political re-education." China continues to impose harsh penalties on political dissenters (Eckholm, 1998).

Our use of China as an example of a totalitarian political system should not be taken to mean, however, that totalitarianism is found only in socialist societies. Although a society's economic and political systems are connected, there are many examples of totalitarian governments in societies with capitalist economies: Chile and Iraq, for instance.

Democracy

Democracy is a political system in which governing is done by the people, either directly or through elected representatives. In a *direct democracy*, all the people who would be affected by a decision come together, voice their concerns, and reach an agreement about what should be done. Such a system is at least theoretically possible, but in practice a direct democracy does not exist on a national level in any society with a formal government. The only societies in which decision making approaches direct democracy are hunting and gathering societies, but recall some of the defining traits of these societies: They are very small, so all members can meet in one place and discuss an issue in a reasonable amount of time. Also, the simplicity and routine of life in hunting and gathering societies means that few things need to be decided.

So far, it's been difficult, if not impossible to bring all citizens together for decision making in a modern industrial society such as our own. Town meetings are one way that direct democracy has been accomplished at the local level. Some analysts believe that computers and telecommunications technology, such as video conferencing, will make direct democracy feasible on a larger scale, perhaps even at the national level of decision making. Other analysts, though, are skeptical, arguing that the sheer numbers of people involved would make direct democracy impractical, even in cities and towns of moderate size. Consider, for example, the single issue of whether liquor should be taxed to pay for drug and alcohol rehabilitation programs. Telecommunications might make a state-level meeting on this issue possible without having everyone physically present in the same place, but imagine what the discussion would be like. Even if participation were restricted to adults, aged eighteen and older, there would still be at least 775,000 people eligible to voice their opinions in a small state, such as Rhode Island and about 23 million in a large state, such as California. It would be difficult for everyone to be heard and to arrive at a decision on this single issue, let alone the numerous other complex and divisive issues that must be decided to keep a large, modern industrial society operational.

Most democracies, including the United States, have a system of *representative democracy*, in which people give decision-making authority to individuals they elect to represent them. Thus, elected officials are accountable to their constituency; they have rational-legal authority. Democracies are usually based on rational-legal authority. Elections are carried out, for example, according to rules and procedures that specify who may vote, who may run for office, how often elections must be held, and how ballots may be cast. Although all citizens in a democracy theoretically have a voice in government through voting, the rules and procedures used to regulate voting may exclude some people. Originally, for instance, the right to vote in our country was limited to White male property owners. African American men were denied the right to vote until after the Civil War. In fact, the U.S. Constitution declared an African American to be three-fifths a person. African American and White women, however, continued to be denied voting rights until passage of the Nineteenth Amendment in 1920.

Voting, however, is not the sole component of democracy. Many societies claim to be democratic and point to elections as evidence, but is a country with only a single candidate for office really democratic? Or, suppose voters have a choice of candidates, but all come from the same party or are hand-picked by party leaders? Such is the case in Albania and Iran today, where even though citizens vote in elections, people have no real choice in deciding who governs them.

As our examples show, democracy in the United States and elsewhere does not always function ideally. Let's take a closer look at the U.S. political system, and along the way consider how political practices in other societies compare with our own.

REFLECTING ON

Types of Government

1. Have you or anyone you know lived in a society with a government different from that of the United States? What type of government was it, and what are some of the ways it differed from the U.S. system?

2. It is easy for us to see how authoritarian and totalitarian governments are repressive, but can repression occur in democracies? Can you give an example of a repressive practice or policy enacted by a democratic government?

3. Why do you think rational-legal authority tends to be predominant in democratic societies? Can you think of any examples of traditional or charismatic authority in a democratic society?

POLITICS AND GOVERNMENT IN THE UNITED STATES

The framers of the U.S. Constitution called for a democratic government in which decisions are made consensually by elected representatives. However, research that we will examine in this section indicates that our governing process is often disproportionately influenced by those with certain social characteristics, especially wealth. If the wealthy have more input into political decision making than other citizens, they have a greater likelihood of seeing their interests and viewpoints represented in law and public policy.

To understand the differential political influence of the wealthy and other groups in the United States, we will look at key aspects of the U.S. political process, including political parties, political attitudes and activities, and the role of special interest groups.

Political Parties

A **political party** is an organization that supports and promotes particular principles and candidates for public office. Most democracies throughout the world have three or more influential political parties. In Australia, for example, the major parties are the Labor Party, the Liberal Party, and the National Party. In the United States, however, just two political parties—the Republican Party and the Democratic Party—play a major role in national politics. The last third-party candidate to win a national election in the United States was Abraham Lincoln in 1860. Since then, although every national election has had at least one third-party candidate on the ballot, in only five elections has a third-party presidential candidate received more than 10 percent of the vote. The most recent instance was in 1992, when Ross Perot, the candidate of the United We Stand Party, won 19 percent of the vote. But in the 1996 election, Perot received just 8 percent of the vote. (In 1998, a member of Perot's Reform Party was elected to state office; Jesse "The Body" Ventura was elected governor of Minnesota, becoming the first Reform Party candidate to win a statewide election and consequently the highest-ranking elected official in the party.)

The United States operates under a winner-takes-all system: The candidate who receives the majority of votes, even if it is a slim 51 percent, wins the election, while the opposing candidate, who may have received 49 percent of the vote, loses. Compare this with the system in most European democracies. Most European democracies operate under a system of **proportional representation,** in which legislative seats go to candidates from all the political parties represented in the election according to the percentage of votes each party received. So, if one party received 30 percent of the votes, they get 30 percent of the legislative seats. A party winning 20 percent of the votes, gets 20 percent of the seats, and so on. Proportional representation is more democratic than the winner-takes-all model because it gives small constituencies a voice in government. It also increases competition, so that the chances of any one party totally dominating decision making are lessened. Moreover, proportional representation encourages the formation of *coalitions* within government because a party with a large percentage of seats but not the majority must win the support of one of the smaller parties to get its positions enacted. The need to form coalitions, however, can also be a disadvantage of proportional representation, since small parties can refuse to align themselves with any of the larger parties, pushing only their own agenda. When coalition building fails, decision making becomes snarled and inefficient.

In the United States, as in other democracies, each major party is associated with a particular position on important social and economic issues. These positions constitute the party's *platform*. In general, the differences between the Democratic and Republican parties center around the question of how much government should be involved in solving specific social problems. Since the Great Depression of the 1930s, the Democratic position has favored broad government intervention to do for people what they cannot do for themselves. Consequently, the Democratic Party has supported government spending on programs, such as Medicaid (public health insurance) and has also favored legislation to promote equality among social groups, such as affirmative action and public benefits for legal immigrants. The Republican Party is associated with a "hands-off" position regarding government involvement in solving certain social problems. So, for example, Republicans have not supported gun control legislation and have favored limited regulation of the environment.

Despite their ideological differences, in practice, the Democratic and Republican parties are more similar than they appear at first. Their similarity stems from the fact that they must appeal to voters, and the majority of voters consider themselves moderate, rather than extreme in their political views. Thus, candidates from both parties often temper their views on most issues in order to attract more voters (Lemann, 1998). Nevertheless, evidence in-dicates increasing dissatisfaction among voters with both major parties. In recent years, for example, the percentage of voters who identify themselves as independent has increased. In 1972, only 13 percent of voters identified as Independents, rather than as Democrats or Republicans, whereas in 1998, a little more than 25 percent of voters identified as Independents ("A Look at Voting Patterns," 1998; U.S. Department of Commerce, Bureau of the Census, 1997). Some political analysts think this growing independence stems from voters' perceptions that neither major party adequately represents their interests (Lorch, 1996).

Political Attitudes and Activities

Political attitudes fall along a continuum from radically "liberal" (sometimes called the *far left*) to radically "conservative" (the *far right*), but as we've already noted, most people consider themselves moderate or "middle of the road." Researchers have identified several social factors that influence people's political attitudes. One factor is social class. Since the 1930s, for instance, Democratic candidates have had a good deal of support from the poor, working class, and lower-middle class. Most trade unions have also consistently backed Democratic office seekers. These findings are not especially surprising, given Democrats' positions during this period favoring government regulation of business and federal spending on programs to assist the poor. These positions, though, did not win Democrats much support from the upper-middle class and the wealthy. In the late 1970s, a sizeable percentage of Democratic voters supported Ronald Reagan and continued to vote Republican during the 1980s. In the 1992 presidential election, however, working class and poor voters once again voted strongly Democratic and, as Table 14.2 shows, this trend continued in 1996. In the 1996 election, for example, 59 percent of voters with an annual family income under $15,000 voted for Bill Clinton, while just 28 percent voted for Bob Dole. In contrast, 38 percent of voters with an annual family income over $100,000 voted for Clinton and 54 percent for Dole. This pattern continued, but was somewhat weaker, in the 1998 midterm congressional elections when 59 percent of voters with an annual family income under $15,000 voted Democratic, while 55 percent of voters with an annual family income over $100,000 voted Republican ("A Look at Voting Patterns," 1998).

Race and ethnicity are also related to political attitudes. For several decades, the majority of racial and ethnic minorities have identified with the Democratic party. Recent Democratic support by racial and ethnic minorities is related to Democratic candidates' position in favor of civil rights laws and programs designed to counteract the effects of prejudice and discrimination against people of color. Table 14.2 on page 372 shows that this support played a major role in the 1996 presidential election, when 84 percent of African American voters and 72 percent of Hispanic American voters backed the Democratic ticket. Interestingly, White voters were more evenly split: 43 percent voted Democratic, while 46 percent voted Republican. Among Whites, it appears that social class has a greater impact on political attitudes than race.

In the 1998 congressional elections, race and ethnicity also figured prominently. Among African American voters, 89 percent voted Democratic, and among Hispanic American voters, 63 percent voted Democratic. Among White voters, however, 43 percent voted Democratic ("A Look at Voting Patterns," 1998). The votes of people of color were a deciding factor for many candidates in the 1998 congressional elections when, for the first time since 1934, a President's party gained congressional seats in the middle of his term (Holmes, 1998).

Some of the most interesting research on political attitudes, however, has concentrated on gender. Gender differences in political attitudes captured the attention of

researchers in the 1980 presidential election when, for the first time since winning the franchise in 1920, more women than men cast ballots. Also in 1980, women voted significantly differently from men, resulting in an 8 percentage-point gap in women's and men's votes, the largest gender difference in voting since 1952 when gender statistics were first collected. Political analysts weren't sure at first whether these differences were just a one-time difference or a genuine shift in women's and men's voting patterns. But subsequent elections confirmed the existence of what has come to be known as the **gender gap**: differences in the voting patterns and political attitudes of women and men. As Table 14.2 shows, in the 1996 presidential election, the gender gap was the largest it has ever been: 11 percentage points (54 percent of women voted for Clinton, while only 43 percent of men did). Moreover, a gender gap was found across all age groups, with the widest gap being among voters under age thirty (17 percentage points), and across racial and ethnic groups. For instance, although African Americans strongly backed

TABLE 14.2   Voters in the 1996 Presidential Election

Voters	Percent of Total Vote	PERCENT WHO VOTED FOR		
		Clinton	Dole	Perot
Men	48	43	44	10
Women	52	54	38	7
White	83	43	46	9
African American	10	84	12	4
Hispanic American	5	72	21	6
Asian American	1	43	48	8
White men	40	38	49	11
White women	43	48	43	8
African American men	5	78	15	5
African American women	5	89	8	2
Family income was:				
< $15,000	11	59	28	11
$15,000–$29,999	23	53	36	9
$30,000–$49,999	27	48	40	10
> $50,000	39	44	48	7
> $75,000	18	41	51	7
> $100,000	9	38	54	6
18–29 years old	17	53	34	10
30–44 years old	33	48	41	9
45–59 years old	26	48	41	9
60 or older	24	48	44	7

Source: "Portrait of the electorate." *New York Times* (1996, November 10), p. 28. Copyright © 1996 by The New York Times Co. Reprinted by Permission.

Clinton, 11 percent more African American women than men voted for him in 1996. Thus, women played a major role in Clinton's 1996 victory.

Similarly, in the 1998 congressional elections, significantly more women (53 percent) than men (46 percent) voted Democratic. A gender gap of 5 to 11 percentage points held for all age groups, although a majority of men and women aged sixty and older voted Republican. The gender gap was also present across racial and ethnic groups. For instance, although more Whites voted Republican than Democratic, 5 percent more White women than White men voted Democratic. Although more African Americans voted Democratic than Republican, 8 percent more African American women than African American men voted Democratic ("A Look at Voting Patterns," 1998).

The Doing Sociology feature explores the gender gap in greater detail. Let's turn our attention now to the topic of political activities.

Political Activities.   When you think of political activities, you probably think of voting, but voting is just one of many forms of political activity. Political scientist Lester Millbrath (1965) identified three levels of political activism. Millbrath called the lowest level spectator activities, which include wearing campaign buttons or putting a bumper sticker on your car. He considers voting in elections a spectator activity because it requires minimal effort. The middle level of political activism is transitional activities, such as writing to public officials, making campaign contributions, and attending rallies or meetings. The highest level of political activity Millbrath

DOING SOCIOLOGY

Is There a Political Gender Gap on Your Campus?

To say that the gender gap in politics is about voting behavior is to look at only the tip of the iceberg. Research shows that at the heart of the gender gap are issues of economics, social welfare, foreign policy, and, to a lesser extent, environmental protection and public safety. How do the sexes differ on these issues? Let's look at some examples.

Women feel more economically vulnerable than men (and rightfully so). In public opinion polls, this vulnerability is revealed when more women than men express concern about health care (especially long-term care), child care, education, poverty, and homelessness. In contrast, more men than women express concern about the federal deficit, taxes, energy, defense, and foreign policy. Over the last two decades, women have also expressed greater pessimism about the economic condition of the United States and have tended to favor government spending on programs to help families, even if these programs require tax increases (Goldberg, 1996; Lake & Breglio, 1992; Sciolino, 1996; see also Gidengie, 1995).

A strong and consistent gender gap emerges on issues of war and peace. This difference in the political opinions of women and men can be traced as far back as World War I. More women than men thought the United States's entry into both world wars was a mistake; they also voiced greater opposition to the Korean and Vietnam Wars (Abzug, 1984; Baxter & Lansing, 1983). During the Persian Gulf War, more women than men favored a negotiated settlement over military action, and fewer women than men felt that the loss of life, both military and civilian, was worth the victory (Dowd, 1990; Lake & Breglio, 1992).

However, while women advocate peaceful solutions over military solutions to international conflicts and advocate domestic social spending over military spending, they express greater distrust of other nations, and, more than men, think current international relations pose a risk for the United States (Goldberg, 1996). This perspective carries over into issues of public safety, with more women than men expressing concern about crime (Lake & Breglio, 1992). Although support for the death penalty is high among both women and men, there is nevertheless a significant gender gap with fewer women than men favoring the death penalty. Women are also more likely than men to favor gun

control laws (Goldberg, 1996; U.S. Department of Justice, Bureau of Justice Statistics, 1998).

Despite sex differences on economic issues, war and peace, and public safety, men's and women's opinions on other topics converge more. For instance, about as many men as women favor government regulations to protect the environment. Interestingly, women's and men's opinions on women's rights issues are more similar than you might predict, although there are some topics on which they disagree. One is abortion. While a majority of women and men support a woman's right to an abortion under at least some circumstances, more women than men report that a political candidate's position on this issue would affect their vote. This view is held by both pro-choice and anti-abortion women (Lake & Breglio, 1992; Sciolino, 1996).

Conduct your own political opinion poll to measure the gender gap on your campus. Develop a survey that asks respondents their opinions on the issues we've discussed here, and then go out and survey male and female students on your campus. How do their opinions differ overall? Do other factors, such as race/ethnicity and social class, seem to influence men's and women's opinions? How do you explain your findings?

calls *gladiator activities*. These include working on a political campaign, taking an active role in a political party, or running for public office. Gladiator activities require maximum effort and commitment.

A substantial segment of the American population is uninvolved in politics at any level. Consider, for example, one of the most basic forms of political activity: voting. Nationally, less than two-thirds (62 percent) of the voting-age population is registered to vote, and since 1932, just 56 percent of registered voters on average have cast ballots in presidential elections. Even fewer registered voters go to the polls for midterm congressional elections: an average of 45 percent since 1932, but in 1998, voter turnout reached a record low of just over 30 percent (U.S. Department of Commerce, Bureau of the Census, 1996). Voter turnout in other major industrial countries is significantly higher: for instance, almost 89 percent in Italy, 84 percent in Germany, 79 percent in Israel, 75 percent in Britain, and 71 percent in Japan ("Is There a Better Way," 1988). In Australia, voting is mandatory and nonvoters are fined.

Why do relatively few Americans exercise their right to vote? Recent research comparing voters and nonvoters found that nonvoters simply don't think voting is important. They don't feel their vote matters, and they don't believe elections make much difference in determining how the country is run (Berke, 1996; Johnson, 1998). These findings reflect the problem of **voter apathy**, the feeling that voting is not worthwhile because it makes no difference in election outcomes and governance. Voter apathy is partly the result of the lack of choice voters have in elections. As we noted earlier, there are only two major political parties in the United States, and in order to appeal to the largest number of people, candidates from both parties often sound more alike than different. In 1992, when Ross Perot ran for President as a third-party candidate, voter turnout rose to nearly 50 percent, perhaps because voters felt they had an alternative to "politics as usual."

Voter apathy also results from citizens' perceptions that the political system does not benefit them. Compared to voters, nonvoters are younger, less educated, and have lower incomes. Members of these groups are alienated from government, feeling that politicians do not represent their interests or address the problems they face in their everyday lives, such as medical expenses, credit card debt, and difficulty collecting child support (Johnson, 1998). The Starr investigation and subsequent impeachment of President Clinton by the House of Representatives also prompted a large number of potential voters in the 1998 congressional elections to stay away from the polls. Some were angry with President Clinton for his indiscretions with Monica Lewinsky; others were angry with their congressional representatives whom they felt had wasted too much time and money on the investigation (Johnson, 1998).

Given Americans' lack of involvement in spectator political activities, it's not surprising that involvement in transitional and gladiator activities is also low. And while it is true that many second- and third-level activities require certain resources (such as discretionary income to contribute to a political campaign), it is possible to be politically active with a low income by participating in such transitional activities as rent strikes, school boycotts, and petition drives. In fact, some experts think studies of political activism focus too narrowly on elections and office holding and overlook these other efforts (Bookman & Morgen, 1988).

Indeed, a good deal of political research focuses on the gladiator activities of working on a political campaign, serving as a party delegate, and running for public office. Interestingly, studies show that women are almost twice as likely as men to work for a political party or a campaign by canvassing door-to-door, for example, or stuffing envelopes and distributing campaign literature. However, White men have traditionally dominated party conventions and public officeholding. At the 1996 Republican National Convention, for instance, only 52 of the 1,990 delegates were African Americans; 91 percent of the convention delegates were White. Women were better represented at the Republican convention; 36 percent of the delegates were women. In contrast, 32.2 percent of the delegates at the 1996 Democratic National Convention were racial and ethnic minorities, and 49.8 percent were women. The greater diversity of Democratic delegates is partly a result of a plan adopted by the Democrats in 1972 to increase the number of racial and ethnic minorities and women at their conventions (Bennet, 1996; Democratic National Committee, 1997).

As U.S. Secretary of State during the Clinton administration, Madeline Albright participated in critical negotiations for peace in the Middle East. She achieved her position through appointment. Why, historically, have women and racial and ethnic minorities been underrepresented in both elected and appointed political officeholding? What is involved in getting elected to public office in the United States?

TABLE 14.3   Women and People of Color in Congress, 1995–1998

	House of Representatives, Number	Senate, Number
Females	53	9
People of Color		
African Americans	40	1
Hispanic Americans	17	0
Asian/Pacific Islander	4	2
Native American	1	0

Sources: Center for the American Woman and Politics, 1998; U.S. Department of Commerce, Bureau of the Census, 1995.

Historically, White men have also had a virtual monopoly on officeholding. Although women and minorities have made significant progress in winning public office recently, they are still underrepresented, given their numbers in the general population. As Table 14.3 shows, only 53 of the 435 seats in the House of Representatives are held by women. Just nine of 100 U.S. senators are women. These numbers mean that women make up less than 11 percent of the U.S. Congress, when they are 51 percent of the U.S. population. Racial and ethnic minorities do not fare much better. As Table 14.3 shows, only about 12 percent of Congress is non-White, compared with 27 percent of the general population.

One major stumbling block for women and minorities seeking political office has been incumbency. Incumbents already hold political office, but seek another term. Incumbents have several advantages in an election, including high public visibility, voter recognition, and the opportunity to campaign throughout their term in office. Because fewer women and minorities are in office, when they do run, it is more often as challengers than incumbents, and like most challengers, they are more likely to lose to an incumbent than if they were running for an open seat.

Incumbent or not, every political candidate needs money to run a campaign, and the more prestigious the office sought, the more money they need. Traditionally, political campaigns have been financed through personal wealth subsidized by party funds. But since women and minorities have had fewer financial resources than White men, if they did run for office, their campaigns were not likely to have sufficient funds to be successful. And today, even more than in the past, money is essential to winning elections. Consider, for example, that in 1998 the average amount spent by U.S. senatorial candidates was over $3.6 million. In effect, this means that to run for the Senate an individual had to raise about $10,000 a week for six years or be a multimillionaire (Wayne, 1998). These figures are misleading, however, because the money was not distributed equally among candidates. In general, incumbents had more campaign funds at their disposal than chal-

lengers, and in 94 percent of Senate races and 95 percent of House races, the candidate who spent the most money won the election. In fact, the percentage of elections won by the biggest spending candidates has increased in recent years. In 1992, 89 percent of House candidates and 86 percent of Senate candidates who spent the most won the election (Wayne, 1998). It is estimated that in the 2000 Presidential election, candidates who have a reasonable chance of winning will need to raise at least $22 million (or $50,000 a day) before convention delegates are even selected (Abramson, 1998).

Where do such enormous sums of money come from? Certainly, most candidates for national office continue to be individuals with substantial personal wealth, but the lion's share of campaign funds today comes from private contributions by corporations and groups representing special interests. Let's look at this issue more closely.

Political Action Committees and Lobbyists

People who wish to advocate a particular position on an issue and influence politicians to enact laws and set public policy that favor their position often organize a special interest group. The range of special interest groups in the United States is enormous, but examples include cigarette manufacturers, health care providers, feminists, the automobile industry, and teachers. Sometimes the focus and membership of interest groups overlap, as when feminists join with health care providers to pressure Congress to pass legislation helping victims of domestic violence.

One way special interest groups influence law and public policy is by making campaign contributions. In fact, some special interest groups dedicate themselves to fundraising and distributing contributions to the political campaigns of candidates who support the group's cause. These special interest groups are called **political action committees** or **PACs**. PACs contribute millions of dollars to campaigns, making them a powerful force on the political scene. And as Figure 14.1 on page 376 shows, the number of PACs has increased substantially as campaigning has become more expensive.

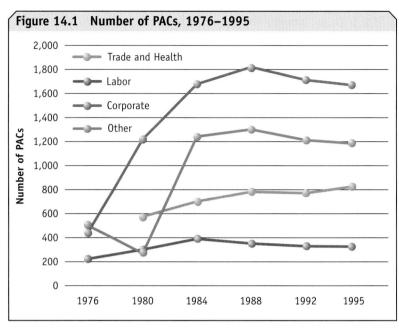

Figure 14.1 Number of PACs, 1976–1995

Source: U.S. Department of Commerce, Bureau of the Census, 1991, p. 274; 1994, p. 291; 1997, p. 292.

Although the Federal Election Commission closely regulates the activities of PACs and campaign financing laws limit PAC contributions to individual candidates, PACs often find ways to skirt regulations. For instance, while they may give only $5,000 directly to a candidate, PACs may give as much as they want to a political party, which, in turn, can use the money to finance their candidates' campaigns. During 1996, for example, Philip Morris, one of the largest tobacco, food, and alcohol corporations, donated more than $1.6 million to the Republican Party, stating that they have a responsibility to their employees and shareholders to support candidates who share their political views (Wayne, 1996). But the PACs are not entirely to blame since the parties themselves seek out these donations, which they call "soft money," because its use is discretionary. During the 1996 Democratic National Convention, for instance, the Democratic Party held a luncheon to honor executives and businesses who had made party contributions of at least $10,000. Many guests were from firms directly affected by various governmental decisions (Wayne, 1996; see also Wayne, 1997).

Elections, then, can be heavily influenced by monied special interest groups, but the special interest groups' power is not limited to elections. Many special interest groups hire lobbyists to influence the lawmaking process. A **lobbyist** is a paid professional who pressures elected officials to pass or defeat proposed legislation. Lobbyists keep track of proposed legislation to determine what effect, if any, it might have on the interest groups they represent. They also suggest to lawmakers legislative changes that would benefit their groups. In fact, lobbyists may actually help a congressional representative or assist in

drafting a specific piece of legislation. Many lobbyists are recruited from government because of their valuable contacts and their intimate knowledge of the legislative process.

Currently, there are more than 7,500 registered lobbyists in Washington, DC, and countless others who are not registered. Together, they represent interests as diverse as the National Rifle Association and the Parent-Teachers Association. Lobbyists may also represent the governments and businesses of other countries. For instance, Japan spends $60 million a year, more than any other country, lobbying U.S. officeholders to support policies, such as reduced tariffs on Japanese-made products. Ironically, Japan prohibits lobbying by foreigners in its country. Like PACs, lobbyists can seriously influence the political process by exerting pressure on officeholders not only through personal visits and organized letter writing campaigns from constituents, but also through their financial resources.

R E F L E C T I N G   O N

Politics and Government in the United States

1. How would you characterize your political attitudes? Do you think of yourself as conservative, liberal, or moderate? Which political party, if any, best represents your views?

2. How do you think voter turnout in the United States might be increased? For example, should voting in national elections be made mandatory? If so, how could such a statute be enforced?

3. Besides money, what are some other obstacles to the election of women and racial and ethnic minorities to political office?

4. People who don't vote typically think their vote doesn't make a difference in how the government is run. Do you think that the prevalence of PACs and lobbyists reinforces this attitude? What would you say to a nonvoter to counter this attitude? And how would you attempt to curb the political influence of PACs and lobbyists?

SOCIOLOGICAL THEORIES OF THE POLITICAL PROCESS

The influence of special interest groups raises questions about how political power is distributed and exercised in the United States. Do some groups dominate political decision making while others are excluded? Two major theories address this question. One, the pluralist model, was developed largely by structural functionalist theorists; the other, the elitist model, was developed by conflict theorists.

The Pluralist Perspective

What if there were no government? Social life would probably be disorganized and unpredictable. Disputes would have to be resolved between individuals with no help from the courts, and many conflicts could easily erupt into violence. According to structural functionalists, it's for these reasons that governments are formed. People living together want order and predictability in their lives, and they want protection from one another and "outsiders." So the members of a society give government the authority to make decisions, distribute resources, and resolve disputes, using force if necessary. Granted, bestowing such power on an institution is risky, since it could be used against the citizens themselves, but this is a risk most people are willing to take. And usually the risk pays off: Government functions to organize social life and protect a society's members.

One factor that contributes to the smooth operation of government is **pluralism**, the diffusion of political influence among numerous interest groups with no single group dominating (Dahl, 1982). Although all groups in a society share a set of core values, the diversity inherent in modern societies means that groups with competing interests often form. At first glance, this competition might seem harmful to the society because it could cause disorder and conflict, but functionalists maintain that the competition actually generates balance. The demands of one group are offset by the demands of another group. The role of government is to ensure that each group gets to voice its position so that none has a disproportionate share of influence in the decision-making process. Sometimes, competing interest groups are brought together to sort out their differences and reach a compromise, a process that lessens conflict.

A major proponent of pluralism is Robert Dahl, a political scientist who studied political decision making in New Haven, Connecticut. Dahl (1961, 1982) observed many different groups with leaders from diverse segments of the community, each of whom had access to various types of political resources. Some of the groups formed quickly in response to a specific issue and disbanded once the issue had been resolved. Other groups, such as labor unions and business organizations, outlived individual issues. But none of these groups seemed more able than any of the others to gain access to and unduly influence government decision makers (see also Lerner et al., 1996).

In short, structural functionalists depict government—at least in a modern industrial society—as a neutral arbitrator in the political struggles of competing interest groups. It is through this competition that government is made responsive to the needs of its citizens, balancing the interests of diverse groups against one another and showing partiality toward none.

Evaluating the Pluralist Perspective.   The pluralist perspective highlights the importance of government in maintaining social order and the role of competing interest groups in the political process. Critics of pluralism have identified several serious weaknesses in the model.

One major problem with the pluralist perspective is that it assumes everyone's interests are represented by at least one interest group. However, as we have seen, the majority of the general public does not get involved in the political process, and those who do, are typically middle and upper class, so the views of the poor and working class are underrepresented.

A second criticism of the pluralist perspective is that it inaccurately depicts interest groups as equally powerful. For instance, a small group of citizens who band together to prevent their housing project from being torn down so that a shopping center can be built are hardly equal in size or resources to large corporations such as Wal-Mart, which ranks fourth in the Fortune 500 listing. According to critics of pluralism, it is such corporations, along with well-financed associations (such as the American Medical Association, the American Bar Association, and the National Rifle Association), that dominate the political landscape.

A third criticism of the pluralist perspective focuses on the role of government as neutral arbitrator. According to critics, governments often show favoritism toward monied interests to the detriment of the poor, racial and ethnic minorities, and other disadvantaged groups. Compare, for instance, pending tax reform bills with recently enacted welfare reform legislation. Each of the tax laws under consideration gives money to the middle and upper classes by lowering their taxes, while the welfare reform law takes money from the poor by limiting eligibility and decreasing benefits. As we will see next, some critics argue that such policies reflect the biases of government decision makers, who are themselves members of the upper classes (see also Sanger, 1998).

The Elitist Perspective

Elitism, the perspective developed by conflict theorists, argues that decisions are made by a small but powerful minority of society's members. According to this model, government is controlled by economic elites—the people with the most money—so national policy reflects their best interests, not the general public's.

C. Wright Mills (1956), a major proponent of elitism, identified two basic classes in U.S. society: the power elite and the passive majority who are manipulated by the power elite. According to Mills, the **power elite** is made up of three subgroups: the government elite, the military elite, and the corporate elite. These three subgroups constitute a *ruling class* that dominates society from their structural "command posts." They are "ruthlessly exploitative . . . driven by the quest for ever-renewed profit, arrayed against the downtrodden and the poor who are denied access to the political levers by which change can be achieved" (Mills, 1956, p. 29).

Other elitist theorists, such as sociologist G. William Domhoff, have also described government as a tool of the ruling class. According to Domhoff (1978, 1990), the ruling class in the United States is made up of the richest 1 percent of the population. Members of the ruling class know one another because they travel in the same social circles. Some choose to run for political office, and many are appointed to high-level government positions. They are therefore well positioned to influence public policy in such a way as to preserve their wealth and dominance. In fact, Domhoff and others (Useem, 1984; Zweigenhaft & Domhoff, 1998) are careful to point out that elite control is not the outgrowth of a conspiracy by the rich, but rather a reflection of their common interests and backgrounds. In other words, if we were in their position we would probably do just as they do.

Evaluating the Elitist Perspective. The data on PACs and lobbyists that we discussed earlier lend support to the elitist perspective. However, while critics of the elitist position concede that wealth often translates into political influence, they argue that depicting government as a tool of the upper class is too narrow.

First, critics maintain that the term *ruling class* inaccurately portrays elites as a strongly unified group when, in fact, they often have divergent interests and positions. The American Medical Association, for instance, has long been at odds with cigarette manufacturers, such as Philip Morris, over government regulation of the tobacco industry.

Critics also argue that public policy does not consistently favor elite interests. They point to numerous instances in which government decisions go against the interests of corporations and the wealthy, favoring the "common" people instead. For example, consumer protection laws, such as food inspections, no-smoking ordinances in public buildings, and required use of seat belts in cars cost corporations money and therefore cut into profits. But in each case, the government has acted to protect its citizens. Research shows that some government decisions clearly favor elites, others clearly favor the "masses," and still others contain concessions to both (Chambliss & Zatz, 1994; Curran, 1993). The political process, then, is rarely as simplistic as the elite perspective makes it out to be.

International "power elites" often emerge in historical contexts. Before World War I, for instance, European heads of state collaborated and competed to divide up Africa in building their colonial empires, and after World War I, the heads of state of the victorious countries were hailed as great world powers. How might adherents of the elitist perspective interpret these events? Do you think there is a global power elite today? Would you consider the United Nations as a power elite in geopolitics today? Why or why not? Do you think the United States has a ruling class?

REFLECTING ON
....
Sociological Theories of the Political Process

1. Which theoretical perspective—pluralist or elitist—do you find most persuasive? Why?

2. Can you think of an example of a law or policy that advantages a particular interest group over the majority of the population? Can you see *any* benefits to the general population from this law or policy?

WARFARE AND THE MILITARY

Our nation's founders tried to create a political system in which power was balanced across the three branches of government: legislative, executive, and judicial. However, with the exception of granting Congress the power to declare war, the Constitution does not address warfare. The military is entrusted with protecting national security and waging war. The military falls under the purview of the executive branch of the government, but some critics charge that the military has become so independent in recent years that, in effect, it constitutes a fourth branch of the federal government. To conclude our discussion of government, then, let's take a closer look at the military.

The Composition of the U.S. Military

The armed forces of the United States are made up of three main branches: the army, the navy, and the air force. The number of active-duty military personnel numbers about 1.4 million, with about 240,000 of these based in over 100 countries abroad. About 44 percent of military personnel assigned overseas are in Europe, the majority in Germany which, before the fall of socialism in the Soviet Union and Eastern Europe, was considered the first line of defense against a Soviet or Eastern Bloc invasion. An additional 33.5 percent are stationed in Asia, primarily in Japan and South Korea (U.S. Department of Commerce, Bureau of the Census, 1997).

Although all American men over age eighteen are required to register for the military draft, today's armed forces are almost entirely composed of volunteers. One concern about an all-volunteer army has been that the enlistees may not have as much schooling on average as the general population, and a poorly educated military can pose a threat to national security. For at least a decade, there didn't seem to be any problem, though: The percentage of recruits who were high school graduates increased from 68 percent in 1980 to 95 percent in 1995 (Applebome, 1991). But in 1997, the army announced that it was lowering its educational standards to accept more recruits without high school diplomas because enlistment had declined substantially. Although the armed forces offer enlistment bonuses and money toward college to appeal to high school graduates, the low average salary of a recruit—about $769 a month (U.S. Department of Commerce, Bureau of the Census, 1996)—means

that well-educated or highly skilled young people will look for better paying, more prestigious civilian jobs instead (Myers, 1998). To make the military a more attractive option, however, the federal government is increasing salaries for all service members and offering merit bonuses for service members midway through their military careers. In addition, the government will give service members a retirement package that includes a pension at 50 percent of base pay plus more education benefits (Becker, 1999).

As Table 14.4 on page 380 shows, today's military is more diverse than in the past. Since 1980, the proportion of women in the military, both officers and enlisted personnel, has risen dramatically. During the same period, the proportion of military officers who are racial and ethnic minorities also increased. In fact, African Americans are overrepresented in the military: African Americans are 12.6 percent of the general population, but 18.4 percent of active duty military personnel. Some observers are concerned that women and minorities are entering the military in greater numbers not because they freely choose to, but because they are the most economically vulnerable segments of the population, with fewer alternative opportunities available to them. The military appeals to these groups because it provides benefits they may have difficulty getting in the society at large, including a steady income, health insurance, education, and job training (Enloe, 1987; Wilkerson, 1991).

Racism has long been a problem in the military. Until the mid-1950s, the armed forces were racially segregated.

What political and economic factors contribute to the increasing representation of women and racial and ethnic minorities in the armed forces? What have been the experiences of these groups in the military? What are the issues surrounding the participation of lesbians and gays in the military?

TABLE 14.4 Men and Women on Active Military Duty by Race, 1985, 1990, and 1997

	1985	1990	1997
Men			
Officers	278,816	262,645	197,834
White	252,348	233,326	169,504
Black	16,054	16,366	13,892
Hispanic	4,222	5,427	6,311
Other*	6,192	7,526	8,127
Enlisted	1,649,233	1,623,714	1,031,231
White	1,261,842	1,138,985	781,701
Black	251,704	336,151	182,581
Hispanic	66,301	78,856	72,214
Other*	69,386	69,722	57,535
Women			
Officers	30,321	34,241	31,204
White	25,096	27,519	23,986
Black	3,728	4,602	4,349
Hispanic	546	753	988
Other*	951	1,367	1,881
Enlisted	179,049	108,700	163,317
White	114,421	136,219	79,204
Black	53,059	64,677	60,852
Hispanic	5,719	8,364	12,144
Other*	5,850	7,172	11,117

*Includes other races/ethnicities and those for whom racial/ethnic identification is unknown.

Source: U.S. Department of Defense, *Military manpower statistics,* 1997.

Although racial discrimination is now outlawed in the military, there is evidence that it has not completely disappeared. One recent study by the General Accounting Office, for example, found that, compared with Whites, African Americans were promoted less often than one would expect on the basis of their numbers in the military. Some analysts attribute this disparity to racial discrimination ("Blacks Found Less Likely," 1995).

Sexism is also a serious problem in the military. One way women have been discriminated against in the military is by being excluded from combat positions. Combat jobs pay significantly higher salaries than support jobs and are critical for promotion to the highest ranks of the military. As a result, women military personnel have been concentrated in the bottom and middle ranks. In 1993, the Secretary of Defense, acting on behalf of the Clinton Administration, ordered the armed services to allow women to fly aircraft in combat. In 1994, the Air Force and Navy announced they had female pilots who were combat-ready. Also in 1994, the Army and Marine Corps opened

some combat jobs to women, but continued to exclude them from direct combat, such as armor, infantry, and field artillery on the ground that they lack the physical strength needed for these jobs and their presence would disrupt morale (Schmitt, 1994). Despite several other exceptions—for example, women cannot serve in units where the cost of renovations to accommodate them would be prohibitively expensive and in support jobs that operate and remain with direct ground combat troops— it is estimated that about 95 percent of military jobs are now open to women. However, the Intersecting Inequalities box discusses another problem stemming from sexism in the military: sexual harassment.

The increased diversity of military personnel has not extended to homosexuals. Historically, gay men and lesbians have been banned from military service because their presence—like women's in combat—was believed to be disruptive. It was also argued that homosexuals in the military would discourage heterosexuals from enlisting and endanger national security because homosexuals

INTERSECTING INEQUALITIES

Is Sexual Harassment a Serious Problem in the Military?

In 1994, the U.S. Defense Department announced that it was opening thousands of military positions, including combat positions, to women. Although many in the military and the general public praise the Defense Department's greater openness to women, some observers caution that simply permitting women to hold more military jobs does not adequately address the problem of sexism that plagues the military. One of the most serious manifestations of sexism in the military is widespread sexual harassment of female military personnel.

A survey of 47,000 women conducted by the Pentagon in 1996 found that 55 percent reported experiencing some form of sexual harassment, ranging from sexual assault to offensive remarks, during the past year. Half of those reporting harassment said they were harassed by superior officers. Sixty percent of the women who were harassed did not file a formal complaint primarily because they felt nothing would be done, they would be blamed, or their superiors would retaliate against them. According to this report, most of the women believed that reporting the harassment would end their military careers (Egan, 1996).

The problem of sexual harassment in the military first got widespread media attention in 1991, when an official government investigation revealed widespread abuse of female naval officers by at least 175 male Navy pilots during their annual convention known as Tailhook (Gordon, 1993). More recently, in 1996, a military jury convicted an Army drill sergeant of raping six trainees, and he was sentenced to twenty-five years in prison and was dishonorably discharged. Eleven other staff members at the Army training center where these rapes occurred were also charged with sexual misconduct. However, the drill sergeant's conviction and the charges against the other staffers also raised concerns about racism, since all of the accused were African Americans and the majority of the accusers White. Army investigators denied racist motives and widened their investigation to all Army training facilities in the United States and abroad ("Sergeant Gets 25-Year Term," 1997).

In response to these sexual harassment scandals, a special panel appointed by Defense Secretary William Cohen recommended in 1997 that the Army, Navy, and Air Force segregate men's and women's core units of both basic and ad-

vanced training, although field and classroom training could remain coed (Myers, 1997). Interestingly, however, a second advisory committee, which inspected twelve military training schools and interviewed military personnel, found strong support for greater sex *integration* since such conditions more accurately mirror the real-life conditions under which recruits will eventually work (Shenon, 1998). In March 1998, Defense Secretary Cohen announced that armed forces training would not be sex segregated, but he also ordered increased supervision of recruits, especially in barracks, and an increase in the number of women serving as recruiters and drill sergeants (Myers, 1998).

The impact of Cohen's orders remains to be seen, but the scandals themselves raise questions about the future role of women in the military. Many feminist social scientists have cautioned that women's greater involvement in the military is not necessarily a positive development. This is because women are not so much transforming the military as they are being forced to participate on men's terms, and many are enduring tremendous hardships, including sexual harassment, to do so (Enloe, 1993).

could be blackmailed into disclosing military secrets (Wells-Petry, 1993). However, there is no empirical support for any of these objections, and studies commissioned by the Pentagon itself have not been able to document that homosexuals negatively affect military discipline or morale. In fact, the Pentagon studies show that if job performance is used as a criterion for evaluation, there is no reason to ban homosexuals from military service. In other countries where gays and lesbians are permitted to serve in the military—for example, Denmark, the Netherlands, Canada, and Australia—there have been no morale or recruitment problems that can be attributed to their presence (Shilts, 1993).

During his first campaign, President Clinton promised to lift the ban on homosexuals serving in the military. His position won him the support of gay and lesbian rights

groups, but unleashed a heated debate among politicians, military personnel, and the heterosexual public. What eventually emerged from the controversy was a political compromise among the Clinton administration, Congress, and the Pentagon. The Social Policy box on page 382 discusses the new policy that went into effect February 5, 1994.

The Military and the International Political Scene

Although it may seem that 1.4 million military personnel is an enormous number, military staffing has actually declined significantly since the demise of communism in the Soviet Union and Eastern Europe. In 1991, the United States and Russia agreed to reduce not only their weapons

The Issue

On February 5, 1994, the federal government implemented its new policy toward homosexuals in the military. The policy, known as "Don't Ask, Don't Tell," basically permits lesbians and gay men to serve in the military as long as they are not open about their sexual orientation and do not engage in homosexual acts. A homosexual act is defined broadly as human contact to satisfy sexual desires between members of the same sex as well as any bodily contact that a reasonable person would see as demonstrating a propensity toward homosexual behavior (such as holding hands with a person of the same sex). Under the new policy, men and women who join the military will no longer be asked if they are homosexuals, nor will they be discharged from the military if they admit to being homosexual. However, such an admission would be enough to allow military officials to begin investigating the individual to determine if he or she is engaging in homosexual acts.

The Debate

Critics of the new policy say it is not significantly different from the old one (Directive No. 1332.14), which prohibited "persons who engaged in homosexual conduct," or who "demonstrate a propensity" to do so, from serving in the military. Under the old policy, military officials investigated individuals suspected of being homosexual, and suspects were often harassed, subjected to humiliating interrogations, and coerced into naming others in the military who might be homosexual. Such investigations resulted in about 1,400 women and men being discharged annually from military service without the benefit of judicial proceedings. Many of these women and men had outstanding service records and were decorated veterans (Cammermeyer, 1994; Shilts, 1993).

Supporters of the new policy maintain that it prevents the military from launching aggressive and arbitrary investigations to find homosexuals. Early evaluations of the new policy did show that the number of homosexuals discharged from the military declined in 1994: That year, 597 homosexuals were discharged compared with 682 in 1993 and 708 in 1992 (Schmitt, 1995). However, a more recent study showed that the number of service members discharged for homosexuality has actually increased since the new policy went into effect: 850 women and men were discharged in 1996, an 18 percent increase over 1995 and a 42 percent increase over 1994 (Shenon, 1997). In 1998, 1,145 gay men and lesbians were discharged from the military, nearly double the number in 1993, the last year before the current policy went into effect (Myers, 1999).

The reasons for the increase in homosexual discharges is also being debated. The Pentagon maintains that many of the discharges are the result of service members volunteering information about their sexual orientation, often as a ploy to get out of the military. However, some homosexual service members and their advocates argue that the increase shows that the "Don't Ask, Don't Tell" policy is a failure and that gay men and lesbians in the military are still being harassed and persecuted. They believe that many commanders do not fully understand the new policy or are intentionally misusing it. "Don't ask, don't tell" gives commanders greater discretion in handling reports of homosexual service personnel, and many commanders are homophobic. As a result, some commanders are still initiating aggressive investigations of individuals on the basis of unreliable information or accusations from coworkers. Some analysts also argue that the controversy generated over the policy itself caused a backlash against homosexuals in the military by focusing attention on them (Myers, 1999; Schmitt, 1994; Shenon, 1997).

What Do You Think?

What is your opinion of the "don't ask, don't tell" policy? Do you think homosexuals should be permitted to serve in the military without fear of harassment or discharge on the basis of their sexual orientation? If "don't ask, don't tell" is not working, what policy would you suggest to replace it?

---

arsenals, but also the number of troops stationed throughout Europe. This agreement represents a major change in relations between the United States and Russia, who since the Korean War (1950–1953) were engaged in a *cold war*. That is, while the two countries never fought one another directly in a military conflict, they battled one another indirectly: through military assistance to other countries, in verbal sparring, and by stockpiling weapons. Let's look at several components of the cold war and the changes brought about by its end in the 1990s.

The Arms Race. During the cold war, the United States and the Soviet Union competed in a deadly game of military chess, an *arms race*. For each advance in defense technology or for every new deployment of weapons by one country, there was a corresponding advance or deployment by the other country. The rationale for this simultaneous build-up of weapons was the **deterrence doctrine**, the belief that an increase in military might would prevent war because no rational political leader would enter into a war that could not be won due to the opponent's military superiority.

At first glance, the deterrence doctrine makes sense, and it may have actually worked for a time. But with the development of nuclear weapons, the deterrence doctrine was replaced by a condition of mutually assured destruction. A nuclear war would immediately devastate the earth, eventually destroying the planet's entire ecosystem. Military superiority becomes meaningless in such a war, since there can be no winners in an all-out nuclear confrontation.

Nevertheless, during the cold war, the United States and the Soviet Union stockpiled huge arsenals of nuclear weapons. By 1990, U.S. nuclear missiles and bombs outnumbered those of the Soviet Union, 12,000 to 11,000, and each warhead had a destructive power 1,000 times greater than the atomic bomb dropped on Hiroshima in 1945. The arms negotiations of the 1990s produced agreements that both the United States and Russia would reduce their nuclear arsenals by several thousand missiles and bombs (Myers, 1998) Although the U.S.–Russian agreement is significant, it does nothing to control the development and use of nuclear arms by other countries. Great Britain, France, China, Pakistan, and India already have nuclear weapons. Libya, Iraq, North Korea, and other nations have often tried to buy or produce material to develop their own nuclear weapons. Currently, there are about 50,000 nuclear weapons worldwide, more than enough to kill each person on earth many times over (Whitney, 1994).

The Military-Industrial Complex.

The sale of weapons and war technology is big business for several countries, including the United States, France, Great Britain, China, Germany, and since the end of the cold war, Russia and many Eastern European countries, such as Bulgaria (Bonner, 1998). Between 1990 and 1994, the United States alone sold $49 billion worth of arms to other countries; total arms sales worldwide from 1992 to 1994 was $80.5 billion (U.S. Department of Commerce, Bureau of the Census, 1997). Who besides the U.S. government buys the products and services of defense contractors? Among the countries spending the most on arms purchases between 1984 and 1994 were Saudi Arabia ($20.5 billion), Egypt ($4.1 billion), Turkey ($3.1 billion), and South Korea ($3.0 billion) (U.S. Department of Commerce, Bureau of the Census, 1997). The large sum spent by Saudi Arabia during this period is in part the result of that country's defense concerns following the Persian Gulf War.

Very few companies produce weapons and military equipment. In the United States, for example, the majority of U.S. defense contracts are held by only three companies: Lockheed Martin Corporation, Boeing, and Raytheon (Wayne, 1998). Thus, in the arms business, there is very limited competition among contractors and few clients (national governments) looking for goods and services. A closed, mutually dependent relationship develops: The government depends on a select number of suppliers to provide the military equipment it needs, and the suppliers depend on the government for a significant percentage of their business. This closed relationship is usually referred to as the **military-industrial complex**, a term first used by President Dwight Eisenhower in the late 1950s. Although some analysts argue that a closed relationship between defense contractors and the government is unavoidable, given the products—weapons—and the fact that few companies have the expertise and technical equipment to produce them, other analysts see serious problems concentrating such power in the hands of a few "experts," especially with a lack of cost and quality control.

In the late 1990s, following the Gulf War and bombings of Baghdad, the United States conducted air strikes in no-fly zones over Iraq. Why might Iraq and other less industrialized and lower-income or oil-rich countries be regarded as threats to regional stability? to world peace? What are some other examples? What roles might technological developments and an international military-industrial complex play in perpetuating threats of war?

Concerns about cost and quality control certainly appear justified. Research indicates that the final cost of a defense contract frequently exceeds the original price. For instance, the cost of producing the M-1 tank was 220 percent more than the contractor's original estimate; the F-15 fighter plane cost 250 percent more. In addition, many products are overpriced. For instance, Navy officials paid $127 for an aluminum washer that could be purchased at a hardware store for less than a dollar. A gas bottle was also purchased for $1,975, even though it was available through the government's own supply store for $103 (DeFazio, 1996). Although the responsibility for these problems must be shared by the military and the contractors, the closed nature of the military-industrial complex sets the stage by allowing a small group of people to control information and set prices without outside scrutiny or competition.

The military-industrial complex is closed not only in terms of suppliers and customers, but also in the exchange of personnel between government and the defense industry. High-ranking public officials (Pentagon officials,

Cabinet members, presidential advisors) often go to work for the defense industry when they leave their government posts, and it is just as common for defense industry employees to take jobs in government. This practice means that important information, including that pertaining to pending and future contracts, is often informally exchanged between the government and the defense industry, further limiting competition and objective evaluation. Moreover, to ensure the flow of contracts, the defense industry and the Pentagon spend millions of dollars each year lobbying government officials to support military expenditures. Large defense contractors are among the biggest PAC contributors because more contracts means greater profits (Wayne, 1998).

The Continued Threat of Conventional War. In 1997, there were eighteen ongoing military conflicts worldwide, down from twenty-one in 1996. Most of these conflicts were internal or civil, rather than international. Some had been going on for many years: twenty years in Afghanistan, fifteen years in Sudan, fourteen years in Sri Lanka, and ten years in Somalia. Civilian casualties have increased from 5 percent of war-related deaths at the turn of the twentieth century to more than 90 percent in many wars of the 1990s. Indeed, targeting civilians, including children, has increasingly become a part of military strategy, with the goal of demoralizing the enemy. Wars during the 1990s have claimed the lives of 2 million children, disabled 4 to 5 million children, left 1 million children orphaned or separated from their parents, and made 12 million children homeless (U.N. Development Programme, 1998).

At the same time, new weapons have been developed for fighting wars and military conflicts. Of growing concern is the use of chemical and biological weapons. Chemical weapons were first used extensively during World War I, but their use in subsequent conflicts has been increasing. Chemical weapons are poisons that kill when they come into contact with skin. Chemical weapons, however, can ony be used in limited geographic areas. More alarming is the development of bioweapons, which can infect a great number of people across a large geographic area. Bioweapons contain bacteria or viruses, such as smallpox and Ebolapox, that invade the body, multiply inside it, and eventually cause death. It is believed that Iraq, Iran, North Korea, India, Israel, Russia, China, the United States, and probably Libya and Syria have bioweapons in their national arsenals (Preston, 1998).

This information should give us reason to pause. Although many observers look to the twenty-first century as holding the potential for a new era of global diplomacy, ongoing conventional wars, as well as the threat of biological warfare and the continued risk of nuclear war, threaten our future as a world community.

REFLECTING ON

Warfare and the Military

1. It has been said that the military is a masculine institution. What is the traditional image of a "military man," and how might this image make the military an inhospitable environment for heterosexual women, gay men, and lesbians?
2. What is your opinion of the deterrence doctrine? Does it apply at all to contemporary international politics?
3. How might the power of the military-industrial complex be better controlled? Do you think the military-industrial complex will become more or less powerful in the twenty-first century?
4. Some observers say that most wars are unavoidable. What do you think? Is there a way to prevent the outbreak of war? Can you give a specific example?

 For useful resources for study and review, run Chapter 14 on your *Living Sociology* CD-ROM.

CONNECTIONS

Power and authority	Review the definitions of types of authority as introduced in Chapter 6. Then preview the section on "Power and Authority" in the family in Chapter 15. What are some variations in the distribution of power and authority in families? Which types of authority outlined in Chapters 6 and 14 are involved in family structure and the dynamics of family interaction?
Leadership	Review the discussion of leaders and leadership styles in Chapter 6. How does that discussion relate to the section on "Types of Govenment" in Chapter 14?

CONNECTIONS

Types of government and types of society	Review the information on types of societies and economic systems in Chapters 3 and 13 and on social institutions in Chapter 6. What types of government and what political institutions are associated with each type of society? How do political and economic systems interact in each type of society?
Conformity and dissent	Chapter 6 describes the group dynamics involved in conformity, or obedience to authority, and dissent. What specific examples can you find of connections between those topics and political and military activities within a society?
Collective behavior	Preview the section on "Collective Behavior" in Chapter 20. What are the different types of collective behavior that influence the way a society operates? What collective behaviors are involved in political participation? What roles might rumor, riots, and public opinion play in political activities?
Social stratification and power	Reread the section on "Political Power" in Chapter 12. In what ways are elders a politically powerful group? Also review Chapters 10 and 11. How do age, sex and gender, and race and ethnicity relate to the distribution of political power in a society? How do they relate to political participation? Now review Chapters 8 and 9. How do systems of social stratification, such as social class and caste, relate to the distribution of power in a society?
Social control	Review Chapter 7 on deviance and social control. What are some specific examples of links between issues of social control and the exercise of power and authority by the state or government?
Power elites	C. Wright Mills's concept of the power elites was introduced in Chapter 1 in the section on "Conflict Theory." Also review the section on "The Wealthy" in Chapter 8. Whom might you identify as members of a "ruling class" in the United States? Do you favor the elitist or the pluralist perspective on the political process? How might you reconcile these two views in a new theory?
Political protest and social change	Find information in Chapter 8 on the anti-apartheid movement, and in Chapters 10 and 11 on the feminist, gay and lesbian, and civil rights movements in the United States. Also preview the sections on the environmental conservation movement in Chapter 19 and "Social Movements" in Chapter 20. How do these examples illustrate the role of political protest and social movements in bringing about lasting social change?
International relations	Review Chapter 9 on global stratification and Chapter 11 on race and ethnicity. How do global inequalities, racism, and nativism threaten world peace? Also preview Chapter 17 on the sociology of religion. What examples can you find of the influence of religion on domestic and global politics?

SUMMING UP CHAPTER 14

Power, Authority, and the State

1. Max Weber studied how power is exercised. Power may be imposed by force or by the threat of force and compliance obtained involuntarily. However, leaders who rule through force are not regarded as legitimate. Authority is power perceived as legitimate by those being led.

2. There are three types of authority: rational-legal (bestowed by legally enacted rules, regulations, or contracts, and

most often found in bureaucratic organizations and modern industrial societies); traditional (bestowed by custom and most often found in preindustrial societies whose populations are homogeneous); charismatic (derives from the extraordinary personal virtues or skills of the people on whom it is bestowed and may be found in all types of societies). These, though, are ideal types; in real life, combinations of these forms of authority are likely to be found.

Types of Government

1. Different types of political systems are prevalent in particular types of societies. It was not until the emergence of agricultural societies that political systems familiar to us today first developed. The first European nation-states emerged in the twelfth century. The modern nation-state attempts to unify its citizens under the banner of a single governmental authority, a difficult task given the diversity in societies. The modern nation-state is also characterized by the rule of law, whereby every aspect of social life is regulated by law and citizens are given specific legal rights and responsibilities.
2. The governments of independent nation-states in the world today may be classified into four types: monarchy (one family rules from one generation to the next, inheriting power), authoritarianism (authority is concentrated solely in the hands of rulers who severely restrict popular participation in government), totalitarianism (government regulates nearly all significant aspects of people's lives), and democracy (governing is done by the people, either directly or through elected representatives).

Politics and Government in the United States

1. Political parties are organizations that support and promote particular principles and candidates for public office. In the United States, there are two major political parties, the Republican and Democratic parties, with a winner-takes-all system, whereas in most other Western democracies, there are three or more parties and a system of proportional representation. The two major parties in the United States have different political platforms that reflect each party's position on how much government should be involved in solving specific social problems.
2. Political attitudes fall along a continuum from radically liberal to radically conservative, but most people identify themselves as moderate. A number of social factors influence political attitudes, including social class, race and ethnicity, and gender. In fact, there is a gender gap in political attitudes and voting patterns.
3. There are three levels of political activism: spectator activities (wearing a campaign button), transitional activities (writing to an office holder), and gladiator activities (working on a political campaign). Most Americans are relatively uninvolved in politics to the point of not even exercising their right to vote. Voter apathy, or the feeling that voting is not worthwhile because it makes no difference in election outcomes and governance, is one major reason for low voter turnout in the United States.

With respect to office holding (a gladiator activity), we find some groups—women and racial and ethnic minorities—systematically underrepresented.

4. The political process is influenced by special interest groups, including political action committees (PACs) and lobbyists. PACs contribute millions of dollars to campaigns, making them a powerful force on the political scene. Lobbyists keep track of proposed legislation to determine what effect, if any, it might have on the special interest groups they represent and pressure elected officials to pass or defeat the proposed legislation.

Sociological Theories of the Political Process

1. There are two major sociological theories of the political process. The pluralist (structural functionalist) perspective assumes that society is made up of numerous interest groups competing to influence government decision making, but with no single group dominating the process. This diffusion of power contributes to the smooth operation of government by generating balance and minimizing conflict. Government acts as a neutral arbitrator among the competing interest groups. But critics of the pluralist perspective argue that it inaccurately assumes everyone's interests are represented by at least one interest group, and that all interest groups are equally powerful. In addition, critics maintain that empirical evidence shows that government often favors some groups over others in the decision-making process.
2. The elitist (conflict) perspective sees government as a tool of the wealthy, acting to preserve elite interests. Elites are well-positioned to protect their interests because they know one another and often hold political office themselves. Although there is empirical support for the elitist perspective, critics argue that the theory inaccurately portrays elites as a strongly unified group, when in fact they often disagree among themselves. At the same time, public policy does not consistently favor elite interests.

Warfare and the Military

1. The armed forces are made up mostly of volunteers. There are concerns that a lowering of educational requirements will diminish the military's effectiveness. In addition, while the military is more diverse today than in the past, racial and ethnic minorities, women, and gay men and lesbians confront serious problems in the military, including sexism, racism, and homophobia.
2. During the cold war, the United States and the Soviet Union competed in an arms race, stockpiling large arsenals that included nuclear weapons. Following the end of the cold war, this arms race ended and the United States and Russia agreed to reduce their nuclear arsenals. However, both countries continue to hold numerous nuclear weapons and their agreement does not cover other countries who also possess nuclear weapons.
3. The government and military contractors have developed a closed, mutually dependent relationship, which con-

tributes to a concentration of power in the hands of a few "experts," cost inefficiency, and overcharging.

4. Although there is reason to be concerned about nuclear weapons, conventional warfare continues to pose a serious threat to the world's security and well-being. Of growing concern is the development and use of chemical and biological weapons.

KEY PEOPLE AND CONCEPTS

authoritarianism: a political system in which authority is concentrated solely in the hands of rulers who severely restrict popular participation in government

authority: power perceived as rightful or legitimate by those being led

charismatic authority: derives legitimacy from the extraordinary personal virtues or skills of the people on whom it is bestowed

democracy: a political system in which governing is done by the people, either directly or through elected representatives

deterrence doctrine: the belief that an increase in military might would prevent war because no rational political leader would enter into a war that could not be won due to the opponent's military superiority

elitism: the perspective developed by conflict theorists, which sees the political process as dominated by a small, but wealthy and powerful minority of society's members

gender gap: differences in the voting patterns and political attitudes of women and men

government: the social institution with formal authority to distribute power, allocate resources, make decisions for the society, and regulate relationships among the society's members as well as between the society itself and other societies

lobbyist: a paid professional who pressures elected officials to pass or defeat proposed legislation

military-industrial complex: the closed, mutually dependent relationship between government and military contractors

monarchy: a political system in which one family rules from one generation to the next, inheriting political power

nation-state: a unit of political organization in which the governed are citizens with specific legal rights and responsibilities who reside within recognized national boundaries

pluralism: the diffusion of political influence among numerous interest groups with no single group dominating

political action committees (PACs): special interest groups dedicated to fundraising and distributing contributions on political campaigns, making them a powerful force on the political scene

political party: an organization that supports and promotes particular principles and candidates for public office

power: the ability to get others to do one's will even if they do not want to

power elite: a term coined by C. Wright Mills to describe the segments of society that dominate the political process: the government elite, the military elite, and the corporate elite

proportional representation: legislative seats go to candidates from all political parties represented in an election according to the percentage of votes each party received

rational-legal authority: authority bestowed by legally enacted rules, regulations, or contracts

routinization of charisma: the replacement of charismatic authority with some combination of traditional and rational-legal authority

state: the sole political entity with the legally recognized right to use force within its territory

totalitarianism: a political system in which government regulates nearly all the significant aspects of people's lives

traditional authority: authority bestowed by custom

voter apathy: the feeling that voting is not worthwhile because it makes no difference in election outcomes and governance

LEARNING MORE

Dyer, G. (1985). *War.* New York: Crown Publishers, Inc. A study of how warfare and military strategy have changed throughout human history, highlighting in particular developments since World War II and the advent of nuclear weapons.

Foerstel, K., & Foerstel, H. N. (1996). *Climbing the hill: Gender conflict in Congress.* Westport, CT: Greenwood. Using historical records and personal interviews with members of Congress, the authors trace the history and status of Congresswomen and female staffers.

Shilts, R. (1993). *Conduct unbecoming: Gays and lesbians in the military.* New York: St. Martin's Press. A look at the historical ban on homosexuals serving in the military, including an analysis of traditional arguments in support of the ban, the evidence that refutes them, and the personal stories of gay and lesbian military personnel.

Stern, P. M. (1988). *The best Congress money can buy.* New York: Pantheon. An examination of the role of monied interests in the political process. Although the statistics are dated, the analysis remains useful.

 Run Chapter 15 on your *Living Sociology* CD-ROM for interesting and informative activities, web links, videos, practice tests, and more.

Families and Intimate Relationships

S haron Kowalski and Karen Thompson exchanged rings and pledged to be life partners. Of course, they were not—could not be—legally married because homosexual marriages are not permitted in the United States. But their legal standing didn't matter to them. What mattered was that they were deeply in love. In 1983, Sharon was severely disabled in a car accident. Unable to care for herself, she wanted Karen to care for her in the home they shared. But Sharon's parents, who strongly disapproved of her lesbian relationship, convinced a court that Karen might sexually abuse their daughter. The Kowalskis won the right to remove Sharon from her home, put her in a nursing home, and bar Karen from even visiting her. Karen appealed the lower court's decision, and in 1991 was finally appointed Sharon's guardian by a Minnesota appellate court. In its decision, the appellate court stated that Sharon Kowalski and Karen Thompson were a "family of affinity," that is, a family established because the members choose to be together and identify themselves as family. And, the court added, this type of family deserves to be respected.

The case of Sharon Kowalski and Karen Thompson raises the important question, "What is a family?" A **family** is a long-term, exclusive relationship in which members identify themselves as related, usually by ancestry, marriage, or adoption, and are committed to one another emotionally as well as financially. A family is a kind of **intimate relationship**, a relationship of intense emotional attachment. Typically, families are established through **marriage**, a socially approved union of two or more people in which each is expected to fulfill specific economic, sexual, and caregiving responsibilities. However, as the story of Sharon Kowalski and Karen Thompson illustrates, families may be established without the legal sanction of marriage, and families are diverse—not only in how they are formed, but also in their composition, resources, and the interactions of their members. In this chapter, we'll examine the rich diversity of family life in contemporary societies.

We'll begin with a broad overview of various types of family structures and characteristics, discuss sociological perspectives on families, and then focus on families in the United States.

FAMILIES THROUGHOUT THE WORLD: STRUCTURES AND CHARACTERISTICS

In hunting and gathering societies, the primary social unit is the family. All social activity in hunting and gathering societies, from food distribution to decision making, is organized around **kinship**, a social network of individuals and families joined by ancestry, marriage, or adoption. As societies develop, families continue to provide basic necessities as well as important social services for their members—food, shelter, health care, education—but they also become critical in the intergenerational transfer of wealth and power. In pastoral, horticultural, and agricultural societies, money, property, and even the right to rule are passed on through inheritance, so families are important for the preservation of wealth and political power.

In industrial societies, families continue to pass on wealth through family inheritance, but they lose many of their social service responsibilities. Health care and education, for example, are taken over by social institutions (hospitals and schools). Industrialization also transforms the family into a primary unit of consumption, since goods and services previously made or provided at home now have to be purchased. At the same time, in industrial societies, the family becomes, as historian Phillippe Aries (1965) put it, the center of emotional specialization. The family is responsible for regulating sexual behavior and reproduction; socializing and caring for children; and providing emotional support, affection, and nurturing for all its members. This is not to say, though, that all families look the same or do the same things, as we'll see next.

Given Families and Chosen Families

Each of us is born into a family, what sociologists call our **family of origin**. Because we are born into it, our family of origin is given, not chosen. Most people grow up in their family of origin; it introduces them to the world and socializes them into the culture of their society. For those who are adopted, however, the family in which they grow up is usually different from the family into which they were born. For example, Aidan, the younger of our two sons, was born in Korea; he never saw his father and he was with his mother for only a few days. He spent his first three months with a foster mother and became a member of our family more than nine years ago, when he was just eight months old. His adoptive family has provided almost all his socialization experiences. Although we are not his family of origin, we are his **family of orientation**, the family with whom he identifies as a member and who socializes him.

Someday, Aidan may grow up and choose to have or adopt children of his own. The family a person forms by having or adopting children is called a **family of procreation**. Chances are that if Aidan does form a family of procreation, he will live separately from us, his parents. This doesn't mean that we will cease being family. It simply means that he will establish a separate household from ours; he and his children will constitute a **nuclear family**, a family composed of one or two parents and their dependent children who live together in a household separate from other relatives. Had Aidan remained in Korea with his birth parents or even his foster mother, he likely would have lived in or grown up to form an **extended family**, a family composed of one or two parents, their dependent children, and other relatives who live together in the same household. Extended families are more common in Asia than in the United States (Baca Zinn & Eitzen, 1993).

These categories—family of origin, family of orientation, nuclear family, and extended family—are the basic ways sociologists classify families and family relationships. But four categories are hardly adequate for capturing the diversity of contemporary family life. For instance, in her study of working-class families, sociologist Judith Stacey found that the composition of a household often changes as the needs of family members (siblings, adult children, even divorced spouses and their parents) change. Stacey (1990) calls these families *accordian families* because they expand and contract over time, with family members pooling resources, including shelter, as a survival strategy as well as a demonstration of caring and love.

Many families also contain some *fictive kin*, people not related by ancestry, marriage, or adoption, but who are nonetheless considered members of the family. Perhaps you have fictive kin, such as an "Uncle" or "Aunt" who is not a sibling of your parents, but a close friend of theirs. Sometimes families are constructed completely through fictive kin. For instance, gay men and lesbians are sometimes shunned by their parents, siblings, and other relatives when they reveal their sexual orientation. But they create new families—what Weston (1991) calls *families of choice*, and the judge who decided Sharon Kowalski's fate called *families of affinity*—with a partner, close friends, and sometimes ex-lovers who provide intimacy, companionship, and financial support (see also Stacey, 1998).

How else do families differ? They differ in marriage patterns, residential patterns, ways of determining descent and inheritance, and assignment of power and authority among family members.

Marriage Patterns

Since most families are still formed through marriage, we should consider some of the diverse forms of marriage found throughout the world. The form of marriage with which we are most familiar is **monogamy**, marriage to one partner. This is the only form of marriage legally recognized in the United States, but interestingly, we are in a minority of the world's cultures in this respect: Only about 20 percent of cultures worldwide insist on monogamous marriage (Lamanna & Riedmann, 1994). Many societies may officially endorse monogamy, but they permit **polygamy**, marriage to multiple partners concurrently. For instance, while doing fieldwork in the Republic of Guinea in West Africa during the 1980s, we found that although government policy discouraged polygamy, many men had more than one wife and some had as many as four.

You don't have to travel outside the United States to find polygamy, however. Although polygamy was outlawed in Utah in 1896, polygamous marriages have been increasing there since 1950 among Mormon fundamentalists, very traditional members of the Church of Jesus Christ of Latter-day Saints. The church's founder, Joseph Smith, taught that one way to attain the highest level of heaven was to have as many children as possible, so he encouraged men to marry more than one woman. Today, some Mormon fundamentalist men have as many as ten wives and it is estimated that about 2 percent of Utah's population (that is, about 40,000 people) are involved in polygamous marriages. Utah officials have decided not to prosecute Mormons for polygamy per se, but rather to more vigorously police and prosecute polygamists for problems associated with polygamy in Utah: statutory rape, incest, child abuse, and welfare fraud (Brooke, 1998; Williams, 1997).

There are two types of polygamy. The most common is **polygyny**, in which one man is married concurrently to two or more women. This was the practice we observed in Guinea and we find in Utah. Polygyny has been found historically in many different societies throughout the world, including Iran, Iraq, and China. People practice polygyny to increase offspring, especially male offspring and to show off a man's wealth. Since men must be able to adequately support all their wives and children, polygyny is sometimes practiced by only the wealthiest men in the society. When practiced by men of lesser means, polygyny may impoverish the family (Brooke, 1998).

Polygyny benefits men by increasing their status, but how does it affect women? Some experts maintain that the presence of multiple wives in a household eases the domestic workload for all the women and gives them a system of mutual emotional support. Others, though, think polygyny is divisive for women, especially if co-wives must compete for their husband's attention and resources. Polygyny can also affect co-wives differently; for instance, the first wife may be accorded special status and privileges, or she may be considered a servant to her husband and his later wives (Brooke, 1998; O'Kelly & Carney, 1986).

The second form of polygamy is **polyandry**, in which one woman is married concurrently to two or more men. Polyandry is rare and is found only in very poor societies where a lack of financial resources makes marriage an unattainable goal for many, especially if the norm is for husbands to be the economic providers (Lamanna & Riedmann, 1994). In such cases, brothers may share a wife. Polyandry may also be found in societies where female infanticide (the systematic killing of female babies) is practiced. As the Global Insights box shows, female infanticide causes a sex imbalance in the population, which in turn eventually leads to a shortage of female marriage partners (see also Shenon, 1994).

Polygamy may seem strange to many of us, but keep in mind that most adults in our population marry more than once. About half of all first marriages end in divorce within seven years, but almost 60 percent of those who divorce remarry, some more than once. In light of these high rates of divorce and remarriage, it could be said that we actually practice *serial monogamy*, not monogamy.

Apart from how many marriage partners a person may have is the question of who can marry. In most societies, including our own, the social norm for choosing a partner is **endogamy**, marrying within one's social stratum or group. In other words, in most societies people are expected to choose marriage partners from the same social class, race (and to a less extent, ethnicity), religion, and even educational background as themselves. There is evidence, however, that in the United States endogamy is weakening somewhat, especially given the sharp increase in interracial marriages—more than 400 percent—since 1970 (Jaret, 1995; U.S. Department of Commerce, Bureau of the Census, 1997). However, for some groups, the expectation of endogamy remains strong (see, for exam-

GLOBAL INSIGHTS   Where Have All the Young Women Gone?

In the United States and Europe, even among women and men who have a preference for sons, there is still strong disapproval of the use of medical technology, such as ultrasound and amniocentesis, to select for sex (Kolker & Burke, 1992). But in some countries, such as China and India, where son preference is exceptionally strong, technology is increasingly being used not for diagnostic purposes, but to identify the sex of a fetus (Burns, 1994; Gargan, 1991). If the fetus is the "wrong" sex—that is, a female—the parents frequently opt for an abortion. A Chinese publication recently quoted a man from a rural community who said, "Ultrasound is really worthwhile, even though my wife had to go through four abortions to get a son" (Kristof, 1991, p. C12).

In these societies, sons are favored over daughters because tradition dictates that property is passed on from father to son, and also because sons provide financial security for their parents in old age. Before the widespread availability of ultrasound and amniocentesis, sex selection was accomplished through infanticide: female infants were often killed by being left exposed to the elements or by suffocation, or else they died early in childhood from neglect and lack of food (Hegde, 1999).

However, regardless of the means used, sex selection produces a sex imbalance in a country's population. As the table shows, in many of these countries, males outnumber females; in most countries throughout the world, there are slightly more females than males.

In countries where the sex ratio is skewed in favor of males, it becomes increasingly difficult for some men to find marriage partners. In China, for example, there are now 120 males for every 100 females (Fang, 1998; She-non, 1994). One outcome of this imbalance is a growing market in kidnapped young women who are sold as brides to male farmers from rural villages where the sex ratio is even more skewed than in the cities. Human rights groups and even the Chinese government estimate that tens of thousands of young women have been kidnapped and sold. Despite recent campaigns to break up kidnapping rings and severely punish the bride traffickers, the problem is expected to worsen. In 1998 alone, 1 million Chinese boys were born whom experts believe will not be able to find wives when they grow up.

Actual and Expected Ratios of Males to Females for Selected Countries

| | RATIO OF MALES TO FEMALES | |
Country	Actual Ratio	Expected Ratio[*]
China	1.066	1.010
India	1.077	1.020
Pakistan	1.105	1.025
Bangladesh	1.064	1.025
Nepal	1.050	1.025
Egypt	1.047	1.020

[*]Based on a model of stable population and assuming 1.059 as the sex ratio at birth.

Source: Coale, 1991, p. 522.

ple, Glaser, 1997; Niebuhr, 1997). For instance, a lesbian friend who is Jewish told us about her mother's reaction to meeting her new lover, who happens to be Catholic: "What," her mother asked, "you couldn't find a nice Jewish girl?"

The opposite of endogamy is **exogamy**, a social norm that prescribes people marry outside their social stratum or group. In some societies, exogamy is encouraged to strengthen alliances among villages (O'Kelly & Carney, 1986). Exogamy may also be encouraged by some groups within a society. For instance, in the United States, young women have traditionally been encouraged to seek a marriage partner from a higher social class as a means of upward mobility. Marrying "down" or "out," however, can lead to ridicule or even ostracism. Among the Old Order Amish, for example, marrying someone who is not Amish is cause for imposing the *Meidung* (shunning from the community) (Kephart & Zellner, 1991).

Residential Patterns

Residential patterns refer to customs governing where newly formed families will live. One option is for a married couple to live with the husband's family, or at least in his village or community. This residential pattern, called **patrilocality**, is still common in the nonindustrialized world. In rural India, for example, a newly married woman leaves her family and village and moves in with their husband's family, where she is under the strict control of her mother-in-law. Her mother-in-law directs all household work and keeps close watch on all her movements. The bride must show respect and deference not only to her mother-in-law, but also to her new male kin. Any norm violation on her part brings shame to her family, and can result in physical punishment or even death for her (O'Kelly & Carney, 1986; Stone & James, 1995; Waters, 1999).

In the less common residential pattern of **matrilocality**, a married couple lives with the wife's family, or at least in her village or community. Matrilocality is most often found in horticultural societies, where men must often travel long distances to engage in warfare or trade. With men away for extended periods of time, mothers, daughters, and sisters are left to mind the property and handle all domestic affairs, so it is important that they know one another well and have strong allegiances to each other (O'Kelly & Carney, 1986).

In our society and other industrialized societies, the common residential pattern is **neolocality**, in which the married couple establishes its own residence apart from either the husband's or wife's family. With our geographic mobility, this can mean living across the country, but many couples still choose to live close to one or both spouses' parents or relatives, sometimes in the same neighborhood. Sometimes, because of the high cost of hous-

ing, newlyweds move in with one spouse's parents to save money for their own residence. In this way, they temporarily form a kind of extended family.

Descent and Inheritance

During the 1970s, the television miniseries, *Roots*, won critical acclaim from historians, educators, and filmmakers, but on a more practical level it inspired thousands of people to try to trace their ancestry. The way the members of a society trace descent is important because it determines who will be identified as kin and who is eligible for inheritance.

Descent may be traced through either parent, or *unilineally*. There are two types of unilineal descent. The most common is **patrilineal descent**, in which descent is traced through the father's side of the family. In societies that practice patrilineal descent, fathers pass to their sons (usually the first-born son) property, and sometimes a title or position as well, when they die. The wife/mother has no claim to her husband's property, and, with her husband's death, her well-being is also entrusted to the son (O'Kelly & Carney, 1986).

The second type of unilineality is **matrilineal descent**, in which descent is traced through the mother's side of the family. Among the Akan of Ghana, for instance, sons and daughters share privileges and responsibilities based on their descent from a common mother. Matrilineality is most often found in horticultural societies probably for the same reason that matrilocality developed in these societies: Men are often absent for long periods of time and property is safeguarded by women who remain behind (O'Kelly & Carney, 1986).

If descent is traced through both parents it is called **bilateral descent**. Although hunting and gathering societies do not have inheritance, most use a bilateral descent system to trace kin. Bilateral descent results in a larger kin network, which comes in handy during times of crisis or need. In the United States, we also use a bilateral system of descent, although some of our descent norms are patrilineal. For example, although a woman may now legally retain her surname when she marries, that surname is her father's. Her children, in turn, will bear the surname of their father, a practice that has been upheld by the courts (Lindgren & Taub, 1993).

Power and Authority

When we think of marriages and families, we think of partnerships, not power struggles. We like to think that each family member, or at least each spouse, has input into decision making, and if there is disagreement, everyone tries to compromise. We call this kind of family an **egalitarian family** because power and authority are shared by family members. Research shows that in the United

These Amish children grow up in patriarchal nuclear families in closely cooperating communities united by both religion and way of life. According to the structural functional perspective, what basic functions do all families perform? According to the conflict and feminist perspectives, what specific social placements or social locations do families provide for their members? How does social location relate to social inequality?

States and other industrialized societies, egalitarianism in families has increased during the past twenty-five years, especially in households where both spouses work (Blumstein & Schwartz, 1983; Pyke, 1994). But in most families in most societies, family members are vested with different levels of power and authority.

If most power and authority are held by the wife/mother or eldest female family member, the family is **matriarchal.** Single-parent families in which only a mother is present are often described as matriarchal, but in such cases, the woman's authority derives only from the fact that there is no man present to be in charge. But on a societal level, single mothers can hardly be considered powerful. In our society, for example, single mothers are typically regarded negatively and are disproportionately represented among the poor. Even in societies with matrilocality and matrilineality, research shows that women do not accrue enough power and authority to be considered matriarchs (O'Kelly & Carney, 1986).

The most common family structure throughout the world is the **patriarchal family,** where most power and authority are held by the husband/father or eldest male family member. Even in our own society, where individual families try to be more egalitarian, norms, including those enacted into law, continue to reinforce patriarchy. Consider, for example, that most states continue to give husbands the legal right to decide domicile (where the family will live), although some courts have made exceptions for women determined to be the family's chief breadwinner. In fact, most states automatically assign women to their husbands' domicile when they marry, even if they live apart from their husbands because of their careers or to attend school. The consequences for a woman can be serious, especially if her husband's domicile is in a different state than her premarital domicile.

For instance, she must reregister to vote, she may lose the right to attend a university in her home state as a resident student (thereby losing in-state tuition benefits), and she may be ineligible to run for public office in her home state (Lindgren & Taub, 1993).

Later in the chapter we will discuss other problems that arise from our society's patriarchal family structure. First, though, let's review several theoretical perspectives on families to see how sociologists have come to understand this social institution.

REFLECTING ON

Families throughout the World

1. Many people in the United States grow up in a household where at least one grandparent lives with them or a grandparent raises them. If you've had this experience, what did you like and dislike about it? If you haven't had this experience, what do you think the advantages and disadvantages of living with a grandparent might be?

2. Do you know any accordian families or families of choice? What are they like?

3. Do you think polygyny benefits women? Why or why not?

4. Think about your own family. Do you live near relatives? Would you describe your family as patrilocal, matrilocal, or neolocal? What do you like or dislike about your family's residence pattern?

5. Did you ever try to trace your ancestry? If so, how did you do it and what did you find out?

6. What is your idea of the ideal family? Why?

SOCIOLOGICAL PERSPECTIVES ON FAMILIES

Structural functionalists, conflict theorists, feminists, and symbolic interactionists have all developed theories about families. Let's consider each perspective in turn.

Structural Functionalism

Every type of society has families. They may be nuclear or extended; patriarchal, matriarchal, or egalitarian. Regardless of their type or structure, the family is universal. To explain the universality of the family, structural functionalists look at the common functions all families perform, instead of focusing on the diversity among families. Functionalists have identified five basic functions that families perform:

1. *Regulation of sexual behavior and reproduction.* No society permits its members to have sex whenever and with whomever they choose. All societies have norms to regulate sexual behavior, and the family is the social institution through which these norms are enforced. Marriage and family norms specify who may have sex with whom and under what conditions. Although the reasons for these norms vary from society to society, one shared reason is to ensure that children are cared for. Consequently, the family's function of regulating sexual behavior and reproduction also ensures that the population of the society will be replaced over time.

2. *Socialization.* Within the family, children, the newest members of society, are given their first instructions in the society's norms. Children are also taught language, values, customs, and the skills needed to be productive members of their society. In preindustrial societies, the family is the primary educational institution. But even in modern industrial societies, the family shares the education function with schools by, for example, reinforcing values and customs taught in school, helping children with homework, and providing educational toys and books.

3. *Social location.* Membership in a family bestows on an individual specific social locations, including membership in a social class, a racial or ethnic identity, and usually a religious affiliation. And, as we have seen many times in this book, a person's social location opens or closes doors to certain opportunities. For instance, social class and race or ethnicity strongly influence the quality of one's education, health care, and housing.

4. *Financial support and physical security.* People need food and shelter to survive, and these most basic needs are provided by the family. The family functions as a system for sharing resources, and it offers some insurance during times of financial hardship. This is as true in industrial societies as in preindustrial societies. If, for instance, a family member cannot find a job or cannot work because of disability, as in Sharon Kowalski's case at the opening of this chapter, the rest of the family will support and help them.

5. *Emotional support and caring.* The family has been described as a "haven in a heartless world" (Lasch, 1977), a private place where family members can be themselves (even their worst selves) without being criticized or ridiculed, and where they can express their feelings and receive love and affection. There is no other social institution that fulfills this uniquely human need.

Although functionalists focus on the functions of families, they do acknowledge that the family has problems. From their perspective, families are weakened when other social institutions fail to reinforce or support family functions. For instance, laws that make it easy for families to dissolve devalue family life and relationships. Still, for functionalists, even divorce has positive functions. Divorce can be a corrective for poor marriage choices by freeing individuals to seek more compatible partners and thus improving the quality of marriage generally (Parsons & Bales, 1955).

Evaluating Structural Functionalism. The universality of family cannot be denied, nor can we overlook the fact that families perform important social functions. However, critics of the functionalist perspective point out that by emphasizing what is supposedly common to all families, functionalists downplay the tremendous diversity among families. For example, while families provide financial support and physical protection for their members, the fact that they do so in many different ways has important consequences not only for family members, but for society as a whole. In some cultures, male family members are fed first, most, and best; if food is left over, the females may eat it. Within the family, then, females are not afforded the same support and security males are, and within the society, females have higher illness and death rates than males do. In these circumstances, the family is dysfunctional for females.

A related criticism has to do with functionalists' focus on the positive functions of families. Critics argue that by depicting the family as a "haven in a heartless world," functionalists mask the tension and violence that often occur in families. Later in the chapter, we will discuss the problem of family violence in more detail.

Conflict and Feminist Theories

Conflict and feminist theorists agree that the family serves important functions in society, but they think functionalists overlook how the family reproduces social inequality.

Conflict theorists are interested in the family's role of social placement. You know already that families give people social class standing and a racial or ethnic identity that in turn affects their access to various opportunities in life. At the same time, the family is also one of the primary ways that wealth and power are passed on intergenerationally. Inheritance thus preserves a society's stratification system and protects the wealth and power of individual families. A family's social class also affects whether they will have particular problems. Poor families, for instance, are more likely than wealthy families to have a family member die by street violence or a drug overdose. Conflict theorists attribute these problems not to weaknesses in poor families, but to the disadvantaged conditions in which they live (Collins, 1989; Mirandé, 1990).

Conflict theorists also look at inequality within the family, especially gender inequality. Drawing on the work of Frederich Engels (1942), a friend and colleague of Karl Marx, conflict theorists consider the relationship between husbands and wives similar to the relationship between capitalists and workers. Just as workers exchange their labor power for a wage, so do wives exchange their domestic labor and sexuality for the economic support of their husbands. And husbands, like capitalists, enjoy greater rights and privileges (Zaretsky, 1976). For instance, husbands have traditionally had an absolute right to the sexual services of their wives, so a husband could not be charged with raping his wife, no matter how brutally he behaved toward her. Today, even though all states have laws that allow husbands to be charged with rape, thirty-three states exempt husbands from rape charges under certain circumstances. For example, in some states a wife can file rape charges against her husband only if the couple has been living apart (Bergen, 1996).

Feminist theorists also see the family as an institution of social inequality, but they believe gender inequality in the family predates capitalism and exists in noncapitalist societies as well. Consequently, they focus more on patriarchy than on social class. The family, according to feminists, is the basis of all male domination over women. Women's subordination in the home is reinforced by other social institutions, such as the economy, which pays women less than men for similar work, and the legal system, which grants husbands greater family authority (such as the right to determine domicile). As we will see shortly, the legal system has also failed to protect women against men's violence in the home. According to feminist theorists, men use violence to control women. In fact, research shows that a wife's attempt to be independent of her husband (for example, by getting a job or returning to school) sometimes triggers domestic violence, as the man seeks to reinstate his dominance and authority in the family (Walby, 1986; Yllö, 1993).

Evaluating Conflict and Feminist Theories. The conflict and feminist perspectives are valuable for highlighting how inequality affects families and how family relationships reinforce social inequalities. However, critics maintain that conflict and feminist theorists give too much attention to family problems and overlook the positive aspects of family life. Not all families are oppressive, and some women and men are challenging traditional gender relations by forming more egalitarian marriages. Some studies, for example, report more men sharing housework and child care with their wives (Harrell, 1995; Snarey, 1993; Wilkie, 1993). The Doing Sociology box takes a closer look at other characteristics of "successful" families.

Symbolic Interactionism

Sociologist Jesse Bernard (1972) once wrote that within every marriage there are really two marriages—his and hers. What Bernard recognized was that the social actors in marriage, as in any form of social interaction, often give different meanings or interpretations to particular situations and events. The construction of meaning by family members as they interact with one another is the focus of symbolic interactionist theory. While functionalist, conflict, and feminist theorists look at the family in the context of the larger social structure, symbolic interactionists concentrate on the dynamics of interaction within the family. Indeed, interactionists argue that it is through their communication and daily interactions with

Blended families are formed when a couple with children divorces and one or both partners remarry and combine their families with the children over whom they have custody. The blended family may also include additional children from the new marriage. What factors in U.S. society have contributed to the dramatic increase in blended families? What are some other types of diversity in family forms in the United States?

DOING SOCIOLOGY

What Makes for Happy Families?

Although there are various ways to define *success*, we usually think of successful families as those who manage the stresses and strains of life together and who resolve the inevitable family conflicts fairly for everyone involved. In other words, successful families are happy families. Researchers who have studied successful families have identified a number of characteristics that they believe contribute to the families' success. Among the most important factors are:

Accord. Family members have developed ways for resolving their disagreements so that everyone feels satisfied with the outcome.

Communication. Successful families share information with one another. Family members talk openly about their ideas and beliefs and tell one another their feelings, including that they love and care for one another.

Financial management. Most families have limited resources that must be shared. Planning expenses and equitably distributing resources within the family build family members' sense of well-being. Of course, money management is especially difficult for poor families, and financial instability is a major contributor to family break-ups.

Health. Although we can take steps toward good health, illness and accidents can strike at anytime. Researchers have found that a physically or mentally ill family member imposes tremendous strain on the rest of the family and can lead to additional problems, including conflict between family members.

Support network. Families are usually thought of as support networks, but researchers emphasize the importance of extending the network beyond immediate family members. Successful families have support networks that include in-laws, cousins, and family friends, who can be counted on in times of crisis, but who also join the family in celebrations.

Celebrations. Observing special occasions, such as birthdays, graduations, and retirements builds bonds among family members. The celebrations need not be elaborate or expensive. What is important is that the event—and the family member—are acknowledged as special.

Traditions. In addition to celebrating special events, successful families develop special ways to celebrate an occasion that they repeat year after year, across generations. All family members, for instance, may gather every year at the eldest relatives' house to observe Passover with a Seder supper. Or on Thanksgiving, everyone might gather at a park for a family football game. Traditions are a way to honor family experiences and thus also solidify family bonds.

Time and routine. Apart from special events, successful families spend time together each day: They might have dinner together every night, with each family member responsible for a particular mealtime chore. Or they might spend time together watching a favorite TV show or talking about how their day went. Time spent together performing routine activities as well as having fun contributes to family stability.

Hardiness. Hardiness refers to family members' sense that all members of the family are committed to the family. In successful families, members feel they have control over their lives, but are committed to one another as well.

While some of these characteristics are more difficult to pinpoint than others, researchers tell us that they are the key ingredients in making a family resilient in times of crisis or strain.

Do you agree with these findings? Let's see what others think. Ask a sample of your peers what they consider to be the most important factors in making a family happy and why. Compare their responses with the researchers' findings and share the results with your class.

Sources: Cox, 1993; McCubbin & Patterson, 1981; Olson et al., 1983.

---

one another that partners, parents, and children construct "family."

For example, when two people marry and begin living together, they begin to construct a new merged identity, a *couple identity*. Although they retain some aspects of their individual selves, their daily interaction as a married couple, with one another and with others, changes both how they see themselves and how others see them. Their relationships with friends and their families of orientation also change. For instance, each partner probably had a friendship network before marriage. After marriage, partners often combine friendship networks, so that one partner doesn't perceive a network as a competitor for the spouse's attention.

Family and couple identities change over the course of a lifetime. Acquiring new roles, such as parent, affects other roles, such as spouse. The birth or adoption of a child, for example, often means that partners have less time for one another and for pursuing personal interests, and more financial and household responsibilities (Cowan

& Cowan, 1992). Symbolic interactionists look at the various ways family members adjust their individual and family identities in response to changing roles and crises (Davis, 1991). Some families adapt to change by reshaping their self-concepts and family images, while other families unravel. Divorce dismantles the couple identity and often restructures parental identities and roles (Vaughn, 1986). Men and women who divorce acquire new identities and roles (for example, divorcee, exhusband or ex-wife). If they remarry, they acquire a couple identity again, and if they marry someone who has children, they acquire yet another identity and role: stepmother or stepfather. Each family role also has norms attached to it. For example, a widow or widower is expected to wait a "respectable" amount of time after their spouse's death before dating again.

Evaluating Symbolic Interactionism.   Symbolic interactionism helps explain why, despite the commonalities among families, each family is still unique. Each family is a mosaic of individual personalities and personal histories, so that it develops its own identity with its own traditions and patterns of interaction. At the same time, symbolic interactionism helps explain commonalities across families within a society by looking at the norms governing family roles. Critics, however, charge that by focusing on the internal dynamics of individual families, symbolic interactionists don't see the bigger picture. They overlook both the impact of social structural conditions on the family and how families reinforce particular structural arrangements, such as social class and gender inequality. The criticisms are very important because symbolic interactionism may give the impression that families dissolve because of miscommunication or personality clashes between spouses. While these factors may certainly contribute to family breakdown, we must not overlook the strain imposed by external factors, such as work demands or the stress of living in poverty. Social structural conditions generate family conflict as much as, if not more than, incompatible personalities, but these conditions are largely ignored by symbolic interactionists.

REFLECTING ON

Sociological Perspectives on Families

1. Can you think of any other functions families perform that structural functionalists did not identify?
2. What are gender relations like in your own family? Do the members of your family seem satisfied with these relations? How about you? Would you like to see gender relations in your family changed in any way?

3. Symbolic interactionists believe that as family members interact, individual identities take shape and each person assumes a role that reflects his or her personality and interactions with others. For instance, one family member may emerge as the peacemaker in family conflicts, while another seems to make everyone laugh. In your family, do particular family members fill certain roles such as these? Can you explain the development of these roles as a symbolic interactionist would?

FAMILIES AND INTIMATE RELATIONSHIPS IN THE UNITED STATES

When we were growing up, television families were all alike: They were White and lived in a roomy house in a quiet suburban neighborhood. The television Mom stayed home and was happy about it, while Dad went off each day to a professional job. The youngsters (usually two) might get into mischief, but it was never anything serious. On one level, we knew that most people didn't live like that—certainly we didn't as the daughter of a car salesman and the son of a truck driver. But there was a lot to envy in those images. Money never seemed to worry the television families. In fact, when they had a problem, they solved it with good humor and understanding—and in only a half hour.

These media images distorted and idealized family life, but they were accurate in depicting most married women as stay-at-home moms: In 1960, fewer than 7 percent of women with children under eighteen worked outside the home. Moreover, about 90 percent of family households had two parents present. Only about 20 percent of the population was single/never married, and only about 4 percent was divorced (U.S. Department of Commerce, Bureau of the Census, 1995).

Figure 15.1 illustrates how American households have changed over the last several decades. Although married couples with children make up the second highest household category, only a minority of the women in those households are stay-at-home moms; 70 percent of married women with children under eighteen work outside the home. About 73 percent of family households with children under eighteen have two parents present. About 23 percent of the adult population is single/never married, and more than 9 percent are divorced (U.S. Department of Commerce, Bureau of the Census, 1997).

These statistics indicate not only how families have changed in the United States, but also how the diversity of American families has increased. In the remaining sec-

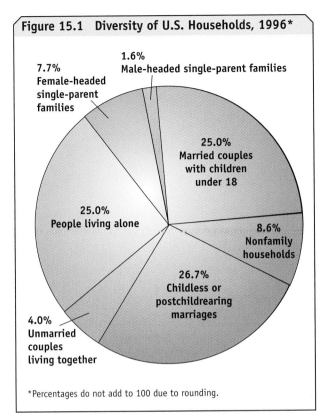

Figure 15.1 Diversity of U.S. Households, 1996*

7.7%
Female-headed
single-parent
families

1.6%
Male-headed single-parent families

25.0%
Married couples
with children
under 18

25.0%
People living alone

8.6%
Nonfamily
households

26.7%
Childless or
postchildrearing
marriages

4.0%
Unmarried
couples
living together

*Percentages do not add to 100 due to rounding.

Source: Compiled from U.S. Department of Commerce, Bureau of the Census, 1997.

tions of this chapter, we will consider diversity in a number of ways: diversity of intimate relationships, the diversity of problems in intimate relationships, and family diversity by race and ethnicity. Let's begin, however, by discussing how intimate relationships develop and the role of sexuality in intimate relationships.

Love, Romance, and Sex

Most of us can't conceive of two people who are not in love getting married. However, the natural connection we see between love and marriage is a relatively recent social development. Historically, love and marriage were viewed as separate concerns. Among the wealthy, marriage was too important an economic and political matter to be left to the whimsical emotion of love. Marriages were often carefully arranged so that land holding could be consolidated or political alliances forged. Even among peasants, arranged marriages were the norm and it was a good match if the families achieved some economic gain. It was not until the colonial period in the United States that arranged marriages for economic and political reasons became less important, and mutual attraction and feelings of love were gradually recognized as the bases for marriage (Aulette, 1994). Arranged marriages are still the norm in some societies, such as Pakistan and Turkme-

nistan (a small country bordering Iran, Afghanistan, and Uzbeskistan) (Hoge, 1997; Stanley, 1995).

We also tend to associate love and marriage with sex. But like love and marriage, norms regarding sex vary historically and cross-culturally. According to Aulette (1994), for example, in classical Greece, men married women, but took teenage boys as lovers. Among the Hagen, a contemporary horticultural society, sex is considered unclean and dangerous for women and men, married or unmarried, and both are expected to abstain from it as much as possible. In contrast, among the Nuer, a pastoral society of sub-Saharan Africa, adolescent girls and boys are expected to have many premarital sexual affairs, although once married, adultery is acceptable only for men (O'Kelly & Carney, 1986).

In the United States, sex norms have also varied. In the early 1970s, for example, 37 percent of respondents to a national survey said premarital sex is always wrong. By 1988, 26 percent expressed this attitude, but in the early 1990s, only 19.7 percent felt that premarital sex is always wrong (Kain, 1990; Michael et al., 1994). Moreover, today, half of young women and three-fourths of young men have sexual intercourse before age eighteen. These rates are about 20 percent higher than 1970s' rates. The average age of first intercourse is sixteen for boys and seventeen for girls (Children's Defense Fund, 1997; 1998). Such statistics raise concerns that Americans, especially young Americans, are promiscuous. But research indicates that U.S. teens are not more sexually active than their European peers, although they have less access to contraceptives, counseling services, and sex education programs (Children's Defense Fund, 1997; Jones, 1989).

Attitudes toward homosexuality have also changed in recent years, although our society's sex norms still consider heterosexual relationships normal and homosexual relationships deviant. In 1976, 47 percent of college freshmen surveyed favored laws prohibiting homosexual relationships. Ten years later, the figure had risen to 53 percent, but after 1987, there was a steady decline in support for such laws, reaching a low of 30.6 percent in 1995 (U.S. Department of Justice, Bureau of Justice Statistics, 1995). Overall, about 70 percent of Americans think homosexual sex is wrong, but more than 73 percent believe homosexuals should have equal rights in terms of job opportunities (Michael et al., 1994; Schmalz, 1993; Wolfe, 1998). Despite slowly liberalizing attitudes toward homosexuals, homophobia remains strong, and gay men and lesbians experience disproportionately greater physical violence than members of other minority communities (Cage, 1993).

Increasingly, then, our intimate relationships have become a matter of personal choice, although these choices are made within the constraints of prevailing social norms. Let's discuss some of the family forms and intimate relationships that are currently part of our social landscape.

Why are gay and lesbian couples denied legal rights to marriage and often parenting opportunities? What does research show about the psychological and social adjustments of children in families created by homosexual parents compared to children of heterosexual parents? Are heterosexual children raised in homosexual families more likely to experience gender identity problems?

Singles and Domestic Partners

When we think of singles, most of us probably think of young heterosexual women and men who have not yet married. However, the single population in the United States is far more diverse. In addition to never-married heterosexuals, the single population includes gay men and lesbians who are not in a committed relationship; women and men, heterosexual and homosexual, who are not married but living with an intimate partner in what is called a *domestic partnership*; and divorced, separated, and widowed women and men with or without dependent children. We will consider the special concerns of divorce and single parenting later in this chapter. In this section, we will focus on heterosexual and homosexual never-married singles and domestic partners.

Heterosexual Singles and Domestic Partners In our society, the word *bachelor* conjures up images of hip young men who "play the field," and cherish their independence. But what comes to mind when we think of unmarried women? Unmarried women are often depicted as lonely, "on the prowl" for a "good catch," and willing to use sex to get men to marry them before their biological clocks stop ticking. Of course, all these images are stereotypes, and, like most stereotypes, they bear little resemblance to real-life experiences.

For most heterosexual young adults, male and female, singlehood is a temporary status. The vast majority eventually marry, but they are delaying marriage longer than in the past. In 1970, for instance, the median age at first marriage was 20.6 for women and 22.5 for men; by 1990, it was 24.0 for women and 25.9 for men (U.S. Department of Commerce, Bureau of the Census, 1997). Still, as

Table 15.1 shows, the number of people who have never married has increased across age groups in recent years.

Singles delay and postpone marriage for several reasons, including more positive social attitudes toward singlehood; greater reluctance to marry given high divorce rates and awareness of domestic violence; and greater availability of contraceptives, which means fewer marriages from unwanted pregnancy. But one of the most important reasons young people give for delaying marriage is economic constraints (Bedard, 1992). In the last thirty years, housing prices have increased significantly, while the number of jobs that pay a wage adequate for establishing an independent household has declined (Children's Defense Fund, 1998). Consequently, in contrast to the image of the swinging single's "pad," a substantial percentage of young adults—53 percent of those aged eighteen to twenty-four and 12 percent of those aged twenty-five to thirty-four—are living with their parents (Lehmann-Haupt, 1999; U.S. Department of Commerce, Bureau of the Census, 1997).

Some people also have difficulty finding suitable marriage partners. Women and men who are physically or mentally disabled, for example, need intimacy and sexual gratification the same as other people, but their needs may go unfulfilled because others view them as deviant, unattractive, or sexless (Hall, 1992; Kelly, 1995). African American women also face some difficulty finding marriage partners for several reasons. One reason is the high mortality rate of young African American men. The death rate of African American men aged fifteen to twenty-four is 249 per 100,000, whereas for White men of the same age, the death rate is 123 per 100,000 (U.S. Department of Health and Human Services, 1998). A second reason

TABLE 15.1 Never-Married Persons as a Percent of the Total Population, by Sex and Age, 1970 and 1996

	MALE		FEMALE	
Age	1970	1996	1970	1996
Total	18.9%	26.8%	13.7%	19.9%
18–19 years old	92.8	97.6	75.6	92.2
20–24 years old	54.7	81.0	35.8	68.5
25–29 years old	19.1	52.0	10.5	37.6
30–34 years old	9.4	29.6	6.2	20.5
35–39 years old	7.2	20.8	5.4	13.1
40–44 years old	6.3	14.2	4.9	9.7
45–54 years old	7.5	8.1	4.9	6.3
55–64 years old	7.8	5.0	6.8	4.7
65 years old and over	7.5	7.7	7.7	8.2

Source: U.S. Department of Commerce, Bureau of the Census, 1995, pp. 54-55; 1997, p. 56.

is the disproportionate number of young African American men who are in prison. Although African American men make up only about 6 percent of the U.S. population, they are nearly 47 percent of the prison population (U.S. Department of Justice, Bureau of Justice Statistics, 1995). A third reason fewer African American than White women marry is that African American men have poor economic prospects, which makes them less desirable partners (Lloyd & South, 1996; Tucker & Mitchell-Kernan, 1995; Wilson, 1987).

Instead of marrying, some heterosexual singles choose a **domestic partnership**, a cohabiting relationship between intimate partners not married to each other. Domestic partnerships appear to be an increasingly popular lifestyle choice. In 1996, more than 4 million unmarried heterosexual couples were living together in the United States, an increase of more than 2 million since 1980 and more than 3 million since 1970 (U.S. Department of Commerce, Bureau of the Census, 1997). The numbers are small (just over 6 percent of U.S. couples) compared with both the number of married couples and the number of domestic partnerships in countries such as Sweden and Norway, where 12 percent of heterosexual couples live in domestic partnerships (Blanc, 1987; Kammeyer, 1987). Still, the increase over the past twenty-five years has been substantial, and current counts may actually be underestimates, since many people do not report their cohabitation status to census takers (Bedard, 1992).

Our knowledge of heterosexual domestic partnerships is limited by the fact that most of the research focuses on college students and other young people. However, only

20.1 percent of domestic partnerships involve couples under age twenty-five. Most (58.6 percent) cohabiting partners are aged twenty-five to forty-four; 15.3 percent are aged forty-five to sixty-four; and 5.6 percent are sixty-five and older (U.S. Department of Commerce, Bureau of the Census, 1997). Although domestic partnerships vary considerably with people at different stages of life, sociologists have nevertheless identified several trends.

First, researchers report that most domestic partnerships are impermanent, usually lasting two years or less (Bumpass & Sweet, 1991). Most domestic partners either break up within this period of time or marry instead of adopting cohabitation as a permanent lifestyle. Most heterosexual domestic partners are also childless, although each partner may have one or more children from a previous marriage. Overall, 36 percent of domestic partners have children under fifteen years old living with them (U.S. Department of Commerce, Bureau of the Census, 1997). In the past, when domestic partners considered adding children to their household, they usually decided to marry first (Blumstein & Schwartz, 1983), but recent research indicates that the decision by cohabitors to marry is no longer influenced by a desire to begin having children (Manning, 1995).

A majority of domestic partners (56 percent) have never been married, and many have divorced parents (U.S. Department of Commerce, Bureau of the Census, 1991). Young adults whose parents are divorced express greater support for cohabitation than those whose parents are married (Black & Sprenkle, 1991). About a third of domestic partners are divorced themselves and say they prefer cohabitation to traditional marriage, at least temporarily, because it affords them the benefits of intimacy without the legal and economic entanglements of marriage. However, some domestic partners come to discover that legal "entanglements" can actually be legal protections. For example, if the domestic partners break up, one partner may lose out financially if property and assets have been acquired jointly but joint ownership cannot be proven. Even if the relationship endures, partners may confront other legal difficulties. For instance, if one partner gets sick or is disabled, the other may be barred from hospital visits and have no say in medical decisions. If one partner dies without a will, property that was intended for the surviving partner may end up with relatives, since they are the ones with legal standing (Rankin, 1987).

However, while difficulties sometimes arise for heterosexual domestic partners, they at least have the option to legally marry. Gay and lesbian partners do not have that option, and as we saw in the story of Sharon Kowalski and Karen Thompson, the problems posed by domestic partnerships are compounded by the social stigma attached to gay and lesbian relationships.

Gay and Lesbian Singles and Domestic Partners.   There is no way to determine how many gay men and lesbians live in the United States. Because of the social stigma attached to homosexuality, many hide or "closet" their sexual orientation, at least from some people or in certain situations, such as at work. For this reason, and because social science research has traditionally focused on heterosexuals, accurate knowledge and genuine appreciation of gay and lesbian relationships are still goals rather than achievements.

Much of the research that is being done on gay and lesbian relationships is by gay and lesbian social scientists, and the findings indicate that there is as much diversity as there is among heterosexual men and women; there is no "homosexual lifestyle." The research also refutes many common myths about gay and lesbian relationships, such as that gays and lesbians are sexually promiscuous and unable to form committed intimate relationships. Studies show that although gay men do have more partners on average than straight men, most also establish enduring intimate relationships (Kelly, 1995; Meredith, 1986). Research even indicates that lesbian couples have more stable relationships than either heterosexual couples or gay male couples (Blumstein & Schwartz, 1983).

Some researchers feel that gay and lesbian relationship stability is held to a higher standard than stability in heterosexual relationships. For example, about half of all heterosexual marriages end in divorce within seven years, hardly an ideal of relationship stability. In contrast, in her research on gay and lesbian families, Kath Weston (1991) found that when gay and lesbian partners break up, they often maintain a close relationship by making a transi-

tion from lovers to friends. Weston argues, therefore, that gay and lesbian relationships are actually more stable on average than heterosexual marriages: "If two people cease being lovers after six years but remain friends and family for another forty, they have indeed achieved a relationship of long standing" (Weston, 1991, p. 120).

Gay and lesbian partners may not legally marry in the United States. In 1993, a lesbian couple in Hawaii challenged that state's ban on homosexual marriage, arguing that it was unconstitutional. The state Supreme Court ordered the government to demonstrate a compelling interest to support the ban. In 1996, a Circuit Court judge ruled that no compelling reason had been established and ordered the state to grant marriage licenses to same-sex couples. The state appealed the decision and, in 1998, the issue was put to a public vote in a ballot initiative. Voters in Hawaii decided by an overwhelming majority to allow the legislature to amend the state constitution to outlaw same-sex marriages. But even if Hawaii had allowed same-sex marriage, a new federal law, the Defense of Marriage Act, relieves other states from the legal obligation of recognizing same-sex marriages performed elsewhere (Goldberg, 1996). Meanwhile, an increasing number of municipal governments, universities, and corporations, including Lotus Development Corporation and Disney, are openly recognizing gay and lesbian domestic partnerships, and some cities allow gay and lesbian partners to officially register their relationships. Some people think registration is important because such public recognition lends legitimacy to the relationship. Registration may also have practical benefits, including insurance coverage for partners, family leaves, family membership rates, and inheritance protection. However, critics of domestic partnership registration worry about the consequences for those who choose not to register. Will a certificate of registration—or a marriage certificate—become evidence of a committed intimate relationship so that those who choose not to register are denied rights and benefits (Robson, 1992; Stacey, 1998)?

Heterosexual Marriages

A marriage is a legally binding contractual agreement. However, unlike most contracts, the conditions of the agreement cannot be changed or negotiated by the two parties involved. Only the state has the right to set the terms of the marriage contract. In fact, the contracting parties rarely even review the conditions of the agreement before entering into it.

Historically, a marriage contract specified an exchange relationship between husband and wife. A wife's obligations included caring for the marital household and complying with her husband's requests for sex. In return, the husband was expected to financially support his wife in a manner he deemed appropriate. The husband was

In about 20 percent of two-parent families with young children and working mothers, fathers are the sole caregivers while the mothers are at work. In what ways, and why, are fathers' roles changing in U.S. families? In any given year, about what percentage of single-parent families is headed by fathers?

legally granted all decision-making authority in the family (Lindgren & Taub, 1993). Today, we tend to think of marriage as a partnership rather than an exchange relationship, but vestiges of the traditional marriage contract exist in many contemporary marriages.

Consider, for example, the division of labor within the home. Studies conducted for more than a decade show that wives may spend as much as five times more hours per week on housework than their husbands (Shelton & John, 1993). This may not seem unfair if spouses are exchanging services according to the traditional marriage contract—she does the housework, and he works in the paid labor force to support them financially—but this model applies to only a minority of contemporary families in the United States. Most married women today are employed outside the home, and although husbands in two-earner households spend more time on housework than men who are sole breadwinners, they still do significantly less than their wives. Husbands today express a greater willingness to "help" their wives with the housework, but even in two-earner households, the prevailing attitude of both women and men is that housework is primarily the woman's responsibility no matter what other demands she has on her time (Harrell, 1995; Shelton, 1992; Wilkie, 1993). In fact, research shows that men are more critical of gender inequality in the workplace than they are of gender inequality in the home (Kane & Sanchez, 1992). Consequently, employed wives shoulder a *double work load.* They work what sociologist Arlie Hochschild (1989) calls the **second shift**: They are wage earners *and* they do significantly more housework than their husbands.

Regardless of the amount of time spent on housework, the division of labor in the home differs in terms of which chores each spouse typically does. Wives do most of the daily chores, such as cooking and cleaning. The chores men do are done less regularly and are less repetitive. So, for example, most wives prepare their families' meals, which must be done at least once or twice every day, whereas husbands usually mow the lawn and do minor home repairs—occasional chores. Thus, wives' work in the home binds them to a fairly fixed schedule, while husbands have more control over when they will do their chores (Hochschild, 1989; Shelton, 1992).

The differences between women's and men's work in the home have important consequences, especially for wives. For example, working the "second shift" lessens wives' leisure time. One study, in fact, found that husbands spend much of their leisure time watching television or listening to the radio, while many wives' leisure time could actually be classified as housework, such as sewing, canning and preserving fruits, baking, and preparing meals to freeze for future use (Shelton, 1992). Working wives must also strike a balance between home and employment in ways that men are not required to face. Husbands' relative freedom from household labor affords them more time to pursue employment opportunities, whereas wives' greater responsibility at home may restrict their employment opportunities (Shelton, 1992; but for a different perspective, see Hochschild, 1997).

Of course, some marriages are relatively egalitarian, with a more equal division of household labor between the spouses. One of the most important factors in egalitarian marriage is that both wife and husband believe that housework is not "women's work," but rather something family members do for one another (Coltrane, 1989; Harrell, 1995). However, even among couples striving for an egalitarian marriage, an equal division of housework usually ends when children join the household. Let's consider, then, families with children.

Families with Children

In the United States, as in most other societies throughout the world, married couples are expected to have children. Historically, couples without children were either regarded as selfish or pitied for their "barrenness." Most couples do conform to cultural expectations: 85 percent of American couples have children and, according to Baca Zinn and Eitzen (1993), about two-thirds of couples without children want them, but are infertile (see also May, 1995).

The birth rate and average number of children born to women in the United States have declined significantly since 1800, as Table 15.2 on page 404 shows. We see, too, that both birth rate and family size have varied only slightly over the last three decades. Most couples today have only one or two children.

What has also changed in recent years is the way people can go about having children, as we'll discuss next.

TABLE 15.2 Birth Rate and Average Number of Births per Adult Woman, United States, 1800–1996

Year	Births per 1,000 Population	Average Number of Births per Adult Woman
1800	58.0	7.0
1850	48.0	5.4
1900	32.0	3.5
1925	25.1	3.0
1936	18.4	2.1
1950	24.1	3.2
1957	25.0	3.6
1970	18.4	2.4
1975	14.8	1.7
1980	15.8	1.9
1985	15.8	1.8
1991	16.4	2.1
1992	15.9	1.9
1993	15.7	1.8
1994	15.6	1.8
1995	15.3	1.7
1996	14.5	1.6

Source: Population Today, March, 1997, p. 6; M. Baca Zinn & D. S. Eitzen (1993). *Diversity in families.* NY: HarperCollins, p. 296; U.S. Department of Commerce, Bureau of the Census, 1997, p. 9.

New Reproductive Technologies. It is estimated that of the 60.2 million women of reproductive age in the United States, 10 to 13 percent are unable to conceive or maintain a pregnancy (Altman, 1998). There are also women with physical disabilities who wish to have children, but for whom pregnancy and childbirth pose severe health risks (Asch, 1989). Postmenopausal women who want to have a child are unable to become pregnant because they are no longer fertile. Physically able single women may also wish to have children, but do not want to marry or even enter into an intimate relationship with a man in order to become pregnant. Also, an increasing number of lesbian and gay couples wish to become parents (Feigenbaum, 1996). Just three decades ago, these groups faced an unsolvable problem, but today, **new reproductive technologies (NRTs)**, which include a variety of laboratory techniques, allow members of all these groups to become parents.

Following the birth of the first "test tube" baby in 1978, reproductive technology developed rapidly. Today, there are an array of options available, including *in vitro* ("test tube") fertilization (IVF). In the standard IVF procedure, a woman takes a prescribed dosage of a fertility drug in order to stimulate the production of eggs, which are subsequently removed and fertilized with the woman's husband's sperm. Some of the embryos that result from the laboratory fertilization are then implanted in the woman's uterus; remaining embryos are usually frozen. An infertile woman can also use IVF by using eggs donated (often anonymously) by another woman. The donor eggs are then fertilized in the laboratory with the husband's or a donor's sperm and the embryos implanted in the infertile woman's uterus. This was the form of IVF used by a sixty-three-year-old California woman who gave birth to a healthy baby girl in 1996 (Kolata, 1997).

Male infertility accounts for about 40 percent of fertility problems, but in such cases IVF is still an option since eggs can be fertilized using donated sperm, typically from a sperm bank. Donated sperm is also often used in *artificial insemination,* a less complicated technique in which sperm is injected into a woman's vagina or uterus, allowing fertilization to take place inside her body.

Another NRT is *surrogacy,* in which a couple contracts with a woman who agrees to undergo embryo implantation or artificial insemination and to carry the resulting pregnancy to term. The surrogate mother also agrees to give up her parental rights when the baby is born and to give sole custody to the baby's father so that his partner can then legally adopt the baby. In 1992, about 4,000 babies in the United States were born through surrogacy (Belkin, 1992).

Not surprisingly, NRTs have generated considerable controversy. The Social Policy box discusses some of the legal and ethical issues posed by various NRTs. Let's now consider what happens to family life after a baby arrives.

Two-Parent Families. Despite the widespread belief that the birth of a child brings marriage partners closer together, research shows that children increase stress and may lower marital satisfaction (Larson, 1988). New parents are usually excited about the arrival of their baby, but they are rarely prepared for the disruption a baby causes in their lives: the loss of sleep, spontaneity, and time to pursue personal interests; the increased financial pressures and household chores (Cowan & Cowan, 1992; 1998). However, these problems are not experienced in the same way by women and men. Although most men today are present at the birth of their children, they are significantly less involved than women in primary child care (bathing, changing clothes, and feeding).

Fathers today are expected to be more nurturing and involved with their children than fathers in the past, and today's fathers, especially in two-earner households, do

Social Policy
Should New Reproductive Technologies Be Regulated?

The Issue

The new reproductive technologies (NRTs) are miracles to some people who have had difficulty conceiving a child. However, each NRT is also accompanied by a host of legal and ethical questions. Let's consider some of them.

The Debate

One question that arises about IVF and related procedures is what to do with unused embryos. For example, frozen embryos are now accumulating at a rate of about 10,000 per year (Kolata, 1997). Prospective parents pay a fee to store their frozen embryos for future use. But suppose a couple divorces, or one partner dies, and there is disagreement over the fate of the stored embryos? In one such case that reached the Supreme Court of Tennessee in 1992, a divorced couple fought over the custody of seven frozen embryos, the products of *in vitro* fertilization using the former spouses' eggs and sperm. The ex-wife wished to donate the embryos to an infertile couple; the ex-husband wished to have the embryos destroyed. The court ultimately found in favor of the partner wishing to destroy the embryos, reasoning that no one should be forced to become a biological parent even if that individual was not being asked to raise the child. However, the court did note that had the biological mother sought to use the embryos

herself because she had no other means of bearing a child, her concerns would have carried greater weight in the decision (Becker et al., 1994).

In another case, a woman died before she and her husband were able to use the embryos they had frozen. Before her death, this woman stated that she wanted the embryos destroyed if she died, and her husband agreed. Following her death, her husband changed his mind and began looking for a surrogate who would have the embryos implanted and carry them to term. The hospital staff where the embryos were stored now faced a dilemma: Should they honor the wishes of the dead woman or turn the embryos over to the husband to use as he pleased? (Kolata, 1997).

Situations such as these will probably continue to be handled on a case-by-case basis, since no government agency has been charged with regulating *in vitro* fertilization or the storage and disposition of frozen embryos. In 1992, Congress passed legislation to establish federal standards for fertility clinics, but these are primarily "truth in advertising" laws, requiring fertility clinics to provide "consumers" with accurate information on their success rates. Meanwhile, scientific "progress" in reproductive technologies continues to expand the boundaries of the possible. After the announcement in 1997 that scientists had successfully cloned a sheep, many people became con-

cerned that humans might be cloned. Human cloning would allow a couple to give birth to identical twins, with each twin born several years apart. If they don't like the first child, they might have the cloned frozen embryo destroyed. Or, since embryos can be frozen indefinitely, a woman could give birth to her own identical twin (Kolata, 1997). In 1998, researchers in South Korea announced that they had successfully cloned a human cell. They halted their experiments for ethical reasons, but pointed out that their work demonstrates that human cloning is possible in the more immediate rather than distant future (Wu Dunn, 1998). As one scientist recently remarked, human cloning "is going to happen sooner or later... you'd better get used to it" (quoted in Kolata, 1998, p. A12).

What Do You Think?

Clearly NRTs are changing the traditional meanings of the words *family, parent,* and *offspring.* But should our government develop legislation to limit or regulate the use of NRTs? What kinds of laws would you propose, and who should be charged with enforcing them? And what about cloning? What do you see as the potential benefits as well as detriments of human cloning? Do you think human cloning should be completely banned, or is there some way it could be successfully regulated?

---

spend more time caring for their children than fathers did even two decades ago. For instance, in 20 percent of households with preschool-age children and employed mothers, fathers provide sole care while the mothers are working (Chira, 1993a; Lawlor, 1998). Research also shows that most fathers are least involved in primary care when their children are infants; become more involved when their children are about eighteen months old and walking and talking; and are most involved during the middle childhood period (five to fifteen years old). Even during middle childhood, however, the time fathers spend with their children typically involves recreation or academics (playing, reading to them, teaching them some-

thing), as opposed to primary caregiving (Snarey, 1993). Consequently, it is mothers, even those employed full-time, who still provide most of the primary care needed by their children, in addition to caring for their husbands and their homes (Bond et al., 1998; Walzer, 1996).

Some theorists argue that women's greater role in parenting reflects a natural predisposition for caregiving, but there is no conclusive empirical evidence that human females are born with a "maternal instinct" (Eyer, 1993; Rossi, 1984). Other social scientists believe that women take primary responsibility for caregiving because of socialization. In other words, from the time they are young children, women, not men, are taught to be caregivers.

Although socialization undoubtedly plays an important role in the gendered division of caregiving, keep in mind that particular social arrangements also restrict people's attempts to change this behavior. For instance, many men say they would like to be more involved in the care of their children, but that their jobs make it difficult, if not impossible (Snarey, 1993; Walzer, 1996; Weisner et al., 1994). The occupational structure of our society operates on the ideology that men are the economic providers of families, while women are the caretakers. Consequently, even though federal law now requires companies with more than fifty employees to provide women *and* men with family leave, most employers say it's inappropriate for male employees to take family leaves (Chira, 1993b; Silverstein, 1996). At the same time, many families cannot afford to have fathers assume full-time caregiving responsibilities given that women, on average, earn only 76 percent of what men earn (Erikson & Garcia, 1990).

Gay and lesbian couples experience the same problems in caring for children, but they also have serious normative constraints on even becoming parents. In fact, it is in the area of parental rights that gay and lesbian couples face the greatest hostility and resistance (Stacey, 1998; Wolfe, 1998). To a large extent, negative attitudes toward homosexuals as parents stem from widespread myths about relationships between homosexuals and children. For instance, many heterosexuals believe that gay men try to seduce young boys, but the data on child molesters show that about 90 percent are heterosexual men (Greenfeld, 1996; Prentky et al., 1997). Many heterosexuals also think that homosexuals try to "recruit" children to their "lifestyle," and that simply seeing homosexual couples together leads children into immorality. Such beliefs have been used repeatedly to prevent lesbians and gay men from becoming foster or adoptive parents and to deny them custody or visitation rights to their own children (Ayres, 1993; Robson, 1992). In 1996, for example, an appeals court in Florida upheld a lower court's ruling denying a lesbian mother custody of her daughter and awarding custody to her ex-husband who had been imprisoned for killing his first wife. The judge who originally decided the case said he wanted to give the child a chance to live in a "non-lesbian world" (Epstein, 1996).

Currently, only six states permit adoptions by same-sex couples, raising legal problems if a partner has custody of children from a previous heterosexual marriage, has adopted children as a single parent, or has given birth to children using an NRT. Despite persistent myths, however, research consistently shows that children raised by gay and lesbian parents are emotionally healthy and well-adjusted (Bozett, 1988; Patterson, 1992; Silverstein, 1996).

Single-Parent Families. In single-parent families, only one parent must meet all the needs of the children. Although the percentage of children living with only their fathers has more than doubled since 1970, 86 percent of

Most single-parent families are headed by women who struggle to fulfill job demands without sacrificing the well-being of their children. Unlike the mother in this photograph, however, low-income women have far fewer resources for accomplishing this. What are the costs of divorce or single parenthood for women? for children? for society?

children living in single-parent households live with their mothers: 83 percent of White children in single-parent families, 92 percent of African American children in such families, and 88 percent of Hispanic American children in single-parent families (U.S. Department of Commerce, Bureau of the Census, 1997).

The number of single-parent families has increased dramatically during the past thirty years, from 13 percent of families with dependent children in 1970 to 29 percent of families with dependent children in 1993 (U.S. Department of Commerce, Bureau of the Census, 1997). Part of the increase reflects the growing number of women who have children, but remain unmarried. In 1970, unmarried mothers represented only 0.8 percent of families with dependent children, but by 1996 they constituted nearly 10 percent. Some of these women had children as a result of unintended or unwanted pregnancies, and many of these women (about 30 percent) are teenagers (U.S. Department of Commerce, Bureau of the Census, 1997). Some, however, are well educated, gainfully employed, financially secure heterosexual or lesbian women who use one of the NRTs we discussed earlier, adopt a child, or choose to have a child but not marry the father. For these women, single parenthood is a viable alternative to marriage because they have the financial resources, but they must still juggle career and caregiving responsibilities like married women do (Miller, 1992).

Although both women and men may become single parents by being widowed, the most common way is

SOCIOLOGY LIVE

University of Kansas, Lawrence KS
Course: Elements of Sociology, Susan C. Cooper, Instructor
Students: (left to right) Trisha Reuber, Jackie Dowell, Lynne Whitaker, Elizabeth Greer Hutchinson, Erin McGee, Cara Corcoran, Emily VinZant, Kelly McWhite, and (not shown) Thad Petry

How do students at our school define a successful intimate relationship?

In response to this question, as a group we defined the term "successful intimate relationship" to mean a relationship that exemplifies open communication, endures over time, is physical, honors loyalty, and values differing interests.

Our Method: To determine the "successful" elements of intimate relationships, we created a survey and administered it to the members of our Elements of Sociology class. The survey consisted of Likert-type questions with answers ranging from 1 = Strongly Disagree to 4 = Strongly Agree. Basic demographic information also was solicited. The surveys were distributed, with consent forms, on a test day to ensure the greatest possible response rate. Five extra-credit points were offered to class members answering the survey. Forty-two students completed the survey, 21 males and 21 females. The nine members of our sociology research group met outside of class time to analyze the data and discuss the results, and then we presented the findings.

Our Findings: We tallied responses to the survey questions and calculated the distribution of responses on the basis of respondents' sex, age, and religious affiliation. To get a picture of a "successful intimate relationship," we grouped together questions that measured similar concepts. Respondents' age and religious affiliation proved not to be important distinctions, but respondents' sex was. Males and females differ slightly in their descriptions of a successful intimate relationship.

All the females in the sample strongly agreed that open communication is imperative, while only 90 percent of males strongly agreed. Males and females both tended to disagree that people involved in an intimate relationship must come

from similar religious backgrounds. A higher proportion of males strongly agreed that maintaining self-esteem is beneficial in keeping a relationship successful. Forty-eight percent of females strongly agreed that they must be in love to be in a successful relationship, while only 33 percent of males strongly agreed that love is necessary.

Although 60 percent of the class agreed that independence is beneficial to a successful intimate relationship, 48 percent of females agreed with this strongly. No females disagreed, yet 10 percent of males did disagree. It also appears that respondents distinguished between "sexual" and "physical" components of a relationship. Twenty-four percent of females and 24 percent of males agreed that an important part of the definition is that the relationship is "sexual." However, 47 percent of females and 43 percent of males agreed that an important part of the definition is that the relationship is "physical." Finally, 76 percent of the females agreed that they would "never continue an intimate relationship with a partner who

was unfaithful," and 72 percent of the males also agreed.

Discussion and Conclusions: Generalizability of the results of this survey is limited due to the small and homogeneous sample. There were no respondents who identified themselves as persons of color and only one who identified as other than heterosexual. Nevertheless, it is possible to sketch an outline of a "successful intimate relationship" from this study on which both males and females basically agree. The only significant difference we found was between males and females on the questions of how important "love" is in a relationship. We also found it noteworthy that females valued independence more than did males, while males valued self-esteem more than did females. We concluded that additional data would be needed to explore the significance of sex and sexual orientation and other demographic variables in people's ideas about what constitutes a successful intimate relationship.

through **divorce**, the legal dissolution of a marriage that frees former spouses to marry someone else if they choose to. Today, 50 percent of couples divorce within 7.2 years of pronouncing their wedding vows (U.S. Department of Commerce, Bureau of the Census, 1997).

Before the Industrial Revolution, fathers were usually awarded legal custody of their children both because children were considered their property and because fathers more likely had the financial means to support their children. However, as the Industrial Revolution progressed

INTERSECTING INEQUALITIES

The Costs of Divorce for Women and Children

In 1957, Oklahoma became the first state to adopt *no-fault divorce*. Before no-fault divorce, couples who sought to dissolve their marriages had to demonstrate that one partner had broken the marriage contract, for example, by being unfaithful or deserting the family. The wronged partner was given monetary rewards and other special considerations in the divorce settlement. In contrast, under no-fault statutes, either partner may file for divorce on the grounds of "irreconcilable differences," neither is blamed for the failure of the marriage, and all property and assets are divided equally. Today, all fifty states have some form of no-fault divorce, but the pendulum may be swinging in the opposite direction once again: Legislators in Iowa, Colorado, Michigan, Pennsylvania, and Georgia have proposed revisions to their states' divorce laws that would

eliminate the no-fault divorce option, at least for couples with children. The reason? Although no-fault divorce has made marital dissolution somewhat easier, research shows that it hurts women and children (Johnson, 1996). Let's see how.

First, researchers tell us, women are hurt economically by no-fault divorce, and because they are most likely to have custody of their children, the children also suffer the negative economic consequences of the divorce. Under no-fault divorce, financial awards such as alimony and child support are determined primarily by need, the spouses' ability to work and be self-supporting, and the spouses' relative ability to pay. Alimony awards, however, are now frowned on by the courts. However, if a woman has been out of the labor force for an extended period of time, her ability to support herself and her children will likely

be impaired. Even if she has been working full time, her salary is rarely equal to that of her husband.

Adding to the financial difficulties women and children face is the fact that in dividing marital property, the courts usually consider only tangible assets, such as the family's home, car(s), and furniture. Given that most divorcing couples have mortgages and other debts, by the time the bills are paid, there may be little left to divide. The equal division of property often forces the sale of the family home. However, there are other types of assets—for example, pensions and retirement benefits, licenses to practice a profession, medical insurance, or the value of a business—that only infrequently figure into property settlements. This means that one spouse (usually the husband) retains control of some of the family's most valuable assets (Lindgren & Taub, 1993).

and production and education moved away from home, the ideology of childhood changed. Instead of being viewed as miniature adults, children came to be seen as helpless dependents in need of nurturing, and childrearing experts believed mothers were better caregivers than fathers. By the turn of the twentieth century, there was a dramatic shift in custody decisions against fathers and in favor of mothers (Lindgren & Taub, 1993). Today, although most courts favor joint custody awards that give both parents equal decision-making authority in their

children's rearing, the mother is still usually awarded physical custody.

Research indicates that the single-parenting experiences of men and women are different (see Table 15.3). For one thing, single fathers, on average, have higher incomes than single mothers. They also are often better educated and they are typically employed full-time, so they have fewer financial problems. Single fathers also usually receive considerable support from friends, relatives, and neighbors who consider them extraordinary for parent-

TABLE 15.3 Median Income of Families by Type of Family and Race/Ethnicity, 1997

Type of Family	MEDIAN INCOME($)			
	All Families	White	African American	Hispanic American
Married couple families	51,591	52,098	45,372	33,914
Wife in paid labor force	60,669	61,441	51,702	42,280
Wife not in paid labor force	36,027	36,343	28,757	23,748
Male householder, wife absent	32,960	34,802	25,054	25,543
Female householder, husband absent	21,023	22,999	16,879	14,994

Source: U.S. Department of Commerce, Bureau of the Census, 1998a, pp. 13–16.

How do no-fault settlements add up in terms of dollars and cents? One researcher concluded that in the first year after a divorce, women and their dependent children suffer a 73 percent drop in their standard of living, while men enjoy a 42 percent rise (Weitzman, 1985). Others estimate the decline in income for women following divorce is between 30 and 50 percent (Holden & Smock, 1991).

Besides the financial costs of divorce, there are studies about the emotional costs, especially for children. Opponents of no-fault divorce argue that it has contributed to a rise in the divorce rate which, in turn, has caused a rise in emotional and behavioral problems of children. They cite research that shows children of divorced parents have low academic achievement, elevated high school dropout rates, high rates of single parenthood, low self-esteem, high rates of admission to psychiatric hospitals, higher rates of prison incarceration and high teen suicide rates (Harper & McLanahan, 1998; Harris, 1998; Nicholi, 1991). Other researchers caution that these findings come from faulty studies. That is, the studies do not make clear whether the problems emerged after the divorce or during the marriage. When children of divorced parents are compared with children from intact marriages, the differences in emotional and behavioral problems are actually small (Amato, 1994; Furstenberg & Cherlin, 1991). Indeed, some researchers maintain that children living in homes with high levels of conflict between parents suffer as many, if not more, negative consequences as children of divorced parents (Kurz, 1995). According to two researchers, the best indicators of a child's level of emotional adjustment are the child's relationship with his or her mother and the level of conflict between the child's parents (Furstenberg & Cherlin, 1991; see also Wallerstein, 1998). However, one recent study, which looked at the negative effects of parental divorce on children as they grow up, found that although some negative effects were the result of factors present before the parents' divorce, others were attributable to the divorce itself. Moreover, these negative effects were evident even when the children were adults in their twenties and thirties (Cherlin et al., 1998).

Contradictory research findings have fueled, not quenched, the debate over no-fault divorce. This debate is not likely to be settled soon, regardless of the outcome of pending legislative proposals.

---

ing alone, but needy when it comes to handling housework and childcare (Casper & Bryson, 1998; Teltsch, 1992). In fact, single fathers' most frequent complaints are that they are treated as incompetent parents (for example, teachers may ask to meet with their ex-wives instead of them), and they feel their social lives and careers are restricted because of parenting responsibilities (Hanson, 1988).

In contrast, single mothers tend to receive less help from others; many, in fact, report feeling socially isolated (Kamerman & Kahn, 1988). Single mothers, like their male counterparts, also must struggle to fulfill employment demands without sacrificing the well-being of their children. However, since women are less likely than men to hold high-status, high-income jobs, they more often have problems with inflexible work schedules, inadequate salaries, and unaffordable childcare facilities. Simply finding a job is sometimes difficult for a single mother, especially if she has been out of the labor force as a full-time homemaker for a number of years, has little work experience, or has developed few marketable skills. Not surprisingly, then, the biggest problem of most single mothers is money (Holden & Smock, 1991; Kurz, 1995).

We can get a good sense of the financial problems of single-parent, female-headed families from Table 15.3. Here we see that in 1997, the median income of married couple families was more than $18,000 greater than that of male-headed, single-parent families, but more than double the median income of female-headed, single-parent families. For minority female-headed families, financial resources are even more limited.

The Intersecting Inequalities box takes a closer look at the financial consequences of divorce for women and men and also considers the psychological impact of divorce on children.

Another serious problem families may confront is domestic violence, which we'll examine next.

R E F L E C T I N G   O N

Families and Intimate Relationships in the United States

1. Sex norms today are generally more liberal than they were in the past, but are they the same for males and females? On your campus, for example, are men and women held to the same standards of sexual conduct by their peers?
2. Do you favor or oppose the legalization of homosexual marriages? Give the rationale for your position.

Continued on p. 410

3. Why do you think many men express greater opposition to gender inequality in the workplace than at home? How could their attitudes be changed to support greater egalitarianism at home?
4. Most women and men work out of economic necessity. But let's assume that you have the option of leaving your job if you have children so you can be with them full-time until they start school. Would you choose to exercise that option? Why or why not?
5. Single-parent, female-headed families face numerous problems. Choose one and develop a practical strategy for solving it.

VIOLENCE IN FAMILIES

The image of the family as a "haven in a heartless world" is tarnished today by widespread reports of family violence. According to the U.S. Department of Justice (1995), about 450,000 incidents of family violence occur in the United States each year. About 57 percent of these cases involve married couples or ex-spouses. Many victims, however, are reluctant or unable to report the abuse, so the statistics probably underestimate the problem. Let's examine what is known about three forms of family violence: partner abuse, child abuse, and elder abuse.

Partner Abuse in Heterosexual Relationships

National surveys using random samples of married and cohabiting heterosexual couples show that each year, about 12 percent of adult intimates experience at least one incident of physical abuse at the hands of their partners. In one of the best known studies, sociologist Murray Straus found that for every 1,000 couples in the United States, there are 122 assaults by husbands and 124 assaults by wives each year (Straus, 1993).

On the surface, Straus's findings suggest that partner abuse is usually *mutual abuse* by husbands and wives, an exchange of physical and psychological abuse between partners (Straus, 1993). Other researchers, however, feel the data are misleading because they do not indicate motives (such as control of the partner, punishment, self-defense, retaliation) for the assaults. For instance, studies show that in most cases, husbands initiate the violence to control or punish their wives, and husbands kill their partners in self-defense less often than wives (Barnett et al., 1997; Saunders, 1989). Husbands are also more likely to seriously injure or kill their wives during an assault (Crowell & Burgess, 1996; Dobash et al., 1998).

Early research on the causes of partner abuse focused on the personal characteristics of batterers. According to one hypothesis, batterers were uneducated, lower-class

men, usually members of racial minority groups, whose poor status made violence the only way they could assert dominance in relationships. However, research shows that although partner abuse among lower-class and minority couples is more likely to come to the attention of the police, the problem is found among all racial and ethnic groups, and crosses social class and education lines as well. Nevertheless, research does show that battering is more frequent in low-income families (Moore, 1997; Schwartz, 1988).

Many people believe that alcohol and drug abuse cause battering. Although there is a relationship between substance abuse and family violence, it does not appear to be causal. Instead, drinking and drug use are often used to justify or excuse battering: "I didn't know what I was doing; I was drunk" (Gelles, 1993).

Some people argue that women provoke men into assaulting them. Consider, for instance, a 1994 case in which a Maryland judge sentenced a defendant, a man who had killed his wife after he found her in bed with another man, to just eighteen months probation, stating that most men would have felt compelled to "punish" their partners under such circumstances ("Punishment is 18 Months," 1994).

Some people are unsympathetic to abused women because they believe the woman should leave the relationship

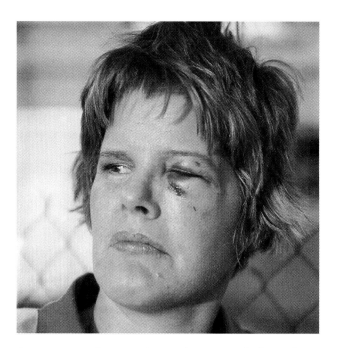

In most cases of partner abuse in heterosexual relationships, men initiate the violence in order to control or punish their partners or to exploit them sexually. They often inflict serious injury. Why do so many women stay with abusive partners? What do you think could be done to reduce domestic violence in the United States?

as soon as the abuse begins. "If it's so bad," they ask, "why does she stay?" Recent research indicates that abused women typically do leave their partners, sometimes more than once, but that leaving is more difficult than most people think (Brown, 1997). For one thing, they must have some place to go; relatives may not be supportive, and battered women's shelters may not have space for them and their children. Second, they must be able to support themselves and their children if they leave. Women who are quick to leave an abusive relationship tend to be gainfully employed or to have good chances for employment, possess above-average resources, and have relatives nearby who are willing and able to help them (Pagelow, 1981). Finally, leaving an abuser does not guarantee that the abuse will stop; in fact, research shows that abuse often escalates when a woman tries to leave or after she has left (DeKeseredy, 1997; Kurz, 1995).

It is important, too, to keep in mind that partner abuse takes place in the context of a violent society; until the late 1800s, husbands were legally permitted to beat their wives. Although the law has changed, attitudes remain remarkably the same: Many people who see violence as a normal part of everyday life believe that under certain circumstances, men are justified in hitting their wives or girlfriends (DeKeseredy & MacLeod, 1997).

Partner Abuse in Gay and Lesbian Relationships

Much less is known about partner abuse in gay and lesbian relationships. For one thing, we cannot do studies using large, national samples of gay and lesbian couples because many gay men and lesbians are not open about their sexual orientation. Therefore, it is impossible to estimate with much accuracy the incidence of violence in same-sex relationships. Some researchers argue that it occurs at about the same rate as violence in heterosexual relationships (Island & Letellier, 1991). However, these claims are based on studies of lesbians and gay men who volunteer for the research and who therefore may not be representative of the general lesbian and gay populations. What we do know is that research documents that partner abuse does occur in same-sex relationships and that, like heterosexual domestic violence, the abuse is recurring and likely to grow more severe over time (Renzetti, 1992).

Many people assume that it is easier for abused lesbians and gay men to leave their partners because they are not married. However, there are few shelters and services specifically for victims of same-sex domestic violence, and many lesbians and gay men do not feel welcome at shelters and services designed for heterosexual abused women. For example, when abused lesbians and gay men call the police for help, the police often do not take their complaints seriously, or they respond with hostility (Renzetti, 1992).

Child Abuse

We often tell children to be wary of strangers, but the fact is they are more likely to be harmed by someone they know, especially a family member. Estimates of child abuse and neglect range from about 1 million to nearly 3 million cases per year (U.S. Department of Health and Human Services, 1998). As many as one-third of all child abuse and neglect cases probably go unreported or undetected. Nevertheless, the incidence and severity of child abuse appears to be increasing (Children's Defense Fund, 1997). Girls are slightly more likely than boys to be abused; 52 percent of abuse victims are girls. Boys are more likely to be physically abused and neglected, whereas girls are more likely to be emotionally abused and they are three times more likely than boys to be sexually abused (U.S. Department of Health and Human Services, 1998). Sexual exploitation of children may be perpetrated by strangers, but most victims know their abusers. The abuser is usually a relative, stepparent, family friend, or close neighbor. Accurate estimates of child sexual abuse are difficult to calculate, but research indicates that about 19 percent of girls and 9 percent of boys have been sexually abused by the time they turn eighteen, and about 40 percent of them by a relative (Hodson & Skeen, 1987; Holmes & Slap, 1998; Russell, 1986).

What are some of the factors that contribute to child abuse and neglect? There is evidence that children from unwanted or unplanned pregnancies are at high risk of all forms of abuse and neglect (Zuravin, 1987). Most studies also show that mothers are more likely than fathers to physically and psychologically abuse their children. This finding may simply reflect the greater time mothers spend with their children, but it may also be caused in part by

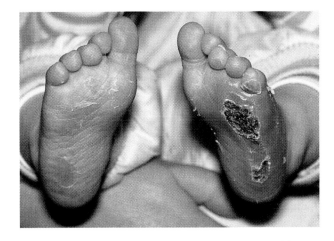

Who perpetrates the physical and sexual abuse of children? Who neglects them? What social factors contribute to child abuse and neglect? What social factors inhibit the effective prevention and intervention of child abuse and neglect in the United States?

the greater social isolation of mothers. Parents who are socially isolated are more likely to abuse their children (Straus & Smith, 1990). Finally, we must not forget that child abuse occurs in a specific social context. Most people approve of parents exercising strict control over children and physically punishing children for misbehavior (Dibble & Straus, 1990). This social approval, along with the idea that what parents do in their homes is their own business, helps perpetuate child abuse and neglect.

Elder Abuse

Elder abuse refers to the physical, psychological, or financial maltreatment, neglect, or exploitation of a senior citizen by an adult caretaker. Obviously, such abuse can be inflicted by anyone entrusted with the care of an elderly person (such as nurses, physicians, bankers, or lawyers), but research shows that the typical abuser is a family member (Kosberg, 1988; Mates, 1997; Pillemer & Finkelhor, 1988). An estimated 700,000 to 1 million elderly people are abused in the United States each year (Pillemer & Finkelhor, 1988).

Although research into elder abuse did not really begin until the 1980s, the work that has been done shows who is at greatest risk of being abused and who are the likely abusers. Women who are aged seventy-five and older and who are infirm and physically or financially dependent on others for meeting their basic daily needs are most susceptible to abuse (Kosberg, 1988; Pillemer & Finkelhor, 1988). Women may have higher rates of victimization simply because they outnumber elderly men, but also they are less able to resist abuse, they are more vulnerable to sexual assault, and they have lower social status than elderly men.

Research on abusers shows that they are often adult daughters who have brought severely impaired aged parents into their home to care for them. The daughters continue to care for their own families and often work outside the home as well. They typically receive little or no outside help in caring for their parents, and eventually the psychological and financial stress become so great that they use violence to control their parents or to express their resentment about the situation (Mates, 1997; Steinmetz, 1993). Abusers may also be the elderly person's spouse, continuing a pattern of abuse in the marriage or taking revenge for previous abuse by the now-impaired partner (Kosberg, 1988; Pillemer & Finkelhor, 1988).

What can be done to reduce elder abuse? Advocates for the elderly believe adult children should receive greater professional assistance and support in caring for their parents. In addition, if elder abuse is a continuation of earlier family violence, then it must be addressed along with partner abuse and child abuse. Finally, the elderly in our society are devalued, which not only increases their vulnerability to abuse, but to other serious problems, such as poverty, as well.

REFLECTING ON

Violence in Families

1. What would you say to someone who claims that husbands are as likely as wives to be abused?
2. How would you go about improving domestic violence services for lesbians and gay men?
3. Do you think corporal punishment is an appropriate method for disciplining children? If so, how do you draw the line between acceptable corporal punishment and child abuse?
4. At least thirty-seven states have enacted laws that make reporting incidents of elder abuse or neglect mandatory. However, some experts say that such laws are ineffective because they address the problem after the fact. What do you think? How would you propose handling the problem of elder abuse?

RACIAL AND ETHNIC DIVERSITY IN U.S. FAMILIES

What will families and intimate relationships look like as the twenty-first century progresses? This is an important question for many of you, especially if you are in your late teens or early twenties. Chances are you will be establishing intimate relationships and families of your own in the near future, if you haven't done so already. What will they look like?

Most analysts tell us that the family will remain an integral part of our society, but that diversity in family forms will probably increase. For example, the United States is currently experiencing what some observers are calling a "lesbian baby boom." It's expected that over the next few decades we will see an increasing number of lesbians, as well as gay men, becoming parents (Kantrowitz, 1996). Another expected change is related to the growing number of racial and ethnic minority groups in the United States. Early in the twenty-first century, racial and ethnic minorities are expected to make up about a third of the U.S. population. Family life varies in important ways across and within racial and ethnic groups. So to conclude this chapter, let's briefly consider some research on racial and ethnic diversity in U.S. families.

African American Families

Looking at Figure 15.2, we see that more than 39 percent of African American women and men have never married. This rate is about 18 percent higher than that for the White population. Sociologists offer a variety of reasons for the high rate of singlehood among African Americans (Tucker & Mitchell-Kernan, 1995). As we

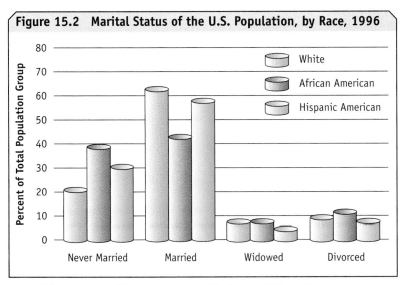

Figure 15.2   Marital Status of the U.S. Population, by Race, 1996

Source: U.S. Department of Commerce, Bureau of the Census, 1997, p. 55.

noted earlier, the mortality rate of young African American men reduces the pool of marriage partners for African American women. The disproportionately high unemployment rate of African American men also makes it difficult for them to marry. In addition, African American parents often encourage their children to delay marriage in favor of education (Higginbotham & Weber, 1995).

At the same time, a significant number of never-married African American women have children. African American women represented about 35 percent of unmarried women who gave birth in 1994. About 47 percent of African American families are single-parent, female-headed households. Single-parent, female-headed families are especially vulnerable to poverty, so it isn't surprising that almost 42 percent of African American children under the age of eighteen live in poverty (compared with just 16 percent of White children); the majority of these children live in single-parent, female-headed households (U.S. Department of Commerce, Bureau of the Census, 1997).

Some sociologists say that the large number of single-parent, female-headed African American families is to blame for poverty among African Americans, as well as other social problems, including crime, drug abuse, and alcoholism. But other sociologists have documented that the African American female-headed family has historically been a source of strength and resistance to oppression. Within many African American families, there is an ethic of care that allows family members to draw on the resources and support of their relatives in an extended family network: Family members may lend one another money, provide each other with transportation, and take care of one another's children (Collins, 1990; Higginbotham & Weber, 1995). Any analysis of the relationship between social problems and African American families

must therefore take into account the intersection of sexism, racism, and social class inequality. The kinds and levels of stress experienced by African American families, as well as other minority families, and the families' methods and chances of success in dealing with this stress, is affected by these other factors (Jayakody & Chatters, 1997; Neighbors, 1997).

Hispanic American Families

It is difficult to draw conclusions about Hispanic American families because the Hispanic American population is made up of many culturally and economically diverse groups. Let's consider some of the available data on Hispanic Americans in general to trace a broad picture of Hispanic American families.

Looking again at Figure 15.2, we see that about 30 percent of Hispanic Americans are single, never married, a statistic that surprises many people because of the popular stereotype of Hispanics as romantics. Most Hispanic Americans, like the general population, do eventually marry, but a significant number are delaying marriage longer than in the past for many of the same reasons—including education and finances—as other young Americans.

According to another widely held image of Hispanic American families, men are considered the unquestioned head of the household and women the caregivers. However, some researchers argue that Hispanic women wield considerable power in the home, which is considered their realm of authority (O'Kelly & Carney, 1986).

Hispanic American families are also often characterized by an extended family network that includes not only parents and their children, grandparents, and siblings, but also aunts, uncles, cousins, and godparents.

How would you describe family diversity in the United States? What may be some areas of cultural variation in family structure and family relations? Do you think similarities are more important than differences? Why or why not?

The extended family creates a system of emotional and financial support that family members can count on in times of crisis (such as the loss of a job or a death) as well as times of joy (such as a marriage or the birth of a child) (Williams, 1990).

Despite the strong bonds of the extended Hispanic American family, some researchers have begun to document increasing intergenerational family conflict over sexuality and marriage. Among middle-class and wealthy Hispanic American families, in particular, many traditions appear to be breaking down as young women and men adopt the norms of the dominant White culture, such as having many different dating partners before marrying and cohabiting with a potential marriage partner (Lorch, 1996; Oropesa, 1996; Williams, 1990). Given that Hispanic Americans are expected to make up nearly 20 percent of the U.S. population by 2050, these changes in

family structure and tradition may offer us a glimpse of the future.

Asian American Families

Asian American families, too, are made up of many diverse ethnic groups, making generalization difficult at best. Overall, however, Asian American families are considered very stable: Nearly eighty percent of Asian American family households are composed of married couples, almost the same percentage as White American family households. Asian Americans have the lowest percentage of single-parent, female-headed households of any racial or ethnic group: 12 percent (U.S. Department of Commerce, Bureau of the Census, 1997). Many Asian families in the United States continue the tradition of extended families common in their home countries. Tradition also engenders a strong sense of ethnic pride, respect for elders, an emphasis on personal achievement, and an obligation to honor one's family.

While many observers believe that traditions and deeply ingrained norms regarding family are major contributing factors to Asian American economic success, others argue that these traditions and norms mask many problems. For example, the strong prohibition against bringing dishonor to one's family is considered the main reason why Asian American wives abused by their husbands do not seek help. To speak to others, especially "outsiders" about one's problems would shame not only the couple, but also each spouse's parents and other relatives (Huisman, 1996).

Little is known about the incidence of domestic violence and other social problems among Asian American families. Future research will no doubt shed light in this area. Meanwhile, the data that are available reflect positively on Asian American families, who have one of the highest median incomes and rates of college enrollment of any racial or ethnic group in the United States (U.S. Department of Commerce, Bureau of the Census, 1997).

Native American Families

Native American families on reservations experience high rates of poverty, unemployment, and other social problems. Among many Native American tribes, the extended family is the norm, and the support it provides is a real survival tool for reservation families. Family members often pool financial resources, and relatives can count on one another for child care and other forms of help. On many reservations, tribal leaders are working to reinstate cultural traditions and ensure that younger generations know their heritage. Within the family, it is the elder members who usually take responsibility for educating the youth about tribal customs and history (Gugliotta, 1999; U.S. Department of Education, 1991).

Among Native Americans living away from reservations, particularly in urban areas, tribal family traditions may fade as family members adopt the dominant culture of the society. Still, many urban Native Americans, especially those who are middle aged or older, report that they hope to someday return to their tribes on reservations. They see the reservation as their "hometown," and although about a third leave the reservation when they are young, over half return to spend their old age there and, with relatives, form an extended family (Weibel-Orlando, 1989).

Multiracial Families

Finally, we can expect an increase in multiracial families over the next several decades if interracial adoptions and interracial marriage rates continue to increase as they have over the past fifty years. Interracial marriage has

How is the racial and ethnic composition of families in the United States changing? Why can we expect to see an increase in multiracial families over the next several decades? What effect do you think increases in multiracial families will have on the U.S. society and culture?

been rare in the United States. In 1970, only 0.7 percent of marriages were between partners of different racial identifications, but by 1996, the number had more than doubled to 2.3 percent (U.S. Department of Commerce, Bureau of the Census, 1997). Intermarriage is more common in Hawaii and the western States, where most interracial marriages are of Asian American and White couples. Interracial marriages occur least often in the southern United States (Jaret, 1995). Native Americans are most likely and African Americans are least likely to marry a partner of a different race; 26.7 percent of interracial marriages are of African Americans and White partners and 3.1 percent are African Americans and other non-White partners (U.S. Department of Commerce, Bureau of the Census, 1997).

Some people think that interracial couples who marry and have children are abandoning their own groups and trying to create a more homogenous or blended population. However, research shows that instead of losing their racial and ethnic identities, interracial families preserve ties to their different heritages. Interracial couples typically transmit multiple cultures to their children, reinforcing not a single racial identity, but a multiracial identity (Jaret, 1995). Professional golfer Tiger Woods is a good example. Woods considers himself "Cablinasian" because his father is African American, Chinese, and Native American, and his mother is Thai, Chinese, and White (Verdi, 1997).

Some social scientists predict that a steady increase in interracial marriages and families will help reduce interracial conflict in our society. So far, though, there is no empirical evidence that bears out this effect (Jaret, 1995). What is more certain is that the growing number of interracial marriages and families will further enrich the already diverse cultural landscape of the United States.

R E F L E C T I N G   O N

Racial and Ethnic Diversity in U.S. Families

1. Why do you think race and ethnicity are important factors influencing family life and intimate relationships? Can you name two ways that race and ethnicity impact family life or intimate relationships?
2. What do you think will be the most significant family issues in the twenty-first century? What do you think the most important changes in families and relationships will be?

 For useful resources for study and review, run Chapter 15 on your *Living Sociology* CD-ROM.

C O N N E C T I O N S

Marriage and the family	Marriage is discussed in Chapter 4 in the context of cultural norms and values. For a recap on the family as a social institution, review the section on "Institutions" in Chapter 6. How does the family relate to the social structure of a society? Also review Chapter 3 on "Types of Societies." How do family characteristics vary among the six different types of society? For a discussion on changes in the family as a consequence of the industrial Revolution, see the section on "Industrial Societies" in Chapter 3.
Endogamy	Reread the sections on "The Caste System" and "The Wealthy" in Chapter 8. How does a marriage rule of endogamy help to preserve a society's system of social stratification? Also review Chapter 11. How might a marriage rule of endogamy help to preserve racial stratification in a society?
Sociological perspectives on families	Compare the structural functional, conflict and feminist, and symbolic interactionist perspectives on the family with the same perspectives on other social institutions, such as the economy (Chapter 13), the government (Chapter 14), education (Chapter 16), religion (Chapter 17), or medicine (Chapter 18). What central ideas of each perspective transfer from one institution to another?
Gender inequality in the home	Review the discussion of gender inequality in the section on "Gender and Sexual Orientation as systems of Stratification" in Chapter 10. See also the section on "Gender and Global Poverty" in Chapter 9. How do the statuses of women as mothers, wage earners, and home makers relate to gender inequality in the home?
Parents as agents of socialization	Review "The Family" as an agent of socialization, discussed in Chapter 5. See also the section on gender role socialization in Chapter 10. In what ways is the family a primary agent of socialization? In what ways do parents tend to perpetuate gender as a system of socialization?
Single-parent families	Reread "Poverty in the United States" in Chapter 8. What is the poverty rate of female-headed families?

C O N N E C T I O N S

Domestic partnerships	Review the sections on "Sexual Orientation" and "Gender, Sexual Orientation, and Social Change" in Chapter 10. What issues of gay and lesbian rights do these sections introduce? How do those issues affect the roles and status of homosexuals as domestic partners?
Domestic violence	Review the section on "Gendered Violence" in Chapter 10. How do the concepts of sexual harassment, acquaintance rape, and sexual assault introduced in Chapter 10 relate to the discussion of marital rape and child sexual abuse in Chapter 15?
Family diversity	Reread the sections in Chapter 11 on African Americans, Hispanic Americans, Asian Americans, and Native Americans. See also the discussion of family diversity in Chapter 4. What are some connections between race and ethnicity, gender, and social class that affect family life?

SUMMING UP CHAPTER 15

Families throughout the World: Structures and Characteristics

1. The functions of the family in society have changed over time as the economy changed. Today, the primary functions of the family are the regulation of sexual behavior and reproduction; socialization and child care; and the provision of emotional support, affection, and nurturing for family members. However, the specific ways families are organized to do these tasks and the way they carry them out vary a great deal across societies. Families differ in their structure, marriage patterns, residential patterns, ways of determining descent and inheritance, and investment of power and authority in family members.

Sociological Perspectives on Families

1. Structural functionalists explain the universality of families in terms of the common functions they perform in all societies: regulation of sexual behavior and reproduction, socialization, social location, financial support and physical security, and emotional support and caring. The functionalist perspective has been criticized for downplaying family diversity and for overlooking the tension and violence that often occur in families.
2. Conflict and feminist theorists are interested in how the family reproduces social inequality. Conflict theorists are especially interested in the family's role of social placement, how the family preserves social class inequality through inheritance, and inequality within the family. Feminist theorists emphasize how families reproduce gender inequality. Critics of both perspectives think they give too much attention to family problems and overlook the positive aspects of family life.
3. Symbolic interactionists are concerned with how family members construct meaning through their everyday in-

teractions with one another. They also look at how family members adjust their individual and family identities in response to changing roles and crises. Critics of symbolic interactionism argue that by focusing on the internal dynamics of individual families, this perspective overlooks the impact of social structural conditions on the family as well as how family members reinforce particular structural arrangments.

Families and Intimate Relationships in the United States

1. Arranged marriages were the norm in the United States until the colonial period, when love and mutual attraction replaced economic and political considerations as the bases for marriage. Norms regarding sex have also varied historically and cross-culturally. In the United States, attitudes toward sexual behavior have become increasingly liberal, but our society's sex norms still promote heterosexual relationships and discourage or stigmatize homosexual relationships.
2. Although the percentage of the never-married heterosexual population has risen in recent years, singlehood continues to be a temporary status for most men and women. The increase in the never-married population and the trend toward delaying marriage longer than in the past are the result of several factors, including more positive attitudes about singlehood, reluctance to marry given high rates of divorce and domestic violence, greater availability of contraception, economic constraints, and for some groups, difficulty in finding a suitable marriage partner. A temporary alternative to marriage is a domestic partnership, an increasingly popular lifestyle choice for heterosexual couples.
3. Recent research on gay and lesbian relationships refutes many common myths. First, there is no gay lifestyle; there

is as much diversity among homosexual couples as heterosexual couples. Second, gay men and lesbians establish enduring intimate relationships that may in fact last longer on average than heterosexual marriages. There is disagreement in the gay and lesbian community over the advantages and disadvantages of domestic partnership registration.

4. Although most people no longer think of the marriage contract as establishing an exchange relationship between partners, the typical division of labor within the home supports traditional gender roles. Women continue to have primary responsibility for housework, even if they work full time outside the home. Husbands and wives not only spend different amounts of time on housework, they also do different household tasks, with this division of labor having important consequences in their everyday lives.

5. New reproductive technologies are allowing couples and individuals with various fertility problems to become parents, although many people object to NRTs on ethical grounds. The presence of children in a household raises stress and lowers marital satisfaction, but men and women experience these problems differently. Mothers are significantly more involved in primary child care than fathers are. The two factors contributing most to this arrangement are gender socialization and the occupational structure of our society. Gay and lesbian couples, however, are often denied their right to parent even though research shows that children raised by gay and lesbian parents are emotionally healthy and well-adjusted.

6. The number of single-parent families has increased substantially over the past two decades, and most children living in such households live with their mothers only. Men and women may become single parents as a result of several different causes, but the most frequent cause is divorce. Single fathers and mothers confront different types of problems. The most common complaints of single fathers are that they are treated as incompetent parents and their social lives and careers are restricted because of parenting responsibilities. The most common complaints of single mothers are employment problems (such as inflexible work hours and lack of affordable child care) and financial problems. Single-parent, female-headed families are more likely than other types of families to be poor.

Violence in Families

1. Violence occurs at a disturbing rate in U.S. families. The majority of instances of domestic violence involve married couples or ex-spouses. Although some researchers claim the abuse is mutual, others have documented that women are by far most often victimized and men are typically the abusers. Partner abuse occurs in families from all racial and ethnic, educational, and social class backgrounds. It also occurs in lesbian and gay relationships. Victims of domestic violence, especially gay men and lesbians, face numerous obstacles when leaving the rela-

tionship, and leaving does not guarantee that the abuse will end.

2. Experts believe that the incidence of child abuse and neglect in the United States is significantly underreported. Moreover, although girls and boys are equally vulnerable to abuse, girls are more likely than boys to be sexually abused. Factors that contribute to child abuse and neglect are: unwanted and unplanned pregnancies, social isolation of parents, and social norms expressing approval of parents physically disciplining their children.

3. Studies indicate that women aged seventy-five and older who are infirm and physically or financially dependent on others for meeting their basic daily needs are most vulnerable to elder abuse. Abusers are usually family members, most often an adult daughter who is caring for a severely impaired aged parent who lives with her.

Racial and Ethnic Diversity in U.S. Families

1. Analysts predict greater diversity in family forms during the next century. The number of racial and ethnic minority families is also expected to increase substantially. Family life varies in important ways across and within racial and ethnic groups.

2. African Americans are signficantly more likely than White Americans to remain single, even if they have children. A disproportionate number of African American families are headed by single mothers, making them vulnerable to many social problems, including poverty. However, the African American female-headed family has also been a source of strength and resistance to oppression.

3. Hispanic Americans are also more likely than White Americans to be single. Although traditions with respect to gender roles, family authority, and responsibilities and obligations have been hallmarks of Hispanic American families, there is evidence that these traditions are breaking down among the younger generations.

4. The majority of Asian American households contain married couples; Asian Americans have the lowest rate of single-parent, female-headed households of any racial or ethnic group. Some observers attribute the educational and economic success of Asian Americans to their strong cultural traditions and family norms, but others warn that these norms also cover serious family problems, such as domestic violence.

5. The extended family is common on Indian reservations and serves as a survival tool for Native American family members. Although family traditions often are not observed by Native Americans living off reservations, especially in cities, many urban Native Americans express a desire to return to their tribes and extended families on reservations.

6. The number of interracial families is growing steadily, although such families are still a small minority of all U.S. families. Multiracial couples do not abandon their different racial heritages, but rather maintain ties to each group and foster a multiracial identity in their children.

KEY PEOPLE AND CONCEPTS

bilateral descent: a system in which descent is traced through both parents

divorce: the legal dissolution of a marriage that frees former spouses to marry someone else if they choose to

domestic partnership: a cohabiting relationship between intimate partners not married to each other

egalitarian family: a family in which power and authority is shared by family members

endogamy: a social norm prohibiting marriage to anyone outside one's own social stratum or group

exogamy: a social norm that prescribes people to marry outside their own social stratum or group

extended family: a family composed of one or two parents, their dependent children, and other relatives who live together in the same household

family: a long-term, exclusive relationship in which members are related by ancestry, marriage, or adoption, and are committed to one another emotionally as well as financially

family of orientation: the family with whom an individual identifies as a member and who socializes her or him

family of origin: the family into which one is born

family of procreation: the family a person forms by having or adopting children

intimate relationship: a relationship of intense emotional attachment

kinship: a social network of individuals and families joined by ancestry, marriage, or adoption

marriage: a socially approved union of two or more people in which each is expected to fulfill specific economic, sexual, and caregiving obligations and responsibilities

matriarchal family: a family in which power and authority are disproportionately held by the wife/mother or eldest female family member

matrilineal descent: a system in which descent is traced through the mother's side of the family

matrilocality: a residential pattern in which a married couple lives with the wife's family, or at least in her village or community

monogamy: marriage to one partner

neolocality: a residential pattern in which a married couple establishes their own residence apart from either the husband's or the wife's family

new reproductive technologies (NRTs): a variety of laboratory techniques that allow people who, for various reasons, cannot conceive children through sexual intercourse to become parents

nuclear family: a family composed of one or two parents and their dependent children who live together in a household separate from other relatives

patriarchal family: a family in which power and authority are disproportionately held by the husband/father or eldest male family member

patrilineal descent: a system in which descent is traced through the father's side of the family

patrilocality: a residential pattern in which a married couple lives with the husband's family, or at least in his village or community

polyandry: a marriage in which one woman is married concurrently to two or more men

polygamy: marriage to multiple partners concurrently

polygyny: a marriage in which one man is married concurrently to two or more women

second shift: the household responsibilities of women who work full time outside the home, but who nevertheless are expected to perform most household chores

LEARNING MORE

Altman, I., & Ginat, J. (1996). *Polygamous families in contemporary society.* New York: Cambridge University Press. A fascinating study of the family relationships of fundamentalist Mormons in the United States, who continue to practice polygamy as prescribed by their religious teachings.

Hochschild, A. (1997). *The time bind.* New York: Metropolitan Books. Based on the author's extensive interviews with men and women working for a major corporation in the Midwest, this book presents the controversial argument that Americans are working longer hours today because they prefer to be at work rather than at home and children are suffering as a result.

Mason, M. A., Skolnick, A., & Sugarman, S. D. (Eds.) (1998). *All our families: New policies for a new century.* New York: Oxford University Press. A highly readable, comprehensive look at different family forms by experts in a variety of fields, including sociology, psychology, and social work.

Weston, K. (1991). *Families we choose: Lesbians, gays, and kinship.* New York: Columbia University Press. A study of lesbian and gay families built largely from fictive kin, who provide one another with an enduring support and affectional network that refutes the negative stereotypes of lesbian and gay relationships.

 Run Chapter 16 on your *Living Sociology* CD-ROM for interesting and informative activities, web links, videos, practice tests, and more.

Education

S uppose we told you that a new program is being developed for use in our nation's elementary schools. It's called the "Program for Educational and Occupational Needs," or PEON for short. PEON is based on research that shows students' race, ethnicity, and social class are good predictors of their future occupations. For example, researchers have found that White middle- and upper-class children have a high probability of entering professional and managerial occupations, while African American and Hispanic American children, who are disproportionately poor, tend to go into unskilled jobs when they grow up. PEON is designed to guide students along certain educational paths based on their race, ethnicity, and social class. White middle- and upper-class children, for instance, will follow a traditional academic curriculum to prepare them for college and then professional careers. Poor and minority children will take physical education classes that will teach them crouching, stooping, and stretching, and they will learn to obey orders by playing games such as "Mother May I?", "Follow the Leader," and "Simon Says."

You've probably already guessed that we're putting you on. PEON, fortunately, is fictitious. Although schools do not—and will not—have PEON programs, the writers who developed the idea were trying to make the point that education in the United States does not give all children equal opportunities (Frazier & Sadker, 1973). Not everyone agrees with this position, of course, as we will see in this chapter.

Our focus in this chapter is **education,** the social institution for instructing a society's members in the knowledge, values, and skills the society deems important. We will discuss major sociological theories of education, problems in education, and the issues that are likely to dominate education in the twenty-first century. But first, let's look at the history of education—that is, how education has changed as societies change.

SCHOOLS AND SOCIETIES

The kind of education that exists in a society has a lot to do with the economy of the society. That's because the society needs to transmit to its members knowledge, values, and skills that will allow them to contribute to economic production. In hunting and gathering societies, for example, education is informal. Children learn by observing adults and trying their hand at various tasks. Children accompany adults on hunting, gathering, and fishing expeditions; help prepare food; and care for younger children. They are also taught the values of sharing and cooperation, which are essential to the survival of the group.

It was only when a surplus accumulated, especially in agrarian societies, that education became more formal. **Formal education** is instruction given by specially trained teachers in designated settings, usually schools. Recall that in agrarian societies, the division of labor is more complex and specialized, so some people can become teachers. Some of history's most famous teachers—Aristotle, Plato, and Socrates in Greece and Confucius in

China—lived in agrarian societies. However, the availability of formal education is limited. Only wealthy children have sufficient leisure time to pursue formal education. (The word *school* comes from a Greek word that means "leisure.") Other children are educated "on the job," much the same as in hunting and gathering, horticultural, and pastoral societies.

Religious groups played an important role in the development of formal education. During the Middle Ages in Europe, for example, monasteries were intellectual centers where monks translated the Bible and ancient church teachings. Through study of the Torah (the first five books of the Hebrew Bible), Jews also fostered the concept of formal education. In the American colonies, Puritan com-

These students are learning catering in a vocational-technical school. Why in industrial and postindustrial societies are information and communication skills increasingly important? Without reading, writing, numeracy, and information processing or programming skills, what do you think workers can expect in the job market of the future?

munities established religious education programs as early as the mid-1600s to teach children to read the Bible so they could resist the devil's temptations. But it was not until industrialization that **mass education**—the extension of formal education to the general public—was introduced. Let's see why and how this occurred in the United States.

Education and Industrialization in the United States

Apart from Bible study, formal education in the American colonies during the seventeenth and much of the eighteenth centuries was available to only a privileged few. The educated man—formal education was restricted to males until 1786—was schooled in the classics, moral philosophy, mathematics, and rhetoric, and he acquired his knowledge as often through private study, tutoring, and travel as in a classroom (Graham, 1978). The educated young man was also expected to be trained in self-discipline and moral piety, so he could take his place among the White "ruling class" when the time came (Howe, 1984). Upper-class White women, when educated, were taught at home, but "education" meant something different than for men. Women studied music and were given "a taste" of literature and perhaps a foreign language. Their education was designed to prepare them for their "natural" role in life as demure, witty, well-groomed partners for their elite husbands (Schwager, 1987).

In the post–Revolutionary War period, formal education came to be seen as a necessity for instilling patriotism and "civic virtue" in citizens who would now be voting for political leaders. Keep in mind, however, that voting was restricted to White, male, property holders, so formal education continued to be their privilege, too. Schools were opened for young women—the first, the Young Ladies Academy, was established in Philadelphia in 1786 —but they were set up to prepare women for their domestic roles. It was believed that American women would play a vital role in the future of the republic as the first educators of sons who would grow up to be citizens (Schwager, 1987). Most wealthy young men and women attended private schools, although public schools existed for White children of all social classes; public schools, however, also charged tuition, which put them out of reach for most families. And it was illegal to educate slaves (Hellinger & Judd, 1991; Howe, 1984).

As industrialization displaced agriculture as the primary means of production, **literacy**, that is, basic reading, writing, and numeracy skills, became increasingly important. Such skills were not needed for the manual labor predominant in agricultural societies, but were necessary for such newly created industrial jobs as operating machinery, marketing and selling products, keeping track of inventory and sales, negotiating contracts, and designing new products. Also, as work moved away from

The first public schools in the United States opened in New England in the 1830s. As the public school movement spread across the country, a tax-supported school often was headed by a single female teacher who instructed students of all ages and grades in one room. Why was free public education important in an industrializing democracy peopled by waves of immigrants? In less developed and low-income countries, why might education be seen as a privilege rather than as an entitlement?

the home and into factories, so did responsibilities traditionally fulfilled by the family, including education, which became public. Finally, as immigration from Europe increased, mass education came to be seen as a means of insuring that American values were not corrupted by foreign influences (Bowles & Gintis, 1976; Hellinger & Judd, 1991).

In the 1830s, the first public schools providing mass education free of charge were opened in Massachusetts. The schools were paid for by tax revenues, and soon all the states established government-supported elementary schools to educate children of all social classes, although schools were segregated by race. In rural areas, schools often consisted of a single room with one teacher responsible for instructing students of all ages and grade levels. Within twenty years, mass public education was extended to the secondary level, and most states enacted laws making at least six years of schooling compulsory.

As Table 16.1 on page 424 shows, by the turn of the twentieth century, over half the boys and girls in the U.S. population were enrolled in school, with the majority in elementary school. Most students completed their formal education after eight years of elementary school; only 10 percent received a high school diploma.

As industrialization progressed, technology grew even more complex and service occupations, which require mental rather than physical labor, became more prevalent. The United States and other industrialized societies increasingly looked to education as a means of preparing people for the labor force, and educational attainment became a major qualification for employment. In fact,

TABLE 16.1 Percentage of the U.S. Population Enrolled in Elementary and Secondary School (Males/Females), 1870–2000

Year	Percent of Population Enrolled (M/F)
1870	49.8/46.9
1880	59.2/56.5
1890	54.7/53.8
1900	50.1/50.9
1910	59.1/59.4
1920	64.1/64.5
1930	70.2/69.7
1940	74.9/69.7
1950	79.1/78.4
1960	84.9/83.8
1970	88.5/87.2
1980	95.5/95.5
1990	96.3/95.9
2000 (projected)	96.2*

*A breakdown by sex is unavailable for 2000.

Sources: P. A. Graham (1978). Expansion and exclusion: A history of women in American higher education. Signs 3, pp. 759–773; U.S. Department of Commerce, Bureau of the Census, 1975; 1995.

according to sociologist Randall Collins (1979), the United States can be called a **credential society** because employment and social status are so heavily based on educational credentials—certification that a specific level of education has been attained. The stakes have gone up, too: Today, an elementary school education qualifies a person for only the most menial jobs. Even low-level service jobs require at least some high school, although a high school diploma is preferable, and many jobs now require a college degree. Accordingly, as Figure 16.1 shows, the percentage of the population made up of high school and college graduates has more than doubled since 1960. Having educational credentials doesn't necessarily mean that the best qualified person gets the job; it means that education has become a shortcut for matching people with jobs. As a result, education has a significant impact on income and, therefore, social class, as Table 16.2 shows.

Education in Other Societies

Compared with other industrialized countries, the United States has the highest rate of high school graduates pursuing higher education: 61.9 percent of U.S. high school graduates go to college (U.S. Department of Commerce, Bureau of the Census, 1997). In other industrialized countries, admission to college is more competitive than in the United States. In Japan, for example, only about 40 percent of high school graduates go on to college, and admission is determined almost solely by students' scores on rigorous national exams. In the United States, college-bound youth must also take an exam, the Scholastic Aptitude Test, but students who do not score in the top fortieth percentile can still attend college, especially if they have the financial means or if they are recruited because of their athletic ability. In Japan, though, no matter how wealthy or athletically gifted a student is, entrance to college depends strictly on test scores (White, 1987).

In economically undeveloped countries—the low-income countries in the World Bank stratification system—access to formal education, even at the elementary and secondary levels, is limited for other reasons than test scores or inability to pay. In these societies, especially those in Africa and Asia, the majority of the population works in agriculture, not industry. Thus, like the United States before industrialization, formal education is not considered a necessity for children, who are needed as workers to help support the family. Neither do the governments of these countries have the financial resources to pay for mass education. Consequently, as Table 16.3 on pages 426–427 shows, in most low-income countries, far fewer children attend school than in high-income industrialized countries. This table also shows that males are more likely to attend school than females. Even children who do attend school, though, confront many obstacles to learning, such as a lack of laboratory equipment, books, and basic supplies (U.N. Development Programme, 1998). As a result, the United Nations Children's Fund (UNICEF, 1998) estimates that about 1 billion people—nearly a sixth of the world's population—are entering the twenty-first century without the ability to read, write, or master other skills necessary to hold a job. Illiteracy, in turn, keeps these people locked in extreme poverty. According to UNICEF, education literally makes the difference between life and death in future of the world's children.

In societies where the economy is in transition, education is also directly affected. In the former Soviet Union, for example, beginning in the 1950s, the government provided free mass education for all children. Schools were state-run, and all students wore the same brown uniforms. The curriculum was standardized and included courses in civil defense as well as the usual academic subjects. Although children were supposed to attend the school closest to their homes, the political elite often sent their children to the public schools of their choice since some schools were considered better than others (Stanley, 1994).

When *perestroika* was introduced in the 1980s, teachers and students were given more freedom, including free

Figure 16.1   High School and College Graduates as a Percentage of the U.S. Population, 1910–2000

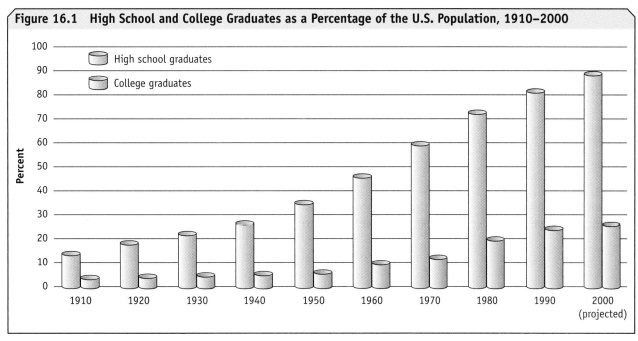

Source: U.S. Department of Commerce, Bureau of the Census, 1975; 1995.

speech and a greater selection of courses. In the post-socialist era, even more educational innovations were introduced, some borrowed from France, Germany, and the United States. For example, in their last two years of high school, students could specialize in humanities, the sciences, or other areas of study. In 1994, the government further liberalized the curriculum for the country's 67,000 public schools, even allowing electives such as English and religious education. However, the new curriculum is not mandatory, and most schools have not adopted it; this creates great disparities in what students are

taught not only from school to school, but also from classroom to classroom in a single school. The most drastic change, however, has been the opening of private, tuition-supported elementary and secondary schools for children of high-ranking political officials and the business elite. In one private school, which charges $3,000 a year (an extraordinary sum by Russian standards) and is subsidized by one of Russia's largest corporations, fifty-seven students are taught by thirty-two teachers, whose salaries are about three times higher than public school teachers. The spread of private schools has some Russian analysts concerned that soon only wealthy children will receive a high-quality education (Stanley, 1994). The remainder of the population will have only basic skills or, worse, will lack even the basic skills needed to be productive workers in the new economy.

TABLE 16.2   Median Annual Income by Educational Attainment

Level of Educational Attainment	Median Annual Income ($)
Not a high school graduate	17,696
High school graduate only	33,779
Some college, no degree	40,015
Associate's degree	45,258
Bachelor's degree	59,048
Master's	68,115
Doctorate	87,232
Professional	92,228

Source: U.S. Department of Commerce, Bureau of the Census, 1998a, p. 6.

REFLECTING ON

Schools and Societies

1. Students are sometimes surprised to hear that the word *school* comes from a word meaning *leisure*. What do you think accounts for their surprise? Is there any way that the association of the two words still makes sense today?
2. Perhaps you or someone you know has attended school in another society. How was education in that society different from education in the United States? How does education in that society reflect the structure of the society as a whole?

TABLE 16.3   Percentage of the School-Age Population Enrolled in School, Twenty Poorest and Twenty Wealthiest Countries, 1993*

Country	ELEMENTARY		SECONDARY	
	Percent Female Population	Percent Male Population	Percent Female Population	Percent Male Population
TWENTY POOREST COUNTRIES (FROM POOREST TO LESS POOR)				
Rwanda	50	50	9	11
Mozambique	51	69	6	9
Ethiopia	19	27	11	12
Tanzania	69	71	5	6
Burundi	63	76	5	9
Sierra Leone**	43	61	8	20
Malawi	77	84	3	6
Chad	38	80	na	na
Uganda	83	99	10	7
Madagascar	72	75	14	14
Nepal	85	129	26	46
Vietnam**	106	111	40	44
Bangladesh	105	128	12	26
Haiti**	70	70	13	14
Niger	21	35	4	9
Guinea-Bissau**	43	94	2	10
Kenya	91	92	23	23
Mali	24	38	6	12
Nigeria	82	105	27	32
Burkina Faso	30	47	6	11

*Percentages may exceed 100 percent because in some countries students enrolled are older or younger than the standard school-age population.

SOCIOLOGICAL THEORIES OF EDUCATION

Given the diversity of education historically and cross culturally, does education have any universal purpose? Some sociologists think so. Let's examine the major sociological theories of education.

The Functionalist Perspective on Education

In line with their analysis of other institutions, structural functionalists study education in terms of how it contributes to the smooth functioning of the society as a whole. According to functionalists, education has both manifest (intended) and latent (unintended) functions. First, we'll consider some of the most important manifest functions.

Transmitting Knowledge, Values, and Skills.   The most significant function of education is found in our definition: instructing a society's members in the knowledge, values, and skills the society deems important. In other words, education is a primary agent of socialization. Every society must impart to younger generations the knowledge and skills they need to be productive members, whether that's how to plow a field, how to read a book, or how to run a computer program. Originally, families fulfilled this function, but once societies industrialize, as we've said, schools take over.

Country	ELEMENTARY		SECONDARY	
	Percent Female Population	Percent Male Population	Percent Female Population	Percent Male Population
TWENTY WEALTHIEST COUNTRIES (FROM RICHEST TO LESS RICH)				
United Arab Emirates	108	112	94	84
Switzerland	102	100	89	93
Japan	102	102	97	95
Denmark	98	97	115	112
Norway	99	99	114	118
United States	106	107	97	98
Germany	98	97	100	101
Austria	103	103	104	109
Sweden	100	100	100	99
France	105	107	107	104
Belgium	100	99	104	103
Singapore**	106	109	59	56
Netherlands	99	96	120	126
Hong Kong**	106	107	65	63
Canada	104	106	103	104
Kuwait	65	65	60	60
Italy	99	98	82	81
Finland	100	100	130	110
United Kingdom	113	112	94	91
Australia	107	108	86	83

**Most recent data available are from 1980.

Source: World Bank, (1996). *World Development Report 1996*, pp. 200–201.

Schools also teach values. When school children pledge allegiance to the American flag before class each morning, they are being taught patriotism and respect for one of our country's cherished symbols. When students are warned to keep their eyes on their own papers, they are being taught not only honesty, but also individualism— they're not to "help" one another; they're on their own. And when they are reprimanded for coming to class after the bell has rung, they are being taught the value our society places on punctuality.

Social Integration. In discussing the history of education, we noted that our nation's early leaders saw schools as a way of teaching citizens the values of the new republic. Later, when scores of immigrants arrived in the United States from Eastern and Southern Europe, education was a way to "Americanize" them. According to structural functionalists, these are examples of the *social integration* function of education: instilling in a large, diverse, and sometimes conflict-ridden group of people a common identity so they form a unified whole.

Schools promote social integration in various ways. One way is through what is taught—the curriculum. For instance, in the former Soviet Union, the largest country in the world in terms of sheer land mass, *all* public schools taught exactly the same subjects. Schools also foster social integration through how the curriculum is taught. Again, in the former Soviet Union, which was composed of numerous ethnic groups, each with its own language and cultural heritage, all subjects were taught in Russian.

In the United States, one of the most ethnically diverse countries in the world, English is the teaching language.

Of course, this is not to say that students and their parents in any of these countries always welcome schools' attempts at social integration. Indeed, the controversy surrounding multicultural education and the English-only movement in the United States is evidence that at the very least, social integration for some people means giving up their racial or ethnic identity and the cultural heritage they attach to it (Traub, 1999).

Social Placement. Educational attainment, we have said, is tied to social stratification. Recall from Chapter 8 that structural functionalists explain stratification in terms of assuring that the best qualified people fill the most important jobs in a society. For functionalists, the educational system is not only the social institution for equipping people with qualifications, but also for identifying who the "best" people are. From the time children enter kindergarten, teachers begin sorting them according to their perceived abilities (Rist, 1970). The brightest students receive the most challenging curriculum, which eventually leads them to challenging—and high-paying and prestigious—jobs. Less gifted students follow a less rigorous course of study that prepares them for a lower place in the labor force, in jobs that require less mental effort and training.

According to functionalists, then, meritocracy begins in school. Through its social placement function, education reinforces social stratification, which functionalists view positively.

Social Change and Innovation. Another function of schools is to foster creative thinking and allow people to pursue their intellectual curiosity. In colleges and universities, in particular, research carried out by faculty adds to the body of knowledge in various fields and can have an enormous practical impact on people's lives. Research on immunization for infectious diseases, for example, was pioneered in university laboratories just as today, medical researchers at some of our country's finest universities are working on an AIDS vaccine. At the same time, sociologists and other social scientists are studying how to educate people about AIDS and HIV transmission, and how to better meet the social needs of people with AIDS. The outcome of all this research could be lower mortality and longer life expectancy for the population as a whole as well as a more productive and comfortable life for people with AIDS.

Latent Functions of Education. Formal education is obviously designed to fulfill many manifest functions for society, but it also serves a number of latent functions. One latent function of formal education is child care. We sometimes hear teachers tell parents of young children that they're not there to babysit, but the reality is that schools provide a safe environment where children are cared for while parents work. As the number of single-parent families and families with two parents in the labor force has increased, so has the number of three-to-five-year-old children enrolled in school. In 1970, for instance, 20.5 percent of three- and four-year-olds were in school, compared to 63.9 percent in 1995 (U.S. Department of Commerce, Bureau of the Census, 1997). Some of the increase comes from greater recognition of the social and intellectual benefits of early childhood education, but it also reflects parents' growing child care needs. Many schools even offer special early morning and aftercare programs so parents can drop off their children on the way to work before the school day officially begins and

According to structural functionalism, what are the manifest and latent functions of education in a society? How does education contribute to social cohesion? According to the conflict and feminist perspectives, in what ways does education reinforce the status quo and perpetuate social inequality?

pick them up on the way home from work several hours after the school day officially ends.

Another latent function of formal education is exposing children to a peer culture. As any parent of a young child will tell you, children pick up new words and behaviors—not all of them desirable—from friends at school. Teenagers, too, for better or for worse, are influenced by classmates in how they talk and dress, what music they listen to, how they spend their leisure time, and so on.

A related latent function of formal education is that it provides children with opportunities to establish social networks. Parents sometimes send children to particular schools so they'll meet the "right" people, that is, people who will supposedly help their children get ahead later in life. Students often meet future life partners at school, so formal education also serves as a dating or matchmaking service. Of course, since most children go to school with others like themselves in terms of social background, the matchmaking function preserves endogamy.

Evaluating the Functionalist Perspective.   Because functionalists look at how education contributes to the stable

SOCIOLOGY LIVE

In our research on this question, we learned that for students at Marshall, attending college serves functions in both life and education. Through the college experience students reported meeting a variety of new people from diverse places and backgrounds. New friends and a new environment lead to new experiences. Thus, college is a primary place for individuals to grow socially. Adaptation is reported as an important part of college life. Time spent away from the parents' home teaches this independence, and school becomes a stepping stone in separating from the family to become independent.

Lessons of the financial world also become very important as students quickly learn how to live on the limited finances they have available. Money management is key, with limited hours for work and new expenses for school and social life. Students build credit and pay loan agencies for the debt that their college attendance may have forced on them. In addition to financial management, the management of time and stress also becomes among the greatest responsibilities that college students must learn. Educationally, college is where students prepare for the good enjoyable job they hope to find after graduation.

College attendance affects the student's family, which must learn to let go and allow the child to grow up. For many students, graduation from college provides an upward intergenerational mobility for their family through a higher level of education. With this mobility, the family also raises its expectations for the student. The most im-

Marshall University, Huntington, West Virginia
Course: Introduction to Sociology, Carolyn U. Nilles, Instructor
Students: (left to right) Ed Slusher, Jane Horton, Erin Dager, Michelle Davis, and (not shown) David Drennen

What functions does college attendance have for students at our university?

portant function of college attendance to the family is the source of pride they find in having a student in college. Difficulties come primarily from the financial realities and hardships that families often face in helping students pay for a college education. In return, graduates may use advantages they gain in the job market to help bring greater financial stability to their families.

For our university as a state institution, student attendance determines the amount of funding that it receives from the government. The numbers of alumni, a reflection of past attendance, also affect the amount of funding and donations. Attendance also affects the programs that the school offers, which affects faculty hiring. Another function of attendance for the school is to heighten its prestige.

Likewise, communities surrounding the school feel direct effects from college attendance. Our university serves as an institution of employment for instructors, administrators, coaches and staff, service workers, and many others, and so serves as a source of revenue for organizations necessary for the function of the school and its parts. Students contribute directly to the community by being a source of employees and by spending money in the community for goods and services.

At a broader level, college is a place where students receive the training that society needs for an educated workforce. Thus, as our sociological inquiry at Marshall University made clear, going to college has a variety of interrelated social functions at all levels—for individuals, for students as a group, for colleges as educational institutions and formal organizations, for local communities, and for the society as a whole.

operation of society, they tend to emphasize its positive aspects. But, critics argue, in focusing on the positive, functionalists overlook the detrimental consequences. For example, functionalists correctly identify socialization and social integration as two functions of education, but critics say that what is taught is typically exclusive rather than inclusive of many groups. Indeed, education has been used to destroy some cultures. In Australia, for instance, Aboriginal children were taken from their parents and put in boarding schools, where they had to dress like Europeans and were forbidden to speak their indigenous languages or practice ancient rituals. Today, most Australian Aboriginal children know little about their cultural heritage, although Aboriginal communities are trying to revitalize ethnic languages and traditions. In the United States, Native Americans have had a nearly identical educational experience (Brooke, 1995; Noley, 1990). Thus, instead of integrating all members of a society, schools can make some groups social outsiders.

Critics also question the extent to which schools foster creative thinking and encourage children to satisfy their intellectual curiosity. While it is true that universities are sources of innovation and even social rebellion, elementary and secondary schools in some countries promote rigid conformity and rote learning. Critics of Japan's school system, for example, say it stifles students' creativity and teaches them to memorize rather than think independently (White, 1987; Wu Dunn, 1995; 1996). On the other hand, education reformers in the United States say we would do well to adopt some Japanese practices, such as aspiring to higher standards and assigning heavier workloads. We rank embarrasingly low on international math, science, and reading tests compared to other modern, industrialized countries (Applebome, 1996).

Finally, critics agree with functionalists that education reinforces a society's stratification system, but they do not believe that the basis for social placement is always—or even often—merited. Research shows, for instance, that students' social class, race and ethnicity, and sex influence teachers' perceptions of their intellectual abilities as much as, if not more than, their objective classroom performance (American Association of University Women [AAUW], 1992; Hartocollis, 1998; Oakes, 1985; Rist, 1970). Therefore, critics argue, social inequality affects education and education preserves social inequality. We look more closely at this point in the next section.

Conflict and Feminist Perspectives on Education

Conflict and feminist sociologists focus on the relationship between education and inequality. They cite ability grouping, bias in testing, the "hidden curriculum," and underfunded schools as areas of potential inequality. We'll look at each in turn.

Schools as "Sorting Machines." Most of us assume that what's taught to children in school is pretty standard. How much or how quickly a child learns may vary, but aren't children at least presented with a common body of knowledge? Conflict theorists say, "no," and point to research showing that education material presented to a student, as well as the way it is presented, depends on the student's assigned *track* in school (Oakes, 1985). **Tracking** is a system of grouping students identified as having similar abilities so they can be taught together. In other words, tracking is a sorting mechanism. It creates an academic hierarchy of fast, average, and slow learners. About 60 percent of elementary schools and 80 percent of secondary schools track students (Strum, 1993).

Educators who support tracking say that by grouping together students who are academically alike, slow learners can get extra help while not feeling inferior to brighter students, and fast learners are not held back by those who learn more slowly. However, empirical research shows that just the opposite is true: Tracking actually lowers the self-esteem of students identified as slow, causing them to do worse, not better, in school. Once placed in the low tracks, these students see themselves as stupid and lose the motivation to work up to their potential (Children's Defense Fund, 1991; Oakes, 1985).

Conflict theorists are even more concerned about how tracking reinforces social inequality. Studies show that poor, working-class, and minority students are significantly more likely than White, middle-class, and wealthy students to be in low tracks (Dreeban & Gamoran, 1986; Paul, 1987; Salmans, 1988) and special education programs (Hartocollis, 1998; U.S. Department of Education, 1997). Once tracked, the students are taught different things. For example, while high-track students are learning Shakespeare and analytic geometry, low-track students are being taught how to fill out forms, figure sales tax, and write checks. Teachers of high-track students say they want these students to learn to think critically, creatively, and independently. Teachers of low-track students say they want these students to learn to "keep themselves clean," "cope with frustration," and "take a directive order and act upon it" (Oakes, 1985). In short, high-track students are taught knowledge and skills that are highly valued in our society, while low-track students are not. Students exposed to only "low-prestige" knowledge and skills are denied certain educational opportunities up the line, such as college, which, in turn, closes other doors to them, including high-level social and economic positions in our society (Bidwell & Friedkin, 1988; Mathews, 1998). As one researcher asks, "In essence, are we teaching kids at the bottom to stay there and kids at the top how to get ahead?" (Oakes, 1985, p. 91). In light of these findings, our earlier story about the PEON program does not seem far-fetched at all. Some schools have changed their tracking policies in response to the charge that tracking perpetuates elitism (Strum, 1993).

Biased Testing.

The debate over tracking is related to another controversy: the fairness of standardized testing. Students in different tracks get differential learning opportunities that over time affect academic performance and eventually job opportunities. Still, some educators argue, if tracking is based on real differences in ability, it makes sense to use it. After all, it would be unfair to expect students of different abilities to do identical work, and teachers should not give low-ability students false hopes about future high-level careers. However, conflict theorists point out that tracking is at least partly determined by students' performance on standardized tests, and these tests have built-in biases that disadvantage particular groups.

Consider, for example, the following question:

Symphony is to composer as _____ is to poet.

a) music
b) sonnet
c) flute
d) paper

The correct answer is *sonnet.* If you got this question wrong, does that mean you are not as intelligent as someone who got it right? Maybe. But an incorrect answer might also mean that you are simply unfamiliar with such things as symphonies and sonnets. Who is most likely to be unfamiliar with symphonies and sonnets? Children from economically disadvantaged backgrounds for one, but also children whose racial and ethnic heritage is not Western European. Yet, this kind of question is common on standardized tests used for tracking *all* students, regardless of social class, race, or ethnicity. Not surprisingly, children from wealthy White families do better on such tests than children from non-White and poorer families (Applebome, 1997a; Jones, 1994).

Conflict theorists argue that while standardized tests provide some measure of students' intellectual abilities, they are a better indicator of a student's background and learning environment. The tests are culturally specific—geared to a child's familiarity with White, middle-class language and experiences—but our society is culturally diverse. Although test preparers claim that they have eliminated biased questions from standardized tests, critics disagree. Still, despite the persistent biases, standardized testing is more popular than ever, not only for sorting students into tracks in elementary and secondary school, but also for determining admission to special programs, colleges, universities, and professional schools. In 1997, President Clinton even proposed national standardized tests in reading (Applebome, 1997b). These developments have led some critics of standardized testing to refer to our society as a "testocracy" rather than a meritocracy (Guinier & Strum, 1996).

The Hidden Curriculum.

Education is about transmitting not only knowledge and skills, but also values. Schools do this explicitly by, for instance, teaching patriotism in civics class, which is part of the official curriculum. Coexisting with the state-required curriculum is the **hidden curriculum,** values transmitted implicitly through education. Both conflict theorists and feminist sociologists believe that the hidden curriculum reinforces social inequality. How?

Suppose we asked you who Abraham Lincoln was? You probably wouldn't have much trouble answering, right? And if we asked who invented the telephone, you'd reply quickly, "Alexander Graham Bell." But suppose we asked you about Matthew Henson, Phillis Wheatley, or Dr. Daniel Hale Williams? Chances are that you don't recognize their names because most students never learn about them in school. Conflict and feminist sociologists would point out that, not coincidentally, Abraham Lincoln and Alexander Graham Bell were both White males, while Matthew Henson, Phillis Wheatley, and Daniel Hale Williams were African Americans. Phillis Wheatley was also a woman.

Although coverage of women and racial and ethnic minorities in textbooks has improved, these groups are still underrepresented (Davis, 1995). The underrepresentation of racial and ethnic minorities and women, as well as lesbians and gay men, in curriculum materials sends an implicit but powerful message to students: It says that members of these groups have rarely made significant contributions to our society. You might think that children don't notice such exclusions, but studies show that children learn the lessons of the hidden curriculum. In a recent survey of 7,500 schoolchildren in grades one through twelve in the Minneapolis–St. Paul, Minnesota area, when asked about a woman being elected President of the United States, the majority said only men can be President; some said women can't even run for the office (Snow, 1992; see also Best, 1983).

By the way, if you're still wondering about Matthew Henson, Phillis Wheatley, and Daniel Hale Williams, we'll quickly fill you in: Matthew Henson was a member of Admiral Perry's North Pole expedition; it was he who planted the American flag at the North Pole on April 6, 1909. Phillis Wheatley wrote the second book published by a woman in America. The book appeared in 1773, and Wheatley received a commendation from President George Washington. Dr. Daniel Hale Williams was a physician who practiced in Chicago, and in 1893, he performed the first successful heart operation.

The hidden curriculum does not operate only through textbooks and other teaching materials. The composition of the education labor force also sends covert messages

What economic, political, social, and cultural factors might account for the differences you see among the schools and students in these photographs? According to the conflict perspective, how do these differences relate to the distribution of wealth and power within a society? How do these differences relate to the distribution of wealth and power among societies globally?

about gender, racial, and ethnic inequalities (Manzo, 1993). For example, 87 percent of elementary school teachers and 83 percent of teachers' aides are women, but only 40 percent of school administrators and 43 percent of principals and assistant principals are women. Among chief state school officers—the leaders of the states' public school systems—only nine out of fifty are women, and women are just 4.8 percent of the country's school superintendents (AAUW, 1992; U.S. Department of Commerce, Bureau of the Census, 1997). Eighty-four percent of public school teachers are White, a statistic that has not changed significantly since 1982. Even in urban areas with a high concentration of minority students, nearly three quarters of teachers identify themselves as White. Of our nation's 1.8 million teachers, 7 percent are African American, 2 percent Hispanic American, 1 percent Native

American, and 1 percent Asian American ("Study of Teachers," 1996). As Table 16.4 shows, this distribution persists at the college and university level, too.

Unequal Schools.   Conflict theorists are concerned not only about unequal treatment of students in schools, but also about inequality between schools. Private elementary and secondary schools, for example, are still available for families who can afford them. These schools rely largely on tuition and other fees to meet their expenses. Average annual tuition at private elementary schools ranges from $1,628 at Catholic parish schools to $4,693 at nonsectarian schools; at the secondary school level, the range is $3,643 to $9,525 (U.S. Department of Commerce, Bureau of the Census, 1997). But these are averages; at some elite private schools, tuition for kindergar-

TABLE 16.4   Percentage Distribution of Full-Time Instructional Faculty at Institutions of Higher Education, by Sex and Race

Race/Ethnic Group	SEX (%)*	
	Women	Men
White	28.4	57.4
Black/African American	2.2	2.5
Hispanic American/Latino	0.8	1.4
Asian/Pacific Islander	1.2	3.5
American Indian/Alaskan Native	0.14	0.23
Nonresident alien	0.45	1.5
Race/Ethnicity unknown	0.06	0.14

*Percentages do not add to 100 percent due to rounding.
Source: U.S. National Center for Education Statistics, 1996, p. 231

ten is $10,000 or more a year. The teacher–student ratio at private schools is usually lower than at public schools, and private school graduates are more likely than public school graduates not only to go on to college, but to be admitted to the top colleges and universities in the country, many of which are also private (Coleman & Hoffer, 1987; U.S. Department of Commerce, Bureau of the Census, 1997).

Only about 10 percent of all elementary and secondary students attend private schools. The vast majority attend public schools that are financed largely with local property tax revenues with some state and federal appropriations. States vary greatly in the amount of money they spend on education. In general, the Northeastern states spend the most per student and the Southern states the least, with a national average of $5,949 per student (U.S. Department of Commerce, Bureau of the Census, 1997).

These between-state differences mask important within-state differences across school districts. Even students living in states with high educational spending do not necessarily go to well-funded schools because public schools get most of their money from their local tax bases. Relying on community property taxes makes public schools vulnerable to citizen tax revolts. Taxpayers trying to control government spending and prevent tax increases often vote against additional funding for financially strapped public schools (Hernandez, 1995). Moreover, school districts with a strong tax base can spend more money on their schools than poorer districts. In other words, school districts with a high concentration of low-income homeowners and renters generate less school revenue than districts with wealthier homeowners whose properties have greater value. Residents in many city school districts actually pay a higher-than-average portion of their incomes toward education, but because their incomes are low, their schools lag behind schools in suburban districts where incomes are higher. In fact, per-student spending in well-to-do school districts is, in some cases, more than nine times greater than per-student spending in inner city school districts (Children's Defense Fund, 1991; Kozol, 1991; see also the Doing Sociology box).

In summary, conflict theorists maintain that unequal schools lead to unequal schooling. Poorly funded schools must cut back on staff and programs as well as upkeep of facilities, which generally translates into lower-quality education. Since students in these school districts come from poor families and are disproportionately members of

DOING SOCIOLOGY

How Does Your State Finance Its Public Schools?

We have already noted that a state's use of local property taxes to fund the lion's share of educational expenses usually results in schools in poor neighborhoods being underfinanced. During the 1990s, a number of parents' and citizens' groups challenged this funding strategy in court, resulting in at least twelve states having their school financ-

ing systems declared unconstitutional. In these decisions, the courts ruled that such funding strategies deny students in poor neighborhoods equal educational opportunity relative to their peers who live in wealthier neighborhoods. But importantly, in a number of cases, the courts also ruled that educational equity between poor and affluent schools cannot be achieved simply by states giving each school the same amount of money. Instead, schools in poor districts should be given *greater* state funds than schools in wealthier districts, keeping in mind that economically disadvantaged chil-

dren have special needs (for example, early enrichment programs, health services, a lower teacher-to-student ratio) that require extra funds (Sullivan, 1994).

How does your state fund public education? On your own or with your classmates, research how funds are allocated to school districts in your state. Which school districts get the most money using your state's current funding strategy? Is the system equitable? If it appears inequitable, brainstorm with your classmates about ways your state could more equitably distribute education funds.

minority groups, the socially and economically disadvantaged are once again denied educational opportunities that lead to upward social mobility (see the Intersecting Inequalities box).

Evaluating the Conflict and Feminist Perspectives.
Critics say the conflict and feminist position on tracking is overstated, that students are grouped by academic ability, not by social class, sex, race, and ethnicity. Research

has not consistently supported the conflict and feminist perspectives (Hurn, 1985), but in general, these two perspectives on education do have considerable empirical support.

Critics also point out that conflict and feminist sociologists downplay the extent to which education helps the poor, women, and minorities move ahead in our society. They grant that the educational system reproduces stratification, but it is not simply a means of keeping the

INTERSECTING INEQUALITIES

Who Goes to College?

We know that good grades and high SAT scores are important for getting into college, but sociologists have found that going to college is also strongly related to family income. As the table below shows, children from high-income families are significantly more likely to attend college than children from low-income families.

The relationship between family income and college enrollment is in part a function of the fact that children in high-income families usually go to well-financed schools, which better prepare them for the SATs and college-level work; they are more likely to be admitted to college. But the relationship between family income and college enrollment also reflects the cost of a college education. For the 1997–1998 academic year, tuition at public four-year colleges averaged $3,111, while at private four-year colleges the average tuition was $13,664. Tuition at some elite colleges and universities now exceeds $20,000 (Bronner, 1997). The cost of room, board, and other fees further raises the price of a college education by several thousand dollars (U.S. Department of Commerce, Bureau of the Census, 1997). But what disturbs many students and parents is that college tuition has been increasing at a rate of 5 percent or more a year, which is higher than the rate of inflation as well as the growth in average family income (1–2 percent a year) (Bronner, 1997).

Student Debt

To meet these expenses, most students (more than 60 percent) need financial aid, which usually turns out to be a combination of scholarships, grants, work-study arrangements, and loans. In fact, the number of federal student loans rose from 8,900 in 1966 when the federal loan program began to over 5 million in 1998—more than the number of beneficiaries of any other social program except Medicare and Social Security (Honan, 1998). By the time a student at a four-year college graduates, she or he has an average debt of $10,146 (Hershey, 1996).

The prospect of such indebtedness causes some students to postpone college; others enroll at least initially at a two-year college, where tuition and other

expenses are usually lower than at four-year colleges, or attend a four-year public college near their home. Over 50 percent of full-time undergraduates now attend colleges where the tuition is under $4,000. Less than 5 percent attend colleges where the tuition is $20,000 or more (Arenson, 1996). Moreover, although most colleges and universities are offering more scholarships than in the past, the majority of these scholarships are merit-based rather than need-based. Although most of the financial aid provided by colleges and universities is still need-based, the proportion of merit-based aid—the aid that goes to academically outstanding students regardless of their ability to pay—grew at an annual rate of 13 percent during the 1980s. This shift raises concerns that the pool of money available to needy students will shrink and that students from working-class families who do not qualify for merit-based or need-based aid will find college education out of their financial reach (Children's Defense Fund, 1997; Passell, 1997).

Student Elite?

The cost of a college education has risen faster than the inflation rate every year for nearly two decades. If this trend continues, some analysts think that educational opportunity in the early twenty-first century will be a lot like that of the early twentieth century, with higher education available only to an elite characterized not so much by its scholarly ability as by its ability to pay (McCarty, 1985).

College Enrollment by Family Income, 1993

Family Income	Percent of Families with Children 18–24 Who Have at Least One Child Enrolled in College
< $10,000	19.1%
$10,000–$19,999	26.1
$20,000–$29,999	36.2
$30,000–$39,999	43.5
$40,000–$49,999	50.7
$50,000–$74,999	57.1
$75,000 & >	67.7

Source: U.S. Department of Commerce, Bureau of the Census, 1994.

disadvantaged in their places. There is upward social mobility in advanced industrial societies, including the United States, and education is a major contributor to this mobility.

The Symbolic Interactionist Perspective on Education

While structural functionalists and conflict theorists study education at the macro level, symbolic interactionists focus on the micro level, looking at interactions in the classroom. Some feminist sociologists also study education at the micro level. Let's see what these theorists have to say.

Education and Self-Concept.   Do you remember Charles Horton Cooley's concept of the looking-glass self that we discussed in Chapter 5? According to Cooley, how we see ourselves—that is, our self concepts—depends largely on how we think others see us. One interest of symbolic interactionists, therefore, is how teachers' labeling of students affects students' self-concepts, and consequently, their academic performance. Symbolic interactionists have found that differences in students' academic performance are not only the result of real differences in ability, but they are also the product of a **self-fulfilling prophecy,** that is, something comes true because people believe it to be true and act accordingly. When teachers predict how individual students will do, their predictions may come true not because of the intellectual differences among students, but because the students and their teachers believe the differences are true and act accordingly (Aronson & Gonzalez, 1988).

The classic study of the self-fulfilling prophecy in education was conducted by Richard Rosenthal and Lenore Jacobson (1968). They gave all first through sixth graders at a San Francisco elementary school a standardized test at the beginning of the school year and reported the scores to their teachers. But Rosenthal and Jacobson also *randomly* selected 20 percent of the students and identified them as having "unusual intellectual promise." What Rosenthal and Jacobson wanted to see was whether the teachers treated these "gifted" students differently and what impact the differential treatment would have on their learning. At the end of the school year they retested all the students and found that the scores of the children who had been identified as "promising" improved on average twice as much as the other students, and the youngest children showed the greatest gains.

Subsequent research confirmed these findings across racial and ethnic groups and in other societies as well (see, for example, Willis, 1990). In one well-known follow-up study, for instance, sociologist Ray Rist (1970) observed teacher–student interaction in a kindergarten with mostly African American teachers and students. Rist found that by the second week of school, the teacher had divided the children into three groups based on her perceptions of their intellectual abilities. The students she labeled bright were seated at the front of the classroom, closest to her, and she interacted most with them. The "slow learners" were seated in the back and received the least positive interaction with the teacher. Rist believed that the children in each group quickly internalized the teacher's perceptions of them and performed in ways congruent with the label. The bright students actively participated in class, were enthusiastic about school, and did well. The slow students withdrew from class participation, showed little interest in school, and did poorly. As the children moved through the grades, Rist found that the labels stuck with them and were thus further reinforced.

Symbolic interactionists conclude from these findings that students adjust their self-concepts to teachers' expectations of them. Students labeled "slow" come to believe they will not excel in school and, sooner or later, their academic record confirms the prediction. The initial labeling sets up a vicious cycle for these children, as one analyst explained:

> For every day in the classroom, the children who are considered less able fall further behind their contemporaries and give the teacher further reason to handle them differently. Thus, the small differences between children in the early years of school expand quickly to the drastic forms of differential performance which become obvious in the later years. (quoted in Hurn, 1985, p. 189)

Some feminist sociologists have also looked at how teacher–student interactions differ by gender and what effect this has on boys' and girls' learning experiences. So, before we evaluate the symbolic interactionist perspective as a whole, let's briefly look at this feminist research.

Gender Labels.   Research shows that teachers interact differently with girls than boys. Boys, for example, get more feedback from teachers than girls, and they are praised more for the intellectual quality of their work. However, boys also engage in more negative interaction with teachers, who perceive them as more disruptive and less attentive (AAUW, 1992; Farkas et al., 1990; Sadker & Sadker, 1994). One result of this perception is that boys more often than girls are labeled "learning disabled" and placed in special education programs.

As Table 16.5 on page 436 shows, boys greatly outnumber girls in special education classes: More than two-thirds of special education students are male. To some extent, this statistic reflects the greater number of boys born with disabling conditions, but feminist researchers have found that congenital problems do not fully explain the sex difference. Instead, it appears that teachers consider students' attitudes and behavior, as well as their academic

TABLE 16.5   Elementary and Secondary School Students Identified with Learning Problems, by Race/Ethnicity and Sex

Race/Ethnicity & Sex	LEARNING PROBLEM		
	Mental Retardation	Serious Emotional Disturbance	Specific Learning Disability
White			
Male	33.34	51.85	46.55
Female	24.43	13.69	20.50
African American			
Male	19.05	19.32	11.94
Female	12.39	5.20	5.28
Hispanic American			
Male	4.78	6.20	8.77
Female	3.47	1.60	4.24
Asian American/Pacific Islander			
Male	0.77	0.68	0.93
Female	0.58	0.17	0.42
American Indian			
Male	0.68	1.00	0.94
Female	0.50	0.29	0.43

Source: U.S. Department of Education, 1997, p.1.

performance, when deciding who should be placed in special education programs. Girls are typically perceived as more cooperative than boys. Even though research shows boys and girls are equally disruptive in class, boys are more often labeled as "acting out" (AAUW, 1992; Serbin et al., 1973). Moreover, feminist research shows that sex interacts with race and ethnicity in influencing teachers' labels of students (Fordham, 1996). For instance, studies show that African American girls are more likely than all other students to be ignored by teachers (AAUW, 1992; Cox, 1998; Reid, 1982).

What are the consequences of inaccurate and excessive labeling? On the one hand, boys who are inaccurately labeled learning disabled carry the label with them throughout their school years, which often limits their educational opportunities. On the other hand, girls with learning disabilities who are not placed in special education programs are denied services they need to improve academically. Moreover, it appears that minority students are harmed more by this labeling process than White students (AAUW, 1992).

Evaluating the Symbolic Interactionist Perspective.   Education research by symbolic interactionists reinforces many of the observations made by macro-level theorists. However, some critics feel that symbolic interactionists do not go far enough in their analyses; they stop short of explicitly drawing connections between micro-level and macro-level processes. How do teachers' expectations of students develop in the first place, critics ask? How are teachers' expectations of students influenced by social in-

equalities inherent in society as whole? By failing to answer such questions, symbolic interactionists ignore the fact that the parameters of most teacher–student interactions are defined by existing (and taken-for-granted) social structural arrangements.

Other critics say that symbolic interactionism puts too much emphasis on the negative consequences of labeling and overlooks other factors that affect students' learning. For example, students' enthusiasm for school is inspired not only by teachers, but also by parents. Thus, critics argue, more attention needs to be given to the role parents play in developing their children's self-concepts as students. Research shows that students with parents who are enthusiastic about learning, who are active learners themselves, and who show interest in their children's education perform better academically than students with disinterested and uninvolved parents (Hannon, 1987; Pelligrini et al., 1991). In short, critics maintain, even students not negatively labeled by teachers can develop poor academic self-concepts if their home environment is not supportive.

R E F L E C T I N G   O N

Sociological Theories of Education

1. Can you think of any other manifest or latent functions of education besides those discussed by the authors of the chapter and the Sociology Live box?

2. Were you tracked in elementary or secondary school? If so, was your experience positive or negative?

3. Do you think it's possible to develop a standardized test completely free of cultural biases? Why or why not? If you believe such a test is possible, what do you think it would look like?

4. Some sociologists think the Rosenthal and Jacobson experiment was unethical. Recalling our discussion of research ethics in Chapter 2, do you think this study raises ethical concerns? If so, what are they, and how would you resolve them?

5. Have you ever been labeled by a teacher in a way you considered unfair or inaccurate? If so, did the labeling affect your self-concept or academic performance in any way? How?

PROBLEMS IN EDUCATION

In our discussion so far, we have identified several problems that contradict the popular image of our education system as equitable and democratic: These are the negative effects of tracking; biases in standardized testing; unequal educational opportunities for the poor, females, and minorities; and arbitrary and inaccurate labels that lower students' self-concepts and school performance. We'll continue our discussion by considering three other persistent problems in education: racial segregation, educational quality, and crime and violence in schools.

Racial Segregation

Segregation refers to physically and socially separating and keeping apart different racial and ethnic groups. Today, segregation is illegal, but it still characterizes our nation's schools.

In 1954, the U.S. Supreme Court ruled in the case of *Brown* v. *Board of Education of Topeka* that racially segregated schools are unconstitutional. "It is doubtful," the Court said, "that any child may reasonably be expected to succeed in life if he or she is denied the opportunity of education. Such an opportunity is a right which must be available to all on equal terms" (quoted in Cole, 1985, p. 148). Still, more than forty years later, minority children continue to attend separate and usually unequal schools. Nationally, almost 75 percent of Hispanic American students and 67 percent of African American students are enrolled in schools with minority populations of more than 50 percent. In 1997, the typical African American student attended a school where only about one-third (33.9 percent) of the students were White; the typical Hispanic American student attended a school where just 30.6 percent of the students were White. Although many of these students attend urban schools, a troubling finding of recent research is that segregation is increasing in the suburban schools, as more families of color move from urban areas to the suburbs (Orfield et al., 1996).

Why does racial segregation persist in schools? One reason is residential segregation. Most students attend public schools, and the public school they attend depends on the neighborhood in which they live. United States neighborhoods continue to be highly segregated. As long as schools are assigned by neighborhoods and neighborhoods are racially segregated, schools will be racially segregated, too (Orfield & Montfort, 1993).

Another reason that racial segregation persists in schools is that attempts to achieve racial balance have failed. Following the *Brown* decision, the courts recognized that desegregation was not occurring rapidly enough on a voluntary basis, so they took further steps. One strategy was court-ordered busing of students across school districts, but busing was strongly opposed by White parents. White parents who favored school integration did not want their children sent on long bus rides, and those who openly opposed school integration on racist grounds protested or took their children out of public schools and enrolled them in private schools to avoid busing. Many minority parents also opposed busing, largely because it was usually minority students who had to bear the burden of long bus rides. For example, in one famous desegregation case involving the Charlotte-Mecklenburg, North Carolina, school districts, equal numbers of African American and White students were bused, but the White students were bused for only two years and the African American students for four. Similarly, in Milwaukee, Wisconsin, nine times more African American than White students were bused (Willie, 1987). Critics of

The majority of students in the United States continue to attend racially segregated schools despite the fact that the Supreme Court ruled in 1954 that racial segregation in education is illegal. What desegregation measures have been tried? Why have most state- and community-based school desegregation plans failed? In what ways do students in racially integrated schools actually contribute to resegregation? How will school choice initiatives and the demise of affirmative action in the United States affect the racial balance of schools? What do you think will be some consequences of racial imbalances for the future?

busing also point out that it often does not improve the educational experiences and opportunities of minority students because placing these students in all-White schools does not prevent them from being segregated once again in their new schools (Hacker, 1992).

In another strategy for promoting desegregation, some school systems created *magnet schools*, public schools designed to attract high-achieving students of diverse backgrounds by offering high-quality, specialized programs. Magnet schools focus on science, music and the performing arts, or other specialties, such as foreign languages. The first magnet schools were opened in urban neighborhoods with large minority populations, but now, with more than 5,000 in operation across the country, many are located in suburban districts (Hacker, 1992; Toch, 1991).

Magnet schools are appealing because they are based on voluntarism; a family *selects* a magnet school because of what it offers students academically and socially. There is evidence that magnet schools are an effective and academically sound way to foster integration, but the programs are small and accessible to only the "best and the brightest" (Hacker, 1992; Lyons & Walton, 1988). Consequently, many educators believe that magnet schools alone cannot achieve racial integration throughout a school system, although they disagree on what is the most practical and effective means to achieve this goal. Research does show that desegregation has a positive impact on education under specific conditions, including:

- When it takes place early in a child's education before racial prejudices become too ingrained (Hawley, 1985);
- When teachers are trained in multicultural education and have inner city teaching experience;
- When a multicultural curriculum is adopted and teachers use a variety of teaching techniques, especially cooperative learning in small groups (Aronson & Gonzalez, 1988);
- When minority teachers and counselors are available to help minority students and serve as role models; and
- When interracial extracurricular activities are offered and encouraged (Cole, 1985; Hawley, 1985).

The benefits of integrated schools include improved minority student academic performance, but not at the expense of White students; improved employment prospects for minority students; and improved racial and ethnic relations as students learn from and about people who are different from themselves (Hawley 1985; Hawley & Smylie, 1988).

Educational Quality

In 1983, the National Commission on Excellence in Education issued a report on the quality of education in the United States. The Commission had spent two years collecting data and hearing testimony, and its findings were alarming. For example, U.S. students scored well below their peers in other industrialized countries on international tests of math, science, and reading. The vast majority of seventeen-year-olds (80 percent) could not write a persuasive essay; about 67 percent could not solve a math problem requiring several steps; and about 60 percent could not draw inferences from written material. The Commission concluded that our country had been committing "an act of unthinking, unilateral educational disarmament" and called for reforms to improve the quality of education in the United States (National Commission on Excellence in Education, 1983, p. 5).

More recent studies show some improvements in U.S. students' performance. The United States now ranks close to the international average in math, but still below the international average in science. On tests of advanced math and physics, the United States scored lower than all other countries that participated in the International Mathematics and Science Study, including Greece, Cyprus, and Latvia (Bronner, 1998). In reading and writing, U.S. students also lag behind students in other countries ("Slight Rise in Math and Science Scores," 1996).

What accounts for U.S. students' poor academic showing? Not surprisingly, experts disagree on the answer to this question and, consequently, on how to solve the problem. Some analysts blame poorly trained teachers. In one recent study, for example, a group of education specialists evaluated lesson transcripts and videotapes of German, Japanese, and American math teachers instructing students. Eighty-seven percent of American teachers received low grades and none received high grades. In contrast, 13 percent of Japanese teachers got low grades and 30 percent were given high grades (Applebome, 1996b). In Japan (as well as in Great Britain and in a number of European countries), teacher training programs have more selective admissions than in the United States and once admitted, Japanese teachers-in-training follow a challenging curriculum and do not get to teach until they have apprenticed with an experienced teacher (Phillips, 1991; White, 1987). Most U.S. teachers do not rate their training as challenging or even intellectually stimulating (Fiske, 1987), and apart from a semester of student teaching, most enter the classroom immediately after college graduation, with no mentoring from experienced colleagues (Applebome, 1996b). Not surprisingly, a 1998 survey of 4,000 U.S. teachers found that only about one in five (20 percent) felt well prepared to teach in the nation's schools (Honan, 1999).

Other analysts feel that teachers' salaries are problematic, being too low to attract and retain the most qualified individuals to the profession. In Japan, for example, teaching commands significantly higher pay and prestige than in the United States. The average starting salary of

Japanese teachers is $2,000 to $3,000 more than the average starting salary of other Japanese public-sector workers and is comparable to the salaries of Japanese college graduates who pursue corporate careers (White, 1987). In the United States, teachers' pay raises have outpaced inflation since the 1980s, but as Table 16.6 shows, the average annual salary of a public school teacher is well below the salaries of most other professions requiring a college degree.

Other education analysts blame the schools for students' poor performance, specifically criticizing a weak and inconsistent curriculum. First, they say, the work that U.S. students do is not very challenging. The curriculum in most schools covers too many subjects, and each is watered down to provide only superficial knowledge. At the same time, U.S. schools allow students to take too many electives—more than 50 percent of the curriculum in some high schools—which means basic skills and knowledge needed for college and the work world are neglected (Mosle, 1996). In fact, one study likened U.S. high schools to shopping malls where students choose courses the way shoppers hunt for bargains. For shoppers, the best buy is the item with the lowest price; for students, the best course is often the one that requires minimal effort, but still applies to graduation. Why struggle with Chaucer and Poe when you can take "Sports Literature"? Who needs calculus when "Consumer Mathematics" fulfills the third-year math requirement just as well (Powell et al., 1985)?

TABLE 16.6   Average Starting Salary of Public School Teachers Compared with Salaries in Private Industry, Selected Professions, 1993

College Graduates in (profession)	Average Starting Salary ($)
Public school teaching	22,505
Engineering	35,004
Computer science	31,164
Mathematics/statistics	30,756
Chemistry	30,456
Economics/finance	28,584
Sales/marketing	28,536
Accounting	28,020
Business administration	27,564
Liberal arts*	27,216

*Excluding chemistry, mathematics, economics, and computer science

Source: U.S. Department of Commerce, Bureau of the Census, 1996, p. 167.

Many of those who see schools as the cause of students' poor academic performance advocate *school choice programs,* programs that allow parents to choose the public schools their children will attend or use federal "vouchers" to pay for private schooling. The rationale behind school choice programs is simple: Forcing schools to compete for students motivates them to improve. Critics think that school choice programs would create greater educational inequality because underfunded inner city public schools do not have the resources to compete with their better funded suburban counterparts and private schools. The best schools will skim the best students from the pool, leaving behind poor, non-English speaking, and learning disabled students (Children's Defense Fund, 1991; Chira, 1991). Another concern is that school choice programs allow parents from similar social class, racial and ethnic, and religious backgrounds to concentrate their children in a specific school, thus increasing school segregation (Mosle, 1996).

One recent study, though, indicates that these concerns may be overstated. The study found that two-thirds of parents who used vouchers to send their children to private or parochial schools with the goal of improving their children's education were very satisfied with the program. Parents who did not participate in the program cited transportation and financial problems as two major reasons for not participating. Although participants and nonparticipants did not differ in terms of ethnicity, family size, religion, or mother's education or employment, the children of nonparticipants were more likely to be in special education classes or classes for the gifted (Lewin, 1997; see also Brooke, 1997).

An alternative solution is a standard national curriculum for all U.S. schools. As one analyst explains, U.S. students are taking more standardized tests than ever before, but our schools have no consistent standards, that is, "no agreed-on expectations of what students should know at each level of schooling" (Mosle, 1996, p. 46). Almost all other industrialized countries in the world—including those that outscore the United States on international tests—have a national curriculum that specifies what students must learn in core subjects such as math, science, literature, and history. Before students can progress to the next level, they must pass a standardized test. Unlike most school standardized tests in the United States, which try to measure general ability, these tests are content-based, measuring what students have learned in school (Mosle, 1996). Opponents believe that having all children learn exactly the same things in school is undesirable. They favor local control of schools, allowing teachers, parents, and local school officials the freedom to decide what students in their schools should be taught. Some point to disagreement over what constitutes a core curriculum and worry that adopting a standard curriculum nationwide might exclude the history and culture of minorities.

Social Policy
Can Charter Schools Improve Education?

The Issue

In 1988, a group of parents, educators, and policy makers concerned about the declining quality of public education in the United States developed the idea of *charter schools*, that is, public schools run by parents or community groups free to establish their own missions, curricula, and teaching strategies. In 1991, Minnesota became the first state to pass legislation permitting charter schools, and the first charter school opened in 1992. By 1999, there were over 1,100 charter schools in operation across the country, educating about 250,000 students (Hartocollis, 1999). Can parents and community groups really run schools better than state and school district officials who are usually responsible for designing the curriculum and establishing educational practice and policy?

The Debate

Supporters of charter schools argue that parents and community groups know their children's learning patterns and specialized needs better than state or school district officials. Charter schools get parents and the neighborhood involved in education by making them responsible for educational outcomes. In order for charter schools to remain open, they must demonstrate that their students are learning at least as well as students in traditional public schools. Supporters point to the results of a recent study of thirty-one charter schools as evidence that such schools are successful. Twenty-one of the schools in the study reported improvements in students' standardized test scores (the remaining ten schools, however, did not report any data) (Archibold, 1998).

Critics of charter schools are skeptical of these research findings. They argue that the study was based on too limited a sample, since only the top-ranked charter schools were included. They also think that the schools have not been established long enough for them to be adequately evaluated; at least five years worth of data are required, they say, for a sound assessment. Critics acknowledge that some schools may be successful in raising students' standardized test scores, but by 1999, about 3 percent of all charter schools had been closed, most because they had not demonstrated that their students were learning as well as students in traditional public schools.

Another concern is that charter schools alone cannot solve the problem of educational quality, especially in poor neighborhoods, since they also often confront difficulties posed by underfunding. Charter schools receive funds to cover operating expenses from the public school system, but they do not receive money for construction, renovation, and sometimes, equipment. Compounding the funding problem, most charter schools are not permitted to issue bonds like traditional public schools can. As a result, charter schools must raise money from private sources and so are dependent on the generosity of local businesses, organizations, and philanthropists (Hartocollis, 1999). If this money dries up or private funders decide to invest their money elsewhere, the charter school would likely be in serious financial trouble.

What Do You Think?

Do you think the potential benefits of charter schools outweigh their potential risks? Do you foresee any other problems that might arise by allowing parents or community groups to run local schools? Some states have turned the management of their charter schools over to for-profit companies in the hope of keeping them financially sound. Do you think this is a good idea? Of the school choice programs we have discussed, which do you favor most: magnet schools, the voucher system, or charter schools?

The Social Policy box discusses another solution that builds on the idea that parents and teachers should take control of schools and the curriculum.

Crime and Violence in Schools

Regardless of what a school's curriculum is, teachers can't teach and students can't learn if they feel unsafe. During the 1990s, student murders at schools in Arkansas, Kentucky, Oregon, Colorado, and elsewhere in the United States increased many teachers' and students' fears for their safety. However, research indicates that such incidents, while horrifying, are actually rare. In fact, one study showed that children are generally safer on school grounds than off them ("Schools Are Relatively Safe," 1995). When crime does occur in school, it is typically property crime, not violent crime. In fact, the number of violent crimes committed in schools has declined in recent years (Chandler et al., 1998; Lively, 1997).

Nevertheless, while the overall picture of crime in schools is optimistic, problems remain. For one thing, the incidence of violent crime is not evenly distributed across school districts. Students who live in impoverished, high-crime neighborhoods attend schools where they are at greater risk of violent victimization than students in higher income neighborhoods. For instance, more than 30 percent of students living in impoverished, high-crime neighborhoods report they have stayed home from school because of fear of crime, and almost 40 percent say they have carried a weapon to school for protection (Applebome, 1996a; Chandler et al., 1998). Thus, students who are already multiply disadvantaged are more

Educational quality and student performance are affected by characteristics of the school environment. Research shows, for example, that learning does not occur when students feel unsafe or threatened by the behavior of classmates. What factors contribute to violent juvenile crime? What factors contribute to violence and crime on college campuses?

likely to have to deal with violence as an additional obstacle to education.

On college and university campuses nationwide, crime has also decreased, with two exceptions. One exception is drug arrests, which rose 18 percent at major universities in 1995. The second exception is sexual assault, which increased slightly (by about 3 percent) in 1995. In both cases, however, officials are uncertain whether these figures represent real increases or simply better law enforcement efforts and a greater willingness of sexual assault victims to report the crime (Lively, 1997; Schwartz & DeKeseredy, 1997).

Some observers point out that although violent crime has decreased for the nation as a whole, violent crime by juveniles remains a serious problem (Butterfield, 1998). They warn, therefore, that we cannot afford to grow complacent about safety in schools. Let's conclude this chapter by considering other important educational issues for the twenty-first century.

R E F L E C T I N G   O N

Problems in Education

1. How would you solve the problem of school segregation?
2. Do you favor a national standardized curriculum for U.S. schools? Why or why not?
3. Do you feel safe at your school? If safety is a concern for you, what do you think could be done to make your campus safer?

EDUCATIONAL CHALLENGES IN THE TWENTY-FIRST CENTURY

What challenges await educators of the twenty-first century? Certainly, one challenge will be meeting the education needs of an increasingly diverse population. The United States is already one of the most diverse countries in the world, and this diversity is expected to grow during the first half of the next century. By 2050, only about 52.8 percent of the U.S. population will be White, compared with nearly 75 percent today, while the percentage of the population that is Hispanic will increase from 10 percent today to almost 25 percent, and Asian from 3 percent to over 8 percent (U.S. Department of Commerce, Bureau of the Census, 1997). A significant portion of these minority populations will be school age, and for many, English will not be their first language. Educators will need to design programs that effectively meet the educational needs of these students.

Currently, about 3.5 million children in the United States are non-English speakers, and 75 percent of these are Hispanic. Because they lack proficiency in English, these children need special academic help. However, research shows that at least 25 percent of non-English-speaking students receive no additional educational services. Instead, many are placed in education programs for the learning disabled and speech impaired. Both parents and educators are divided over whether bilingual education—that is, teaching children some subjects in their native language until they are proficient in English—is beneficial (Terry, 1998; Traub, 1999). Even students who do receive bilingual education are often placed in English-only classes before they are adequately prepared, and then they do not receive supplemental help. Studies show that non-English-speaking children have greater academic difficulties and higher dropout rates than English-speaking children (Children's Defense Fund, 1991). If our national goal is equitable, high-quality education for all students, then these problems must be remedied, especially given the fact that the number of non-English-speaking students will likely increase over the next several decades.

Race and ethnicity are just one kind of diversity that educators must consider. Children with physical, emotional, and developmental disabilities also add to the diversity of the school-age population. Approximately 20 percent of children under eighteen have a disability that impairs their education (U.S. Department of Education, 1997). Poor children are among those at highest risk for

One of the major challenges of the twenty-first century will be meeting the educational needs of children with physical, emotional, and developmental disabilities. The 1970s and 1980s saw demands for equal rights for people with disabilities, which led to calls for educational reform. As a consequence, mainstreaming and inclusion initiatives nationwide have resulted in classrooms in which children with disabilities are educated alongside their nondisabled peers. What are some advantages and disadvantages of this practice?

learning problems because of their prenatal and early childhood environments: 40 percent of their mothers had no prenatal care during the first three months of pregnancy; their mothers were more likely to abuse drugs and alcohol while pregnant; 13 percent were born underweight; many receive no routine medical care because they lack health insurance, which means that common infant and childhood illnesses, such as ear infections, go untreated and can cause hearing damage and other health problems that interfere with learning; and they are more

likely to live in houses and apartments with lead paint, increasing their risk of lead poisoning and consequently brain damage and other problems (Boyer, 1991; Carnegie Corporation, 1994). To address the educational needs of these children, educators will not only have to increase and improve special education programs, but also work with other public and private sector leaders to lower child poverty rates.

Finally, educators in the twenty-first century will continue to confront the question of what constitutes high-quality education. It is a primary function of education to equip students with the knowledge and skills they need to be productive citizens. Recently, however, the nature of productivity in the United States has changed dramatically as the service sector of the economy has grown. In the twenty-first century, most jobs will be service jobs, which, even if they are low level, require a literate workforce. Currently, though, an estimated one-third of American adults are **functionally illiterate:** Their reading, writing, and computation skills are below the level needed to carry out basic everyday activities, such as reading directions for preparing packaged food, using a map, and figuring out price differences in a supermarket (Kozol, 1985; U.S. Department of Education, 1993). If the literacy level of the population does not improve, an increasing number of people will be shut out of all but the most menial jobs in the future. Already, a growing number of companies, such as Diamond-Star Motors and Honda, require job applicants to pass a basic skills test before they are even interviewed for a job. Also, jobs increasingly require computer literacy, which means at the minimum, reading and understanding the keyboard and screen and accurately spelling out commands (Levy, 1996).

In short, the job market of the twenty-first century will require workers in jobs paying middle-class incomes to have higher reading, writing, and mathematics skills than many high school graduates today. Whether or not educators can meet this challenge depends on decisions made now, not in the distant future.

REFLECTING ON

Educational Challenges in the Twenty-First Century

Can you think of other challenges twenty-first-century educators will confront? What would be the best way to meet each of these challenges?

For useful resources for study and review, run Chapter 16 on your *Living Sociology* CD-ROM.

CONNECTIONS

Education and types of societies	Review the discussion in Chapter 3 about types of societies. With what types of society is formal education associated? In what way did that type of economy permit the development of formal education? Also see education as a social institution in Chapter 6. How is education a part of a society's social structure?
Education in the United States	See Chapter 13 on the impact of industrialization in the United States. How did industrialization lead to mass public education and compulsory schooling? How does an educational system of this kind help meet the needs of an industrializing society?
Education and social stratification	Review the discussion in Chapter 8 on the role of education in the U.S. class system. How does education affect occupation, employment, and income or wages? Why is equal access to education a continuing goal of educational reform in the United States?
Global education	Review the discussion in Chapter 9 of the role of education in global inequalities. What basic outcome of education is most significant in efforts to reduce global inequalities?
Schools as agents of socialization	Chapter 5 discusses schools as agents of socialization. How do schools reinforce the manifest social functions of education, such as social integration, social placement, and social change? How do schools serve latent functions of education through their hidden curricula?
AIDS education	See "The Social Epidemiology of AIDS" in Chapter 18. In what ways is education critical to AIDS prevention? What are some other examples of educational services that are essential to public health and to individual decisions about personal health and well being?
Peer culture	See "Peers" as agents of socialization in Chapter 5. Also review the discussions of youth subcultures and countercultures in Chapter 4, "Behavior in Groups" in Chapter 6, and "Subcultural Theories" of deviance in Chapter 7. Why is exposure to peer culture a significant outcome of the U.S. educational system?
Education, social class, and gender inequality	Assess the conflict and feminist perspectives on education in relation to information in Chapters 8 and 10 on class and gender inequalities. In what ways do teachers, schools, and curricula tend to perpetuate class and gender inequalities?
Education and racial and ethnic inequality	Review Chapter 11 on race and ethnicity in relation to education. How has the history of education in the United States reflected and reinforced the ethnocentrism, racism, discrimination, and segregation of the wider society?
Education, learning, and self-concept	Review the theories of symbolic interactionists Cooley and Mead in Chapter 5. By what means do teachers and schools provide mirrors for the "looking-glass" selves of learners? How does the educational system reflect the learning theories and theories of development presented in Chapter 5?
Education in Japan	See the feature on Japanese cram schools in Chapter 5. How do cultural values and social institutions shape education in Japan? Do you think the educational performance of Japanese students compared to American students makes the United States less competitive globally?

CONNECTIONS

School violence and crime	Review the information in Chapter 7 about violent crime in the United States. Are the young more or less likely to be victims of violent crime? See also the discussion in Chapter 19 of conditions that promote urban violence. How might anomie as a feature of inner city schools create a climate of violence?
Education in a diverse society	Preview Chapter 19 on projected population diversity in the United States. How do you think increased cultural diversity will affect the educational system? In what ways do curricula reflect the principles of multiculturalism or pluralism? Also see the feature on bilingual education in Chapter 4. What are some other educational issues that relate to diversity?
Education in a postindustrial society	Reread the section on "Work in the United States" in Chapter 13. What kind of educational system do postindustrial societies need? What kinds of knowledge and skills do you think postindustrial workers need?

SUMMING UP CHAPTER 16

Schools and Societies

1. The education system of a society is strongly influenced by the economy of the society, since one purpose of education is to prepare the members of society for their roles in economic production. Formal education emerges once the accumulation of a surplus is possible, but it is available only to a wealthy few.

2. When the United States was primarily agrarian, access to education was limited to the wealthy: elite White men to prepare them for leadership positions, elite White women to groom them to be partners of elite husbands. After the American Revolution, formal education was used to instill patriotism, but availability remained restricted. It was not until industrialization that literacy became important for the general population, and in the 1830s, the first public schools for mass education were opened. Eventually, education became a screening device to identify qualified job applicants, as the United States became a credential society.

3. Education in other societies differs from education in the United States in important ways. Japanese education is more rigorous and competitive. In economically undeveloped societies where the majority of the population works in agriculture, access to formal education is limited because education is not considered a necessity and the governments of these countries do not have the financial resources to pay for mass education. In societies in economic transition, such as Russia, education is also in transition.

Sociological Theories of Education

1. Structural functionalists study education in terms of how it contributes to the smooth functioning of society as a whole. Manifest functions of education include transmitting knowledge, values, and skills; social integration; social placement; and social change and innovation. Latent functions include child care, exposing children to a peer culture, and opportunities to develop social networks. Critics of functionalism say it overlooks the detrimental consequences of formal education, such as exclusion of minority groups and destruction of their culture, the promotion of rigid conformity and rote learning, and reinforcement of a society's stratification system.

2. Conflict and feminist sociologists emphasize the relationship between education and inequality. They see schools as "sorting machines" that disadvantage poor, working-class, and minority students. Much of the sorting, or tracking, in schools is based on standardized tests, which, these theorists say, are culturally biased, further disadvantaging the poor and minorities. Conflict and feminist sociologists also look at how schools' hidden curriculum reinforces social inequality by excluding, underrepresenting, or stereotyping women, minorities, and homosexuals. And conflict and feminist sociologists show that unequal funding of schools prevents students in poor neighborhoods from obtaining a high-quality education. Critics of the conflict and feminist perspectives argue that research does not consistently support all their claims and that these theorists downplay the positive role education plays in the lives of disadvantaged people.

3. Symbolic interactionists study teacher–student interaction and how labeling students affects their self-concepts. Their research shows that students adjust their self-concepts and performance according to teachers' expectations of them. Some feminist sociologists take a symbolic interactionist approach in studying how labeling differs by gender. Their work shows that these labels can cause boys to be misidentified as learning disabled and girls with learning disabilities to be ignored. Critics of symbolic interactionism say the theory does not link

teacher expectations to social structural arrangements and does not consider such factors as parents' interest and involvement in education.

Problems in Education

1. One of the most persistant problems in U.S. education is racially segregated schools. Although segregation is illegal, schools remain segregated largely because of residential segregation. Strategies to desegregate schools, including busing and magnet schools, have had limited success. Research shows, however, that desegregation can have a positive impact on education when it takes place under specific conditions.

2. Recent studies show that U.S. students still lag behind their peers in other industrial countries in math, science, reading, and writing. Some analysts blame inadequate teacher training for this problem, while others blame schools with inconsistent and watered-down curricula. Some experts think school choice programs will improve education quality because schools will have to compete for students. Others say school choice programs further disadvantage underfunded schools and foster segregation. An alternative way to improve education quality is adopting a national standardized curriculum, which proponents say will specify basic skills and knowledge in core subjects that students at different levels should know.

However, some critics of this approach maintain it will take control of schools out of the hands of parents, teachers, and local administrators who know what's best for their children, while other critics worry that a standardized curriculum will further exclude the history and culture of nondominant groups.

3. Schools are relatively safe; students are at greater risk of becoming crime victims off school grounds than on them. But some schools have more reason to be concerned about crime and violence than others. In particular, students who attend schools in impoverished, high-crime neighborhoods are more likely to be victimized at school than students in higher income neighborhoods. Crime on college and university campuses has declined overall except for drug arrests and sexual assault.

Educational Challenges in the Twenty-First Century

1. Educators in the twenty-first century will need to meet the education needs of a more diverse student population, including non-English-speaking students, poor students, and students with disabilities. Educators will also need to raise the literacy levels of the population, as a growing service economy demands workers with higher skills in reading, writing, and math.

KEY PEOPLE AND CONCEPTS

credential society: a society in which eligibility for employment and social status derive from credentials certifying completion of a specific level of education

education: the social institution for instructing a society's members in the knowledge, values, and skills the society deems important

formal education: instruction given by specially trained teachers in designated academic settings, usually schools

functionally illiterate: people whose reading, writing, and computation skills are below the level needed to carry out basic everyday activities

hidden curriculum: the values transmitted implicitly through education

literacy: basic reading, writing, and numeracy skills

mass education: the extension of formal education to the general public

segregation: physically and socially separating and keeping apart different racial and ethnic groups

self-fulfilling prophecy: something comes true because people believe it to be true and act accordingly

tracking: a system of grouping students identified as having similar abilities so they can be taught together

LEARNING MORE

Hirsch, E. D. (1996). *The schools we need: And why we don't have them.* New York: Doubleday. A well-known commentator on U.S. education argues against school choice programs and in favor of a standard national curriculum to improve educational quality in the United States.

Loewen, J. W. (1996). *Lies my teacher told me.* New York: Touchstone. In part, an analysis of the hidden curriculum of high school American history texts, showing that although the books are interesting to read, they are often inaccurate in their presentation of historical facts.

Mathews, J. (1998). *Class struggle.* New York: Time Books/Random House. A study of the educational inequalities

of U.S. schools through a careful examination of several elite high schools across the country. Mathews makes a strong case for "detracking" schooling.

Sadker, M., & Sadker, D. (1994). *Failing at fairness.* New York: Charles Scribner's Sons. A comprehensive analysis of gender inequality in education, focusing primarily on elementary and secondary schools.

Sizer, T. R. (1996). *Horace's hope: What works for the American high school.* Boston: Houghton Mifflin. A look at the innovative approaches to education used at a group of highly successful public schools.

 Run Chapter 17 on your *Living Sociology* CD-ROM for interesting and informative activities, web links, videos, practice tests, and more.

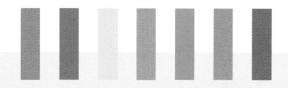

447

Dear Friends,

Last year I lost my brother, my first best friend, to brain cancer. Six months later, my second best friend, my schoolmate since sixth grade, died of breast cancer. Both of my friends were good people. They hadn't done anything bad to anyone; they certainly didn't deserve to die when they did (my brother was 37 and my girlfriend was 42), and in such a painful way. When they died, something died in me, too. Although I had been raised in a religious household and had gone to church on a pretty regular basis, I stopped believing in God. How could there be a Supreme Being who lets such awful things happen? But then, just two months ago, I found you, and you've changed my life. From watching you, I've learned that God does things for reasons we may never understand. And I know that my brother and my friend are safe in heaven. You, the angels, took them there. I know, too, that I have an angel looking after me. I fact, I believe I found you because my angel guided me to you one Sunday night. Thanks for everything, and keep up the good work.

Sincerely,
Peggy Martin

Some of you may think this letter represents the delusional rantings of a woman thrown into emotional turmoil by tragedy and grief. However, this letter is typical of hundreds of letters received each week by the cast of the popular television drama, *Touched by an Angel,* in which angels in human form tell the troubled and the downtrodden that God loves them. Viewers write in with personal stories of loss, addiction, illness, and numerous other problems, thanking the cast for giving them hope and renewing their faith. Some people so deeply identify with the show that they even write to chastise a cast member for any "unangelic" behavior (Lipton et al., 1999).

Research shows that the 20 million fans of *Touched by an Angel* are not unique in their beliefs. According to the Princeton Religion Research Center (Gallup, 1996), 72 percent of Americans believe in angels and 90 percent believe there is a heaven where people who have led good lives are eternally rewarded. This research also shows that the majority of Americans feel that religion fills a need in their lives.

It appears that people have been turning to religion for answers to difficult and troubling questions—What is the meaning of life? What happens after death?—for a very long time. Every known society has some form of religion, and archeologists have found what they think are religious artifacts dating back to the earliest cave-dwelling humans. Interestingly, these artifacts appear to be related to funeral practices: items buried with the dead so they would have them in the afterlife.

In this chapter, we will discuss what religion is and how sociologists study religion. We'll look at types of religious organizations and the six major world religions. We'll also look at religion in the United States and other countries, with special attention to how religion both contributes to and is affected by social change. Let's begin by examining what religion means sociologically.

THE SOCIOLOGY OF RELIGION

Sociologists have long recognized the importance of religion in society. It was Emile Durkheim (1954), in fact, who gave us one of the first sociological definitions of religion that is still in use today: **Religion** is a social institution composed of a unified system of beliefs and practices about sacred things. By **sacred** Durkheim meant things regarded by a community of believers as extraordinary and awe-inspiring. The sacred inspires reverence, respect, even fear. The **profane,** on the other hand, is anything regarded as ordinary. People may value it because of its usefulness, but typically, it inspires little more than indifference.

As Durkheim emphasized, nothing is inherently sacred or profane: An object becomes one or the other because of the meaning the community of believers attaches to it. Thus, wine is a popular dinner beverage, but for Catholics attending Mass, wine represents the blood of Christ. For these same Christians, a cow is a farm animal and source of food, but for Hindus in India, the cow is sacred, signifying the unity of all living things. So, even though most of the population of India is poorly nourished, over 100 million cows roam freely across the countryside and through city streets in no danger of being slaughtered for food.

Because of the special qualities imbued to sacred things, people never approach them the way they approach the profane. Instead, a community of believers develops **ritual**—formal, stylized ceremony—for approaching the sacred. Rituals include chants, prayers, and special movements of the body. Before entering a mosque, for example, Muslims wash their hands, face, and feet three times; they remove their shoes, then they kneel and bow down. The performance of ritual often requires religious leaders and believers to wear special clothes. So, for instance, when attending synagogue, Jewish men don a *yarmulke* (skull-

How Do People Image God?

What does God look like? Your answer to this question depends to a large extent on the dominant culture of your society. For example, most Western Christians and Jews image God as a White male. To envision God as Black or a female seems silly to some, heretical to others. Despite the fact that Jesus was Middle Eastern and, therefore, likely dark-skinned with dark hair and eyes, he is usually depicted in the United States as White and blond. So hostile are many White Christians to the idea of a Black Jesus that when, in 1997, a Catholic performing arts center in New Jersey announced that a Black actor would portray Jesus in the annual Easter play, the center was flooded with complaints. Ironically, the same actor was also appearing as Lucifer in a play at a nearby theater. He noted that no one had objected to a Black man being cast as the Devil (McQuiston, 1997).

In many African American churches, we do find statues and portraits of God and Jesus as Black men. Some women have begun to pray to God personified as female (Steinfels, 1994), and they report a number of positive psychological effects, including improved self-esteem (Saussy, 1991). However, as the table to the right shows, the number of people who image God as female remains small (Root & Root, 1984).

How do the students on your campus image God? Use the question and categories in the table to find out. After you've surveyed a sample of the student body, examine your results to see if they differ by race, ethnicity, and gender.

Gendered Images of God

Question: Which of the following images do you associate with God? (You may select more than one.)

Image	Percent Surveyed Who Image God This Way
Master	48.3
Father	46.8
Judge	36.5
Redeemer	36.2
Creator	29.5
Friend	26.6
King	20.6
Healer	8.3
Lover	7.3
Liberator	5.5
Mother	3.2
Spouse	2.6

Source: National Opinion Research Center, *General Social Survey*, 1989, pp. 156–159.

cap) and drape a *tallith* (prayer shawl) over their shoulders before reading *Torah* (the first five books of the Hebrew bible).

Sociologists studying religion today, like Durkheim before them, are not so much interested in individual religious experiences or beliefs as they are in the collective practice of religion. Although individual sociologists may hold a personal commitment to a particular religion, or perhaps not identify with any religion at all, their goal is not to decide if one religion is better or one set of beliefs more true than another. Instead, as with all other aspects of social life, sociologists study religion in terms of how it affects social organization and interaction. Sociologists also look at how other social institutions affect religion in a society. For example, as the Doing Sociology box shows, sociologists have found that religions typically reflect major social structural features of the society in which they are practiced, including the society's stratification system.

Of course, not all sociologists explain the relationship between religion and society the same way. Let's discuss, then, the major sociological perspectives on religion.

The Sociology of Religion

1. Have you ever been in a situation where something you regard as sacred was considered ordinary by someone else? Or perhaps the reverse occurred: Something you treat as ordinary was held sacred by someone else. What were your reactions, and why do you think you felt the way you did?
2. Think of your personal religious identification, if you have one. What are your favorite rituals? Why?
3. Some people think that sociologists should not study religion because the sacred is a matter of faith that shouldn't be subjected to scientific scrutiny. How would you respond to this argument?

SOCIOLOGICAL THEORIES OF RELIGION

Each of the four major sociological perspectives that we have discussed throughout this book make an important contribution to understanding the relationship between religion and society. We'll consider each theory in turn.

Structural Functionalism

Early sociologists such as Auguste Comte believed that science would displace religion as the primary source of explaining social as well as natural phenomena in the modern world. Emile Durkheim disagreed, and in his classic study, *The Elementary Forms of Religious Life* (1954), which was first published in 1912, he explained

What social functions do religions serve? What kinds of symbols and rituals do religious communities develop for expressing or imitating conditions they regard as sacred? How do the conflict and feminist perspectives on religion differ from Durkheim's view?

why. Durkheim pointed out that religion is a cultural universal, and the reason for religion's universal appeal is that it plays an essential role in preserving social order. More specifically, Durkheim saw religion as a source of social solidarity, a social glue that binds people together. Even before the emergence of nation-states, people were unified by religious observances that gave them a sense of purpose. Religious beliefs and rituals, then, reinforce group identity, offer solace in times of crisis, and promote morality. Indeed, Durkheim was concerned that any weakening of traditional religion would be dysfunctional for society because without the collective moral belief system that religion offers, people would become too individualistic and self-centered.

Contemporary structural functionalists have elaborated on Durkheim's ideas, saying that religion serves four major social functions:

1. *Social solidarity.* Like Durkheim, today's structural functionalists believe that religion unites a community of believers, establishing them as an in-group. Religious rituals underscore this unity. At many religious services, for example, the congregation recites prayers aloud, speaking the words together as if in one voice. Similarly, the Catholic Mass follows basically the same pattern throughout the world, so that Catholics can attend Mass

anywhere and still feel at home with the ritual, even if it's performed in a foreign language. The common beliefs and practices of a religion foster in members a common identity that binds them together even if they are geographically dispersed.

2. *Social control.* You now know that social control is an essential part of social life. Social control maintains social order, which makes social life predictable and more secure for a society's members. The legal system is an important social control mechanism, but so is religion. Think for a moment about the most important norms in our society. All are codified not only in secular law, but in religious teachings as well. Take for example the commandments: Thou shalt not kill and thou shalt not covet thy neighbor's property. Religion also functions as a social control mechanism by legitimating government. One historical example is medieval European monarchs' claims to rule by divine right. Closer to home, in the United States today, when we pledge allegiance to the flag, we also pledge allegiance to the republic for which it stands, "one nation under God."

3. *Providing meaning and purpose to life.* Religion offers answers to some of the most perplexing questions about human existence: Why are we here? What happens after we die? A desire to answer these questions seems to be a fundamental human trait. Humans have a basic need for coherence in their lives. They don't want to think of their existence as a series of random events with no real purpose. Moreover, as we have already noted, when something happens that seems to have no rational explanation, religion provides one. We may no longer believe that floods and droughts are punishments from angry spirits, but it is not uncommon to answer the question, "Why did this happen to me?" with "It was God's will."

4. *Psychological/emotional support.* Religion can offer people tremendous psychological comfort during critical periods in their lives. In fact, most major life events, such as birth, marriage, and death, are marked by religious ritual (a baptism, wedding, or funeral). People often turn to religion during times of crisis (Newman, 1996), and there is empirical evidence that praying actually has positive physical as well as psychological effects. Researchers from the Harvard Medical School, for example, report that praying can lower brain wave activity and heart and breathing rates, which, in turn, can relieve pain and reduce the need for invasive surgery (Wronski, 1995).

Despite their emphasis on the functions of religion, structural functionalists recognize that religion can be dysfunctional. One major dysfunction of religion is that it can lead to severe social conflict, even war. Religious differences have sparked violent conflicts throughout history; for recent examples, we need only look at the daily headlines: Fighting continues between Jews, Muslims, and

Christians in the Middle East; between Hindus, Muslims, and Christians in India; and between Catholics and Protestants in Northern Ireland, despite attempts to negotiate peace. These conflicts have some economic and political bases, but religion is the rallying point: People are fighting in the name of their faith, not their country.

Evaluating Structural Functionalism. Structural functionalists draw our attention to the important contributions religion makes to maintaining social order. However, while they acknowledge that religion can also be dysfunctional, they downplay the role religion plays in legitimating and preserving inequality. In the Catholic church, for example, one of the grounds for excluding women from the priesthood is the claim that Jesus Christ called twelve men to be his disciples (the first priests), not twelve women or twelve women and men. However, some theologians argue that Jesus did, in fact, include women among his disciples, and women and men shared the leadership of the early Christian church (Carmody, 1989). Nevertheless, functionalists overlook that religious teachings came to be used to subordinate women.

Conflict and Feminist Theories

Karl Marx, who wrote at about the same time as Emile Durkheim, had a very different view of religion. Religion, Marx said, is the "opium of the people" (1964, p. 27). In other words, the ruling class uses religion to maintain its position of dominance over the lower classes, keeping them from rebelling against oppressive conditions by promising them a better life in "heaven."

Contemporary conflict theorists continue to examine the relationship between religion and social inequality. Religion, they point out, is often used to justify inequal-

ity. During the sixteenth century, for example, followers of the Protestant reformer, John Calvin, were mostly entrepreneurs who believed that their prosperity was a sign from God of their salvation, and that the misery of the masses, was God's way of informing them of their eternal damnation (Weber, 1958). Slavery was often justified in southern White churches of the United States, with preachers proclaiming the White race "God's chosen people." Such ideas have not disappeared. In 1996, for example, an Alabama state senator argued that the Bible supports slavery because in the book of Leviticus it says, "You may acquire male and female slaves from the pagan nations that are around you" ("Bible Backed Slavery," 1996). Also in 1996, the pastor of a White Baptist church in Georgia tried to have the body of a mixed-race baby removed from the church cemetery. Although he eventually backed down, he refused to marry the baby's mother (who is White) and father (who is Black) or let them join the church ("Church Faces a New Dispute," 1996). Actually, most churches are racially segregated, to some extent reflecting residential segregation, but also because of simple racism (Barrett, 1987). Many White people, it seems, firmly believe God is White and, feminist sociologists add, a White man at that.

In studying religion and inequality, feminist sociologists consider not only social class, race, and ethnicity, but also gender and sexual orientation. According to feminist sociologists, many major religions, including Christianity, Islam, and Judaism are male-dominated and heterosexist. The leadership of most congregations is all male, and the official teachings say that women are subordinate to men. Islam, for example, has such rigid rules of sex segregation that women have restricted access to public life and are secluded at home (*purdah*). In some Islamic societies, such as Saudi Arabia, a woman may not

Many Christian denominations ordain women as clergy, but the Roman Catholic Church continues to exclude women from the priesthood, an issue that has created dissention among Catholic congregations. How might a symbolic interactionist interpret this social reality in terms of individuals' religious identity?

appear alone in public unless she has written permission from her father, brother, or another close male relative. Even then, she may not drive, and she must dress "modestly," that is, be completely covered by a veil and *chador* (a loose-fitting gown). The Saudi religious police (the Committee for Commendation of Virtue and Prevention of Vice) patrol streets and shopping malls to ensure that women adhere to religious teachings (Brooks, 1996; Goodwin, 1994). The major religions openly condemn homosexuality as well. This is not to say that feminists reject religion. Rather, many feminists have developed religious rituals and symbols to challenge and reform patriarchal traditions (Anderson & Hopkins, 1991; Steinfels, 1994). The Intersecting Inequalities box discusses heterosexism in two major religions, Christianity and Judaism.

Evaluating Conflict and Feminist Theories.

Conflict and feminist sociologists recognize the importance of religion in society, but emphasize that it does not benefit everyone. Critics say that conflict and feminist theorists overstate the negative aspects of religion. They point out that religion does not always support oppression and, in fact, religion has been a powerful advocate on behalf of the oppressed in many societies. For example, the Black Protestant churches in the United States have been at the forefront of the civil rights movement. Many prominent social activists and political leaders were first ministers

in Black churches, including the late Rev. Martin Luther King, Jr., Rev. Leon Sullivan, and Rev. Jesse Jackson (Lincoln & Mamiya, 1990; Patillo-McCoy, 1998). Similarly, Catholic clergy have fought alongside the poor and disenfranchised in Latin America to end political repression and secure a more equitable distribution of resources (Batstone, 1994). Thus, say critics, religion does not always uphold the status quo. It can be a potent force for social change. We'll take a closer look at how religion contributes to social change later in the chapter.

Symbolic Interactionism

Earlier, we said that whether something is sacred or profane depends entirely on the meaning people give to it. Symbolic interactionsts are interested in how religious meaning is constructed and how religious belief shapes people's identities.

According to symbolic interactionists, people create religious meaning out of their need to explain events in their lives and the world around them. The most important events, experiences, and values are given special—supernatural—significance and translated into religious principles, a unified set of beliefs. Symbols are then used as a kind of shorthand for expressing these beliefs. A cross hanging on the wall of someone's living room tells others that the resident is a Christian who believes Jesus Christ was the son of God, sent to atone for our sins. Besides a

INTERSECTING INEQUALITIES

Gay Rights in the Church and Synagogue

Many religious denominations and sects have struggled in recent years with shaping an official position on homosexuality. Most continue to express disapproval. In 1996, for example, the General Conference of the United Methodist Church, the second largest Protestant denomination in the United States, voted to retain its official position that homosexuality is incompatible with Christian teaching (Niebuhr, 1996a). Several Baptist churches have been expelled from their regional religious organizations because they have welcomed homosexuals as church members without teaching that homosexual activity is sinful (Niebuhr, 1996b). Similarly, the Roman Catholic church has called homosexuality a serious "disorder," and although the church says discrimination

against homosexuals is unjust, its bishops are directed to actively oppose any legislation that would promote public acceptance of homosexuality (Steinfels, 1992; Williams, 1987).

Some denominations and sects welcome homosexuals not only as members, but also as clergy. In 1988, the United Church of Canada, the country's largest Protestant denomination, voted to admit gay men and lesbians to its clergy, and in 1996, a court of the Episcopal church ruled that gay men and lesbians could be ordained as both priests and bishops (Niebuhr, 1996c). Reform Judaism's Central Conference of American Rabbis voted to accept sexually active gay men and lesbians into its rabbinate in 1990 (Goldman, 1990), but the Orthodox and Conservative denomina-

tions still prohibit the ordination of homosexuals as rabbis. Conservative Judaism does welcome gay men and lesbians as members, although it leaves the decision of whether to hire homosexuals as teachers or youth leaders up to individual rabbis.

The usual argument against admitting homosexuals to a congregation or the clergy is that Scripture condemns homosexuality. However, according to one Christian analyst, only about ten verses in the Bible deal with homosexuality. He then raises an important question: "How do these become the sum and substance of the faith, over which there is no compromise?" (Niebuhr, 1996b). What do you think? Is there room for compromise on this issue in most religions?

set of beliefs, the symbol conveys a fundamental component of an individual's identity—in this case, "I am a Christian." An individual's identity, in turn, influences how that person interacts with others and they with her or him. For instance, a friend of ours recently told us about meeting the grandmother of one of her son's classmates. Both children attend a private Episcopal school, although our friend is Jewish and there are only a handful of Jewish children at the school. The adults happened to sit next to one another at a school function. Their conversation was cordial until our friend mentioned that she had to leave the event early to take her older child to Hebrew class. That's when, she said, the conversation ended; the grandmother stopped smiling and did not speak to her for the rest of the afternoon, only nodding when our friend got up to leave. Although we're not positive our friend's Jewish identity influenced this interaction, that certainly appears to be the case. And because, as symbolic interactionists tell us, our identities our shaped by how we think others see us, what transpired here affected our friend: She was angry and sad, but most of all, she felt like an unwelcome outsider.

Evaluating Symbolic Interactionism. The micro-level approach of symbolic interactionism gives us insight into why religious beliefs take hold and how they affect individuals' lives. Nevertheless, this perspective is criticized for overlooking how one's religious beliefs and identity are constrained by the historical and social structural context in which one lives. Our Jewish friend's experience, for example, is not an isolated incident. It reflects a pattern of inequality with a long history that has been reinforced through institutionalized discrimination (for example, historically, elite social clubs refused to admit Jews as members). According to critics, then, in neglecting to analyze the historical and structural context in which religious meaning is constructed, symbolic interactionists overlook an essential dimension for understanding the role of religion in society.

REFLECTING ON

Sociological Theories of Religion

1. Can you think of other manifest functions of religion that we haven't covered? Are there any latent functions of religion?
2. Can you give some examples of how religion reinforces the status quo? How about examples of how religion challenges the status quo?
3. How do you think your interactions with others have influenced, for better or worse, your religious identity? How does your religious identity influence your interactions with others?

TYPES OF RELIGIOUS ORGANIZATIONS

Hundreds of religious organizations exist in the United States alone, thousands throughout the world. How can sociologists manage to study all of them? Many use a classification system that originated with Max Weber (1921) and was more fully developed by one of his students, Ernst Troeltsch (1931). They designated four types of religious organization—ecclesia, denomination, sect, and cult—which can be thought of in terms of a continuum. Table 17.1 on page 454 summarizes the major characteristics of each type, but let's discuss them briefly in turn. Keep in mind, however, that some sociologists feel that because this classification system developed out of studies of Western religious traditions, it is useful for understanding religious organizations in North America and Europe, but has limited applicability to much of the rest of the world.

Ecclesia

An **ecclesia** is a religious organization that is formally part of the state and claims all citizens as members. People, then, don't join an ecclesia—they are born into it; they become members by virtue of their membership in the society. Needless to say, religious diversity and tolerance of religious differences are not typically found in societies with an ecclesia.

Ecclesiae tend to be bureaucratic, with specially trained officials arranged in a hierarchy of authority. The hallmark of an ecclesia is its ties to government. The ecclesia basically represents the state and helps ensure compliance with government dictates. In turn, ecclesiastic officials receive the total support of the government. Thus, the principle of "separation of church and state," so familiar to us is unknown in societies with strong ecclesia. Indeed, in some of these societies, such as Iran, the head of the ecclesia is also the head of the government. But in some societies with an ecclesia, the ties between government and religion are much weaker than what we've been describing. Sweden is a good example. Lutheranism is the official state religion in Sweden, but the religious hierarchy is not active in government. While most Swedes identify as Lutherans, attendance at religious services is lower than in the United States, and there is considerable religious diversity. Certainly, although the Anglican church, or the Church of England as it is also known, is still the official religion of Great Britain, it is far less politically powerful today than it was when it was established by Henry VIII in the sixteenth century.

Denominations

A **denomination,** or **church** as it is sometimes called, is a religious organization independent of the state that is

TABLE 17.1   Types of Religious Organization: A Summary

Type	Size	Formally Trained Clergy	Tolerance of Religious Diversity	"Respectability"	Examples
Ecclesia	Large: all citizens of the society are members	Yes	Usually low	High	Islam in Iran; Anglican Church in Great Britain
Denomination	Large	Yes	High	High	Roman Catholic Church; Methodist Church; Orthodox Judaism
Sect	Medium-small	Usually no	Low	Medium-low	Church of the Lord Jesus (the "snakehandlers"); Jehovah's Witnesses
Cult	Small	No	Low	Low	Heaven's Gate; the Unification Church

generally tolerant of religious diversity and accepts voluntary membership. Denominations are large, well-established, and, like ecclesiae, bureaucratically organized. But unlike societies with an ecclesia, societies with denominations officially separate church and state. Moreover, the denomination's tolerance of religious diversity means that there will be not one, but many religious organizations in the society.

Most people who belong to a denomination become members at birth; that is, their parents are members and have them baptized, circumcised, or officially received into the denomination in some way. Denominations also accept people who choose to join. These "converts" usually receive formal religious instruction, and a ritual marks their official acceptance as members of the church. Because denominations accept voluntary membership and there are multiple denominations in a society, they may compete with one another for members. Again, however, the general tolerance of religious diversity among most denominations means that competition is subtle and recruitment fairly passive.

The United States is a society with many denominations, which include the Roman Catholic, Greek Orthodox, and Russian Orthodox churches; the Episcopalian, Lutheran, Methodist, Baptist, and other large Protestant churches; and the three major branches of Judaism—Orthodox, Conservative, and Reform.

Sects

A **sect** is a religious organization that sets itself apart from the larger society, sometimes even rejecting the values and norms of the society. In fact, sect members hold strongly to the notion that theirs is the "one true religion," and

may, like the Old Order Amish, cut themselves off from the larger society to practice their religion more privately (Kephart & Zellner, 1991). Tolerance of religious diversity is generally low among sect members.

Sects are smaller than denominations and usually more loosely organized. There are few, if any, trained clergy, and services are typically emotionally charged events with a high level of participation by the congregation. The rather unusual beliefs and practices of many sects makes them less "respectable" than denominations. For example, some sects, such as the Church of the Lord Jesus, be-

Why are snake handlers regarded as a religious sect? In what ways are sects and cults similar and different? What is the role of charismatic leadership in these types of religious organizations? Why is it said that ecclesiae and denominations often begin as sects or cults? How might you describe the transformations that would change a cult into a denomination?

lieve that if congregants are "saved, sanctified, and filled with the Holy Ghost," they can handle deadly rattle-snakes without being harmed. Rattlesnakes are brought to services in boxes, and when congregants feel "anointed by the Spirit," they take out the snakes and dance while holding them in their hands. Some snake handlers have been bitten more than one hundred times and some have died, but sect members are not deterred (Sims, 1988; "When the Faithful Tempt the Serpent," 1992).

The religious zeal of sect members prompts them to actively recruit new members through proselytizing (dramatic conversion). Some sects, such as the Jehovah's Witnesses, go door to door, eagerly sharing their beliefs in an effort to attract new members to the sect. However, because of the lower respectability accorded sects, they generally attract people from marginalized groups, not integrated members of society's mainstream.

Many sects are relatively short-lived, but if sect members are good recruiters, the organization grows and some develop into denominations. When a sect tranforms itself into a denomination, it gains respectability, but it also becomes more bureaucratic as well as less spontaneous and zealous. These changes may actually motivate some members to break away from the church and form a new sect. This phenomenon seems to be occurring in Japan, where Buddhism is experiencing a growth in "splinter sects" because members do not think the mainstream church is adequately meeting their religious needs (Davis, 1991).

Cults

Of all the types of religious organizations, the cult elicits the most negative reactions. Many people associate cults with brainwashing, communes, weird chants, and even bizarre sexual rituals. The mass suicide by members of the Heaven's Gate U.F.O. cult in 1997 certainly reinforced this image. But cults are not necessarily bizarre or dangerous. A **cult** is simply a religious organization whose teachings and practices put it outside the sphere of the society's conventional religious traditions. In fact, some researchers prefer to use the term *new religious movements* to avoid the stigma attached to cults (Ayella, 1993). However, as the Global Insights box shows, some cults are hardly new, having developed a following and a set of rituals long ago. We also often forget that the largest denomination in the world today—Christianity—began as a cult. The beliefs and practices of the followers of Jesus Christ (that he was the son of God and that he rose from the dead) set them far outside the mainstream religious practices of their day.

GLOBAL INSIGHTS   Voodoo: A Blending of Cultural Traditions

When they hear the word *voodoo*, many Americans think of animal sacrifices, dolls with pins stuck through them, and magical potions for bringing good luck or bad. But voodoo is actually a healing-based religion that blends various African religious traditions with French colonial Catholicism. *Vodou* (the Creole spelling for the African word *spirit*) was developed in the eighteenth century by African slaves who had been transported to Haiti to work in the sugar plantations. Using found objects from the environment—pieces of fabric, feathers, candles, shells, discarded bottles—the slaves created a religion rich in symbolism and ritual (Brown, 1991).

Haitian immigrants to the United States have brought the practice of voodoo with them, setting up small altars in the basements of their homes. In fact, the choice of the basement is not to hide the altar or keep it out of the way, but rather to locate it as close to the earth as possible. In practicing voodoo, priests and priestesses call the spirits to "possess" them, to temporarily inhabit their bodies. They believe that the spirits have difficulty traveling through concrete; being close to the earth gives the priest or priestess more power to work with the spirits. Thus,

basements have become sacred spaces, centers of religious ritual where various spirits from different spirit families are served and called and where "spiritual recipes" for influencing human behavior and earthly events—charms, libations—are created (Brown, 1998).

No one knows how many voodoo devotees there are in the United States because most people practice the religion in secret. In fact, one researcher likens the home altars of voodoo practitioners today with the home churches of early Christians (Brown, 1991). Most voodoo devotees also continue to practice some form of Christianity, usually Catholicism. And some people do not practice voodoo consistently, but instead seek the help of voodoo priests and priestesses for dealing with specific problems, such as an ailing child or a cheating spouse. These more "casual" voodoo devotees include not only Haitians, but also other African Americans, Koreans, Japanese, and Italian Americans. Voodoo appears to be enjoying a revival among the descendents of Haitian immigrants who are looking to rediscover their roots, but is also finding broader, cross-cultural appeal (Brown, 1998).

Cults are usually small and revolve around a *charismatic* leader (Storr, 1996). **Charismatic leadership** is based on the extraordinary talents and personal qualities of an individual leader. Cult leaders—the Rev. Sun Myung Moon of the Unification Church and David Koresh of the Branch Davidians, for example—have strong personal appeal, and their followers believe they are endowed with exceptional or supernatural gifts. Most cults allow anyone to join who wants to, but membership usually requires some break with society and an absolute commitment to a radically new way of life. The new lifestyle does not necessarily require followers to live separately from the dominant society, though some cults do establish communes or another type of collective residence. However, many cults have very basic requirements, such as attending weekly meetings, donating 2 percent of income, eating only certain foods, and practicing nonviolence. Some people add cult rituals, such as healing with crystals, to

Millenialist cults believe that the apocalyptic prophecies of the book of Revelation in the Bible—which predict earthquakes and other catastrophes signaling the end of the world—will begin to be fulfilled in the year 2000. Other members of new religious movements believe that aliens with more advanced spirituality are coming (or are already here) to convert humans to a new, universal, superior, cosmology-based religion. How might you explain the origins or rise of these religious cults?

their traditional religious practices but do not consider themselves members of a cult. Cults usually attract people who feel alienated from the more established religions (Finke & Stark, 1992), but despite the negative publicity that cults receive, research shows that cult membership has no detrimental effects on most people (Beckford, 1985; Robbins, 1988).

R E F L E C T I N G   O N

Types of Religious Organizations

1. Although we emphasize separation of church and state in the United States, can you give any examples of ties between church and state in this country?
2. Do you belong to a religious organization? If so, what are some of its essential features? Would you classify it as a denomination, sect, or cult?
3. Why do you think cults are viewed so negatively by most people?

WORLD RELIGIONS

Every society has some form of religion, and, as some governments have found, religious traditions are often very hard to suppress. Even when religious practices are officially prohibited, believers often continue their traditions secretly.

Sociologists and anthropologists have studied literally thousands of religions throughout the world, documenting tremendous diversity in beliefs and rituals. Some religions are characterized by **monotheism**, belief in a single Supreme Being, while others are based on **polytheism**, belief in many gods. Despite the large number of religions, most of the world's population—about 4 billion people or 75 percent of the world's inhabitants—belong to one of just six religions: Christianity, Islam, Hinduism, Buddhism, Judaism, and Confucianism. These are known as world religions because they have members in many parts of the world and because they have large numbers of members. Let's look at each of these religions individually, from the largest in terms of membership to the smallest.

Christianity

Christianity is the largest religion in the world today: Almost 2 billion people (about 34 percent of the world's population) identify themselves as Christian. Most Christians, though, live in North and South America and Europe, making Christianity a distinctly Western religious tradition (U.S. Department of Commerce, Bureau of the Census, 1997).

Christianity in the United States encompasses Catholic and Protestant denominations and sects. Protestant denominations and sects, for example, are many and diverse, including Baptists, Lutherans, Calvinists, Methodists, Mormons, Congregationalists, Presbyterians, Unitarians, Jehovah's Witnesses, and many others. What do all Christians have in common? In the United States, how is Christianity expressed and restricted in the relationship between church and state? What are some examples of modern states in which religion is actually the basis of government?

Christianity began as a cult in the Middle Eastern country of Palestine nearly two thousand years ago. It developed in response to the teachings of a charismatic leader, Jesus of Nazareth, who told people to stop behaving sinfully, love one another, and treat everyone as they themselves would want to be treated. Christianity got its name because Jesus's followers believed that he was the Christ or Messiah, whose coming the prophets of the Hebrew Bible had foretold. They referred to him as their "King" and the son of God, and when he preached, he often spoke of his Father in heaven. Jesus came to be seen as a serious political threat and he was eventually arrested as a traitor and crucified. Two fundamental beliefs of all Christians are that Jesus's death was a blood sacrifice to atone for humans' sins and that three days after his death he was resurrected (brought back to life).

Early Christians endured extreme persecution, often being cruelly executed. Within four centuries, Christianity grew from a cult to an ecclesia, becoming the official religion of the Roman Empire, often called the *Holy Roman Empire*. Disagreements among religious leaders led to a split in the eleventh century, resulting in the establishment of the Eastern Orthodox Church headquartered in Constantinople (today, Istanbul, Turkey). Another split occurred in the sixteenth century, when reformers such as Martin Luther spoke out against the growing corruption of church officials (including affairs by supposedly celebate clergy, which resulted in the birth of children, and the sale of indulgences, that is, forgiveness of sins). Their rebellion led to the establishment of the Protestant branches of Christianity.

Today, many different Christian denominations, sects, and cults exist, but they all continue to share the belief that Jesus Christ was the son of God, their Savior, whose death and resurrection ensures their salvation if they live according to his teachings. Still, even within a single Christian denomination, the diversity is remarkable, with some Christians accepting their church's teachings literally as the word of God, and others seeing their church as providing broad guidelines for everyday living.

Islam

Islam, which means submission to Allah (God), is the second largest world religion. There are more than 1 billion Muslims (followers of Islam), representing about 19 percent of the world's population (U.S. Department of Commerce, Bureau of the Census, 1997). Christianity may be the largest religion, but Islam is the world's fastest growing religion, adding 25 million new members each year (Marty & Appleby, 1992).

Islam was founded by Muhammad in the seventh century. Muhammad was born in Mecca (now in Saudi Arabia), but fled to Medina around 622, when he learned of a plan to murder him. In Medina (also now in Saudi Arabia), he gathered followers and established himself as a powerful religious leader. He returned to conquer Mecca in 630.

Muhammad is not considered God or the son of God the way Christians view Jesus. Rather, Muhammad was a prophet, a descendent of Abraham, to whom the word of God was revealed. God's word as spoken to Muhammad is recorded in the *Qur'an* (Koran), the sacred book of Islam. Besides the Qur'an, however, Muslims also rely on the *sharia,* the way, to guide their daily lives. The *sharia* is based in part on the Qur'an, but also on records of how Muhammad lived his life, Muslim traditions that have developed over the centuries, and the dictates of current Islamic leaders. The *sharia* spells out Islamic prescriptions for all aspects of social and personal life, including daily prayer and worship, child rearing, gender roles, and government. Muslims must adhere to the Five Pillars of Islam:

1. Accept Allah as the only true God and Muhammad as Allah's messenger.

2. Observe the ritual of worship, which includes daily prayers recited with body bowed, facing Mecca, at five special times a day.

3. Observe *Ramadan,* a month of special prayer and ritual, including daily fasting. During *Ramadan,* Muslims may only eat and drink before sunrise and after sundown; during the day, the especially devout will not even swallow their own saliva in order not to break the fast.

4. Give alms (donations) to the needy.

5. Make a pilgrimage to the Sacred House of Allah in Mecca at least once during one's life.

As a result of press coverage of conflicts in Iran, Iraq, and Kuwait, as well as between Arabs and Israelis, and because Mecca is in Saudi Arabia, most Westerners associate Islam with the Middle East. It is true that most people in the Middle East are Muslims, but so are the majority in Northern Africa and western Asia. There are also many Muslims in India, Pakistan, China, and Indonesia, and, because of recent immigration, there are more than half a million Muslims in the United States.

Hinduism

Hinduism is one of the oldest religions in the world, predating the birth of Christ by about two thousand years. Today, there are about 790 million Hindus—about 13.7 percent of the world's population—and most live in India and Pakistan (U.S. Department of Commerce, Bureau of the Census, 1997). Even though Hinduism is largely an Eastern religion, more than a quarter of a million Hindus live in the United States.

Unlike the other world religions we've discussed, the founding of Hinduism is not associated with any single charismatic leader. Moreover, Hindus have no sacred texts like the Christian Bible, the Qur'an, or the Torah. Instead, Hindus are obligated to fulfill specific religious responsibilities called *dharma.* The dharma include living according to particular virtues, such as honesty, courage, purity, and nonviolence.

One Hindu principle that many in the West have at least heard of is *karma.* Karma is perhaps best summed up by the saying, "What goes around, comes around." Hindus believe that everything a person does has spiritual consequences, not in this life, but in the next. However, Hindus do not think, as Christians do, that following death, a person is judged by God and subsequently welcomed into heaven or banished to hell. Rather, Hindus believe in **reincarnation,** a process of birth, death, and rebirth. When the body dies, the soul continues to live, and eventually is reborn in a form determined by the individual's moral progress in his or her previous life. The goal of every Hindu is to achieve spritual perfection or *nirvana,* which ends the cycle of reincarnation and unites the soul with the universe.

The beliefs and practice of Hinduism are closely tied to the caste system. In fact, one of the most important dharma is to act in accordance with the prescriptions of one's caste. Thus, members of the upper castes (the Brahmins and the Kshatriyas) tend to be monotheistic, believing in a moral Absolute, with all other gods a part of the One. Members of the lower castes (the Vaisyas, Shudras, and outcasts) tend to be polytheistic, worshipping not only the deities of Hinduism (Brahma, Shiva, and Vishnu), but also local spirits and godlings (Johnstone, 1988). One ritual that all Hindus except the outcasts practice is ritual cleansing after contact with someone of a lower caste. Most Hindus also try to participate in *Kumbh Mela,* a ritual occurring every twelve years during which the faithful make a pilgrimage to bathe in the purifying water of the sacred Ganges River.

Hinduism was largely unfamiliar to most Westerners until the 1940s, when Mhatma Ghandi led India's struggle for independence from Great Britain. Ghandi's com-

Islam was inspired by early Christianity and includes many people described in the Bible, including John the Baptist and Christ. Like Orthodox Judaism, Islam is strongly monotheistic and incorporates many secular rules, traditional practices, and practical advice for food preparation, family relations, and the conduct of daily life. How might a structural functionalist analyze Islam's Five Pillars of Faith?

mitment to nonviolence, as well as his personal courage, simplicity, and self-control won him, and Hinduism, the admiration and respect of people not only in India, but in other parts of the world as well.

Buddhism

Buddhism developed out of Hinduism, and the two religions continue to have much in common. The founder of Buddhism was Siddhartha Gautama, who lived in Nepal nearly six hundred years before the birth of Christ. Gautama was born into an upper-caste Hindu family, but when he was twenty-nine years old, he gave up his comfortable lifestyle, left home, and became a wanderer in search of higher meaning. Through meditation and self-denial, he achieved enlightenment and became Buddha, which means "enlightened one."

Gautama Buddha was a charismatic leader who quickly gained many followers. His teachings, or *dhamma,* are basically guidelines for leading a moral life, rather than principles based on belief in a Supreme Being. Buddhists believe in Karma and reincarnation. They also believe that all living creatures experience suffering because of their attachment to or desire for earthly things. Suffering continues through every rebirth unless a person follows Buddha's Eightfold Path, which includes giving up carnal and material pleasures and practicing self-denial, meditation, and doing no harm to other living creatures.

Today, more than 325 million people identify as Buddhists, with the majority (322 million) living in Asian countries, including Burma, Thailand, Cambodia, Sri Lanka, and Japan (U.S. Department of Commerce, Bureau of the Census, 1997). Large numbers of Buddhists also live in India and China, especially in Tibet. Many Buddhist sects exist because believers often combine Buddha's teachings with indigenous customs. Immigration has also brought Buddhism to the United States, and tiny Buddhist shrines can be found in many Asian restaurants (De Silva, 1996). Some Buddhists in the United States routinely release into the wild captive fish, turtles, and other animals they buy from pet shops because they believe that freeing those creatures complies with one of the tenets of the Eightfold Path and leads to good karma (West, 1997). But environmental experts are afraid this practice can cause overpopulation of some species and spread diseases among others. Many Buddhists in the United States and elsewhere, however, are less demonstrative of their religious beliefs and consider their religion a very private matter. Unfortunately, sociologists have no way of knowing how many "hidden Buddhists" there are.

Judaism

About 14.1 million people throughout the world identify themselves as Jews (U.S. Department of Commerce, Bureau of the Census, 1997). Judaism is one of the smallest of the six world religions, but it receives a good deal of attention for a number of reasons. First, Israel, the Jewish state, is prominent in world affairs. Second, Judaism is generally considered the first monotheistic religion, setting it apart from other ancient religions that worshipped many gods. Finally, a third reason Judaism commands our attention is the large number of Jews who live in the United States—about 2 percent of the U.S. population, or 3.1 million people, are Jewish (U.S. Department of Commerce, Bureau of the Census, 1997).

Judaism's history spans about four thousand years. Jews trace their ancestry to Abraham, who is believed to have entered into a *covenant* (relationship) with God, who named Jews as His chosen people. Abraham's descendants included Isaac, Jacob, and Joseph, who, along with Moses, play prominent roles in Jewish history. When Moses was born, the Jews were living as slaves in Egypt. Moses was adopted by an Egyptian princess and, according to Jewish history, was selected by God to lead the Jews out of Egypt. It was to Moses that God gave the Ten Commandments. The early history of the Jews is recorded in the *Torah,* composed of the first five books of the Hebrew Bible.

The Torah contains Jewish history, and the *Talmud* contains Jewish religious laws (*halakhah*). The Talmud, thought to have been compiled around the year 200, collects the ancient *rabbis'* (teachers) interpretations of scripture. Over the years however, in response to changing social conditions and political conflicts, Jewish leaders have modified and reinterpreted Jewish law (Hyman, 1979).

Today, Judaism is composed of three major denominations. Orthodox Jews adhere most closely to the teachings and rituals of the Torah and Talmud and follow strict rules of daily living. There are separate religious obligations (*mitzvot*) for women and men, but everyone carefully observes dietary rules (*kosher*), which prescribe that only certain foods may be eaten and that separate dishes and utensils must be used for meat and dairy products. The Sabbath, from sunset on Friday to sunset on Saturday, is strictly observed. Orthodox Judaism includes a number of sects, such as Hasidism, which establishes separate residential communities for its members (Johnstone, 1988).

In the mid-1800s, some Jews felt the need to make Judaism more "up-to-date." They rejected the authority of the Talmud and also the Judaic principle that God would send a Messiah to lead the Jews back to the promised land: "a Messiah . . . is neither expected nor desired by us; we know no fatherland but that to which we belong by birth or citizenship" (quoted in Johnstone, 1988, p. 241). Reform Judaism emphasizes the importance of developing a personal standard of ethics rather than following rabbinic laws. Another hallmark of Reform Judaism is equality between women and men (Neuberger, 1983). In 1972, Reform Judaism opened rabbinical ordination to

These images represent diversity of expression in the world's great religions. To ward off evil, the Hindu child has had limes sewn to his body without spilling his blood. Avoiding the contamination of evil will have a positive effect on the child's next reincarnation. The Buddhist priest folding an American flag is not in Asia but at a Buddhist temple in California. Reading from the Torah in Hebrew, a rabbi helps a girl prepare for her Bat Mitzvah. And disciples of K'ung Fu-tzu participate in a formal ceremony of respect, moral learning, and self-discipline. In what social contexts did the world's great religions arise?

women, and in 1990, homosexuals were accepted into the rabbinate (Goldman, 1990).

The third Jewish denomination, Conservative Judaism, was deliberately established as a middle-of-the-road alternative to Orthodoxy and Reform Judaism. Conservative Judaism originated in the United States in the 1880s, but gained members in the 1920s and 1930s as it appealed to European Jewish immigrants who had become "Americanized" and wished to "modernize" their worship (such as by praying in English), but did not want to give up all their religious traditions (Martin, 1978). They

adapted some non-Jewish religious practices for their own use. For instance, they established religious education programs similar to Protestant Sunday schools, so Jewish children could learn religious history and traditions but continue to attend public schools. They also developed a confirmation ceremony for girls, the *Bat Mitzvah*, to parallel the ceremony for boys, the *Bar Mitzvah* (Johnstone, 1988).

In the 1960s, a fourth Jewish denomination, Reconstructionist Judaism, was established. Reconstructionist Judaism rejects all the doctrines of traditional Judaism, including the Torah and Talmud; stories in the Bible are considered myths. Instead, Reconstructionist Jews emphasize humanistic values and the cultural heritage of Judaism. Not surprisingly, Reconstructionist Judaism is highly egalitarian—for example, about 20 percent of Reconstructionist rabbis are women—but, being new, Reconstructionism is still small compared with the three other Jewish denominations (Carmody, 1989).

One thing that all Jews have in common is a history of severe persecution. From slavery in Egypt to the *ghettos* (segregated residential districts) in the twelfth century to the most horrific of all persecutions, the Holocaust during World War II, Jews have endured intense prejudice and discrimination. Unfortunately, research shows that prejudice and discrimination against Jews, called **anti-Semitism,** continues today and often manifests itself in the form of hate crimes (Niebuhr, 1996).

Confucianism

Of the six world religions, Confucianism is the most secular. That is, Confucianism has no concept of other-worldliness and largely rejects notions of the supernatural. The founder of Confucianism, K'ung Fu-tzu (which English speakers pronounce as *Confucius*), refused to speculate on death and spirits, maintaining that understanding life and human existence is more important (Tu, 1984). Consequently, Confucianism, more than any of the religions we have discussed, is primarily a program of self-discipline designed to improve life on earth, not to ensure peace or eternal rest in the hereafter.

K'ung Fu-tzu lived in China about five hundred years before Christ's birth. Worried by the corruption he saw in Chinese social and political life, he developed a code of moral conduct and urged everyone to follow it. K'ung Fu-tzu was a great teacher who emphasized "learning for the sake of the self." Some people mistakenly think he was advocating the pursuit of individualism, but K'ung Fu-tzu meant just the opposite because he saw the self as the center of relationships. Self-understanding, then, was a communal quality, not an isolated, individual one (Tu, 1984). Thus, the Confucian concept of *jen,* or humaneness, treating everyone justly and with respect is very important. K'ung Fu-tzu believed that humane conduct begins at home in family members' interactions with one another, then carries over to the local community, and eventually infuses the entire society.

K'ung Fu-tzu's teachings had enormous appeal in China, and his followers compiled them in a book called the *Analects.* Within two hundred years, Confucianism had become an ecclesia, the official religion of China. The communist revolution in 1949 and the new government of the People's Republic of China suppressed Confucianism, but its influence can still be found among the Chinese today. Moreover, immigration following the revolution helped spread Confucianism to other countries, mostly in Asia (such as Taiwan and Singapore), but also to the United States. Nevertheless, because most people who follow Confucianism practice it clandestinely, it is difficult to estimate how many adherents there are today. A conservative estimate puts the number at 5.1 million (U.S. Department of Commerce, Bureau of the Census, 1997).

REFLECTING ON

World Religions

1. Thinking as a sociologist (not as a theologian or even as a believer), how would you explain the tremendous popularity of Christianity?
2. Many Americans hold negative stereotypes of Islam. What do you see as the source of these stereotypes? Based on what you've learned about Islam, how would you respond to people who hold such stereotypes?
3. Many people who do not consider themselves Hindus or Buddhists nevertheless believe in both karma and reincarnation. Why do you think these ideas are so appealing? How do you feel about these two ideas?
4. Some people argue that Reconstructionist Judaism is more of a sect than a denomination. Let's assume you agree with them. Do you think Reconstructionist Judaism can achieve the status of denomination? Why or why not?
5. Some experts claim that Confucianism has played a major role in fostering rapid economic development in several Asian countries, such as Singapore. What do you think? In what ways could Confucianism contribute to economic development?

RELIGION IN THE UNITED STATES

The United States has been described as one of the most religious industrialized countries in the world. Why? For one thing, there are more than 1,300 different religious denominations, sects, and cults in the United States. A second reason is that public opinion polls consistently show that Americans express more favorable attitudes toward religion than people in most other industrialized countries. For example, 79 percent of the U.S. population says that religion gives them strength and comfort compared with 62 percent in Canada, 45 percent in Great Britain, and 41 percent in Japan (Inter-University Consortium for Political and Social Research, 1994). About 69 percent of Americans are church or synagogue members, and 96 percent profess a belief in a personal God (Gallup, 1996). A closer look at the data reveals some interesting religious differences, as well as several trends that may signal a split in the population's commitment to a religious belief system. Let's examine the data in more detail to see what they tell us about religion in the United States.

Religious Affiliation

We've said that 69 percent of the U.S. population belong to a church or synagogue. This number has declined only slightly over the past thirty years. In 1965, the figure was 73 percent; in 1975 and 1985, it was 71 percent (Gallup, 1996; U.S. Department of Commerce, Bureau of the Census, 1997). Still, as Table 17.2 shows, there are differences in religious affiliation by both sex and race and ethnicity.

First, although most people—regardless of sex and race/ethnicity—are affiliated with a religion, slightly more women than men belong to a particular religion. Of those who are unaffiliated, 69 percent are men. In addition, the majority of unaffiliated Americans are White. Race and ethnicity also appear to influence the religion to which a person belongs. African Americans are more likely to belong to a Protestant church than either White or Hispanic Americans. Hispanic Americans, though, are more likely to be Catholic than either White or African Americans.

Another factor related to religious affiliation is social class. Wealthy Americans tend not only to be Protestant, but also to belong to particular Protestant denominations: the Episcopal Church, the Presbyterian Church, and the United Church of Christ. A large percentage of Jews are also members of the upper classes, especially the upper-middle class. The middle class is more likely to be Catholic or to belong to the Methodist or Congregationalist Protestant denominations. Among the working class and the poor, there are many Catholics, but the Baptist and Lutheran Protestant denominations, as well as the Protestant sects, are also popular. These affiliations by social class are, of course, trends and do not mean that there are no wealthy Catholics and no poor Episcopalians; within each group, there are variations (Waters et al., 1995).

Finally, age is correlated with religious affiliation. People aged eighteen to twenty-nine are least likely to be affiliated with a particular religion (59 percent), whereas people who are age fifty and older are most likely to affiliate (76 percent). The age group of greatest interest to sociologists of religion is the baby boom generation—individuals born in the post–World War II era between 1946 and 1964. Although many baby boomers stopped affiliating with a religion in their late teens, especially if they were in college, today most, but particularly those

TABLE 17.2 Religious Identification by Sex, Race/Ethnicity, and Age, United States

	RELIGIOUS IDENTIFICATION (%)			
	Protestant	*Catholic*	*Jewish*	*Other*
Sex*				
Men	*56*	*27*	*2*	*1*
Women	*60*	*26*	*2*	*2*
Race/Ethnicity				
White	*58*	*27*	*2*	*2*
Black	*73*	*11*	****	****
Hispanic	*24*	*63*	*2*	*2*
Household Income				
Under $20,000	*60*	*23*	*1*	*2*
$20,000–$29,999	*61*	*24*	*1*	*2*
$30,000–$49,999	*58*	*27*	*1*	*1*
$50,000 or >	*54*	*30*	*4*	*1*
Age				
Under 30	45	32	1	2
30–49	57	26	2	1
50–64	64	26	2	1
65 and older	69	22	2	1

*These figures are for individuals who report church/synagogue affiliation. More women (73 percent) than men (64 percent) are affiliated.

**Less than 0.05 percent

Source: Gallup, 1996, pp. 41–42.

with children, say they have a strong interest in religion and desire a system of ethics to guide their lives (Gallup, 1992; 1996; Roof, 1993).

But religious affiliation isn't always equivalent to religious commitment. In other words, identifying oneself as a member of a specific religion does not necessarily mean one *practices* his or her religion. Let's examine this issue next.

Religiosity

Sociologists use the term **religiosity** to describe an individual's or group's intensity of commitment to a religious belief system. Sociologists measure religiosity in a number of ways. One way we have already discussed is church or synagogue membership. But another—and some would argue, better—way to measure religiosity is to look at church and synagogue attendance, since a person may belong to a church or synagogue, but never go there to pray or worship. Church or synagogue attendance measures what some sociologists call the *ritualistic dimension* of religiosity (Glock, 1968; Stark & Glock, 1968). Overall, while 69 percent of the population claims church or synagogue membership, just 31 percent attend religious services on at least a weekly basis (Gallup, 1996). Importantly, researchers have found that twice as many people say they attended religious services on a given day than actually attended, which probably reflects people's desire to give a socially approved answer (Hadaway et al., 1993).

Another dimension of religiosity is *experiential*, that is, how strongly a person feels attached to their religion. One simple way to measure experiential religiosity is to ask people how important religion is in their lives. Public opinion polls show that Americans' experiential religiosity is somewhat higher than their ritualistic religiosity: About 58 percent say religion is very important in their lives. However, there are large differences by sex, with 66 percent of women, but only 49 percent of men reporting that religion is very important in their lives (Gallup, 1996).

There are three other dimensions of religiosity: *Ideological religiosity* is how committed a person is to religious doctrine or teachings. *Consequential religiosity* is the extent to which religion affects the way a person conducts his or her daily life. And *intellectual religiosity* is a person's knowledgeability of the history and teachings of a religion. To completely understand religiosity, a researcher must consider all five dimensions, since an individual could be high on one and thus appear to be very religious, but low on the other four and actually be irreligious (Johnstone, 1988). Catholics, for example, tend to score high on intellectual religiosity, having been taught church doctrine from an early age, but lower on ideological religiosity, often disagreeing with church teaching on major issues, such as contraception (Gallup, 1996; Hout & Greeley, 1987; Steinfels, 1994).

These findings tell us that religiosity is a complex social phenomenon that requires multidimensional measurement and shows that religiosity varies greatly within subgroups of the population and the population as a whole.

Religious Trends in the United States

How has religion changed in the United States in recent years, and what does the future hold? We'll answer these questions by examining two recent religious trends in the United States, secularization and fundamentalism.

Secularization. Sociologists of religion pay close attention to **secularization,** the process by which sacred beliefs are weakened over time and religion becomes less influential in society. Secularization can occur in an individual religion as it changes from a sect to a denomination, or as church leaders try to make the religion more up-to-date, more relevant to members, or more in line with the way members lead their daily lives. Until the 1960s, for instance, the Catholic Church required that members fast before taking Communion and not eat meat on Friday; female members had to cover their heads before entering a church. Today, none of these rules remain. We saw another example of secularization when we discussed the establishment of Reform Judaism.

Secularization can occur on a broader level as well, affecting the role of religion in the society generally. As a society industrializes and scientific advances change the scope of what is possible, a belief in supernatural powers becomes less appealing, less rational. Members of modern societies increasingly turn to scientific experts, not religious authorities, for solutions to problems. In response—and in an effort to retain members—religions often modernize, too, placing less emphasis on the hereafter and more on practical responses to social problems, including offering treatment programs for substance abusers or opening a soup kitchen or homeless shelter (De Witt, 1994). Researchers have documented the increase in secularization in the United States since the 1960s (Hammond, 1992; Roof, 1993).

One consequence of secularization is the growth of **civil religion,** a term coined by the sociologist Robert Bellah (1975) to describe how religious meaning spreads into politics and eventually helps reinforce the legitimacy of the state. Citizenship in a society also comes to be imbued with quasi-religious significance. In the United States, examples of civil religion are abundant. Most Americans, for instance, consider the "American way" just and moral —even if they also disagree on what exactly constitutes the American way. On hearing the "Star Spangled Banner," Americans stand respectfully, men remove their hats, many people place their right hand over their heart, and some sing the anthem. The bald eagle and the Stars and

SOCIOLOGY LIVE

Creighton University, Omaha Nebraska
Course: Self and Society, Dr. Lisa A. Riley
Students: (left to right) Tenzin Jigme, Patrick Gilger, Zachary D. Russell, James E. (Mac) Thompson, Kennina J. Ceasar, and (not shown) Frank N. Gomez

What religious organizations are represented in our student community?

We are freshman students at Creighton University who decided to immerse ourselves in the sociology of our very own campus. Our teacher encouraged us to take surveys of interested students, which is known as a convenience sample.

For this research question, the class as a whole totaled 60 surveys. Of the respondents, 35.6 percent were female and 64.4 percent male. Students ranged in age from 17 to 26, with a majority between 18 and 19. Forty-one of the 60 students were Caucasian Americans. Of the rest, 3.3 percent classified themselves as African American, 11.7 percent as Asian American, and 5.0 percent as Hispanic American. We classed 15.0 percent as "Other." Many of these "Others" checked all the races/ethnicities that they felt applied to them. Finally, two students did not respond to the question about race. We analyzed our data on religious organizations represented in our college community in terms of these sociological variables, race being the trickiest to work with.

Creighton University is a Jesuit college, and our convenience sample predictably showed that most students who attend are Catholic. We did find, however, that fewer than half the respondents reported that Creighton's religious affiliation affected in any way their decision to attend. In addition to 58.3% Catholic, the sample included 1.7% Protestant, 1.7% Presbyterian, 6.7% Hindu, 1.7% Muslim, 3.3% Lutheran, 1.7% Pentecostal, 3.3% Christian, 3.3% Methodist, 3.3% Baptist, and 1.7% Charismatic. The percentage of those reporting no church affiliation was 8.3.

In our analysis we found one missing tally, so only 59 of the 60 students were recorded. We noted that while this would make no difference at all in a larger survey,

it could skew the results of such a small sample as ours. For instance, the 6.7% for Hindus represents only four individuals and the 1.7% for Charismatic represents only one person!

We asked a number of other questions about religion, ran some correlations, and found generally that students tend not to be involved in campus religious organizations and are not concerned or worried about influences from cults or religious fundamentalism. We were very surprised to find significant differences between students' religious affiliations and those of their parents, but we're still working on that and how to explain it. We think we need more detailed data.

Stripes are as sacred to many Americans as the cross or star of David.

Growing secularization does not mean that politics eventually replaces religion in people's lives, or that belief in the power of science eliminates belief in God. We have already considered data that show that religiosity in the United States is strong on many measures. Moreover, a 1997 survey found that 40 percent of scientists believe in a God who actively communicates with people and to whom one prays and expects an answer. This is the same percentage as in 1916, when the survey was first conducted. Furthermore, in both 1916 and 1997, only 15 percent of respondents said they had no definite be-

lief in God (Angier, 1997). Still, some people are alarmed by the growth in secularization, seeing it as evidence of the moral breakdown of our society. Instead of wanting religion "modernized" and doctrine liberalized, they want religion to put greater emphasis on tradition and the supernatural realm. Many of these people turn to religious fundamentalism.

Religious Fundamentalism. Fundamentalism is a religious orientation that denounces secular modernity and attempts to restore traditional spirituality through selective retrieval of doctrines, beliefs, and practices from a sacred past (Marty, 1992). Most religious fundamentalists in the United States belong to Protestant sects and denominations, such as the Southern Baptist and Assemblies of God churches. There are also Shi'ite Muslims and numerous fundamentalist Catholic groups (see Dinges & Hitchcock, 1991; Marty & Appleby, 1992), and researchers have noted an increase in Jewish fundamentalism (Kaufman, 1991).

Sociologist Nancy Ammerman (1991) has identified four central features of religious fundamentalism in North America. The first feature is *evangelism,* zealously preaching God's Word. Christian fundamentalists, for example, believe that they are saved because they have been born again—that is, they have repented their sins, entered into a personal relationship with God, and try to follow the teachings of Jesus Christ in their everyday lives. They also, however, consider it their responsibility to try to save others by evangelizing through books, television and radio broadcasts, door-to-door canvassing, and even political lobbying.

A second feature of fundamentalism is a belief in the *inerrancy* of holy Scripture. To Christian fundamentalists, the Bible not only teaches religious doctrine and moral principles, but also renders an accurate account of history and science (Ammerman, 1991). A true believer unquestioningly accepts what is written in the Bible as Truth and understands it literally. Thus, the earth was created in seven days by God, and the theory of evolution is heresy. As two observers put it, if you ask fundamentalists about the source of their beliefs, the likely response will be, "The Bible says. I believe it. That settles it" (Marty & Appleby, 1992, p. 87; see also Woodberry & Smith, 1998).

A third feature of fundamentalism is a belief in *premillennialism.* Scripture not only teaches history and morality, it also prophecies future world events. For Christian fundamentalists, the Book of Revelation (the last book of the New Testament) teaches that Christ will return to earth and rule for one thousand years, gathering up the faithful to enter heaven with Him. The prophetic teachings of the Bible, though, require interpretation and are not taken literally the way the moral, historic, and scientific teachings are. For example, to fundamentalists a week is interpreted as a period of seven years, and invading armies from the North are Russian troops. Various political events are believed to be predicted in the Book of Revelation and all are taken as signs of Christ's second coming (Ammerman, 1991; Heard & Klebnikov, 1998).

Finally, the fourth feature of fundamentalism is *separatism.* Fundamentalists see themselves as the only true believers, and they try to distance themselves from nonbelievers, those who don't take Scripture literally. While nonfundamentalists are usually tolerant of other religious perspectives, fundamentalists believe that tolerating religious diversity leads to the false belief that any form of religious expression is permissible, and any conception of morality acceptable. Such relativism separates those who

are outside of God's kingdom (nonfundamentalists) from those who are welcome in God's kingdom (fundamentalists) (Marty & Appleby, 1992).

Sociologists of religion are careful to distinguish fundamentalists from people who are simply religious traditionalists or conservatives (Woodberry & Smith, 1998). As Marty and Appleby (1992) point out, for example, the Amish are traditionalists, but they are not fundamentalists because they don't evangelize or oppose non-Amish beliefs. Rather, the Amish simply wish to be left alone to practice what they believe. What sets fundamentalists apart from traditionalists is that fundamentalists will fight to make their world view dominant in society. Fundamentalists "sincerely believe that society would be better off were it run, or at least heavily influenced, by people of explicit religious convictions who are willing to act morally and politically on those convictions" (Marty & Appleby, 1992, p. 15). Thus, in the United States, religious fundamentalists have formed their own political parties and lobbying groups to get their positions represented in law and public policy. These positions tend to be highly conservative. For instance, 65 percent of fundamentalists maintain that abortion should not be available under any circumstances, whereas only 14 percent of the general population expresses this view. About 75 percent of fundamentalists believe homosexual relations should be outlawed compared with less than 50 percent of the general population (Berke, 1994; Schmalz, 1993).

Fundamentalism has grown in strength and numbers in the United States over the last thirty years. One area in which this growth is evident is education. Between 1965 and 1983, for instance, enrollment in private Christian (evangelical, fundamentalist) schools increased by 600 percent, and the number of such schools surpassed 10,000. It is also estimated that about 100,000 fundamentalist children are educated at home (Ammerman, 1991; Marty & Appleby, 1992; Sachs, 1998). Some observers attribute this growth to fundamentalists' skillful use of electronic media to get their message across to large audiences. As Woodberry and Smith (1998) point out, fundamentalists' rejection of modernity can be selective. We'll consider the role of the media and other technology in the future of religion in the last section of this chapter.

R E F L E C T I N G O N

Religion in the United States

1. Why do you think the level of religious affiliation has remained relatively stable in the United States over the last three decades? Do you think this trend will continue? If so, why? If not, how do you think it will change?

Continued on p. 466

2. How religious do you consider yourself? On which dimensions of religiosity do you think you score highest? How about lowest?
3. What impact do you think scientific advances such as cloning will have on religion in the United States during the twenty-first century?
4. Do you think religious fundamentalism has a mostly positive or mostly negative effect on politics in the United States? Explain your position.

RELIGION, TECHNOLOGY, AND SOCIAL CHANGE

Sociologist Max Weber first emphasized the role of religion in bringing about social change. In this concluding section, we'll look first at Weber's classic research, and then at other ways religion contributes to social change. Finally, we'll consider how technology can affect religious beliefs and practices.

Max Weber on Religion and Social Change

Although Weber agreed with Marx that changes in the economy generate changes in ideas, he also believed that revolutionary or innovative ideas can produce social structural change, including economic change. Weber's classic statement of this theory appears in his first major writing, *The Protestant Ethic and the Spirit of Capitalism* (1958).

The Protestant Ethic is a study of how a particular set of religious beliefs known as *Calvinism* motivated people in the seventeenth and eighteenth centuries to pursue profits and accumulate wealth, thereby giving rise to capitalism. More specifically, the followers of John Calvin (1509–1564), a leader of the Protestant Reformation, believed that trying to achieve salvation through prayer, ritual, or good works was futile since God had already decided who was saved and who was damned. In short, Calvinists believed in predestination. Only God knew who was saved and who was damned, and there was nothing a person could do to change her or his eternal fate since it was decided before birth. Weber hypothesized that the fear of the unknown inherent in the doctrine of predestination created a great deal of psychological distress for Calvinists. Since no amount of prayer or ritual could help, people turned to work for a sign, some kind of assurance, that they were among the saved. They worked hard, reinvested profits, and saved their money. When they almost inevitably became wealthy, wealth could be taken as a sign of salvation. Thus, Weber theorized, the religious teachings of Calvinism, especially the doctrine of predestination, led people to develop a very positive and individualistic attitude toward work—the

Protestant work ethic. The Protestant work ethic, in turn, produced successful capitalist entrepreneurs and spurred the Industrial Revolution.

The Protestant Ethic remains a fascinating study of the impact of religion on the economy, but critics have found flaws in Weber's work. Many are methodological. For example, Weber relied on the writings of prominent Calvinists, including John Calvin himself as evidence of the Protestant ethic, but he had little data showing that the Calvinist rank-and-file incorporated the religious ideals into their daily lives. In fact, there is considerable evidence that many Calvinist leaders themselves did not act on the doctrine, spending a good bit of their money on alcohol and good times (Finke & Stark, 1992). Moreover, industrial capitalism did not emerge until about two hundred years after Calvinism was established, and it developed in areas dominated by many religious groups, not just Calvinists, or even Protestants for that matter. Consequently, some critics question not only the extent to which Calvinism played a role in the emergence of capitalism, but also the very existence of a Protestant work ethic.

Despite these criticisms, Weber's work draws attention to the important relationship between religion and social change. There are other ways that this relationship is visible today, as we'll see next.

Liberation Theology

We said earlier that conflict theorists criticize religion for its tendency to focus the attention of the poor on a better life in the hereafter rather than organize them in a revolt against their earthly oppressors. Some religious groups, however, have allied themselves with the poor and are actively engaged in justice projects to bring about social change. One such group is made up of Christian clergy and lay women and men who have made liberation theology part of their core religious belief system. **Liberation theology** merges the religious teachings and social functions of the Christian church with a critical analysis of the history and current experience of human suffering. It originated in Latin America in the 1960s, when Catholic clergy there declared that the inhumane treatment of millions of people was not a product of fate, but a willful act of the powerful against the powerless. And because such behavior goes against the teachings of Christ, it should be addressed not simply through prayer, but through social activism (Batstone, 1994).

Liberation theology has had some successes in Latin America. In El Salvador, for instance, liberation theologians have established agricultural cooperatives; organized unions of sugar refinery and coffee plantation workers; and staged successful protests to get bank credit for indigenous farmers and lower prices on agricultural products, such as fertilizers. These successes, however, have come at a high price: Thousands of people have "dis-

What are the core beliefs of Liberation Theology? How does this religious movement relate to social, political, and economic change in Latin American countries? Do you think that Liberation Theology is a good fit with religious trends in the United States? Why or why not? How might Weber analyze Liberation Theology in relation to the Protestant Reformation? How might Liberation Theology be evaluated from the perspective of religious fundamentalism?

appeared" or been killed by government authorities, including the priests and nuns, who were considered the leaders behind the mass movement (Batstone, 1994). Some within mainstream Christianity, including the Pope, have also criticized liberation theology because of its Marxist leanings. Still, the criticism and even the violence have not stopped liberation theology from spreading beyond Latin America to other oppressed communities in the world.

Religion and Technology

We've said that some observers credit fundamentalists' use of the media, especially telecommunications, for their growing popularity. The *electronic church*, as it has come to be called, transmits the sermons, prayers, and healing rituals of evangelists (now known as "televangelists") into the homes of millions of Americans each week. Fundamentalist preachers such as Pat Robertson, Robert Schuler, and Jerry Falwell are considered national celebrities. According to public opinion polls, nearly 50 percent of adults report having watched religious programming at least once, and 21 percent (more than 40 million people) are weekly viewers (Colasanto & De Stefano, 1989). The fundamentalists' telecommunications network also gen-

erates contributions that provide organizations such as the Christian Coalition (televangelist Pat Robertson's political organization) with an annual budget of $8 million to $10 million (Sullivan, 1993).

The fundamentalists are not the only religious group that has turned to technology to spread the "Good News." Some groups have their own cable channels, broadcasting religious talk shows, Bible study, and even church services. Many groups also use computer technology. In 1997, for instance, Temple Emanuel, a New York synagogue, celebrated Passover online with a Cyber-Seder. The temple's Web site had 250,000 visitors, who clicked on Passover songs and prayers and toured the temple ("Passover cyber-seder," 1997). And just as in the sixth century, when Benedictine monks created beautiful hand-lettered books and illuminated them with intricate designs, a Benedictine monastery in the New Mexico desert today creates beautiful hand-lettered Web sites (Cohen, 1996). Even Pope John Paul II has a Web page, where he can receive and send e-mail, including his papal speeches translated into six languages (Bohlen, 1996; see also Kalish, 1998).

It is too early to tell what impact computer technology will have on religion in the twenty-first century, but if the fundamentalists' experience with telecommunications is any indication, computers could substantially increase religious participation. Computers can reach people in remote areas, where perhaps few people of a particular faith live; in this way, those who might not have an opportunity to attend services or talk with others who hold similar beliefs can participate online. The same would be true for people who are sick or who have no transportation to services or religious meetings. In the future, communities of believers throughout the world are likely to be linked by computers. Thus, instead of science displacing religion, it may actually strengthen religion.

R E F L E C T I N G   O N

Religion, Technology, and Social Change

1. If Max Weber were alive today, what would you tell him about the effects of religion on the economy and other social institutions?
2. Why do you think mainstream Christianity objects to liberation theologians embracing some of Marx's ideas?
3. Besides those we have discussed here, can you think of other ways that technology might impact religion in the future?

For useful resources for study and review, run Chapter 17 on your *Living Sociology* CD-ROM.

CONNECTIONS

Emile Durkheim	Review the discussion in Chapter 1 on Durkheim's analysis of social facts and the incidence of social behavior. See also Durkheim's definition of deviance in Chapter 7. What did he determine about the relationship between religious denomination and the incidence of suicide?
Social solidarity and social control	Durkheim's concept of social solidarity is defined in Chapter 3 in the section on "Industrial Societies," and social control is defined in Chapter 7 in the section on "Social Control." How exactly does religion relate to these two factors?
Religion and social stratification	Review the discussion of systems of social stratification in Chapter 8. How can religion reinforce caste systems of social stratification? What might be some links between religion and social class in the United States?
Social inequality and religion	Survey Chapter 11. What specific examples can you find of the use of religion to justify racial and ethnic prejudice and discrimination? What might Robert Merton call this "function" of religion? What might conflict theorists point out about the role of religion in social injustices?
Symbolic interaction and identity formation	Review the discussion of socialization and families as agents of socialization in Chapter 5. According to the developmental psychologists, how and when does morality develop? How and when do people establish their religious identity?
Ecclesia and denominations	Review the sections on "Power, Authority, and the State" and "Types of Government" in Chapter 14. What are some specific examples of links between religion and political systems?
Cults	Preview the section on "Social Movements" in Chapter 20. What characteristics of religious or redemptive movements can you relate to the examples given in Chapter 17? What is the role of religion in social change?
Charismatic leaders	Chapters 6 and 14 both have sections on charismatic leadership. What specific examples can you find of both positive and negative outcomes of this kind of leadership? What are some characteristics of religious leadership that other kinds of charismatic leadership might not share?
Secularization	What examples of secularization can you find in the chapter on political systems, Chapter 14? Does secularization mean that politics replaces religion?
Education and religion	Survey Chapter 16 on educational systems. What are some examples of how the explicit curriculum in public schools might convey both religious and secular values? How might the hidden curriculum convey those kinds of values? How do alternative educational systems serve the needs of ecclesia and denominations?
The Protestant Ethic and the Spirit of Capitalism	Max Weber's views on religion were introduced in Chapter 1, and his concept of the ideal type as an analytic tool is explained in Chapter 3 in the section on "Types of Societies." Review the definition and discussion of capitalism as an ideal type of economy in Chapter 3 in the section on "Industrial Societies," in Chapter 9 in the section on "Modernization Theory," and in Chapter 13 in the section on "Types of Economic Systems."

The Sociology of Religion

1. Religion is a social institution composed of a unified system of beliefs and practices relative to sacred things. The sacred is anything a community of believers defines as extraordinary and awe-inspiring. It is distinguished from the profane, which is ordinary. The sacred is approached through ritual.
2. The sociological study of religion is separate from sociologists' individual religious beliefs. Sociologists are interested in the collective practice of religion; the effect of religion on social organization and interaction; and the way other social institutions affect religion.

Sociological Theories of Religion

1. Structural functionalists explain the universal appeal of religion in terms of its role in preserving social order. Religion serves four major functions: social solidarity, social control, provision of meaning and purpose to life, and psychological/emotional support. Religion can also be dysfunctional by causing social conflict. Critics of structural functionalism maintain that the theory downplays the role of religion in legitimating and preserving inequality.
2. Conflict theorists examine the relationship between religion and social inequality. Feminists also analyze this relationship, but look at the intersection of social class, race and ethnicity, gender, and sexual orientation. Both conflict and feminist sociologists recognize the importance of religion in society, but emphasize that it does not always function for everyone's benefit. Critics of the two theories think that both overstate the negative aspects of religion and overlook how religion is sometimes a powerful advocate for the oppressed.
3. Symbolic interactionists focus on how religious meaning is constructed and the way this common meaning shapes people's identities. Symbolic interactionists also look at how people use religious symbols to express their beliefs. Symbolic interactionism has been criticized for overlooking the way one's religious beliefs and identity are constrained by the historical and social structural context in which a person lives.

Types of Religious Organizations

1. Although there are thousands of religious organizations, sociologists classify them into four major types. One type is the ecclesia, a religious organization that is formally part of the state and claims all citizens as members. Ecclesia have strong ties to government, and there is little tolerance of religious diversity.
2. A second type of religious organization is a denomination or church. A denomination is independent of the state, generally tolerant of religious diversity, and accepts voluntary membership. Denominations are large and enjoy considerable respectability.
3. A sect is a religious organization that sets itself apart from the larger society. Sects are smaller than denominations, more loosely organized, and have less respectability. Sect practices stress a high level of personal participation and emotion. Many sects are short-lived, but some grow into denominations.
4. Cults are religious organizations whose teachings and practices put them outside the society's conventional religious traditions. Cults are regarded negatively by most people, largely because of media attention to the most unusual cults. Most cults, however, do no harm to their members and vary in the degree they require members to separate themselves from the larger society.

World Religions

1. There are thousands of religions in the world. Some are characterized by belief in a single Supreme Being (monotheism), and others by belief in many gods (polytheism). But there are only six world religions—religions that have a large number of adherents in many parts of the world.
2. The largest world religion is Christianity, which started as a cult nearly two thousand years ago. Today, Christianity is highly diverse, with many different denominations, sects, and cults, but they all share a belief in Jesus Christ as the son of God, who died for their sins and rose from the dead.
3. Islam is the second largest world religion. It was founded in the seventh century by Muhammad and today has adherents not only in the Middle East, but also in North Africa, western Asia, east Asia, and the United States.
4. Hinduism is one of the oldest religions in the world, dating back about four thousand years. Hinduism is largely an Eastern religion, with a central belief in karma and reincarnation.
5. Buddhism developed out of Hinduism and the two religions continue to have much in common. Buddhism is also an Eastern religion, with belief in karma and reincarnation. There are about 338 million Buddhists today, although there are also many "hidden Buddhists" who practice their religion privately.
6. Judaism is one of the smallest world religions, but it enjoys international prominence. Judaism's history spans four thousand years. Today, it is composed of three major denominations—Orthodox, Reform, and Conservative—and a smaller denomination, Reconstructionist Judaism. Jews endured severe persecution throughout history and continue to experience anti-Semitism.
7. Confucianism is the most secular of the world religions, emphasizing self-knowledge and discipline on earth and rejecting notions of the supernatural. Confucianism is

found largely in Asia, where it is estimated that there are 6.3 million adherents.

Religion in the United States

1. The United States is considered one of the most religious industrialized countries in the world. A majority of the population is affiliated with a church or synagogue, and 79 percent say that religion gives them strength and comfort.
2. Religious affiliation differs across social groups. Slightly more women than men are affiliated with a religion, and proportionately more minorities are affiliated than White people. Religious affiliation also varies by social class, with some religions having a higher concentration of wealthy Americans, and others having mostly middle-class, working-class, or poor Americans. Finally, religious affiliation varies by age, with the young (those eighteen to twenty-nine) having the lowest rate of membership in a church or synagogue.
3. Religiosity, an individual's or group's intensity of commitment to a religious belief system, is multifaceted with ritualistic, experiential, ideological, consequential, and intellectual dimensions. An individual or group may score high on some dimensions and low on others.
4. Sociologists have found a trend toward secularization in the United States, which was expected because as industrialization and scientific development progress, belief in the supernatural declines. One consequence of secularization is the growth of civil religion, but another consequence has been the growth of fundamentalism, which is a response to modernized and liberalized religion. Fundamentalists actively try to recruit others to their posi-

tion by evangelizing them. Fundamentalists also believe in the inerrancy of holy Scripture, although Scripture prophecies must be interpreted and are not to be taken literally. Fundamentalists seek to separate themselves from nonfundamentalists, but believe that society would be better off if more fundamentalists held political power. They actively work to get their positions enacted into public policy and law.

Religion, Technology, and Social Change

1. In his classic study, *The Protestant Ethic and the Spirit of Capitalism*, Max Weber showed how a particular set of religious beliefs known as *Calvinism*, but especially the Calvinist belief in predestination, contributed to the emergence of capitalism by creating an attitude toward work that fostered production and the accumulation of wealth. Although Weber's work has been criticized for a number of reasons, *The Protestant Ethic* continues to be an important study of the impact of religion on the economy.
2. Some religious groups, such as liberation theologians, actively work on behalf of the oppressed and attempt to better their social condition, which they consider unjust and in opposition to Christ's teaching. Although liberation theology began in Latin America, it has spread in recent years to other countries, including the United States.
3. It is likely that technology will have a major impact on religion in the twenty-first century, as more religious groups use computers to recruit new believers and reach out to those believers who are socially or geographically isolated.

KEY PEOPLE AND CONCEPTS

anti-Semitism: prejudice and discrimination against Jews

charismatic leadership: leadership based on the extraordinary talents and personal qualities of an individual leader

civil religion: religious meaning spreads into politics, eventually helping to reinforce the legitimacy of the state, and citizenship in a society is imbued with quasi-religious significance

cult: a religious organization whose teachings and practices put it outside the sphere of the society's conventional religious traditions

denomination (church): a religious organization independent of the state, generally tolerant of religious diversity, and accepting of voluntary membership

ecclesia: a religious organization that is formally part of the state and claims all citizens as members

fundamentalism: a religious orientation that denounces secular modernity and attempts to restore traditional spirituality through selective retrieval of doctrines, beliefs, and practices from a sacred past

liberation theology: a religious orientation that merges the religious teachings and social functions of the Christian church with a critical analysis of the history and current experience of human suffering

monotheism: belief in a single Supreme Being

polytheism: belief in many gods

profane: anything regarded as ordinary

reincarnation: a process or cycle of birth, death, and rebirth

religion: a social institution composed of a unified system of beliefs and practices relative to sacred things

religiosity: an individual's or group's intensity of commitment to a religious belief system

ritual: a formal, stylized ceremony for approaching the sacred

sacred: things regarded by a community of believers as extraordinary and awe-inspiring

sect: a religious organization that sets itself apart from the larger society, sometimes even rejecting the values and norms of the society

secularization: the process by which sacred beliefs are weakened over time and religion becomes less influential in society

LEARNING MORE

Carmody, D. L. (1996). **Chr istian feminist theology: A co n-structive interpretation.** New York: Blackwell Publishers. An introduction to the ways feminism can be blended with traditional Christianity, written in a style accessible to undergraduate students.

Hartman, M., & Hartman, H. (1996). **Ge nder equality and American Jews.** Buffalo: State University of New York Press. This is the first major study that looks at the issue of gender equality by comparing American Jews with the U.S. population in general and with Israeli Jews of similar socioeconomic backgrounds. The book also teaches a great deal about Judaism beyond the question of gender equality.

Kimbrough, D. L. (1995). **T aking up serpents: Snake handlers of eastem K entucky.** Chapel Hill: University of North Carolina Press. A fascinating participant-observation study of a snake handling sect in Appalachia.

Lean, M. (1995). **Br ead, bricks, and belief: Com munities in charge of their future.** New York: Kumarian. A study of how religion contributes to economic growth and positive social change in diverse communities throughout the world, including communities of Hindus, Buddhists, and Christians.

Marty, M. E., & Appleby, R. S. (1992). **The glory and the powe r.** Boston: Beacon Press. A thorough, but very readable analysis of various fundamentalist movements throughout the world, including Protestant fundamentalism in the United States, Gush Emunism in Israel, and Islam in the Middle East.

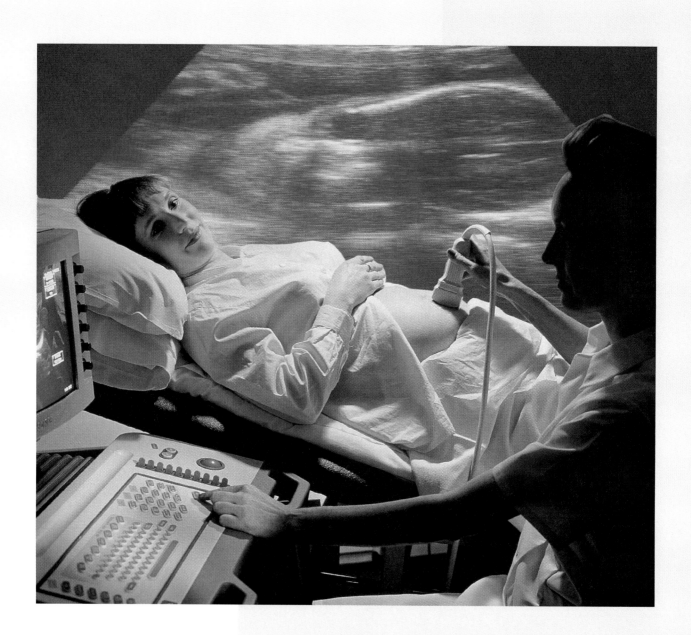

 Run Chapter 18 on your *Living Sociology* CD-ROM for interesting and informative activities, web links, videos, practice tests, and more.

C H A P T E R

18

Health and Medicine

eventeen-year-old Jim Davis (a pseudonym) was checked into the rehab center two days ago by his parents. Today, he is curled into a fetal position on the bed in his room, his body convulsing. Periodically, he gets up screaming and tears the sheets off his bed or throws a chair against the wall. Jim is going through withdrawal, but from what? Is he addicted to heroin, perhaps, or cocaine, alcohol, or even nicotine? No, Jim's psychologist explains that Jim is an Internet addict. A high school senior and, until recently, an honors student, Jim spends more than six hours a day on-line. He quit long-distance running and withdrew from other extracurricular activities to have more time for the Internet. Then he began skipping classes and calling in sick to his part-time employer. His parents insisted that he cut down his time on-line, but Jim couldn't seem to do it. When they removed Jim's computer from his room, he at first became depressed, but then he went into a rage, threatening to kill himself if his parents did not return his computer. That's when they decided to seek professional help, which eventually led to Jim's admission to a rehabilitation center that usually treats drug and alcohol abusers (Belluck, 1996a).

Clinicians report that they are seeing an increasing number of people with Internet addiction, a compulsive disorder similar to uncontrollable gambling, binge eating, and drug and alcohol abuse. But sociologists see these reports as the latest example of **medicalization,** the process of defining a behavior or condition as an illness in need of medical treatment. Sociologists believe that illness is not simply a biological or physiological condition. Rather, illness is *socially constructed.* What gets defined as illness has as much to do with a society's culture as with objective symptoms.

This chapter is about the sociology of health and medicine. We will discuss not only how illness is socially constructed, but also how illness is distributed among different groups in a society and among different societies. We will also look at the medical profession and the health care system in the United States. First, though, let's define some basic concepts and examine the major sociological theories of health and medicine.

DEFINING HEALTH AND MEDICINE

What is health? Some people define *health* as simply the absence of illness, but this vague definition raises more questions than it answers. For example, when should we consider a person ill—when that person says he or she feels ill or when the person is unable to perform normal social roles? On the one hand, an individual's assessment can be problematic because research shows that while most people consider their health very good or excellent, only a small percentage is completely free of physical ailments at any given time (U.S. Department of Health and Human Services, 1997). On the other hand, if we define health solely in terms of the absence of disability or in-

capacitation, we overlook the thousands of people who are ill but who continue to carry out their daily activities for a variety of reasons, such as economic necessity.

As these examples illustrate, health is multidimensional. In addition to a physiological dimension, health also has psychological and social dimensions. Consequently, sociologists have adopted the World Health Organization's (1961) definition of **health** as a state of physical, mental, and social well-being. This definition makes the point that we cannot consider a person healthy if she or he is emotionally distressed or living in a hazardous environment, even if the person is free of physical illness.

Health and Society

What is the relationship between health and society? We answer this question throughout the chapter, but for now, we can identify several factors that connect health to both culture and social structure:

- *Standards of health vary cross-culturally.* What is considered healthy or wholesome in one society may be regarded as unhealthy or harmful in another. For instance, physical conditions that would be diagnosed as serious skin diseases by U.S. physicians are not considered even symptoms of illness by the Kuba of Sumatra (Kane et al., 1976). Definitions of health and illness may also be manipulated for political reasons. For example, in Japan, where the national government owns the country's largest cigarette manufacturing company, any medical reports that warn of the health hazards of smoking must also include claims about cigarettes' benefits, such as how smoking cigarettes contributes to creativity (Sterngold, 1993). In some societies, medical diagnoses, especially of mental illness, have also been used to justify institutionalizing political dissenters in psychiatric hospitals. Such was the case in the former Soviet Union (Krause, 1973).

- *Standards of health vary over time.* Little more than a century ago, physicians believed that hysteria was caused by the uterus breaking free and moving through the body. Thus, by definition, all hysterics were women, and the "cure" was removal of the uterus (hysterectomy). Hysteria, which is today called *histrionic personality,* is still a medically recognized disorder, but it is not thought to have a physical cause, nor is it only diagnosed in women; 25 to 50 percent of individuals with histrionic personality are men (Chambless & Goldstein, 1980; Tavris, 1992).

- *Standards of health reflect the dominant values and norms of a society.* Consider that in the United States, where individualism is highly prized, some people develop a phobia of being embarrassed, whereas in Japan, where group welfare is valued over the individual, some people develop a fear that they might embarrass others. Health standards may also be used to enforce norms. In many West African countries, for example, young women are expected to be virgins when they marry. To guarantee marriageability, parents usually have their daughters "circumcised" (their external genitals are removed and the vagina is sewn closed except for a small opening to allow the passage of menstrual blood), even though the procedure often results in complications, including shock, hemorrhage, and tetanus. In these countries, the circumcised woman is considered healthy, wholesome. The circumcision serves as a means of social control to ensure young women's conformity to their society's sexuality norms (Renzetti & Curran, 1986).

- *Health is affected by a society's level of economic development.* Economically undeveloped societies have high rates of illness and death, especially from preventable infectious diseases. As a society develops, death from infectious diseases declines dramatically, so that industrialized societies enjoy the highest standards of health. This does not mean that industrialized societies are illness-free, however. Infectious diseases may be under control, but industrialization generates other health problems. Workers in industrialized societies, for example, contract life-threatening illnesses because of occupational exposure to cotton fibers, coal dust, asbestos, mercury, and numerous chemicals. And today, as industrial societies enter the postindustrial era with a growing service economy, new health problems are emerging. Workers are prone to radiation exposure from copying machines and computer monitors, and eye strain, carpal tunnel syndrome, and elevated risk of miscarriage from working long hours at video display terminals.

Medicine and Society

Just as health reflects the culture and structure of a society, so does medicine. **Medicine** is the social institution established to identify and treat illness and promote health. We usually think of medicine after the fact—that is, once we have gotten sick, we rely on medicine to make us better. This kind of medicine, **curative medicine,** focuses on treating people who are already ill. In contrast, **preventive medicine** seeks to establish conditions that keep illness from occurring. In the United States, preventive medicine has been getting more attention in recent years. We are all familiar with the campaigns to quit smoking and "eat heart healthy." But for the most part, medicine in the United States has traditionally emphasized cure over prevention, an emphasis that follows logically from our society's values of individualism and free enterprise. The individual is supposed to determine his or her own health needs, find a source of health care, and pay for that care (Kurtz & Chalfont, 1991).

Health care in the United States is a business, sharing many of the same features as other businesses, including profit-making. Doctors set their own hours and prices, providing care on a fee-for-service basis. Doctors with specialized knowledge and skills reap the highest monetary rewards. Government regulation has primarily consisted of licensing and prohibiting practices such as fee-splitting, which would give some physicians an unfair advantage over others in the competition for patients.

With a basic understanding of the relationships among health, culture, medicine, and society in mind, let's look at the major sociological perspectives on health and medicine.

R EFLECTING ON

Defining Health and Medicine

1. Using the World Health Organization's definition of health, can you give an example of how well-being can be jeopardized by social conditions without causing a physical illness?
2. Can you think of other examples of how standards of health in the United States or elsewhere have changed over time?
3. Besides individualism, what other values are reflected in our country's standards of health?
4. Why do you think preventive medicine has not been more popular in the United States until recently?

SOCIOLOGICAL PERSPECTIVES ON HEALTH AND MEDICINE

Each of the four major sociological perspectives—structural functionalism, conflict theory, feminist sociology, and symbolic interactionism—offers a theoretical framework for understanding health and medicine. Let's look at each perspective in turn.

The Structural Functionalist Perspective

The structural functionalist perspective on health and medicine was formulated largely by Talcott Parsons (1951). According to Parsons, a healthy population is essential to society. Healthy people can perform the social roles necessary to keep society functioning optimally. Illness, then, is dysfunctional because it prevents people from performing their social roles, at least temporarily. Thus, the social institution of medicine plays a vital role in the overall functioning of a society by making members healthy.

Of course, everyone gets sick sometimes and when they do, Parsons argued, they follow a socially prescribed role. Physicians also have specific role expectations. Let's examine these roles more closely.

The Sick Role. Parsons identified four characteristics of the **sick role,** the behaviors defined by a society as appropriate for people who are sick. First, sick people are excused from their usual responsibilities, such as attending class or working. However, while saying you're sick might initially evoke sympathy, you won't be excused from your obligations for long unless your illness is verified by a recognized expert, such as the school health service or your physician.

Second, sick individuals are considered "worthy" of others' sympathy only if they did nothing to precipitate their illness. Consider, for example, the recent lawsuits brought against the tobacco industry by smokers with serious illnesses. Juries have been reluctant to award damages because the plaintiffs knew smoking was harmful to their health, but kept doing it anyway. Lawyers for the plaintiffs had to show that the tobacco companies, not smokers, were at fault. Compare this response to the way people react when they learn someone who never smoked has cancer.

Third, the sick person must display a sincere desire to be well. Someone who claims to be ill to avoid work, get out of a sociology exam, or be pampered by others is not considered legitimately sick by society.

Finally, the sick person must do everything possible to get well. If the sick person makes no attempt to get medical help or ignores "doctor's orders," he or she relinquishes legitimate claim to the sick role.

The help-seeking element of the sick role leads us to consider the role of the help provider, the physician.

The Physician's Role. According to Parsons, the physician's role has two components. One is to evaluate people's claims of illness, assessing whether they are really sick and, if so, determining the cause of their ailment. The second component of the physician's role is to cure the sick so they can carry out their normal social roles. But, as Parsons points out, the physician's role and the sick role are interdependent. First, patients must supply their medical history and symptoms in order for the physician to fulfill the first component of his or her role. Then, to fulfill the second component, the physician depends on the patient to follow instructions. Despite this interdependence, the specialized knowledge of the physician

Health and illness are both objective conditions and social constructs that are defined and managed by the social institution of medicine. What social and cultural factors will determine if this American child is sick enough to stay home from school? Sociologist Talcott Parsons showed how people learn to act when they are ill, behaving in predictable, socially prescribed ways. How would you expect this child to perform "the sick role"? According to the structural functionalist perspective, what is the role of the child's father in this case, and what is the role of the physician?

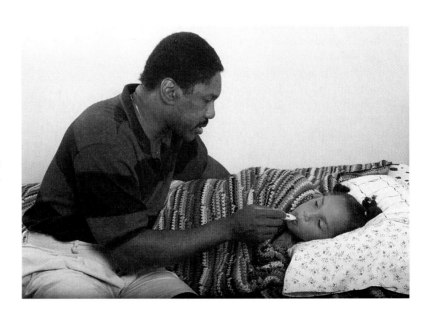

makes the physician–patient relationship unequal. The level of inequality varies cross-culturally, but the physician always has the upper hand in the relationship. Parsons did not view patient–physician inequality negatively, though. The physician simply knows what is necessary for a person to get better, so the patient should defer to him or her.

Evaluating the Structural Functionalist Perspective.
Parsons's analysis of the sick role shows how social norms impinge on both health and illness. Parsons also correctly depicts the physician as the gatekeeper to the sick role. Despite an individual's claims, the physician ultimately decides who may legitimately assume the sick role.

But Parsons's ideas have also been criticized. Some, for example, say that Parsons's concept of the sick role implies that a person is only temporarily ill and can be restored to normal functioning relatively quickly. This is true if the person is suffering from an acute illness, which, though often serious, is curable. But chronic illness—prolonged illness that may be controlled, but not cured—is permanently incapacitating and prevents a person from ever resuming normal social roles.

Parsons is also criticized for putting too much emphasis on individual responsibility while downplaying the social structural factors that can affect health. For instance, Parsons's claim that people who contribute to their own affliction have no legitimate claim to the sick role overlooks the fact that social structural factors also shape people's behavioral choices. Advertising, for example, promotes a great deal of unhealthy behavior, including smoking and alcohol consumption.

Finally, Parsons has been criticized for ignoring the negative consequences of social inequality for health and medicine. Sick people may wish to get well, for example, but their access to medical care may be limited by their financial status. The extent to which inequality in the physician–patient relationship benefits healing has also been questioned.

We'll return to the physician–patient relationship later in the chapter. For now, let's consider the other three sociological perspectives on health and medicine.

The Conflict and Feminist Perspectives

Conflict and feminist sociologists focus on how social inequality affects health and medicine. Drawing on Marx's claim that all aspects of social life in capitalist societies are reduced to commodity relations, conflict theorists analyze health and medicine as commodities that can be bought and sold. Recall our earlier discussion of medicine as a business enterprise with a profit motive. Conflict theorists examine how the quest for profits affects health care. For example, doctors may order unnecessary tests performed at laboratories where they have made a fi-

nancial investment (Relman, 1997). Or sophisticated, and very expensive, technology may be used to treat a patient despite evidence that treatment may not be effective (Waitzkin, 1997).

At the same time, conflict theorists are quick to point out that not everyone in a capitalist society has an equal chance of undergoing tests or receiving state-of-the-art treatment. Rather, because health and medicine are commodities, those with the greatest financial resources have the most access to care, and the best care available at that. Recent research shows that "during the last 50 years, Western men and women of higher status have lived longer and have been healthier and saner than the people they outclass" (Schweder, 1997, p. E5; see also Haynes & Smedley, 1999). Furthermore, patients who are poor get less care than wealthier patients when admitted to hospitals (Kahn et al., 1994). Unlike functionalists, conflict theorists consider inequality in medical care detrimental to the healing process.

Feminist sociologists extend conflict theory by examining how social class inequality intersects with other inequalities. They are especially interested in the effects of sexism on health and medicine. Studies show, for example, that physicians treat male and female patients differently, even when they exhibit comparable physical symptoms. In one study, researchers found that most physicians do not respond to female patients' symptoms of heart disease as quickly as they respond to male patients' symptoms. Physicians typically assume that women's symptoms are caused by a problem other than heart disease, so women must prove their problem is with their hearts by being significantly sicker than the men (Nechas & Foley, 1994; Rochon et al., 1998; Schrott et al., 1997). As a result, by the time women are identified as candidates for heart surgery, their condition has worsened to the point of substantially lowering their chances of surviving the operation (Kahn et al., 1990). Feminist research also documents a legacy of negative and stereotypic attitudes among physicians toward poor women, women of color, elderly women, and, as the Intersecting Inequalities box shows, lesbians. These women's health concerns are often trivialized, so they end up receiving less effective and less respectful medical care (Nechas & Foley, 1994).

Evaluating the Conflict and Feminist Perspectives.
Critics of the conflict perspective think it focuses too narrowly on capitalist societies and the United States in particular. They point to data showing that the health status of populations in capitalist societies is far higher than in socialist societies, largely because of the higher standard of living in capitalist societies. Moreover, in most capitalist societies, including the United States, access to health care is signficantly greater for all segments of the population than in socialist societies. Indeed, even in the

INTERSECTING INEQUALITIES

How Does Sexual Orientation Affect Health Care?

When choosing a physician, what characteristics do you look for? Most likely, you consider the physician's credentials: medical school attended, board certification, years practicing, perhaps even awards and honors. You may also ask around to see what kind of reputation the physician has. But if you are a lesbian or gay man, one of the most important characteristics to you as a patient is that the physician feel comfortable with homosexuals and be knowledgeable about the special health needs of gays and lesbians. Research indicates that homosexuals often do not disclose their sexual orientation to health care providers because they fear rejection, ridicule, and disrespect (Tiemann, et al., 1998). Many believe their care will be negatively affected if providers are aware of their sexual orientation (Johnson, et al., 1981).

Studies show that these fears are not unfounded. Consider, for example, the lesbian who went to a neurologist be-

cause she was having severe headaches and occasional memory loss. While taking this woman's medical history, the physician questioned why she did not use contraception. When she replied that she is a lesbian, the neurologist reassessed all her symptoms in light of this information and decided she should have psychological testing and be evaluated by a clinical psychologist. Her physical problem was redefined as a psychological disorder stemming from her sexual orientation. Another lesbian, who disclosed her sexual orientation to her allergy specialist was told that her lesbianism might be caused by her allergies and that perhaps a series of injections would "cure" her (Tiemann et al., 1998). Other gay men and lesbians report that although their health care providers don't explicitly state their disapproval or discomfort with their patients' homosexuality, their behavior betrays their feelings: They are startled, become nervous, and can no longer

maintain eye contact, preferring to look at the floor or past the patient. The providers may also stop talking with the patient or not engage in extensive questioning, which in turn, could result in misdiagnoses or inadequate treatment (Stevens, 1998).

Heterosexual physicians typically assume that their patients are also straight. A substantial number—40 percent in one study—admit that they are sometimes or often uncomfortable providing care to gay and lesbian patients (Matthews, et al., 1986). The heterosexism and homophobia that characterizes health care, however, has a negative impact on gays and lesbians. Some forego care altogether. Most, though, simply hide their sexual orientation from medical professionals even though their failure to disclose this information could mean that they do not get the care they need (White & Dull, 1998).

United States, which, as we will see, is one of the only industrialized countries without some form of universally available health care, the health status of the population improved steadily during the twentieth century.

Critics of the feminist perspective argue that if women's health care is so inferior to men's, why do women live on average seven years longer than men? And although most critics concede that sexism and other forms of prejudice and discrimination are pervasive in medicine, they believe the problem will lessen as more women and minorities enter the medical profession (Franks & Clancey, 1993; Lurie et al., 1993; but see also Fee, 1983).

All these criticisms have some merit, but much of the data we will examine in this chapter support the conflict and feminist perspectives.

The Symbolic Interactionist Perspective

Symbolic interactionists are primarily concerned with the meanings people give to their social interactions, so they focus on how health and medicine are socially constructed. Quite apart from objective symptoms, health and illness are *socially* defined by the members of a society. In

Lithuania, for example, there are about as many rear-end car collisions as in Norway and the United States, but Lithuanians never report the lingering neck pain, called whiplash, commonly reported by Norwegian, and American accident victims. Lithuanians don't have stronger neck muscles and their cars aren't safer, so why don't they get whiplash? Researchers believe the answer lies in how the situations are socially defined. In Lithuania, people are not accustomed to suing one another for any reason, let alone accident liability. Lithuanians do not have personal injury insurance; if they are injured in an accident, the government's public health insurance program pays the medical bills. When a rear-end collision occurs, they define it as a major inconvenience, not because they will miss work because of neck pain, but because it is so difficult to get spare car parts in Lithuania. In contrast, in Norway, which has the highest number of whiplash cases in the world, there is much to be gained from defining a rear-end collision as an injury-producing event because insurance companies generously compensate individuals for chronic disability caused by whiplash. Similarly, in the United States, where personal injury suits are commonplace, rear-end collisions are defined as injury-producing events and whiplash is part of 50 to 66 percent of all injury claims, even though objective medical evidence shows that in 90 percent of cases, neck injuries heal on their own within a few days or weeks and require little or no treatment (Grady, 1996; Schrader et al., 1996). This is not to say that accident victims in Lithuania never experience neck pain, or that people in Norway and the United States only pretend to be in pain. Rather, according to symbolic interactionists, the social expectations that individuals attach to an event shape how they experience it and the meanings they give to the experience (see also Blakeslee, 1998).

Symbolic interactionists are also interested in how medical treatment is socially constructed. Think about your most recent visit to a physician's office. After being seated in a waiting area, you were probably escorted to an examining room by a nurse, who took some basic medical information (your weight, temperature, and blood pressure). Once the nurse finished, you were left to wait for the doctor. The doctor wasn't difficult to recognize since she or he had several props that designated the status *doctor*. For example, the doctor probably wore a white lab coat with a stethoscope protruding from the pocket. The two of you may have initially exchanged small talk, but the conversation was likely limited to you answering the doctor's questions. Although the doctor may have addressed you by your first name, you invariably used the title "Doctor" when addressing her or him. The doctor also probably used a specialized vocabulary, referring to your sore throat as "pharyngitis" or your swollen pinky finger as your "fifth digit" (Rosenthal, 1993a). Each element of the interaction, including the props and the language, contribute to the social construction of the statuses *physician* and *patient* and the physician–patient relationship. The relationship itself is clearly hierarchical, with the doctor assuming the role of authority. Is it any wonder that 33 percent of patients say they feel uninformed about their medical care and uninvolved in medical decisions that affect them? The Global Insights box on page 480 provides another example of how health and medicine are socially constructed.

Evaluating the Symbolic Interactionist Perspective. The symbolic interactionist perspective is valuable for emphasizing the social nature of health and medicine, which we typically think of only in biological terms. In fact, the definitions people attach to particular behaviors or conditions—labeling them healthy or unhealthy, well or sick—often derive as much from nonmedical factors as from medical ones.

Nevertheless, the symbolic interactionist perspective has been criticized for downplaying the objective reality of health and illness. After all, people do get sick and suffer debilitating physical illness, regardless of whether they are professionally diagnosed or socially labeled sick. Ill-

ness can also exist independent of self-definitions. For example, an underweight woman who considers herself overweight and refuses to eat will experience harmful physical changes that can eventually cause death, even as she defines her dramatic weight loss as healthy. Finally, critics charge that symbolic interactionists overlook how social inequality affects who and what gets defined as sick or well, and how a person so defined is treated by the medical community.

REFLECTING ON

Sociological Perspectives on Health and Medicine

1. Have others ever considered you unworthy of the sick role despite your claim to be ill? Why were you thought unworthy? How did you handle the situation?
2. Do you think if more women and minorities enter the medical professions, the problems identified by conflict and feminist sociologists will be resolved? Why or why not?
3. Can you think of other examples of how health or medical treatment are socially constructed?
4. Of the theoretical perspectives we have discussed, which best explains your personal experiences with health, illness, and medicine?

HEALTH AND MEDICINE ACROSS SOCIETIES

Despite variations in the social construction of health and illness, there are objective measures that allow us to gauge the well-being of a population. When we use these measures to compare health across types of societies, we find that health is related to economic development.

Health and Economic Development

Table 18.1 on page 481 shows various health indicators for different types of societies using the World Bank's stratification system. The first measure is **life expectancy,** the average number of years of life remaining to an individual at a given age, in this case, at birth. As the data show, there is a positive relationship between economic development and life expectancy: The populations of high-income countries live on average nearly twenty years longer than the populations of low-income countries.

The next indicator in the table is inversely related to economic development. The **infant mortality rate,** the number of deaths of children under one year of age per 1,000 live births, also declines dramatically as one moves from low-income to high-income countries.

Can a Folk Healer Cure What Ails You?

Suppose you went to see your doctor because you've been having severe headaches. After a thorough examination and a series of tests, no physical cause for the headaches can be established. Your doctor prescribes a mild tranquilizer, assuming that the headaches might be stress-induced, but you don't like taking the medication because it makes you drowsy. Meanwhile, your friend Marta, originally from Mexico, suggests you visit her Uncle Luis, who is a folk healer. Willing to do just about anything to stop the headaches, you accompany Marta to Uncle Luis's apartment.

Uncle Luis is a tall, slim man about sixty years old. He asks you to sit on a wooden chair in the center of the room and places a necklace of coconut shells around your neck to see if an evil spirit is causing your headaches. It turns out not to be a spirit, but rather, that someone has put a spell on you. Uncle Luis begins the "cure": He walks around your chair chanting, but you don't understand the words. He leaves the room momentarily and returns with a live chicken. Holding the bird above your head, he plucks several feathers and lets them fall on you. Then, in the blink of an eye, he grasps the chicken's neck and twists. Your treatment is complete. You pay the ten-dollar fee and leave the apartment. You try to joke with Marta about what happened, but it's clear that she takes her uncle's healing ceremonies seriously. You have to admit it: You do feel better. Within a week, in fact, the headaches have stopped.

The influx of immigrants to the United States from countries such as Mexico, Haiti, and Cambodia has brought a corresponding increase in the number of folk healers as well as patients seeking their services. More surprising, though, is the number of physicians who are referring their patients to folk healers. These doctors are taking into account their patients' cultural backgrounds in determining their treatments. Although most physicians still consider folk healers "purveyors of superstitious quackery, ineffective at best, dangerous at worst," some doctors accept their patients' use of folk medicine and even consult with the folk healers (Belluck, 1996b, pp. B1, B4). Allowing patients to combine folk medicine with conventional medicine, they say, fosters trust between physician and patient, improves patients' attitudes toward their illnesses and treatment, enourages patients to follow doctors' orders, and calms patients' fears, all of which are critical to good health (Belluck, 1996b). In 1998, the prestigious *Journal of the American Medical Association* devoted an entire issue to "alternative" medicine.

So was your cure by Uncle Luis purely coincidence, or did the folk healer really know what he was doing? Folk healers combine their knowledge of nature with aspects of various religions. There is a growing body of research showing the therapeutic benefits of patients' spirituality (Bilu & Witztum, 1996). Moreover, when no physical cause for an illness can be established despite extensive examinations and testing, a visit to a folk healer may be just what the doctor should order to relieve symptoms.

The remaining indicators in Table 18.1 help explain the differences in life expectancy and infant mortality across the three types of societies. First, we see that less than three quarters of the population of low-income countries has access to safe water, compared to eight of ten people in middle-income countries and nearly 100 percent of the population of high-income countries. Similarly, less than a third of the population of low-income countries has access to sanitation, compared to just over a third of the population of middle-income countries and 92 percent of the population of high-income countries. These are important statistics because unsafe water and poor sanitation spread infectious diseases, a leading cause of death, especially among children, in low-income countries. Moreover, disease preys on malnourished bodies, and as the data in Table 18.1 show, malnutrition is a major problem in low-income countries but is extremely low in high-income countries.

Also contributing to the poor health status of the population of low-income countries is limited access to health care. As Table 18.1 shows, low-income countries spend significantly less on health care than high-income countries. Low-income countries have greater health care needs than high-income countries, but significantly fewer economic resources to address them. Only 58.5 percent of the population of low-income countries has access to health care compared to 86.1 percent of the population of middle-income countries and 96.6 percent of the population of high-income countries (World Bank, 1996).

Finally, one factor that does not appear in Table 18.1, but that has substantially diminished the health status of people in low-income countries is the spread of the human immunodeficiency virus (HIV), which causes AIDS (acquired immune deficiency syndrome). According to the United Nations, 37 million people worldwide are infected with HIV, and 95 percent of them live in low-

TABLE 18.1   A Comparison of Health: Low-Income, Middle-Income, and High-Income Countries

Health Indicator	WORLD BANK CATEGORY		
	Low income	Middle income	High income
Life expectancy at birth (years)	59	68.5	77.5
Infant mortality rate (per 1,000 live births)	80	35	6
Percent population with access to safe water	71	84	99.8
Percent population with access to sanitation	30	36	92
Prevalence of malnutrition (percent under 5 years old)	30.8	15.4	<5
Public expenditures on health care (percent of GDP)	0.9	3.0	6.9

Source: World Bank, 1999, pp. 192–193, 202–203; 1996, pp. 198–199.

income countries. In Sub-Saharan Africa alone, 22.5 million people (8.0 percent of the adult population) have HIV or AIDS (Altman, 1998; U.N. Development Programme, 1998). AIDS is adding to the economic prob-

Diseases such as cholera, which have been virtually eliminated in high-income countries, still occur at epidemic rates in low-income countries, usually because of the lack of safe water and sanitation systems. What are some outcomes of widespread poor health in a country? What are the factors tracked by organizations such as the World Bank that contribute to the poor health of people in low-income countries?

lems of low-income countries because those most likely to be infected are in their prime productive and reproductive years; half of new infections are among those aged fifteen to twenty-four. "Households headed by children have begun to appear in some African villages, and in an increasing number of communities the strain is proving too great for traditional coping systems" (U.N. Development Programme, 1998, p. 34). It is estimated that the AIDS epidemic has reduced life expectancy in low-income countries by about ten years (Altman, 1996).

The poverty of low-income countries prevents them from effectively addressing the health problems of their populations. While health in high-income countries is significantly better, good health and access to medical care are not equally available to all groups, as we will see when we discuss the United States in the next section.

REFLECTING ON

Health and Medicine across Societies

Suppose you were asked by policy makers how to improve the health status of people in low-income countries. What advice would you give them?

HEALTH IN THE UNITED STATES

In general, Americans enjoy exceptionally good physical health, and health in the United States has improved considerably since mid-century.

First, consider life expectancy. An individual born in the United States at the turn of the century could expect to live just 47.3 years. By 1950, life expectancy had risen to 68.2 years, and then life expectancy increased an additional seven and a half years to 75.8 in 1995 (U.S. Department of Health and Human Services, 1997). Improvements in life expectancy are a major factor in the growth of the elderly population in the United States. In fact, today, the over-sixty-five age group is the fastest growing age group in the country.

Consider also the **mortality rate,** the number of deaths in proportion to a given population. In 1950, there were 840.5 deaths per 100,000 people in the population, but by 1995, the U.S. death rate was 508.2 per 100,000 people in the population. Deaths from some diseases such as diptheria, whooping cough, and polio are virtually unheard of today. Heart disease is the leading cause of death in this country, and even the heart disease mortality rate has decreased by more than 50 percent since 1950. Unfortunately, the mortality rates for cancer, stroke, and homicide have increased since 1950. Each of these causes of death is linked to environmental and lifestyle factors, indicating that our modern industrial—and often violent—society may be our worst enemy (U.S. Department of Health and Human Services, 1997).

Finally, the infant mortality rate, like the mortality rate in general, has declined sharply since mid-century. In 1950, the infant mortality rate was 29.2 per 1,000 live births, but in 1995, it reached a record low of 7.6 (U.S. Department of Health and Human Services, 1997).

The statistics on health in the United States paint a very positive picture, but our society has a highly diverse population, and health and illness are not distributed proportionately across groups. The study of the distribution of health and illness across population groups is called **social epidemiology,** and the work of social epidemiologists reveals important differences in the health status of various groups of U.S. citizens. Let's look at some of their findings.

Sex and Health

Since the turn of the century, there has been a gap in women's and men's life expectancies, and this gap has widened over the years. In 1900, women could expect to live just two years longer than men. By 1950, the difference had increased to five and a half years. In 1995, it was about 6.4 years (U.S. Department of Health and Human Services, 1997).

Analysts offer several reasons to explain the gender gap in life expectancy. The gap may be partly the result of genetic or chromosomal differences between the sexes (Stillion, 1995). Hormonal differences also contribute. In particular, the female sex hormones (the estrogens) appear to give women some protection against heart disease, the number one cause of death in the United States (Waldron, 1995). Many experts believe that the gap is also largely a result of behavioral differences between the

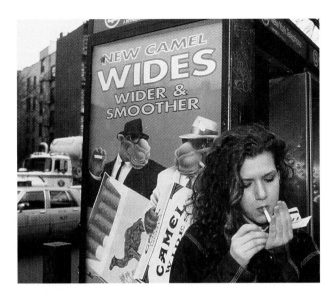

What trends in cigarette smoking have affected the health of males and females and people of different ages? How can cigarette smoking be seen as an example of the social and cultural determination of health and illness? What other risks contribute to the cancer mortality rate in the United States?

sexes. That is, conforming to traditional gender norms affects life expectancy, and, specifically, gender norms having to do with smoking, alcohol consumption, risk-taking behavior, and hazardous jobs.

Table 18.2 shows sex-specific mortality rates for various causes. First, male deaths from heart disease and stroke (cerebrovascular diseases) are about 84 percent higher than female deaths from these causes. One reason is that men are more likely than women to smoke, and among smokers, twice as many men as women are considered heavy smokers, and smoking is associated with heart disease (Waldron, 1995). However, when age is taken into account, as many women as men die from heart disease and related illnesses. Although heart attacks are rare for premenopausal women under fifty, the heart attack rate of postmenopausal women climbs quickly, soon equaling the heart attack rate for men over fifty. It appears that women develop heart disease at a rate comparable to men, but six to ten years later in life. Why this is so is not well understood, because until recently, most studies of heart disease focused almost exclusively on men (Nechas & Foley, 1994).

Looking again at Table 18.2, we see that men's cancer mortality rate is 58 percent higher than that of women. Again, men's smoking habits contribute to this difference, since smoking is a leading cause of lung cancer (Waldron, 1995). Smoking by both men and women has declined substantially since 1965, but women's rate of decline has been slower than men's. The percentage of young people

TABLE 18.2   Mortality Rates for Selected Causes of Death for White and Black Males and Females, 1993

Cause of Death	White Males	Black Males	White Females	Black Females
All causes	627.5	1,052.2	367.7	578.8
Natural causes	554.3	905.2	342.8	542.1
Diseases of the heart	190.3	267.9	99.2	165.3
Cerebrovascular diseases	26.8	51.9	22.7	39.9
Malignant neoplasms	156.4	238.9	110.1	135.3
Chronic obstructive pulmonary diseases	28.2	26.6	17.8	12.2
Pneumonia & influenza	16.6	25.9	10.4	13.5
Chronic liver disease & cirrhosis	10.8	16.1	4.6	6.6
Diabetes mellitus	12.2	26.3	10.0	26.9
Human immune deficiency virus	19.0	70.0	1.9	17.3
External causes	73.1	147.1	24.8	36.7
Unintentional injuries	42.9	59.8	16.6	20.1
Motor vehicle crashes	22.5	25.3	9.7	8.5
Suicide	19.7	12.9	4.6	2.1
Homicide and legal intervention	8.9	70.7	3.0	13.4
Drug-induced causes	6.2	13.0	2.8	4.4
Alcohol-induced causes	9.7	21.3	2.7	5.5

Source: U.S. Department of Health and Human Services, 1996, pp. 110–111.

aged twelve to twenty-one who smoke has also increased in recent years (a 32 percent rise among high school students between 1991 and 1997), and more girls than boys are smoking (Rosenbaum, 1998). As a result, women's mortality rate from lung cancer and respiratory diseases rose 600 percent from the 1960s through the 1980s, and it is expected to rise further during the first quarter of the twenty-first century (Thun et al., 1995; U.S. Department of Health and Human Services, 1997).

Adding to the risk of developing cancer are industrial hazards, especially the inhalation of certain dusts, such as asbestos, and exposure to toxic fumes and chemicals. Jobs with high exposures to carcinogens have traditionally been dominated by men (Staples, 1995; Waldron, 1986).

For the remaining causes of death listed on Table 18.2, only two (diabetes mellitus, and pneumonia and influenza) are not associated with behavioral differences between the sexes. Chronic liver disease and cirrhosis of the liver, for example, are often caused by alcoholism and alcohol-induced malnutrition. Men are four times more likely than women to drink excessively. Men's drinking

habits also contribute to their higher accidental death rate (Waldron, 1995).

Race and Health

Table 18.2 shows that there is also a race gap in mortality. In fact, race accounts for a greater share of the difference in mortality than sex does and, as Table 18.3 on page 484 shows, much of the race gap in mortality comes from excessively high rates among African Americans. African American women have a lower mortality rate for all causes of death than African American men, but when women and men are considered together, African Americans have significantly higher mortality rates than Whites. Overall, the African American death rate is almost 64 percent higher than the White death rate.

The higher mortality rate among African Americans is due in large part to heart disease. African Americans are twenty times more likely than Whites to suffer from high blood pressure, a condition that contributes to heart disease. Research links elevated blood pressure in African

TABLE 18.3 Mortality Rates (all causes) by Sex and Race, 1995

Race & Sex	Mortality rate
White males	610.5
Black males	1016.7
Hispanic males	515.0
Asian/Pacific Islander males	384.4
American Indian/Alaskan Native males	580.4
White females	364.9
Black females	571.0
Hispanic females	274.4
Asian/Pacific Islander females	231.4
American Indian/Alaskan Native females	368.0

Source: U.S. Department of Health and Human Services, 1997, pp. 127–129.

Americans to the stress of dealing with racial discrimination in everyday life. In fact, one study found that stress induced by racial discrimination has as much or more of an impact on blood pressure as smoking, lack of exercise, and a high-fat, high-sodium diet (Kreiger & Sidney, 1996). Once African Americans are diagnosed with heart disease, they are 40 percent less likely than Whites to undergo bypass surgery or angioplasty, a statistic that some researchers also attribute in part to racism: Most cardiologists are White, and they may have difficulty communicating effectively with Black patients, making it harder for the patients to trust them (Haney, 1996). Kidney disease, also caused by high blood pressure, is another leading cause of death among African Americans. African Americans are six times more likely than Whites to die from kidney disease, and they make up 31 percent of all patients in dialysis because of kidney failure ("CDC head urges minorities," 1996). African Americans are also more likely than White Americans to develop and die from various kinds of cancer, including prostate cancer among men and breast cancer among women (Haynes & Smedley, 1998).

Perhaps the most striking racial difference in mortality, however, is the homicide rate. African American women are more than four times more likely than White women to be murdered, and the African American male homicide rate is more than seven times higher than the White male rate. Since 1978, homicide has been a leading cause of death for Black males aged fifteen to twenty-four (U.S. Department of Health and Human Services, 1997). About 20 percent of the difference in life expectancy between White and Black men is attributed to differences in their homicide rates (Staples, 1995).

Race also intersects with social class to affect health. For example, in the study linking racial discrimination with high blood pressure, the researchers found that middle- and upper-class Blacks were no more likely than Whites of the same social classes to have elevated blood pressure. This does not mean middle- and upper-class Blacks do not experience racial discrimination, but rather that their greater economic and social resources probably allow them to cope more successfully with the stress and also to challenge the discrimination (Kreiger & Sidney, 1996). African Americans are disproportionately represented among the poor and are therefore more likely to live in unhealthy, stressful, high-crime environments that breed not only disease, but also violence. Their higher rates of poverty also mean that they are less likely to receive early and adequate medical treatment (Geiger, 1996; Gornick et al., 1996). Let's consider, then, the relationship between social class and health.

Social Class and Health

Health status varies not only by sex and race, but by social class. Indeed, as one observer noted, "There is an incestuous relationship between poverty and ill health" (Holloman, 1983, p. 86). Members of low-income families (annual income of less than $14,000) are significantly more likely to rate their health as fair or poor than members of high-income families (annual income of $50,000 or more): 20.4 percent compared to 3.9 percent (U.S. Department of Health and Human Services, 1997).

Other statistics support these self-assessments. For example, the poor are considerably more likely than the wealthy to have their everyday activities (work, cleaning, cooking) restricted because of chronic illness. About 21 percent of people with annual family incomes below $14,000 are limited in or unable to carry on major activities because of chronic illness, compared to only 5.5 percent of people with annual family incomes above $50,000 (U.S. Department of Health and Human Services, 1997). Although the poor and nonpoor are afflicted with many of the same chronic illnesses, the incidence and severity of the illnesses are greater among the poor (President's Commission on the Study of Ethical Problems in Medicine and Biomedical and Behavioral Research, 1983). There is a significant relationship between social class and health: As one moves up the social class hierarchy, health improves. The higher one's social class, the lower the probability of suffering a range of ailments, including cancer, headaches, varicose veins, hypertension, insomnia, and schizophrenia (Haynes & Smedley, 1998; Schweder, 1997).

Researchers believe that a number of factors contribute to social class disparities in health. First, the poor often live in conditions that are crowded, unsafe, and unsanitary, which not only contributes to the spread of disease, but also increases the probability of accidents and violence (Short & Shea, 1995; Syme & Berkman, 1997). Also, the jobs and working conditions of the poor are associated with greater risk of particular illnesses, including heart disease and cancer (Marmot & Theorell, 1997); however, unemployment also elevates mortality (Bartley, 1996; Lewis & Sloggett, 1998). People with low incomes are also more likely than the more affluent to have unhealthy lifestyles: They are more likely to smoke, drink excessively, use drugs, get little physical exercise, and eat high-fat, high-sodium foods (Short & Shea, 1995; Schweder, 1997). Another important reason for the social class disparity in health is that people with low incomes are less likely to receive preventive medical care. When they do obtain medical assistance, they are usually sicker than more affluent individuals seeking care (Gornick et al., 1996; Kahn et al., 1994).

We will return to the issue of access to medical care, but first, to see how the intersection of sex, race, and social class affect the distribution of illness within a population, let's examine the incidence of AIDS in the United States.

The Social Epidemiology of AIDS

The Centers for Disease Control reported the first cases of AIDS in the United States in June 1981. By June 1996, more than 530,000 AIDS cases had been reported in this country, a rate of 26.7 per 100,000 people in the population. By 1993, AIDS was the second leading cause of death of Americans aged twenty-five to forty-four (U.S. Department of Health and Human Services, 1997). However, as with other diseases, not everyone is at equal risk of becoming infected with HIV, and the groups at greatest risk appear to be changing. Let's take a closer look at the data.

There are only a few ways that HIV is transmitted. HIV is carried through blood, semen, and vaginal secretions, so one of the most common ways for the disease to be transmitted is by sexual contact with an infected person. The riskiest form of sexual contact is anal intercourse because it frequently causes tears in the rectal lining and blood vessels, allowing the virus to pass from the semen of the infected partner into the blood of the other partner. Gay and bisexual men account for 52 percent of total AIDS cases reported since 1985, but the percentage of people with AIDS who are gay or bisexual men has declined in recent years. In 1985, for example, 66.8 percent of people with AIDS were gay and bisexual men, but by 1995, the percentage had dropped to 43.5 (U.S. Department of Health and Human Services, 1997). Experts attribute this decline to successful education campaigns in the gay community about AIDS prevention.

A second common way of contracting HIV is by using contaminated needles to inject drugs. The disease can be transmitted if a drug user injects himself or herself with a used needle that has traces of blood containing HIV. People with AIDS who are injection drug users increased from 17.2 percent in 1985 to nearly 26 percent in 1995. Research indicates that impoverished racial and ethnic minorities are more likely than Whites to be injection drug users, so their risk of infection is greater. In 1995,

Although the number of people infected with AIDS continues to grow, the number of AIDS deaths in the United States declined in 1997 and 1998 for the first time since the disease was first identified. To what factors can this decline be attributed? How do comparatively higher increases in HIV infection among women and children reflect changes in social patterns of transmission?

for example, 14 percent of Whites with AIDS had contracted the disease through injection drug use, compared to 36 percent of African Americans and 32.9 percent of Hispanic Americans (U.S. Department of Health and Human Services, 1997). AIDS is already the leading cause of death among African Americans aged twenty-five to forty-four. Early in the twenty-first century, more than half of all people with AIDS will be African Americans; an African American will be nine times more likely to be diagnosed with AIDS than someone who is not African American (Rimer, 1996). Efforts to curb HIV transmission among injection drug users by establishing needle exchange programs have not been widely supported by federal, state, and local governments because some people believe such programs encourage illegal drug use.

Vaginal intercourse, though less risky than anal intercourse and injection drug use, is also a means of HIV transmission. About 66 percent of those who have contracted HIV through heterosexual sex are women, and the majority of them through unprotected vaginal intercourse with an infected partner. Between 1985 and 1995, the percentage of people with AIDS who were women tripled, increasing from 6.5 percent to 18.6 percent (U.S. Department of Health and Human Services, 1997). Hispanic American and African American women are especially at risk, since so many more Hispanic American and African American men are infected than White men. African American women, for example, make up two-thirds of all women infected with HIV (Rimer, 1996).

The risk of HIV infection is also high for poor women, a disproportionate number of whom are women of color (Valleroy et al., 1998). For some poor women, sex is a source of income (Osmond et al., 1993). Health experts are also concerned that the growing use of crack cocaine and rising incidence of other sexually transmitted diseases in poor urban areas contributes to HIV infection. Female crack users often engage in unprotected sex in exchange for money or drugs (Inciardi et al., 1993). And the presence of other sexually transmitted diseases, such as syphilis, can facilitate HIV transmission (Barringer, 1993).

Given the greater likelihood of infection among women of color, it is not surprising that most children with AIDS are non-White. Although African American children make up about 15 percent of the child population in the United States (the population under thirteen), they make up 64.7 percent of children with AIDS. Hispanic American children represent 10 percent of the U.S. child population, but 17.7 percent of children with AIDS (U.S. Department of Health and Human Services, 1997).

The number of people infected with HIV is stable at about 40,000 per year in the United States, but the number of AIDS deaths declined in 1997 for the first time since the epidemic began. The decline indicates that peo-

ple who become infected with HIV are not developing AIDS as quickly as in the past and that people with AIDS are living longer. Most experts credit new HIV treatments, particularly drugs called protease inhibitors. However, researchers are concerned that the lack of decline in the infection rate means that those living with HIV/AIDS may still be infecting others (National Center for Health Statistics, 1998; Sack, 1999).

HIV infection and AIDS are severely stigmatized. To a large extent, the social stigma stems from people's misunderstandings about HIV transmission. Despite efforts to educate the general public, the level of misinformation is still high, and widespread myths and stereotypes often lead to prejudice and discrimination against people with HIV/AIDS (Herek & Glunt, 1997). Research shows that factual knowledge about HIV and AIDS is highest among the general gay male population and among heterosexual and homosexual college students (Ames et al., 1992; Bearden, 1992). The Doing Sociology box gives you an opportunity to test the level of HIV/AIDS awareness on your campus.

R EFLECTING ON

Health in the United States

1. About four times as many men as women commit suicide each year. Two-thirds of men who commit suicide use firearms, whereas just one-third of women use them. Based on your knowledge of gender norms, how would you explain this sex difference in mortality?

2. What strategies would you propose for closing the race gap in mortality?

3. Can you think of other examples of how social class affects health?

4. A physician recently wrote that prejudice and discrimination against people with HIV or AIDS stems in part from the fact that most people consider themselves far removed from these diseases. Thus, since everyone will soon know someone who has either HIV or AIDS, prejudice and discrimination will diminish. Do you agree with the doctor's prediction? Why or why not?

MEDICINE IN THE UNITED STATES

In preindustrial societies and even in societies in the early stages of industrialization, health care is largely a part of family caregiving. As with other social institutions, such as education, highly specialized formal roles do not emerge until a society produces enough surplus to sustain members who are not engaged in production. When the

DOING SOCIOLOGY

What Do Students Know about AIDS Prevention?

Recent research indicates that factual knowledge about HIV transmission and AIDS is greatest in the gay community and among heterosexual and homosexual college students, although there is still a high level of risk-taking behavior among these groups (Ames et al., 1992; Bearden, 1992; Osmond et al., 1993; Sack, 1999). To gauge the accuracy of HIV/AIDS knowledge on your campus, test a sample of students with the following true/false quiz:

1. HIV cannot be transmitted through oral sex. True or false?
2. HIV cannot be transmitted by kissing. True or false?
3. There is no need to use a condom when having sex with a partner who has recently tested negative for HIV. True or false?
4. There is no risk of contracting HIV by donating blood. True or false?
5. To prevent HIV transmission, never eat off the same plate or share eating utensils with someone who is HIV-positive or has AIDS. True or false?

Obtain demographic information from your respondents, too: their sex, race or ethnicity, age, and if you and they feel comfortable about disclosure, their sexual orientation. Compile your results and combine them with the results of your classmates. Are there differences in the responses among different social groups? Who appears to be most knowledgable about HIV transmission?

The correct answers are: (1) F; (2) T; (3) F; (4) T; (5) F.

role of *healer* or *doctor* does emerge, treatment is usually based on nature (for example, herbs and other plants) and spiritual beliefs. As shown earlier in the Global Insights box, even today, traditional healers blend herbal remedies with spirituality in their medical treatments, often engendering more trust from patients than professionally trained physicians (Belluck, 1996b).

Traditional healers and their practices are shunned as "unscientific" and "superstitious" by many people in industrial and postindustrial societies. Advanced industrial societies are "credential societies," and tremendous faith is placed in sophisticated technology to solve human problems. This is no less true of medicine: Health care is controlled by an elite group of specially trained, officially licensed medical practitioners who have a vast array of synthetic drugs, finely calibrated instruments, and complicated machines for treating patients. We can see the transition from traditional healer to scientific medical practitioner well by examining the professionalization of medicine in the United States.

The Professionalization of Medicine

Imagine that you lived in the United States in the early 1800s and had a small lump growing on your neck or a throbbing toothache. Whom would you go to for help? Chances are, you would devise your own remedy first, and if that failed, you'd seek advice from a relative or friend who might know a "cure," such as packing your neck in coarse salt to shrivel the lump or pulling the tooth out with their bare hands. Or, you might pay a visit to the local barber, not so you would look nicer as you suffered, but because barbers doubled as surgeons and dentists. The barber might actually cut the lump from your neck or have a tool for extracting the tooth—without the benefit of an anesthetic. If you're in a lot of pain, an herbalist could mix up a potion to ease your misery, although you could also buy various bottled remedies, many containing opium, at the corner grocery. And of course, you could always see a physician, that is, someone who had attended a medical school. This is not to say that the physician's credentials were more prestigious than the barber's or the herbalist's. Medical schools in the early 1800s offered only a few courses and no clinical experience. There wasn't even an agreed-upon science of medicine (the germ theory of disease—that microbes or germs cause disease—wasn't proven until 1876). Needless to say, medicine in the early 1800s was largely unlicensed and unregulated; and the barber, the herbalist, and the physician competed with one another for patients (Starr, 1982).

Advances in science played a major role in professionalizing medicine, but how did it come to be the doctor and not the barber or the herbalist that we go to today when we're ill? The answer lies in the professionalization of medicine. *Professionalizing* any field results in important changes: (1) to enter the profession, people must have extensive education or training, and master a body of theoretical knowledge; (2) people in the profession regulate themselves, deciding, for example, who is qualified to practice the profession; (3) professionals have authority over their clients because of their specialized training and knowledge; and (4) professionals maintain that their work serves some public good, not simply their own self-interest (Greenwood, 1962). In medicine, physician training grew lengthier and more complex as scientific knowledge of the body and disease grew. To set themselves apart from other "unscientific" medical practitioners, doctors trained at medical schools formed a professional organization in 1847 called the American Medical Association (AMA). The AMA established standards for medical education and medical practice. Individuals, as well as medical schools, who did not meet these standards were discredited as "quacks." A major turning point in the professionalization of medicine occurred in 1910 with the publication of the *Flexner Report*. A famous educator, Abraham Flexner, personally visited every medical school in the country and concluded that only about half the schools provided adequate physician training. He recommended licensing physicians who were graduates of these schools only, and he encouraged philanthropic organizations to award generous grants to these institutions so they could further upgrade their facilities. Thereafter, the best and the brightest faculty and students went to the Flexner-approved medical schools along with the funding. The nonapproved schools were forced to close, including nearly all of those with an exclusively Black or female student body. At the same time, individual states adopted strict licensing laws prohibiting anyone who had not graduated from an approved school from practicing medicine. This put many healers, including midwives and herbalists, out of business and eventually gave M.D.'s a monopoly on medical practice (Nechas & Foley, 1994; Starr, 1982).

Although a substantial number of people are once again seeking alternative treatments for illness, ranging from healing crystals to acupuncture to macrobiotic diets, physicians continue to dominate the practice of medicine (Eisenberg, 1990). Let's take a closer look, then, at medicine in the United States today.

The Practice of Medicine

Physicians today enjoy high prestige as well as high incomes. Indeed, physicians are among the highest paid professionals in the country, with an average annual income of about $182,000. Those in particular specialties, such as surgery, radiology, and anesthesiology, earn considerably more (U.S. Department of Commerce, Bureau of the Census, 1997). There are over 681,000 active physicians in the United States, more than triple the number in 1950; early in the twenty-first century, the number is expected to reach over 724,000 (U.S. Department of Health and Human Services, 1997). Applications to medical schools have risen steadily, from 27,000 in 1988 to 45,000 in 1994 (Fein, 1995a). This dramatic growth has led both the AMA and leaders of U.S. medical schools to ask the federal government to develop strategies for limiting the number of people who enter the medical profession each year. They believe there are too many physicians (Pear, 1997) and already research shows that almost 25 percent of physicians have significant difficulty finding jobs after they complete their residencies (Miller et al., 1998). However, research also indicates that the problem is not too many doctors, but too many doctors concentrated in particular specialties and geographic areas.

The first problem—too many doctors concentrated in particular specialties—is known as **overspecialization.** More than two-thirds of all office-based physicians have a specialty practice, such as cardiology, neurology, or psychiatry. This means that of the more than 600,000 professionally active physicians in this country, only about 59,000 are general or family practitioners; an additional 72,000 are internists. Yet, these are the kinds of doctors most people depend on for their primary health care. For every 10,000 people in the population, there are only about 12 primary care physicians (U.S. Department of Health and Human Services, 1996; 1997). Although the number of medical school graduates interested in general medicine rose from 14.6 percent in 1992 to 27.6 percent in 1995, the vast majority of medical school graduates are still attracted to specialty medicine, largely because of the greater prestige and financial rewards (Fein, 1995b). Consider, for example, that the average income of surgeons in 1995 was $255,200 compared to $121,200 for family practitioners, the lowest mean income of any subgroup of practicing physicians (U.S. Department of Commerce, Bureau of the Census, 1997).

The second problem—the concentration of physicians in particular geographic areas—is known as **maldistribution.** Rural areas and inner city neighborhoods with large low-income and minority populations have the fewest physicians. Doctors tend to be concentrated in more affluent urban and suburban areas, leaving some nonmetropolitan regions and impoverished inner city neighborhoods with no primary care physicians. According to the U.S. public health service, there are 2,100 medically underserved areas in the United States with a total population of over 30 million. Two-thirds of these people are women of childbearing age and children (Children's Defense Fund, 1991; Rosenthal, 1993b). Geographic and professional isolation are two reasons many physicians are reluctant to practice in rural locations. But whether the medically underserved live in rural or urban areas, they share two characteristics: They are usually poor and non-White. Besides geographic location, then, economic and racial factors also influence physicians' decisions about where to practice.

There are not only few physicians serving minority neighborhoods, but also few minority physicians in general. The practice of medicine, in fact, is organized hier-

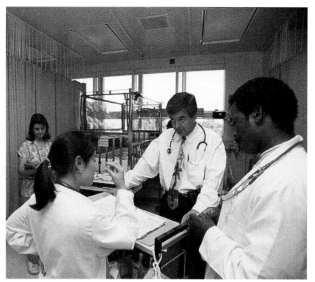

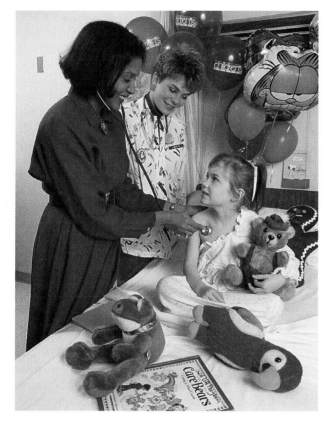

Over the last fifty years, what patterns and trends have developed in the field of medicine and medical practice in the United States? What have been some social outcomes of these patterns and trends? How do sex and race and ethnicity affect health care and employment in health care occupations? How might the hierarchy of health care occupations and physicians' interactions with nurses and patients be interpreted from the perspective of conflict theory?

archically, with White males concentrated at the top. Let's look at the hierarchy of health care occupations more closely.

The Hierarchy of Health Care Occupations.   Physicians are at the top of the health care occupational hierarchy. Most physicians are White men, although the number of physicians who are women has increased in recent years. In 1996, for instance, women were 26.4 percent of physicians, up from 15.8 percent in 1983. The representation of racial and ethnic minorities showed less improvement.

In 1996, 4.5 percent of physicians were African American compared to 3.2 percent in 1983, and the percentage of physicians who were Hispanic Americans increased from 4.5 percent in 1983 to 5.1 percent in 1996 (U.S. Department of Commerce, Bureau of the Census, 1997). As Table 18.4 shows, medical school enrollments have followed a similar pattern, indicating that although more women may be practicing medicine in the future, most will be White. In fact, in 1997, there was an 11-percent drop in minority medical school enrollments, which most experts attribute to the dismantling of affirmative action

TABLE 18.4 Medical School Enrollments by Sex and Race, 1980–1981 & 1994–1995

Percent of total students enrolled in medical school who are:	1980–1981	1994–1995
Women	26.5	41.1
White (non-Hispanic)	85.0	67.7
Black (non-Hispanic)	5.7	7.6
Hispanic	4.2	6.2
American Indian	0.3	0.6
Asian	3.0	16.5

Source: U.S. Department of Health and Human Services, 1997, p. 242.

programs in some states. The backlash against affirmative action has discouraged some minority students from applying to medical school and caused some administrators to be overly cautious in admissions decisions to avoid charges of "reverse discrimination" ("Minority Enrollment Drops," 1997; but see also Davidson & Lewis, 1998).

Moving down the health care occupational hierarchy, the number of women and racial and ethnic minorities is significantly higher. Health care historically has been an area of high female employment because many health care jobs are considered an extension of women's roles in the home. Not surprisingly, then, women made up over 87 percent of health care workers in 1996, including 93.3 percent of registered nurses, 98.2 percent of dental hygienists, 90.2 percent of dieticians, and 88.4 percent of nurses aides (U.S. Department of Commerce, Bureau of the Census, 1997). Workers who hold these positions have much less prestige and lower incomes than physicians. The lower the prestige and income, the greater the representation of racial and ethnic minorities (Glenn, 1992). For example, African Americans were 8.6 percent and Hispanic Americans 2.6 percent of registered nurses in 1996, but African Americans were 33.2 percent and Hispanic Americans 8.1 percent of nurses aides and orderlies (U.S. Department of Commerce, Bureau of the Census, 1997).

The acute shortage of registered nurses during the 1980s helped raise nursing salaries and benefits. These changes, in turn, attracted more men to nursing, although the profession has consistently remained more than 90 percent female.

Physicians' Interactions with Patients. Do sex and race or ethnicity affect physicians' interactions with their patients? There is evidence that these factors do influence the physician–patient relationship. We have already discussed, for example, how physicians may misdiagnose women's symptoms of heart disease because women are considered at lower risk than men. More generally, many physicians treat women in stereotyped ways. Even in medical school, sexual remarks and jokes are commonly made at the expense of women (Nechas & Foley, 1994). One recent study found that advertisements in widely read medical journals portray women and men in gender-stereotyped ways, with men appearing more serious than women, and female models being younger than males (Leppard et al., 1993). Reseachers have also found that female physicians appear to care for female patients better than male physicians, especially when the practices of younger female and male physicians are compared (Franks & Clancy, 1993; Lurie et al., 1993).

Race and ethnicity can also affect the physician–patient relationship. As we mentioned earlier, some researchers believe that because most physicians are White, they sometimes have difficulty communicating with and winning the trust of non-White patients. Other researchers have found that assumptions about patients' race and ethnicity can lead to misdiagnoses. For example, doctors diagnosed a Black patient's upper abdominal pain as sickle cell anemia, a disease found predominantly among African Americans, when in fact it was caused by a bleeding ulcer (Witzig, 1996). Other studies have found that psychiatric diagnoses are often affected by racial and ethnic stereotypes. For instance, Black patients are more likely than White patients to be diagnosed as violent even when all other circumstances of their cases are identical (Loring & Powell, 1988; see also Littlewood & Lipsedge, 1989).

Apart from sex and race and ethnicity, however, a significant number of patients report they are dissatisfied with their interactions with physicians. In one study, 23 percent of patients reported that their physicians appeared unprepared, having failed to review their medical charts; 26 percent said their physicians were not thorough in taking their medical histories; and 30 percent said their physicians did not perform a thorough examination (Kravitz et al., 1996). Research also shows that physicians and patients generally disagree about what constitutes good health care. In ranking nine factors, both physicians and patients felt that a doctor's clinical skill was most important, but patients rated effective communication second, while physicians rated it sixth (Laine et al., 1996). Physicians have a vested interest in taking patients' ratings seriously, since other studies show that when technical expertise is held constant, it is doctors whom patients feel treat them rudely, rush their visits, and fail to answer their questions who are most likely to be sued for malpractice (Hickson, et al., 1994).

The practice of medicine in the United States is undergoing dramatic change. For example, in 1996, for the first time, more doctors were working as employees in large-group practices than as solo practitioners or with one or two colleagues. Employee-physicians now outnumber self-employed physicians by a ratio of almost three to two, reflecting important changes in the delivery of health care overall (Kletke et al., 1996). Let's look more closely at U.S. health care.

The Medical-Industrial Complex

For much of the twentieth century, health care has been considered a social service, but since the 1970s, it has increasingly become a corporate industry. Health care delivery is now dominated by corporately owned, for-profit medical practices, hospitals, and freestanding emergency rooms. As the for-profit sector of health care grows, the nonprofit, and in particular, the public, sector shrinks, causing many urban, public hospitals to close (Conrad, 1997). It is also common today for hospitals and medical practices to advertise their services, touting their advantages over their "competitors." In short, health care has become what physician Arnold Relman calls the *medical-industrial complex* (Relman, 1997).

It is unclear whether the corporatization of medicine results in higher quality care, but it is clear that health care has become a "good investment." In recent years, in fact, the health care sector of the economy has outperformed the economy as a whole in all aspects of "production." During the first half of the 1980s, for example, when the rest of the U.S. economy was in a slump, employment and work hours in the health care industry showed solid gains. In 1995, consumer medical prices rose 3.5 percent, while the Consumer Price Index for all items rose by only 3.0 percent. During the first half of the 1990s, consumer medical prices increased an average of 6.3 percent, while the CPI for all items increased an average of 3.4 percent (U.S. Department of Commerce, Bureau of the Census, 1997).

While investors benefit from for-profit medicine, there is some question about whether the corporatization of health care is in the public interest (Gray, 1991; Relman, 1997). The growth of for-profit health care facilities at the expense of nonprofit and public facilities limits access to health care for some groups of people. Corporately owned facilities tend to be located in middle-class and more affluent urban and suburban areas. They charge, on average, more than their nonprofit and public competitors, and they usually have no problem collecting payments because of their favorable locations and preadmission screening for patients with private insurance. The uninsured or patients insured by government programs for the poor are often directed to the remaining nonprofit and public facilities, thus increasing their burden and thereby further jeopardizing their financial stability (Corn-

The medical-industrial complex includes multinational pharmaceutical companies that manufacture, import, and export drugs, including drugs not approved for use in the United States. Profit-seeking pharmaceutical companies have driven up the cost of both medical treatment and medical insurance, essentially ensuring that some segments of society do not receive the medicine they need to be well. What might be some other ethical issues involved in the corporatization of medical care?

well et al., 1996; Weissman, 1996). In the final analysis, the growth of the medical-industrial complex favors society's haves over the have-nots.

The debate over the corporatization of medical care is inseparable from the debate over how to pay for health care. To conclude this section, then, we'll discuss health insurance programs, which are the primary means of paying for health care in the United States.

Insuring Health

People in the United States spend more on health care than people anywhere else in the industrialized world,

Figure 18.1 Health Care Expenditures in the United States, 1960–1995

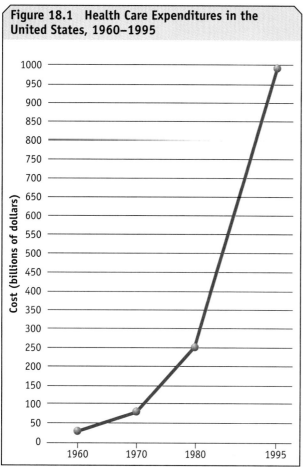

Source: U. S. Department of Commerce, Bureau of the Census, 1997, p. 112.

and these expenditures have risen dramatically since 1960, as Figure 18.1 shows. More than $3,700 per person is spent on health care in the United States, which is 55 percent more than in Canada, 58 percent more than in Germany, and more than double what is spent in Japan, Sweden, and the United Kingdom (U.S. Department of Commerce, Bureau of the Census, 1997). Yet, as Tables 18.5 and 18.6 show, the populations of these countries have a higher life expectancy and lower infant mortality rate than we do. Why?

The answer to this question rests with the fact that health care in the United States is a **direct-fee system,** in which patients pay directly for medical services. Unlike every other industrialized country, the United States has no public, nationwide health care system that ensures all citizens basic care. Instead, our health care system is private, which means that those who can afford it buy the best, most technologically sophisticated medical care available in the world, and those who can't afford it often go without any care at all. As we observed earlier, health is strongly associated with social class. Let's discuss what health insurance programs are available in the United States.

Private Insurance. About 71 percent of the U.S. population under age sixty-five had private health insurance in 1995, down from 77 percent in 1984 (U.S. Department of Health and Human Services, 1997). The majority receive health insurance as an employment benefit, but employers are increasingly unwilling to extend insurance

TABLE 18.5 Life Expectancy at Birth for Selected Countries, 1993

Country	LIFE EXPECTANCY (IN YEARS)		Country	LIFE EXPECTANCY (IN YEARS)	
	Males	*Females*		*Males*	*Females*
Japan	76.5	83.1	Costa Rica	73.3	77.8
Sweden	75.5	80.8	Singapore	73.2	78.9
Greece	75.0	80.4	Austria	72.9	79.5
Switzerland	75.0	81.7	Cuba	72.9	76.8
Canada	74.9	81.4	Germany	72.8	79.3
Australia	74.7	80.8	New Zealand	72.8	79.2
Israel	74.7	78.5	Northern Ireland	72.7	78.7
Netherlands	74.3	80.5	Denmark	72.7	77.9
Norway	74.2	80.5	Ireland	72.6	78.2
England & Wales	73.9	79.5	United States	72.2	78.8
France	73.8	82.3	Finland	72.1	79.6
Italy	73.7	80.5	Scotland	71.7	77.4
Spain	73.4	80.7	Portugal	70.6	77.9

Source: U.S. Department of Health and Human Services, 1997, pp. 106–107.

TABLE 18.6   Infant Mortality Rates for Selected Countries, 1993

Country	Infant Mortality Rate	Country	Infant Mortality Rate
Japan	4.35	Austria	6.49
Finland	4.40	Scotland	6.50
Singapore	4.68	France	6.82
Hong Kong	4.76	Northern Ireland	7.07
Sweden	4.84	Italy	7.16
Norway	5.11	Spain	7.19
Denmark	5.40	New Zealand	7.24
Switzerland	5.55	Israel	7.80
Germany	5.84	Belgium	8.20
Ireland	5.99	Greece	8.30
Australia	6.11	United States	8.37
England & Wales	6.24	Czech Republic	8.49
Netherlands	6.27	Cuba	9.40
Canada	6.30	Portugal	9.57

Source: U.S. Department of Health and Human Services, 1997, p. 105.

benefits to workers' family members, so some people also purchase private insurance on their own (Children's Defense Fund, 1997). The self-employed, unemployed, individuals working for small businesses that do not offer insurance benefits, and early retirees who are too young to be eligible for Medicare (the federal insurance program for the elderly) and not poor enough for Medicaid (the federal insurance program for the impoverished) must also buy individual policies. Individual health insurance coverage is about twice as expensive as group coverage (available through employers) (Kilborn, 1998).

Private insurance programs rarely cover all medical costs. At least two-thirds have patient deductibles, and most exclude certain kinds of care, such as dental care, infertility treatments, experimental procedures, and drugs. Most also limit hospital stays to a certain number of days and set a ceiling on how much they will pay for various procedures.

Growing in popularity are **health maintenance organizations (HMOs)**, which provide medical services to subscribers at a fixed rate and emphasize preventive medicine. In 1996, nearly 53 million people were enrolled in HMOs, an increase of more than 500 percent since 1980 (U.S. Department of Health and Human Services, 1997). HMOs are less expensive than other private insurance plans, especially if one subscribes through an employer

rather than individually, but they usually have more restrictions on coverage. Sometimes patients cannot keep the physician they have been using; they might be required to choose a physician from the HMO's staff, their physician may not accept their HMO, or their physician's practice may have already accepted its quota of HMO subscribers. Physicians usually limit the number of HMO patients they treat because HMO reimbursements are lower than reimbursements from other private insurers.

Private health insurance coverage varies by race and social class. While 78.2 percent of White Americans have private health insurance, 53.5 percent of African Americans and 47.2 percent of Hispanic Americans are privately insured. Not surprisingly, 93.6 percent of individuals with annual family incomes of $50,000 or more have private health insurance, whereas 55.7 percent of those with annual family incomes of $14,000 to $24,999 and only 24.3 percent of those with annual family incomes below $14,000 are privately insured.

Public Insurance.   The United States has two public health insurance programs, both financed by the federal government. Compared with the public health insurance programs of other industrialized countries, both are relatively recent—established by Congress in 1965—and less generous in coverage.

The effectiveness of HMOs became the subject of a government investigation in 1998, in which it was uncovered that some for-profit health maintenance organizations may seek to save money by denying or delaying treatment and referral and by generally undertreating patients. What are some abuses that have been uncovered relating to public insurance? Who are the uninsured, and what do they do when they become ill?

Medicare is a public health insurance program primarily covering people aged sixty-five and older. The program has two parts: Part A, hospital insurance, is financed through the Social Security payroll tax and is designed to defray the costs of hospitalization and aftercare. Part B, Supplementary Medical Insurance (SMI), covers other forms of medical treatment, including physician visits and diagnostic tests. Enrollment in SMI is voluntary and requires payment of a monthly premium. Medicare actually covers less than half the health care expenses of the elderly (Pear, 1984). Medicare has patient deductibles and it also limits the portion of specific charges it will pay. Some services, such as prescription drugs and many nursing home costs, are not covered at all (Holahan & Palmer, 1988). To fill the gaps, some elderly people also purchase private insurance, but those who are poor can use one of

four "safety-net" programs established by the federal government to prevent the impoverished elderly from being medically uninsured. These programs exempt the impoverished elderly from SMI premiums and pays for about 20 to 30 percent of the health care costs Medicare does not cover. However, studies show that a minimum of 40 percent of the elderly who are eligible for these programs are not enrolled in them, largely because they do not know about them or they find the application procedures too difficult or demeaning (individuals must apply through state agencies that supervise welfare services) (Kilborn, 1999).

With the projected growth of the elderly population in the twenty-first century, a major concern is whether Medicare can remain financially solvent. Many analysts predict that unless immediate changes are made to the program, it will be bankrupt early in the twenty-first century. Proposed changes include raising premiums for higher-income beneficiaries and giving beneficiaries a fixed sum of money with which to buy insurance coverage from either the government or private insurers (Pear, 1999).

Individuals under sixty-five years old who are poor may qualify for another public health insurance program, Medicaid.

Medicaid is a public assistance program designed to pay the health care costs of the poor, including the elderly poor for whom Medicare is inadequate. Medicaid is jointly financed by the federal government and individual states, with the federal government contributing 50 to 80 percent of the cost, depending on per capita state income. In 1994, 10.9 percent of the population under age sixty-five was insured by Medicaid (U.S. Department of Health and Human Services, 1997).

Research indicates that Medicaid has improved the health of the poor by increasing their access to medical care. Unfortunately, the percentage of the poverty population covered by Medicaid declined between the 1970s and the 1990s (Lewin, 1991). Why aren't all poor people covered? Medicaid, like other welfare programs, has specific eligibility requirements. Each state is responsible for administering its own Medicaid program and for establishing its eligibility standards within broad guidelines issued by the federal government. All states are required to provide Medicaid to recipients of Temporary Aid to Needy Families (TANF)—mostly single mothers and their dependent children—and to recipients of Supplemental Security Income (SSI), which includes the impoverished elderly and disabled. However, coverage does not have to be extended to poor people who do not receive TANF (with the exception of children and pregnant women), the homeless, and formerly illegal aliens who have obtained legal status. Because of the wide discretion afforded states, there is substantial variation in Medicaid eligibility requirements and benefits, and states with large minority populations typically have the strictest eligibility standards (Children's Defense Fund, 1997; Lundberg, 1991).

The Uninsured. Although the majority of people in the United States have some form of health insurance even if it does not cover all of their medical expenses, 16.5 percent of the population under sixty-five—more than 39 million people—are medically uninsured, a 14 percent increase since 1984 (U.S. Department of Health and Human Services, 1997). An additional 25 to 48 million people are underinsured, and about 63 million people during any two-year period temporarily lose their health insurance (Hilts, 1991; Weissman, 1996). More than 75 percent of

TABLE 18.7   Who Are the Uninsured?

Social characteristic	Percent uninsured, 1995
Total (age-adjusted)	16.5
Age	
Under 15 years	14.2
Under 5 years	13.2
5–14 years	14.7
15–44 years	20.7
45–64 years	11.5
Sex	
Male	17.6
Female	15.5
Race & Ethnicity	
White (non-Hispanic)	13.4
Black (non-Hispanic)	19.9
Hispanic	31.5
Family Income	
< $14,000	33.5
$14,000-$24,999	28.0
$25,000-$34,999	17.2
$35,000-$49,999	8.3
$50,000 or >	4.6
Geographic Region	
Northeast	13.8
Midwest	12.0
South	20.1
West	18.4

Source: U.S. Department of Health and Human Services, 1997, p. 269.

the uninsured are employed or are the dependents of an employed householder. As Table 18.7 shows, 14.2 percent of the uninsured are children under age fifteen, representing more than 8.1 million children. Most of these children (92 percent) live with at least one parent who is working. Most are also in young families; more than one in five children in families headed by a person under age thirty and one in four children in families headed by a person under age twenty-five are uninsured. Although many of their parents are in the labor force, almost one-third work in low-paying services jobs, retail industries, or small businesses where insurance benefits are rarely provided. Other parents might only be employed part time. The number of part-time workers has risen considerably in recent years, but part-timers are least likely to receive insurance benefits (Children's Defense Fund, 1997; 1998; Schneider, 1997).

Of course, lack of insurance coverage does not indicate less need for health care. Indeed, as one recent study found, sick newborns who were uninsured received significantly less care than sick newborns covered by either public or private insurance, even though the uninsured infants were in greater need of care (Braveman et al., 1991). A lack of insurance often worsens ill health, since the uninsured receive little or no primary care and must delay treatment until they are severely ill. They then typically seek care at hospital emergency rooms, which are increasingly refusing to treat uninsured patients and are transferring them to public hospitals (Cornwell et al., 1996). Thus, lack of insurance sets in motion a spiral of events that ultimately limits care for many who need it most.

There are no easy solutions to the health insurance problem, but most experts agree that reforms are needed. The Social Policy box on page 496 discusses some recent proposals.

R E F L E C T I N G   O N

Medicine in the United States

1. How can the federal government encourage physicians to enter family medicine and practice in medically underserved areas?
2. Have you ever thought that your interaction with a physician was influenced in any way by your sex, race or ethnicity, social class, or sexual orientation? How did the encounter make you feel? How did you handle the situation?
3. Can you think of ways that the corporatization of health care may benefit patients?
4. What reforms would you suggest for improving the U.S. health care system?

Social Policy
Alternative Health Care Reforms in the United States

The Issue

The large number of uninsured Americans, coupled with the dramatic rises in health care costs over the last several decades, have prompted politicians, policy makers and citizens to call for reforms in how we pay for health care in the United States. A variety of plans have been proposed, and, not suprisingly, there is disagreement over which is the best. Let's briefly review some of them.

The Debate

Managed competition. This is the plan that was proposed by the Clinton administration. It would have established a national health program based on an HMO model. All citizens would enroll in an HMO of their choice, but would be restricted to the doctors and hospitals in their HMO. The government would subsidize the cost of medical care, but the program would be financed largely by the premiums paid by patients for the health insurance. Because all citizens would be enrolled in an HMO, however, these premuims would be lower than they are now, making it affordable for most Americans and thus dramatically reducing the number of uninsured. The HMOs would be owned and operated by private insurance companies, as they are now. Individuals who chose to, could still buy health care outside the

HMO system, but they would not be exempt from enrolling in an HMO and paying the premiums. The Clinton plan was defeated in Congress in 1994 (Starr, 1995). At this point, its future is uncertain.

An individual mandate and tax credit. This plan is based on the idea that just as all car owners are required to carry liability insurance, all patients should be required to carry health insurance. Under this plan, all citizens would be required to purchase health insurance from a private health insurance company, but would receive a tax credit to pay for it. The tax credit would be sufficient for most people to buy a basic plan. Additional coverage could be purchased at an individual's own expense out of after-tax income. The tax credit would be progressive; the more a person's annual income, the lower their tax credit. The wealthiest segments of the population would receive no tax credit at all and would be personally responsible for paying their medical expenses or insurance premiums. The insurance premiums of people at the lowest income levels would be paid by state and local governments directly to the insurance carriers. Medicare and Medicaid could be integrated into this plan (Cadette, 1997). This plan has received considerable support from the insurance industry, but critics are concerned that

those with minimal coverage would be unable to obtain adequate care because any out-of-pocket expenses could be prohibitive for them.

A national health service. Modeled after the Canadian system, this plan proposes to replace private insurance with universal public health insurance financed by the federal government and the states through various types of taxes. A uniform national fee schedule for all hospitals and physicians would be set by the government. Although this plan has received support from the general public, it is opposed by many physicians who argue that it would too severely restrict their medical decisions and limit the personal choices of their patients. It is also opposed by some policy analysts and politicians who argue that it would be too expensive or that it would lower the quality of available medical care. Not surprisingly, it is also opposed by the insurance industry since it would eliminate their health insurance business (Eckholm, 1991).

What Do You Think?

Which plan do you favor? Can you suggest alternative plans for reforming the U.S. health care system?

HEALTH CARE CHALLENGES FOR THE TWENTY-FIRST CENTURY

Health care costs in the United States have increased dramatically, partly because of the growing availability of highly sophisticated, but extraordinarily expensive medical technology. Dialysis, for example, which has extended life for people with chronic kidney failure and renal disease, is extremely expensive. In fact, given that only 70,000 people are affected by these illnesses, med-

ical sociologist Peter Conrad (1997) questions whether the $2 billion a year cost for their treatment is an effective use of medical resources.

Dialysis is just one example of advanced medical technology that prolongs life for small numbers of people at great cost. Conrad (1997) goes on to say that the health care industry will soon be able to provide more medical care than our society can afford. But the economic issues are just one dimension of the dilemma. We must consider quality of life issues as well. Should a person be kept alive

A terminally ill patient committed suicide using a self-administered drug supplied by Dr. Jack Kervorkian, shown here during his trial. The growing "right to die" movement aims to take decisions about quality of life and timing of death out of the hands of physicians and family members and into the hands of dying individuals. What are the issues surrounding the practice of physician-assisted suicide? In what ways is death, like health and illness, a social product? What are some other controversies about health care relating to advances in medical technology?

through the use of machinery, such as a respirator, even though his or her brain and body will never again be able to function normally? Should physicians use extraordinary medical interventions to keep people alive no matter how old or infirm they are? Medical technology's

potential to prolong life has even more fundamental questions: What is death? When does death occur?

Such questions are likely to be at the center of health care policy debates in the twenty-first century, generating social, legal, and ethical as well as medical dilemmas. Some analysts argue for explicitly rationing health care, that is, prioritizing services based on cost and effectiveness as well as a patient's age and likelihood of recovery. Many people in this country balk at the idea of rationing, holding fast to the notion that every individual should have the freedom to decide the level of care he or she wants. The fact is that rationing already exists, albeit in implicit form (Covinsky et al., 1996). According to Conrad (1997), we currently ration health care on the basis of ability to pay. If you can't pay, you don't get the care. The greatest health care challenge of the twenty-first century, then, is likely to revolve around the equitable distribution of medical resources. How well we meet this challenge is literally a matter of life and death.

REFLECTING ON
....

Health Care Challenges for the Twenty-First Century

1. Do you favor rationing medical care? Why or why not? Do you think it's possible to equitably ration health care? If so, how?
2. Can you think of other health care challenges our society will have to address in the twenty-first century? How do you think each of these challenges can best be met?

 For useful resources for study and review, run Chapter 18 on your *Living Sociology* CD-ROM.

CONNECTIONS

Culture and health	Review Chapter 4. What examples can you suggest of intersections between health and illness, health care practices, and cultural norms, beliefs, and values?
Female circumcision	Reread the feature on female circumcision in Chapter 11. How might this be an example of Durkheim's notion of normative deviance, explained in Chapter 7? What norms and values does female circumcision aim to protect?
Health and social stratification	Review Chapter 8 to find some specific examples of impacts of social class on health and illness and quality of life within a society. Then review Chapter 9 to find examples of impacts of wealth and poverty in global stratification. What unifying concepts do conflict and feminist perspectives offer for understanding inequality in access to health?

CONNECTIONS

Symbolic interactionist approaches to illness	Socially labeling people as "sick" is part of the medicalization of deviance discussed in Chapter 7. See also the section on "The Homeless" in Chapter 8. How might a symbolic interactionist interpret stereotypes of homelessness as a symptom of sickness or insanity? See also the section on "Sexual Orientation" in Chapter 10. According to the symbolic interactionist perspective, why might homosexuality be seen as illness?
Infant mortality and life expectancy	In Chapter 9, review the definitions of infant mortality and life expectancy and the discussion of the other stratification indicators used by the World Bank. Then reread the section on "Children and Global Poverty." How does global stratification relate to infant mortality, life expectancy, and general health and well-being?
Sex and health	Review Chapter 10. What are some specific examples of the impacts of sex and gender and sexual orientation on health care in the United States? How do you think sexism and homophobia might affect medical research and the treatment or care that health care professionals provide? How might sexism affect employment opportunities in medicine?
Race and ethnicity and health	Review Chapter 11. Why do you think racism and ethnocentrism might occur in interactions between health care providers with patients? How might racism and ethnocentrism lead to injustices in medical insurance and treatment? How might racism affect employment opportunities in medicine?
Age and health	Review Chapter 12. What are some myths and realities about health and illness in the elderly population? How do social constructs concerning old age and those concerning illness overlap, and how do they affect the medical system's treatment and care of the elderly?
Families and health	Reread the section on "Violence in Families" in Chapter 15. How does the medical system as a social institution interact with other social institutions to address the problems of partner abuse, child abuse and neglect, and elder abuse in a violent society such as the United States?
Healers	Chapter 3 discusses the role of healers in preindustrial and traditional societies, and Chapter 17 refers to the role of religious experience in health and illness, as in the case of faith healing or healing through prayer or the laying on of hands. Why are these kinds of healing often effective? How do they differ from the development of modern medicine?
Medicine as a profession	Review the discussions of the hierarchy of occupations in Chapters 8 and 13. How would you relate the hierarchy of occupations to specific jobs in the medical profession and health care industry? How might you rank jobs in medicine in terms of occupational prestige and general salary?
Medical-industrial complex	Compare the medical-industrial complex with the military-industrial complex, described in Chapter 14. What features do they have in common? What are the costs and of these relationships to society?

SUMMING UP CHAPTER 18

1. Illness is not simply a biological or physiological condition. Both health and illness are socially constructed. Medicalization is the process of defining a specific behavior or condition as an illness in need of medical treatment.

Defining Health and Medicine

1. Health is multidimensional. Health is a state of physical, mental, and social well-being.
2. Health is linked with culture and social structure in several ways: Standards of health vary cross-culturally; standards of health vary over time; standards of health reflect the dominant values and norms of a society; and health is affected by a society's level of economic development.
3. Medicine also reflects the culture and structure of the society in which it is practiced. Curative medicine focuses on treating people who are already ill, whereas preventive medicine focuses on establishing conditions that preclude the onset of illness. Curative medicine has been dominant in our society because it is most compatible with our culture's values of individualism and free enterprise.

Sociological Perspectives on Health and Medicine

1. The structural functionalist perspective, developed by Talcott Parsons, sees medicine as vital to the overall functioning of society by making members healthy. When people get sick, they must conform to the society's sick role in order for their condition to be considered legitimate. The sick role has four characteristics. The sick person is: excused from usual responsibilities, not at fault for becoming ill, sincere in his or her desire to get well, and doing all he or she can to get well. Parsons also identified a physician role, based on the physician's specialized knowledge. The physician role has two components: to evaluate people's claims of illness and determine the cause of the illness, and to cure the sick. The structural functionalist perspective has been criticized for focusing on acute illness, placing too much emphasis on individual responsibility, and ignoring the negative consequences of inequality.
2. The conflict and feminist perspectives focus on how inequality affects health and medicine. Conflict theorists look at how health and medicine are treated as commodities in capitalist societies and at their unequal distribution across social classes. Feminist sociologists extend this analysis by examining how social class inequality intersects with other inequalities, especially sexism, racism, and heterosexism, to affect health and medicine. The conflict perspective has been criticized for focusing too narrowly on capitalist societies and for overlooking the fact that the populations of capitalist societies are healthier than the populations of socialist societies. The feminist perspective has been criticized for downplaying the beneficial effects of medicine for women in our society despite prejudice and discrimination.
3. Symbolic interactionists examine how health and medicine are socially constructed, both in a society and across societies. Symbolic interactionism is valuable for emphasizing the social nature of health and medicine, but has been criticized for downplaying the objective reality of health and illness.

Health and Medicine across Societies

1. The well-being of a population as measured by different health indicators varies dramatically across societies and is related to a society's level of economic development. As one moves from low-income countries to high-income, industrialized countries, the health of the population improves significantly.

Health in the United States

1. Health in the United States, as in other high-income, industrialized societies, is very good, although the United States ranks lower than many other industrialized countries in terms of both life expectancy and infant mortality. Social epidemiologists have found that the distribution of health and illness varies among groups in the U.S. population.
2. Sex is a factor related to health. Women have longer life expectancy than men and lower rates of mortality for most causes of death. Sex differences in health are strongly associated with traditional gender norms.
3. There is also a race gap in mortality, most of which is accounted for by excess mortality of African Americans, especially African American men. Some of this excess mortality is the result of racial discrimination as well as the intersection of racial inequality with social class inequality. African Americans are disproportionately represented among the poor and are therefore more likely to live in unhealthy, stressful, high-crime environments that breed disease and violence. They also have less access to medical care.
4. Illness is inversely related to social class: The higher one's social class, the fewer one's ailments. Factors that contribute to social class disparities in health include differences in living conditions, work conditions, lifestyle, and access to health care.
5. AIDS is a leading cause of death in the United States, but like other diseases, the risk of contracting HIV, the virus that causes AIDS, is not the same across social groups, and the groups at greatest risk appear to be changing. The percentage of AIDS cases attributable to gay and bisexual men is declining, while the percentage of cases attributable to injection drug users is increasing. The percentage of people with AIDS who are women is also

rising, with poor and minority women at especially high risk. The social stigma attached to HIV/AIDS stems in part from misinformation about HIV transmission, but these misunderstandings generate prejudice and discrimination against people with HIV and AIDS.

Medicine in the United States

1. Health care in the United States has developed over the past two hundred years from a mosaic of diverse healing practices performed by many different people, including but not limited to physicians, to a system controlled by an elite group of specially trained, officially licensed and certified medical practitioners, who have at their disposal an array of sophisticated technology with which to treat patients.
2. Advances in science played a major role in the professionalization of medicine. Efforts by the American Medical Association, backed by the Flexner Report, also led to professional distinctions between specially trained physicians and other healers, with physicians identified as the only legitimate medical practitioners. This change contributed to a decline in the number of women and racial and ethnic minorities practicing medicine.
3. Physicians are highly paid and enjoy high prestige. There has been a dramatic increase in the number of physicians in the United States over the past twenty years, leading some experts to call for policies to limit entrance to the medical profession. However, research shows that the problems of overspecialization and maldistribution are more serious than simply the number of practicing physicians.
4. Health care occupations are organized hierarchically, with physicians at the top. Most physicians are White men. Although the number of women entering medicine has increased, there has been little change in the number of racial and ethnic minorities. As one moves down the occupational hierarchy to jobs with less pay and less prestige, the number of women and people of color increases. Racial and ethnic minorities are concentrated at the bottom of the health care occupational hierarchy.
5. Sex as well as race and ethnicity affect physicians' interactions with patients. Apart from sex and race and ethnicity, though, a significant number of patients are dissatisfied with their interactions with physicians. A major source of patient dissatisfaction is physicians' lack of effective communication, although physicians consider communication less important than patients do.
6. Health care has become more of an industry than a social service during the past two decades, with health care delivery being dominated by corporately owned, for-profit practices and facilities constituting a medical-industrial complex. The corporatization of health care has made for sound business and investment, but some observers question whether it is in the public interest since it further limits access to health care for some social groups, especially the poor.
7. Unlike the health care systems of other industrialized societies, the United States has a largely private, direct-fee system. Although most people are covered by some form of insurance—private, public, or a combination of the two—more than 17 percent of the population under age sixty-five is uninsured. Most uninsured people are working or are the dependents of a working householder. The working uninsured are employed in the types of jobs and businesses that rarely offer health insurance benefits, or they work part time. Even with insurance, most people must still pay a substantial portion of health care costs themselves because of deductibles, limits on coverage, and eligibility requirements for public insurance.

Health Care Challenges for the Twenty-First Century

1. A major challenge facing our society in the twenty-first century will be how to most effectively and fairly use health care resources, especially given the growing availability of sophisticated medical technology that prolongs life, but at great expense and with no consideration for quality of life issues.

KEY PEOPLE AND CONCEPTS

curative medicine: medicine that focuses on treating people who are already ill

direct-fee system: a system of health care in which patients pay directly for medical services

health: a state of physical, mental, and social well-being

health maintenance organization (HMO): a type of private medical insurance that provides medical services to subscribers at a fixed rate and emphasizes preventive medicine

infant mortality rate: the number of deaths of children under one year of age per 1,000 live births

life expectancy: the average number of years of life remaining to an individual at a given age

maldistribution: the concentration of physicians in particular geographic areas

medicalization: the process of defining a specific behavior or condition as an illness in need of medical treatment

medicine: the social institution established to identify and treat illness and promote health

mortality rate: the number of deaths in proportion to a given population

overspecialization: the concentration of physicians in particular specialties

preventive medicine: medicine that establishes conditions that preclude the onset of illness

sick role: the behaviors defined by a society as appropriate for people who are sick

social epidemiology: the study of the distribution of health and illness across population groups

LEARNING MORE

Gesler, W. M. (1992). *The cultural geography of health care.* Pittsburgh: University of Pittsburgh Press. A fascinating look at the social construction of health, illness, and medicine across diverse societies.

Haynes, M. A., & Smedley, B. D. (Eds.). (1999). *The unequal burden of cancer: An assessment of NIH research and progress for ethnic minorities and the medically underserved.* Washington, DC: National Academy Press. A report by the National Research Council's Institute of Medicine that examines data from numerous studies of who gets cancer, showing strong evidence that Americans of color and the poor are more likely to develop the disease and less likely to survive it than White Americans and the financially secure.

Hilfker, D. (1994). *Not all of us are saints: A doctor's journey with the poor.* New York: Hill and Wang. The moving autobiography of a physician who committed himself to providing health care to the medically underserved poor.

Nechas, E., & Foley, D. (1994). *Unequal treatment.* New York: Simon & Schuster. A thorough analysis of sexism in medical care and its effects on the physical and psychological health of women.

Sabo, D., & Gordon, D. F. (Eds.). (1995). *Men's health and illness.* Thousand Oaks, CA: Sage. A review of the current research on gender differences in illness and mortality (and the reasons for them) by some of the leading experts in medical sociology and public health.

 Run Chapter 19 on your *Living Sociology* CD-ROM for interesting and informative activities, web links, videos, practice tests, and more.

Population, Urbanization, and the Environment

In 1970, an astronaut orbiting the earth looked down from his craft to see the Amazon region in Brazil. He was overwhelmed by the immense, virtually untouched emerald green forest. Not having a camera handy to capture the view, he carefully wrote down the longitude and latitude so that on a later flight he could photograph it. Unfortunately, he never participated in another mission. In 1997, he approached a crew member of an upcoming space shuttle flight and told about his missed opportunity to photograph what he considered to be one of the most dramatic sights of his life. He gave the shuttle astronaut the longitude and latitude he had recorded more than twenty-five years earlier, and she agreed to take the photograph. Upon her return, the two met and she presented several photographs of a heavily populated area cleared in a grid pattern. Looking at the pictures, the man thought she had made a mistake: This simply could not be the same place. She said she, too, had been so surprised that she'd asked another astronaut to doublecheck the coordinates. This was the place, and the man's paradise was lost not only for him but for all humanity.

This account is fictitious, but the facts about the Amazon region are true. In 1970, the state of Rondonia had a population of 110,000 people and was basically a vast stretch of rainforest. To encourage development, the Brazilian government built Road 364, and ranchers and farmers moved into the region. They aggressively cleared land in a grid pattern, converting forest to pasture and farmland. The environmental loss is almost unthinkable. According to the National Academy of Sciences, by 1997, the Rondonia area was highly developed with over 1.4 million people living there, and the population is expected to continue to grow during the twenty-first century. At the same time, the development is fundamentally altering the natural habitat of 750 species of trees, 400 varieties of birds, 125 types of mammals, 160 kinds of reptiles and amphibians, and more than 400 species of insects. Environmentalists fear that many of the species now face extinction.

The loss of vast tracts of the Amazon rainforest illustrates the relationship among population, urbanization, and the environment—the three topics of this chapter. Governmental efforts to develop Rondonia and thereby improve the Brazilian economy resulted in increased regional population density at the expense of the environment. This is not to say that there is a set pattern to how these three variables interact, but rather that in order to fully understand any one of them, all three must be taken into account. In fact, in an ideal scenario, economic development should produce balanced population growth, and at the same time, protect or enhance the environment.

We begin this chapter by looking at the dynamics of population growth and control. Then we will look at how urban areas have developed historically and review some of the major issues confronting city dwellers today. Finally, we discuss environmental issues and threats to the natural environment. Throughout, we stress how humans and the environment interact and how that interaction can preserve or endanger our future.

POPULATION: GROWTH AND CONTROL

Picture a world in which there are so many people that there aren't enough fish in the ocean to feed them all, enough land for them to live on and grow food, or enough water for them to drink. In the world you are picturing, there are so many children that there are not enough schools and teachers to educate them all, and there are so many adults of working age that there are not enough jobs to go around. All of these people must compete with one another for the scarce resources available. Divisions form along racial, ethnic, and religious lines, and soon the physical and social stresses from the intense competition erupt into armed conflict among these groups.

Have we asked you to imagine a scene from a science fiction movie? No, this scenario represents what some analysts believe is in store for some countries in the future if their governments and citizens do not act now to curb population growth (Brown et al., 1998). Of course, not all population experts share this view, and to a large extent, their disagreement revolves around how population growth is measured and the accuracy of population projects. Before we evaluate this scenario, then, let's take a look at these measurement issues.

Demography: Counting the People

Demographers are sometimes described as "people counters," but this is only one dimension of what they actually do. **Demography** is the study of population size, distribution, composition, and movement or migration. While the most basic demographic analysis focuses on the population count, most research is aimed at understanding changes in population in order to gauge future change and develop population policies.

Undoubtedly, the most significant policy issue is population growth or decline. Globally, growth and decline reflect the number of people who are born and die dur-

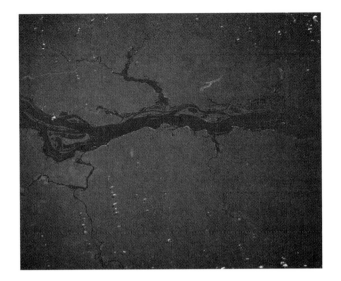

The NASA satellite photographs illustrate the areas of untouched rainforest that remain in northwestern Brazil and the effects of roadbuilding, clearcutting, and intensive settlement on deforestation. In 1970, only 110,000 people were living in the state of Rondonia in Brazil. By 1995 the population was 1.4 million. What are some consequences of rainforest destruction? What do these photographs show about the relationship between societies and their environments?

ing a specific period of time, usually a year. Demographers use the term **fertility** to refer to the incidence of live births and **mortality** to refer to the incidence of deaths. They measure fertility and mortality by dividing the number of live births or deaths by the total population and then multiplying by 1,000. This statistic is called the *crude rate*. Thus, the **crude birth rate** is the number of live births per 1,000 people in a year, and the **crude death rate** is the number of deaths per 1,000 people in a year.

For example, the U.S. Bureau of the Census projects that in the year 2010 the number of births in the United States will be about 4.2 million and the total population in the United States will be 296 million. Dividing 4.2 million by 296 million equals .0142, and when this figure is multiplied by 1,000, the result is a crude birth rate of 14.2 births per 1,000 people. The statistic is called "crude" because it is a very general indicator of fertility based on total population; it does not take into account the number of women of childbearing age or differences

between subgroups in a society. A more accurate fertility rate is calculated using such factors as age, race, and socioeconomic status.

Demographers use fertility and mortality rates to construct a **population pyramid,** a visual representation of a population by age and sex. Figure 19.1 on page 506 shows two population pyramids, one for the United States and one for less developed countries. Population pyramids are important because they show how economic development affects the population distribution of a nation. As Figure 19.1 illustrates, developing countries are typically bottom-heavy, most closely resembling a pyramid. High fertility rates and moderate mortality rates cause a population concentration in the younger age groups. Industrialized countries tend to have a more balanced distribution because of lower birth and mortality rates.

Life expectancy also plays a significant role in the way a country's population pyramid looks. **Life expectancy** is the average number of years a person can expect to live

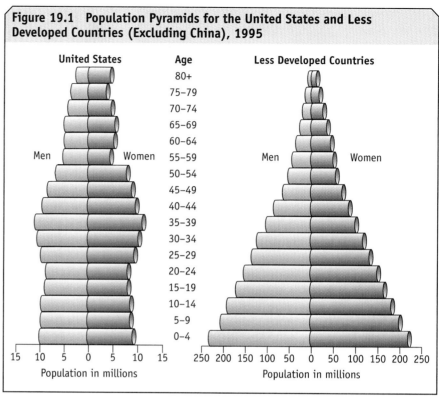

Figure 19.1 Population Pyramids for the United States and Less Developed Countries (Excluding China), 1995

Sources: Population Today, January 1997, p. 4; U.S. Department of Commerce, Bureau of the Census, 1996; p. 16.

after reaching a certain age. Obviously, a nation's average life expectancy is linked to its mortality rate and, as we learned in previous chapters, both correlate highly with the country's level of development.

Migration

Demographers study not only population size, composition, and distribution, but also movement of populations, or migration. Since there is no movement on or off our planet (that has been officially documented), the earth's population changes are determined exclusively by fertility and mortality. This is not the case for national (or regional) population growth, since people often move from area to area, both legally and illegally. **Net migration** is determined by comparing in-migration (the number of individuals entering an area) with out-migration (the number of people departing). A country's population growth or decline, therefore, is established by considering births, deaths, and net migration. In the United States, for example, the number of births declined in 1997 and 1996, and the number of deaths was just slightly higher in 1997 than in 1996, but the population growth rate remained stable largely because of international immigration (in-migration) which exceeded out-migration (U.S. Department of Commerce, Bureau of the Census, 1998).

In the United States, debate over immigration, especially illegal immigration along the U.S.–Mexican border, has raised public awareness of migration. The U.S. Immigration and Naturalization Service (INS) reports that between 1980 and 1995, 12.6 million people legally emigrated to the United States. The INS estimates that 5 million undocumented immigrants have entered the United States (U.S. Department of Commerce, Bureau of the Census, 1997). But U.S. immigration is only a small portion of a larger global phenomenon. Today, between 100 and 130 million people are living in a country different from the one in which they were born (United Nations High Commissioner for Refugees [UNHCR], 1995).

Many variables contribute to migration, but one of the most important is population growth. As population increases, the demand for jobs exceeds the availability of jobs. Consequently, people without employment, typically young adults, move someplace that they believe will provide them with a livelihood, sometimes across international borders, but often within a country from a rural area to an urban area. Population growth can also produce environmental conditions that cause people to migrate. For example, soil degradation resulting from overuse of land or a shortage of water can reduce crop production, forcing people to move to more fertile areas.

In addition to people who voluntarily move to enhance their life conditions, a growing number of people are being forced to flee their homes. **Refugees** are people who leave their home country because of such factors as international or civil war, political repression, or famine. As Table 19.1 shows, the volume of refugees has risen dramatically since the 1960s. In the 1960s, an average of 1.6 million refugees received United Nations assistance. During the 1970s, the number rose to 2.8 million, and in the 1980s, the figure was 10.8 million. In the early 1990s, the number was 19.7 million, and by 1995, a record high number of 27.4 million refugees received U.N. aid. Africa has the largest number of refugees (11.8 million), surpassing Asia (7.9 million). But Europe has also experienced a surge in refugees from about 1 million annually in the 1980s and early 1990s to 6.5 million in 1995 (Kane, 1997). Keep in mind, however, that these figures include only the refugees who receive U.N. assistance; thousands —perhaps millions—of others do not get U.N. support.

Approximately seventy countries have at least 10,000 refugees living within their borders, but the vast majority come from relatively few countries. For example, if we count both international and internal refugees, 65 percent of the population of Liberia has been uprooted; in Bosnia and Rwanda, about 45 percent (Renner, 1997). Populations can be displaced not only because of war, famine, and similar problems, but because their governments force them to move to make room for development projects. Between 1985 and 1995, as many as 90 million people were forced to leave their homes because of the construction of dams, roads, and other development projects (Renner, 1997). If this trend continues, the refugee population will rise even more dramatically during the first quarter of the twenty-first century.

In addition to analyzing changes, demographers also develop theories to explain patterns of population growth. Let's consider those theories now.

Malthus's Theory of Population and Its Natural Limits

One of the earliest and best known models of population growth and its consequences was proposed by an English economist named Thomas Malthus (1766–1834). Malthus's theory was based on the relationship between growth and the food supply. He used an **exponential population growth** model. That is, if growth is left unchecked, population increases exponentially: 1, 2, 4, 8, 16, 32, 64, and so on, but the food supply only increases arithmetically: 1, 2, 3, 4, 5, 6, 7, and so on. Today, demographers often refer to exponential growth as **doubling time,** the amount of time it takes a population to double itself, given a constant rate of growth.

To understand the impact of exponential growth, think about how a water lily grows. Let's say you plant a water lily in a pond, knowing that it will double its size every day. The first day, the water lily doubles to become two water lilies; the second day, there are four water lilies, and so on. Growth is slow but steady until one day, water lilies cover about a quarter of the pond. When you return

TABLE 19.1 Refugees Receiving United Nations Aid, 1961–1995

Year	Total (millions)	Year	Total (millions)	Year	Total (millions)
1961	1.4	1973	3.3	1985	10.5
1962	1.3	1974	4.6	1986	11.6
1963	1.3	1975	5.7	1987	12.4
1964	1.3	1976	2.6	1988	13.3
1965	1.5	1977	2.8	1989	14.8
1966	1.6	1978	3.3	1990	14.9
1967	1.8	1979	4.6	1991	17.2
1968	2.0	1980	5.7	1992	17.0
1969	2.2	1981	8.2	1993	19.0
1970	2.3	1982	9.8	1994	23.0
1971	2.6	1983	10.4	1995	27.4
1972	2.8	1984	10.9		

Source: Kane, 1997, p. 83.

According to Thomas Malthus, why are these babies hungry? Do you agree with his ideas about the relationship between population growth and food supply? Why or why not? What other factors cause hunger in the world? What other factors affect population growth, and what means are available to control birth rate and population size?

two days later, you find the entire pond covered with water lilies. They have overwhelmed all the other plants and the pond is totally unbalanced ecologically. If you understand the concept of doubling time, you are not surprised. The doubling time for the water lily was one day. Therefore, once it covered 25 percent of the pond, the next day it would cover half and the next, the entire pond. The only way to avoid this outcome would be to control the growth of the water lily.

Similarly, Malthus believed that without certain types of "checks," the population would inevitably exceed the food supply. The checks could be positive or preventive. A positive check was anything that could cause wide-scale death, such as disease, famine, and war. Preventive measures were conscious actions to limit population growth. For Malthus, living in the late 1700s, the principal preventive measures were celibacy and marriage at a late age.

Evaluating Malthus's Theory. Does population growth really work the way Malthus described? Could what happened in the pond happen to earth? Figure 19.2 shows world population growth. Let's consider the doubling time of the world's population. It took between two and five billion years for the earth's population to reach one billion in 1804. One hundred and twenty-three years later, the population had doubled, and less than fifty years after that, it doubled again. In 1974, the demographer A. J. Coale warned that if the growth rate continued, in seven decades there would be only one square foot of land for each person on earth. The growth rate has slowed, but we will see shortly that there is still reason for concern.

Today, the world's population is increasing by one million people every four or five days. According to the United Nations, the earth's population reached the 5 bil-

---

Figure 19.2 World Population Growth by Billions

	Time Taken to Reach	Year Attained
One Billion	2–5 billion years	About C.E. 1800
Two Billion	About 130 years	1930
Three Billion	30 years	1960
Four Billion	15 years	1975
Five Billion	12 years	1987
Six Billion	11 years	1998

Source: Population Reference Bureau, 1988; Worldwatch Institute, 1991, 1997.

lion mark in 1987. At the start of the twenty-first century, we number over 6 billion; by 2011, 7 billion; and we will reach 8 billion in 2025. However, population is not evenly distributed over the earth and growth rates vary significantly from region to region, as we will soon see.

Food supplies also vary. The United States and other industrial nations have an abundance of food that could support a much larger population, a situation that goes counter to Malthus's prediction. However, in undeveloped and developing areas of Asia, Africa, and South America, the supply of food does not meet the current needs of the population because not enough food is produced and the geographic isolation of some segments of the population makes food distribution difficult (see Table 19.1). Moreover, as population grows, less land is available per person for food production. In the final analysis, then, Malthus's basic warning is a valid one. If population growth is not controlled, the earth at some point will not be able to support all of its inhabitants, and starvation or conflict may intervene to restore population to a sustainable size (Brown et al., 1998).

Global Population Growth: Reasons, Trends, and Challenges

Another way to understand population growth is to examine it historically. World population rose gradually in early periods, with periodic declines resulting from wars and disease. It is estimated that 300 million people inhabited the earth in the year 1 C.E. (Common Era), and it was not until the 1500s that this figure doubled. This slow but steady growth is in stark contrast to the rapid growth patterns that began in the mid-1700s. Two growth spurts in particular stand out. First, as Figure 19.2 shows, in the 130-year period from 1800 to 1930, the population doubled to 2 billion. Second, unprecedented growth

occurred between 1960 and the present, with the earth's population doubling again from 3 billion to almost 6 billion people. To put it another way, there was more growth during the second half of the twentieth century than during the 4 million years prior to 1950 (Brown et al., 1998). The first population growth spurt occurred primarily in industrial nations, and the second in low-income countries, although both are the result of the two demographic concepts we discussed at the beginning of the chapter—the birth rate and the death rate.

Accurate data on the first doubling period are unavailable, but it is safe to say that it was probably caused by a combination of a decreasing death rate as infectious diseases were brought under control, and the maintenance of a high birth rate for some time. For example, in the late eighteenth century, the smallpox vaccine was discovered, and in the 1890s, vaccinations against diphtheria were first administered. As Malthus would have said, one of the positive checks on population growth—disease—had been significantly lowered. Advocates of the theory of demographic transition, however, would have another interpretation.

The Theory of Demographic Transition

The theory of **demographic transition** was developed in 1945 by demographer Frank Notestein. According to this theory, population growth is tied to the technological development of a society. Demographic transition has three stages. In the initial stage, a society has a high birth rate and a high death rate, so population size remains stable or grows slowly (see Figure 19.3). Preindustrial societies are at this stage; the birth rate is high because children help fill work demands. Put another way, in preindustrial societies, a large family is an economic necessity and thus is culturally defined as desirable. At the same time, though,

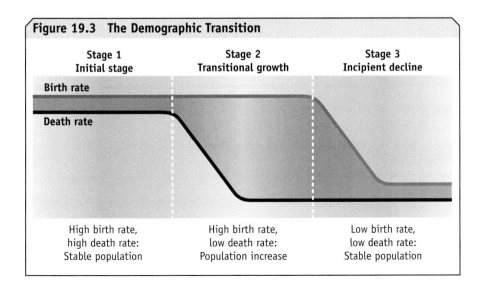

Figure 19.3 The Demographic Transition

Stage 1 Initial stage	Stage 2 Transitional growth	Stage 3 Incipient decline
Birth rate		
Death rate		
High birth rate, high death rate: Stable population	High birth rate, low death rate: Population increase	Low birth rate, low death rate: Stable population

living standards are poor and infectious diseases pose a major threat, so life expectancy is low.

Stage two, the *transitional growth stage,* occurs with industrialization; the death rate declines but the birth rate remains high, producing a population explosion. The major factor that precipitates the change from stage one to stage two is a significant improvement in the standard of living that follows industrialization. The food supply becomes more stable, and the quality of housing and sanitation improves dramatically. The most significant factor in lowering the death rate is medical advances. As medicine improves, the incidence of infectious diseases goes down, the rate of infant and child mortality decreases, and life expectancy increases. Overall, people in this stage live longer, healthier lives, but the cultural belief that a large family is desirable and necessary does not change. Thus, the combination of a high birth rate and a declining death rate results in rapid population growth. It was this situation that Malthus observed and that precipitated his theory of exponential growth. People were living longer, having many children, and facing what Malthus perceived to be limited food supplies. Today, many developing countries are in stage two.

As industrialization progresses, countries move into the third stage of demographic transition, the *stage of incipient decline.* During this period, both the birth rate and the death rate are low, so population growth is minimal. Although industrialized countries rarely have a **zero growth rate,** where the number of births does not exceed the number of deaths, most have significantly lower population increases than the rest of the world. Demographers consider any country with an annual growth rate under 0.4 percent to have stabilized its population. By 1998, only thirty-two countries in the world had stable populations; all are industrialized countries (Brown et al., 1998).

How does the transition to stage three occur? First, as societies industrialize, both the demand for labor and the nature of work change. In industrial societies, work becomes specialized, it takes place largely in factories and not in fields, and children are no longer employed. In fact, children are no longer considered economic assets, rather they become financial liabilities—they stop being a source of income and instead must be supported by their parents' income. If a family is large, the financial burden is obviously greater, and over time cultural norms shift to favor a smaller family. The increasing need for women to work outside the home also plays a role in lowering the birth rate, as does the availability of contraception and rising educational attainment (Brown et al., 1998).

Evaluating the Theory of Demographic Transition. The theory of demographic transition appears to make sense, at least from a Western industrial perspective. It does basically describe our experience, our history. Proponents of demographic transition see industrialization and its ac-

companying technological advances as the driving forces for social change, having the potential to resolve social and economic problems.

Critics question the factual accuracy of the theory, however. For example, one recent study shows that basic but profound changes in personal and public health practices, not medical discoveries, caused the rapid population growth in industrialized countries at the turn of the twentieth century (Kolata, 1997). Although several major vaccinations were discovered in the eighteenth and nineteenth centuries, there was little change in the death rate. There were few major medical innovations in the early 1900s; sulfa drugs to kill bacteria were introduced in the late 1930s, and penicillin not until the late 1940s. What, then, accounts for the population spurt? According to the study, the public's acceptance of the germ theory of disease was the key factor. Once it was proven that diseases were caused by invisible microorganisms—germs—that were everywhere, people began to wash their hands and food, isolate the sick, and not drink water with sewage in it. The technological component of the medical advance, then, may have played a more limited role in population growth.

Critics also say that the theory of demographic transition fails to account for cross-cultural differences. While it may apply to population growth in countries that modernized during the Industrial Revolution, the population growth pattern of developing societies today is more com-

As in many low-income countries today, India's death rate has declined, but the birth rate remains very high, leading to high population growth. How would the theory of demographic transition account for this fact? What accounts for the decline in the death rate in India? What would need to happen for India or any country to achieve zero population growth? How do late industrial and postindustrial societies favor trends toward zero growth rate?

plex. Let's compare population in developed and developing countries.

Population in Industrialized and Developing Countries

Most industrialized countries have had low population growth in the post–World War II period, but the same cannot be said for developing countries. For the majority of developing countries, the death rate began dropping significantly during the 1950s, but while the birth rate declined somewhat, it did not go down enough to prevent population increases. As a result, the world's population overall has grown rapidly since World War II.

The difference is easy to see: In industrialized countries, the average number of children per family is about two, whereas most families in developing countries have at least four children. In rural regions of developing countries, it is common to have five or more children. Why do couples in developing countries have so many children? From a Western perspective, it is often hard to understand why parents would compound an already difficult situation with more mouths to feed. Actually, there are several reasons parents in developing countries have many children.

- In preindustrial societies, children's labor helps the family economically. Children are economic assets in these societies.
- In many developing countries, boys are valued more than girls. Consequently, parents have many children to increase the chances that at least one son survives.
- Since most developing countries do not have a social security or public pension system to help sick and old people, parents rely on their children to support them in sickness and old age. Children form a social safety net for the parents.
- In some developing countries, high fertility is encouraged for religious and political reasons.
- In many countries, information about and access to birth control is limited. People with the highest incomes are most likely to use contraception. In some cases, contraception is not used because the women lack the power to convince men that it should be used, and in other cases, sex is coerced or forced.
- As we learned in Chapter 9, in most developing countries, women's autonomy and opportunities are limited. They are less likely than men to be educated and many jobs are closed to them. Childbearing, especially at an early age, is one of the few roles open to women in many of these societies (Brown et al., 1998; Mensch et al., 1998).

Table 19.2 shows the population difference between developing and industrialized countries of the world. No low-income country, except Sri Lanka (1.1 percent), has a projected birth rate close to the birth rates of industrialized countries. China, which now ranks as a lower-middle income country, has an annual growth rate of 1.0 percent. Analysts expect that most developing countries will

TABLE 19.2 Average Growth Rates by Selected Groupings, 1970–2000

Country Group	AVERAGE PERCENT OF ANNUAL GROWTH		
	1970–1980	1980–1990	1990–2000
World	2.2	1.7	1.5
Low-income economies[1]	2.6	2.7	2.3
Sub-Saharan Africa	2.8	3.0	2.8
East Asia	1.9	1.6	1.2
South Asia	2.4	2.2	1.9
Middle East and N. Africa	2.8	3.1	2.5
Latin America and Caribbean	2.4	2.0	1.6
China	1.8	1.5	1.0
India	2.3	2.1	1.7
Middle-income economies	3.1	1.8	1.5
High-income economies	0.8	0.6	0.6

[1]Excluding China and India.

Source: World Bank, 1994, pp. 210–211; 1996, pp. 194–195.

China's one child family policy has been spectacularly successful in controlling population growth in China. This success was achieved through strong social sanctions, rigorous resocialization, and free birth control, including state-sponsored or state-mandated abortion and sterilization. How might a one child per family policy affect the ratio of males and females in a traditionally patriarchal society? How does China's projected population growth rate now compare to that of high-income industrialized countries such as the United States?

continue to have an annual population increase of over 2 percent during the first half of the twenty-first century. Table 19.3 shows that of the ten countries expected to be most populous by the mid-twenty-first century, only one—the United States—is a high-income country. Brazil is the only upper-middle income country in Table 19.3. Of the remaining eight countries in the table, three—China, Indonesia, and Iran—are lower-middle income. The rest are low-income countries. Because of continuously high fertility and lowered infant mortality rates in low- and lower-middle income countries in recent years, a considerable portion of the populations of these countries (about 40 percent) is between the ages of fifteen and forty. In more economically developed countries, only about 20 to 25 percent of the population is in this age group. Consequently, even if the number of births per woman is reduced, the large number of women of childbearing age will nevertheless keep birth rates high.

One factor that may cause a significant decline in population growth in many low-income countries is HIV/AIDS. As we noted in Chapter 18, the rate of HIV infection and the AIDS mortality rate in low-income African countries is already dramatically lowering life expectancy in those countries. The majority of individuals infected with HIV are in their prime reproductive years and neither they nor their government can afford the costly drug treatments available to HIV/AIDS patients in high-income countries. As the AIDS death rate increases in these countries, it will offset the high birth rates, thereby stabilizing population growth. For example, in Zimbabwe, where 26 percent of the adult population has HIV, the overall population is expected to stabilize by 2002. Other countries in this situation include Botswana (25 percent of the adult population is HIV-positive), Namibia (20 percent is HIV-positive), Zambia (19 percent is HIV-positive), and Swaziland (18 percent is HIV-positive) (Brown et al., 1998).

The stabilization of population as a result of rising death rates from infectious diseases which offset birth rates is cause for serious concern. These countries are experiencing a reversal in economic and social development. If we return to the theory of demographic transition, for instance, these countries are moving *backwards* from stage two to stage one, a negative rather than a positive trend that threatens the sustainability of entire communities (Brown et al., 1998; U.N. Development Programme, 1998). As the United Nations points out, "Just as poverty fuels the epidemic, the epidemic intensifies poverty. . . . Striking the poorest countries of the world—already burdened with other socio-economic problems, low resources and inadequate social services—the HIV/AIDS epidemic is becoming one of the main development challenges facing the world community" (U.N. Development Programme, 1998, p. 35).

A Conflict Perspective on Population

Karl Marx, the classic theorist whose work serves as the foundation of contemporary conflict theory, was highly critical of Malthus's basic assumption that uncontrolled population growth would be a source of hardship for the masses. Instead, Marx believed the unequal distribution of resources was a far more significant factor in the lives of people. At the individual level, Marx argued, a small group of people would control the majority of the wealth and power in a capitalist society, leaving the rest of the population with little. The same principle applied to countries.

Conflict theorists today take a similar approach to the problem. More important than numbers of people is the way resources are distributed among people. As we saw in Chapter 9, there is a wide gap between the wealth—and well-being—of people in low-income countries and high-income countries. Moreover, we observed that this

TABLE 19.3   Ten Most Populous Countries in 2050

Rank	Country	1998 Population (millions)	Projected 2050 Population (millions)
1	India	976	1,533
2	China	1,255	1,517
3	Pakistan	148	357
4	United States	247	348
5	Nigeria	122	339
6	Indonesia	207	318
7	Brazil	165	243
8	Bangladesh	124	218
9	Ethiopia	62	213
10	Iran	73	170

Source: Brown et al., 1998, p. 10.

gap has been widening in recent years. A higher concentration of wealth translates into a greater ability to *consume* resources. Not surprisingly, then, we find that 20 percent of the world's population living in the highest-income countries account for 86 percent of private consumption, whereas the 20 percent living in the poorest countries account for only 1.3 percent of private consumption. Consider, for instance, that the wealthiest fifth of the world's people consumes 45 percent of all meat and fish, while the poorest fifth consumes just 5 percent. The wealthiest fifth consumes 58 percent of total energy resources, but the poorest fifth consumes less than 4 percent of these resources. Since 1950, the populations of high-income countries have accounted for over half the increase in world resource use because their higher incomes allow them to consume more. However, while the world's biggest consumers live in the highest-income countries, they also do the greatest environmental damage: A child born in a high-income industrial country adds more to resource consumption and pollution during his or her lifetime than thirty to fifty children born in developing countries (U.N. World Development Programme, 1998). Thus, conflict theorists maintain that the current world population of 6 billion people—and even as many as 8 billion people—could be supported if the world's resources and technology were distributed and used more equitably (Lappe & Collins, 1979; Meadows et al., 1992).

Evaluating the Conflict Perspective.   Conflict theorists are correct in arguing that to understand the relationship between population and food supply, the distribution of resources must be taken into account. However, they underestimate the potential threat of population growth it-

self. While most experts agree that the earth can provide adequate food for its current population, they also say that unlimited population cannot be supported over time.

Conflict theorists also downplay the impact of uneven population growth as a *contributing* factor to global inequality. Consider that during the 1990s, about 94 percent of the population growth occurred in developing countries where 78 percent of the world's population now lives. These countries' large populations are already

This Mexican couple is receiving counseling in family planning. How might their religion and social class status affect the size of their family? How might those factors affect the size of their country's population? How, in turn, might Mexico's population growth contribute to its status in global stratification compared to other countries? How could these social facts be interpreted from a Marxian perspective?

straining their land and water supplies. India, for example, which increases its population by about 18 million per year, currently faces severe water shortages. By 2050, when the country's population reaches nearly 1.6 billion, available grainland will be only one-fourth of an acre per person (a size significantly smaller than an average suburban building lot in the United States) (Brown et al., 1998). These are not resources that can simply be redistributed. Therefore, a doubling or tripling of the populations of low-income countries such as India will further lower their standard of living, widening the inequality gap between them and high-income countries (Brown et al., 1998).

While a redistribution of the world's resources and wealth toward greater equity for low-income countries is an important goal, it alone cannot solve the problems these countries face because of uncontrolled population growth. It is clear that all countries must work together to slow population growth. The Social Policy box discusses several strategies.

REFLECTING ON

Population: Growth and Control

1. Can you think of other factors, besides the ones discussed here, that contribute to population growth or decline?
2. Have you ever migrated to a new country, or even a different region of this country? What kinds of adjustments did you need to make as you established your new home?
3. Which of the theories we've discussed do you think best explains population growth and decline?

THE URBAN ENVIRONMENT

One of the most significant developments linked to population growth is the emergence of cities. Over the centuries, cities have stood for advanced cultures, centers of progress, the seats of government, and the hubs of commercial activities. The "great" cities were also centers for the arts. While urban areas in economically developed countries still serve these functions, they have lost considerable luster if population is the measure. Internationally, major cities have been losing population over the past decade: New York, Chicago, and Philadelphia in the United States as well as London, Paris, and Moscow overseas. The "great" cities of the late twentieth century are in developing countries, and their greatness is measured primarily in terms of numbers of residents, not cultural or economic contributions.

A **city** is a large, permanent community of people who rely on one another for food, goods, and services. Let's briefly review the historical development of the city, and then discuss some classic sociological analyses of urban life.

The Development of Cities

While estimates vary, it is safe to say that the first cities appeared between 7,000 and 10,000 years ago. Many scholars think Jericho, a settlement north of the Dead Sea, was the first city. Jericho had a population of only about six hundred people, which may lead you to wonder why it would be considered a city, but its establishment, along with other settlements, marked a dramatic change in lifestyle. First, although a small town by contemporary standards, in 8000 B.C.E. (Before the Common Era), Jericho's six hundred residents formed an enormous community, and the fact that it was a permanent settlement also made it unique. Second, to establish these early cities, people had to first domesticate animals and cultivate crops. Mastering these skills provided a predictable source of food and yielded a surplus to support nonagricultural city laborers. Third, because of their permanence, many of the settlements were vulnerable to attacks by outsiders, so residents took defensive measures, usually by building a wall around the city.

Larger cities began to appear by about 4000 B.C.E. in several parts of the world, beginning with Mesopotamia (what is today mostly Iraq). Then, there was an explosion of major settlements, some with populations over 50,000, along the Nile, Indus, and Yangtze Rivers, around the Mediterranean Sea, in Central and South America, and in West Africa. These cities were the first wave of global urbanization. **Urbanization** is the process whereby members of a society become concentrated in cities, and urban areas exert a significant influence on the society. However, in this pre-industrial period, cities served as centers of commerce, but the society itself remained agrarian. The emergence of cities at this time was largely a result of improved farming techniques which freed people for other roles than agriculture, and nonagricultural workers became concentrated in one place. It wasn't until industrialization that urban jobs grew dramatically. At that time, unprecedented numbers of workers moved into the city for employment in the factories, and urbanization increased.

Cities and the Industrial Revolution

Before the Industrial Revolution, the vast majority of cities were relatively small, with only a few having populations over 100,000. There were some exceptions. When it was most influential, Rome's population may have reached 1 million (Flanagan, 1995). Changan, China around 800 C.E.

Social Policy
Slowing Population Growth

The Issue

History shows that as economic development progresses, the rate of population growth declines. But the acute population crisis in low-income countries has prompted some governments to take immediate action. What is the best strategy for slowing population growth in developing countries?

The Debate

Usually, action is in the form of educational programs. Few countries have tried to enact legislation to regulate fertility, but China has.

In 1950, confronted with massive population increases, China legislated minimum marriage ages of eighteen for women and twenty for men. Delaying the entry of young women of childbearing age into the marriage market not only reduced the overall number of children born, but more women continued their education or entered the labor force, benefitting both them and the general economy.

In 1971, China expanded its population control policies to encourage longer spacing between births and fewer children. Later in the 1970s, officials realized that even these requirements would not reduce the population to the national goal of 1.2 billion by 2000. Consequently, they established the country's controversial one-child family policy. Following the lead of Sichuan province, which instituted such a policy in 1979, the one-child family principle became national policy in 1980. The government made contraceptives widely available and promoted their use as well as the use of abortion to terminate unwanted pregnancies. But the government did not leave family planning up to indi-

vidual citizens. Instead, couples are required to get "pregnancy permits" from a local government agency and from the woman's employer. Each neighborhood and employer is allotted a quota of births per year, so couples may be turned down if their neighborhood or company has reached or exceeded its annual birth quota.

To guarantee compliance with this strict policy, which goes counter to cultural values stressing a large family, a system of rewards and punishments was established. Basically, couples choosing to have a second child forfeit certain privileges such as advanced education; they may also have to pay fines, they may lose their jobs, and they can even be detained by the police. Couples who follow the law receive bonuses, such as increased food allowances and low-interest business loans (Rosenthal, 1998).

Can laws effectively change birth patterns? By 1982, in China's three largest cities—Beijing, Shanghai, and Tianjin—80 percent of all births reported were first children. More significantly, since 1950, China has reduced its growth rate to 1.1 percent, half that of other developing nations. In 1988, the Chinese government relaxed its one-child family policy, but without an adverse effect on population control. Exceptions to the law were made for those who belong to ethnic minority groups, rural couples whose only child is a girl, couples who are themselves only children, and couples whose first child is disabled. In 1998, the policy was also amended in limited areas (primarily Shanghai, Beijing, and wealthy regions) to allow couples who wish to have a second child to do so without punishment by simply paying a "family planning fee" to cover the expense of an "extra" citizen (Rosenthal, 1998).

Even though legislation has proven effective in China, most countries shy away from such measures and depend instead on educational programs to lower the birth rate. Education programs can take many forms. Providing extended formal education is in itself a way to delay younger women's entry into childbearing. In addition, education empowers women, which, in turn, appears to lead to a reduced birth rate (Brown et al., 1998; Chira, 1994).

Other methods to reduce the birth rate are even more basic than education. For example, some programs provide information about breastfeeding. Extended breastfeeding significantly delays the resumption of menstruation and lowers the probability of pregnancy. (Only about 7 percent of women conceive without having resumed menstruation.) Breastfeeding has health benefits for infants, as well.

What Do You Think?

Epidemiological research shows that if adequate family planning programs were available, there would be 150,000 fewer maternal deaths each year. And if family planning needs were met globally, there would be a drop of at least 60,000 abortion-related deaths (MacFarquhar, 1994). Yet, 120 million women worldwide do not have access to family planning services (Brown et al., 1998).

Can you think of other strategies for reducing population growth and increasing access to family planning services? Which strategy do you think is most effective: legislation, education, or a combination of the two?

and Baghdad, Persia about 900 C.E. also reached populations of more than a million. But all three of these cities lost residents as the power of their rulers declined. At the start of the Industrial Revolution two hundred years ago, there were probably only two cities with a population of

1 million—London, England and Beijing, China (Chandler & Fox, 1974). By 1900, sixteen cities had more than 1 million residents.

England provides an excellent example of the pace of urbanization during the Industrial Revolution. In the early

1800s, there were approximately one hundred towns that had populations over 5,000; by 1900, there were more than six hundred towns in this category. London, the center of industry, grew from about 1 million in 1800 to 6.5 million in 1900 (Chandler & Fox, 1974). As cities grew during the Industrial Revolution, the role of the city changed. In fact, cities and rural regions pretty much reversed roles, with cities becoming the centers of economic activity and rural regions serving a supportive function by providing food and the raw materials needed for industrial production. Life in these big, newly industrialized cities became a subject of interest and concern for early sociologists.

Sociologists and the City

Living conditions in cities were deplorable, even by nineteenth-century standards. People lived in crowded, unsanitary shanties. One outbreak of disease—cholera, dysentery, typhoid—was followed by another. Men, women, and children toiled long hours, for low wages, in unsafe factories. Among the first sociologists to study the changes brought by urbanization were Emile Durkheim and Ferdinand Toennies.

Toennies and Durkheim: Focusing on the Societal Transformation.
In the late nineteenth century, the work of two sociologists dominated the study of the new urban community. One was Emile Durkheim (1858–1917), whose work on other areas of social life you have already read much about. The other was a German sociologist, Ferdinand Toennies (1855–1937). Durkheim and Toennies took a similar approach to the study of urbanization, but they arrived at somewhat different conclusions. Let's consider Toennies's analysis first.

For Toennies, the transformation from a predominantly rural society to an urban society was best understood in terms of two concepts: *gemeinschaft* and *gesellschaft*. The German word *gemeinschaft* roughly translates as "community." Sociologically, the **gemeinschaft** is a type of social organization characterized by close intimate relationships, a strong sense of kinship and community, and strong mores and traditions. In other words, the *gemeinschaft* is a unified community with a common identity where primary groups are the center of social life.

Toennies contrasts the *gemeinschaft* with the **gesellschaft** or "association" where social relationships are impersonal, family and community ties are weak, and the community orientation is replaced by the pursuit of individual goals and desires. Toennies felt that urban life destroys primary social relations and replaces them with the short-term, impersonal relationships of secondary groups. For Toennies, urbanization was clearly detrimental to social life.

Durkheim, we said, also studied urbanization. Durkheim organized his analysis around the concept of **social**

Industrialization greatly quickens the pace of urbanization in developing countries. Can you identify the city shown in this photograph? You might be surprised to learn that it is Saigon, Vietnam. According to Toennies and Durkheim, what societal transformations do urbanizing communities like Saigon undergo? How are social relations different in cities than in rural agricultural communities?

solidarity, the unifying force that holds members of a society together, and he identified two types of social solidarity, mechanical and organic. These types closely parallel Toennies's *gemeinschaft* and *gesellschaft*. Societies with mechanical solidarity are homogenous. People have the same values and traditions, and for the most part perform the same roles. Rural societies are characterized by mechanical solidarity. With urbanization, mechanical solidarity is replaced by organic solidarity, and the members of society are held together by their interdependence and specialization. The diversity of roles in urban societies makes the members dependent on one another for necessary goods and services. Their bonds are different from the bonds in rural societies, but they are still strong. So Durkheim, like Toennies, recognized that urbanization dramatically changed social life, but he did not think this transformation was negative. Instead, Durkheim felt modern urban life allowed for differences and freedom that were not possible in rural agricultural communities, and that these changes were largely beneficial, unless they occurred too rapidly.

If urbanization occurred too rapidly, both the values and norms governing the newly emerging social relations could not sufficiently evolve. Then a condition Durkheim called *anomie* would develop. **Anomie** is a state of norm confusion, where traditional norms no longer make sense, but new norms haven't developed to replace them. It was the rapid pace of urbanization, then, that worried Durkheim, because it produced anomie, which he saw as the source of such urban social problems as crime, alcoholism, poverty, and family breakdown.

Simmel and Wirth: Two More Views of Urban Life.   As the problems of the modern city became increasingly apparent around the turn of the century, negative views of urban life began to dominate sociological analysis. The work of noted sociologists, such as Georg Simmel (1858–1918) in Germany and later Louis Wirth (1897–1952) in the United States, are two prominent examples. In an essay entitled "The Metropolis and Mental Life," (1964/1902), Simmel argued that people who lived in cities were constantly subjected to "nervous stimulation," which, he said, hardened people to the world around them. They developed a "blasé attitude," a mentality that shut out others as a way of coping with the overwhelming stimulation of urban living.

Similarly, Wirth (1938), a member of the Chicago School, believed that urban life loosened traditional social bonds. He felt that three factors were primarily responsible: the size of cities, the density of urban populations, and the population's diversity. Taken together, these factors meant that people did not have to rely on each other on a personal level and were consequently less apt to develop close personal relationships. Thus, although specialization leads to interdependence, as Durkheim also argued, it is an interdependence based on social roles rather than personal connections. Wirth believed that social relations between urban residents was largely impersonal, self-interested, and transitory.

The Chicago School and Urban Ecology

One of Louis Wirth's best-known colleagues at the University of Chicago was Robert Ezra Park (1864–1944). Park viewed the city as a social organism that must be directly observed. He called his approach to studying the city *human ecology,* because he borrowed heavily from the discipline of ecology and emphasized the interplay between humans and their environment. More specifically, **human ecology** is the study of the spatial distribution of people in an urban environment. Park saw the city not as a single large, impersonal entity, but as a grouping of smaller units, each with distinctive characteristics, that he called *natural areas.* Researchers found that in some natural areas, ethnic communities thrived with close, intimate relationships among members. Other researchers showed that rates of crime, vice, and delinquency varied from one neighborhood to another.

In 1925, Ernest Burgess, a student and colleague of Park's, presented a model of urban growth that he called the **concentric zone theory.** As Figure 19.4 shows, Burgess portrayed the city as a series of five rings, each constituting a zone. The innermost ring, the first zone, is the central business district, the hub of political and commercial activities. The second zone is a zone of transition, characterized by poverty, deteriorating housing, disease, vice, and crime. This is where immigrants and other newcomers to the city first live because of the low housing costs. Next comes the zone of working-class homes, where people who have managed to save money move to escape the conditions of the zone of transition. These are not expensive houses, but they are significantly better than the apartments and boarding houses of the transitional zone.

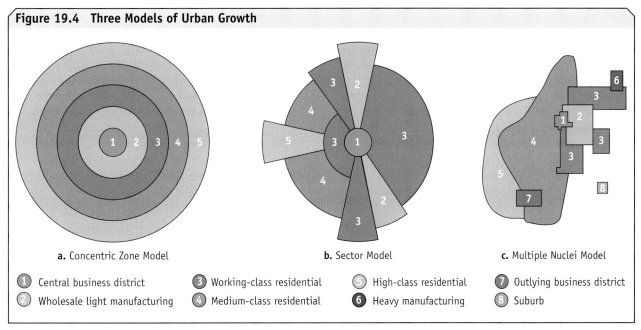

Figure 19.4   Three Models of Urban Growth

a. Concentric Zone Model   b. Sector Model   c. Multiple Nuclei Model

1 Central business district   3 Working-class residential   5 High-class residential   7 Outlying business district
2 Wholesale light manufacturing   4 Medium-class residential   6 Heavy manufacturing   8 Suburb

Source: Adapted from Harris & Ullman, 1945, p. 13.

The fourth ring, the residential zone, is where wealthy people live, typically in single-family dwellings and other more expensive forms of housing. The final ring is the commuter zone, which consists of suburban areas and smaller satellite communities that develop along expanding public transportation routes.

For Burgess, the concentric zone model illustrated how cities tend to expand outward from their business centers. It also showed how patterns of succession work in a city: One group enters an area as prior residents leave for better living conditions.

Figure 19.4 also shows two other models of growth. In 1939, Homer Hoyt adapted Burgess's theory to account for the fact that the zones do not usually form complete circles. In Hoyt's model, the zones become sectors that expand unevenly. Hoyt's *sector theory* allowed for the development of different types of housing side by side. Another model of growth—the *multiple-nuclei model*—was developed by two geographers, Chauncey Harris and Edward Ullman (1945). In the mid-1940s, Harris and Ullman found that cities tended to have several central areas with specialized functions. Heavy industrial enterprises tend to group together in the cities because of similar needs, such as access to transportation. More affluent residents live in areas where housing costs are high; this type of residential development tends to locate far from industrial areas. Consequently, rather then concentric zones, Harris and Ullman's model is organized into irregularly shaped clusters.

Keep in mind that all of these models were written at a specific period in the development of U.S. cities. But not all cities were alike, nor did they develop at the same pace or in identical ways. As the development of cities continued, some problems of urban life declined, but others persisted and new problems emerged, as we will see next.

The Plight of the U.S. City

Take a drive through any one of America's major cities and you will find that many are in a sad state, to say the least. What used to be the industrial center of the city is now an eyesore of abandoned buildings and vacant lots. The deterioration of urban centers didn't happen overnight. Rather, it is the end-product of years of exploitation by property owners, along with decades of governmental neglect. While it is easy to blame the victim—the poor who cannot afford to live somewhere else—the primary responsibility lies elsewhere.

Government efforts to "renew" the city date back to the 1930s, when agencies such as the Federal Housing Administration (FHA) were established to help people find adequate housing. Over the years, the names of these well-intended projects have often changed, but their meager results have not. For example, between 1949 and 1967, various urban renewal programs built 107,000 new housing units and renovated another 75,000 dwellings,

while federal agencies demolished more than 380,000 units (U.S. Department of Health, Education, and Welfare, 1969). Thus, these attempts to provide housing actually resulted in fewer available houses. In late 1967, the Johnson administration launched the Model Cities Program, in response to urban ghetto riots. Considered by some experts to be the most comprehensive attempt by the federal government to address the needs of the urban poor, this program also ended up reducing housing in many of the low-income urban neighborhoods it was established to serve (Weltner, 1977).

Many analysts argue that the major reason these programs failed was they minimized community participation (Keating et al., 1990). Decisions about the amount and kind of housing that was needed, as well as the need for other neighborhood services, were typically made by mayors and their staff in conjunction with urban planners. The people who lived in the targeted neighborhoods were excluded from planning and decision making, even though they knew from firsthand experience what the greatest obstacles to urban renewal were.

From the 1970s into the 1990s, the number of houses for low-income urban families continued to decline. In 1970, there were almost 6 million low-rent units, but by the early 1990s there were less than 3 million. The emphasis of the federal government's urban renewal efforts has been more on keeping and attracting businesses to cities than providing housing for the urban poor. At times, federal programs have actually displaced the poor by encouraging investment by businesses and the affluent (Siegel, 1997).

Thanks to a strong economy in the late 1990s, a number of American cities are undergoing revitalization. Downtowns are once again becoming centers of tourism, the arts, entertainment, and sports. The city is also becoming more attractive to some people as a place to live. As the Intersecting Inequalities box shows, however, not all segments of the population are benefitting from this renaissance. Although home ownership in cities increased during the 1990s, only about 50 percent of city residents own their homes (compared to 70 percent of suburban residents). There has also been a sharp decline in affordable urban housing during the 1990s, and while the overall poverty rate declined slightly between 1993 and 1996, poverty has become more concentrated in the most distressed urban neighborhoods (U.S. Department of Housing and Urban Development, 1998).

Suburbanization

Despite the urban resurgence of the 1990s, suburbanization has not declined. **Suburbanization** is the movement of people from the city to communities outside the city. The introduction of the automobile in the 1920s first stimulated the growth of the suburbs, but a massive expansion occurred after World War II, when low-interest

INTERSECTING INEQUALITIES

Who Lives in the City?

As we begin the twenty-first century, it appears that American cities are experiencing a "comeback." After decades of persistent decay, many U.S. cities are undergoing renovation and a building boom. Young, well-educated professionals are moving back to the city along with older professional couples whose children have grown up and moved out of their parents' homes. Their return has pushed city home ownership up to their highest level in fifteen years. But what kinds of homes are these groups buying? And what are the consequences of their move into the city for older and less well-off city dwellers?

Gentrification is the renewal of old neighborhoods by affluent professionals, resulting in improved housing stock and commercial opportunities in selected areas of cities. Gentrification usually leads to a significant increase in housing purchase and rental prices. In Boston, for example, rents in old working-class neighborhoods in the North End and South Boston have increased about 70 percent between 1996 and 1998. Apartments that previously rented for $800 a month now rent for $2,000 a month. Buildings that sold for $200,000 in the 1980s now sell for $600,000 (Goldberg, 1998).

While gentrification raises the quality of urban housing and reinvigorates business, it also squeezes out poorer residents. People on fixed incomes, those earning the minimum wage, and newly arrived immigrants are being displaced. Between 1993 and 1995 alone, there was a 9 percent decline in low-income rental housing units in the nation's cities. Put differently, there was a loss of 900,000 rental units affordable to low-income families during this two-year period.

Housing affordable to the poorest poor declined even more: 16 percent between 1993 and 1995. Moreover, Congress has provided no new housing vouchers to families on waiting lists for housing assistance since 1994 (U.S. Department of Housing and Urban Development, 1998). As a result, a record 5.3 million poor renters used over 50 percent of their income for rent or lived in substandard housing, and the most severe housing problems were experienced by central city renters. At the same time, poverty became even more concentrated in certain inner city neighborhoods, and homelessness increased (Goldberg, 1998; U.S. Department of Housing and Urban Development, 1998). If these trends continue, American cities in the twenty-first century are likely to be demographically divided between the affluent and the poor.

---

mortgages provided by the Federal Housing Authority and the Veterans Administration made it possible for returning veterans and most other middle-income families to purchase homes outside the cities.

Suburbanization has shown no sign of declining since the 1950s. Since 1970, about 6 million middle- and high-income families have moved out of central cities. Between 1975 and 1985, in fact, the number of affluent families (those with incomes 150 percent higher than the national median) living in the suburbs rose 16 percent (U.S. Department of Housing and Urban Development, 1998). But families are not the only participants in suburbanization; the greatest growth in jobs has occurred in the suburbs and "exurbs" (areas farther out from the city beyond the suburbs) (Goldberg, 1998).

Suburbanization has important consequences for cities. First, it contributes to the residential segregation of racial and ethnic minorities as well as the poor in cities, since White upper- and middle-class families have the financial resources to purchase suburban housing. Second, suburbanization contributes to a loss in tax revenues for city governments. Starting in the 1950s, the eroding urban tax base meant that cities had to continue to provide basic services, such as education, fire and police protection, sanitation, and social services, while the number of taxpayers available to finance these services declined. Suburbanites who work in the city "use" the streets and rely on city services such as sanitation and snow plowing, but they don't pay for them. As a result, the cities had to spend money on services, but they were getting back less revenues. Facing a fiscal crisis, many city governments

What has been the impact of suburbanization on cities in the United States? In each of the three models of urban growth discussed in this chapter (see Figure 19.4), how might you show suburbanization as an extension of cities? What factors have encouraged the development of suburbs, and what factors are leading to the revitalization of some cities today?

have resorted to cutting social services to the poor and raising taxes and charges for basic services. According to a study by the National League of Cities (1991), 15 percent of U.S. city officials said they reduced services, while 80 percent with populations over 100,000 increased charges for basic services and 41 percent increased property taxes. Thus, city governments are not the only ones paying more and getting less in return: The burden of higher charges and taxes but fewer social services falls disproportionately on low-income city residents.

Even as the population and prestige of U.S. cities is in flux, new cities are emerging globally. Some will become the commercial hubs of the world economy in the twenty-first century, but this growth will not be without problems, as we will see next.

The World's New Cities

According to some experts, the most important demographic trend of the second half of the twentieth century, other than world population growth, was global urbanization (Brown et al., 1998). The United Nations Conference on Human Settlement predicts that by 2005, half the earth's population will live in urban areas. By 2025, the majority of people on all major continents will live in a metropolitan region (Crossette, 1996). Each week, the world's urban population grows by slightly more than 1 million people, but perhaps most important, the greatest urban growth is occurring in developing countries.

Table 19.4 shows the ten largest urban areas in terms of population for the years 1950 and 1980, as well as estimates for 2000. In 1950, only New York and London had populations over 10 million, and seven of the ten

largest cities were in industrialized nations. In 1980, seven of the largest cities were in developing countries. In 2000, twenty-five urban areas are estimated to have populations over 10 million, and only four are in high-income industrialized countries. London, the second largest city in 1950, will not be among them.

Some cities in high-income industrial and postindustrial societies are becoming **global cities**, metropolitan areas that serve as centers of international commerce, finance, and culture. Global cities, such as Hong Kong, London, New York, Singapore, and Tokyo, are part of an interconnected global system that exerts great economic and political power (Friedman & Wolff, 1982; Sassen, 1991). The role of the global cities in economics and politics will expand in the twenty-first century as the influence of multinational corporations and international finance continue to grow and the significance of national boundaries declines. Keep in mind, however, that global cities are not necessarily the largest cities in terms of population.

The most rapid urbanization is occurring in low- and lower-middle income countries, especially Mexico, China, India, Indonesia, and Brazil. In these countries, cities are growing almost twice as fast as the overall population (World Bank, 1999). Three factors contribute most to this rapid growth: (1) more births than deaths, (2) high migration from rural to urban areas, and (3) the development of new urban areas in formerly rural regions. Twenty-eight percent of the population in low-income countries and 42 percent of the population in lower-middle income countries now live in cities (World Bank, 1999). Unfortunately, the emerging cities of these countries cannot accommodate the massive influx of new residents. Good housing is either unavailable or too expensive, so

TABLE 19.4 Ten Largest Metropolitan Areas, 1950, 1980, and 2000 (in millions of people)*

	1950		*1980*		*2000*	
1.	New York	12.3	Tokyo	16.9	Tokyo	28.0
2.	London	10.4	New York	15.6	**Mexico City**	18.1
3.	Tokyo	6.7	**Mexico City**	14.5	**Bombay**	18.0
4.	Paris	5.4	**Sao Paulo**	12.1	**Sao Paulo**	17.7
5.	**Shanghai**	5.3	**Shanghai**	11.7	New York	16.6
6.	**Buenos Aires**	5.0	**Buenos Aires**	9.9	**Shanghai**	14.2
7.	Chicago	4.9	Los Angeles	9.5	**Lagos**	15.5
8.	Moscow	4.8	**Calcutta**	9.0	Los Angeles	13.1
9.	**Calcutta**	4.4	**Beijing**	9.0	Seoul	12.9
10.	Los Angeles	4.0	**Rio de Janeiro**	8.8	**Beijing**	12.4

*Cities in developing nations in bold print.

Source: O'Meara, 1999, p. 135; United Nations, *World Urbanization Prospects 1990.* New York: United Nations, 1991.

slums, shantytowns, and squatter settlements develop throughout the city (Brown et al., 1998). It is estimated that 25 percent of the residents in metropolitan areas in low-income countries are squatters, and in some cities, including Cartagena (Colombia, South America), Colombo (Sri Lanka, Asia), and Kinshasa (Zaire, Africa), the figure is between 50 and 70 percent (Barros, 1979; Palen, 1975).

Shantytowns are built almost anywhere there is space to construct shelter. Most are constructed illegally, so local governments do not feel compelled to provide basic services to squatters: Water, power, and sanitation are usually nonexistent. Health care and schools are also rare. Since over 50 percent of the city dwellers come from rural agricultural regions, newcomers are typically young and unskilled, and therefore have trouble finding jobs. Food is also a critical problem because cities serve as commercial centers and land for cultivating crops is scarce. Even when there aren't food shortages, most diets are inadequate. People who move to cities in low-income countries because rural land can no longer produce enough food to support them find themselves facing the same problems and many others (Brown et al., 1998). The declining productivity of the land is a direct result of the deterioration of the natural environment. Let's conclude this chapter, then, with a discussion of the natural environment.

R E F L E C T I N G   O N

The Urban Environment

1. Did you grow up in a rural or an urban area? What were the advantages and disadvantages of growing up in this type of environment?
2. If you ever lived in a city, which of the models of urban life discussed in the chapter best describes where you lived?
3. If you had the opportunity to speak with government officials, what advice would you give them about revitalizing U.S. cities?
4. Suppose the opportunity to offer advice was expanded to include policy makers from low-income countries. What strategies would you urge them to adopt to reduce the problems urbanization is creating in their societies?

THE NATURAL ENVIRONMENT

Only relatively recently have we become aware of the destruction of our natural habitat, but the deterioration is a consequence of centuries of misuse. The science of *ecology* emerged during the second half of the nineteenth century, when naturalists became concerned that industry was depleting natural resources. Ecologists study the interrelationships between living things and their environment.

A group of living things that interact with each other and with their environment are an **ecosystem.** An ecosystem, then, includes living and nonliving things, and together, they form a complete unit. Ecosystems exist on many levels. The earth is one big ecosystem, but so is a lake or a pond an ecosystem because each exists as a complete unit. In an ecosystem, all of the components have relationships with each other, so every single component affects the others and is affected by the others. If all the components interact in harmony, the ecosystem is said to be in balance. When components conflict with one another, the ecosystem changes. Natural events can alter an ecosystem, just as the Ice Age radically altered the earth's ecosystem. But it is humans who have caused the most significant and potentially dangerous changes to the earth's ecosystem.

Basically, people have negatively affected the environment in three ways. One way is through population growth. A second way is the human appetite for natural materials. Coupled with increased population, the need for natural materials has reached a critical point where certain resources are already becoming depleted. Wood and water, in particular, are in increasingly short supply (Brown et al., 1998). The third way people affect the environment is through the rapid development of technology. While new technology generally means an improved standard of living, the improvement often comes at great environmental cost. The Global Insights box on page 522 gives some idea of the human impact on the environment. Let's take a closer look at how our uncontrolled appetite for resources and shortsighted, unregulated technological development have caused long-term environmental damage.

Human Intrusion into the Natural Environment

Humans' intrusion into the natural environment dates back about 50,000 years, when our species first mastered the use of fire and developed weapons. Since the earliest cultures were basically nomadic hunters and gatherers who lived off what the earth naturally offered them, they represented no major threat to the natural environment. Humans' transformation of the earth began with the introduction of agriculture, although the environmental problems that resulted, such as soil erosion, were relatively limited. The most serious environmental problems developed from the Industrial Revolution, and the human threat has increased dramatically since then because of the unregulated use of advanced technology. This is not to say that technological advances are inherently bad for the environment, but that the development of technology without environmental awareness inevitably leads to environmental problems, such as pollution. Of course, we all contribute to the pollution problem in our own way. For instance, most of us use many products—cleaners, containers, toxic chemicals, aerosol sprays—that damage

GLOBAL INSIGHTS   How Is the Earth's Physical Environment Changing?

The ecosystem we know as planet earth is changing dramatically, and these environmental changes will have a significant impact on our everyday lives in the twenty-first century. Let's consider some of them:

- **Climate** The buildup of "greenhouse" gases, primarily carbon dioxide, in the atmosphere is causing the earth's temperature to rise. The fifteen warmest years on record all occurred after 1979, with 1998 being the warmest. This climate change leads to more intense heat waves, more extreme weather conditions (drought, flooding, and destructive storms, such as hurricanes), as well as increased forest fires and shifts in rainfall that threaten food production.
- **Fresh Water** In parts of Africa, China, India, and North America, the underground water tables are falling as the demand for water exceeds the rate at which the earth naturally supplies it. In addition, the quality of groundwater is deteriorating. In the United States, for instance, more than fifty different types of pesticides contaminate the groundwater in thirty-two states. Worldwide, thousands of lakes are biologically dead because of contamination.
- **Ozone Layer** Human-produced pollution has resulted in a growing hole in the earth's ozone layer over Antarctica, which most experts believe marks

the beginning of a global depletion of ozone. Ozone blocks the sun's harmful ultraviolet rays. With depletion, increased rates of skin cancer are predicted.
- **Forest Cover** Each year, 11 million hectares of tropical forests are lost and more than 30 million hectares of forest land in industrial countries are damaged from pollution. It is estimated that 75 percent of the loss in forested areas worldwide occurred during the twentieth century. Much of this loss is the result of increased consumption of wood and wood products and byproducts. It is also an outcome of population growth in that more people need cleared land to build housing, to farm, and to provide pastureland for their livestock.
- **Species Diversity** As human population growth has risen, the populations of other species have declined dramatically. Experts tell us that we are living through the greatest period of plant and animal extinction since the disappearance of the dinosaurs about 65 million years ago. If extinction of plant and animal species continues at the present rate, which is 100 to 1,000 times the natural rate, within just two decades, one-fifth of all species will be lost.

Sources: Achayara, 1995; Brown et al., 1998; French, 1997; Gardner, 1995; Tuxill, 1997.

---

the environment. In addition, according to the Environmental Protection Agency (EPA), each year the United States generates about 208 million tons of waste material. This means that a ton of waste is produced annually for each adult in this country. Only about 27 percent of this waste is recovered or recycled (U.S. Department of Commerce, Bureau of the Census, 1997). The Doing Sociology box is designed to raise your awareness of your contribution to the pollution problem.

The impact of individual pollution pales compared to industrial pollution, however. We'll discuss three byproducts of industrial pollution—acid rain, ozone depletion, and the greenhouse effect—to get a better sense of its impact on the environment.

Acid Rain.   When we burn fossil fuels in our homes, cars, or factories, they release gases, all of which fall back to the earth, with two exceptions. Sulfur dioxide and nitrogen oxide enter the atmosphere to become two of the major pollutants responsible for the increased acidity of rainfall, commonly referred to as **acid rain.** Sulfur dioxide combines with oxygen and water in the atmosphere to form sulfuric acid, and nitrogen oxide combines with

water to form nitric acid. These acids return to the earth in rain and snow, which are at times as acidic as vinegar.

A major source of sulfur dioxide emissions are coal-burning power plants. Wind and clouds carry the pollutants so that acid rain occurs in both surrounding and distant areas. The major source of nitrogen oxide pollution is automobiles, although electrical utilities also emit nitrogen oxide and are the second major source of the pollutant. In industrialized countries, environmental laws have had an impact on newly built power plants and new technology, such as flue gas desulfurization units, has significantly reduced sulfur dioxide. Unfortunately, unregulated use of fossil fuels in developing countries, particularly in Asia and Eastern Europe, has increased, offsetting the gains made. In fact, world carbon, sulfur, and nitrogen emissions continued to rise during the 1990s (Dunn, 1997; O'Meara, 1997; U.N. Development Programme, 1998).

What are the effects of acid rain? Drinking water contains unsafe levels of certain heavy metals, a clear threat to human health. The problem can be so bad that aluminum saucepans and water pipes corrode. When the copper content of the ground water is particularly high,

DOING SOCIOLOGY

How Much Waste Do You Generate in One Day?

Industrial pollution does far more damage to the environment than individual pollution, but that does not excuse us from being environmentally responsible. There are many ways that we as individuals can help clean up the environment. One way is to cut down on the amount of waste we produce daily.

Most people assume that they personally generate little waste, but if each of us produces one ton of waste each year, our daily contribution is not insignificant.

Do you know how much waste you generate in a single day? To find out, keep track of all the waste you produce in one day, from the time you get up until the time you go to sleep. Everytime you're ready to throw something out—a bottle or can, a piece of paper, uneaten food or food scraps—put it in a trash bag. If possible, carry the bag with you everywhere you go that day, or save all your waste and deposit it in the bag when you can. At the end of the day, weigh the bag. Or, if your class is doing this together as a project, everyone can bring their bags to class to be weighed. Now you'll know how much waste you generate in a single day, but you're not finished yet. Sort the waste that's in the bag. How much of it can be recycled? Do

you know what the local recycling regulations are, and how to go about recycling particular types of waste? If not, find out.

Keep in mind that in this exercise you really only measured your personal contribution of waste in the form of garbage. We also create waste by unnecessarily using up resources. Think, for example, about how many times a day you flush the toilet, how much water you use when you take a shower, and how many times you leave the faucet running or the lights or TV on even though you've finished with them. Can you now think of at least three specific ways you can reduce daily waste? Share these strategies with your class and compile a list of ideas for waste reduction that can be circulated on campus or posted in public facilities and residence centers.

---

blond hair can turn temporarily green. Acid rain also contributes to soil erosion and deforestation by altering the chemical and nutrient balance of the soil. Trees die, and many plant species worldwide have already disappeared. Increased acidity slows the growth of crops and requires added chemicals, such as lime, to counteract the acidity. Acid rain also corrodes stone structures, such as build-

Human ecology includes people's relationships with the natural physical environment as well as their manufactured and social environments. These relationships are ongoing and complex and have long term effects on people's quality of life. How is this family both contributing to and reducing environmental problems associated with human waste? On what four other sources of environmental pollution does this chapter focus?

ings and statues, and exposed or unprotected metals on buildings, bridges, fences, and steel railings.

Ozone Depletion. The environmental threat from pollution is not limited to the earth's surface, as evidenced by two extremely serious atmospheric conditions, ozone depletion and the gradual warming of earth called the *greenhouse effect.* For some time now, scientists have known that certain industrial chemicals (such as chlorofluorocarbons and holons) have been causing smog and destroying the earth's protective ozone layer. The ozone layer is a thin veil in the earth's stratosphere that protects the earth and its population from harmful ultraviolet radiation. Scientists estimate that tons of chemicals released into the atmosphere have already burned away more than 2 percent of the ozone shield (Worldwatch Institute, 1990).

In the Antarctic, the damage is so severe that environmentalists refer to a "hole" in the ozone. This ozone hole, first detected in 1979, is approximately twice the size of the continental United States and already extends into the southernmost region of South America, where higher rates of skin cancer and eye diseases are being reported (Glick, 1988; Nash, 1991). In the United States, the EPA estimates that if the ozone continues to deteriorate at the current rate, the increased ultraviolet exposure will result in an additional 155 million skin cancer cases in the U.S. population and more than 3 million additional cancer deaths (Shabecoff, 1988).

In 1987, the world's scientists met and developed the "Montreal Protocol on Substances That Deplete the Ozone

Layer," which established far-reaching standards to control ozone pollutants. A decade after this meeting, the global production of chlorofluorocarbons is down 76 percent (French, 1997). This is an encouraging sign that humans can reverse their destructive behavior. At the same time, we must keep in mind that the ozone that has been depleted can never be replaced, and that even if there were a total halt in the emission of chemicals into the atmosphere, the damage to the ozone would continue for a significant period of time. Gases used today take seven to ten years to reach the stratosphere, and once there, many of the chemicals are active for up to 125 years.

The Greenhouse Effect.   Another of our environmental legacies to future generations is a warmer global climate, called the **greenhouse effect.** The greenhouse effect is basically a two-step process, one natural and essential to life itself, and the other the result of human action. First, sunlight—solar radiation—warms the earth and some of it is trapped to keep the planet's temperature stable. Excess radiation escapes through the atmosphere. However, modern industrial society has disturbed the normal process because of gaseous emissions from cars and factories. Now, in a second step, the volume of gases, especially carbon dioxide, from burning fossil fuels is so great that the molecules are accumulating in our atmosphere and blocking the release of solar radiation.

The direct consequence of this process is an increase in the earth's temperature. The 1990s was the warmest decade since data collection began in 1866, with four of the five warmest years ever recorded (Monastersky, 1997). As the greenhouse effect worsens, sweltering weather will be the norm, but this will be the least of our worries. Global warming is an ecological crisis. Warming causes the global sea level to rise, which will eventually claim thousands of acres of coastal land. In the United States, for example, Louisiana alone will lose 100,000 acres of wetlands to the rising ocean, and New York City will have to build levees to contain the growing Hudson and East Rivers. In the Great Lakes regions, the greenhouse effect will be just the opposite: Increased evaporation will reduce the size of the lakes, which will change the distribution of productive farming areas. The midwestern parts of the United States, traditionally the heartland of the nation's farm industry, will become desertlike, while colder areas, such as Canada and Siberia, will produce bumper crops (Begley et al., 1988; Worldwatch Institute, 1994).

Many scientists think the impact of the greenhouse effect is unavoidable, but this does not mean we cannot slow the pace of global warming (Worldwatch Institute, 1994). One obvious strategy would be to sharply cut back on the burning of fossil fuels. This would also help lessen ozone depletion and acid rain production. In 1997, the industrialized countries of the world agreed to reduce their emissions of greenhouse gases by 5 percent by 2007. However, to cut fossil fuel use, alternative energy sources must

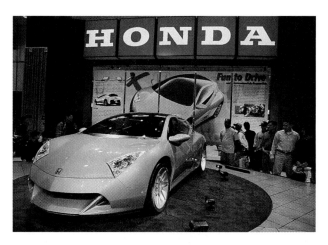

To ensure reliability, this state-of-the-art electric car also has an internal combustion engine that kicks in when needed. The technology for reducing or eliminating pollution from the burning of fossil fuels has been in existence for some time. Why do you think manufacturers have been slow to adopt this technology? Why have consumers been slow to demand it? How might electric and solar cars affect industries based on the exploitation of nonrenewable energy resources?

be explored. Other countries have successfully developed alternative energy sources, including Japan, where solar collectors are used to heat water in more than two million buildings. This number is steadily increasing so that soon one-third of Japanese buildings will be heated this way. In Brazil, alcohol-based fuel from sugar cane powers about 20 percent of the country's vehicles. And in Germany, a hydrogen-powered transportation system is being developed that will use power imported from solar collectors in southern Europe and northern Africa (Flavin, 1991). But in the United States, support for such options has been limited. Also, attempts to regulate fossil fuel use have not had a major impact, as evidenced by the fact that most major metropolitan areas fail to meet EPA ozone safety standards (U.S. Department of Commerce, Bureau of the Census, 1997). Significantly, more than half the population of the United States resides in these regions. In 1994, new federal Clean Air standards forced the introduction of reformulated gasoline to decrease smog and related pollutants. The new rule affects 30 percent of the nation's gasoline market, including the Boston–New York–Washington megalopolis (Wald, 1994). It is hoped that these tougher standards will help reduce ozone depletion and the greenhouse effect.

Acid rain, ozone depletion, and the greenhouse effect are the direct results of pollution caused by industrial production. It can be argued that atmospheric changes were unanticipated byproducts of production, and that they were difficult to foresee. But the same cannot be said for pollution resulting from toxic wastes, which are known to be hazardous and continue to be released into the environment.

Toxic Waste.   Toxic **waste** is any by-product of production or other processes that is of no use, but is hazardous to humans and the environment. Every production process, whether it is the production of clothing, food, drugs, or textbooks, creates materials that are of no use. Before the Industrial Revolution, these waste products were, for the most part, harmless, with only a small percentage presenting a threat to people and the environment. As industrialization progressed, though, the problem of waste became more acute, particularly following World War II when the production of plastics and synthetic chemicals rose dramatically. The problem has only become worse. At the end of World War II, U.S. industries produced 1 billion pounds of hazardous waste annually. Today, we generate about 180 million tons of hazardous waste and another 11 billion tons of industrial waste that is not subject to hazardous waste regulations each year (Organization for Economic Cooperation and Development, 1993).

Why has the problem grown so great? The most obvious reason is the sheer number of new materials developed that produce toxic wastes. As the supply of natural resources declines and public demand for cheaper, longer-lasting goods increases, industry turns to synthetic substitutes. Wood, cotton, and wool have been replaced by plastic, polyester, and other human-made products. Despite the fact that this chemical revolution started a half century ago, we still don't know much about how these substances affect people, plants, or animals. In fact, we have no information at all about the possible toxic effects of over 80 percent of the approximately 50,000 industrial chemicals—for example, pesticides, food additives, cosmetics—that are used in the United States (Misch, 1995).

The EPA estimates that more than 750,000 businesses generate toxic waste, and between 100,000 and 200,000 industrial firms of varying size dump their waste directly into sewers. Hazardous waste management is now big business, grossing $6.0 billion in revenues in 1996 (U.S. Department of Commerce, Bureau of the Census, 1997). There are over 51,000 transporters who move toxic waste for treatment or disposal at an undetermined number of legal and illegal dump sites.

Unfortunately, while considerable time and money have been committed to the development of new synthetics, little attention has been paid to properly disposing of them. It is generally accepted that only 10 percent of hazardous waste is disposed of properly. Waste has been placed in unlined lagoons and ponds, and in nonsecure landfills, and has been dumped into water (sewers, wells, rivers, and even in the ocean). These high-risk sites are responsible for a wide range of environmental and health problems, including contamination of water supplies and/or groundwaters; destruction of natural habitats and soil contamination resulting in fish and livestock kills; damage to sewer systems and public treatment

Hundreds of thousands of businesses in the United States alone face the problem of disposing of toxic or radioactive waste. Some dump these wastes illegally into sewers, waterways, or landfills, where they poison soil and water, plants and animals, and people. Toxic waste disposal companies use officially designated sites, such as these disused missile silos in Idaho, but still face opposition to dumping from nearby communities. What are the long term effects of toxic waste on a population? Why is burying toxic waste not a long-term solution?

works, rendering them unsafe or inoperable; fires and explosions; and finally and most significantly, damage to human health, such as cancer, infertility, and even death. What is more, the danger created by these toxic dumps extends beyond the area of the site. In Love Canal, New York, for example, waste was disposed near a residential area, a school was built directly on the toxic site itself, and underground streams carried the toxic threat to neighboring communities.

In the United States, cleanup of toxic waste is coordinated by the EPA. As of 1998, the EPA had 1,353 sites on its "national priority list" because they represent an immediate threat to public health (General Accounting Office, 1998). The cleanup of dumps and other contaminated areas has grown into a major economic problem for the government. In Times Beach, Missouri, for example, the cleanup of dioxin-contaminated soil cost the federal government approximately $200 million; 2,240 residents were permanently evacuated in 1983 at a cost

Portland Community College–Portland, Oregon

Course: Social Change and Social Institutions, Dr. S. Rowan Wolf

Students: (not shown) Jason Buelt, Willow Fee, Robyn Heinecke, Eric Jozwiak, Teresa Morescalchi, Lindsey Myers, Amy Newton, Nicole Pourpak, Jessica Ravitsky, Nadege Rettier, Tuyen Tran, Mandy Workman

How does our college affect the environment?

We examined several areas of environmental concern—recyclable items, toxic waste, and transportation. We found that, while a number of initiatives are already in place for reducing and reusing materials and for discouraging the use of private cars, perhaps more can be done.

Portland Community College uses a lot of paper. In fact, last year the college ordered 39,200 reams of paper. This was for all usages. The use of recycled paper is relatively low. We were told this is because recycled paper seems to jam the machines more and costs more than regular paper. The school has accessible recycling boxes in classrooms, offices, and libraries; however, we were unable to get figures on how much paper is actually recycled. Less paper could be used by allowing two-sided printing of papers, single-spacing rather than double-spacing of reports, and printing drafts on used paper.

Food Services decreases its impact on the environment by recycling and reusing items. Less than one percent of the food bought by the college actually goes to waste. Leftover food from lunch is incorporated into another meal or sent to a local teen homeless shelter. The cafeteria also recycles polystyrene, glass, and #2 plastic. Fifty percent of polystyrene that comes into the school is recycled. This recycling effort has decreased the waste from Food Services by roughly two-thirds.

After all the attempts by the school to cut back on waste by setting up recycling centers, some students still throw away items that could be recycled. Many students throw their recyclables into the trash when there is a bin less than two feet away. It would be interesting to find out who behaves this way and why. We need to increase awareness of the effects of not recycling. This could be done with the help of student-run recycling centers, or a composting project using students' leftover food.

A number of classes (e.g., art, nursing, dental, and sciences) use toxic materials. We were concerned about both how much was being used and how it was being stored.

The College has reduced the amount of toxic material used in courses significantly by using "microscale" techniques in a number of areas. Currently, roughly fifty pounds of toxic material is used for every 300 students in science classes. The College's toxic materials are collected with other Portland metropolitan public sources for safe disposal or storage.

Another large issue was the use of private transportation. Programs have been initiated to reduce the use of private transportation to and between campuses. These include a multi-van shuttle service that has various city pick-up points and runs between the College's three campuses and multiple centers, and a car pool program that offers reduced parking fees and prime parking places. In addition, TriMet (the local mass transit company) has special runs to all campuses, and a small number of discounted passes are available to students. We can reduce our impact on the environment by encouraging each other to car pool, take the bus, and bike to school. We could also encourage TriMet to increase the number of student passes available to college students.

---

of over $33 million. Nevertheless, government funding for such cleanups is inadequate. In 1980, a $1.6 billion Superfund was established by Congress to clean up the country's estimated 16,000 waste sites. In 1986, government officials finally conceded that the amount was insufficient and Congress increased the funding to $8.6 billion. By the end of the 1990s, more than 40,000 locations were listed by the EPA as hazardous waste sites. The EPA estimates it will cost $31 billion to clean up its 1,353 priority sites alone (Worldwatch Institute, 1998).

The cumulative effect of hazardous waste and pollution creates a major threat to the ecosystem in our contemporary world. In addition to these problems, the world faces an energy crisis.

Energy: The Universal Resource

The potential for a global energy crisis is linked to the types of energy the world uses. Energy can be divided into three categories: perpetual, renewable, and nonrenewable. *Perpetual energy resources* are inexhaustible and will exist regardless of the level of human usage. The sun provides a perpetual energy resource in the form of solar power. *Renewable energy resources* (also called *flow resources*) are reproducible, so they can be replaced as they are used. Wood is an example of a renewable energy resource. *Nonrenewable energy resources* (also called *stock resources*) exist in a finite amount and cannot be replaced once they are used. Today, three nonrenewable fossil fuels account for 85 percent of the world's commercial energy—oil, coal, and gas. In the United States, over 90 percent of our energy is derived from nonrenewable sources (Brown, 1997). Throughout this century, industrialized nations have depended on cheap fossil fuel to power the economy, ignoring the fact that from the time the first coal mines were dug and the first oil wells drilled, these resources were slowly but surely being exhausted. Indeed, it was not until the 1970s, when oil prices rose and coal was found to be a major contributor to air pollution, that we began to recognize there was a problem.

Industrial production consumes more of the world's commercial energy than either housing or transportation, and there is a clear relationship between the wealth of a nation and the level of energy used (Goldenberg, 1987). If energy is to be saved, the responsibility rests with the economically developed countries, and certainly if one nation were to be pointed out as excessive in its energy use, it would be the United States. Consider, for example, that China has 21 percent of the world's population and consumes 10 percent of the world's energy, whereas the United States, with less than 5 percent of the world's population, consumes 24 percent of all energy (U.S. Department of Commerce, Bureau of the Census, 1997). As Table 19.5 indicates, the United States has been the major consumer of energy for some time, although the percentage share has been declining. The greatest increase in energy use has been in Asia with its growing economies.

What if the world continues its current energy practices? If there is no change in policy, by the year 2025, the demand for oil will increase from 135 million barrels per day to 300 million barrels per day. International coal production would have to triple. About 350 new nuclear power plants would be needed and about four times as many rivers would have to have hydroelectric dams. Environmentally, acid rain would probably triple under these conditions and the level of carbon dioxide would double, possibly causing an even more rapid greenhouse effect (Flavin & Lenssen, 1991). However, this scenario is not inevitable. With a significant shift toward conservation, renewable energy sources could provide between 50 and 70 percent of energy in the United States by 2030 (Flavin & Lenssen, 1991).

Even with successful efficiency measures in place, the problem remains that industrial societies are and will continue to depend on nonrenewable fossil fuels. Replacing fossil fuels with renewable energy sources, therefore, is also key to creating an environmentally secure society. Alternatives, as we have seen, are being developed, but unfortunately, the United States and most other countries have not yet taken full advantage of them.

Clearly, conserving energy and our natural environment are major challenges for the world community as we begin the twenty-first century, but we must rise to these challenges if we want to ensure the future survival of our societies.

REFLECTING ON

The Natural Environment

1. Why do you think people in the United States have been reluctant to embrace alternative energy sources to reduce acid rain, ozone depletion, and the greenhouse effect? Can you suggest ways to promote alternative energy use?
2. It's expected that as the global economy develops, disposal of toxic waste will become even more critical, especially in developing countries where the manufacturing stage of production is increasingly taking place. Is this environmental crisis inevitable, or do you think it can be avoided? Explain your position.
3. How would you explain the relationship between a country's wealth and its level of energy use? What do you think can be done to make worldwide energy use more equitable across societies?

TABLE 19.5 United States and World Energy Consumption, 1960–1994

Region	CONSUMPTION IN MILLION METRIC TONS*					PERCENT DISTRIBUTION				
	1960	1970	1980	1990	1994	1960	1970	1980	1990	1994
World total	3,924	6,440	8,544	10,826	11,258	100.0	100.0	100.0	100.0	100.0
United States	1,454	2,217	2,364	2,687	2,969	37.1	34.4	27.2	24.8	26.4
Europe	1,039	1,770	2,145	2,346	3,413	26.5	26.7	25.1	21.7	30.3
Russia	595	999	1,592	1,919	**	15.2	15.5	17.2	17.7	**
Asia	514	903	1,579	2,624	3,455	13.1	14.0	18.5	24.2	30.7
Rest of world	322	551	983	1,258	1,421	8.2	9.4	11.5	11.5	12.6

*In tons of coal equivalent.
**In 1994, Russia was included in Europe.
Source: U.S. Department of Commerce, Bureau of the Census, 1995, p. 592; 1997, p. 589.

For useful resources for study and review, run Chapter 19 on your *Living Sociology* CD-ROM.

C O N N E C T I O N S

Mortality rate and life expectancy	These demographic indicators were introduced and defined in Chapter 18 in the sections on "Health and Medicine across Societies" and "Health in the United States." See also the tables in Chapter 18, which focus on mortality rates and life expectancy. What generalizations can you draw from these data? What are the implications of these data for population growth?
Population and migration	Review the section on "Race and Ethnicity in the United States" in Chapter 11. For the groups discussed, what are some specific examples of immigration and internal migration? Also preview the section on "Population Fluctuation and Social Change" in Chapter 20. What can be the effects of migration on a society's population?
Population and types of societies	Review the discussion of types of societies in Chapter 3. See also the section on "Economies in Historical Perspective" in Chapter 13. What population characteristics are typical of each of the six "ideal types" of societies? For instance, what family size and population size does each type of society favor, and why? Does the theory of demographic transition adequately explain the differences you find? Why or why not?
Population and economic development	Review Chapter 9 on Global Stratification. What population characteristics are common in low-income countries, and how might those characteristics affect a country's per capita GNP? How does the Human Development Index relate to population?
Families and population size	Review the section on "Families throughout the World: Structures and Characteristics" in Chapter 15. What "structures and characteristics" of families potentially affect the demographics of societies' populations? What are some examples of differences these demographics might show?
Karl Marx on population and wealth	Review the introduction to Marx's ideas in Chapter 1. Which of his core concepts are most applicable to a sociological investigation of population? How does his criticism of Malthus's view of population growth reflect the conflict perspective in sociology?
Social solidarity and anomie	Review these concepts as they are introduced and in Chapter 3. How do Durkheim's notions of organic and mechanical solidarity relate to Toennies's concepts of *gemeinshaft* and *gesellschaft*? In what ways does the urbanization of industrializing societies lead to anomie? How do the views of Simmel and Wirth build on these observations?
Chicago School	Review the section on "Sociology in the United States" in Chapter 1. Who were the sociologists of the Chicago School? What were some criticisms of their work? How did their work affect the study of population, urbanization, and the condition of cities in the United States and abroad? What are some specific examples in Chapter 19 of the Chicago School's focus on social problems of the city?
Cities in developing countries	Review again Chapters 9 and 13 on factors affecting global stratification and economic development. How does Chapter 19's discussion of "The World's New Cities" relate to those factors? For instance, according to modernization theory, how might urbanization in low-income countries contribute to the spread of slums around central cities?

CONNECTIONS

Technology and the environment   Review the discussions of types of societies in Chapter 3 and of technology and material culture in Chapter 4. How would you describe the ecosystem of each of the six types of society? In each case, how does cultural ecology, including technology, affect the natural environment, and with what consequences?

SUMMING UP CHAPTER 19

Population: Growth and Control

1. Demography is the study of population size, distribution, composition, and movement or migration. Demographers not only count people, but also try to understand population changes in order to gauge future trends and develop sound population policies. Demographers use two indicators to measure population growth and decline: fertility and mortality. Demographers construct population pyramids as visual representations of a society's population distribution.

2. National or regional population changes are also affected by fertility and mortality, but in addition, net migration produces population growth or decline. People migrate for a number of reasons, including to obtain jobs; to escape war and political repression; to search for food during periods of famine; and to make room for development projects.

3. Thomas Malthus's theory of population focuses on the relationship between population growth and the food supply. Malthus believed that population increases exponentially, while the food supply increases only arithmetically. Consequently, if population growth is not controlled by either positive or preventive checks, the population's demand for food will exceed the supply. But Malthus's theory has been criticized because it does not take into account significant regional differences in population growth and in the food supply.

4. The theory of demographic transition links population growth with the technological development of a society. Demographic transition occurs in three stages. In the first stage, characteristic of preindustrial societies, there is a high birth rate and a high death rate, which keep population size fairly stable. In the second stage, called the *transitional growth stage*, the death rate declines while the birth rate stays high, causing a population explosion. The second stage is characteristic of societies at the onset of industrialization. In the third stage, called the *stage of incipient decline*, both the birth and death rates are low, so population growth is minimal. This stage is characteristic of the most economically developed countries. Although the theory of demographic transition has common-sense appeal, it has been criticized for its Western bias, failing to account for cross-cultural differences. It has also been criticized for being too simplistic and for overemphasizing the role of technology in population change, which in some cases appears to be factually inaccurate.

5. There are stark contrasts in population growth between low-income countries and high-income, industrialized countries. In low-income countries, the birth rate is much higher than in high-income countries for several reasons, including that in low-income countries children are considered economic assets; infant and child mortality remain high; there is a higher value placed on sons over daughters; children are a form of "social security" for elderly parents; religious and political values emphasize children; and there is limited access to birth control.

6. In his analysis of population, Karl Marx emphasized that the maldistribution of resources in a society was a more important factor in determining people's status than unchecked population growth. Marx felt that this maldistribution occurred not only in capitalist societies, but also between capitalist and economically undeveloped societies. This position implies that there are adequate resources for the world's population and that control of population growth is unnecessary if these resources are equitably distributed and more carefully developed. But Marx's argument overlooks the serious threat posed by population growth itself, since even though the earth's resources are plentiful, there is not enough to sustain an unlimited population. Moreover, uneven population across countries reinforces global inequality.

The Urban Environment

1. A city is a large, permanent community of people who rely on one another for food, goods, and services. The first cities emerged between 7,000 and 10,000 years ago. Most of these cities were small by today's standards, though. The first wave of urbanization, in which members of a society came to be concentrated in cities, occurred about 4,000 years ago with the growth of larger cities with populations of over 50,000. Still, prior to the Industrial Revolution, the populations of most cities did not exceed 100,000. Industrialization was an important contributing factor to rapid urbanization.

2. Early sociological studies of urbanization focused on the problems of city life. Toennies felt that urbanization

weakened traditional community ties found in the *gemein-schaft,* replacing them with individualism and short-term impersonal relationships (*gesellschaft*), a change that was detrimental to social life. In contrast, Durkheim maintained that all societies, rural and urban, had social solidarity, but this solidarity took different forms. With urbanization, mechanical solidarity was replaced by organic solidarity, holding the members of society together through their specialization and interdependence. For Durkheim, urbanization was not detrimental to social life unless it occurred too quickly for new norms to take hold. In that case, the result would be anomie, or norm confusion, which was dysfunctional for the society. The work of Georg Simmel is similar to that of Toennies in that Simmel felt that the "nervous stimulation" of city life causes people to shut others out in order to cope. Louis Wirth also believed that urbanization caused a loosening of traditional social bonds. According to Wirth, urban dwellers come to view one another in terms of their social roles rather than as unique individuals.

3. Robert Park of the Chicago School developed an approach to studying cities that he called *human ecology,* which focused on the spatial distribution of people in cities. Park saw the city as organized into natural areas, each with distinctive characteristics. Ernest Burgess expanded on Park's work with his concentric zone theory, which portrayed the city as a series of five rings or zones. The innermost zone was the central business district, followed by the zone of transition where social problems were widespread. Moving out from these two zones, housing and living conditions improved. Homer Hoyt adapted Burgess's theory to show that instead of circles, cities were organized into sectors that tended to expand unevenly. Chauncey Harris and Edward Ullman also developed a model of urban growth called the *multiple-nuclei model,* which focused on the specialized functions of each area of a city.

4. U.S. cities today are plagued by serious problems. Government attempts to renew the cities have largely failed for a number of reasons, including inadequate funding of the renewal projects, the exclusion of urban residents from program planning and decision making, and an overemphasis on commercial rather than residential development.

5. Following World War II, the United States experienced a surge in suburbanization. Suburbanization adds to the problems of U.S. cities by reinforcing residential segregation and eroding the tax base.

6. Urbanization is a worldwide trend that will result in half of the earth's population living in cities shortly after the turn of the twenty-first century. One result of this urbanization is the emergence of global cities, which serve as centers of international commerce, finance, and culture. The greatest urban growth is occurring in low-income countries, causing many problems: inadequate housing, a rise in the unemployment rate, food shortages, and the spread of disease.

The Natural Environment

1. The ecosystem is a set of interrelated environmental components, which often conflict with one another, creating crises and environmental change. Many of these changes are brought about naturally, but others are caused by humans' demands on and intrusion into the natural environment. This intrusion dates back about 50,000 years, but it has created the most serious environmental problems only since the Industrial Revolution, increasing dramatically in recent years because of our failure to regulate advanced technology; the overproduction of wastes, including hazardous wastes; and our excessive use of natural materials.

2. Acid rain, ozone depletion, and the greenhouse effect are three outcomes of environmental pollution. These environmental problems harm humans and other living creatures as well as our built environment. New regulations may help to remedy these problems and reduce their effects.

3. The problem of toxic waste has increased significantly since the end of World War II because of the increased production and use of plastics and synthetic materials. However, the detrimental effects of the toxic waste created by the manufacture of the vast majority of these products is either unknown or not well understood. Much of the waste is not disposed of properly, and improper or illegal disposal has resulted in a wide range of environmental and health problems as well as enormous financial costs for government cleanups.

4. Energy and energy use are fundamental to the economic well-being of the world community, but if current energy use patterns are maintained, serious environmental problems such as acid rain and the danger of exhausting some energy sources are likely outcomes. Industrial production consumes the lion's share of the world's commercial energy, and wealthier countries use a disproportionate share of the world's energy. Efforts to conserve energy and our natural environment are being undertaken through cooperative agreements among countries and an international commitment to sustainable development. Although these efforts have achieved some success, there have also been serious setbacks.

KEY PEOPLE AND CONCEPTS

acid rain: the combination of two major pollutants—sulfur dioxide and nitrogen oxide—to form nitric acid in the atmosphere that returns to the earth in rain and snow

anomie: a state of norm confusion, where traditional norms no longer make sense, but new norms haven't developed to replace them

city: a large, permanent community of people who rely on one another for food, goods, and services

concentric zone theory: a theory that portrays the city as a series of five rings, each constituting a zone

crude birth rate: the number of live births per 1,000 people per year, unadjusted for differences between subgroups in a society

crude death rate: the number of deaths per 1,000 people per year, unadjusted for differences between subgroups in a society

demographic transition: a theory that sees population growth as tied to the technological development of a society

demography: the study of population size, distribution, composition, and movement or migration

doubling time: the amount of time it takes a population to double itself, given a constant rate of growth

ecosystem: the interrelationships between living things and their environments

exponential population growth: the theory that if growth is left unchecked, the population will increase exponentially (1, 2, 4, 8, 16, 32, 64, and so on)

fertility: the incidence of live births

gemeinschaft: a type of social organization characterized by close intimate relationships, a strong sense of kinship and community, and strong mores and traditions

gentrification: the renewal of old neighborhoods by affluent individuals that results in significant improvement in selected areas of the city, but also causes many low-income families and the elderly to lose their homes

gesellschaft: a type of social organization where social relationships are impersonal, family and community ties are weak, and the community orientation is replaced by the pursuit of individual goals and desires

global cities: metropolitan areas that serve as centers of international commerce, finance, and culture; part of an interconnected global system that exerts great power on the economic and political decision-making process

greenhouse effect: the warming of the earth because of trapped solar radiation due to a build-up of gases in the atmosphere

human ecology: the study of the spatial distribution of people in an urban environment

life expectancy: the average number of years a person can expect to live after reaching a certain age

mortality: the incidence of deaths

net migration: determined by comparing in-migration (the number of individuals entering a country or area) with out-migration (the number of people departing a country or area)

population pyramid: a device used by demographers to make a visual presentation of population variation

refugees: people who leave their home country because of such factors as international or civil war, political repression, or famine

social solidarity: the unifying force that holds members of a society together

suburbanization: the movement of people from the city to communities outside the city called suburbs

toxic waste: any byproduct of production or other processes that are of no use, but are hazardous to humans and the environment

urbanization: the process whereby the members of a society are concentrated in cities and urban areas exert a significant influence on the society

zero growth rate: the number of births do not exceed the number of deaths

LEARNING MORE

Carson, R. (1962). *Silent spring*. Boston: Houghton Mifflin. This classic marks the beginning of the "green revolution." Carson discusses the threats of chemical pollution, enlightening the United States and the world about its dangers.

Ehrlich, P. (1968). *The population bomb*. New York: Ballantine Books and Ehrlich, P. & Ehrlich, A. (1990). *The population explosion*. New York: Simon & Schuster. The 1968 publication was central in starting the debate regarding overpopulation. While some of the predictions of the author did not occur, it is still a classic. The 1990 text addresses some of the early work's shortcomings and adds more insights into the issue of the "population explosion."

Harr, J. (1995). *A civil action*. New York: Random House. Now recommended reading in many law schools, this book recounts the legal struggle to force two major corporations to take responsibility for polluting the water supply of Woburn, MA, which resulted in illness and death of residents.

Rees, W., & Wackernagel, M. (1996). *Ecological footprint: Reducing the human impact on the earth*. Philadelphia, PA: New Society Publishers. This work gives a historical account of the negative consequences of human intrusion into the environment. The author argues that issues such as overpopulation were concerns of society long before the industrial period.

Sassen, S. (1991). *The global city: New York, London, Tokyo*. Princeton, NJ: Princeton University Press. This book provides one of the best presentations of the "global city" argument. It focuses on three of the world's major urban centers and shows their interrelatedness in the global economy.

Silliman, J., & King, Y. (Eds.). (1999). *Dangerous intersections*. Cambridge: South End Press. A collection of essays by international scholars who look at environmental, population, and development problems from a multicultural feminist perspective.

Worldwatch Institute. (annually). *State of the world*. New York: W.W. Norton and Co. An annual collection of writings that focuses on a variety of environmental issues. The anthology takes a truly global perspective and provides excellent international data on the environment. The Watchwatch Institute also publishes *Vital Signs* each year.

 Run Chapter 20 on your *Living Sociology* CD-ROM for interesting and informative activities, web links, videos, practice tests, and more.

CHAPTER

20

Social Change, Collective Behavior, and Social Movements

It was 5 A.M., April 26, 1994, in Katlehong township, South Africa, and Christina Vanqa was waiting in line to vote for the first time in her life. She was eighty years old and she stood with hundreds of others, most, like herself, were Black and newly enfranchised by sweeping constitutional reforms in the South African government. Although it would be hours more before they actually cast their ballots, Christina and her neighbors were happy to wait because on this historic day, they would elect South Africa's first Black president. Nelson Mandela's victory wiped out the last official vestige of the racist system known as *apartheid* and three centuries of White rule in their country (Cline, 1994).

Although White domination of South Africa dates back about three hundred years, its more recent manifestation, *apartheid*—a set of official policies to segregate the races in all aspects of life—was enacted by the South African government in 1950. Under apartheid, 23 million Black South Africans, about 77 percent of the country's population, were forced to live in rural "homelands" and townships covering just 13 percent of the country's geographic area, while vast stretches of prime residential real estate were reserved for Whites. Black South Africans were required to carry passbooks for identification and certification to enter specific areas of White South Africa. Failure to present a valid passbook when stopped by the police was cause for imprisonment, and 17 million Blacks were arrested for entering areas reserved for Whites during apartheid. Black South Africans had to observe curfews, and were forbidden to gather in public. Police were permitted to detain anyone merely suspected of violating the security laws. During apartheid, 80,000 Black South Africans were detained without trial and about 40,000 were forced into foreign exile.

It is little wonder that Black South Africans rebelled against apartheid. Some, such as Steven Biko, lost their lives in the struggle; others, such as Nelson Mandela, spent many years in prison. However, through their courageous activism and sacrifice, apartheid was finally repealed in March, 1990, and free elections were held in April, 1994, bringing Christina Vanqa and millions of other Black South Africans to the polls for the first time.

Black South Africans' struggle against apartheid is a dramatic example of the human role in bringing about social change. **Social change** is the transformation of culture, social structure, and social behavior over time. Social change is a constant part of social life, but it occurs at different rates in different societies. The fight for social change in South Africa took three hundred years, which is a long time, but social change in hunting and gathering societies can take centuries longer. In general, industrial societies change faster than preindustrial societies. Of course, some changes have a greater impact on social life and social structure than others. The introduction of the mini-skirt, for example, was said to have "revolutionized" fashion, but, like most fashion changes, its impact on society was at most weak and transitory. In contrast, the repeal of apartheid fundamentally altered social relations within South Africa as well as international relations between that country and other countries throughout the world.

Our focus in this chapter is on social change. We will consider sociological theories of social change and sources of change. Social change can be brought about in many ways, but one of the most important is human action. Consequently, the lion's share of the chapter is given to a discussion of **collective behavior:** voluntary activity, often spontaneous and goal-oriented, by a large number of people who are typically violating dominant norms and values with their behavior. We will discuss various forms and theories of collective behavior, giving special attention to organized efforts to bring about social change through social movements. Let's begin by looking at how sociologists explain social change.

THEORIES OF SOCIAL CHANGE

Sociologists are interested in how and why social change occurs. Sociologists who study social change may focus on changes in a particular social group such as fluctuations in the Black infant mortality rate during the twentieth century. Or they may look at changes that affect an entire society such as China's transition from a socialist agricultural economy to an industrial market economy. They may even look at changes across societies such as the economic development of low-income countries in Africa. Regardless of the change studied, sociologists generally use one of two theoretical models—structural functionalist or conflict—to explain how and why social change takes place. Let's look at each model in turn.

Structural Functionalist Perspectives

Functionalists often describe society as an organism. Organisms change, but very slowly and only when it's necessary and adaptive. In other words, they evolve. Thus, functionalist theories of social change have traditionally characterized it as an evolutionary process.

Herbert Spencer, for example, writing in the late nineteenth century, argued that societies evolve from simple social systems characterized by sameness to complex social systems characterized by diversity. In simple societies, the tasks that must be completed require basic skills that all members possess. Since everyone performs the same roles, people can survive independently of one another. However, success in meeting survival needs means that the society gets bigger. Growth also results when members come in contact with people from other societies and the societies merge. More people means more work, which produces greater role differentiation. Greater role differentiation leads to greater complexity, with institutions emerging to meet needs that members can no longer take care of on their own. This growing complexity also generates interdependence among the society's members. No longer can individuals perform all necessary tasks; they must rely on each other for survival (Spencer, 1860).

This view of social change is probably familiar to you, since it resembles Durkheim's idea that societies evolve from mechanical solidarity, characterized by sameness, to organic solidarity, characterized by diversity. Durkheim also believed that change occurs as a result of internal and external pressures, such as population growth or cross-cultural contacts. According to Durkheim, societies ideally achieve a state of equilibrium or balance, until some internal or external pressure prompts change. Sociologist Talcott Parsons (1966) shared the view that as societies change, they become more complex. Parsons believed that growing complexity is functional because it is basically an adaptation mechanism, a response to internal or external forces. Change, then, does not necessarily disrupt a society's equilibrium, since it occurs in order to preserve social stability.

Other functionalist theorists accept the idea that change brings greater differentiation, but argue that differentiation can produce independence instead of interdependence. In modern industrial societies, for example, social life becomes more impersonal, giving people a sense that they can't depend on anyone but themselves. This increasing independence can be a source of social conflict and tension. However, differentiation is not an inevitable outcome of social change, and not all parts of a society undergo change at the same rate or to the same extent. In fact, instead of growing more complex, some institutions can become less complex or outdated as a result of resisting change or not keeping up with changes in other parts of the society. This outcome, too, can generate tension and conflict (Alexander & Colomy, 1990; Merton, 1968).

Evaluating Structural Functionalist Perspectives. Societies often become more complex as they change, with an increase in social roles and institutions. Critics of structural functionalism, especially the earlier evolutionary theories, point out that social change is not always "progressive." Such an assumption is based on the ethno-

centric view that Western industrial societies are more "evolved" and, therefore, better than more "primitive" non-Western preindustrial societies. As we have seen, however, social changes such as industrialization bring many problems, including environmental pollution and bureaucratic depersonalization. Moreover, the diversity that characterizes modern industrial societies does not necessarily lead to greater interdependence among people, but rather often generates hostility, conflict, and even violence. More recent functionalist theories of social change take these dysfunctional outcomes into account, but some critics believe they still don't go far enough.

Another criticism of structural functionalism is that it overemphasizes such factors as population growth and cross-cultural contact, and downplays the organized efforts of a society's members to bring about change.

The Conflict Perspective

Instead of viewing societies as relatively stable, changing only when it's necessary or adaptive, conflict theorists see social change as a built-in feature of social life. According to conflict theorists, social change is the result of the conflicts between competing groups in a society. Recall, for example, that Karl Marx believed that class conflict inevitably arises in capitalist societies and leads to wholesale social change through a socialist revolution. Thus, instead of slow, evolutionary change, conflict theorists think change can be abrupt and often violent. Moreover, conflict theorists emphasize that, for better or for worse, much social change is the result of planned, organized human action rather than "natural" processes such as population growth or environmental factors. Change is not always positive or progressive either, since some changes (such as the colonization of Africa and Latin America by the Europeans) result in the subordination of some groups by others. Change impacts different groups in different ways.

Evaluating the Conflict Perspective. Conflict theory addresses many of the issues that functionalist theories overlook, but it also has its share of critics. For example, Marx's view of social change is criticized for being evolutionary in its own right. According to Marx, societies move through various stages until they ultimately reach communism, the classless society resulting from the workers' revolution against the capitalists. In general, however, Marx's version of conflict theory has not proven to be an accurate predictor of revolutionary change in capitalist societies.

More recent conflict theories take into account that organized efforts can bring about change and that change affects various groups differently, but they are criticized for focusing almost exclusively on economic conflict as a source of change. Critics point out that racial and ethnic, religious, and gender-based conflicts, along with conflicts stemming from differences in sexual orientation, can be as important as economics in triggering social change.

Let's look at some of the sources of social change more closely.

REFLECTING ON

Theories of Social Change

1. In July 1997, the governance of Hong Kong reverted from Great Britain to China. How would structural functionalists explain this change? What about conflict theorists?

2. Think about a social change that you consider very significant for our society. Which theoretical perspective—structural functionalist or conflict—best explains this change?

SOURCES OF SOCIAL CHANGE

There are many sources of social change. Social change can be caused by fluctuations in population, changes in the natural environment, elements of culture, and social conflict. We'll consider each source in turn, but keep in mind that in real life, these sources are interrelated and continuously influence one another.

Population Fluctuation and Social Change

Fluctuations in a society's population—that is, significant increases or decreases in the number of people in a society—can dramatically alter the social life and organization of the society. Population growth, for example, increases the demand for housing, for jobs, and for various social services, such as education. On an institutional level, these expanding needs can place considerable strain on the society, as in low-income countries, where rapid population growth is causing rising unemployment rates and housing shortages. The shantytowns that spring up provide no services, not even basic sanitation, medical facilities, or schools.

Changes in the composition of a society's population also bring about social change. We are currently witnessing the "graying" of the U.S. population. The percentage of the population over sixty-five grew from 4 percent in 1900 to 16.5 percent in 1996, and senior citizens are expected to make up nearly 25 percent of the population by the mid-twenty-first century (Taeuber, 1992). Most people over sixty-five get some—or all—of their income from Social Security, which is supported by the working population. Unfortunately, at the same time that the older population is growing, the working population is shrink-

ing, which could eventually mean reduced Social Security payments. Our society needs to devise strategies for sustaining economic as well as social supports for the elderly. The graying of the population is also increasing the demand for gerontological services, a need that will continue to expand well into the next century, another problem that requires immediate attention.

Finally, population migrations can also cause significant social change. The swell in immigrants to the United States in recent years (from 531,000 in 1980 to 720,500 in 1995) has exposed Americans to many new cultures, and is a driving force of the multiculturalism movement, which encourages an appreciation of diversity and supports programs such as bilingual education. But the influx of immigrants has also led to the "English-only" movement, which emphasizes assimilation into the dominant culture and sole use of the English language in schools, businesses, and public facilities (U.S. Department of Commerce, Bureau of the Census, 1997).

The Natural Environment

Sometimes natural events stimulate social change. Natural disasters are one type of event that can produce organizational and behavioral changes. When one of your authors was in graduate school, for example, she took part in a research project that looked at how people deal with natural disasters, such as floods, hurricanes, and tornados. Your author visited a small midwestern town that floods every spring because it is located at the base of some mountains and the confluence point of two large rivers. You might think the residents of this town would just pack up and move, but instead, they've developed institutionalized responses to the annual flooding. For instance, when the flood is imminent, the townspeople move their belongings to the highest point in their houses. They open their basement windows so the local fire company can fill the basements with clean water. When the flood waters rush through the streets, the clean water acts as a countervailing force, keeping the mud and debris out of the basements. When the flood ends, the fire company returns to pump out the water and the basements just dry out. Meanwhile, residents forced to evacuate their homes usually go to the school up on the hill, where they wait out the flood and socialize with long-time neighbors. Some residents even describe the atmosphere as "festive."

Many environmental changes, however, are not the result of nature's whimsy; rather, they are the byproducts or intended consequences of human action. Environmental pollution, overuse of natural resources, and the damming of rivers and clearing of forests for residential and commercial development are examples of how human intervention can change the natural environment. But just as people can act to change their environment, the environmental changes that result often force changes in human

What sources of social change do these photographs represent? In each case what social changes occur and with what consequences for society? How could each of these situations be understood from the perspectives of structural functionalism and conflict theory?

behavior and social organization. One dramatic example occurred in London in 1952. Heavy industrialization and residential development over the decades produced a thick green-yellow smog that Londoners came to accept as part of their environment. The smog was a combination of fog and high concentrations of sulfur dioxide released from the burning of sulfurous coal, oil, and fossil fuels in homes and factories. When the smog was particularly dense, people referred to it as a "real peasouper." In 1952, over the course of just five days, one of the worst smogs killed over 4,000 people, the world's deadliest air pollution disaster on record. This tragedy prompted Londoners to take action to clean their air. The entire city, and many other cities in Great Britain, were declared smoke-free zones and no one was permitted to burn a coal fire unless a pre-

processed, sulfur-free fuel or a "smoke-eating" furnace was used. Both ordinary citizens and industrial leaders had to change their thinking about the environment and their behavior. Methods of industrial production were also changed. The result was a significant improvement in London's air quality (Hillary, 1984).

This example also shows the *dynamics* of change: One source of change (human intervention into the natural environment) can produce another source of change (environmental pollution), which leads to social change (actions taken to clean the environment), which leads to still further environmental change (improved air quality), and so on.

A more recent example of how the interaction between humans and the environment can lead to social change occurred in Love Canal, New York. During the 1950s, the town of Love Canal was built on a filled-in dump site previously owned by the Hooker Chemicals Corporation. During the 1960s and 1970s, however, toxic chemicals that had been improperly disposed of began to ooze to the surface, at first killing grass and trees, but eventually causing elevated cancer rates, infertility, and birth defects. Eventually, the area was determined unsafe for habitation, and all the town's residents were forced to move. Besides the social changes caused by population relocation, the Love Canal residents banded together to force the chemical company and the government to take responsibility for the problem. Their actions generated new social relationships as well as institutional change.

Culture

A society's culture is also an important source of social change. Three types of cultural change are particularly instrumental in producing more widespread social change: discoveries, inventions, and diffusion.

A discovery is the perception of something that already exists, such as gravity or a continent. Throughout history, discoveries have caused profound changes in social life and social structure. Electricity, for example, has always been part of the earth's atmosphere, but it had to be discovered to have an impact on social life. To appreciate the impact of electricity on social life, you need only consider how life changes during an extended power failure. A more dramatic historical example is the colonization of Africa. People lived on the African continent for thousands of years, but when they were discovered by the Europeans and subsequently colonized, the entire course of world history changed. This event caused the destruction of many indigenous cultures and resulted in the enslavement of African people; however, European economic development soared as a result of this single discovery.

Inventions, which are the result of people using existing knowledge to produce something new, also cause significant social change. Consider, for example, the changes brought about by the invention of the automobile. One of the most obvious was increased mobility, allowing people to live farther from work and contributing to the process of suburbanization. Work and home became increasingly separate, not only ideologically, but also geographically. Automobiles also helped foster individualism and a growing sense of anonymity. People began spending less time walking about their neighborhoods and towns, meeting and greeting one another. As cars became more affordable, people also spent less time with one another on public transportation. Automobiles also became a symbol of social stratification. At first, simply having a car was a status symbol, but today, owning particular makes and models denotes a person's status.

Inventions derive from existing knowledge, other inventions, and discoveries, so that a single invention or dis-

covery can spawn many others. The rate of invention in a society depends on the knowledge base members have to work with. The more knowledge accumulates, the greater and faster the rate of inventions. Think of the multitude of inventions that followed the introduction of the computer. A new language has even been invented that includes words such as *Internet, e-mail, information superhighway,* and *cyberspace.* Today, computers run everything from electrical power plants to air traffic control to bank machines. They generate paychecks, regulate lifesaving equipment in hospitals, even flush toilets (Feder & Pollack, 1998). In fact, some scientists believe that technological change in our contemporary society is occurring at a rate one million times faster than the rate of humans' ability to adjust to new situations (Mariott, 1996).

Computers play a special role in the third type of cultural change—diffusion—the spread of culture from one society or group to another. Diffusion can occur through travel, migration, and conquest, but in recent years, nothing has aided diffusion more than telecommunications and computers. Today, the Internet links over 50 million computers in at least 175 countries, allowing people of diverse cultures to do business, share ideas, or just chat. This information exchange means that an unprecedented number of people are exposed to elements of other societies' cultures previously unknown to them; this knowledge, in turn, can change their worldviews as well as their behavior. For example, one significant social change that has resulted from cultural diffusion over the Internet is an increasing number of people who use English as a second language (Specter, 1996).

Diffusion, however, can generate social conflict, and conflict itself can produce far-reaching social change.

Conflict

Strain and conflict within a society as well as between societies can generate significant social change. Indeed, new societies can be born and established societies destroyed by social conflict. Consider, for example, the former Soviet Union. What was formerly known as "Soviet society" is now fifteen societies that differ in language, government, and ethnic composition.

Conflict among groups in a society can also lead to important social changes. Conflict resulting from racism in the United States, for instance, gave rise to the abolitionist movement in the 1800s and the civil rights movement in the 1950s and 1960s. Similarly, conflict that grew out of gender inequality prompted the women's movement in the 1840s and its resurgence in the 1960s.

These examples underscore the importance of human action in bringing about social change, a point we have emphasized from the outset of this chapter and throughout the text. Let's examine more closely the human role in social change by discussing collective behavior.

REFLECTING ON

Sources of Social Change

1. The "greenhouse effect" is expected to alter the distribution of productive farm land in the United States by the middle of the twenty-first century. The Midwest will become a desert, while colder regions in the North will become ideal for farming. What social changes will likely result from this environmental change?
2. Can you think of cultural changes besides those we've discussed that have caused significant social change? Name one and describe the social changes it generated.
3. Have you ever been involved in a conflict—for example, in your neighborhood or school—that resulted in an important change? Describe the conflict, your role in it, and the changes that resulted.

COLLECTIVE BEHAVIOR

Recall our definition of collective behavior: voluntary activity, often spontaneous and goal-oriented, by a large number of people who are typically violating dominant norms and values. If we think about this definition for a moment, it's not difficult to see why collective behavior is sometimes hard to study. First, this voluntary activity encompasses a wide range of behavior, from mass hysteria to public opinion to fads. Second, because some collective behavior is spontaneous, it can also be short-lived, so there is little—or no—opportunity for long-term, systematic study. A third problem is that collective behavior is sometimes unstructured, making it hard for sociologists to discern patterns that allow them to generalize across incidents.

Despite these difficulties, sociologists have undertaken numerous studies of collective behavior and have developed explanations of why it occurs. They begin by distinguishing collectivities from other social groups. A **collectivity** is a large number of people engaged in limited interaction guided by weak or unconventional norms. In short, *collectivity* refers to the actors engaged in a behavior. There are important differences between social groups and collectivities: (1) Social groups engage in direct and frequent interaction, whereas the interaction of collectivities is usually temporary and, in some cases, face-to-face interaction does not occur at all. (2) People in social groups have a common identity that derives from their membership, whereas members of collectivities do not usually feel this sense of "belonging." (3) Social groups are governed by a set of norms defining conventional behavior, whereas the norms guiding behavior in collectivities are weak because they are newly emerging and often

unconventional, developing in response to uncertainty, strain, or threat.

Sociologists also distinguish two types of collectivities. In a **localized collectivity,** people who are in close physical proximity to one another act together. The localized collectivities that we will discuss are crowds, mobs and riots, and panics and hysteria. In a **dispersed collectivity,** the actions of people who are not in close physical proximity nevertheless affect one another. The activity of dispersed collectivities is sometimes referred to as *mass behavior* because it involves large numbers of people who are spread out geographically—even throughout the world—but engaged in basically the same behavior or concerned with the same phenomenon. The dispersed collectivities that we will discuss are rumor and gossip, public opinion, and fashions and fads. Because social movements are a special form of collective behavior, we will discuss them separately later in the chapter.

Crowds

Each of us has, at some time, been part of a **crowd,** a temporary gathering of people with a common focal point who influence one another. If you've ever attended a rock concert or a university or professional sporting event, you've witnessed—and taken part in—crowd behavior. In fact, the size of a crowd is sometimes a source of pride; your school newspaper may report, for example, that 25,000 people turned out for a basketball or football game. The size of a crowd can also be cause for concern, especially among social control agents. Managing the behavior of large numbers of people, particularly when emotions may run high, is extremely difficult. But that is not to say that a large crowd is necessarily an unmanageable crowd.

In studying crowds, sociologist Herbert Blumer (1970) identified four main types of crowds:

1. A casual crowd forms spontaneously around a specific incident, but people in the gathering engage in little, if any, interaction with one another. For example, while we were at the beach one summer, a life guard was struck by lightning. A crowd of about fifty people collected at the scene and watched as another life guard gave mouth-to-mouth resuscitation. Most people were silent, and those who spoke whispered only briefly to one another. When the ambulance arrived to take the injured life guard to the hospital, the crowd dispersed.
2. A **conventional crowd** collects for a specific event, but their gathering is planned, not spontaneous. When students pack the lecture hall of a favorite professor or art lovers fill a convention center for a juried art show, they form a conventional crowd. Conventional crowds abide by the norms that govern such occasions.

3. An **expressive crowd** gathers for an event that is highly emotional or exciting. In fact, it's the expected emotional charge or promised excitement that draws people to the gathering. For example, every August an expressive crowd numbering tens of thousands gathers at Graceland, the estate of Elvis Presley in Memphis, Tennessee, for "Elvis week." These seven days leading up to the anniversary of Presley's death have been described by fans throughout the world as a "pilgrimage" of prayer, music, and other activities to venerate the memory of "the King" (Rosenbaum, 1995).

4. An **acting crowd** is emotion-charged and forms spontaneously for one specific purpose. The emotion that characterizes an acting crowd is more intense than the emotion of an expressive crowd, so acting crowds have the greatest likelihood of being unmanageable. A crowd that has waited in line all night to buy concert tickets, only to be told the concert is sold out may erupt into an acting crowd and storm the ticket office.

These political demonstrators in Hong Kong expressed dissatisfaction with specific government policies concerning public security and citizens' rights. According to Herbert Blumer's classification, which type of crowd was involved in this collective behavior? How would you define collective behavior?

To this list, some sociologists add a fifth type, **protest crowds,** who purposely gather to express dissatisfaction with particular conditions or events (McPhail & Wohlstein, 1983). Political demonstrations and strikes by workers are examples of protest crowds. However, other sociologists consider protest crowds simply a subtype of conventional crowds. Part of the disagreement stems from the fact that, like other crowds, protest crowds can quickly change in character during an event. Consider, for example, the crowd that gathered on the streets of Chicago during the 1968 Democratic National Convention. Some observers might have considered this a protest crowd, since there were demonstrations against the Vietnam War. Others would label it a conventional crowd, since the people gathered peacefully for a planned special event. But when the police arrived dressed in riot gear and armed with tear gas and clubs, the gathering was quickly transformed into an expressive crowd. When police and protestors began taunting each other, pushing and shoving ensued, and a violent clash erupted. The crowd changed again—to an acting crowd. Within a brief period, many protestors, who were unarmed, were seriously injured and hundreds were taken into police custody.

Mobs and Riots

If an acting crowd becomes violent, it can turn into a **mob,** an intensely emotional crowd set on doing violence to specific others or property. Mobs are relatively short lived because their intense emotion is difficult to sustain; however, usually a mob does not disperse until it has at least partially achieved its goal or agents of social control—police, guards, military personnel—prevent it from achieving its goal.

Lynchings are the most frequently cited example of mob behavior. In the South, after the Civil War, the mere accusation by a White woman that a Black man had made sexual advances toward her was enough to rouse a lynch mob. There are also recent examples of lynchings and similar mob behavior. In 1994, for instance, on the steps of a Northeast Philadelphia church, a sixteen-year-old boy was beaten to death by boys from a nearby neighborhood who alleged that a boy from the victim's neighborhood had tried to rape one of their girlfriends (Kershaw, 1996). In this case, vengeance, not race, was the primary motivator of the mob.

A **riot** is another intensely emotional crowd, but its violent behavior is not purposefully directed like that of a mob. Riots erupt when a triggering incident ignites a crowd's emotions and they lash out in frenzied, seemingly unfocused violence and destruction. Sometimes riots stem from longstanding, but repressed anger, as in the riots that erupted in Los Angeles following the announcement of the not-guilty verdict in the trial of the police officers charged with beating motorist Rodney King. But riots can also erupt during celebrations, as when football fans surge from stadium stands after a championship win and proceed to rip up the field, knock down goal posts, pull out benches, and loot snack bars.

Panics and Hysteria

When faced with a crisis or serious threat, we are often told, "Don't panic!" Panic is a feeling of overwhelming fear or terror that can lead to impulsive actions that put people in even greater danger. These feelings can grip a collectivity just as they can an individual. Sociologists use the term **panic** to describe the collective behavior that occurs when people who are confronted with a crisis or serious threat respond irrationally and actually worsen their situation.

During one of our field visits to Guinea, for example, the military staged a coup. People who had supported the defeated political leaders feared retribution, so many decided to leave the country while they were still free to do so. The few scheduled airline flights in and out of Guinea all became quickly overbooked. Since we had tickets for one of the flights, we arrived at the airport to make our departure, only to find three hundred people also holding tickets on a plane with less than two hundred seats. No one was issued a boarding pass. Instead, we were instructed to wait in a large room that was ground level with the runway. As the room filled with passengers, it became clear that many of us would not be leaving the country that night and that we would have to wait almost a week for another flight. Of course, the political situation could change dramatically during that time. The tension mounted as the flight was delayed several hours. Finally, we were told that passengers would be boarded on a first-come, first-served basis. When the outside doors opened, we were supposed to walk in an orderly fashion to the stairs of the plane. Immediately, passengers started jostling for position. Suddenly, one passenger flung the doors open and started to run toward the plane. Panic ensued. Everyone ran, and people were trampled. Some were seriously injured, including several children. As passengers tried to mount the stairs, others pulled them back or tried to climb over them. On board, fights broke out over seats, causing more injuries. When the flight was finally ready to take off, the plane was less than full because so many people had to be left behind for treatment.

Another form of collective behavior that involves fear and irrational behavior is **hysteria**. With hysteria, however, the behavior is usually a response to an imagined event or a real event that has been misinterpreted or distorted. The most famous example of hysteria arose from a radio broadcast dramatizing H. G. Wells's story *War of the Worlds*. On October 30, 1938, a music program was suddenly interrupted by a special news report informing the American public that Martians were invading earth. Although at various points in the broadcast, listeners were

How would you describe this crowd compared to the Hong Kong protest march in the previous photograph? How would you determine if the situation in the photograph portrays a mob action or riot or a reaction of panic or hysteria? What role might rumor and gossip play in these kinds of collective behavior?

told that it was a dramatization, it seemed real enough to over 1 million people who jammed roadways trying to escape, overloaded telephone lines trying to call relatives to warn them, and filled the streets as they ran from their houses crying and praying.

More recently, hysteria broke out in Puerto Rico. In 1996, more than twenty people claimed to have seen a vampire-like predator that they believed had been killing animals by draining their blood. According to witnesses, the "monster" was four to five feet tall, had large, elongated red eyes, spikes down its back, and a pointy tongue that shot in and out of its mouth. It changed colors, hopped like a kangaroo but could also fly, and exuded a sickening, sulfur-like odor. However, autopsies performed on some of the monster's alleged victims revealed that many had been killed by parasites and a few had been killed by wild dogs. Nevertheless, people organized armed search parties to capture the monster, animal owners moved their pets and livestock indoors, and tourists cancelled visits to the island. Some residents were so hysterical they had to be hospitalized. No monster was ever found, and eventually the hysteria subsided (Navarro, 1996; see also Kristof, 1998).

Rumor and Gossip

The collective behavior we have discussed so far occurs in localized collectivities. Let's consider collective behavior found among dispersed collectivities, although this does not mean that localized collectivities cannot participate in them as well.

One form of collective behavior engaged in by both localized and dispersed collectivities is **rumor,** information transmitted among people, usually informally and from unconfirmed sources. It may be true or false, but typically as it spreads, it becomes a little of both, because in the telling and retelling, distortions, omissions, and embellishments frequently occur.

To understand how rumor works, you can play a game our children enjoy called "Pass It On." Sit in a circle with some of your friends or classmates and whisper some information in the ear of the person seated to your right. That person then whispers what you've said to the person on his or her right, and so on around the circle. The last person in the circle shares the information aloud with the group, and the person who started the "rumor" can confirm whether or not that's what was actually said. The reason the game is so much fun is that the outcome is often hilarious; what finally gets shared with the group often bears little resemblance to the original information.

A less lighthearted game of "Pass It On" was played by students who participated in an experiment in the 1940s. A student was asked by the experimenters to look at a photograph that showed two men in a subway car. One man was White, and he appeared to be threatening the second man, who was Black. The student then described the photo to another student, who passed the information on to a third student, and so on. The researchers found that the more the photo was described, the more it changed. Eventually, the photo was described as showing a Black man threatening a White man on a subway (Allport & Postman, 1947).

As this example illustrates, a major problem with rumor is not only that people don't verify the information before passing it on, but they typically alter it according to their own prejudices. Whether true or false, rumor is important because it can lead to other forms of collective behavior, including crowds, mobs, and riots. In fact, recognizing the power of rumor to generate social unrest, many state and local governments open "rumor hotlines" in the wake of a politically or emotionally charged event, so citizens can call to verify information or obtain facts before taking action.

Gossip is rumor about individuals' personal lives, rather than an issue or event. Sociologist Charles Horton Cooley (1962/1909), writing shortly after the turn of the century, said that gossip is spread by a small group of people personally associated with the individual they're gossiping about. Cooley's description, however, doesn't entirely fit the "information age" in which we live today. People still gossip about others in their social or professional networks, but spreading gossip about people one doesn't know personally—especially famous people, such as entertainers and politicians—appears to be a national pastime nowadays. Consider the popularity of tabloid newspapers and magazines, such the *Star*, the *National Enquirer*, and *People*. Television programs, such as *Entertainment Tonight* and *Inside Hollywood*, have millions of viewers. The growing use of the Internet means that

gossip and other rumors can be spread to millions of people throughout the world in a matter of seconds.

Like many rumors, once gossip is spread, it is often difficult to retract even in the face of factual information that discredits it. Of course, not everyone accepts rumor and gossip without question. Some people express doubt about the accuracy of the information as they pass it on; others relay the information, but argue against it or offer a different interpretation; and still others refuse to spread a particular rumor or piece of gossip. The research shows that rumor and gossip considered exciting or emotionally charged will most likely be spread, and it is these kinds of rumor and gossip that are most distorted in the process (Allport & Postman, 1947).

Public Opinion

Throughout the text, we've cited statistics to show the public's opinion on a variety of issues, ranging from support for the death penalty to belief in God. **Public opinion** consists of the attitudes expressed by members of a society, or those selected to represent them. Since researchers and pollsters usually cannot study everyone belonging to a group they're interested in, let alone an entire society, they select a sample, and the opinions of those sampled are generalized to the whole population. It is very important, though, to get an inclusive sample so that diverse opinions can be heard. When we speak about "the public," therefore, we must keep in mind that there really is no single public, but many publics. These publics differ in terms of sex, race and ethnicity, social class, age, sexual orientation, and a host of other factors.

Public opinion, then, is rarely, if ever, unified. People, and the issues on which they express opinions, are di-

In 1999 an impeached President Clinton was acquitted of criminal charges in a sex scandal that fueled speculation, riveted media attention for nearly a year, and set Republicans against Democrats. The public had tired of the debacle and its perceived undermining of the national interest. What roles did rumor and gossip, political partisanship, media propaganda, and public opinion play in this complex event?

verse, as are the opinions themselves. Moreover, on any given issue, some people say they have no opinion at all. The issue simply may not be important to them, or they may feel they don't know enough about it to express an opinion. Interestingly, however, lack of knowledge does not usually keep people from offering an opinion on the subject. In one experiment, for example, researchers asked people they stopped on a city street if they supported or opposed U.S. aid to the rebels in Eastern Alphacenturi. Most respondents offered strong opinions, many sounding quite knowledgeable, even though Eastern Alphacenturi is not real (Annenberg/CPB Collection, 1989).

Public opinion also changes over time. Table 20.1 shows, for example, how public opinion about the most important problem facing the United States has changed since 1977. In 1977, the public was most concerned about economic issues, including the high cost of living, taxes, and unemployment. In 1998, however, the chief concerns were crime and violence; followed by moral decline, which was cited by only 4 percent of the public surveyed in 1977.

Public opinion is influenced not only by current events, but by other factors as well. One of the most important is a society's "opinion makers," which include politicians, special-interest groups, and the media. Opinion makers often use propaganda to shape public opinion. **Propaganda** is information designed to persuade people to adopt a particular opinion on a specific issue. Consider, for example, advertisements by the National Rifle Association to sway public opinion against gun control legislation. In one ad, a young woman walking to her car alone late at night is stalked by a menacing male figure, and we're told that if Congress has its way, only the criminals will have guns. The ad's message is clear: If you don't oppose gun control, you or someone you love could soon become the victim of a crime because the "bad guys" will always find ways to get guns, while law-abiding citizens will be left with no effective means to defend themselves. The millions of dollars spent on propaganda by special-interest groups such as the NRA is a good indicator, though, of the importance of public opinion. Opinion makers realize that by influencing public opinion, they can also often influence public policy.

Fashions and Fads

Have you ever told anyone they're old-fashioned? Essentially, you were telling them that their look or behavior

TABLE 20.1 Public Opinion on the Most Important Problem Facing the United States, 1977, 1987, 1998

Problem	*PERCENT CITING AS MOST SERIOUS PROBLEM IN*		
	1977	1987	1998
High cost of living/taxes	32	5	7
Unemployment	17	13	5
Energy problems	15	NA	NA
International problems/foreign affairs	10	NA	4
Crime; violence	6	3	20
Fear of war/nuclear war	NA	23	NA
Moral decline in society	4	5	16
Dissatisfaction with government	3	5	8
Excessive government spending	3	11	5
Drug abuse	2	11	12
Race relations	2	NA	NA
Poverty	2	10	10
Education; quality of education	NA	NA	13
Health care	NA	NA	6
Can't say; don't know; no opinion	8	4	4

Sources: U.S. Department of Justice, Bureau of Justice Statistics, *Sourcebook of Criminal Justice Statistics,* 1978, p. 296; *Sourcebook of Criminal Justice Statistics,* 1998, p. 100.

was not up to date, that they are out of style. Sociologists use the term **fashion** in a similar way: to refer to currently favored styles of appearance or behavior. The word *currently* in the definition reveals an important characteristic of fashions: that they are short-term. At the turn of the century, sociologist Georg Simmel (1904/1971) pointed out that fashions are an expression of people's contradictory needs to be unique on the one hand, but to fit in with the group on the other. In other words, by adopting the latest fashion, one is not just a trendsetter, but part of a group of trendsetters. However, once the fashion is adopted on a large scale, there's no longer anything special about it, so it loses its appeal and is replaced by a new fashion.

Of course, fashions do not just appear spontaneously. Many fashions are carefully developed and marketed. Moreover, when a new fashion first appears, it is often very expensive, which is why historically, trendsetters have been members of the upper class, although the particular fashions they favor usually vary by age. As the fashion becomes more widespread, less expensive versions become available, but as we've already noted, a fashion's popularity breeds contempt for it among the most fashionable.

Fashions are a form of collective behavior unique to economically developed societies. The garments and bodily adornments worn by members of preindustrial societies usually signify their sex and age, although some members may wear particular clothing or ornamentation because they have a special role, such as shaman. However, this style of appearance changes little from year to year, or even from generation to generation. Compare this situation with our own society, where clothing styles change every *season* and automobile styles change annually, to give just two examples. The economies of preindustrial societies simply do not allow for such rapid change. There is little or no surplus, so most items, such as clothing, are prized for their function, not the status they confer. It is when societies develop and surpluses grow that many items become valued for the status they bestow on owners. This trend can be seen in many developing societies that are exposed to Western culture and products. In Guinea, for example, women traditionally wore long, wrap-around skirts that they tied at their waist, leaving their breasts uncovered. Over the course of our field visits, we saw an increasing number of women wearing bras, but no blouses, with their skirts. Bras had become a status symbol because they were associated with Western culture.

A **fad** is more temporary than a fashion and at least mildly unconventional. Fads have tremendous mass appeal and catch on very quickly, but they tend to disappear just as fast. Fads are also unique to high-income industrial societies because these populations have more discretionary money to spend on typically useless, but often entertaining products. One recent fad among children was the Furby, a stuffed animal that resembled a gremlin and spoke its own language. When this fad first appeared, each "pet" cost about $30, but within a year, they could be purchased for as little as $12. Fads of earlier decades include the pet rock, the mood ring, and the hula hoop. Fads may not require the purchase of anything, because a behavior can also be a fad. "Moshing" is a recent example of faddish behavior. Earlier examples include "streaking" (running naked in public), which was popular briefly in the early 1970s, and cramming people into phone booths in the 1950s.

Although people of all ages usually pay attention to fashions, fads appeal mostly to the young. Sociologists think fads help young people distinguish themselves from their elders and give them a distinctive identity of their own (Turner & Killian, 1993). How do sociologists ex-

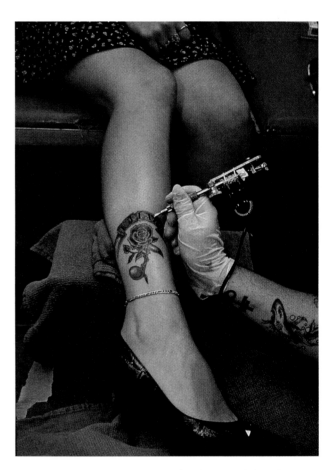

Is this woman participating in a fashion or a fad? What would determine the difference between fashion and fad as forms of collective behavior? From your own observations and experience, what are some examples of each? How do contagion theory, emergent-norm theory, and value-added theory attempt to explain collective behavior?

TABLE 20.2 Types of Collective Behavior*

Type	Definition	Examples
LOCALIZED COLLECTIVITIES		
Crowd	Temporary gathering of people with a common focal point who exercise influence over one another	Rock concert, professional sporting event, Oscar awards night in Hollywood
Mob	Intensely emotional crowd set on doing violence to specific others or property	Lynchings
Riot	Intensely emotional crowd whose violent behavior is not purposefully directed	Los Angeles riots following the announcement of the verdict in the Rodney King case
Panic	Collective behavior that emerges when people who are confronted with a crisis or serious threat respond in irrational and uncoordinated ways that may worsen their situation	Rushing exits when someone shouts, "Fire!"
Hysteria	Collective behavior in which people react fearfully and irrationally to an imagined event or a real event that has been misinterpreted or distorted	1938 Orson Welles radio broadcast of the *War of the Worlds*, the 1996 vampire predator in Puerto Rico
DISPERSED COLLECTIVITIES		
Rumor	Information transmitted among people, usually informally and from unsubstantiated sources	Without first verifying the facts, a man tells some of his neighbors that a teenager from their community has been shot by police. These neighbors tell others, also before verifying the facts, until most residents of the community confront the police chief, demanding an explanation of why the police "gunned down an innocent child."
Gossip	Rumor about individuals' personal lives	Tabloid stories about politicians' and celebrities' extramarital affairs
Public opinion	Attitudes expressed by members of a society, or those selected to represent them	Responses to social surveys, responses to exit polls on election day
Fashion	Currently favored styles of appearance	Mini-skirts; ponytails and earrings worn by men
Fad	An object or behavior that is at least mildly conventional, that has tremendous mass appeal and catches on and disappears quickly	Electronic pets, mood rings, hula hoops, moshing, streaking

*Because social movements constitute a special type of collective behavior they are not included in this table. See Table 20.3 for a summary of the types of social movements.

plain other forms of collective behavior? We'll consider theories of collective behavior next. First, however, Table 20.2 provides a summary of the types of collective behavior we have discussed so far.

REFLECTING ON

Collective Behavior

1. Most of us have been part of a casual crowd, a conventional crowd, and even expressive and protest crowds, but have you ever been involved in an acting crowd? Describe what happened. Did the acting crowd arise from one or more of the other types of crowds? Describe how the crowd changed over time.

2. College campuses are often the site of rumor. Can you think of a rumor that recently circulated on your campus? Did information get distorted as the rumor spread? Was the rumor eventually verified as fact, or was it finally discredited as a falsehood?

3. What do you think is one of the most important issues of public concern today? How do opinion makers try to influence public opinion on this issue?

4. What fads have you participated in? Which was your favorite? Why? How long did the fad last?

Sociologists have developed several theories of collective behavior, including contagion theory, convergence theory, emergent-norm theory, and value-added theory. We'll discuss each in turn.

Contagion Theory

Contagion theory emphasizes the emotional nature of collective behavior. This theory was originally developed by French social psychologist Gustave Le Bon (1960/1896) and focused primarily on crowds, including mobs and riots, though it could also be applied to panics and outbreaks of hysteria. Essentially, Le Bon argued that when people congregate in large numbers, a "collective mind" emerges that releases them from inhibitions and encourages them to behave irrationally. In a crowd, individuals feel relieved of personal responsibility for their actions and easily get caught up in emotion and frenzy.

Although many theorists later rejected Le Bon's notion of the "collective mind," they remained fascinated by the imitative nature of collective behavior, even when it is harmful and irrational. American sociologist Herbert Blumer (1951), for example, used the concept of *circular reaction* to explain how some forms of collective behavior escalate out of control. According to Blumer, if just a few members of a crowd become agitated or excited, their feelings are picked up by people around them who react with similar feelings, thus intensifying the emotions of the original actors. Within a short time, the collective mood—anger, fear, or some other intense emotion—spirals out of control and irrational behavior ensues. In short, people in crowds and other forms of collective behavior behave more like a herd of animals than rational human beings.

Evaluating Contagion Theory. If you've ever been part of a large crowd, you probably agree that the anonymity it offers can lower inhibitions and spark intense emotions. Moreover, laughter, as well as fervor and anger, does sometimes seem "infectious." However, contagion theory simply describes these phenomena; it doesn't explain why they occur except to say that people turn into animals. But while people may copy one another or look to others for indications of how to behave, this doesn't mean that they lose their rationality when in a crowd or similar type of collectivity. In fact, there is no empirical evidence to support the notion that collectivities take on lives of their own, independent of the concerns or goals of the individuals that make them up (McPhail, 1991; Polletta, 1998).

Convergence Theory

While contagion theory emphasizes the effect of the collectivity on individuals, *convergence theory* holds that people who think basically the same way, or share the same attributes, come together—or, converge—in collectivities. Collective behavior is simply a way for like-minded people to express their common attitudes and beliefs. Thus, collective behavior is not irrational at all; it makes sense in light of the sentiments of the people engaged in it.

For example, a few years ago in Philadelphia, a protest crowd demonstrating against the lack of funding for AIDS research became a riot. The protest began peacefully, but when police who were called to disperse the protestors donned rubber gloves before touching them, the crowd became violent. It might seem that the protestors reacted irrationally—after all, the police used no excessive force in trying to move them—but a convergence theorist would say the violence was a predictable reaction given the collectivity's longstanding concerns about discrimination against people with AIDS fueled by myths about HIV transmission. The plastic gloves were a powerful symbol for this collectivity who shared very strong attitudes and emotions about HIV/AIDS.

Evaluating Convergence Theory. One strength of convergence theory is that it depicts people in collectivities as rational, purposeful social actors. Moreover, the idea that like-minded people tend to band together for collective behavior has common-sense appeal. But critics point out that empirical research does not identify any significant attitudinal differences between those who participate in collective behavior and those who do not (McPhail, 1991). Critics also charge that convergence theory puts too much emphasis on attitudes and emotions, while overlooking the structural conditions that give rise to collective behavior.

Emergent-Norm Theory

Sociologists Ralph Turner and Lewis Killian (1993) draw on the principles of symbolic interactionism to explain collective behavior. Their perspective, known as *emergent-norm theory*, maintains that although collective behavior often appears irrational, it is actually governed by norms just like other forms of social interaction. The difference is that the norms emerge as the behavior unfolds. As in other social situations, people try to give meaning to what is happening around them: They consciously evaluate what they see, as well as their own feelings and motivations. The norms that emerge, therefore, are a product of the collectivity's definition of the situation, which of course may change as the interaction continues.

Let's return to the AIDS protest as an example of how a collectivity defines a situation. The protestors believed the police were insulting them and, at the same time, contributing to myths about HIV/AIDS transmission. Violence was therefore perceived as a just response, although certainly it was not defined that way by the police. In fact, all the protestors may not have defined the situation similarly, but the norm that emerged prescribed violent behavior, which the collectivity then adhered to.

Evaluating Emergent-Norm Theory.

An important aspect of emergent-norm theory is its emphasis on the rationality of social actors in collectivities. It portrays the members of collectivities as conscious decision makers, rather than unthinking automatons. Moreover, it allows for differing definitions of a situation among the participants. That is, although similar attitudes or beliefs initially bring people together in a collectivity, they do not all think the same way about the activity that eventually develops or have the same reasons for participating in it. Some people participate because of a personal commitment to a particular issue, while others may not know what to do and turn to others for cues as to how to behave. When norms emerge, not everyone will support them to the same degree; there will be leaders, followers, passive observers, and perhaps even some opponents. It will be the emergent norms, however, that ultimately determine the course of action taken by most of the collectivity.

Despite these valuable contributions to our understanding of collective behavior, emergent-norm theory has been criticized on several grounds. First, some critics point out that norms do not govern all collective behavior, that spontaneous outbursts of impulsive, frenzied behavior occur that emergent-norm theory cannot explain. Participants in such situations often claim afterward that they cannot account for their behavior; they are embarrassed and bewildered, unable to explain why they behaved as they did since it was so out of character for them. An emergent-norm theorist might counter that norms were present, but these social actors simply couldn't identify or articulate them. However, that raises a second problem with this perspective: Emergent-norm theory is difficult to evaluate empirically because it does not specify precisely what constitutes a norm, the process by which norms emerge in a collectivity (apart from the vague notion that people are trying to define the situation), and how a norm gets conveyed and adopted so quickly (in some cases, almost instantaneously) by the members of a collectivity. Finally, like the other theories we have discussed so far, emergent-norm theory is criticized for not taking into account the structural conditions that give rise to collective behavior. In the example of the AIDS protestors, for instance, emergent-norm theory focuses on the situation at hand and the collectivity's reaction to it; however, to fully understand the conditions that gave rise to the violence, one must also examine outside factors, such as widespread homophobia in our society.

Smelser's Value-Added Theory

Neil Smelser (1962), one of the most prominent researchers of collective behavior, developed what he called *value-added theory* because it takes into account not only the characteristics and decision-making processes of collectivities, but also the structural factors that generate collective behavior. According to Smelser, collective behavior occurs when people try to change their environment because they are faced with uncertainty, strain, or threat; but basic conditions must be met for collective behavior to emerge:

1. *Structural conduciveness* refers to the presence of specific structural conditions. For example, residential segregation contributed to the outbreak of riots following the not-guilty verdict in the trial of police officers accused of beating Black motorist Rodney King. Had the Black population of Los Angeles been more geographically dispersed, the riots may not have happened so quickly, or at all. Or if the incident had occurred two decades earlier, it might have gone unnoticed since few people then owned portable video cameras such as the one used by a passerby who recorded King's beating.

2. *Structural strains* refers to stress-inducing social conditions that motivate people to take action to relieve the problem. The Los Angeles riots are again a good example, since they arose in response not only to the trial verdict, but more generally to the structural strains of police brutality and racism experienced by the city's Black population.

3. *Generalized belief* refers to shared ideas about the source of the problem and how to address it that are held by people experiencing structural strain. The existence of racism in Los Angeles, for instance, was not sufficient in itself to trigger the riots there. Black residents must also have developed generalized beliefs about the source of racist oppression and ways of responding to it. These beliefs, then, justified the riots.

4. *Precipitating factors* refers to a triggering event. Structural conditions and strains can be present along with generalized beliefs, but it is a specific event that ultimately triggers the collective behavior. In Los Angeles, it was the announcement of the trial verdict.

5. *Mobilization for action* refers to actions by some people that encourage others to join in. Even if a precipitating factor occurs, collective behavior will not emerge unless some people do something in response to it. In Los Angeles, the first people who took to the streets, throwing rocks, setting fires, and smashing windows, encouraged others to follow their example.

6. *Failure of social control* refers to weak or nonexistent control mechanisms that allow the emergence of collective behavior. Even if all five of the preceding conditions are present, collective behavior will not occur if some form of social control intervenes to inhibit it. The Los Angeles riots, for instance, might have been prevented if community leaders had pleaded for calm before or immediately after the announcement of the verdict. A heavy

police presence in the community might also have inhibited the rioting.

Evaluating Value-Added Theory. Smelser's perspective is more thorough than the other theories we have discussed. Rather than relying solely on micro-level factors and processes such as shared attitudes and emerging definitions, Smelser also considers macro-level factors, including structural conduciveness, structurally induced strains, and a breakdown in social control. Smelser's theory also has broader applicability than the other theories in that it explains a wider range of collective behavior. Whereas the other theories focus primarily on crowds, mobs, riots, and panics, Smelser's theory has been used to explain collective behavior in such diverse situations as self-help groups (Smith & Pillemer, 1983) and welfare organizations (Smith & Moses, 1980).

Nevertheless, Smelser's theory is criticized for continuing the emphasis on collective behavior as largely *reactive,* even though what produces the reaction involves structural conditions as much as situational interactions. Critics say that Smelser's theory needs to take better account of the role people play as initiators of social change, rather than simply as *de facto* participants venting their frustration over untenable circumstances.

Sociologists who focus on the role of people as initiators of social change usually study a special form of collective behavior, the social movement. Let's turn, then, to a discussion of social movements.

REFLECTING ON

Explaining Collective Behavior

Think of collective behavior you've participated in. In light of your experiences, which of the four theories we have discussed—contagion, convergence, emergent-norm, or value-added—do you think best explains collective behavior? Why?

SOCIAL MOVEMENTS

A **social movement** is an issue-oriented group specifically organized to bring about or prevent social change through collective action. Social movements are considered a special type of collective behavior because they differ in important ways from the other types we have discussed:

1. *Social movements endure for a significant period of time.* While the other forms of collective behavior we have discussed are usually short-lived, social movements last comparatively longer. This is not to say that once a social movement is organized, it never disbands, but rather that social movements have a considerably greater longevity than other types of collective behavior.

2. *Social movements often have long-lasting and far-reaching consequences.* Although riots and mobs can produce significant social change, most other types of collective behavior are inconsequential. Social movements, however, have a greater potential for significantly affecting society as a whole. Social movements form around major issues of public concern. Because their underlying goal is to bring about or prevent change in relation to these issues, the outcome of social movement activity can be both significant and enduring. Consider the women's movement, for example. The women's movement was instrumental in bringing larger numbers of women than ever before into the paid labor force. Today, the typical working-age woman, even if she has young children, is in the wage-labor force, a dramatic change that occurred over the course of less than thirty years and is unlikely to be undone.

3. *Social movements typically have a well-defined and high level of internal organization.* Although leaders can emerge in any type of collective behavior, the fleeting nature of most types does not allow for the development of much internal organization. A social movement, though, tends to develop an internal structure for organizing and directing activities. In fact, as we will see shortly, the internal organization of a social movement can be a critical factor in its longevity and success.

Despite these differences, social movements are like the other forms of collective behavior that we've discussed in that they occur most often in industrialized societies. Recall for a moment the characteristics of hunting and gathering societies: These societies are small, homogenous, and highly egalitarian. Decisions are reached through consensus. In short, there are too few people and no significant areas of disagreement to give rise to a social movement. Even in other types of preindustrial societies, social movements are unlikely to form, given the high value placed on tradition and the firm control that rulers have. In contrast, industrial societies have very large, geographically dispersed populations with markedly diverse backgrounds, interests, and attitudes. Subcultures and countercultures are plentiful. Moreover, the inequality that is characteristic of industrial societies generates conflict: There are those who seek a more equitable share of resources and opportunities and those who wish to preserve the status quo. It is in democratic industrialized societies that we find the greatest number of social movements, since these societies give their members considerable freedom to organize and publicly express their opinions. We cannot even begin to count, for example, the number of social movements currently active in the United States.

Types of Social Movements

Given the large number of social movements and the diverse people who join them, it is not surprising that there are different types of social movements. One widely used system of classifying social movements was developed in the 1960s by David Aberle (1966). Aberle's typology includes four types of social movements based on the type of change sought (individual versus macro level) and the amount of change sought. We'll discuss five types of social movements—reform movements, revolutionary movements, resistance movements, religious movements, and alterative movements—but retain Aberle's focus on type and amount of change sought.

Reform Movements.   A **reform movement** tries to bring about limited social change by working within the existing system. Reform movements usually target policy makers and the courts, with the purpose of influencing legislation so that it reflects their interests. Legislation is considered a tool to force people to change their behavior. Reform movements also invest considerable energy in education to raise awareness of their concerns and to persuade others to adopt their position. Education can also be a way to reject stigma and instill pride in members.

The early civil rights movement is an example of a reform movement. Through nonviolent demonstrations, such as lunch-counter sit-ins and street marches, members of the movement sought to outlaw both segregation and discrimination. They also legally challenged existing laws in the courts. Speeches by such famous civil rights leaders as Rev. Martin Luther King, Jr. advocated not wholesale replacement of the social system, but equal access to that system by people of color. Movement activities were designed to raise public awareness of the problem of discrimination and to encourage African Americans to stand up for their rights and not be ashamed of their skin color. Rev. Jesse Jackson, for instance, visited schools, teaching young children racial pride. During his inspirational talks, Jackson would ask the students to shout with him, "I *am* somebody!"

The civil rights movement, like many reform movements, won impressive legislative victories. The 1964 Civil Rights Act prohibited, among other things, employment discrimination on the basis of race, and the 1965 Voting Rights Act removed all remaining obstacles to Black voter registration, effectively enfranchising thousands of Black citizens, especially in the South. Nevertheless, these successes also speak to the major drawbacks of reform movements. Legislation and education do not necessarily change people's attitudes or behavior. As we noted in Chapter 11, for example, racial and ethnic prej-

Courageous individuals such as Rosa Parks played a major role in raising public awareness about racial discrimination in the United States in the 1950s, which fueled an emerging civil rights movement. What characteristics of a social movement were evident in the American civil rights movement? According to David Aberle's typology, which type of social movement did the civil rights movement represent? How were the outcomes of that movement characteristic of the type? What other types of social movements are there and how do they promote or thwart social change?

udice is alive and well in the United States, and many forms of discrimination, including residential segregation, persist, despite the laws.

Revolutionary Movements.   The limits of reform movements lead some members to use drastic measures to bring about sweeping social change. A **revolutionary movement** seeks to replace the existing system with a fundamentally different one. Members of revolutionary movements work outside the system to cause change, using radical—and often illegal—tactics. They target the people and places they consider the major sources and symbols of oppression. For example, revolutionaries might kidnap the political leaders of a government they consider repressive or organize a boycott of the railway system that transports products made by exploited workers.

Sometimes revolutionary movements resort to violence to achieve their goals. The evening news never seems short of reports of terrorist bombings, hijackings, hostage takings, and assassinations. Terrorists inspire fear not only because of their lethal impact, but also because they usually

In 1999, Sinn Fein leaders told the press that they could not deliver IRA disarmament. What type of social movement is represented by the ongoing threat of violence of factions of the Irish Republican Army? Are all movements of this type violent? What are some examples of how violence may become a part of any of the types of social movements described in this chapter? How would you explain the actions of the Irish Republican Army as a social movement? Which sociological theory do you think offers the best explanation: mass society theory, relative deprivation theory, resource mobilization theory, or new social movements theory?

strike with little or no warning and their victims are often innocent people. Revolutionary movements that engage in terrorism and other forms of violence today include the Irish Republican Army in Northern Ireland, the Islamic Jihad in the Middle East, and the Shining Path in Peru.

Not all revolutionary movements use terrorism or other forms of violence. The revolutionary movement for democracy in China in 1989, for example, was nonviolent, although the military, acting on behalf of the government, used violence to suppress the movement. Other examples of nonviolent revolutionary movements are *communtarian movements*, which attempt to establish a radically different society from the dominant one by forming communities based on their ideologies. Several utopian socialist communities arose in the United States in the late nineteenth century and again during the 1960s. Both times, however, the effort proved daunting and most disbanded within a relatively short period of time. One surviving example, however, is the Rainbow Family, a nomadic utopian community begun in the early 1970s in the southwestern United States, which continues to follow a communitarian philosophy of nonviolence and decision making by consensus (Niman, 1997).

Resistance Movements. A **resistance movement**, also called a **reactionary movement**, seeks to maintain the sta-

tus quo or to restore conditions that existed prior to social change. Of course, most movements trying to bring about change meet with resistance from those who believe life is better left as is. But a resistance or reactionary *movement* is different from general opposition because it is an organized effort to turn back the clock. Typically, these movements present a previous era when their values and beliefs were dominant as a "Golden Age." Their picture of the past is usually more fiction than fact, but it provides a powerful impetus for action.

Resistance movements use many of the same strategies as revolutionary movements, including violence. Consider, for example, Operation Rescue, one of the most extreme groups in the anti-abortion movement. Members of Operation Rescue have assassinated physicians and clinic workers, fire-bombed clinics, thrown bottles supposedly containing aborted fetuses at women arriving at clinics, and made threatening phone calls to physicians and their families (Sydell, 1993). Other examples of resistance movements based in the United States are the Ku Klux Klan, the White Aryan Resistance, and various militia groups. Timothy McVeigh, who was found guilty of the 1995 bombing of the Oklahoma City federal building, was an active militia member.

Religious Movements. A **religious movement**, also sometimes referred to as a **redemptive movement**, focuses more on changing individuals than social systems, but it nevertheless seeks profound change deriving from unconventional spiritual or supernatural beliefs. Members of religious movements sometimes live apart from nonmembers and devote their lives to "the cause." They usually recruit new members by proselytizing. New religious movements are also referred to as cults and include the Hare Krishnas, the Church of Scientology, and various Christian millennialists, such as the Brethren, who believe that Christ's second coming—and Armageddon or the fiery end of the world—will occur early in the twenty-first century (Heard & Klebnikov, 1998).

Alterative Movements. An **alterative movement** seeks limited change in a specific segment of society (Aberle, 1966). Because of their limited focus and goals, alterative movements rarely, if ever, threaten the existing social system. There are numerous alterative social movements in our society, reflecting the tremendous diversity of the population. For example, the feminist health care movement, which began during the 1960s, encourages women to "take charge of their health." Its activities include "know-your-body" courses in which women learn about their bodies and how to provide themselves with basic care, such as breast and pelvic self-exams (Ruzek, 1987). Mothers Against Drunk Driving is another example of an alterative movement. MADD lobbies legislators to enact stiffer penalties for people convicted of drunk dri-

TABLE 20.3 Types of Social Movements

Movement Type	Definition	Examples
Reform movement	Tries to bring about limited social change by working within the existing system	Suffrage movement, civil rights movement, disabilities rights movement
Revolutionary movement	Seeks to replace the existing system with a fundamentally different one, using radical (sometimes illegal) tactics	Irish Republican Army, prodemocracy movement in China, the Rainbow Family
Resistance movement (Reactionary movement)	Seeks to maintain the status quo or restore conditions that existed prior to social change	Operation Rescue, Ku Klux Klan
Religious movement (Redemptive movement)	Seeks to profoundly change individuals through unconventional spiritual or supernatural beliefs	Hare Krishnas, Church of Scientology, the Brethren
Alterative movement	Seeks limited change among a specific segment of a society's population	Feminist health care movement, Mothers Against Drunk Driving

ving and works to educate the public about the consequences of drunk driving.

Table 20.3 summarizes the various types of social movements we've discussed. At this point, let's look at several theories that explain how social movements emerge.

Explaining Social Movements

The features that distinguish social movements from other forms of collective behavior have caused sociologists to develop separate theories to explain them, although you may recognize ideas common to both. However, one theory—Smelser's value-added theory—can be applied to social movements as well as most of the other forms of collective behavior we discussed earlier. Since we have already presented Smelser's perspective, we will not discuss it again here. You may want to review value-added theory in light of what you learned about social movements. Now let's turn to four other theories: mass society theory, relative deprivation theory, resource mobilization theory, and new social movements theory.

Mass Society Theory.   Mass society theory was developed in the 1950s by William Kornhauser (1959), who argued that social movements are an outgrowth of the anonymity and alienation fostered by large, complex societies that he called "mass societies." According to Kornhauser, the people who are most likely to join social movements are those who feel socially isolated and belong to few social networks. After all, maintained Kornhauser, the individual who is well integrated into the society, with many social contacts, would be satisfied with life and not want to change it.

Evaluating Mass Society Theory.   Kornhauser's point that the alienation generated by life in a large, complex society can lead to the emergence of social movements is well taken. However, critics of mass society theory say that instead of systematically analyzing the causes and consequences of alienation, Kornhauser focuses on individual social psychology. In other words, Kornhauser emphasizes the personal, rather than the political aspects of social movements. Some critics, in fact, take offense at his characterization of movement members as social misfits, and point out that most empirical research doesn't support such a profile (see, for example, McAdam, 1989; Sears & McConahay, 1973).

Relative Deprivation Theory.   According to relative deprivation theory, social movements develop when people feel deprived in some fundamental way. They do not have enough money or food to survive, for example, or they are denied basic political rights, such as the right to vote or the right to voice dissenting opinions. These people organize a social movement to try to change the situation so it is more equitable (Rose, 1982).

The idea that deprivation leads to the formation of social movements seems to make sense, but relative deprivation theorists add another twist to their argument. They say that what people consider deprivation is relative. In other words, **relative deprivation** is an individual's or group's perception that they are disadvantaged compared to those they use as their reference group. Interestingly, then, the theory holds that by objective standards, the members of a social movement may not appear severely deprived. In fact, movements are most likely to emerge when a period of decline follows a period of increasing prosperity, since such circumstances lead people to expect a better life, but these rising expectations end up being unfulfilled (Davies, 1962).

Evaluating Relative Deprivation Theory.

Relative deprivation helps explain why some people, who by objective measures should be satisfied with their circumstances, join movements to bring about social change. For example, during the past thirty years, the women's movement has been dominated by White, middle- and upper-class women. To some observers, including poor women and women of color, these women seem highly privileged, but their personal perception is that they are oppressed by sexism. To a poor woman, not being admitted to an all-male dining club is irrelevant as she struggles simply to feed her family. Her experience of deprivation is absolute. But to an upper-middle class professional woman striving to rise to the highest level of her corporation, being shut out of the dining club because of her sex is a disadvantage. Her experience of deprivation is relative. Some feminist sociologists point out that these dramatically different concerns help explain why the women's movement is often viewed as a White, middle-class women's movement (Hood, 1984; King, 1988).

Still, relative deprivation theory is criticized on several grounds. For one thing, it doesn't explain why some people who experience relative deprivation still do not join a social movement. In addition, empirical research on the roles of various factors in motivating people to join social movements shows that relative deprivation often plays no part at all. The strongest predictors that a person will become involved in a movement appear to be previous activism, having friends and family who are involved, and "moral shocks," visual and verbal messages that convey the scope and seriousness of a problem the movement addresses (Jasper & Poulsen, 1995; Ohlemacher, 1996).

Resource Mobilization Theory.

Resource mobilization theory takes into account the factors researchers have identified as the best predictors of social movement involvement. Resource mobilization theorists refer to these factors as resources. Previous activism translates into resources in the form of experience and skills. Involved friends and family are human resources. And communicating verbal and visual images depends on access to such resources as the media, computers, copiers, fax machines and, perhaps the most important resource of all, money. Another vital resource identified by resource mobilization theorists is support from people outside the movement. The support of sympathetic outsiders is particularly important for social movements mostly composed of people who are economically or socially disadvantaged. Research also shows that social movements connected to traditional segments of a community or society enjoy greater success (Breyman, 1998; Mesch & Schwirian, 1996; Ohlemacher, 1996; Tarrow, 1994).

In short, resource mobilization theory maintains that no matter how deprived people feel, there can be no social movement without essential resources. The ability to mobilize resources is critical to the success of any social movement. And if the opposition to the movement has greater resources—such as the military personnel and weapons mobilized by the Chinese government against the prodemocracy student movement in 1989—the movement is also likely to fail.

Evaluating Resource Mobilization Theory.

The fundamental message of resource mobilization theory is that it takes more than emotional commitment to build a social movement. It takes different kinds of resources, including outsiders who can add legitimacy to the movement and may have access to valuable resources not available to members.

Critics, however, point out that resource mobilization theory doesn't account for the success of social movements that have minimal resources. Sometimes, groups with relatively few resources accomplish a great deal if they are well organized and can draw on the intense emotional commitment of their members. In rural Louisiana, for example, residents of two small, poor communities of color successfully joined together to prevent the building of a uranium processing facility in their area. They had little in the way of financial resources, but they had a firm commitment to their cause. They also enlisted the assistance of national environmental organizations, including Greenpeace and the Sierra Club, as well as prominent civil rights leaders ("United They Stand," 1997).

A second criticism of resource mobilization theory is that it gives too much credit to elite outsiders. In many cases, critics maintain, the support of the privileged for the causes of the disadvantaged is equivocal at best. In the Louisiana case, for example, several relatively affluent White people from a nearby community also opposed building the uranium processing plant, but their support did not offset the harassment and threats of violence from the larger White community that wanted the facility ("United They Stand," 1997).

New Social Movements Theory.

The most recent social movement theory focuses on how social movements today differ from movements of the past (Laraña et al., 1994; Pichardo, 1997). According to *new social movements theory,* social movements in societies on the brink of postindustrialism differ in three significant ways from movements of earlier periods.

First, whereas earlier social movements were often locally based with relatively few reaching a national level, the new social movements are not only national, but international. Two examples are the human rights movement and the environmental movement. Both recognize the multinational causes and global effects of the problems they address. Their global reach is greatly enhanced, too,

Which type of social movement does the women's health care movement represent? What have been some outcomes? How might the women's health care movement be understood in terms of the four theories of social movements presented in this chapter? In what ways might the women's health care movement change as it is carried forward into the twenty-first century?

by postindustrial technology such as the Internet, which makes it possible to communicate important information and mobilize members throughout the world more quickly and less expensively than by telephone or mail (Harmon, 1998; Herszenhorn, 1995).

A second difference between earlier movements and new social movements is that the former tended to focus mainly on economic problems, whereas the latter are more concerned with cultural and political issues and problems affecting social and physical well-being (Melucci, 1996). Amnesty International, for instance, works to free political prisoners, end torture, and abolish the death penalty worldwide.

A final difference between earlier movements and new social movements involves their constituencies. While earlier social movements attracted members primarily from economically disadvantaged groups, the new social movements appeal more to members of the middle and upper classes. We have already mentioned the women's movement as one example. Other examples include the gay rights movement, the animal rights movement and the environmental or "green" movement (Breyman, 1998; Kriesi et al., 1995).

Evaluating New Social Movements Theory. New social movements theorists' emphasis on the globalization of social problems, and their efforts to address them provide an important contribution to our understanding of how movements change over time in response to changing structural conditions. Critics, however, say that this perspective overstates the differences between earlier movements and contemporary ones (Pichardo, 1997; Scott, 1990). For instance, although international in scope, many new social movements are most successful because of involvement at the local level. Moreover, many of the problems that the new social movements address have

economic roots or connections. Animal rights activists, for example, oppose the fur trade and the use of animals by corporations testing new products, issues that are tied to economics and international commerce. Some critics also point out that while these movements may claim to focus on universal goals to improve social and physical well-being, the benefits they seek are often economic and class-based (Pichardo, 1997; Rose, 1997).

Although sociologists may explain the emergence of social movements differently, they tend to agree that all movements develop in much the same way. To conclude this section, then, let's briefly examine the developmental stages of social movements.

The Life Course of a Social Movement

Sociologists who study social movements have identified four developmental stages in a social movement. We can think of these developmental stages as the life course of the movement. The four stages are:

1. *Emergence.* In the initial stage, people begin expressing their dissatisfaction with existing conditions. They recognize that the problem concerning them is not private or individual, but public and shared by others. From this recognition, leaders step forward to encourage collective action to bring about change.

2. *Coalescence.* The focus of the second stage is on building the movement. Important decisions must be made during this stage: How will the movement be organized? What is the movement's official mission? What do movement members consider acceptable strategies for achieving their goals? How will new members be recruited? Who are potential movement allies, and who are the movement's

opponents? It is also during this stage that members begin raising public awareness of the problem that concerns them. They may do this in various ways, such as holding a press conference or a demonstration, doing a mass mailing, or handing out flyers in public places.

3. *Institutionalization.* The third stage is also sometimes called *bureaucratization* because the movement develops an organizational structure that has many elements of a bureaucracy. For instance, a membership hierarchy develops, with paid staff replacing volunteers in most positions. Paid staff have greater authority and command more respect than volunteers. The activities of the movement become routinized, which can diminish the enthusiasm of some members. In fact, as the structure of the movement becomes more like the structure of any large organization, some early supporters may withdraw, or form or join another movement that retains some of the ideals they feel were lost as a result of institutionalization.

4. *Decline.* Most movements eventually experience decline. Some disappear completely, while others simply weaken, becoming less visible or vocal. Ironically, one factor contributing to decline is success. As the movement achieves its goals, members may become content and no longer see the need for change. Other reasons for decline are that the movement may run out of money, or internal conflicts and power struggles may diminish members' ability and willingness to stay focused on the movement's goals. Each of these factors, for example, is thought to have contributed to the decline of the international environmental organization, Greenpeace. First, the problem for which the movement became known, "Save the Whales," has largely been solved. Second, membership and donations dropped dramatically. Third, the movement experienced internal conflict over what its new mission should be. Consequently, in 1997 Greenpeace began closing all ten of its U.S. branch offices and laying off 335 of its 400 staff members (Goldberg, 1997).

As some social movements decline, others are in the early stages of development. What role will social movements play in our future? Let's conclude the text by addressing this question.

REFLECTING ON

Social Movements

1. Have you ever participated in a social movement? If so, what kind? Are you still involved? If so, why? If not, what were your main reasons for dropping out?

2. Each of the theories we discussed accounts for some aspects of social movements, but overlooks or inaccurately portrays others. Can you think of a way to synthesize these perspectives into a single, comprehensive theory? If you don't believe such a synthesis is possible, explain your rationale.

SOCIAL MOVEMENTS, SOCIAL CHANGE, AND OUR FUTURE

Some of the most profound changes in our society have been brought about by the collective action of social movements. Indeed, the collective behavior of colonists protesting British rule in the 1700s—from the riots triggered by the Boston Tea Party to the declaration of independence on July 4, 1776 that remains cause for celebration today—led to the very birth of our country. In recent years, we have witnessed the birth or rebirth and demise of other societies through collective efforts of segments of their populations. The actions of crowds, mobs, and social movements, for example, played a major role in the division of the former Yugloslavia into five new societies. Social movements were also instrumental in bringing about the collapse of communism in the former Soviet Union and Eastern Europe and the end of the Cold War. The example that opened this chapter—the end of apartheid and the beginning of Black rule in South Africa—marks the success of such revolutionary movements as the African National Congress (ANC).

Of course, whether one cheers the members of these collectivities as freedom fighters or denounces them as fools or traitors depends to a large extent on whether one gained or lost through the conflict. Labeling collective behavior as "good" or "bad" nearly always has a political dimension to it. What is clear, however, is that ordinary people cannot create the society they desire without acting collectively. Frederick Douglass, who grew up in slavery and became a famous antiracism activist, recognized this fact more than a hundred years ago when he said:

> Those who profess to favor freedom, and yet deprecate agitation, are [people] who want crops without plowing up the ground. They want rain without thunder and lightning. They want the ocean without the awful roar of its many waters. This struggle may be a moral one; or it may be a physical one; or it may be both moral and physical; but it must be a struggle. Power concedes nothing without a demand. It never did and it never will.

DOING SOCIOLOGY

Shaping the Future: What Part Will You Play?

College students have a long history of activism in social movements. During the 1950s and early 1960s, for example, college students participated in the civil rights movement, particularly in the Deep South, where they helped organize sit-ins at segregated facilities and registered Black voters. Later in the 1960s and into the 1970s, students staged rallies and demonstrations to protest U.S. involvement in what they judged to be an unjust war in Southeast Asia (Zaroulis & Sullivan, 1984).

Today, students continue to organize and collectively act to address pressing social issues, such as homelessness, environmental conservation, and human rights. Many join social movements to improve conditions for various disadvantaged groups (Herszenhorn, 1995; Zane, 1992). In fact, despite all the talk about student apathy, national surveys show that a majority of college freshmen (over 60 percent) consider it essential or very important to help people who are in difficulty, and that the number who feel it is essential or very important to influence social values has been growing in recent years (*Chronicle of Higher Education*, 1991). Based on these findings, we feel we can predict with some confidence that students who feel strongly about particular social issues today will join social movements that work to address those concerns in the future.

How committed to social activism is the student body on your campus? Ask a sample of your peers if they are currently involved in any social movement activities. Ask them, too, whether they see personal participation in social movements essential or very important for shaping the future. And finally, ask them what it would take for them to get involved in a social movement. Before you compile your results, however, ask yourself these same questions and take some time to reflect on how you can make a difference in shaping the future of our society.

What are the implications of Douglass's words as we begin the twenty-first century? What part will social movements and other forms of collective behavior play? As our own society grows increasingly diverse and inequality remains a feature of social life, differing beliefs and value systems and differential access to resources and opportunities will no doubt continue to cause conflict. Social movements and other forms of collective behavior will therefore be important for voicing concerns and taking action to address our social problems (see the Doing Sociology box). Given that the problems of our society are inextricably connected to the problems of other societies, social movements and other types of collective behavior will have to grow more international in scope. Computers and other telecommunications technology are already breaking down national barriers, but we must keep in mind that the unequal distribution of this technology can, in fact, widen the gap between developed and undeveloped societies as well as between groups in these societies.

One question remains: What part will *you* play in shaping the future? There is an old adage that says knowledge is power. But that's only true if knowledge serves as the basis for action. That is, after all, how we *live* sociology. Our goal in this text has not been to convert you to a particular point of view, but to equip you with usable knowledge for evaluating diverse views and making decisions about how you want to help shape the world. Our future depends largely on our willingness as members of a global community to become actively involved today in collectively building a better world.

 For useful resources for study and review, run Chapter 20 on your *Living Sociology* CD-ROM.

CONNECTIONS

Conflict perspective on social change	Review the discussions of Marx's predictions for capitalist societies in the sections on "Industrial Societies" in Chapter 3, "Explaining Stratification" in Chapter 8, and "Types of Economic Systems" in Chapter 13. Which *type* of social movement and which *theory* of social movements described in Chapter 20 might best apply to Marx's prediction of a communist revolution?

CONNECTIONS

Social change and population	Review the discussion of population changes such as population growth and migration in Chapter 19. What specific examples can you find of demographic factors that lead to social change? Also review the discussion of the aging of the U.S. and world populations in Chapter 12. In what ways might the demographic factor of aging act as a source of social change?
Social change and environment	Review the discussion of the natural environment in Chaper 19. In each case, how might acid rain, ozone depletion, the greenhouse effect, toxic waste, and energy crises act as sources of social change?
Cultural change	Review the discussion in Chapter 4 on the types of cultural change. What are some other specific examples of cultural lag, invention, and diffusion as sources of social change? For instance, what social and cultural changes do you predict for the Internet? What are some elements of culture other than technology that are affected by social change?
Conflict and social change	Review Chapter 14 on politics and government. What are some specific examples of sources of conflict described in that chapter that led to social change? What examples can you find in Chapters 10 and 11 of group conflict as a source of social change?
Collective behavior	Review the information in Chapters 6 and 7 on people's behavior in groups. How do conformity and deviance relate to the study of collective behavior? What group dynamics are evident in collectives such as crowds and riots? How might group size be a factor in panics and rumors?
Charles Horton Cooley	Review Chapter 5 on socialization and the contributions of symbolic interactionists to the study of people's learned social behavior. In what sense are rumor and gossip and public opinion "agents" of socialization? How is collective behavior an extension of Cooley's concept of the looking-glass self?
Fashions and fads	Review the discussion in Chapter 7 of youth gangs as subcultures. What role do fashions and fads play in youth subcultures? What specific examples can you find of sociologist Georg Simmel's observation that people use fashion both to be unique and to fit in? Also review the information in Chapter 5 on identity development. How can fashions and fads contribute to individual identity development across the lifespan?
Theories of collective behavior	What examples of collective behavior can you identify in Chapter 14? Which theory of collective behavior described in Chapter 20 best explains these examples? For instance, which theory of collective behavior do you think best explains voting in an election, participating in a labor union strike, and marching on Washington in a protest for animal rights?
Smelser's value-added theory	How does the discussion of Merton's strain theory in Chapter 7 relate to the discussion of Smelser's value-added theory in Chapter 20?
Minorities and social movements	Review Chapters 10, 11, and 12. What specific examples can you find of each of the types of social movements described in Chapter 20? Which theory of social movements do you think best explains each example?
Religion and social movements	Review Chapter 17. In what sense can it be said that all the world's great religions began as redemptive social movements?
Institutionalization of social movements	Review the discussion of bureaucracies in Chapter 6 in the section on formal organizations. What are the benefits and dangers of bureaucratization in the life course of a social movement?

1. Social change is the transformation of culture, social structure, and social behavior over time. It is a consistent feature of social life, although it occurs at different rates in different societies, with industrial societies changing at a much faster rate than preindustrial societies. In addition, some social changes have a more significant and long-lasting effect than others.

Theories of Social Change

1. Most sociologists use one of two theoretical models—structural functionalism and conflict theory—to explain how and why social change takes place. Some structural functionalist perspectives describe social changes in terms of evolution—that is, societies change slowly and only when it is necessary and adaptive for them to change. More recent functionalist theories take into account different types and rates of change as well as the fact that change can sometimes be dysfunctional. Critics of evolutionary functionalist perspectives see them as ethnocentric. More recent functionalist perspectives are criticized for not fully analyzing the dysfunctional outcomes of social change. Finally, functionalist perspectives are criticized for downplaying the role of organized efforts to create change by members of a society.

2. Conflict theory sees social change as a built-in feature of social life, which grows out of the conflicts between competing groups in society. Although conflict theorists recognize many sources of social change, they pay particular attention to the human role in social change. They also examine how change impacts different groups in different ways. Conflict theory is criticized for focusing almost exclusively on economic conflict as a source of change, while neglecting other conflicts, such as those based on racial and ethnic, religious, and gender differences.

Sources of Social Change

1. Social change can be caused by fluctuations in population, including fertility and mortality rates, changes in population composition, and migration; changes in the natural environment, including natural disasters and changes caused by human intervention; elements of culture, especially discoveries, inventions, and diffusion; and social conflict, including conflict between societies as well as in a society.

Collective Behavior

1. Collective behavior is voluntary activity, often spontaneous and goal-oriented, by a large number of people who are typically violating dominant norms and values. Collective behavior is sometimes difficult to study because it encompasses a wide range of behavior, it is short-lived, and it is sometimes unstructured.

2. A collectivity differs from a social group because it is temporary and sometimes involves no face-to-face interaction; members usually do not share a common identity deriving from membership; and norms are weak. There are two types of collectivities: localized collectivities, which involve activity by people in close physical proximity to one another; and dispersed collectivities, which involve activity by people who are geographically spread out, often across great distances. Localized collectivities include crowds, mobs and riots, and panics and hysteria. Dispersed collectivities include rumor and gossip, public opinion, and fashions and fads.

3. A crowd is a temporary gathering of people with a common focal point who exercise influence over one another. There are five types of crowds: casual crowds, conventional crowds, expressive crowds, acting crowds, and protest crowds. Crowds can change from one type to another relatively quickly during the course of an event.

4. A mob is an intensely emotional crowd set on doing violence to specific others or property. Mobs are short-lived, but they often do not disperse unless they have at least partially accomplished their goals or have been suppressed by social control agents. A riot is also an intensely emotional crowd, but its violent behavior is not purposefully directed. Riots erupt when a triggering incident ignites a crowd's emotions and they lash out in frenzied, seemingly unfocused violence and destruction.

5. A panic occurs when people who are confronted with a crisis or serious threat respond in irrational ways that actually can worsen their situation. Hysteria occurs when people react with fear and irrational behavior to an imagined or real event that has been misinterpreted or distorted.

6. Rumor is information transmitted among people, usually informally and from unconfirmed sources. It may be true or false, but typically as it spreads, it becomes a little of both because in the telling and retelling, distortions, omissions, and embellishments frequently occur. Gossip is rumors about individuals' personal lives. Like many rumors, once gossip is spread, it is often difficult to retract even in the face of factual information to discredit it.

7. Public opinion consists of the attitudes expressed by members of a society or those selected to represent them. There are actually many publics, differing in terms of a number of social locating variables. Public opinion, then, is rarely unified, and it also changes over time. Public opinion may be influenced by many factors, including current events and opinion makers. Opinion makers may use propaganda to influence public opinion.

8. Fashion refers to currently favored styles of appearance or behavior. Fashions are short-lived and express people's contradictory need to be unique, but also to fit into a group. A fad is more temporary than a fashion and at least mildly unconventional. Fads have tremendous mass appeal and catch on very quickly, but they tend to disappear just as fast. Both fashions and fads are found primarily in economically developed societies. Although people of all ages usually pay attention to fashions, fads appeal most to young people as they try to distinguish themselves from their elders and establish a distinctive identity.

Explaining Collective Behavior

1. Contagion theory, first developed by Le Bon and later modified by Blumer, emphasizes the emotional nature of collective behavior. Le Bon argued that when people congregate in large numbers, a collective mind develops that releases them from inhibitions and causes them to behave irrationally. Blumer and other sociologists rejected the notion of the collective mind, but Blumer used the concept of circular reaction to explain how if just a few members of a crowd become agitated or excited, they can incite the same feelings in others, who then reinforce the feeling in the original actors, causing emotions to spiral out of control. Contagion theories are criticized for being too descriptive and for a lack of empirical evidence to support them.

2. Convergence theory holds that collective behavior is a way for like-minded people to express their common attitudes and beliefs. Although convergence theory depicts people in collectivities as rational, purposeful social actors, critics point out that it overlooks structural conditions that give rise to collective behavior and lacks empirical evidence to support it.

3. Emergent-norm theory maintains that collective behavior is governed by norms just like other forms of social interaction, but these norms emerge as people in collectivities try to give meaning to what's happening around them. Emergent-norm theory makes valuable contributions to our understanding of collective behavior, but it has been criticized because norms do not govern all incidents of collective behavior and the theory is difficult to test empirically. Moreover, emergent-norm theory emphasizes reaction to circumstances, downplaying structural conditions that contribute to the emergence of collective behavior.

4. Smelser's value-added theory takes into account characteristics and decision-making processes of collectivities as well as structural factors that generate collective behavior. Collective behavior occurs when people try to change their environment because they are faced with uncertainty, strain, or threat. Six conditions must be met for collective behavior to emerge: structural conduciveness, structural strains, generalized belief, precipitating factors, mobilization for action, and failure of social control. Smelser's theory is criticized for continuing to emphasize the reactive nature of collective behavior, instead of focusing on people as initiators of social change.

Social Movements

1. A social movement is an issue-oriented group purposefully organized to bring about or prevent social change through collective action. Social movements differ from other types of collective behavior in three ways: They endure for a significant period of time, they have long-lasting and far-reaching consequences, and they typically have a well-defined and high level of internal organization. Like other forms of collective behavior, though, social movements are prevalent in industrialized societies.

2. There are five types of social movements: reform movements, which try to bring about limited social change by working within the existing system; revolutionary movements, which seek to replace the existing system with a fundamentally different one using radical (and sometimes illegal) tactics; resistance or reactionary movements, which try to maintain the status quo or restore conditions that existed prior to social change; religious movements, which focus on changing individuals rather than social systems through typically unconventional spiritual or supernatural beliefs; and alterative movements, which seek limited change among a specific segment of the society's population.

3. Sociologists have developed several theories to explain social movements. One is Smelser's value-added theory discussed earlier. Another theory is Kornhauser's mass society theory developed in the 1950s, which argues that social movements attract people who feel socially isolated because of the anonymity and alienation fostered by mass societies. Mass society theory has been criticized for its negative view of social movement members and for its emphasis on personal over political sources of social movements.

4. Relative deprivation theory maintains that social movements develop when people feel disadvantaged when they compare themselves with others whom they use as a reference group. This theory predicts that social movements are most likely to emerge when a period of decline follows a period of increasing prosperity because such circumstances lead people to expect a better life, and their rising expectations end up being unfulfilled. Relative deprivation is helpful in explaining why some people, who by objective measures should be satisfied with their circumstances, join social movements. The theory is criticized because it doesn't explain why some people who experience relative deprivation do not join social movements. In addition, empirical research has not found relative deprivation to be a good predictor of involvement in social movements.

5. Resource mobilization theory maintains that there can be no social movement unless essential resources, including support from sympathetic outsiders, are acquired. The ability to mobilize resources is critical to the success of any social movement. Critics of this theory point out that it cannot account for the success of social movements with minimal resources, and it gives too much credit to elite outsiders in terms of their support of movements for social change.

6. New social movements theory focuses on how social movements today differ from movements of earlier periods. New social movements are national and international in scope; focus less on economic problems and more on cultural and political issues as well as problems affecting social and physical well-being; and attract members mostly from the middle- and upper-middle classes. Critics of new social movements theory maintain that this perspective overstates the differences between earlier and new social movements, and also downplays the fact that many of the problems that new social movements address have economic roots or connections.

7. Social movements pass through four developmental stages: emergence, coalescence, institutionalization (bureaucratization), and decline.

KEY PEOPLE AND CONCEPTS

acting crowd: an emotion-charged crowd that forms spontaneously for one intense purpose

alterative movement: a social movement that seeks limited change among a specific segment of a society's population

casual crowd: a crowd that forms spontaneously around a specific incident, but the people involved engage in little, if any, interaction with one another

collective behavior: voluntary activity, often spontaneous and goal-oriented, by a large number of people who are typically violating dominant norms and values with their behavior

collectivity: a large number of people engaged in limited interaction guided by weak or unconventional norms

conventional crowd: a planned gathering that comes together for a special event

crowd: a temporary gathering of people with a common focal point who exercise influence over one another

dispersed collectivity: activity by people who are not in close physical proximity, but who affect one another nevertheless

expressive crowd: a crowd that gathers for an event that is considered highly emotional or exciting

fad: an object or behavior that is at least mildly unconventional, with tremendous mass appeal that catches on and disappears quickly

fashion: currently favored styles of appearance or behavior

gossip: rumor about individuals' personal lives

hysteria: a form of collective behavior in which people respond fearfully and irrationally to either an imagined or real event that has been misinterpreted or distorted

localized collectivity: activity by people who are in close physical proximity to one another

mob: an intensely emotional crowd set on doing violence to specific others or property

panic: a form of collective behavior that emerges when people who are confronted with a crisis or serious threat respond in irrational ways that actually worsen their situation

propaganda: information designed to persuade people to adopt a particular opinion on a specific issue

protest crowd: a crowd that gathers purposely to express dissatisfaction with particular conditions or events

public opinion: the attitudes expressed by members of a society, or those selected to represent them

reform movement: a social movement that tries to bring about limited social change by working within the existing system

relative deprivation: the perception by an individual or group that they are disadvantaged compared with others whom they use as their reference group

religious movement (redemptive movement): a social movement that seeks to bring about profound change in individuals based on unconventional spiritual or supernatural beliefs

resistance movement (reactionary movement): a social movement that seeks to maintain the status quo or to restore conditions that existed prior to social change

revolutionary movement: a social movement that seeks to replace the existing system with a fundamentally different one, often by using radical (and sometimes illegal) tactics

riot: an intensely emotional crowd whose violent behavior is not purposefully directed

rumor: information transmitted among people, usually informally and from unconfirmed sources

social change: the transformation of culture, social structure, and social behavior over time

social movement: an issue-oriented group purposefully organized to bring about or prevent social change

LEARNING MORE

Breyman, S. (1998). *Movement genesis: Social movement theory and the 1980s West German peace movement.* Boulder, CO: Westview. An interesting test of new social movements theory in a study of West German citizens' activism to prevent the placement by NATO of intermediate-range nuclear missles in western Europe.

DeFronzo, J. (1991). *Revolutions and revolutionary movements.* Boulder, CO: Westview. A well-written and balanced evaluation of theories of social change through the use of case studies of revolutions in Russia, China, Vietnam, Cuba, Nicaragua, and Iran, and revolutionary movements in South Africa.

Erikson, K. T. (1976). *Everything in its path.* New York: Plenum. A now-classic study of how a disaster can bring about significant social change. Erikson analyzes the effects of the 1972 flood of Buffalo Creek, West Virginia, on the residents of the community.

McPhail, C. (1994). *Acting together: The social organization of crowds.* Hawthorne, NY: Aldine de Gruyter. A thorough discussion of crowd research that also evaluates theories of crowd behavior and draws on many interesting and insightful examples.

References

Abelson, R. (1996, February 11). Tax reformers, take your mark. *New York Times*, pp. F1, F12.

Abelson, R. (1998, November 2). Part-time work for some adds up to full-time job. *New York Times*, pp. A1, A18.

Aberle, D. F. (1966). *The peyote religion among the Navaho*. Chicago: Aldine.

Abramson, J. (1998, December 6). By any name, it's still c.a.s.h. *New York Times*, p. WK4.

Abzug, B. (1984). *Gender gap*. Boston: Houghton Mifflin.

Acharya, A. (1995). Tropical forests vanishing. In L. R. Brown, N. Lenssen, & H. Kane (Eds.), *Vital signs, 1995* (pp. 116–117). New York: W. W. Norton.

Achenbaum, W. A. (1985). Societal perceptions of aging and the aged. In R. H. Binstock & E. Shanas (Eds.), *Handbook of aging and the social sciences* (pp. 129–148). New York: Van Nostrand Reinhold.

Achenbaum, W. A. (1991). Putting ADEA into historical context. *Research on Aging, 13*, 463–469.

Adler, F. (1975). *Sisters in crime*. New York: McGraw-Hill.

Adler, P. A., & Adler, P. (1998). *Peer power: Preadolescent culture and identity*. New Brunswick, NJ: Rutgers University Press.

Adorno, T. W., Frenkel-Brunswik, E., Levinson, D. J., & Sanford, R. N. (1950). *The authoritarian personality*. New York: Harper and Row.

Agnew, R., & Peterson, D. M. (1989). Leisure and delinquency. *Social Problems, 36*, 332–350.

Akers, R. L. (1968). Problems in the sociology of deviance: Social definitions and behavior. *Social Forces, 46*, 455–465.

Alba, R. (1985). *Italian Americans*. Englewood Cliffs, NJ: Prentice-Hall.

Aldag, R. J., & Fuller, S. R. (1993). Beyond fiasco: A reappraisal of the groupthink phenomenon and a new model of group decision processes. *Psychological Bulletin, 113*, 533–552.

Alexander, J. C., & Colomy, P. (1990). *Differentiation theory and social change*. New York: Columbia University Press.

Alfino, M., Caputo, J. S., & Wynyard, R. (Eds.) (1998). *McDonaldization revisited: Critical essays on consumer culture*. New York: Praeger.

Allen, L. S., & Gorski, R. A. (1992). Sexual orientation and the size of the anterior commissure of the human brain. *Proceedings of the National Academy of Sciences, 89*, 7199–7202.

Allport, G., & Postman, L. (1947). *The psychology of rumor*. New York: Holt.

A look at voting patterns of 115 demographic groups in House races. (1998, November 9). *New York Times*, p. A20.

Altman, I., & Ginat, J. (1996). *Polygamous families in contemporary society*. New York: Cambridge University Press.

Altman, L. K. (1996, November 28). U.N. reports 3 million new HIV cases worldwide for '96. *New York Times*, p. A10.

Altman, L. K. (1997, February 28). U.S. reporting sharp decrease in AIDS deaths. *New York Times*, pp. A1, A24.

Altman, L. K. (1998, November 24). Dismaying experts, HIV infections soar. *New York Times*, p. F7.

Alvarez, L. (1995, October 1). Interpreting new worlds for parents. *New York Times*, pp. 29, 36.

Amato, P. (1994). Life-span adjustment of children to their parents' divorce. *The Future of Children: Children and Divorce, 1*, 149–152.

American Association of Retired Persons (AARP). (1998). *Aging everywhere*. Washington, DC: Author.

American Association of University Women (AAUW). (1992). *How schools shortchange girls*. Washington, DC: AAUW Educational Foundation.

American Council on Education. (1994). *Minorities in higher education*. Washington, DC: Author.

American Council on Education. (1998). *Minorities in higher education*. Washington, DC: Author.

American Friends Service Committee (1985, March-April). *World hunger actionletter*.

American Psychiatric Association (1995). Practice guidelines for psychiatric evaluation of adults. *Supplement to the American Journal of Psychiatry, 11*, 65–80.

Ames, L. J., Atchinson, A. N., & Rose, D. T. (1992, August). *Love, lust, and fear: Safe sex decision making among gay men*. Paper presented at the Annual Meeting of the American Sociological Association, Pittsburgh, PA.

Ammerman, N. T. (1991). North American Protestant fundamentalism. In M. E. Marty & R. S. Appleby (Eds.), *Fundamentalisms observed* (pp. 1–65). Chicago: University of Chicago Press.

Amnesty International. (1991). *Women on the front lines*. New York: Author.

Amott, T. L., & Matthaei, J. A. (1991). *Race, gender, and work*. Boston: South End Press.

Anastas, J. W. (1998). Working against discrimination: Gay, lesbian, and bisexual people on the job. *Journal of Gay and Lesbian Social Services*, 83–98.

Andersen, M. L., & Renzetti, C. M. (1980). Rape crisis counseling and the culture of individualism. *Contemporary Crises, 4*, 323–339.

Anderson, S. R., & Hopkins, P. (1991). *The feminine face of God*. New York: Bantam.

Andrews, L. B. (1989). Alternative modes of reproduction. In S. Cohen & N. Taub (Eds.), *Reproductive laws for the 1990s* (pp. 361–403). Clifton, NJ: Humana Press.

Angier, N. (1996, January 2). Variant gene tied to a love of new thrills. *New York Times*, pp. A1, B11.

Angier, N. (1997, April 3). Survey of scientists finds a stability of faith in God. *New York Times*, p. A14.

Annenberg CPB Collection. (1989). *Against all odds: Inside statistics. #14, Samples and surveys*. (Videotape). Available from Intellimotion, Santa Barbara, CA.

Appelbaum, R. P., & Gereffi, G. (1994). Points of profit in the garment commodity chain. In E. Bonacich et al. (Eds.), *Global production* (pp. 42–62). Philadelphia: Temple University Press.

Applebome, P. (1991, March 16). Victory in Gulf a boon for military recruiters. *New York Times*, p. 9.

Applebome, P. (1996a, March 3). Shootings at schools prompt new concerns about violence. *New York Times*, p. 12.

Applebome, P. (1996b, November 21). Americans straddle "average" mark in math and science. *New York Times*, p. B14.

Applebome, P. (1997, April 8). Schools see re-emergence of "separate but equal." *New York Times*, p. A10.

Applebome, P. (1997a, May 4). Tests, too, have their failings. *New York Times*, p. E4.

Applebome, P. (1997b, May 4). U.S. pupils score high on science facts but falter on reasoning. *New York Times*, p. 36.

A progress report on reform. (1998, September/October). *Global Aging Report*, p. 4.

Archer, D. (1985). Social deviance. In G. Lindsey & E. Aronson (Eds.), *Handbook of social psychology* (pp. 743–804). New York: Random House.

Archibold, R. C. (1998, March 16). Charter schools said to raise pupils' performance on tests. *New York Times*, p. A10.

Arenson, K. W. (1996, September 26). College tuition rates show steady growth, report says. *New York Times*, p. A18.

Arenson, K. W. (1998, November 11). Questions about future of those many Ph.D.'s. *New York Times*, p. B14.

Aries, P. (1965). *Centuries of childhood: A social history of family life*. New York: Knopf.

Aronson, E., & Gonzalez, A. (1988). Desegregation, jigsaw, and the Mexican-American experience. In P. A. Katz & D. A. Taylor (Eds.), *Eliminating racism* (pp. 301–314). New York: Plenum.

Asch, A. (1989). Reproductive technology and disability. In S. Cohen & N. Taub (Eds.), *Reproductive laws for the 1990s* (pp. 69–124). Clifton, NJ: Humana Press.

Asch, S. E. (1955, November). Opinions and social pressure. *Scientific American*, 31–35.

Asimov, E. (1997, September 14). Close your eyes. Hold your nose. It's dinner time. *New York Times*, p. 12WK.

Associated Press. (1991, November 20). 397 earn at least $200,000, pay no taxes.

At leisure: Americans' use of down time. (1993, May 9). *New York Times*, p. E2.

Attie, I., & Brooks-Gunn, J. (1987). Weight concerns as chronic stressors in women. In R. C. Barnett, L. Biener, & G. K. Baruch (Eds.), *Gender and stress* (pp. 218–254). New York: Free Press.

Aulette, J. R. (1994). *Changing families*. Belmont, CA: Wadsworth.

Axtell, R. E. (1991). *Gestures: The do's and taboos of body language around the world*. New York: Wiley.

Ayella, M. (1993). "They must be crazy": Some of the difficulties in researching "cults." In C. M. Renzetti & R. M. Lee (Eds.), *Researching sensitive topics* (pp. 108–124). Newbury Park, CA: Sage.

Ayres, B. D. (1993, September 9). Judge's decision in custody case raises concerns. *New York Times*, p. A16.

Ayres, E. (1996, July/August). The expanding shadow economy. *Worldwatch*, pp. 10–23.

Babbie, E. (1995). *The practice of social research*. Belmont, CA: Wadsworth.

Baca Zinn, M., & Eitzen, D. S. (1993). *Diversity in families*. New York: HarperCollins.

Bailey, J. M., & Pillard, R. C. (1991). A genetic study of male sexual orientation. *Archives of General Psychiatry, 48*, 1089–1096.

Bailey, J. M., & Pillard, R. C. (1993). Heritable factors influence sexual orientation in women. *Archives of General Psychiatry, 50*, 217–223.

Bailey, J. M., Pillard, R. C., Neale, M. C., & Agyei, Y. (1993). Heritable factors influence sexual orientation in women. *Archives of General Psychiatry, 50*, 217–223.

Baker, S. W. (1980). Biological influences on human sex and gender. *Signs, 6*, 80–96.

Baltzell, E. D. (1979/1958). *Philadelphia gentlemen: The making of a national upper class*. Philadelphia: University of Pennsylvania Press.

Baltzell, E. D. (1988, September). The WASP's last gasp. *Philadelphia Magazine*, pp. 104–107, 184–188.

Bane, M. J. (1986). Household composition and poverty. In S. H. Danziger & D. H. Weinberg (Eds.), *Fighting poverty: What works and what doesn't* (pp. 209–231). Cambridge, MA: Harvard University Press.

Banfield, E. C. (1974). *The unheavenly city revisited*. Boston: Little, Brown.

Banner, L. (1986). Act one. *Wilson Quarterly, 10*, 90–98.

Barber, B. L., & Eccles, J. S. (1992). Long-term influence of divorce and single parenting on adolescent family- and work-related values, behaviors, and aspirations. *Psychological Bulletin, 111*, 108–126.

Barboza, D. (1999, January 10). Measuring floor space and cyberspace. *New York Times*, p. 4WK.

Bardwell, J. R., Cochran, S. W., & Walker, S. (1986). Relationship of parental education, race, and gender to sex role stereotyping in five-year-old kindergartners. *Sex Roles, 15*, 275–281.

Barlett, D. L., & Steele, J. B. (1996). *America: Who stole the dream?* Kansas City: Andrews and McMeel.

Barnett, O. W., Lee, C. Y., & Thelan, R. E. (1997). Gender differences in attributions of self-defense and control in interpartner aggression. *Violence Against Women, 3*, 462–481.

Barrett, S. A. (1987). *Is God a racist?* Toronto: University of Toronto Press.

Barringer, F. (1991, March 22). Despite problems, the Census Bureau hails its first count of the homeless. *New York Times*, p. B12.

Barringer, F. (1993, April 1). 1 in 5 in U.S. have sexually caused viral disease. *New York Times*, pp. A1, B9.

Barringer, F. (1993, April 25). Measuring sexuality through polls can be shaky. *New York Times*, p. 28.

Barringer, H. R., Gardner, R. W., & Levin, M. J. (1993). *Asians and Pacific Islanders in the United States*. New York: Russell Sage Foundation.

Barros, F. (1979). Cradled in hunger. *UNESCO Courier, 32*, 9–12.

Bartley, M. (1996). Unemployment and health selection. *The Lancet, 348*, 904–905.

Basow, S. A. (1990). Effectiveness of teacher expressiveness: Mediated by sex-typing? *Journal of Educational Psychology, 82*, 599–602.

Bass, B. M. (1990). *Bass and Stogdill's handbook of leadership: Theory, research, and managerial applications*. New York: Free Press.

Batstone, D. B. (1994). Liberation theology in Latin America. In D. J. Curran & C. M. Renzetti (Eds.), *Contemporary societies: Problems and prospects* (pp. 333–344). Englewood Cliffs, NJ: Prentice-Hall.

Baxter, S., & Lansing, M. (1983). *Women and politics*. Ann Arbor: University of Michigan Press.

Bearden, J. (1992, August). *Attitudes and knowledge about AIDS and college student sexual behavior*. Paper presented at the Annual Meeting of the American Sociological Association, Pittsburgh, PA.

Becker, E. (1999, January 28). Senate panel passes bill to increase military pay and benefits. *New York Times*, p. 18.

Becker, H. S. (1967). Whose side are we on? *Social Problems, 14*, 239–247.

Becker, H. S. (1973). *Outsiders*. New York: Free Press.

Becker, M., Bowman, C. G., & Torrey, M. (1994). *Feminist jurisprudence: Taking women seriously*. Minneapolis: West.

Beckford, J. A. (1985). *Cult controversies*. New York: Tavistock.

Bedard, M. E. (1992). *Breaking with tradition*. Dix Hills, NY: General Hall.

Begley, S., Miller, M., & Hager, M. (1988, July 11). The endless summer. *Newsweek*, 18–20.

Belkin, L. (1992, July 28). Childless couples hang on to last hope, despite law. *New York Times*, pp. A1, B2.

Bell, A., Weinberg, M. S., & Hammersmith, S. K. (1981). *Sexual preference and its development in men and women*. Bloomington, IN: Indiana University Press.

Bell, D. (1973). *The coming crisis of postindustrial society: A venture in social forecasting.* New York: Basic Books.

Bell, D. (1989, Spring). The third technological revolution and its possible socioeconomic consequences. *Dissent,* 164–176.

Bellah, R. (1975). *The broken covenant.* New York: Seabury.

Bellah, R. N., Madsen, R., Sullivan, W. M., Swidler, A., & Tipton, S. M. (1985). *Habits of the heart: Individualism and commitment in American life.* New York: Harper and Row.

Belluck, P. (1996, February 18). New to the U.S., back in school. *New York Times,* pp. 37, 41.

Belluck, P. (1996a, December 1). The symptoms of Internet addiction. *New York Times,* p. E5.

Belluck, P. (1996b, May 9). Mingling two worlds of medicine. *New York Times,* pp. B1, B4.

Belluck, P. (1998, March 17). Omaha tribe turns to cigarettes for a better life. *New York Times,* p. A12.

Belz, H. (1991). *Equality transformed: A quarter-century of affirmative action.* New Brunswick, NJ: Transaction Books.

Bennet, J. (1996, August 12). The delegates: Where image meets reality. *New York Times,* p. A1.

Berenbaum, S. A., & Hines, M. (1992). Early androgens are related to childhood sex-typed toy preferences. *Psychological Science, 3,* 203–206.

Bergen, R. K. (1993). Interviewing survivors of marital rape: Doing feminist research on sensitive topics. In C. M. Renzetti & R. M. Lee (Eds.), *Researching sensitive topics* (pp. 197–211). Newbury Park, CA: Sage.

Bergen, R. K. (1996). *Wife rape: Understanding the response of survivors and service providers.* Newbury Park, CA: Sage.

Berger, P. (1963). *Invitation to sociology.* New York: Anchor.

Berger, P. (1986). *The capitalist revolution: Fifty propositions about prosperity, equality, and liberty.* New York: Basic Books.

Berke, R. L. (1988, December 16). Census Bureau girding for bid to count homeless. *New York Times,* p. B6.

Berke, R. L. (1994, July 22). Christian right defies categories. *New York Times,* pp. A1, A16.

Berke, R. L. (1996, March 30). Nonvoters are no more alienated than voters, a survey shows. *New York Times,* p. A21.

Bernard, J. (1972). *The future of marriage.* New York: Bantam.

Bernstein, N. (1997, September 15). On line, high-tech sleuths find private facts. *New York Times,* pp. A1, A20.

Berreman, G. D. (1991). Race, caste, and other invidious distinctions in social stratification. In N. R. Yetman (Ed.), *Majority and minority* (pp. 30–48). Boston: Allyn & Bacon.

Bessant, J., & Watts, R. (1999). *Sociology Australia.* Sydney: Allen and Unwin.

Best, R. (1983). *We've all got scars: What boys and girls learn in elementary school.* Bloomington, IN: Indiana University Press.

Bianco, R. (1999, August 6). The world according to TV. *USA Today,* pp. E1, E2.

Bible backed slavery, says a lawmaker. (1996, May 10). *New York Times,* p. A20.

Bickerton, D. (1995). *Language and human behavior.* Seattle: University of Washington.

Bickerton, D. (1995, May 21). Get smart. *New York Times Book Review,* p. 9.

Biddle, W. (1985, March 10). Pentagon puts a ripple into defense contractor's cash flow. *New York Times,* p. E3.

Bidwell, C. E., & Friedkin, N. E. (1988). The sociology of education. In N. J. Smelser (Ed.), *Handbook of sociology* (pp. 449–471). Newbury Park, CA: Sage.

Bilson, J. M. (1995). *Keepers of the culture: The power of tradition in women's lives.* New York: Lexington Books.

Bilu, Y., & Witztum, E. (1996). Between sacred and medical realities. *Science in Context, 8,* 159–173.

Binstock, R. (1978, November). Federal policy toward the aging—Its inadequacies and its politics. *National Journal,* 1838–1845.

Birke, L. (1992). Transforming biology. In H. Crowley & S. Himmelweit (Eds.), *Knowing women: Feminism and knowledge* (pp. 66–77). Cambridge: Polity Press.

Bjorkqvist, K. (1994). Sex differences in physical, verbal, and indirect aggression: A review of recent research. *Sex Roles, 30,* 177–188.

Black, L. E., & Sprenkle, D. H. (1991). Gender differences in college students' attitudes toward divorce and their willingness to marry. In S. S. Volgy (Ed.), *Women and divorce, men and divorce* (pp. 47–60). New York: Haworth.

Black, N. (1988, August 14). Military contractors targeted. *Philadelphia Inquirer,* p. A9.

Blacks found less likely than Whites to be promoted in military. (1995, November 22). *New York Times,* p. A20.

Blackwell, J. E. (1982). Persistence and change in intergroup relations: The crisis upon us. *Social Problems, 29,* 325–346.

Blakeslee, S. (1998, October 13). Placebos prove so powerful even experts are surprised. *New York Times,* p. F1.

Blanc, A. K. (1987). The formation and dissolution of second unions: Marriage and cohabitation in Sweden and Norway. *Journal of Marriage and the Family, 49,* 391–400.

Blau, J., & Blau, P. (1982). The cost of inequality: Metropolitan structure and violent crime. *American Sociological Review, 47,* 114–129.

Blau, P., & Meyer, M. (1987). *Bureaucracy in modern society.* New York: Random House.

Blau, P. M., & Duncan, O. D. (1967). *The American occupational structure.* New York: Wiley.

Blauner, R. (1972). *Racial oppression in America.* New York: Harper and Row.

Bleier, R. (1984). *Science and gender.* New York: Pergamon Press.

Blum, D. (1997). *Sex on the brain.* New York: Viking.

Blumer, H. (1951). Collective behavior. In A. M. Lee (Ed.), *Principles of sociology* (pp. 165–222). New York: Barnes & Noble.

Blumer, H. (1969). *Symbolic interactionism: Perspective and method.* Englewood Cliffs, NJ: Prentice-Hall.

Blumer, H. (1970). *Human nature and collective behavior.* Englewood Cliffs, NJ: Prentice-Hall.

Blumstein, P., & Schwartz, P. (1983). *American couples.* New York: William Morrow.

Bohlen, C. (1995, November 26). Catholics defying an infallible church. *New York Times,* p. E3.

Bohlen, C. (1996, January 7). Pope John Paul @ Vatican: How many angels can dance . . . ? *New York Times,* p. 6.

Bohlen, C. (1998, November 15). Where Russians are hurting, racism takes root. *New York Times,* p. 3.

Bok, S. (1979). *Lying: Moral choice in public and private life.* New York: Vintage Books.

Bok, S. (1998). *Mayhem: Violence as public entertainment.* Reading, MA: Addison-Wesley.

Bonacich, E. (1991). Class approaches to ethnicity and race. In N. R. Yetman (Ed.), *Majority and minority* (pp. 59–76). Boston: Allyn & Bacon.

Bond, J. T., Goelnsky, E., & Swanberg, J. E. (1998). *The 1997 National Study of the Changing Workforce.* New York: Families and Work Institute.

Bonner, R. (1998, December 6). New weapons sales to Africa trouble arms-control experts. *New York Times,* p. 14.

Bookman, A., & Morgen, S. (Eds.) (1988). *Women and the politics of empowerment.* Philadelphia: Temple University Press.

Booth, A., Shelley, G., Mazur, A., Tharp, G., & Kittock, R. (1989). Testosterone and winning and losing in human competition. *Hormones and Behavior, 23,* 556–571.

Boswell, J. E. (1990). Sexual and ethical categories in premodern Europe. In D. P. McWhirter, S. A. Sanders, & J. M. Reinisch (Eds.), *Homosexuality/heterosexuality: Concepts of sexual orientation* (pp. 15–31). New York: Oxford University Press.

Bourque, L. B. (1989). *Defining rape.* Durham, NC: Duke University Press.

Bower, J. E., Kemeny, M. E., & Taylor, S. E. (1998). Cognitive processing, discovery of meaning, CD4 decline and AIDS-related mortality among bereaved HIV-seropositive men. *Journal of Consulting and Clinical Psychology, 66,* 979–986.

Bowles, S., & Gintis, H. (1976). *Schooling in capitalist America: Educational reform and the contradictions of economic life.* New York: Basic Books.

Boxer, S. (1997, November 8). It seems art is indeed monkey business. *New York Times,* pp. A1, B11.

Boyer, E. L. (1991). *Ready to learn: A mandate for the nation.* Princeton, NJ: Carnegie Foundation for the Advancement of Teaching.

Bozett, F. W. (1988). Gay fatherhood. In P. Bronstein & C. P. Cowan (Eds.), *Fatherhood today: Men's changing role in the family* (pp. 214–235). New York: John Wiley.

Bragg, R. (1996, March 5). Big holes where the dignity used to be. *New York Times,* pp. A1, A16.

Bramson, L. (1961). *The political context of sociology.* Princeton, NJ: Princeton University Press.

Brannon, E. M., & Terrace, H. S. (1998). Ordering the numerosites 1 to 9 by monkeys. *Science, 282,* 746–749.

Braveman, P. A., Egerter, S., Bennett, T., & Showstack, J. (1991). Differences in hospital resource allocation among sick newborns according to insurance coverage. *Journal of the American Medical Association, 266,* 3300–3304.

Brewer, R. M. (1988). Black women in poverty: Some comments on female-headed families. *Signs, 13,* 331–339.

Brewster, K. L. (1992). *Race differences in adolescent sexual activity: Another piece of the puzzle.* Paper presented at the Annual Meeting of the American Sociological Association, Pittsburgh, PA.

Breyman, S. (1998). *Movement genesis: Social movement theory and the 1980s West German peace movement.* Boulder, CO: Westview.

Bridges, J. S. (1989). Sex differences in occupational values. *Sex Roles, 20,* 205–211.

Brief, A. P. (1998). *Attitudes in and around organizations.* Thousand Oaks, CA: Sage.

Brien, P. M., & Beck, A. (1996). *HIV in prisons, 1994.* Washington, DC: U.S. Department of Justice, Bureau of Justice Statistics.

Brink, S. (1995, May 15). New research suggests that folks from 8 to 80 can shape up their brains with aerobic exercise. *U.S. News & World Report,* pp. 76–81.

Brody, J. E. (1996, February 28). Good habits outweigh genes as key to a healthy old age. *New York Times,* p. C9.

Bronner, E. (1997, September 25). College tuitions climb 5 percent, survey finds. *New York Times,* p. A18.

Bronner, E. (1998, February 25). U.S. trails the world in math and science. *New York Times,* p. B10.

Bronner, E. (1998, November 7). U. of Washington will end race-conscious admissions. *New York Times,* p. A12.

Bronner, E. (1998, December 1). For more textbooks, a shift from printed page to screen. *New York Times,* pp. A1, A27.

Bronstein, P. (1988). Father-child interaction. In P. Bronstein & C. P. Cowan (Eds.), *Fatherhood today: Men's changing role in the family* (pp. 107–124). New York: John Wiley.

Brooke, J. (1995, November 27). A bid to redefine Indian education. *New York Times,* p. A10.

Brooke, J. (1997, December 27). Minorities flock to cause of vouchers for schools. *New York Times,* pp. A1, A7.

Brooke, J. (1998, August 23). Utah struggles with a revival of polygamy. *New York Times,* p. 12.

Brooks, G. (1996). *Nine parts of desire: The hidden world of Islamic women.* New York: Anchor Books/ Doubleday.

Brooks-Gunn, J., Duncan, G. J., & Maritato, N. (1997). Poor families, poor outcomes: The well- being of children and youth. In G. Duncan & J. Brooks-Gunn (Eds.), *Consequences of growing up poor* (pp. 1–17). New York: Russell Sage Foundation.

Brooks-Gunn, J., & Matthews, W. S. (1979). *He and she.* Englewood Cliffs, NJ: Prentice-Hall.

Broome, R. (1982). *Aboriginal Australians.* Sydney: Allen and Unwin.

Brown, D. E. (1991). *Human universals.* Philadelphia, PA: Temple University Press.

Brown, J. (1997). Working toward freedom from violence: The process of change in battered women. *Violence Against Women, 3,* 5–26.

Brown, K. M. (1991). *Mama Lola: A vodou priestess in Brooklyn.* Berkeley: University of California Press.

Brown, L. R. (1997). Overview: A year of contrasts. In L. R. Brown, M. Renner, & C. Flavin (Eds.), *Vital signs 1997* (pp. 15–22). New York: W. W. Norton & Company.

Brown, L. R., Gardner, G., & Halweil, B. (1998). *Beyond Malthus: Sixteen dimensions of the population problem.* Washington, DC: Worldwatch Institute.

Brown, P. L. (1998, December 31). Where the spirits feel at home. *New York Times,* pp. F1, F5.

Browne, A., & Bassuk, S. S. (1997). Intimate violence in the lives of homeless and poor housed women. *American Journal of Orthopsychiatry, 67,* 261–278.

Brownmiller, S. (1975). *Against our will.* New York: Simon & Schuster.

Bruni, F. (1995, November 5). For gay couples, ruling to cheer on adoption. *New York Times,* p. 41.

Bumpass, L. L., & Sweet, J. E. (1991). The role of cohabitation in declining rates of marriage. *Journal of Marriage and the Family, 53,* 913–927.

Burbank, V. (1994). *Fighting women.* Berkeley, CA: University of California Press.

Burns, A., & Homel, R. (1989). Gender division of tasks by parents and their children. *Psychology of Women Quarterly, 13,* 113–125.

Burns, A. L., Mitchell, G., & Obradovich, S. (1989). Of sex roles and strollers: Female and male attention to toddlers at the zoo. *Sex Roles, 20,* 309–315.

Burns, J. F. (1994, August 27). India fights abortion of female fetuses. *New York Times,* p. A3.

Bush, D. M. (1987). *The impact of family and school on adolescent girls' aspirations and expectations: The public-private split and the reproduction of gender inequality.* Paper presented at the Annual Meeting of the American Sociological Association, Chicago, IL.

Butler, D., & Geis, F. L. (1990). Nonverbal affect responses to male and female leaders: Implications for leadership. *Journal of Personality and Social Psychology, 58,* 48–59.

Butler, R. N., & Lewis, M. (1972). *Aging and mental health.* St. Louis, MO: C. V. Mosby.

Butterfield, F. (1998, December 10). Guns blamed for rise in homicides by youths in 80s. *New York Times,* p. A29.

Butterfield, F. (1999, January 11). Inmates serving more time, Justice Department reports. *New York Times,* p. A10.

Byrne, J. A. (1993, December 20). The horizontal corporation: It's about managing across, not up and down. *Business Week,* pp. 76–81.

By the numbers. (1998, October 12). *Forbes,* p. 4.

Cadette, W. M. (1997, May). *Prescription for health care policy.* Public Policy Brief, No. 30A. Annandale-on-Hudson, NY: The Jerome Levey Economics Institute of Bard College.

Cage, M. C. (1993, March 10). Openly gay students face harassment and physical assaults on some campuses. *Chronicle of Higher Education,* pp. A22-A24.

Calavita, K., & Pontell, H. N. (1993). Savings and loan fraud as organized crime: Toward a conceptual typology of corporate crime. *Criminology, 31,* 519–548.

Calavita, K., Tillman, R., & Pontell, H. N. (1997). The savings and loan debacle, financial crime and the State. *Annual Review of Sociology, 23,* 19–38.

Cammermeyer, M. (1994). *Serving in silence: The story of Margarethe Cammermeyer.* New York: Penguin.

Campbell, G. R. (1989). The changing dimension of Native American health: A critical understanding of contemporary Native American health issues. *American Indian Culture and Research Journal, 13,* 1–20.

Cann, A., & Siegfried, W. D. (1990). Gender stereotypes and dimensions of effective leader behavior. *Sex Roles, 23,* 413–419.

Carmody, D. (1988, September 21). Head Start gets credit for rise in scores. *New York Times,* p. B9.

Carmody, D. L. (1989). *Women and world religions.* Nashville, TN: Abingdon.

Carnegie Corporation. (1994). *Starting points: Meeting the needs of our youngest children.* Princeton, NJ: Carnegie Foundation.

Casper, L. M., & Bryson, K. (1998). *Household and family characteristics: March 1998.* Washington, DC: U.S. Department of Commerce, Bureau of the Census.

Cassel, C. (1995). *Approaching death: Improving care at the end of life.* NY: National Academy Press.

CDC head urges minorities: Exercise is a key to health. (1996, July 17). *Chicago Tribune,* p. 7.

Center for Women Policy Studies. (1991). *Violence against women as bias motivated hate crime: Defining the issues.* Washington, DC: Center for Women Policy Studies.

Cernkovich, S. A., & Giordano, P. C. (1980). Family relationships and delinquency. *Criminology, 25,* 295–321.

Chafetz, J. S. (1997). Feminist theory and sociology: Underutilized contributions for mainstream theory. *Annual Review of Sociology, 23,* 97–120.

Chambless, D. L., & Goldstein, A. J. (1980). Anxieties: Agoraphobia and hysteria. In A. M. Brodsky & R. Hare-Mustin (Eds.), *Women and psychotherapy* (pp. 113–134). New York: Guilford Press.

Chambliss, W. J. (1973). The saints and the roughnecks. *Society, 2,* 24–31.

Chambliss, W. J., & Zatz, M. (1994). *Making law: Law, state, and structural contradiction.* Bloomington: Indiana University Press.

Champion, D. J. (1989). Private counsels and public defenders: A look at weak cases, prior records, and leniency in plea bargaining. *Journal of Criminal Justice, 17,* 253–263.

Chan, S. (1991). *Asian Americans.* Boston: Twayne.

Chandler, K. A., Chapman, C. D., Rand, M. R., & Taylor, B. M. (1998). *Students' reports of school crime: 1989 and 1995.* Washington, DC: U.S. Department of Education and U.S. Department of Justice.

Chandler, T. & Fox, G. (1974). *3000 years of urban history.* New York: Academic Press.

Chapman, J. (1990). Violence against women as a violation of human rights. *Social Justice, 17,* 54–70.

Chasin, B. H. (1997). *Inequality and violence in the United States: Casualties of capitalism.* New York: Humanities Press.

Chavez, L. (1998). *The color bind: California's battle to end affirmative action.* Berkeley: University of California Press.

Cherlin, A. J., Chase-Lansdale, P. L., & McRae, C. (1998). Effects of parental divorce on mental health throughout the life course. *American Sociological Review, 63,* 239–249.

Chesney-Lind, M., & Sheldon, R. G. (1992). *Girls' delinquency and juvenile justice.* Pacific Grove, CA: Brooks/Cole.

Children Now & the Kaiser Family Foundation. (1997). *A national survey of children: Reflections of girls in the media—a summary of findings and toplines.* Menlo Park, CA: Author.

Children's Defense Fund. (1988). *Teenage pregnancy: An advocate's guide to the numbers.* Washington, DC: Adolescent Pregnancy Prevention Clearinghouse.

Children's Defense Fund. (1991). *The state of America's children.* Washington, DC: Author.

Children's Defense Fund. (1993). *Decade of indifference: Maternal and child health trends, 1980–1990.* Washington, DC: Author.

Children's Defense Fund. (1993). *The state of America's children.* Washington, DC: Author.

Children's Defense Fund. (1994). Examples of possible "pathways" from poverty to adverse child outcomes. *CDF Reports, 15*(11), 7.

Children's Defense Fund. (1997). *The state of America's children—Yearbook 1997.* Washington, DC: Author.

Children's Defense Fund (1998). *The state of America's children—Yearbook 1998.* Washington, DC: Author.

China's growing reliance on caregiving contracts. (1998, July/August). *Global Aging Report,* p. 6.

Chira, S. (1988, July 31). The melting pot is a confounding idea to the Japanese. *New York Times,* p. 9E.

Chira, S. (1991, March 24). How to translate the talk about school reform into action. *New York Times,* p. E1.

Chira, S. (1991, June 12). The rules of the marketplace are applied to the classroom. *New York Times,* pp. A1, B5.

Chira, S. (1993a, September 23). Census data show rise in child care by fathers. *New York Times,* p. B1.

Chira, S. (1993b, October 21). Fathers who want time off for families face uphill battle. *New York Times,* p. C6.

Chira, S. (1994, April 13). Women campaign for new plan to curb world's population. *New York Times,* pp. A1, A12.

Chiricos, T., & Bales, W. (1991). Unemployment and punishment: An empirical assessment. *Criminology, 29,* 701–724.

Christakis, N. A., & Escarce, J. J. (1996). Survival of Medicare patients after enrollment in hospice programs. *New England Journal of Medicine, 36,* 172–178.

Christie, I. (1999, January). Sociology's new golden age. *Prospect Magazine.* Available at: http://www.prospect-magazine.co.uk/highlights/return_sociology/index.html

Chronicle of Higher Education. (1991). *Chronicle of Higher Education almanac.* Washington, DC: Author.

Church faces a new dispute involving race. (1996, April 3). *New York Times,* p. 12.

Churchill, W., & LaDuke, W. (1992). Native North America: The political economy of radioactive colonialism. In M. A. Jaimes (Ed.), *The state of Native America* (pp. 241–266). Boston: South End Press.

Cialdini, R. B., & Trost, M. R. (1998). Social influence: Social norms, conformity, and compliance. In D. T. Gilbert, S. T. Fiske, & G. Lindsey (Eds.), *Handbook of social psychology* (pp. 151–192). New York: Random House.

Citing drop in welfare rolls, Clinton to seek further cuts. (1999, January 25). *New York Times,* p. A14.

Clancy, P. (1987, July 22). Cops battle stress; "I'm hurting." *USA Today,* p. 1A.

Clark, R., Lennon, R., & Morris, L. (1993). Of Caldecotts and kings: Gendered images in recent American children's books by Black and non-Black illustrators. *Gender & Society, 7,* 227–245.

Clark, R. L. (1990). Income maintenance policies in the United States. In R. H. Binstock & L. K. George (Eds.), *Handbook of aging and the social sciences* (pp. 382–397). New York: Academic Press.

Clarke, R. L., Passel, J. S., & Fix, M. E. (1994). Fiscal impacts of undocumented immigrants. *Government Finance Review, 11,* 20–22.

Clinard, M. B. (1964). The theoretical implications of anomie and deviant behavior. In M. B. Clinard (Ed.), *Anomie and deviant behavior* (pp. 1–56). New York: Free Press.

Cline, F. X. (1994, February 27). The Pequots. *New York Times Magazine,* pp. 49–52.

Cline, F. X. (1994, April 27). The South African vote: The overview. *New York Times,* pp. A1, A8.

Cloward, R. A., & Ohlin, L. E. (1960). *Delinquency and opportunity.* New York: The Free Press of Glencoe.

Coale, A. J. (1974). The history of human population. In Scientific America (Eds.), *The human population.* San Francisco, CA: Freeman & Co.

Coale, A. J. (1991). Excess female mortality and the balance of the sexes in the population: An estimate of the number of "missing females." *Population and Development Review, 17,* 517–523.

Cochran, S. D., & Mays, V. M. (1988). Issues in the perception of AIDS risk and risk reduction activities by Black and Hispanic/Latina women. *American Psychologist, 43,* 949–957.

Cohen, A. K. (1955). *Delinquent boys.* New York: Free Press.

Cohen, E. (1996, March 17). 21st century scribes: Monks designing web pages. *New York Times,* pp. 1, 22.

Colasanto, D., & De Stefano, L. (1989). *Public image of TV evangelists deteriorates as Bakker trial continues.* Princeton, NJ: Gallup Polling Organization, Inc.

Cole, B. P. (1985). The state of education for Black Americans. In F. Schultz (Ed.), *Annual editions: Education 85/86* (pp. 148–151). Guilford, CT: The Dushkin Publishing Group.

Cole, S. (1994). Why sociology doesn't make progress like the natural sciences. *Sociological Forum, 9,* 133–154.

Cole, T. B. (1999). Ebbing epidemic: Youth homicide rate at 14-year low. *Journal of the American Medical Association, 281,* 25–26.

Coleman, J. (1989). *The criminal elite.* New York: St. Martin's Press.

Coleman, J. S., & Hoffer, T. (1987). *Public and private high schools: The impact of communities.* New York: Basic Books.

Collins, P. H. (1986). Learning from the outsider within: The sociological significance of Black feminist thought. *Social Problems, 33,* 514–532.

Collins, P. H. (1989). A comparison of two works on Black family life. *Signs, 14,* 875–884.

Collins, P. H. (1990). *Black feminist thought.* Cambridge, MA: Unwin and Hyman.

Collins, R. (1979). *The credential society: An historical sociology of education.* New York: Academic Press.

Collins, R., & Makowsky, M. (1989). *The discovery of society.* New York: Random House.

Coltrane, S. (1989). Household labor and the routine production of gender. *Social Problems, 36,* 473–490.

Commission on Professionals in Science and Technology. (1992). *Professional women and minorities.* Washington, DC: Author.

Comstock, G. (1991). *Television and the American child.* San Diego, CA: Academic Press.

Condry, J. C. (1989). *The psychology of television.* Hillsdale, NJ: Lawrence Erlbaum Associates.

Connor, W. (1993). Beyond reason: The nature of the ethnonational bond. *Ethnic and Racial Studies, 16,* 373–389.

Conover, T. (1997, May 11). Border vigilantes. *New York Times Magazine,* pp. 44–46.

Conrad, P. (Ed.). (1997). *The sociology of health and illness.* New York: St. Martin's Press.

Cooley, C. H. (1962/1909). *Social organization.* New York: Schocken Books.

Cooley, C. H. (1964). *Human nature and the social order.* New York: Schocken.

Coombs, L. C. (1977). Preferences for sex of children among U.S. couples. *Family Planning Perspectives, 9,* 259–265.

Corbett, K., Gentry, C. S., & Peterson, W., Jr. (1993). Sexual harassment in high school. *Youth and Society, 25,* 93–103.

Corcoran, M., & Adams, T. (1997). Race, sex, and the intergenerational transmission of poverty. In G. J. Duncan & J. Brooks-Gunn (Eds.), *Consequences of growing up poor* (pp. 461–517). New York: Russell Sage Foundation.

Cornell, S., & Kalt, J. P. (1990). Pathways from poverty: Economic development and institution building on American Indian reservations. *American Indian Culture and Research Journal, 14,* 89–125.

Cornia, G. A., & Danziger, S. (Eds.). (1997). *Child poverty and deprivation in the industrialized countries, 1945–1995.* New York: Oxford University Press.

Cornwell, E. E., Berne, T. V., Belzberg, H., Asensio, J., Velmahos, G., Murray, J., & Demetriades, D. (1996). Health care crisis from a trauma care perspective. *Journal of the American Medical Association, 276,* 940–947.

Corsaro, W. A., & Eder, D. (1990). Children's peer cultures. *Annual Review of Sociology, 16,* 197–220.

Cortes, J. B. (1972). *Delinquency and crime.* New York: Seminar Press.

Cose, E. (1993). *The rage of a privileged class.* New York: HarperCollins.

Coser, L. A. (1977). *Masters of sociological thought.* New York: Harcourt Brace Jovanovich.

Cott, N. F. (1987). *The grounding of modern feminism.* New Haven, CT: Yale University Press.

Council of Economic Advisors (1991, 1994). *Economic report of the President.* Washington, DC: U.S. Government Printing Office.

Couric, E. (1989, December 11). An NLJ/West survey, women in the law: Awaiting their turn. *National Law Journal,* pp. S1, S12.

Covinsky, K. E., Landefeld, C. S., & Phillips, R. S. (1996). Is economic hardship on the families of the seriously ill associated with patient and surrogate care preferences? *Archives of Internal Medicine, 156,* 1737–1745.

Cowan, C. P., & Cowan, P. A. (1992). *When parents become partners.* New York: Basic Books.

Cowan, P., & Cowan, C. P. (1998). New families: Modern couples as new pioneers. In M. A. Mason, A. Skolnick, & S. D. Sugarman (Eds.), *All our families* (pp. 169–192). New York: Oxford University Press.

Cowell, A. (1996, May 28). Old Catholic Church offers new Catholic ways. *New York Times,* p. A4.

Cowgill, D. (1986). *Aging around the world.* Belmont, CA: Wadsworth.

Cowgill, D., & Holmes, L. (1972). *Aging and modernization.* New York: Appleton-Century-Crofts.

Cowie, P. (Ed.). (1995). *Variety international film guide.* Hollywood, CA: Samuel French Trade.

Cox, F. D. (1993). *Human intimacy: Marriage, the family and its meaning.* Minneapolis: West.

Cox, R. S. (1998, Winter). Speaking out for those "loud Black girls." *Outlook,* pp. 8–11.

Crandall, C. S. (1995). Do parents discriminate against their heavyweight daughters? *Personality and Social Psychology Bulletin, 21,* 724–735.

Crime drops in '97; murders are at 30-year low. (1998, November 23). *New York Times,* p. A16.

Crocker, J., Major, B., & Steele, C. (1998). Social stigma. In D. T. Gilbert, S. T. Fiske, & G. Lindsey (Eds.), *Handbook of social psychology* (pp. 504–553). New York: Random House.

Crossette, B. (1996, November 17). World is less crowded than expected, the U.N. reports. *New York Times,* p. 3.

Crowell, N. A., & Burgess, A. W. (1996). *Understanding violence against women.* Washington, DC: National Academy Press.

Cruikshank, M. (1992). *The gay and lesbian rights movement.* New York: Routledge, Chapman, and Hall.

Cumming, E. C., & Henry, W. E. (1961). *Growing old: The process of disengagement.* New York: Basic Books.

Cupach, W., & Metts, S. (1994). *Facework.* Thousand Oaks, CA: Sage.

Curran, D. J. (1993). *Dead laws for dead men: The politics of federal coal mine health and safety legislation.* Pittsburgh: University of Pittsburgh Press.

Curran, D. J. (1996, November). *Economic reform, the floating unemployed, and crime: The contradictions and conflicts of China's development strategy.* Paper presented at the annual meeting of the American Society of Criminology, Chicago, IL.

Curran, D. J., & Renzetti, C. M. (1996). *Social problems: Society in crisis.* 4th ed. Boston: Allyn & Bacon.

Curtis, J. E., Grabb, E. G., & Baer, D. (1992). Voluntary association membership in fifteen countries: A comparative analysis. *American Sociological Association, 57,* 139–152.

Curtiss, S. (1977). *Genie: A psycholinguistic study of a modern day "wild child."* New York: Academic Press.

Cushman, J. H. (1994, October 6). Congress forgoes its bid to speed cleanup of dumps. *New York Times*, pp. A1, A22.

Dahl, R. A. (1961). *Who governs?* New Haven, CT: Yale University Press.

Dahl, R. A. (1982). *Dilemmas of pluralist democracy: Autonomy vs. control.* New Haven, CT: Yale University Press.

Daly, K. (1989). Gender varieties in white-collar crime. *Criminology, 27*, 769–793.

Daly, K. (1989). Neither conflict nor labeling nor paternalism will suffice: Intersections of race, ethnicity, gender, and family in criminal court decisions. *Crime and Delinquency, 35*, 136–168.

Dannefer, D. (1989). Human action and its place in theories of aging. *Journal of Aging Studies, 3*, 1–20.

Das Dasgupta, S., & Warrier, S. (1996). In the footsteps of "Arundhati": Asian Indian women's experiences of domestic violence in the U.S. *Violence Against Women, 2*, 238–259.

David, D. (1987). *Intellectual women and Victorian patriarchy.* Ithaca, NY: Cornell University Press.

Davidson, R. C., & Lewis, E. L. (1997). Affirmative action and other special consideration admissions at the University of California, Davis, School of Medicine. *Journal of the American Medical Association, 278*, 1153–1158.

Davies, C. (1987). Things to come: The NHS in the next decade. *Sociology of Health and Illness, 9*, 302–317.

Davies, J. C. (1962). Toward a theory of revolution. *American Sociological Review, 27*, 5–19.

Davis, E. A. (1995). *Sex bias in United States history textbooks.* Paper presented at the Annual Meeting of the Eastern Sociological Society, Philadelphia, PA.

Davis, F. (1991). *Passage through crisis: Polio victims and their families.* New Brunswick, NJ: Transaction.

Davis, J. A. (1994). What's wrong with sociology? *Sociological Forum, 9*, 179–197.

Davis, K. (1940). Extreme social isolation of a child. *American Journal of Sociology, 45*, 554–564.

Davis, K. (1947). Final note on a case of extreme isolation. *American Journal of Sociology, 50*, 432–437.

Davis, K. (1948). *Human society.* New York: Macmillan.

Davis, K., & Moore, W. (1945). Some principles of stratification. *American Sociological Review, 10*, 242–249.

Davis, K., Grant, P., & Rowland, D. (1990, Summer). Alone and poor: The plight of elderly women. *Generations, 14*, 43–47.

Davis, W. (1991). Fundamentalism in Japan: Religious and political. In M. E. Marty & R. S. Appleby (Eds.), *Fundamentalisms observed* (pp. 782–813). Chicago: University of Chicago Press.

Davis-Kimball, J. (1997). Warrior women of the Eurasian steppes. *Archeology, 50*, 44–48.

Day, D. (1996). *Claiming a continent: A history of Australia.* Sydney: Harper Collins.

De Silva, C. (1996, September 25). The silent partners inside restaurants. *New York Times*, pp. C1, C6.

De Witt, K. (1994, March 27). Cold shoulder to churches that practice preachings. *New York Times*, pp. 1, 11.

De Witt, K. (1995, September 22). Student loans show sharp rise, report says. *New York Times*, p. A16.

Deaux, K., & Kite, M. F. (1987). Thinking about gender. In B. B. Hess & M. M. Ferree (Eds.), *Analyzing gender* (pp. 92–117). Newbury Park, CA: Sage.

Deegan, M. I. (1988). *Jane Addams and the men of the Chicago School, 1892–1918.* New Brunswick, NJ: Transaction Books.

DeFazio, P. (1996). *More Pentagon follies.* Available at: http://www.taxpayer.net/tcs/Pentagonfollies

DeKeseredy, W. S. (1997). Post-separation woman abuse. A special issue of *Violence Against Women*, V. 3, #6.

DeKeseredy, W. S., & MacLeod, L. (1997). *Woman abuse: A sociological story.* Toronto: Harcourt Brace Canada.

DeKeseredy, W. S., & Schwartz, M. D. (1993). Male peer support and woman abuse: An explanation of DeKeseredy's model. *Sociological Spectrum, 13*, 393–413.

Delmar, R. (1986). What is feminism? In J. Mitchell & A. Oakley (Eds.), *What is feminism? A re-examination* (pp. 8–33). New York: Pantheon.

DeLoache, J. S., Cassidy, D. J., & Carpenter, C. J. (1987). The three bears are all boys: Mothers' gender labeling of neutral picture book characters. *Sex Roles, 17*, 163–178.

Democratic National Committee (1997). Personal communication.

DeMott, B. (1996, January 7). Sure, we're all just one big happy family. *New York Times*, pp. H1, 31.

Dennehy, K., & Mortimer, J. T. (1992). *Work and family orientations of contemporary adolescent boys and girls in a context of social change.* Paper presented at the Annual Meeting of the American Sociological Association, Pittsburgh, PA.

DePalma, A. (1996, December 15). Three countries face their Indians. *New York Times*, p. E3.

DePalma, R. (1988, May 15). Reassessment hits homeowners hard. *New York Times*, pp. A1, A14.

DeParle, J. (1992, March 1). Why marginal changes don't rescue the welfare system. *New York Times*, p. E3.

Deutsch, C. H. (1997, January 7). Services becoming the goods in industry. *New York Times*, pp. D1, D4.

Devine, P. G. (1989). Stereotypes and prejudice: Their automatic and controlled components. *Journal of Personality and Social Psychology, 56,* 5–18.

Devine, P. G., & Monteith, M. J. (1993). The role of discrepancy-associated affect in prejudice reduction. In D. E. Mackie & D. L. Hamilton (Eds.), *Affect, cognition, and stereotyping: Interactive processes in group perception* (pp. 317–344). San Diego, CA: Academic Press.

Diamond, I. (1988). Medical science and the transformation of motherhood: The promise of reproductive technologies. In E. Boneparth & E. Strooper (Eds.), *Women, power and policy: Toward the year 2000* (pp. 155–167). New York: Pergamon.

Diamond, M., & Sigmundson, K. H. (1997). Sex reassignment at birth: Long-term review and clinical implications. *Archives of Pediatrics and Adolescent Medicine, 151,* 298–305.

Diaz, W. A. (1984). *Hispanics: Challenges and opportunities.* New York: The Ford Foundation.

Dibble, U., & Strauss, M. A. (1990). Some social structure determinants of inconsistency between attitudes and behavior: The case of family violence. In M. A. Strauss & R. J. Gelles (Eds.), *Physical violence in families* (pp. 167–180). New Brunswick, NJ: Transaction.

Diener, E., Lusk, R., DeFour, D., & Flax, R. (1980). Deindividuation: Effects of group size, density, number of observers, and group member similarity on self-consciousness and disinhibited behavior. *Journal of Personality and Social Psychology, 39,* 449–459.

Dinges, W. D., & Hitchcock, J. (1991). Roman Catholic traditionalism and activist conservatism in the United States. In M. E. Marty & R. S. Appleby (Eds.), *Fundamentalisms observed* (pp. 66–141). Chicago: University of Chicago Press.

Dittman, R. W., Kappes, M. H., Kappes, M. E., Borger, D., Mayer- Bahlberg, H. F. L., Stenger, H., Willig, R. H., & Wallis, H. (1990a). Congenital hyperplasia I: Gender-related behavior and attitudes in female patients and sisters. *Psychoneuroendocrinology, 15,* 401–420.

Dittman, R. W., Kappes, M. H., Kappes, M. E., Borger, D., Mayer-Bahlberg, H. F. L., Stenger, H., Willig, R. H., & Wallis, H. (1990b). Congenital hyperplasia II: Gender-related behavior and attitudes in female salt-wasting and simple-virilizing patients. *Psychoneuroendocrinology, 15,* 421–434.

Dobash, R. P., Dobash, R. E., Cavanagh, K., Lewis, R. (1998).Separate and intersecting realities: A comparison of men's and women's accounts of violence against women. *Violence Against Women, 4,* 382–414.

Dobrzynski, J. H. (1996, November). When directors play musical chairs. *New York Times,* pp. F1, F8–F9.

Dobson, D. (1983). The elderly as a political force. In W. P. Brown & L. K. Olson (Eds.), *Aging and public policy* (pp. 123–142). Westport, CT: Greenwood.

Domhoff, G. W. (1970). *The higher circles.* New York: Random House.

Domhoff, G. W. (1990). *The power elite and the state: How policy is made in America.* New York: Aldine de Gruyter.

Dovidio, J. F., Brigham, J. C., Johnson, B. T., & Gaertner, S. L. (1996). Stereotyping, prejudice, and discrimination: Another look. In N. Macrae, C. Stangor, & M. Hewstone (Eds.), *Stereotypes and stereotyping* (pp. 276–319). New York: Guilford.

Dowd, M. (1990, November 20). Americans more wary of Gulf policy, poll finds. *New York Times,* p. A12.

Doyal, L. (1990). Hazards of hearth and home. *Women's Studies International Forum, 13,* 501–517.

Doyle, J. A. (1983). *Sex and gender.* Dubuque, IA: Wm. C. Brown.

Draper, P. (1975). !Kung women: Contrasts in sexual egalitarianism in foraging and sedantary contexts. In R. R. Reiter (Ed.), *Toward an anthropology of women* (pp. 77–109). New York: Monthly Review Press.

Dreeban, R., & Gamoran, A. (1986). Race, instruction, and learning. *American Sociological Review, 51,* 660–669.

Dressel, P. L. (1988). Gender, race, and class: Beyond the feminization of poverty in later life. *The Gerontologist, 28,* 177–180.

Dresser, N. (1996). *Multicultural manners.* New York: John Wiley and Sons.

Dublin, T. (1994). *Transforming women's work.* Ithaca, NY: Cornell University Press.

Dugger, C. W. (1996, October 12). New law bans genital cutting in United States. *New York Times,* pp. 1, 28.

Dugger, C. W. (1997, October 20). Immigration law's fine print emerges, setting off a debate about welfare provisions. *New York Times,* p. A14.

Duncan, G. J., Yeung, W. J., & Brooks-Gunn, J. (1998). The effects of childhood poverty on the life chances of children. *American Sociological Review, 63,* 406–423.

Dunn, S. (1997). Carbon emissions set new record. In L. R. Brown, M. Renner, & C. Flavin (Eds.), *Vital signs 1997* (pp. 58–59). New York: W. W. Norton & Company.

Durkheim, E. (1954). *The elementary forms of religious life.* Glencoe, IL: Free Press.

Durkheim, E. (1966, 1897). *Suicide.* New York: Free Press.

Dweck, C. S., Davidson, W., Nelson, S., & Enna, B. (1978). Sex differences in learned helplessness. *Developmental Psychology, 14,* 268–276.

Dzeich, C. S., & Weiner, L. (1990). *The lecherous professor*. Boston: Beacon Press.

Eagley, A. H., & Johnson, B. T. (1990). Gender and leadership style: A meta-analysis. *Psychological Bulletin, 108,* 233–256.

Eagley, A. H., & Karau, S. J. (1991). Gender and the emergence of leaders: A meta-analysis. *Journal of Personality and Social Psychology, 60,* 687–710.

Eagly, A. H., Karau, S. J., & Makhijani, M. G. (1995). Gender and the effectiveness of leaders: A meta-analysis. *Psychological Bulletin, 117,* 125–145.

Earthscan (1984). *Natural disasters: Acts of God or acts of man?* Washington, DC: Author.

Earle, T. (1997). *How chiefs come to power: The political economy of prehistory.* Palo Alto, CA: Stanford University Press.

Ebomoyi, E. (1987). Prevalence of female circumcision in two Nigerian communities. *Sex Roles, 17,* 139–151.

Eckholm, E. (1991, May 2). Rescuing health care. *New York Times,* pp. A1, B12.

Eckholm, E. (1998, November 15). Not (yet) gone the way of all Asia. *New York Times,* p. 6.

Eckholm, E. (1999, January 19). China tightens rein on writers and publishers. *New York Times,* pp. A1, A4.

Eckholm, E. (1999, February 1). Spreading protests by China's farmers meet with violence. *New York Times,* pp. A1, A10.

Eder, D. (1995). *School talk.* New Brunswick, NJ: Rutgers University Press.

Edin, K., & Lein, L. (1997). *Making ends meet.* New York: Russell Sage Foundation.

Edwards, S. S. M. (1986). Neither bad nor mad: The female violent offender reassessed. *Women's Studies International Forum, 9,* 79–87.

Egan, T. (1996, November 15). Sexual conflict in Army can be undisciplined. *New York Times,* p. A14.

Ehrhardt, A. A., & Meyer-Bahlburg, H. F. L. (1981). Effects of prenatal sex hormones on gender-related behavior. *Science, 211,* 1312–1318.

Eisenberg, D. M. (1990). Alternative therapies and medical practices. *New England Journal of Medicine, 322,* 65–69.

Elkin, S., & Greenstein, R. (1998). *The budget surplus, tax cuts, and Social Security.* Washington, DC: Center on Budget and Policy Priorities.

Elkind, D. (1981). *The hurried child.* Reading, MA: Addison-Wesley.

Eller, T. J., & Fraser, W. (1995). Asset ownership of households: 1993. *Current Population Reports.* Washington, DC: U.S. Department of Commerce.

Ellis, H. (1915). *The criminal.* New York: Scribner.

Ellison, C. G., Bartkowski, J. P., & Segal, M. L. (1996). Conservative Protestantism and the parental use of corporal punishment. *Social Forces, 74,* 1003–1029.

Ellison, C. G., & Sherkat, D. E. (1993). Conservative Protestantism and support for corporal punishment. *American Sociological Review, 58,* 131–144.

Ellwood, D. T., & Bane, M. J. (1994). *From rhetoric to reform.* Cambridge, MA: Harvard University Press.

El Nasser, H. (1994, March 25). On border, life is a sewer for "tunnel rat" orphans. *USA Today,* p. 2A.

Engels, F. (1942/1884). *The origin of the family, private property, and the state.* New York: International Publishers.

Enloe, C. H. (1987). Feminist thinking about war, militarism, and peace. In B. Hess & M. M. Ferree (Eds.), *Analyzing gender* (pp. 536–548). Newbury Park, CA: Sage.

Enloe, C. H. (1993). *The morning after.* Berkeley: University of California Press.

Epstein, G. A. (1996, August 31). Judges rule against lesbian mom. *Tampa Tribune,* p. 1.

Epstein, R. A. (1998). *Principles for a free society.* Reading, MA: Perseus Books.

Equal Employment Opportunity Commission. (1991). *Job patterns for minorities and women in private industry 1990.* Washington, DC: Author.

Erikson, R. J., & Garcia, V. (1990). Social class and fatherhood. In F. W. Bozett & S. M. H. Hanson (Eds.), *Fatherhood and families in cultural context* (pp. 114–137). New York: Springer.

Erlanger, H. S. (1974). The empirical status of the subculture of violence thesis. *Social Problems, 22,* 280–292.

Essed, P. (1991). *Understanding everyday racism.* Newbury Park, CA: Sage.

Estioko-Griffin, A. (1986, May). Daughters of the forest. *Natural History, 95,* p. 5.

Estrada, L. F., Garcia, F. C., Macias, R. F., & Maldonado, L. (1981). Chicanos in the United States: A history of exploitation and resistance. *Daedalus, 110,* 103–131.

Estrich, S. (1987). *Real rape.* Boston: Harvard University Press.

Etzioni, A. (1975). *A comparative analysis of complex organizations.* Glencoe, IL: Free Press.

Euthanasia favored in poll. (1991, November 4). *New York Times,* p. A 16.

Expenditures: How to plan a budget. (1996, April 1). *China News Analysis,* p. 4.

Eyer, D. (1994). *Mother-infant bonding: A scientific fiction.* New Haven, CT: Yale University Press.

Fagot, B. I. (1985). Beyond the reinforcement principle: Another step toward understanding sex role development. *Developmental Psychology, 21,* 1097–1104.

Fagot, B. I., & Leinbach, M. D. (1983). Play styles in early childhood: Social consequences for boys and girls. In M. B. Liss (Ed.), *Social cognitive skills: Sex roles and children's play* (pp. 93–116). New York: Academic Press.

Faison, S. (1996, October 9). As towns lose allure, nomads are nomads again. *New York Times,* p. A4.

Fang, B. (1998, October 12). China's stolen wives. *U.S. News and World Report,* pp. 35–38.

Farkas, G., Sheehan, D., & Grobe, R. P. (1990). Coursework mastery and school success: Gender, ethnicity and poverty groups within an urban school district. *American Educational Research Journal, 27,* 807–827.

Farkas, S., & Johnson, J. (1997). *Kids these days: What Americans really think about the next generation.* New York: Public Agenda.

Fausto-Sterling, A. (1985). *Myths of gender.* New York: Basic Books.

Fazlollah, M., Matza, M., & McCoy, C. R. (1998, November 1). How to cut city's crime rate: Don't report it. *Philadelphia Inquirer,* pp. A1, A26-A27.

Feagin, J. R., & Feagin, C. B. (1993). *Racial and ethnic relations.* Englewood Cliffs, NJ: Prentice-Hall.

Feagin, J. R., & Sikes, M. P. (1994). *Living with racism: The Black middle-class experience.* Boston: Beacon Press.

Featherman, D., & Hauser, R. M. (1978). *Opportunity and change.* New York: Academic Press.

Featherstone, M. (Ed.) (1990). *Global culture: Nationalism, globalization, and modernity.* London: Sage.

Feder, B. J., & Pollack, A. (1998, December 27). Computers and 2000: Race for security. *New York Times,* pp. 1, 22–23.

Federal Bureau of Investigation. (1996). *Crime in America.* Washington, DC: U.S. Government Printing Office.

Federal Bureau of Investigation. (1995). *Crime in the United States, 1995.* Washington, DC: U.S. Government Printing Office.

Federal Bureau of Investigation. (1997). *Crime in America.* Washington, DC: U.S. Government Printing Office.

Fee, E. (1983). Women and health care: A comparison of theories. In E. Fee (Ed.), *Women and health: The politics of sex in medicine* (pp. 17–34). Farmdale, NY: Baywood.

Feigenbaum, N. (1996, July 23). Lesbian baby boom? Increase in same-sex parents kindles debate. *Orlando Sentinel,* p. C1.

Fein, E. B. (1995a, November 17). Medical schools are urged to cut admissions by 20%. *New York Times,* p. D2.

Fein, E. B. (1995b, October 16). More young doctors forsake specialty for general practice. *New York Times,* pp. A1, B2.

Feiring, C., & Lewis, M. (1987). The child's social network: Sex differences from three to six years. *Sex Roles, 17,* 621–636.

Fejes, F. J. (1992). Masculinity as fact. In S. Craig (Ed.), *Men, masculinity and media* (pp. 9–22). Newbury Park, CA: Sage.

Feminist Scholars in Sociology. (1995). What's wrong is right: A response to the state of the discipline. *Sociological Forum, 10,* 493–498.

Ferguson, T., & Dunphy, J. S. (1992). *Answers to the mommy track.* Far Hills, NJ: New Horizon Press.

56 executions this year are most since 1957. (1995, December 30). *New York Times,* p. 28.

Finke, R., & Stark, R. (1992). *The churching of America.* New Brunswick, NJ: Rutgers University Press.

First-half imports up for all major products. (1995, September 4). *Consumer Electronics,* p. 8.

Fischer, D. H. (1977). *Growing old in America.* New York: Oxford University Press.

Fiske, E. B. (1987, April 12). Redesigning the American teacher. *New York Times Education Supplement,* pp. 18–21.

Fiske, S. T. (1998). Stereotyping, prejudice, and discrimination. In D. T. Gilbert, S. T. Fiske, & G. Lindsey (Eds.), *Handbook of social psychology* (pp. 357–411). New York: Random House.

FitzPatrick, C. S., & Lazere, E. (1999). *The poverty despite work handbook.* Washington, DC: Center on Budget and Policy Priorities.

Fivush, R. (1989). Exploring sex differences in the emotional content of mother-child conversations about the past. *Sex Roles, 20,* 675–691.

Flaherty, D. (1989). *Protecting privacy in surveillance societies.* Chapel Hill, NC: University of North Carolina Press.

Flanagan, W. G. (1995). *Urban sociology: Images and structure.* Boston: Allyn & Bacon.

Flavin, C. (1991). Conquering U.S. oil dependence. *Worldwatch, 4,* 28–35.

Flavin, C., & Lenssen, N. (1991). Here comes the sun. *Worldwatch, 4* (5), 10–18.

Forbes top 40 athletes. (1997). Available at: http://www.forbes.com

Fordham, S. (1996). *Blacked out: Dilemmas of race, identity, and success at Capital High.* Chicago: University of Chicago Press.

Fortune 500 largest U.S. corporations. (1998, April 27). *Fortune,* pp. F1-F6.

Frank, A. G. (1969). *Latin America: Underdevelopment or revolution?* New York: Monthly Review Press.

Frankenberg, R. (1993). *White women race matters: The social construction of Whiteness.* Minneapolis, MN: University of Minnesota Press.

Franks, P., & Clancy, C. M. (1993). Physician gender bias in clinical decisionmaking: Screening for cancer in primary care. *Medical Care, 31,* 213–218.

Frazier, N., & Sadker, M. (1973). *Sexism in school and society.* New York: Harper and Row.

Frederick D. Patterson Research Institute (1997). *The African American education data book, V. 1.* Fairfax, VA: Author.

Freedman, R. (1986). *Beauty bound.* Lexington, MA: Lexington Books.

French, H. F. (1997). Learning from the ozone experience. In Worldwatch Institute (Ed.), *State of the world 1997* (pp. 151–171). New York: W. W. Norton & Company.

French, H. F. (1997). Ozone response accelerates. In L. R. Brown, M. Renner, & C. Flavin (Eds.), *Vital signs, 1997* (pp. 102–103). New York: W. W. Norton.

French, H. W. (1997, February 2). Africa's culture war: Old customs, new values. *New York Times,* pp. E1, E4.

Freud, S. (1983/1933). Femininity. In M. W. Zak & P. A. Motts (Eds.), *Women and the politics of culture* (pp. 80–92). New York: Longman.

Friedan, B. (1963). *The feminine mystique.* New York: W. W. Norton.

Friedmann, J., & Wolff, G. (1982). World city formation: An agenda for research and action. *International Journal of Urban and Regional Research, 6,* 309–344.

Furstenberg, F. F., & Cherlin, A. (1991). *Divided families.* Cambridge, MA: Harvard University Press.

Gabe, J. (1997). Continuity and change in the British National Health Service. In P. Conrad (Ed.), *The sociology of health and illness* (pp. 492–504). New York: St. Martin's Press.

Gailey, C. W. (1987). Evolutionary perspectives on gender hierarchy. In B. B. Hess & M. M. Ferree (Eds.), *Analyzing gender* (pp. 32–67). Newbury Park, CA: Sage.

Galaty, J. G., Hjortaf Ormas, A., Ndagala, D. (1994). Special issue of *Nomadic Peoples, 34/35.*

Gallup, G. H. (1992). *Emerging trends.* Princeton, NJ: Princeton Religious Research Center.

Gallup, G. H. (1996). *Religion in America 1996.* Princeton, NJ: Princeton Religious Research Center.

Gallup, G., & Castelli, J. (1989). *The people's religion.* New York: Macmillan.

Gans, H. J. (1973). *More equality.* New York: Pantheon.

Gans, H. J. (1992). Comment: Ethnic invention and acculturation: A bumpy-line approach. *Journal of American Ethnic History, 12,* 42–52.

Gardner, G. (1995). Water tables falling. In L. R. Brown, N. Lenssen, & H. Kane (Eds.), *Vital signs, 1995* (pp. 122–123). New York: W. W. Norton.

Gardner, H. (1991). *The unschooled mind.* New York: Basic Books.

Garfinkel, H. (1967). *Studies in ethnomethodology.* Englewood Cliffs, NJ: Prentice-Hall.

Gargan, E. A. (1991, December 13). Ultrasound skews India's birth ratio. *New York Times,* p. A13.

Garreau, J. (1987, November 29). A middle class without precedent: Transcending race barriers and living the American dream. *Washington Post,* pp. A1, A17.

Geiger, H. J. (1996). Race and health care—An American dilemma? *New England Journal of Medicine, 335,* 815–816.

Geis, F. L., Brown, V., Jennings (Walstedt), J., & Porter, N. (1984). TV commercials as achievement scripts for women. *Sex Roles, 10,* 513–525.

Gelles, R. J. (1993). Alcohol and drugs are associated with violence—they are not its cause. In R. J. Gelles & D. R. Loseke (Eds.), *Current controversies on family violence* (pp. 182–196). Newbury Park, CA: Sage.

Gelles, R. J., & Cornell, C. P. (1985). *Intimate violence in families.* Beverly Hills, CA: Sage.

General Accounting Office (1998). *SUPERFUND: Times to complete site listing and cleanup.* Washington, DC: Author.

George, J. M., & Brief, A. P. (1992). Feeling good—doing good: A conceptual analysis of the mood at work-organizational spontaneity relationship. *Psychological Bulletin, 112,* 310–329.

George, S. (1990). *A fate worse than debt.* New York: Grove Weiderfeld.

Gerbner, G. (1993). *Women and minorities on television: A study in casting and fate.* A Report to the Screen Actors Guild and the American Federation of Radio and Television Artists. Available from the author, Annenberg School for Communication, University of Pennsylvania.

Gerbner, G. (1995). *The cultural environment of violence against women.* Unpublished manuscript, Annenberg School for Communication, University of Pennsylvania.

Gereffi, G. (1992). New relations of industrial development in East Asia and Latin America: Global, regional, and national trends. In R. Applebaum & J. Henderson (Eds.), *States and development in the Asian Pacific rim* (pp. 85–112). Newbury Park, CA: Sage.

Gershon, R., Escamilla, A., LaFon, D., Karkashian, C., & Vlahov, D. (1999). *The public health and law en-*

forcement stress. Washington, DC: National Institute of Justice.

Gidengil, E. (1995). Economic man—social woman? The case of the gender gap in support for the Canada–United States Free Trade Agreement. *Comparative Political Studies, 28,* 384–408.

Gilbert, D., & Kahl, J. A. (1993). *The American class structure: A new synthesis.* Belmont, CA: Wadsworth.

Gilbert, N. (1993). Examining the facts: Advocacy research overstates the incidence of date and acquaintance rape. In R. J. Gelles & D. R. Loseke (Eds.), *Current controversies on family violence* (pp. 120–132). Newbury Park, CA: Sage.

Gilligan, C. (1982). *In a different voice: Psychological theory and women's development.* Cambridge, MA: Harvard University Press.

Gilligan, C. (1990). *Making connections: The relational worlds of adolescent girls at Emma Willard School.* Cambridge, MA: Harvard University Press.

Gilligan, C., Taylor, J. M., & Sullivan, A. (1995). *Between voice and silence: Women and girls, race and relationships.* Cambridge, MA: Harvard University Press.

Gilmore, D. O. (1990). *Manhood in the making.* New Haven, CT: Yale University Press.

Gimlin, D. (1996). Pamela's place: Power and negotiation in the hair salon. *Gender & Society, 10,* 505–526.

Giordano, P., Cernkovich, S., & Pugh, M. (1986). Friendships and delinquency. *American Journal of Sociology, 91,* 1170–1202.

Glaser, G. (1997). *Strangers to the tribe.* Boston: Houghton Mifflin.

Glass Ceiling Commission. (1995). *A solid investment: Making full use of the nation's human capital.* Washington, DC: U.S. Government Printing Office.

Glenn, E. N. (1992). From servitude to service work: Historical continuities in the racial division of paid reproductive labor. *Signs, 18,* 1–43.

Glick, J. (1988, March 1). Even with action today, ozone loss will increase. *New York Times,* pp. 1, 30.

Glock, C. Y. (1968). On the study of religious commitment. *Religious Education, 6* (4), 98–110.

Glueck, S., & Glueck, E. (1950). *Unraveling juvenile delinquency.* Cambridge, MA: Harvard University Press.

Glueck, S., & Glueck, E. (1956). *Physique and delinquency.* New York: Harper.

Goering, L. (1996, May 21). Fighting lucrative sex trade a losing battle. *Chicago Tribune,* p. 4.

Goetting, A., & Fenstermaker, S. (Eds.). (1995). *Individual voices, collective visions: Fifty years of women in sociology.* Philadelphia: Temple University Press.

Goffman, E. (1959). *The presentation of self in everyday life.* New York: Anchor/Doubleday.

Goffman, E. (1961). *Asylums: Essays on the social situation of mental patients and other inmates.* Garden City, NY: Anchor Books.

Golant, S. M. (1984). *A place to grow old.* New York: Columbia University Press.

Goldberg, C. (1995, September 21). Choosing the joys of the simplified life. *New York Times,* pp. C1, C9.

Goldberg, C. (1995, November 26). Debutantes and bachelors preparing to meet, and be, the elite. *New York Times,* p. 44.

Goldberg, C. (1996, October 5). Political battle of the sexes is sharper than ever: Suburbs' soccer moms, fleeing the GOP, are much sought. *New York Times,* pp. 1, 24.

Goldberg, C. (1996, December 4). Hawaii judge ends gay-marriage ban. *New York Times,* pp. A1, A26.

Goldberg, C. (1997, September 16). Downsizing activism: Greenpeace is cutting back. *New York Times,* pp. A1, A24.

Goldberg, C. (1997, September 21). How political theater lost its audience. *New York Times,* P. 6WK.

Goldberg, C. (1998, November 3). Boston leading a renewal of old northern cities. *New York Times,* pp. A1, A20.

Goldberg, C. (1998, December 15). Children and violent video games. *New York Times,* p. A16.

Golden, S. (1992). *The women outside: Meanings and myths of homelessness.* Berkeley, CA: University of California Press.

Goldenberg, J. (1987). *Energy for a sustainable world.* Washington, DC: World Resource Institute.

Goldman, A. L. (1990, June 26). Reform Judaism votes to accept active homosexuals in rabbinate. *New York Times,* pp. A1, A21.

Goldstein, L. F. (1979). *The constitutional rights of women.* New York: Longman.

Goleman, D. (1995). *Emotional intelligence.* New York: Bantam.

Goleman, D. (1995, December 5). Making room on the couch for culture. *New York Times,* pp. C1, C3.

Goleman, D. (1996, February 26). Studies suggest older minds are stronger than expected. *New York Times,* pp. A1, A10.

Goleman, D. (1996, March 19). Anthropology group takes activist stand to protect cultures. *New York Times,* p. C11.

Golombok, S., & Fivush, R. (1994). *Gender development.* Cambridge: Cambridge University Press.

Gonzalez, A. (1982). Sex roles of the traditional Mexican family. *Journal of Cross-cultural Psychology, 13,* 330–339.

Goodchilds, J., & Zellman, G. (1984). Sexual signalling and sexual aggression in adolescent relationships. In N. Malmuth & E. Donnerstein (Eds.), *Pornography and sexual aggression* (pp. 233–243). Orlando, FL: Academic Press.

Goodenough, R. G. (1990). Situational stress and sexist behavior among young children. In P. R. Sanday & R. G. Goodenough (Eds.), *Beyond the second sex* (pp. 225–252). Philadelphia: University of Pennsylvania Press.

Goodwin, J. (1994). *Price of honor.* Boston: Little, Brown.

Gordon, D. R. (1984). Equal protection, unequal justice. In L. W. Dunbar (Ed.), *Minority report* (pp. 118–151). New York: Pantheon.

Gordon, M. (1995, November 23). Lawmakers target sales of medical records. *Chattanooga Times,* p. I5.

Gordon, M. M. (1964). *Assimilation in American life.* New York: Oxford University Press.

Gordon, M. R. (1993, April 24). Pentagon report tells of aviators' debauchery. *New York Times,* pp. 1, 9.

Gordon, M. R. (1998, November 30). Soviet mindset defeating capitalism. *New York Times,* pp. A1, A6.

Gorham, J., Kafka, P., & Neelakantan, S. (1998, October 12). The *Forbes* 400: The richest people in America. *Forbes,* pp. 165–361.

Gorman, C. (1992, January 20). Sizing up the sexes. *Time,* pp. 42–51.

Gornick, M. E., Eggers, P. W., Reilly, T. W., Mentneck, R. M., Fitterman, L. K., Kucken, L. E., & Vladeck, B. C. (1996). Effects of race and income on mortality and use of services among Medicare beneficiaries. *New England Journal of Medicine, 335,* 791–799.

Gornick, V. (1982, April). Watch out: Your brain may be used against you. *Ms,* pp. 14–20.

Gortmaker, S. L., Must, A., Perrin, J. M., Sobol, A. M., & Dietz, W. H. (1993). Social and economic consequences of overweight in adolescence and young adulthood. *New England Journal of Medicine, 329,* 1008–1012.

Gough, K. (1975). The origin of the family. In R. R. Reiter (Ed.), *Toward an anthropology of women* (pp. 51–76). New York: Monthly Review Press.

Gould, S. J. (1980). *The panda's thumb.* New York: W. W. Norton.

Gould, S. J. (1981). *The mismeasure of man.* New York: W. W. Norton.

Gould, S. J. (1984, July). Carrie Buck's daughter. *Natural History,* pp. 14–18.

Grady, D. (1996, May 7). In one country, chronic whiplash is uncompensated (and unknown). *New York Times,* p. C3.

Graham, E. (1986, June). African women fight clitoris cutting. *off our backs,* pp. 18–19.

Graham, P. A. (1978). Expansion and exclusion: A history of women in American higher education. *Signs, 3,* 759–773.

Gray, B. H. (1991). *The profit motive and patient care.* Cambridge, MA: Harvard University Press.

Gray, F. D. (1989). *Soviet women: Walking the tightrope.* New York: Doubleday.

Green, J. (1993, June 13). Out and organized. *New York Times,* pp. V1, V7.

Greenfeld, L. A. (1996). *Child victimizers: Violent offenders and their victims.* Washington, DC: U.S. Department of Justice, Bureau of Justice Statistics.

Greenfeld, L. A. (1997). *Sex offenders and offenses.* Washington, DC: U.S. Department of Justice.

Greenfield, S. (1997, January 19). Enhanced memory? Forget about it. *The Independent* (London), p. 42.

Greenhouse, L. (1998, March 5). High court widens workplace claims in sex harassment. *New York Times,* pp. A1, A18.

Greenhouse, S. (1987, November 15). Industrial nations await the pensioner boom: In Europe, the bill's due next century. *New York Times,* p. 8E.

Greenhouse, S. (1996, January 29). Strikes decrease to a 50-year low. *New York Times,* pp. A1, A12.

Greenhouse, S. (1997a, February 14). Sporting goods concerns agree to combat sale of soccer balls made by children. *New York Times,* p. A12.

Greenhouse, S. (1997b, October 1). Measure to ban import items made by children in bondage. *New York Times,* p. A1.

Greenhouse, S. (1999, January 26). Union membership rose in '98, but unions' percentage of work force fell. *New York Times,* p. A20.

Greenstein, R. (1996). *Raising families with a full-time worker out of poverty: The role of an increase in the minimum wage.* Washington, DC: Center on Budget and Policy Priorities.

Greenwood, E. (1962). Attributes of a profession. In S. Nosow & W. H. Form (Eds.), *Man, work, and society* (pp. 206–218). New York: Basic Books.

Griffin-Nolan, E. (1994). Dealing glue to third world children. In D. J. Curran & C. M. Renzetti (Eds.), *Contemporary societies: Problems and prospects* (pp. 57–62). Englewood Cliffs, NJ: Prentice-Hall.

Gross, L. (1991). Out of the mainstream: Sexual minorities and the mass media. *Journal of Homosexuality, 21,* 19–46.

Gruber, J. E., & Bjorn, L. (1982). Blue-collar blues: Sexual harassment of women auto-workers. *Work and Occupations, 9,* 271–298.

Gugliotta, G. (1999, August 9). Saying the words that save a culture. *Washington Post,* pp. A1, A8.

Guinier, L., & Strum, S. (1996). The future of Affirmative Action: Reclaiming the innovative ideal. *California Law Review, 84,* 953–1037.

Gustavsson, N. S., & MacEachron, A. E. (1998). Violence and lesbian and gay youth. *Journal of Gay and Lesbian Social Services, 8,* 41–68.

Haberman, C. (1987, November 15). For retirees, Tokyo is relying on self-reliance. *New York Times,* p. 8E.

Hacker, A. (1992). *Two nations: Black and White, separate, hostile, unequal.* New York: Ballantine Books.

Hadaway, C. K., Marler, P. L., & Chaves, M. (1993). What the polls don't show: A closer look at U.S. church attendance. *American Sociological Review, 58,* 741–752.

Hagan, J. (1989). *Structural criminology.* New Brunswick, NJ: Rutgers University Press.

Hakim, R. B., Teno, J. M., & Lynn, J. (1996). Factors associated with Do-Not-Resuscitate Orders: Patients' preferences, programs, and physicians' judgments. *Annals of Internal Medicine, 125,* 284–293.

Hale-Benson, J. E. (1986). *Black children: Their roots, culture, and learning styles.* Provo, UT: Brigham Young University Press.

Hall, L. (1992). Beauty quests—a double disservice: Beguiled, beseeched and bombarded—challenging the concept of beauty. In D. Driedger & S. Gray (Eds.), *Imprinting our image* (pp. 134–139). Charlottetown, PEI, Canada: Gynergy Books.

Hall, R. M., & Sandler, B. R. (1985). A chilly climate in the classroom. In A. G. Sargent (Ed.), *Beyond sex roles* (pp. 503–510). New York: West.

Hamer, D. H., & Copeland, P. (1994). *The science of desire: The search for the gay gene and the biology of behavior.* New York: Simon & Schuster.

Hamer, D. H., Hu, S., Magnuson, V. L., & Pattatucii, A. M. (1993). A linkage between DNA markers and male sexual orientation. *Science, 261,* 321–327.

Hammond, P. E. (1992). *Religion and personal autonomy: The third disestablishment in America.* Columbia, SC: University of South Carolina Press.

Hancock, G. (1989). *Lords of poverty: The power, prestige, and corruption of the international aid business.* New York: Atlantic Monthly Press.

Handler, J. F., & Hasenfeld, Y. (1997). *We the poor people: Work, poverty, and welfare.* New Haven, CT: Yale University Press.

Haney, D. Q. (1996, March 28). Heart disease worse for blacks. *Chattanooga Times,* p. F4.

Hannon, P. (1987). A study of the effects of parental involvement in the teaching of reading on children's reading test performance. *British Journal of Educational Psychology, 57,* 56–72.

Hansell, S. (1998, August 16). Big web sites to track stops of their users. *New York Times,* p. 1.

Hanson, S. M. H. (1988). Divorced fathers with custody. In P. Bronstein & C. P. Cowan (Eds.), *Father-hood today: Men's changing role in the family* (pp. 166–194). New York: John Wiley.

Harbeck, K. M. (1992). Introduction. In K. M. Harbeck (Ed.), *Coming out of the classroom closet* (pp. 1–7). New York: Haworth.

Hardin, R. (1995). *One for all: The logic of group conflict.* Princeton, NJ: Princeton University Press.

Harlow, H. F. (1962). The heterosexual affectional system in monkeys. *American Psychologist, 17,* 1–9.

Harlow, H. F., & Zimmerman, R. R. (1958). The development of affectional responses in infant monkeys. *Proceedings of the American Philosophic Society, 102,* 501–509.

Harmon, A. (1998, October 31). "Hacktivists" of all persuasions take their struggle to the web. *New York Times,* pp. A1, A6.

Harper, C., & McLanahan, S. (1998, August). *Father absence and youth crime.* Paper presented at the annual meeting of the American Sociological Association, San Francisco, CA.

Harr, J. (1995). *A civil action.* New York: Random House.

Harrell, W. A. (1995). Husbands' involvement in housework: Effects of relative earning power and masculine orientation. *Psychological Reports, 77,* 1331–1337.

Harrington, A. (1987). *Medicine, mind, and the double brain.* Princeton, NJ: Princeton University Press.

Harrington, M. (1984). *The new American poverty.* New York: Holt, Rinehart, and Winston.

Harris, C. D., & Ullman, E. L. (1945). The nature of cities. *Annals of the Academy of Political and Social Sciences, 242,* 7–17.

Harris, J. R. (1998). *The nurture assumption.* New York: Free Press.

Harris, M. (1975). *Cows, pigs, wars and witches: The riddles of culture.* New York: Vintage.

Harris, M. (1977). *Cannibals and kings: The origins of cultures.* New York: Random House.

Harris, M. (1993). The evolution of human gender hierarchies: A trial formulation. In B. D. Miller (Ed.), *Sex and gender hierarchies* (pp. 57–80). New York: Cambridge University Press.

Hart, P. (1991). Groupthink, risk-taking and recklessness: Quality of process and outcome in policy decision making. *Politics and the Individual, 1,* 67–90.

Hartocollis, A. (1998, November 21). U.S. questions the placement of city pupils. *New York Times,* pp. B1, B7.

Hartocollis, A. (1999, January 3). Test-tube babies: Private public schools. *New York Times,* p. WK3.

Haskins, R. (1989). Beyond metaphor: The efficacy of early childhood education. *American Psychologist, 44,* 274–282.

Hawley, W. D. (1985). Achieving quality integrated education—with or without federal help. In F. Schultz (Ed.), *Annual editions: Education 85/86* (pp. 142–145). Guilford, CT: Dushkin Publishing Group.

Hawley, W. D., & Smylie, M. A. (1988). The contribution of school desegregation to academic achievement and racial integration. In P. A. Katz & D. A. Taylor (Eds.), *Eliminating racism* (pp. 281–297). New York: Plenum Press.

Haynes, M. A., & Smedley, B. D. (Eds.) (1999). *The unequal burden of cancer: An assessment of NIH research and programs for ethnic minorities and the medically underserved.* Washington, DC: National Academy Press.

Heard, A., & Klebnikov, P. (1998, December 27). Apocalypse now. No, really. Now! *New York Times,* pp. 40–43.

Hedges, C. (1998, March 10). On a garage floor in Kosovo, a gruesome Serbian harvest. *New York Times,* pp. A1, A10.

Hegde, R. S. (1999). Marking bodies, reproducing violence: A feminist reading of female infanticide in South India. *Violence Against Women, 5,* 507–524.

Helgesen, S. (1990). *The female advantage: Women's ways of leadership.* New York: Doubleday Currency.

Hellinger, D., & Judd, D. R. (1991). *The democratic facade.* Pacific Grove, CA: Brooks/Cole.

Hendricks, J. (1992). Generation and the generation of theory in social gerontology. *Aging and Human Development, 35,* 31–47.

Henriques, D. B. (1995, November 26). Black mark for a "good citizen." *New York Times,* pp. 1, 11.

Herbert, B. (1996, July 12). Trampled dreams. *New York Times,* p. A8.

Herek, G. M., & Berrill, K. T. (1992). *Hate crimes.* Newbury Park, CA: Sage.

Herek, G. M., & Glunt, E. K. (1997). An epidemic of stigma: Public reaction to AIDS. In P. Conrad (Ed.), *The sociology of health and illness* (pp. 125–132). New York: St. Martin's Press.

Hernandez, R. (1995, January 18). Revolt against school spending reaches the wealthiest suburbs. *New York Times,* pp. A1, B7.

Herrmann, G. M. (1996). Women's exchange in the U.S. garage sale: Giving gifts and creating community. *Gender & Society, 10,* 703–728.

Herrnstein, R. J., & Murray, C. (1994). *The bell curve: Intelligence and class structure in American life.* New York: The Free Press.

Hersey, P., Blanchard, K., & Natemeyer, W. (1987). *Situational leadership, perception, and the use of power.* Escondido, CA: Leadership Studies.

Hershey, R. D. (1995, April 27). Bias hits Hispanic workers. *New York Times,* pp. D1, D3.

Hershey, R. D. (1995, December 19). Statistic that gets no respect. *New York Times,* pp. D1, D17.

Hershey, R. D. (1996, November 10). At college, many learn how to plunge into debt. *New York Times,* p. 38.

Hershey, R. D. (1999, January 4). How the U.S. consumer feels . . . and how the economy is doing. *New York Times,* p. C7.

Herszenhorn, D. M. (1995, March 29). Students turn to Internet for nationwide protest planning. *New York Times,* p. A20.

Hetherington, E. M., Stanley-Hagan, M., &. Anderson, E. R. (1989). Marital transitions: A child's perspective. *American Psychologist, 44,* 303–312.

Hewitt, J. P. (1998). *The myth of self-esteem: Finding happiness and solving problems in America.* New York: St. Martin's.

Hickson, G. B., Clayton, E. W., Entman, S. S., Miller, C. S., Githens, P. B., Whetson-Goldstein, K., & Sloan, F. A. (1994). Obstetricians' prior malpractice experience and patients' satisfaction with care. *Journal of the American Medical Association, 272,* 1583–1587.

Higginbotham, E., & Weber, L. (1995). Moving up with kin and community: Upward social mobility for Black and White women. In M. L. Andersen & P. H. Collins (Eds.), *Race, class, and gender: An anthology* (pp. 134–147). Belmont, CA: Wadsworth.

High-profile violence against gays. (1998, October 13). Associated Press.

Hillary, E. (Ed.). (1984). *Ecology 2000: The changing face of earth.* New York: Beaufort Books.

Hilts, P. J. (1991, May 19). Demands to fix U.S. health care reach a crescendo. *New York Times,* p. E1.

Hirsch, M., & Keller, E. F. (Eds.). (1990). *Conflicts in feminism.* New York: Routledge.

Hirschi, T. (1969). *Causes of delinquency.* Berkeley, CA: University of California Press.

Hirschman, C., & Wong, M. G. (1991). The extraordinary educational attainment of Asian Americans: A search for historical evidence and explanations. In N. R. Yetman (Ed.), *Majority and minorty* (pp. 169–184). Boston: Allyn & Bacon.

Hobbs, F. B. (1996). *65+ in the United States.* Washington, DC: U.S. Department of Commerce, Bureau of the Census.

Hochschild, A .R. (1989). *The second shift.* New York: Viking.

Hochschild, A. R. (1997). *The time bind.* New York: Metropolitan Books.

Hodson, D., & Skeen, P. (1987). Child sexual abuse: A review of research and theory with implications for family life educators. *Family Relations, 36,* 215–221.

Hoecker-Drysdale, S. (1992). *Harriet Martineau: First woman sociologist.* Oxford, England: Berg.

Hofferth, S. L., & Sandberg, J. (1998). *Changes in children's time, 1981–1997.* A working paper based on the Panel Study of Income Dynamics, University of Michigan, Ann Arbor, MI.

Hoffman, D. L., & Novak, T. P. (1998). Bridging the racial divide on the Internet. *Science, 280,* 390–391.

Hoge, W. (1997, October 18). Women marked for death by their own families. *New York Times,* p. A4.

Hoge, W. (1998, November 25). Hereditary peers feel the winds of obsolescence. *New York Times,* p. A4.

Holahan, J., & Palmer, J. L. (1988). Medicare's fiscal problems: An imperative for reform. *Journal of Health, Politics, Policy, and Law, 13,* 53–82.

Holden, C. (1980). Identical twins reared apart. *Science, 207,* 1323–1325.

Holden, C. (1987). Why do women live longer than men? *Science, 238,* 158–160.

Holden, K. C., & Smock, P. J. (1991). The economic costs of marital dissolution: Why do women bear a disproportionate cost? *Annual Review of Sociology, 17,* 51–78.

Holloman, J. L. S. (1983). Access to health care. In President's Commission for the Study of Ethical Problems in Medicine and Biomedical Research (Eds.), *Securing access to health care* (pp. 79–106). Washington, DC: U.S. Government Printing Office.

Holmes, S. A. (1994, July 8). Federal government is rethinking its system of racial classification. *New York Times,* p. A18.

Holmes, S. A. (1995, September 25). Congress plans stiff new curb on immigration. *New York Times,* pp. A1, A12.

Holmes, S. A. (1996, November 18). Quality of life is up for many Blacks, data say. *New York Times,* pp. A1, B10.

Holmes, S. A. (1997, May 16). Poll finds few support label of multiracial. *New York Times,* p. A20.

Holmes, S. A. (1998, March 16). Administration cuts affirmative action while defending it. *New York Times,* p. A17.

Holmes, S. A. (1998, November 8). Why both parties wooed Black voters this year. *New York Times,* p. 4WK.

Holmes, S. A. (1998, November 11). Children study longer and play less, a report says. *New York Times,* p. A16.

Holmes, W. C., & Slap, G. B. (1998). Sexual abuse of boys: Definition, prevalence, correlates, sequelae, and management. *Journal of the American Medical Association, 280,* 1855–1862.

Holusha, J. (1995, October 7). Down on the farm with R2D2. *New York Times,* pp. D1, D38.

Honan, W. H. (1994, October 16). Acorns sprout where mighty oaks grew. *New York Times,* p. E3.

Honan, W. H. (1998, March 4). Heated debate is expected over rate for student loans. *New York Times,* p. B9.

Honan, W. H. (1999, January 29). Nearly fifth of teachers say they feel unqualified. *New York Times,* p. A12.

Hood, E. F. (1984). Black women, White women: Separate paths to liberation. In A. M. Jagger & P. S. Rothenberg (Eds.), *Feminist frameworks* (pp. 189–201). New York: McGraw-Hill.

Hopcke, R. H., Carrington, K. L., & Wirth, S. (1994). *Same-sex love and the path to wholeness.* Boston: Shambhala Publications.

Hout, M., & Greeley, A. M. (1987). The center doesn't hold: Church attendance in the United States, 1940–1984. *American Sociological Review, 52,* 325–345.

How the U.S. consumer feels. (1999, January 4). *New York Times,* p. C7.

Howe, F. (1984). *Myths of coeducation.* Bloomington, IN: Indiana University Press.

Hoyenga, K. B., & Hoyenga, K. T. (1993). *Gender-related differences.* Boston: Allyn & Bacon.

Hu, S., Pattatucci, A. M. L., Patterson, C., Li, L., Fulker, D. W., Cherny, S. S., Kruglyak, L., & Hamer, D. H. (1995). Linkage between sexual orientation and chromosome X_q28 in males but not in females. *Nature Genetics, 11,* 248–256.

Hubbard, R. (1979). Have only men evolved? In R. Hubbard, M. S. Heniffin, & B. Fried (Eds.), *Women looking at biology looking at women* (pp. 7–36). Cambridge, MA: Schenkman.

Hubbard, R., & Wald, E. (1993). *Exploding the gene myth.* Boston: Beacon Press.

Hübler, E. (1999, January 3). The new faces of retirement. *New York Times,* pp. 1BU, 12BU.

Hudson, R. B., & Gonyea, J. G. (1990, Summer). Political mobilization and older women. *Generations, 14,* 67–72.

Huisman, K. A. (1996). Wife battering in Asian American communities: Identifying the service needs of an overlooked segment of the U.S. population. *Violence Against Women, 2,* 260–283.

Humphreys, L. (1970). *Tearoom trade: Impersonal sex in public places.* Chicago: Aldine.

Hurn, C. J. (1985). *The limits and possibilities of schooling.* Boston: Allyn & Bacon.

Hurtig, A. L., & Rosenthal, I. M. (1987). Psychological findings in early treated cases of female pseudohermaphroditism caused by virilizing congenital adrenal hyperplasia. *Archives of Sexual Behavior, 16,* 209–223.

Hyman, P. (1979). The other half: Women in the Jewish tradition. In E. Koltun (Ed.), *The Jewish woman* (pp. 105–113). New York: Schocken Press.

Inciardi, J. A., Lockwood, D., & Pottieger, A. E. (1993). *Women and crack-cocaine.* New York: Macmillan.

Institute for Research on Poverty. (1992). *Measuring poverty.* Madison, WI: Institute for Research on Poverty.

Institute for Research on Poverty. (1998, Spring). Improving the measurement of American poverty. *Focus,* pp. 2–5.

Inter-University Consortium for Political and Social Research. (1994). *World values survey, 1990–1993.* Ann Arbor, MI: Author.

Is there a better way to run an American election? (1988, November 13). *New York Times,* pp. E1, E3.

Isaaks, L. (1980). *Sex role stereotyping as it relates to ethnicity, age, and sex in young children.* Unpublished doctoral dissertation, East Texas State University.

Island, D., & Lettellier, P. (1991). *Men who beat the men who love them.* New York: Haworth.

Jablon, R. (1996, August 19). Computer banking is feared as a hardship to poor people. *Chattanooga Times,* p. C2.

Jacobs, B. (1990). Aging and politics. In R. H. Binstock & L. K. George (Eds.), *Handbook of aging and the social sciences* (pp. 349–361). New York: Academic Press.

Jacobs, J. A., & Lim, S. T. (1995). Trends in occupational and industrial sex segregation in 56 countries, 1960–1980. In J. A. Jacobs (Ed.), *Gender inequality at work* (pp. 259–293). Thousand Oaks, CA: Sage.

Janis, I. (1989). *Crucial decisions: Leadership in policymaking and crisis management.* New York: Free Press.

Janis, I. L. (1982). *Groupthink.* Boston: Houghton Mifflin.

Japp, P. M. (1991). Gender and work in the 1980s: Television's working women as displaced persons. *Women's Studies in Communication, 14,* 49–74.

Jaret, C. (1995). *Contemporary racial and ethnic relations.* New York: HarperCollins.

Jasper, J. M., & Poulsen, J. D. (1995). Recruiting strangers and friends: Moral shocks and social networks in animal rights and anti-nuclear protests. *Social Problems, 42,* 493–512.

Jayakody, R., & Chatters, L. M. (1997). Differences among African American single mothers: Marital status, living arrangements, and family support. In R. J. Taylor, J. S. Jackson, & L. M. Taylor (Eds.), *Family life in Black America* (pp. 167–184). Thousand Oaks, CA: Sage.

Jeffrey, P., Jeffrey, R., & Lyon, A. (1988). *Labor pains and labor power: Women and childbearing in India.* London: Zed Books.

Jehl, S. H. (1997, September 25). King cotton exacts a tragic toll from the young. *New York Times,* p. A4.

Jencks, C., et al. (1972). *Inequality: A reassessment of the effects of family and schooling in America.* New York: Basic Books.

Jenkins, R. (1994). Rethinking ethnicity: Identity, categorization, and power. *Ethnic and Racial Studies, 17,* 197–223.

John, R. (1991). The state of research on American Indian elders' health, income security, and social support networks. In *Minority elders: Longevity, economics, and health* (pp. 38–50). Washington, DC: The Gerontological Society of America.

Johnson, D. (1996, February 12). No-fault divorce is under attack. *New York Times,* p. A10.

Johnson, D. (1996, May 20). Bid to auction killer's tools provokes disgust. *New York Times,* p. A10.

Johnson, D. (1998, November 3). Bored, dispirited, disgusted, most won't vote. *New York Times,* pp. A1, A23.

Johnson, K. (1996, March 7). In the class of '70, wounded winners. *New York Times,* pp. A1, A20-A21.

Johnson, R. E., Marcos, A. C., & Bahr, S. J. (1987). The role of peers in the complex etiology of adolescent drug use. *Criminology, 25,* 323–340.

Johnson, S., Guenther, S., Laube, D., & Keettel, W. (1981). Factors influencing lesbian gynecologic care: A preliminary study. *American Journal of Obstetrics and Gynecology, 140,* 20–28.

Johnston, D. (1992, April 24). Survey shows number of rapes far higher than official figures. *New York Times,* p. A14.

Johnstone, R. L. (1988). *Religion in society.* Englewood Cliffs, NJ: Prentice-Hall.

Jones, C. (1994, July 8). Test scores show gaps by ethnicity. *New York Times,* pp. B1, B3.

Jones, E. F. (1989). *Pregnancy, contraception, and family planning services in industrialized countries.* New Haven, CT: Yale University Press.

Jones, M. G., & Wheatley, J. (1990). Gender differences in teacher-student interactions in science classrooms. *Journal of Research in Science Teaching, 27,* 861–874.

Kahn, K. L., Pearson, M. L., & Harrison, E. R. (1994). Health care for Black and poor hospitalized Medicare patients. *Journal of the American Medical Association, 271,* 1169–1174.

Kahn, S. S., Nessim, S., Gray, R., Czer, L. S., Chaux, A., & Matloff, J. (1990). Increased mortality of women in coronary bypass surgery: Evidence of referral bias. *Annals of Internal Medicine, 112,* 561–567.

Kain, E. (1990). *The myth of family decline.* Lexington, MA: Lexington Books.

Kalish, J. (1998, December 31). For the oldest lessons, the newest tools. *New York Times,* p. G8.

Kameda, T., & Sugimori, S. (1993). Psychological entrapment in group decision making: An assigned decision rule and a groupthink phenomenon. *Journal of Personality and Social Psychology, 65,* 282–292.

Kamerman, S. B., & Kahn, A. J. (1988). *Mothers alone.* Dover, MA: Auburn House.

Kammeyer, K. C. W. (1987). *Marriage and family.* Boston: Allyn & Bacon.

Kane, E. W., & Sanchez, L. (1992). *Pushing feminism out?: Family status and criticism of gender inequality at home and work.* Paper presented at the Annual Meeting of the American Sociological Association, Pittsburgh, PA.

Kane, H. (1995). Leaving home. In Worldwatch Institute, (Ed.), *State of the world 1995* (pp. 132–149). New York: W. W. Norton & Company.

Kane, H. (1996). Refugees on the rise again. In Worldwatch Institute, (Ed.), *Vital signs 1996* (pp. 96–97). New York: W. W. Norton & Company.

Kane, J. (1995). *Savages.* New York: Alfred A. Knopf.

Kane, R. L., Kasteller, J. M., & Gray, R. M. (1976). *The health gap: Medical services and the poor.* New York: Springer.

Kanter, R. M. (1977). *Men and women of the corporation.* New York: Basic Books.

Kanter, R. M. (1983). *The change masters: Innovation and entrepreneurship in the American corporation.* New York: Simon and Schuster.

Kantrowitz, B. (1996, November 4). Gay families come out. *Newsweek,* pp. 50–57.

Kart, C. S. (1985). *The realities of aging.* Boston: Allyn & Bacon.

Kasof, J. (1993). Sex bias in the naming of stimulus persons. *Psychological Bulletin, 113,* 140–163.

Kaspar, A. S. (1986). Consciousness re-evaluated: Interpretive theory and feminist scholarship. *Sociological Inquiry, 56,* 30–49.

Kaufman, D. R. (1991). *Rachel's daughters: Newly Orthodox Jewish women.* New Brunswick, NJ: Rutgers University Press.

Kay, F. M., & Hagan, J. (1995). The persistent glass ceiling: Gendered inequalities in the earnings of lawyers. *British Journal of Sociology, 46,* 279–310.

Kay, F. M., & Hagan, J. (1998). Raising the bar: The gender stratification of law-firm capital. *American Sociological Review, 63,* 728–743.

Kaye, E. (1993, June 6). So weak, so powerful. *New York Times,* pp. V1, V10.

Keating, W. D., Rasey, K. P., & Krumholz, N. (1990). Community development in the United States. In W. van Vliet & J. van Weesep (Eds.), *Government and housing* (pp. 206–219). Newbury Park, CA: Sage.

Keenen, J. S. (1996, April 29). The end of integration. *Time,* pp. 38–45.

Keith, J. (1990). Age in social and cultural context: Anthropological perspectives. In R. H. Binstock & L. K. George (Eds.), *Handbook of aging and the social sciences* (pp. 91–111). New York: Academic Press.

Keith, J., & Associates. (1994). *The aging experience.* Thousand Oaks, CA: Sage.

Kelly, G. F. (1996). *Sexuality today: The human perspective.* Dubuque, IA: Brown and Benchmark.

Kent, S. (Ed.) (1996). *Cultural diversity among twentieth-century foragers: An African perspective.* New York: Cambridge University Press.

Kephart, W. M., & Zellner, W. W. (1991). *Extraordinary groups.* New York: St. Martin's Press.

Kerber, L. K., Greeno, C. G., Maccoby, E. E., Luria, Z., Stack, C. B., & Gilligan, C. (1986). On *In a Different Voice:* An interdisciplinary forum. *Signs, 11,* 304–333.

Kershaw, S. (1996, January 1). As 7 go to trial in a fatal beating, a Philadelphia neighborhood still grieves. *New York Times,* p. 10.

Kifner, J. (1998, October 21). Protestors say the police created 'havoc' at rally. *New York Times,* p. B5.

Kijakazi, K., & Greenstein, R. (1998). *How would various Social Security reform plans affect Social Security benefits?* Washington, DC: Center on Budget and Policy Priorities.

Kilborn, P. T. (1994, May 1). College seniors find more jobs but modest pay. *New York Times,* pp. 1, 26.

Kilborn, P. T. (1995, December 5). Union capitulation shows strike is now dull sword. *New York Times,* pp. A18.

Kilborn, P. T. (1996, March 8). And how do unions fit into all of this? *New York Times,* p. A22.

Kilborn, P. T. (1997, June 11). For poorest Indians, casinos aren't enough. *New York Times,* pp. A1, B11.

Kilborn, P. T. (1998, December 5). Premiums rising for individuals. *New York Times,* p. A7.

Kilborn, P. T. (1999, January 23). Medicare safety nets fail to catch many of the poor. *New York Times,* p. A9.

King, D. R. (1988). Multiple jeopardy, multiple consciousness: The context of a Black feminist ideology. *Signs, 14,* 42–72.

Kitano, H. H. L. (1985). *Race relations.* Englewood Cliffs, NJ: Prentice-Hall.

Kitfield, J. (1988, July-August). For industry, turmoil and change. *Military Logistics Forum,* 10–26.

Kitzinger, C. (1995). Social constructionism: Implications for lesbian and gay psychology. In A. R. D'Augelli & C. J. Patterson (Eds.), *Lesbian, gay, and bisexual identities over the lifespan* (pp. 136–161). New York: Oxford University Press.

Kleinfield, N. R. (1995, January 3). Yearning to breathe free: Urban Indians long for lives left behind. *New York Times,* pp. B1, B3.

Kleinfield, N. R. (1996, March 4). The company as family, no more. *New York Times,* pp. A1, A12–A14.

Kleinmuntz, B. (1982). *Personality and psychological assessment.* New York: St. Martin's Press.

Kletke, P. R., Emmons, D. W., & Gillis, K. D. (1996). Current trends in physicians' practice arrangements: From owners to employees. *Journal of the American Medical Association, 276,* 555–560.

Klockars, C. B. (1979). The contemporary crises of Marxist criminology. *Criminology, 16,* 477–515.

Kohn, M. (1965). Social class and parent-child relationships: An interpretation. *American Journal of Sociology, 68,* 471–480.

Kohn, M. (1976). Occupational structure and alienation. *American Journal of Sociology, 82,* 111–130.

Kohn, M. (1977). *Class and conformity.* Homewood, IL: Dorsey.

Kolata, G. (1993, October 26). Cloning human embryos: Debate erupts over ethics. *New York Times,* pp. A1, C3.

Kolata, G. (1994, January 6). Fetal ovary transplant is envisioned. *New York Times,* p. A16.

Kolata, G. (1996, February 27). New era of robust elderly belies the fears of scientists. *New York Times,* pp. C1, C3.

Kolata, G. (1997, January 7). Model shows how medical changes let population surge. *New York Times,* p. C3.

Kolata, G. (1997, April 24). A record and big questions as woman gives birth at 63. *New York Times,* pp. A1, A25.

Kolata, G. (1997). *Clone.* New York: William Morrow.

Kolker, A., & Burke, B. M. (1992). *Sex preference and sex selection: Attitudes of prenatal diagnosis clients.* Paper presented at the Annual Meeting of the American Sociological Association, Pittsburg, PA.

Kolker, C. (1998, May 6). More women, children seek shelters, study says. *Houston Chronicle,* p. 1.

Konner, M. (1982). *The tangled wing: Biological constraints on the human spirit.* New York: Harper Colophon Books.

Korn, D. A. (1988). *Ethiopia, the United States, and the Soviet Union.* Carbondale, IL: Southern Illinois University Press.

Kornhauser, W. (1959). *The politics of mass society.* New York: Free Press.

Kosberg, J. I. (1988). Preventing elder abuse: Identification of high-risk factors prior to placement decisions. *The Gerontologist, 28,* 43–50.

Koss, M., Gidcycz, C., & Wisniewski, N. (1987). The scope of rape: Incidence and prevalence of sexual aggression in a sample of higher education students. *Journal of Consulting and Clinical Psychology, 55,* 162–170.

Kozol, J. (1985). *Illiterate America.* Garden City, NY: Anchor/Doubleday.

Kozol, J. (1988). *Rachel and her children: Homeless families in America.* New York: Fawcett Columbine.

Kozol, J. (1991). *Savage inequalities: Children in America's schools.* New York: Crown.

Kozol, J. (1995). *Amazing grace: The lives of children and the conscience of a nation.* New York: Harper Perennial.

Krafka, C., Linz, D., Donnerstein, E., & Penrod, S. (1997). Women's reactions to sexually aggressive mass media depictions. *Violence Against Women, 3,* 149–181.

Kramer, R. (1986). The third wave. *Wilson Quarterly, 10,* 110–129.

Krause, E. A. (1977). *Power and illness.* New York: Elsevier.

Kravitz, R. L., Callahan, E. J., & Lewis, C. E. (1996). Prevalence and sources of patients' unmet expectations for care. *Annals of Internal Medicine, 125,* 730–736.

Kraybill, D. B., & Nolt, S. M. (1996). *Amish enterprise: From plows to profits.* Baltimore: Johns Hopkins University Press.

Krieger, N., & Sidney, S. (1996). Racial discrimination and blood pressure: The CARDIA study of young Black and White adults. *American Journal of Public Health, 86,* 1370–1378.

Kriesi, H., et al. (1995). *New social movements in Western Europe: A comparative analysis.* Minneapolis: University of Minnesota Press.

Krisberg, B. (1975). *Crime and privilege.* Englewood Cliffs, NJ: Prentice-Hall.

Kristof, N. D. (1991, November 5). Stark data on women: 100 million are missing. *New York Times,* pp. C1, C12.

Kristof, N. D. (1995, April 30). Japan hunts gas terrorists with self-imposed restraint. *New York Times,* pp. 1A, 8A.

Kristof, N. D. (1996, March 24). Morning in America in Japan. *New York Times,* pp. E1, E16.

Kristof, N. D. (1996, April 14). Asian childhoods sacrificed to prosperity's lust. *New York Times,* pp. 1, 8.

Kristof, N. D. (1996, September 22). Aging world, new wrinkles. *New York Times,* pp. E1, E5.

Kristof, N. D. (1998, October 20). Fears of sorcerers spur killings in Java. *New York Times,* pp. A1, A6.

Kristof, N. D. (1998, October 26). Japanese are torn between efficiency and egalitarian values. *New York Times,* pp. A1, A10.

Kübler-Ross, E. (1969). *On death and dying.* New York: Macmillan.

Kunitz, S. J., & Levy, J. E. (1991). *Navajo aging: The transition from family to institutional support.* Tucson, AZ: University of Arizona Press.

Kurtz, R. A., & Chalfant, H. P. (1984). *The sociology of medicine and illness.* Boston: Allyn & Bacon.

Kurtz, R. A., & Chalfant, H. P. (1991). *The sociology of medicine and illness.* Boston: Allyn & Bacon.

Kurz, D. (1993). Physical assaults by husbands: A major social problem. In R. J. Gelles & D. R. Loseke (Eds.), *Current controversies on family violence* (pp. 88–103). Newbury Park, CA: Sage.

Kurz, D. (1995). *For richer, for poorer: Mothers confront divorce.* New York: Routledge.

Kutner, N. G., & Levinson, R. M. (1978). The toy salesperson: A voice for change in sex-role stereotypes? *Sex Roles, 4,* 1–8.

Kuznets, S. (1955). Economic growth and income inequality. *The American Economic Review, XLV,* 1–28.

Labaton, S. (1995, May 1). Data show federal agents seldom employ surveillance authority against terrorists. *New York Times,* p. B6.

Labaton, S. (1998, November 22). The debacle that buried Washington. *New York Times,* pp. BU1, BU12.

Labaton, S. (1998, December 13). Merger wave spurs a new scrutiny. *New York Times,* p. 38.

Lackey, P. N. (1989). Adults' attitudes about assignments of household chores to male and female children. *Sex Roles, 20,* 271–281.

Laine, C., Davidoff, F., Delbanco, T. L. (1996). Important elements of outpatient care: A comparison of patients' and physicians' opinions. *Annals of Internal Medicine, 125,* 640–645.

Lake, C. C., & Breglio, V. J. (1992). Different voices, different views: The politics of gender. In P. Ries & A. J. Stone (Eds.), *The American woman, 1992–93* (pp. 178–201). New York: W. W. Norton.

Lakoff, R. (1991). You are what you say. In E. Ashton-Jones & G. A. Olson (Eds.), *The gender reader* (pp. 292–298). Boston: Allyn & Bacon.

Lamanna, M. A., & Riedmann, A. (1994). *Marriages and families.* Belmont, CA: Wadsworth.

Lamb, D. (1982). *The Africans.* New York: Random House.

Lambert, B. (1998). Secret surveillance cameras growing in city, report says. *New York Times,* p. 61.

Lane, A. I. (1995). *Return of the buffalo: The story behind America's Indian gaming explosion.* New York: Bergin and Garvey.

Lane, D. (1984). Social stratification and class. In E. P. Hoffman & R. F. Laird (Eds.), *The Soviet polity in the modern era* (pp. 563–605). New York: Aldine.

Lane, D. (1990). *Soviet society under Perestroika.* Winchester, MA: Unwin Hyman.

Langan, P. A., & Harlow, C. W. (1994). *Child rape victims, 1992.* Washington, DC: U.S. Department of Justice.

Lanis, K., & Covell, K. (1995). Images of women in advertisements: Effects of attitudes related to sexual aggression. *Sex Roles, 21,* 639–649.

Lappe, F. M., & Collins, J. (1979). *Food first.* New York: Ballantine.

Larana, E., Johnston, H., & Gusfield, J. R. (Eds.) (1994). *New social movements: From ideology to identity.* Philadelphia: Temple University Press.

Larson, J. H. (1988). The marriage quiz: College students' beliefs in selected myths about marriage. *Family Relations, 37,* 3–11.

Lasch, C. (1977). *Haven in a heartless world: The family besieged.* New York: Basic Books.

Laslett, B., & Thorne, B. (Eds.) (1997). *Feminist sociology: Life histories of a movement.* New Brunswick, NJ: Rutgers University Press.

Laumann, E. O., Gagnon, J. H., Michael, R. T., & Michaels, S. (1994). *The social organization of sexuality.* Chicago: University of Chicago Press.

Lav, I. J. (1998). *IRS Reform Bill includes new salvo of tax cuts for wealthy.* Washington, DC: Center on Budget and Policy Priorities.

Lawlor, J. (1998, April 26). For many blue-collar fathers, child care is shift work, too. *New York Times,* p. BU11.

Le Bon, G. (1896/1960). *The crowd: A study of the popular mind.* New York: Viking Press.

Leacock, E. (1971). *The culture of poverty: A critique.* New York: Simon and Schuster.

Leacock, E. B. (Ed.) (1972). *The origin of the family, private property and the state by Frederick Engels.* New York: International Publishers.

Lee, R. M. (1995). *Dangerous fieldwork.* London: Sage.

Lee, S. M. (1993). Racial classifications in the U.S. census: 1890–1990. *Ethnic and Racial Studies, 16,* 75–94.

Lehmann-Haupt, R. (1999, January 24). Rooming with a guy named mom. *New York Times,* pp. ST1, ST2.

Lemann, N. (1998, November 1). The new American consensus. *New York Times Magazine,* pp. 37–47, 74.

Lemert, E. M. (1964). Social structure, social control, and deviation. In M. B. Clinard (Ed.), *Anomie and deviant behavior* (pp. 57–97). New York: Free Press.

Lemert, E. M. (1967). *Human deviance, social problems, and social control.* New York: Prentice-Hall.

Lenski, G., Nolan, P., & Lenski, J. (1995). *Human societies.* New York: McGraw-Hill.

Leonard, J. S. (1991). The federal anti-bias effort. In E. P. Hoffman (Ed.), *Essays on the economics of discrimination* (pp. 85–113). Kalamazoo, MI: W. E. Upjohn Institute for Employment Research.

Lepowsky, M. (1990). Gender in an egalitarian society: A case study from the coral sea. In P. R. Sanday & R. G. Goodenough (Eds.), *Beyond the second sex* (pp. 169–224). Philadelphia: University of Pennsylvania Press.

Lepowsky, M. (1994). Women, men and aggression in an egalitarian society. *Sex Roles, 30,* 199–211.

Leppard, W., Ogletree, S. M., & Wallen, E. (1993). Gender stereotyping in medical advertising: Much ado about something? *Sex Roles, 29,* 829–838.

Lerner, G. (1972). *Black women in White America.* New York: Vintage.

Lerner, R., Nagai, A. K., & Rothman, S. (1996). *American elites.* New Haven, CT: Yale University Press.

LeVay, S. (1991). A difference in the hypothalamic structure between heterosexual and homosexual men. *Science, 253,* 1034–1037.

Levin, J., & Levin, W. C. (1980). *Ageism: Prejudice and discrimination against the elderly.* Belmont, CA: Wadsworth.

Levine, J. M., & Moreland, R. L. (1998). Small groups. In D. T. Gilbert, S. T. Fiske, & G. Lindsey (Eds.), *Handbook of social psychology* (pp. 415–469). New York: Random House.

Levy, F. (1996). *Teaching the new basic skills: Principles for educating children to thrive in a changing economy.* New York: Free Press.

Levy, F. (1998). *The new dollars and dreams.* New York: Russell Sage Foundation.

Lewin, T. (1991, April 28). The ailing health care system: A question of access. *New York Times,* p. 28.

Lewin, T. (1991, July 21). Communities and their residents age gracefully. *New York Times,* pp. 1, 16.

Lewin, T. (1997, September 15). Women losing ground to men in widening income difference. *New York Times,* pp. A1, A12.

Lewin, T. (1997, September 18). School voucher study finds satisfaction. *New York Times,* p. A16.

Lewis, D. L. (1993). *W. E. B. Du Bois: Biography of a race, 1868–1919.* New York: Henry Holt and Co.

Lewis, O. (1966, October). The culture of poverty. *Scientific American,* 19–25.

Lewis, P. (1988, June 28). World hunger still growing. *New York Times,* p. 3.

Lewis, P. (1991, March 22). U. N. survey calls Iraq's war damage near-apocalyptic. *New York Times,* pp. A1, A9.

Lewis, G., & Sloggett, A. (1998). Suicide, deprivation, and unemployment: Record linkage study. *British Journal of Medicine, 317,* 1283–1286.

Lieberman, P. (1991). *Uniquely human.* Cambridge, MA: Harvard University Press.

Lieberman, P. (1998). *Eve spoke: Human language and human evolution.* New York: W. W. Norton.

Lightfoot-Klein, H. (1989). *Prisoners of ritual: An odyssey into female genital circumcision in Africa.* New York: Harrington Park Press.

Lim, L. L. (1998). The economic and social bases of prostitution in Southeast Asia. In L. L. Lim (Ed.), *The sex sector* (pp. 1–28). Geneva: International Labour Office.

Lin, N., Ensler, W. M., & Vaughn, J. C. (1981). Social resources and strength of ties: Structural factors in occupational status attainment. *American Sociological Review, 46,* 393–405.

Lincoln, C. E., & Mamiya, L. H. (1990). *The Black church in the African American experience.* Durham, NC: University of North Carolina Press.

Lindesmith, A. R., & Gagnon, J. (1964). Anomie and drug addiction. In M. B. Clinard (Ed.), *Anomie and deviant behavior* (pp. 158–188). New York: Free Press.

Lindgren, J. R., & Taub, N. (1993). *The law of sex discrimination.* Minneapolis: West.

Lindner, R. (1996). *The reportage of urban culture: Robert Park and the Chicago School.* New York: Cambridge University Press.

Lines, W. J. (1991). *Taming the great south land.* Berkeley: University of California Press.

Linton, R. (1937, April). One hundred percent American. *The American Mercury, 40,* 427–429.

Lipset, S. M. (1994). The state of American sociology. *Sociological Forum, 9,* 199–220.

Lipton, M. A., Leonard, E., & Tomashoff, C. (1999, February 22). Heaven help us. *People,* pp. 86–94.

Liska, A. E., & Reed, M. D. (1985). Ties to conventional institutions and delinquency: Estimating reciprocal effects. *American Sociological Review, 50,* 547–560.

Littlewood, R., & Lipsedge, M. (1989). *Aliens and alienists: Ethnic minorities and psychiatry.* London: Unwin Hyman.

Lively, K. (1997, March 21). Campus drug arrests increased 18 percent in 1995; Reports of other crimes fell. *Chronicle of Higher Education,* pp. A44–A46.

Livingston, J. (1992). *Crime and criminology.* Englewood Cliffs, NJ: Prentice-Hall.

Lloyd, K. M., & South, S. J. (1996). Contextual influences on young men's transition to first marriage. *Social Forces, 74,* 1097–1119.

Lobel, T. E., Bempechat, J., Gewirtz, J. C., Shoken-Topaz, T., & Bashe, E. (1993). The role of gender-related information and self-endorsements of traits in preadolescents' inferences and judgments. *Child Development, 64,* 1285–1294.

Lock, J., & Kleis, B. N. (1998). A primer on homophobia for the child and adolescent psychiatrist. *Journal of the American Academy of Child and Adolescent Psychiatry, 37,* 671–672.

Lockhart, L. L. (1991). Spousal violence: A cross-racial perspective. In R. L. Hampton (Ed.), *Black family violence* (pp. 85–101). Lexington, MA: Lexington Books.

Lofland, L. H. (1975). The "thereness" of women: A selective review of urban sociology. In M. Millman & R. M. Kanter (Eds.), *Another voice* (pp. 144–170). New York: Anchor/Doubleday.

Lohr, S. (1996, December 29). Though upbeat on the economy, people still fear for their jobs. *New York Times*, pp. 1, 22.

Lorber, J. (1998). *Gender inequality: Feminist theories and politics*. Los Angeles: Roxbury.

Lorch, D. (1996, March 30). Young voters, diverse and disillusioned, are unpredictable in '96 race. *New York Times*, p. 8.

Lorch, D. (1996, April 11). Is America any place for a nice Hispanic girl? *New York Times*, pp. C1, C10.

Loring, M., & Powell, B. (1988). Gender, race and DSM-III: A study of psychiatric behavior. *Journal of Health and Social Behavior, 29*, 1–22.

Lott, B. (1987). *Women's lives*. Monterey, CA: Brooks/Cole.

Love, A. A. (1998, June 9). Wage gap between the sexes narrowing. *Atlanta Constitution*, p. 1.

Lowest violent U.S. crime rate in 25 years in '97. (1998, December 27). Reuters. (Internet)

Luker, K. (1996). *Dubious conceptions: The politics of teen pregnancy*. Cambridge, MA: Harvard University Press.

Lundberg, G. D. (1991). National health care reform: An aura of inevitability is upon us. *Journal of the American Medical Association, 265*, 2566–2567.

Lurie, A. (1991). *Imaginary friends*. New York: Avon.

Lurie, N., Slater, J., McGovern, P., Ekstrum, J., Quam, L., & Margolis, K. (1993). Preventive care for women: Does the sex of the physician make a difference? *New England Journal of Medicine, 329*, 478–482.

Lykken, D. T., McGue, M., Tellegen, A., & Bouchard, T. J. (1992). Emergenesis. *American Psychologist, 47*, 1565–1577.

Lynch, M. J., & Groves, W. B. (1986). *A primer in radical criminology*. New York: Harrow and Heston.

Lyons, J. E., & Walton, K. O. (1988). Magnetic attractions: Desegregating a minority school district. *Educational Record, 68/69*, 32–34.

MacDonald, K., & Parke, R. D. (1986). Parent-child physical play: The effects of sex and age on children and parent. *Sex Roles, 15*, 367–378.

MacFarquhar, E. (1994, September 12). Population wars. *U.S. News and World Report*, pp. 54–57.

MacFarquhar, N. (1996). Mutilation of Egyptian girls: Despite ban, it goes on. *New York Times*, p. A3.

Macke, J. P., et al. (1993). Sequence variation in the androgen receptor gene is not a common determinant of male sexual orientation. *American Journal of Human Genetics, 53*, 844–852.

Madriz, E. I. (1997). Images of criminals and victims: A study of women's fear and social control. *Gender & Society, 11*, 342–356.

Maguire, P. (1987). *Doing participatory research: A feminist approach*. Amherst, MA: The Center for International Education, School of Education, University of Massachusetts.

Maier, M. H. (1991). *The data game: Controversies in social science statistics*. New York: M. E. Sharpe.

Malmgren, H. B. (1990). Technology and the economy. In W. E. Brock & R. D. Hormats (Eds.), *The global economy: America's role in the decade ahead* (pp. 92–119). New York: W. W. Norton.

Mamdani, M. (1996). *Citizen and subject: Contemporary Africa and the legacy of late colonialism*. Princeton: Princeton University Press.

Mankoff, M. (1971). Societal reaction and career deviance: A critical analysis. *Sociological Quarterly, 12*, 204–218.

Mann, C. R. (1993). *Unequal justice: A question of color*. Bloomington, IN: Indiana University Press.

Manning, W. D. (1995). Cohabitation, marriage, and entry into motherhood. *Journal of Marriage and the Family, 57*, 191–200.

Mannix, M. (1996, April 29). It's a jungle out there. *U.S. News and World Report*, pp. 73–75.

Manton, K. G., & Vaupel, J. W. (1995). Survival after the age of 80 in the United States, Sweden, France, England, and Japan. *New England Journal of Medicine, 333*, 1232–1235.

Manzo, K. K. (1993, November 18). Latino student failures tied to lack of Latino teachers. *Black Issues in Higher Education*, pp. 17, 20.

Marable, M. (1986). *W. E. B. Du Bois: Black radical democrat*. Boston: Twayne Publishers.

Mares, M. (1996). *Positive effects of television on social behavior: A meta-analysis*. Paper presented at the Annenberg Washington Conference on Children and Television, Washington, DC.

Marmor, T. R., & Mashaw, J. L. (1997). Canada's health insurance and ours: The real lessons, the big choices. In P. Conrad (Ed.), *The sociology of health and illness* (pp. 482–492). New York: St. Martin's Press.

Marmot, M., & Theorell, T. (1997). Social class and cardiovascular disease: The contribution of work. In P. Conrad (Ed.), *The sociology of health and illness* (pp. 93–105). New York: St. Martin's Press.

Marriott, M. (1996, January 24). In a cashless future, robots will cook. *New York Times*, pp. C1, C4.

Marsiglio, W., & Donnelly, D. (1991). Sexual relations in later life: A national study of married persons. *Journals of Gerontology: Social Science, 46,* S338–S334.

Martin, B. (1978). Conservative Judaism and Reconstructionism. In B. Martin (Ed.), *Movements and issues in American Judaism* (pp. 103–157). Westport, CT: Greenwood Press.

Martin, C. L. (1989). Children's use of gender-related information in making social judgements. *Developmental Psychology, 25,* 80–88.

Martin, M. K., & Voorhies, B. (1975). *Female of the species.* New York: Columbia University Press.

Martin, R., Mutchnick, R. J., & Austin, W. T. (1990). *Criminological thought: Pioneers past and present.* New York: Macmillan.

Marty, M. E. (1992). Fundamentals of fundamentalism. In L. Kaplan (Ed.), *Fundamentalism in comparative perspective* (pp. 15–23). Amherst, MA: University of Massachusetts Press.

Marty, M. E., & Appleby, R. S. (1992). *The glory and the power.* Boston: Beacon Press.

Marx, K. (1964). *Karl Marx: Selected writings in sociology and social philosophy.* (T. B. Bottomore, Ed.). New York: McGraw-Hill.

Mason, M. A., Skolnick, A., & Sugarman, S. D. (Eds.) (1998). *All our families.* New York: Oxford University Press.

Massey, D. S., & Denton, N. A. (1993). *American apartheid: Segregation and the making of the underclass.* Cambridge, MA: Harvard University Press.

Mates, R. (1997, April 4). Financial abuse of elderly hits close to home. *Toronto Globe and Mail,* p. 1.

Mathews, J. (1998). *Class struggle: What's wrong (and right) with America's best public high schools.* New York: Times Books/Random House.

Matsueda, R. L. (1988). The current state of differential association theory. *Crime and Delinquency, 34,* 277–306.

Matsui, T., & Onglatco, M. L. U. (1990). Relationships between employee quality circle involvement and need fulfillment in work as moderated by work type: A compensatory or spillover model? In U. Kleinbeck, H. Quast, H. Thierry, & H. Hacker (Eds.), *Work motivation.* Hillsdale, NJ: Lawrence Erlbaum.

Matthews, W., Booth, M., Turner, J., & Kessler, L. (1986). Physicians' attitudes toward homosexuality—survey of a California County Medical Society. *Western Journal of Medicine, 144,* 106–110.

May, E. T. (1995). *Barren in the promised land: Childless Americans and the pursuit of happiness.* New York: Basic Books.

Mazur, A., & Lamb, T. A. (1980). Testosterone, status, and mood in human males. *Hormones and Behavior, 14,* 236–246.

McAdam, D. (1989). The biographical consequences of activism. *American Sociological Review, 54,* 744–760.

McAdoo, H. P. (1986). Societal stress: The Black family. In J. B. Cole (Ed.), *All American women* (pp. 187–197). New York: Free Press.

McAdoo, H. P. (1988). Changing perspectives on the role of the Black father. In P. Bronstein & C. P. Cowan (Eds.), *Fatherhood today* (pp. 79–92). New York: John Wiley.

McCartney, J. (1985, February 3). Accused of abuses, 10 largest defense firms are under fire. *Philadelphia Inquirer,* pp. 1, 20.

McCarty, B. (1985, January 27). Torpedoing higher education. *New York Times,* p. E21.

McCauley, C. (1989). The nature of social influence in groupthink: Compliance and internalization. *Journal of Personality and Social Psychology, 57,* 250–260.

McCubbin, H. I., & Patterson, J. M. (1981). *Systematic assessment of family stress, resources, and coping.* St. Paul, MN: Family Stress and Coping Project, University of Minnesota.

McDonald, L. (1993). *The early origins of the social sciences.* Montreal: McGill-Queens University Press.

McFadden, R. (1991, April 22). Degrees and stacks of resumes yield few jobs for class of '91. *New York Times,* pp. A1, B6.

McGregor, R., & Lawnham, P. (1993, August 5). Japan apologizes to sex slaves. *The Australian,* p. 8.

McKee, V. (1996, June 9). Blue blood and the color of money. *New York Times,* pp. 49–50.

McKinley, J. C. (1996, May 4). In peace, warrior women rank low. *New York Times,* p. 4.

McKinley, J. C. (1999, January 11). In Cuba's new dual economy, have-nots far exceed haves. *New York Times,* pp. A1, A6.

McKinney, K., Saxe, P., & Cobb, L. (1998). The 1996 Hans O. Mauksch award presentation: Are we really doing all we can for our undergraduates? Professional socialization via out-of-class experiences. *Teaching Sociology, 26,* 1–13.

McPhail, C. (1991). *The myth of the maddening crowd.* New York: Aldine.

McPhail, C., & Wohlstein, R. T. (1983). Individual and collective behaviors within gatherings, demonstrations, and riots. *Annual Review of Sociology, 9,* 579–600.

McQuiston, J. T. (1997, March 16). Caller objects to integration of lead role in Passion play, but threat report is denied. *New York Times,* p. B6.

McWhirter, D. P. (1993). Biological theories of sexual orientation. *American Psychiatric Press Review of Psychiatry, 12,* 41–57.

Mead, G. H. (1934). *Mind, self, and society.* Chicago: University of Chicago Press.

Mead, M. (1935). *Sex and temperament in three primitive societies.* New York: Dell.

Meadows, D. H., Meadows, D. L., & Randers, J. (1992). *Beyond the limits.* Post Mills, VT: Chelsea Green.

Meet the class of 1996. (1996, October 14). *Forbes Magazine,* pp. 100–320.

Megargee, E. I. (1972). *The California psychological inventory handbook.* San Francisco: Jossey-Bass.

Meier, M. S. (1990). North from Mexico. In C. McWilliams (Ed.), *North from Mexico* (pp. 309–331). New York: Greenwood Press.

Meier, R. F., & Geis, G. (1997). *Victimless crime? Prostitution, drugs, homosexuality, and abortion.* Los Angeles: Roxbury Publishing Co.

Meigs, A. (1990). Multiple gender ideologies and statuses. In P. R. Sanday & R. G. Goodenough (Eds.), *Beyond the second sex* (pp. 99–112). Philadelphia: University of Pennsylvania Press.

Melucci, A. (1996). *Challenging codes: Collective action in the information age.* New York: Cambridge University Press.

Mensch, B. S., Bruce, J., & Green, M. E. (1998). *Uncharted passage: Girls' adolescence in the developing world.* New York: Population Council.

Mercer, R. T., Nichols, E. G., & Doyle, G. C. (1989). *Transitions in a woman's life.* New York: Springer.

Meredith, N. (1986). The gay dilemma. In L. Simkins (Ed.), *Alternative sexual lifestyles* (pp. 113–117). Acton, MA: Copley Publishing Group.

Mergenhagen, P. (1996, January). What can the minimum wage buy? *American Demographics,* 32–36.

Merton, R. K. (1949). Discrimination and the American creed. In R. M. MacIver (Ed.), *Discrimination and national welfare* (pp. 99–126). New York: Institute for Religious Studies.

Merton, R. K. (1968). *Social theory and social structure.* New York: Free Press.

Merton, R. K. (1975). *Social theory and social structure.* Glencoe, IL: The Free Press of Glencoe.

Mesch, G. S., & Schwirian, K. P. (1996). The effectiveness of neighborhood collective action. *Social Problems, 43,* 467–483.

Metzger, G. (1992, November). TV is a blonde, blonde world. *American Demographics,* p. 51.

Michael, R. T., Gagnon, J. H., Laumann, E. O., & Kolata, G. (1994). *Sex in America: A definitive study.* Boston: Little, Brown.

Michels, R. (1949/1911). *Political parties.* Glencoe, IL: Free Press.

Mifflin, L. (1998, April 17). Increase seen in number of violent TV programs. *New York Times,* p. A16.

Milgram, S. (1965). Liberating effects of group pressure. *Journal of Personality and Social Psychology, 1,* 127–134.

Millbrath, L. (1965). *Political participation.* Chicago: Rand McNally.

Miller, B. D. (1993). The anthropology of sex and gender hierarchies. In B. D. Miller (Ed.), *Sex and gender hierarchies* (pp. 3–31). New York: Cambridge University Press.

Miller, K. F., & Baillargeon, R. (1990). Length and distance: Do preschoolers think that occlusion brings things together? *Developmental Psychology, 26,* 103–114.

Miller, N. (1992). *Single parents by choice.* New York: Plenum.

Miller, N., & Brewer, M. B. (Eds.). (1984). *Groups in contact: The psychology of desegregation.* Orlando, FL: Academic Press.

Miller, R. S., Dunn, M. R., Richter, T. H., & Whitcomb, M. E. (1998). Employment-seeking experiences of resident physicians completing training during 1996. *Journal of the American Medical Association, 280,* 777–783.

Miller, W. B. (1958). Lower class culture as a generating milieu of gang delinquency. *Journal of Social Issues, 14,* 5–19.

Millman, M., & Kanter, R. M. (Eds.). (1975). *Another voice.* New York: Anchor/Doubleday.

Mills, C. W. (1956). *The power elite.* New York: Oxford University Press.

Mills, C. W. (1959). *The sociological imagination.* New York: Oxford University Press.

Milner, D. (1983). *Children and race.* Beverly Hills, CA: Sage.

Min, P. G. (Ed.). (1994). *Asian Americans: Contemporary trends and issues.* Thousand Oaks, CA: Sage.

Mink, G. (1998). *Welfare's end.* Ithaca, NY: Cornell University Press.

Minority enrollment drops. (1997, November 2). *Atlanta Constitution,* p. 1.

Mirandé, A. (1990). Ethnicity and fatherhood. In F. W. Bozett & S. M. H. Hanson (Eds.), *Fatherhood and families in cultural context* (pp. 53–82). New York: Springer.

Misch, A. (1995). Assessing environmental health risks. In Worldwatch Institute, (Ed.), *State of the world 1995* (pp. 117–136). New York: W. W. Norton & Company.

Mitford, J. (1998). *The American way of death revisited.* New York: Knopf.

Moffitt, T. E. (1997). Adolescence-limited and life-course-persistent offending: A complementary pair of developmental theories. In T. P. Thornberry Ed.), *Developmental theories of crime and delinquency* (pp. 11–54). New Brunswick, NJ. Transaction Publishers.

Mohan, R. P., & Wilke, A. S. (Eds.) (1994). *International handbook of contemporary developments in sociology*. New York: Greenwood.

Mohawk, J. (1992). Looking for Columbus: Thoughts on the past, present, and future of humanity. In M. A. Jaimes (Ed.), *The state of Native America* (pp. 439–444). Boston: South End Press.

Molotch, H. (1994). Going out. *Sociological Forum, 9,* 221–239.

Monastersky, R. (1997, January 18). Year of warmth and weather reversals. *Science News,* p. 1.

Money, J., & Ehrhardt, A. A. (1972). *Man and woman, boy and girl.* Baltimore: Johns Hopkins University Press.

Money, J., & Matthews, D. (1982). Prenatal exposure to virilizing progestins: An adult follow-up study on twelve young women. *Archives of Sexual Behavior, 11,* 73–83.

Moore, M. A. (1997). Intimate violence: Does socioeconomic status matter? In A. P. Cardarelli (Ed.), *Violence between intimate partners* (pp. 90–100). Boston: Allyn and Bacon.

Moore, R. (1994). Permanently temporary: The new employment relationship in U.S. society. In D. J. Curran & C. M. Renzetti (Eds.), *Contemporary societies: Problems and prospects* (pp. 37–48). Englewood Cliffs, NJ: Prentice-Hall.

Moreau, C. (1995, April 28). "English only" comment draws suspension. *Hartford Courant,* p. A3.

Morris, J. (1996). Prediction of probable Alzheimer's disease in memory-impaired patients: A prospective longitudinal study. *Neurology, 46,* 661–667.

Mosle, S. (1996, October 27). The answer is national standards. *New York Times Magazine,* pp. 45–47, 56, 68.

Moyer, I. L. (1991). *Women's prisons: Issues and controversies.* Paper presented at the Annual Meeting of the American Society of Criminology, San Francisco, CA.

Mulenga, M. (1996, October 21). World increases in number of ages. *Pan African News Agency Press Release.*

Mullen, B., Anthony, T., Salas, E., & Driskell, J. E. (1994). Group cohesiveness and quality of decision making: An integration of tests of the Groupthink hypothesis. *Small Group Research, 25,* 189–204.

Murdoch, M., & Nichol, K. L. (1995). Women veterans' experiences with domestic violence and with sexual harassment while in the military. *Archives of Family Medicine, 4,* 411–418.

Murdock, G. P. (1949). *Social structure.* New York: Free Press.

Murphy, M. E. (1985). *World population: Toward the next century.* Washington, DC: Population Reference Bureau.

Murray, S. O. (1996). *American gay.* Chicago: University of Chicago Press.

Myers, D. J., & Dugan, K. B. (1996). Sexism in graduate school classrooms: Consequences for students and faculty. *Gender & Society, 10,* 330–350.

Myers, S. L. (1997, December 16). Pentagon is urged to separate sexes. *New York Times,* pp. A1, A26.

Myers, S. L. (1998, November 3). Good times mean hard sell for the military. *New York Times,* p. A16.

Myers, S. L. (1998, November 23). Pentagon ready to shrink arsenal of nuclear bombs. *New York Times,* pp. A1, A10.

Myers, S. L. (1999, January 23). Despite "don't ask" policy, gay ousters rose in '98. *New York Times,* p. A15.

Nagel, J. (1996). *American Indian ethnic renewal: Red power and the resurgence of identity and culture.* New York: Oxford University Press.

Nakanishi, D. T. (1988). Seeking convergence in race relations research: Japanese-Americans and the resurrection of the internment. In P. A. Katz & D. A. Taylor (Eds.), *Eliminating racism* (pp. 159–180). New York: Plenum.

Nanda, S. (1990). *Neither man nor woman: The Hijras of India.* Belmont, CA: Wadsworth.

Nasar, S. (1992, March 5). Even among the well-off, the richest get richer. *New York Times,* pp. A1, D24.

Nash, N. C. (1991, July 23). Unease grows under the ozone hole. *New York Times,* p. C4.

National Center for Health Statistics. (1998). *Births and deaths: Preliminary data for 1997.* Washington, DC: Author.

National Commission on Excellence in Education. (1983). *A nation at risk.* Washington, DC: U.S. Government Printing Office.

National Council on Aging. (1998). *Sexuality and older adults.* Available at: http://www.ncoa.org

National League of Cities. (1991). *Annual report: National League of Cities.* Washington, DC: Author.

National Opinion Research Center. (1989). *General Social Survey.* Chicago: Author.

National Opinion Research Center. (1994). *General social surveys, 1972–1994: Cumulative codebook.* Chicago: Author.

Navarro, M. (1996, January 26). A monster on the loose? Or is it fantasy? *New York Times,* p. A10.

Navarro, M. (1999, January 8). Youth says he got idea for sexual abuse from Springer show. *New York Times,* p. A10.

Nechas, E., & Foley, D. (1994). *Unequal treatment.* New York: Simon & Schuster.

Negative stereotypes feed anti-gay violence. (1998, August 18). Reuters. (Internet)

Neighbors, H. W. (1997). Husbands, wives, family and friends: Sources of stress, sources of support. In R. J. Taylor, J. S. Jackson, & L. M. Chatters (Eds.), *Family life in Black America* (pp. 277–292). Thousand Oaks, CA: Sage.

Nelson, J. I. (1994). Work and benefits: The multiple problems of service employment. *Social Problems, 41,* 240–256.

NetVote '98. (1998, July/August). *Global Aging Report,* p. 2.

Neuberger, J. (1983). Women in Judaism: The fact and the fiction. In P. Holden (Ed.), *Women's religious experience: Cross-cultural perspectives* (pp. 132–142). London: Croom Helm.

Newman, A. (1996, September 26). When letters roll in, the prayers flow out. *New York Times,* pp. B1, B8.

New York Times poll. (1996, March 3). *New York Times,* pp. 27–28.

Nicholi, A. M. (1991). The impact of family dissolution on the emotional health of children and adolescents. In B. J. Christensen (Ed.), *When families fail . . . The social costs* (pp. 27–41). New York: University Press of America.

Niebuhr, G. (1996, January 17). In fight against bigotry, good news in a bad time. *New York Times,* p. 10.

Niebuhr, G. (1996a, April 25). Methodists keep rule against homosexuality. *New York Times,* p. A16.

Niebuhr, G. (1996b, May 8). Open attitude on homosexuality makes pariahs of some churches. *New York Times,* pp. A1, B13.

Niebuhr, G. (1996c, May 28). Episcopal bishop hails victory on gay priests. *New York Times,* p. B4.

Niebuhr, G. (1997, October 12). Rabbis still resist interfaith marriage, study shows. *New York Times,* p. 28.

Nikolic-Ristanovic, V. (1999). Living without democracy and peace: Violence against women in the former Yugoslavia. *Violence Against Women, 5,* 63–80.

Nilsen, A. P. (1991). Sexism in English: A 1990s update. In E. Ashton-Jones & G. A. Olson (Eds.), *The gender reader* (pp. 259–270). Boston: Allyn & Bacon.

Niman, M. I. (1997). *People of the rainbow: A nomadic utopia.* Knoxville: University of Tennessee Press.

Noble, H. B. (1998, October 20). A secret of health in old age: Muscles. *New York Times,* p. F18.

Noble, K. B. (1995, December 13). Attacks on Asian-Americans on the rise, especially in California. *New York Times,* p. B13.

Noel, D. L. (1991). A theory of the origin of ethnic stratification. In N. R. Yetman (Ed.), *Majority and minority* (pp. 113–125). Boston: Allyn and Bacon.

Noley, G. (1990). The foster child of American education. In G. E. Thomas (Ed.), *Race relations in the 1980s and 1990s* (pp. 239–248). New York: Hemisphere.

O'Kelly, C. G., & Carney, L. S. (1986). *Women and men in society: Cross-cultural perspectives on gender stratification.* Belmont, CA: Wadsworth.

O'Meara, M. (1997). Sulfur and nitrogen emissions unchanged. In L. R. Brown, M. Renner, & C. Flavin (Eds.), *Vital signs 1997* (pp. 60–61). New York: W. W. Norton & Company.

O'Meara, M. (1999). Exploring a new vision for cities. In L. R. Brown & C. Flavin (Eds.), *State of the world, 1999* (pp. 133–150). New York: W. W. Norton.

O'Neill, M. (1992, March 18). As the rich get leaner, the poor get french fries. *New York Times,* pp. C1, C6.

O'Neill, W. L. (1969). *Everyone was brave.* New York: Quadrangle.

Oakes, J. (1985). *Keeping track: How schools structure inequality.* New Haven, CT: Yale University Press.

Oakley, A. (1981). Interviewing women: A contradiction in terms. In H. Roberts (Ed.), *Doing feminist research* (pp. 30–61). London: Routledge and Kegan Paul.

O'Connell, J. (1996, February 15). Suicide rate is worrisome. *The Patriot Ledger,* p. 17.

Office of the President of the United States. (1995). *Budget of the United States government: Fiscal year.* Washington, DC: U.S. Government Printing Office.

Ogburn, W. F. (1964). *On culture and social change.* Chicago: University of Chicago Press.

Ohlemacher, T. (1996). Bridging people and protest: Social relays of protest groups against low-flying military jets in West Germany. *Social Problems, 43,* 197–218.

Oishi, G. (1985, April 28). The anxiety of being a Japanese American. *New York Times Magazine,* pp. 54–65.

Oliver, M. L., & Shapiro, T. M. (1995). *Black wealth/White wealth: A new perspective on racial inequality.* New York: Routledge.

Olson, D. H., et al. (1989). *Families: What makes them work.* Newbury Park, CA: Sage.

Olson, L. K. (1982). *The political economy of aging.* New York: Columbia University Press.

Olson, L. K. (1994). *The graying of the world.* New York: Haworth.

Ong, P. E., Bonacich, E., & Cheng, L. (Eds.) (1994). *The new Asian immigration in Los Angeles and global restructuring.* Philadelphia: Temple University Press.

Onishi, N. (1996, May 30). New sense of race rises among Asian-Americans. *New York Times,* pp. A1, B6.

Orfield, G., Eaton, S. E., & the Harvard Project on School Desegregation. (1996). *Dismantling desegregation:*

The quiet reversal of Brown *v.* Board of Education. New York: The New Press.

Orfield, G., & Montfort, F. (1993). *The status of school desegregation.* Washington, DC: National School Boards Association.

Organization for Economic Cooperation and Development (1993). *OECD environmental data 1993.* Paris: Author.

Oropesa, R. S. (1996). Normative beliefs about marriage and cohabitation: A comparison of non-Latino Whites, Mexican Americans, and Puerto Ricans. *Journal of Marriage and the Family, 58,* 49–62.

Osmond, M. W., Wambach, K. G., Harrison, D. F., Byers, J., Levine, P., Imershein, A., & Quadragno, D. M. (1993). The multiple jeopardy of race, class, and gender for AIDS risk among women. *Gender & Society, 7,* 99–120.

Ostrander, S. A. (1984). *Women of the upper class.* Philadelphia: Temple University Press.

Ouchi, W. (1981). *Theory Z: How American business can meet the Japanese challenge.* Reading, MA: Addison-Wesley.

Padevic, I. A. (1992). White-collar work values and women's interest in blue-collar jobs. *Gender & Society, 6,* 215–230.

Pagelow, M. D. (1981). Secondary battering and alternatives of female victims to spouse abuse. In L. H. Bowker (Ed.), *Women and crime in America* (pp. 277–298). New York: Macmillan.

Palen, J. (1975). *The urban world.* New York: McGraw-Hill.

Palmore, E. (1981). What can the USA learn from Japan about aging? In H. J. Wershow (Ed.), *Controversial issues in gerontology* (pp. 133–139). New York: Springer.

Parker, L. (1999, February 23). New avenues aiding hate groups. *USA Today,* p. 1.

Parrott, S. (1998). *Welfare recipients who find jobs: What do we know about their employment and earnings?* Washington, DC: Center on Budget and Policy Priorities.

Parsons, T. (1951). *The social system.* New York: Free Press.

Parsons, T. (1966). *Societies: Evolutionary and comparative perspectives.* Englewood Cliffs, NJ: Prentice-Hall.

Parsons, T., & Bales, R. F. (Eds.). (1955). *Family, socialization, and interaction process.* Glencoe, IL: The Free Press.

Passas, N., & Agnew, R. (1997). *The future of anomie theory.* Boston: Northeastern University Press.

Passell, P. (1995, September 19). The wealth of nations: A "greener" approach turns list upside down. *New York Times,* pp. C1, C12.

Passell, P. (1997, April 9). Rise in merit-based aid alters college market landscape. *New York Times,* p. B10.

Passover cyber-Seder fills need in remote areas. (1997, April 22). *Seattle Times,* p. A9.

Paternoster, R., & Triplett, R. (1988). Disaggregating self-reported delinquency and its implications for theory. *Criminology, 26,* 591–625.

Patillo-McCoy, M. (1998). Church culture as a strategy of action in the Black community. *American Sociological Review, 63,* 767–784.

Patterson, C. J. (1992). Children of lesbian and gay parents. *Child Development, 63,* 1025–1042.

Paul, F. (1987). *Declining access to educational opportunities in metropolitan Chicago 1980–1985.* Chicago: Metropolitan Opportunity Project, University of Chicago.

Pear, R. (1984, February 20). Linking Medicare and ability to pay. *New York Times,* p. A11.

Pear, R. (1991, December 12). Federal auditors report rise in abuses in medical billings. *New York Times,* pp. A1, B6.

Pear, R. (1996, June 1). Thousands rally in capitol on children's behalf. *New York Times,* p. 10.

Pear, R. (1997, March 1). Doctors assert there are too many of them. *New York Times,* p. 9.

Pear, R. (1998, December 30). Most states meet work requirement of welfare law. *New York Times,* pp. A1, A12.

Pear, R. (1999, January 23). Income-based Medicare proposal is offered. *New York Times,* p. A16.

Peck, S. (1985). *Halls of jade, walls of stone: Women in China today.* New York: Franklin Watts.

Pellingrini, A. D., et al. (1991). Joint reading between Black Head Start children and their mothers. *Child Development, 61,* 443–453.

Pereira, M. A., Kriska, A. M., Day, R. D., Cauly, J. A., LaPorte, R. E., & Kuller, L. H. (1998). A randomized walking trial in postmenopausal women: Effects on physical activity and health 10 years later. *Archives of Internal Medicine, 158,* 1695–1701.

Perkins, D. (1995). *Outsmarting IQ.* New York: Free Press.

Perlez, J. (1991, July 29). Kenyans do some soul-searching after the rape of 71 schoolgirls. *New York Times,* pp. A1, A7.

Peter, L. J., & Hull, R. (1969). *The Peter principle: Why things always go wrong.* New York: William Morrow.

Peters, J. F. (1998). *Life among the Yanomani: The story of change among the Xilixana on the Mucajai River in Brazil.* New York: Broadview Press.

Pettigrew, T. F. (1998). Intergroup contact theory. In J. T. Spence, J. M. Darley, & D. J. Foss (Eds.), *Annual review of psychology* (pp. 65–85), Palo Alto, CA: Annual Reviews.

Pettigrew, T. F., & Meertens, R. W. (1995). Subtle and blatant prejudice in western Europe. *European Journal of Social Psychology, 25,* 57–75.

Phillips, N. (1991, December 1). Teacher program woos grads outside education. *Philadelphia Inquirer,* pp. 1A, 6A.

Phillips, S. P., & Schneider, M. S. (1993). Sexual harassment of female doctors by patients. *New England Journal of Medicine, 329,* 1936–1939.

Pichardo, N. A. (1997). New social movements: A critical review. *Annual Review of Sociology, 23,* 411–430.

Pickering, M. (1993). *Auguste Comte: An intellectual biography, V. 1.* New York: Cambridge University Press.

Pillemer, K., & Finkelhor, D. (1988). The prevalence of elder abuse: A random sample survey. *The Gerontologist, 28,* 51–57.

Pinderhughes, D. M. (1987). Civil rights and the future of the American presidency. In J. E. Jacobs (Ed.), *The state of Black America* (pp. 39–60). New Brunswick, NJ: Plenum.

Piven, F. F., & Cloward, R. A. (1977). *Poor peoples' movements.* New York: Pantheon.

Pizzo, S. P., & Muolo, P. (1993, May 9). Take the money and run. *New York Times Magazine,* pp. 26–28, 56, 60–62.

Platt, J. (1996). *A history of sociological research methods in America, 1920–1960.* New York: Cambridge University Press.

Pollack, A. (1995, November 28). The life force in the briefcase. *New York Times,* pp. D1, D6.

Pollack, A. (1996, May 7). It's see no evil, have no harassment in Japan. *New York Times,* p. D1.

Polletta, F. (1998). "It was like a fever . . . " Narrative and identity in social protest. *Social Problems, 45,* 137–159.

Polsby, D. D. (1994, March). The false promise of gun control. *The Atlantic Monthly,* special reprint.

Population Reference Bureau. (1994). *World population data sheet.* Washington, DC: Author.

Porter, B. (1998, November 8). Is solitary confinement driving Charlie Chase crazy? *New York Times Magazine,* pp. 52–58.

Porter, K. (1997). *Improvements in poverty and income in 1995 tempered by troubling long-term trends.* Washington, DC: Center on Budget and Policy Priorities.

Portes, A., & Manning, R. D. (1991). The immigrant enclave: Theory and empirical examples. In N. R. Yetman (Ed.), *Majority and minority* (pp. 319–333). Boston: Allyn & Bacon.

Portes, A., & Truelove, C. G. (1991). Making sense of diversity: Recent research on Hispanic minorities in the United States. In N. R. Yetman (Ed.), *Majority and minority* (pp. 402–420). Boston: Allyn & Bacon.

Portrait of the Electorate. (1996, November 10). *New York Times,* p. 28.

Posner, R. A. (1996). *Aging and old age.* Chicago: University of Chicago Press.

Poussaint, A. F., & Comer, J. P. (1993). *Raising Black children.* New York: Plume.

Powell, A. G., Farrar, E., & Cohen, D. K. (1985). *The shopping mall high school.* Boston: Houghton Mifflin.

Power, T. (1981). Sex typing in infancy: The role of the father. *Infant Mental Health Journal, 2,* 226–240.

Prentice-Dunn, S., & Rogers, R. W. (1984). Effects of deindividuating situational cues and aggressive models on subjective deindividuation and aggression. *Journal of Personality and Social Psychology, 39,* 104–113.

Prentky, R. A., Knight, R. A., & Lee, A. F. S. (1997). *Child sexual molestation: Research issues.* Washington, DC: U.S. Department of Justice, National Institute of Justice.

President's Commission on the Study of Ethical Problems in Medicine and Biomedical Research. (1983). *Securing access to health care, V. 1.* Washington, DC: U.S. Government Printing Office.

Press, A. L. (1991). *Women watching television: Gender, class, and generation in the American television experience.* Philadelphia: University of Pennsylvania Press.

Preston, R. (1998, March 9). The bioweaponeers. *The New Yorker,* pp. 52–65.

Price-Bonham, S., & Skeen, P. (1982). Black and White fathers' attitudes toward children's sex roles. *Psychological Reports, 50,* 1187–1190.

Princeton Religious Research Center. (1992, April-June). *Emerging trends.* Princeton, NJ: Author.

Prus, R. C. (1975). Resisting designations: An extension of attribution theory into a negotiated context. *Sociological Inquiry, 45,* 3–14.

Puente, M., & Morello, C. (1998, November 13). Bilingual battle still rages in classrooms. *USA Today,* p. 4A.

Punishment is 18 months for killing cheating wife. (1994, October 19). *New York Times,* p. A20.

Purdy, M. (1995, November 6). A kind of sexual revolution. *New York Times,* pp. B1, B6.

Pyke, K. D. (1994). Women's employment as gift or burden? *Gender & Society, 8,* 73–91.

Quadango, J., & Hardy, M. (1991). Regulating retirement through the Age Discrimination in Employment Act. *Research on Aging, 13,* 470–475.

Ragins, B. R., & Scandura, T. A. (1995). Antecedents and work-related correlates of reported sexual harassment: An empirical investigation of competing hypotheses. *Sex Roles, 32,* 429–455.

Raley, R. K. (1996). Cohabitation, marriageable men, and racial differences in marriage. *American Sociological Review, 61,* 973–983.

Rankin, D. (1987, May 31). Living together as a way of life. *New York Times,* p. F11.

Rankin, J. H., & Wells, L. E. (1990). The effect of parental attachments and direct controls on delinquency. *Journal of Research in Crime and Delinquency,* 140–160.

Rasinski, K. A. (1989). The effect of question wording on public support for government spending. *Public Opinion Quarterly, 53,* 388–394.

Rayman, P. (1993). *Pathways for women in the sciences.* Wellesley, MA: Center for Research on Women.

Reich, R. B., & Nussbaum, K. (1994). *Working women count! A report to the nation.* Washington, DC: Women's Bureau & U.S. Department of Labor.

Reid, G. M. (1994). Maternal sex-typing of newborns. *Psychological Reports, 75,* 1443–1450.

Reid, P. T. (1982). Socialization of Black female children. In P. Berman (Ed.), *Women: A developmental perspective* (pp. 137–155). Bethesda, MD: National Institutes of Health.

Reid, T. (1998, October 4). Professor finds key to lasting happiness. *London Telegraph,* p. 1.

Reilly, M. E., Lott, B., & Gallogly, S. M. (1986). Sexual harassment of university students. *Sex Roles, 15,* 333–358.

Reiman, J. (1995). *The rich get richer and the poor get prison.* Boston: Allyn & Bacon.

Reinharz, S. (1992). *Feminist methods in social research.* New York: Oxford University Press.

Relman, A. S. (1997). The health care industry: Where is it taking us? In P. Conrad (Ed.), *The sociology of health and illness* (pp. 240–246). New York: St. Martin's Press.

Renner, M. (1997). Transforming security. In Worldwatch Institute (Ed.), *State of the world 1997* (pp. 115–131). New York: W. W. Norton & Company.

Renzetti, C. M. (1992). *Violent betrayal: Partner abuse in lesbian relationships.* Newbury Park, CA: Sage.

Renzetti, C. M., & Curran, D. J. (1986). Structural constraints on legislative reform. *Contemporary Crises, 10,* 137–155.

Renzetti, C. M., & Lee, R. M. (Eds.). (1993). *Researching sensitive topics.* Newbury Park, CA: Sage.

Reskin, B. F. (1993). Sex segregation in the workplace. *Annual Review of Sociology, 19,* 241–270.

Reskin, B. F., & Hartmann, H. I. (Eds.). (1986). *Women's work, men's work: Sex segregation on the job.* Washington, DC: National Academy Press.

Reverse discrimination of Whites is rare, labor study reports. (1995, March 31). *New York Times,* p. A23.

Rheingold, H. L., & Cook, K. V. (1975). The content of boys' and girls' rooms as an index of parents' behavior. *Child Development, 46,* 459–463.

Rhoades, L. (1981). *A history of the American Sociological Association: 1905–1980.* Washington, DC: American Sociological Association.

Rhoads, E. C. (1984). Reevaluation of aging and modernization theory. *The Gerontologist, 24,* 243–250.

Rice, G., Anderson, C., & Risch, N. (1999). Male homosexuality: Absence of linkage to micro-satellite markers at Xq28. *Science, 284,* 665–667.

Richardson, L. W. (1981). *The dynamics of sex and gender.* Boston: Houghton Mifflin.

Ridgeway, C. L. (1983). *The dynamics of small groups.* New York: St. Martin's Press.

Riding, A. (1993, January 9). European inquiry says Serbs' forces have raped 20,000. *New York Times,* pp. 1, 4.

Riger, S. (1988). Comment on "Women's history goes to trial: EEOC v. Sears, Roebuck and Company." *Signs, 13,* 897–903.

Riger, S., & Gordon, M. T. (1988). The impact of crime on urban women. In A. W. Burgess (Ed.), *Rape and sexual assault II* (pp. 293–316). New York: Garland.

Rimer, S. (1996, October 23). Blacks urged to act to increase awareness of the AIDS epidemic. *New York Times,* p. A1, A16.

Rimer, S. (1998, November 22). Seattle's elderly find a home for living, not dying. *New York Times,* pp. 1, 36–37.

Ringer, B. B. (1983). *"We the People" and others: Duality and America's treatment of racial minorities.* London: Tavistock.

Ringer, F. (1997). *Max Weber's methodology: The unification of the cultural and social sciences.* Cambridge, MA: Harvard University Press.

Riportella-Muller, R. (1989). Sexuality in the elderly: A review. In K. McKenny & S. Sprecher (Eds.), *Human sexuality: The societal and interpersonal context* (pp. 210–236). Norwood, NJ: Ablex.

Risch, N., Wheeler, E. S., & Keats, B. J. B. (1993). Male sexual orientation and genetic evidence. *Science, 262,* 2063–2065.

Rist, R. (1970). Student, social class, and teacher expectations: The self-fulfilling prophecy in ghetto education. *Harvard Educational Review, 40,* 411–451.

Ritzer, G. (1993). *The McDonaldization of society.* Thousand Oaks, CA: Pine Forge Press.

Robbins, T. (1988). *Cults, converts, and charisma.* Newbury Park, CA: Sage.

Roberts, S. (1995, December 24). Alone in the vast wasteland. *New York Times,* p. E3.

Robertson, J., & Fitzgerald, L. F. (1990). The (mis)treatment of men: Effects of client gender role and lifestyle on diagnosis and attribution of pathology. *Journal of Counseling Psychology, 37,* 3–9.

Robson, R. (1992). *Lesbian (out)law.* Ithaca, NY: Firebrand Books.

Rochon, P. A., Anderson, G. M., & Tu, J. V. (1998). Age- and gender-related low-dose therapy: The need to manufacture low-dose therapy and evaluate the minimum effective dose. *Journal of the American Geriatrics Society, 47,* 954–959.

Rodriquez, C. E. (1989). *Puerto Ricans: Born in the U.S.A.* Boston: Unwin Hyman.

Rogers, J. W., & Buffalo, M. D. (1974). Fighting back: Nine modes of adaptation to a deviant label. *Social Problems, 22,* 101–118.

Rogoff, B., & Morelli, G. (1989). Perspectives on children's development from cultural psychology. *American Psychologist, 44,* 343–348.

Roiphe, K. (1993). *The morning after.* Boston: Little, Brown.

Romero, M. (1992). *Maid in America.* New York: Routledge.

Roof, W. C. (1993). *A generation of seekers: The spiritual journeys of the baby boom generation.* San Francisco: Harper.

Roof, W. C., & Roof, J. L. (1984). Review of the polls: Images of God among Americans. *Journal for the Scientific Study of Religion, 23,* 201–205.

Rooks, N. M. (1996). *Hair raising: Beauty, culture, and African American women.* New Brunswick, NJ: Rutgers University Press.

Roopnarine, J. L. (1984). Sex-typed socialization in mixed-age preschool classrooms. *Child Development, 55,* 1078–1084.

Roscoe, W. (1991). *The Zuni man-woman.* Albuquerque: University of New Mexico Press.

Roscoe, W. (1998). *Changing ones: Third and fourth genders in Native North America.* New York: St. Martin's.

Rose, A. (1971). History and sociology of the study of social problems. In E. O. Smigel (Ed.), *Handbook on the study of social problems* (pp. 3–18). Chicago: Rand McNally.

Rose, F. (1997). Toward a class-cultural theory of social movements: Reinterpreting new social movements. *Sociological Forum, 12,* 461–494.

Rose, J. D. (1982). *Outbreaks.* New York: Free Press.

Rosenbaum, D. E. (1998, November 18). Smoking by college students is on the rise, research finds. *New York Times,* p. A28.

Rosenbaum, D. E. (1999, January 28). Social security: The basics, with a tally sheet. *New York Times,* p. A21.

Rosenbaum, J. L., & Lasley, J. R. (1990). School, community context, and delinquency: Rethinking the gender gap. *Justice Quarterly, 7,* 493–513.

Rosenbaum, R. (1995, September 24). Among the believers. *New York Times Magazine,* pp. 50–64.

Rosenfeld, R. A., & Spenner, K. I. (1992). Occupational sex segregation and women's early-career job shifts. *Work and Occupations, 19,* 424–449.

Rosenthal, D. (1995, December 10). Demons get a fast checkout on Bali. *New York Times,* p. 29.

Rosenthal, E. (1991, April 30). In Canada, a government system that provides health care to all. *New York Times,* pp. A1, A16.

Rosenthal, E. (1993a, November 28). How doctors learn to think they're doctors. *New York Times,* pp. E1, E4.

Rosenthal, E. (1993b, May 24). Medicine suffers as fewer doctors join front lines. *New York Times,* pp. A1, B7.

Rosenthal, E. (1998, December 10). In North Korean hunger, legacy is stunted children. *New York Times,* pp. A1, A14.

Rosenthal, R., & Jacobson, L. (1968). *Pygmalion in the classroom.* New York: Holt, Rinehart & Winston.

Rossi, A. S. (1984). Gender and parenthood. *American Sociological Review, 49,* 1–18.

Rossi, P. (1989). *Down and out in America: The origins of homelessness.* Chicago: University of Chicago Press.

Rostow, W. W. (1978). *The world economy: History and prospect.* Austin: University of Texas Press.

Roszak, T. (1969). *The making of a counter-culture: Reflections on the technocratic society and its youthful opposition.* New York: Doubleday.

Roth, J. A. (1994, February). Psychoactive substance abuse and violence. *National Institute of Justice Research in Brief.* Washington, DC: U.S. Government Printing Office.

Rubin, G. (1975). The traffic in women. In R. R. Reiter (Ed.), *Toward an anthropology of women* (pp. 157–211). New York: Monthly Review Press.

Russell, D. E. H. (1986). *The secret trauma.* New York: Basic Books.

Rustad, M. (1982). *Women in khaki.* New York: Praeger.

Ruzek, S. (1987). Feminist visions of health: An international perspective. In J. Mitchell & A. Oakley (Eds.), *What is feminism? A re-examination* (pp. 184–207). New York: Pantheon.

Ryan, W. (1981). *Equality.* New York: Pantheon.

Rymer, R. (1993). *Genie: A scientific tragedy.* New York: HarperCollins.

Sachs, A. (1994, March-April). Men, sex, and parenthood in an overpopulated world. *Worldwatch,* 12–19.

Sachs, C. E. (1996). *Gendered fields: Rural women, agriculture, and environment.* Boulder, CO: Westview.

Sachs, S. (1998, November 10). Muslim schools in U.S. a voice for identity. *New York Times,* pp. B1, B10.

Sack, K. (1999, January 29). HIV peril and rising drug use. *New York Times,* p. A10.

Sacks, K. (1979). *Sisters and wives.* Westport, CT: Greenwood Press.

Sacks, O. (1995). *An anthropologist on Mars.* New York: Knopf.

Sadker, M., & Sadker, D. (1994). *Failing at fairness.* New York: Charles Scribner's Sons.

Sahlins, M. D. (1972). *Stone age economics.* Chicago: Aldine.

Salmans, S. (1988, April 10). The tracking controversy. *New York Times Education Supplement,* pp. 56–62.

Samuels, P. D. (1996, May 12). Who's reading your e-mail? Maybe the boss. *New York Times,* p. F11.

Sanday, P. R. (1981). *Female power and male dominance: On the origins of sexual inequality.* New York: Cambridge University Press.

Sanday, P. R. (1996). Rape-prone versus rape-free campus cultures. *Violence Against Women, 2,* 191–208.

Sanger, D. E. (1994, May 27). Job-seeking women in Japan finding more discrimination. *New York Times,* p. A9.

Sanger, D. E. (1998, October 21). U.S. trade deficit shows the effect of global turmoil. *New York Times,* pp. A1, C4.

Sanger, D. E. (1998, December 6). From trustbusters to trust trusters. *New York Times,* pp. WK1, WK4.

Sarre, R. (1994). The concept of native title to land: An Australian perspective. *Humanity and Society, 18,* 97–104.

Sarre, R. (1996). Aboriginal Australians: Current criminological themes. In M. Schwartz & D. Milovanovic (Eds.), *Race, gender, and class in criminology: The intersection* (pp. 193–218). New York: Garland.

Sarre, R. (1998). Aboriginal Australians struggle to preserve their land and their culture. In C. M. Renzetti & D. J. Curran, *Living Sociology* (p. 87). Boston: Allyn and Bacon.

Sassen, S. (1991). *The global city: New York, London, Tokyo.* Princeton: Princeton University Press.

Saunders, D. G. (1989). *Who hits first and who hurts most? Evidence for the greater victimization of women in intimate relationships.* Paper presented at the Annual Meeting of the American Society of Criminology, Reno, NV.

Saussy, C. (1991). *God images and self esteem.* Louisville, KY: Westminster/John Knox.

Schaie, K. W. (1994). The course of adult intellectual development. *American Psychologist, 49,* 304–313.

Schaie, K. W., & Willis, S. L. (1986). *Adult development and aging.* Boston: Little, Brown.

Schmalz, J. (1993, March 5). Poll finds an even split on homosexuality's cause. *New York Times,* p. A14.

Schmemann, S. (1995, April 30). Overseas, Oklahoma City bombing is seen through prism of experience. *New York Times,* p. 28.

Schmitt, E. (1988, December 26). Suburbs wrestle with steep rise in the homeless. *New York Times,* pp. 1, 36.

Schmitt, E. (1994, May 9). Gay troops say the revised policy is often misused. *New York Times,* pp. A1, A14.

Schmitt, E. (1994, July 31). Army and Marine corps offer women more yet less. *New York Times,* p. E2.

Schmitt, E. (1995, March 13). The new rules on gay soldiers: A year later, no clear results. *New York Times,* pp. A1, A16.

Schneider, A. (1997). *Reducing the number of uninsured children.* Washington, DC: Center on Budget and Policy Priorities.

Schneider, K. (1995, April 29). Manual for terrorists extols "greatest coldbloodedness." *New York Times,* p. 10.

Schools are relatively safe, U.S. study says. (1995, November 19). *New York Times,* p. 40.

Schrader, H., Obelieniene, D., & Sand, T. (1996). Natural evolution of late whiplash syndrome outside the medicolegal context. *The Lancet, 347,* 1207–1211.

Schrott, H. G., Bittner, V., Vittinghoff, E., Herrington, D. M., & Hulley, S. (1997). Adherence to National Cholesterol Education Program treatment goals in postmenopausal women with heart disease: The Heart and Estrogen/Pregestin Replacement Study (HERS). *Journal of the American Medical Association, 277,* 1281–1286.

Schur, E. M. (1965). *Crimes without victims: Deviant behavior and public policy.* Englewood Cliffs, NJ: Spectrum.

Schur, E. M. (1973). *Radical nonintervention.* Englewood Cliffs, NJ: Spectrum.

Schur, E. M. (1979). *Interpreting deviance: A sociological introduction.* New York: Harper and Row.

Schur, E. M. (1984). *Labeling women deviant.* New York: Random House.

Schwabe, C. W. (1979). *Unmentionable cuisine.* University of Virginia Press.

Schwager, S. (1987). Educating women in America, *Signs, 12,* 333–372.

Schwartz, F. N. (1989, January-February). Management women and the new facts of life. *Harvard Business Review*, 65–76.

Schwartz, M. D. (1988). Ain't got no class: Universal risk theories of battering. *Contemporary Crises, 12*, 373–392.

Schwartz, M. D., & DeKeseredy, W. (1997). *Sexual assault on the college campus*. Thousand Oaks, CA: Sage.

Schweder, R. A. (1997, March 9). It's called poor health for a reason. *New York Times*, p. E5.

Sciolino, E. (1996, October 5). Political battle of the sexes is sharper than ever. *New York Times*, pp. 1, 24.

Scott, A. (1990). *Ideology and the new social movements*. New York: Unwin Hyman.

Scott, A. J., & Storper, M. (1986). The geographical anatomy of industrial capitalism. In A. J. Scott & M. Storper (Eds.), *Production, work, territory* (pp. 301–312). Boston: Allen & Unwin.

Scott, K., & Schau, C. (1985). Sex equity and sex bias in instructional material. In S. Klein (Ed.), *Handbook for achieving sex equity through education* (pp. 218–260). Baltimore, MD: Johns Hopkins University Press.

Scully, D., & Marolla, J. (1985). "Riding the bull at Gilley's": Convicted rapists describe the rewards of rape. *Social Problems, 32*, 251–263.

Sears, D. O., & McConahay, J. B. (1973). *The politics of violence: The new urban Blacks and the Watts riot*. Boston: Houghton Mifflin.

Sears, J. T. (1992). Educators, homosexuality, and homosexual students: Are personal feelings related to professional beliefs? In K. M. Harbeck (Ed.), *Coming out of the classroom closet* (pp. 29–79). New York: Haworth.

Sebald, H. (1992). *Adolescence: A social psychological analysis*. Englewood Cliffs, NJ: Prentice-Hall.

Senior, J. (1994, January 3). Language of the deaf evolves to reflect new sensibilities. *New York Times*, pp. A1, A12.

Serbin, L. A., Moller, L., Powlishta, K., & Gulko, J. (1991). *The emergence of gender segregation and behavioral compatibility in toddlers' peer preferences*. Paper presented at the Annual Meeting of the Society for Research in Child Development, Seattle, WA.

Serbin, L. A., O'Leary, D. K., Kent, R. M., & Tonick, I. J. (1973). A comparison of teacher response to the preacademic and problem behavior of boys and girls. *Child Development, 44*, 776–784.

Sergeant gets 25-year term for 6 rapes at Aberdeen. (1997, May 7). *New York Times*, p. A18.

Sexual harassment: Little boys, big corps. (1996, October 4). Washington, DC: Reuters. (Internet).

Shabecoff, P. (1988, June 26). The heat is on: Calculating the consequences of a warmer planet earth. *New York Times*, p. E1.

Shakin, M., Shakin, D., & Sternglanz, S. H. (1985). Infant clothing: Sex labeling for strangers. *Sex Roles, 12*, 955–964.

Shanab, M. E., & Yahya, K. A. (1978). A cross-cultural study of obedience. *Bulletin of the Psychonomic Society, 11*, 267–269.

Shanklin, E. (1993). *Anthropology and race*. Belmont, CA: Wadsworth.

Shapiro, I. (1995). *Unequal shares: Recent income trends among the wealthy*. Washington, DC: Center on Budget and Policy Priorities.

Shapiro, J., Sheler, J. L., & Gest, T. (1985, January 28). How our government works. *U.S. News and World Report*, pp. 37–50.

Shatz, M., & Gelman, R. (1973). *The development of communication skills: Modifications in the speech of young children as a function of listener*. Chicago: University of Chicago Press.

Shaw, C. R., & McKay, H. D. (1969). *Juvenile delinquency in urban areas*. Chicago: University of Chicago Press.

Shaywitz, B. A., et al. (1995). Sex differences in the functional organization of the brain for language. *Nature, 373*, 607–608.

Shea, M. (1995). Dynamics of economic well-being: Poverty, 1991 to 1993. *Current Population Reports*. Washington, DC: U.S. Department of Commerce.

Shedler, J., & Black, J. (1990). Adolescent drug use and psychological health: A longitudinal study. *American Psychologist, 45*, 612–630.

Sheehan, T. (1976). Senior esteem as a factor in socioeconomic complexity. *The Gerontologist, 16*, 433–440.

Sheldon, W. (1949). *Varieties of delinquent youth*. New York: Harper and Brothers.

Shelton, B. A. (1992). *Women, men, and time: Gender differences in paid work, housework, and leisure*. Westport, CT: Greenwood.

Shelton, B. A., & John, D. (1993). Does marital status make a difference? *Journal of Family Issues, 14*, 401–420.

Shenon, P. (1994, August 16). China's mania for baby boys creates surplus of bachelors. *New York Times*, pp. A1, A8.

Shenon, P. (1997, February 26). New study faults Pentagon's gay policy. *New York Times*, p. A10.

Shenon, P. (1998, January 21). New finding on mixing sexes in military. *New York Times*, p. A12.

Shephard, R. J., & Rode, A. (1996). *The health consequences of "modernization": Evidence from circumpolar peoples*. New York: Cambridge University Press.

Shepperd, J. A. (1993). Productivity loss in performance groups: A motivation analysis. *Psychological Bulletin, 113,* 67–81.

Sherry, A., Lee, M., & Vatikiotis, M. (1995, December 14). For lust or money. *Far Eastern Economic Review,* pp. 22–28.

Shiao, J. L. (1994). *An examination of class stratification and the model minority thesis in high school and beyond dataset.* Paper presented at the Annual Meeting of the American Sociological Association, Los Angeles, CA.

Shilts, R. (1993). *Conduct unbecoming: Gays and lesbians in the military.* New York: St. Martin's Press.

Shipman, P. (1994). *The evolution of racism.* New York: Simon and Schuster.

Short, K., & Shea, M. (1995, November). Beyond poverty, extended measures of well-being. *Current Population Reports.* Washington, DC: U.S. Department of Commerce.

Shostak, M. (1981). *Nisa: The life and words of a !Kung woman.* Cambridge, MA: Harvard University Press.

Sidel, R. (1986). *Women and children last.* New York: Penguin.

Sidel, V. W., & Sidel, R. (1983). *A healthy state.* New York: Pantheon.

Sidoti, C. (1997). *Young people and racism.* Paper presented at the Youth and Racism Conference, Australian Catholic University, Ascot Vale.

Sieber, J. E. (1993). The ethics and politics of sensitive research. In C. M. Renzetti & R. M. Lee (Eds.), *Researching sensitive topics* (pp. 14–32). Newbury Park, CA: Sage.

Siegel, F. (1997). *The future once happened here.* New York: Free Press.

Sigelman, L., & Welch, S. (1991). *Black Americans' views of racial inequality: The dream deferred.* Cambridge: Cambridge University Press.

Signorelli, N. (1997). *A content analysis: Reflections of girls in the media.* Menlo Park, CA: Children Now and the Kaiser Family Fund.

Silliman, J., & King, Y. (1999). *Dangerous intersections.* Cambridge: South End Press.

Silverstein, L. B. (1996). Fathering is a feminist issue. *Psychology of Women Quarterly, 20,* 3–37.

Simmel, G. (1964/1905). The metropolis and mental life. In K. Wolff (Ed.), *The sociology of Georg Simmel* (pp. 409–424). New York: Free Press.

Simmel, G. (1971). Fashion. In D. N. Levine (Ed.), *On individuality and social forms* (pp. 294–323). Chicago: University of Chicago Press.

Simmons, J. L. (1969). *Deviance.* Berkeley, CA: Glendessary Press.

Simons, M. (1993a, November 23). French prosecutor fighting girl-mutilation by immigrants. *New York Times,* p. A13.

Simons, M. (1993b, January 11). France jails woman for daughters' circumcision. *New York Times,* p. A8.

Sims, G. (1988, August 24). Robots to make fast food chains still faster. *New York Times,* p. D5.

Sims, P. (1988, March 27). The snake-handlers of Carson Springs. *Philadelphia Inquirer Magazine,* pp. 17, 28, 30, 38–43.

Since coming out is in, a guide for the TV audience. (1997, February 23). *New York Times,* p. E7.

Singapore's snack? Termites, of course. (1995, December 31). *New York Times,* p. 31.

Slight rise in math and science scores, less in reading. (1996, October 13). *New York Times,* p. 28.

Smart, C. (1982). The new female offender: Reality or myth? In B. R. Price & N. J. Sokoloff (Eds.), *The criminal justice system and women* (pp. 105–116). New York: Clark Boardman.

Smelser, N. J. (1962). *Theory of collective behavior.* New York: Free Press.

Smith, A. F. (1994). *The tomato in America.* Chapel Hill: University of North Carolina Press.

Smith, A. K. (1995, October 9). Does coverage depend on color? With homeowner's insurance, it might. *U.S. News & World Report,* 85.

Smith, D. H., & Pillemer, K. (1983). Self-help groups as social movement organizations. *Research in Social Movements, Conflicts and Change, 5,* 203–233.

Smith, J. R., Brooks-Gunn, J., & Klebanov, P. K. (1997). Consequences of living in poverty for young children's cognitive and verbal ability and early school achievement. In G. J. Duncan & J. Brooks-Gunn (Eds.), *Consequences of growing up poor* (pp. 132–189). New York: Russell Sage Foundation.

Smith, M. J., & Moses, B. (1980). Social welfare agencies and social reform movements: The case of the single parent family. *Journal of Sociology and Social Welfare, 7,* 125–136.

Smith, P. M. (1985). *Language, society, and the sexes.* New York: Basil Blackwell.

Smith, R. E. (1996, September 8). The true terror is in the card. *New York Times Magazine,* p. 58–59.

Smothers, R. (1996, January 30). Unions try to push past workers' fears to sign up poultry plants in south. *New York Times,* p. A10.

Snarey, J. (1993). *How fathers care for the next generation.* Cambridge: Harvard University Press.

Snipp, C. M. (1989). *American Indians: The first of this land.* New York: Russell Sage Foundation.

Snipp, C. M. (1991). American Indians and natural resource development: Indigenous people's land, now sought after, has produced new Indian-White problems. In N. R. Yetman (Ed.), *Majority and minority* (pp. 457–469). Boston: Allyn & Bacon.

Snow, M. (1992, October 6). Mindworks: Question on gender brings out stereotypes. *New York Times*, pp. 1E, 3E.

Sokoloff, N. J. (1992). *Black women and White women in the the professions: Occupational sex segregation by race and gender, 1960–1980.* New York: Routledge, Chapman and Hall.

Sontag, D. (1993, September 27). Women asking U.S. asylum expand definitions of abuse. *New York Times*, pp. A1, A13.

Sorenson, E. (1994). *Comparable worth: Is it worthy policy?* Princeton, NJ: Princeton University Press.

Sowell, T. (1990). *Preferential policies.* New York: William Morrow.

Spanier, B. (1995). Biological determinism and homosexuality. *NWSA Journal, 7,* 54–71.

Spates, J. L., & Perkins, H. W. (1982). American and English student values. *Comparative Social Research, 5,* 245–268.

Specter, M. (1996, April 14). World, wide, web: 3 English words. *New York Times*, pp. E1, E5.

Spencer, H. (1860). *The social organism.* London: Greenwood.

Spindler, A. M. (1996, June 9). It's a face-lifted, tummy-tucked jungle out there. *New York Times*, pp. F1, F8–9.

Spitzer, S. (1983). Marxist perspectives in the sociology of law. *Annual Review of Sociology, 9,* 103–124.

Stacey, J. (1990). *Brave new families.* New York: Basic Books.

Stacey, J. (1998). Gay and lesbian families: Queer like us. In M. A. Mason, A. Skolnick, & S. D. Sugarman (Eds.), *All our families* (pp. 117–143). New York: Oxford University Press.

Stanley, A. (1994, May 22). In Russian education, growing class distinction. *New York Times*, p. 3.

Stanley, A. (1995, December 7). In the land of arranged wedlock, love steals in. *New York Times*, p. A4.

Stansell, C. (1986). *City of women.* New York: Alfred A. Knopf.

Staples, R. (1995). Health among African American males. In D. Sabo & D. F. Gordon (Eds.), *Men's health and illness* (pp. 121–138). Thousand Oaks, CA: Sage.

Stark, R., & Glock, C. Y. (1968). *American piety: The nature of religious commitment.* Berkeley, CA: University of California Press.

Starr, P. (1982). *The social transformation of American medicine.* New York: Basic Books.

Starr, P. (1995, Winter). What happened to health care reform? *American Prospect,* 20–31.

Steele, C. H. (1985). The acculturation/assimilation model in urban Indian studies: A critique. In N. R.

Yetman (Ed.), *Majority and minority* (pp. 332–339). Boston: Allyn & Bacon.

Steinbacher, R., & Gilroy, F. D. (1985). Preference for sex of child among primiparous women. *The Journal of Psychology, 119,* 541–547.

Steinberg, R. J. (1990). The social construction of skills. *Work and Occupations, 17,* 449–482.

Steiner, I. D. (1982). Heuristic models of groupthink. In M. Brandstatter, J. H. Davis, & G. Stocker-Kreichgauer (Eds.), *Group decision making* (pp. 503–524). New York: Academic Press.

Steinfels, P. (1992, July 19). Vatican condones some discrimination against homosexuals. *New York Times*, p. 7.

Steinfels, P. (1994, May 14). Female concept of God is shaking Protestants. *New York Times*, p. 8.

Steinfels, P. (1994, May 29). Ancient rock in crosscurrents of today. *New York Times*, pp. 1, 20–21.

Steinfels, P. (1996, May 12). New York to hear Mass in Latin, language of Catholic discontent. *New York Times*, pp. 1, 16.

Steinmetz, S. K. (1993). The abused elderly are dependent: Abuse is caused by the perception of stress associated with providing care. In R. J. Gelles & D. R. Loseke (Eds.), *Current controversies on family violence* (pp. 222–236). Newbury Park, CA: Sage.

Stephan, W. G., & Stephan, C. W. (1984). The role of ignorance in intergroup relations. In N. Miller & M. B. Brewer (Eds.), *Groups in contact: The psychology of desegregation* (pp. 229–250). New York: Praeger.

Stephenson, J. S. (1985). *Death, grief, and mourning.* New York: Macmillan.

Sterngold, J. (1993, October 17). When smoking is a patriotic duty. *New York Times*, pp. F1, F6.

Sterngold, J. (1998, December 29). A racial divide widens on network TV. *New York Times*, pp. A1, A12.

Stevens, P. E. (1998). The experiences of lesbians of color in health care encounters: Narrative insights for improving access and quality. *Journal of Lesbian Studies, 2,* 77–94.

Stevenson, R. W. (1996, September 7). Trying to figure out how low unemployment figures can go. *New York Times*, pp. 35–36.

Stillion, J. M. (1995). Premature death among males. In D. Sabo & D. F. Gordon (Eds.), *Men's health and illness* (pp. 46–67). Thousand Oaks, CA: Sage.

Stimulating supply with preferred mortgages. (1998, November/December). *Global Aging Report,* p. 5.

Stinchcombe, A. L. (1994). Disintegrated disciplines and the future of sociology. *Sociological Forum, 9,* 279–291.

Stock, R. W. (1996, April 18). Alcohol lures the old. *New York Times*, pp. C1, C2.

Stone, L., & James, C. (1995). Dowry, bride-burning, and female power in India. *Women's Studies International Forum, 18,* 125–134.

Stoneman, Z., Brody, G. H., & MacKinnon, C. E. (1986). Same-sex and cross-sex siblings: Activity choices, roles, behavior, and gender stereotypes. *Sex Roles, 15,* 495–511.

Straus, M. A. (1993). Physical assaults by wives: A major social problem. In R. J. Gelles & D. R. Loseke (Eds.), *Current controversies on family violence* (pp. 67–87). Newbury Park, CA: Sage.

Straus, M. A., & Gelles, R. J. (1990). How violent are American families? Estimates from the National Family Violence Resurvey and other studies. In M. S. Straus & R. J. Gelles (Eds.), *Physical violence in American families* (pp. 95–132). New Brunswick, NJ: Transaction.

Straus, M. A., & Smith, C. (1990). Family patterns and child abuse. In M. A. Straus & R. J. Gelles (Eds.), *Physical violence in American families* (pp. 245–262). New Brunswick, NJ: Transaction.

Straus, M. A., & Sugarman, D. B. (1997). Spanking by parents and subsequent antisocial behavior. *Archives of Pediatrics and Adolescent Medicine, 151,* 761–767.

Streib, G. F., & Binstock, R. H. (1990). Aging and the social sciences: Changes in the field. In R. H. Binstock & L. K. George (Eds.), *Handbook of aging and the social sciences* (pp. 1–16). New York: Academic Press.

Strum, C. (1993, April 1). Schools' tracks and democracy. *New York Times,* pp. B1, B7.

Study of teachers finds almost 90 percent are white. (1996, October 17). *Orlando Sentinel,* p. A20.

Sudarkasa, N. (1988). Black enrollment in higher education: The unfulfilled promise of equality. In J. E. Jacob (Ed.), *The state of Black America* (pp. 7–22). New Brunswick, NJ: Transaction Books.

Sullivan, J. F. (1994, July 13). Top Jersey court orders new plan for school funds. *New York Times,* pp. A1, B6.

Sullivan, R. (1993, April 25). An army of the faithful. *New York Times Magazine,* pp. 32–35, 40–44.

Surprisingly sunny, for seniors. (1996, January 7). *New York Times Education Life,* p. 8.

Survey: Patients unsatisfied. (1997, January 28). *Dayton Daily News,* p. 3A.

Sutherland, E. H. (1940). White collar criminality. *American Sociological Review 5,* 1–12.

Sutherland, E. H. (1947). *Principles of criminology.* Philadelphia: J. B. Lippincott Company.

Swaab, D. F., Gooren, L. J. G., & Hofman, M. A. (1995). Brain research, gender, and sexual orientation. *Journal of Homosexuality, 28,* 283–302.

Swazy, J. P., Anderson, M. S., & Lewis, K. S. (1993). Ethical problems in academic research. *American Scientist, 81,* 542–553.

Sydell, L. L. (1993, August). The right to life rampage. *The Progressive,* pp. 24–27.

Syme, S. L., & Berkman, L. F. (1997). Social class, susceptibility, and sickness. In P. Conrad (Ed.), *The sociology of health and illness* (pp. 29–35). New York: St. Martin's Press.

Taeuber, C. M. (1992). *Sixty-five plus in America.* Current Population Reports, Series P-23–178. Washington, DC: U.S. Government Printing Office.

Takaki, R. (1989). *Strangers from a different shore: A history of Asian Americans.* Boston: Little, Brown.

Takaki, R. (Ed.). (1987). *From different shores: Perspectives on race and ethnicity in America.* New York: Oxford University Press.

Tallichet, S. E. (1995). Gendered relations in the mines and the division of labor underground. *Gender & Society, 9,* 697–711.

Talty, S. (1996, February 25). The method of a neo-Nazi mogul. *New York Times Magazine,* pp. 40–43.

Tarrow, S. (1994). *Power in movement: Social movements, collective action and politics.* New York: Cambridge University Press.

Tavakolian, B. (1984). Women and socioeconomic change among Sheikhanzai nomads of western Afghanistan. *Middle East Journal, 36,* 433–453.

Tavris, C. (1992). *The mismeasure of woman.* New York: Simon & Schuster.

Taylor, I., Walton, P., & Young, J. (1973). *The new criminology.* New York: Harper and Row.

Taylor, V. (1990). The continuity of the American women's movement: An elite-sustained stage. In G. West & R. L. Blumberg (Eds.), *Women and social protest* (pp. 277–301). New York: Oxford University Press.

Teachman, J. D., & Schollaert, P. T. (1989). Gender of children and birth timing. *Demography, 26,* 411–426.

Teltsch, K. (1991, July 22). New study of older workers finds they can become good investments. *New York Times,* pp. B1, B4.

Teltsch, K. (1992, July 22). As more people need care, more men help. *New York Times,* pp. B1, B4.

Templeton, A. R. (1998). Human races: A genetic and evolutionary perspective. *American Anthropologist, 100,* 632–650.

Terry, D. (1996, March 22). Minnesotans split on bill requiring "living wage." *New York Times,* p. A12.

Terry, D. (1996, March 29). Suit says schools failed to protect a gay student. *New York Times,* p. A14.

Terry, D. (1996, December 2). Cultural tradition and law collide in middle America. *New York Times,* p. A10.

Terry, D. (1998, March 10). Bilingual education facing toughest test. *New York Times,* pp. A1, A15.

Terry, R. M. (1978). *Trends in female crime: A comparison of Adler, Simon, and Steffensmeier.* Paper presented at the Annual Meeting of the Society for the Study of Social Problems, San Francisco, CA.

The *Forbes* 400. (1998, October 12). *Forbes,* pp. 165–361.

The perilous cost of early retirement. (1998, September/October). *Global Aging Report,* p. 3.

The soul catcher. (1999). Available at: http://home.sprynet.com/~eastwood01/soulcat.htm

The year of the Michaels. (1996, December 16). *Forbes Magazine,* pp. 244–249.

Thorne, B. (1982). Feminist rethinking of the family: An overview. In B. Thorne (Ed.), *Rethinking the family* (pp. 1–24). New York: Longman.

Thorne, B. (1993). *Gender play: Girls and boys in school.* New Brunswick, NJ: Rutgers University Press.

Thun, M. J., Day-Lally, C. A., Calle, E. E., Flanders, W. D., & Heath, C. W., Jr. (1995). Excess mortality among cigarette smokers: Changes in a 20-year interval. *American Journal of Public Health, 85,* 1223–1230.

Thurow, L. C. (1996). *The future of capitalism.* New York: William Morrow.

Tiemann, K. A., Kennedy, S. A., & Haga, M. P. (1998). Rural lesbians' strategies for coming out to health care professionals. *Journal of Lesbian Studies, 2,* 61–75.

Tjaden, P., & Thoennes, N. (1998). *Prevalence, incidence, and consequences of violence against women: Findings from the National Violence Against Women Survey.* Washington, DC: U.S. Department of Justice, Office of Justice Programs, National Institute of Justice.

Toby, J. (1979). The new criminology is the old sentimentality. *Criminology 16,* 516–526.

Toch, H., & Adams, K. (1989). *The disturbed violent offender.* New Haven, CT: Yale University Press.

Toch, T. (1991). *In the name of excellence: The struggle to reform the nation's schooling: Why it's failing and what should be done.* New York: Oxford University Press.

Top 40 entertainers. (1998, September 21). *Forbes,* pp. 220–237.

Torry, B. B., Kinsella, K., & Taeuber, C. M. (1987). *An aging world.* Washington, DC: U.S. Government Printing Office.

Torry, S. (1997, August 5). ABA leader criticizes admissions policies. *Washington Post,* p. A7.

Touby, J. (1994, May-June). In the company of thieves. *Journal of Business Strategy,* 24–50.

Traub, J. (1988, July 24). Into the mouths of babes. *New York Times Magazine,* pp. 18–20, 37–38, 52–53.

Traub, J. (1999, January 31). The bilingual barrier. *New York Times Magazine,* pp. 32–35.

Triandis, H. C. (1988). The future of pluralism revisited. In P. A. Katz & D. A. Taylor (Eds.), *Eliminating racism* (pp. 31–50). New York: Plenum Press.

Trimble, J. E. (1988). Stereotypical images, American Indians, and prejudice. In P. A. Katz & D. A. Taylor (Eds.), *Eliminating racism* (pp. 181–202). New York: Plenum Press.

Troeltsch, E. (1931). *The social teaching of the Christian churches.* New York: Macmillan.

Tu, W. (1984). The Confucian tradition: A Confucian perspective in learning to be human. In F. Whaling (Ed.), *The world's religious traditions* (pp. 55–71). Edinburgh, Scotland: T. & T. Clark Ltd.

Tucker, M. B., & Mitchell-Kernan, C. (1995). *The decline in marriage among African Americans.* New York: Russell Sage Foundation.

Tumin, M. M. (1953). Some principles of stratification: A critical analysis. *American Sociological Review, 18,* 387–393.

Turner, C. S. V., & Thompson, J. R. (1993). Socializing women doctoral students: Minority and majority experiences. *The Review of Higher Education, 16,* 355–370.

Turner, R. H., & Killian, L. M. (1993). *Collective behavior.* Englewood Cliffs, NJ: Prentice-Hall.

Turner, S. P., & Turner, J. H. (1990). *The impossible science.* New York: Harper and Row.

Tuxill, J. (1997). Primate diversity dwindling worldwide. In L. R. Brown, M. Renner, & C. Flavin (Eds.), *Vital signs, 1997* (pp. 100–101). New York: W. W. Norton.

2 million orphans. (1998, November 19). *New York Times,* p. 15.

Tyler, P. (1991, March 3). "Clean win" in the war with Iraq drifts into a bloody aftermath. *New York Times,* pp. E1, E3.

Tyler, P. E. (1995, December 27). Deng's economic drive leaves vast regions of China behind. *New York Times,* pp. A1, A6.

Tyler, T. R., & Smith, H. J. (1998). Social justice and social movements. In D. T. Gilbert, S. T. Fiske, & G. Lindsey (Eds.), *Handbook of social psychology* (pp. 595–629). New York: Random House.

U.S. Conference of Mayors. (1986, 1993). *Annual report.*

U.S. Department of Commerce, Bureau of the Census. (1975). *Historical statistics of the United States, colonial times to 1970, Part I.* Washington, DC: U.S. Government Printing Office.

U.S. Department of Commerce, Bureau of the Census. (1994, 1995, 1996, & 1997). *Statistical abstract of the United States.* Washington, DC: U.S. Government Printing Office.

U.S. Department of Commerce, Bureau of the Census. (1996a). *Educational attainment in the United States:*

March, 1995. Washington, DC: U.S. Government Printing Office.

U.S. Department of Commerce, Bureau of the Census. (1996b). *Population projections of the United States by age, sex, race and Hispanic origin: 1995 to 2050.* Washington, DC: U.S. Government Printing Office.

U.S. Department of Commerce, Bureau of the Census. (1998a). *Money income in the United States: 1997.* Washington, DC: U.S. Government Printing Office.

U.S. Department of Commerce, Bureau of the Census. (1998b). *Poverty in the United States: 1997.* Washington, DC: U.S. Government Printing Office.

U.S. Department of Commerce, Bureau of the Census. (1999). *Poverty threshholds, 1998.* Available at: http://www.cenus.gov

U.S. Department of Education. (1991). *Indian nations at risk: An educational strategy for change.* Washington, DC: U.S. Government Printing Office.

U.S. Department of Education. (1993). *Adult literacy in America.* Washington, DC: National Center for Education Studies.

U.S. Department of Education. (1997). *1994 Elementary and secondary school civil rights compliance report.* Washington, DC: Author.

U.S. Department of Health and Human Services. (1996). *Health United States, 1995.* Washington, DC: U.S. Government Printing Office.

U.S. Department of Health, Education, and Welfare. (1969). *Toward a social report.* Washington, DC: U.S. Government Printing Office.

U.S. Department of Housing and Urban Development. (1998). *The state of the cities 1998.* Washington, DC: Author.

U.S. Department of Justice. (1994). *Violence against women.* Washington, DC: Author.

U.S. Department of Justice, Bureau of Justice Statistics. (1993, 1994, 1995, 1996, & 1998). *Sourcebook of criminal justice statistics.* Washington, DC: U.S. Government Printing Office.

U.S. Department of Justice, Bureau of Justice Statistics. (1994). *Criminal victimization in the United States: National Crime Survey Report.* Washington, DC: U.S. Government Printing Office.

U.S. Department of Justice, Bureau of Justice Statistics. (1994). *HIV in U.S. prisons and jails.* Washington, DC: U.S. Government Printing Office.

U.S. Department of Justice, Bureau of Justice Statistics. (1997). *Criminal victimization in the United States, 1994.* Washington, DC: Author.

U.S. Department of Labor. (1993). *Employment and earnings, November.* Washington, DC: U.S. Government Printing Office.

U.S. Department of Labor. (1995). *Report on the American workforce.* Washington, DC: U.S. Government Printing Office.

U.S. Department of Labor. (1997). *Employment and earnings, March 1997.* Washington, DC: U.S. Government Printing Office.

U.S. Department of Labor. (1997). *The glass ceiling initiative: Are there cracks in the ceiling?* Washington, DC: Author.

U.S. Department of Labor. (1998a). *The employment situation: May 1998.* Washington, DC: U.S. Government Printing Office.

U.S. Department of Labor. (1998b, January). *Employment and earnings.* Washington, DC: Author.

U.S. Department of Labor, Bureau of Labor Statistics. (1991). *Employment and earnings.* Washington, DC: U.S. Government Printing Office.

U.S. Department of State. (1994). *Country reports on human rights practices for 1993.* Washington, DC: U.S. Government Printing Office.

U.S. Department of State. (1995). *Patterns of global terrorism: 1994.* Washington, DC: U.S. Government Printing Office.

U.S. House of Representatives, Select Committee on Children, Youth and Families. (1987). *The crisis in homelessness: Effects on children and families.* Washington, DC: U.S. Government Printing Office.

U.S. Senate, Committee on the Judiciary. (1993). *The response to rape: Detours on the road to equal justice.* Washington, DC: U.S. Government Printing Office.

U.S. Senate, Special Subcommittee on Aging. (1991). *Aging America: Trends and projections.* Washington, DC: U.S. Government Printing Office.

Uchitelle, L. (1996, July 31). Workers' pay rises again, but benefits lag behind. *New York Times,* pp. D1, D4.

Uchitelle, L. (1996, December 8). More downsized workers are returning as rentals. *New York Times,* pp. 1, 34.

Uchitelle, L. (1998, December 7). Downsizing comes back, but the outcry is muted. *New York Times,* pp. A1, A16.

Uchitelle, L., & Kleinfield, N. R. (1996, March 3). On the battlefields of business, millions of casualties. *New York Times,* pp. 1, 26–27.

UN sees new famine in Africa. (1991, July 20). *New York Times,* p. 5.

UN sharply increases estimate of youngsters at work full time. (1996, November 12). *New York Times,* p. A6.

United Nations. (1997). *Report on the world social situation, 1997.* New York: Author.

United Nations Children's Fund. (1994). Squandered opportunities. In R. Reoch (Ed.), *Human rights: A new consensus* (pp. 80–83). London: Regency Press.

United Nations Children's Fund. (1998). *The state of the world's children, 1999.* New York: Author.

United Nations Commission on the Status of Women. (1980). *Report of the world conference of the United Nations decade for women.* Copenhagen, A/CONF.94/35.

United Nations Development Programme. (1996). *Human development report 1996.* New York: Oxford University Press.

United Nations Development Programme. (1998). *World development report 1998.* New York: Oxford University Press.

United Nations High Commissioner for Refugees [UNHCR]. (1995).*The state of the world's refugees.* New York: Oxford University Press.

United they stand. (1997, Spring). *Greenpeace Quarterly,* pp. 6–8.

Updegrave, W. L. (1994, June). You're safer than you think. *Money,* pp. 114–133.

Upham, F. (1988). *Law and equality in other cultures: Japan.* Paper presented at the IV Annual Education Conference of the American Bar Association, April, Bedford, MA.

Urciuoli, B. (1996). *Exposing prejudice: Puerto Rican experiences of language, race, and class.* Boulder, CO: Westview.

Uribe, V., & Harbeck, K. M. (1992). Addressing the needs of lesbian, gay and bisexual youth: The origins of PROJECT 10 and school-based intervention. In K. M. Harbeck (Ed.), *Coming out of the classroom closet* (pp. 9–28). New York: Haworth.

Useem, M. (1984). *The inner circle.* New York: Oxford University Press.

Valian, V. (1998). *Why so slow? The advancement of women.* Boston: MIT Press.

Vallas, S. P., & Beck, J. P. (1996). The transformation of work revisited: The limits of flexibility in American manufacturing. *Social Problems, 43,* 339–361.

Valleroy, L. A., et al. (1998). HIV infection in disadvantaged out-of-school youth: Prevalence for U.S. Job Corps entrants, 1990–1996. *Journal of Acquired Immune Deficiency Syndromes and Human Retrovirology, 19,* 67–73.

van den Berghe, P. L. (1978). Race and ethnicity: A sociobiological perspective. *Ethnic and Racial Studies, 1,* 401–411.

Vander Zanden, J. (1983). *American minority relations.* New York: Knopf.

Vanderstaay, S. (1992). *Street lives.* Philadelphia: New Society Publishers.

Vanishing act. (1998, May). *The Progressive,* pp. 8–9.

Van Poppel, F., & Day, L. H. (1996). A test of Durkheim's theory of suicide—without committing the "ecological fallacy." *American Sociological Review, 61,* 500–507.

Vaughn, D. (1986). *Uncoupling: Turning points in intimate relationships.* New York: Oxford University Press.

Vaughn, J., & Kappeler, V. (1987). The denial of bail: Pretrial preventive detention. *Criminal Justice Research Bulletin, 3*(6), 1–5.

Verdi, B. (1997, May 6). Eggheads would do well to leave Woods alone. *Chicago Tribune,* pp. 1–2.

Verhovek, S. H. (1997, December 14). In poll, Americans reject means but not ends of racial diversity. *New York Times,* pp. 1, 32.

Verhovek, S. H. (1998, December 31). Plugged-in students help adults stymied by games. *New York Times,* pp. A1, A14.

Video: Trooper threatens speeder. (1996, March 9). *Dubuque Telegraph Herald,* p. B11.

Videotape of beating by authorities jolts Los Angeles. (1996, April 3). *New York Times,* p. A10.

Vincent, J. A. (1995). *Inequality and old age.* New York: St. Martin's Press.

Vivian, J. (1993). *The media of mass communication.* Boston: Allyn & Bacon.

Voelker, R. (1998). Teen health risks. *Journal of the American Medical Association, 279,* 1599.

Vold, G. B., & Bernard, T. J. (1986). *Theoretical criminology.* New York: Oxford University Press.

Wacquant, L. J. D., & Wilson, W. J. (1991). The cost of racial and class exclusion in the inner city. In N. R. Yetman (Ed.), *Majority and minority* (pp. 498–512). Boston: Allyn & Bacon.

Wade, N. (1998, October 23). Study suggests monkeys have ability to think. *New York Times,* p. A6.

Waite, T. L. (1992, December 8). Sexual behavior levels compared in studies in Britain and France. *New York Times,* p. C3.

Waitzkin, H. (1997). A Marxian interpretation of the growth and development of coronary care technology. In P. Conrad (Ed.), *The sociology of health and illness* (pp. 247–259). New York: St. Martin's Press.

Walby, S. (1986). *Patriarchy at work: Patriarchal and capitalist relations in employment.* Minneapolis: University of Minnesota Press.

Walcott, J., & Duffy, B. (1994, July 4). The CIA's darkest secrets. *U.S. News and World Report,* pp. 34–47.

Wald, M. L. (1994, November 9). Fuel prices rise with clean-air rule. *New York Times,* p. A18.

Waldron, I. (1995). Contributions of changing gender differences in behavior and social roles to changing gender differences in mortality. In D. Sabo & D. F. Gordon (Eds.), *Men's health and illness* (pp. 22–45). Thousand Oaks, CA: Sage.

Waldron, I. W. (1986). Why do women live longer than men? In P. Conrad & R. Kern (Eds.), *The sociology of health and illness* (pp. 34–44). New York: St. Martin's Press.

Walewski, S. (1999, January 7). Teens charged with molesting sister. Associated Press Wire Service. (Internet)

Walker, A., & Parmar, P. (1993). *Warrior marks: Female genital mutilation and the sexual blinding of women*. New York: Harcourt Brace.

Wallerstein, I. M. (1974). *The modern world system*. New York: Academic Press.

Wallerstein, I. M. (1990). *The modern world system II*. New York: Academic Press.

Wallerstein, J. S. (1998). Children of divorce: A society in search of policy. In M. A. Mason, A. Skolnick, & S. D. Sugarman (Eds.), *All our families* (pp. 66–94). New York: Oxford University Press.

Wallerstein, J. S., & Blakeslee, J. (1989). *Second chances*. New York: Ticknor and Fields.

Walzer, S. (1996). Thinking about the baby: Gender and divisions of infant care. *Social Problems, 43,* 219–234.

Warner, W. L. (1963). *Yankee city*. New Haven, CT: Yale University Press.

Warr, M. (1985). Fear of rape among urban women. *Social Problems, 32,* 238–250.

Warr, M., & Stafford, M. (1991). The influence of delinquent peers: What they think or what they do? *Criminology, 29,* 851–866.

Warren, B. (1980). *Imperialism: Pioneer of capitalism.* London: Verso.

Warren, M. A. (1985). *Gendercide: The implications of sex selection.* London: Rowman and Allanheld.

Waters, A. B. (1999). Domestic dangers: Approaches to women's suicide in contemporary Maharashtra, India. *Violence Against Women, 5,* 525–547.

Waters, M. S., Heath, W. C., & Watson, J. K. (1995). A positive model of the determination of religious affiliation. *Social Science Quarterly, 76,* 105–123.

Wayne, L. (1996, September 6). Loopholes allow presidential race to set a record. *New York Times,* pp. 1, 26.

Wayne, L. (1997, March 13). Congress uses leadership PACs to wield power. *New York Times,* p. B10.

Wayne, L. (1998, November 6). If no guarantee of victory, money sure makes it easier. *New York Times,* p. A29.

Webb, P. (1997, August 23). U.S. politics of genocide in Rwanda. Available at: http://www.earlham.edu/ear/hamc...obalprobs/rwanda/Pollypols.html

Weber, M. (1921). *The sociology of religion.* Boston: Beacon Press.

Weber, M. (1958/1904–05). *The protestant ethic and the spirit of capitalism.* New York: Charles Scribner's Sons.

Weibel-Orlando, J. (1989). Elders and elderly well-being in Indian old age. *American Indian Culture and Research Journal, 13,* 149–170.

Weisner, T. S., Garnier, H., & Loucky, J. (1994). Domestic tasks, gender egalitarian values and children's gender typing in conventional and nonconventional families. *Sex Roles, 30,* 23–54.

Weissman, J. (1996). Caring for the uninsured and underinsured. *Journal of the American Medical Association, 276,* 823–828.

Weitzman, L., Eifler, D., Hokada, E., & Ross, C. (1972). Sex-role socialization in picture books for preschool children. *American Journal of Sociology, 77,* 1125–1150.

Weitzman, L. J. (1985). *The divorce revolution.* New York: Free Press.

Wellings, K., Field, J., Johnson, A. M., & Wadsworth, J. (1994). *Sexual behavior in Britain.* London: Penguin.

Wells-Petry, M. (1993). *Exclusion.* New York: Regnery Gateway, Inc.

Weltner, C. (1977, Fall). The Model Cities Program: A sobering scorecard. *Policy Review,* 73–87.

Werthheimer, B. M. (1979). "Union is Power": Sketches from women's labor history. In J. Freeman (Ed.), *Women: A feminist perspective* (pp. 339–358). Palo Alto, CA: Mayfield.

West, C. (1993). *Race matters.* New York: Random House.

West, D. (1997, January 11). Good for karma. Bad for fish? *New York Times,* pp. 27, 31.

Westley, L. A. (1982). *A territorial issue: A study of women in the construction trades.* Washington, DC: Wider Opportunities for Women.

Weston, K. (1991). *Families we choose: Lesbians, gays, kinship.* New York: Columbia University Press.

Weyler, R. (1982). *Blood of the land.* New York: Vintage.

When the faithful tempt the serpent. (1992, September 11). *New York Times,* p. A14.

Whitbourne, S. K. (1990, Summer). Sexuality in the aging male. *Generations, 14,* 28–30.

White, J. C., & Dull, V. T. (1998). Room for improvement: Communication between lesbians and primary care providers. *Journal of Lesbian Studies, 2,* 95–110.

White, M. (1987). *The Japanese educational challenge.* New York: Free Press.

Whitehead, H. (1981). The bow and the burden strap: A new look at institutionalized homosexuality in Native North America. In S. B. Ortner & H. Whitehead (Eds.), *Sexual meanings* (pp. 31–79). New York: Cambridge University Press.

Whitney, C. R. (1994, August 21). Who will buy: Plutonium for sale. Call 1-800-TERROR. *New York Times,* pp. 1, 6.

Wigdor, A. K., & Hartigan, J. A. (1990, March/April). The case for fairness. *Society,* pp. 12–16.

Wikan, U. (1984). Shame and honour: A contestable pair. *Man, 19,* 635–652.

Wilcox, W. B. (1998). Conservative Protestant childrearing: Authoritarian or authoritative. *American Sociological Review, 63,* 796–809.

Wilford, J. N. (1997, February 25). Ancient graves of armed women hint at Amazons. *New York Times,* pp. C1, C6.

Wilken, E. (1995). Soil erosion's toll continues. In L. R. Brown, N. Lenssen, & H. Kane (Eds.), *Vital signs, 1995* (pp. 118–119). New York: W. W. Norton.

Wilkerson, I. (1991, January 25). Blacks wary of their big role in military. *New York Times,* pp. A1, A2.

Wilkie, J. R. (1993). Changes in U.S. men's attitudes toward the family provider role, 1972–1989. *Gender and Society, 7,* 261–279.

Williams, A. P., Vayda, E., Cohen, M. L., Woodward, C. A., & Ferrier, B. (1995). Medicine and the Canadian state: From the politics of conflict to the politics of accommodation. *Journal of Health and Social Behavior, 36,* 303–321.

Williams, B. (1987). Homosexuality: The new Vatican statement. *Theological Studies, 48,* 259–277.

Williams, C. L. (1992). The glass escalator: Hidden advantages for men in the "female" professions. *Social Problems, 39,* 253–267.

Williams, C. L. (1995). *Still a man's world: Men who do women's work.* Berkeley: University of California Press.

Williams, C. W. (1991). *Black teenage mothers.* Lexington, MA: Lexington Books.

Williams, F. (1997, December 11). A house, 10 wives: Polygamy in suburbia. *New York Times,* pp. F1, F7.

Williams, J. E. (1985). Mexican American and Anglo attitudes about sex roles and rape. *Free Inquiry in Creative Sociology, 13,* 15–20.

Williams, L. (1992, February 6). Woman's image in the mirror: Who defines what she sees? *New York Times,* pp. A1, B7.

Williams, N. (1990). *The Mexican American family: Tradition and change.* Dix Hills, NY: General Hall.

Williams, R. M. (1970). *American society: A sociological interpretation.* New York: Alfred A. Knopf.

Williams, W. L. (1986). *The spirit and the flesh.* Boston: Beacon.

Williamson, J. B., Evans, L., & Powell, L. A. (1982). *The politics of aging.* Springfield, IL: Charles C. Thomas.

Williamson, N. E. (1976a). *Sons or daughters.* Beverly Hills, CA: Sage.

Williamson, N. E. (1976b). Sex preference, sex control, and the status of women. *Signs, 1,* 847–862.

Willie, C. V. (1987). The future of school desegregation. In J. E. Jacob (Ed.), *The state of Black America* (pp. 71–80). New Brunswick, NJ: Transaction Books.

Willie, C. V. (1989). The inclining significance of race. In C. V. Willie (Ed.), *Caste and class controversy on race and poverty* (pp. 10–21). New York: General Hall.

Willis, P. (1990). *Common culture.* Boulder, CO: Westview.

Wilson, E. O. (1978). *On human nature.* New York: Bantam Books.

Wilson, J. Q., & Herrnstein, R. (1985). *Crime and human nature.* New York: Simon & Schuster.

Wilson, K. L., & Portes, A. (1985). Immigrant enclaves: An analysis of the labor market experiences of Cubans in Miami. In N. R. Yetman (Ed.), *Majority and minority* (pp. 305–319). Boston: Allyn & Bacon.

Wilson, S., & Greider, J. (1995). Social cleansing in Colombia: The war on street children. In R. J. Kelly & J. Maghan (Eds.), *Hate crime: Global politics of polarization* (pp. 167–186). Chicago: Office

Wilson, W. J. (1990). *The truly disadvantaged: The inner city, the underclass, and public policy.* Chicago: University of Chicago Press.

Wilson, W. J. (1996). *When work disappears.* New York: Alfred A. Knopf.

Wines, M. (1998, November 19). Siberians' coming winter: Hungry, cold and broke. *New York Times,* pp. A1, A10.

Wirth, L. (1938). Urbanism as a way of life. *American Journal of Sociology, 44,* 1–24.

Witelson, S. F. (1989). Hand and sex differences in the isthmus and genu of the human corpus collusum: A postmortem morphological study. *Brain, 112,* 799–835.

Witzig, R. (1996). The medicalization of race: Scientific legitimization of a flawed social construct. *Annals of Internal Medicine, 125,* 675–678.

Wolf, N. (1991). *The beauty myth.* New York: William Morrow.

Wolfe, A. (1998). *One nation, after all.* New York: Viking.

Women's Institute for Freedom of the Press. (1982, September 1). NIMH reports 10 years of studies on TV: TV violence doesn't reflect society. *Media Report to Women,* p. 9.

Woodberry, R. D., & Smith, C. S. (1998). Fundamentalism et al.: Conservative Protestants in America. *Annual Review of Sociology, 24,* 25–56.

Woodruff, D. (1992, August 17). Saturn. *Business Week,* pp. 85–91.

Woods, J. D. (1993). *The corporate closet: The professional lives of gay men in America.* New York: Free Press.

Woog, D. (1995). *School's out.* Los Angeles: Alyson Publications.

Wooley, S. C., & Wooley, O. W. (1980). Eating disorders: Obesity and anorexia. In A. M. Brodsky & R. Hare-

Mustin (Eds.), *Women and psychotherapy* (pp. 135–158). New York: The Guilford Press.

Woollett, A., White, D., & Lyon, L. (1982). Fathers' involvement with their infants: The role of holding. In N. Beail & J. McGuire (Eds.), *Fathers: Psychological perspectives* (pp. 72–91). London: Junction.

Words that work. (1998, November/December). *Global Aging Report*, p. 2.

World Bank. (1990, 1993, 1995, 1996, & 1999). *World development report*. New York: Oxford University Press.

World Health Organization. (1961). *Constitution*. Geneva: Palais des Nations.

World Health Organization. (1996). *The world health report 1996*. Geneva: World Health Organization.

Worldwatch Institute. (1990). *State of the world, 1990*. New York: W. W. Norton & Company.

Worldwatch Institute. (1994). *State of the world, 1994*. New York: W. W. Norton.

Wright, J. C., Huston, A. C., Truglio, R., Fitch, M., Smith, E., & Piemyat, S. (1995). Occupational portrayals on television: Children's role schemata, career aspirations, and perceptions of reality. *Child Development, 66*, 1706–1718.

Wright, L. (1998). *Twins*. New York: John Wiley.

Wright, R., & Jacobs, J. A. (1995). Male flight from computer work: A new look at occupational resegregation and ghettoization. In J. A. Jacobs (Ed.), *Inequality at work* (pp. 334–376). Thousand Oaks, CA: Sage.

Wronski, R. (1995, December 6). Experts sing praises of prayer. *Chicago Tribune*, p. 14.

Wu Dunn, S. (1995, May 22). Japanese critics say schools led best and brightest into arms of the sect. *New York Times*, p. A6.

Wu Dunn, S. (1996, September 8). For Japan's children, a Japanese torment. *New York Times*, p. E3.

Wu Dunn, S. (1996, January 23). In Japan, even toddlers feel the pressure to excel. *New York Times*, p. A3.

Wu Dunn, S. (1997, October 9). Incubators of creativity. *New York Times*, pp. D1, D21.

Wu Dunn, S. (1998, December 17). South Korean scientists say they cloned a human cell. *New York Times*, p. A12.

Yahoo! box office reports. (1999). Available at: http://dir.Yahoo.com/Entertainment/Movies_and_Film/BoxOffice_Reports/

Ybarra, M. J. (1996, June 9). Limitations of statutes in light of today. *New York Times*, p. 4E.

Yee, B. W. K. (1990, Summer). Gender and family issues in minority groups. *Generations, 14*, 39–42.

Yetman, N. R. (Ed.) (1991). *Majority and minority*. Boston: Allyn & Bacon.

Yinger, J. M. (1985). Assimilation in the United States: The Mexican Americans. In W. Connor (Ed.), *Mexican Americans in comparative perspective* (pp. 30–55). Washington, DC: Urban Institute Press.

Yllö, K. A. (1993). Through a feminist lens: Gender, power, and violence. In R. J. Gelles & D. R. Loseke (Eds.), *Current controversies on family violence* (pp. 47–62). Newbury Park, CA: Sage.

Yoder, J. D., & McDonald, T. W. (1998). Empowering token women leaders: The importance of organizationally legitimated credibility. *Psychology of Women Quarterly, 22*, 209–222.

Young, K. (Ed.). (1993). *Bodylore*. Memphis: University of Tennessee Press.

Younger workers in Russia found more likely to be poor. (1998, November 19). New York Times, p. A5.

Yussen, S. R. (1977). Characteristics of moral dilemmas written by adolescents. *Developmental Psychology, 13*, 162–163.

Zane, J. P. (1992, January 6). As social need rises, so does volunteerism. *New York Times*, pp. A1, B9.

Zaretsky, E. (1976). *Capitalism, the family, and personal life*. New York: Harper and Row.

Zaroulis, N., & Sullivan, G. (1984). *Who spoke up? American protest against the war in Vietnam, 1963–1975*. New York: Holt, Rinehart & Winston.

Zeitlin, I. M. (1968). *Ideology and the development of sociological theory*. Englewood Cliffs, NJ: Prentice-Hall.

Zhou, J., Hofman, M. A., Gooren, L. J. G., & Swaab, D. F. (1995). A sex difference in the human brain and its relation to transsexuality. *Nature, 378*, 68–70.

Zhou, M., & Bankston, C. L. (1998). *Growing up American: How Vietnamese children adapt to life in the United States*. New York: Russell Sage Foundation.

Zicklin, G. (1992, August). *Re-biologizing sexual orientation: A critique*. Paper presented at the Annual Meeting of the Society for the Study of Social Problems, Pittsburgh, PA.

Zigler, E. F. (1987). Formal schooling for four-year-olds? No. *American Psychologist, 42*, 254–260.

Zimbardo, P. G. (1972, April). Pathology of imprisonment. *Society, 9*, pp. 4–8.

Zuber, J. A., Crott, H. W., & Werner, J. (1992). Choice shift and group polarization: An analysis of the status of arguments and social decision schemes. *Journal of Personality and Social Psychology, 62*, 50–61.

Zuravin, S. J. (1987). Unplanned pregnancies, family planning problems, and child maltreatment. *Family Relations, 36*, 135–139.

Zweigenhaft, R. L., & Domhoff, G. W. (1998). *Diversity in the power elite: Have women and minorities reached the top?* New Haven: Yale University Press.

Glossary

absolute poverty: the poor lack the basic resources necessary to sustain life

accommodation: in Piaget's theory, the mental strategy by which we use a new piece of information or an experience to change or adapt an idea or behavior in our existing repertoire

achieved status: a status one works to acquire

acid rain: the combination of two major pollutants—sulfur dioxide and nitrogen oxide—to form nitric acid in the atmosphere that returns to the earth in rain and snow

acquaintance rape: a case of sexual assault in which the victim knows or is familiar with her assailant

acting crowd: an emotion-charged crowd that forms spontaneously for one intense purpose

activity theory: the symbolic interactionist position that in order for people to age successfully, they must remain socially active throughout the life course

adrenogenital syndrome (AGS): a prenatal abnormality that occurs when the adrenal glands of a pregnant woman or her fetus malfunction, exposing the fetus to excessive amounts of male hormones and causing female babies to be born with female internal reproductive organs, but masculinized external genitalia

age in place: the phenomenon of continuing to live in the home one occupied while still in the labor force after one reaches retirement age

age stratification: the social ranking of individuals at different stages of the life course who, in turn, are given differential access to society's resources, rewards, or opportunities

ageism: the use of age to define an individual's capabilities and social roles, and to determine the individual's access to societal resources, rewards, and opportunities

agents of socialization: individuals, groups, and institutions that have as one of their primary functions the socialization of new members of the society by providing them with explicit instruction in or modeling of social expectations

aggregate: a collection of people who happen to be in the same place at the same time

agricultural society (agrarian society): a society in which the subsistence strategy is based on cultivating crops using plows, draft animals, and other technology such as irrigation

alterative movement: a social movement that seeks limited change among a specific segment of a society's population

anal stage: in Freud's theory, the second stage of personality development during which the focus of satisfaction as well as frustration centers on the child learning to control bodily functions

androcentrism: a disproportionate focus on men's perspectives and concerns; male-centered

androgen-insensitive syndrome: a prenatal abnormality that occurs when a genetically male fetus is insensitive to male hormones, causing the baby to be born with female genitals and undescended testes even though it is a genetically normal male.

anomie: according to Durkheim, a state of norm confusion, where traditional norms no longer make sense, but new norms haven't developed to replace them; according to Merton, an imbalance between the goals of a society and the means to achieve these goals

anti-Semitism: prejudice and discrimination against Jews

anticipatory socialization: learning and adopting the behavior patterns and social traits of a group one wishes to join

artifacts: the physical things that the members of a society make when they apply their technology to the physical environment

ascribed status: a status one acquires by birth or that is imposed on an individual by nature or by chance

assimilation: in Piaget's theory, the mental strategy by which we incorporate a piece of new information into our existing repertoire of thoughts and behaviors and then use it later in situations we identify as similar or appropriate; the process by which a racial or ethnic group gradually loses its distinctiveness and separateness and becomes absorbed into the culture and interaction of its host society

attributes: the descriptive categories or values that comprise variables

authoritarian leadership: a leadership style in which leaders make decisions on their own and then inform group members what they are expected to do

authoritarian personality: a personality type made up of traits including insecurity and intolerance, rigid conformity to tradition, superstition, and submission to authority

authoritarianism: a political system in which authority is concentrated solely in the hands of rulers who severely restrict popular participation in government

authority: power perceived as rightful or legitimate by those being led

bail: a court requirement that a defendant post a specified sum of money to guarantee his or her return to court for a hearing

berdache: individuals who adopt the gender behavior ascribed to members of the opposite sex; a part of the culture and gender relations of some societies in Asia and the South Pacific and among some North American Indian societies

bilateral descent: a system in which descent is traced through both parents

bisexuality: a sexual orientation in which individuals are sexually and affectionally attracted to members of both sexes

blue-collar jobs: jobs that require mostly physical rather than mental labor, which got their name because of the way most workers who hold them dress for work (in denim)

bourgeoisie: the social class composed of wealthy property holders and bankers

bureaucracy: a form of organization based on written rules and procedures and designed for managing and coordinating the actions of large numbers of people

bureaucratic ritualism: when the rules and procedures of an organization take on greater importance than the organization's purpose and goals

capitalism: an economic system in which the means of production are privately owned and operated

caste system: a stratification system in which movement between strata is virtually closed, so individuals stay in the stratum into which they were born for their entire lives

casual crowd: a crowd that forms spontaneously around a specific incident, but the people involved engage in little, if any, interaction with one another

causal relationship: an empirically measured relationship between two variables in which a change in one variable causes a change in a second variable

charismatic authority: derives legitimacy from the extraordinary personal virtues or skills of the people on whom it is bestowed

charismatic leadership: leadership based on the extraordinary talents and personal qualities of an individual leader

Chicago School: developed at the first academic department of sociology in the United States, the University of Chicago, and focused on the study of the problems of urban life experienced by particular segments of the population as a result of social disorganization

city: a large, permanent community of people who rely on one another for food, goods, and services

civil religion: religious meaning spreads into politics, eventually helping to reinforce the legitimacy of the state, and citizenship in a society is imbued with quasireligious significance

class system: a stratification system in which movement between strata is possible, so individuals can change strata over the course of their lives

coercive organization: an organization that one is forced to join, or that one joins by choice but cannot easily withdraw from

collective behavior: voluntary activity, often spontaneous and goal-oriented, by a large number of people who are typically violating dominant norms and values with their behavior

collective conscience: an underlying set of moral norms that gives the members of a society the shared feeling that they belong to something larger than themselves as individuals

collectivity: a large number of people engaged in limited interaction guided by weak or unconventional norms

colonialism: the conquest of one country by another, resulting in the former ruling the latter, claiming its natural resources, and exploiting the population as cheap or slave labor

communism: a classless or nonstratified society in which all property is collectively owned and controlled

Comte, Auguste (1798–1857): considered to be the founder of sociology

concentric zone theory: theory that portrays the city as a series of five rings, each constituting a zone

concept: a mental representation of some aspect of our environment or the people in that environment

concrete operations stage: the second stage of cognitive development in Piaget's theory, during which children learn more complex rules of behavior and the reasons underlying them; develop the ability to see and evaluate a situation from a number of different viewpoints; and are able to anticipate events and other people's behavior

conflict theory: a contemporary sociological perspective that focuses on how inequality in society produces advantages or disadvantages for particular segments of the population, thus generating social conflict and sometimes social change

conformity: an individual's willingness to go along with an opinion or action undertaken by others in a group

conglomeration: the process of corporate mergering

conservation: in Piaget's theory, the understanding that an object may change in appearance, but remain the same weight, substance, or volume

consumer price index: a measure that gauges the cost of products, services, and other items that are essential to everyday living

content analysis: a research method in which the content of some form of communication is analyzed

control: to neutralize in some way the effects of a variable on the other variables being studied

control theory: a theory developed by Travis Hirschi that proposes that deviance results when an individual has weak social bonds to conventional institutions

conventional crowd: a planned gathering that comes together for a special event

conventional morality: the second level of moral development in Kohlberg's theory, during which a behavior is evaluated not only in terms of its consequences, but also in terms of whether it will please others whose opinions are important to the actor

Cooley, Charles Horton (1864–1929): the social theorist who postulated that the development of the individual self grows out of our interactions with others and our perceptions of how others see us

corporation: a group of people who own a business and have a special legal status that grants them rights, privileges, and responsibilities separate and distinct from those they hold as individuals

correlational relationship: an empirically measured relationship between variables in which the variables are found to change together

counterculture: a subgroup within a society that develops in opposition to the dominant culture, openly rejecting it and sometimes attempting to change it or at least live an alternative lifestyle

credential society: a society in which eligibility for employment and social status derive from credentials certifying completion of a specific level of education

crime: the violation of norms a society considers so important that it enacts laws to force compliance with them

Crime Index Offenses: eight crimes spotlighted by the FBI in the Uniform Crime Reports; these crimes are homicide and nonnegligent manslaughter, forcible rape, robbery, aggravated assault, burglary, larceny-theft, motor vehicle theft, and arson

crimes against property: crimes involving theft or damage to an individual's possessions

crimes against the person: crimes that cause or threaten to cause physical injury to an individual

cross-sectional study: a study that examines behavior or attitudes at one fixed point in time

crowd: a temporary gathering of people with a common focal point who exercise influence over one another

crude birth rate: the number of live births per 1,000 people per year, unadjusted for differences between subgroups in a society

crude death rate: the number of deaths per 1,000 people per year, unadjusted for differences between subgroups in a society

cult: a religious organization whose teachings and practices put it outside the sphere of the society's conventional religious traditions

cultural assimilation (behavioral assimilation, acculturation) a form of assimilation that occurs over the course of several generations and involves cultural changes (such as changes in dress and language) until eventually the cultural expression of the members of a specific racial or ethnic group is indistinguishable from that of the dominant or core group

cultural diversity: variations in culture between societies as well as within a society

cultural integration: the interdependence among the elements of a culture

cultural lag: when changes in one dimension of culture (typically material culture) outpace changes in another dimension of culture (typically nonmaterial culture)

cultural relativism: the practice of judging a culture in terms of how well it helps the members of a society meet their survival needs

cultural transmission: the process by which culture is passed on from one generation to the next

cultural universals: cultural traits common to all cultures

culture: the shared set of values, beliefs, behavioral expectations, and artifacts that comprise the way of life of a people

curative medicine: medicine that focuses on treating people who are already ill

deductive model: a method of conducting research in which the researcher develops hypotheses from a particular theory and conducts research to test these hypotheses

deindividuation: the process of losing one's sense of personal responsibility and individuality to the group

democracy: a political system in which governing is done by the people, either directly or through elected representatives

democratic leadership: a leadership style in which leaders seek input from all group members before arriving at a decision

democratic socialism: an economic system in which there is substantial public ownership of production and government intervention into economic activity, but there is also considerably more political freedom (including democratic elections) than what is typically associated with socialist societies

demographic transition: a theory that sees population growth as tied to the technological development of a society

demography: the study of population size, distribution, composition, and movement or migration

denomination (church): a religious organization independent of the state, generally tolerant of religious diversity, and accepting of voluntary membership

dependency theory: a theory that explains the poverty of low-income countries as the result of the policies and practices that high-income countries pursue to amass greater wealth while putting low-income countries in a position of relative dependency on them

dependent variable: a variable whose value depends on the value of the independent variable; in a cause-and-effect relationship, this variable represents the effect

descriptive statistics: statistics used to describe specific variables; however, descriptive statistics cannot be used for drawing conclusions about the relationships between variables

determinate task: a task that can be accomplished in only one or two correct ways

deterrence doctrine: the belief that an increase in military might would prevent war because no rational political leader would enter into a war that could not be won due to the opponent's military superiority

deviance: any act, attribute, or belief that violates a norm and elicits from others a negative or positive reaction

differential association: the process of social interaction by which definitions favorable and unfavorable to deviation are taught and learned

diffusion: the spread of one society's culture to another

direct-fee system: a system of health care in which patients pay directly for medical services

discretion: the power of criminal justice officials to decide for themselves how to handle a specific case

discrimination: any actions, policies, or practices that have the effect of denying an individual or group equal access to the society's resources, rewards, and opportunities

disengagement theory: a structural functionalist position that when people reach old age they disengage from their work roles and responsibilities, relinquishing them to younger workers so as to keep the society running smoothly

dispersed collectivity: activity by people who are not in close physical proximity, but who affect one another nevertheless

division of labor: the differentiation of people according to the roles and tasks for which they are responsible

divorce: the legal dissolution of a marriage that frees former spouses to marry someone else if they choose to

domestic partnership: a cohabiting relationship between intimate partners not married to each other

doubling time: the amount of time it takes a population to double itself, given a constant rate of growth

downward intergenerational mobility: the movement of adult children to a social stratum lower than that of their parents

downward vertical mobility: movement to a lower position in the stratification hierarchy

dramaturgical analysis: the sociological study of social interaction as theatrical performance

drives: basic physiological needs that must be met in order for humans to survive

dual labor market: a labor market composed of essentially two types of jobs: high-paying, high-prestige jobs with extensive benefits, and low-paying, low-prestige jobs with few, if any, benefits

Durkheim, Emile (1858–1917): the sociologist whose work essentially established sociology as an independent scientific discipline; focused on the fundamental question of what makes social order possible

dyad: a group of two people

dysfunctions: consequences or outcomes of institutional operations that lessen social adaptation and weaken the social system

ecclesia: a religious organization that is formally part of the state and claims all citizens as members

economic culture: the system of values, beliefs, and traditions in which economic activities and economic institutions exist

economy: the social institution that produces, manages, and distributes a society's human and material resources

ecosystem: the interrelationships between living things and their environments

education: the social institution for instructing a society's members in the knowledge, values, and skills the society deems important

egalitarian family: a family in which power and authority is shared by family members

ego: in Freud's theory, the element of the personality that operates on the reality principle, trying to satisfy the needs of the id in socially acceptable ways

elitism: the perspective developed by conflict theorists, which sees the political process as dominated by a small, but wealthy and powerful minority of society's members

empirical evidence: information that is directly verifiable

endogamy: the prohibition against marriage or the formation of an intimate relationship with anyone outside one's own social stratum or group

equalitarian pluralism: the maintenance of racial and ethnic diversity in a society that simultaneously involves the development of an appreciation of and respect for the cultures of groups other than one's own

Erikson, Erik (1902–1990): the psychologist who proposed a theory of human development as a lifelong process divided into eight stages, during each of which the individual struggles to resolve a basic psychological conflict

establishment sex segregation: a form of occupational sex segregation in which women and men have the same job, but they work for different types of establishments, which are unequal in pay and prestige

ethics: principles of right or good conduct in research

ethnic group: a group whose members share a common cultural heritage and a sense of peoplehood that they pass on from one generation to the next

ethnicity: the characteristics of an ethnic group, that is, the ways they express their cultural heritage and sense of belonging to the group

ethnocentrism: regarding the values and behavior of one's own group as "correct" or "best" and judging other groups' values and practices as inferior; the practice of judging another culture by the standards of one's own

Eurocentrism: a disproportionate focus on beliefs and concerns of relevance to Western societies with European roots

exclusion: a form of institutional discrimination that involves restricting the entry of a group into society or preventing its full participation in the society

exogamy: a social norm that prescribes people to marry outside their own social stratum or group

experiment: a research method through which the researcher tests hypotheses about the relationship between an independent variable and a dependent variable, while controlling for the effects of other variables; usually conducted in a laboratory setting

exponential population growth: the theory that if growth is left unchecked, the population will increase exponentially (1, 2, 4, 8, 16, 32, 64, and so on)

expressive crowd: a crowd that gathers for an event that is considered highly emotional or exciting

expressive leader: a leader who is people-oriented and whose primary concern is the well-being of the group as a whole

expulsion: a form of institutional discrimination that involves the forced removal of a group from an area or the harassment of a group to compel migration

extended family: a family composed of one or two parents, their dependent children, and other relatives who live together in the same household

fad: an object or behavior that is at least mildly unconventional, with tremendous mass appeal that catches on and disappears quickly

family: a long-term, exclusive relationship in which members are related by ancestry, marriage, or adoption, and are committed to one another emotionally as well as financially

family of orientation: the family with whom an individual identifies as a member and who socializes her or him

family of origin: the family into which one is born

family of procreation: the family a person forms by having or adopting children

fashion: currently favored styles of appearance or behavior

feminist sociology: a contemporary sociological perspective that examines gender as a central organizing factor in the social world

feminist sociology of gender: a theoretical perspective that acknowledges the importance of both biology and social learning in the acquisition of gender, but that sees gender as primarily a social construction

fertility: the incidence of live births

field observation: a research method in which the researcher watches the social phenomenon he or she is studying unfold in its natural setting

folkways: relatively weak norms that bring only mild sanctions when violated, since adherence is not considered essential to the well-being of the society

formal education: instruction given by specially trained teachers in designated academic settings, usually schools

formal operations stage: the final stage of cognitive development in Piaget's theory, when children can think abstractly and use deductive logic and during which time children can engage in hypothetical or future-oriented thinking

formal organization: a large, secondary group whose members interact for the purpose of achieving their common goals as efficiently and effectively as possible

frequency distribution: a table that shows the number of times each attribute of a variable occurs in a sample or population

Freud, Sigmund (1856–1939): the psychologist who developed a psychosocial theory of human development that focuses on the struggles between three interrelated components of the personality

functionally illiterate: people whose reading, writing, and computation skills are below the level needed to carry out basic everyday activities

fundamentalism: a religious orientation that denounces secular modernity and attempts to restore traditional spirituality through selective retrieval of doctrines, beliefs, and practices from a sacred past

game stage: the third stage of socialization in Mead's theory, during which children internalize the values and expectations of the larger society and come to understand the complex interrelationship of roles in the social network

gemeinschaft: a type of social organization characterized by close intimate relationships, a strong sense of kinship and community, and strong mores and traditions

gender: the socially constructed cluster of behavioral patterns and personality traits associated with masculinity and femininity

gender gap: differences in the voting patterns and political attitudes of women and men

gender identification: in Freud's theory of personality development, when children adopt the behavior and attributes of their same-sex parent

gender identity: the set of gendered characteristics that an individual adopts as an integral part of her or his self

gender inequality: (see **sexism**)

gender roles: the behavioral requirements or expectations that are prescribed for a society's members depending on their sex

gender socialization: teaching individuals what is expected of them as males and females; teaching masculinity and femininity

gender stereotype: simplistic descriptions of the supposedly "masculine male" or "feminine female"

generalized other: in Mead's theory, the values and expectations of the larger society

genital stage: in Freud's theory, the final stage in personality development, when children enter adolescence and become increasingly independent of their parents and learn to develop mature social and sexual relationships with members of the opposite sex

genocide: a form of institutional discrimination that involves the deliberate attempt to exterminate an entire race or ethnic group

gentrification: the renewal of old neighborhoods by affluent individuals that results in significant improvement in selected areas of the city, but also causes many low-income families and the elderly to lose their homes

gerontology: the scientific study of aging

gerontophilia: respect and reverence for the aged

gerontophobia: a strong dislike or hatred of aging and the aged

gesellschaft: a type of social organization where social relationships are impersonal, family and community ties are weak, and the community orientation is replaced by the pursuit of individual goals and desires

Gilligan, Carol: psychologist who critiqued and elaborated on Kohlberg's theory of moral development by replicating his research using female research subjects and thereby showing gender differences in moral reasoning

global cities: metropolitan areas that serve as centers of international commerce, finance, and culture; part of an interconnected global system that exerts great power on the economic and political decision-making process

global stratification: the ranking of the nations of the world in terms of wealth and political power and, to a lesser extent, prestige

Goffman, Erving (1922–1982): sociologist who studied the construction of social reality by developing dramaturgical analysis, the analysis of social interaction as theatrical performance

gossip: rumor about individuals' personal lives

government: the social institution with formal authority to distribute power, allocate resources, make decisions for the society, and regulate relationships among the society's members as well as between the society itself and other societies

greenhouse effect: the warming of the earth because of trapped solar radiation due to a build-up of gases in the atmosphere.

group polarization: the tendency for individuals in a group to adopt opinions or engage in behaviors that are more extreme or risky than those they would normally support or do alone

groupthink: the process by which the members of a group support one another during decision making, with the primary goal of preserving group harmony and unity

Hawthorne effect: when research participants change their behavior to what they perceive are the researcher's expectations of them

health: a state of physical, mental, and social well-being

health maintenance organization (HMO): a type of private medical insurance that provides medical services to subscribers at a fixed rate and emphasizes preventive medicine

heterosexism: the privileging of heterosexuality over homosexuality

heterosexuality: a sexual orientation in which the source of an individual's affectional preferences, sexual arousal, and sexual gratification are persons of the sex opposite them

hidden curriculum: the values transmitted implicitly through education

high culture: the beliefs, values, expectations, and artifacts of a society's elites

high-income countries: industrial countries with an annual per capita GNP above US$9,656

homeless: the segment of the poverty population without private living space or adequate shelter

homosexuality: a sexual orientation in which the source of an individual's affectional preferences, sexual arousal, and sexual gratification are persons of their same sex

horizontal merger: the acquisition of a company by another company in the same industry or business

horizontal mobility: movement from one position to another of equal wealth, status, and political power

horticultural society: a society in which the subsistence strategy is based on cultivating plants using relatively simple technology such as digging sticks and the slash-and-burn method

human ecology: the study of the spatial distribution of people in an urban environment

hunting and gathering society: a society in which the subsistence strategy in based on hunting game, fishing, and gathering vegetation and other types of food from the surrounding environment

hypothesis: a statement of the expected relationship between two variables

hysteria: a form of collective behavior in which people respond fearfully and irrationally to either an imagined or real event that has been misinterpreted or distorted

I: in Mead's theory, the spontaneous, free-willed dimension of the self

id: in Freud's theory, the unconscious element of the personality, composed of powerful forces called *drives* and *wishes*

ideal culture: made up of the shared values, beliefs, and norms that the members of a society claim as their culture

ideal type: an analytic tool that sociologists construct by carefully studying various examples of the phenomenon they are interested in, and from this, identifying what they consider to be its essential features

ideology: a set of beliefs

imitation stage: the first stage of socialization in Mead's theory, during which children begin to imitate or mimic the people with whom they interact most

income fifths (quintiles): the division of a population into five equal segments, ranked according to their income, from the lowest or poorest 20 percent to the highest or wealthiest 20 percent

independent variable: a variable that produces or causes change in another variable; in a cause-and-effect relationship, this variable is the cause

indeterminate task: a task that can be accomplished correctly in many different ways

indicator: shows the presence or absence of the variable being studied

inductive model: a method of conducting research in which the researcher begins by collecting data on the topic of interest and subsequently builds theory through data analysis

industry sex segregation: a form of occupational sex segregation in which the representation of women and men in a particular industry as a whole is relatively balanced, but within the industry, women and men hold different kinds of jobs that are unequal in pay and prestige

industrial society: a society in which the subsistence strategy is based on mechanized systems of production

inequality: the differential allocation of rewards, opportunities, and other resources among members of a society

infant mortality rate: the number of deaths of children under one year of age per 1,000 live births

inflation: an increase in the price of goods and services

ingroup: a social group whose members express intense loyalty, respect, and pride in the group

instincts: biologically programmed directions for living

institutional discrimination: policies and practices of the central institutions in a society that systematically disadvantage members of particular groups

instrumental leader: a leader who is task-oriented and focuses on getting a job done as efficiently and effectively as possible

intercorporate control: a network of connections among corporations that allows them to coordinate their activities so as to maintain or enhance their economic position

intergenerational mobility: the degree to which the social standing of adult children is different from that of their parents

interlocking directorate: a network of associations formed through simultaneous memberships on the boards of directors of multiple corporations

intimate relationship: a relationship of intense emotional attachment

intragenerational mobility: movement across the stratification system during a single individual's lifetime

kinship: a social network of individuals and families joined by ancestry, marriage, or adoption

Kohlberg, Lawrence (1927–1987): the social psychologist whose work focused on how children develop a sense of morality and engage in moral reasoning

Kuznets curve: the theory that during the transitional stage of development from agriculture to industry, inequality will increase, but conditions will improve once industrialization is established

labeling theory: a symbolic interactionist theory of deviance that sees deviance not as a result of some quality of an act, attribute, or belief, but rather as the product of others applying rules or sanctions to a particular person

labor union: an organization of workers who seek to improve wages and working conditions in their trade

laissez-faire leadership: a leadership style in which leaders avoid intervention and simply wait for problems or crises to resolve themselves over time

language: a system of patterned sounds, often with corresponding written symbols, that the members of a society use to communicate their thoughts and feelings to one another

latency stage: in Freud's theory, the period from five to twelve years of age, during which sexual impulses become dormant

latent functions: observable, unintended consequences or outcomes of institutional operations

laws: norms that a governing authority within a society officially adopts as rules to regulate the behavior of the members of that society

legitimate authority: power that is perceived as rightful by those being led

liberation theology: a religious orientation that merges the religious teachings and social functions of the Christian church with a critical analysis of the history and current experience of human suffering

life expectancy: the average number of years a person can expect to live after reaching a certain age

life expectancy at birth: the average number of years a person can expect to live after birth

literacy: basic reading, writing, and numeracy skills

literature review: reading what other researchers have learned about the research problem

lobbyist: a paid professional who pressures elected officials to pass or defeat proposed legislation

localized collectivity: activity by people who are in close physical proximity to one another

longitudinal study: a study in which data are gathered over an extended period of time, either continuously or at specific intervals

looking-glass self: Cooley's notion that we derive our self-concepts from our perceptions of how others see us

lower-middle income countries: countries with a per capita GNP of between US$786 and US$3,125; also referred to as *developing countries*

low-income countries: countries with a per capita GNP of US$785 or less per year; also referred to as *underdeveloped countries*

macro-level theory: a theory that conceptualizes society in broad, abstract terms and emphasizes the role of institutional structures in shaping social life

magnet schools: public schools designed to attract high-achieving students of diverse backgrounds by offering high-quality, specialized programs

maldistribution: the concentration of physicians in particular geographic areas

manifest functions: observable, intended consequences or outcomes of institutional operations

marriage: a socially approved union of two or more people in which each is expected to fulfill specific economic, sexual, and caregiving obligations and responsibilities

Marx, Karl (1818–1883): the revolutionary social theorist whose life's work was dedicated to the study of class conflict, especially in capitalist societies; believed that a fundamental restructuring of the social system was necessary to end inequality

mass education: the extension of formal education to the general public

mass media: the impersonal means by which information is communicated to a large audience

master status: a status that takes on greater significance in the eyes of others than any other aspect of an individual's identity

material culture: all the tangible or physical products that the members of a society create

matriarchal family: a family in which power and authority are disproportionately held by the wife/mother or eldest female family member

matriarchy: a sex/gender system in which women dominate men and that which is considered feminine is more highly valued than that which is considered masculine

matrilineal descent: a system in which descent is traced through the mother's side of the family

matrilocality: a residential pattern in which a married couple lives with the wife's family, or at least in her village or community

matrix of domination: an interlocking system of control in which each type of inequality reinforces others, so that the impact of one cannot be fully understood without considering the others

Me: in Mead's theory, the dimension of the self formed by the stable, internalized values and norms of one's community

Mead, George Herbert (1863–1931): the social theorist who focused on how language, gestures, and other symbolic systems of communication allow for the development of the individual and make social order possible

mean: the average value in a distribution

mechanical solidarity: the sense of belonging that the members of a society develop because of their similarity to one another

median: the midpoint of a distribution; 50 percent of the distribution falls below this value and 50 percent falls above this value

medicalization: the process of defining a specific behavior or condition as an illness in need of medical treatment

medicalization of deviance: the assignment of various acts, attributes, and beliefs considered deviant to the realm of psychiatric medicine and psychology for treatment and "cure"

medicine: the social institution established to identify and treat illness and promote health

micro-level theory: a theory that focuses on contextualized patterns of social interaction and communication

middle class: the largest social class in the United States, encompassing 40 to 45 percent of the population and composed of two groups: a small segment (the upper-middle class) and a large segment (the lower-middle class)

military-industrial complex: the closed, mutually dependent relationship between government and military contractors

minority groups: racial and ethnic groups who are singled out for unfair treatment

mob: an intensely emotional crowd set on doing violence to specific others or property

mode: the most frequent value in a distribution

modernization theory: a theory that focuses on the conditions that are necessary for a country to become economically developed—that is, fully modern; the idea that the economic transformation of a society from agriculture to industry produces a progressive devaluation of aging

monarchy: a political system in which one family rules from one generation to the next, inheriting political power

monogamy: marriage to one partner

monotheism: belief in a single Supreme Being

mores: norms that carry a strong sanction if violated because the members of a culture consider adherence essential to the well-being of the society

mortality: the incidence of deaths

mortality rate: the number of deaths in proportion to a given population

multiculturalism: respect for and appreciation of the cultural contributions, practices, and experiences of diverse groups

multinational corporations: large corporations that engage in production and marketing in numerous countries throughout the world

nation-state: a unit of political organization in which the governed are citizens with specific legal rights and responsibilities who reside within recognized national boundaries

National Crime Victimization Survey (NCVS): a survey of a sample of the general population conducted by the U.S. Department of Justice that asks about experiences of criminal victimization during a specific period of time and whether these experiences were reported to the police

nativism: an anti-immigrant position that those already settled in an area are racially superior to newcomers

naturally occurring retirement communities (NORCs): neighborhoods, towns, or even just single apartment buildings that were not intended as residential areas for older people but where, because of the population's aging, at least half the residents are over sixty years old

neocolonialism: the relationships between multinational corporations and low-income countries in which the economic power of the multinationals dominates low-income countries in ways similar to the political control previously exercised by foreign governments

neolocality: a residential pattern in which a married couple establishes their own residence apart from either the husband's or the wife's family

net migration: determined by comparing in-migration (the number of individuals entering a country or area) with out-migration (the number of people departing a country or area)

network: a chain of associations that links people with common interests who otherwise would not have the opportunity to interact

new reproductive technologies (NRTs): a variety of laboratory techniques that allow people who, for various reasons, cannot conceive children through sexual intercourse to become parents

nomadic: having to move from one locale to another, without permanent settlement

nonmaterial culture: all the nontangible or nonphysical products that the members of a society create

normative consensus: a set of agreed-upon values, customs, and expectations for appropriate behavior shared by the members of a society

norms: the behavioral rules of a culture

nuclear family: a family composed of one or two parents and their dependent children who live together in a household separate from other relatives

object permanence: in Piaget's theory, the ability to understand that when a person or object is out of sight, it still exists

objectivity: the extent to which research is free from the personal values or biases of the researcher

occupational crime: the willful attempt of an individual or group to take advantage of their professional position to illegally secure something of value

occupational sex segregation: the degree to which men and women are concentrated in occupations in which workers of one sex predominate

oligarchy: occurs when the resources and decision-making authority of a bureaucracy are controlled by a tiny faction of members

oligopoly (shared monopoly): a small group of corporations that enjoys a disproportionate share of the market for specific goods or services

operationalizing a variable: the process of developing measures to be used to gauge the existence of a particular variable in the real world

oral stage: in Freud's theory, the first stage of personality development during which the mouth, tongue, and lips are the areas of gratification and desire

organic solidarity: social integration built on a specialized division of labor

organizational crime: crimes committed by major decision makers of a corporation or government who, in the pursuit of profits or in the name of national security, engage in illegal activity

outgroup: a group that is viewed as the competitor or rival of another group

overspecialization: the concentration of physicians in particular specialties

panic: a form of collective behavior that emerges when people who are confronted with a crisis or serious threat respond in irrational ways that actually worsen their situation

particular other: in Mead's theory, the perspectives of people who are significant in the child's environment

pastoral society: a society in which the subsistence strategy is based on domesticating and herding animals

patriarchal family: a family in which power and authority are disproportionately held by the husband/father or eldest male family member

patriarchy: a sex/gender system in which men dominate women and that which is considered masculine is more highly valued than that which is considered feminine

patrilineal descent: a system in which descent is traced through the father's side of the family

patrilocality: a residential pattern in which a married couple lives with the husband's family, or at least in his village or community

peers: those individuals who are about the same age, share the same social position in the status hierarchy, and have similar interests

per capita gross national product (per capita GNP): the total value of the goods and services produced in a country each year divided by the number of people in the country's population

personality: a set of behavioral and emotional characteristics that describe a person's reactions to various situations or events in the environment

phallic stage: in Freud's theory, the third stage of personality development during which gender identification takes place

Piaget, Jean (1892–1980): the social psychologist who focused his life's work on examining how children think and interpret the world around them

pink-collar jobs: jobs primarily in the service sector with a high concentration of women workers, which got their name not because of the way workers dress for work, but because the jobs are associated with females and femininity

play stage: the second stage of socialization in Mead's theory, during which children distinguish a variety of social roles and spend time in play that involves role taking

plea bargaining: a process whereby the accused agrees to plead guilty in exchange for a reduction in the charges or the sentence

pluralism: the diffusion of political influence among numerous interest groups with no single group dominating; the maintenance of racial and ethnic diversity in a society

political action committees (PACs): special interest groups dedicated to fundraising and distributing contributions on political campaigns, making them a powerful force on the political scene

political party: an organization that supports and promotes particular principles and candidates for public office

political power: the decision-making component of stratification, referring to an individual's relationship to government and the ability to influence political decisions

political socialization: the development of political values and attitudes over time in response to various environmental influences, including one's social locations and experiences of political events

politics of research: the ways in which research may be used to promote or support a particular interest or partisan position

polyandry: a marriage in which one woman is married concurrently to two or more men

polygamy: marriage to multiple partners concurrently

polygyny: a marriage in which one man is married concurrently to two or more women

polytheism: belief in many gods

popular culture: the beliefs, values, expectations, and artifacts of a society's masses

population: the entire group that a researcher is interested in studying; all possible subjects of relevance to a study

population pyramid: a device used by demographers to make a visual presentation of population variation

positional mobility: movement through the stratification hierarchy as a result of individual causes, such as hard work and luck

positivism: the position that knowledge must be derived from observable facts, not from superstition, fantasy, or some other nonempirical (nonverifiable) source

postconventional morality: the highest level of moral development in Kohlberg's theory, during which people evaluate behavior in terms of whether they consider it to be in the best interests of their community or their society

postindustrial economy: a system for producing, managing, and distributing services and information, with the help of electronic technology, especially computers

postindustrial society: a society in which work is devoted primarily to the production of services and information rather than to the physical production of goods

poverty line: the federal government's measure of poverty, calculated by multiplying by three the amount of money needed for a minimally nutritional diet, while also taking into account factors such as size of the family and age of the household head

power: the ability to get others to do one's will even if they do not want to do it

power elite: a term coined by C. Wright Mills to describe the segments of society that dominate the political process: the government elite, the military elite, and the corporate elite

preconventional morality: the first stage of moral development in Kohlberg's theory, during which behavior is evaluated in terms of whether it will be punished or rewarded

prejudice: biased beliefs or attitudes about individuals based on their membership in a particular group; in the context of race and ethnic relations, biased beliefs about individuals based on their membership in a particular racial or ethnic group

preoperational stage: the second developmental stage in Piaget's theory, during which the child builds on language and reasoning skills and learns to represent the world symbolically

presentation of self: the careful control of one's appearance and behavior in order to convey to others a specific image of one's self

preventive medicine: medicine that establishes conditions that preclude the onset of illness

primary deviation: rule breaking

primary group: a social group, typically small in size, that is characterized by strong emotional attachments among the members and that endures over time

primary labor market: made up of high-paying, high-prestige jobs with extensive benefits

primary sector (of the economy): the segment of the economy made up of activities that extract products directly from the natural environment

primordialist perspective: a theory that explains race and ethnic stratification as a product of humans' natural preference for those whom they perceive as being most like themselves

profane: anything regarded as ordinary

profession: an occupation that requires extensive, specialized training in a particular field

proletariat: the social class consisting mostly of workers who sell their labor to the bourgeoisie in exchange for wages

propaganda: information designed to persuade people to adopt a particular opinion on a specific issue

proportional representation: legislative seats go to candidates from all political parties represented in an election according to the percentage of votes each party received

protest crowd: a crowd that gathers purposely to express dissatisfaction with particular conditions or events

pseudohermaphroditism: a condition in which a person's sexual differentiation is ambiguous or incomplete

public opinion: the attitudes expressed by members of a society, or those selected to represent them

qualitative analysis: the analysis of data in which the researcher focuses on specific qualities (distinct descriptive categories) within the data that show patterns of difference or similarity among the study participants, but do not allow the formulation of precise numerical statements about or measurements of these similarities or differences

quantitative analysis: the analysis of data in which the researcher translates study participants' responses into numerical categories that subsequently can be analyzed using various statistical techniques, usually via a computer

quintile (see **income fifths**)

race: a group whose members share a real or supposed biological heritage that is thought to give rise to a set of fixed physical, mental, emotional, and moral characteristics; members of a race also share common customs, values, and traditions and develop a sense of peoplehood

racism: a form of inequality in which one racial group dominates another and legitimates this domination by proclaiming itself physically, intellectually, and/or socially superior, and instituting laws or practices to protect its dominance

random sampling: the method of selecting a sample for a study that ensures that each member of the population has an equal chance of being selected for participation in the study

rape: when a person uses force or the threat of force to have some form of sexual intercourse (vaginal, oral, or anal) with another person

rational-legal authority: authority bestowed by legally enacted rules, regulations, or contracts

real culture: the values, beliefs, and norms that are reflected in the actual behavior and social practices of a society's members

reference group: a group that serves as a point of reference in personal decision making

reform movement: a social movement that tries to bring about limited social change by working within the existing system

refugees: people who leave their home country because of such factors as international or civil war, political repression, or famine

reincarnation: a process or cycle of birth, death, and rebirth

relative deprivation: the perception by an individual or group that they are disadvantaged compared with others whom they use as their reference group

relative poverty: the poor lack many of the resources available to the rest of the population, but nevertheless have the basic necessities of life

reliability: the ability of a measure to yield consistent results each time it is used

religion: a social institution composed of a unified system of beliefs and practices relative to sacred things

religiosity: an individual's or group's intensity of commitment to a religious belief system

religious movement (redemptive movement): a social movement that seeks to bring about profound change in individuals based on unconventional spiritual or supernatural beliefs

replication: repeating a study that was conducted at an earlier time

representative sample: a sample that closely resembles the population in terms of aggregate characteristics that are important for a specific study

research method: a technique or procedure used to collect data

resistance movement (reactionary movement): a social movement that seeks to maintain the status quo or to restore conditions that existed prior to social change

resocialization: the systematic stripping of an individual of much of what she or he learned in the past and replacing it with drastically different norms, values, behaviors, and attitudes

reverse socialization: the process by which aspects of a culture are transmitted from the young to their elders

revolutionary movement: a social movement that seeks to replace the existing system with a fundamentally different one, often by using radical (and sometimes illegal) tactics

riot: an intensely emotional crowd whose violent behavior is not purposefully directed

ritual: a formal, stylized ceremony for approaching the sacred

role: the behaviors, responsibilities, and privileges expected of individuals occupying a specific status

role conflict: the clash between roles attached to different statuses occupied by a single individual

role model: an individual who serves as an example to be emulated

role strain: the clash between multiple roles attached to a single status occupied by an individual

routinization of charisma: the replacement of charismatic authority with some combination of traditional and rational-legal authority

rumor: information transmitted among people, usually informally and from unconfirmed sources

sacred: things regarded by a community of believers as extraordinary and awe-inspiring

sample: a subgroup of the larger group one is interested in studying

sampling: the process of selecting a subgroup for study from the entire group of interest

Sapir-Whorf hypothesis: the position that language shapes perception and affects how we experience and understand reality

scapegoats: relatively powerless people whom others unjustly blame for their own or society's problems

school choice programs: programs that allow parents to choose the public schools their children will attend or use federal "vouchers" to pay for private schooling

science: a logically organized method of obtaining information through direct, systematic observation

second shift: the household responsibilities of women who work full time outside the home, but who nevertheless are expected to perform most household chores

secondary analysis: the analysis of data that were gathered by others

secondary deviation: deviation that results from social reaction

secondary group: a social group that may be large or small in size, but that is characterized by members' orientation to achieving the same goal rather than members' emotional attachments to one another

secondary labor market: made up of low-paying, low-prestige jobs with few, if any benefits

secondary sector (of the economy): the segment of the economy composed of activities that transform material resources into goods or products

sect: a religious organization that sets itself apart from the larger society, sometimes even rejecting the values and norms of the society

secularization: the process by which sacred beliefs are weakened over time and religion becomes less influential in society

sedentary: settled with respect to residence

segregation: physically and socially separating and keeping apart different racial and ethnic groups; the physical separation of social groups or strata

self-fulfilling prophecy: something comes true because people believe it to be true and act accordingly; expectations about how the individual will behave are fulfilled, not so much because the person is truly deviant, but because both the person and others have come to believe that he or she is deviant and behave accordingly

semisedentary: semisettled with respect to residence

sensorimotor stage: the first (and most important) developmental stage in Piaget's theory, during which time the child begins to interact socially and develops object permanence

sex: the genetic determination of maleness and femaleness

sex/gender system: the institutionalized traits, behaviors, and patterns of social interaction that are prescribed for a society's members on the basis of their sex; composed of three interrelated components: the social construction of gender, a sexual division of labor, and the social regulation of sexuality

sexism: differentially valuing people's traits or abilities on the basis of their sex and without regard for their attributes as individuals

sexual harassment: any unwanted leers, comments, suggestions, or physical contact of a sexual nature, as well as unwelcome requests for sexual favors

sexual orientation: the source of an individual's affectional preferences, sexual arousal, and sexual gratification

sick role: the behaviors defined by a society as appropriate for people who are sick

social category: a collective of people who occupy the same status

social change: the transformation of culture, social structure, and social behavior over time

social class: an economic status determined by one's role in the production process; as defined by Marx, one's socioeconomic position in society, which is determined by one's role in production

social control: responses aimed at inhibiting or punishing deviation and promoting or rewarding conformity

social epidemiology: the study of the distribution of health and illness across population groups

social facts: phenomena that endure beyond the life span of particular individuals, are caused by factors external to individuals, and exercise a coercive power over individuals

social group: two or more people who interact with one another on a regular basis and share common expectations and a common identity

social institution: a set of relatively stable rules and relationships that serve to regulate the social activities in which the members of a society engage in order to meet their survival needs

social mobility: movement within the stratification system of a society

social movement: an issue-oriented group purposefully organized to bring about or prevent social change

social solidarity: the unifying force that holds members of a society together

social stratification: a system of ranking people in a hierarchy according to certain attributes

social structure: stable patterns of interaction in a society

socialism: an economic system in which the means of production are publically owned and operated

socialization: the process by which a society's culture is taught and learned and human personalities are developed

society: a collectivity of interacting people who share the same culture

sociobiological perspective of gender: a theoretical perspective that holds that the differences we may observe in women's and men's personalities and behavior are directly traceable to the difference in their physical makeup, especially their reproductive abilities

sociology: the scientific study of human societies; the scientific study of the collective interactions of social actors within a particular social structure and the collective meanings these actors give to their interactions with one another

spurious: when an observed relationship between two variables is not real and the change in both is actually the result of a third variable

state capitalism: an economic system in which the means of production are privately owned and operated, but there is a high level of government intervention in economic activity

state: the sole political entity with the legally recognized right to use force within its territory

status: particular social positions held by members of a society interacting in social institutions; the prestige component of stratification, determined by how others perceive an individual or group in terms of respect and deference

status degradation ceremony: the process of publicly attaching an official label of deviant to an individual

status offense: a behavior which if engaged in by an adult would not be considered illegal, such as running away from home, incorrigibility, and being in danger of becoming "morally depraved"

status set: all the social positions held by an individual at any one time

stereotype: an oversimplified summary description, usually negative in nature, of a particular group

structural assimilation: a form of assimilation that occurs when the members of a racial or ethnic group have full access to the same structural opportunities and social activities as the members of the dominant group

structural functionalism: a contemporary sociological perspective that sees society as being made up of interrelated parts, each of which contributes to the overall functioning of the society as a whole

structural mobility: movement through the stratification hierarchy as a result of factors external to individual control, such as changes in the economy or occupational structure of the society

subculture: a group within a society's dominant culture that shares some of its elements, but at the same time differentiates itself from the dominant culture in a specific way

suburbanization: the movement of people from the city to communities outside the city called suburbs

superego: in Freud's theory, the element of the personality that represents the internalization of the values and norms of the society; also called the *conscience*

surplus: the accumulation of more resources than are necessary to meet daily subsistence

survey: a research method in which the researcher selects a sample of respondents and asks them questions about specific topics

sustainable development: a balance of economic development, improved social equity, and environmental preservation, requiring changes in production and consumption patterns as well as economic development strategies for low-income countries that do not disrupt the ecological balance

symbol: anything that has been given representational meaning by the members of a cultural group

symbolic annihilation: the practice of the media to ignore, trivialize, ridicule, or condemn women and homosexuals and the issues that are of particular concern to them

symbolic interactionism: a contemporary sociological perspective that focuses on how social reality is constructed through the daily communications and rituals in which people engage with one another

taboos: norms so strongly held that to violate them is inconceivable to virtually all members of the society

taking the role of the other: Mead's concept of the ability of all members of the social group to visualize the world and themselves from the points of view of one another

technology: the body of knowledge that the members of a society apply to their physical environment to help them meet their survival needs

tertiary sector (of the economy): the segment of the economy devoted to providing services rather than producing tangible goods; also called the *service sector*

thanatology: the interdisciplinary study of death and dying

theory: a set of interrelated propositions that explain how two or more phenomena are related to one another

total institution: a place where individuals live for a specific period of time, isolated from the rest of society and under the near-total control of a group of officials charged, in part, with resocializing them

totalitarianism: a political system in which government regulates nearly all the significant aspects of people's lives

toxic waste: any byproduct of production or other processes that are of no use, but are hazardous to humans and the environment

tracking: a system of grouping students identified as having similar abilities so they can be taught together

trade deficit (or **trade gap**): occurs when a country imports more goods than it exports

traditional authority: authority bestowed by custom

trained incapacity: the inability to think independently and creatively, which results from the removal of autonomy in one's job within an organization

triad: a group of three people

underemployment: taking a job below one's educational background, abilities, or experience

unemployment rate: the percentage of the working-age population currently out of work but actively looking for a job

Uniform Crime Reports (UCR): statistics on the number of crimes reported to the police as compiled by the Federal Bureau of Investigation

upper-middle income countries: countries with an annual per capita GNP between about US$3,126 and US$9,655 per year

upward intergenerational mobility: movement of adult children to a stratum higher than their parents

upward vertical mobility: involves movement to a higher position in the stratification hierarchy

urbanization: the process whereby the members of a society are concentrated in cities and urban areas exert a significant influence on the society

utilitarian organization: an organization one joins because of the material gains to be had from membership

validity: the extent to which a measure accurately gauges what it was intended to measure

values: cultural standards or judgments of what is right, good, or desirable

variable: a concept whose value varies or changes

verstehen: in sociology, a research method requiring the sociologist to take an empathic stance toward understanding research subjects, thus interpreting the significance of specific interactions and events in terms of the meanings that they have for people who live them

vertical merger: the acquisition of a company by another company whose business activities are unrelated or only marginally related

vertical mobility: movement up or down the stratification hierarchy

victimless crimes: offenses that involve willing exchanges of strongly desired, but illegal goods and services in which none of the participants consider themselves victims

voluntary association: an organization one joins because of its moral appeal and the personal satisfaction attained from participating in it; also called *normative association*

voter apathy: the feeling that voting is not worthwhile because it makes no difference in election outcomes and governance

wealth: the material component of stratification, determined by income and other assets

the wealthy: the society's upper class, representing only about 3 percent of the U.S. population, with yearly incomes of hundreds of thousands of dollars

Weber, Max (1864–1920): classical social theorist who, like Marx, studied the problems of capitalist society and who advocated the use of interpretative understanding (*vertstehen*) in sociological research

white-collar jobs: jobs that require mostly mental labor rather than physical labor, which got their name because of the way most workers who hold them dress for work (in suits)

working class: composed of 30 to 35 percent of the U.S. population, with average annual incomes between $15,000 and $25,000

workplace crime: crimes against employers by employees

world systems theory: a theory that emphasizes the interconnections of countries in the global capitalist production process, which results in an uneven distribution of profits across the countries depending on their participation in core or peripheral production activities

zero growth rate: the number of births do not exceed the number of deaths

Name Index

Subject Index

Photo Credits

Chapter 1

xxvi, © Bob Daemmrich/Stock Boston; 9, top left, Corbis/Bettmann; 9, top middle, Corbis/Bettmann; 9, top right, © Roger Viollet/Gamma Presse; 9, bottom left, Culver Pictures; p. 13, top left, Archive Photos; p. 13, middle, Archive Photos; p. 13, top right, Culver Pictures; p. 13, bottom left, Corbis/Bettmann; p. 15, Klaus Lahnstein/Tony Stone Images; p. 18, © Michael Newman/PhotoEdit; p. 19, © Michael Newman/PhotoEdit.

Chapter 2

24, © R. Lord/The Image Works; p. 27, Mark Romine/Tony Stone Images; p. 30, © Bruce Hands/Stock Boston; p. 32, © Bill Horsman 1993/Stock Boston; p. 39, top left, © Michael Newman/PhotoEdit; p. 39, top right, © Bob Daemmrich/Stock Boston; p. 39, bottom left, © Michael Newman/Photo Edit; p. 39, bottom right, © Jeff Isaac Greenberg/Photo Researchers; p. 42, courtesy Dr. Philip G. Zimbardo; p. 43, © Michael Newman/PhotoEdit.

Chapter 3

56, PhotoEdit; p. 59, top, © Michael Newman/PhotoEdit; p. 59, bottom, © Fred Mayer/Magnum; p. 65, top left, © I. Devore/AnthroPhoto; p. 65, top right, © J. Scherschel/Photo Researchers; p. 65, bottom left, © Antonio Mari/The Gamma Liaison Network; p. 65, bottom right, © Bonnie Kamin/PhotoEdit; p.68, Reuters/Anuruddha/Lokuhapuarachchi/Archive Photos; p. 69, Hulton Getty/Tony Stone Images; p. 71, © James Schnepf/Liaison International; p. 72, Andrew Sacks/Tony Stone Images.

Chapter 4

78, © A. Ramey/PhotoEdit; p. 81, Reuters/Natalie Behring/Archive Photos; p. 82, © J. O. Atlanta 1966/Gamma Liaison; p. 84, © Michael Newman/PhotoEdit; p. 86, © Patrick Ward/Stock Boston; p. 89, top left, © 1994 Peter Gunter/Material World; p. 89, top right, © 1994, Leong Ka Tai/Material World; p. 89, bottom, © 1994, David Reed/Material World; p. 92, © C. Gatewood/The Image Works; p. 93, © Richard Lord/The Image Works; p. 99, © David R. Frazier/Photo Researchers.

Chapter 5

104, © Robert Eckert/Stock Boston; p. 107, © T. K. Wanstal/The Image Works; p. 108, Martin Rogers/Stock Boston; p. 112, © David Young-Wolff/PhotoEdit; p. 115, © Laura Dwight/PhotoEdit; p. 117, © Michael Newman/PhotoEdit; p. 119; © D. Young-Wolff/PhotoEdit; p. 124, top left, © Jeffrey W. Myers/Stock Boston; p. 124, top right, Ric Feld/AP/Wide World Photos; p. 124, bottom left, Penny Tweedie/c Tony Stone Images; p. 124, bottom right, © Richard Shock/Liaison International; p. 128, © Gary A. Conner/PhotoEdit.

Chapter 6

134, Bob Daemmrich/Stock Boston; p. 136, © Mark Richards/PhotoEdit; p. 139, top left, © Raghu Rai/Magnum Photos, Inc.; p. 139, top right, courtesy of St. Joseph's University; p. 139, bottom left, Frank Orel/c Tony Stone Images; p. 139, bottom right, © Cindy Charles/PhotoEdit; p. 144, Will Hart; p. 146, Copyright 1965 by Stanley Milgram. From the film Obedience, distrubuted by Penn State, Media Sales. Courtesy The Milgram Estate; p. 150, © David Young-Wolff/PhotoEdit; p. 151, © Herb Snitzer/Stock Boston; p. 153, © M. Granitsas/The Image Works; p. 157, © Diego Goldberg/Sygma.

Chapter 7

163, © A. Ramey/PhotoEdit; p. 165, top left, © 1998 North Wind Pictures; p. 165, top right, Archive Photos; p. 165, bottom, © Dagmar Fabricius/Stock Boston; p. 169, © A. Tannenbaum/SYGMA; p. 171, © John Van Hasselt/SYGMA; p. 188, AP/Wide World Photos; p. 181, Christopher Berkey/AP/Wide World Photos; p. 185, © 1996 David Hurn/Magnum Photos, Inc.; p. 188, © Shelly Katz/The Gamma Liaison Network.

Chapter 8

194, © A. Ramey/PhotoEdit; p. 196, © Mark Richards/PhotoEdit; p. 198, © David Austen/Stock Boston; p. 199, Reuters/Pool/Archive Photos; p. 203, left, Mark J. Terrill/AP/Wide World Photos; p. 203, middle, Gary Holscher/© Tony Stone Images; p. 203, right, © Michael Newman/PhotoEdit; p. 205, top left, © Tannenbaum/SYGMA: p. 205, top right, © Bachmann/PhotoEdit; p. 205, bottom, © Robert Brenner/PhotoEdit; p. 210, © Bob Daemmrich/Stock Boston; p. 216, © Tony Freeman/PhotoEdit.

Chapter 9

224, © Lionel Delevigne/Stock Boston; p. 227, top left, © Bruce Paton/Impact Visuals; p. 227, top right, David and June Smith; p. 227, bottom, © John Neubauer/PhotoEdit; p. 232, © Les Stone/SYGMA; p. 233, Reuters/David Ahmed/Archive Photos; p. 236, © Jack S. Grove/PhotoEdit; p. 237, © Steven Rubin/The Image Works; p. 239, Reuters/Corbis-Bettmann; p. 241, © Kees/SYGMA; p. 243, © L. DeMatteis/The Image Works.

Chapter 10

250, © Jeff Greenberg/PhotoEdit; p. 255, left, Culver Pictures; p. 255, right, © Mary Ellen Lepionka; p. 258, UPI/Corbis-Bettmann; p. 259, Bagish/AnthroPhoto; p. 261, © A. Ramey/Stock Boston; p. 263, © Chip Hines/The Gamma Liaison Network; p. 265, © Michael Newman/PhotoEdit; p. 266, © Bob Daemmrich/Stock Boston; p. 269, © Tom McCarthy/PhotoEdit; p. 275, © J. Jones/SYGMA.

Chapter 11

284, © Myleen Ferguson/PhotoEdit; p. 285, Reuters/Jeff Topping/Archive Photos; p. 289, © Jim Bourg/The Gamma Liaison Network; p. 291, © 1984 Eve Arnold/Magnum Photos, Inc.; p. 292, Hulton Getty/Tony Stone Images; p. 293, Reuters/Nick Sharp/Archive Photos; p. 295, top left, © B. Daemmrich/The Image Works, p. 295, top right, © D. Young-Wolff/PhotoEdit; p. 295, bottom, © Lawrence Migdale/Stock Boston; p. 296, AP/Wide World Photos; p. 299, © Deborah Davis/PhotoEdit; p. 301, © J. C. Labbe/Gamma-Liaison; p. 303, © R. Lord/The Image Works; p. 304, © Jean-Marc Giboux.

Chapter 12

312, © A. Ramey/PhotoEdit; p. 315, © Owen Franken/Stock Boston; p. 317, Will and Demi McIntyre/Photo Researchers; p. 318, © Bob Daemmrich/Stock Boston; p. 320, © Alan Oddie/PhotoEdit; p. 321, © M. Greenlar/The Image Works; p. 324, top left, Brooks Kraft/SYGMA; p. 324, top right, © Joe Polillio/Liaison International; p. 324, bottom, © Christopher Brown/Stock Boston; p. 325, © Hector L. Delgado/Impact Visuals; p. 328, © M. Granitsas/The Image Works; p. 329, © Frank Siteman/Stock Boston.

Chapter 13

334, © M. Benjamin/The Image Works; p. 337, © 1997 Raghu Rai/Magnum Photos, Inc. p. 338, Earl Dotter Historic/Impact Visuals; p. 339, © Joe Sohm/The Image Works; p. 341, AP/Wide World Photos; p. 342, © Phyllis Picardi/Stock Boston; p. 346, top left, AP/Wide World Photos; p. 346, top right, © Matthew Neal McVay/Stock Boston; p. 346, bottom, © Richard Kalvar/Magnum Photos, Inc.; p. 353, © Joseph Nettis, Stock Boston; p. 355, © P. Howell/Gamma-Liaison.

Chapter 14

362, © Bob Daemmrich/Stock Boston; p. 366, AP/Wide World Photos; p. 367, top left, AP/Wide World Photos; p. 367, top right, © Gamma; p. 367, bottom left, © 1996 Hiroji Kubota/Magnum Photos, Inc.; p. 367, bottom right, Reuters/Kimimasa Mayama/Archive Photos; p. 374, © Dirk Halstead/The Gamma Liaison Network; p. 378, © Chip Hires/Gamma Liaison; p. 379, © John Chiasson/Gamma Liaison; p. 383, Reuters/Archive Photos.

Chapter 15

388, © Bachmann/Photo Researchers; p. 394, © Renato Rotolo/The Gamma Liaison Network; p. 396, © Chromosohn/Sohm/Stock Boston; p. 400, © Chris Hayward/The Gamma Liaison Network; p. 403, © Pete Souza/Liaison International; p. 406, © Seth Resnick/Liaison International; p. 410, © Michael Newman/PhotoEdit; p. 411, Science Photo Library/Photo Researchers; p. 414, top left, © Jim Vecchione/Liaison International; p. 414, top right, © Michael Newman/PhotoEdit; p. 414, bottom left, © Tony Freeman/PhotoEdit; p. 414, bottom right, © Bob Daemmrich/Stock Boston; p. 415, © William Cochrane/Impact Visuals.

Chapter 16

420, © James D. Wilson/The Gamma Liaison Network; p. 422, © Bob Daemmrich/The Image Works; p. 423, Archive photos; p. 428, © Brian Smith/Stock Boston; p. 432, top left, © Yvonne Hemsey/The Gamma Liaison Network; p. 432, top right, © Bob Daemmrich/The Image Works; p. 432, bottom left, © Robert Caputo/Stock Boston; p. 432, bottom right, The Image Works; p. 437, © Will and Demi McIntyre/Photo Researchers, Inc.; p. 441, © Bob Daemmrich/Stock Boston; p. 442, © Spencer Grant/ Stock Boston.

Chapter 17

446, © Hugh Sitton/Tony Stone Images; p. 450, © Tony Freeman/PhotoEdit; p. 451, © Jack Kurtz/Impact Visuals; p. 454, © M. Schwartz/The Image Works; p. 456, © 1994 North Wind Pictures; p. 457, © Mike Malysko/Stock Boston; p. 458, Reuters/Corbis-Bettmann; p. 460, top left, Reuters/Sunil Malhotra/Archive Photos; p. 460, top right, © Steve Liss/Gamma Liaison; p. 460, bottom left, © Hazel Hankin/Stock Boston; p. 460, bottom right, © Forrest Anderson/The Gamma Liaison Network; p. 467, AP/Wide World Photos.

Chapter 18

472, © Tim Brown/Tony Stone Images; p. 476, © Ellen B. Senisi/Photo Researchers; p. 481, © A. Balaguer/SYGMA; p. 482, © Stacy Rosenstock/Impact Visuals; p. 485, © David Young-Wolff/PhotoEdit; p. 489, top left, © Spencer Grant/PhotoEdit; p. 489, top right © Stephen Ferry/Gamma Liaison; p. 489, bottom, © Joseph Nettis/Stock Boston; p. 491, © Mitch Kerr/Tony Stone Images; p. 494, AP/Wide World Photos; p. 497, AP/Wide World Photos.

Chapter 19

502, © Peterson/Gamma-Liaison; p. 505, top left and bottom left, 1996 Corbis; Original image courtesy NASA; p. 505, top right, © Herve Collart/Gamma Liaison; p. 508, © Kilcullen/Trocaire/SYGMA; p. 510, c Sujoy Das/Stock Boston; p. 511, © Owen Franken/Stock Boston; p. 513, © Michael Newman/PhotoEdit; p. 516, © Jeff Greenberg/PhotoEdit; p. 519, © Stacy Pick/Stock Boston; p. 523, © Bob Daemmrich/The Image Works; p. 524, © A. Ramey/PhotoEdit; p. 525, © David R. Frazier/Photo Researchers.

Chapter 20

532, © Joe McBride/Tony Stone Images; p. 537, top left, © Jackson Archives/The Image Works, p. 537, top right, © Michael Newman/PhotoEdit; p. 537, bottom left, John Ibbotson/ © Tony Stone Images; p. 537, bottom right, © Paula Bronstein/Impact Visuals; p. 540, © Dan Groshong/SYGMA; p. 541, AP/Wide World Photos; p. 542, © Michael Newman/ PhotoEdit; p. 544, © Steve McCurry/Magnum Photos, Inc. p. 549, © Bob Daemmrich/Stock Boston; p. 550, © Kelvin Buyes/Gamma Liaison; p. 553, © Marilyn Humphries/Impact Visuals